More information about this series at https://link.springer.com/bookseries/558

Lecture Notes in Computer Science 1341

Guang Yang · Angelica Aviles-Rivero ·
Michael Roberts ·
Carola-Bibiane Schönlieb (Eds.)

Medical Image Understanding and Analysis

26th Annual Conference, MIUA 2022
Cambridge, UK, July 27–29, 2022
Proceedings

 Springer

Editors
Guang Yang ⓘ
Imperial College London
London, UK

Angelica Aviles-Rivero ⓘ
University of Cambridge
Cambridge, UK

Michael Roberts ⓘ
University of Cambridge
Cambridge, UK

Carola-Bibiane Schönlieb ⓘ
University of Cambridge
Cambridge, UK

ISSN 0302-9743   ISSN 1611-3349 (electronic)
Lecture Notes in Computer Science
ISBN 978-3-031-12052-7   ISBN 978-3-031-12053-4 (eBook)
https://doi.org/10.1007/978-3-031-12053-4

This Springer imprint is published by the registered company Springer Nature Switzerland AG
The registered company address is: Gewerbestrasse 11, 6330 Cham, Switzerland

Preface

We are very pleased to present the proceedings of the 26th Conference on Medical Image Understanding and Analysis (MIUA 2022), a UK-based international conference for the communication of image processing and analysis research and its application to biomedical imaging and biomedicine. The conference was held at the University of Cambridge, UK, during July 27–29, 2022, and featured presentations from the authors of all accepted papers. The conference also featured the Women in MIUA (WiMIUA) workshop.

This year's edition was co-chaired by Dr. Guang Yang, Dr. Angelica Aviles-Rivero, Dr. Michael Roberts, and Prof. Carola-Bibiane Schönlieb at the Centre for Mathematical Sciences, University of Cambridge (http://www.cms.cam.ac.uk/) together with the Department of Applied Mathematics and Theoretical Physics (DAMTP, http://www.damtp.cam.ac.uk/), the Cambridge Mathematics of Information in Healthcare Hub (CMIH, https://www.cmih.maths.cam.ac.uk/), the Isaac Newton Institute for Mathematical Sciences (INI, https://www.newton.ac.uk/), and the A. Yang Lab (AYL, https://www.yanglab.fyi/). One of the General Chairs is from Imperial College London.

The conference was organized with sponsorship received from Microsoft Research (https://www.microsoft.com/en-us/research/lab/microsoft-research-cambridge/, gold level and diamond level for WiMIUA), Aiforia (https://www.aiforia.com/, gold level), MathWorks (https://uk.mathworks.com/, gold level and diamond level for WiMIUA), the Multidisciplinary Digital Publishing Institute (https://www.mdpi.com/, bronze level), Frontiers Media (https://www.frontiersin.org/, bronze level), Nvidia (https://www.nvidia.com, GPU prize), the Institute of Engineering and Technology (https://www.theiet.org/, student prize), and The British Machine Vision Association (https://britishmachinevisionassociation.github.io/). The conference proceedings were published in partnership with Springer (https://www.springer.com).

The diverse range of topics covered in these proceedings reflects the growth in the development and application of biomedical imaging. The conference proceedings feature the most recent work in the fields of (1) Biomarker Detection; (2) Novel Imaging, Image Registration, and Reconstruction; (3) Image Interpretation; (4) Image Segmentation; (5) Generative Adversarial Networks, Transformers, and New Models; (6) Image Classification; (7) Image Enhancement, Quality Assessment, and Data Privacy; (8) Radiomics, Predictive Models, and Quantitative Imaging; and (9) Image-Guided Intervention.

Despite the COVID-19 pandemic, this year's edition of MIUA received a large number of high-quality submissions making the review process particularly competitive. In total, 129 submissions were submitted to the Conference Management Toolkit (CMT), and after an initial quality check, the papers were sent out for the peer-review process completed by the Program and Scientific Review Committees consisting of 83 reviewers. To keep the quality of the reviews consistent with the previous editions of MIUA, the majority of the reviewers were selected from (i) a pool of previous MIUA conference reviewers and (ii) authors and co-authors of papers presented at past MIUA conferences.

All submissions were subject to double-blind review by at least three members of the Program Committee and meta-reviewed by at least one member of the Scientific Review Committee. Based on their recommendations, a ranking was created and the best 65 papers (50%) were accepted as full papers for presentation at the conference. Furthermore, the papers included in the proceedings were revised by the authors following feedback received from the reviewers.

Submissions were received from authors at 108 different institutes from 26 countries across 6 continents, including Argentina (3), Australia (3), Austria (1), Bangladesh (2), Canada (1), China (8), Colombia (1), Egypt (1), France (6), Germany (9), Hungary (1), India (10), Iraq (1), Italy (2), Japan (1), Morocco (1), Nigeria (1), Pakistan (2), South Africa (1), Spain (3), Sweden (1), Switzerland (1), Turkey (2), the UK (31), the United Arab Emirates (2), and the USA (13). Papers were accepted from a total of 184 authors, with an average of ~3 co-authors per paper.

We thank all members of the MIUA 2022 Organizing, Steering, Program, and Scientific Review Committees. In particular, we sincerely thank all who contributed greatly to the success of MIUA 2022: the authors for submitting their work, the reviewers for insightful comments improving the quality of the proceedings, the sponsors for financial support, and all participants in this year's hybrid MIUA conference.

We also thank our exceptional keynote speakers Alejandro Frangi (Diamond Jubilee Chair in Computational Medicine at the University of Leeds), Polina Golland (Professor of Electrical Engineering and Computer Science and principal investigator in the CSAIL at MIT), and Sotirios Tsaftaris (Chair and Full Professor in Machine Learning and Computer Vision at the University of Edinburgh) for sharing their success, knowledge, and experiences.

July 2022

Guang Yang
Angelica Aviles-Rivero
Michael Roberts
Carola-Bibiane Schönlieb

Organization

General Chairs

Guang Yang   Imperial College London, UK
Angelica Aviles-Rivero   University of Cambridge, UK
Michael Roberts   University of Cambridge, UK
Carola-Bibiane Schönlieb   University of Cambridge, UK

Steering Committee

Ke Chen   University of Liverpool, UK
Víctor González-Castro   University of León, Spain
Tryphon Lambrou   University of Lincoln, UK
Sasan Mahmoodi   University of Southampton, UK
Stephen McKenna   University of Dundee, UK
Mark Nixon   University of Southampton, UK
Nasir Rajpoot   University of Warwick, UK
Constantino Carlos   City, University of London, UK
    Reyes-Aldasoro
Maria del C. Valdes-Hernandez   University of Edinburgh, UK
Bryan M. Williams   Lancaster University, UK
Xianghua Xie   Swansea University, UK
Xujiong Ye   University of Lincoln, UK
Yalin Zheng   University of Liverpool, UK
Reyer Zwiggelaar   Aberystwyth University, UK
Guang Yang   Imperial College London, UK
Angelica Aviles-Rivero   University of Cambridge, UK
Michael Roberts   University of Cambridge, UK
Carola-Bibiane Schönlieb   University of Cambridge, UK

Scientific Review Committee

Angelica Aviles-Rivero   University of Cambridge, UK
Guang Yang   Imperial College London, UK
Lei Zhu   The Hong Kong University of Science and
    Technology (Guangzhou), China
Shujun Wang   University of Cambridge, UK
Xi Wang   Stanford University, USA
Yingying Fang   Imperial College London, UK

Local Organizing Committee

Claire Bonner	Newton Gateway to Mathematics, UK
Clare Merritt	Newton Gateway to Mathematics, UK
Josh Stevens	University of Cambridge, UK
John Aston	University of Cambridge, UK
Zhening Huang	University of Cambridge, UK
Lihao Liu	University of Cambridge, UK
Christina Runkel	University of Cambridge, UK

Program Committee

Adrian Galdran	Universitat Pompeu Fabra, Spain
Alaa Bessadok	University of Sousse, Tunisia
Ali Karaali	Trinity College Dublin, Ireland
Amaya Gallagher-Syed	Queen Mary University of London, UK
Ander Biguri	University of Cambridge, UK
Anna Breger	University of Cambridge, UK
Aras Asaad	University of Buckingham, UK
Carlos Moreno-Garcia	Robert Gordon University, UK
Cesar Veiga	Instituto de Investigacion Sanitaria Galicia Sur (IISGS), Spain
Chaoyan Huang	Nanjing University of Posts and Telecommunications, China
Charalambos Rossides	Radii Devices, UK
Cheng Xue	The Chinese University of Hong Kong, China
Chenyu You	Yale University, USA
Cian Scannell	King's College London, UK
Cohen Ethan	Ecole Normale Supérieur, France
Constantino Reyes-Aldasoro	City, University of London, UK
Damian Farnell	Cardiff University, UK
David Rodriguez Gonzalez	CSIC, Spain
Elena Loli Piccolomini	University of Bologna, Italy
Francisco Lopez-Tiro	Tecnológico de Monterrey, Mexico
Fuying Wang	Carnegie Mellon University, USA
Gilberto Ochoa-Ruiz	Tecnológico de Monterrey, Mexico
Giovanna Dimitri	University of Siena, Italy
Hok Shing Wong	The Chinese University of Hong Kong, China
Jaidip Jagtap	Mayo Clinic, USA
Jason Dou	University of Pittsburgh, USA
Jiahao Huang	Imperial College London, UK
Jialu Li	Shenzhen Institutes of Advanced Technology, Chinese Academy of Sciences, China

Jinah Park	KAIST, South Korea
Jing Zou	The Hong Kong Polytechnic University, China
Jorge Novo	University of A Coruña, Spain
Juan Arribas	Valladolid University, Spain
Krassimira Ivanova	Institute of Mathematics and Informatics, Bulgarian Academy of Sciences, Bulgaria
Larbi Boubchir	University of Paris 8, France
Laurent Cohen	Université Paris Dauphine-PSL, France
Lei Qi	Iowa State University, USA
Lei Zhu	The Hong Kong University of Science and Technology (Guangzhou), China
Lihao Liu	University of Cambridge, UK
Linde Hesse	University of Oxford, UK
Michael Tanzer	Imperial College London, UK
Mike Roberts	University of Cambridge, UK
Ming Li	Imperial College London, UK
Neda Azarmehr	University of Sheffield, UK
Nicolas Basty	University of Westminster, UK
Omnia Alwazzan	Queen Mary University of London, UK
Pablo Tahoces	Universidad de Santiago de Compostela, Spain
Qiangqiang Gu	Mayo Clinic, USA
Rakkrit Duangsoithong	Prince of Songkla University, Thailand
Rihuan Ke	University of Cambridge, UK
Said Pertuz	Universidad Industrial de Santander, Colombia
Sarah Lee	Amallis Consulting, UK
Shujun Wang	University of Cambridge, UK
Simone Saitta	Politecnico di Milano, Italy
Sungho Hwang	Korea University, South Korea
Timothy Cootes	University of Manchester, UK
Tryphon Lambrou	University of Aberdeen, UK
Veronika Cheplygina	ITU, Switzerland
Victor Gonzalez	Universidad de León, Spain
Weiqin Zhao	The University of Hong Kong, China
Weiwei Zong	University of Michigan, USA
Xiaodan Xing	Imperial College London, UK
Xiaohui Zhang	University of Illinois Urbana-Champaign, USA
Xin Yang	Shenzhen University, China
Xujiong Ye	University of Lincoln, UK
Xurui Jin	Mindrank AI, China
Yang Nan	Imperial College London, UK
Yann Gavet	Mines Saint-Etienne, France
Yanwu Xu	Baidu Inc, China

Contents

Biomarker Detection

Neck Fat Estimation from DXA Using Convolutional Neural Networks 3
Emily Cresswell, Fredrik Karpe, and Nicolas Basty

Multimodal Cardiomegaly Classification with Image-Derived Digital
Biomarkers 13
*Benjamin Duvieusart, Felix Krones, Guy Parsons, Lionel Tarassenko,
Bartłomiej W. Papież, and Adam Mahdi*

Proton Density Fat Fraction of Breast Adipose Tissue: Comparison
of the Effect of Fat Spectra and Initial Evaluation as a Biomarker 28
*Isobel Gordon, George Ralli, Carolina Fernandes, Amy Herlihy,
and Sir Michael Brady*

Revisiting the Shape-Bias of Deep Learning for Dermoscopic Skin Lesion
Classification 46
*Adriano Lucieri, Fabian Schmeisser, Christoph Peter Balada,
Shoaib Ahmed Siddiqui, Andreas Dengel, and Sheraz Ahmed*

Novel Imaging, Image Registration and Reconstruction

Joint Group-Wise Motion Estimation and Segmentation of Cardiac Cine
MR Images Using Recurrent U-Net 65
Pengfang Qian, Junwei Yang, Pietro Lió, Peng Hu, and Haikun Qi

Recursive Deformable Image Registration Network with Mutual Attention 75
*Jian-Qing Zheng, Ziyang Wang, Baoru Huang, Tonia Vincent,
Ngee Han Lim, and Bartłomiej W. Papież*

Spatiotemporal Attention Constrained Deep Learning Framework
for Dual-Tracer PET Imaging 87
Dankun Lian, Yue Li, and Huafeng Liu

Faster Diffusion Cardiac MRI with Deep Learning-Based Breath Hold
Reduction 101
*Michael Tänzer, Pedro Ferreira, Andrew Scott, Zohya Khalique,
Maria Dwornik, Ramyah Rajakulasingam, Ranil de Silva,
Dudley Pennell, Guang Yang, Daniel Rueckert,
and Sonia Nielles-Vallespin*

Preoperative CT and Intraoperative CBCT Image Registration
and Evaluation in Robotic Cochlear Implant Surgery 116
   Chenxi Lu, Bo Dong, Xi Hu, Yang Zhao, Hongjian He, and Jing Wang

Simultaneous Semantic and Instance Segmentation for Colon Nuclei
Identification and Counting 130
   Lihao Liu, Chenyang Hong, Angelica I. Aviles-Rivero,
   and Carola-Bibiane Schönlieb

Point2Mask: A Weakly Supervised Approach for Cell Segmentation
Using Point Annotation 139
   Nabeel Khalid, Fabian Schmeisser, Mohammadmahdi Koochali,
   Mohsin Munir, Christoffer Edlund, Timothy R Jackson, Johan Trygg,
   Rickard Sjögren, Andreas Dengel, and Sheraz Ahmed

Image Interpretation

Class Distance Weighted Cross-Entropy Loss for Ulcerative Colitis
Severity Estimation 157
   Gorkem Polat, Ilkay Ergenc, Haluk Tarik Kani, Yesim Ozen Alahdab,
   Ozlen Atug, and Alptekin Temizel

Procrustes Analysis of Muscle Fascicle Shapes Based on DTI Fibre
Tracking 172
   Lei Ye, Eugenie Hunsicker, Baihua Li, and Diwei Zhou

Weakly Supervised Captioning of Ultrasound Images 187
   Mohammad Alsharid, Harshita Sharma, Lior Drukker,
   Aris T. Papageorgiou, and J. Alison Noble

Computerised Methods for Monitoring Diabetic Foot Ulcers on Plantar
Foot: A Feasibility Study 199
   Manu Goyal, Neil D. Reeves, Satyan Rajbhandari, and Moi Hoon Yap

CellCentroidFormer: Combining Self-attention and Convolution for Cell
Detection 212
   Royden Wagner and Karl Rohr

GPU-Net: Lightweight U-Net with More Diverse Features 223
   Heng Yu, Di Fan, and Weihu Song

Self-supervision and Multi-task Learning: Challenges in Fine-Grained
COVID-19 Multi-class Classification from Chest X-rays 234
   Muhammad Ridzuan, Ameera Bawazir, Ivo Gollini Navarrete,
   Ibrahim Almakky, and Mohammad Yaqub

Image Segmentation

Ultrasonography Uterus and Fetus Segmentation with Constrained
Spatial-Temporal Memory FCN 253
    Bin Kong, Xin Wang, Yi Lu, Hao-Yu Yang, Kunlin Cao, Qi Song,
    and Youbing Yin

Thigh and Calf Muscles Segmentation Using Ensemble of Patch-Based
Deep Convolutional Neural Network on Whole-Body Water-Fat MRI 262
    Zhendi Gong, Rosemary Nicholas, Susan T. Francis, and Xin Chen

Fitting Segmentation Networks on Varying Image Resolutions Using
Splatting 271
    Mikael Brudfors, Yaël Balbastre, John Ashburner, Geraint Rees,
    Parashkev Nachev, Sébastien Ourselin, and M. Jorge Cardoso

Rotation-Equivariant Semantic Instance Segmentation on Biomedical
Images 283
    Karl Bengtsson Bernander, Joakim Lindblad, Robin Strand,
    and Ingela Nyström

Joint Learning with Local and Global Consistency for Improved Medical
Image Segmentation 298
    Md. Atik Ahamed and Abdullah Al Zubaer Imran

LKAU-Net: 3D Large-Kernel Attention-Based U-Net for Automatic MRI
Brain Tumor Segmentation 313
    Hao Li, Yang Nan, and Guang Yang

Attention-Fused CNN Model Compression with Knowledge Distillation
for Brain Tumor Segmentation 328
    Pengcheng Xu, Kyungsang Kim, Huafeng Liu, and Quanzheng Li

Lung Segmentation Using ResUnet++ Powered by Variational Auto
Encoder-Based Enhancement in Chest X-ray Images 339
    Samar Ibrahim, Kareem Elgohary, Mahmoud Higazy,
    Thanaa Mohannad, Sahar Selim, and Mustafa Elattar

A Neural Architecture Search Based Framework for Segmentation
of Epithelium, Nuclei and Oral Epithelial Dysplasia Grading 357
    Neda Azarmehr, Adam Shephard, Hanya Mahmood, Nasir Rajpoot,
    and Syed Ali Khurram

STAMP: A Self-training Student-Teacher Augmentation-Driven Meta
Pseudo-Labeling Framework for 3D Cardiac MRI Image Segmentation 371
    S. M. Kamrul Hasan and Cristian Linte

Implicit U-Net for Volumetric Medical Image Segmentation 387
Sergio Naval Marimont and Giacomo Tarroni

A Deep-Learning Lesion Segmentation Model that Addresses Class
Imbalance and Expected Low Probability Tissue Abnormalities in Pre
and Postoperative Liver MRI 398
*Nora Vogt, Zobair Arya, Luis Núñez, Kezia Hobson, John Connell,
Sir Michael Brady, and Paul Aljabar*

Utility of Equivariant Message Passing in Cortical Mesh Segmentation 412
*Dániel Unyi, Ferdinando Insalata, Petar Veličković,
and Bálint Gyires-Tóth*

A Novel Framework for Coarse-Grained Semantic Segmentation
of Whole-Slide Images 425
*Raja Muhammad Saad Bashir, Muhammad Shaban,
Shan E. Ahmed Raza, Syed Ali Khurram, and Nasir Rajpoot*

Generative Adversarial Network, Transformer and New Models

How Effective is Adversarial Training of CNNs in Medical Image Analysis? ... 443
Yiming Xie and Ahmed E. Fetit

A U-Net Based Progressive GAN for Microscopic Image Augmentation 458
Qifan Zhou and Hujun Yin

A Deep Generative Model of Neonatal Cortical Surface Development 469
*Abdulah Fawaz, Logan Z. J. Williams, A. David Edwards,
and Emma C. Robinson*

A Generative Framework for Predicting Myocardial Strain
from Cine-Cardiac Magnetic Resonance Imaging 482
*Nina Cheng, Rodrigo Bonazzola, Nishant Ravikumar,
and Alejandro F. Frangi*

An Uncertainty-Aware Transformer for MRI Cardiac Semantic
Segmentation via Mean Teachers 494
Ziyang Wang, Jian-Qing Zheng, and Irina Voiculescu

SF-SegFormer: Stepped-Fusion Segmentation Transformer for Brain
Tissue Image via Inter-Group Correlation and Enhanced Multi-layer
Perceptron 508
Jinjing Zhang, Lijun Zhao, Jianchao Zeng, and Pinle Qin

Polyp2Seg: Improved Polyp Segmentation with Vision Transformer 519
Vittorino Mandujano-Cornejo and Javier A. Montoya-Zegarra

Multi-resolution Fine-Tuning of Vision Transformers 535
*Kerr Fitzgerald, Meng Law, Jarrel Seah, Jennifer Tang,
and Bogdan Matuszewski*

From Astronomy to Histology: Adapting the FellWalker Algorithm
to Deep Nuclear Instance Segmentation 547
Michael Yeung, Todd Watts, and Guang Yang

Image Classification

Leveraging Uncertainty in Deep Learning for Pancreatic Adenocarcinoma
Grading 565
Biraja Ghoshal, Bhargab Ghoshal, and Allan Tucker

A Novel Bi-level Lung Cancer Classification System on CT Scans 578
Shubham Dodia, B. Annappa, and Mahesh A. Padukudru

Jointly Boosting Saliency Prediction and Disease Classification on Chest
X-ray Images with Multi-task UNet 594
Hongzhi Zhu, Robert Rohling, and Septimiu Salcudean

Deep Bayesian Active-Learning-to-Rank for Endoscopic Image Data 609
*Takeaki Kadota, Hideaki Hayashi, Ryoma Bise, Kiyohito Tanaka,
and Seiichi Uchida*

Improving Image Representations via MoCo Pre-training for Multimodal
CXR Classification 623
*Francesco Dalla Serra, Grzegorz Jacenków, Fani Deligianni,
Jeff Dalton, and Alison Q. O'Neil*

Multi-scale Graph Neural Networks for Mammography Classification
and Abnormality Detection 636
*Guillaume Pelluet, Mira Rizkallah, Mickael Tardy, Oscar Acosta,
and Diana Mateus*

TransSLC: Skin Lesion Classification in Dermatoscopic Images Using
Transformers 651
*Md Mostafa Kamal Sarker, Carlos Francisco Moreno-García,
Jinchang Ren, and Eyad Elyan*

Image Enhancement, Quality Assessment, and Data Privacy

Privacy Preserving and Communication Efficient Information
Enhancement for Imbalanced Medical Image Classification 663
   Xiaochuan Li and Yuan Ke

Contrastive Pretraining for Echocardiography Segmentation with Limited
Data 680
   Mohamed Saeed, Rand Muhtaseb, and Mohammad Yaqub

High-Quality 4D-CBCT Imaging from Single Routine Scan 692
   Huihui Li, Pengfei Yang, Xin Ge, and Tianye Niu

Non-iterative Blind Deblurring of Digital Microscope Images
with Spatially Varying Blur 703
   *Furkan Kaynar, Peter Geißler, Laurent Demaret, Tamara Seybold,
   and Walter Stechele*

Low-Effort Re-identification Techniques Based on Medical Imagery
Threaten Patient Privacy 719
   Laura Carolina Martínez Esmeral and Andreas Uhl

Removing Specular Reflection in Multispectral Dermatological Images
Using Blind Source Separation 734
   Mustapha Zokay and Hicham Saylani

A Multi-scale Self-supervision Method for Improving Cell Nuclei
Segmentation in Pathological Tissues 751
   Hesham Ali, Mustafa Elattar, and Sahar Selim

Radiomics, Predictive Models, and Quantitative Imaging

Correlation Between IBSI Morphological Features
and Manually-Annotated Shape Attributes on Lung Lesions
at CT 767
   *Francesco Bianconi, Mario Luca Fravolini, Giulia Pascoletti,
   Isabella Palumbo, Michele Scialpi, Cynthia Aristei, and Barbara Palumbo*

Large-Scale Patch-Wise Pathological Image Feature Dataset
with a Hardware-agnostic Feature Extraction Tool 778
   *Zheyu Zhu, Ruining Deng, Quan Liu, Zuhayr Asad, Can Cui,
   Tianyuan Yao, and Yuankai Huo*

Predicting Myocardial Infarction Using Retinal OCT Imaging 787
Cynthia Maldonado García, Rodrigo Bonazzola, Nishant Ravikumar,
and Alejandro F. Frangi

On the Feasibility of Radiomic Analysis for the Detection of Breast
Lesions in Speed-of-Sound Images of the Breast 798
Andres F. Vargas, Angie Hernández, Ana Ramirez, and Said Pertuz

Oral Dental Diagnosis Using Deep Learning Techniques: A Review 814
Asmaa Elsayed, Hanya Mostafa, Reem Tarek, Kareem Mohamed,
Abdelaziz Hossam, and Sahar Selim

Computational Image Analysis Techniques, Programming Languages
and Software Platforms Used in Cancer Research: A Scoping Review 833
Youssef Arafat and Constantino Carlos Reyes-Aldasoro

Image-Guided Intervention

A User Interface for Automatic Polyp Detection Based on Deep Learning
with Extended Vision 851
Adrian Krenzer, Joel Troya, Michael Banck, Boban Sudarevic,
Krzysztof Flisikowski, Alexander Meining, and Frank Puppe

Using Deep Learning on X-ray Orthogonal Coronary Angiograms
for Quantitative Coronary Analysis 869
Laura Busto, José A. González-Nóvoa, Pablo Juan-Salvadores,
Víctor Jiménez, Andrés Íñiguez, and César Veiga

Efficient Pipeline for Rapid Detection of Catheters and Tubes in Chest
Radiographs 882
Hossam Mohamed Sarhan, Hesham Ali, Eman Ehab, Sahar Selim,
and Mustafa Elattar

FCN-Transformer Feature Fusion for Polyp Segmentation 892
Edward Sanderson and Bogdan J. Matuszewski

Correction to: Faster Diffusion Cardiac MRI with Deep Learning-Based
Breath Hold Reduction C1
Michael Tänzer, Pedro Ferreira, Andrew Scott, Zohya Khalique,
Maria Dwornik, Ramyah Rajakulasingam, Ranil de Silva,
Dudley Pennell, Guang Yang, Daniel Rueckert,
and Sonia Nielles-Vallespin

Author Index 909

Biomarker Detection

Neck Fat Estimation from DXA Using Convolutional Neural Networks

Emily Cresswell[1], Fredrik Karpe[1,2,3], and Nicolas Basty[3(✉)]

[1] Oxford Centre for Diabetes, Endocrinology and Metabolism,
University of Oxford, Oxford, UK
[2] NIHR Biomedical Research Centre, OUH Foundation Trust, Oxford, UK
[3] Research Centre for Optimal Health, School of Life Sciences,
University of Westminster, London, UK
n.basty@westminster.ac.uk

Abstract. Expansion of neck adipose tissue (NAT) is an understudied trait in obesity biology. NAT can be quantified using dual X-ray absorptiometry (DXA), a tool commonly used in body composition studies. However, the neck region is not defined in standard regional outputs from a body composition DXA acquisition; instead, quantifying NAT relies on a scanner-dependent software, where manual input is required to define a non-standard region of interest. This makes specialised body composition studies at scale very time-consuming. We thus developed an automated pipeline for NAT estimation from DXA using convolutional neural networks. We investigated whether predicting measurements with a prior step of cropping a region of interest, using automatic landmark prediction, was better than directly predicting from the entire image. We then compared our proposed architecture to the ResNet50 architecture, a well known model used as a basis for transfer learning experiments in many tasks including classification and regression. For the direct and the two-step prediction, both models displayed high performance accuracy. The anatomical landmark placement model performed within three pixels accuracy, and NAT estimation errors for both models were within less than 2.5% points of mean absolute error. However, the proposed model outperformed ResNet50 in the direct prediction, where ours had a mean absolute error of 2.42 against 5.58 for ResNet50. To ensure that the direct predictions are specifically focusing on neck fat, and that the results did not arise from chance correlations with other adipose tissue depots, we generated activation maps which highlighted that the network is focusing on the neck region. This work will enable large-scale population analyses of non-standard regions of interests across a variety of DXA analyses.

Keywords: DXA · Convolutional neural networks · Body composition · Adipose tissue · Neck fat

1 Introduction

The expansion of upper body fat depots is strongly associated with adverse metabolic outcomes; opposite to those of the lower body [11]. In certain

G. Yang et al. (Eds.): MIUA 2022, LNCS 13413, pp. 3–12, 2022.
https://doi.org/10.1007/978-3-031-12053-4_1

adiposity redistribution syndromes, such as Cushing's disease, obesity hypoventilation syndrome and familial partial lipodystrophy, there is a marked accumulation of neck adipose tissue (NAT), also accompanied by elevated cardiometabolic risk [17]. The neck region is an upper body fat depot comprising both white and thermogenic brown adipose tissue (BAT), the latter of which appears positively associated with metabolic health [2]. It has been speculated that abdominal adiposity is linked to BAT transdifferentiation and replacement by white tissue [3,13]. In the absence of easy and reproducible methods to quantify NAT at scale, investigators have used neck circumference (NC) as a proxy measure. NC has demonstrated strong relationships with visceral adipose tissue; an ectopic fat depot associated with adverse cardiometabolic consequences [16], and type 2 diabetes [4]. NC, however, does not delineate tissue composition, confounding direct NAT measurements due to the effect of neck lean tissue. In addition, studies directly assessing NAT using computed tomography (CT) at a single slice neck vertebral level have suggested positive relationships between NAT volume and cardiometabolic risk [1,21]. However, these small studies did not examine the full length of the neck region, and were limited to healthy cohorts. Dual X-ray Absorptiometry (DXA) is a reliable modality for determining tissue composition [22], specifying the weight and ratios of fat to lean tissue, as opposed to CT-based NAT.

DXA is commonly used for body composition analyses, allowing efficient all-around quantification of fat and lean tissue. It is fast, inexpensive and involves a low radiation dose exposure, which has made it a standard tool for measuring body composition in large cohorts such as the Oxford Biobank (OBB) [12] and the UK Biobank [20]. The standard regional body composition output, automatically included in DXA scans, consists of arm, leg, trunk as well as further subdivisions such as the abdominal and gluteofemoral regions. Additional algorithms within the scanner platforms are used for the quantification of visceral fat content. The neck region is not part of any standard output, requiring the manual definition and construction of regions of interest (ROI) for analysis, which renders it difficult and time-intensive to perform NAT estimations at scale.

Although DXA imaging is commonly used in body composition, it is a less commonly studied imaging modality in the image processing literature. DXA image processing studies generally deal with the skeletal system, for example covering bone segmentation [9], scoliosis prediction [10] or osteoporosis detection [8].

In this study, we have developed and evaluated a two-stage automated end-to-end pipeline for estimation of NAT fat to lean mass ratio in % from DXA images acquired from the OBB, enabling automated estimation of NAT at scale. Analysing these values alongside biochemical parameters from the OBB will thence allow for an in-depth investigation into the role of NAT in metabolic health.

2   Methods

We used the DXA images of 495 OBB participants for this study, including 72 type 2 diabetics. Each individual data set consisted of two images, one low energy X-ray (mostly delineating the soft tissue) and one high energy (mostly delineating the skeletal structure), as well as the NAT mass percentage within a manually defined ROI. The quantitative image software output used as labels in this study came from the GE Lunar iDXA enCORE platform. For each set of images, we manually placed the neck ROI defined at four anatomical landmarks and saved their coordinates: first, two at the level of the right and left lung apices and second, two at the lowest margins of the mandible on the right and the left hand sides. An example of the two X-ray images acquired during a DXA scan are shown in Fig. 1A-B, and the respective neck ROIs for the same subject in Fig. 1C-D. For model training, we performed tenfold data augmentation. This included horizontal flipping, translations of a random number of pixels (-16 to 16), and also small random rotations (-2 to $2°C$), in order to realistically simulate different subjects of various heights and positioned in various orientations. We kept the data for 95 subjects completely apart for final evaluation and we performed all prototyping and parameter tuning experiments with the 400 other data using an 80–20 training and validation split.

In this study, we compare two pipelines for NAT estimation, one predicting the measurement from the entire image and one using a prior step of cropping a ROI of the neck region, as previous studies have shown deep learning tasks to improve when an intermediate step of localisation is added into the pipeline [6, 14].

The pipeline using cropped data for prediction consists of two parts: first, the ROI placement, and second; estimation of NAT using the cropped neck ROI, as delineated by the four landmarks. For the first part, we trained a U-net [18] to predict the four coordinates of the neck ROI landmarks. We created label ROI images using the neck landmark coordinates, where each coordinate was represented by a point spread function (PSF) consisting of a Gaussian blur with standard deviation of four pixels, centred on the four landmark coordinates, as has been done by others for landmark detection [23]. We also normalised the two channels of input data as well as the ROI label image. We show an example ROI label image in Fig. 2A. Our U-net-based model has six resolution levels, doubling the number of convolution filters from 64 to 512 in the first four encoding levels, and 512 filters for the fifth, sixth, and the bottom. Each convolutional block has a filter size 3, stride of 2 instead of pooling, batch normalisation and a leaky ReLU activation. The decoding blocks at the same resolution levels match the encoding blocks in terms of filter numbers, and have deconvolutions instead of convolutions. The output layer has a sigmoid activation. We trained the models for 15 epochs minimising a F1 score loss function using the Adam optimiser and a learning rate of 0.002 with decay 0.005. We then calculated the centroids of the final output map predicted by the ROI placement model. We repeated training ten times for the ROI placement-model and assessed performance through mean absolute error (MAE) of euclidean distance in pixels for each of the four landmarks compared to the ground truth coordinates on a held out test set of 95 images.

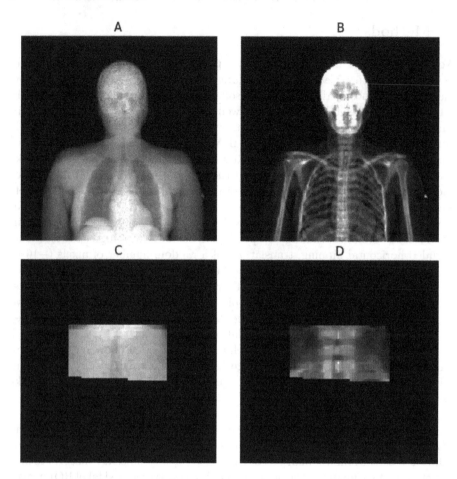

Fig. 1. Example of DXA images and corresponding neck ROI: A) low attenuation energy X-ray, B) high energy X-ray, C) neck ROI of low and D) high attenuation energy X-ray.

For NAT estimation, we adapted a recently published methodology for brain age prediction by Peng et al. [15]. The authors propose a simple fully convolutional neural network that predicts a probability for the age of the subject from 3D brain MRI. Their proposed architecture consists of five convolutional layers followed by two fully connected layers. Our proposed model is constructed using two kinds of convolutional blocks. First: RC_X, a residual block made up of two successive convolutions with X filters of size 3, batch normalisation and ReLU activation where the input and the output of the block are connected by a skip-connection followed by max-pooling. Second: two fully convolutional layers (convolutions of filter size 1), FC_X. The architecture is as follows: $RC_{64} - RC_{128} - RC_{256} - RC_{512} - RC_{1024} - FC_{256} - FC_{65}$. The first FC has ReLU activation, and average pooling as in [15], and the final output has a softmax activation. The network input consists of the neck ROIs of both channels extracted

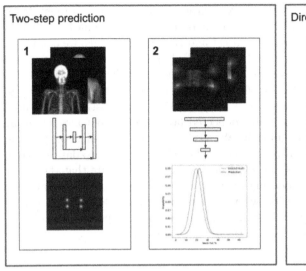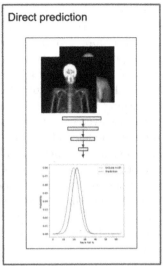

Fig. 2. Graphic representation of the pipelines. Left: two-step prediction showing ROI placement using U-Net (A) and Neural network output estimation of NAT (B). The green distribution represents the true value and magenta for our estimation. Right: direct prediction.

from X-ray images of input size 128 × 128. The final layer predicts a probability distribution, between 0 and 65, instead of 0 to 50 as in [15]. We selected the range from 0 to 65 to capture the range of the ground truth labels (which ranged from NAT of 7.3% to 53.6%) that we converted into Gaussian distribution centred around the value used as labels. We found the model performance to improve when training was performed minimising categorical cross-entropy and not the Kullback-Leibler divergence loss, as used in Peng et al. [15]. During model prototyping experiments, we explored various values of standard deviation, σ, for the Gaussian distribution around the NAT estimation label (1, 3, 5, 7.5, 10) and found the most robust and repeatable results to be obtained from $\sigma = 5$. We set the number of epochs to 65, after observing that the exploratory training runs, which went on for 100 epochs, converged around epoch 65. We trained the NAT estimation model using the Adam optimiser and a learning rate of 0.01 and decay of 0.001. The output of the network is a probability distribution, and we calculate the final predicted NAT percent values as the mean of the distribution. We repeated training ten times and assessed performance via MAE and root mean square error (RMSE) in percentage points using the 95 held out testing set. Figure 2 shows a graphic describing the pipeline, 1A) showing the ROI placement, 1B) the NAT estimation, and 2) showing the direct prediction pipeline.

We also trained models predicting NAT from the entire top half (containing the neck region) of the DXA images without performing a landmark prediction and ROI cropping step. For both the direct and two-step methods, we compared our proposed architecture against ResNet50 [7]. ResNet50 is a version with 50 layers of the well-known ResNet architecture, which was the first to introduce residual learning. For our ResNet50 comparison experiments, we used transfer learning to retrain the model for NAT prediction. We substituted the final activation layer with the same fully connected layer with 65 outputs as in our proposed model, before retraining it. We also performed visual checks of the activation maps generated using guided back-propagation [19] (adapting code from https://github.com/experiencor/deep-viz-keras/) to ensure that the direct predictions are specifically focusing on neck fat, and that the results are not arising from a chance correlation with other adipose tissue depots. All experiments presented in this paper, including transfer learning experiment using the pre-trained ResNet50 model, were performed using Keras [5].

3   Results

The ROI placement metrics are summarised in Table 1, where we give the MAE for each landmark in pixels (euclidean distance) when compared to the manual placement on the held out test set of 95 data. The results show that the network is able to predict the four landmarks within less than three pixels accuracy. The NAT estimation metrics for both methods using our model and ResNet50 are summarised in Table 2, where we show that the networks in all experiments are able to predict NAT within a few percentage points. We show examples of low, medium, and high NAT out-of-sample subjects in Fig. 3. The first column are the low attenuation X-ray images, the middle columns show the predicted landmark PSF centroids in red superimposed on top of the manually placed ground truth PSFs in white, and the third column shows the network output (magenta) and the distribution centred on the ground truth NAT value (green). We can see in those examples that the network slightly overestimates (by 1.1% points) the low NAT and slightly underestimates (by 2.36% points) the high NAT. We show activation maps using our proposed direct prediction model in Fig. 4.

Table 1. ROI placement performance metrics. The error of the coordinates of the four individual landmarks are given in euclidean distance in pixels (resolution $0.23\,\mathrm{mm}^2$).

Landmark	Top left	Top right	Bottom right	Bottom left
Mean absolute error	2.0	2.5	1.9	2.1

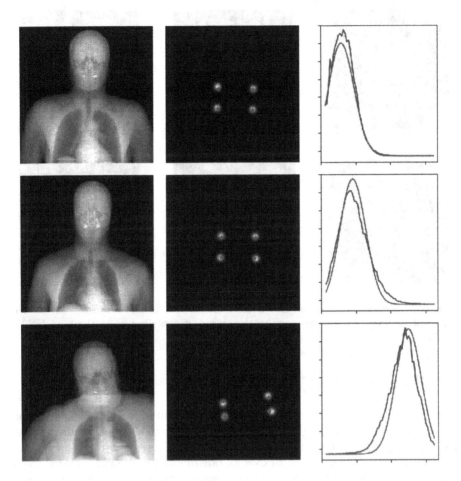

Fig. 3. ROI and NAT estimation on three out-of-sample data for the two-step model. First column is the low energy X-ray, second the four landmarks (red = estimation, white = PSFs centred on manual landmarks), third the predicted distribution (magenta) and ground truth label (green).

Table 2. Root Mean Square Error and Mean Absolute Error of NAT prediction from two-step and direct methods using the model proposed in this work and ResNet50. The values shown in the table are in percentage points.

Model	Root mean square error	Mean absolute error
ResNet50 (two-step)	3.03	2.26
This work (two-step)	2.97	2.36
ResNet50 (direct)	6.68	5.58
This work (direct)	3.04	2.42

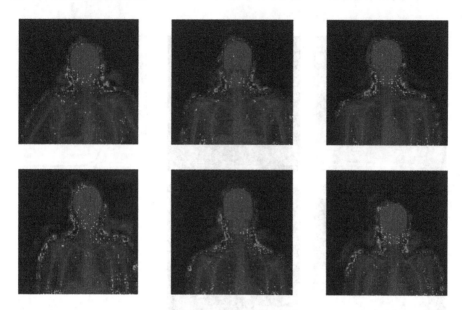

Fig. 4. Activation maps for six examples of direct NAT estimation using our model, highlighting areas around the neck as the strongest contributors to the model NAT output.

4   Discussion and Conclusion

In this study, we have developed an automatic solution for NAT composition estimation from DXA imaging. We have shown through our experiments that the two proposed methods are able to perform NAT predictions within a small margin of error. Compared to ResNet50, our model to performed better when predicting NAT using the entire image foregoing the cropping step, for which both models performed similarly well. In order to further increase confidence when applying our model to a large cohort, we will increase the training dataset, with a focus on enriching with more extreme NAT values. This method of predicting parameters from DXA images using deep learning will enable a fast way to estimate NAT in the Oxford Biobank at scale, which would have otherwise required many months of manual labour. There is further potential to apply this to other DXA-containing Biobanks, allowing the investigation of specific disease cohorts where NAT is of interest (e.g. Cushing's, familial partial lipodystrophy, obesity hypoventilation syndrome). On top of that, we can easily measure neck diameter using the distance between the predicted landmarks from the ROI model. As most of the existing data is on NC, we will use this to confirm previously established relationships between NC and metabolic health [1,21]. Our research may enable additional parameters to be learnt, and further regions to be predicted in other large-scale image analyses.

Acknowledgments. This research was supported by a BHF program grant to FK [RG/17/1/32663]. EC was supported by the Rokos Internship Grant (Pembroke College Oxford) and the OxKen studentship scheme.

References

1. Arias-Tellez, M.J., et al.: Neck adipose tissue accumulation is associated with higher overall and central adiposity, a higher cardiometabolic risk, and a pro-inflammatory profile in young adults (2021)
2. Becher, T., Palanisamy, S., Kramer, D.J., Eljalby, M., Marx, S.J., Wibmer, A.G., Butler, S.D., Jiang, C.S., Vaughan, R., Schöder, H., Mark, A., Cohen, P.: Brown adipose tissue is associated with cardiometabolic health. Nat. Med. **27**(1), 58–65 (2021)
3. Chait, A., den Hartigh, L.J.: Adipose tissue distribution, inflammation and its metabolic consequences, including diabetes and cardiovascular disease. Front. Cardiovasc Med. **7**, 22 (2020)
4. Cho, N.H., et al.: Neck circumference and incidence of diabetes mellitus over 10 years in the Korean genome and epidemiology study (KoGES). Sci. Rep. **5**, 18565 (2015)
5. Chollet, F., et al.: Keras (2015). https://github.com/fchollet/keras
6. Fitzpatrick, J.A., Basty, N., Cule, M., Liu, Y., Bell, J.D., Thomas, E.L., Whitcher, B.: Large-scale analysis of iliopsoas muscle volumes in the UK biobank. Sci. Rep. **10**(1), 1–10 (2020)
7. He, K., Zhang, X., Ren, S., Sun, J.: Deep residual learning for image recognition. In: Proceedings of the IEEE Conference on Computer Vision and Pattern Recognition, pp. 770–778 (2016)
8. Hussain, D., Han, S.M.: Computer-aided osteoporosis detection from DXA imaging. Comput. Methods Programs Biomed. **173**, 87–107 (2019)
9. Hussain, D., Naqvi, R.A., Loh, W.K., Lee, J.: Deep learning in DXA image segmentation (2021)
10. Jamaludin, A., Kadir, T., Clark, E., Zisserman, A.: Predicting scoliosis in DXA scans using intermediate representations (2019)
11. Karpe, F., Pinnick, K.E.: Biology of upper-body and lower-body adipose tissue-link to whole-body phenotypes. Nat. Rev. Endocrinol. **11**(2), 90–100 (2015)
12. Karpe, F., Vasan, S.K., Humphreys, S.M., Miller, J., Cheeseman, J., Dennis, A.L., Neville, M.J.: Cohort profile: the oxford biobank. Int. J. Epidemiol. **47**(1), 21–21g (2018)
13. Kotzbeck, P., et al.: Brown adipose tissue whitening leads to brown adipocyte death and adipose tissue inflammation. J. Lipid Res. **59**(5), 784–794 (2018)
14. Oktay, O., et al.: Attention u-net: Learning where to look for the pancreas. arXiv preprint arXiv:1804.03999 (2018)
15. Peng, H., Gong, W., Beckmann, C.F., Vedaldi, A., Smith, S.M.: Accurate brain age prediction with lightweight deep neural networks. Med. Image Anal. **68**, 101871 (2021)
16. Preis, S.R., et al.: Neck circumference as a novel measure of cardiometabolic risk: the framingham heart study. J. Clin. Endocrinol. Metab. **95**(8), 3701–3710 (2010)
17. Resende, A.T.P., Martins, C.S., Bueno, A.C., Moreira, A.C., Foss-Freitas, M.C., de Castro, M.: Phenotypic diversity and glucocorticoid sensitivity in patients with familial partial lipodystrophy type 2. Clin. Endocrinol. **91**(1), 94–103 (2019)

18. Ronneberger, O., Fischer, P., Brox, T.: U-Net: Convolutional networks for biomedical image segmentation (2015)
19. Springenberg, J.T., Dosovitskiy, A., Brox, T., Riedmiller, M.: Striving for simplicity: The all convolutional net. arXiv preprint arXiv:1412.6806 (2014)
20. Sudlow, C., et al.: UK biobank: an open access resource for identifying the causes of a wide range of complex diseases of middle and old age. PLoS Med. **12**(3), e1001779 (2015)
21. Torriani, M., Gill, C.M., Daley, S., Oliveira, A.L., Azevedo, D.C., Bredella, M.A.: Compartmental neck fat accumulation and its relation to cardiovascular risk and metabolic syndrome. Am. J. Clin. Nutr. **100**(5), 1244–1251 (2014)
22. Vasan, S.K.: Comparison of regional fat measurements by dual-energy x-ray absorptiometry and conventional anthropometry and their association with markers of diabetes and cardiovascular disease risk. Int. J. Obes. **42**(4), 850–857 (2018)
23. Xue, H., Artico, J., Fontana, M., Moon, J.C., Davies, R.H., Kellman, P.: Landmark detection in cardiac MRI by using a convolutional neural network (2021)

Multimodal Cardiomegaly Classification with Image-Derived Digital Biomarkers

Benjamin Duvieusart[1], Felix Krones[2], Guy Parsons[3], Lionel Tarassenko[1],
Bartłomiej W. Papież[4,5], and Adam Mahdi[2(✉)]

[1] Department of Engineering Science, University of Oxford, Oxford, UK
[2] Oxford Internet Institute, University of Oxford, Oxford, UK
adam.mahdi@oii.ox.ac.uk
[3] Intensive Care Registrar, Thames Valley Deanery, NIHR Academic Clinical Fellow
at Oxford University, Oxford, UK
[4] Big Data Institute, Li Ka Shing Centre for Health Information and Discovery,
University of Oxford, Oxford, UK
[5] Nuffield Department of Population Health, University of Oxford, Oxford, UK

Abstract. We investigate the problem of automatic cardiomegaly diagnosis. We approach this by developing classifiers using multimodal data enhanced by two image-derived digital biomarkers, the cardiothoracic ratio (CTR) and the cardiopulmonary area ratio (CPAR). The CTR and CPAR values are estimated using segmentation and detection models. These are then integrated into a multimodal network trained simultaneously on chest radiographs and ICU data (vital sign values, laboratory values and metadata). We compare the predictive power of different data configurations with and without the digital biomarkers. There was a negligible performance difference between the XGBoost model containing only CTR and CPAR (accuracy 81.4%, F1 0.859, AUC 0.810) and black-box models which included full images (ResNet-50: accuracy 81.9%, F1 0.874, AUC 0.767; Multimodal: 81.9%, F1 0.873, AUC 0.768). We concluded that models incorporating domain knowledge-based digital biomarkers CTR and CPAR provide comparable performance to black-box multimodal approaches with the former providing better clinical explainability.

Keywords: Cardiomegaly · Multimodal approach · Domain knowledge · Digital biomarkers · Data fusion · Deep learning · Chest X-ray · Cardiothoracic ratio · Segmentation · Detection

1 Introduction

There is a worldwide shortage of trained radiologists [27,28]. The application of automated radiograph labelling and diagnosis algorithms to support clinical staff has the potential to increase the efficiency of clinical workflows and reduce demand on radiology services. A tool which accurately identifies pathology, as part of an appropriate care pathway, has the potential to increase the quality

G. Yang et al. (Eds.): MIUA 2022, LNCS 13413, pp. 13–27, 2022.
https://doi.org/10.1007/978-3-031-12053-4_2

of care worldwide. This paper approaches the problem of creating an automatic labelling tool for cardiomegaly.

Cardiomegaly, an abnormal enlargement of the heart, may result from many cardiac conditions, such as coronary artery disease or congenital heart disorders. Often cardiomegaly is first identified by examining a patient's cardiothoracic ratio (CTR), calculated by taking the ratio of the cardiac width to the thoracic width on a posterior-anterior projection of a chest X-ray. The cardiac width is measured as the horizontal distance between the leftmost and rightmost extremes of the cardiac shadow, and the thoracic width is measured as the horizontal distance from the inner margin of the ribs at the level of the hemidiaphragm. A CTR of 0.5 is usually classed as the upper limit for normal cardiac size and hence commonly used as the delimiter of cardiomegaly.

The increased availability of large publicly-available clinical imaging datasets has accelerated the use of computer vision and machine learning techniques to identify the CTR by using edge detection [14] or convolutional neural networks [25,33]. While CTR is an important and widely accepted first metric to identify cardiomegaly, there are inherent limitations. CTR values are prone to inaccuracies as both the cardiac and thoracic widths are dependant on many factors, such as the dilation of cardiac chambers, respiratory phase and body posture. It is known that this method risks flagging false-positives, causing many patients with suspected cardiomegaly to be subjected to further imaging. Despite these concerns, the CTR is still a fundamental tool for identifying cardiomegaly due to its simplicity and since false-positives are considered a more acceptable error type in clinical settings.

A clinician can compensate for the uncertainties associated with using only CTR values by synthesising all available patient data from multiple modalities, including patient metadata, vital signs and blood test results to refine a diagnosis of cardiomegaly and identify the underlying pathology. Multimodal approaches in machine learning have been tested to various degrees, such as through combining medical images with basic demographics to predict endovascular treatment outcomes [30], or classifying skin lesions using a combination of dermoscopic images and patient age and sex [7]. There have also been efforts to use multimodal data to classify cardiomegaly by combining imaging data, with extensive non-imaging data (patient metadata, lab results, and vital signs) [10].

In this paper, we consider the classification of cardiomegaly by mimicking existing diagnostic pathways - we combine domain knowledge in the form of two image-derived digital biomarkers with imaging and non-imaging data from the Intensive Care Unit (ICU). The digital biomarkers used here are CTR and the cardiopulmonary area ratio (CPAR), the latter being a proxy for the cardiothoracic area ratio which has been used to evaluate cardiac function [19]. While CTR is the classic clinical value, it only measures horizontal expansion, while the CPAR provides a more holistic measure of cardiac enlargement. We assess the predictive power of models using different combinations of data modalities: imaging data, non-imaging ICU data and combination of imaging and non-imaging data. Finally, we compare models incorporating domain knowledge-based digital biomarkers CTR and CPAR with the black-box multimodal approaches.

2 Data and Methods

2.1 Data Sources

We used four publicly available databases: MIMIC-CXR [9,17], MIMIC-IV [9, 16], JSRT [31] and Montgomery County [2,15].

MIMIC-IV Database. This database contains medical data for 382,278 patients from the Beth Israel Deaconess Medical Center Intensive Care Units between 2008 and 2019. MIMIC-IV is structured into three sections: *core* (patient metadata, ward transfers), *icu* (vital sign time series, ICU procedures), and *hosp* (laboratory results, prescriptions).

MIMIC-CXR Database. This is a large publicly available database which contains 227,835 studies for 65,379 patients (a subset of the MIMIC-IV patients) from 2011 to 2016 collected from the Beth Israel Deaconess Medical Center Emergency Department. Each study contains one or more chest radiographs taken from different positions for a total of 377,110 images. Additionally, each study is accompanied by a semi-structured free-text radiology report describing the the findings of the radiologist. In this study we primarily use MIMIC-CXR-JPG [18] which is derived from MIMIC-CXR, containing the same images in the JPG format instead of the original DICOM format. While there is a certain loss of information by using JPG, the DICOM format can be difficult to use and comprehend, hence JPG format is preferred.

JSRT Database. The Japanese Society of Radiological Technology (JSRT) database is a publicly available database of posterior-anterior chest radiographs collected from medical centers in Japan and the USA. The database consists of 247 chest radiographs. The associated database, Segmentation Chest Radiographs [8], provides segmentation masks of lungs and heart.

Montgomery County Database. This is a publicly available database of chest radiographs collected from the Tuberculosis control program by the Department of Health and Human Services of Montgomery County, USA. It contains 138 chest radiographs, and contains segmentation masks of lungs.

2.2 Dataset Preparation

We prepared two new datasets, described below, one to train and test digital biomarkers models and the second to train and test the cardiomegaly classifiers.

CTR Dataset. The CTR dataset was created to train and test the models used to calculate the image-based digital biomarkers CTR and CPAR. It combines the JSRT, Montgomery County and MIMIC-CXR databases containing a total of 585 chest radiographs (247 from JSRT, 138 from Montgomery County, and 200 from MIMIC-CXR), and their associated segmentation masks for the heart and lungs. The JSRT database has an associated database, Segmentation Chest Radiographs, which contains segmentations of the heart and lungs. For Montgomery County Database, we used the included lung segmentations and supplemented this with manual, clinician supervised, segmentations of the heart. For MIMIC-CXR, we selected 200 random posterior-anterior chest radiographs with labels *fracture, consolidation* and *support devices*. Any samples also present in the cardiomegaly dataset, described below, were removed. Lung and heart segmentation masks for MIMIC-CXR images were manually completed under the supervision of a clinician. The manually completed segmentations will be released in due course.

Cardiomegaly Dataset. The cardiomegaly dataset was used to train and test the cardiomegaly classifiers. It combines data from MIMIC-CXR-JPG and MIMIC-IV. MIMIC-CXR-JPG comes with four cardiomegaly labels: *positive, negative, uncertain* and *no mention*. These labels were extracted from two natural language processing tools, NegBio [23] and CheXpert [13]. We only used images where both tools agreed on the label and further removed all *uncertain* and *no mention* labels, since in the last case we could not exclude cardiomegaly. This criteria reduced the size of the MIMIC-CXR dataset to 54,954 studies (81,346 radiographs) for 23,303 patients.

Cardiomegaly is identified from posterior-anterior radiographs, to avoid the unnatural enlargement of the cardiac silhouette which may occur from the anterior-posterior view. As such, we linked ICU stays from MIMIC-IV with the closest radiographic study containing a posterior-anterior chest radiograph, within a window of 365 days before the patient entered the ICU and up to 90 days after the discharge (see Fig. 1). This was completed using a unique patient across the MIMIC-CXR-JPG and MIMIC-IV datasets. This produced a dataset of 2,774 multimodal samples, each sample contains chest radiographs and ICU vital sign values, laboratory results and patient metadata. For more details see [10].

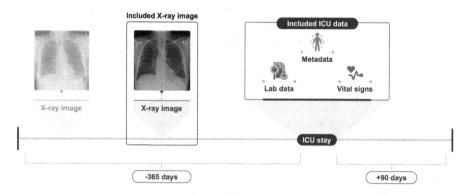

Fig. 1. We merged the closest radiographic study within a time window of 365 days prior to ICU admission and 90 days after release to the data collected during the patient's ICU stay.

2.3   Pre-processing

Imaging Data. To improve model robustness images were re-sized to squared images (244 pixels for cardiomegaly prediction, 256 for segmentation) and pixel values were normalized before input to models under both test and train conditions. Under train conditions only, we also performed standard data augmentation steps including random vertical and horizontal flips and random rotation up to $10°$.

Non-imaging Data. Patient metadata was combined with time-series data such as vital sign recordings, using summary statistics such as minimum, maximum, and mean values.

2.4   Models

Heart and Lung Detection. For the detection of hearts and lungs from chest radiographs, we implemented a Faster R-CNN [26] architecture with a ResNet-50 backbone [12] which was pre-trained on ImageNet [5]. Faster R-CNN has shown previously to perform well in clinical object detection tasks [29]. Independent models were trained for heart and lung detection, each model was trained for 300 epochs using the Adam optimiser [20] with a learning rate reduced by a factor of 0.5 on validation intersection over union (IoU) loss plateau. The model iteration with the lowest validation IoU loss was saved.

Heart and Lung Segmentation. For the segmentation of heart and lungs from chest radiographs we implemented a Mask R-CNN [11] architecture with a ResNet-50 backbone which was pre-trained on ImageNet. Mask R-CNN architectures have shown to provide good results in clinical segmentation tasks [6]. For detection, independent models were trained for heart segmentation and lung segmentation. Each model was trained for 300 epochs using the Adam optimiser and with a learning rate which reduced by a factor of 0.5 on validation IoU loss plateau. In order for the loss to be comparable to the detection, bounding boxes were used to calculate IoU loss. To find the bounding boxes the output masks were made into binary masks using Otsu thresholding [22]. The model iteration with the lowest validation IoU loss was saved. In order to have a metric to evaluate the masks, Dice loss [21] was also calculated for predicted masks.

Cardiomegaly Classification with Non-imaging Data. For cardiomegaly classification using non-imaging ICU data as well as the derived digital biomarkers CTR and CPAR (all stored in tabular format), we implemented XGBoost algorithms [4]. XGBoost is known to perform well for similar classification tasks, especially on sparse data [3,24]. A weighted cross-entropy loss was implemented for training. For these XGBoost models we optimised learning rate, maximum tree depth, and tree sub-sample (the fraction of the database sampled to train each tree) through grid search. The XGBoost model which used only CTR and CPAR values as features had a lower max tree depth, than XGBoost models using the ICU non-imaging data. The exact numerical values of the model hyperparameters can be found in Table 1.

Cardiomegaly Classification with Imaging Data. For cardiomegaly classification using images only, we implemented a ResNet-50 architecture pre-trained on ImageNet. This architecture was shown to provide state-of-the-art results with radiology classification tasks, achieving 0.84 accuracy in classifying cardiomegaly on the CheXpert database [1]. The ResNet-50 algorithm uses a cross-entropy loss function with an Adam optimizer and cyclical learning rates [32]. The network was trained in two stages, for the first 15 epochs we trained only the fully connected layers, before unfreezing the convolutional layers and training the full network at a lower maximum learning rate as the optimal maximum learning rate bounds vary [32]. The numerical values for the learning rate bounds can be found in Table 1.

Cardiomegaly Classification with Multimodal Imaging and Non-imaging Data. For classification of cardiomegaly using the multimodal dataset we implemented the network structure proposed in Grant et al. [10]. This architecture combines imaging (chest radiographs) and non-imaging data (metadata, vital sign values, laboratory values and digital biomarkers) by concatenating outputs of the X-ray feature block and the ICU feature block into the joint feature block (shown in Fig. 2). This method has provided good performance [10] and was used to integrate the digital biomarkers, CTR and CPAR, into the classification process. The training was again completed using the Adam optimizer, cyclical learning rates, binary cross-entropy and was completed in two stages. The convolutional layers of the ResNet in the X-ray feature block are frozen and all fully connected layers in the network are trained for 15 epochs with cyclical learning rates. Once the ResNet layers were then unfrozen, the model was trained for 45 epochs with cyclical learning rates using a lower max learning rate. As above, the numerical values for the learning rate bounds and other parameters describing the multimodal network can be found in Table 1. The concatenation layer used to merge the two modalities uses 32 nodes from the X-ray feature block and 16 nodes from the ICU feature block.

2.5 CTR and CPAR: Computation and Model Integration

To compute the CTR and CPAR values, we trained the segmentation and detection models described in Sect. 2.4. To do this we split the CTR dataset into train (80%), validation (10%) and test (10%) subsets; each subset containing a consistent proportion of the JSRT, Montgomery County, and MIMIC databases. Individual models were trained for heart detection, heart segmentation, lung detection and lung segmentation.

CTR Computation. The CTR was computed as the ratio of the widths of the cardiac and pulmonary bounding boxes. To find cardiac and pulmonary bounding boxes we investigated four methods: detection, segmentation, best score ensemble, and average ensemble. For the detection method, bounding boxes output by the Faster R-CNN models were used directly. For the segmentation method, masks output by the Mask R-CNN models were first passed though Otsu thresholding to give a binary mask. From the binary masks cardiac and pulmonary

Table 1. Numerical values of hyperparameters used in different models.

Model	Hyperparameter	Value
XGBoost	Learning rate	0.1
	Tree sub-sample	0.75
	Max tree depth	8 (Tabular models)
		3 (CTR only model)
ResNet	Network depth	ResNet-50
	Learning rate bounds	1e−05–1e−02 (stage 1)
		2e−05–1e−03 (stage 2)
Multimodal	CNN depth	ResNet-50
	ICU Network size	3 Fully connected layers
	Learning rate bounds	1e−05–1e−02 (stage 1)
		2e−05–1e−03 (stage 2)

bounding boxes for the heart and the lungs were found. For the best score ensemble method each sample was passed through both the Faster R-CNN and Mask R-CNN models. The cardiac and pulmonary predictions with the highest score were then selected as the final heart/lung bounding box. For the average ensemble method, each X-ray image was passed through both the Faster R-CNN and Mask R-CNN models. The cardiac and pulmonary predictions were found by producing a point wise average of the bounding box corner coordinates. The methods with the highest IoU on the test set were used to select the final cardiac and pulmonary bounding boxes in the multimodal network.

CPAR Computation. CPAR was computed using the area of the Otsu thresholded masks produced from the segmentation models. The areas of binary masks were used as the cardiac and pulmonary areas and the CPAR was calculated by finding the ratio of the two areas.

Integration of CTR and CPAR into the Multimodal Network. To combine the image-derived digital biomarkers CTR and CPAR with the cardiomegaly classifiers the two methods described above were integrated into the pre-processing stage of our multimodal approach as shown in Fig. 2. CTR and CPAR are combined with the pre-processed ICU data and passed either to the XGBoost models (non-imaging data only) or to the multimodal network via a feedforward neural network in the ICU feature block.

When training the various modality combinations for cardiomegaly classification we used 5-fold stratified cross-validation, each fold is independent of the others with no image repeated between folds and each fold having a similar positive/negative label distribution. When training each combination, four folds were combined for train data and the last fold was split in half for the validation and test data.

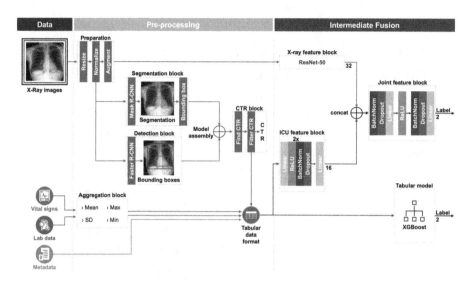

Fig. 2. In the pre-processing step, data is split into tabular (non-imaging ICU data and digital biomarkers) and imaging formats. To generate the biomarkers radiographs are normalised and passed into the segmentation and detection blocks to extract cardiac and pulmonary bounding boxes and masks; then, the CTR bock uses the results from assembled model to find the CTR and CPAR values. The digital biomarker values (CTR and CPAR) are subsequently combined with the non-imaging ICU data (metadata, vital signs, and lab results) into a tabular format. Next, the image data and the combined tabular data are handled either by intermediate or early fusion approach. For the intermediate fusion approach, the image data is augmented and features are extracted by a ResNet-50 in the X-ray feature block. The tabular data is handled via a feedforward neural network in the ICU feature block. Finally, the imaging features are combined with the non-imaging features in the joint feature block via a concatenation layer. Alternatively, for the early fusion approach, predictions are obtained from the tabular data alone via an XGBoost model.

3   Results

3.1   CTR Computation

The performance of the R-CNN model configurations on the CTR test sets is summarised in Table 2 in the form of average IoU scores calculated on the bounding boxes and average precision scores (i.e. area under the curve on a smoothed precision-recall curve) at threshold IoU values of 0.75, 0.85, and 0.95. Additionally, the Dice scores of heart and lung Mask R-CNN models on test sets using the thresholded binary masks were calculated; the heart and lung segmentation models having Dice scores of 0.906 and 0.937, respectively.

For cardiac bounding boxes the best score ensemble model showed the strongest performance with an average IoU score of 0.836 over the test set. For pulmonary bounding boxes the strongest model is the averaged prediction ensemble model with an average IoU score of 0.908 over the test set. As such, these two ensemble models were integrated in the multimodal cardiomegaly classification network to find cardiac and thoracic widths and CTR values. An example of output predictions by each model type and by a combination of the best models is given in Fig. 3.

Table 2. IoU score and AP at IoU thresholds of 0.75, 0.85, and 0.95 for bounding boxes found using Fast R-CNN, Mask R-CNN, and ensemble models on test data.

Model	IoU score	AP@0.75	AP@0.85	AP@0.95
Heart Detection	0.810	0.900	0.398	0.020
Heart Segmentation	0.834	0.963	0.678	**0.028**
Heart Ensemble (best)	**0.836**	**0.966**	**0.681**	**0.028**
Heart Ensemble (avg)	0.833	0.954	0.572	–
Lungs Detection	0.853	0.970	0.636	0.100
Lungs Segmentation	0.894	**1.0**	0.963	0.088
Lungs Ensemble (best)	0.852	0.970	0.638	0.100
Lungs Ensemble (avg)	**0.908**	**1.0**	**0.938**	**0.218**

3.2 Multimodal Classification

The performance of models with and without the image-derived digital biomarkers CTR and CPAR are summarised in Table 3 using accuracy (Acc), F1-Score (F1), and area under the receiver operating characteristic curve (AUC). The results scores are averaged over 5-fold cross-validation.

The XGBoost model on non-imaging ICU data showed a distinctly weaker performance (72.4% accuracy) compared to the ResNet-50 on imaging data only (81.9% accuracy), and multimodal network using imaging and non-imaging ICU data (81.9% accuracy). All models which included the digital biomarkers (CTR and CPAR) had comparable performance with accuracy ranging from 81.0% (multimodal network with digital biomarkers) to 82.1% (non-imaging ICU data with digital biomarkers). Overall, all models which included image derived information, either in the form of the digital biomarkers, or direct input of images, had similar level of performance with a accuracy range of 1.1%.

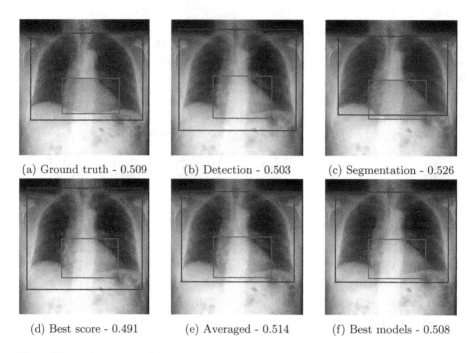

(a) Ground truth - 0.509   (b) Detection - 0.503   (c) Segmentation - 0.526

(d) Best score - 0.491   (e) Averaged - 0.514   (f) Best models - 0.508

Fig. 3. Example output of different methods for finding the bounding boxes and their corresponding calculated CTR values. The best output uses the best score model for cardiac bounding box and averaged model for pulmonary bounding boxes.

Table 3. Performance for different modality combinations with and without digital biomarkers, values averaged over 5-fold cross-validation, with standard deviation in brackets. *includes both digital biomarkers, CTR and CPAR. **includes images, ICU data, and digital biomarkers

Data used	Model type	Acc	F1	AUC
Images	ResNet-50	0.819 (0.015)	0.874 (0.010)	0.767 (0.029)
ICU data	XGBoost	0.723 (0.030)	0.807 (0.022)	0.651 (0.034)
Images + ICU data	Multimodal	0.819 (0.017)	0.873 (0.013)	0.768 (0.018)
CTR*	XGBoost	0.814 (0.014)	0.859 (0.011)	0.810 (0.012)
ICU data + CTR*	XGBoost	0.821 (0.019)	0.860 (0.012)	0.813 (0.011)
All**	Multimodal	0.810 (0.012)	0.872 (0.009)	0.732 (0.014)

4   Discussion

4.1   Principal Findings

In this work, we considered the classification of cardiomegaly by combining domain knowledge digital biomarkers CTR and CPAR with imaging and non-imaging ICU data. Our results suggest that the multimodal and image-based models are unable to extract additional information beyond what is captured by models trained on CTR and CPAR only. Thus, in the context of cardiomegaly, complicated black-box models may be replaced with carefully curated digital biomarkers, which convey critical clinical information.

4.2   Comparison to Related Works

Sogancioglu et al. [33] compared the predictive power of a black box image classifier to a CTR-based model for cardiomegaly classification, and achieved state of the art results with the later. The CTR-based model outperformed the classic image classification, with AUC values of 0.977 and 0.941, respectively. The conclusions presented in Sogancioglu et al., are in line with the results produced in this work, as the XGBoost model using only CTR and CPAR had an AUC of 0.810, outperforming the ResNet-50 (AUC of 0.767). However, there is a significant difference in the performance of the models in this work compared to their counterparts in Sogancioglu et al., this may be attributed to larger training datasets, cleaner data, and better models. Firstly, the classifiers in Sogancioglu et al. were trained on $65,205$ samples, this contrast to the $2,774$ samples used in this work. Additionally, Sogancioglu et al. excluded any samples where the cardiac boundary was difficult to find, these samples were a notable cause of misclassifications in this work. Lastly, Sogancioglu et al. claimed that the quality of the segmentation models is the most important factor in determining the performance of the CTR-based classifier. Their models performed well achieving IoU scores of 0.87 and 0.95 for heart and lung segmentation respectively. This compares favourably to the IoU scores achieved in this work, 0.836 for heart and 0.907 for lung detection. This may partially be attributed to a larger amount of higher quality data, as Sogancioglu et al. again excluded challenging samples; they used a total of 778 filtered samples to train the segmentation models, compared to 585 unfiltered samples in this work.

For multimodal classification of cardiomegaly, Grant et al. [10] is most relevant, comparing unimodal and multimodal approaches. The multimodal approaches included images, patient metadata, as well as extensive ICU data. The multimodal approach (accuracy of 0.837 and AUC of 0.880) marginally outperformed the image-only ResNet-50 (accuracy of 0.797 and AUC of 0.840), and greatly outperformed the non-imaging only model (accuracy of 0.700 and AUC of 0.684). Results achieved by Grant et al. are comparable to the results from this work, as the multimodal approaches outperform unimodal ones, with a large drop in performance if no images or image-derived data is included (i.e. no raw images or image-derived biomarkers).

4.3   Strengths and Weaknesses of the Study

Automated Image Classification. An advantage of automatic image labelling tools is that they often avoid cognitive biases. For instance, after making an initial pathological finding on a radiograph, a clinician is less likely to identify further pathological features - a form of premature conclusion bias. Since automatic tools are not subject to this bias, their addition to clinical workflows may increase the pick-up rates of secondary pathologies. In the specific context of this paper, cardiomegaly may be an indicator of many underlying cardiac pathologies and is associated with higher short-term mortality [34], hence the early identification of cardiomegaly is vital. The automatic identification of cardiomegaly can therefore serve as preventative care and a screening tool for cardiac pathologies.

Domain-Based Digital Biomarkers. The CTR (and CPAR) are a clinically valuable diagnostic tools showing high performance when used with classification models (e.g. XGBoost). Since they contain clinically relevant information, their use alongside patient medical data allows the models to more closely imitate the holistic approach taken by clinicians and more accurately reflects existing diagnostic pathways. Hence, leading to a higher degree of confidence in model predictions.

Misclassification Errors. We estimated the digital biomarkers CTR and CPAR values using Mask R-CNN and Fast R-CNN models. Figure 4 shows common cases of false positives and negatives from the XGBoost model trained using the digital biomarkers. The common causes of misclassification are interference from other pathologies leading to inaccurate cardiac and thoracic widths and models' failures to accurately identify the heart.

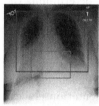 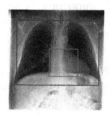 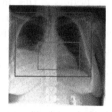 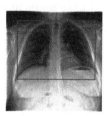

  (a) False negative   (b) False negative   (c) False positive   (d) False positive

Fig. 4. False positive and false negative classifications from XGBoost model trained using only digital biomarkers. Suspected causes of error for the respective images are: (a) area of parenchymal opacity around heart hides heart boundary leading to inaccurate cardiac bounding box; (b) R-CNN models failed to correctly identify image-right boundary of heart; (c) pleural effusion in image-left lung causing pulmonary bounding box width to be smaller than thoracic width; (d) R-CNN models failed to identify heart.

Label Errors. The cardiomegaly labels were derived from the free text reports associated with chest radiographs. These labels may contain errors since the radiographs alone may be insufficient for definitive cardiomegaly diagnosis. Also, the automatic label extraction from the free test reports may be another source of error [13,23]. It is known that these procedures can introduce noise and affect model performance [18]. We took steps to mitigate these errors by employing the procedures described in Sect. 2.2.

Acknowledgements. BWP acknowledges Rutherford Fund at Health Data Research UK (HDR UK) (MR/S004092/1) and Nuffield Department of Population Health (NDPH) Senior Research Fellowship.

References

1. Bressem, K.K., Adams, L.C., Erxleben, C., Hamm, B., Niehues, S.M., Vahldiek, J.L.: Comparing different deep learning architectures for classification of chest radiographs. Sci. Rep. **10**(1), 13590 (2020)
2. Candemir, S., et al.: Lung segmentation in chest radiographs using anatomical atlases with nonrigid registration. IEEE Trans. Med. Imaging **33**(2), 577–590 (2014)
3. Chang, W., et al.: A machine-learning-based prediction method for hypertension outcomes based on medical data. Diagnostics **9**(4), 178 (2019)
4. Chen, T., Guestrin, C.: XGBoost: a scalable tree boosting system. In: Proceedings of the 22nd ACM SIGKDD International Conference on Knowledge Discovery and Data Mining, pp. 785–794. KDD 2016. ACM, New York, NY, USA (2016)
5. Deng, J., Dong, W., Socher, R., Li, L.J., Kai, L., Li, F-F.: ImageNet: a large-scale hierarchical image database. In: Institute of Electrical and Electronics Engineers (IEEE), pp. 248–255 (2010)
6. Durkee, M., Abraham, R., Ai, J., Fuhrman, J., Clark, M., Giger, M.: Comparing mask r-CNN and u-net architectures for robust automatic segmentation of immune cells in immunofluorescence images of lupus nephritis biopsies. In: Leary, J., Tarnok, A., Georgakoudi, I. (eds.) Imaging, Manipulation, and Analysis of Biomolecules, Cells, and Tissues XIX. SPIE, March 2021
7. Gessert, N., Nielsen, M., Shaikh, M., Werner, R., Schlaefer, A.: Skin lesion classification using ensembles of multi-resolution EfficientNets with meta data. MethodsX **7**, 100864 (2020)
8. van Ginneken, B., Stegmann, M., Loog, M.: Segmentation of anatomical structures in chest radiographs using supervised methods: a comparative study on a public database. Med. Image Anal. **10**(1), 19–40 (2006)
9. Goldberger, A.L., et al.: PhysioBank, PhysioToolkit, and PhysioNet: components of a new research resource for complex physiologic signals. Circulation **101**(23), e215–e220 (2000)
10. Grant, D., Papież, B., Parsons, G., Tarassenko, L., Mahdi, A.: Deep learning classification of cardiomegaly using combined imaging and non-imaging ICU data. In: Medical Image Understanding and Analysis, pp. 547–558. Springer International Publishing, July 2021. https://doi.org/10.1007/978-3-030-80432-9_40
11. He, K., Gkioxari, G., Dollár, P., Girshick, R.: Mask R-CNN (2017)
12. He, K., Zhang, X., Ren, S., Sun, J.: Deep residual learning for image recognition. In: Proceedings of the IEEE Computer Society Conference on Computer Vision and Pattern Recognition, vol. 2016-Decem, pp. 770–778. IEEE Computer Society (2016)
13. Irvin, J., et al.: CheXpert: a large chest radiograph dataset with uncertainty labels and expert comparison. In: 33rd AAAI Conference on Artificial Intelligence. AAAI 2019, 31st Innovative Applications of Artificial Intelligence Conference, IAAI 2019 and the 9th AAAI Symposium on Educational Advances in Artificial Intelligence, EAAI 2019, vol. 33, pp. 590–597. AAAI Press (2019)

14. Ishida, T., Katsuragawa, S., Chida, K., MacMahon, H., Doi, K.: Computer-aided diagnosis for detection of cardiomegaly in digital chest radiographs. In: Medical Imaging 2005: Image Processing, vol. 5747, p. 914. SPIE (2005)
15. Jaeger, S., et al.: Automatic tuberculosis screening using chest radiographs. IEEE Trans. Med. Imaging **33**(2), 233–245 (2014)
16. Johnson, A., Bulgarelli, L., Pollard, T., Horng, S., Celi, L.A., Mark, R.: MIMIC-IV v0.4. Tech. rep., MIT Laboratory for Computational Physiology (2020)
17. Johnson, A.E.W., et al.: MIMIC-CXR, a de-identified publicly available database of chest radiographs with free-text reports. Sci. Data **6**(1), 1–8 (2019)
18. Johnson, A.E.W., et al.: MIMIC-CXR-JPG, a large publicly available database of labeled chest radiographs. arXiv (2019)
19. Karaman, S.: Cardiothoracic area ratio for evaluation of ejection fraction in patients. J. Clin. Anal. Med. **10**, 188–192 (2019)
20. Kingma, D.P., Ba, J.L.: Adam: a method for stochastic optimization. In: 3rd International Conference on Learning Representations, ICLR 2015 - Conference Track Proceedings. International Conference on Learning Representations, ICLR (2015)
21. Milletari, F., Navab, N., Ahmadi, S.: V-Net: fully convolutional neural networks for volumetric medical image segmentation. In: 2016 Fourth International Conference on 3D Vision (3DV), pp. 565–571 (2016)
22. Otsu, N.: A threshold selection method from gray-level histograms. IEEE Trans. Syst. Man Cybern. **9**(1), 62–66 (1979)
23. Peng, Y., Wang, X., Lu, L., Bagheri, M., Summers, R., Lu, Z.: NegBio: a high-performance tool for negation and uncertainty detection in radiology reports (2017)
24. Pimentel, M.A.F., et al.: Detecting deteriorating patients in hospital: development and validation of a novel scoring system. Am. J. Respir. Crit. Care Med. **204**, 44–52 (2021)
25. Que, Q., et al.: CardioXNet: automated detection for cardiomegaly based on deep learning. In: Proceedings of the Annual International Conference of the IEEE Engineering in Medicine and Biology Society, EMBS, vol. 2018-July, pp. 612–615. Institute of Electrical and Electronics Engineers Inc. (2018)
26. Ren, S., He, K., Girshick, R., Sun, J.: Faster R-CNN: towards real-time object detection with region proposal networks (2015)
27. Rimmer, A.: Radiologist shortage leaves patient care at risk, warns royal college. BMJ **359**, j4683 (2017)
28. Rosman, D., et al.: Imaging in the land of 1000 hills: Rwanda radiology country report. J. Glob. Radiol. **1**(1), 5 (2015)
29. Sa, R., et al.: Intervertebral disc detection in x-ray images using faster R-CNN. In: 2017 39th Annual International Conference of the IEEE Engineering in Medicine and Biology Society (EMBC). IEEE, July 2017
30. Samak, Z.A., Clatworthy, P., Mirmehdi, M.: Prediction of thrombectomy functional outcomes using multimodal data. In: Papież, B.W., Namburete, A.I.L., Yaqub, M., Noble, J.A. (eds.) MIUA 2020. CCIS, vol. 1248, pp. 267–279. Springer, Cham (2020). https://doi.org/10.1007/978-3-030-52791-4_21
31. Shiraishi, J., et al.: Development of a digital image database for chest radiographs with and without a lung nodule. Am. J. Roentgenol. **174**(1), 71–74 (2000)
32. Smith, L.N.: Cyclical learning rates for training neural networks. In: Proceedings - 2017 IEEE Winter Conference on Applications of Computer Vision, WACV 2017, pp. 464–472. Institute of Electrical and Electronics Engineers Inc. (2017)
33. Sogancioglu, E., Murphy, K., Calli, E., Scholten, E.T., Schalekamp, S., Van Ginneken, B.: Cardiomegaly detection on chest radiographs: segmentation versus classification. IEEE Access **8**, 94631–94642 (2020)

34. Yen, T., Lin, J.L., Lin-Tan, D.T., Hsu, K.H.: Cardiothoracic ratio, inflammation, malnutrition, and mortality in diabetes patients on maintenance hemodialysis. Am. J. Med. Sci. **337**(6), 421–428 (2009)

Proton Density Fat Fraction of Breast Adipose Tissue: Comparison of the Effect of Fat Spectra and Initial Evaluation as a Biomarker

Isobel Gordon[1,2]([✉]) ⓘ, George Ralli[2] ⓘ, Carolina Fernandes[2] ⓘ, Amy Herlihy[2] ⓘ, and Sir Michael Brady[2,3] ⓘ

[1] Nuffield Department of Women's and Reproductive Health, University of Oxford, Oxford, England
isobel.gordon@new.ox.ac.uk
[2] Perspectum Ltd., Oxford, England
[3] Department of Oncology, University of Oxford, Oxford, England

Abstract. The composition of breast adipose tissue has been shown to vary according to disease state. Proton density fat fraction (PDFF) is a quantitative MR biomarker which has not yet been thoroughly examined in the characterisation of breast fat; this work therefore explores the estimation of breast-specific PDFF. An MR spectrum derived from healthy breast fat is shown to perform significantly better in PDFF calculation of breast adipose tissue amongst a healthy cohort than either 6-peak or 9-peak subcutaneous fat spectra. Calculated PDFF values of breast adipose tissue suggest a similar composition between healthy breast fat and gluteal fat and a reference value of $91.6 \pm 3.0\%$ PDFF is found for healthy breast adipose tissue. Early results indicate that localised regions of lowered adipose PDFF are visible in proximity to both invasive and non-invasive breast cancer; this may be indicative of the inflammation and browning of mammary fat around tumour cells.

Keywords: Breast cancer · Proton density fat fraction · MRI

1 Introduction

Breast cancer is the single most common cancer in the UK [1] and the worldwide leading cause of cancer death amongst women [24]. Early detection of breast cancer greatly improves prognosis; this has led to nationwide screening of asymptomatic women. These screening initiatives exclusively use mammography and are restricted to postmenopausal women typically above the age of 50. The effectiveness of mammography is dramatically reduced in radiologically 'dense'

Supported by the Royal Commission for the Exhibition of 1851 and Perspectum Ltd. We also gratefully acknowledge the provision of MR spectral data by Gene Kim and Pippa Storey at New York University Grossman School of Medicine.

G. Yang et al. (Eds.): MIUA 2022, LNCS 13413, pp. 28–45, 2022.
https://doi.org/10.1007/978-3-031-12053-4_3

breasts [16], which have a high proportion of fibrous, functional tissue compared to fatty tissue. Breast density has been found to be the single most important risk factor for breast cancer in postmenopausal women [6] and thus the reporting of breast density is mandatory in most US states and several other territories.

High-risk younger women and postmenopausal women with dense breasts are increasingly offered 'abbreviated' MRI with protocols which include dynamic contrast enhanced MRI (DCE-MRI). DCE-MRI is primarily used to aid visualisation of increased localised vascularity that may indicate the presence of a tumour. This scan requires the injection of a contrast agent which is poorly tolerated by many patients and has a wide array of side effects. DCE-MRI also takes a substantial proportion of the MR imaging time, even in 'abbreviated' protocols, and is at best semi-quantitative. Current breast MRI protocols focus on detecting localised potential tumour regions despite increasing evidence showing that the composition of the breast parenchyma is important for assessing both pathology and cancer risk [6,28]. Quantitative characterisation of the whole breast parenchyma, rather than only the tumour, could enable the health of the whole breast to be examined and thereby lead to improved estimation of risk and improved patient care.

Proton density fat fraction (PDFF) is a quantitative MR biomarker which has been used extensively in the diagnosis, staging, and monitoring of non-alcoholic fatty liver disease (NAFLD) [22] and non-alcoholic steatohepatitis (NASH) [8]. Henze Bancroft et al. [4] recently demonstrated the use of proton density water fraction (PDWF) as a biomarker of mammographic breast density. However, PDFF has not yet been thoroughly studied as a useful metric in breast tissue characterisation itself. Initial work in this area is promising; a recent study by Hisanaga et al. [13] found that the fat fraction of adipose tissue around invasive breast cancer was associated with lymph node metastasis.

PDFF is typically quantified from multi-echo chemical shift encoded (CSE) MRI acquisitions, which exploit the different precession frequencies of fat and water to estimate fat content. These acquisitions are typically short and entirely non-invasive. Analysis of CSE-MRI acquisitions has typically used both the magnitude and phase information of the MRI signal to determine PDFF. However, such complex information may not be readily available in the clinical setting, and the inclusion of complex data can introduce artefacts which may impact PDFF quantification. Triay Bagur et al. [3] recently introduced a magnitude-only method (MAGO) to estimate liver PDFF which has been demonstrated to be robust to imaging artefacts.

To date, the incorporation of a breast-specific fat spectrum into PDFF calculation has not been studied. For example, Henze Bancroft et al. [4] assumed breast fat and subcutaneous fat to be equivalent, whilst the IDEAL-IQ fat fraction maps used in Hisanaga et al. [13] employ a liver-specific fat spectrum.

Human adipose tissue may generally be classified into two subtypes: brown adipose tissue (BAT), which is primarily used for heat generation, and white adipose tissue (WAT) which is predominantly used for energy storage. The PDFF of white and brown adipose tissue has been approximated through determination of PDFF in supraclavicular and gluteal adipose tissue [9]. BAT was found to have significantly lower PDFF than WAT; this is reflective of the lower lipid content and higher intracellular water content of BAT.

White adipocytes may differentiate into brown-like ('beige') adipocytes in a process referred to as 'browning'. Importantly, breast cancer tumour growth has been associated with the browning of mammary fat close to the tumour [23,26]. Moreover, Bos et al. [5] found larger volumes of BAT throughout the body in patients with cancer whilst Cao et al. [7] found three times as much BAT in breast cancer patients compared to patients with other cancers.

Furthermore, the release of proinflammatory cytokines has been associated with decreased lipid content in cancer-adjacent adipose tissue [18] and inflammation of adipose tissue has been found to be associated with both ductal carcinoma in situ [2] and invasive breast cancer [25]. Moreover, perilesional oedema may be found in proximity to invasive breast cancer; this may correlate to the aggressiveness of the disease [19].

We hypothesise that lower PDFF in breast adipose tissue may be associated with the browning and inflammation of mammary fat, or with perilesional oedema, and thereby associated with tumour growth. This may either be localised, further aiding the detection and categorisation of tumours, or spread through the breast, improving assessment of breast cancer risk.

This work explores the estimation of breast-specific PDFF. Firstly, adipose tissue is segmented within the highly heterogeneous breast structure. Next, the performance of five different fat spectra in the calculation of breast adipose PDFF is examined and values are reported across a healthy cohort. Finally, PDFF is examined in the adipose tissue immediately surrounding both cysts and cancerous lesions.

2   Methods

2.1   Data Acquisition

Participants were imaged in the prone position on a Siemens Magnetom Aera 1.5T scanner (Siemens Healthineers AG, Erlangen, Germany) using a bilateral 18-channel breast coil (Siemens Healthineers AG, Erlangen, Germany). Participants were scanned with a 3D axial 6-echo (TE1 = 1.81 ms, delta TE = 1.95 ms) gradient echo protocol designed to minimize T1 bias with a small flip angle (5°). The following additional acquisition parameters were used: TR = 15.0 ms, reconstructed in-plane resolution $1.7 \times 1.7\,\mathrm{mm}^2$, slice thickness 2.0 mm, acquired matrix size 128×128, FOV $440 \times 399\,\mathrm{mm}^2$, bandwidth 1560 Hz/Px. Typically, 80 slices covered the whole of both breasts, though this number was adjusted to ensure full coverage of larger breasts. For a scan with 80 slices, the acquisition time was 2 min and 19 s. Nine participants were additionally scanned with a multi-slice 2D axial 6-echo gradient echo sequence. The parameters were: TE1 = 1.30 ms, delta TE = 2.00 ms, TR = 14.0 ms, flip angle 5°, reconstructed in-plane resolution $1.7 \times 1.7\,\mathrm{mm}^2$, slice thickness 10.0 mm, slice distance factor 50%, acquired matrix size 128×128, FOV $440 \times 399\,\mathrm{mm}^2$, bandwidth 1560 Hz/Px, acquisition time 8 s. Five slices were acquired in the breasts with the position of the central slice matching that of the 3D CSE sequence described above. This sequence, referred to as 'LMS IDEAL' in Triay Bagur et al. [3], has been used extensively for quantification of PDFF in the liver and was acquired for comparative purposes; note that full coverage of the breast is not obtained with this 2D acquisition. In addition to these two gradient echo sequences, a high resolution T1-weighted volumetric scan was obtained for purposes of localisation and anatomical identification.

Forty-six female volunteers were scanned for this study; ethical approval was granted by South Central Ethics (NHS REC 20/WS/0110). Forty-two participants were healthy with no known breast lesions, whilst two volunteers had known breast cysts but were otherwise healthy. The healthy cohort was defined as these forty-four women. In addition, one participant had confirmed ductal carcinoma in situ (DCIS) in the left breast and one participant had confirmed invasive ductal carcinoma (IDC) in the right breast. Both participants with confirmed cancer underwent biopsy on a date at least 4 weeks prior to the MRI scan. The mean age of participants was 41 years (range 24–78 years). Written informed consent was obtained from all subjects prior to scanning.

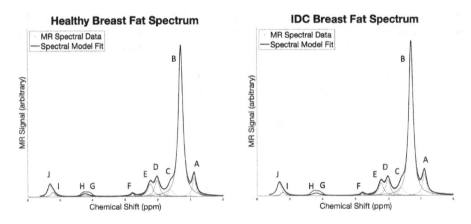

Fig. 1. MR spectra of a participant with no suspicious findings in MR images (designated 'healthy') (left) and a participant with invasive ductal carcinoma (IDC) (right).

2.2 Spectroscopic Analysis

Breast adipose MR spectroscopic data was derived from Freed et al. [10]. The group acquired a three-dimensional sagittal 144-echo gradient-echo sequence with a low flip angle and a bandwidth 694 Hz. A Fourier transform was applied to each voxel with corrections for phase and eddy currents to produce an MR spectrum. A region of interest (ROI) was drawn in the breast adipose tissue; the final spectrum for each patient was found by averaging across all voxels in the

ROI. As Freed et al.'s work concentrated on determining the relative amplitudes of just five select peaks in breast fat, we re-analysed the spectra to determine the relative amplitude of all peaks. We analysed two MR spectra provided by Freed et al.: one from the breast adipose tissue of a woman with no suspicious findings in MR images (designated 'healthy') and one from the breast adipose tissue of a woman with known invasive ductal carcinoma (IDC) (Fig. 1).

To minimize differences in linewidth, the free induction decay (FID) of the spectra were first multiplied by an exponential filter so that the methylene ('B') peak in both spectra had the same linewidth. A spectral model was fitted to the data consisting of a linear baseline and 10 Lorentizian line profiles, each of which corresponded to one of the 10 fat peaks identified by Freed et al. The data was fitted to this model using a non-linear least squares approach. The positions of the Lorentzian peaks were initially set to literature values but allowed to vary during the fit. The R^2 of the final fit to the spectral data was 0.997 in the spectrum taken from the participant with IDC, and 0.998 in the spectrum taken from the healthy participant. Finally, the area under each peak was found through integrating the Lorentzian equation associated with each peak across the whole spectrum (Table 1).

Table 1. Chemical shift values and relative areas of the fitted fat peaks in the MR spectra of the breast adipose tissue of a participant with no suspicious findings in MR images (designated 'healthy') and a participant with invasive ductal carcinoma (IDC).

Peak label	Healthy		IDC	
	Chemical shift (ppm)	Relative area (%)	Chemical shift (ppm)	Relative area (%)
J	5.32	4.15	5.32	5.25
I	5.22	1.90	5.21	1.42
H	4.24	1.07	4.29	0.43
G	4.16	1.06	4.17	1.82
F	2.77	0.87	2.79	0.64
E	2.23	6.67	2.23	6.32
D	2.02	7.81	2.03	6.96
C	1.61	3.38	1.59	4.26
B	1.30	66.73	1.30	64.64
A	0.89	6.37	0.89	8.26

2.3   PDFF Map Generation

The 6-echo gradient echo CSE data were processed using the MAGO algorithm [3] to produce maps of proton density fat fraction (PDFF) (Fig. 2). This confounder-corrected CSE method uses an input of a multi-peak spectral model for fat. The raw echo data was processed 5 separate times, each time using a different multi-peak spectral model. The spectral models included the two ten-peak breast fat spectra derived above, a nine-peak spectrum derived from subcutaneous adipose tissue [11], a six-peak spectrum derived from subcutaneous adipose tissue [21] and a six-peak spectrum derived from liver fat [12]. Whilst the composition of liver fat and breast adipose tissue are different, the liver fat spectrum is readily available in the clinical setting and well described in literature, therefore it was included in this analysis to enable assessment of its applicability to breast fat in PDFF quantification.

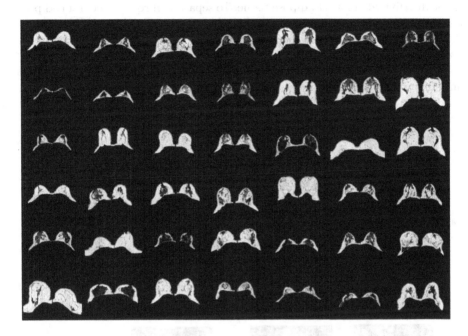

Fig. 2. Examples of central slices of PDFF maps calculated from 3D CSE-MRI.

2.4   Body Masking

A body masking approach was used to separate the breasts from surrounding noise in the PDFF maps. Initial masks were computed in the water and fat images separately by first square-root transforming the image intensities and computing an Otsu threshold. The two masks were morphologically opened using a spherical structuring element with a radius of 3 pixels and then combined into one mask with a logical OR operation. Morphological closing was then applied to the combined mask using the same spherical structuring element to produce the body mask shown in Fig. 3a.

To segment the breasts away from the body outline, the chest wall was manually delineated on the central slice of the proton density fat image. A line was drawn beneath each breast which extended out to the tip of the axillae, as shown in Fig. 3b. A mask was produced to include all pixels above this delineation which was then combined with the body mask calculated in Fig. 3a. This produced a mask of both breasts as shown in Fig. 3b. Figure 3c shows the resulting whole breast segmentation for the 3D CSE acquisition across three different participants.

2.5   Segmentation of Adipose Tissue from Fibrous Tissue

Breast tissue is highly heterogeneous, often containing thin strands of fibrous tissue distributed amongst adipose tissue. To separate fibrous tissue from adipose tissue, the monogenic signal was used as described in Ralli et al. [20] using a log-Gabor filter. Five filters were used with wavelengths 2, 3, 4, 5 and 6 pixels and a σ/f_0 ratio of 0.5 was used. For each CSE acquisition, phase symmetry was computed for the echo image that provided the highest contrast between fibrous and fatty tissue; this was the first echo time in the 3D CSE acquisition and the fourth echo time in the 2D CSE acquisition.

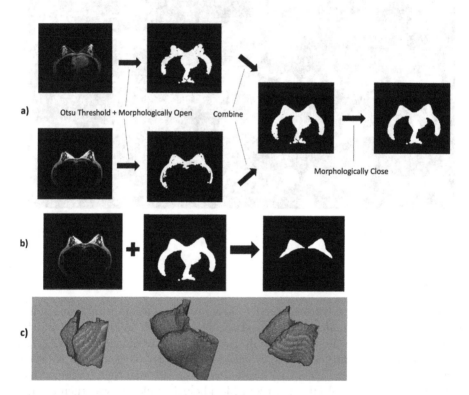

Fig. 3. Overview of segmentation of the whole breast a) Body mask produced from proton density water and fat images using morphology - one example slice shown b) Manual chest delineation combined with body mask to form mask of each breast c) Example whole breast masks produced using 3D CSE acquisitions.

Phase symmetry is computed from the responses of the even (log-Gabor) and odd (Riesz-transformed log-Gabor) filters. Phase symmetry measures the extent to which the even filter response dominates the odd response, and thus quantifies the extent to which a given voxel contains a symmetric feature. It was hypothesised that thin pieces of fibrous tissue surrounded by adipose tissue would have high phase symmetry values. An Otsu threshold was applied to the calculated phase symmetry map to provide a mask which identified thin strands of fibrous tissue.

Whilst the use of phase symmetry maps provided excellent identification of thinner segments of fibrous tissue, larger homogeneous clumps of fibrous tissue in the breast exist, and are especially prevalent amongst younger women. The edges of these areas are readily identified in the phase symmetry maps but the phase symmetry within a homogeneous region of fibrous tissue is approximately equal to the phase symmetry within a homogeneous region of fatty tissue. Therefore a purely phase-symmetry-based approach cannot readily identify these larger areas of fibrous tissue. This is demonstrated in the phase symmetry maps shown in the second column of Fig. 4, where thin strands of fibrous tissue are clearly identified but larger areas of fibrous tissue are not. An additional step ensured larger areas of fibrous tissue were identified and excluded from the masking of breast adipose tissue.

Fig. 4. Overview of adipose tissue segmentation, shown in a single slice of the 3D CSE acquisition for a participant with fatty breasts (top) and a participant with dense breasts (bottom). Left to right: the raw echo image; the phase symmetry map; the PDFF map with the breast mask calculated in Fig. 3b applied; the PDFF map with the threshold determined from multi-modal Gaussian histogram analysis applied; the PDFF map with both the histogram threshold applied and the phase symmetry mask applied.

For each dataset, the whole breast mask (Fig. 3b) was applied to the central slice of the PDFF map calculated using the healthy breast fat spectrum. A histogram was plotted of all PDFF values within this slice. As shown in Fig. 5, a multi-modal Gaussian model with three peaks was fitted to a kernel-smoothed estimate of the histogram using a non-linear least squares approach. The three peaks were hypothesised to correspond to: fibrous tissue (lowest PDFF values), adipose tissue (highest PDFF values) and mixed voxels. A threshold to exclude remaining areas of fibrous tissue was found by calculating the three sigma upper boundary for the central peak as shown in Fig. 5. This was hypothesised to correspond to the PDFF value at which 99.7% of fibrous-tissue-containing voxels were excluded. For each case, the calculation of this threshold value from the histogram distribution was reviewed, and when the multi-modal Gaussian model did not fit well (for example, in very fatty breasts where the two peaks containing fibrous tissue are sparsely populated), a manual threshold was selected through examination of the histogram distributions.

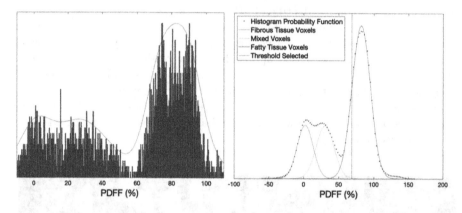

Fig. 5. Left: Example histogram of PDFF values within the central slice of the breast along with the probability density function of the histogram (not to scale). Right: Multi-modal Gaussian fitting to the probability density function of the histogram of PDFF values, showing identification of the threshold value.

To produce the final PDFF maps containing only breast adipose tissue the whole breast mask, the phase symmetry mask and the thresholding value determined from histogram analysis were all applied to the calculated PDFF maps. An overview of this process is shown for two example cases in Fig. 4.

3   Results

3.1   Variation in PDFF with Different Fat Spectra

The variation in PDFF resulting from the use of different fat spectra was measured through examination of the mean PDFF value in the breast adipose tissue of the healthy cohort, using the 3D CSE acquisition for each case. The mean R^2 value for the fit in the breast adipose tissue was also calculated. To obtain a measure of the PDFF of breast fat in each case, the mean PDFF value was calculated within the adipose tissue in the central 40 slices, corresponding to an axial slice stack of 8 cm. This central slice stack was used to exclude the effect of a phase-encoded motion artefact observed in the peripheral slices of the acquisition which contained minimal breast tissue.

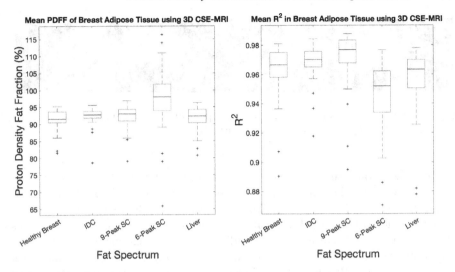

Fig. 6. Left: Box plot displaying variation in mean PDFF of breast adipose tissue as measured with 3D CSE-MRI using different fat spectra. Right: Box plot displaying variation in mean R^2 of PDFF fitting using different fat spectra. Left to right: Healthy breast fat spectrum, breast fat spectrum from participant with IDC, 9-peak subcutaneous fat spectrum, 6-peak subcutaneous fat spectrum, liver fat spectrum.

Figure 6 shows the distribution in measurement of breast adipose tissue PDFF and R^2 values across five different fat spectra. A significant difference was found in PDFF values calculated using the healthy breast fat spectrum and those calculated using the IDC fat spectrum (Wilcoxon rank sum test, p = 0.028). Additionally, a significant difference was found in PDFF values calculated using the healthy breast fat spectrum and those calculated using the 9-peak subcutaneous fat spectrum (p = 0.043). The 6-peak subcutaneous fat spectrum described by Ren et al. [21] demonstrated a very clear over-estimation of PDFF compared to all four other fat spectra (p << 0.001 for all comparisons). The PDFF values produced using the liver fat spectrum were not found to be significantly different to those produced using healthy breast fat (p = 0.238).

The overestimation in PDFF calculation of the 6-peak subcutaneous spectrum is reflected in its significantly lower distribution of R^2 values compared to other fat spectra (p = 0.0029 compared to liver fat spectrum, p << 0.001 for all other comparisons). Utilising the 6-peak liver fat spectrum was found to have significantly poorer R^2 performance than using the healthy breast fat spectra (p = 0.0456) or the 9-peak subcutaneous fat spectrum (p << 0.001). Though the 9-peak subcutaneous fat spectrum was found to have the highest median R^2, manual review of PDFF images showed that use of this spectrum often resulted in areas of artificially low PDFF due to poor fitting, as shown in Fig. 7. However, as these areas of artificially low PDFF were typically segmented out during the thresholding step described in the Sect. 2.5, such areas of poor fitting are not reflected in Fig. 6.

Fig. 7. Example PDFF map showing region of poor fitting using 9-peak subcutaneous fat spectrum (right) compared to using healthy breast fat spectrum (left).

To demonstrate this, for each case the mask calculated from the PDFF map generated with the healthy breast fat spectrum was applied to all the PDFF maps fitted with different spectra. This mask was manually reviewed against the high resolution T1-weighted acquisition to ensure that it excluded only regions of fibrous tissue and that any areas of adipose tissue which may be poorly fitted would still be included in the mask. As shown in Fig. 8, using the same mask across the different PDFF maps did indeed force these areas of poor fitting to be included. This resulted in the R^2 of PDFF fitting using the 9-peak subcutaneous fat spectrum (median R^2 0.951) being significantly lower than that using the healthy breast fat spectrum (median R^2 0.960, p-value of Wilcoxon rank sum test = 0.0085).

Utilising the healthy breast fat spectra, the median PDFF across breast adipose tissue in a healthy cohort was found to be $91.6 \pm 3.0\%$ (IQR 90.5–93.7%).

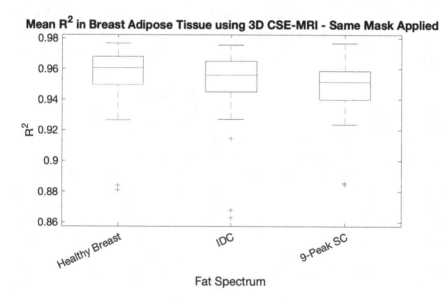

Fig. 8. Box plot displaying variation in mean R^2 of PDFF fitting in breast adipose tissue using the 3D CSE sequence and different fat spectra whilst applying the same adipose tissue mask derived from the use of the healthy breast fat spectrum to all data.

Franz et al. [9] found the PDFF of gluteal fat to be $90.8 \pm 4.5\%$ (IQR 81.4–96.2%) when measured with 3D 6-echo CSE-MRI, therefore suggesting similar adipose composition between healthy mammary and gluteal fat.

3.2 Variation in PDFF Calculation Between 2D and 3D CSE Acquisitions

Agreement between the 2D and 3D 6-echo gradient echo CSE acquisitions was assessed through calculation of the 95% Bland-Altman limits of agreement across the nine participants in the healthy cohort who were scanned with both acquisitions (Fig. 9). The mean PDFF value in the central slice was calculated for the 2D and 3D acquisitions, using the healthy volunteer breast fat spectrum. The 95% limits of agreement were -0.72% to 5.54% PDFF, with a bias of 2.41% ($2.41 \pm 3.13\%$), suggesting that the 3D acquisition typically measures a higher PDFF value within adipose tissue compared to the 2D acquisition. No trend was observed across the Bland-Altman plot, suggesting that the bias remains reasonably constant across varying PDFF values.

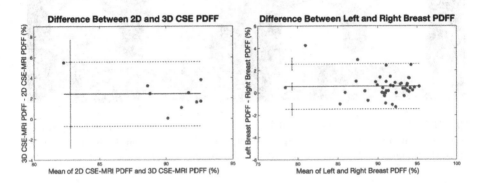

Fig. 9. Bland-Altman plots showing agreement between PDFF values of the breast adipose tissue in a healthy cohort calculated in the central slice of the 2D and 3D CSE acquisitions (left) and agreement between PDFF values of the breast adipose tissue in a healthy cohort calculated in left and right breasts (right). The 95% upper and lower limits of agreement are displayed (dotted lines), along with the confidence intervals for each limit of agreement (solid vertical lines).

3.3 Variation in PDFF Between Left and Right Breast

Agreement in PDFF measurement between left and right breast adipose tissue was assessed in the healthy cohort through calculation of the 95% Bland-Altman limits of agreement (Fig. 9). The mean PDFF value across the central slice stack of the 3D-CSE acquisition described in Sect. 3.1 was calculated for each participant's left breast and right breast, using the healthy volunteer breast fat spectrum. The 95% limits of agreement were -1.46% to 2.60% PDFF with a bias of 0.57% (0.57 ± 2.03%), demonstrating high agreement between the PDFF in breast adipose tissue found in each breast. No trend was observed in left-right breast PDFF agreement across varying PDFF values.

3.4   Variation in PDFF of Perilesional Adipose Tissue

The PDFF of breast adipose tissue immediately surrounding breast lesions was measured through application of user-drawn ROIs to single slices in the 3D CSE acquisition (Fig. 10). This was carried out in one participant with DCIS, one participant with IDC and in two participants with known breast cysts. The mean PDFF values extracted from the ROI in the adipose tissue around each lesion and the mean PDFF of the adipose tissue across the whole slice are displayed in Table 2. Breast cysts which were adjacent to adipose tissue were selected for measurement; note that cyst 2 and cyst 3 were present in the same participant, whilst cyst 1 was taken from a separate participant.

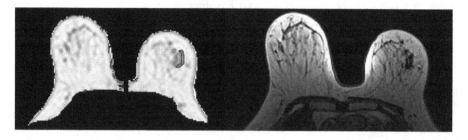

Fig. 10. Example images showing DCIS lesion: PDFF map (left) with user-drawn ROI (shown in blue) in surrounding adipose tissue and high resolution T1-weighted image at most similar slice location (right). (Color figure online)

ROIs were drawn in two adjacent PDFF slices where DCIS was identified and four adjacent slices where IDC was identified. Regions of partial voluming were excluded from the user-drawn ROIs, and inclusion of fibrous tissue was avoided through comparison to the high resolution T1-weighted images acquired at the most similar slice location. The difference in the PDFF of mammary fat around the lesion to the PDFF of mammary fat across the whole slice was found to be larger with DCIS than cysts, with a mean difference of 4.5% PDFF compared to 0.4% PDFF. The difference between the PDFF of perilesional adipose tissue and the PDFF of adipose tissue across the whole slice was found to be largest of all in the participant with IDC, with a mean difference of 5.6%.

Table 2. Table showing mean PDFF of breast adipose tissue surrounding different lesion types alongside the mean PDFF of all breast adipose tissue in the slice containing the lesion. The difference between these values for each lesion is shown, as well as the mean difference for each lesion type.

	DCIS		IDC				Cysts		
	Slice 1	Slice 2	Slice 1	Slice 2	Slice 3	Slice 4	Cyst 1	Cyst 2	Cyst 3
Mean PDFF around lesion (%)	87.5	87.1	86.2	84.3	85.3	83.5	88.6	90.1	91.6
Mean PDFF throughout slice (%)	91.8	91.8	90.3	90.7	90.4	90.3	89.2	89.8	92.5
Difference (%)	4.3	4.7	4.1	6.4	5.1	6.8	0.6	−0.2	0.9
Mean Difference (%)	4.5		5.6				0.4		

4 Discussion

An MR spectrum derived from the adipose tissue of a participant designated as healthy was shown to perform significantly better in breast adipose PDFF calculation than either 6-peak or 9-peak subcutaneous fat spectra. Calculated PDFF values of breast adipose tissue in a healthy cohort suggested a similar composition between breast fat and gluteal fat and the median PDFF across a healthy cohort was found to be $91.6 \pm 3.0\%$; this may have use as a reference value to compare pathology against. Early results indicated that adipose tissue surrounding both invasive and non-invasive cancers demonstrated lowered PDFF values which may be reflective of the browning or inflammation of mammary fat.

Phase symmetry maps enabled identification of thinner strands of fibrous tissue but did not identify larger areas of fibrous tissue such as those often seen in dense breasts. Whilst the use of multi-modal Gaussian fitting of histograms to provide a threshold for the exclusion of larger areas of fibrous tissue was successful, often voxels containing adipose tissue were excluded along with the fibrous tissue. Since the aim of this paper was to examine the PDFF of adipose tissue, exclusion of adipose voxels is preferable to inclusion of voxels containing fibrous tissue. However, for future work where precise identification of areas fibrous tissue may be required, we will explore other methods which do not dispose of spatial information, for example the use of phase asymmetry (rather than phase symmetry) to identify larger areas of homogeneous tissue.

Whilst the 9-peak subcutaneous fat spectrum showed the best R^2 performance when masks were individually calculated for the different PDFF maps, application of the same mask across the PDFF maps demonstrated the increased prevalence of regions of poor fitting when using this subcutaneous fat spectrum. This suggests that an alternative fat spectrum should be used in breast adipose PDFF calculation to ensure accurate quantification throughout the whole breast. When the same mask was applied to all PDFF maps, the R^2 performance was distinctly highest when using the healthy breast fat spectrum.

A significant difference was found amongst a healthy cohort in the PDFF values calculated with a healthy breast fat spectrum and a breast fat spectrum taken from a participant with invasive ductal carcinoma. This finding may prove to be an issue for the use of PDFF as a biomarker of the breast, as it may suggest the need for a fat spectrum particular to the patient's disease state. However, before this conclusion can be made, PDFF calculation with these two spectra would need to be evaluated in a cohort of patients with breast cancer and the effect of spectra from other participants, both those who are healthy and those who have cancer, should be examined. Additionally, the effect of this difference on disease identification with PDFF would need to be assessed; any bias incurred by use of an imperfect spectrum may not effect the sensitivity of PDFF to disease. For example, in Sect. 3.4, the same fat spectrum was used in PDFF calculation across a cohort with varying disease states and a differentiation between benign and malignant lesions was still observed.

The performance of the PDFF fitting was lowest when using the 6-peak liver fat spectrum and the 6-peak subcutaneous fat spectrum which may suggest that identification of more peaks within the fat spectrum leads to improved PDFF fitting within breast adipose tissue. However, the actual PDFF values calculated using the healthy breast fat spectrum were not significantly different from those calculated when using the liver fat spectrum. This suggests potential utility of the liver fat spectrum in measurement of breast adipose PDFF, thereby supporting the IDEAL-IQ maps used in the work of Hisanaga et al. [13].

High agreement and negligible bias were observed between left and right breast adipose PDFF in a healthy cohort, suggesting similar tissue composition. The bias seen in the comparison of 3D CSE PDFF to 2D CSE PDFF could result from the substantially thicker slice used in the 2D CSE acquisition. This may result in the inclusion of small pieces of fibrous tissue within voxels which are identified as containing only adipose tissue, thus lowering the estimate of PDFF compared to that of the 3D CSE acquisition.

Early results from a single invasive ductal carcinoma case agree with the findings of Hisanaga et al. [13] that the fat fraction of breast adipose tissue is distinctly lowered around invasive cancers. Excitingly, perilesional adipose fat fraction was also found to be distinctly lowered around ductal carcinoma in situ, suggesting potential utility of breast adipose PDFF as a biomarker of early-stage, non-invasive cancer.

Whilst these lowered fat fraction values could be caused by the inclusion of voxels with partial voluming artefact in the ROI, the difference between breast adipose PDFF across the whole slice and the PDFF around the lesion was found to be distinctly greater in both cancer cases than in the cases with cysts. This result agrees with the finding that increased browning of mammary fat occurs in proximity to cancerous lesions compared to benign lesions [26]. The lowered fat fraction values in proximity to cancer may also be reflective of inflammation or possibly oedema in the case of the participant with invasive cancer. Data from more participants with cancer, particularly non-invasive subtypes, must be processed and a less variable method of identifying the ROIs around lesions must be found before this result can be reported as significant. An improved method would account for varying amounts of fibrous tissue in proximity to the lesions.

There are several limitations associated with this study. Firstly, the segmentation of whole-breast adipose tissue is currently semi-automatic, requiring user intervention to delineate the chest wall and identify the tips of the axillae. An improved method could use machine learning to identify these anatomical markers, such as that demonstrated by Wei et al. [27]. Secondly, whilst R^2 has proven to be a valuable metric in assessing both the quality of PDFF maps [17] and the performance of different spectral models in PDFF map generation [14], it is not a definitive metric of the accuracy of PDFF calculation. This is not possible without ground truth measurement of fat content, such as that acquired histologically. Computation of other metrics such as the Cramer-Rao lower bound would further aid evaluation of the different spectral models in PDFF calculation. Thirdly, when the same adipose tissue mask was applied to PDFF maps generated with different spectra for the analysis shown in Fig. 8, the mask chosen was that calculated from the PDFF map processed with the healthy breast fat spectrum. This mask was chosen as it was manually reviewed to accurately include breast adipose tissue and not to exclude any regions of artificially lowered PDFF, such as those shown in Fig. 7. To avoid bias which may be incurred by applying an adipose tissue mask calculated using a particular fat spectrum, an improved method would apply a mask calculated from a separate MR sequence and co-register back to the CSE-MRI sequence. Finally, biopsy-induced effects such as oedema may affect the PDFF of adipose tissue adjacent to lesions. The biopsy for both participants with confirmed cancer was completed at least 4 weeks prior to their MRI scan, compliant with the guidelines in Ko et al. [15], though future work should include assessment of fat adjacent to needle-naive tumours.

To our knowledge, this work is the first to implement a breast-specific fat spectrum into the calculation of breast adipose PDFF and the first to have reported this parameter in a healthy cohort. We believe that with additional work across a more varied patient cohort, this parameter has exciting potential to characterise the breast parenchyma and identify early-stage cancer growth.

References

1. Breast cancer incidence (invasive) statistics, July 2021. https://www.cancerresearchuk.org/health-professional/cancer-statistics/statistics-by-cancer-type/breast-cancer/incidence-invasive

2. Almekinders, M.M., et al.: Breast adipocyte size associates with ipsilateral invasive breast cancer risk after ductal carcinoma in situ. npj Breast Cancer **7** (2021). https://doi.org/10.1038/s41523-021-00232-w

3. Bagur, A.T., Hutton, C., Irving, B., Gyngell, M.L., Robson, M.D., Brady, M.: Magnitude-intrinsic water-fat ambiguity can be resolved with multipeak fat modeling and a multipoint search method. Magn. Reson. Med. **82**, 460–475 (2019). https://doi.org/10.1002/mrm.27728

4. Bancroft, L.C.H., et al.: Proton density water fraction as a reproducible MR-based measurement of breast density. Magn. Reson. Med. (2021). https://doi.org/10.1002/mrm.29076, https://onlinelibrary.wiley.com/doi/10.1002/mrm.29076

5. Bos, S.A., Gill, C.M., Martinez-Salazar, E.L., Torriani, M., Bredella, M.A.: Preliminary investigation of brown adipose tissue assessed by PET/CT and cancer activity. Skeletal Radiol. **48**, 413–419 (2019). https://doi.org/10.1007/S00256-018-3046-X, https://link.springer.com/article/10.1007/s00256-018-3046-x

6. Boyd, N.F., Martin, L.J., Yaffe, M.J., Minkin, S.: Mammographic density and breast cancer risk: current understanding and future prospects. Breast Cancer Res. BCR **13** (2011). https://doi.org/10.1186/BCR2942, https://pubmed.ncbi.nlm.nih.gov/22114898/

7. Cao, Q., et al.: A pilot study of FDG PET/CT detects a link between brown adipose tissue and breast cancer. BMC Cancer **14**, 126 (2014). https://doi.org/10.1186/1471-2407-14-126, https://www.ncbi.nlm.nih.gov/pmc/articles/PMC3937456/

8. Caussy, C., Reeder, S.B., Sirlin, C.B., Loomba, R.: Non-invasive, quantitative assessment of liver fat by MRI-PDFF as an endpoint in NASH trials. Hepatology (Baltimore, Md.) **68**, 763 (2018). https://doi.org/10.1002/HEP.29797, https://www.ncbi.nlm.nih.gov/pmc/articles/PMC6054824/

9. Franz, D., et al.: Differentiating supraclavicular from gluteal adipose tissue based on simultaneous PDFF and T2* mapping using a 20-echo gradient-echo acquisition. J. Magn. Resonan. Imaging **50**, 424 (2019). https://doi.org/10.1002/JMRI.26661, https://www.ncbi.nlm.nih.gov/pmc/articles/PMC6767392/

10. Freed, M., et al.: Evaluation of breast lipid composition in patients with benign tissue and cancer by using multiple gradient-echo MR imaging. Radiology **281**, 43–53 (2016). https://doi.org/10.1148/radiol.2016151959

11. Hamilton, G., et al.: In vivo triglyceride composition of abdominal adipose tissue measured by 1H MRS at 3T. J. Magn. Resonan. Imaging **45**, 1455–1463 (2017). https://doi.org/10.1002/jmri.25453

12. Hamilton, G., et al.: In vivo characterization of the liver fat ^{1}H MR spectrum. NMR Biomed. **24**, 784–790 (2011). https://doi.org/10.1002/NBM.1622, https://pubmed.ncbi.nlm.nih.gov/21834002/

13. Hisanaga, S., et al.: Peritumoral fat content correlates with histological prognostic factors in breast carcinoma: a study using iterative decomposition of water and fat with echo asymmetry and least-squares estimation (IDEAL). Magn. Reson. Med. Sci. **20**, 28–33 (2021). https://doi.org/10.2463/mrms.mp.2019-0201

14. Hong, C.W., et al.: MRI proton density fat fraction is robust across the biologically plausible range of triglyceride spectra in adults with nonalcoholic steatohepatitis. J. Magn. Reson. Imaging **47**, 995–1002 (2018). https://doi.org/10.1002/jmri.25845

15. Ko, Y.H., Song, P.H., Moon, K.H., Jung, H.C., Cheon, J., Sung, D.J.: The optimal timing of post-prostate biopsy magnetic resonance imaging to guide nerve-sparing surgery. Asian J. Androl. **16**, 280–284 (2014). https://doi.org/10.4103/1008-682X.122190

16. Kolb, T.M., Lichy, J., Newhouse, J.H.: Comparison of the performance of screening mammography, physical examination, and breast us and evaluation of factors that influence them: an analysis of 27,825 patient evaluations. Radiology **225**, 165–175 (2002). https://doi.org/10.1148/RADIOL.2251011667, https://pubmed.ncbi.nlm.nih.gov/12355001/

17. Middleton, M., et al.: A quantitative imaging biomarker assessment metric for MRI-estimated proton density fat fraction. Hepatology, AASLD Abstracts **66**, 1113–1114 (2017)

18. Nieman, K.M., et al.: Adipocytes promote ovarian cancer metastasis and provide energy for rapid tumor growth. Nat. Med. **17**, 1498–1503 (2011). https://doi.org/10.1038/nm.2492

19. Panzironi, G., Moffa, G., Galati, F., Marzocca, F., Rizzo, V., Pediconi, F.: Peritumoral edema as a biomarker of the aggressiveness of breast cancer: results of a retrospective study on a 3 T scanner. Breast Cancer Res. Treat. **181**(1), 53–60 (2020). https://doi.org/10.1007/s10549-020-05592-8

20. Ralli, G.P., Ridgway, G.R., Brady, S.M.: Segmentation of the biliary tree from MRCP images via the monogenic signal. Commun. Comput. Inf. Sci. 1248 CCIS, 105–117 (2020). https://doi.org/10.1007/978-3-030-52791-4_9. https://link.springer.com/chapter/10.1007/978-3-030-52791-4_9

21. Ren, J., Dimitrov, I., Sherry, A.D., Malloy, C.R.: Composition of adipose tissue and marrow fat in humans by 1H NMR at 7 Tesla. J. Lipid Res. **49**, 2055–2062 (2008). https://doi.org/10.1194/jlr.D800010-JLR200

22. Rodge, G.A., Goenka, M.K., Goenka, U., Afzalpurkar, S., Shah, B.B.: Quantification of liver fat by MRI-PDFF imaging in patients with suspected non-alcoholic fatty liver disease and its correlation with metabolic syndrome, liver function test and ultrasonography. J. Clin. Exp. Hepatol. **11**, 586–591 (2021). https://doi.org/10.1016/J.JCEH.2020.11.004

23. Sun, S., et al.: Exosomes from the tumour-adipocyte interplay stimulate beige/brown differentiation and reprogram metabolism in stromal adipocytes to promote tumour progression. J. Exp. Clin. Cancer Res. CR **38** (2019). https://doi.org/10.1186/S13046-019-1210-3, https://pubmed.ncbi.nlm.nih.gov/31138258/

24. Torre, L.A., Islami, F., Siegel, R.L., Ward, E.M., Jemal, A.: Global cancer in women: burden and trends. Cancer Epidemiol. Biomarkers Prevention : a publication of the American Association for Cancer Research, cosponsored by the American Society of Preventive Oncology **26**, 444–457 (2017). https://doi.org/10.1158/1055-9965.EPI-16-0858, https://pubmed.ncbi.nlm.nih.gov/28223433/

25. Vaysse, C., et al.: Inflammation of mammary adipose tissue occurs in overweight and obese patients exhibiting early-stage breast cancer. npj Breast Cancer **3** (2017). https://doi.org/10.1038/s41523-017-0015-9

26. Wang, F., et al.: Mammary fat of breast cancer: gene expression profiling and functional characterization. PloS One **9** (2014). https://doi.org/10.1371/JOURNAL.PONE.0109742, https://pubmed.ncbi.nlm.nih.gov/25291184/

27. Wei, D., Weinstein, S., Hsieh, M.K., Pantalone, L., Kontos, D.: Three-dimensional whole breast segmentation in sagittal and axial breast MRI with dense depth field modeling and localized self-adaptation for chest-wall line detection. IEEE Trans. Biomed. Eng. **66**, 1567–1579 (2019). https://doi.org/10.1109/TBME.2018.2875955

28. Zhu, Z.R., et al.: Fatty acid composition of breast adipose tissue in breast cancer patients and in patients with benign breast disease. Nutrition Cancer **24**, 151–160 (1995). https://doi.org/10.1080/01635589509514403, https://pubmed.ncbi.nlm.nih.gov/8584451/

Revisiting the Shape-Bias of Deep Learning for Dermoscopic Skin Lesion Classification

Adriano Lucieri[1,2]([✉])[ID], Fabian Schmeisser[1][ID], Christoph Peter Balada[2][ID],
Shoaib Ahmed Siddiqui[2][ID], Andreas Dengel[1,2][ID], and Sheraz Ahmed[2][ID]

[1] Department of Computer Science, Technische Universität Kaiserslautern,
Erwin-Schrödinger-Straße 52, 67663 Kaiserslautern, Germany
{adriano.lucieri,fabian.schmeisser,andreas.dengel}@dfki.de
[2] Smart Data and Knowledge Services (SDS), German Research Center for Artificial
Intelligence GmbH (DFKI), Trippstadter Straße 122, 67663 Kaiserslautern, Germany
{christoph.balada,shoaib.siddiqui,sheraz.ahmed}@dfki.de

Abstract. It is generally believed that the human visual system is biased towards the recognition of shapes rather than textures. This assumption has led to a growing body of work aiming to align deep models' decision-making processes with the fundamental properties of human vision. The reliance on shape features is primarily expected to improve the robustness of these models under covariate shift. In this paper, we revisit the significance of *shape-biases* for the classification of skin lesion images. Our analysis shows that different skin lesion datasets exhibit varying biases towards individual image features. Interestingly, despite deep feature extractors being inclined towards learning entangled features for skin lesion classification, individual features can still be decoded from this entangled representation. This indicates that these features are still represented in the learnt embedding spaces of the models, but not used for classification. In addition, the spectral analysis of different datasets shows that in contrast to common visual recognition, dermoscopic skin lesion classification, by nature, is reliant on complex feature combinations beyond *shape-bias*. As a natural consequence, shifting away from the prevalent desire of shape-biasing models can even improve skin lesion classifiers in some cases.

Keywords: Dermatology · Digital dermatoscopy · Skin lesion analysis · Spectral analysis · Robustness · Deep learning

1 Introduction

For over a decade now, Deep Neural Networks (DNNs) outperformed conventional techniques in various research areas including language translation [27], image classification [17] and image synthesis [11]. Although new state-of-the-art performances are being reported continuously for areas like Melanoma detection [12,29], an unconstrained application of Deep Learning (DL) in real-world,

© The Author(s), under exclusive license to Springer Nature Switzerland AG 2022
G. Yang et al. (Eds.): MIUA 2022, LNCS 13413, pp. 46–61, 2022.
https://doi.org/10.1007/978-3-031-12053-4_4

high-stakes medical decision-making is still considered questionable due to a lack of robustness and intelligibility. Several works have revealed weak spots of the current technology like the presence of adversarial examples [28], the influence of distribution shifts [23] and the bias-variance tradeoff [10]. In this work we consider the term bias as the systematic decision-making behaviour of an algorithm, utilizing (a combination of) statistically relevant features, which might or might not be desired by the stakeholders, to solve a given problem.

Geirhos et al. [9] disproved the widespread *shape hypothesis*, which states that Convolutional Neural Networks (CNNs) hierarchically combine lower-lever features into higher-level features for generating the final predictions. Instead the authors propose the *texture hypothesis*, stating that an inherent *texture-bias* in the dataset can lead to a lack of robustness in CNNs. Similarly, other works [34] have reported a higher importance of texture-like high-frequency input features, which aligns with the vulnerability to high-frequency adversarial attacks [31]. Through expensive modification of the training dataset, exchanging the dataset's *texture-bias* to a *shape-bias*, the authors of [9] achieve improved classification robustness. Along similar lines, recent works [5,33] exploit the idea that the phase spectrum of a Fourier-transformed image mainly encodes semantic information resembling edges and outlines used by humans for object identification. The authors propose different data augmentation strategies for improved robustness, inducing explicit focus on the phase spectra of images, shifting the networks' focus towards shape information. The common idea in these works is the explicit alignment of a network's non-functional requirements with those used in analytical, human decision-making (i.e. focusing on shape more than on texture).

Despite recent efforts towards suppressing high-frequency texture features in DL, Ilyas et al. [13] argue that datasets can contain robust features which are indeed imperceptible to humans. This alternative perspective is particularly interesting when dealing with complex medical problems which are yet to be fully understood by human experts and cannot be easily solved through intuition. One of such high-stakes use-cases of DL in medicine is the classification of Melanoma, which is mainly driven by non-analytic clinical reasoning (i.e. pattern analysis [16]).

The statistical relevance of shapes, textures and colors in dermoscopic images for Melanoma detection has been extensively investigated in different studies. Marques et al. [20] reported that color and texture features individually have a high relevance for skin lesion classification, but their combination is even more informative. In other works [2,25] the superior role of color features is reported. Ruela et al. [24] investigate the importance of shape features, concluding that, although shape is relevant for classification, the use of texture and color descriptors is more effective. Beyond texture, shape, and color, other studies indicate a high relevance of spectral features for predictive performance [3,19]. However, the influence of individual features, as well as the effect of the *shape-bias* on DL-based skin lesion classifiers has not yet been explored.

In this paper, we revisit the *shape-bias* and it's effect on the analysis of dermoscopic images using DL-based models. To that end, we explore the relevance of individual image features known to be relevant in dermoscopy (i.e. *Texture, Shape*, and *Color*). A spectral analysis on different datasets is performed to investigate the distribution of relevant image features in the spectral domain, and to revisit the effectiveness of robustness methods enforcing explicit *shape-bias* on deep feature extractors. Lastly, a new variant of the Amplitude-Phase Recombination [5] robustness method is introduced, which is more aligned with the complex needs of dermoscopic skin lesion analysis. We argue that the current trend of focusing network robustness in Deep Learning purely on the *shape-bias* is to narrow-minded, and that medical imaging tasks (like dermoscopy) in particular, have radically different requirements when it comes to non-functional properties of their decision-making.

Section 2 gives a brief introduction into the notions of *Texture, Shape*, and *Color* in dermoscopy and describes image ablations used to isolate these different features. The datasets used throughout our work, as well as the general experimentation setting is outlined in Sect. 3. In Sect. 4, the individual importance of isolated image features is investigated, and their encoding in the DL-based models' feature space. A spectral analysis on different datasets is performed in Sect. 5, followed by an investigation of shape-focused robustness methods. Finally, the results are discussed in Sect. 6, followed by the concluding remarks.

2 Definition and Isolation of Texture, Shape, and Color in Skin Lesions

To properly investigate the influence of individual image features, we need to isolate image features and feature combinations from the input images. We follow the previous lines of work and concentrate on the *Texture, Shape* and *Color* features as the main components descriptive of skin lesion images. First, the individual features are briefly defined, based on the relevant literature. Then, the transformations achieving the different feature isolations are elaborated and presented.

Texture. Marques et al. [20] define textures in skin lesions as conveying *"information about the differential structures (pigment network, dots, streaks, etc.) present in the lesion"*. We therefore argue that textures are solely encoded in structures such as fine edges, and color contrasts.

Shape. Shape descriptors are computed in [24] based on the segmented lesion outline. The measures include simple shape descriptors such as the lesion's area, compactness, and rectangularity, but also more advanced features such as symmetry-related features and moment invariants. In this work, we define the shape of a lesion by the size and area of a lesion's segmentation, as well as the regularity and overall shape of it's outline. For the sake of simplicity, we omit information regarding the smoothness of a lesion's transition.

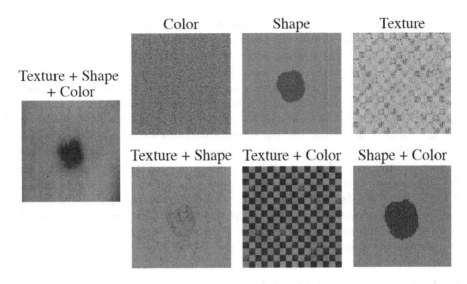

Fig. 1. Illustration of the different augmentations designed to isolate individual image features in skin lesion images. The original image is provided on the left. The first row shows augmentations for isolated images, while the second row shows combinations of two individual features.

Color. In [20], color features are defined as containing *"information about the color distribution and number of colors in the skin lesion"*. Ruela et al. [25] compute different color descriptors based on different color spaces. Most descriptors contain only information about the quantitative distribution of color in an image, whereas one descriptor also encodes information about the spatial location. We argue that color information is not only encoded in the absolute color values, but also in the contrast information of broader surfaces. However, we do not regard spatial color information for the sake of simplicity.

2.1   Feature Ablations

To isolate the effect of individual features, we design different data augmentation strategies, each representing one of the seven unique feature combinations. An illustration of the different transformations is provided in Fig. 1. The original images combine all three features and serve as the baseline. An ablation representing only the *Color* feature is obtained by randomly scrambling the spatial ordering of individual image pixels, while preserving the sample's original color distribution. A combination of *Texture* and *Shape* is achieved by explicitly removing the *Color* cues. This is done by changing the style of a sample to a sketch-like image, in order to remove color value and contrast information, while maintaining the characteristic edges necessary to identify textures and shapes.

A DL-based segmentation model[1] is tuned for the computation of lesion segmentation maps, representing the isolated *Shape* feature. The *Shape* feature is removed from the original image with the help of the segmentations as well. Therefore, the segmentation map is divided in equally-sized patches to identify image regions containing information about the lesion's outline (i.e. containing both lesion and background pixels). After removing all outline patches, a new image is assembled by alternatingly sampling random patches from the lesion and the background, to ensure that no information about the lesion's absolute size is retained. A similar procedure is followed to obtain the isolation of the *Texture* feature. Instead of scrambling image patches of the original image, the sketch transformation is used in order to spare color information. A combination of *Shape* and *Color* is obtained by separately scrambling the spatial ordering of individual image pixels within the lesion region, and the background. Images with radical domain shifts (through sketch transformation or segmentation) are shaded with the channel-wise average of the dataset's color.

3 Datasets and Methodology

3.1 Datasets

ISIC & ISIC-b. The International Skin Imaging Collaboration (ISIC) organized several skin cancer classification challenges over the last decade. The challenge datasets are hosted on the ISIC's online archive[2], which is the largest public database of dermoscopic skin images to date. The complete archive consists of over 69.000 clinical and dermoscopic images of different provenance. We follow Cassidy et al. [4], who propose a duplicate removal strategy for the ISIC challenge datasets to avoid overlap between training and evaluation sets. For experimentation, we combine all duplicate-free challenge training sets and generate new training, validation and testing splits under stratification.

The complete ISIC dataset has annotations for eight classes, i.e. Actinic Keratosis (AK), Basal Cell Carcinoma (BCC), Benign Keratosis (BKL), Dermatofibroma (DF), Melanoma (MEL), Nevus (NV), Squamous Cell Carcinoma (SCC) and Vascular Lesions (VASC). We generate a multi-class variant of the dataset (henceforth referred to as *ISIC*) comprising of 23.868 training, 2.653 validation and 2.947 testing samples. In addition, a binary variant consisting of only NV and MEL samples (henceforth referred to as *ISIC-b*) is generated comprising of 10.543 training, 4.519 validation and 6.456 testing samples.

D7P & D7P-b. The seven-point checklist criteria dataset (*D7P*) proposed in [14] consists of clinical and dermoscopic images of 1.011 skin lesions. Each image is annotated with regards to its diagnostic class, several dermoscopic criteria as well as further clinical data. In this work, we only consider the subset of

---

[1] BA-Transfomer architecture proposed by Wang et al. [30], trained on ISIC2016-2018 challenge datasets.

[2] https://www.isic-archive.com/.

dermoscopic images along with the respective annotations of dermoscopic criteria and final diagnosis. We follow the original work, categorizing the fine-grained annotations into BCC, NV, MEL, Sebbhoreic Keratosis (SK) as well as a miscellaneous (MISC) classes. Again, we generate a stratified binary variant of only NV and MEL samples (henceforth referred to as *D7P-b*) comprising of 371 training, 183 validation and 273 testing samples. For concept detection experiments, we follow the same splitting procedure for each dermoscopic concept.

3.2 Experimental Setup

If not mentioned otherwise, all experiments are conducted with a ResNet50, pre-trained on *ImageNet*. Training is conducted using softmax cross-entropy loss and AdamW optimizer. The learning rate and weight decay are determined by hyperparameter tuning on the baseline setting. A plateau learning rate scheduler is used in conjunction with an early stopping scheme to ensure convergence of the models. Each training and respective evaluation is run 10 times with varying random seeds to ensure significance of the reported results.[3]

4 Deep Feature Extractors for Dermoscopy Can Encode Disentangled Features

In this section, we perform an extensive study on the influence of individual features for the DL-based classification of dermoscopic skin lesions. We show that even within the dermoscopy domain, biases are dataset-dependent. Moreover, we show that although feature extractors are inclined towards learning entangled features, last-layer retraining can recover at least some features successfully.

4.1 Different Dermoscopic Skin Lesion Datasets Have Different Biases

In a first experiment, we train separate classifiers on the individual ablations introduced in Sect. 2. By training and testing on a specific ablation, we want to quantify the CNN-based feature extractor's capability to leverage individual, interpretable features from the images. We consider both binary and multiclass skin lesion datasets to account for possible effects of varying task complexity.

Figure 2 shows the macro averaged F1-scores on the test set of the respective ablations. When providing only single features in isolation, we observe that both binary and multiclass datasets based on *D7P*, show a stronger bias towards *Shape*, whereas the *ISIC* datasets are more sensitive with respect to *Texture*. This is indicated by the lower decrease in F1-scores when training on the respective isolated feature. It can also be observed that *Color* is the most important of all three features, resulting in the lowest performance decline.

---

[3] Reproducible code available on GitHub https://github.com/adriano-lucieri/shape-bias-in-dermoscopy.

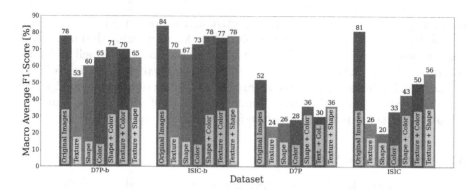

Fig. 2. Macro averaged F1-scores from models trained and tested on individual *Texture*, *Shape* and *Color* feature ablations. The first bar of each group represents the reference F1-score achieved by models trained on unaltered data, followed by the three feature isolation and feature removal ablations.

Training on a pair of two individual features can be considered as the removal of the absent feature, and therefore serves as an inverted indicator for feature importance. The previous observations are also confirmed by the results of removing *Texture* and *Shape*, except for *ISIC-b* which is influenced almost equally. Surprisingly, removing the *Color* did not indicate similar relevance as indicated by the isolation experiment. A reason for this behaviour could be that the combination of *Shape* and *Texture* information forms stronger higher-level features as compared to combinations including *Color*.

4.2 Dermoscopic Skin Lesion Classifiers Learn Entangled Features

The previous results showed that for some datasets, decent classification performances can be achieved even if only one or two features are present in the data. We now investigate the ability of trained classifiers to transfer their features in ablated scenarios. Therefore, the performance of each classifier trained in the previous experiment is measured across all ablations, as well as the original data.

Figure 3 shows a comparison of the results obtained by the models trained on the original input data, when evaluated on the test sets of all individual ablations (blue bars) with the inverse case, where different models trained on individual ablations are evaluated only on the original test set (orange bars). The data clearly shows that the baseline classifier is unable to properly transfer it's learned features to the classification of ablated data, representing isolated input features. However, the increased scores of the ablation-trained classifiers on the original data indicates the validity of the features even on unablated data. Hence, we conjecture that the baseline models are not capable of making decisions purely based on the remaining features, but are instead overrelying on an entangled representation of different features.

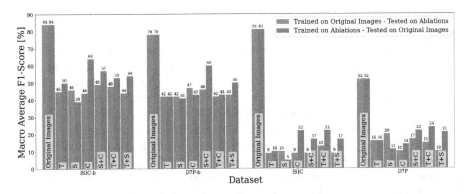

Fig. 3. Comparison of macro averaged F1-scores from models trained and tested on different data ablations. Blue bars show results of models trained on original images, and tested on different ablations. Orange bars show results of models trained on individual ablations, and tested on original images. *T, S, C* refer to *Texture, Shape* and *Color* features, respectively. (Color figure online)

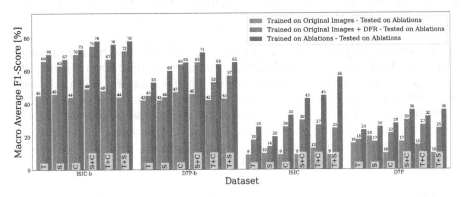

Fig. 4. Comparison of macro averaged F1-scores from models tested on different feature ablations. Blue bars show results of a baseline model trained on original images, and tested on all ablations. Orange bars show results of the same models after *Deep Feature Reweighting*. Green bars show results of models trained and tested on ablations. *T, S, C* refer to *Texture, Shape* and *Color* features, respectively. (Color figure online)

4.3   Feature Extractors Are only Partially Feature Biased

Inspired by *Deep Feature Reweighting* (DFR) proposed in [15], we explore the level of entanglement in the skin lesion classifiers' feature spaces. We again utilise the models trained on the original images from Sect. 4.1 but retrain the fully connected classification layers using the respective feature-ablated training and test sets. In Fig. 4, the macro averaged F1-scores of baseline models with naive transfer, and DFR is compared to the accuracies of the models trained end-to-end on the ablated data.

It can be seen that in some cases (e.g. *Color, Shape + Color* and partially *Texture + Color* as well as *Texture + Shape* for *ISIC-b*) DFR is able to achieve classification performances near the ideal values represented by the results of models trained and tested on ablations. For models trained on different skin lesion datasets, the successfully recovered features vary significantly. In contrast to *D7P* and *D7P-b* models, where only *Color* could be recovered, models trained on *ISIC-b* were able to recover all individual features to a sufficient degree. A similar observation can be made when inspecting the results of multiclass *ISIC* trained models. Another striking observation is that combinations of two features resulted in higher DFR performance across all datasets. The results indicate that the feature extractor is always inclined towards learning entangled features. However, the fact that individual features are additionally encoded, particularly in more complex and feature-rich datasets, confirms the results reported in [15]. This also suggests that an abundance of mostly redundant features in a dataset allows networks to learn alternative, isolated representations.

5   Dermoscopy Relies on Complex Feature Combinations in Spectral Domain

In this section, we investigate the difference between feature entanglement in skin lesion classification tasks and common visual recognition. For comparability, we consider the distinction of features in the spectral domain, which has been commonly examined in previous studies [5,33,34]. We show that, compared to conventional visual recognition tasks, dermoscopy is more reliant on features across both amplitude and phase spectra. To contrast the spread of dermoscopic features to those used in common visual recognition tasks, we utilize two subsets of *ImageNet* [6], namely *Imagenette* and *Imagewoof*[4].

5.1   Dermoscopy Features Are Spread over Phase and Amplitude

First, we implement phase- and amplitude-randomization augmentations which are applied to train, validation and test images alike. Phase-randomization (i.e. retaining *Amplitude-Only*) is applied by replacing the phase spectrum of an image, with the phase spectrum of a randomly sampled image of Gaussian noise in Fourier domain. The same procedure is followed analogously for Amplitude-randomization (i.e. retaining *Phase-Only*).

Table 1 shows the test results of models trained in the *Amplitude-* and *Phase-Only* settings in comparison to the baseline classification accuracies over five different datasets. It can be observed that *Amplitude-Only* always leads to comparatively high deterioration of accuracy for all datasets. However, *Phase-Only* results in comparable accuracy drops over all skin lesion datasets, even causing a higher relative performance decrease for *D7P-b*. Both visual recognition datasets instead show a significantly higher decrease in accuracy when providing only amplitude information, as compared to the *Phase-Only* setting.

---

[4] https://github.com/fastai/imagenette.

Table 1. Resulting testing accuracies from retraining ResNet50 with different spectral randomizations. For both spectral randomizations, the performance decrease with respect to the baseline training is provided in a separate row.

Dataset	D7P-b	D7P	ISIC-b	ISIC	Imagenette	Imagewoof
Baseline	82.01	69.13	88.45	85.93	97.77	92.53
Amplitude-Only	69.71	36.53	78.42	52.94	50.28	26.86
Δ Baseline	−15.00	−47.16	−11.34	−38.39	−48.57	−70.97
Phase-Only	67.66	45.45	80.78	69.29	91.98	81.53
Δ Baseline	−17.50	−34.25	−08.67	−19.36	−05.92	−11.89

The results indicate that skin lesion datasets rely heavily on both amplitude- and phase-spectra, therefore potentially considering a more complex composition and variety of features beyond simple shape information. In contrast, both *ImageNet* subsets show a significant bias towards the phase spectra of the images. The higher drop in accuracy when training *Imagewoof Phase-Only* indicates that a combination of phase and color is extremely important to achieve high performance in some classes, although phase being mostly sufficient. Interestingly, an inspection of the confusion matrices reveals that in the *Phase-Only* setting, networks tend to most often confuse *Beagles* with *English Foxhounds*, which share many features in their physique. A similar observation was made for the *Amplitude-Only* setting, where *Rhodesian Ridgebacks* and *Dingos* where confused most often, sharing a similar fur color.

5.2   Focusing on Amplitude Can Improve Performance

Amplitude-Phase Recombination (*APR*) has been proposed in [5] as a method to increase the robustness of DL classifiers by focusing the feature extraction on the phase-spectrum of images. $\mathcal{F}_x$ is the spatial Discrete Fourier Transform (DFT) of an image x over each individual channel. This frequency representation can be decomposed into an amplitude component ($\mathcal{A}_x$) and a phase component ($\mathcal{P}_x$) as follows:

$$\mathcal{F}_x = \mathcal{A}_x \otimes e^{i \cdot \mathcal{P}_x}, \tag{1}$$

Amplitude-Phase Recombination for pair samples (*APR-P*) [5] augments a given input image x_j by replacing its amplitude spectrum $\mathcal{A}_{x_j}$ with the spectrum of another randomly selected image from the batch ($\mathcal{A}_{x_k}$).

$$x_{j,aug} = iDFT(\mathcal{A}_{x_k} \otimes e^{i \cdot \mathcal{P}_{x_j}}), \tag{2}$$

Table 2. Average test results of random retraining with different variants of *APR* augmentation. Statistical significance of average accuracy to the baseline training is indicated by asterisks.

Dataset	D7P-b	ISIC-b	D7P	ISIC	Imagenette	Imagewoof
Baseline	82.01	88.45	**69.13**	**85.93**	**97.77**	**92.53**
APR-P	80.4*	88.62	66.05*	82.79	96.52	91.47
AF-APR-P	**82.42**	**89.23****	67.43	84.18	97.06**	91.91***
MIX-APR-P	81.5	89.16	68.62	84.22	97.3**	91.68

*** $p < 0.01$, ** $p < 0.05$, * $p < 0.1$

Instead, we propose two new variations of *APR-P*, namely Amplitude-Focused *APR-P* (*AF-APR-P*) and Mixed *APR-P* (*Mix-APR-P*). *AF-APR-P* swaps the phase spectrum of images as follows:

$$x_{j,aug} = iDFT(\mathcal{A}_{x_j} \otimes e^{i \cdot \mathcal{P}_{x_k}}),\tag{3}$$

Therefore, the ground truth label corresponding to the original image's amplitude spectrum is preserved. Using a random variable p, uniformly distributed between 0 and 1, *Mix-APR-P* randomly selects the spectral component from which to assign the respective label as follows:

$$x_{j,aug} = \begin{cases} iDFT(\mathcal{A}_{x_j} \otimes e^{i \cdot \mathcal{P}_{x_k}}) & p \geq 0.5 \\ iDFT(\mathcal{A}_{x_k} \otimes e^{i \cdot \mathcal{P}_{x_j}}) & p < 0.5 \end{cases}\tag{4}$$

forcing the network to independently extract both phase and amplitude features during training.

Table 2 shows the test performance of models trained with different variations of *APR-P* augmentation. *AF-APR-P* outperformed the other variations in the case of binary skin lesion classification, although statistical significance is only achieved in case of *ISIC-b*. When classifying skin lesions in multiple disease classes, neither augmentation showed any benefit. However, it can be seen that *APR-P* decreased the average test accuracy in all skin classification tasks. For both visual recognition datasets, neither *APR* augmentation improved the results. As expected, *AF-APR-P* and *Mix-APR-P* even led to a significant decrease in most cases.

6   Discussion

We have shown that there exist different, dataset-dependend biases with respect to *Texture*, *Shape* and *Color* features in dermoscopy. *D7P* datasets seem to be more biased towards *Shape* as compared to *Texture*. One possible explanation for this finding is that the significant difference in training size between *ISIC* and *D7P* (×28 for binary and ×53 for multiclass) allows the *ISIC*-trained models to pick up more nuanced features including fine-grained textures. This effect requires further investigation and is of special importance for the robustness and explainability of skin lesion classifiers in clinical use.

The results in Sect. 4.3 show differences between the feature entanglement of binary and multiclass classification tasks and indicat that a partial or even full encoding of disentangled features is possible depending on the complexity of the target task. However, it has also been shown that the end-to-end trained classifier does not necessarily use these features independently, potentially suffering a loss in robustness. Additional experimentation is required to investigate potential mechanisms leading to disentangled classification layers from end-to-end training. One possible way would be the explicit data augmentation with the different feature isolations proposed in Sect. 2. Another interesting direction would be the application of contrastive losses from self-supervised learning to achieve a better alignment of different feature-isolated ablations.

Section 5.1 revealed that features relevant for dermoscopic classification are spread across different components in the spectral domain, whereas visual recognition classifiers are deliberately biased towards only the phase component in order to increase robustness. A reason for this phenomenon might lie in the relevance of *Texture*, *Shape* and *Color* in skin lesion classification. The phase spectrum is known to encode mainly edges, which often correspond to coarse structures as outlines, but also fine-grained structures resembling textures. On the other hand, color is mainly encoded in the amplitude spectrum, as it contains information about the magnitude of specific frequency components in the respective color channels.

These findings indicate that common methods for increased robustness, which reinforce the *shape-bias*, are not necessarily suitable for skin lesion classification. However, skin lesion classification has been shown to significantly benefit from our proposed Amplitude-Focused *APR* augmentation. Multiclass skin lesion classification seem to not benefit, or even suffer from the Fourier-domain augmentation. A reason for this behaviour might be the increasing relevance of *Texture* and *Shape* features in multiclass settings, as reported in Sect. 4.3. The intuition behind the *Mix-APR-P* augmentation was that a random exposure to phase- or amplitude-randomized samples might implicitly force the network to learn individual features. Yet, this assumption has been disproved.

A very important but underexplored problem in dermoscopic and dermatological skin lesion classification is the effect of ethnic biases in datasets and the resulting inequalities in diagnostic performance for different minorities [32]. Our work again confirms that color and thus skin tone play a crucial role in modern DL classifiers. Based on previous insights from works like Ruela et al. [25], the involvement of lesion color is indeed very crucial for reliable diagnosis and should not be ignored. Therefore, we argue that the effect of bias related to the skin tone, in contrast to bias related to lesion color needs further investigation. Our experiments focused on the isolated effect of colour on the complete image. In further experiments, we will investigate the effect of colour in distinct image regions to separate the effect of skin tone and lesion color. Another relevant consideration is the fact that depending on the skin tone, the presentation of a disease can vary significantly [18]. The exclusion of skin tone related information could thus even lead to decreased diagnostic performances, further reinforcing inequalities.

Overall, the findings of this work indicate an inherent complexity of the dermoscopic skin lesion classification task. Indeed, the process of clinical reasoning has already been shown to be fundamentally different from other human decision-making such as visual recognition, based mostly on analytical reasoning. Norman et al. [22] describe the process of clinical reasoning as an iterative approach, combining non-analytical with analytical operations to varying degrees, depending upon personal style preferences, experience, and awareness of the diagnostic task [7]. Commonly applied diagnostic procedures in dermoscopy are manual algorithms like the ABCD rule [26], the Menzies method [21], the seven-point checklist [1] as well as the method of pattern analysis [16]. Methods like the seven-point checklist and pattern analysis are based on the identification of complex dermoscopic features such as Blue-Whitish-Veil or Pigment Networks. The successful application of pattern analysis requires years of extensive training. Evidence suggest, that clinical reasoning in dermoscopy puts more emphasis on the non-analytical, unconscious description of overall patterns as compared to analytical processes [8,35].

The *shape-bias* has been introduced to increase the alignment between the automated decision-making of modern AI algorithms and analytical human reasoning as applied in many visual object recognition tasks. Our work suggests that dermoscopic skin lesion classification and many other medical imaging tasks require considerable amounts of intuition and non-analytical reasoning, posing particularly interesting challenges upon the whole computer vision community. This means that *shape-biasing* classifiers is not a general solution for robustness, but algorithms must be modeled according to the needs of the task at hand. To properly disentangle features and align explanations with the human clinical reasoning processes in medical imaging tasks, the AI researching community must pay special attention to the complexity and peculiarities of these complex reasoning processes.

7   Conclusion

In this paper, we revisit the utility of developing *shape-biased* models for recognition beyond natural image recognition. Therefore, we consider the domain of dermoscopic skin lesion classification in particular. Through a range of different experiments, we have shown that deep features learnt for the classification of skin lesions are inherently entangled due to the complexity of the underlying task. At the same time, our analysis reveals that feature disentanglement can be achieved even on networks trained without constraints, and found that an increasing task complexity as well as a higher number of training samples leads deep feature extractors to learn a more diverse set of redundant and isolated features. Additionally, we showed that dermoscopic features are spread over different spectral components in contrast to common visual recognition tasks like *Imagenet*. This indicates that the commonly desired *shape-bias* for improved model robustness does not apply in dermoscopy, and that complex medical imaging tasks like these require specifically tailored solutions. We demonstrated a first step towards dermoscopy-specific robustness measures beyond *shape-bias* by introducing Amplitude-Focused Amplitude-Phase Recombination, showing improved performance on binary skin lesion classification tasks. More importantly, this work highlights the importance of scrutinizing a given computer vision task in order to find relevant, and robust requirements for the decision-making. Dermoscopy is only one out of plenty use-cases with unique requirements which extend beyond the simple analytical procedures of visual object recognition. These kind of considerations are particularly important for pivotal areas such as self-supervised learning, where an adequate requirement engineering will potentially lead to enormous performance improvements.

References

1. Argenziano, G., Fabbrocini, G., Carli, P., De Giorgi, V., Sammarco, E., Delfino, M.: Epiluminescence microscopy for the diagnosis of doubtful melanocytic skin lesions: comparison of the ABCD rule of dermatoscopy and a new 7-point checklist based on pattern analysis. Arch. Dermatol. **134**(12), 1563–1570 (1998)
2. Barata, C., Ruela, M., Mendonça, T., Marques, J.S.: A bag-of-features approach for the classification of melanomas in dermoscopy images: The role of color and texture descriptors. In: Scharcanski, J., Celebi, M. (eds.) Computer Vision Techniques for the Diagnosis of Skin Cancer, pp. 49–69. Springer, Heidelberg (2014). https://doi.org/10.1007/978-3-642-39608-3_3
3. Betta, G., Di Leo, G., Fabbrocini, G., Paolillo, A., Sommella, P.: Dermoscopic image-analysis system: estimation of atypical pigment network and atypical vascular pattern. In: IEEE International Workshop on Medical Measurement and Applications, 2006. MeMea 2006. pp. 63–67. IEEE (2006)
4. Cassidy, B., Kendrick, C., Brodzicki, A., Jaworek-Korjakowska, J., Yap, M.H.: Analysis of the ISIC image datasets: usage, benchmarks and recommendations. Med. Image Anal. **75**, 102305 (2022)
5. Chen, G., Peng, P., Ma, L., Li, J., Du, L., Tian, Y.: Amplitude-phase recombination: Rethinking robustness of convolutional neural networks in frequency domain. In: Proceedings of the IEEE/CVF International Conference on Computer Vision, pp. 458–467 (2021)
6. Deng, J., Dong, W., Socher, R., Li, L.J., Li, K., Fei-Fei, L.: Imagenet: a large-scale hierarchical image database. In: 2009 IEEE Conference on Computer Vision and Pattern Recognition, pp. 248–255. IEEE (2009)
7. Dinnes, J., et al.: Visual inspection and dermoscopy, alone or in combination, for diagnosing keratinocyte skin cancers in adults. Cochrane Database Syst. Rev. **12**(12), CD011901 (2018)
8. Gachon, J., Beaulieu, P., Sei, J.F., Gouvernet, J., Claudel, J.P., Lemaitre, M., Richard, M.A., Grob, J.J.: First prospective study of the recognition process of melanoma in dermatological practice. Arch. Dermatol. **141**(4), 434–438 (2005)
9. Geirhos, R., Rubisch, P., Michaelis, C., Bethge, M., Wichmann, F.A., Brendel, W.: Imagenet-trained cnns are biased towards texture; increasing shape bias improves accuracy and robustness. arXiv preprint arXiv:1811.12231 (2018)
10. Geman, S., Bienenstock, E., Doursat, R.: Neural networks and the bias/variance dilemma. Neural Comput. **4**(1), 1–58 (1992)
11. Goodfellow, I., et al.: Generative adversarial nets. In: Advances in Neural Information Processing Systems 27 (2014)

12. Hasan, M.K., Elahi, M.T.E., Alam, M.A., Jawad, M.T., Martí, R.: Dermoexpert: skin lesion classification using a hybrid convolutional neural network through segmentation, transfer learning, and augmentation. Informatics in Medicine Unlocked, p. 100819 (2022)
13. Ilyas, A., Santurkar, S., Tsipras, D., Engstrom, L., Tran, B., Madry, A.: Adversarial examples are not bugs, they are features. In: Advances in Neural Information Processing Systems 32 (2019)
14. Kawahara, J., Daneshvar, S., Argenziano, G., Hamarneh, G.: Seven-point checklist and skin lesion classification using multitask multimodal neural nets. IEEE J. Biomed. Health Inf. **23**(2), 538–546 (2019). https://doi.org/10.1109/JBHI.2018.2824327
15. Kirichenko, P., Izmailov, P., Wilson, A.G.: Last layer re-training is sufficient for robustness to spurious correlations. arXiv preprint arXiv:2204.02937 (2022)
16. Kittler, H., Rosendahl, C., Cameron, A., Tschandl, P.: Dermatoscopy: an algorithmic method based on pattern analysis. facultas (2016)
17. Krizhevsky, A., Sutskever, I., Hinton, G.E.: Imagenet classification with deep convolutional neural networks. In: Advances in Neural Information Processing Systems 25 (2012)
18. Kundu, R.V., Patterson, S.: Dermatologic conditions in skin of color: part i. special considerations for common skin disorders. Am. Family Phys. **87**(12), 850–856 (2013)
19. López-Leyva, J.A., Guerra-Rosas, E., Álvarez-Borrego, J.: Multi-class diagnosis of skin lesions using the fourier spectral information of images on additive color model by artificial neural network. IEEE Access **9**, 35207–35216 (2021)
20. Marques, J.S., Barata, C., Mendonça, T.: On the role of texture and color in the classification of dermoscopy images. In: 2012 Annual International Conference of the IEEE Engineering in Medicine and Biology Society, pp. 4402–4405. IEEE (2012)
21. Menzies, S.W., Ingvar, C., Crotty, K.A., McCarthy, W.H.: Frequency and morphologic characteristics of invasive melanomas lacking specific surface microscopic features. Arch. Dermatol. **132**(10), 1178–1182 (1996)
22. Norman, G., Barraclough, K., Dolovich, L., Price, D.: Iterative diagnosis. Bmj 339 (2009)
23. Quiñonero-Candela, J., Sugiyama, M., Schwaighofer, A., Lawrence, N.D.: Dataset Shift in Machine Learning. Mit Press (2008)
24. Ruela, M., Barata, C., Mendonca, T., Marques, J.S.: On the role of shape in the detection of melanomas. In: 2013 8th International Symposium on Image and Signal Processing and Analysis (ISPA), pp. 268–273. IEEE (2013)
25. Ruela, M., Barata, C., Mendonça, T., Marques, J.S.: What is the role of color in dermoscopy analysis? In: Sanches, J.M., Micó, L., Cardoso, J.S. (eds.) IbPRIA 2013. LNCS, vol. 7887, pp. 819–826. Springer, Heidelberg (2013). https://doi.org/10.1007/978-3-642-38628-2_97
26. Stolz, W.: Abcd rule of dermatoscopy: a new practical method for early recognition of malignant melanoma. Eur. J. Dermatol. **4**, 521–527 (1994)
27. Sutskever, I., Vinyals, O., Le, Q.V.: Sequence to sequence learning with neural networks. In: Advances in Neural Information Processing Systems 27 (2014)
28. Szegedy, C., et al.: Intriguing properties of neural networks. In: International Conference on Learning Representations (2014). http://arxiv.org/abs/1312.6199
29. Tang, P., Yan, X., Nan, Y., Xiang, S., Krammer, S., Lasser, T.: Fusionm4net: a multi-stage multi-modal learning algorithm for multi-label skin lesion classification. Med. Image Anal. **76**, 102307 (2022)

30. Wang, J., Wei, L., Wang, L., Zhou, Q., Zhu, L., Qin, J.: Boundary-aware transformers for skin lesion segmentation. In: de Bruijne, M., Cattin, P.C., Cotin, S., Padoy, N., Speidel, S., Zheng, Y., Essert, C. (eds.) MICCAI 2021. LNCS, vol. 12901, pp. 206–216. Springer, Cham (2021). https://doi.org/10.1007/978-3-030-87193-2_20
31. Wang, Z., Yang, Y., Shrivastava, A., Rawal, V., Ding, Z.: Towards frequency-based explanation for robust CNN. arXiv preprint arXiv:2005.03141 (2020)
32. Wen, D., et al.: Characteristics of publicly available skin cancer image datasets: a systematic review. The Lancet Digital Health (2021)
33. Xu, Q., Zhang, R., Zhang, Y., Wang, Y., Tian, Q.: A fourier-based framework for domain generalization. In: Proceedings of the IEEE/CVF Conference on Computer Vision and Pattern Recognition, pp. 14383–14392 (2021)
34. Yin, D., Gontijo Lopes, R., Shlens, J., Cubuk, E.D., Gilmer, J.: A fourier perspective on model robustness in computer vision. In: Advances in Neural Information Processing Systems 32 (2019)
35. Zalaudek, I., et al.: Time required for a complete skin examination with and without dermoscopy: a prospective, randomized multicenter study. Arch. Dermatol. **144**(4), 509–513 (2008)

Novel Imaging, Image Registration and Reconstruction

Joint Group-Wise Motion Estimation and Segmentation of Cardiac Cine MR Images Using Recurrent U-Net

Pengfang Qian[1] , Junwei Yang[1,2] , Pietro Lió[2] , Peng Hu[1], and Haikun Qi[1(✉)]

[1] School of Biomedical Engineering, ShanghaiTech University, Shanghai, China
qihk@shanghaitech.edu.cn
[2] Department of Computer Science and Technology, University of Cambridge, Cambridge, UK

Abstract. Cardiac segmentation and motion estimation are two important tasks for the assessment of cardiac structure and function. Studies have demonstrated deep learning segmentation methods considering the valuable dynamics of the heart have more robust and accurate segmentations than those treating each frame independently. The former methods require annotations of all frames for supervised training, while only end-systolic (ES) and end-diastolic (ED) frames are commonly labeled. The issue has been addressed by integrating motion estimation into the segmentation framework and generating annotations for unlabeled frames with the estimated motion. However, the current pair-wise registration method with the ED frame as the template image may result in inaccurate motion estimation for systolic frames. We therefore, propose to use a group-wise registration network where the template image is learned implicitly for optimal registration performance, with the assumption that more accurate motion estimation leads to improved segmentation performance. Specifically, a recurrent U-Net based network is employed for joint optimization of group-wise registration and segmentation of the left ventricle and myocardium, where the dynamic information is utilized for both tasks with the recurrent units. In addition, an enhancement mask covering the heart is generated with the segmentation masks, which is expected to improve the registration performance by focusing the motion estimation on the heart. Experimental results in a cardiac cine MRI dataset including normal subjects and patients show that the group-wise registration significantly outperforms the pair-wise registration which translates to more accurate segmentations. The effectiveness of the proposed enhancement mask is also demonstrated in an ablation study.

Keywords: Nonrigid registration · Segmentation · Cine MRI · Deep learning

1 Introduction

Cardiac cine MRI is an important tool of assessing the anatomical structure and function of the heart noninvasively, and has been widely used in the clinical practice to diagnose

---

P. Qian and J. Yang—These authors have contributed equally to this work and share first authorship.

G. Yang et al. (Eds.): MIUA 2022, LNCS 13413, pp. 65–74, 2022.
https://doi.org/10.1007/978-3-031-12053-4_5

various cardiovascular diseases [1]. Motion estimation and segmentation are two important tasks of analyzing cardiac cine images for calculating functional parameters and evaluating myocardial elasticity and contractility. In this regard, extensive deep learning methods have been developed, especially for cardiac image segmentation, while most approaches consider registration and segmentation individually, ignoring the fact that they are closely related. Considering the two tasks together may help to improve the performance of both.

Deep convolutional neural networks (CNN) have demonstrated exceptional accuracy for automatic segmentation of the left ventricle and myocardium [2]. However, most CNN methods treat each frame of cine images individually without leveraging the dynamics of heart motion. Then, recurrent neural network-based methods have been developed to consider the temporal information for dynamic image segmentation, which have shown improved accuracy and robustness [3–7]. However, the dynamic image segmentation methods require annotations of all frames for supervised training which are time-consuming and laborious, and in practice only end-systolic (ES) and end-diastolic (ED) frames are labeled.

To facilitate training of dynamic segmentation networks with sparsely annotated data, Qin et al. propose to integrate motion estimation into the segmentation framework, and generate annotations for unlabeled frames with the estimated motion [8], where a pairwise registration and a segmentation network are trained jointly. The results demonstrate the effectiveness of guiding the dynamic segmentation network with another motion estimation network for sparsely annotated cardiac cine images. However, the adopted pair-wise registration using the ED frame as the reference image may result in inaccurate motion estimation for systolic frames due to the large difference between those frames and the ED frame. On the other hand, the group-wise registration [9] has shown superior performance than the pair-wise registration in registering a set of images by searching for an implicit template image which usually lies in the geometric center. In the joint learning model, more accurate motion estimation should provide more effective supervision for the segmentation network. Therefore, we assume that combing the group-wise registration with the dynamic segmentation network may help to improve the segmentation performance.

In this study, we propose a recurrent U-Net based network for joint motion estimation and segmentation of cardiac cine MRI, consisting of a diffeomorphic group-wise registration network and a dynamic segmentation network, which have shared encoder for exploration of the redundancy of the feature representation for both tasks. The recurrent unit of gated recurrent unit (GRU) [10] is adopted to capture the dynamic information of the heart. And the diffeomorphic image registration [11, 12] is used to obtain invertible motion fields for generation of segmentation masks for unlabeled frames. In addition, an enhancement mask covering the heart is generated with the segmentation masks of labelled ED and ES frames, which is expected to improve the cardiac motion estimation by focusing the registration network on the heart. A composite loss is devised to optimize the two networks jointly.

2 Methods

The proposed joint model consists of a group-wise registration network and a dynamic image segmentation network. Details of the networks and loss function are provided in this section.

2.1 Group-Wise Registration for Cardiac Motion Estimation

Given a set of cine image $\mathcal{J} = \{I_1, \dots, I_{n_T}\}$ with n_T frames, group-wise registration aims to estimate a set of transformations $\mathcal{T} = \{T_1, \dots, T_{n_T}\}$ that warp the dynamic images $\mathcal{J}$ to a common implicit template $\bar{I}$. Any two frames warped to the template with the corresponding transformations should have similar structural and shape features, which can be represented as $T_i \circ I_i \approx T_j \circ I_j \approx \bar{I}, \forall i \neq j$, where $\circ$ is the warping operator.

In order to transform images from the implicit template space to the original dynamic image space to thus facilitate the transformation between any two frames, invertible motion fields are required, and diffeomorphic registration is considered [12]. Instead of directly estimating the motion flow, velocity fields $\mathcal{V} = \{v_1, \dots, v_{n_T}\}$ pointing from the template to the dynamic images are estimated through a learnable mapping. Then, transformations $\mathcal{T}$ and their inverse transformations $\mathcal{T}^{-1} = \{T_1^{-1}, \dots, T_{n_T}^{-1}\}$ can be subsequently obtained by integrating of $\mathcal{V}$ and $-\mathcal{V}$ respectively [11]. The implicit template image is defined as the average of the warped dynamic images [11]: $\bar{I} = \frac{1}{n_T} \sum_{i=1}^{n_T} T_i \circ I_i$.

To enforce the reference image to lie in the geometric center of the group, the average velocity field is subtracted from each of the estimated velocity fields, as proposed in [9]: $\hat{v} = v_i - \frac{1}{n_T} \sum_{i=1}^{n_T} v_i$. The registration network is optimized using a self-supervised loss measuring the intensity-based similarity and the velocity field smoothness:

$$\mathcal{L}_{\text{backward}} = \frac{1}{n} \frac{1}{n_T} \sum_{i=1}^{n_T} \left(\|\bar{I} - T_i \circ I_i\|_2^2 \right) \tag{1}$$

$$\mathcal{L}_{\text{forward}} = \frac{1}{n} \frac{1}{n_T} \sum_{i=1}^{n_T} \left(\|I_i - T_i^{-1} \circ \bar{I}\|_2^2 \right) \tag{2}$$

$$\mathcal{L}_{\text{spatial}} = \frac{1}{n} \frac{1}{n_T} \sum_{i=1}^{n_T} \left(\|\nabla_{xy} v_i\|_2^2 \right) \tag{3}$$

$$\mathcal{L}_{\text{temporal}} = \frac{1}{n} \frac{1}{n_T} \sum_{i=1}^{n_T} \left(\|\nabla_t v_i\|_2^2 \right) \tag{4}$$

$$\mathcal{L}_{\text{reg}} = \mathcal{L}_{\text{backward}} + \mathcal{L}_{\text{forward}} + \alpha \mathcal{L}_{\text{spatial}} + \beta \mathcal{L}_{\text{temporal}} \tag{5}$$

where $\mathcal{L}_{\text{backward}}$ measures the similarity between the implicit reference image and the warped dynamic images; $\mathcal{L}_{\text{forward}}$ measures the similarity between the original dynamic images and the generated dynamic images by transforming the template with the inverse transformations; $\mathcal{L}_{\text{spatial}}$ and $\mathcal{L}_{\text{temporal}}$ respectively measures the spatial and temporal smoothness of the velocity field, and $\nabla_{xy} v_i$ and $\nabla_t v_i$ denotes the gradients of the velocity field in the spatial and temporal dimensions. The total registration loss is a weighted combination of the similarity and smoothness loss terms with regularization parameters of α and β.

2.2   Joint Cardiac Motion Estimation and Segmentation

To estimate cardiac motion and segment the left ventricle and myocardium simultaneously, we construct a joint learning framework with two branches as shown in Fig. 1. The motion estimation and segmentation network share an encoder to explore the redundancy of the feature representation. The encoder and decoders are adapted from U-Net [13]. A short-axis cardiac MR cine images $\mathcal{J}$ are inputted to the shared encoder E frame by frame, generating a set of feature maps for all dynamic frames. Then a shared bidirectional Gated Recurrent Unit (GRU) is applied to the feature maps of the last stage of the encoder to model the dependencies along the temporal dimension. After GRU, the feature maps go through two separate decoders D_{reg} and D_{seg} to output a set of velocity fields $\mathcal{V}$ and a set of segmentations $\hat{S} = \left\{\hat{S}_1 = \hat{S}_{ed}, \ldots, \hat{S}_{es}, \ldots, \hat{S}_{nT}\right\}$, respectively. $\hat{S}_{ed}$ and $\hat{S}_{es}$ denote the segmentations for the ED and ES frames.

For optimization of the segmentation network, a categorical cross-entropy loss is adopted for the labeled ED and ES frames: $\mathcal{L}_{edes} = -\sum_{i \in L} S_i \log\left(\hat{S}_i\right)$, where $L = \{i_{ed}, i_{es}\}$ are the indices of labeled frames in dynamic image and S_i is the ground truth. Then, the motion guided optimization of the segmentation branch is performed by warping segmentations of labeled frames to the implicit template and then to other unlabeled frames with the forward motion and backward motion from the registration branch. Another categorical cross-entropy loss $\mathcal{L}_{warped} = -\sum_{i \in L} \sum_{j \in U} \left(T_j^{-1} \circ T_i \circ S_i\right) \log\left(\hat{S}_j\right)$ is calculated between the warped segmentations and the network output, where U contains the indices of unlabeled frames.

For joint optimization of registration and segmentation networks, the registration loss in Eq. (5) and the segmentation loss are weighted combined: $\mathcal{L} = \mathcal{L}_{reg} + \lambda_1 \mathcal{L}_{edes} + \lambda_2 \mathcal{L}_{warped}$, where λ_1 and λ_2 are the weighting parameters controlling the contributions of the two segmentation loss terms.

2.3   Network Training with Enhancement Mask

Image artifacts and bright signals from other organs tend to compromise the cardiac motion estimation. To focus the registration network on the cardiac region, we propose to generate a mask covering the heart by taking advantages of the ground-truth segmentations of the ED and ES frames. Specifically, a bounding box termed as enhancement mask is generated according to segmentations of the left and right ventricle of the ED and ES frames so that the heart is tightly included in the bounding box. In the enhancement mask, the pixel value inside the bounding box is set to 1, while the pixel value outside the bounding box is exponentially decayed according to its distance to the bounding box. During the optimization, each loss term is element wisely multiplied with the enhancement mask, so as to reduce the influence of regions beyond the heart. It is noted that the enhancement mask is only required in the training stage for loss calculation, and is not needed during inference.

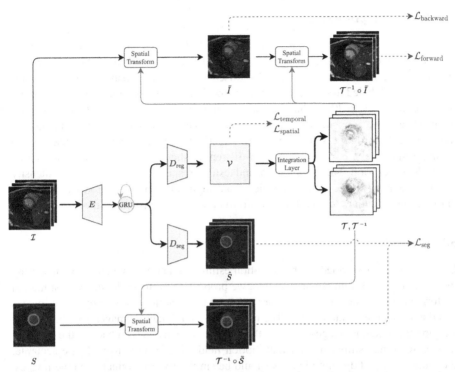

Fig. 1. Overview of the joint diffeomorphic group-wise motion estimation and segmentation framework. E denotes a shared U-Net encoder, D_{reg} and D_{seg} denote the registration and segmentation decoders.

3 Experiments and Results

The joint model is firstly compared with the model with the segmentation only (Seg-only) by training the segmentation network with $\mathcal{L}_{\text{edes}}$. Then, to investigate the influence of the registration method, we also compare the joint model with group-wise registration with that with the pair-wise registration where the ED frame is designated as the reference image to be registered with, as proposed in [8]. Other settings are kept the same for the joint models with different registration methods for fair comparison. In addition, to investigate the benefit of adding the enhancement mask, the proposed joint model is also trained without the enhancement mask.

For the network architecture, the U-Net encoder and decoders have 4 stages and 32 base channels. The hyper parameters for the loss function are optimized with limited number of searches and are set as follows: $\alpha = 0.001$, $\beta = 0.0001$, $\lambda_1 = 2$, $\lambda_2 = 1$. The deep learning model is trained for 100 epochs by the Adam optimizer with the learning rate of 10^{-4} which is halved every 20 epochs. Since the motion estimation network plays an important role in guiding the segmentation branch, we pretrain the motion estimation branch for 100 epochs before the joint optimization.

3.1 Dataset Preprocessing

Methods are evaluated in a public cardiac cine MRI dataset of Automatic Cardiac Diagnosis Challenge (ACDC), which consists of short-axis cine MR images of 150 normal subjects and patients with ischemic and non-ischemic cardiomyopathies, where 100 subjects are semi-labeled in ES and ED frames, and 50 subjects are unlabeled. The number of frames n_T is set to 20, so that the entire cardiac cycle can be covered. To make sure all the slices have equal number of frames, any subjects who have dynamic frames less than 20 are discarded, resulting in 50, 16 and 17 subjects for training, validation and testing, respectively. For each subject, 6–10 central slices are selected, leading to 260, 86 and 85 slices for training, validation, and testing, respectively. The min-max intensity normalization is performed for each slice. Data augmentations are performed on-the-fly during training with random affine-transformations and intensity variations.

3.2 Evaluation

Evaluations are performed for both motion estimation and segmentation. Considering the motion ground truth is not available, we propose to evaluate the motion estimation performance by assessing the similarity between the motion-warped dynamic images and the original dynamic images. The motion-warped dynamic images are obtained by warping the dynamic images firstly to the template image and then back to the dynamic images with the estimated invertible motion fields. If the motion fields are accurate, the motion-warped dynamic images should be similar to the original dynamic images. Here we use peak signal-to-noise ratio (PSNR) and Structural similarity index (SSIM) to measure the similarity. The evaluation of segmentations is performed by calculating the Dice coefficient (DICE) and Hausdorff distance (HD) using our manual segmentations as ground truth. Considering that the segmentation network is optimized with the ground truth of ED and ES frames only, and is motion-guided for other frames, we report the segmentation metrics for the ED, ES frames and other non-EDES frames separately.

3.3 Results

The registration results are reported in Table 1. It can be seen the joint models with the group-wise registration achieve higher PSNR and SSIM than that with the pair-wise registration, indicating the superior performance of group-wise registration over pair-wise registration. By adding the enhancement mask (Group-wise U-Net-GRU EM), the PSNR and SSIM of the joint model are improved further, confirming the effectiveness of the enhancement mask of focusing the learning on the cardiac region.

Example registration results are shown in Fig. 2. For each method, we examine the accuracy of warping the ED frame to the ES frame. The forward transformation T_{ES}^{-1} is performed on the reference image ($\bar{I}$ for the group-wise registration and I_{ED} for the pair-wise registration) to transform the reference image to the ES frame, and then a difference image between the warped image and the original ES frame can be calculated and compared. The smaller intensities of the difference image with the group-wise registration indicate that the group-wise registration with the template image in the geometric center, performs much better than the pair-wise registration in aligning the

ED and ES frames, which is a challenging task due to the large motion between them. Moreover, it is noted the enhancement mask further improves the group-wise registration slightly.

Table 1. Evaluation of the registration branch using the peak signal-to-noise ratio (PSNR) and Structural similarity index (SSIM).

Methods	PSNR	SSIM
Pair-wise U-Net-GRU	31.63 ± 2.180	0.9550 ± 0.0189
Group-wise U-Net-GRU	34.57 ± 3.559	0.9685 ± 0.0169
Group-wise U-Net-GRU EM	**34.82** ± 3.355	**0.9690** ± 0.0165

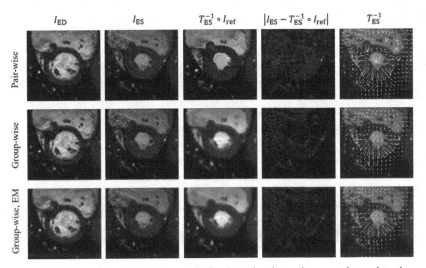

Fig. 2. Visualization of the registration results for the pair-wise and group-wise registration, and the group-wise registration with enhancement mask (EM).

The segmentation metrics of DICE and HD for the ED, ES frames and non-EDES frames are summarized in Table 2 and Table 3, respectively. Overall, the segmentations of the ED, ES frames are more accurate than those of the non-EDES frames. The joint models with motion estimation perform much better than the seg-only method, especially for the ED, ES frames. Comparing between the joint models, the group-wise U-Net-GRU achieves better performance than the pair-wise counterpart with higher DICE and lower HD for both ED, ES frames and non-EDES frames, benefiting from the more accurate motion estimation of group-wise registration. Furthermore, the group-wise U-Net-GRU with enhancement mask (Group-wise U-Net-GRU EM) generally improved the segmentation accuracy regarding DICE, while its HD for the ED and ES frames slightly increased compared with its counterpart without EM, which may be due to increased variations of the predicted segmentation contours caused by the EM which may overemphasize motion in the cardiac region.

Table 2. The average and standard deviation of the Dice coefficient (DICE) and Hausdorff distance (HD) of the myocardium (Myo) and left ventricular (LV) segmentations for the ED and ES frames.

Methods	EDES Myo		EDES LV	
	DICE	HD	DICE	HD
Seg-only	0.8160 ± 0.1001	6.584 ± 10.76	0.9324 ± 0.0394	4.362 ± 9.223
Pair-wise U-Net-GRU	0.8334 ± 0.0866	7.044 ± 12.05	0.9268 ± 0.0982	5.645 ± 12.25
Group-wise U-Net-GRU	0.8645 ± 0.0543	**2.862** ± 1.059	0.9470 ± 0.0239	**2.322** ± 0.894
Group-wise U-Net-GRU EM	**0.8653** ± 0.0726	4.778 ± 10.75	**0.9483** ± 0.0421	3.959 ± 11.20

Table 3. The average and standard deviation of the Dice coefficient (DICE) and Hausdorff distance (HD) of the myocardium (Myo) and left ventricular (LV) segmentations for the non-EDES frames.

Methods	Non-EDES Myo		Non-EDES LV	
	DICE	HD	DICE	HD
Seg-only	0.8154 ± 0.0688	4.395 ± 2.765	0.9157 ± 0.0545	3.526 ± 2.363
Pair-wise U-Net-GRU	0.8190 ± 0.0706	3.993 ± 1.274	0.9215 ± 0.0482	3.089 ± 1.253
Group-wise U-Net-GRU	0.8293 ± 0.0495	3.512 ± 0.954	**0.9306** ± 0.0253	2.636 ± 0.457
Group-wise U-Net-GRU EM	**0.8369** ± 0.0501	**3.218** ± 0.718	0.9304 ± 0.0299	**2.531** ± 0.614

Example segmentations of 4 representative frames for a challenging subject are compared between the three segmentation methods in Fig. 3. The epicardium and endocardium are precisely delineated with the proposed Group-wise U-Net-GRU EM, while erroneous segmentations of the epicardium can be observed for the other two segmentation methods.

4   Conclusion

In this paper, we propose a novel deep learning approach for joint group-wise motion estimation and segmentation of cardiac cine MR images. The joint learning model consists of a diffeomorphic group-wise registration network and a segmentation network, where a recurrent U-Net with bidirectional GRU is adopted to capture the spatial and valuable dynamic information of the heart motion. Experimental results show that the group-wise registration outperforms the pair-wise registration which leads to the better segmentation performance of the joint model with the group-wise registration. In addition, with the segmentation results at hand, we propose to generate an enhancement mask to focus the network learning on the cardiac region, which is proved to be effective in improving the cardiac motion estimation. In the future work, we will explore some self-attention techniques to replace the hand-crafted enhancement mask and validate our method in a larger-scale dataset.

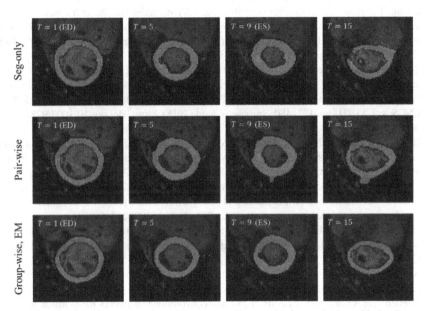

Fig. 3. Visualization of segmentation of the myocardium and left ventricular with the three segmentation methods (Seg-only, Pair-wise U-Net-GRU and Group-wise U-Net-GRU EM) for a representative subject.

References

1. Ripley, D.P., Musa, T.A., Dobson, L.E., Plein, S., Greenwood, J.P.: Cardiovascular magnetic resonance imaging: what the general cardiologist should know. Heart **102**, 1589–1603 (2016). https://doi.org/10.1136/heartjnl-2015-307896
2. Chen, C., et al.: Deep learning for cardiac image segmentation: a review. Front. Cardiovasc. Med. **7**, 25 (2020)

3. Yan, W., Wang, Y., Li, Z., van der Geest, R.J., Tao, Q.: Left ventricle segmentation via optical-flow-net from short-axis Cine MRI: preserving the temporal coherence of cardiac motion. In: Frangi, A.F., Schnabel, J.A., Davatzikos, C., Alberola-López, C., Fichtinger, G. (eds.) Medical Image Computing and Computer Assisted Intervention – MICCAI 2018. Lecture Notes in Computer Science, vol. 11073, pp. 613–621. Springer, Cham (2018). https://doi.org/10.1007/978-3-030-00937-3_70
4. Bai, S., Kolter, J.Z., Koltun, V.: An empirical evaluation of generic convolutional and recurrent networks for sequence modeling. ArXiv Prepr. ArXiv:180301271 (2018)
5. Du, X., Yin, S., Tang, R., Zhang, Y., Li, S.: Cardiac-DeepIED: automatic pixel-level deep segmentation for cardiac bi-ventricle using improved end-to-end encoder-decoder Network. IEEE J. Transl. Eng. Health Med. 7, 1–10 (2019). https://doi.org/10.1109/JTEHM.2019.2900628
6. Savioli, N., Vieira, M.S., Lamata, P., Montana, G.: Automated segmentation on the entire cardiac cycle using a deep learning work - flow. In: 2018 Fifth International Conference on Social Networks Analysis, Management and Security (SNAMS), pp. 153–158 (2018). https://doi.org/10.1109/SNAMS.2018.8554962
7. Zhang, D., et al.: A multi-level convolutional LSTM model for the segmentation of left ventricle myocardium in infarcted porcine cine MR images. In: 2018 IEEE 15th International Symposium on Biomedical Imaging (ISBI 2018), Washington, DC, pp. 470–473. IEEE (2018). https://doi.org/10.1109/ISBI.2018.8363618
8. Qin, C., et al.: Joint learning of motion estimation and segmentation for cardiac MR image sequences. In: Frangi, A.F., Schnabel, J.A., Davatzikos, C., Alberola-López, C., Fichtinger, G. (eds.) Medical Image Computing and Computer Assisted Intervention – MICCAI 2018. LNCS, vol. 11071, pp. 472–480. Springer, Cham (2018). https://doi.org/10.1007/978-3-030-00934-2_53
9. Li, B., Niessen, W.J., Klein, S., Ikram, M.A., Vernooij, M.W., Bron, E.E.: Learning unbiased group-wise registration (LUGR) and joint segmentation: evaluation on longitudinal diffusion MRI. In: Landman, B.A., Išgum, I. (eds.) Medical Imaging 2021: Image Processing, p. 14. SPIE, Online Only, United States (2021). https://doi.org/10.1117/12.2580928
10. Cho, K., van Merrienboer, B., Bahdanau, D., Bengio, Y.: On the properties of neural machine translation: encoder-decoder approaches. Cs Stat. ArXiv:14091259 (2014)
11. Dalca, A.V., Balakrishnan, G., Guttag, J., Sabuncu, M.R.: Unsupervised learning of probabilistic diffeomorphic registration for images and surfaces. Med. Image Anal. 57, 226–236 (2019)
12. Ashburner, J.: A fast diffeomorphic image registration algorithm. NeuroImage 38, 95–113 (2007). https://doi.org/10.1016/j.neuroimage.2007.07.007
13. Ronneberger, O., Fischer, P., Brox, T.: U-net: convolutional networks for biomedical image segmentation. In: Navab, N., Hornegger, J., Wells, W.M., Frangi, A.F. (eds.) MICCAI 2015. LNCS, vol. 9351, pp. 234–241. Springer, Cham (2015). https://doi.org/10.1007/978-3-319-24574-4_28

Recursive Deformable Image Registration Network with Mutual Attention

Jian-Qing Zheng[1,2]([⊠]) [iD], Ziyang Wang[3] [iD], Baoru Huang[4] [iD], Tonia Vincent[1] [iD],
Ngee Han Lim[1] [iD], and Bartłomiej W. Papież[2,5] [iD]

[1] The Kennedy Institute of Rheumatology, University of Oxford, Oxford, UK
jianqing.zheng@kennedy.ox.ac.uk
[2] Big Data Institute, University of Oxford, Oxford, UK
bartlomiej.papiez@bdi.ox.ac.uk
[3] Department of Computer Science, University of Oxford, Oxford, UK
[4] Department of Surgery and Cancer, Imperial College London, London, UK
[5] Nuffield Department of Population Health, University of Oxford, Oxford, UK

Abstract. Deformable image registration, estimating the spatial transformation between different images, is an important task in medical imaging. Many previous studies have used learning-based methods for multi-stage registration to perform 3D image registration to improve performance. The performance of the multi-stage approach, however, is limited by the size of the receptive field where complex motion does not occur at a single spatial scale. We propose a new registration network combining recursive network architecture and mutual attention mechanism to overcome these limitations. Compared with the state-of-the-art deep learning methods, our network based on the recursive structure achieves the highest accuracy in lung Computed Tomography (CT) data set (Dice score of 92% and average surface distance of 3.8 mm for lungs) and one of the most accurate results in abdominal CT data set with 9 organs of various sizes (Dice score of 55% and average surface distance of 7.8 mm). We also showed that adding 3 recursive networks is sufficient to achieve the state-of-the-art results without a significant increase in the inference time.

Keywords: Deformable image registration · Recursive network · Mutual attention

1 Introduction

Deformable image registration (DIR) is an essential computer vision task which has been widely studied [18]. In medical imaging, DIR enables the estimation of the non-linear correspondence between different acquisitions over time to monitor progress of treatment, or between different types of scanners (e.g. multi-modal image fusion) to provide complementary disease information. The classical registration algorithms have been developed as continuous optimization [2, 15, 20], or discrete optimization problems [8]. Their computational performance, however, is limited due to highly dimensional, non-convex problem, and low capability to capture complex, global and local deformations [16]. Recently, researchers have shifted interest to deep-learning-based

© The Author(s), under exclusive license to Springer Nature Switzerland AG 2022
G. Yang et al. (Eds.): MIUA 2022, LNCS 13413, pp. 75–86, 2022.
https://doi.org/10.1007/978-3-031-12053-4_6

unsupervised learning methods in deformable image registration, becuase data-driven methods benefit significantly from a large amount of given paired/unpaired images compared with classical methods [1,12,22]. A fast learning-based approach, VoxelMorph, is presented in [4], where convolutional neural networks (CNN) and spatial transformer layers [11] are used to register two images by regressing directly dense displacement field. Other deep learning approaches investigated different representations of the transformation e.g. diffeomorphism [14], which preserve the topology of the transformation. The direct regression of the spatial transformation via neural networks however, only gives one prediction on registration without any progressive refinement.

Multi-stage architecture is one of the solutions that is beneficial to CNN [10,22,25]. A weakly supervised multi-model registration method [10], utilizing an end-to-end convolution based network, aims to predict displacement fields to align multiple labelled corresponding structures for individual image pairs. Alternatively, an end-to-end multi-stage networks [24] are proposed for a deep recursive cascade architecture that allows unlimited number of cascades that can be built on the backbone networks. All of these multi-stage cascaded network structures, however, are still potentially suffering from the limited capture range of the receptive field.

The attention mechanism [21] addresses the limited receptive field of CNNs and has been widely utilized in transformer networks. Optimal correspondence matching was studied in [13] for a stereo matching task, where self-attention-based transformer is proposed to relax the limitation of a fixed disparity range. Local feature matching can also benefit from self and cross attention, because transformer networks are proved to obtain feature descriptors that are conditioned on both images [19]. The attention-based mechanism was applied to registration [5,17,23] previously, however is computationally expensive, and thus has not been explored in recursive deformable image registration.

In this paper, we propose a Recursive Mutual Attention Network (RMAn), combining the Mutual Attention (MA) based module with a recursive architecture to increase the size of the receptive field. The recursive architecture provides the progressive refinement to 3D image deformable registration so that MA module can expand the global receptive field on a pair of low-resolution feature maps without extra cost of computation. Our contributions in this paper are as follows.

1. A Mutual Attention based Recursive Network (RMAn) is proposed for deformable image registration, combining the mutual attention [21] into recursive networks [24];
2. The proposed network achieves the best performance against the state-of-the-art deep learning network structures respectively in lung Computed Tomography (CT) data set (Dice similarity coefficient of 92% and average surface distance for of 3.8 mm lung) and comparable performance in abdomen (9 organs) CT data set.

2   Methods

2.1   Image Registration

Image registration can be defined as estimation of the spatial transformation $\phi : \mathbb{R}^n \rightarrow \mathbb{R}^n$, represented by the corresponding parameters or a series of displacements denoted

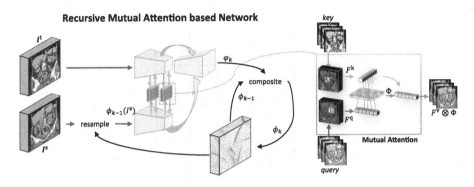

Fig. 1. Proposed framework of Recursive Mutual Attention based Network, including a Siamese Encoder-Decoder structure with Mutual Attention interconnected, and the network structure detailed in Fig. 2, where $k \in [1, K] \cap \mathbb{Z}$ denotes the recursive index and $K \in \mathbb{Z}_+$ denotes the total recurrent number. (Color figure online)

by $\phi[\boldsymbol{x}] \in \mathbb{R}^d$ at the spatial position $\boldsymbol{x} \in \mathbb{Z}^d$ of a target image $\boldsymbol{I}^t \in \mathbb{R}^n$ from a source image $\boldsymbol{I}^s \in \mathbb{R}^n$, where n is the size of a 3D image defined as $n = H \times W \times T$, and d, T, H, W denoting the image dimension, thickness, height, and width, respectively. Originally, image registration was solved as an optimization problem by minimization of a dissimilarity metric $\mathcal{D}$ and a regularization term $\mathcal{S}$:

$$\hat{\phi} = \underset{\phi}{\operatorname{argmin}} \big(\mathcal{D}(\phi(\boldsymbol{I}^s),\, \boldsymbol{I}^t) + \lambda \mathcal{S}(\phi, \boldsymbol{I}^t) \big) \tag{1}$$

where $\hat{\phi}$ denotes the estimated spatial transformation, λ denotes the weight of the regularization. More recently, the registration is performed via CNN $\mathcal{R}$ directly regressing the spatial transformation e.g. using the Dense Displacement Field (DDF) [3,14]:

$$\phi = \mathcal{R}(\boldsymbol{I}^s, \boldsymbol{I}^t; w) \tag{2}$$

with the training process based on minimizing the loss function (e.g. given in Eq. (1)) with the trainable weights w (w is omitted in the following part of the paper to simplify the formula). However the direct regression of spatial transformations via convolution neural networks could suffer due to limited capture range of the receptive field of convolutional layers when dealing with large motion.

2.2 Recursive Registration Networks

Inspired by [24], we proposed a recursive network structure for coarse-to-fine registration of a pair of images as shown in Fig. 1. In coarse-to-fine approach, the residual transformation φ_k between the target image $\boldsymbol{I}^t$ and the warped source feature map based on previous level $k - 1$ registration $\phi_{k-1}(\boldsymbol{I}^s)$ is estimated via $\mathcal{R}$ and accumulated via composition:

$$\begin{cases} \phi_k = \phi_{k-1} \circ \varphi_k \\ \varphi_k = \mathcal{R}(\phi_{k-1}(\boldsymbol{I}^s), \boldsymbol{I}^t) \end{cases} \tag{3}$$

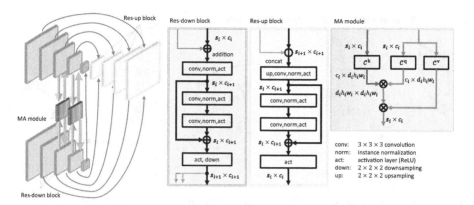

Fig. 2. The subnetwork in Fig. 1 including three main components, a Siamese Encoder consists of four pairs of Residual Downsampling (Res-down) blocks, Residual Upsampling (Res-up) block, and two Mutual Attention (MA) modules. (Color figure online)

where $\circ$ denotes the composition of two spatial transformations, and ϕ_0 is initialized as the identity transform. The subnetwork used in Fig. 1 including a weight-sharing two-branch Siamese encoder interconnected with a Mutual Attention module to extract and retrieve the common features, and a decoder to estimate the DDF φ_k, where each component of the network structure is shown in Fig. 2, and where the convolution layers in each Res-down and Res-up blocks are set with the kernel size of 3, and atrous rate (1,1,3) following the theoretical optimization of receptive field size in [27].

2.3 Mutual Attention

Similar to the idea from [7, 13, 19, 26], Mutual Attention (MA) mechanism [21] is used in the RMAn to obtain the global receptive field and use so-called indicator matrices to quantify the relationship between each pair of pixels from two images, and the usage of multiple indicator matrices is called multi-head. The feature maps $F^k, F^q \in \mathbb{R}^{c \times n}$ are extracted from two stream of the two images I^s, I^t via the encoder part as shown in Fig. 1, where c denotes the feature channel number. Each element of F^k (yellow arrow in Figs. 1 and 2) as a key vector is retrieved in the query vectors via correlation from F^q (blue arrow) in an indicator matrix $\Phi \in \mathbb{R}^{n \times n}$ which can be formulated as:

$$\Phi = \text{softmax}(\mathcal{C}^q(F^k)^\top \mathcal{C}^k(F^q)) \tag{4}$$

Then the vector from F^q is passed through the corresponding linear mapping to the other stream via the Φ:

$$\begin{cases} F^v = \mathcal{C}^v(F^k) \\ F^{k \to q} = F^v \otimes \Phi \end{cases} \tag{5}$$

where $F^{k \to q}$ denotes the feature maps passed from one stream to the other (green arrow in Figs. 1 and 2), $\mathcal{C}^q$, $\mathcal{C}^k$ and $\mathcal{C}^v$ denote the linear transformation for query, key and value feature vectors, respectively. Because the MA module is used bi-directly, the feature forwarded as both the key and query features are denoted as half blue half yellow arrows in Figs. 1 and 2, and the corresponding green arrow always point to the branch of the query stream.

3 Experiments

3.1 Datasets

We evaluated the proposed RMAn for unsupervised deformable registration problem using two publicly available data sets with the ground truth annotations for 9 organs in abdomen CT data set and lung volumes annotations in lung CT data set.

Unpaired Abdomen CTs are selected from [6]. The ground truth segmentation of spleen, right kidney, left kidney, esophagus, liver, aorta, inferior vena cava, portal, splenic vein, and pancreas are annotated for all CT scans. The inter-subject registration of the abdominal CT scans is challenging due to large inter-subject variations and great variability in organ volume, from 10 ml (esophagus) to 1.6 l (liver). Following the previously presented works, each volume is resized to $2 \times 2 \times 2 \, \text{mm}^3$ in the pre-processing step. From totally 30 subjects, 23 and 7 are respectively used for training and testing, forming 506 and 42 different pairs of images.

Unpaired Chest (Lung) CTs are selected from [9]. The CT scans are all acquired at the same time point of the breathing cycle with a slice thickness of 1.00 mm and slice spacing of 0.70 mm. Pixel spacing in the X-Y plane varies from 0.63 to 0.77 mm with an average value of 0.70 mm. The ground truth annotations of lungs for all scans are provided. Following the previously presented works, each volume is resized to $1 \times 1 \times 1 \, \text{mm}^3$ in the pre-processing step. We perform inter-subject registration from the total of 20 subjects, 12 and 8 are respectively used for training and testing, forming 132 and 56 different pairs of images.

3.2 Training Details

We normalize the input image into 0–1 range and augment the training data by randomly cropping input images during training. For the experiments on inter-subject registration of abdomen and lung CT, the models are first pre-trained for 50k iteration on synthetic DDF, with the loss function set as:

$$\mathcal{L}_{\text{syn}} = \sum \|\phi - \tilde{\phi}\|_2^2 + \lambda \sum \|\nabla \phi\|_2^2 \tag{6}$$

Then the models are trained on real data for 100k iterations with the loss function:

$$\mathcal{L} = \mathcal{D}(\boldsymbol{I}^{\text{t}} - \phi(\boldsymbol{I}^{\text{s}})) + \lambda \|\nabla \phi \odot \text{e}^{-\|\nabla \boldsymbol{I}^{\text{t}}\|_2^2}\|_2^2 \tag{7}$$

where normalized cross correlation and mean squared error are used in abdomen and lung CT respectively for $\mathcal{D}$ following [4]. The whole training takes one week, including the data transfer, pretraining and fine-tuning. With a training batch size of 3, The model was end-to-end trained with Adam optimizer with the initial learning rate set as 0.001.

3.3   Implementation and Evaluation

Implementation: The code for inter-subject image registration tasks was developed based on the framework of [3] in Python using Tensorflow and Keras. It was run on Nvidia Tesla P100-SXM2 GPU with 16 GB memory, and Intel(R) Xeon(R) Gold 6126 CPU @ 2.60 GHz.

Baselines: We compared RMAn with the relevant state-of-the-art networks. The Voxelmorph [4] is adopted as the representative state-of-the-art, deep learning method of direct regression (DR). The composite network combing CNN (Global-net) and U-net (Local-net) following to [10], recursive cascaded network (RCN) [24] were also adopted into the framework as the relevant baselines representing multi-stage (MS) networks, as well as D-net [26] was adopted for DIR based on the MA mechanism.

Evaluation Criterion: Following [22], we calculated the Dice Coefficient Similarity (DSC), Hausdorff Distance (HD), and Average Surface Distance (ASD) on annotated organs for the performance evaluation of nine organs in abdomen CT and one organ (lung) in chest CT. We additionally calculated the negative number of Jacobian determinant in tissues' region (detJ) for rationality evaluation on prediction. The model size and running time for comparison with the previous methods on inter-subject registration of lung and abdomen are shown in Table 1.

4   Results

Table 1. Average of Dice Similarity Coefficient (DSC), Average Surface Distance (ASD), Hausdorff Distance (HD) and negative number of Jacobian determinant in tissues' region (detJ) for unsupervised inter-subject registration of abdomen and chest CT using the Voxelmorph (VM1) [4] and its enhanced version with double number of feature channels (VM2), D-net [26] adopted for deformable registration, convolution networks cascaded with U-net (Cn+Un) [10], 5-recursive cascaded network based on the structure of the Voxelmorph (RCn) [24], and our RMAn network, with different registration (reg.) types and varying Parameter Number (#Par), and Time cost per Pair of Images (TPI).

Model	Reg. type	Abdomen (9 organs)				Chest (lung)				Efficiency	
		DSC↑	HD↓	ASD↓	detJ↓	DSC↑	HD↓	ASD↓	detJ↓	#Par↓	TPI↓
		(%)	(mm)	(mm)	(e3)	(%)	(mm)	(mm)	(e3)	(e6)	(sec)
Initial	–	30.9	49.5	16.04	–	61.9	41.6	15.86	–	–	–
VM1	DR	44.7	**43.8**	9.24	2.23	84.0	32.9	6.38	5.94	0.36	0.23
VM2	DR	51.9	45.0	8.40	4.03	88.8	32.0	5.02	15.58	1.42	0.25
Dnet	MA	47.4	47.6	8.72	5.28	88.3	33.2	5.01	10.38	0.40	0.41
Cn+Un	MS	53.6	44.6	7.84	4.13	91.1	**29.7**	3.84	4.23	2.11	0.36
RCn	MS	**55.6**	44.9	7.79	2.91	89.8	33.1	4.68	5.68	0.36	0.44
RMAn	MS+MA	55.2	45.1	**7.78**	4.32	**92.0**	31.8	**3.83**	4.53	0.40	0.67

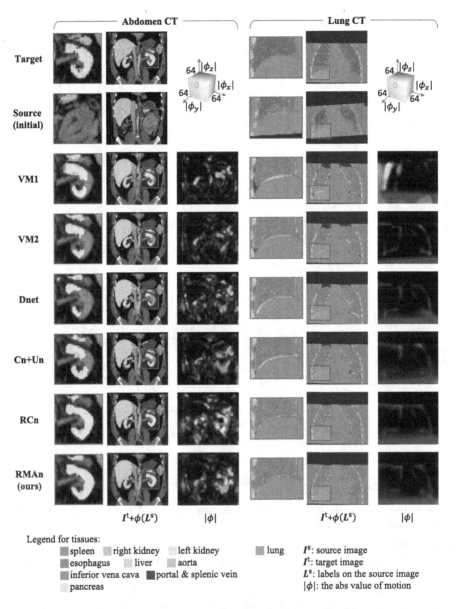

Fig. 3. Qualitative example in chest CT shows our network achieves plausible registration, with a significant improvement, especially at the edge area of the left kidney and the lung.

Comparison with the State-of-the-Art Networks: Our proposed RMAn is compared with other methods on unsupervised DIR of abdomen and chest CT using all 10 organs. With an intuitive qualitative results shown in Fig. 3, RMAn achieves better performance on registration with an improvement in the area of lung boundaries (as depicted by the

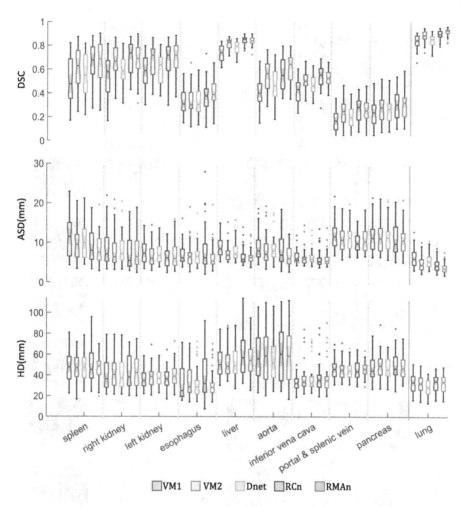

Fig. 4. RMANs achieve the best registration of the lung in chest CT scans as well as one of the best in the abdomen CT scans.

Table 2. Ablation study on recursive structure by inter-subject image registration of abdomen CT and lung CT using, with varying setting of recursive number (Rec. No.) for training and testing.

Model	Rec. no.		Abdomen (9 organs)				Chest (lung)				Efficiency	
	K_{train}	K_{infer}	DSC↑ (%)	HD↓ (mm)	ASD↓ (mm)	detJ↓ (e3)	DSC↑ (%)	HD↓ (mm)	ASD↓ (mm)	detJ↓ (e3)	#Par↓ (e6)	TPI↓ (sec)
MAn	1	1	47.4	47.6	8.72	5.28	88.3	33.2	5.01	10.38	0.40	0.41
RMAn	2	2	52.2	45.5	8.35	5.20	91.2	**31.6**	4.16	6.74	0.40	0.64
RMAn	3	3	54.4	44.9	7.91	5.01	91.4	32.6	4.01	5.36	0.40	0.65
RMAn	3	5	**55.2**	45.1	**7.78**	**4.32**	**92.0**	31.8	**3.83**	**4.53**	0.40	0.65

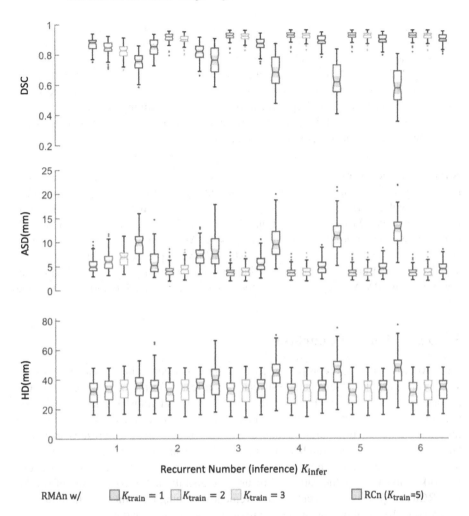

Fig. 5. The registration results on chest CT using our RMANs and the baseline RCn, with varying recursive number both for training and inference, shows that, with the increase of recursive number (inference), the model with recursive number (training) 2 and 3 achieve higher accuracy and converge closely, while it get worse with recursive number (training) 1, and RMAn outperform RCN with each K_{infer} in terms of DSC and ASD.

red box) and a plausible registration on the nine organs in the abdomen CT scans. The quantitative results shown in Fig. 4 illustrate that our RMAn achieves the best on lung and one of the best on the other nine abdominal organs. More numerical results are shown in Table 1, which demonstrates our network achieved comparable performance in this task with lower computational cost.

Ablation Study: Comparing VM1 and D-net in Table 1, the MA based architecture outperforms the pure encoder-decoder structure in two dataset with comparable network scale. To validate the effect of recursive architecture, we also tried several combination on varying recursive number for training and testing stage respectively on experiments of abdomen and lung CT as shown in Table 2 and Fig. 5. Comparing RMAn ($K_{\text{train}} = 1, K_{\text{infer}} = 1$) with others, the results show recursive architecture used in both training and testing phase results in the improved accuracy both in chest and abdomen CT scans, and the larger recurrent number for training could bring significant improvement. In addition, architecture reduces the negative number of Jacobian determinant, which thus improves the rationality of registration.

Number of Recurrent Stages: Furthermore, RMAn is tested with varying recurrent number for both training and inference as shown in Fig. 5. Surprisingly, the performance of RMAn with recurrent number $K_{\text{train}} = 1$ and $K_{\text{infer}} > 1$ for training and inference is even worse than MAn ($K_{\text{train}} = 1$ and $K_{\text{infer}} = 1$). This is probably due to the lack of recursive pattern during training for $K_{\text{train}} = 1$. As shown in Fig. 5, the RMAn with $K_{\text{train}} = 2$ and $K_{\text{train}} = 3$ as well as the RCn achieve improvement with more K_{infer}. We also compare our RMAn with baseline RCn based on varying K_{infer} as shown in Fig. 5. It shows RMAn outperform RCn for varying $K_{\text{infer}} \in [1, 8]$ in terms of DSC and ASD.

5 Discussion and Conclusion

The novel RMAn design is proposed based on the MA structure incorporated in a recursive architecture. It achieves the best registration results in the inter-subject lung CT registration and one of the best on other 9 organs in abdominal CT scans compared with the state of the art networks. The recursive architectures for registration are also investigated via varying training and inference recurrent number. The results show that larger inference recurrent number can improve the registration results, and on the other hand, also implies a small influence of the training recurrent number as long as the sub-network is able to learn the pattern of recursive registration. The comparison of RMAn with RCn also proves the accuracy improvement stemming from the MA. In future, the proposed RMAn will be also applied to multi-modal image registration.

Acknowledgements. This work was supported by a Kennedy Trust for Rheumatology Research Studentship, the Centre for OA Pathogenesis Versus Arthritis (Versus Arthritis grant 21621). B. W. Papież acknowledges Rutherford Fund at Health Data Research UK (MR/S004092/1).

References

1. Aggarwal, H.K., Mani, M.P., Jacob, M.: MoDL: model-based deep learning architecture for inverse problems. IEEE Trans. Med. Imaging **38**(2), 394–405 (2018)
2. Avants, B.B., Epstein, C.L., Grossman, M., Gee, J.C.: Symmetric diffeomorphic image registration with cross-correlation: evaluating automated labeling of elderly and neurodegenerative brain. Med. Image Anal. **12**(1), 26–41 (2008)
3. Balakrishnan, G., Zhao, A., Sabuncu, M.R., Guttag, J., Dalca, A.V.: An unsupervised learning model for deformable medical image registration. In: Proceedings of the IEEE Conference on Computer Vision and Pattern Recognition, pp. 9252–9260 (2018)

4. Balakrishnan, G., Zhao, A., Sabuncu, M.R., Guttag, J., Dalca, A.V.: VoxelMorph: a learning framework for deformable medical image registration. IEEE Trans. Med. Imaging **38**(8), 1788–1800 (2019)
5. Chen, J., Du, Y., He, Y., Segars, W.P., Li, Y., Frey, E.C.: TransMorph: transformer for unsupervised medical image registration. arXiv preprint arXiv:2111.10480 (2021)
6. Dalca, A., et al.: Learn2reg-the challenge (2020)
7. Heinrich, M.P.: Closing the gap between deep and conventional image registration using probabilistic dense displacement networks. In: Shen, D., et al. (eds.) MICCAI 2019. LNCS, vol. 11769, pp. 50–58. Springer, Cham (2019). https://doi.org/10.1007/978-3-030-32226-7_6
8. Heinrich, M.P., Jenkinson, M., Papież, B.W., Brady, S.M., Schnabel, J.A.: Towards real-time multimodal fusion for image-guided interventions using self-similarities. In: Mori, K., Sakuma, I., Sato, Y., Barillot, C., Navab, N. (eds.) MICCAI 2013. LNCS, vol. 8149, pp. 187–194. Springer, Heidelberg (2013). https://doi.org/10.1007/978-3-642-40811-3_24
9. Hering, A., Murphy, K., van Ginneken, B.: Learn2Reg challenge: CT lung registration - training data, May 2020. https://doi.org/10.5281/zenodo.3835682
10. Hu, Y., et al.: Weakly-supervised convolutional neural networks for multimodal image registration. Med. Image Anal. **49**, 1–13 (2018)
11. Jaderberg, M., Simonyan, K., Zisserman, A., et al.: Spatial transformer networks. Adv. Neural. Inf. Process. Syst. **28**, 2017–2025 (2015)
12. Jia, X., et al.: Learning a model-driven variational network for deformable image registration. IEEE Trans. Med. Imaging **41**(1), 199–212 (2021)
13. Li, Z., Liu, X., Drenkow, N., Ding, A., Creighton, F.X., Taylor, R.H., Unberath, M.: Revisiting stereo depth estimation from a sequence-to-sequence perspective with transformers. In: Proceedings of the IEEE/CVF International Conference on Computer Vision, pp. 6197–6206 (2021)
14. Mok, T.C., Chung, A.: Fast symmetric diffeomorphic image registration with convolutional neural networks. In: Proceedings of the IEEE/CVF Conference on Computer Vision and Pattern Recognition, pp. 4644–4653 (2020)
15. Rueckert, D., Sonoda, L.I., Hayes, C., Hill, D.L., Leach, M.O., Hawkes, D.J.: Nonrigid registration using free-form deformations: application to breast MR images. IEEE Trans. Med. Imaging **18**(8), 712–721 (1999)
16. Schnabel, J.A., Heinrich, M.P., Papież, B.W., Brady, J.M.: Advances and challenges in deformable image registration: from image fusion to complex motion modelling. Med. Image Anal. **33**, 145–148 (2016)
17. Song, X., et al.: Cross-modal attention for MRI and ultrasound volume registration. In: de Bruijne, M., et al. (eds.) MICCAI 2021. LNCS, vol. 12904, pp. 66–75. Springer, Cham (2021). https://doi.org/10.1007/978-3-030-87202-1_7
18. Sotiras, A., Davatzikos, C., Paragios, N.: Deformable medical image registration: a survey. IEEE Trans. Med. Imaging **32**(7), 1153–1190 (2013)
19. Sun, J., Shen, Z., Wang, Y., Bao, H., Zhou, X.: LoFTR: detector-free local feature matching with transformers. In: Proceedings of the IEEE/CVF Conference on Computer Vision and Pattern Recognition, pp. 8922–8931 (2021)
20. Thirion, J.P.: Image matching as a diffusion process: an analogy with Maxwell's demons. Med. Image Anal. **2**(3), 243–260 (1998)
21. Vaswani, A., et al.: Attention is all you need. In: Advances in Neural Information Processing Systems, pp. 5998–6008 (2017)
22. de Vos, B.D., Berendsen, F.F., Viergever, M.A., Sokooti, H., Staring, M., Išgum, I.: A deep learning framework for unsupervised affine and deformable image registration. Med. Image Anal. **52**, 128–143 (2019)

23. Zhang, Y., Pei, Y., Zha, H.: Learning dual transformer network for diffeomorphic registration. In: de Bruijne, M., et al. (eds.) MICCAI 2021. LNCS, vol. 12904, pp. 129–138. Springer, Cham (2021). https://doi.org/10.1007/978-3-030-87202-1_13

24. Zhao, S., Dong, Y., Chang, E.I., Xu, Y., et al.: Recursive cascaded networks for unsupervised medical image registration. In: Proceedings of the IEEE/CVF International Conference on Computer Vision, pp. 10600–10610 (2019)

25. Zhao, S., Lau, T., Luo, J., Eric, I., Chang, C., Xu, Y.: Unsupervised 3D end-to-end medical image registration with volume tweening network. IEEE J. Biomed. Health Inform. **24**(5), 1394–1404 (2019)

26. Zheng, J.-Q., Lim, N.H., Papież, B.W.: D-net: Siamese based network for arbitrarily oriented volume alignment. In: Reuter, M., Wachinger, C., Lombaert, H., Paniagua, B., Goksel, O., Rekik, I. (eds.) ShapeMI 2020. LNCS, vol. 12474, pp. 73–84. Springer, Cham (2020). https://doi.org/10.1007/978-3-030-61056-2_6

27. Zhou, X.Y., Zheng, J.Q., Li, P., Yang, G.Z.: ACNN: a full resolution DCNN for medical image segmentation. In: 2020 IEEE International Conference on Robotics and Automation (ICRA), pp. 8455–8461. IEEE (2020)

Spatiotemporal Attention Constrained Deep Learning Framework for Dual-Tracer PET Imaging

Dankun Lian[1], Yue Li[1], and Huafeng Liu[1,2,3(✉)]

[1] State Key Laboratory of Modern Optical Instrumentation,
College of Optical Science and Engineering,
Zhejiang University, Hangzhou 310027, China
`liuhf@zju.edu.cn`
[2] Jiaxing Key Laboratory of Photonic Sensing and Intelligent Imaging,
Jiaxing 314000, China
[3] Intelligent Optics and Photonics Research Center, Jiaxing Research Institute,
Zhejiang University, Jiaxing 314000, China

Abstract. Dual-tracer positron emission tomography (PET) imaging can provide the concentration distribution of two tracers in the body in a single scan, helping to better diagnose and understand diseases. However dual-tracer PET imaging separation is a challenging problem because of indistinguishable gamma photon pairs. In this work, we propose a two-dimensional convolutional network to separate the reconstructed mixed activity images, with the aid of channel attention modules to pay attention to both spatial and temporal information, which play an important role in the separation. Simulation experiments with different tracer pairs, scanning times, and phantoms are conducted to verify the generalization and robustness of the method to noise and individual differences. And its performance is also evaluated with real datasets. These results demonstrate the proposed method might have strong potential for the dual-tracer PET imaging.

Keywords: Dual-tracer PET imaging · Separation · Deep learning · Spatiotemporal information

1 Introduction

Positron Emission Tomography (PET), a powerful medical imaging technique, is often used to identify distribution of radiolabeled probes at molecular level and becomes an extremely effective diagnostic aid. Dynamic dual-tracer PET can provide more comprehensive spatiotemporal information than single-tracer PET in one scan, which saves time and cost while improving the accuracy of diagnosis and helping doctors choose more effective treatment options [1]. However, since the gamma photon pairs emitted by different tracers have the same energy (both 511 keV), it is difficult to distinguish different tracer signals in dual-tracer

G. Yang et al. (Eds.): MIUA 2022, LNCS 13413, pp. 87–100, 2022.
https://doi.org/10.1007/978-3-031-12053-4_7

PET imaging. Currently, methods for imaging the concentration distribution of two tracers in one scan are mainly divided into traditional methods and deep learning methods. Traditional methods [2–4] require additional information and are affected by tracer pairs and injection intervals. In contrast, deep learning methods do not suffer from these limitations and can achieve good separation effect because of their powerful feature learning capabilities.

At present, deep learning methods to achieve dual-tracer signal separation are mainly divided into two categories. The first method starts from mixed images, reconstructed from EM or MAP methods. Time activity curves (TACs) show the changes in the concentration value of a pixel on the image at different time frames, and TACs are extracted from these images for separation, such as stacked auto-encoder (SAE) [5], deep belief network (DBN) [6,7] and mask-based bidirectional gated recurrent unit (MB-BGRU) [8]. The limitation of these methods is to separate the signal of each pixel without considering the spatial information. Another type of method is to use a three-dimensional convolutional network to reconstruct and separate the activity images of a single tracer directly from the mixed sinogram, such as FBP-CNN [9] and multi-task learning three-dimensional convolutional network [10]. Although these methods can focus on both temporal and spatial information, the large amount of parameters in the network makes training difficult. Considering that reconstruction in a neural network consumes a lot of memory, or there are no constraints, the generalization is limited and a large amount of data is required [11]. This work proposes a method starting from the reconstructed activity images, that can focus on both temporal and spatial information, and has fewer network parameters, low training cost, and stronger generalization and robustness.

This work proposes a two-dimensional convolutional neural network based on U-net to separate two single-tracer activity images from the reconstructed dual-tracer activity images. Convolutional networks can handle spatial information. Considering that temporal information is as important as spatial information during dynamic dual-tracer PET imaging, we input the activity images of a series of time frames into the network and take the number of time frames as the initial number of feature channels, and focus on the time information by adding channel attention mechanisms to the network. Compared with 3D-CNN (the separation network part in FBP-CNN) which simultaneously focuses on spatiotemporal information, this network has ten times fewer parameters. We set up four sets of simulation experiments to verify the generalization of the network to sampling protocol, tracer pair and phantom shape, robustness to noise and kinetic parameter variation range, and the performance of the method is demonstrated with real experiments. We compare this method with MB-BGRU method and 3D-CNN method, using different evaluation metrics, our method can outperform with about 10 times faster.

2   Methodology

2.1   Dual-Tracer PET Imaging Model

The model for simultaneous injection of dual-tracer PET imaging can be described as:

$$X^{dual}(t) = GY^{dual}(t) + e(t) \qquad (1)$$

$$Y^{dual}(t) = Y^I(t) + Y^{II}(t) \qquad (2)$$

where t represents time, X^{dual} is the dual-tracer sinogram obtained by PET scan, G is the system matrix, Y^{dual} is the dual-tracer activity images, which is composed of Y^I and Y^{II} of the two tracers injected separately, and e is the noise generated by sampling process. This work starts from the mixed activity images reconstructed from the sinogram and uses the proposed network to obtain Y^I and Y^{II}.

2.2   Network Architecture

We designed the network structure on the basis of U-net [12], as shown in Fig. 1. Considering dynamic PET imaging, we input the dual-tracer activity images of the same slice at different time frames into the network. Because it is a two-dimensional convolution network, the number of feature map channels at the beginning is the number of time frames. The convolutional layers in the network are followed by a batch normalization layer and a Leaky ReLU activation layer, except the activation function of the last convolutional layer is softplus. There are two convolutional layers before and after each change in the number of feature channels. The convolutional layer will eliminate some details of the image, so we add a skip connection pointing from the input of the first convolutional layer to the output of the second convolutional layer. At the end of U-net, two channel attention modules [13] are added. Because the channel dimension is initially represented by the number of time frames, the channel attention module is designed to improve the utilization of temporal information. Finally, the network outputs a stacked activity images of the two tracers.

2.3   Loss Function and Evaluation Metrics

Loss Function. The loss function we used in the training process was composed of mean square error (MSE) and structural similarity index (SSIM), as follows:

$$L = \alpha[MSE(\hat{y}_1, y_1) + MSE(\hat{y}_2, y_2)] - \beta[ln\frac{1 + SSIM(\hat{y}_1, y_1)}{2} + ln\frac{1 + SSIM(\hat{y}_2, y_2)}{2}] \qquad (3)$$

where α and β are weighting factors that balance MSE and SSIM, we tested the performance of different combinations using grid search and finally set to 1 and 0.02 respectively in the training process; $\hat{y}_1$ and $\hat{y}_2$ represent the predicted image and y_1 and y_2 are the ground truth image, where subscripts 1 and 2 represent two tracers, respectively. MSE evaluates the difference between each pixel in the predicted image and the ground truth image, SSIM measures image similarity in terms of luminance, contrast and structure. MSE and SSIM can be calculated as:

$$MSE(\hat{y}, y) = \frac{\sum_{i=1}^{N}(\hat{y}_i - y_i)^2}{N} \qquad (4)$$

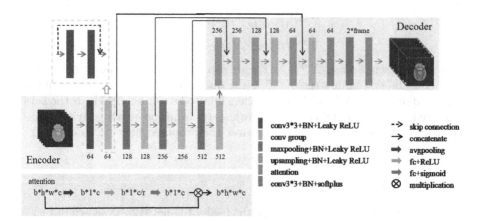

Fig. 1. A schematic diagram of the network structure, the feature channels will change each time downsampling or upsampling, and the number of feature channels in each layer is marked in the figure. Two channel attention mechanisms are added at the end of the network (see the lower left corner for details), and finally a stacked activity images of the two tracers is output.

$$SSIM(\hat{y}, y) = \frac{(2\mu_y\mu_{\hat{y}} + c_1)(2\sigma_{y\hat{y}} + c_2)}{(\mu_y^2 + \mu_{\hat{y}}^2 + c_1)(\sigma_y^2\sigma_{\hat{y}}^2 + c_2)} \qquad (5)$$

where N is the number of pixels, μ_y, σ_y and $\sigma_{y\hat{y}}$ are mean of y, standard deviation of y and covariance of y and $\hat{y}$, c_1 and c_2 are constants used to prevent the denominator from being zero, related to the range of pixel value in ground truth image.

Evaluation Metrics. We used MSE, Multi-scale SSIM (MS-SSIM) [14] and Peak Signal to Noise Ratio (PSNR) to assess the separated activity images quality. MS-SSIM considers the resolution, and is a combination of SSIM calculated separately after scaling the two pictures from large to small. PSNR is defined as:

$$PSNR = 10 \cdot log_{10}[\frac{y_{max}^2}{MSE(\hat{y}, y)}] \qquad (6)$$

where y_{max} is the maximum value of the image.

The image has singular points due to noise, so before calculating the loss function and evaluating the results, the image should be normalized to a common range. The normalization method is as follows:

$$y_{norm} = \frac{y - min(y)}{max(y) - min(y)} \qquad (7)$$

where $min(\cdot)$ gets the minimum value of the image pixel value, $max(\cdot)$ gets the maximum value of the image pixel value.

3   Experiments and Results

3.1   Simulation Datasets and Implementation Details

The three-dimensional Zubal phantom (128 pixel $\times$ 128 pixel $\times$ 40 slice) [15] is mainly used in the simulation, and this phantom has five regions of interest (ROI). We used the parallel compartment model to simulate the dynamic spatial distribution of the tracer. The kinetic parameters describing the velocity of the tracer movement between different ROIs are obtained in real experiments in the literature [16–18]. To generate more data, we randomly select kinetic parameters from a Gaussian distribution with mean values of the true experimental values. In the simulation experiment, we used different tracer pairs with different half-lives. Tracers with long half-lives require longer scanning time. Each scanning time has 18 time frames. The details of sampling protocol setting are shown in Table 1. Each set of experiments generates 1200 sets of dynamic PET data, each set of data contains 18 time frames, of which 960 sets are used for training, 120 sets are used for validation, and 120 sets are used for testing. The training set, validation set and test set have different kinetic parameter. Since the sinogram needs a system matrix to reconstruct the activity images, which consumes a lot of memory in the network, we use the Filtered Back-projection (FBP) reconstruction algorithm to obtain the activity image (128 pixel $\times$ 128 pixel $\times$ 18 frame) and input it into the network for subsequent separation.

Table 1. Details of sampling protocol setting

Tracer	Scanning time	Scanning protocol
^{18}F-FDG/^{11}C-FMZ	40 min	$2 \times 60\,s + 2 \times 90\,s + 14 \times 150\,s$
	50 min	$3 \times 60\,s + 7 \times 140\,s + 8 \times 230\,s$
	60 min	$2 \times 60\,s + 6 \times 180\,s + 10 \times 240\,s$
^{11}C-FMZ/^{11}C-acetate	30 min	$4 \times 30\,s + 12 \times 110\,s + 2 \times 180\,s$

We input the dual-tracer activity images into the network for separation, and the respective activity images of the two tracers are used as the ground truth of the network. The optimizer of the network is Adam, the learning rate is set to 0.0002 during the training process, the batch size is 8, and a total of 100 epochs are trained.

3.2   Simulation Experiments

^{18}F-FDG+^{11}C-FMZ. For the first and second sets of experiments, we selected the tracer pair ^{18}F-FDG and ^{11}C-FMZ. Due to the large difference in half-life of these two tracers (110 min and 20.4 min), we set the scanning time to 40 min, 50 min and 60 min, and generated 1200 sets of data (10 group kinetic parameters

× 3 scanning time × 40 slice) to form the datasets with a ratio of 8:1:1 for training, validation and testing. We trained and tested it using proposed network and 3D-CNN network, considering that this phantom has the first two ROIs per slice, we calculated the average pixel value on the first two ROIs of each frame for both methods, resulting in six TAC curves. Figure 2 shows these TAC curves, it can be seen that both methods apply different sampling protocols, but for the first tracer (^{18}F-FDG), the 3D-CNN method deviates seriously, our method is closer to the ground truth, and it can be seen that using the channel attention module can better focus on temporal information.

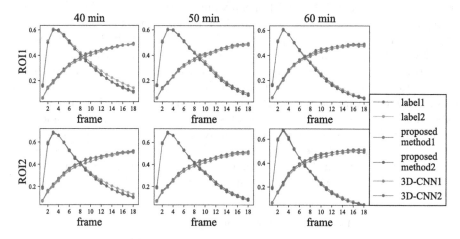

Fig. 2. TAC curve comparison chart. Each row is an ROI area, followed by 40 min, 50 min and 60 min. There are six TAC curves in each figure, blue and orange represent ground truth, green and red represent the results of the proposed method, and purple and brown represent 3D-CNN results. (Color figure online)

We superimpose random noise on the simulated sinogram, the signal-to-noise ratios (SNR) are 19 dB, 12 dB and 6 dB respectively, and trained and tested them respectively. Each data set has 1200 sets of data as before. The results are shown in Fig. 3, which shows the activity images of the 17th, 26th and 35th slices, with two ROIs, three ROIs, and five ROIs, respectively. It can be seen that as the signal-to-noise ratio decreases, the noise artifacts become larger, but still present a clear and smooth image, which is not much different from the ground truth. It reflects the high robustness of the network to noise.

^{11}C-FMZ+^{11}C-acetate. For the third set of experiments, we selected the tracer pair ^{11}C-FMZ and ^{11}C-acetate. The difference from the previous group is that the half-life of the previous group of tracers is about 5 times different, this group of tracers has the same half-life. Because of the short half-life of this set of tracer pair, we set the scanning time to 30 min. We randomly generate varying kinetic parameters by Gaussian to simulate physiological differences between individuals. In order to explore the performance of the network in the

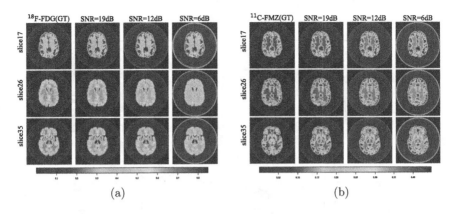

Fig. 3. Separation results of the 17th, 26th and 35th slices at SNR of 19 dB, 12 dB and 6 dB. (a) ^{18}F-FDG, (b) ^{11}C-FMZ.

case of large individual differences, we set the variance of Gaussian random to 10%, 15% and 20% of the mean, and each group has 1200 sets of data (30 group kinetic parameters × 40 slice). Figure 4(a)–(c) shows the profile of the separation results using the proposed network and MB-BGRU network. It can be seen that when the variation range of the kinetic parameters becomes larger, the deviation between the activity images and the ground truth of the two networks becomes larger, but the proposed network has less deviation and clearer boundaries than the MB-BGRU network, which shows that the network has good robustness to the differences between individuals, demonstrating the importance of paying attention to spatial information. Figure 4(d) and (e) show the evaluation metrics MS-SSIM and PSNR of the two networks in each group of experiments. The larger the value, the better the effect. It can be seen that our method outperforms MB-BGRU in both metrics, further verifying the superiority of proposed method.

Three Two-Dimensional Phantoms. In the fourth set of experiments, we selected another three two-dimensional phantoms. They are two-dimensional Zubal complex brain phantom, Zubal thorax phantom and Hoffman simple brain phantom (64 pixel × 64 pixel). Each phantom has different ROIs, corresponding to different tissues or organs. We chose three tracer pairs ^{18}F-FDG and ^{18}F-FLT, ^{62}Cu-ATSM and ^{11}C-DTBZ, ^{18}F-FLT and ^{11}C-FMZ. These tracer pairs have the same or very different half-lives, the shorter half-life of the radionuclide adopts the shorter scanning time, and a total of 90 sets of data (10 group kinetic parameters × 3 scanning time × 3 phantoms) are generated. The ratio for training and testing is 4:1. The results are shown in Fig. 5. It can be seen that for each phantom, the network achieves a certain separation effect, which proves the generalization of the network to different organ structures.

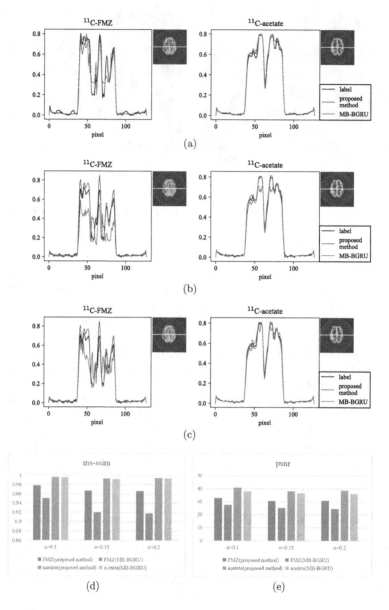

Fig. 4. Profiles of separation results using the proposed network and MB-BGRU network at different ranges of kinetic parameters. The black line represents the label, the green line represents the proposed method, and the red line represents the MB-BGRU method. The range from top to bottom is (a) 10%, (b) 15%, (c) 20%. (d) The MS-SSIM values of the proposed method and the MB-BGRU method on different tracers for different ranges of kinetic parameters. (e) Similar to (d), the value of PSNR. (Color figure online)

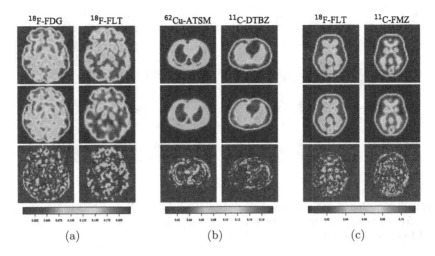

Fig. 5. The separation results of the three phantoms, the first row is the ground truth, the second row is the separation result of the proposed network, and the third row is the absolute error map.

3.3 Real Experiments

Studies have shown that in certain brain regions, mitochondria-related energy exhaustion may precede glycolysis-related hypometabolism due to pathologically confirmed early neurodegeneration in Alzheimer's disease [19]. ^{18}F-BCPP-EF can image the activity of mitochondrial complex I, and ^{18}F-FDG can measure the local brain glucose metabolism rate, so the simultaneous use of these two tracers can obtain more information in the study of neurodegenerative diseases, which has clinical significance. We used a high-resolution small animal PET scanner (SHR-38000; Hamamatsu Photonics KK, Hamamatsu, Japan) to perform dynamic PET scans of five male rhesus monkeys (rhesus macaques) weighing 4.7–8.7 kg, sequentially injected with two tracers and at intervals of more than one week to ensure complete metabolism of the tracer in the body. We used a scanning time of 120 min ($6 \times 10\,s + 2 \times 30\,s + 8 \times 60\,s + 10 \times 300\,s + 6 \times 600\,s$) to obtain 32 frames of dynamic PET data. The acquired raw data is listmode, converted to sinogram and reconstructed with Iterative 3D Dynamic Raw-Action Maximum Likelihood Algorithm (3D-DRAMA). Considering that the reconstructed image may be noisy, we performed Gaussian smoothing on the reconstruction result as the ground truth for network separation. To reduce errors caused by multiple scans, we summed the unsmoothed data from two single-tracer scans as a dual-tracer activity images. We chose the data of four monkeys as the training set and the data of the other monkey as the test set.

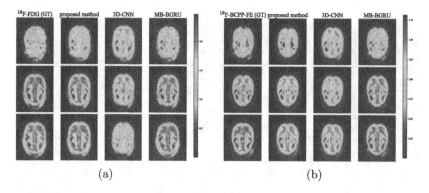

Fig. 6. Separation results of the proposed method, 3D-CNN and MB-BGRU on real data, from top to bottom are the 6th, 18th and 30th frames of the same slice. (a) ^{18}F-FDG, (b) ^{18}F-BCPP-EF.

The experimental results are shown in Fig. 6. The proposed network, 3D-CNN and MB-BGRU are used for training and testing respectively, and the activity images of frames 6, 18 and 30 are shown in turn. It can be seen that the separation results of 3D-CNN are somewhat blurred, and even obvious noise appears. Our method and MB-BGRU perform better, but for the 6th frame, the proposed method is closer to the ground truth than MB-BGRU. Table 2 shows the quantitative results of the three networks, although the proposed network has a lower average of some metrics in ^{18}F-FDG than the MB-BGRU network, it has a smaller standard deviation. At the same time, for the same amount of data, the training time is less, the speed is about 10 times that of the other two. The proposed method can obtain better quality separation results in less time.

4   Discussion

The network proposed in this work is designed on the basis of U-net, mainly adding channel attention mechanisms to focus on time information. In order to prove that the proposed method is more effective than U-net, we use the original U-net and our method to train and test on the first set of simulation data, respectively, and obtain their respective evaluation metrics as shown in Fig. 7(a)–(c). The smaller the MSE, the better, and the larger the MS-SSIM and PSNR, the better. It can be seen that the proposed method is superior to the original U-net in evaluation metrics, and has a smaller standard deviation. Figure 7(d) shows the TAC curves of ROI1 and ROI2 at different sampling times, for the tracer ^{18}F-FDG, both methods perform well, but for another tracer, our method is closer to the ground truth than the original U-net, especially after the fourth frame. The proposed method performs better on separation and also demonstrates the importance of considering temporal information.

Table 2. The evaluation metrics of the three methods in the real experiment. The value in front is the average, the $\pm$ is followed by the standard deviation

Metrics	Tracer	Proposed method	3D-CNN	MB-BGRU
MSE	^{18}F-FDG	0.0016 ± 0.00031	0.00026 ± 0.00084	0.0016 ± 0.00051
	^{18}F-BCPP-EF	$0.00085 \pm 6.56e\text{-}5$	0.0019 ± 0.00054	0.0025 ± 0.00067
MS-SSIM	^{18}F-FDG	0.952 ± 0.0024	0.923 ± 0.0067	0.956 ± 0.0061
	^{18}F-BCPP-EF	0.968 ± 0.0012	0.947 ± 0.0045	0.945 ± 0.0080
PSNR	^{18}F-FDG	28.04 ± 0.81	26.08 ± 1.23	28.24 ± 1.47
	^{18}F-BCPP-EF	30.71 ± 0.33	27.34 ± 1.20	26.20 ± 1.21

The loss function of this method uses two weighting factors α and β to balance MSE and SSIM. We set α to 1, and β to 0.1, 0.05, 0.02 and 0.01 in turn, and use loss functions of different proportions to train and test on the first set of simulation data. Figure 7(e) and (f) represent the MSE and PSNR under different proportions, it can be seen that the best performance is obtained when α is set to 1 and β is set to 0.02.

However, there are some problems to be solved. First, the method is to separate the dual-tracer signals from the reconstructed mixed activity images, so the result is limited by the accuracy of the traditional reconstruction algorithm. Second, considering the problems of tracer dose matching and physiological differences caused by multiple scans, the mixed activity images that we input into the network in both simulation and real experiments are reconstructed from the addition of two tracer sinograms. However, in practice, the scanning results obtained after the simultaneous injection of two tracers may not be the simple addition of two single tracers after injection. It is possible that the concentration of one tracer is higher than the concentration of another tracer due to the dose of tracer, human absorption, etc. Third, this work is mainly to prove the availability of the proposed method in dual-tracer PET imaging. The experiments are mainly based on phantom images, and no specific clinical application is analyzed. In future work, we can consider adding reconstruction modules and constraints to the neural network to improve the accuracy of the reconstructed activity images with less memory loss, and also need to consider the injection dose ratio of the tracer concentration. At the same time, the analysis of the specific physiological structure should be considered, whether it meets the clinical requirements needs further research.

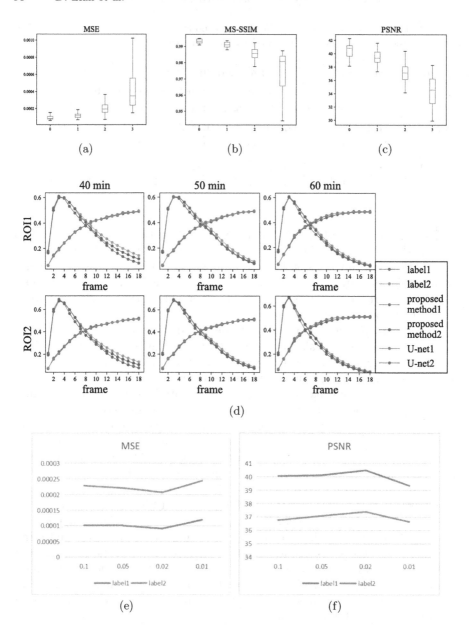

Fig. 7. Boxplots of evaluation metrics obtained using the proposed method and the original U-net, each boxplot from left to right is ^{18}F-FDG (the proposed method), ^{18}F-FDG (original U-net), ^{11}C-FMZ (proposed method), ^{11}C-FMZ (original U-net). (a) MSE, (b) MS-SSIM, (c) PSNR. (d) TAC curves of ROI1 and ROI2 under different sampling protocols, blue and orange represent ground truth, green and red represent the results of the proposed method, and purple and brown represent original U-net results. (e) and (f) represent the MSE and PSNR obtained using different scaled loss functions, and the two lines represent different tracers.

5 Conclusion

This paper proposed a deep learning network framework based on U-net to separate the mixed dual-tracer activity images into two single-tracer activity images. Compared with the method that separates TACs after extracting TACs from the mixed activity images, this method takes spatial information into account. Compared with the 3D convolutional network, by adding channel attention modules to pay attention to temporal information, it can take less time to obtain a good-quality single-tracer activity images. We verify the superiority of this method in simulation experiments and real experiments. Four sets of simulation experiments verify the generalization of the network to sampling protocols, tracer pairs, and phantom shapes, and robustness to noise and kinetic parameter variations. Real experiments also prove that this method outperforms other networks in evaluation metrics and image quality.

Acknowledgements. This work was supported by the Talent Program of Zhejiang Province (2021R51004).

References

1. Kadrmas, D.J., Hoffman, J.M.: Methodology for quantitative rapid multi-tracer pet tumor characterizations. Theranostics **3**(10), 757 (2013)
2. Huang, S., Carson, R., Hoffman, E., Kuhl, D., Phelps, M.: An investigation of a double-tracer technique for positron computerized tomography. J. Nucl. Med. **23**(9), 816–822 (1982)
3. Koeppe, R.A., Raffel, D.M., Snyder, S.E., Ficaro, E.P., Kilbourn, M.R., Kuhl, D.E.: Dual-[11c] tracer single-acquisition positron emission tomography studies. J. Cereb. Blood Flow Metab. **21**(12), 1480–1492 (2001)
4. Kudomi, N., Hayashi, T., Teramoto, N., Watabe, H., Kawachi, N., Ohta, Y., Kim, K.M., Iida, H.: Rapid quantitative measurement of CMRO2 and CBF by dual administration of 15o-labeled oxygen and water during a single pet scan - a validation study and error analysis in anesthetized monkeys. J. Cereb. Blood Flow Metab. **25**(9), 1209–1224 (2005)
5. Ruan, D., Liu, H.: Separation of a mixture of simultaneous dual-tracer pet signals: a data-driven approach. IEEE Trans. Nucl. Sci. **64**(9), 2588–2597 (2017)
6. Xu, J., Liu, H.: Deep-learning-based separation of a mixture of dual-tracer single-acquisition pet signals with equal half-lives: a simulation study. IEEE Trans. Radiat. Plasma Med. Sci. **3**(6), 649–659 (2019)
7. Qing, M., Wan, Y., Huang, W., Xu, Y., Liu, H.: Separation of dual-tracer pet signals using a deep stacking network. Nucl. Instrum. Methods Phys. Res. Sect. A **1013**, 165681 (2021)
8. Tong, J., Wang, C., Liu, H.: Temporal information-guided dynamic dual-tracer pet signal separation network. Med. Phys. (2022)
9. Xu, J., Liu, H.: Three-dimensional convolutional neural networks for simultaneous dual-tracer pet imaging. Phys. Med. Biol. **64**(18), 185016 (2019)
10. Zeng, F., Liu, H.: Dual-tracer pet image direct reconstruction and separation based on three-dimensional encoder-decoder network. In: Optics in Health Care and Biomedical Optics X, vol. 11553, p. 115530X. International Society for Optics and Photonics (2020)

11. Wang, B., Liu, H.: FBP-net for direct reconstruction of dynamic pet images. Phys. Med. Biol. **65**(23), 235008 (2020)

12. Ronneberger, O., Fischer, P., Brox, T.: U-net: convolutional networks for biomedical image segmentation. In: Navab, N., Hornegger, J., Wells, W.M., Frangi, A.F. (eds.) MICCAI 2015. LNCS, vol. 9351, pp. 234–241. Springer, Cham (2015). https://doi.org/10.1007/978-3-319-24574-4_28

13. Hu, J., Shen, L., Sun, G.: Squeeze-and-excitation networks. In: Proceedings of the IEEE Conference on Computer Vision and Pattern Recognition, pp. 7132–7141 (2018)

14. Wang, Z., Simoncelli, E.P., Bovik, A.C.: Multiscale structural similarity for image quality assessment. In: 2003 The Thirty-Seventh Asilomar Conference on Signals, Systems and Computers, vol. 2, pp. 1398–1402. IEEE (2003)

15. Zubal, I.G., Harrell, C.R., Smith, E.O., Rattner, Z., Gindi, G., Hoffer, P.B.: Computerized three-dimensional segmented human anatomy. Med. Phys. **21**(2), 299–302 (1994)

16. Cheng, X., et al.: Direct parametric image reconstruction in reduced parameter space for rapid multi-tracer pet imaging. IEEE Trans. Med. Imaging **34**(7), 1498–1512 (2015)

17. Koeppe, R., Holthoff, V., Frey, K., Kilbourn, M., Kuhl, D.: Compartmental analysis of [11c] flumazenil kinetics for the estimation of ligand transport rate and receptor distribution using positron emission tomography. J. Cereb. Blood Flow Metab. **11**(5), 735–744 (1991)

18. Chen, S., Ho, C., Feng, D., Chi, Z.: Tracer kinetic modeling of/sup 11/c-acetate applied in the liver with positron emission tomography. IEEE Trans. Med. Imaging **23**(4), 426–432 (2004)

19. Terada, T., et al.: In vivo mitochondrial and glycolytic impairments in patients with Alzheimer disease. Neurology **94**(15), e1592–e1604 (2020)

Faster Diffusion Cardiac MRI with Deep Learning-Based Breath Hold Reduction

Michael Tänzer[1]([⊠])(iD), Pedro Ferreira[1,2]([⊠])(iD), Andrew Scott[1,2](iD),
Zohya Khalique[1,2](iD), Maria Dwornik[1,2](iD), Ramyah Rajakulasingam[1],
Ranil de Silva[2], Dudley Pennell[1,2](iD), Guang Yang[1,2](iD), Daniel Rueckert[1,3](iD),
and Sonia Nielles-Vallespin[1,2](iD)

[1] Imperial College London, London, UK
{m.tanzer,m.dwornik,ramyah.rajakulasingam05,
r.desilva,d.pennell,g.yangd.rueckert,s.nielles-vallespin}@imperial.ac.uk
[2] Royal Brompton and Harefield Hospital, London, UK
{P.Ferreira,A.Scott,z.khalique}@rbht.nhs.uk
[3] Technische Universität München (TUM), Munich, Germany

Abstract. Diffusion Tensor Cardiac Magnetic Resonance (DT-CMR) enables us to probe the microstructural arrangement of cardiomyocytes within the myocardium in vivo and non-invasively, which no other imaging modality allows. This innovative technology could revolutionise the ability to perform cardiac clinical diagnosis, risk stratification, prognosis and therapy follow-up. However, DT-CMR is currently inefficient with over six minutes needed to acquire a single 2D static image. Therefore, DT-CMR is currently confined to research but not used clinically. We propose to reduce the number of repetitions needed to produce DT-CMR datasets and subsequently de-noise them, decreasing the acquisition time by a linear factor while maintaining acceptable image quality. Our proposed approach, based on Generative Adversarial Networks, Vision Transformers, and Ensemble Learning, performs significantly and considerably better than previous proposed approaches, bringing single breath-hold DT-CMR closer to reality.

Keywords: MRI · Deep learning · Diffusion · Cardiac

1 Introduction

Diffusion Tensor Cardiac Magnetic Resonance (DT-CMR) is the only medical imaging modality that allows us to non-invasively interrogate the micro-structure of the beating heart at a scale and resolution that other modalities cannot achieve [16]. In clinical research studies, DT-CMR has been shown to be useful in phenotyping several cardiomyopathies such as hypertrophic cardiomyopathy (HCM)

This work was supported in part by the UKRI CDT in AI for Healthcare http://ai4health.io (Grant No. EP/S023283/1), the British Heart Foundation (RG/19/1/34160), and the UKRI Future Leaders Fellowship (MR/V023799/1).
G. Yang, D. Rueckert and S. Nielles-Vallespin—Co-last senior authors.
The original version of this chapter has been revised: the names and details of two additional authors have been inserted into the header of the paper. The correction to this chapter can be found at https://doi.org/10.1007/978-3-031-12053-4_66

G. Yang et al. (Eds.): MIUA 2022, LNCS 13413, pp. 101–115, 2022.
https://doi.org/10.1007/978-3-031-12053-4_8

and dilated cardiomyopathy (DCM) by quantitatively analysing the microstructural organisation and orientation of cardiomyocytes within the myocardium. DT-CMR also has the additional advantage of not requiring any contrast agent, which may be burdensome for patients with reduced kidney function [19].

In its current state, the acquisition time prevents clinical translation as around six minutes are needed to acquire a single 2D slice. For a typical acquisition protocol we require a minimum of three slices (basal, mid, apical), at least 7 different diffusion encoding steps and two time points of the cardiac cycle (systole and diastole), totalling 60 breath-holds and 90 min and making it clinically unfeasible. The long scan times have various source, but, most importantly, the protocol acquires multiple repetitions of each image to increase the signal-to-noise ratio (SNR) and to reduce motion-related artefacts. In this study, we will tackle the problem by reducing the number of repetitions.

Our contribution, shown in Fig. 1, is a novel deep-learning framework that can be used to reduce the number of repetitions used in the DT-CMR acquisition. Using fewer averages leads to lower SNR, and deep learning can be used to recover the original full-repetition data. This allows us to greatly reduce the total acquisition time with minimal loss of image quality. This method could potentially be adopted to acquire a DT-CMR scan in only one breath hold while maintaining acceptable quality, reducing the scan time from several minutes to well under a minute.

2   Background

2.1   DT-CMR

DT-CMR measures the diffusion pattern of water molecules in every voxel of the imaged tissue and approximates it with a 3D tensor. As the free diffusion of water in the tissue is constrained by the shape of cardiac muscle microstructure for every voxel, studying the extracted 3D tensors has been shown to give us information related to the shape and orientation of the cardiomyocytes in the imaged tissue.

In-vivo DT-CMR requires the rapid acquisition of multiple single-shot diffusion-weighted images with diffusion encoded in at least six different 3D directions. Single-shot encoding acquisitions translate to low SNR images. Low SNR is also an inherent issue in DT-CMR as we measure the signal lost due to diffusion. Therefore, multiple repetitions are commonly acquired to increase the quality of the signal. While improving the SNR, this also translates to longer acquisition times and extra breath-holds for the patient. Our clinical research protocol requires approximately 12 breath-holds for every single DT-CMR slice at a single time point in the cardiac cycle. The series of signal intensities is then fitted to a rank-2 diffusion tensor using a linear least-square (LLS) [11] fitting or alternatively more advanced linear and non-linear iterative methods [6].

The cardiac diffusion tensor information is commonly visualised and quantified through four per-voxel metric maps: Mean Diffusivity (MD) that quantifies the total diffusion in the voxel (higher corresponds to more diffusion), Fractional Anisotropy (FA) that quantifies the level of organisation of the tissue (higher corresponds to a higher organisation), Helix Angle (HA) and Second Eigenvector

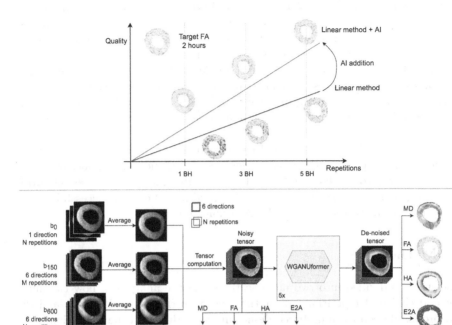

Fig. 1. Proposed deep learning framework. From left to right, we can see the original input data comprised of several repetitions that are then averaged to increase the SNR and reduce artefacts. This averaged data is then used to compute (noisy) diffusion tensors using a least squares tensor fit. From the noisy tensors we can then compute noisy DT-CMR maps (lower central part of the image). In our proposed framework we use an ensemble of deep-learning models to de-noise the diffusion tensors and therefore obtain better DT-CMR maps (shown on the right).

(E2) Angle (E2A) that quantify the 3D orientation and shape of the tissue in the voxel [2,12].

2.2 De-noising in DT-CMR

There are several ways to approach the task of reducing the number of repetitions used to compute the DT-CMR maps. In our proposed approach, we will see how we treat it as de-noising task where the goal is to produce de-noised diffusion tensors from noisy tensors.

De-noising is the process of removing noise from a given signal with the aim of restoring the original noise-free version of the signal. In a number of studies the noise is assumed to come from a known distribution, giving rise to models that work on this assumption to remove it [25], while some other studies instead do not make any assumption on the source of the noise and produce models that are more robust to real-world noise [3]. In recent years, deep learning-based de-noising has been extremely popular, both applied to photographs [23] and to other types of signals, such as MRI data [10,15], CT data [5], audio data [23], and point clouds [9]. Focusing on de-noising models designed for imaging data, Batson et al. [3] used a U-Net model and a self-supervised approach to blindly de-noise images without using an assumed noise distribution. Park et al. [17] trained a de-noising model on unpaired CT data using a GAN model. More recently, Vision Transformers have also been used to tackle the de-noising problem [4,13,20,24].

Phipps et al. [18] used a residual-learning approach to de-noise the diffusion weighted images prior to the tensor calculation to reduce the number of acquisitions required to produce high-quality DT-CMR maps. In our previous work [21], our group also showed how a U-NET-based model can be successfully used to predict de-noised tensors directly from noisy images.

3   Methods

The study is divided into two main sections: (1) the analysis of how the number and choice of repetitions affect the quality of the DT-CMR maps and (2) our proposed deep-learning-based de-noising procedure and the validation of its results.

3.1   Data Acquisition

All data used in this work was approved by the National Research Ethics Service. All subjects gave written informed consent.

All the data were acquired using a Siemens Skyra 3T MRI scanner and more recently a Siemens Vida 3T MRI scanner (Siemens AG, Erlangen, Germany) with diffusion weighted stimulated echo acquisition mode (STEAM) single shot echo planar imaging (EPI) sequence with reduced phase field-of-view and fat saturation, $TR = 2RR$ intervals, $TE = 23\,ms$, SENSE or GRAPPA $R = 2$, echo train duration $= 13\,ms$, at a spatial resolution of $2.8 \times 2.8 \times 8.0\,mm^3$. Diffusion was encoded in six directions with diffusion- weightings of $b = 150$ and $600\,s/mm^2$ in a short-axis mid-ventricular slice. Additionally, reference images were also acquired with minimal diffusion weighting, named here as "b_0" images. All diffusion data were acquired under multiple breath-holds, each with a duration of 18 heartbeats. We used a total of 744 DT-CMR datasets, containing a mixture of healthy volunteers (26%, $n = 197$) and patient (74%, $n = 547$) scans acquired in either the diastolic pause (49%, $n = 368$) or end-systole (51%, $n = 376$). The patient data comes from several conditions including 31 amyloidoses, 45 dilated cardiomyopathy (DCM), 11 Fabry's disease, 48 HCM genotype-positive-phenotype-negative (HCM G+P-), 66 hypertrophic cardiomyopathies (HCM), 4 hypertensive DCM (hDCM), 246 acute myocardial infarction (MI), 7 Marfan's syndrome, and 89 in-recovery DCM (rDCM).

3.2 Data Preparation

The mean number of repetitions was 12 ± 2.0 for b_0 images; 10 ± 2.2 for $b = 600\,s/mm^2$ images; and 2 ± 0.6 for $b = 150\,s/mm^2$. These datasets, containing all acquired data, were used to calculate the reference tensor results for each subject using a newly developed tool written in Python and validated against our previous post-processing software [22] . Before tensor calculation, all the diffusion images were assessed visually, and images corrupted with bulk motion artefacts were removed. Subsequently, all remaining images were registered with a multi-resolution rigid sub-pixel translation algorithm [8], manually thresholded to remove background features. Lastly, the left ventricle (LV) myocardium was segmented excluding papillary muscle.

Tensors were calculated with an LLS fit of all the acquired repetitions and respective diffusion weightings and directions [11]. The tensors were then used to compute the DT-CMR maps that we considered as the ground truth for all the comparisons in the study.

We were also able to dynamically create three new datasets with an increasingly reduced number of repetitions. We assessed the quality or the DT-CMR maps produced from different subsets of repetitions (e.g., using the first N repetitions vs using the last N repetitions, see Sect. 3.3). We proposed three choices for the numbers of repetitions that result in three datasets:

- 5BH. Four repetitions of b_0 and b_{600}, and one repetition of b_{150}. This acquisition would require 5 breath-holds.
- 3BH. Two repetitions of b_0 and b_{600}, and one repetition of b_{150}. This acquisition would require 3 breath-holds.
- 1BH. One repetition of b_0 and b_{600} only. This acquisition would require 1 breath-hold.

For the purpose of training a deep-learning model, the data was also randomly augmented with random rotation and random cropping.

3.3 The Effect of Repetitions

In a standard DT-CMR acquisition, we acquire several repetitions to reduce the effect of noise and motion. To do so, we ask the patient to hold and resume their breathing at fixed intervals.

First, we quantitatively studied how the number of repetitions (and breath-holds) affects the quality of the maps. We compared the maps produced from all available breath-holds with maps computed from M repetitions where M represents a number smaller than the number of available repetitions for the patient. We repeated the process separately for the four maps.

Secondly, we analysed how choosing different repetition subsets affects the final quality of the DT-CMR acquisition. We defined five different methods to select a subset from the eight original repetitions: (1) we selected the first M repetitions (First, F); (2) we selected the central M repetitions (Centre, C); (3) we used the last M repetitions (Last, L); (4) uniformly random repetition sampling (Random, R); (5) based on the clinician's observation that the first breath-hold is usually lower-quality due to the patient adjusting to holding and resuming their breath, we selected the first $M + 1$ repetitions and discarded the first one (First+1, F1).

3.4 Deep-Learning-Based De-noising

In this study, we developed and trained a deep-learning model based on the current state-of-the-art architectures for image de-noising to improve the quality of noisy DT-CMR tensors produced from the low-breath-holds datasets described above.

Input and Output. The output of all the models reported here is the diffusion tensor components. As the tensors are represented by a rank-2 symmetric matrix, they only contain six unique components: for a 3×3 matrix D we only need the upper triangular elements to represent it. All input and output images were cropped to be 128×128 pixels in size. Thus, the output is a 128×128 image with 6 channels. For the input we compared different approaches: building on our previous work, we used the average diffusion weighted images as input, resulting in 13 channels for the 5BH and 3BH datasets ($1 b_0 + 6 b_{600} + 6 b_{150}$) and 7 channels for the 1BH dataset ($1 b_0 + 6 b_{600}$). Alternatively, we also experimented with de-noising diffusion tensors directly, which translated to a six-channel input image.

We had two types of inputs: diffusion-weighted images (DWI) or diffusion tensors. In the case of DWI, the images were normalised in the range $[0, 1]$ by dividing them by the maximum value present in the dataset. The background pixels were also replaced with zeros. The diffusion tensors were instead either normalised by a fixed amount (500) that was empirically found to make most values in the range $[-1, 1]$ or normalised by performing channel-wise z-score normalisation across the whole dataset. In the latter case, the normalisation was undone before computing the maps.

The data were randomly divided into three parts: a training set, a validation set, and a test set with ratios of 80:10:10 respectively. In order to ensure consistency, all the experiments maintained the same random split.

Model. We compared our new model with our previous work as the setting is extremely similar to the one proposed here and we had obtained promising results. In our previous setting, we used a U-Net model with six encoders and six decoders. Each encoding layer consisted of two blocks, each containing a convolution layer, a batch normalisation layer and the leaky ReLU activation function; after the two blocks, a max-pooling operator was applied. Each decoding layer consisted of two blocks: the first one contained a transpose convolution, a concatenation operation, batch normalisation, and the leaky ReLU activation; the second one instead consisted of a convolution, batch normalisation, and the leaky ReLU activation. The concatenation was between encoding and decoding layers as per the original U-Net formulation. This baseline model contained a total of 31 million trainable parameters.

We proposed several modifications to the baseline above. To show the effect of these changes, we progressively introduced them on the baseline model to show how they affected the quality of the output. In these experiments, we kept the main structure of the model unchanged and we did not modify the training hyperparameters. Specifically, in order, we experimented with:

1. U-NET image-to-tensor baseline model.
2. Baseline with channel normalisation (BL+CN): the output tensors were normalised with a channel-wise z-score normalisation.
3. Baseline with tensor-to-tensor training (BL+T2T): the input type was changed from images to tensors, making the task a tensor de-noising task. This also allowed us to use residual learning for our training, improving convergence and performance. For this experiment, the tensors were only normalised by dividing all the values by a fixed amount.
4. BL+CN with tensor to tensor (BL+CN+T2T): similarly to BL+T2T, the training was performed on a tensor-to-tensor de-noising task, but in this case, the input and target tensors were normalised with z-score normalisation.
5. BL+CN+T2T with multiple datasets (BL+CN+multiT2T): multiple repetition strategies were used simultaneously for the training (First, Centre, Last). This made significantly better use of the available training data and effectively increased the size of the dataset by a factor of 3 (although using non-independent data for the training).

State of the art (SOTA) models in image de-noising and image restoration were also investigated: Restormer [24] and Uformer [20]. These models were trained with Channel Normalisation and multi tensor-to-tensor.

Finally, we investigated a novel model that made use of all the additions proposed above based on SOTA models. Specifically, we expanded on the Uformer architecture by using it as the generator of a generative adversarial network. The Uformer is a U-Net-like Transformer-based architecture that uses LeWin blocks and residual connections to form a hierarchical encoder-decoder network.

We, therefore, proposed the WGANUformer (WGUF) by adding a Patch-GAN discriminator [7] and an adversarial loss to a Uformer. The model was trained with a Wasserstein objective function and with weight clipping as per Arjovsky et al. [1] as it combats mode collapse and has been proved to converge to optimality, unlike other GAN formulations.

A schematic representation of the architecture and training procedure can be found in Fig. 1.

Training. All training was performed using a workstation with Ubuntu 18.04, CPU Intel i7-10700k, 64 GB of RAM, and an NVIDIA RTX 3080 GPU (Python 3.8 with PyTorch 1.9). The training required a total of 215 GPU-hours, resulting in an estimated 30 kg CO_2eq.

During training, a mean absolute error was used as the loss function. For the baseline-based models, other parameters included an Adam optimiser with a learning rate $= 10^{-4}$, beta1 $= 0.9$, beta2 $= 0.999$; a batch-size of 8 images and 500 epochs. These parameters and CNN design were optimised empirically based on our pilot study results. The WGANUformer was trained as per Loshchilov et al. with the AdamW optimiser [14], a learning rate $= 10^{-4}$, beta1 $= 0.9$, beta2 $= 0.999$, weight decay alpha $= 0$, a batch-size of 8 tensors for 500 epochs. All models were trained from scratch without any pre-training.

In all our experiments, we report the metrics computed on the never-seen-before test set using the model that produced the lowest validation loss.

3.5   DT-CMR Post-processing

For the computation of all metrics and maps, we post-processed the data with an in-house developed software written in Python. For the post-processing, each subject in the dataset was processed several times:

- Initially to obtain the reference tensor parameter results using all available repetitions.
- Every time we computed a dataset with a reduced number of repetitions we performed the same steps (image registration, thresholding, and segmentation). When training the models using images as input, we replaced the tensor calculation process with the model prediction.
- To produce a comparison, we also computed the conventional LLS tensor fit from the reduced datasets. All the comparisons are voxel-wise.

3.6   DT-CMR Maps Comparison

Four DT-CMR maps representing different aspects of the diffusion of water within the tissue were chosen as output. These maps represent different physical properties and need to be compared with appropriate metrics.

HA and E2A are angular maps with values between $-90°$ and $90°$. When comparing these maps, we were interested in the direction of the vector corresponding to the angle but not its orientation. This means that any two angles with a $180°$ difference should be identical and two angles with a $90°$ difference should have the maximum distance. For HA and E2A we then reported the Mean Angle Absolute Error (MAAE):

$$\text{MAAE}(X,Y) = \frac{1}{NM} \sum_{i=0}^{N} \sum_{j=0}^{M} \begin{cases} \left|X^{(i,j)} - Y^{(i,j)}\right|, & \text{if } \left|X^{(i,j)} - Y^{(i,j)}\right| < 90° \\ 180° - \left|X^{(i,j)} - Y^{(i,j)}\right|, & \text{otherwise} \end{cases}$$

(1)

For MD and FA, as they are scalar maps, we therefore reported the Mean Absolute Error (MAE) between de-noised and target maps.

In the experiments below, we reported the MAAE and MAE across all the voxels in the left ventricle (i.e., ignoring the background and the right ventricle).

Statistical Analysis. We treated all results as non-parametric as we were unable to assure normal distributions in the test subjects. The statistical significance threshold for all tests was set at P = 0.05. Intersubject measures are quoted as *median [interquartile range]*.

4 Results

4.1 The Effect of Repetitions

From Table 1, no significant differences were found between the distribution of errors for HA, E2A, and FA for all the pairs of strategies only containing First, Centre, First+1, and Last. There is, instead, a significant difference (P < 0.05) in distributions between the Random strategy compared to the other strategies for these metrics (with few non-significant exceptions for FA in 3BH and 5BH). When analysing the MD MAE errors, we found that the pairwise significance pattern we had observed for the other metrics does not hold and we did not recognise any clear pattern.

4.2 Deep-Learning-Based De-noising

We report the results of our experiments on tensor de-noising in Table 2.

Training Additions. Channel normalisation brought an overall improvement compared to the baseline, especially when considering metrics computed from datasets with a higher number of repetitions. On the other hand, tensor-to-tensor training on its own appeared to be unstable, greatly benefiting some metrics while making some others worse (e.g., HA for 1BH compared to FA for 5BH) with no discernible pattern. By combining the two, we obtained a model that was more stable than one with T2T only but with slightly worse performance than using only CN. Nonetheless, T2T opened the doors to multi-tensor-to-tensor training, which brought a remarkable improvement to all metrics compared to a naive T2T approach.

State-of-the-Art Models. Between the two explored SOTA models, Restomer consistently outperformed Uformer at the cost of a much longer and computationally-expensive training (13 h vs 3 h on our machine). For this reason, the Uformer was chosen for further exploration.

GAN Uformer and Ensemble Learning. The addition of a discriminator and its associated loss to the training produced tensors that better encoded angular information but that encode scalar information marginally worse.

The best possible model given our training additions and architectural choices was produced by an ensemble of five Wasserstein GAN Uformer models

Table 1. MAAE and MAE for HA, E2A, MD and FA for the different sampling scheme choices compared to using all the available repetitions. We also report the statistical significance of comparing the distributions of pairs of repetitions strategies. This provides information on whether two repetitions-sampling strategies produce the same distribution of errors across our dataset or not. In this context, a green background signifies that we can reject the null hypothesis that the errors belong to the same distribution according to the Kolmogorov–Smirnov test.

Dataset	Scheme	HA MAAE					E2A MAAE				
1BH	First	25.69 [4.95]	C	L	F1	R	33.66 [4.77]	C	L	F1	R
	Centre	25.93 [5.26]	F	L	F1	R	33.86 [4.57]	F	L	F1	R
	Last	25.94 [4.91]	F	C	F1	R	33.87 [4.33]	F	C	F1	R
	First+1	25.69 [4.82]	F	C	L	R	33.57 [4.70]	F	C	L	R
	Random	26.60 [4.78]	F	C	L	F1	34.36 [4.48]	F	C	L	F1
3BH	First	20.10 [4.62]	C	L	F1	R	28.13 [5.45]	C	L	F1	R
	Centre	20.12 [4.75]	F	L	F1	R	28.24 [5.04]	F	L	F1	R
	Last	20.23 [4.89]	F	C	F1	R	28.22 [4.94]	F	C	F1	R
	First+1	20.09 [4.63]	F	C	L	R	28.23 [5.33]	F	C	L	R
	Random	21.02 [4.74]	F	C	L	F1	29.03 [5.07]	F	C	L	F1
5BH	First	13.90 [4.13]	C	L	F1	R	20.98 [5.28]	C	L	F1	R
	Centre	13.97 [4.08]	F	L	F1	R	21.02 [5.30]	F	L	F1	R
	Last	14.07 [4.05]	F	C	F1	R	20.89 [5.08]	F	C	F1	R
	First+1	14.06 [4.00]	F	C	L	R	21.07 [5.27]	F	C	L	R
	Random	14.68 [4.26]	F	C	L	F1	21.78 [5.51]	F	C	L	F1

Dataset	Scheme	MD MAE ($\times 10^5$)					FA MAE ($\times 10^2$)				
1BH	First	14.69 [5.51]	C	L	F1	R	19.50 [4.59]	C	L	F1	R
	Centre	15.75 [6.39]	F	L	F1	R	19.80 [4.72]	F	L	F1	R
	Last	15.58 [6.52]	F	C	F1	R	19.45 [4.82]	F	C	F1	R
	First+1	14.44 [5.30]	F	C	L	R	19.50 [4.57]	F	C	L	R
	Random	15.72 [6.52]	F	C	L	F1	20.41 [5.01]	F	C	L	F1
3BH	First	9.76 [3.93]	C	L	F1	R	14.13 [3.92]	C	L	F1	R
	Centre	9.63 [3.76]	F	L	F1	R	13.99 [4.04]	F	L	F1	R
	Last	10.12 [4.36]	F	C	F1	R	14.03 [3.72]	F	C	F1	R
	First+1	9.64 [3.91]	F	C	L	R	14.05 [3.92]	F	C	L	R
	Random	8.85 [3.38]	F	C	L	F1	14.49 [4.05]	F	C	L	F1
5BH	First	6.24 [2.68]	C	L	F1	R	9.05 [3.05]	C	L	F1	R
	Centre	6.32 [2.76]	F	L	F1	R	8.93 [3.02]	F	L	F1	R
	Last	6.50 [2.92]	F	C	F1	R	8.90 [2.96]	F	C	F1	R
	First+1	6.16 [2.69]	F	C	L	R	8.90 [3.05]	F	C	L	R
	Random	5.86 [2.42]	F	C	L	F1	9.27 [2.85]	F	C	L	F1

(WGUFx5). Using even a naive bagging ensemble greatly improved all metrics for all datasets compared to using a single model.

All metrics except for MD for 1BH and MD for 5BH were significantly improved by our final model compared to the baseline (Wilcoxon signed-rank test, P < 0.05). Our best performing model is the result of a naive bagging ensembling of five WGANUformer models (WGUFx5). The results show that even a naive bagging ensemble improves stability and validation performance, and reduces the variance of the output, all desirable properties in a medical setting.

Table 2. DT-CMR maps errors for all the deep-learning models we experiment with. The table is divided into three sections, one per dataset (1BH, 3BH, 5BH) and also include the error for the linear approximation method of the maps (Least squares). In bold and underlined we report, respectively, the best and second best results for each metric and dataset.

	Model	HA	E2A	MD ($\times 10^5$)	FA ($\times 10^2$)
	WGUFx5 + CN + multi T2T	**11.55 [4.45]**	**21.79** [7.28]	6.45 [3.35]	9.16 [4.32]
	WGUF + CN + multi T2T	12.03 [4.51]	22.82 [8.61]	7.12 [3.20]	**8.62 [3.71]**
	Restomer + CN +multi T2T	12.07 [4.85]	22.88 [7.61]	6.49 [3.35]	9.70 [4.07]
	Uformer + CN +multi T2T	12.18 [4.47]	23.08 [6.27]	6.52 [3.36]	8.91 [4.12]
1BH	BL + CN + multi T2T	<u>11.92 [4.30]</u>	<u>22.17 [7.18]</u>	6.44 [3.57]	9.26 [4.04]
	BL + CN + T2T	12.73 [5.11]	25.04 [8.38]	6.16 [3.05]	10.15 [4.73]
	BL + T2T	13.03 [4.74]	26.16 [8.10]	**6.03 [3.03]**	10.70 [4.86]
	BL + ChanNorm	13.60 [5.05]	24.80 [8.94]	6.30 [6.14]	9.44 [3.99]
	Baseline (BL)	13.86 [4.36]	25.90 [7.69]	<u>6.14 [2.98]</u>	8.93 [3.45]
	Least squares	20.80 [8.06]	31.62 [7.00]	11.40 [3.25]	17.06 [4.65]
	WGUFx5 + CN + multi T2T	**10.05 [3.86]**	**18.81 [6.04]**	**5.02 [2.11]**	7.69 [3.72]
	WGUF + CN + multi T2T	10.25 [4.21]	19.56 [6.33]	5.31 [2.04]	8.06 [3.57]
	Restomer + CN + multi T2T	10.38 [4.11]	<u>19.41 [5.82]</u>	5.72 [2.04]	<u>7.48 [3.20]</u>
	Uformer + CN + multi T2T	10.42 [4.18]	19.86 [7.13]	5.43 [2.11]	**7.26 [3.36]**
3BH	BL + CN + multi T2T	<u>10.73 [5.01]</u>	20.21 [6.92]	5.57 [2.01]	8.38 [3.19]
	BL + CN + T2T	11.33 [5.30]	22.12 [7.84]	5.54 [2.75]	9.55 [5.17]
	BL + T2T	12.57 [5.65]	22.46 [7.40]	5.96 [2.53]	10.09 [4.01]
	BL + ChanNorm	12.85 [4.90]	21.62 [6.86]	5.37 [1.93]	8.57 [3.17]
	Baseline (BL)	12.00 [5.25]	24.34 [6.56]	5.39 [1.78]	8.35 [3.12]
	Least squares	15.11 [7.56]	23.85 [6.61]	7.88 [3.39]	12.09 [4.07]
	WGUFx5 + CN + multi T2T	**8.39 [3.80]**	**15.56 [6.46]**	4.67 [1.89]	**6.30 [2.85]**
	WGUF + CN + multi T2T	8.54 [4.15]	16.58 [6.07]	4.53 [2.00]	6.61 [3.11]
	Restomer + CN + multi T2T	8.66 [3.82]	<u>15.57 [6.67]</u>	4.73 [1.81]	6.79 [2.80]
	Uformer + CN + multi T2T	8.75 [4.03]	16.07 [6.43]	4.48 [1.75]	<u>6.44 [2.48]</u>
5BH	BL + CN + multi T2T	<u>8.45 [4.25]</u>	16.30 [6.99]	4.79 [2.03]	6.71 [2.79]
	BL + CN + T2T	9.54 [5.44]	17.20 [7.34]	5.71 [2.69]	9.23 [3.91]
	BL + T2T	9.77 [4.90]	17.77 [7.15]	4.59 [1.80]	7.78 [3.12]
	BL + ChanNorm	10.81 [4.11]	18.92 [6.60]	4.16 [1.74]	6.96 [2.43]
	Baseline (BL)	10.94 [3.80]	19.61 [5.37]	**4.11 [2.14]**	8.03 [3.34]
	Least squares	9.79 [4.26]	17.20 [5.51]	6.10 [2.67]	8.30 [2.93]

5 Discussion

5.1 Breath-Hold Choice

From our results on the breath-hold repetition sampling patterns, we can draw several conclusions on how the patient behaviour affects the quality of the maps:

- Despite the clinician's intuition, no significant conclusion can be drawn about the difference in errors between the First and the First+1 protocols.
- There is no clear pattern for the pairwise significance of the results within a dataset, suggesting that there are other factors that affect the quality of the maps besides the sampling pattern.
- Lower numbers of breath-holds produce far fewer significant results compared to higher-breath-holds datasets (44/80 for BH1, 46/80 for BH3 and 48/80 for BH5). This can be attributed to the higher variability of errors due to the effect of the singular bad acquisition on the final quality of the maps. Such effect is instead smoothed out when considering the maps produced from a larger number of repetitions, making the error distributions more similar to each other.

Keeping the statistical significance in mind, First, Centre, or Last sampling strategies seem a reasonable choice as they have lower error and no significant difference in error distributions. The exception is for MD, for which the difference is sometimes significant. For this reason, we decided to train our models on the First, Centre, and Last strategies, but to only use the First strategy for the validation and test sets. Notice that the data acquired with the First+1 strategy was not used for the training as it contains a considerable amount of redundancy with that acquired with the First scheme. This also mirrors a real clinical acquisition situation, where choosing the first M repetitions is the shortest option in terms of the number of breath-holds for the patient. Any other strategy would require us to acquire and discard some data, which is not feasible in a clinical setting where the aim is to minimise the scan time for the patient.

5.2 Deep-Learning-Based De-noising

Our proposed additions to the training (channel normalisation, tensor-to-tensor training and multi-tensor-to-tensor training) have a beneficial effect if we consider the errors on the DT-CMR derived maps. This is due to various reasons:

- Channel normalisation simplifies the training, allowing the network to not focus on rescaling the output to match the input range for each channel individually.
- Tensor-to-tensor training completely changes the training objective. In our previous work, we had trained a model to compute de-noised tensors from noisy images, effectively replacing the linear optimisation problem (LSS). This corresponds to training the model on two tasks simultaneously: de-noising and tensor computation, making the overall convergence harder. In

our new proposed setting, we simplify the training objective by removing the tensor-computation aspect and only leaving the de-noising part of the training. Moreover, this allowed us to make use of the existing literature in the well-studied field of image de-noising, while our previous approach (image-to-tensor) proposed a model for a completely novel task with no existing literature.
- Making use of multiple sampling patterns from our available data also gave us an advantage over previous work by allowing us to greatly increase the size of the dataset used for the training without the need to scan additional patients.

Our final model, WGUFx5, draws from the SOTA in camera images de-noising uses several novel blocks to encode local information by using local self-attention and hierarchical feature encoding. All these additions produce a definite improvement in our tensor de-noising task.

Finally, according to the literature, a bagging ensemble reduces the variance of the prediction and therefore suggests that previous models were inadvertently overfitting to the training set, despite our efforts to prevent it. The ensemble strategy in our setting can be therefore interpreted to act as a regulariser.

6 Conclusion

DT-CMR has the potential to revolutionise the ability to non-invasively image and assess the microstructural organisation of the myocardium underlying cardiac pathology, but it is held back from clinical translation by its long acquisition times. Here, we proposed to tackle the problem by reducing the number of repetitions used in a classical DT-CMR acquisition protocol, which linearly reduced the total acquisition time, but also decreased SNR. When choosing the repetition selection scheme, we demonstrated that the choice of breath-hold had no statistically significant effect on the final quality of the DT-CMR maps. We also proposed several improvements on existing deep learning models, that, combined, may lead to a significant and considerable step towards single-breath-hold DT-CMR acquisition for clinical use.

References

1. Arjovsky, M., Chintala, S., Bottou, L.: Wasserstein GAN. arXiv:1701.07875 [cs, stat], December 2017
2. Basser, P.J.: Inferring microstructural features and the physiological state of tissues from diffusion-weighted images. NMR Biomed. **8**(7), 333–344 (1995)
3. Batson, J., Royer, L.: Noise2Self: blind denoising by self-supervision. In: Proceedings of the 36th International Conference on Machine Learning, pp. 524–533. PMLR, May 2019
4. Chen, H., et al.: Pre-trained image processing transformer. In: 2021 IEEE/CVF Conference on Computer Vision and Pattern Recognition (CVPR), Nashville, TN, USA, pp. 12294–12305. IEEE, June 2021. https://doi.org/10.1109/CVPR46437.2021.01212

5. Chen, H., et al.: Low-dose CT denoising with convolutional neural network. In: 2017 IEEE 14th International Symposium on Biomedical Imaging (ISBI 2017), pp. 143–146, April 2017. https://doi.org/10.1109/ISBI.2017.7950488

6. Collier, Q., Veraart, J., Jeurissen, B., den Dekker, A.J., Sijbers, J.: Iterative reweighted linear least squares for accurate, fast, and robust estimation of diffusion magnetic resonance parameters (2015)

7. Demir, U., Unal, G.: Patch-based image inpainting with generative adversarial networks. arXiv:1803.07422 [cs] (Mar 2018)

8. Guizar-Sicairos, M., Thurman, S.T., Fienup, J.R.: Efficient subpixel image registration algorithms. Opt. Lett. **33**(2), 156–158 (2008). https://doi.org/10.1364/OL.33.000156

9. Hermosilla, P., Ritschel, T., Ropinski, T.: Total denoising: unsupervised learning of 3D point cloud cleaning. In: Proceedings of the IEEE/CVF International Conference on Computer Vision, pp. 52–60 (2019)

10. Jiang, D., Dou, W., Vosters, L., Xu, X., Sun, Y., Tan, T.: Denoising of 3D magnetic resonance images with multi-channel residual learning of convolutional neural network. Jpn. J. Radiol. **36**(9), 566–574 (2018). https://doi.org/10.1007/s11604-018-0758-8

11. Kingsley, P.B.: Introduction to diffusion tensor imaging mathematics: Part II. Anisotropy, diffusion-weighting factors, and gradient encoding schemes. Concepts Magn. Reson. Part A **28**(2), 123–154 (2006)

12. Kung, G.L., et al.: The presence of two local myocardial sheet populations confirmed by diffusion tensor MRI and histological validation. J. Magn. Reson. Imaging **34**(5), 1080–1091 (2011)

13. Liang, J., Cao, J., Sun, G., Zhang, K., Van Gool, L., Timofte, R.: SwinIR: image restoration using Swin transformer. In: 2021 IEEE/CVF International Conference on Computer Vision Workshops (ICCVW), Montreal, BC, Canada, pp. 1833–1844. IEEE, October 2021. https://doi.org/10.1109/ICCVW54120.2021.00210

14. Loshchilov, I., Hutter, F.: Decoupled weight decay regularization. arXiv:1711.05101 [cs, math], January 2019

15. Manjón, J.V., Coupe, P.: MRI denoising using deep learning. In: Bai, W., Sanroma, G., Wu, G., Munsell, B.C., Zhan, Y., Coupé, P. (eds.) Patch-MI 2018. LNCS, vol. 11075, pp. 12–19. Springer, Cham (2018). https://doi.org/10.1007/978-3-030-00500-9_2

16. Mori, S., Zhang, J.: Principles of diffusion tensor imaging and its applications to basic neuroscience research. Neuron **51**(5), 527–539 (2006). https://doi.org/10.1016/j.neuron.2006.08.012

17. Park, H.S., Baek, J., You, S.K., Choi, J.K., Seo, J.K.: Unpaired image denoising using a generative adversarial network in X-ray CT. IEEE Access **7**, 110414–110425 (2019). https://doi.org/10.1109/ACCESS.2019.2934178

18. Phipps, K., et al.: Accelerated in Vivo cardiac diffusion-tensor MRI using residual deep learning-based denoising in participants with obesity. Radiol. Cardiothorac. Imaging **3**(3), e200580 (2021). https://doi.org/10.1148/ryct.2021200580

19. Schlaudecker, J.D., Bernheisel, C.R.: Gadolinium-associated nephrogenic systemic fibrosis. Am. Fam. Physician **80**(7), 711–714 (2009)

20. Wang, Z., Cun, X., Bao, J., Zhou, W., Liu, J., Li, H.: Uformer: a general U-shaped transformer for image restoration. arXiv:2106.03106 [cs], November 2021

21. Ferreira, P.F., et al.: Accelerating cardiac diffusion tensor imaging with a U-Net based model: toward single breath-hold. J. Magn. Reson. Imaging (2022)

22. Ferreira, P.F., et al.: In vivo cardiovascular magnetic resonance diffusion tensor imaging shows evidence of abnormal myocardial laminar orientations and mobility in hypertrophic cardiomyopathy. J. Cardiovasc. Magn. Reson. **16**(1), 1–16 (2014)

23. Xie, J., Xu, L., Enhong, C.: Image denoising and inpainting with deep neural networks. In: Advances in Neural Information Processing Systems, vol. 3, pp. 183–189. Morgan-Kaufmann (2012)

24. Zamir, S.W., Arora, A., Khan, S., Hayat, M., Khan, F.S., Yang, M.H.: Restormer: efficient transformer for high-resolution image restoration. arXiv:2111.09881 [cs], November 2021

25. Zhang, K., Zuo, W., Chen, Y., Meng, D., Zhang, L.: Beyond a Gaussian denoiser: residual learning of deep CNN for image denoising. IEEE Trans. Image Process. **26**(7), 3142–3155 (2017). https://doi.org/10.1109/TIP.2017.2662206

Preoperative CT and Intraoperative CBCT Image Registration and Evaluation in Robotic Cochlear Implant Surgery

Chenxi Lu[1,2], Bo Dong[1,2], Xi Hu[3], Yang Zhao[4], Hongjian He[1,2] 📷, and Jing Wang[5(✉)]

[1] Center for Brain Imaging Science and Technology, College of Biomedical Engineering and Instrumental Science, Zhejiang University, Hangzhou, Zhejiang, People's Republic of China
[2] Key Laboratory for Biomedical Engineering of Ministry of Education, Zhejiang University, Hangzhou, Zhejiang, People's Republic of China
[3] Department of Radiology, Sir Run Shaw Hospital, Zhejiang University School of Medicine, Hangzhou, People's Republic of China
[4] Chinese Academy of Medical Sciences & Peking Union Medical College, Beijing, People's Republic of China
[5] Sir Run Shaw Hospital, Zhejiang University School of Medicine, Hangzhou, People's Republic of China
fwjing@zju.edu.cn

Abstract. Robotic cochlear implantation is an effective way to treat deafness and severe losses in hearing, which can reduce errors caused by human factors. It requires the pre-operative CT and intra-operative CBCT image registration to map the preoperatively computed drilling trajectory into the intra-operative space, and has extremely high requirements for registration speed and accuracy. At present, the research on the registration method is mature, while the evaluation method is not effective. The current evaluation metrics are mostly limited to the similarity, lacking of geometric information. Whereas in clinical surgery, we are more concerned with the target registration error (TRE). In this work, we complete the CT-CBCT registration by the commonly used intensity-based method and do the process with the open source tool Elastix. We do experiment on 2 cadaver head datasets with 8 screws implanted and 14 human head datasets. We calculate the centroid distance of the screws in CBCT image and registered CT image. Meanwhile, we use SIFT to extract key points in images and calculate the average Euclidean distance between corresponding points. Results show that the registration time is less than one minute. The average centroid distances of the screws in two cadaver heads are 0.19 mm and 0.12 mm, and the average Euclidean distances of the key points in two cadaver heads are 0.196 mm and 0.239 mm. TRE of all 16 datasets are within one voxel. The TRE calculated by SIFT key points is very close to the result obtained from implanted screws. We can use SIFT feature extraction method to evaluate the registration accuracy instead of implanting screws into the patient's head during pre-operation period, which will greatly simplify surgical procedure and avoid unnecessary injury.

Keywords: CT-CBCT registration · SIFT feature extraction · Evaluation

G. Yang et al. (Eds.): MIUA 2022, LNCS 13413, pp. 116–129, 2022.
https://doi.org/10.1007/978-3-031-12053-4_9

1 Introduction

Thousands of people around the world suffer from cochlear damage which affects their hearing ability. Cochlear implant (CI) surgery is currently an effective method for the treatment for deafness and severe losses in hearing [1]. Doctors use a manual procedure, which costs time and effort, to get relevant information from medical images of the cochlea before CI surgery, and then work at the limits of their visual-tactile feedback and dexterity. Robotic cochlear implantation can reduce the instability of man-made operations in traditional surgery [2]. While automating this manual procedure is a challenging problem due to the small size and complicated structure of the cochlea. Combining cochlea images from different modalities using image registration and fusion techniques may help in the automation of cochlea structure identification, more accurate measurements of the cochlea, drilling path planning and implementation relevant to CI surgery.

Preoperative imaging is performed before CI surgery. A CT scan of the patient is done to identify ear anatomy and segment facial nerve [3]. An optimally safe drilling trajectory is computed based on the identified structures. During surgery, a Cone-beam computed tomography (CBCT) scan of the patient is obtained to help ensure the patient positioning and present the anatomy during treatment, which is a common on-treatment imaging method owning to its fast acquisition, cost-effectiveness, and low dose to patients. Registration between the planning CT and the intra-operative CBCT is crucial to match the drilling path and cochlear structures between two time points.

In general, the existing medical image registration methods are mainly classified into feature-based, intensity-based, segmentation-based and fluoroscopy-based [4]. Segmentation-based registration need to define a region of interest, and fluoroscopy-based registration is used for 2D-3D registration. So we mainly talk about the first two kinds. Feature-based registration has been used for CT-CBCT or other modalities image registrations in [5–7], it is computationally efficient, but the quality of registration largely depends on the accuracy of extracting and matching features. Usually, manual participation is required, even not, how to precisely match corresponding points is a problem to be solved. Intensity-based registration directly operate on voxel values, thus without manual intervention. This method achieves the purpose of aligning the two images by maximizing the similarity measures of the two images. These similarity measures include the sum of squared differences (SSD) for monomodal registration, mutual information (MI) or correlation coefficient (CC) for multimodal registration. CBCT intensity is inconsistent with CT due to artifacts from various sources such scatter, truncation. So even though CT and CBCT use the same imaging modality, X-ray, the CT-CBCT registration can be regarded as a special case of multimodal registration [8], where MI or CC is widely used. Even though intensity-based registration is widely used for its simplicity and easy-operability, it is limited by time and computing resources. Fortunately, with a hierarchical system (adoption of pyramid structure on images, eg. the method in [9]), computing time and memory can be greatly reduced. Furthermore, a large number of software have been presented for medical image registration based on intensity, such as ITK, 3D Slicer, Elastix or other commercial software. Most of them are based on C++ or shell language to improve coding performance and speed. In our study, we used Elastix for intensity-based CT-CBCT registration.

How to measure the registration effect is a more critical issue, because if there is no accurate value, no matter how advanced the algorithm is, it has no practical value. The most common method of performance evaluation is similarity measures between the whole images or outlined structures, it is the criteria to evaluate how much two or more images are similar. Among various similarity measures, root mean square error (RMSE) is the simplest, others include structural similarity index (SSIM), dice similarity coefficient (DSC), etc. While study shows that these measures, even when used in combination, cannot distinguish accurate from inaccurate registrations [10]. In addition, these measures often have no geometric significance. More reliable measure is target registration error (TRE). It evaluates the registration accuracy based on points correspondence, by computing Euclidean distance between corresponding points. It has more physical meaning, but how to choose and correspond to these points is a problem. In our study, we will comprehensively use the similarity measures and TRE to evaluate the registration error. Among them, the similarity measure is used to evaluate the overall registration effect, and the TRE is used to make up for the limitations of the similarity measures and provide a more intuitive judgment. We will discuss the methods in detail in the following sections.

2   Methods

In this section, we present a detailed description of the process we use to perform automatic registration of pre-operative CT images and intra-operative CBCT images. Most importantly, we propose specific evaluation metrics for the registration accuracy requirements, which needs to pay attention to in the actual surgery.

2.1   CT-CBCT Registration

Image Preprocessing. The raw data has different voxel size and dimensions, and contains patient bed which may be a disruptive factor in subsequent registration processes. So firstly, we need to resample the data to the same resolution. And then, remove patient bed from CT and CBCT images, consist of intensity normalization, binarization, and morphological processing operations, as shown in Fig. 1.

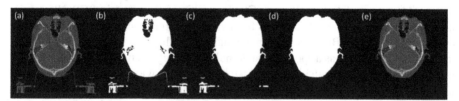

Fig. 1. Remove patient bed from the image (take one of the slices as an example) (a) the original image; (b) binary segmentation; (c) morphological processing: opening operation, filling holes; (d) extract the largest connected component and generate mask; (e) using the mask on (a)

Intensity-Based Image Registration. The algorithm and the components of intensity-based image registration used in our study are described in the flowchart in Fig. 2.

The preprocessed images act as input images. When starting the iteration process, it is necessary to sample, that is to say, adopt a hierarchical strategy. If not, it is time-consuming for large images. Then, in each level of the pyramid, the images go into the registration process, computing the cost function, e.g. the advanced mattes's mutual information (AMMI). The regular step gradient descent (RSGD) optimizer modifies parameters of the affine transform to minimize the cost function. When AMMI is maximum or it has reached the maximum iteration, optimization process ends, and outputs the transformation matrix. The transformation matrix is applied to the moving image to obtain the registered image.

We do this process using Elastix [11], which is an open-source intensity-based medical image registration software, based on the well-known Insight Segmentation and Registration Toolkit (ITK). The software allows the user to set various parameters to quickly configure, test, and compare different registration methods for a specific application. In previous studies, Elastix has been widely used for mono-modal or multi-modal, rigid or non-rigid registration [12–15], but rarely used for CT and CBCT registration.

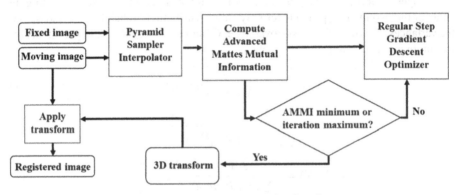

Fig. 2. Intensity-based registration flowchart

2.2 Evaluation

For robotic cochlear implant surgery, the registration speed and accuracy are the issues we focus on, otherwise, a little carelessness can cause damage to the nerve around the cochlea, since for a facial nerve a margin of up to 1.0 mm is available and an accuracy of at least 0.3 mm is required, depending on the navigation system [16]. In terms of time, from the start of timing after reading the dicom image to the stop of generating the registration image or registration matrix, this time should be less than 2 min as a project metric. There is currently no convincing gold standard for measuring registration accuracy. As is mentioned above, similarity measures cannot always distinguish accurate from inaccurate registrations, only used as a reference indicator. At present, the more reliable, intuitive, and widely used evaluation metric is target registration error (TRE). While in our study, in order to comprehensively evaluate the registration results, we use both similarity measures and TRE to evaluate registration result.

For TRE, we evaluate registration accuracy from the following two aspects: on the one hand, segment a specific structure in the two images and calculate the distance of centroid distance [17]. To ensure the accuracy of the segmentation, we used implanted titanium screws as the target structure, because in the image, the brightness and contrast of the screws is much higher than the surrounding tissue. On the other hand, determine the corresponding points in the two images and calculate the average Euclidean distance. Points can usually be manually selected by experienced doctors, however, this is more affected by human factors and cannot be accurate to a single voxel. So we adopted the method of automatically selecting points, based on the SIFT feature operator. Then we filter out some of these landmarks based on manual experience. We will discuss these two aspects in detail in the sections below.

Similarity Metrics. Similarity metrics include root mean square error (RMSE), correlation coefficient (CC), normalized mutual information (NMI), structural similarity index (SSIM). The calculation formula of each metric is as follows. X, Y represent the two images, x_i and y_i are the gray value of the ith voxel, μ_x and μ_y are the mean gray value of the two images, p stands for gray value distribution probability, σ_x^2 and σ_y^2 are the variances, and σ_{xy} is the cross-covariance. C_1 and C_2 are regularization constants for the luminance and contrast respectively.

$$\text{RMSE} = \sqrt{\frac{1}{n}\sum(x_i - y_i)^2} \tag{1}$$

$$\text{CC} = \frac{\sum(x_i - \mu_x)(y_i - \mu_y)}{\sqrt{\sum(x_i - \mu_x)^2}\sqrt{\sum(y_i - \mu_y)^2}} \tag{2}$$

$$\text{NMI(X, Y)} = 2\frac{\sum p(x_i, y_i)\log\frac{p(x_i,y_i)}{p(x_i)p(y_i)}}{\sum p(x_i)\log p(x_i) + p(y_i)\log p(y_i)} \tag{3}$$

$$\text{SSIM(X, Y)} = \frac{(2\mu_x\mu_y + C_1)(2\sigma_{xy} + C_1)}{(\mu_x^2 + \mu_y^2 + C_1)(\sigma_x^2 + \sigma_y^2 + C_1)} \tag{4}$$

Screws Centroid Position. The TRE is defined as the mean Euclidean distance between the centroid of the eight corresponding screws implanted in the specimens. The local positions of eight screws are shown in Fig. 3. They can be easily identified using threshold segmentation [18]. Then centroid position in a volume image is calculated as the equation below, where g(i, j, k) is the gray value at the voxel (i, j, k).

$$x = \frac{\sum g(i, j, k) * i}{\sum g(i, j, k)} \tag{5}$$

$$y = \frac{\sum g(i, j, k) * j}{\sum g(i, j, k)} \tag{6}$$

$$z = \frac{\sum g(i, j, k) * k}{\sum g(i, j, k)} \tag{7}$$

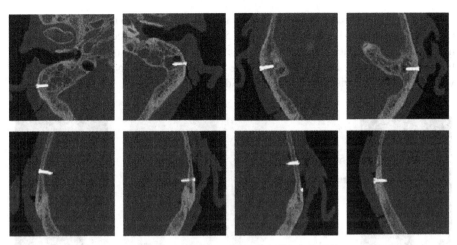

Fig. 3. Local positions of eight screws

Feature Points Extraction. To compute the average distance between the points of the reference and the registered images, we need to extract feature points and match corresponding points. The scale invariant feature transform (SIFT) is invariant to rotation, scaling, and brightness changes [19]. So it is capable of extracting and matching stable and characteristic points between two images. The SIFT-feature-based registration has been used in [7, 20, 21]. In our study, we use SIFT feature not for registration, but for evaluation.

SIFT feature extraction includes extreme detection in scale space, keypoints localization, orientation and generating a features vector called "descriptors". The whole process is shown in Fig. 4 and Fig. 5. Scale-space refers to the space formed by the convolution of a Gaussian function with the original image at different resolutions called 'octave'. The general principle of extreme value detection is to find local extremes based on the difference of Gaussians (DoG) in each octave, as shown in Fig. 4(b). The points corresponding to these found extremes, comparing each voxel to its neighbors, are called keypoints, shown in Fig. 4(c). In order to match feature points in two images, the directions of keypoints should firstly be determined, that is, the direction in which the gray value decreases the fastest, and the gradient direction and amplitude of all voxels within a certain range with the feature point as the center of the circle are counted. The angle with the highest amplitude is the main direction (Fig. 4(d)), (in order to increase robustness, an auxiliary direction is usually determined). Rotate the image to the main orientation, calculate the gradient direction histogram of eight directions in sub-region, and draw the accumulated value of each gradient direction to for a seed point (Fig. 4(e)).

For registration accuracy, the most similar SIFT descriptors in reference images and registered images need to be identified (Fig. 5). We computed the nearest and the second nearest distance neighbor in two feature descriptors. If the ratio is below a threshold [7], the feature having the lowest distance value is chosen to corresponding points, and the value is TRE. Otherwise, no association is identified.

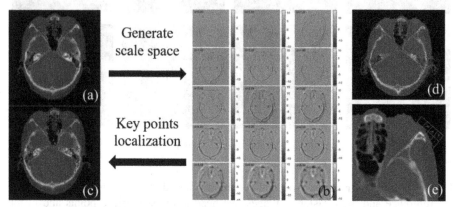

Fig. 4. (a) Original image; (b) DoG in each octave: each column stands for a resolution (from left to right, the resolution decreases) and each row stands for a Gaussian coefficient (from top to bottom, the coefficients increase, and the image becomes blurry); (c) Keypoints detection. (d) Orientation; (e) Generate descriptors (one of descriptors is shown)

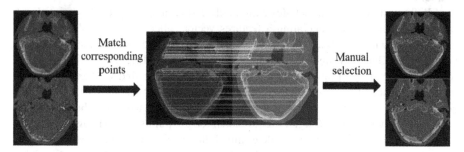

Fig. 5. The process of matching corresponding points

3 Experiments

3.1 Datasets

In this study, we conducted experiments on 16 pairs of pre-operative CT scans and intra-operative CBCT scans, of which 14 pairs were human data and 2 pairs were cadaveric data. Detailed data information is shown in Table 1. The institutional review board has approved this study.

Table 1. (a) Image-acquisition settings (CBCT). (b) Image-acquisition settings (CT)

(a)

DataID	Manufacturer	Voxelsize (mm^3)	Dimensions
corpse_head1	Imaging Sciences International	$0.250 \times 0.250 \times 0.250$	$640 \times 640 \times 528$
corpse_head2	GE Medical Systems	$0.533 \times 0.533 \times 0.400$	$512 \times 512 \times 711$
human1–7	Varian Medical Systems (OBI Cone-beam CT)	$1.172 \times 1.172 \times 2.500$	$384 \times 384 \times 64$
human8		$1.172 \times 1.172 \times 2.500$	$384 \times 384 \times 64$
human9		$0.651 \times 0.651 \times 2.500$	$384 \times 384 \times 70$
human10		$0.488 \times 0.488 \times 2.500$	$512 \times 512 \times 64$
human11		$0.488 \times 0.488 \times 2.500$	$512 \times 512 \times 116$
human12		$0.488 \times 0.488 \times 1.000$	$512 \times 512 \times 174$
human13		$0.488 \times 0.488 \times 1.000$	$512 \times 512 \times 174$
human14		$0.488 \times 0.488 \times 1.000$	$512 \times 512 \times 174$

(b)

DataID	Manufacturer	Voxelsize (mm^3)	Dimensions
corpse_head1	SIEMENS (SOMATOM Definition Flash)	$0.396 \times 0.396 \times 0.600$	$512 \times 512 \times 391$
corpse_head2	GE Medical Systems	$0.484 \times 0.484 \times 0.600$	$512 \times 512 \times 400$
human1–7	SIEMENS (Sensation Open)	$0.781 \times 0.781 \times 3.000$	$512 \times 512 \times 88$
human8		$0.977 \times 0.977 \times 3.000$	$512 \times 512 \times 122$
human9		$0.781 \times 0.781 \times 3.000$	$512 \times 512 \times 93$
human10	SIEMENS (SOMATOM Definition AS)	$0.635 \times 0.635 \times 3.000$	$512 \times 512 \times 66$
human11		$0.738 \times 0.738 \times 1.500$	$512 \times 512 \times 138$
human12		$0.787 \times 0.787 \times 3.000$	$512 \times 512 \times 70$
human13		$0.600 \times 0.600 \times 2.000$	$512 \times 512 \times 97$
human14		$0.820 \times 0.820 \times 3.000$	$512 \times 512 \times 64$

3.2 Experimental Setup

Registration was done by using Melastix Toolbox, which is a collection of MATLAB wrappers for Elastix. Program runs on MATLAB version 2021a based on Intel(R) Core(TM) i7-9750H CPU (2.60 GHz, 2592 MHz, 6 cores, 12 logical processors).

3.3 Registration Parameters

The main registration parameters we use based on Elastix are shown in Table 2.

Table 2. CT-CBCT registration parameters

Similarity measure	Advanced mattes mutual information
Optimizer	Regular step gradient descent
Maximum number of iterations	1000
Maximum step length	0.1
Number of resolutions	6
Image pyramid	Recursive image pyramid
Interpolator	BSpline interpolator
Initial translation	Aligning the geometric centers
Transform	Affine transform

4   Results

Some visual results of the registration are shown in Fig. 6, showing three slices of corpse_head1 and corpse_head2, human4 and human10. From left to right, they are the reference images, registered images and fusion display of them.

In the fusion image map, gray regions have the same intensities, while magenta and green regions show where the intensities are different. For the reason that CT and CBCT have different gray value ranges, we can see most of the area is colorful. The images are aligned, which is reflected in the overlapping of magenta and green. Among them, the corpse_head2 was deformed due to the long soaking time and incorrect placement. We used affine transformation because in the actual operation, the head will not deform greatly.

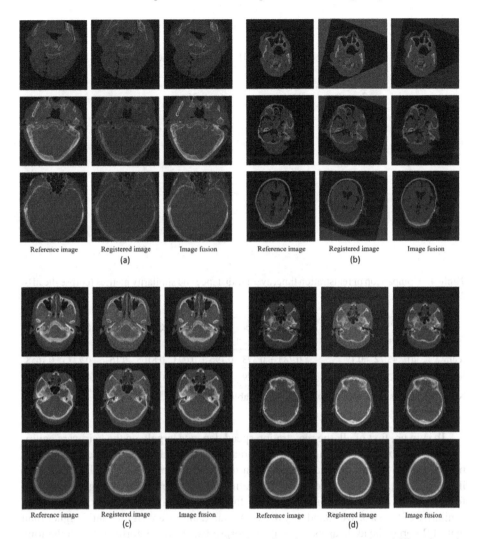

Fig. 6. Three of the slices are shown, the left column is reference image, the middle column is registered image, and the right column is fusion display, where magenta and green regions show different intensities. (a) corpse_head1 (b) corpse_head2. (c) human4. (d) human10. (Color figure online)

The centroid distances of the eight screws implanted in the two cadaver heads are shown in Table 3, and Table 4 shows registration time, average distance of the corresponding feature points (AveDis) and similarity of the two cadaver heads. Human's results are shown In Table 5.

Table 3. Centroid distance of the eight screws (mm)

Screws	Corpse_head1	Corpse_head2
1	0.12	0.10
2	0.09	0.26
3	0.14	0.12
4	0.22	0.10
5	0.22	0.15
6	0.19	0.09
7	0.32	0.04
8	0.24	0.10
Mean	0.19	0.12

Table 4. Comparison of registration time, average distance and similarity metrics (corpse_head1–2)

	CPU time/s	MS_Dis/mm	AveDist/voxel	AveDist/mm	CC	NMI	SSIM	RMSE
corpse_head1	43.72	0.19	0.783 ± 0.373	0.196 ± 0.093	0.8105	0.1646	0.2273	0.1658
corpse_head2	43.62	0.12	0.448 ± 0.329	0.239 ± 0.175	0.4781	0.1336	0.1925	0.1868

Note: MS_Dis is the mean screws distance in Table 3

To sum up, first of all, the registration speed depends largely on the hardware equipment. In our experiments, the entire registration process can be completed within one minute for all 16 sets of data. Secondly, in terms of accuracy, we calculated the similarity metrics, the centroid distance of the implanted screws and average distance of feature points. About the similarity metrics, the larger the value, the higher the grayscale similarity of the two. We found that the 14 human datasets are significantly higher than that of 2 corpse head datasets. One of the corpse heads was deformed due to the long soaking time, and the other had limited field of view during scanning, and part of the voxel information was missing. These may be the reasons for the low similarity metrics.

For corpse data, from Table 3 and Table 4, a good alignment is achieved during the registration process. The average centroid distance of implanted screws is 0.19 mm and 0.12 mm respectively, which can basically meet the requirements of surgical precision. In the extraction of corresponding feature points, key points are automatically extracted and matched based on SIFT. After obtaining the corresponding points, combined with manual experience, another selection is carried out to remove the obviously non-corresponding points on the image to ensure that the final results are not affected by individual abnormal points. Results show that TRE obtained by implanted titanium screws is very close to that obtained by SIFT feature points. So SIFT feature extraction can be used to replace titanium screws implanting during the pre-operation period for registration results evaluation, which will greatly simplify surgical procedure and avoid unnecessary injury.

Table 5. Comparison of registration time, average distance and similarity metrics (human1–14)

	CPU time/s	AveDist/voxel	AveDist/mm	CC	NMI	SSIM	RMSE
human1	9.10	0.648 ± 0.325	0.759 ± 0.381	0.9891	0.5928	0.9399	0.1047
human2	19.13	0.487 ± 0.335	0.571 ± 0.392	0.9916	0.5748	0.9543	0.0891
human3	18.87	0.413 ± 0.317	0.484 ± 0.371	0.9939	0.6151	0.9529	0.1172
human4	18.36	0.913 ± 0.360	1.070 ± 0.422	0.9865	0.6005	0.9508	0.0949
human5	18.99	0.943 ± 0.355	1.105 ± 0.416	0.9889	0.5872	0.9491	0.1185
human6	17.80	0.375 ± 0.315	0.439 ± 0.369	0.9930	0.6183	0.9574	0.1015
human7	19.58	0.504 ± 0.307	0.590 ± 0.359	0.9878	0.4957	0.7816	0.2108
human8	25.70	0.430 ± 0.384	0.650 ± 0.450	0.9865	0.6005	0.9033	0.0969
human9	20.20	0.680 ± 0.375	0.443 ± 0.244	0.9689	0.4425	0.7723	0.1255
human10	6.35	0.866 ± 0.374	0.422 ± 0.183	0.9878	0.4957	0.7816	0.2108
human11	10.86	0.964 ± 0.366	0.470 ± 0.179	0.9863	0.5810	0.7546	0.1059
human12	14.26	0.880 ± 0.369	0.429 ± 0.180	0.9475	0.3736	0.7280	0.1575
human13	14.82	0.865 ± 0.367	0.422 ± 0.179	0.9609	0.4779	0.7122	0.1946
human14	13.18	0.861 ± 0.368	0.420 ± 0.180	0.9613	0.4686	0.6900	0.2177

For human data, the average feature points distances of 14 datasets are less than one voxel. Furthermore, as can be seen from Table 5, although the similarity metrics seem great, the TRE results do not coincide with them. Therefore, we cannot estimate registration quality only from the similarity, for it reflects the difference of the overall gray value, but the difference in image structure cannot be seen.

5 Conclusion

Cochlear implant surgery requires the registration of the pre-operative CT and intra-operative CBCT images to map the preoperatively computed drilling trajectory into the intra-operative space. For robotic surgery, registration speed and precision are especially important. In this paper, we use Elastix to perform intensity-based image registration, which can complete the entire process in one minute. In terms of accuracy, the similarity metrics cannot reflect the geometric difference characteristics, and is easily affected by the gray value. The target registration error of the two corpse head datasets are both below 0.3 mm, whether it is the distance of the screw centroid or feature points. We also find that results of implanted titanium screws and SIFT feature points are very close. So SIFT feature extraction can be used to replace titanium screws implanting during the pre-operation period for registration results evaluation, which will greatly simplify surgical procedure and avoid unnecessary injury. For the 14 human datasets, the similarity metrics are relatively high, and the average point distance is less than one voxel size, which is a reasonable result of image registration. In clinical surgery, when high registration distance accuracy is required, high resolution image should be obtained correspondently.

Acknowledgments. This work was supported in part by the National Key Research and Development Program of China under Grant 2019YFB1311800, in part by the Fundamental Research Funds for the Central Universities under Grant 2021FZZX002-19, in part by the Major Scientific Project of Zhejiang Lab under Grant No. 2020ND8AD01, and in part by the Youth Innovation Team Project of the College of Biomedical Engineering & Instrument Science, Zhejiang University.

References

1. Eshraghi, A.A., Nazarian, R., Telischi, F.F., Rajguru, S.M., Truy, E., Gupta, C.: The cochlear implant: historical aspects and future prospects. Anat. Rec. (Hoboken) **295**, 1967–1980 (2012)
2. Caversaccio, M., et al.: Robotic middle ear access for cochlear implantation: first in man. PLoS ONE **14**, e0220543 (2019)
3. Dong, B., Lu, C., Hu, X., Zhao, Y., He, H., Wang, J.: Towards accurate facial nerve segmentation with decoupling optimization. Phys. Med. Biol. **67**, 065007 (2022)
4. Alam, F., Rahman, S.U., Ullah, S., Gulati, K.: Medical image registration in image guided surgery: issues, challenges and research opportunities. Biocybern. Biomed. Eng. **38**, 71–89 (2018)
5. Xie, Y.Q., Chao, M., Lee, P., Xing, L.: Feature-based rectal contour propagation from planning CT to cone beam CT. Med. Phys. **35**, 4450–4459 (2008)
6. Koutouzi, G., Nasihatkton, B., Danielak-Nowak, M., Leonhardt, H., Falkenberg, M., Kahl, F.: Performance of a feature-based algorithm for 3D–3D registration of CT angiography to cone-beam CT for endovascular repair of complex abdominal aortic aneurysms. BMC Med. Imaging **18**, 42 (2018)
7. Paganelli, C., et al.: Scale invariant feature transform in adaptive radiation therapy: a tool for deformable image registration assessment and re-planning indication. Phys. Med. Biol. **58**, 287–299 (2013)
8. Park, S., Plishker, W., Quon, H., Wong, J., Shekhar, R., Lee, J.: Deformable registration of CT and cone-beam CT with local intensity matching. Phys. Med. Biol. **62**, 927–947 (2017)
9. Xu, P., Yao, D.: A study on medical image registration by mutual information with pyramid data structure. Comput. Biol. Med. **37**, 320–327 (2007)
10. Rohlfing, T.: Image similarity and tissue overlaps as surrogates for image registration accuracy: widely used but unreliable. IEEE Trans. Med. Imaging **31**, 153–163 (2012)
11. Klein, S., Staring, M., Murphy, K., Viergever, M.A., Pluim, J.P.: elastix: a toolbox for intensity-based medical image registration. IEEE Trans. Med. Imaging **29**, 196–205 (2010)
12. Ishida, T., et al.: Evaluation of performance of pelvic CT-MR deformable image registration using two software programs. J. Radiat. Res. **62**, 1076–1082 (2021)
13. Broggi, S., et al.: A comparative evaluation of 3 different free-form deformable image registration and contour propagation methods for head and neck MRI: the case of parotid changes during radiotherapy. Technol. Cancer Res. Treat. **16**, 373–381 (2017)
14. Styner, M.A., et al.: ACIR: automatic cochlea image registration. In: Medical Imaging 2017: Image Processing (2017)
15. Chiaruttini, N., Burri, O., Haub, P., Guiet, R., Sordet-Dessimoz, J., Seitz, A.: An open-source whole slide image registration workflow at cellular precision using Fiji, QuPath and Elastix. Front. Comput. Sci. Switz **3**, 8 (2022)

16. Schipper, J., et al.: Navigation as a quality management tool in cochlear implant surgery. J. Laryngol. Otol. **118**, 764–770 (2004)

17. So, R.W.K., Chung, A.C.S.: A novel learning-based dissimilarity metric for rigid and non-rigid medical image registration by using Bhattacharyya Distances. Pattern Recogn. **62**, 161–174 (2017)

18. Wang, M.Y., Maurer, C.R., Fitzpatrick, J.M., Maciunas, R.J.: An automatic technique for finding and localizing externally attached markers in CT and MR volume images of the head. IEEE Trans. Biomed. Eng. **43**, 627–637 (1996)

19. Lowe, D.G.: Distinctive image features from scale-invariant keypoints. Int. J. Comput. Vis. **60**(2), 91–110 (2004)

20. Rister, B., Horowitz, M.A., Rubin, D.L.: Volumetric image registration from invariant keypoints. IEEE Trans. Image Process. **26**, 4900–4910 (2017)

21. De Silva, T., Hotaling, N., Chew, E.Y., Cukras, C.: Feature-based retinal image registration for longitudinal analysis of patients with age-related macular degeneration. In: Proceedings of SPIE (2020)

Simultaneous Semantic and Instance Segmentation for Colon Nuclei Identification and Counting

Lihao Liu[1]([✉]), Chenyang Hong[2], Angelica I. Aviles-Rivero[1],
and Carola-Bibiane Schönlieb[1]

[1] DAMTP, University of Cambridge, Cambridge, UK
`ll610@cam.ac.uk`
[2] CSE, Chinese University of Hong Kong, Hong Kong, China

Abstract. Nucleus segmentation and classification within the Haematoxylin and Eosin stained histology images is a key component in computer-aided image analysis, which helps to extract features with rich information for cellular estimation and following diagnosis. Therefore, it is of great relevance for several downstream computational pathology applications In this work, we address the problem of automatic nuclear segmentation and classification. Our solution is to cast as a simultaneous semantic and instance segmentation framework, and it is part of the Colon Nuclei Identification and Counting (CoNIC) Challenge. Our framework is a carefully designed ensemble model. We first train a semantic and an instance segmentation model separately, where we use as backbone HoverNet and Cascade Mask-RCNN models. We then ensemble the results with a customized Non-Maximum Suppression embedding algorithm. From our experiments, we observe that the semantic segmentation part can achieve an accurate class prediction for the cells whilst the instance information provides a refined segmentation. We enforce a robust segmentation and classification result through our customized embedding algorithm. We demonstrate, through our visual and numerical experimental, that our model outperforms the provided baselines by a large margin. Our solution ranked as the 4th solution on the Grand Challenge CoNIC 2022.

Keywords: Semantic segmentation · Instance segmentation · Histology images · Colon nuclei identification and counting

1 Introduction

Computational pathology plays an important role in accurate cellular estimation and also in diagnosis. Specifically, by extracting rich and interpretable cell-based features, nuclei segmentation and classification are becoming a significant asset in the downstream explainable models in computational pathology. Researchers have studied automatic methods for colon nuclei segmentation and classification in Haematoxylin and Eosin stained histology images for decades. In recent years, the advent of convolutional

© The Author(s), under exclusive license to Springer Nature Switzerland AG 2022
G. Yang et al. (Eds.): MIUA 2022, LNCS 13413, pp. 130–138, 2022.
https://doi.org/10.1007/978-3-031-12053-4_10

neural networks (CNN) has revolutionised this field yielding state-of-the-art segmentation and classification results. Although promising results have been reported, this task is still challenging due to the large difference in shape between different types of cells. Traditional methods perform cell segmentation based on hand-crafted features e.g. [2,7]. However, due to the lack of highly semantic information, i.e. a global understanding of the images, traditional methods are still limited in performance.

Most recently, CNN-based methods [8–10, 12], have demonstrated remarkable segmentation and classification accuracy. By extracting highly semantic features, CNN-based methods are capable of learning a strong and robust representation of the images, hence, achieving better performance than traditional methods. In particular, existing CNN-based segmentation techniques can be mainly categorised into semantic segmentation and instance segmentation. Semantic segmentation focus on giving the image contents different classes. By contrast, instance segmentation treats multiple objects of the same class as distinct entities.

The body of literature on semantic segmentation has reported several potential methods, where the most widely used model is U-Net [14]. That model uses an encoder-decoder architecture to reconstruct segmentation masks from CNN features. Based on U-Net, Ψ-Net [11] achieve better senmantic segmentation accuracy bu stacking densely convolutional LSTMs. Another well-known model is Hover-Net [5]. It further leverages the instance information encoded within the vertical and horizontal distances of nuclear pixels to their centers of mass to perform instance segmentation.

Unlike semantic models, instance techniques usually utilise a two-stage architecture to detect and segment each instance. A well-established technique is Faster RCNN [13]. It is composed of a region proposal stage and a bounding box regression stage, which is effective for detection tasks. Mask-RCNN [6] extends Faster R-CNN by adding a mask prediction branch, in parallel to the bounding box recognition branch, to perform instance detection and segmentation simultaneously. Cascade Mask R-CNN [1] achieves better segmentation and classification performance than previous models. By adding a sequence of detectors trained with increasing IoU thresholds on Mask-RCNN.

Contributions. From our observations, semantic models are able to do highly accurate class predictions for cells; as these types of techniques provide a global understanding of the image content. Whilst instance models provide a refined segmentation as they consider the segmentation on each instance. Motivated by the aforementioned advantages of each family of techniques, we propose a simultaneous semantic and instance segmentation framework for Colon Nuclei identification and Counting. Particularly, we firstly train a semantic and instance segmentation model separately. We use as backbone the HoverNet and the Cascade Mask-RCNN. Secondly, we ensemble the results with a customized Non-Maximum Suppression embedding algorithm. The output of our framework is the colon nuclei identification and counting. Our framework ranked 4th out of 373 submissions on the Grand Challenge CoNIC 2022.

2   Proposed Framework

Our framework is composed of three key parts (see Fig. 1). i) an instance segmentation model, ii) a semantic segmentation model and iii) a customised Non-Maximum Suppression (NMS) embedding algorithm. We describe in detail these parts next.

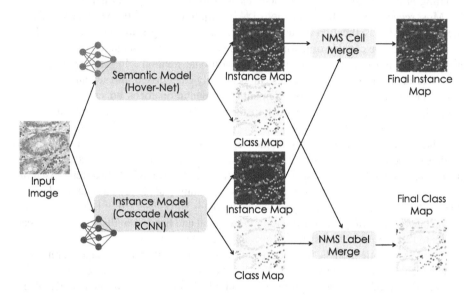

Fig. 1. The schematic illustration of the proposed simultaneous semantic and instance segmentation framework. We first train a semantic and instance segmentation models separately. We then ensemble the results via our customised Non-Maximum Suppression embedding algorithm.

2.1   Every Single Nucleus Matters: Instance Segmentation Model

Instance segmentation [6,13] seeks to detect and localise objects from a set of predefined classes in an image. Unlike semantic segmentation, instance segmentation treats the objects of the same class as different instances. One of the most well-established models is the so-called Cascaded Mask-RCNN [1], where a multi-stage object detection model is proposed. Because of the simplicity yet the high performance offered by Cascade R-CNN, we select it as our backbone.

We follow the work of that [1,11], where we seek to optimise the following the element-wise cross entropy loss over all voxels and all categories:

$$\mathcal{L}_{instance} = -\frac{1}{M \times K} \sum_{m=1}^{M} \sum_{k=1}^{K} y_m^k \, \log(p_m^k) \,, \tag{1}$$

where M denotes the total number of pixels in an input image, and K is the cell categories in our application we have seven categories including the background (details on the categories are displayed in the experimental section). Moreover, y_m^k refers to the

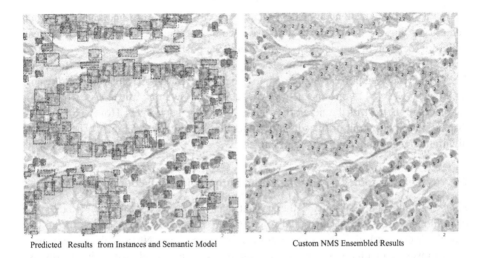

Predicted Results from Instances and Semantic Model   Custom NMS Ensembled Results

Fig. 2. Illustration of the ensemble process from the NMS. The left side figure displays the predicted bounding boxes from the semantic model (black bounding boxes) and the instance model (blue bounding boxes), respectively. We then ensemble the results using our customised NMS algorithm. The final output is displayed, on the right side, showing the ensemble results visualised on the yellow bounding boxes. (Color figure online)

ground truth label at the m-th pixel in the k-th category; p_m^k is the softmax output value, which represents a predicted probability indicating the m-th voxel belongs to the k-th category.

We provide the detailed setting of the Cascaded Mask-RCNN for our purpose. To extract meaningful feature maps, we select ResNeXt-152 [1] as the backbone for the Cascaded Mask-RCNN. For natural images, instance segmentation models usually take a large-sized image as input, e.g. 1300 × 800. If the image is too small, then the segmentation is coarse. To meet this specification, we set the input as 512 × 512, which is currently the smallest image size for instance segmentation models. Moreover, we decrease the original anchor size setting from (32, 64, 128, 256, 512) to (8, 16, 32, 64, 128) due to the smaller size of the images and their targets (nucleus). With these changes, the model is more robust when detecting smaller objects like the nucleus. We display a sample output of the instance model on the left side of Fig. 2. Most notable, the output is marked using the blue bounding boxes.

2.2 Denser Predictions for Better Performance: Semantic Segmentation Model

Semantic segmentation is to provide a denser prediction than instance segmentation models. As the goal is to predict pixel-wise the label of objects related to a set of defined classes. To apply a semantic segmentation model on instance segmentation tasks, an additional post-processing step is needed. This post-processing process can split the semantic segmentation result into multiple single objects from the same class (i.e. into instance segmentation). To avoid re-implement this function, we directly select Hover-

Net as a semantic training model. That is, we seek to optimise another loss, which definition follows (1). For clarity purposes, we denote the loss as $\mathcal{L}_{semantic}$. We can therefore focus on the model design rather than the post-processing.

To keep the same setting as the instance segmentation model, we select ResNeXt-152 [15] as the backbone for our semantic segmentation model, and we use the same input size 512×512 for consistency. We remark that we only did these two modifications, and the rest of the network remains unchanged following Hover-Net [5]. We display a sample output of the semantic model on the left side of Fig. 2. The output is highlighted using the black bounding boxes.

2.3   Model Ensemble: A Non-Maximum Suppression Embedding Algorithm

After obtaining the results from the semantic and instance segmentation models, we then adopted a custom NMS model to ensemble the detected instances from the two models. We remark that this step is not a learning process. NMS seeks to find overlapped instance results based on the position of the detected cells bounding boxes. By setting an Intersection over Union (IoU) threshold, it can be determined if two or more cells from the two models identify the same cell. We highlight that the standard NMS only eliminates multiple excessive cells and keep only one cell. In this work, *we proposed a customised* NMS, which not only detects multiple cells but also merges the segmentation mask and the classification labels.

We first detected the overlapped segmentation results for one cell/one position. We then take as a final segmentation output the merge of such overlapped regions of a cell. Then, we assign a classification label to the merged segmentation results by a weighted voting mechanism, which details are as follows. The semantic segmentation model is capable of a great understanding of the global information content. Hence, it can achieve a great classification performance in cells with a small number such as neutrophils, plasma, and eosinophils. For the label merging process, the weight of the neutrophil, epithelial, lymphocyte, plasma, eosinophil, and connective tissue cells is taken from the semantic segmentation model, and set to (2, 1, 1, 2, 2, 1). Whilst the weight of neutrophil, epithelial, lymphocyte, plasma, eosinophil, and connective tissue cells is taken from the instance segmentation model and set to (1.5, 1.5, 1.5, 1.5, 1.5, 1.5). We assign 1.5 to the weight of the instance model's prediction to avoid the same voting number. For example, two cells overlapped in the NMS stage, where the semantic model predict it as neutrophil and the instance model as epithelial. Then the final label for this cell is assigned as a neutrophil. We underline that we did not use any other further post-processing techniques to refine the results. On the right side of Fig. 2, we display a visual sample output from the ensemble model.

3   Experimental Results

In this section, we detail all experiments and conditions that we follow to evaluate our framework.

Challenge Dataset Description. The Colon Nuclei Identification and Counting (CoNIC) Challenge [4] dataset is forked from the Lizard dataset [3], which is the largest known publicly available dataset in the computational pathology area for instance segmentation. The dataset is composed of Haematoxylin & Eosin stained histology images from six different data sources, with a unified cropped size of 256×256. Visual samples of the dataset are displayed in Fig. 3. For each target nucleus, an instance mask and a classification mask are provided, where each nucleus is assigned to one of the following categories: 1–Neutrophil, 2–Epithelial, 3–Lymphocyte, 4–Plasma, 5–Eosinophil, and 6–Connective tissue.

Pre-processing and Data Augmentation. For a robust training process, we use a four steps augmentation process to enrich the training data. [Step 1] We firstly enlarged the image to twice its original size 512×512. This step is necessary for our instance model training as we described in Sect. 2. [Step 2] We adopted a random scale to resize the images to 0.8–1.2 of the size drawn from Step 1. We then randomly cropped, using a fixed size of 512×512, regions with zero padding. [Step 3] We used random flip to augment the data from different views. [Step 4] We randomly selected Gaussian blur, median

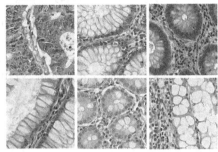

Fig. 3. Visual samples of the histology images used in our experiments. We display selected samples to show the diversity and complexity of the dataset.

blur, and additive Gaussian noise. We used the imgaug package[1] to enhance the pixels sensitivity of the input.

Implementation Details. Our code is built based on Hover-Net and detectron2 repositories. For the loss function, we use binary cross-entropy loss for mask prediction, and cross-entropy loss for label prediction in both repositories. For the instance model, SGD optimiser is used during training with the initial learning rate setting as 10^{-4}. Whilst, for the semantic model, Adam optimiser is used with the same learning rate 10^{-4}. All models are run on an NVIDIA A100 GPU with 80 GB RAM, which takes around 12 h to train the instance model for 60 epochs, and 96 h to train the semantic models for 100 epochs. To evaluate our model, we first use the multi-class panoptic quality (PQ) and multi-class PQ^{+} metrics to evaluate the segmentation and classification tasks. Whilst for the counting (cellular composition) the multi-class coefficient of determination R^{2}.

3.1 Results and Discussion

We followed the official data splitting, which uses 3900 images as the training set and 1081 images as the testing set. We compare our ensembled results against: i) the Baseline and Semantic Model (we modified the backbone and input size) provided by the CoNIC challenge [4], and ii) Detectron2[2] (Instance Model).

---

[1] https://github.com/aleju/imgaug.
[2] https://github.com/facebookresearch/detectron2.

Table 1. Experimental result on the discovery phase. We refer to 'S' and 'I' as the semantic and instance models respectively, and 'B' as the baseline provided by the challenge organizers. 'DataAug' refers to data augmentation. The **best results** are highlighted in bold and blue colour. Whilst the second best is denoted in orange colour.

Model	DataAug	R^2	PQ	mPQ^+	PQ^+_{neu}	PQ^+_{epi}	PQ^+_{lym}	PQ^+_{pla}	PQ^+_{eos}	PQ^+_{con}
B	✗	0.8585	0.6149	0.4998	0.2435	0.6384	0.6832	0.5066	0.3946	0.5707
S	✗	0.8697	0.6235	0.5195	0.3024	0.6133	0.7079	0.5136	0.3954	0.5843
S	✓	0.8801	0.6310	0.5338	0.3498	0.6011	0.7233	0.5326	0.4007	0.5955
I	✗	0.7933	0.6369	0.5158	0.2858	0.6421	0.6955	0.5076	0.3546	0.6090
I	✓	0.8020	0.6457	0.5294	0.3208	0.6491	0.7070	0.5073	0.3750	0.6167
Ours	✓	**0.9048**	**0.6658**	**0.5655**	**0.3781**	0.6225	**0.7373**	**0.5621**	**0.4293**	**0.6272**

The results are reported in Table 1, where our framework outperformed all compared models. In a closer inspection, we observe that our modified Semantic Model performs better than the baseline model. The performance improvement comes from the data augmentation and better backbone model. Moreover, one interesting finding is that the Instance Model performs better than the Semantic Model in terms of PQ evaluation metrics, whilst the Semantic Model outperforms the instances model in terms of mPQ+ and R^2 evaluation metrics. This is because, when performing segmentation, the Instance Model focuses only on the nucleus region. Hence, it has a better segmentation accuracy (PQ). While the Semantic Model has a great semantic understanding of the content of the image, i.e. how many cells are in the images. Hence, the classification accuracy (R^2) is better. Also, even with a low PQ, the Semantic Model can also outperform the Instance Model regarding the final mPQ+.

Our ensembled model (Ours) deals with the inherent problems from the baseline and the Semantic and Instance Models. By providing a good trade-off between the image content and the nucleus region information. As consequence, our framework outperforms all compared models for all metrics. We highlight the positive performance impact of combining both semantic and instance information, see the visual result of our NMS ensemble in Fig. 2. We further support our numerical results with a set of visual comparisons (see Fig. 4) reflecting the advantage of our framework.

Test Stage Performance. There are three main phases for the CoNIC Challenge: Discovery phase, Preliminary test phase, and Final test phase. The results from Table 1 are from the discovery phase. At the time of submitting this paper, we had the test phase results, which details are as follows. In the preliminary testing stage, we use 5-fold cross-validation, and trained 5 models. We ensemble the 5 models and submit them using docker. However, due to the limited testing time, we are only able to submit the instance model, since currently, the semantic model is taking longer than expected to test (see Fig. 1). Our instance model has reached an mPQ+ of 0.47540 on the preliminary testing dataset for the segmentation task, and an R^2 of 0.67599 on the preliminary testing dataset for the counting task.

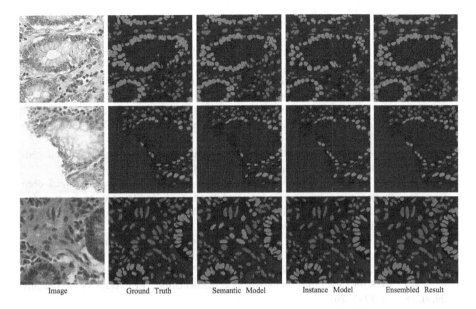

Fig. 4. Visual comparison of the outputs produced by the Semantic Model, Instance Model, and our Proposed Ensemble framework. The color code represents different classes that the cell belongs to (e.g. Neutrophil and Plasma).

4   Conclusion

In this paper, we introduce a framework for colon nuclei identification and counting. Our solution is framed as a simultaneous semantic and instance segmentation framework. Our carefully designed solution is an ensemble that considers simultaneously the nucleus regions and the semantics of the images; this ensures focus on relevant regions on the image content and therefore boosts the performance. Our ensemble is achieved via a customised Non-Maximum Suppression embedding algorithm. Our results outperformed the challenge baseline. We highlighted the relevance of considering semantic and instance information for the task at hand. We underline that our framework ranked as the 4th solution out of 373 submissions on the Grand Challenge CoNIC 2022.

References

1. Cai, Z., Vasconcelos, N.: Cascade r-CNN: Delving into high quality object detection. In: Proceedings of the IEEE Conference on Computer Vision and Pattern Recognition. pp. 6154–6162 (2018)
2. Cheng, J., Rajapakse, J.C., et al.: Segmentation of clustered nuclei with shape markers and marking function. IEEE Trans. Biomed. Eng. **56**(3), 741–748 (2008)
3. Graham, S., et al.: Lizard: a large-scale dataset for colonic nuclear instance segmentation and classification. In: Proceedings of the IEEE/CVF International Conference on Computer Vision, pp. 684–693 (2021)

4. Graham, S., et al.: Conic: Colon nuclei identification and counting challenge 2022. arXiv preprint arXiv:2111.14485 (2021)
5. Graham, S., et al.: Hover-net: Simultaneous segmentation and classification of nuclei in multi-tissue histology images. Med. Image Anal. **58**, 101563 (2019)
6. He, K., Gkioxari, G., Dollár, P., Girshick, R.: Mask r-CNN. In: Proceedings of the IEEE International Conference on Computer Vision, pp. 2961–2969 (2017)
7. Jung, C., Kim, C.: Segmenting clustered nuclei using h-minima transform-based marker extraction and contour parameterization. IEEE Tran. Biomed. Eng. **57**(10), 2600–2604 (2010)
8. Liu, L., Aviles-Rivero, A.I., Schönlieb, C.B.: Contrastive registration for unsupervised medical image segmentation. arXiv preprint arXiv:2011.08894 (2020)
9. Liu, L., Dou, Q., Chen, H., Olatunji, I.E., Qin, J., Heng, P.-A.: MTMR-net: multi-task deep learning with margin ranking loss for lung nodule analysis. In: Stoyanov, D., et al. (eds.) DLMIA/ML-CDS -2018. LNCS, vol. 11045, pp. 74–82. Springer, Cham (2018). https://doi.org/10.1007/978-3-030-00889-5_9
10. Liu, L., Dou, Q., Chen, H., Qin, J., Heng, P.A.: Multi-task deep model with margin ranking loss for lung nodule analysis. IEEE Trans. Med. Imaging **39**(3), 718–728 (2019)
11. Liu, L., Hu, X., Zhu, L., Fu, C.W., Qin, J., Heng, P.A.: ψ-Net: stacking densely convolutional LSTMS for sub-cortical brain structure segmentation. IEEE Trans. Med. Imaging **39**(9), 2806–2817 (2020)
12. Liu, L., Hu, X., Zhu, L., Heng, P.-A.: Probabilistic multilayer regularization network for unsupervised 3D brain image registration. In: Shen, D., et al. (eds.) MICCAI 2019. LNCS, vol. 11765, pp. 346–354. Springer, Cham (2019). https://doi.org/10.1007/978-3-030-32245-8_39
13. Ren, S., He, K., Girshick, R., Sun, J.: Faster r-CNN: towards real-time object detection with region proposal networks. Adv. Neural Inf. Process. Syst. **28** (2015)
14. Ronneberger, O., Fischer, P., Brox, T.: U-net: convolutional networks for biomedical image segmentation. In: Navab, N., Hornegger, J., Wells, W.M., Frangi, A.F. (eds.) MICCAI 2015. LNCS, vol. 9351, pp. 234–241. Springer, Cham (2015). https://doi.org/10.1007/978-3-319-24574-4_28
15. Xie, S., Girshick, R., Dollár, P., Tu, Z., He, K.: Aggregated residual transformations for deep neural networks. In: IEEE Conference on Computer Vision and Pattern Recognition. pp. 1492–1500 (2017)

Point2Mask: A Weakly Supervised Approach for Cell Segmentation Using Point Annotation

Nabeel Khalid[1]([✉])[iD], Fabian Schmeisser[2][iD],
Mohammadmahdi Koochali[1][iD], Mohsin Munir[1][iD], Christoffer Edlund[3][iD],
Timothy R Jackson[4][iD], Johan Trygg[3,5][iD], Rickard Sjögren[3,5][iD],
Andreas Dengel[1,2][iD], and Sheraz Ahmed[1][iD]

[1] German Research Center for Artificial Intelligence (DFKI) GmbH,
Kaiserslautern 67663, Germany
{nabeel.khalid,mohammadmahdi.koochali,mohsin.munir,andreas.dengel,
sheraz.ahmed}@dfki.de
[2] Technische Universität Kaiserslautern, Kaiserslautern 67663, Germany
[3] Sartorius Corporate Research, Umea, Sweden
{nabeel.khalid,fabian.schmeisser,mohammadmahdi.koochali,mohsin.munir,
christoffer.edlund,timothy.jackson,johan.trygg,rickard.sjogren,
andreas.dengel,sheraz.ahmed}@sartorius.com
[4] Arthrex California Technology, Santa Barbara, CA, USA
[5] Computational Life Science Cluster (CLiC), Umeå University, Umeå, Sweden

Abstract. Identifying cells in microscopic images is a crucial step toward studying image-based cell biology research. Cell instance segmentation provides an opportunity to study the shape, structure, form, and size of cells. Deep learning approaches for cell instance segmentation rely on the instance segmentation mask for each cell, which is a labor-intensive and expensive task. An ample amount of unlabeled microscopic data is available in the cell biology domain, but due to the tedious and exorbitant nature of the annotations needed for the cell instance segmentation approaches, the full potential of the data is not explored. This paper presents a weakly supervised approach, which can perform cell instance segmentation by using only point and bounding box-based annotation. This enormously reduces the annotation efforts. The proposed approach is evaluated on a benchmark dataset i.e., LIVECell, whereby only using a bounding box and randomly generated points on each cell, it achieved the mean average precision score of 43.53% which is as good as the full supervised segmentation method trained with complete segmentation mask. In addition, it is 3.71 times faster to annotate with a bounding box and point in comparison to full mask annotation.

Keywords: Weakly supervised · Cell segmentation · Point annotation · Deep learning

© The Author(s), under exclusive license to Springer Nature Switzerland AG 2022
G. Yang et al. (Eds.): MIUA 2022, LNCS 13413, pp. 139–153, 2022.
https://doi.org/10.1007/978-3-031-12053-4_11

1   Introduction

Cell segmentation is regarded as the cornerstone of image-based cellular research. Studying cell migration, cell count, cell proliferation, cell morphology, cellular interactions, and cellular events like cell death are all possible with adequate cell segmentation. Deep learning approaches for instance cell segmentation [3,7,8,16,17,19,20] are showing promising results, but they rely heavily on precise full mask supervision for training. Manually annotating a groundtruth mask for each cell is a very labor-intensive, expensive, complex, and time-consuming task. For the natural object dataset like COCO [10], it takes on average 79.2 s per instance to create a polygon-based object mask. The bounding box for the objects is approximately 11 times faster i.e., 7 s [13]. When it comes to image-based cellular research, the LIVECell dataset [3] is the largest dataset of its kind to date. LIVECell is composed of more than 1.6 million cells. On average it contains more than 313 cells per image, which is way more than any other label-free cell segmentation dataset [17,19]. Some images in the LIVECell dataset contain

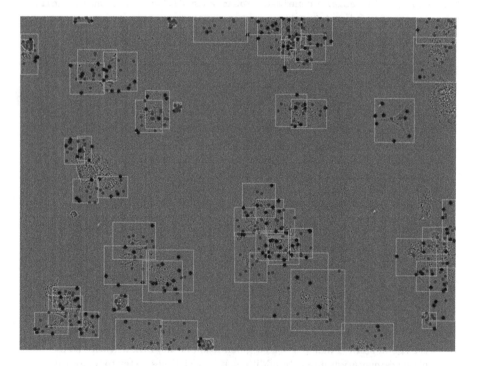

Fig. 1. Point2Mask-based instance annotation combines object bounding boxes with points that are sampled randomly inside each box and annotated as the cell (blue) or background (red). We demonstrate that 6 annotated points per instance are faster to collect than the standard cell masks and such groundtruth is sufficient to train the proposed pipeline to achieve 99.2% of its fully supervised performance on the LIVECell dataset. (Color figure online)

Table 1. Annotation time for different supervision types on the LIVECell dataset. Labeling as many as 6 points per cell instance instead of the fully supervised (segmentation mask) annotation takes 26.96% of the total time spent on annotating the full mask for each cell and is 3.71x faster, assuming that it takes 7 and 0.9 s to draw the bounding box and point annotation respectively.

Annotation supervision	Total time (sec) (mask/bbox+points)	Percentage of time spent on full mask	Times faster than full mask (x)
Full mask	46	100%	-
1-point	7.9	17.17%	5.82
2-point	8.8	19.13%	5.23
4-point	10.6	23.04%	4.34
6-point	12.4	26.96%	3.71
8-point	14.2	30.87%	3.24
10-point	16	34.78%	2.88

more than 3,000 cell instances, which can be overly complex, time-consuming, and labor-intensive to manually annotate each cell in a high cell density environment with overlapping cells. Annotating cells in microscopic images is more challenging than the objects in natural images [10] because cells overlap, and the cell boundaries are also very difficult to identify in crowded images. When preparing LIVECell, it took 46 s on average to create segmentation masks, which if we consider the total number of cells in the training data for the LIVECell dataset is more than 13,213 h spent on annotating the masks.

It is important to mention that LIVECell dataset (which is the largest annotated microscopic cell dataset) contains only 8 type of cells which is only a fraction of more then 200 different cells types found in human body [14]. This means that an ample amount of unlabeled image-based cellular data is available in the cell biology domain, but due to the tedious and exorbitant nature of annotations required for the cell instance segmentation approaches, the data is not being used to its full potential. To boost the research in cell biology, it is pivotal to have high-performing systems, which can accurately segment cells and for these methods, it is necessary to have a large number of labeled datasets, which are unfortunately labor-intensive. To tackle that issue, we have proposed a pipeline for weakly supervised cell segmentation, Point2Mask, which considers the bounding box for each cell and the point labels instead of the full mask. The point labels are sampled randomly inside each bounding box as shown in Fig. 1. The annotation required for the proposed Point2Mask can be divided into three steps. First, the bounding boxes need to be drawn, which takes ~7 s per cell. After that, random point annotations inside each bounding box are automatically generated. As the last step, random points generated inside each bounding box are classified by an annotator as belonging to the foreground (cell) or background, which takes around ~ 0.9 seconds per point. Table 1 provides insights into the annotation time required for different supervision types. If we only consider a single point for each cell and the bounding box for training, it takes 17.17% of the total time spent on the full mask annotation for all the cells in the LIVECell dataset and is 5.82x faster. For 6 points per cell type, it takes 26.96% of the fully supervised annotation time. The main contributions of this study are as follows:

1. An end-to-end pipeline for weakly supervised point-based cell segmentation using Mask R-CNN [5], Feature pyramid Network with ResNet-50 [6], and bilinear interpolation.
2. Extensive evaluation of the proposed method by increasing point labels for each cell instance to analyze the impact on the performance. Achieved 96.51% to 99.16% of the fully supervised performance using Point2Mask weakly supervised cell segmentation with only 1- to 6-points label per cell instance with a significant reduction in the time required for annotating the data for training.
3. Performed per cell type evaluation to analyze the relationship between the morphological characteristics of different cell cultures like size and the number of point labels required.

2   Related Work

Deep learning-based cell segmentation has evolved drastically in the last decade with the development of the U-net proposed by Ronneberger et al. [16] in 2015. With only 35 images trained U-net model, it outperformed all the other contestants in the 2015 ISBI cell tracking and segmentation challenge. The success of U-net prompted a chain of valuable research in the image-based cellular research with the development of algorithms like DeepCell [22] and Usiigaci [20]. Khalid et al. (2021) [7] proposed a pipeline for cell and nucleus segmentation using the EVICAN dataset [17]. Edlund et al. (2021) proposed anchor-free and anchor-based pipelines for the cell segmentation using the LIVECell dataset [3]. Khalid et al. (2021) [8] proposed a pipeline to perform cell-type aware segmentation in microscopic images using the EVICAN dataset.

Weakly supervised cell segmentation is an active area of research with many different variations of the weak supervision i.e., image tags [12,25], points [2,24], missing annotations [4]. Zhou et al. (2018) [25] proposed a promising method for weakly supervised instance segmentation using only class labels of objects appearing in an image. Although this work does not primarily concern itself with cell instance segmentation but object segmentation in general, the approach was also tested on microscopy images and some underlying ideas were developed further to fit the domain [12]. In this method, image regions that produce a particularly high prediction response for a class called class peak responses are backpropagated through a network and mapped to object regions that are high in information. This procedure then allows for full instance masks to be retrieved. Another popular method to make use of weak labels for cell segmentation is using point annotations instead of full pixel-wise mask annotations. Zhao et al. (2020) [24] propose weakly supervised training schemes that only use point annotations to achieve results comparable to those of fully supervised models. In their paper, they propose three distinct methods and compare them to several baseline methods, such as U-Net [16] and the Pyramid-Based fully convolutional network [18]. The first approach, a self-training scheme, updates the output segmentation mask by feeding back the current prediction of the network. For this task, the network is pre-trained using the initial point annotations and a cross-entropy loss, and then a self-training loss is introduced which composes the network's previous prediction with the previous label and uses it as a new label in a feedback loop. The second approach is a co-training scheme that uses two subsets of the initial dataset and self-trains two networks on them separately. The resulting models then supervise each other's learning process, guided by a newly defined co-training loss that combines the predictions of both models. A third approach is a hybrid approach, leveraging the advantages of the better-converging self-training approach and the potentially better segmentation results of the co-training scheme. Guerrero-Pena et al. (2019) [4] introduce a method to tackle the frequent problem of missing or incorrect annotations in microscopy images. The method introduced in the paper proposes three key points to improve the effectiveness of deep learning models when trained on incomplete annotation. The first point is to introduce a loss function that helps separate cells by operating in three distinct classes and classifying underrepresented regions. The second point is introducing a weight-aware map model which is especially useful for contour detection and generalization. The third point consists of data augmentation specifically crafted for the weaknesses of a typical microscopy dataset, i.e. strengthening potentially weak signals on edges by adjusting the intensity of regions that contain shared edges of multiple cells.

All these approaches for weakly supervised cell segmentation are trained on small scale datasets like the PHC [11,21] and Phase100 [23] dataset used in [24], contains 230 and 100 images respectively. This amount of data is too small to enable a trained CNN (Convolutional Neural Network) model to generalize to images beyond its training dataset or for a valid comparison between different supervision approaches. In addition to that, these approaches for weakly supervised cell segmentation are overly complex.

3   Point2Mask: The Proposed Approach

Figure 2 provides a system overview of our Point2Mask weakly supervised cell segmentation approach. The proposed pipeline is composed of Feature Pyramid Network [9] with ResNet-50 [6], Region Proposal Network, and Mask R-CNN [5] as the prediction head, which is detailed below.

3.1   Backbone Network for Feature Extraction

The purpose of this block is to extract feature maps from the input image at different scales. The feature extraction module of the proposed methodology is composed of Feature Pyramid Network [9] along with ResNet-50 [6]. Feature

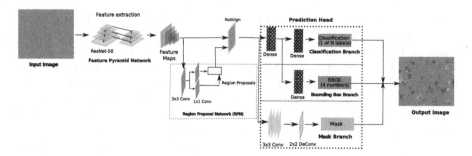

Fig. 2. System overview of the Point2Mask pipeline for weakly supervised cell segmentation. Input image is passed to the proposed pipeline and the output image with cell detection and segmentation is produced.

Pyramid Network (FPN) extracts features from the images using a pyramid scheme. It utilizes deep convolutional networks (CNNs) for computing features. FPN combines low resolution, semantically strong features with high resolution, semantically weak features. It takes a single-scale image as an input and outputs feature maps of proportional size at multiple levels by operating on a bottom-up pathway, top-down pathway, and lateral connections. The bottom-up pathway uses a normal feed-forward CNN architecture to compute a hierarchy of features consisting of feature maps at various scales. The output of each CNN layer is used later in the top-down pathway via lateral connections. The output of each convolution layer of ResNet-50 is used in the top-down pathway which constructs higher resolution layers from the semantic rich layer. As the final task, the FPN applies a 3×3 convolution operation on each merged map to overcome the aliasing effect after the upsampling to generate the final feature map.

3.2   Region Proposal Network for Cell Region Detection and Groundtruth Matching

Following the extraction of multi-scale features from the backbone network, these features are then passed onto a Regional Proposal Network (RPN) [15]. The primary focus of RPN is to detect regions that contain objects and match them to the groundtruth. This process is performed by generating anchor boxes on the input image which are then matched to the groundtruth by taking Intersection over Union (IoU) between anchors and groundtruth. If IoU is larger than the defined threshold of 0.7, the anchor is linked to one of the groundtruth boxes and assigned to the foreground. If the IoU is greater than 0.3 and smaller than 0.7, it is considered background and otherwise ignored. The anchor strides and aspect ratio parameter used to detect and segment objects in MS-COCO [10] dataset overlooks most of the small cell instances when transferred to this task. Unlike MS-COCO [10] and other commonly used image datasets, the area of some cells especially BV-2 cell culture in the LIVECell [3] dataset is exceedingly small.

After extensive experimentation, the anchor sizes and anchor aspect ratios were selected that fit adequately for the task. The details about the anchor parameters are given in Sect. 6. Now that we have the anchor boxes which are assigned to the foreground having shapes like the groundtruth boxes, the next step is anchor deltas calculation which is the distance between groundtruth and anchors. At the final stage of RPN, we choose 3,000 region proposal boxes from the predicted boxes by using non-maximum suppression [1].

3.3 Prediction Head

After the successful generation of proposals, the next block in our pipeline is the prediction head. At the prediction head, we have groundtruth boxes, proposal boxes from RPN, and feature maps from FPN. The job of the prediction head is to predict the class, bounding box, and binary mask for each region of interest. We are using Mask R-CNN [5] as the prediction head, which is an extension of Faster R-CNN [15] by adding a mask branch. Faster R-CNN gives two outputs for each object in an image, classification of the object in an image, and a bounding box around the object. In Mask R-CNN, a third branch is added that outputs an object mask in addition to the other two outputs. The extra branch is composed of Fully Convolutional Network (FCN) which predicts the mask for each RoI in a pixel-to-pixel manner.

In a fully supervised training setting with a mask available for each cell, Mask R-CNN is trained by extracting a matching regular grid of labels from groundtruth masks. On the contrary, for point supervision, predictions are approximated in the locations of groundtruth points from the prediction on the grid using bilinear interpolation (see Fig. 3). Bilinear interpolation is a resampling method that estimates a new pixel value by using the distance weighted average of the four nearest pixel values. When we have prediction and the groundtruth labels at the same points, similar loss as with full supervision can be applied and its gradient will be propagated with bilinear interpolation. Once we have predictions and groundtruth labels at the same points, a loss can be applied in the same way as with full supervision and its gradients will be propagated through bilinear interpolation. In our experiments, we use cross-entropy loss on points.

4 Dataset

LIVECell dataset [3] has been used in this study, which is the largest fully annotated dataset in image-based cellular research. It contains more than 1.6 million cells in 5,239 images. The images in the dataset are from eight morphologically distinct cell cultures. On average, the LIVECell dataset contains 313 cells per image which is exceedingly high as compared to the EVICAN dataset [17], which contains an average of 5.7 cells per image. That is the reason we opted for the LIVECell dataset for this study. LIVECell train set contains 3,188 images with over 1.03 million cell instances. The validation and the test data contain 539 and 1,512 images with 1,84,371 and 4,67,874 instances, respectively.

Fig. 3. Point2Mask supervision illustration. For a 6 × 6 prediction mask on the regular grid (green color indicates foreground prediction i.e., cell), the predictions are obtained at the exact location of the groundtruth points (Cell and the background groundtruth points are indicated by red and blue respectively) with bilinear interpolation. The cell contour line is only for illustration purposes. (Color figure online)

For fully supervised training, original LIVECell data with full masks are used for training. For Point2Mask, the mask from the LIVECell dataset is discarded and six different point labels (1, 2, 4, 6, 8, 10) are generated automatically and randomly for each cell of the training data. The point can either be on the cell or anywhere inside or on the edge of the bounding box. If the point annotation is on the cell, it is assigned a point label of 1, and otherwise 0.

5   Evaluation Metrics

To evaluate the performance of the proposed pipeline we are following the standard COCO evaluation protocol [10] with some modifications as reported in [3] for the area ranges. Average Precision (AP) is the precision averaged across all unique recall levels. Mean Average Precision (mAP) is the mean of average precision across all N classes. For the evaluation, we have reported mean average precision for both object detection and segmentation tasks at different IoU thresholds of 0.5 (mAP50), 0.75 (mAP75), and 0.5:0.95 in the steps of 0.05 (mAP). To identify the performance of the model on objects of varied sizes, we have also included mAP for different area ranges. Objects with area less than $320\,\mu m^2$ (corresponding to 500 pixels) belong to APs (small). APm (medium) is for the objects in area ranges of $320\,\mu m^2$ to $970\,\mu m^2$ (corresponding to 1500 pixels) and APl (large) is for objects with area larger than $970\,\mu m^2$.

6   Experimental Setup

We have designed two different experimental settings to evaluate the performance of the proposed pipeline for the point-supervised weak cell segmentation. In the first experimental setting, namely point2Mask vs fully supervised method and impact of validated annotated points, we have performed several experiments with different annotation supervisions using the LIVECell dataset. In the second experimental setting, namely impact of validated annotated points on different cell cultures, the models trained in the first experimental setting under different annotation supervisions are evaluated on test sets of individual cell cultures to analyze the performance of the different numbers of point annotations for each cell culture.

Training for all the experiments used a stochastic gradient descent-based solver with a base learning rate of 0.02 and momentum of 0.9. The anchor sizes and aspect ratios for all settings were set after careful consideration of the cell's pixel area in the images. Anchor sizes and aspect ratios were set to 8, 16, 32, 64, 128, and 0.5, 1, 2, 3, 4 for all the settings, respectively. The checkpoints for evaluation were chosen based on the higher validation average precision.

The pixel means and pixel standard deviation for the dataset were calculated as 128 and 11.58, respectively. For data augmentation, images are flipped horizontally on a random basis to reduce the risk of over-fitting. All training used multi-scale data augmentation, meaning that image sizes were randomly changed from the original 520×704 pixels to size with the same ratios, but the shortest side was set to one of (440, 480, 520, 580, 620) pixels.

6.1   Point2Mask vs Fully Supervised Method and Impact of Validated Annotated Points

In this experimental setting, the objective is to perform weakly supervised cell segmentation for different point annotations as well as fully supervised cell segmentation with a full mask for each cell. All the experiments are performed under the same settings. For point-supervised cell segmentation, six different training experiments are performed with 1-,2-,4-,6-,8-, and 10-point labels per cell instance instead of a full mask.

The checkpoints at 3,000 have been chosen for 1-, 10-points, and full mask training settings, and 2,9500 for 4-,6-, and 8-point training settings on the basis of higher validation average precision.

Results. Table 2 shows the overall detection and segmentation average precision scores of the proposed pipeline on the LIVECell dataset. For the full mask supervision setting, we are getting detection and segmentation AP scores of 43.12% and 43.90% respectively. The area ranges scores show that the model is performing best for the cells of larger areas. For the 1-point supervision, we are getting AP scores of 42.67% and 43.27% for detection and segmentation tasks, respectively. 1.01% improvement in performance is seen for 2-point supervision

Table 2. Overall detection and segmentation results on different Intersection over union threshold and area range for full mask supervision and $\mathcal{N}$-point supervision. The best results are represented in bold.

Train supervision	AP		AP50		AP75		APs		APm		APl	
	Det.	Seg.	Det.	Seg.	Det.	Seg.	Det.	Seg.	Det.	Seg.	Det.	Seg.
Full mask	43.12	43.90	78.94	78.07	43.26	45.75	44.31	42.30	43.01	43.33	47.01	51.92
1-point	42.67	42.37	78.71	77.58	42.46	42.96	43.91	41.33	42.16	41.37	46.19	48.64
2-point	42.75	42.86	78.49	77.62	42.81	43.79	43.95	41.53	42.81	42.30	46.61	50.38
4 points	43.01	43.17	79.50	77.91	42.96	44.60	43.97	41.68	43.07	42.77	**47.24**	51.40
6 points	**43.32**	**43.53**	**79.69**	**78.18**	**43.31**	**44.93**	**44.54**	**42.06**	**43.31**	**43.31**	46.97	51.52
8 points	42.97	43.41	78.86	78.00	43.18	44.83	43.95	41.83	42.54	42.77	46.94	51.44
10 points	42.93	43.40	78.71	77.97	43.10	44.81	44.12	41.80	42.81	43.04	47.01	**51.65**

in comparison to the 1-point supervision. Similarly, 1.01% gain in performance is achieved for the 4-point supervision as compared to the 2-point supervision. For the 6-point supervision, we are getting the best results with an AP score of 43.53% for segmentation. For the 8- and 10- point supervision, we are getting a decline in the performance for cell segmentation.

6.2   Impact of Validated Annotated Points on Different Cell Cultures

In this experimental setting, we are mostly concerned with finding the inter-link between the morphological properties of the cells and the number of point annotations required for each different cell culture. The models trained in experimental setting 1 are evaluated on the individual test set of each cell culture.

Table 3. Per class mask average precision results for full mask supervision and $\mathcal{N}$-point supervision. The best results are represented in bold.

Train supervision	A172	BT-474	BV2	Huh7	MCF7	SH-SY5Y	SkBr3	SK-OV-3
Full mask	35.45	38.13	52.88	49.90	34.66	21.56	65.20	50.67
1-point	33.39	37.24	51.99	46.98	33.64	19.26	64.03	47.29
2-point	34.80	37.43	51.97	48.89	34.07	20.55	64.08	48.97
4-point	35.17	37.97	52.23	49.61	34.07	20.92	64.65	49.82
6-point	**35.26**	**38.78**	52.20	49.57	34.91	21.32	**64.80**	49.82
8-point	35.11	37.67	**52.27**	49.65	**34.29**	21.08	64.52	49.83
10-point	35.18	38.01	52.13	**49.76**	34.31	**21.61**	64.66	**50.21**

Results. Table 3 gives insights into per class AP scores for different point-supervised training settings. For the cell culture A172 and BT-474, the best performance is achieved by 6-point supervision. When we analyze the area of the A172 cells in the LIVECell dataset, it is observed that more than 50% of the cells belong to the medium area range ($320\,\mu\mathrm{m}^2$ to $970\,\mu\mathrm{m}^2$). The best performance is achieved by the 10-point supervision for the cell cultures Huh7 and SK-OV-3 because more than 48% and 59% of the cells in these cell cultures respectively have cells in a large area range (larger than $970\,\mu\mathrm{m}^2$). For the cell culture BV-2, the best performance is seen across the 6-point supervision, but the interesting thing to notice is that for the 1-point supervision, we are getting 99.5% of 6-point annotation performance with 6x less time spent on the annotation. From these observations, we can conclude that the morphological characteristics like the size of the cells in the dataset can give insights into how many points are enough to achieve the best performance for each cell culture.

7   Analysis and Discussion

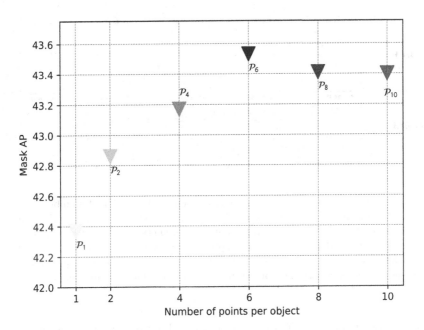

Fig. 4. Training with a different number of points. Proposed approach trained on LIVECell with as few as 6 labeled points per cell instance ($\mathcal{P}_6$) achieves 43.53% mask AP with decline in the score for more labeled points.

In this section, we discuss the results of the point-supervised weak cell segmentation pipeline for both experimental settings. In experimental setting 1 (Point2Mask vs Fully supervised method and impact of validated annotated points), 6 different points and full mask annotation were used for training. Results in Table 2 show that we have achieved 96.51% to 99.16% of the fully supervised performance by using weakly supervised cell segmentation with only 1- to 6-points label per cell instance with a significant reduction in the time

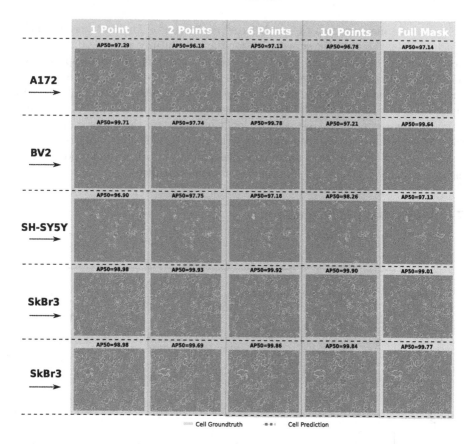

Fig. 5. Inference results using the models trained on the different number of point annotations and full mask. The solid yellow line represents the groundtruth mask for each cell and the dotted red line represents the prediction made by the model. The red, green, blue, and purple columns represent the inference results obtained from the models trained on 1,2,6,10-point annotations and full mask respectively. Each row represents the inference result from an image from different cell culture. (Color figure online)

required for annotating the data for training. Figure 4 presents the mask AP scores on the LIVECell test set with a different number of points used for training. For the 1-point supervision $(\mathcal{P}_1)$, we have achieved a mask AP score of 42.37%, which is 96.51% of the fully supervised trained model performance under the same settings. Similarly, for 2- $(\mathcal{P}_2)$ and 4-point supervisions $(\mathcal{P}_4)$, we have achieved 97.63% and 98.34% of the full supervision performance. For the 6-point supervision $(\mathcal{P}_6)$, we have achieved the best performance in terms of mask AP with the score of 43.53%, which is 99.16% of the fully supervised performance. For the 8-$(\mathcal{P}_8)$ and 10-point$(\mathcal{P}_{10})$ supervision, the performance starts to decline compared to 6-point$(\mathcal{P}_6)$ with mask AP scores of 43.41% and 43.40% respectively.

In experimental setting 2 (Impact of validated annotated points on different cell cultures), we aimed to find the connection between the morphological characteristics of the cells and the $\mathcal{N}$ point supervision required to get the optimal performance. From the analysis of the results in Table 3, it can be seen that for the cultures which contain cells in the small area ranges like BV2, minimal point supervision yields optimal results. For the cells in the medium area ranges like A172, BT-474, and SkBr3, the best performance is achieved with 6-point supervision. Similarly, 10-point supervision outputs the best performance for the cell cultures in large area ranges like Huh7 and SK-OV-3. These findings can help the annotators and the biologists in targeted point annotation according to the morphological characteristics of the different cell cultures.

Figure 5 shows the inference results on some samples using the models trained on the different number of point annotations and full mask. The solid yellow lines are the groundtruth mask for each cell and the dotted red lines are the predictions made by the model. The red, green, blue, and purple columns are the inference results obtained from the models trained on 1-,2-,6-,10-point annotations, and full mask, respectively. Each row shows the qualitative performance of different supervisions on the identical image from different cell culture for comparison. AP50 on top of every prediction sub-image is the segmentation average precision score at the IoU threshold of 0.5. For the image in the first row belonging to cell culture A172, the 1-point supervision model performs best with an AP50 score of 97.29%. The best performance for the image in the second row (BV-2) is seen across the model trained with 6-point supervision. For the image in the third row belonging to the SH-SY5Y cell culture, the best performance is recorded against the 10-point supervision model. The last 2 images in the fourth and the fifth row belong to SkBr3 cell culture. The best performance for both the images can be seen against the model trained on 1- and 6-point supervision, respectively.

We have achieved close to the full supervision performance by reducing the time required to annotate the data by a significant amount compared to the full mask annotation. In this study, quality assurance time has not been considered for both the full mask and the point annotations. Quality assurance for point labels in overlapping cells in crowded images can sometimes take more time than drawing the full mask. Even with the 1-point supervision for training, we are getting more than 96% of the fully supervised performance. As explained earlier, annotation of cells in microscopic images is a very labor-intensive and expensive task and requires expert knowledge of the biomedical staff. One single image of the cell culture BV2 can contain up to 3,000 cell instances, which can be very time-consuming and complex to annotate. With the help of the proposed pipeline, we can annotate the data semi-automatically by using the proposed pipeline for weakly supervised cell segmentation to generate a mask for each cell, which can then be improved by the annotators in case of false positive or missed detection. Also, the findings of experimental setting 2 can help us decide how many point annotations are required for specific cell culture according to its morphological properties.

8   Conclusion

In this study, we have proposed a pipeline for weakly supervised cell segmentation using point annotations. Point2Mask generates a mask for the cell, providing just the bounding box and the point labels. With the help of the proposed pipeline, we have achieved 99.16% of the fully supervised performance with just 6-point labels instead of drawing a full mask. With only 0.84% loss in the performance compared to the fully supervised setup, significant amount of time required for the fully supervised training can be saved. The performance achieved for a 1-point label per cell instance e, 96.51%, is still adequate and can save an ample amount of time spent on labeling the full mask for each cell. The findings of this paper can help biologists and doctors to save enough time in labeling the data and can expedite the field of medicine and disease diagnosis to a great extent. With the help of the results in this study, we have proved that we can not only reduce the time and the cost required for the full annotation, but we can also reduce the amount of expert knowledge required from the biologists to draw the boundaries of each cell. An abundant amount of unlabeled image-based cellular data is available, which can be semi-automatically annotated using the proposed pipeline for weakly supervised cell segmentation. Furthermore, we have also pointed out the relationship between morphological characteristics of different cell cultures and the number of point annotations required. These findings can help biologists to design the targeted point annotation for specific cell cultures.

References

1. Cai, Z., Vasconcelos, N.: Cascade R-CNN: delving into high quality object detection. In: Proceedings of the IEEE Conference on Computer Vision and Pattern Recognition (2018)
2. Chen, Z., et al.: Weakly supervised histopathology image segmentation with sparse point annotations. IEEE J. Biomed. Health Inform. **25**, 1673–1685 (2020)
3. Edlund, C., et al.: Livecell-a large-scale dataset for label-free live cell segmentation. Nat. Methods **18**, 1038–1045 (2021)
4. Guerrero-Peña, F.A., Fernandez, P.D.M., Ren, T.I., Cunha, A.: A weakly supervised method for instance segmentation of biological cells. In: Wang, Q., et al. (eds.) DART/MIL3ID -2019. LNCS, vol. 11795, pp. 216–224. Springer, Cham (2019). https://doi.org/10.1007/978-3-030-33391-1_25
5. He, K., Gkioxari, G., Dollár, P., Girshick, R.: Mask R-CNN. In: Proceedings of the IEEE International Conference on Computer Vision (2017)
6. He, K., Zhang, X., Ren, S., Sun, J.: Deep residual learning for image recognition. In: Proceedings of the IEEE Conference on Computer Vision and Pattern Recognition (2016)
7. Khalid, N., et al.: Deepcens: an end-to-end pipeline for cell and nucleus segmentation in microscopic images. In: 2021 International Joint Conference on Neural Networks (IJCNN). IEEE (2021)
8. Khalid, N., et al.: Deepcis: an end-to-end pipeline for cell-type aware instance segmentation in microscopic images. In: 2021 IEEE EMBS International Conference on Biomedical and Health Informatics (BHI). IEEE (2021)

9. Lin, T.Y., Dollár, P., Girshick, R., He, K., Hariharan, B., Belongie, S.: Feature pyramid networks for object detection. In: Proceedings of the IEEE Conference on Computer Vision and Pattern Recognition (2017)

10. Lin, T.-Y., et al.: Microsoft COCO: common objects in context. In: Fleet, D., Pajdla, T., Schiele, B., Tuytelaars, T. (eds.) ECCV 2014. LNCS, vol. 8693, pp. 740–755. Springer, Cham (2014). https://doi.org/10.1007/978-3-319-10602-1_48

11. Maška, M., et al.: A benchmark for comparison of cell tracking algorithms. Bioinformatics **30**, 1609–1617 (2014)

12. Nishimura, K., Ker, D.F.E., Bise, R.: Weakly supervised cell instance segmentation by propagating from detection response. In: Shen, D., et al. (eds.) MICCAI 2019. LNCS, vol. 11764, pp. 649–657. Springer, Cham (2019). https://doi.org/10.1007/978-3-030-32239-7_72

13. Papadopoulos, D.P., Uijlings, J.R., Keller, F., Ferrari, V.: Extreme clicking for efficient object annotation. In: Proceedings of the IEEE International Conference on Computer Vision (2017)

14. Regev, A., et al.: Science forum: the human cell atlas. Elife **6**, e27041 (2017)

15. Ren, S., He, K., Girshick, R., Sun, J.: Faster R-CNN: Towards real-time object detection with region proposal networks. arXiv preprint arXiv:1506.01497 (2015)

16. Ronneberger, O., Fischer, P., Brox, T.: U-Net: convolutional networks for biomedical image segmentation. In: Navab, N., Hornegger, J., Wells, W.M., Frangi, A.F. (eds.) MICCAI 2015. LNCS, vol. 9351, pp. 234–241. Springer, Cham (2015). https://doi.org/10.1007/978-3-319-24574-4_28

17. Schwendy, M., Unger, R.E., Parekh, S.H.: Evican-a balanced dataset for algorithm development in cell and nucleus segmentation. Bioinformatics **36**, 3863–3870 (2020)

18. Seferbekov, S., Iglovikov, V., Buslaev, A., Shvets, A.: Feature pyramid network for multi-class land segmentation. In: Proceedings of the IEEE Conference on Computer Vision and Pattern Recognition Workshops (2018)

19. Stringer, C., Wang, T., Michaelos, M., Pachitariu, M.: Cellpose: a generalist algorithm for cellular segmentation. Nat. Methods **18**, 100–106 (2020)

20. Tsai, H.F., Gajda, J., Sloan, T.F., Rares, A., Shen, A.Q.: Usiigaci: instance-aware cell tracking in stain-free phase contrast microscopy enabled by machine learning. SoftwareX **9**, 230–237 (2019)

21. Ulman, V., et al.: An objective comparison of cell-tracking algorithms. Nat. Methods **14**, 1141–1152 (2017)

22. Van Valen, D.A., et al.: Deep learning automates the quantitative analysis of individual cells in live-cell imaging experiments. PLoS Comput. Biol. **12**, e1005177 (2016)

23. Zhao, T., Yin, Z.: Pyramid-based fully convolutional networks for cell segmentation. In: Frangi, A.F., Schnabel, J.A., Davatzikos, C., Alberola-López, C., Fichtinger, G. (eds.) MICCAI 2018. LNCS, vol. 11073, pp. 677–685. Springer, Cham (2018). https://doi.org/10.1007/978-3-030-00937-3_77

24. Zhao, T., Yin, Z.: Weakly supervised cell segmentation by point annotation. IEEE Transa. Med. Imaging **40**, 2736–2747 (2020)

25. Zhou, Y., Zhu, Y., Ye, Q., Qiu, Q., Jiao, J.: Weakly supervised instance segmentation using class peak response. In: Proceedings of the IEEE Conference on Computer Vision and Pattern Recognition (2018)

Image Interpretation

Class Distance Weighted Cross-Entropy Loss for Ulcerative Colitis Severity Estimation

Gorkem Polat[1,2](✉) , Ilkay Ergenc[3] , Haluk Tarik Kani[3] ,
Yesim Ozen Alahdab[3] , Ozlen Atug[3] , and Alptekin Temizel[1,2]

[1] Graduate School of Informatics, Middle East Technical University, Ankara, Turkey
{gorkem.polat,atemizel}@metu.edu.tr
[2] Neuroscience and Neurotechnology Center of Excellence (NÖROM),
Ankara, Turkey
[3] Department of Gastroenterology, Marmara University School of Medicine,
Istanbul, Turkey

Abstract. In scoring systems used to measure the endoscopic activity of ulcerative colitis, such as Mayo endoscopic score or Ulcerative Colitis Endoscopic Index Severity, levels increase with severity of the disease activity. Such relative ranking among the scores makes it an ordinal regression problem. On the other hand, most studies use categorical cross-entropy loss function to train deep learning models, which is not optimal for the ordinal regression problem. In this study, we propose a novel loss function, class distance weighted cross-entropy (CDW-CE), that respects the order of the classes and takes the distance of the classes into account in calculation of the cost. Experimental evaluations show that models trained with CDW-CE outperform the models trained with conventional categorical cross-entropy and other commonly used loss functions which are designed for the ordinal regression problems. In addition, the class activation maps of models trained with CDW-CE loss are more class-discriminative and they are found to be more reasonable by the domain experts.

Keywords: Ordinal regression · Ulcerative colitis · Computer-aided diagnosis · Mayo endoscopic score · Deep learning · Medical imaging

1 Introduction

Deep learning (DL) methods are widely used in the field of gastrointestinal endoscopy for problems such as detection of polyps, artifacts, Barrett's esophagus, and cancer analysis [3,4,11,25,27]. In particular, recent studies have reported successful results for the estimation of the endoscopic activity of ulcerative colitis (UC) from colonoscopy images [19,38]. UC is a chronic condition caused by persistent inflammation of the colon mucosa and accurate assessment of the disease severity plays a key role in monitoring and treating the disease.

G. Yang et al. (Eds.): MIUA 2022, LNCS 13413, pp. 157–171, 2022.
https://doi.org/10.1007/978-3-031-12053-4_12

However, there are substantial intra- and inter-observer variability in the grading of endoscopic severity [22] and use of computer-aided diagnosis of the UC can eliminate subjectivity and help experts in the monitoring process. On the other hand, more work, such as validation on external datasets and providing better explainability, are needed to increase their adoption in clinics [19].

Scoring systems for UC, such as Mayo endoscopic score (MES) [30] or Ulcerative Colitis Endoscopic Index of Severity (UCEIS) [40], have several levels (0–3 for MES and 0–8 for UCEIS), which increase in relation to the severity of the disease. Since there is a ranking between the class scores, this problem can be handled as an ordinal regression (or ordinal classification) problem. Although there are many studies on UC endoscopic activity estimation, only a few of these exploit ordinality information. In this study, we propose a novel non-parametric loss function, which respects the ordinal nature of the problem and calculates the cost accordingly.

The main contributions of this paper are as follows:

1. A new loss function called Class Distance Weighted Cross-Entropy (CDW-CE) is proposed, which can be used in training convolutional neural networks (CNN) estimating the endoscopic severity of UC.
2. Three separate CNN architectures are trained using cross-entropy, CORN framework [33], cross-entropy with an ordinal loss term (CO2) [2], ordinal entropy loss (HO2) [2], and CDW-CE. These networks are used to comparatively evaluate the effect of these particular loss functions in estimation of endoscopic severity of UC.
3. We demonstrate through Class Activation Map (CAM) visualizations that models trained with CDW-CE are more class-discriminative and provide better explainability, which are key factors in adoption of computer-aided diagnosis systems for clinical use.

2   Related Work

There has been increasing interest in automatically estimating the UC severity from colonoscopy images. Alammari et al. [1] proposed a 9-layer simple CNN architecture to classify frames in colonoscopy videos. They reported that the model can process the 128×128 pixel images in real-time with 67.7% test set accuracy. Stidham et al. [34] performed one of the earliest comprehensive studies on a large dataset and employed an advanced CNN architecture Inception-v3 [37] to classify images according to MES. Ozawa et al. [23] used GoogLeNet [36] to classify images into three MES levels (Mayo 0, Mayo 1, and Mayo 2–3) due to lack of severe cases. Takenaka et al. [39] used Inception-v3 [37] to estimate endoscopic remission, histologic remission, and UCEIS score using one of the largest datasets used in studies. Bhambhvani et al. [8] used ResNext-101 model on publicly available HyperKvasir dataset. Yao et al. [41] developed a fully automated system that can estimate MES score for the colonoscopy video. Kani et al. [17] employed ResNet18 model to classify MES, severe mucosal disease diagnosis, and remission. Gottlieb et al. [12] estimated the MES and UCEIS for full-length endoscopy videos where the annotation is only provided for the video itself rather than the individual frames. Schwab et al. [31] used a multi-instance learning approach with ordinal regression methods to estimate UC severity from both frame-level and video-level MES labels. Becker et al. [13] proposed an end-to-end fully automated system to estimate MES from raw colonoscopy videos directly. They employed a quality checking model to extract readable frames and weak MES labels obtained by the colon-segment-wise scores were assigned to them to train the UC grading model. Different to the previous approaches employing the existing DL models, Luo et al. [20], proposed a new architecture called UC-DenseNet which combines CNN, RNN, and attention mechanisms. Sutton et al. [35] compared many state-of-the-art CNN models on HyperKVasir [9] dataset and reported that DenseNet121 [16] outperformed the other models.

Ordinal categories are common in many real-world prediction problems, especially in the healthcare domain. Several loss functions have been introduced recently to use in conjunction with CNNs. Niu et al. [21] transformed an ordinal regression problem into a series of binary classification sub-tasks based on the work of Li et al. [18]. They applied this approach to age estimation from face images and reported better results compared to other ordinal regression approaches such as metric learning and widely used cross-entropy loss function. Although the proposed method provided better results, there were rank inconsistencies in the output classification subtasks. Cao et al. [10] proposed a consistent rank logits (CORAL) framework for rank-consistencies by weight sharing in the penultimate layer. They reported that the CORAL framework provided both rank consistency and superior results compared to the previous approaches. Shi et al. [33] proposed Conditional Ordinal Regression for Neural Network (CORN) framework to relax the constraint on the penultimate layer of the CORAL framework to increase neural network's capacity by introducing conditional probabilities. The authors reported that the CORN approach performs better than previous methods. A major disadvantage of CORN-like approaches is that they require a change in the model architecture (output layer) and labeling structure. Another approach for ordinal regression problems is to integrate unimodality in the loss function [2,7]. This approach enforces unimodality by punishing inconsistencies in the posterior probability distribution among adjacent labels. The punishing term is generally added next to the main loss function, where cross-entropy is used mostly. Albuquerque et al. [2] employed a unimodality approach for the cervical cancer classification by using cross-entropy and entropy losses as main loss functions and reported better performance results compared to other approaches. Through the manuscript, cross-entropy and entropy loss with unimodality loss terms will be referred to as CO2 and HO2 respectively as in [2]. Another class of the methods is to use regression to predict a single continuous value at the output or using sigmoid activation function on top of it to limit prediction in $[0, 1]$, then using thresholds or probability distributions to convert the output into discrete levels [5,6]. However, regression-based approaches assume fixed distances between classes and encoding specific parametric distributions (e.g., Gaussian, Poisson) at the network output restricts the model and prevents scaling to a large number of classes [6]. Moreover, tuning parameters in parametric distributions presents another challenge. Regression-based approaches or methods enforcing parametric distributions have been shown to be inferior to other methods in many studies [2,7].

Among the studies in the literature, only Schwab et al. [31] employed two ordinal regression approaches. In their first approach, they applied a CORN-like framework by transforming the output layer into multiple binary subtasks. In their second approach, their models output a continuous value between 0 and 3, and classes are assigned according to the thresholds; however, optimum class thresholds are determined using a search on the dataset, which limits the generalizability of the proposed method. Furthermore, it is not trivial to derive a confidence value for the assessment due to the numeric value, and the method is not compatible with the CAM visualization techniques as it has a single node at the output layer which is responsible for all classes.

In this study, we propose a novel non-parametric loss function called CDW-CE. CDW-CE can be used in conjunction with any model and does not require any changes in the model architecture or labeling structure. Moreover, it does not require setting any thresholds or enforcing a probability distribution and is compatible with CAM visualization techniques.

3   Class Distance Weighted Cross-Entropy

3.1   Motivation

Cross-entropy loss function, which is widely used in classification tasks, does not take into account how probabilities of the predictions are distributed among the non-true classes (Eq. 1):

$$\mathbf{CE} = -\sum_{i=0}^{N-1} y_i \times \log \hat{y}_i = -\log \hat{y}_c \tag{1}$$

where i is the index of the class in the output layer, c is the index of ground-truth class, y is the ground-truth label, and $\hat{y}$ is the prediction. Since one-hot encoding is used for the ground-truth labels of the classes at the output layer, $y_i = 0$ $\forall i \neq c$. Eventually, cross-entropy loss only evaluates the predicted confidence of the true class. However, when there is a ranking among the output classes, class mispredictions become important, too. For example, in an ordinal class structure from 0 to 9, predicting 0 for class 9 is much worse than predicting 8. A better loss function would evaluate this ranking and penalize more if the predictions are away from the true class (see Table 1). Since the predictions farther from the correct classes are not penalized more than the closer classes, cross-entropy is not an optimum loss function for the ordinal classes.

Table 1. Three sample cases that result in the same cross-entropy loss where Class 0 is the true class. Assuming that the classes have an ordinal relation, a more suitable loss function should favor Case 1 by assigning the lowest cost and Case 3 should have the highest cost.

Classes	Case 1	Case 2	Case 3
0	0.6	0.6	0.6
1	0.3	0.1	0
2	0.1	0.3	0.1
3	0	0	0.3

3.2 Class Distance Weighted Cross-Entropy Loss Function

We propose a non-parametric loss function CDW-CE that evaluates the confidences of non-true classes instead of the true class confidence as in cross-entropy (Eq. 2). Firstly, we penalize how much each misprediction deviates from the true value using log loss. Since one-hot encoding is used for encoding the class labels for multi-class classification problems, predicted confidences for the non-true classes should be equal to zero. Secondly, we introduce a coefficient for the loss of each class, which utilizes the distance to the ground-truth class and increases in relation to that distance.

$$\textbf{CDW-CE} = - \sum_{i=0}^{N-1} \log(1 - \hat{y}_i) \times |i - c|^{\alpha} \tag{2}$$

where c is the index of the ground-truth class and power term α is a hyperparameter that determines the strength of the coefficient. Eventually, the logarithmic function inside the summation is calculated for every non-true class.

4 Experiments

4.1 Dataset

LIMUC dataset [26], a publicly available UC dataset labeled according to the MES, was used to train CNN models that employ different loss functions. There are 11276 images from 564 patients in the LIMUC dataset and all images have been reviewed and annotated by at least two expert gastroenterologists. All images have a size of 352×288 and Mayo score distribution is as follows: 6105 (54.14%) Mayo 0, 3052 (27.7%) Mayo 1, 1254 (11.12%) Mayo 2, and 865 (7.67%) Mayo 3. 15% of the images (1686 images from 85 patients) have been used as the test set and the rest (9590 images from 479 patients) for the 10-fold cross-validation by forming train-validation set pairs. All splittings have been performed at the patient-level, randomly, and preserving class ratios.

Table 2. Experiment results for all Mayo scores.

	Loss function	ResNet18	Inception-v3	MobileNet-v3-Large
QWK	Cross-entropy	0.8296 ± 0.014	0.8360 ± 0.011	0.8302 ± 0.015
	CORN	0.8366 ± 0.007	0.8431 ± 0.009	0.8412 ± 0.010
	CO2	0.8394 ± 0.009	0.8482 ± 0.009	0.8354 ± 0.009
	HO2	0.8446 ± 0.007	0.8458 ± 0.010	0.8378 ± 0.007
	CDW-CE	**0.8568 ± 0.010**	**0.8678 ± 0.006**	**0.8588 ± 0.006**
F1	Cross-entropy	0.6720 ± 0.026	0.6829 ± 0.023	0.6668 ± 0.028
	CORN	0.6809 ± 0.014	0.6832 ± 0.013	0.6847 ± 0.020
	CO2	0.6782 ± 0.014	0.6846 ± 0.016	0.6793 ± 0.012
	HO2	0.6856 ± 0.016	0.6901 ± 0.008	0.6741 ± 0.030
	CDW-CE	**0.7055 ± 0.021**	**0.7261 ± 0.015**	**0.7254 ± 0.010**
Accuracy	Cross-entropy	0.7566 ± 0.015	0.7600 ± 0.012	0.7564 ± 0.011
	CORN	0.7591 ± 0.009	0.7600 ± 0.008	0.7613 ± 0.012
	CO2	0.7601 ± 0.008	0.7654 ± 0.008	0.7572 ± 0.009
	HO2	0.7625 ± 0.011	0.766 ± 0.010	0.7583 ± 0.005
	CDW-CE	**0.7740 ± 0.011**	**0.7880 ± 0.011**	**0.7759 ± 0.010**
MAE	Cross-entropy	0.2581 ± 0.018	0.2526 ± 0.013	0.2563 ± 0.012
	CORN	0.2517 ± 0.012	0.2497 ± 0.010	0.2480 ± 0.012
	CO2	0.2497 ± 0.011	0.2404 ± 0.008	0.2524 ± 0.010
	HO2	0.2460 ± 0.011	0.2424 ± 0.011	0.2487 ± 0.005
	CDW-CE	**0.2300 ± 0.011**	**0.2147 ± 0.010**	**0.2272 ± 0.011**

4.2 Training Details

Three commonly used CNN architectures, ResNet18 [14], Inception-v3 [37], and MobileNet-v3-large [15] have been trained with different loss functions. ResNet and Inception model families are commonly used architectures for UC severity estimation [8,13,23,31,34,39,41]. MobileNet-v3-large is a more recent model that stands out with its speed and performance, making it a suitable choice for real-time UC severity estimation from video frames. Random rotation (0°–360°) and horizontal flipping were used as data augmentation and weights were initialized from pretrained models on IMAGENET dataset [29]. Adam optimizer with a learning rate of $2e - 4$ and learning rate scheduling with a scaling factor of 0.2 was applied if there were no increase in the validation set accuracy for the last 10 epochs. Early stopping was used to terminate training when performance did not increase in the last 25 epochs. The best model checkpoint on the validation set of each fold is used for the performance measurement on the test set. PyTorch framework [24] were used for the implementation of the study and CNN models were adapted from TorchVision package.

The proposed model has been evaluated against three state-of-the-art approaches specifically designed for the ordinal regression tasks: CORN framework, CO2, and HO2 and cross-entropy (CE) loss function is used as the main baseline. For the training of CO2 and HO2 models, main loss function (either cross-entropy or entropy loss) is scaled with a λ coefficient as in original paper implementation. Hyperparameter tuning for the λ were performed using values in {0.1, 0.01, 0.001} by performing 10-fold cross validation.

Table 3. Experiment results for remission classification.

	Loss function	ResNet18	Inception-v3	MobileNet-v3-Large
Kappa	Cross-entropy	0.8077 ± 0.023	0.8074 ± 0.021	0.8122 ± 0.018
	CORN	0.8191 ± 0.021	0.8077 ± 0.022	0.8203 ± 0.016
	CO2	0.8185 ± 0.020	0.8243 ± 0.011	0.8067 ± 0.020
	HO2	0.8318 ± 0.015	0.8251 ± 0.015	0.8283 ± 0.018
	CDW-CE	$\mathbf{0.8521 \pm 0.016}$	$\mathbf{0.8598 \pm 0.012}$	$\mathbf{0.8592 \pm 0.012}$
F1	Cross-entropy	0.8419 ± 0.018	0.8420 ± 0.017	0.8451 ± 0.016
	CORN	0.8511 ± 0.016	0.8425 ± 0.018	0.8523 ± 0.013
	CO2	0.8513 ± 0.015	0.8561 ± 0.009	0.8404 ± 0.017
	HO2	0.8618 ± 0.012	0.8565 ± 0.011	0.8583 ± 0.015
	CDW-CE	$\mathbf{0.8785 \pm 0.013}$	$\mathbf{0.8847 \pm 0.010}$	$\mathbf{0.8842 \pm 0.010}$
Accuracy	Cross-entropy	0.9436 ± 0.009	0.9432 ± 0.007	0.9456 ± 0.005
	CORN	0.9473 ± 0.007	0.9429 ± 0.008	0.9473 ± 0.006
	CO2	0.9461 ± 0.008	0.9479 ± 0.004	0.9444 ± 0.006
	HO2	0.9507 ± 0.005	0.9485 ± 0.005	0.9504 ± 0.005
	CDW-CE	$\mathbf{0.9566 \pm 0.005}$	$\mathbf{0.9590 \pm 0.003}$	$\mathbf{0.9588 \pm 0.005}$

4.3 Evaluation Metrics

Quadratic Weighted Kappa (QWK) is used as the main performance metric as it is suitable for both imbalanced and ordinal data. In addition, Mean Absolute Error (MAE), which is a commonly used performance metric in ordinal regression problems, accuracy, and macro F1 metrics are given in Table 2. In addition to the MES prediction, inflammatory bowel disease (IBD) experts are also interested in the estimation of endoscopic remission (Mayo 0 or 1) and moderate to severe disease (Mayo 2 or 3) as defined in the European Medicine Agency and the US Food and Drug Administration guidelines on UC drug development [28]. Trained CNN models for MES estimation were used for remission classification performance measurements by grouping the related Mayo subscores, without any new training. Cohen's Kappa, F1, and accuracy scores for remission classification are reported in Table 3.

Each CNN model has been trained on a different fold and performance measurements were obtained on the initially separated test set; as a result, each architecture has ten different results. Reported performance results in Tables 2 and 3 refer to the average and standard deviation of 10 folds. To observe how much the performance of each class changes with CDW-CE compared to cross-entropy for three different models, confusion matrices are demonstrated in Fig. 1 for both all Mayo classes and remission classification. Confusion matrices produced for each fold were normalized across true labels, then, the mean confusion matrix was obtained by getting the average of 10 normalized confusion matrix.

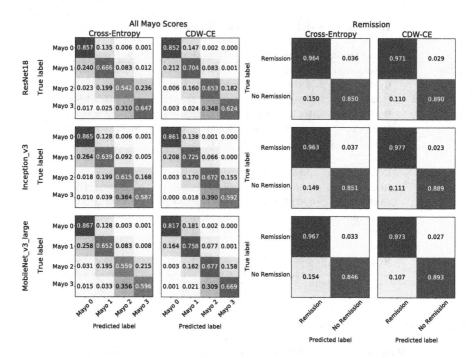

Fig. 1. Mean confusion matrix of each CNN model trained with CE and CDW-CE for all Mayo classes and remission classification.

4.4 Penalization Factor Analysis

Power term α in the CDW-CE loss provides a control over to what extent the more distant classes are penalized. As the α increases, the distant classes are penalized more intensely. However, this penalization factor may vary depending on external factors such as the dataset, number of labels, and the employed CNN model. We have analyzed different α values to determine the optimum for each CNN model. The results in Tables 2 and 3 for CDW-CE are the results of the models trained with the experimentally determined optimum α. For each CNN model, mean and standard deviation of the QWK scores for varying α are given in Fig. 2.

5 Class Activation Maps (CAM)

To make a CNN model's decision more transparent and interpretable, several visualization techniques have been proposed [32,42]. CAM visualizations allow observation of the prominent regions used by the models in making their predictions, which is a particularly important aspect in the medical domain. Models which make their predictions using similar regions with the experts would be more likely to be adopted and build more trust with end-users. Such visualizations can also be used as an another comparison criteria and allow assessing

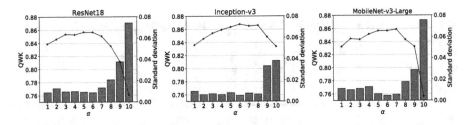

Fig. 2. Change of mean and standard deviation of QWK scores according to varying α for three models.

different models when their performances are similar (i.e., models with more reasonable activation maps can be chosen instead of others even if their performances are exactly the same). In addition, it provides a means for developers to debug their approach and check any potential biases in the model's predictions [32]. We have generated CAM visualizations using the technique in [42]. Since CAM is produced specifically for each class, it highlights the class-specific discriminative regions only for the target class. In Fig. 3, two ResNet18 models trained with CE and CDW-CE losses are used to generate CAMs for different images in the test set. Although both models correctly predict the class scores for the given examples, their CAMs differ considerably.

To make a quantitative evaluation of CAMs produced by two models trained with different loss functions, we asked three IBD experts to choose which one was more compatible with symptomatic areas in the tissue (i.e., more aligned with the regions they considered in their decision making). We also allowed them to specify that both are equally reasonable, when they are not able to decide between two CAM visualizations. We showed the experts a total of 240 images (60 images from each class), which were correctly predicted by the two models. Only the original image and the two CAM visualizations overlaid onto original images were shown to experts. CAM images produced by the models for each new image were randomly named as AI-1 (Artificial Intelligence 1) and AI-2. Clinicians were asked to make a choice between three options without having the knowledge of model-CAM visualization correspondence (Fig. 4).

6   Results and Discussion

Table 2 shows that CE loss is the worst performing among all models, indicating that this widely used loss function is not optimal and approaches taking ordinality into account are more preferable. Unimodality approaches compare favorably to CORN framework for the ResNet18 and Inception-v3 models and only behind for the MobileNet-v3-large model; however, with an insignificant margin. HO2 results are mostly better than CO2, which is aligned with results reported in the literature [2]. CDW-CE outperforms other approaches in all experiments. For all models, CDW-CE results refer to the training with the optimum α, which are 5, 6, and 7 for the ResNet18, Inception-v3, and MobileNet-v3-large, respectively.

Mayo 0	Mayo 1	Mayo 2	Mayo 3

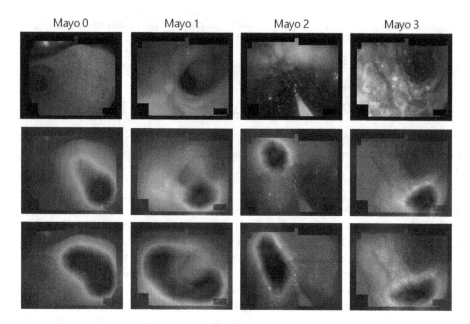

Fig. 3. Original images (top row) and their CAM visualizations of the ResNet18 model trained with CE (middle row) and CDW-CE (bottom row) losses. The model trained with CDW-CE highlights broader and more relevant areas related to the disease.

Similar performance comparison can also be observed for remission classification in Table 3. CO2 and CORN framework have very similar performances. On the other hand, HO2 outperformed CORN framework for all models indicating that it is better at centering estimations around the true class. CDW-CE loss has the highest score for all performance metrics and CNN models. When we observe the individual class performances, Fig. 1 shows that CDW-CE loss significantly reduces the mispredictions which are in two-class distance or more to the true class. Although sensitivity of edge classes (Mayo 0 and Mayo 3) remained the same or even decreased for some models, intermediate classes (Mayo 1 and Mayo 2) are increased significantly for all models. Due to high cost given to farther mispredictions, CDW-CE centers the wrong estimates mostly in classes with one neighborhood distance. Since mispredictions are more close to true classes in CDW-CE, we observe an increase in remission and non-remission sensitivities for the remission classification.

Figure 2 reveals that different models may have different optimum α parameters. While the performance increases as the α increases and gets to the optimum value, the model accuracy decreases sharply beyond it. As the α is an exponential term, increasing it beyond the optimum value results in high cost making the training unstable, resulting in an increase in standard deviation of cross-validation results (Fig. 2). Power analysis shows that a relatively high penalty given to distant classes (that can be counterintuitive at first) allows

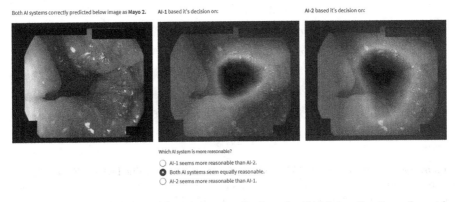

Fig. 4. User interface provided to the experts displays the CAM visualizations alongside the image. Experts are asked to evaluate the spots used in decision making process of CE and CDW-CE and choose the one which they think is more reasonable to them (i.e., more aligned with their decision making).

better optimization of the model training (for $\alpha = 5$, 2-level neighborhood coefficient $(2^5) = 32$ and 3-level neighborhood coefficient $(3^5) = 243$). Nevertheless, α is not a very sensitive parameter for performance as Fig. 2 shows that even the training with non-optimum α values outperforms the baseline and other ordinal approaches.

The experimental results show that using a loss function that penalizes distant mispredictions provides better optimization compared to previous approaches. While CDW-CE penalizes the mispredictions according to their distance to true class, it does not restrict the network to employ a single node at the output layer as it is in metric learning or regression-based approaches. Moreover, CDW-CE does not enforce fixed distances between classes and does not enforce any parametric distribution. Experiments show that, for the given problem where there are four distinct classes, the optimum α value is around six. We speculate that the α is susceptible to dataset, number of classes, and the employed model architecture; therefore, we recommend trying at least a few different values when deciding it. As Fig. 2 shows, as the α increases, network training becomes unstable (i.e., cross-validation results vary a lot), so it is possible to get a high performance randomly from a single training. To avoid this trap, it is necessary to use methods such as cross-validation or multiple training with different seeds when deciding the α.

Training models with the proposed CDW-CE loss does not only improve performance but also provide better explainability through the CAM visualizations. The model trained with CDW-CE highlights more relevant and discriminative regions compared to the model trained with CE for all Mayo scores. Sample CAM visualizations in Fig. 3 show that using CDW-CE loss trains the model to extract more compatible features with the disease symptoms, leading to better performance. The CAM regions extracted by CDW-CE generally appear to be wider; however, these expansions were towards relevant regions rather than unre-

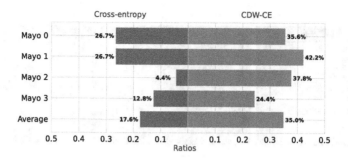

Fig. 5. Assessment results of CAM visualizations of models trained with CE and CDW-CE by experts. The percentage values experts found both visualizations equally reasonable are as follows: 37.7%, 31.1%, 57.8%, 62.8%, 47.4%, respectively.

lated regions. Therefore, it can be said that CDW-CE has semantically captured better features. The average of the three experts' choices is shown in Fig. 5. The experts found that the CAM visualizations of the model trained with CDW-CE are more reasonable than the model trained with CE for all Mayo classes. On average, the experts found nearly half of the images equally reasonable (47.4%) and the rate of selecting CDW-CE is two times more than the Cross-entropy (35.0% vs. 17.6%). Providing more reasonable CAM compatible with disease symptoms along with the high estimation performance increases the trust for the usage of the computer-aided diagnosis systems in clinics. As CDW-CE increases interpretability, transitioning to the clinic will also be accelerated.

MES for UC consists four distinct classes; therefore, experiments performed in this work are only compared for four levels. To what extend CDW-CE loss performs well should be investigated on different datasets, such as cervical cancer (7 levels of diagnosis) or diabetic retinopathy (5 levels of diagnosis) analysis. To test its capability in problems with higher number of classes, non-medical datasets, such as age estimation from face images, can be used. In addition, although the compared ordinal regression approaches are the state-of-the-art, other approaches based on regression setting can be experimented to extend the work.

7   Conclusion

In this study, we have proposed a novel non-parametric loss function designed to penalize the incorrect class predictions for the UC endoscopic severity estimation task. Incorrect classifications are weighted with a term that is in relation to its distance to the true class. Results show that a high penalty to the mispredicted distant classes is very important as experiments show that the optimal α can be a relatively large number. Extensive experiments show that the proposed loss function improves the performance significantly compared to the commonly used cross-entropy and several ordinal regression approaches. Training with CDW-CE does not only provide higher performance but also the models' CAM visualizations are more aligned with the experts opinions, which is expected to contribute positively to their clinical adoption. The proposed approach can be adapted to any problem with an ordinal category structure in medical as well as non-medical applications. In the future, we are planning to investigate its use in other ordinal regression problems.

References

1. Alammari, A., Islam, A.R., Oh, J., Tavanapong, W., Wong, J., De Groen, P.C.: Classification of ulcerative colitis severity in colonoscopy videos using CNN. In: International Conference on Information Management and Engineering, pp. 139–144 (2017)
2. Albuquerque, T., Cruz, R., Cardoso, J.S.: Ordinal losses for classification of cervical cancer risk. PeerJ Comput. Sci. **7**, e457 (2021)
3. Ali, S., et al.: Deep learning for detection and segmentation of artefact and disease instances in gastrointestinal endoscopy. Med. Image Anal. **70**, 102002 (2021)
4. Ali, S., et al.: Assessing generalisability of deep learning-based polyp detection and segmentation methods through a computer vision challenge. arXiv preprint arXiv:2202.12031 (2022)
5. Beckham, C., Pal, C.: A simple squared-error reformulation for ordinal classification. arXiv preprint arXiv:1612.00775 (2016)
6. Beckham, C., Pal, C.: Unimodal probability distributions for deep ordinal classification. In: International Conference on Machine Learning, pp. 411–419 (2017)
7. Belharbi, S., Ayed, I.B., McCaffrey, L., Granger, E.: Non-parametric uni-modality constraints for deep ordinal classification. arXiv preprint arXiv:1911.10720 (2019)
8. Bhambhvani, H.P., Zamora, A.: Deep learning enabled classification of mayo endoscopic subscore in patients with ulcerative colitis. Eur. J. Gastroenterol. Hepatol. **33**(5), 645–649 (2021)
9. Borgli, H., et al.: HyperKvasir, a comprehensive multi-class image and video dataset for gastrointestinal endoscopy. Sci. Data **7**(283), 1–14 (2020)
10. Cao, W., Mirjalili, V., Raschka, S.: Rank consistent ordinal regression for neural networks with application to age estimation. Pattern Recognit. Lett. **140**, 325–331 (2020)
11. Du, W., et al.: Review on the applications of deep learning in the analysis of gastrointestinal endoscopy images. IEEE Access **7**, 142053–142069 (2019)
12. Gottlieb, K., et al.: Central reading of ulcerative colitis clinical trial videos using neural networks. Gastroenterology **160**(3), 710–719 (2021)
13. Gutierrez Becker, B., et al.: Training and deploying a deep learning model for endoscopic severity grading in ulcerative colitis using multicenter clinical trial data. Thera. Adv. Gastrointest. Endosc. **14**, 2631774521990623 (2021)
14. He, K., Zhang, X., Ren, S., Sun, J.: Deep residual learning for image recognition. In: IEEE Conf. on Computer Vision and Pattern Recognition (CVPR), pp. 770–778 (2016)
15. Howard, A., et al.: Searching for mobilenetv3. In: IEEE/CVF International Conference on Computer Vision, pp. 1314–1324 (2019)
16. Huang, G., Liu, Z., Van Der Maaten, L., Weinberger, K.Q.: Densely connected convolutional networks. In: IEEE Conference on Computer Vision and Pattern Recognition (CVPR), pp. 4700–4708 (2017)

17. Kani, H.T., Ergenc, I., Polat, G., Ozen Alahdab, Y., Temizel, A., Atug, O.: P099 evaluation of endoscopic mayo score with an artificial intelligence algorithm. J. Crohn's Colitis **15**(Supplement_1), S195–S196 (2021)
18. Li, L., Lin, H.T.: Ordinal regression by extended binary classification. In: Schölkopf, B., Platt, J., Hoffman, T. (eds.) Advances in Neural Information Processing Systems, vol. 19. MIT Press (2007). https://papers.nips.cc/paper/ 2006/hash/019f8b946a256d9357eadc5ace2c8678-Abstract.html, https://mitpress. mit.edu/books/advances-neural-information-processing-systems-19
19. Limdi, J.K., Farraye, F.A.: Automated endoscopic assessment in ulcerative colitis: the next frontier. Gastrointest. Endosc. **93**(3), 737–739 (2021)
20. Luo, X., Zhang, J., Li, Z., Yang, R.: Diagnosis of ulcerative colitis from endoscopic images based on deep learning. Biomed. Signal Process. Control **73**, 103443 (2022)
21. Niu, Z., Zhou, M., Wang, L., Gao, X., Hua, G.: Ordinal regression with multiple output CNN for age estimation. In: IEEE Conference on Computer Vision and Pattern Recognition (CVPR), pp. 4920–4928 (2016)
22. Osada, T., et al.: Comparison of several activity indices for the evaluation of endoscopic activity in UC: inter-and intraobserver consistency. Inflamm. Bowel Dis. **16**(2), 192–197 (2010)
23. Ozawa, T., et al.: Novel computer-assisted diagnosis system for endoscopic disease activity in patients with ulcerative colitis. Gastrointest. Endosc. **89**(2), 416–421 (2019)
24. Paszke, A., et al.: PyTorch: an imperative style, high-performance deep learning library. Adv. Neural Inf. Process. Syst. **32**, 8026–8037 (2019)
25. Polat, G., Isik-Polat, E., Kayabay, K., Temizel, A.: Polyp detection in colonoscopy images using deep learning and bootstrap aggregation. In: International Workshop on Computer Vision in Endoscopy, IEEE International Symposium on Biomedical Imaging (ISBI). CEUR Workshop Proceedings, vol. 2886, pp. 90–100 (2021)
26. Polat, G., Kani, H.T., Ergenc, I., Alahdab, Y.O., Temizel, A., Atug, O.: Labeled Images for Ulcerative Colitis (LIMUC) Dataset, March 2022. https://doi.org/10. 5281/zenodo.5827695
27. Polat, G., Sen, D., Inci, A., Temizel, A.: Endoscopic artefact detection with ensemble of deep neural networks and false positive elimination. In: International Workshop on Computer Vision in Endoscopy, IEEE International Symposium on Biomedical Imaging (ISBI). CEUR Workshop Proceedings, vol. 2595, pp. 8–12 (2020)
28. Reinisch, W., et al.: Comparison of the ema and FDA guidelines on ulcerative colitis drug development. Clin. Gastroenterol. Hepatol. **17**(9), 1673-1679.e1 (2019)
29. Russakovsky, O., et al.: ImageNet large scale visual recognition challenge. Int. J. Comput. Vis. **115**(3), 211–252 (2015). https://doi.org/10.1007/s11263-015-0816-y
30. Schroeder, K.W., Tremaine, W.J., Ilstrup, D.M.: Coated oral 5-aminosalicylic acid therapy for mildly to moderately active ulcerative colitis. New England J. Med. **317**(26), 1625–1629 (1987)
31. Schwab, E., et al.: Automatic estimation of ulcerative colitis severity from endoscopy videos using ordinal multi-instance learning. Comput. Methods Biomech. Biomed. Eng. Imaging Visual. **10**, 1–9 (2021). https://www.tandfonline. com/doi/full/10.1080/21681163.2021.1997644
32. Selvaraju, R.R., Cogswell, M., Das, A., Vedantam, R., Parikh, D., Batra, D.: Grad-CAM: visual explanations from deep networks via gradient-based localization. In: IEEE Conference on Computer Vision and Pattern Recognition (CVPR), pp. 618–626 (2017)

33. Shi, X., Cao, W., Raschka, S.: Deep neural networks for rank-consistent ordinal regression based on conditional probabilities. arXiv preprint arXiv:2111.08851 (2021)
34. Stidham, R.W., et al.: Performance of a deep learning model vs human reviewers in grading endoscopic disease severity of patients with ulcerative colitis. JAMA Netw. Open **2**(5), e193963–e193963 (2019)
35. Sutton, R.T., Zaiane, O.R., Goebel, R., Baumgart, D.C.: Artificial intelligence enabled automated diagnosis and grading of ulcerative colitis endoscopy images. Sci. Rep. **12**(2748), 1–10 (2022)
36. Szegedy, C., et al.: Going deeper with convolutions. In: IEEE Conference on Computer Vision and Pattern Recognition (CVPR), pp. 1–9 (2015)
37. Szegedy, C., Vanhoucke, V., Ioffe, S., Shlens, J., Wojna, Z.: Rethinking the inception architecture for computer vision. In: IEEE Conference on Computer Vision and Pattern Recognition (CVPR), pp. 2818–2826 (2016)
38. Takenaka, K., Kawamoto, A., Okamoto, R., Watanabe, M., Ohtsuka, K.: Artificial intelligence for endoscopy in inflammatory bowel disease. Intest. Res. **20**(2), 165 (2022)
39. Takenaka, K., et al.: Development and validation of a deep neural network for accurate evaluation of endoscopic images from patients with ulcerative colitis. Gastroenterology **158**(8), 2150–2157 (2020)
40. Travis, S.P., et al.: Reliability and initial validation of the ulcerative colitis endoscopic index of severity. Gastroenterology **145**(5), 987–995 (2013)
41. Yao, H., et al.: Fully automated endoscopic disease activity assessment in ulcerative colitis. Gastrointest. Endosc. **93**(3), 728–736 (2021)
42. Zhou, B., Khosla, A., Lapedriza, A., Oliva, A., Torralba, A.: Learning deep features for discriminative localization. In: IEEE Conference on Computer Vision and Pattern Recognition (CVPR), pp. 2921–2929 (2016)

Procrustes Analysis of Muscle Fascicle Shapes Based on DTI Fibre Tracking

Lei Ye[✉], Eugenie Hunsicker, Baihua Li, and Diwei Zhou

Loughborough University, Loughborough, UK
{L.Ye,E.Hunsicker,B.Li,D.Zhou2}@lboro.ac.uk

Abstract. Diffusion Tensor Imaging (DTI) is a technique developed from Magnetic Resonance Imaging (MRI), which uses a mathematical form diffusion tensor to measure the movement of water molecules in biological tissues in *vivo*. By performing fibre tracking using diffusion tensor data, we can study the micro-structure of biological tissues in a non-invasive way. Skeletal muscle plays a significant role in force and power generation that contribute to maintaining body postures and to controlling its movements. DTI fibre tracking may re-construct the skeletal muscle in a fascicle level. Procrustes analysis is a landmark-based method for studying the shapes of objects. In this paper, we explore using Generalised Procrustes Analysis to study the fascicle shapes that we have collected in medial gastrocnemius muscles from 6 healthy adults by using DTI technology. This is an innovated attempt of using Procrustes analysis to find the trend of the changes of fascicle shape when foot is in plantarflexion and dorsiflexion, by clustering method.

Keywords: Procrustes · Shape · Analysis · DTI · Skeletal muscle · Fascicle

1 Introduction

Shape analysis has been introduced in scientific research for a long time and has been widely used. For example, animal skulls research in biology; postcode recognition in image analysis; steroid molecules in chemistry; MRI and cortical surface shape in medicine; DNA molecules in pharmacy; protein matching in bioinformatics; sand grains in particle science; human movement data in physiotherapy; electrophoretic gels in genetics; Central Place Theory in geography; alignments of standing stones in archaeology and so on [1–7].

As an innovative exploration of applying shape analysis on biological tissues, based on our previous research [8], which uses DTI technology to reconstruct the skeletal muscle of human beings, we try to find the hidden information between foot positions and the muscle fascicle shapes.

G. Yang et al. (Eds.): MIUA 2022, LNCS 13413, pp. 172–186, 2022.
https://doi.org/10.1007/978-3-031-12053-4_13

1.1 DTI and Fibre Tracking

Diffusion Tensor Imaging (DTI) is a technology which uses Diffusion-Weighted Magnetic Resonance Imaging (DWI or DW-MRI) data to describe the movement of water molecules in biological tissues. The movement of water molecules is not free, but is restricted by structures and objects in the tissue such as macromolecules, fibre walls and membranes [9–12]. Therefore, by analysing the movement of water molecules in images, we have the chance to study detailed structures in body tissues, in *vivo*, in a non-invasive way.

DTI provides information on the extent of diffusion anisotropy and its orientation, which can be used to generate a 3D vector field. Generally, at each voxel in DTI, the eigenvectors represent the diffusion directions, and the diffusion strength are proportional to the square roots of eigenvalues associating to the eigenvectors. By studying the connectivities along the vectors within the vector field, we are able to perform fibre tracking and reconstruct fibre tissues from within the human body.

1.2 Skeletal Muscle

Skeletal muscle is one of the most important tissues of the human body, playing a significant role in force and power generation that contribute to maintaining body postures and to controlling its movements [13]. By applying fibre tracking technology on skeletal muscle, we are able to explore its inner structure. Although the tracked fibres cannot be recognized as exactly the same as the muscle fascicles that the tracked fibres follow the orientation of muscle fascicles and therefore we are able to use these fibres as the equivalent of a bundle of muscle fascicles [14]. Figure 1 shows the results of performing fibre tracking within the medial gastrocnemius (MG) of a human calf.

1.3 Shape Analysis

Muscle fascicles can be reconstructed to 3D curves using DTI fibre tracking methods. A fascicle shape can be described by marking a serials points along the contour of a fascicle curve. Specifically a fascicle shape is a collection of k landmarks (points of interest) in an m-dimensional space ($m = 3$ in 3D space). In statistical shape analysis, Procrustes analysis is a landmark-based method for studying the shapes of objects [15]. The principal implementation of Procrustes analysis is to align different shapes in space using translation, rotation, scaling and reflection, then study their relationships. For example, to study the similarity of shapes is of main interest [1,16]. Thus, we would like to explore a method that uses the Procrustes shape analysis to study the muscle fascicles data that we have collected in the human calf.

The aim of our research is to apply statistical shape analysis methods to quantitatively estimate the mean fascicle shapes and to explore the variation of fascicle shapes, and therefore find the connection between fascicle shapes and muscle states.

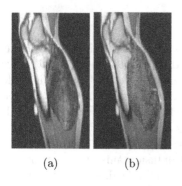

(a)   (b)

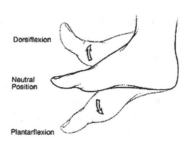

Fig. 1. (a) MG boundary (red) with corresponding MRI. (b) Tracked fascicles (green) within MG with corresponding MRI. (Color figure online)

Fig. 2. Foot plantarflexion and dorsiflexion. In our study, the ankle joint angles are about 67.5° and 107.3°, respectively. Image from www.pinterest.com

2   Procrustes Shape Analysis

The basic stratagem of the Procrustes shape analysis is to align the involved shapes as close as possible by transforming, rotating, scaling or reflecting and then to measure the distance between the shapes. The very first procedure of comparing the shapes of two or multiple objects is called superimpose. This procedure, also known as Procrustes superimposition (PS), is performed by applying optimally translating, rotating and scaling to the involved objects. In 2D or 3D space, the location, orientation, or size of the objects can be adjusted freely in order to make them to fit each other as close as possible. The objective of the operation is to minimize the measurement of the shape difference, which is called Procrustes distance between the objects. Full PS allows translation, rotation and scaling operation. Partial PS means the sizes of the objects keep unchanged. As an extra option, for both full PS and partial PS, there is an operation called 'reflection', which is able to produce a perfect superimposition for the objects with symmetric property (e.g. left ear and right ear, or left hand and right hand, in most of the cases).

Figure 3 shows the three steps to superimpose two object. By labeling four corresponding landmarks, A, B, C, D, and A', B', C', D', on both objects, respectively, we are able to see the procedure of Procrustes superimposition step by step.

2.1   Shape

Procrustes analysis is based on shapes, which exist everywhere and are used to describe the appearance of objects. **Shape** is all the geometrical information that remains when location, scale and rotational effects are removed from an object [1]. A shape is invariant to the Euclidean similarity transformations, which includes translation, scaling and rotation. Two objects can be recognized as in same shape if they match each other after translating, scaling and rotating.

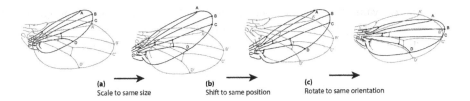

Fig. 3. The three transformation steps of an ordinary Procrustes shape fit for two configurations of landmarks. (a) Scaling of both configurations to the same size; (b) Transposition to the same position of the center point of gravity; (c) Rotation to the orientation that provides the minimum sum of squared distances between corresponding landmarks. Original image based on https://en.wikipedia.org/wiki/Procrustes_analysis

2.2   Landmark and Configuration

Landmarks, a finite number of points selected along the outline of an object, are used to define a shape. A **configuration** is the set of landmarks on a particular object. The **configuration matrix** X is a $k \times m$ matrix of Cartesian coordinates of the k landmarks in m dimensions. The **configuration space** is the space of all landmark coordinates [1].

2.3   Pre-shape

To compute a distance between shapes it is necessary to standardise for size. In this study, we use the centered pre-shape Z_C which is defined by

$$Z_C = CX / \parallel CX \parallel, \tag{1}$$

where

$$C = I_k - \frac{1}{k}\mathbf{1}_k\mathbf{1}_k^T \tag{2}$$

is the centering matrix, I_k is the $k \times k$ identity matrix (diagonal matrix with ones on the diagonal), $\mathbf{1}_k$ is the $k \times 1$ vector of ones and $\parallel A \parallel = \sqrt{trace(A^T A)}$ is the Euclidean norm.

2.4   Procrustes Distances

Procrustes distance is a method to describe the similarity of different shape objects. Consider two configuration matrices from k points in m dimensions X_1 and X_2 with pre-shapes Z_1 and Z_2. We minimize over rotations and scale to find the closest Euclidean distance between Z_1 and Z_2. There are two types of Procrustes distances. The full Procrustes distance between two shapes considers translating, rotating, as well as scaling for superimposition. The partial Procrustes distance applies translating and rotating but not scaling for superimposition. The full Procrustes distance between X_1 and X_2 is

$$d_F(X_1, X_2) = \inf_{\Gamma, \beta, \gamma} \parallel Z_2 - \beta Z_1 \Gamma - \mathbf{1}_k \gamma^T \parallel, \tag{3}$$

where the real value $\beta > 0$ is the scale parameter, $\boldsymbol{\Gamma}$ is an $m \times m$ rotation matrix (in the special orthogonal group $SO(m)$), and the real vector $\boldsymbol{\gamma}$ is an $m \times 1$ location vector. The partial Procrustes distance between $\boldsymbol{X}_1$ and $\boldsymbol{X}_2$ is

$$d_P(\boldsymbol{X}_1, \boldsymbol{X}_2) = \inf_{\boldsymbol{\Gamma}, \boldsymbol{\gamma}} \| \boldsymbol{Z}_2 - \boldsymbol{Z}_1 \boldsymbol{\Gamma} - \boldsymbol{1}_k \boldsymbol{\gamma}^T \| . \tag{4}$$

2.5   Ordinary and Generalised Procrustes Analysis

Procrustes shape analysis aims to match different configurations with similarity transformations to be as close as possible according to Euclidean distance by using the least-squares algorithm. Technically, Procrustes analysis can be further classified into two types, which are Ordinary Procrustes Analysis (OPA) and Generalized Procrustes Analysis (GPA) [1].

OPA is an operation that compares two shapes, or compares a set of shapes with a selected reference shape. The involved shapes need to perform superimposition, which includes removing the translational, rotational and uniform scaling components in order to transform them into a member of an equivalent class which can be used for comparison [17]. The full OPA solution to the minimisation of Eq. 3 is given by $(\hat{\boldsymbol{\gamma}}, \hat{\beta}, \hat{\boldsymbol{\Gamma}})$ where

$$\hat{\boldsymbol{\gamma}} = 0 \tag{5}$$

$$\hat{\boldsymbol{\Gamma}} = \boldsymbol{U}\boldsymbol{V}^T \tag{6}$$

where

$$\boldsymbol{X}_2^T \boldsymbol{X}_1 = \| \boldsymbol{X}_1 \| \| \boldsymbol{X}_2 \| \boldsymbol{V}\boldsymbol{\Lambda}\boldsymbol{U}^T \tag{7}$$

with $\boldsymbol{\Lambda}$ a diagonal $m \times m$ matrix of positive elements, $\boldsymbol{U}$ and $\boldsymbol{V}$ are from the singular value decomposition of $\boldsymbol{X}_2^T \boldsymbol{X}_1$. Furthermore,

$$\hat{\beta} = \frac{trace(\boldsymbol{X}_2^T \boldsymbol{X}_1 \hat{\boldsymbol{\Gamma}})}{trace(\boldsymbol{X}_1^T \boldsymbol{X}_1)} . \tag{8}$$

The partial OPA has the same solution for the location vector and the rotation matrix as in the full OPA.

GPA applies Procrustes analysis to optimally superimpose more than two objects, instead of superimposing them to an arbitrarily selected shape. GPA is able to generate the mean shape of a set shapes automatically by using an iterative approach. OPA and GPA perform the same superimposition operations. The difference between them is the method to determine the reference orientation for the objects, which is arbitrarily selected in OPA but is optimally determined in GPA. When only two shapes are compared, GPA is equivalent to OPA [1,18]. Both OPA and GPA have the options of full and partial sub-types. Their difference is whether a scaling operation is performed.

3   Procrustes Methods for Fascicle Shape Analysis

Muscle fascicles are equivalent to 3D spatial curves. As we have known, a tracked fascicle is composed of a certain number of consecutive voxels, which can be recognized as landmarks along the fascicle shape. To demonstrate the idea of Procrustes analysis, we will carry out experiments using artificial 3D curves.

3.1   Landmark Construction for Fascicle Shapes Using Interpolation

We need to define a configuration matrix for a fascicle shape. The configuration matrix is a $k \times m$ matrix of the k landmarks in m dimensions (in our case $m = 3$). Also, the fascicle shapes need to have the same landmarks (same k value for all fascicle shapes) before performing Procrustes analysis. In this study, we interpolate fascicles which are shorter than the longest fascicle.

Refer to Fig. 4(a). Consider there are three fascicles with different length in muscle. The diamonds on fascicles indicate the original position of voxels, and the fascicles are in the length of 3(red), 5(green) and 7(blue), respectively. Since they are of different lengths, we interpolate the fascicles, for instance, to 20 landmarks. The circle marks on each fascicle show the results of interpolation. By collecting the coordinates of all landmarks on fascicles and storing them into configuration space, which is a $20 \times 3 \times 3$ matrix ($k = 20, m = 3, shape = 3$), we are able to do Procrustes analysis on those artificial curves.

3.2   Example of OPA

Let's perform ordinary Procrustes analysis first. In Fig. 4(a), we choose Fascicle 1 (red) and Fascicle 3 (blue), where Fascicle 3 works as a reference shape. To match Fascicle 1 and 3, all three transformations (translation, rotation and scale) are carried out. The function matches involved configurations by least squares. Figure 4(b) and (c) show the visualized result of full and partial OPA. After performing full OPA, we can get an estimated rotation matrix

$$\hat{\varGamma} = \begin{pmatrix} 1 & 0 & 0 \\ 0 & 0.8618 & -0.5072 \\ 0 & 0.5072 & 0.8618 \end{pmatrix} \tag{9}$$

and an estimated scale factor of $\hat{\beta} = 2.8326$. The centered configuration of Fascicle 3 (blue) and its matched configuration of Fascicle 1 (red) are rendered by 'square' marks and '*' marks at position (b) in the figure, respectively. The black cross is the gravity center (origin) of the superimposed configurations.

Look at the image, compared with the original shapes, the reference shape Fascicle 3 (blue) has no shape change but its location is aligned to the origin according to its gravity center. At the same time, the Fascicle 1 (red) has been translated (matching the origin), rotated (applying matrix $\hat{\varGamma}$) and scaled (applying scale factor $\hat{\beta}$) in order to match with the reference shape.

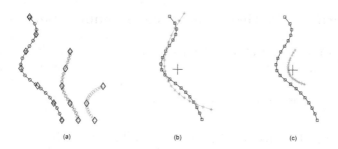

Fig. 4. (a) Example fascicles for performing OPA between Fascicle 1 (red) and Fascicle 3 (blue), where Fascicle 3 (blue) is the reference shape. (b) Re-allocated reference shape (blue) and its matched shape of Fascicle 1 (red) by using full OPA. (c) Re-allocated reference shape (blue) and its matched shape of Fascicle 1 (red) by using partial OPA. The black cross is the common gravity center of them. (Color figure online)

As a comparison, after performing partial OPA, the estimated rotation matrix

$$
\hat{\boldsymbol{\Gamma}} = \begin{pmatrix} 1 & 0 & 0 \\ 0 & 0.8618 & -0.5072 \\ 0 & 0.5072 & 0.8618 \end{pmatrix} \tag{10}
$$

is exactly the same as the $\hat{\boldsymbol{\Gamma}}$ in full OPA. Since there is no scale changing required, the scale factor $\hat{\beta} = 1$. Similarly, the centered configuration of fascicle 3 (blue) and its matched configuration of fascicle 1 (red) are rendered at position (c) in the figure and the black cross is the gravity center (origin) of the superimposed configurations.

From the parameters and image, we can see that in partial OPA, the only difference is that there is no scale factor applied to the configuration (red) which is to be matched with the reference shape (blue).

3.3   Example of GPA

Essentially, GPA performs a series of OPA operations iteratively to find the optimized superimposition as the reference for all involved shapes; we call this the mean shape.

Please refer to Fig. 5, which shows the visualized results of performing a full GPA and a partial GPA, respectively. Similar to above figures, the original fascicles are drawn at left side (a). The black fascicles at the right side, (b) and (c), with square marks, are the mean shapes and the cross signs are the gravity centers. It is notable that mean shapes generated by full and partial GPAs have just a little difference.

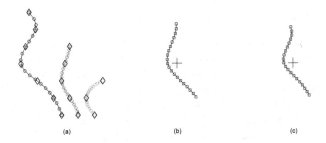

(a)   (b)   (c)

Fig. 5. Performing GPA on the 3 example fascicles at left side (a). The 2 curves on right side are the mean shapes of the example fascicles by using full GPA (b) and partial GPA (c), respectively. Black crosses are the gravity centers of the mean shapes. (Color figure online)

3.4 Example of Procrustes Distance

Once the mean fascicle shape is obtained using the GPA method, we are able to calculate the Procrustes distance d_P between the original example fascicles and their mean shape. Table 1 lists the results based on the GPA example in Fig. 5. It is clear that in full GPA, the mean shape is closest to Fascicle 2 (green) and is very far from Fascicle 1 (red). On the other hand, in partial GPA, the mean shape is most similar to Fascicle 3 (blue) but very different from Fascicle 1 (red).

Table 1. Procrustes distances between the three original fascicles and their mean shape in Fig. 5.

	Fascicle 1 (red)	Fascicle 2 (green)	Fascicle 3 (blue)
Full	0.1211	0.0731	0.0856
Partial	0.1519	0.0642	0.0569

4 Real Application: Mean Fascicle Shapes in Medial Gastrocnemius

In DTI skeletal muscle studies, the number of fascicles which can be tracked is variable, which is determined by the tracking algorithm and parameters chosen. It is also affected significantly by the settings of the MRI machine, as well as by the position and posture of the scanned object. No matter what different results are obtained, the number of fascicles is normally in the thousands or more. In this scenario, we are more interested in the overall appearance of the fascicles than in their one to one relationship. In this context, we would like to perform Generalized Procrustes Analysis in our muscle fascicle research, that is to find the mean shape of the fascicles in a muscle group, and then study the relationship between individual fascicles and this optimal superimposition.

4.1 Data Preparation

The raw DTI data is provided by Dr Bart Bolsterlee [19,20] at Neuroscience Research Australia (NeuRA). The DTI is scanned from the medial gastrocnemius (MG) in the left calf of 6 healthy adults at 2 different ankle positions, respectively. The ankle position is determined by ankle joint angle, which is the angle between the tibia and the sole of the foot. Please refer to Fig. 2. Assuming 90° is a neutral ankle joint orientation, angle values below and above 90° indicate plantarflexion (foot down) and dorsiflexion (foot up), respectively.

After performing fibre tracking [8] based on the DTI data we are able to reconstruct the fascicles within the MG. As above explained, Procrustes analysis can only accept data of the same dimensionality. However, the fascicles obtained by DTI tracking are of different lengths. Therefore, we need to perform data interpolation for the fascicles before Procrustes analysis, as introduced in Sect. 3.1. For these muscle fascicles, the actual solution is finding the longest fascicle first, then interpolating the rest of the fascicles individually in order to reach the identical data points of the longest one. For example, a muscle group has 3000 fascicles in 3D space and the length of the longest fascicle is 50. After interpolation, we will have a $50 \times 3 \times 3000$ data matrix available for Procrustes analysis.

By applying Generalised Procrustes Analysis to all fascicles in the MG, we will find the overall mean fascicle shape of the corresponding muscle. In the meanwhile, the Procrustes distances between each fascicle and the mean shape are calculated as well. As we have performed both full and partial GPA, a total of $6 \times 2 \times 2 = 24$ groups of data are collected. Each data group includes a mean fascicle shape matrix and a distances matrix which indicate the similarity between individual fascicle and the mean shape.

a   b   c   d   e

Fig. 6. Coronal (front-back) view of selected MG fascicle shapes from a participant at foot-down position). (a) is the mean fascicle shape in MG obtained using GPA. (b) to (e) are the fascicles with 25th, 50th, 75th and 100th percentile Procrustes distances from the mean shape. (Color figure online)

4.2 Results Analysis

We would like to treat the mean shape of the fascicles in a MG as the overall fascicle shape of this particular muscle. Figure 6 demonstrates the variability of fascicle shapes in one participant's MG at one foot angle. The left (red) is the mean fascicle shape which has a (nearly) straight line shape. The second left (b) is the fascicle with the 25th percentile Procrustes distance from the mean (red). It is clear that the 25th percentile fascicle is similar to the mean fascicle with a slight difference in orientation. The third left (c) is the fascicle with the median percentile Procrustes distance from the mean. It is shorter than the mean and has a bump in the middle. The fourth left (d) is the fascicle with 75th percentile Procrustes distance which is longer than the mean fascicle and are more curly. The very right (e) is the fascicle with the largest Procrustes distance from the mean fascicle. This fascicle has a hook shape and is the most different one to the mean shape in the MG region.

In order to observe the shape changes of muscle fascicles when the foot is at different positions, we separate the muscle fascicles into two groups by using k-means clustering algorithm, where $K = 2$. Clustering is based on the Procrustes distance, or say shape similarity, between each fascicle and the mean shape. One of the groups includes those fascicles which are more similar (nearer in distance) to the mean shape, while the other group is the fascicles with relatively lower similarity (farther in distance). Here we classify the two groups as 'Group Near' and 'Group Far'.

Figure 7 and Fig. 8 show the visualized results we have obtained for one participant. Figure 7 shows the results of using partial GPA and Fig. 8 shows the full GPA results. In each figure, the columns are different foot positions (left: foot down, right: foot up). To make the figures clearer, we render the fascicles in 'Group Near' in black and the fascicles in 'Group Far' in white. As an initial visual impression, we can see that, compared to the foot is at the 'down' position (left column), when the foot is at the 'up' position (right column), the fascicles in 'Group Near', which are in black, are evidently more than those in 'Group Far'. This phenomenon is applied to all participants.

Table 2. Partial GPA statistics for the muscle fascicles when foot is at 2 positions.

Partial GPA		Obj 1	Obj 2	Obj 3	Obj 4	Obj 5	Obj 6
Foot down	Distance to mean shape	0.0505	0.0532	0.0524	0.0527	0.0524	0.0504
	Fascicles in group near	41.61%	44.67%	43.80%	51.66%	51.88%	46.23%
Foot up	Distance to mean shape	0.0501	0.0519	0.0504	0.0510	0.0509	0.0503
	Fascicles in group near	55.78%	53.25%	54.17%	55.02%	55.65%	56.30%

Table 3. Full GPA statistics for the muscle fascicles when foot is at 2 positions.

Full GPA		Obj 1	Obj 2	Obj 3	Obj 4	Obj 5	Obj 6
Foot down	Distance to mean shape	0.0506	0.0532	0.0525	0.0527	0.0524	0.0505
	Fascicles in group near	42.26%	44.08%	43.58%	50.34%	52.04%	47.88%
Foot up	Distance to mean shape	0.0501	0.0519	0.0504	0.0510	0.0509	0.0503
	Fascicles in group near	56.13%	53.40%	55.08%	55.28%	55.29%	55.16%

Numerically, for each participant, we calculate the mean distance from all fascicles in the muscle to their mean shape, and the percentage of the fascicles in the 'Group Near'. The values are listed in the tables. Table 2 corresponds to Fig. 7 and Table 3 corresponds to Fig. 8.

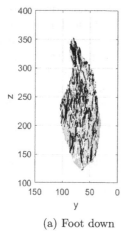

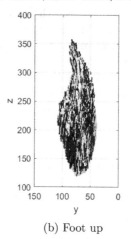

(a) Foot down   (b) Foot up

Fig. 7. Figure shows the percentage of the fascicles which are close to the mean shape. Images show 1 participant × 2 positions, using partial GPA and k-means ($K = 2$) clustering algorithm.

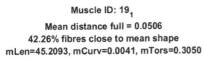

Muscle ID: 19₁
Mean distance full = 0.0506
42.26% fibres close to mean shape
mLen=45.2093, mCurv=0.0041, mTors=0.3050

Muscle ID: 19₃
Mean distance full = 0.0501
56.13% fibres close to mean shape
mLen=54.0400, mCurv=0.0022, mTors=0.2612

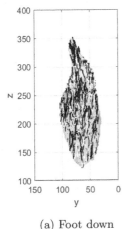

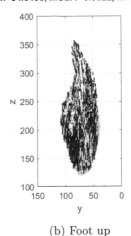

(a) Foot down

(b) Foot up

Fig. 8. Figure shows the percentage of the fascicles which are close to the mean shape. Images show 1 participant × 2 positions, using full GPA and k-means ($K = 2$) clustering algorithm.

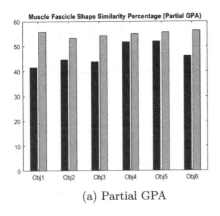

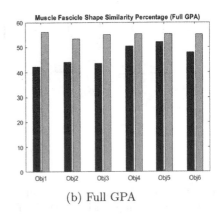

(a) Partial GPA

(b) Full GPA

Fig. 9. Fascicle shape similarity percentage chart while the foot is in different positions, using partial GPA (a) and full GPA (b), respectively. In both plots, blue (on the left): foot at 'down' position; red (on the right): foot at 'up' position. (Color figure online)

From the values in the tables, we can tell that for all participants, when the foot is at the 'up' position, the overall mean Procrustes distance (shape similarity) between fascicles and the mean shape is smaller than that when the foot is at the 'down' position. Meanwhile, the percentage of fascicles in 'Group Near' is higher when the foot is at the 'up' position. We therefore can

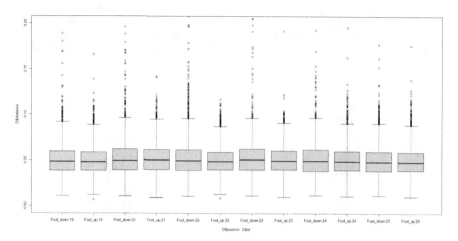

(a) Partial GPA

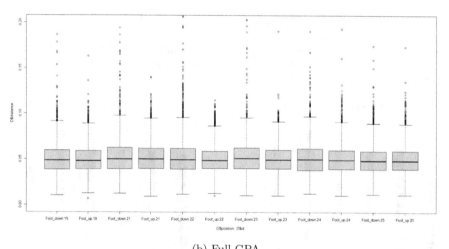

(b) Full GPA

Fig. 10. Boxplots show the distribution of Procrustes distances between each fascicle and the mean shape, using partial GPA (a) and full GPA (b), respectively. Boxes in each plot present 6 participants × 2 foot positions. In both plots, the distances range between 25% and 75% percentile are narrower at the 'up' position.

conclude that when the foot is being raised up, the MG muscles stretch longer, and the fascicles' shapes in the muscle are becoming more similar to each other. In order to give an intuitive understanding for the information in above tables, the percentages of fascicle similarity for all participants with the foot at both positions are visualized by bar charts in Fig. 9a and Fig. 9b.

Furthermore, we verify the collected data using boxplots. Figure 10a and Fig. 10b show the Procrustes distance distribution between each fascicle and the mean shape. The boxplots are based on partial GPA and full GPA, respectively. Each plot presents 6 participants × 2 foot positions. In these plots we can see that the range of distances between 25% percentile and 75% percentile for each participant is narrower when the foot is at the 'up' position. This observation supports the conclusion we have mentioned above. We notice in partial and full GPA, the changes of data distribution are small.

5 Summary and Further Work

Procrustes analysis has been widely used in shape analysis. We have explored the potential application of this technique in DTI skeletal muscle research. In this valuable attempt, we have found some meaningful conclusions which primarily answer what are the mean fascicle shapes in MG region at different ankle positions and how fascicle shape varies within this muscle region. Although the samples used in the research are limited, the results from all participants are obvious and identical.

Procrustes analysis is a useful method to study the shape of objects. A further research topic is to use this technique to observe and analysis more muscle groups, including the shapes of muscle fascicles and muscle boundaries. For example, we are interested in studying the shape properties of same muscle group on different participants, and, different muscle groups on same participant. We are also interested in the relationship between the changing of muscle shape and force generation. Furthermore, applying machine learning in shape analysis is a very attractive research direction.

References

1. Dryden, I.L., Mardia, K.V.: Statistical Shape Analysis: With Applications in R, vol. 995. Wiley, Hoboken (2016)
2. Torres-Tamayo, N., García-Martínez, D., Zlolniski, S.L., Torres-Sánchez, I., García-Río, F., Bastir, M.: 3D analysis of sexual dimorphism in size, shape and breathing kinematics of human lungs. J. Anat. **232**(2), 227–237 (2018)
3. Frelat, M.A., Katina, S., Weber, G.W., Bookstein, F.L.: A novel geometric morphometric approach to the study of long bone shape variation. Am. J. Phys. Anthropol. **149**(4), 628–638 (2012)
4. Sella-Tunis, T., Pokhojaev, A., Sarig, R., O'Higgins, P., May, H.: Human mandibular shape is associated with masticatory muscle force. Sci. Rep. **8**(1), 1–10 (2018)
5. Berge, C., Penin, X., Pellé, É.: New interpretation of Laetoli footprints using an experimental approach and Procrustes analysis: preliminary results. C.R. Palevol **5**(3–4), 561–569 (2006)
6. Andreopoulos, A., Tsotsos, J.K.: Efficient and generalizable statistical models of shape and appearance for analysis of cardiac MRI. Med. Image Anal. **12**(3), 335–357 (2008)

7. de Diego, M., Casado, A., Gómez, M., Martín, J., Pastor, J.F., Potau, J.M.: Structural and molecular analysis of elbow flexor muscles in modern humans and common chimpanzees. Zoomorphology **139**(2), 277–290 (2020). https://doi.org/10.1007/s00435-020-00482-5

8. Ye, L., Hunsicker, E., Li, B., Zhou, D.: Brain fibre tracking improved by diffusion tensor similarity using non-Euclidean distances. In: 2019 IEEE International Conference on Imaging Systems and Techniques (IST), pp. 1–6. IEEE (2019)

9. Hagmann, P., Jonasson, L., Maeder, P., Thiran, J.-P., Wedeen, V.J., Meuli, R.: Understanding diffusion MR imaging techniques: from scalar diffusion-weighted imaging to diffusion tensor imaging and beyond. Radiographics **26**(suppl_1), S205–S223 (2006)

10. Merboldt, K.-D., Hanicke, W., Frahm, J.: Self-diffusion NMR imaging using stimulated echoes. J. Magn. Resonan. (1969) **64**(3), 479–486 (1985)

11. Taylor, D.G., Bushell, M.C.: The spatial mapping of translational diffusion coefficients by the NMR imaging technique. Phys. Med. Biol. **30**(4), 345 (1985)

12. Bhattacharya, P.D.: Diffusion MRI: Theory, Methods, and Applications. Jones, D.K. (ed.) Oxford University Press (2011). 2012

13. Frontera, W.R., Ochala, J.: Skeletal muscle: a brief review of structure and function. Calcif. Tissue Int. **96**(3), 183–195 (2015)

14. Bolsterlee, B., D'Souza, A., Herbert, R.D.: Reliability and robustness of muscle architecture measurements obtained using diffusion tensor imaging with anatomically constrained tractography. J. Biomech. **86**, 71–78 (2019)

15. Webster, M., Sheets, H.D.: A practical introduction to landmark-based geometric morphometrics. Paleontol. Soc. Pap. **16**, 163–188 (2010)

16. Stegmann, M.B., Gomez, D.D.: A brief introduction to statistical shape analysis. Informatics and mathematical modelling, Technical University of Denmark, DTU, 15(11) (2002)

17. Goodall, C.: Procrustes methods in the statistical analysis of shape. J. Roy. Stat. Soc.: Ser. B (Methodol.) **53**(2), 285–321 (1991)

18. Slice, D.E.: Landmark coordinates aligned by procrustes analysis do not lie in Kendall's shape space. Syst. Biol. **50**(1), 141–149 (2001)

19. Bolsterlee, B., Gandevia, S.C., Herbert, R.D.: Effect of transducer orientation on errors in ultrasound image-based measurements of human medial gastrocnemius muscle fascicle length and pennation. PloS One **11**(6), e0157273 (2016)

20. Bolsterlee, B., Finni, T., D'Souza, A., Eguchi, J., Clarke, E.C., Herbert, R.D.: Three-dimensional architecture of the whole human soleus muscle in vivo. PeerJ **6**, e4610 (2018)

Weakly Supervised Captioning
of Ultrasound Images

Mohammad Alsharid[1]($\boxtimes$), Harshita Sharma[1], Lior Drukker[2],
Aris T. Papageorgiou[2], and J. Alison Noble[1]

[1] Institute of Biomedical Engineering, Department of Engineering Science,
University of Oxford, Oxford, UK
mohammad.ali.alsharid@gmail.com
[2] Nuffield Department of Women's and Reproductive Health,
University of Oxford, Oxford, UK

Abstract. Medical image captioning models generate text to describe
the semantic contents of an image, aiding the non-experts in understanding and interpretation. We propose a weakly-supervised approach to
improve the performance of image captioning models on small image-
text datasets by leveraging a large anatomically-labelled image classification dataset. Our method generates pseudo-captions (weak labels) for
caption-less but anatomically-labelled (class-labelled) images using an
encoder-decoder sequence-to-sequence model. The augmented dataset is
used to train an image-captioning model in a weakly supervised learning
manner. For fetal ultrasound, we demonstrate that the proposed augmentation approach outperforms the baseline on semantics and syntax-based
metrics, with nearly twice as much improvement in value on *BLEU-1*
and *ROUGE-L*. Moreover, we observe that superior models are trained
with the proposed data augmentation, when compared with the existing
regularization techniques. This work allows seamless automatic annotation of images that lack human-prepared descriptive captions for training
image-captioning models. Using pseudo-captions in the training data is
particularly useful for medical image captioning when significant time
and effort of medical experts is required to obtain real image captions.

Keywords: Image captioning · Fetal ultrasound · Data augmentation

1 Introduction

Image captioning generates a textual description of the spatial information
present in an image [9]. There has been growing interest recently in medical
image captioning [24], including for ultrasound (US) imaging [8,35,36].

Consider the future where wearable medical technology and seamless sensors
provide consumers with basic information about their health [32]. In this future,
portable US probes would connect to a user's smart mobile device to capture
medical selfies [32] and real-time automated captioning would provide a textual

© The Author(s), under exclusive license to Springer Nature Switzerland AG 2022
G. Yang et al. (Eds.): MIUA 2022, LNCS 13413, pp. 187–198, 2022.
https://doi.org/10.1007/978-3-031-12053-4_14

description of the medical selfie content. While the US probes for this realisation exist today, the technical capability of generating such captions needs to be worked on. This paper takes a preliminary step towards actualizing it.

Data: image-caption pairs and caption-less images with anatomical class labels
Result: caption-less images annotated with pseudo-captions
while *caption-less image i_{cl} exists* **do**

> calculate similarity between i_{cl} and every image with real caption label;
> retrieve caption of most similar image;
> perform parts-of-speech tagging on caption;
> extract words that have been tagged as nouns;
> input label and nouns to seq2seq model to generate pseudo-caption;
> annotate i_{cl} with pseudo-caption;

end
train captioning model

Algorithm 1: The entire pseudo-caption preparation pipeline.

We are interested in understanding the principles of designing US image and video captioning algorithms. Our work is application-agnostic in that the generated captions could be of use to different users, such as amateur observers of ultrasound images. A clinical motivation for automatic US image and video captioning stems from US images being difficult for non-experts to interpret. However, image-to-text translation may encourage greater US use for simple tasks if users do not have domain-specific knowledge of US, for instance, to communicate simple diagnostic findings in text format rather than to expect users to directly interpret the content of an US image. Until recently, methods introduced for automated image captioning typically relied on purely supervised learning requiring large-scale datasets of image-caption pairs for training [11,29, 30,33].

A challenge more specific to medical image captioning is the domain-specific knowledge required to manually prepare image-caption pairs, which makes dataset preparation resource intensive. In contrast, preparing medical imaging datasets for image classification problems is more common and easier to perform. This raises an interesting question: *can we circumvent limitations of the available data for medical image captioning to train captioning models without solely relying on manually prepared image-caption pairs and by leveraging image classification datasets?* In this work, we investigate the potential of using an existing class-labelled classification dataset to augment the small number of available image-caption pairs and train an image captioning model through weakly supervised learning.

Related Works. In the literature, a few studies have addressed the problem of limited image captioning datasets. An image captioning approach that does not require readily available image-caption pairs is introduced in [16]. Another approach identifies concepts in images and tries to find captions that are semantically most similar to those identified concepts [20]. Other studies attempt to first train models on image-caption pairs in one domain, and then transfer the learned knowledge into a second domain that is lacking in paired data [12,37]. Some works identify the concepts exhibited in an image, for example by object identification, and then proceed to build sentence templates around the identified objects in the image [18,19,22,23,31].

However, our work is different from these studies as we do not use a visual concept or object detector. We also do not use the annotated data to train one. A visual concept can refer to an object present in an image and a property pertaining to it (e.g. 'red ball'). In [14], the authors use K-nearest neighbours to identify which image in the dataset is most similar to a target image in a text retrieval-based captioning approach. However, the downside of using text retrieval is that all possible captions are retrieved from the training dataset of image-caption pairs. With text generation, however, novel unseen captions that do not exist in the training dataset can be generated, as proposed in our work. Data augmentation can be considered as a model regularization technique [10]. Some regularization techniques used in NLP include word dropout (WD), where several words in a sequence are randomly chosen to be dropped [17]. Another technique is SwitchOut (SO) which randomly swaps some words in a sequence with other words that exist in the training vocabulary [34]. We compare the proposed augmentation approach with these regularization techniques.

Another different way to make up for the lack of data, as was done in [6], involves using a curriculum learning based approach, where a dual curriculum is used in ranking data points according to their entropy in the image and text modalities and summing their contributions equally to create a new overall ranking. In [7], a natural extension of [6] was investigated where a linear combination of the complexity metrics of a single multi-modal data sample was used. This means that rather than assuming that both metrics contribute equally to the arrangement and ordering of batches in every epoch, one of the complexity metrics is more influential than the other in a given epoch.

Motivation and Contribution. We automatically prepare pseudo-captions for caption-less images by leveraging existing image-caption pairs and anatomically labelled images to use in training the fetal US image captioning model via weakly supervised learning. In the proposed method, nouns are identified in the retrieved caption and then along with the anatomical class label of the target image are fed into a model that generates a sentence given certain keywords. In other work, these keywords would be real concepts that come with the data or could be obtained through object detection. However, in this work, we do not have real concepts associated with our data, and so, we rely on weak labels by generating pseudo-captions from extracted nouns that serve in lieu of concepts acquired through object detection, thereby circumventing two requirements: (1) having to train a visual concept detector, and (2) curating and annotating a dataset to train a visual concept detector on.

Furthermore, the approach makes it possible to introduce an aspect of potential novel caption generation that would be missing if we solely relied on text retrieval, allowing for greater diversity in obtained captions for fetal ultrasound images. Our approach consists of four steps: (1) text retrieval, (2) noun extraction, (3) pseudo-caption creation from anatomical labels and extracted nouns, and (4) caption generation through an image captioning framework.

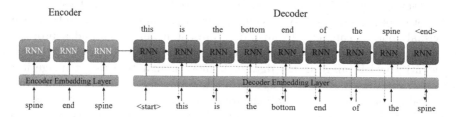

Fig. 1. The sequence-to-sequence model architecture translates the sequence of the anatomical label and the nouns into a pseudo-caption. In the input sequence, the first 'spine' is the label, and 'end' and the second 'spine' are the extracted nouns. Both the encoder and decoder consist of 100 LSTM units. The word embedding size is 300.

2 Methods

Before discussing each step of the proposed method, we briefly describe the available images, captions, and annotations. The images are video frames extracted from second-trimester fetal US scan videos and each image has an image-level anatomical class label associated with the main visible anatomical structure in the image. The associated label is 'abdomen', 'head', 'heart', or 'spine'. These labels are made available through the work of [26]. The images are split into two categories.

The first category consists of images from scan videos with textual descriptions from the transcribed speech of sonographers. These form the training dataset of real image-caption pairs (caption-labelled). The process of annotating and pre-processing this caption-labelled dataset is a cumbersome process. The second category consists of images from different scan videos that form the dataset of the caption-less images (caption-free) or the anatomically labelled image classification dataset. A high-level description of the method is given in Algorithm 1. The subsections below describe each part of the pseudo-caption creation pipeline.

Text Retrieval. We calculate the cosine similarity between caption-less images and every image in the training dataset on the feature domain. Features were extracted from a VGG-16 CNN [27]. The cosine similarity is defined as:

$$similarity_{cos} = \boldsymbol{x_n} \cdot \boldsymbol{t}/|\boldsymbol{x_n}||\boldsymbol{t}|$$

(1)

where x_n is the image feature vector of a data sample from the real image-caption pair dataset and t is the image feature vector of the caption-less image. We retrieve the caption of the image with the highest cosine similarity.

Noun Extraction. After retrieving the caption of the image most similar to the caption-less image, we extract its nouns through the TextBlob Python library [4]. When provided with a string, a list of tuples is returned. Each tuple consists of a word in the original string and its parts-of-speech tag. From the returned list, we create a sublist consisting solely of the nouns that exist in the original string, and we use the parts-of-speech tags to identify those nouns. We hypothesise that these nouns adequately represent the inherent concepts associated with the image feature vector in question and, therefore, are important to use when creating pseudo-captions. Our assumption is based on previous work such as [28] which considers centering the sentence syntax around nouns and [5] which considers nouns to be important in determining the context. This phenomenon coincides with what we have observed in the sonographer recordings, in which most of the verbs (such as 'looking', 'seeing', and 'measuring') are often less correlated to the clinical interpretation of the images. The process by which the input to the pseudo-caption is prepared is demonstrated by Eqs. 2 and 3.

$$C_w = \begin{cases} \{TB(w)\} & if w \in N \\ \{\} & otherwise \end{cases} \tag{2}$$

$$X = \bigcup_{w}^{W}(C_w) \cup \{\alpha\} \tag{3}$$

where C represents a concept associated with a word w, $TB(w)$ represents the parts-of-speech tag of w, N represents the set of tags associated with nouns (including 'NN', 'NNS', 'NNP', 'NNPS'), X represents the extracted nouns and anatomical label α of a data sample, W are all the words in the caption of a single data sample.

Pseudo-Caption Creation. We train an encoder-decoder sequence-to-sequence model to transform a sequence of extracted nouns and the corresponding anatomical label of the caption-less image to a pseudo-caption. This is similar to the con2sen model [16] which generates a pseudo-caption from the objects detected in an image of interest. To train the model (shown in Fig. 1), we perform noun extraction on the real captions. The extracted nouns and the anatomical labels serve as the input while the real captions are the target outputs. Training and deploying the model to create pseudo-captions for caption-less images takes 12 min on a machine with an NVIDIA GeForce GTX 1080.

Caption Generation. Captions are generated for fetal US frames through an image captioning model architecture, as shown in Fig. 2. The image captioning model can be described as a late merge captioning model [6,8,29,30], where image and textual information are merged towards the end of the model to generate the next word in the sequence. The text-focused branch in Fig. 2 is in the left half of the figure. It shows that each word in the input sequence is given a token before being passed through an embedding layer. The embedding layers uses weights from a Word2vec model that has been pretrained on the GoogleNews corpus [1]. The sequence is then passed through a recurrent neural network. The right branch of the captioning model consists of a VGG16 convolutional neural network (CNN) that has been fine-tuned on fetal US images of the same gestational age. The CNN is followed by two fully connected layers. From both branches, a flat feature vector is obtained. The vectors are concatenated together to predict the next word. The process is repeated until the maximum possible length is reached or a special end token ('<end>') is generated. The framework also includes an image feature vector classifier, identical to the right branch of the captioning model, that classifies an image to one of four possible classes, 'abdomen', 'head', 'heart', and 'spine'. In the framework, four variants of the captioning model are trained, one for each of the four structures. By having a separate captioning model for each anatomical structure, generated captions are more likely to be relevant to the ultrasound image. During inference, once

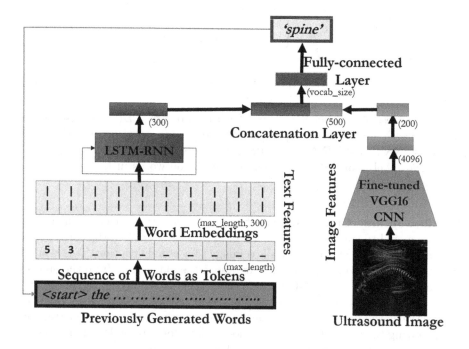

Fig. 2. The image captioning model. Max length represents the maximum number of words a caption of this anatomical structure could consist of. The LSTM-RNN consists of 300 units.

the image feature vector classifier classifies an image, the appropriate captioning model is initiated. Also, at inference, previously generated words are used as input to generate the next word in the sequence. The models are trained with a categorical cross entropy loss. The Adam optimization algorithm [21] is used with a learning rate of 0.001. For the model trained with our approach, we used the real image-caption pairs augmented by the image-pseudo-caption pairs.

3 Experiments

Datasets and Data Preparation. The used data came from the PULSE study [15]. As part of the study, videos of full-length fetal US scans were acquired along with their accompanying audio recordings. For our paper, only part of the data was available. Breakdown of the data used is shown in Table 1. In total, 18 videos are used in this paper. The mean video length is 32 min with standard deviation of 14 min. The shortest video was 8 min long, while the longest was 56 min long. Manually annotating these videos with captions is a time-consuming process. The real image-caption pairs were prepared by transcribing the audio recordings of sonographers from 10 full-length scan videos following the approach of [8]. In this way, we have obtained thousands of image-caption pairs that are rich and representative of the second-trimester fetal ultrasound scan to train the image captioning models (Table 1). As all the scans follow a countrywide scanning protocol, the semantic contents (anatomical categories) are consistent across the different scans, hence, we were able to extract multiple diverse examples of each category from the full-length scan videos (number of samples of each category shown in Table 1).

Table 1. Breakdown of the data used in this work

Dataset	Scans	Pairs	Abdomen	Head	Heart	Spine
Train (real)	7	23,558	3,085	11,145	6,573	2,755
Val (real)	2	17,471	3,003	8,479	4,482	507
Test (real)	1	14,601	2,032	3,710	7,078	1,543
Train (pseudo)	8	2,721	184	614	1,297	553
Entire dataset	18	58,351	8,304	23,948	19,430	5,358

The images from the image-pseudo-caption pairs cover a higher variance having included a step size of 16 between each sampled frame from the scan video. As part of standard pre-processing practice, the images were cropped to remove the user interface and then resized to 224×224 pixels. The text had its punctuation removed, and all letters were made lowercase. The longest video contained the greatest number of samples and, so, was held out as the test set.

Performance Evaluation. The image-captioning evaluation metrics can be divided into two categories: syntax-focused metrics and semantics-focused metrics. The syntax-focused metrics include *BLEU-1 (B1)* [25], *ROUGE-L (RL)* [13] and GrammarBot (*GB*) [3]. *B1* and *RL* look at the degree of overlap between the words of the ground truth and the words of the generated caption. However, they do not take into consideration whether the overlapping words hold any semantic value with respect to the image.

The semantics-focused metrics include the Anatomical Relevance Score (*ARS*) [8] and *F*1 score. *ARS* rewards the model for generating words that are not necessarily synonymous to the words in the ground truth caption, but are anatomically relevant by looking at the degree of word overlap between the words in the generated caption and the vocabulary associated with the anatomical structure depicted in the image of interest. *GB* simply measures the quality of the grammar in the generated captions.

4   Results and Discussion

We trained multiple models to compare our approach (including image-pseudo-caption pairs in the training dataset) with a baseline (no text augmentation or regularization) and other regularization techniques (WD [17] and SO [34]). The quantitative results are shown in Table 2. When comparing between the performance of a model trained on the original dataset and a model trained on the augmented dataset, we can immediately see an increase in *B1*, *RL*, and *ARS* metrics when incorporating the image-pseudo-caption pairs with the exception of *F*1 score where models trained both with and without pseudo-captions obtained the high score 0.97. However, from the *ARS* score, we notice that the model that was trained with pseudo-captions score higher. A higher *ARS* score translates to the model producing higher softmax probabilities for terms that are relevant to an anatomical structure (for e.g. 'brain' and 'nuchal' for the head), so with a high ARS, we can say more confidently that the model generates words that are relevant. With regards to the *B1* score, the models trained with pseudo-captions obtained a score 0.30 which falls within the range that [2] would describe as being 'understandable and good'. On the other hand, the set of models trained without pseudo-captions obtained a *B1* score of 0.13. A score of 0.13 falls within the range that [2] would describe as 'hard to get the gist (of)'. So, our method generates captions with a better sentence structure.

We can see this behavior exemplified in the generated captions in Fig. 3 where qualitative results for four examples are shown. With more data to learn from, a model is more likely to learn an understandable sentence structure, and it is pleasing to see that the pseudo-captions although not provided directly by a sonographer can still help a model to score higher on the metrics, justifying the inclusion of pesudo-captions in the training of a captioning model. All the syntax-focused metrics are better with our proposed approach except *GB*; however, that can be explained by the fact that WD drops words from the sequences

Table 2. Quantitative results comparing our proposed augmentation approach with other regularization techniques

Methods	Syntax-focused			Semantics-focused	
	B1	*RL*	*GB↓*	*ARS*	*F1*
No pseudo-captions (baseline)	0.17	0.24	1.26	0.39	**0.97**
Word dropout token level	0.01	0.03	**0.52**	0.05	0.34
Word dropout vector level [17]	0.07	0.17	0.84	0.03	0.03
SwitchOut [34]	0.11	0.20	2.55	0.08	0.85
Synonym swapping	0.11	0.20	2.62	0.09	0.73
With pseudo-captions (ours)	**0.30**	**0.42**	1.14	**0.77**	**0.97**

GT: we can see normal pulmonary valve
NP: ventricular outflow tract and
WD: this this
WP: this is the heart

GT: this is where we measure the abdominal circumference
NP: measure around the baby's belly
WD: this this let let
WP: let us measure around the baby's belly

GT: this is baby's **head and brain**
NP: this is the posterior lateral ventricle and the anterior lateral ventricle good looking good
WD: (only end token generated)
WP: we are measuring baby **head and brain** side to side and around the perfect **head and brain**

GT: yes now we can see the skin covering all the way to the baby's bottom
NP: the spine
WD: is bottom the the the the the the the
WP: curvature of the spine

Fig. 3. Qualitative results for different images. GT stands for 'Ground Truth' as spoken by a sonographer. 'NP' stands for model trained with 'No Pseudo-captions'. 'WD' stands for model regularized with 'Word Dropout'. 'WP' stands for model trained 'With Pseudo-captions' (our proposed method).

that make up the training samples, and so, the model ends up learning to generate shorter sentences. With shorter sentences, the number of grammatical mistakes decreases. WD and SO have notably lower scores on the semantics-focused metrics. This phenomenon can be explained by the fact that, with WD and SO, anatomically relevant words could be dropped or switched out during training. Even with a WD rate of only 0.2, a caption of, say, five words will lose one word, and that could be the word that refers to the anatomical content. There is a high chance of losing semantically meaningful words in shorter captions when using WD and similar techniques.

5   Conclusion and Future Work

In this paper, we describe a novel approach to create pseudo-captions for fetal US images that lack any captions by leveraging an existing smaller image captioning dataset and an image classification dataset. The practical usefulness of models trained with the extra pseudo-captions allows for better interpretation and relaying of information to laypersons who may be observing an ultrasound scan. We show that these image-pseudo-caption pairs can improve the performance of weakly learnt image captioning models for the fetal US image captioning task. In the future, we will investigate the applicability of the approach for other medical imaging modalities.

5.1   Future Work

One of the future tasks is to use pseudo-captions with other tasks, such as cross-modal retrieval. We intend to work on a transformer-based retrieval of ultrasound images. The architecture would consist of a vision transformer and a BERT encoder to extract an image feature representation and text feature representation. The pooled output from the BERT encoder captures the overall information of the input sequence. To enable retrieval, the cross-modal model would be trained with a ranking loss with the aim of minimizing the distance between the two feature representations of a positive pair and maximizing the distance between the two feature representations of a negative pair in the feature space.

References

1. Google code archive (2018). https://code.google.com/archive/p/word2vec/
2. Evaluating models — automl translation documentation (2020). https://cloud.google.com/translate/automl/docs/evaluate
3. Grammarbot (2020). https://www.grammarbot.io/
4. Textblob (2020). https://textblob.readthedocs.io/en/dev/
5. Context analysis in NLP: why it's valuable and how it's done (2021). https://www.lexalytics.com/lexablog/context-analysis-nlp
6. Alsharid, M., El-Bouri, R., Sharma, H., Drukker, L., Papageorghiou, A.T., Noble, J.A.: A curriculum learning based approach to captioning ultrasound images. In: Hu, Y., et al. (eds.) ASMUS/PIPPI -2020. LNCS, vol. 12437, pp. 75–84. Springer, Cham (2020). https://doi.org/10.1007/978-3-030-60334-2_8
7. Alsharid, M., El-Bouri, R., Sharma, H., Drukker, L., Papageorghiou, A.T., Noble, J.A.: A course-focused dual curriculum for image captioning. In: 2021 IEEE 18th International Symposium on Biomedical Imaging (ISBI), pp. 716–720. IEEE (2021)
8. Alsharid, M., Sharma, H., Drukker, L., Chatelain, P., Papageorghiou, A.T., Noble, J.A.: Captioning ultrasound images automatically. In: Shen, D., et al. (eds.) MICCAI 2019. LNCS, vol. 11767, pp. 338–346. Springer, Cham (2019). https://doi.org/10.1007/978-3-030-32251-9_37
9. Bernardi, R., Cakici, R., Elliott, D., Erdem, A., Erdem, E., Ikizler-Cinbis, N., et al.: Automatic description generation from images: a survey of models, datasets, and evaluation measures. J. Artif. Intell. Res. **55**, 409–442 (2016)
10. Burkov, A.: The Hundred-Page Machine Learning Book, pp. 100–101. Andriy Burkov (2019)
11. Chen, L., et al.: SCA-CNN: spatial and channel-wise attention in convolutional networks for image captioning. In: Proceedings of the IEEE Conference on Computer Vision and Pattern Recognition, pp. 5659–5667 (2017)

12. Chen, T.H., Liao, Y.H., Chuang, C.Y., Hsu, W.T., Fu, J., Sun, M.: Show, adapt and tell: adversarial training of cross-domain image captioner. In: Proceedings of the IEEE International Conference on Computer Vision, pp. 521–530 (2017)

13. Lin, C.Y.: ROUGE: a package for automatic evaluation of summaries. In: Proceedings of the Workshop on Text Summarization Branches Out, Barcelona, Spain, pp. 56–60 (2004)

14. Devlin, J., Cheng, H., Fang, H., Gupta, S., Deng, L., He, X., et al.: Language models for image captioning: the quirks and what works. arXiv preprint arXiv:1505.01809 (2015)

15. Drukker, L., et al.: Transforming obstetric ultrasound into data science using eye tracking, voice recording, transducer motion and ultrasound video. Sci. Rep. **11**(1), 1–12 (2021)

16. Feng, Y., Ma, L., Liu, W., Luo, J.: Unsupervised image captioning. In: Proceedings of the IEEE Conference on Computer Vision and Pattern Recognition, pp. 4125–4134 (2019)

17. Gal, Y., Ghahramani, Z.: A theoretically grounded application of dropout in recurrent neural networks. arXiv preprint arXiv:1512.05287 (2015)

18. Guadarrama, S., et al.: YouTube2Text: recognizing and describing arbitrary activities using semantic hierarchies and zero-shot recognition. In: Proceedings of the IEEE International Conference on Computer Vision, pp. 2712–2719 (2013)

19. Gupta, A., Srinivasan, P., Shi, J., Davis, L.S.: Understanding videos, constructing plots learning a visually grounded storyline model from annotated videos. In: 2009 IEEE Conference on Computer Vision and Pattern Recognition, pp. 2012–2019. IEEE (2009)

20. Hendricks, L.A., Venugopalan, S., Rohrbach, M., Mooney, R., Saenko, K., Darrell, T.: Deep compositional captioning: describing novel object categories without paired training data. In: Proceedings of the IEEE Conference on Computer Vision and Pattern Recognition, pp. 1–10 (2016)

21. Kingma, D.P., Ba, J.: Adam: a method for stochastic optimization. arXiv preprint arXiv:1412.6980 (2014)

22. Krishnamoorthy, N., Malkarnenkar, G., Mooney, R., Saenko, K., Guadarrama, S.: Generating natural-language video descriptions using text-mined knowledge. In: Proceedings of the Workshop on Vision and Natural Language Processing, pp. 10–19 (2013)

23. Kulkarni, G., Premraj, V., Ordonez, V., Dhar, S., Li, S., Choi, Y., et al.: Babytalk: understanding and generating simple image descriptions. IEEE Trans. Pattern Anal. Mach. Intell. **35**(12), 2891–2903 (2013)

24. Lyndon, D., Kumar, A., Kim, J.: Neural captioning for the ImageCLEF 2017 medical image challenges. In: CLEF (Working Notes) (2017)

25. Papineni, K., Roukos, S., Ward, T., Zhu, W.J.: BLEU: a method for automatic evaluation of machine translation. In: Proceedings of the 40th Annual Meeting on Association for Computational Linguistics, pp. 311–318. Association for Computational Linguistics (2002)

26. Sharma, H., Drukker, L., Chatelain, P., Droste, R., Papageorghiou, A.T., Noble, J.A.: Knowledge representation and learning of operator clinical workflow from full-length routine fetal ultrasound scan videos. Med. Image Anal. **69**, 101973 (2021)

27. Simonyan, K., Zisserman, A.: Very deep convolutional networks for large-scale image recognition. arXiv preprint arXiv:1409.1556 (2014)

28. Stuart, L.M., Taylor, J.M., Raskin, V.: The importance of nouns in text processing. In: Proceedings of the Annual Meeting of the Cognitive Science Society, vol. 35 (2013)

29. Tanti, M., Gatt, A., Camilleri, K.: What is the role of recurrent neural networks (RNNs) in an image caption generator? arXiv preprint arXiv:1708.02043 (2017)
30. Tanti, M., Gatt, A., Camilleri, K.P.: Where to put the image in an image caption generator. Nat. Lang. Eng. **24**(3), 467–489 (2018)
31. Thomason, J., Venugopalan, S., Guadarrama, S., Saenko, K., Mooney, R.: Integrating language and vision to generate natural language descriptions of videos in the wild. In: Proceedings of COLING 2014, the 25th International Conference on Computational Linguistics: Technical Papers, pp. 1218–1227 (2014)
32. Topol, E.J.: A decade of digital medicine innovation. Sci. Transl. Med. **11**(498), eaaw7610 (2019)
33. Vinyals, O., Toshev, A., Bengio, S., Erhan, D.: Show and tell: a neural image caption generator. In: Proceedings of the IEEE Conference on Computer Vision and Pattern Recognition, pp. 3156–3164 (2015)
34. Wang, X., Pham, H., Dai, Z., Neubig, G.: SwitchOut: an efficient data augmentation algorithm for neural machine translation. arXiv preprint arXiv:1808.07512 (2018)
35. Zeng, X.H., Liu, B.G., Zhou, M.: Understanding and generating ultrasound image description. J. Comput. Sci. Technol. **33**(5), 1086–1100 (2018)
36. Zeng, X., Wen, L., Liu, B., Qi, X.: Deep learning for ultrasound image caption generation based on object detection. Neurocomputing **392**, 132–141 (2019)
37. Zhao, W., et al.: Dual learning for cross-domain image captioning. In: Proceedings of the 2017 ACM on Conference on Information and Knowledge Management, pp. 29–38 (2017)

Computerised Methods for Monitoring Diabetic Foot Ulcers on Plantar Foot: A Feasibility Study

Manu Goyal[1], Neil D. Reeves[2], Satyan Rajbhandari[3], and Moi Hoon Yap[4(✉)]

[1] Department of Radiology, UT Southwestern Medical Center, 5323 Harry Hines Blvd., Dallas, TX 75390-9085, USA
[2] Musculoskeletal Science and Sports Medicine Research Centre, Manchester Metropolitan University, Manchester M1 5GD, UK
[3] Lancashire Teaching Hospitals NHS Trust, Preston PR2 9HT, UK
[4] Centre for Advanced Computational Science, Department of Computing and Mathematics, Manchester Metropolitan University, Manchester M1 5GD, UK
M.Yap@mmu.ac.uk

Abstract. Recognition and analysis of Diabetic Foot Ulcers (DFU) by computerised methods has been an emerging research area with the evolution of image processing and machine learning algorithms. Precise documentation of wound size over time allows clinicians to gauge responses to treatment, improving healing rates by modifying interventions as required. One of the major issues in the analysis of DFU is non-standardised foot images captured with cameras including factors such as distance of the camera from the foot and orientation of the image. Designing a computerised solution to determine site of DFU and measurements of area for remote assessment and monitoring represents a significant challenge due to the variables involved. In this work, we propose a new computerised solution with the combination of image processing and deep learning algorithms to estimate the site and predict the progress (based on estimated area index) of the DFU irrespective of distance and orientation of the plantar foot. First we segment the foot region and align the foot by fixing the orientation of a series of longitudinal images. Then we localise the region of interest of DFUs and find its relative size to the foot area. We introduce a distribution analysis to determine the site of DFUs. Finally, we introduce an area index ($Area_t$) to predict the healing progress of DFU at different time intervals (t). We demonstrate the feasibility of our proposed method on 154 longitudinal DFUs of plantar foot. We achieved 92.3% on site estimation and 84.7% on healing progress prediction.

1 Introduction

Diabetes Mellitus (DM) causes significant life-threatening complications including potential blindness, cardiovascular, peripheral vascular and cerebrovascular

© The Author(s), under exclusive license to Springer Nature Switzerland AG 2022
G. Yang et al. (Eds.): MIUA 2022, LNCS 13413, pp. 199–211, 2022.
https://doi.org/10.1007/978-3-031-12053-4_15

diseases, kidney failure, and Diabetic Foot Ulcers (DFU) [1,2]. DFU is a major complication of DM, which if not managed properly can lead to lower limb amputation. Patients suffering from DM have a lifetime risk of 15% to 25% of a developing DFU [3], although recent studies suggest that rates can be as high as 34% [4]. Development of a DFU can significantly reduce a patient's capacity for undertaking physical activity. Hence, patients with or at high-risk of developing a DFU require regular foot checks by healthcare professionals, continuous expensive medical care, hygienic personal care, and referral to specialist care to avoid the further consequences [5]. It causes a tremendous financial burden to the patient and their family, especially in developing countries where the cost of treating this disease can be equivalent to 5.7 years of annual income [6]. Also, DFU and their associated consequences represent a significant burden on health-care systems and national economies. It is estimated that healthcare costs for wound management in UK is around £4.5–£5.1 billion a year which accounts for more than 4% of the NHS budget and the cost of treating diabetic foot ulcers makes up around £1 billion of that total.

Currently, healthcare systems are typically composed of primary health care which deals with general medicine, and speciality health care which deals with chronic disease and disorders. It is evident from various studies and surveys [7,8] that current health services are not sufficient to properly handle large numbers of patients due to lack of hospitals, adequately trained medical staff, and available medication. This situation is worse in poor and developing countries [9,10]. High risk patients who do not receive timely treatment will often suffer further consequences due to lack of good communication, collaboration, and clear referral systems between primary and speciality healthcare. Patients with DFU require prompt referral and regular foot evaluation by podiatrists or wound care centres specialising in DFU. Overall, DFU patients constitute 85% of total lower limb amputations within healthcare, with untimely treatment identified as one of the major contributing factors [11,12].

Due to the proliferation of Information Communication Technology (ICT), intelligent systems are often cited as one of the most cost-effective solutions for remote detection and prevention of DFU [13,14]. Telemedicine systems along with current healthcare services can integrate with each other to provide more cost-effective, efficient and quality treatment for DFU to patients. Additionally, internet-enabled telemedicine systems can increase access to patients located in rural and remote locations [13,15]. One study suggests that the management of DFU with the help of remote telemedicine systems is medically equivalent to care at a diabetic foot care program [16]. It is estimated that a reduction in costs associated with visits and appointments of 10% would provide £300 million annual savings to the NHS alone.

According to some studies, the human observers (podiatrists) achieved low reliability for remote assessment of DFU with the help of imaging [17,18]. Reliable remote image monitoring of DFU is difficult due to inconsistencies during image capture, which can result in variations in orientation and distance. Wound surface area reduction is used as an indicator wound healing and treatment efficacy. The variability, of up to 40%, in standard *length* × *width* estimation of wound surface area is unacceptable on a measurement on which care decisions are being based. A description of the two important conditions of DFU [19] is explained below:

Site: The site of the DFU describes the area of the foot where the DFU is located. Usually, DFU occur on the two major sites that are forefoot, or midfoot and hindfoot [20]. The site of the DFU is important to compare against previous ulcerations, to check if it is a recurrence of a previous ulcer, or if the ulcer is new. The mechanism of hind-, mid- and forefoot ulcer is different. Additionally, from simply a categorisation point of view - it is useful to know the location of the foot.

Area: The area of the DFU measures the extent of the 2 dimensional (2D) shape of a DFU. The area of a DFU is classified by whether the DFU is greater than $1\,cm^2$ [19]. Given the inconsistency of the images in the current dataset, a result of distance, orientation, and lighting, DFU images are captured with different magnification and at different angles. Additionally, potentially useful meta-data such as the patient's ethnicity, age, and gender, was not captured at the time of the photos been taken. Accurate wound measurement and tracking is an important aspect of wound care.

Site of ulceration was determined by the podiatrist/consultant during clinical visits. Area (Size of ulcer) has traditionally been determined using a wound ruler to measure wound length and width. However, wound length and width widely overestimate wound area in irregular shaped and are difficult to consistently measure wound shape changes. This is problematic given that serial/timeline wound measurements are a reflection of potential healing. In this work, we propose a new computer method that can estimate the site and the area index of DFUs irrespective of distance and orientation, and predict the progress of DFU, demonstrated a proof-of-concept on a longitudinal dataset.

2 Related Works

Machine Learning (ML) is showing improvements in autonomous and unsupervised learning systems, which is revolutionising many industries, bringing significant shifts in society through developments in healthcare analysis [21–23]. Technological advances in medical imaging over the past three decades have led to greater accessibility to advanced imaging techniques in clinical practice and research settings. Recently, computer vision algorithms were extended to assess different types of abnormal skin lesions, such as skin cancer and DFU, with promising results [24, 25].

Over the past few years, computerised methods for recognition and analysis of DFU have grown rapidly. There are a number of works which address recognition and assessment of DFU which do not take into account distance and orientation. Several studies suggest computer vision methods based on basic image processing approaches and supervised traditional machine learning for the recognition of DFU. Wang et al. [26] used an image capture box to capture image data and determined the area of DFU using cascaded two-stage SVM-based classification. They proposed the use of a superpixel technique for segmentation and extracted the number of features to perform two-stage classification. Although this system reported promising results, it has not been validated on a more substantial dataset. In addition, the image capture box is impractical for data collection as there is a need for the patient's barefoot to be placed directly in contact with the image capture box screen. In a healthcare scenario, such a device would be impractical due to the concerns of infection control. In contrast to traditional machine learning techniques, deep learning methods have demonstrated superiority in object localisation and segmentation of DFU, which suggests that a robust fully automated DFU recognition system may be achievable [23,27–29]. In the field of deep learning, several researchers have made contributions to the classification and segmentation of DFU. Goyal et al. [23] proposed a new deep learning framework called DFUNet, capable of classification and localisation of DFU skin lesions on the plantar surface of the foot. DFUNet identifies skin as two classes - normal skin (healthy skin) and abnormal skin (DFU). In addition, they used deep learning methods for the semantic segmentation of DFU and its surrounding skin with a limited dataset of 600 images [27].

In 2018, the deep localisation networks were optimised to detect the DFU with greater accuracy [14], and these algorithms have been tested on mobile platforms such as smart-phones and the NVIDIA Jetson TX2 low-power embedded AI computing device to assist in remote monitoring. Wang et al. [28] proposed a new deep learning encoder-decoder architecture to perform wound segmentation and analysis to measure the healing progress of the wound. Van et al. [30] proposed the recognition of DFU using infrared thermography. They found that there is a significant temperature difference between the DFU and the surrounding healthy skin. Yap et al. [31,32] developed an iOS mobile app, FootSnap, which can be used to standardise the acquisition of DFU photos to improve longitudinal analysis. This app used basic image processing techniques, such as edge detection, to display a ghost image of the initial foot photo which can be used to align subsequent photos. This system did not perform any automated DFU recognition. At the same time, Brown et al. [33] developed a smart-phone application called MyFootCare, which provides useful guidance to DFU patients as well as keeping a longitudinal record of foot images. In this app, the user has to manually crop the captured image, and with basic colour clustering algorithms it can produce DFU segmentation. For overview of the development of DFU research, please refer to [34].

In the field of wound metrology and planimetry, numerous studies have been conducted to assess the viability of technology to determine size and volume changes to different wound types over time, including DFU. Longitudinal analysis of wound size is an important factor in determining the healing status of DFU. Measurement of wound size gives clinicians insight into the amount of tissue damage, and helps track healing, which assists in auditing and predicting treatment efficacy [35]. Equally important is the ability of clinicians to measure wounds accurately non-invasively so as not to interfere with the healing process.

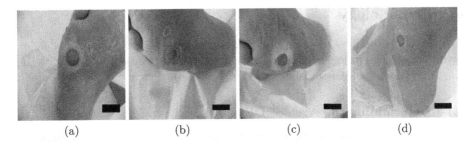

(a)   (b)   (c)   (d)

Fig. 1. The example of timeline dataset with different orientation and angle.

Computerised wound tracking systems have also been shown to provide patient incentive to adhere to prescribed recommendations [36]. They can also allow for patients to self-monitor their condition, which can help to reduce the overall burden to already strained healthcare systems. Most wound measurements are currently completed manually, using a ruler [37,38]. However, this method can prove to be both laborious, inaccurate and carry infection risk. Contact wound measurement techniques include the ruler method, the graph method, the acetate method, and planimetry. All these methods are susceptible to inaccuracy and pose a risk of increased incidence of wound contamination. Also, in the context of self-care, they are highly impractical. Given such factors, it is important that alternative non-contact measurement methods are investigated.

3   DFU Timeline Dataset

To demonstrate the potential of this experiment, 33 cases of patient's feet with DFU obtained over a period of ten years were obtained from the Lancashire Teaching Hospitals. These longitudinal dataset is a subset of larger studies [24,39], in collaboration of Manchester Metropolitan University and Lancashire teaching hospitals. We have received approval from the UK National Health Service Research Ethics Committee (reference number is 15/NW/0539) to use diabetic foot ulcer (DFU) images for research purposes. These images are photographs acquired from the patients during their clinical visits at different time interval. The number of images per patient varies depending on the number of hospital visits made by each patient. In this dataset, the images were captured from different angles and orientations. An example of the non-standardised timeline dataset is demonstrated in Fig. 1.

Meta-data indicating area, site, patient ethnicity, gender, and age is not available for this dataset. The main focus of this work was to test the feasibility of the use of computer vision and machine learning techniques to measure the changes of the wound region over different time intervals.

4   Methodology

This section describes the computer algorithms used for site and area index prediction. Image processing and deep learning methods were used to locate the site and estimate the area of DFU.

4.1   Determining the Area of DFU

Foot images in the dataset do not have standardised focus, distance, angle, or orientation. According to a recent study [17], human observers achieved low reliability for remote assessment of DFU using only photos. Measurement of changes to DFU size is difficult without the use of measurement units or other reference objects of known size being present on foot photos. This is made more difficult by a lack of standardisation of the photos in the dataset. In this work, we develop robust computer methods that can predict the relative location and size of DFU.

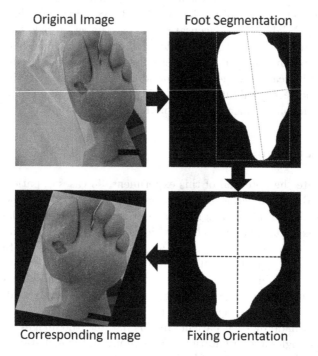

Fig. 2. Stage 1: Fixing the orientation of foot with the image processing algorithms comprised of K-mean clustering, morphological operations, rotation of the image.

This experiment will be limited to locating the site and size of DFU that are present on the plantar surface of the foot (the foot sole) as this is the region where most cases of DFU occur [40]. For this experiment, we utilised the subset of the DFU dataset, which results in 200 usable foot images. This experiment is divided into the following three main steps:

1. Orientation: Image processing techniques are used to fix the different orientation of foot.
2. DFU Localisation: Faster-RCNN algorithm is used to get the ROI of DFU on foot images.
3. Distance and Area Computation: The relative horizontal and vertical size of the DFU is computed with reference to the width of the forefoot.

Stage 1: Fixing Orientation. Since the foot and background have their own distinctive features in the DFU dataset. Hence, to segment the foot from background, we used k-means clustering to separate the image pixels into three clusters in the L*a*b* color space. Furthermore, we used the morphological functions such as fill, majority, dilation, erosion to further refine the foot masks. Then, we calculated the orientation angle of binary foot with regionprops function of Matlab (The MathWorks, Inc., Massachusetts) and rotated the binary foot with calculated orientation angle in image. Similarly, for final step of this stage, we rotated the original image with the same angle for the detection of DFU in the next stage. The whole step is demonstrated by the Fig. 2.

Stage 2: DFU Localisation. In second stage, we used Faster RCNN with Inception-ResNetV2 to localize the DFU on foot images. We used the deep learning algorithm on corresponding foot image with DFU from stage 1 to find the dimensions of bounding box that circumscribed DFU as shown in Fig. 3.

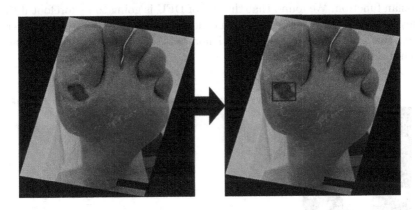

Fig. 3. Localize the DFU on foot images

Stage 3: Distance and Relative Size of DFU. Since there is no meta data regarding the DFU size, foot size, patient's sex about the DFU dataset. In this method, we calculated the horizontal ratio of height of ROI OF DFU and width of the foot. Similarly, the vertical ratio of width of ROI of DFU respectively and for the width of the foot as shown in Fig. 4. Basically, the relative size of DFU is determined with the width of the foot. In this study, the timelines images are mostly focused on the DFU, but there are not many full foot images to determine the height of the foot.

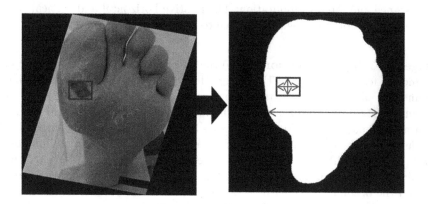

Fig. 4. Finding the relative area of the DFU with width of the foot

4.2 Site of the DFU

After fixing the orientation of foot and finding the ROI of DFU as shown in Fig. 4, we plot the number of horizontal pixels. Then, we smooth the data with Gaussian function. We found that the site of DFU is going to be forefoot if the y values of DFU meet any of the two condition: 1) it has positive gradient overall; 2) negative gradient but value should not be less than 90% of peak value as shown in Fig. 5.

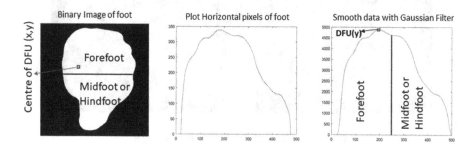

Fig. 5. Finding the relative area of the DFU with width of the foot

4.3 DFU Progress Prediction

We introduce a new progress prediction method of DFUs on Plantar foot. We estimate the progress of the DFU at different time intervals based on the changes of the estimated area index $(Area_t)$ at time (t). Let R_1 represents

$$R_1 = \frac{HeightOfDFUInPixels}{WidthOfFootInPixels} \tag{1}$$

and R_2 denotes

$$R_2 = \frac{WidthOfDFUInPixels}{WidthOfFootInPixels} \tag{2}$$

The area index $(Area_t)$ of the DFU of serial instances of each case at time t is calculated by eq. (3) as follows:

$$Area_t = \frac{R_1}{R_2} * 100 \tag{3}$$

If $Area_{t+1} \geqslant Area_t$, then the DFU is healing. Otherwise, the DFU is deteriorating.

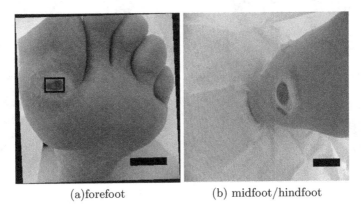

(a)forefoot   (b) midfoot/hindfoot

Fig. 6. The examples of correctly detected forefoot and midfoot/hindfoot sites.

5 Results and Discussion

To evaluate the performance of our proposed method, we used 33 timeline (longitudinal) images of 33 patients. Of 33 longitudinal photographs from 33 patients, there are 23 healing cases and 10 deterioration cases. Each case with 3–7 photos taken at different time interval, with a total of 154 images.

The site accuracy on these 208 images is 92.3%. Figure 6 shows examples of correct site estimation of forefoot and midfoot/hindfoot.

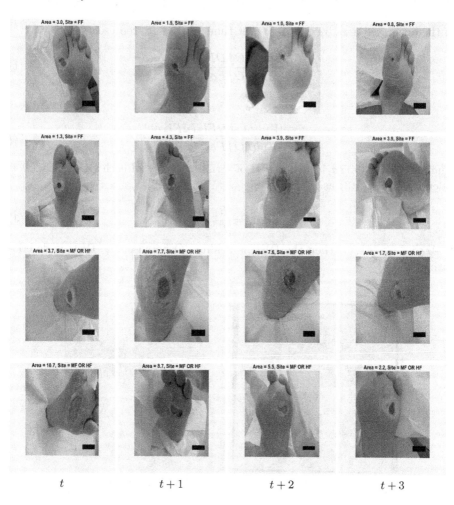

Fig. 7. Illustration of progress prediction four patients at four different time intervals on photographs with different orientation and angle. Area indicates the estimated area, FF represents forefoot, MF represents midfoot and HF represents hindfoot. Row 1 and Row 4 illustrate the healing process, where the Area is reduced on 4 time intervals. Row 2 indicates the deterioration of DFU and Row 3 shows different progress, where the ulcer deteriorate and heal at a later stage.

For DFU progress prediction, our method achieved 84.7% of prediction accuracy to indicate whether DFU is healing (showing reduction of the Area), or growing (showing increase in area), in measuring the progress of the ulcers.

Figure 7 shows four cases of timeline DFU photographs of four patients. For each photo, our method produces the area index prediction and site estimation of timeline DFU images at four time intervals $(t, t+1, t+2, t+3)$. As illustrated in Fig. 7 row 1, $Area_t = 3.0$, $Area_{t+1} = 1.5$, $Area_{t+2} = 1.0$ and $Area_{t+3} = 0.8$, indicates reduction of area index for a healing case. Row 4 shows a healing DFU on midfoot/hindfoot. Figure 7 row 2 depicts a DFU with deteriorate condition at different time intervals. It is noted that the photo on column 2 of row 2 predicted highest area index ($Area_{t+1} = 4.3$) when compared area index of $Area_{t+2} = 3.9$, due to the angle of the camera. This is the main limitation of our method, as it will work best on plantar foot photos with full view. This method is particularly useful for applications with standardised data capturing method for plantar foot, i.e. FootSnap [32].

6   Conclusion

Analysis of DFU conditions using computerised methods is very important for healthcare with high demand and limited resources. This paper demonstrated the feasibility of using computer vision and deep learning techniques to estimate the area and site of DFU on plantar foot. Based on the observation of the area index at different time intervals, our proposed method can be used to monitor the progress of DFUs on plantar foot with a single camera. Followed by the success of this feasibility study, future work will focus on larger scale multimodal dataset and clinical validation.

References

1. Wild, S., Roglic, G., Green, A., Sicree, R., King, H.: Global prevalence of diabetes estimates for the year 2000 and projections for 2030. Diabet. Care **27**(5), 1047–1053 (2004)
2. Armstrong, D.G., Lavery, L.A., Harkless, L.B.: Validation of a diabetic wound classification system: the contribution of depth, infection, and ischemia to risk of amputation. Diabet. Care **21**(5), 855–859 (1998)
3. Apelqvist, J.: The foot in perspective. Diabet. Metab. Res. Rev. **24**(S1), S110–S115 (2008)
4. Armstrong, D.G., Boulton, A.J.M., Bus, S.A.: Diabetic foot ulcers and their recurrence. N. Engl. J. Med. **376**(24), 2367–2375 (2017)
5. Prompers, L., et al.: Delivery of care to diabetic patients with foot ulcers in daily practice: results of the Eurodiale study, a prospective cohort study. Diabet. Med. **25**(6), 700–707 (2008)
6. Cavanagh, P., Attinger, C., Abbas, Z., Bal, A., Rojas, N., Zhang-Rong, X.: Cost of treating diabetic foot ulcers in five different countries. Diabet. Metab. Res. Rev. **28**(S1), 107–111 (2012)
7. Zimmet, P.Z., Magliano, D.J., Herman, W.H., Shaw, J.E.: Diabetes: a 21st century challenge. Lancet Diabet. Endocrinol. **2**(1), 56–64 (2014)
8. Vinicor, F.: The public health burden of diabetes and the reality of limits. Diabet. Care **21**(Supplement 3), C15–C18 (1998)
9. Brim, C.: A descriptive analysis of the non-urgent use of emergency departments. Nurse Res. **15**(3), 72–88 (2008)
10. Lang, T.A., Hodge, M., Olson, V., Romano, P.S., Kravitz, R.L.: Nurse-patient ratios: a systematic review on the effects of nurse staffing on patient, nurse employee, and hospital outcomes. J. Nurs. Adm. **34**(7–8), 326–337 (2004)

11. Singh, N., Armstrong, D.G., Lipsky, B.A.: Preventing foot ulcers in patients with diabetes. Jama **293**(2), 217–228 (2005)

12. Lazzarini, P.A., et al.: Does the use of store-and-forward telehealth systems improve outcomes for clinicians managing diabetic foot ulcers?: a pilot study. Wound Pract. Res. J. Aust. Wound Manag. Assoc. **18**(4), 164 (2010)

13. Chanussot-Deprez, C., Contreras-Ruiz, J.: Telemedicine in wound care: a review. Adv. Skin Wound Care **26**(2), 78–82 (2013)

14. Goyal, M., Reeves, N.D., Rajbhandari, S., Yap, M.H.: Robust methods for real-time diabetic foot ulcer detection and localization on mobile devices. IEEE J. Biomed. Health Inform. **23**(4), 1730–1741 (2018)

15. Currell, R., Urquhart, C., Wainwright, P., Lewis, R.: Telemedicine versus face to face patient care: effects on professional practice and health care outcomes. Cochrane Database Syst. Rev. **2**(2), CD002098 (2000)

16. Wilbright, W.A., Birke, J.A., Patout, C.A., Varnado, M., Horswell, R.: The use of telemedicine in the management of diabetes-related foot ulceration: a pilot study. Adv. Skin Wound Care **17**(5), 232–238 (2004)

17. van Netten, J.J., Clark, D., Lazzarini, P.A., Janda, M., Reed, L.F.: The validity and reliability of remote diabetic foot ulcer assessment using mobile phone images. Sci. Rep. **7**(1), 9480 (2017)

18. Bowling, F.L., et al.: Remote assessment of diabetic foot ulcers using a novel wound imaging system. Wound Repair Regen. **19**(1), 25–30 (2011)

19. Ince, P., et al.: Use of the SINBAD classification system and score in comparing outcome of foot ulcer management on three continents. Diabet. Care **31**(5), 964–967 (2008)

20. Ince, P., Kendrick, D., Game, F., Jeffcoate, W.: The association between baseline characteristics and the outcome of foot lesions in a UK population with diabetes. Diabet. Med. **24**(9), 977–981 (2007)

21. Goyal, M., Oakley, A., Bansal, P., Dancey, D., Yap, M.H.: Skin lesion segmentation in dermoscopic images with ensemble deep learning methods. IEEE Access **8**, 4171–4181 (2019)

22. Yap, M.H., et al.: Breast ultrasound region of interest detection and lesion localisation. Artif. Intell. Med. **107**, 101880 (2020)

23. Goyal, M., Reeves, N.D., Davison, A.K., Rajbhandari, S., Spragg, J., Yap, M.H.: DFUNet: convolutional neural networks for diabetic foot ulcer classification. IEEE Trans. Emerg. Top. Comput. Intell. **4**(5), 728–739 (2018)

24. Yap, M.H., Cassidy, B., Pappachan, J.M., O'Shea, C., Gillespie, D., Reeves, N.D.: Analysis towards classification of infection and Ischaemia of diabetic foot ulcers. In 2021 IEEE EMBS International Conference on Biomedical and Health Informatics (BHI), pp. 1–4. IEEE (2021)

25. Cassidy, B., Kendrick, C., Brodzicki, A., Jaworek-Korjakowska, J., Yap, M.H.: Analysis of the ISIC image datasets: usage, benchmarks and recommendations. Med. Image Anal. **75**, 102305 (2022)

26. Wang, L., Pedersen, P.C., Agu, E., Strong, D.M., Tulu, B.: Area determination of diabetic foot ulcer images using a cascaded two-stage SVM-based classification. IEEE Trans. Biomed. Eng. **64**(9), 2098–2109 (2016)

27. Goyal, M., Yap, M.H., Reeves, N.D., Rajbhandari, S., Spragg, J.: Fully convolutional networks for diabetic foot ulcer segmentation. In: 2017 IEEE International Conference on Systems, Man, and Cybernetics (SMC), pp. 618–623. IEEE (2017)

28. Wang, C., et al.: A unified framework for automatic wound segmentation and analysis with deep convolutional neural networks. In: 2015 37th Annual International Conference of the IEEE Engineering in Medicine and Biology Society (EMBC), pp. 2415–2418. IEEE (2015)

29. Goyal, M., Reeves, N.D., Rajbhandari, S., Ahmad, N., Wang, C., Yap, M.H.: Recognition of Ischaemia and infection in diabetic foot ulcers: dataset and techniques. Comput. Biol. Med. **117**, 103616 (2020)

30. van Netten, J.J., van Baal, J.G., Liu, C., van Der Heijden, F., Bus, S.A.: Infrared thermal imaging for automated detection of diabetic foot complications (2013)

31. Yap, M.H., et al.: Computer vision algorithms in the detection of diabetic foot ulceration a new paradigm for diabetic foot care? J. Diabet. Sci. Technol. **10**(2), 612–613 (2015)

32. Yap, M.H.: A new mobile application for standardizing diabetic foot images. J. Diabet. Sci. Technol. **12**(1), 169–173 (2018)

33. Brown, R., Ploderer, B., Seng, L.S.D., van Netten, J.J., Lazzarini, P.A.: MyFootCare: a mobile self-tracking tool to promote self-care amongst people with diabetic foot ulcers (2017)

34. Yap, M.H., Kendrick, C., Reeves, N.D., Goyal, M., Pappachan, J.M., Cassidy, B.: Development of diabetic foot ulcer datasets: an overview. In: Diabetic Foot Ulcers Grand Challenge: Second Challenge, DFUC 2021, Held in Conjunction with MICCAI 2021, Strasbourg, France, 27 September 2021, Proceedings, p. 1 (2021)

35. Shetty, R., Sreekar, H., Lamba, S., Gupta, A.K.: A novel and accurate technique of photographic wound measurement. Indian J. Plastic Surg. **45**, 425–429 (2012)

36. McCardle, J., Smith, M., Brewin, E., Young, M.: Visitrak: wound measurement as an aid to making treatment decisions. Diabet. Foot J. **8**(4), 207–211 (2005)

37. Molik, M., et al.: Comparison of the wound area assessment methods in the diabetic foot syndrome. Biocybern. Biomed. Eng. **30**(4), 3–15 (2010)

38. Rogers, L.C., Bevilacqua, N.J., Armstrong, D.G., Andros, G.: Digital planimetry results in more accurate wound measurements: a comparison to standard ruler measurements, 799–802 (2010)

39. Cassidy, B., et al.: The DFUC 2020 dataset: analysis towards diabetic foot ulcer detection. touchREVIEWS Endocrinol. **17**(1), 5 (2021)

40. Armstrong, D.G., Boulton, A.J.M., Bus, S.A.: Diabetic foot ulcers and their recurrence. N. Engl. J. Med. **376**, 2367–2375 (2017)

CellCentroidFormer: Combining Self-attention and Convolution for Cell Detection

Royden Wagner$^{(\boxtimes)}$ and Karl Rohr

Biomedical Computer Vision Group, BioQuant, IPMB, Heidelberg University,
Heidelberg, Germany
royden.wagner@bioquant.uni-heidelberg.de, k.rohr@uni-heidelberg.de

Abstract. Cell detection in microscopy images is important to study
how cells move and interact with their environment. Most recent deep
learning-based methods for cell detection use convolutional neural networks (CNNs). However, inspired by the success in other computer
vision applications, vision transformers (ViTs) are also used for this purpose. We propose a novel hybrid CNN-ViT model for cell detection in
microscopy images to exploit the advantages of both types of deep learning models. We employ an efficient CNN, that was pre-trained on the
ImageNet dataset, to extract image features and utilize transfer learning
to reduce the amount of required training data. Extracted image features
are further processed by a combination of convolutional and transformer
layers, so that the convolutional layers can focus on local information
and the transformer layers on global information. Our centroid-based cell
detection method represents cells as ellipses and is end-to-end trainable.
Furthermore, we show that our proposed model can outperform fully convolutional one-stage detectors on four different 2D microscopy datasets.
Code is available at: https://github.com/roydenwa/cell-centroid-former

Keywords: Cell detection · Transformer · Self-attention · Convolution

1 Introduction

Cell detection is an important task when studying biomedical microscopy images
and time-lapse microscopy videos. Main applications are the quantification of
cellular structures as well as studying how cells move and interact with their
environment. Most recent deep learning-based methods for cell detection in
microscopy images use convolutional neural networks (CNNs) (e.g., [5,6,12]).
However, inspired by the success in other computer vision applications, vision
transformers (ViTs) (e.g., [13]) are also used for this purpose.

The comparison of ViTs and CNNs in computer vision applications reveals
that the receptive fields of ViTs and CNNs are fundamentally different [14].
The receptive fields of ViTs capture local and global information in both earlier and later layers. The receptive fields of CNNs, on the other hand, initially

G. Yang et al. (Eds.): MIUA 2022, LNCS 13413, pp. 212–222, 2022.
https://doi.org/10.1007/978-3-031-12053-4_16

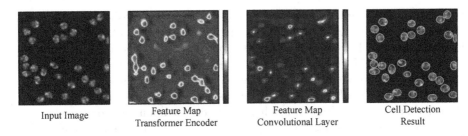

| Input Image | Feature Map
Transformer Encoder | Feature Map
Convolutional Layer | Cell Detection
Result |

Fig. 1. Feature maps and cell detection results for a fluorescence microscopy image. The feature map on the left was generated by a transformer encoder in the neck part of our model, the feature map on the right was generated by an adjacent convolutional layer. The transformer encoder focuses on the overall cell shapes (global features), while the convolutional layer focuses on the cell centroids (local features). Both feature maps have been enlarged, their original size is 48 × 48 pixels.

capture local information and gradually grow to capture global information in later layers. This suggests that ViTs better preserve spatial information across the generated feature maps within the models, which is advantageous for object detection. However, a limitation of most current ViT models is that they require much more training data to reach or surpass the performance of CNNs in computer vision tasks [7]. This is a major limitation for biomedical applications, where annotated training samples are limited. Another limitation of ViTs is that their core mechanism, multi-head self-attention, has a computational complexity of $O(n^2)$, where n is the length of the input sequence. Consequently, large computational resources are required for training such models.

To exploit the advantages of both types of deep learning models, we propose a hybrid CNN-ViT model for cell detection in microscopy images. We employ an efficient CNN, that was pre-trained on the ImageNet [1] dataset, to extract images features and utilize transfer learning to reduce amount of required training data. Extracted image features are further processed by a combination of convolutional and transformer layers, so that the convolutional layers can focus on local information and the transformer layers on global information. We propose a one-stage cell detection method that is end-to-end trainable. Overall, the contributions of our paper are twofold:

1. We introduce a novel deep learning model that combines self-attention and convolution for cell detection in microscopy images.
2. We propose a centroid-based cell detection method that represents cells as ellipses.

2   Related Work

Several related methods use CNNs [3,5,6,9,12,22,24] or combine CNNs with classical image analysis approaches [17] for cell detection in biomedical microscopy images. Amongst these methods, two approaches are common: (i) to perform cell detection by predicting a heatmap for cell positions [3,12,24] or (ii) to perform cell detection by predicting the coordinates of bounding boxes for cells [5,6,9]. The heatmap-based methods are well suited for cell counting, but are unsuitable for morphological studies since they only predict where cells are located and do not provide information on the cell dimensions. The bounding box-based methods are more flexible as they predict the cell positions and the cell dimensions (width and height). However, the bounding box-based methods use a cascade of two CNNs and are therefore not end-to-end trainable. To deal with sparsely annotated or small datasets, semi-supervised learning [3,12] or pre-training with synthetic data [24] is used. Thus complicating the training process, since pseudo-labels must be iteratively generated or synthetic data must be created in advance.

The Cell-DETR [13] model is architecturally most related to ours. Cell-DETR is a hybrid CNN-ViT model for cell detection and segmentation. Prangemeier et al. use a CNN backbone to extract image features, a transformer encoder-decoder block to process image features and a model head with a multi-layer perceptron for cell detection. Due to the high computational complexity of the transformer encoder-decoder block, they use a small input size of 128×128 pixels. Therefore, a considerable amount of information is lost when downsizing high-resolution microscopy images.

3   Method

3.1   Model Architecture

The proposed hybrid CNN-ViT model combines self-attention and convolution for cell detection. For this purpose, we use MobileViT blocks [11], which combine transformer encoders [2,19] with convolutional layers. In MobileViT blocks, input tensors are first processed by convolutional layers, then, the extracted features are unfolded into a sequence and passed through a transformer encoder. Finally, the output tensor of the transformer encoder is folded again into a 3D representation and concatenated with the input tensor. Thereby, the convolutional layers extract local information and the self-attention mechanism in the transformer encoder associates local information from distant features to capture global information. We use MobileViT blocks in the neck part of our proposed model to enhance global information compared to a fully convolutional neck part. MobileViT blocks are a light-weight alternative to the original transformer encoder-decoder design [19]. However, due to their multi-head self-attention layers, MobileViT blocks still have a much higher computational complexity (CC) than convolutional layers:

$$CC_{mhs-attn} \cong \begin{cases} O(n^2) & \text{if } n >> d \cdot h, \\ O(n^2 \cdot d \cdot h) & \text{else} \end{cases} \tag{1}$$

$$CC_{conv} \cong \begin{cases} O(n) & \text{if } n >> d \cdot k \cdot f, \\ O(n \cdot d \cdot k \cdot f) & \text{else} \end{cases} \tag{2}$$

where n is the sequence length, d is the sequence depth, h is the number of self-attention heads, k the size of the convolutional kernels, and f is the number of convolutional filters. Thus, we combine MobileViT blocks in the neck part of our model with convolutional layers to extract more features without increasing the computational complexity excessively. In addition, we add layer normalization layers for regularization and to allow higher learning rates during training.

As backbone of our proposed model, we use parts of an EfficientNetV2S [16] CNN model. EffcientNet models consist of six high-level blocks, we use five of these blocks to extract image features. We initialize the backbone with weights learned from training on the ImageNet dataset to leverage transfer learning and reduce the amount of required training data. EfficientNetV2S models are optimized for a fixed input size of $384 \times 384 \times 3$ pixels. Therefore, we resize all input images to this input size. We represent cells by their centroid, their width, and their height. Our model contains two fully convolutional heads to predict these cell properties. The heads contain 2D convolution, batch normalization, and bilinear upsampling layers. We do not use further MobileViT blocks in the heads to reduce the computational complexity of our model, and since later convolutional layers have a large receptive field that allows them to capture global information [14]. The first head predicts a heatmap for cell centroids, and the second head predicts the cell dimensions (width and height) at the position of the corresponding cell centroid. The output dimensions of our model are 384×384, thus, the output stride is one and we do not need an additional offset head to account for offset errors (as in, e.g., [25]). Figure 2 shows the overall model architecture.

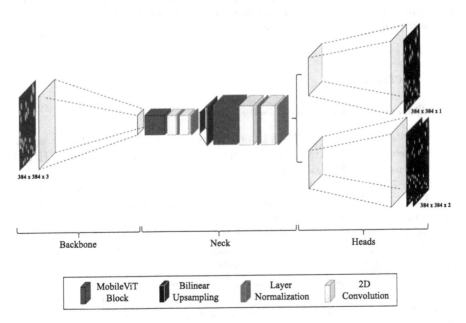

Fig. 2. CellCentroidFormer model. Backbone: Five blocks of an EfficientNetV2S. **Neck:** MobileViT blocks and convolutional layers. **Heads:** Fully convolutional upsampling blocks.

3.2   Bounding Ellipses for Cell Detection

Yang et al. [25] argue that traditional bounding box-based object detection methods are not optimized for biomedical applications. They state that most relevant objects in biomedical applications have round shapes, and thus they propose using bounding circles instead of bounding boxes. We extend this idea and use *bounding ellipses* for cell detection, since most cell types in biomedical applications have an ellipsoidal shape. Figure 3 shows how we generate training samples for the proposed centroid-based cell detection method. We approximate the centroid of a cell by an ellipse with width and height adjusted to the corresponding cell dimensions. We blur the centroid ellipses using a Gaussian kernel to reduce the loss value when a centroid is only missed by a small distance. Similar as in [26], the cell width and cell height are encoded in rectangles located at the position of the cell centroids.

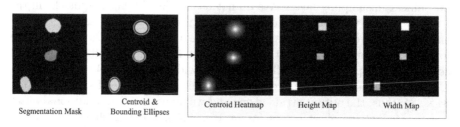

Segmentation Mask   Centroid & Bounding Ellipses   Centroid Heatmap   Height Map   Width Map

Fig. 3. Centroid representation of bounding ellipses. Instance segmentation masks are converted into training samples for cell detection. The training samples contain centroid heatmaps, height maps, and width maps.

4   Experiments

4.1   Datasets and Pre-processing

We evaluate our hybrid CNN-ViT model using four different 2D microscopy datasets from the Cell Tracking Challenge [18]. The Fluo-N2DL-HeLa (HeLa) dataset consists of 2D fluorescence microscopy images of cells stably expressing H2b-GFP. The images of this dataset have a size of 700×1100 pixels. The Fluo-N2DH-SIM+ (SIM+) dataset consists of simulated 2D fluorescence microscopy images of HL60 cells stained with Hoechst dyes. The images of this dataset have a size of 773×739 pixels. The Fluo-N2DH-GOWT1 (GOWT1) dataset consists of 2D fluorescence microscopy images of mouse stem cells. These images have a size of 1024×1024 pixels. The PhC-C2DH-U373 (U373) dataset consists of 2D phase contrast microscopy images of glioblastoma-astrocytoma U373 cells on a polyacrylamide substrate. The images of this dataset have a size of 520×696 pixels. Similar as in [20], we use pseudocoloring to generate input images with three channels suitable for the pretrained backbone. We use the ncar pseudo spectral colormap[1], which is well suited for coloring cell nuclei and their immediate surroundings to distinguish these regions from the background. Figure 4 shows pseudocolored image crops of the SIM+ and GOWT1 datasets.

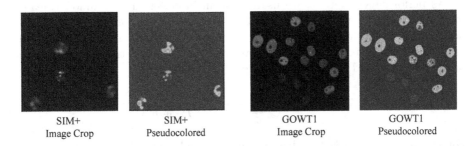

| SIM+ | SIM+ | GOWT1 | GOWT1 |
| Image Crop | Pseudocolored | Image Crop | Pseudocolored |

Fig. 4. Pseudocolored image crops of two considered datasets.

4.2 Baseline Model

Similar to semantic segmentation, our method treats cell detection as a pixelwise regression objective. Therefore, we choose a CNN designed for semantic segmentation as baseline model in the following experiments. The Dual U-Net model [10] has an encoder-decoder architecture with two decoders. Most recently, the Dual U-Net model was used as part of a tracking and segmentation method [15] that achieved multiple top-3 rankings in the Cell Tracking Challenge[2]. Analogously to our model, we use one decoder of the Dual U-Net model to predict the centroid heatmap and the other to predict the cell dimensions.

4.3 Training Setup, Metrics, and Hyperparameters

We use geometric data augmentations such as grid distortion, elastic transformation, shifting, and rotation to increase the size of each dataset to 2150 samples. The resulting datasets are each split into a training dataset (80%), a validation dataset (10%), and a test dataset (10%). All images are normalized using min-max scaling. Our CellCentroidFormer model is trained with pseudocolored training samples, the Dual U-Net model with normalized grayscale training samples. We use three Huber loss functions [4], one loss function per output, to train both models. The total loss is computed by a weighted sum of the three loss values:

$$\mathcal{L}_{Huber}(y,\widehat{y}) = \begin{cases} \frac{1}{2}(y-\widehat{y})^2 & \text{if } y - \widehat{y} \leq 1.0, \\ (y-\widehat{y}) - \frac{1}{2} & \text{else} \end{cases} \tag{3}$$

$$\mathcal{L}_{total} = \mathcal{L}_{heatmap} + \frac{1}{2} \cdot \mathcal{L}_{height} + \frac{1}{2} \cdot \mathcal{L}_{width} \tag{4}$$

---

[1] https://www.ncl.ucar.edu/Document/Graphics/ColorTables/MPL_gist_ncar.shtml.
[2] http://celltrackingchallenge.net/participants/KIT-Sch-GE.

The centroid heatmap loss ($\mathcal{L}_{heatmap}$) contributes the most to the total loss because our method is inherently centroid-based. When decoding the predictions of our model, the width and height of the cells are only looked up at positions where cell centroids are located according to the centroid heatmap prediction.

As performance metrics, we use the mean intersection over union (Mean-IoU) and the structural similarity metric (SSIM) [21]. We convert the centroid heatmaps to binary masks to evaluate the detection performance. Therefore, we apply thresholding to the heatmaps. Afterwards, we compute the MeanIoU value of the predicted and the ground truth centroid mask:

$$MeanIoU = \frac{1}{C} \sum_C \frac{TP_C}{TP_C + FP_C + FN_C} \tag{5}$$

For the two class labels (C), background and cell centroids, the true positive (TP), false positive (FP), and false negative (FN) pixels are determined.

For the cell dimensions (height and width), we use the SSIM metric to quantify the performance. The metric measures the similarity between two images or matrices and is defined as:

$$SSIM(x_1, x_2) = \frac{(2\mu_{x_1}\mu_{x_2} + (0.01L)^2)(2\sigma_{x_1 x_2} + (0.03L)^2)}{(\mu_{x_1}^2 + \mu_{x_2}^2 + (0.01L)^2)(\sigma_{x_1}^2 + \sigma_{x_2}^2 + (0.03L)^2)} \tag{6}$$

For the two inputs (x_1 and x_2), the mean (μ), the variance (σ), and the dynamic range (L) are computed.

We train both models per dataset for 50 epochs with a batch size of 4 using a Nvidia® V100 GPU. We use Adam [8] as optimizer with an initial learning rate of 1^{-4} and reduce the learning rate at plateaus.

4.4 Training Curves and Performance Comparison

Figure 5 shows the training curves for the HeLa dataset.

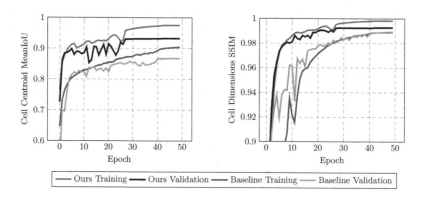

Fig. 5. Training curves for the HeLa dataset.

Our model converges around the 30th epoch, whereas the baseline model converges around the 40th epoch. In these training epochs, the lowest learning rate of 1^{-6} is also reached for both models and, accordingly, the metrics do not change much in the following epochs. Our model converges faster since the pretrained backbone was already trained to extract image features. The performance difference for the cell centroid MeanIoU score is greater than for the cell dimensions SSIM score, but overall our model yields higher values for all considered metrics on both datasets (training and validation).

Table 1. Performance on different microscopy datasets. Metrics are evaluated after training for 50 epochs with the corresponding training datasets.

Dataset	Model	Backbone	Centroid MeanIoU ⇑	Dimensions SSIM ⇑
SIM+ Test	Dual U-Net	–	0.8033	0.9631
	CircleNet	EfficientNetV2S	0.8308	0.9011
	CellCentroidFormer	EfficientNetV2S	**0.8492**	**0.9858**
GOWT1 Test	Dual U-Net	–	0.9278	0.9909
	CircleNet	EfficientNetV2S	0.9108	0.9192
	CellCentroidFormer	EfficientNetV2S	**0.9355**	**0.9959**
U373 Test	Dual U-Net	–	0.9170	0.9908
	CircleNet	EfficientNetV2S	0.8802	0.9241
	CellCentroidFormer	EfficientNetV2S	**0.9256**	**0.9923**
HeLa Test	Dual U-Net	–	0.8675	0.9885
	CircleNet	EfficientNetV2S	0.7650	0.7507
	CellCentroidFormer	EfficientNetV2S	**0.9287**	**0.9937**

Table 1 shows a comparison the performance of the two models on the used *test* datasets. Additionally, we train a CircleNet [25] model with an EfficientNetV2S as backbone. As in [23,26], we combine the backbone with upsampling blocks, such that the CircleNet has an output stride of 4. CircleNets detect bounding circles for cells by predicting a heatmap for cell centers, the circle radius, and a local offset. We train the model with pseudocolored samples, use a Huber loss for the center heatmap predictions, and keep the rest of the training setup as in [25]. To compute the SSIM score for the cell dimensions, we compute the SSIM score for the radius prediction and cell width map, the SSIM score for the radius prediction and cell height map, and average them.

Our CellCentroidFormer model outperforms the Dual U-Net and the CircleNet on all considered datasets. As in Fig. 5, the performance difference for the cell centroid MeanIoU score is greater than for the cell dimensions SSIM score. Our model and the Dual U-Net model yield higher cell dimensions SSIM scores than the CircleNet model since most cells have an ellipsoidal shape, which is more accurately represented by an ellipse than by a circle. On the SIM+ dataset, our model and the CircleNet model outperform the Dual U-Net model on the cell centroid MeanIoU score. On the HeLa dataset, the CircleNet performs worst because this dataset contains many small cells (see Fig. 6), that are challenging to distinguish in a low resolution output of 128×128.

Table 2 shows a comparison of the training times, the inference times, and the overall number of parameters per model. As previously shown [11], vision transformers need more time for training and inference than CNNs. This also applies to our hybrid model, thus, it requires more time to train our model for one epoch (T_{Epoch}), and

Table 2. Model comparison. Inference times (TI_{GPU}) are measured end-to-end and include the data transfer between the host (CPU) and the device (GPU).

Model	T_{Epoch} ⇓	TI_{GPU} ⇓	#Params ⇓
Dual U-Net	106 s	67 ms	33.0 M
CircleNet	64 s	59 ms	24.6 M
CellCentroidFormer	122 s	82 ms	11.5 M

the inference time for one input image is somewhat slower (TI_{GPU}). However, our model only requires one third of the parameters of the Dual U-Net model and roughly half of the parameters of the CircleNet model (11.5 M vs. 33 M vs. 24.6 M) to achieve superior performance.

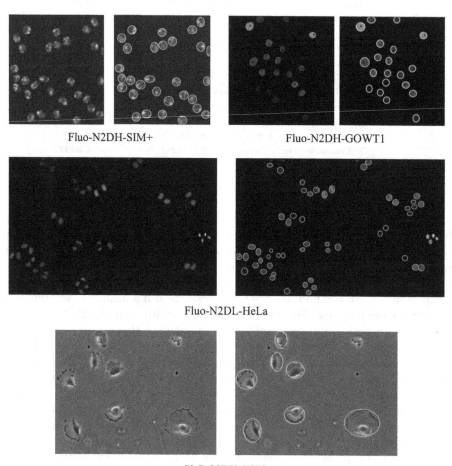

Fluo-N2DH-SIM+   Fluo-N2DH-GOWT1

Fluo-N2DL-HeLa

PhC-C2DH-U373

Fig. 6. Example microscopy images and cell detection results of our proposed method.

Figure 6 shows example images of the considered datasets and the corresponding cell detection results of our model.

5   Conclusion

We have presented a novel hybrid CNN-ViT model that combines self-attention and convolution for cell detection. Our centroid-based cell detection method represents cells as ellipses and is end-to-end trainable. We have shown that the transformer layers in the neck part of our proposed model can focus on the overall cell shapes, while adjacent convolutional layers focus on the cell centroids. Our experiments reveal that pseudocoloring in combination with pretrained backbones improves the cell detection performance, whereas larger output strides worsen the performance. Furthermore, our CellCentroidFormer model outperforms fully convolutional one-stage detectors on four different 2D microscopy datasets despite having less parameters overall.

Acknowledgements. Support of the DFG (German Research Foundation) within the SFB 1129 (project Z4) and the SPP 2202 (RO 2471/10-1), and the BMBF (German Federal Ministry of Education and Research) within the de.NBI is gratefully acknowledged.

References

1. Deng, J., Dong, W., Socher, R., Li, L.J., Li, K., Fei-Fei, L.: ImageNet: a large-scale hierarchical image database. In: Conference on Computer Vision and Pattern Recognition (CVPR), pp. 248–255. IEEE (2009)
2. Dosovitskiy, A., et al.: An image is worth 16x16 words: transformers for image recognition at scale. In: International Conference on Learning Representations (ICLR) (2021)
3. Fujii, K., Suehiro, D., Nishimura, K., Bise, R.: Cell detection from imperfect annotation by pseudo label selection using P-classification. In: de Bruijne, M., et al. (eds.) MICCAI 2021. LNCS, vol. 12908, pp. 425–434. Springer, Cham (2021). https://doi.org/10.1007/978-3-030-87237-3_41
4. Huber, P.J.: Robust estimation of a location parameter. Ann. Stat. **53**, 73–101 (1964)
5. Hung, J., et al.: Keras R-CNN: library for cell detection in biological images using deep neural networks. BMC Bioinform. **21**(1), 1–7 (2020)
6. Jiang, H., Li, S., Liu, W., Zheng, H., Liu, J., Zhang, Y.: Geometry-aware cell detection with deep learning. Msystems **5**(1), e00840-19 (2020)
7. Khan, S., Naseer, M., Hayat, M., Zamir, S.W., Khan, F.S., Shah, M.: Transformers in vision: a survey. ACM Comput. Surv. (2021). https://doi.org/10.1145/3505244
8. Kingma, D.P., Ba, J.: Adam: a method for stochastic optimization. In: International Conference on Learning Representations (ICLR) (2015)
9. Li, X., Xu, Z., Shen, X., Zhou, Y., Xiao, B., Li, T.Q.: Detection of cervical cancer cells in whole slide images using deformable and global context aware faster RCNN-FPN. Curr. Oncol. **28**(5), 3585–3601 (2021)

10. Li, X., Wang, Y., Tang, Q., Fan, Z., Yu, J.: Dual U-Net for the segmentation of overlapping glioma nuclei. IEEE Access **7**, 84040–84052 (2019)
11. Mehta, S., Rastegari, M.: MobileViT: light-weight, general-purpose, and mobile-friendly vision transformer. In: International Conference on Learning Representations (ICLR) (2022)
12. Nishimura, K., Cho, H., Bise, R.: Semi-supervised cell detection in time-lapse images using temporal consistency. In: de Bruijne, M., Cattin, P.C., Cotin, S., Padoy, N., Speidel, S., Zheng, Y., Essert, C. (eds.) MICCAI 2021. LNCS, vol. 12908, pp. 373–383. Springer, Cham (2021). https://doi.org/10.1007/978-3-030-87237-3_36
13. Prangemeier, T., Reich, C., Koeppl, H.: Attention-based transformers for instance segmentation of cells in microstructures. In: International Conference on Bioinformatics and Biomedicine (BIBM). IEEE (2020)
14. Raghu, M., Unterthiner, T., Kornblith, S., Zhang, C., Dosovitskiy, A.: Do vision transformers see like convolutional neural networks? In: Advances in Neural Information Processing Systems (NeurIPS) (2021)
15. Scherr, T., Löffler, K., Neumann, O., Mikut, R.: On improving an already competitive segmentation algorithm for the cell tracking challenge-lessons learned. bioRxiv (2021)
16. Tan, M., Le, Q.: EfficientNetV2: smaller models and faster training. In: International Conference on Machine Learning (ICML), pp. 10096–10106. PMLR (2021)
17. Tyson, A.L., et al.: A deep learning algorithm for 3D cell detection in whole mouse brain image datasets. PLoS Comput. Biol. **17**(5), e1009074 (2021)
18. Ulman, V., et al.: An objective comparison of cell-tracking algorithms. Nat. Methods **14**(12), 1141–1152 (2017)
19. Vaswani, A., et al.: Attention is all you need. In: Advances in Neural Information Processing Systems (NeurIPS) 30 (2017)
20. Wagner, R., Rohr, K.: EfficientCellSeg: efficient volumetric cell segmentation using context aware pseudocoloring. In: Medical Imaging with Deep Learning (MIDL) (2022)
21. Wang, Z., Bovik, A.C., Sheikh, H.R., Simoncelli, E.P.: Image quality assessment: from error visibility to structural similarity. Trans. Image Process. **13**(4), 600–612 (2004)
22. Wollmann, T., Rohr, K.: Deep consensus network: aggregating predictions to improve object detection in microscopy images. Med. Image Anal. **70**, 102019 (2021)
23. Xiao, B., Wu, H., Wei, Y.: Simple baselines for human pose estimation and tracking. In: Ferrari, V., Hebert, M., Sminchisescu, C., Weiss, Y. (eds.) ECCV 2018. LNCS, vol. 11210, pp. 472–487. Springer, Cham (2018). https://doi.org/10.1007/978-3-030-01231-1_29
24. Xie, W., Noble, J.A., Zisserman, A.: Microscopy cell counting and detection with fully convolutional regression networks. Comput. Methods Biomech. Biomed. Eng. Imaging Visual. **6**(3), 283–292 (2018)
25. Yang, H., et al.: CircleNet: anchor-free glomerulus detection with circle representation. In: Martel, A.L., et al. (eds.) MICCAI 2020. LNCS, vol. 12264, pp. 35–44. Springer, Cham (2020). https://doi.org/10.1007/978-3-030-59719-1_4
26. Zhou, X., Wang, D., Krähenbühl, P.: Objects as points. arXiv preprint arXiv:1904.07850 (2019)

GPU-Net: Lightweight U-Net with More Diverse Features

Heng Yu[1(✉)], Di Fan[2], and Weihu Song[3]

[1] Carnegie Mellon University, Pittsburgh, USA
hengyu@andrew.cmu.edu
[2] University of Southern California, Los Angeles, USA
difan@usc.edu
[3] Beihang University, Beijing, China
weihusong@gmail.com

Abstract. Image segmentation is an important task in the medical image field and many convolutional neural networks (CNNs) based methods have been proposed, among which U-Net and its variants show promising performance. In this paper, we propose GP-module (ghost pyramid pooling module) and GPU-Net based on U-Net, which can learn more diverse features by introducing Ghost module and atrous spatial pyramid pooling (ASPP). Our method achieves better performance with more than $4\times$ fewer parameters and $2\times$ fewer FLOPs, which provides a new potential direction for future research. Our plug-and-play module can also be applied to existing segmentation methods to further improve their performance.

Keywords: Segmentation · U-Net · Ghost module · Atrous spatial pyramid pooling

1 Introduction

Recently, the boom of deep learning technology has greatly promoted the development of image segmentation area. Many impressive CNN-based models have been proposed and proved to be very effective. Public datasets such as COCO [16], PASCAL VOC [8] further promote the prosperity of deep learning in this field, considering that pre-trained models on these big datasets can be applied into segmentation task effectively and efficiently using transfer learning. However, it is hard to apply these successful natural image segmentation models into medical image segmentation directly since there exist domain gaps between natural images and medical images such as Computer Tomography (CT), X-ray and Magnetic Resonance Imaging (MRI). The scarcity of medical data and complexity of labeling exacerbates the difficulty of training deeper networks. Aiming at the characteristics of medical images, researchers proposed U-Net [22] and many U-Net based variants, which achieve remarkable performance. These variants mainly focus on optimization of network structure, which introduce

© The Author(s), under exclusive license to Springer Nature Switzerland AG 2022
G. Yang et al. (Eds.): MIUA 2022, LNCS 13413, pp. 223–233, 2022.
https://doi.org/10.1007/978-3-031-12053-4_17

more parameters and generate useful feature maps inefficiently. In this paper, we explore the enhancement that well-learned features can bring and boost U-Net with more higher quality diverse features and fewer parameters. Our main contribution is proposing a lightweight version of U-Net which can achieve competitive and even better performance while significantly reduces the number of parameters and FLOPS. We name our method GPU-Net and experiments show GPU-Net can achieve state-of-the-art performance. To the best of our knowledge, it is the first paper that explore the possibility of learning useful feature maps efficiently through applying ghost-module and its variants into U-Net. We believe our method can be an interest topic to discuss for the medical image segmentation community.

2   Related Work

Image segmentation requires classifying each image pixel on an individual basis and many methods have been proposed to solve this challenging task. In the early days of deep learning era, researchers classify each pixel by training CNNs using the image block around the pixel [6,9,21], which is known as patch-wise training. This method is very inefficient and cannot achieve satisfactory results given that input blocks for adjacent pixels contain redundant information and the receptive field is limited due to the block size. The stagnant situation is changed by FCN method [18], which applies fully convolutional network and provides a new direction for follow-up research. Subsequent methods such as deeplab series [4,5], Mask RCNN [11] and PANet [17] take the advantages of FCN and obtain notable achievement. While the deep learning research in natural image segmentation is in full swing, U-Net [22] is proposed specifically for medical image segmentation. U-Net can be trained with a relatively small number of medical data from scratch and achieve competitive performance. Based on U-Net, a series of compelling methods have been proposed. R2U-Net [3] and Attention U-Net [19] apply recurrent module and attention mechanism into U-Net, respectively. Mixmodule [13] uses multi-size kernels instead of single size kernels. These variants all develop the potential of U-Net from different angles but they ignore the problem of feature redundancy in the network. Redundancy in feature maps can be important but it is better to achieve this kind of redundancy using more efficient ways like getting a set of intrinsic feature maps first and then generating many ghost feature maps based on them as proposed in GhostNet [10]. The intrinsic feature maps can have no redundancy so as to ensure efficiency. The increase in parameters also impair the innovation of architectures in their methods. In this paper, our target is to explore how U-Net can benefit from sufficient diverse features. To get more high quality features with simple operations in network, we borrow and improve the ghost module in GhostNet [10] and propose GP-module, a lightweight module that can boost U-Net with more valuable features and fewer parameters.

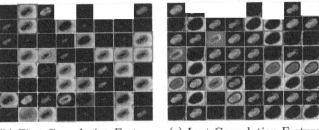

(a) Image   (b) First Convolution Feature   (c) Last Convolution Feature

Fig. 1. Visualization of feature redundancy

3   Methodology

3.1   GP-Module

U-Net and its existing variants have feature redundancy problem as shown in
Fig 1, where we visualize the first and last convolution layer of U-Net segmentation results. This redundancy includes two aspects. On the one hand, some
feature maps contain little or even no useful (green parts in Fig. 1(b)–1(c)) information. On the other hand, there exist similar feature maps (as red, pink and
cyan parts in Fig. 1(b)–1(c)). Redundancy in feature maps can benefit model performance to some extent. However, the existing methods obtain sufficient feature
maps at the expense of efficiency. To solve the problems, we propose GP-module,
an enhanced version of ghost module that is first introduced in GhostNet [10].
Ghost module uses cheap linear operations base on a handful of intrinsic feature
maps to generate comparable features with traditional convolution operation as
shown in Fig. 2. To be specific, ordinary convolution operation can be formulated
as following (We ignore bias term for simplicity here and later):

$$Y = X * f \tag{1}$$

where $X \in \mathbf{R}^{c \times w \times h}$ is the input feature map with c channels and h and w
are the height and width, $*$ is the convolution operation, $f \in \mathbf{R}^{c \times k \times k \times n}$ is
the convolution filters to produce n feature maps and $k \times k$ is the kernel size,
$Y \in \mathbf{R}^{w' \times h' \times n}$ is the output feature map with n channels and h' and w' are
the height and width. In a convolution operation, the number of parameters and
FLOPs required can be calculated as Eq. 2 and Eq. 3, respectively. Both of them
can be very large when c and n are very large, which is the usual case.

$$N_{conv}^{Para} = c \cdot k \cdot k \cdot n \tag{2}$$

$$N_{conv}^{FLOPs} = c \cdot k \cdot k \cdot w' \cdot h' \cdot n \tag{3}$$

We can find out from Fig. 1(b) that there are many similar features and they
can be generate using fewer parameters and FLOPs. Ghost module [10] deal with

this problem by dividing feature maps into two parts. One part is a small number of intrinsic feature maps and the other part of feature maps is "ghosts" of the intrinsic feature maps. They are called ghost feature maps and are produced by using some cheap transformations based on the intrinsic feature maps. The idea is generating m intrinsic feature maps and for each intrinsic feature map, applying several cheap linear operations to get s ghost feature maps. By this way we obtain the $n = m \cdot s$ feature maps desired. The way to generate intrinsic feature maps is the same as ordinary convolution operation and the hyper-parameters (kernel size, padding, stride, etc.) are consistent with ordinary convolution to keep the same output spatial size (Eq. 4). The only difference is that $f' \in \mathbf{R}^{c \times k \times k \times m}$ and $Y' \in \mathbf{R}^{w' \times h' \times m}$, where $m \leq n$ so the number of parameters can be greatly reduced.

$$Y' = X * f' \tag{4}$$

After getting intrinsic feature maps, ghost features can be produced by applying a series of cheap operations on each intrinsic feature as Eq. 5:

$$y_{ij} = G_{ij}(y'_i), \quad \forall i = 1, ..., m, j = 1, ..., s \tag{5}$$

where y'_i is the i-th intrinsic feature map of Y' and G_{ij} is the j-th linear operation (e.g. 3×3 and 5×5 linear kernels) applied on y'_i to generate the j-th ghost feature map y_{ij}. Each y'_i can get s ghost feature maps except that the last one is the identity mapping for preserving the intrinsic feature map for each y'_i. So we can obtain $n = m \cdot s$ output feature maps $Y = [y_{11}, y_{12}, ..., y_{1s}, ...y_{ms}]$. Note that the input and output of G_{ij} are all single-channel feature maps, Eq. 5 can be easily implemented by using depth-wise convolution. Ghost module can produce sufficient ghost features by selecting s and kernel size in G_{ij}. But it uses the same single size kernel in all the s linear operations for each intrinsic feature map y'_i, which is not conducive to generating diverse and informative feature maps. In order to better handle this problem, we introduce atrous spatial pyramid pooling (ASPP) mechanism proposed in [4] and get our GP-module as shown in Fig. 2(c). Our GP-module can be expressed as Eq. 6:

$$y_{ij} = G'_i(y'_i, j), \quad \forall i = 1, ..., m, j = 1, ..., s \tag{6}$$

G'_i is explicitly related to j, which means for each intrinsic feature map y'_i, when generating more than $s > 2$ ghost feature maps, GP-module applies the same kernel size but different dilation rates (except the identity mapping). By introducing ASPP, GP-module can expand the receptive field and capture multi-scale contextual information so as to generate heterogeneous representative ghost feature maps without additional parameters and FLOPs given that GP-module uses the same kernel size as ghost module. For each ghost module/GP-module, there is one ordinary convolution operation to generate m intrinsic feature maps and $m \cdot (s-1) = \frac{n}{s} \cdot (s-1)$ linear operations (one of the s is the identity mapping operation) to get ghost feature maps. Note the kernel size in linear operations is

$d \times d$ and the number of parameters and FLOPs required in ghost module/GP-module can be calculated as Eq. 7 and Eq. 8, respectively. In practice, $d \times d$ and $k \times k$ have the similar magnitude and s can be much smaller than c. So the parameters compression ratio and FLOPs acceleration ratio can be calculated as Eq. 9 and Eq. 10, respectively.

$$N_{gp}^{Para} = c \cdot k \cdot k \cdot \frac{n}{s} + \frac{n}{s} \cdot (s-1) \cdot d \cdot d \tag{7}$$

$$N_{gp}^{FLOPs} = c \cdot k \cdot k \cdot \frac{n}{s} \cdot w' \cdot h' + \frac{n}{s} \cdot (s-1) \cdot d \cdot d \cdot w' \cdot h' \tag{8}$$

$$r_P = \frac{N_{conv}^{Para}}{N_{gp}^{Para}} \approx \frac{c \cdot s \cdot k \cdot k}{c \cdot k \cdot k + (s-1) \cdot d \cdot d} \approx \frac{c \cdot s}{c + s - 1} \approx s \tag{9}$$

$$r_F = \frac{N_{conv}^{FLOPs}}{N_{gp}^{FLOPs}} \approx \frac{c \cdot s}{c + s - 1} \approx s \tag{10}$$

The parameters compression ratio is equal to FLOPs acceleration ratio which means our GP-module does not cost extra computing resources based on ghost module and greatly reduced parameters and FLOPs compared to ordinary convolution operation.

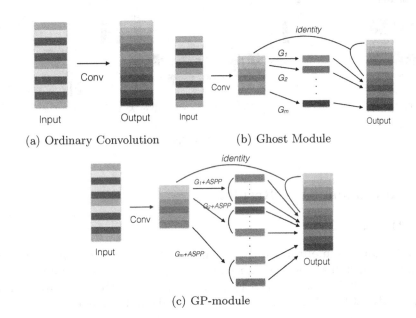

Fig. 2. Diagram of the three modules

3.2   Network Architecture

Based on GP-module, we introduce GP-bottleneck (GP-bneck) as shown in Fig. 3(a), which is similar as G-bneck in [10]. GP-bottleneck has a residual structure proposed in ResNet [12] and two stacked GP-modules, which corresponds to the two continuous convolution operations of each level in U-Net. Batch normalization (BN) [14] is used after each GP-module and ReLU is used only after the first GP-module in GP-bottleneck. After getting GP-bottleneck, we replace the convolution operations in U-Net with our GP-bottleneck and name it GPU-Net, which is a lightweight and powerful (like its name) network for medical image segmentation as shown in Fig 3(b), where the red module indicates the location of the replacement. We use binary cross entropy as loss function to train the whole network.

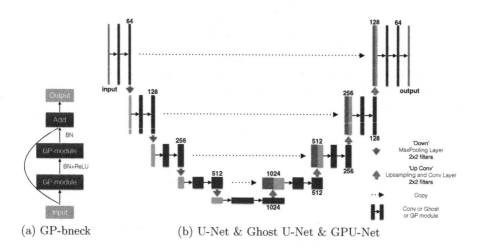

(a) GP-bneck   (b) U-Net & Ghost U-Net & GPU-Net

Fig. 3. Network architecture

4   Experiments and Results

4.1   Dataset

Skin Lesion Segmentation. Skin cancer is the most common cancer and accurate predictions of lesion segmentation boundaries in dermoscopic images can benefit clinical treatment. The dataset is from MICCAI 2018 Workshop - ISIC 2018: Skin Lesion Analysis Towards Melanoma Detection [7,23]

(ISIC for short). ISIC dataset contains 2594 images in total and is split into training set (1814 samples, ~70%), validation set (260 samples, ~10%), and test set (520 samples, ~20%). All the samples are resized into 192×256 given that the original samples are slightly different.

Lung Segmentation. Lung segmentation is important for analyzing lung related diseases, and can be further applied into lung lesion segmentation and other problems. This dataset is from Kaggle Challenge: Finding and Measuring Lungs in CT Data [1] (LUNA for short). LUNA dataset contains 267 2D CT images and is split into training set (186 samples, ~70$), validation set (27 samples, ~10%), and test set (54 samples, ~20%). The original image size is 512×512 and we resize all the images into 256×256 in the experiment.

Nuclei Segmentation. Identifying the cells' nuclei is the starting point of many research and can help researchers better understand the underlying biological processes. This dataset comes from Kaggle 2018 Data Science Bowl [2] (DSB for short). DSB dataset has 670 nucleus images and corresponding masks. The whole dataset is split into training set (469 samples, 70%), validation set (67 samples, 10%), and test set (134 samples, 20%). The original image size is 96×96 and remain the same in the experiment.

4.2 Experimental Setup

We implement all the experiments on a NVIDIA TITAN V GPU using PyTorch [20]. We use a batch size of 4 for ISIC dataset, 2 for LUNA dataset and 16 for DSB dataset since they have different input sizes. We train all the models for 100 epochs with Adam Optimizer [15] and the initial learning rate is 0.001. The two momentum terms in Adam are set to 0.5 and 0.999, respectively. We compare our GPU-Net with original U-Net and Ghost U-Net (replace convolution operations in U-Net with G-bneck in [10]). We set $s = 2$ and $d = 3$ in ghost module of G-bneck according to [10]. For our GP-module, we set $s = 6$, which means $s - 1 = 5$ cheap operations. We set the same $d = 3$ for 4 of the 5 cheap operations and their dilation rates are 1, 6, 12, 18, respectively. The last cheap operation is 1×1 depth-wise convolution, which is proposed in [4]. The other hyper-parameters in GPU-Net/Ghost U-Net are consistent with U-Net. Our code is available and we will release github address if accepted in order not to violate the anonymization rules.

4.3   Results and Discussion

To make a detailed comparison of the model performance, we take Accuracy (AC), F1-score (F1) and Jaccard similarity (JS) as quantitative analysis metrics (Eq. 11). Variables involved in these formulas are: True Positive (TP), True Negative (TN), False Positive (FP), False Negative (FN), Ground Truth(GT) and Segmentation Result (SR).

$$AC = \frac{TP + TN}{TP + TN + FP + FN}, F1 = 2\frac{|GT \cap SR|}{|GT| + |SR|}, JS = \frac{|GT \cap SR|}{|GT \cup SR|} \tag{11}$$

Experimental results are listed as Table 1 and our method can achieve better segmentation performance with significantly reduced parameters and FLOPs. We also show some segmentation results in Fig. 4, where we can find that our GPU-Net can better capture details and have better segmentation results at the edges (red circles). To better demonstrate the important role of our GP-module, we visualize the feature maps in the first level of the three networks as in Fig. 5. We can see that U-Net has many similar and blank feature maps while Ghost U-Net and our GPU-Net can make full use of all feature maps. Our GPU-Net can learn more diverse feature maps since ASPP module guarantees the change of the receptive field. The feature maps in the front part tend to learn textures, and the feature maps in the back tend to learn edges. In this way our method can achieve better performance.

Table 1. Experimental results on three datasets

Dateset	Methods	AC	F1	JS	Params (M)	FLOPs (G)
ISIC	U-Net	0.9554	0.8791	0.8071	34.53	49.10
	Ghost U-Net	0.9605	0.8852	0.8140	9.31	18.78
	GPU-Net	**0.9613**	**0.8926**	**0.8232**	8.27	17.56
LUNA	U-Net	0.9813	0.9785	0.9644	34.53	65.47
	Ghost U-Net	0.9879	0.9796	0.9665	9.31	25.05
	GPU-Net	**0.9892**	**0.9811**	**0.9675**	8.27	23.42
DSB	U-Net	0.9719	0.8698	0.7944	34.53	9.21
	Ghost U-Net	0.9716	0.8731	0.7954	9.31	3.52
	GPU-Net	**0.9727**	**0.8819**	**0.8049**	8.27	3.29

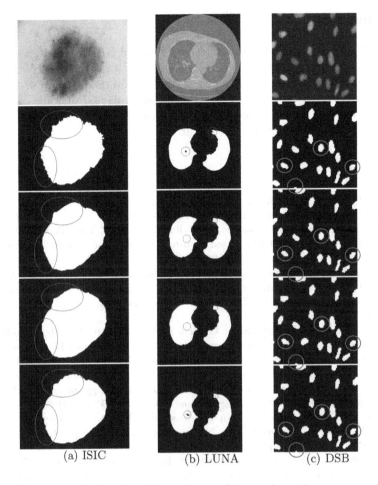

(a) ISIC   (b) LUNA   (c) DSB

Fig. 4. Segmentation result samples. From top to bottom: input images, ground truth, U-Net, Ghost U-Net and GPU-Net outputs

(a) U-Net   (b) Ghost U-Net   (c) GPU-Net

Fig. 5. Visualization of feature maps

5 Conclusion

In this paper, we propose a lightweight model named GPU-Net, which can learn diverse feature maps and get better segmentation performance. We test our method on three dataset and visualize several feature maps to proof the effectiveness and efficiency of our method. Our plug-and-play GP-module can also be applied to existing segmentation methods to further improve their performance, which shed the light on the further research.

References

1. https://www.kaggle.com/kmader/finding-lungs-in-ct-data
2. https://www.kaggle.com/c/data-science-bowl-2018/data
3. Alom, M.Z., Hasan, M., Yakopcic, C., Taha, T.M., Asari, V.K.: Recurrent residual convolutional neural network based on u-net (r2u-net) for medical image segmentation. arXiv preprint arXiv:1802.06955 (2018)
4. Chen, L.C., Papandreou, G., Kokkinos, I., Murphy, K., Yuille, A.L.: Deeplab: semantic image segmentation with deep convolutional nets, atrous convolution, and fully connected crfs. IEEE Trans. Pattern Anal. Mach. Intell. 40(4), 834–848 (2017)
5. Chen, L.C., Zhu, Y., Papandreou, G., Schroff, F., Adam, H.: Encoder-decoder with atrous separable convolution for semantic image segmentation. In: Proceedings of the European Conference on Computer Vision (ECCV), pp. 801–818 (2018)
6. Ciresan, D., Giusti, A., Gambardella, L.M., Schmidhuber, J.: Deep neural networks segment neuronal membranes in electron microscopy images. In: Advances in Neural Information Processing Systems, pp. 2843–2851 (2012)
7. Codella, N., et al.: Skin lesion analysis toward melanoma detection 2018: a challenge hosted by the international skin imaging collaboration (isic). arXiv preprint arXiv:1902.03368 (2019)
8. Everingham, M., Van Gool, L., Williams, C.K., Winn, J., Zisserman, A.: The pascal visual object classes (voc) challenge. Int. J. Comput. Vis. 88(2), 303–338 (2010)
9. Farabet, C., Couprie, C., Najman, L., LeCun, Y.: Learning hierarchical features for scene labeling. IEEE Trans. Pattern Anal. Mach. Intell. 35(8), 1915–1929 (2012)
10. Han, K., Wang, Y., Tian, Q., Guo, J., Xu, C., Xu, C.: Ghostnet: more features from cheap operations. In: Proceedings of the IEEE/CVF Conference on Computer Vision and Pattern Recognition, pp. 1580–1589 (2020)
11. He, K., Gkioxari, G., Dollár, P., Girshick, R.: Mask R-CNN. In: Proceedings of the IEEE International Conference on Computer Vision, pp. 2961–2969 (2017)
12. He, K., Zhang, X., Ren, S., Sun, J.: Deep residual learning for image recognition. In: Proceedings of the IEEE Conference on Computer Vision and Pattern Recognition, pp. 770–778 (2016)
13. Henry, H.Y., Feng, X., Wang, Z., Sun, H.: Mixmodule: mixed CNN kernel module for medical image segmentation. In: 2020 IEEE 17th International Symposium on Biomedical Imaging (ISBI), pp. 1508–1512. IEEE (2020)
14. Ioffe, S., Szegedy, C.: Batch normalization: accelerating deep network training by reducing internal covariate shift. In: International Conference on Machine Learning, pp. 448–456. PMLR (2015)
15. Kingma, D.P., Ba, J.: Adam: a method for stochastic optimization. arXiv preprint arXiv:1412.6980 (2014)

16. Lin, T.-Y., et al.: Microsoft COCO: common objects in context. In: Fleet, D., Pajdla, T., Schiele, B., Tuytelaars, T. (eds.) ECCV 2014. LNCS, vol. 8693, pp. 740–755. Springer, Cham (2014). https://doi.org/10.1007/978-3-319-10602-1_48

17. Liu, S., Qi, L., Qin, H., Shi, J., Jia, J.: Path aggregation network for instance segmentation. In: Proceedings of the IEEE Conference on Computer Vision and Pattern Recognition, pp. 8759–8768 (2018)

18. Long, J., Shelhamer, E., Darrell, T.: Fully convolutional networks for semantic segmentation. In: Proceedings of the IEEE Conference on Computer Vision and Pattern Recognition, pp. 3431–3440 (2015)

19. Oktay, O., et al.: Attention u-net: learning where to look for the pancreas. arXiv preprint arXiv:1804.03999 (2018)

20. Paszke, A., et al.: Pytorch: an imperative style, high-performance deep learning library. In: Wallach, H., Larochelle, H., Beygelzimer, A., d' Alché-Buc, F., Fox, E., Garnett, R. (eds.) Advances in Neural Information Processing Systems, vol. 32, pp. 8024–8035. Curran Associates, Inc. (2019), http://papers.neurips.cc/paper/9015-pytorch-an-imperative-style-high-performance-deep-learning-library.pdf

21. Pinheiro, P.H., Collobert, R.: Recurrent convolutional neural networks for scene labeling. In: 31st International Conference on Machine Learning (ICML), No. CONF (2014)

22. Ronneberger, O., Fischer, P., Brox, T.: U-Net: convolutional networks for biomedical image segmentation. In: Navab, N., Hornegger, J., Wells, W.M., Frangi, A.F. (eds.) MICCAI 2015. LNCS, vol. 9351, pp. 234–241. Springer, Cham (2015). https://doi.org/10.1007/978-3-319-24574-4_28

23. Tschandl, P., Rosendahl, C., Kittler, H.: The ham10000 dataset, a large collection of multi-source dermatoscopic images of common pigmented skin lesions. Sci. Data 5(1), 1–9 (2018)

Self-supervision and Multi-task Learning: Challenges in Fine-Grained COVID-19 Multi-class Classification from Chest X-rays

Muhammad Ridzuan[(⊠)], Ameera Bawazir, Ivo Gollini Navarrete,
Ibrahim Almakky, and Mohammad Yaqub

Mohamed Bin Zayed University of Artificial Intelligence, Abu Dhabi,
United Arab Emirates
{muhammad.ridzuan,ameera.bawazir,ivo.navarrete,ibrahim.almakky,
mohammad.yaqub}@mbzuai.ac.ae

Abstract. Quick and accurate diagnosis is of paramount importance to mitigate the effects of COVID-19 infection, particularly for severe cases. Enormous effort has been put towards developing deep learning methods to classify and detect COVID-19 infections from chest radiography images. However, recently some questions have been raised surrounding the clinical viability and effectiveness of such methods. In this work, we investigate the impact of multi-task learning (classification and segmentation) on the ability of CNNs to differentiate between various appearances of COVID-19 infections in the lung. We also employ self-supervised pre-training approaches, namely MoCo and inpainting-CXR, to eliminate the dependence on expensive ground truth annotations for COVID-19 classification. Finally, we conduct a critical evaluation of the models to assess their deploy-readiness and provide insights into the difficulties of fine-grained COVID-19 multi-class classification from chest X-rays.

Keywords: COVID-19 · X-ray · Classification · Self-supervision · Multi-task learning

1 Introduction

On January 30, 2020, the World Health Organization (WHO) declared a global health emergency due to the *coronavirus disease 2019* (COVID-19) outbreak [5]. Five times more deadly than the flu, SARS-CoV-2 viral infection's main symptoms are fever, cough, shortness of breath, and loss or change of smell and taste [35]. The fast-paced rise in infections and the rate at which it spread

G. Yang et al. (Eds.): MIUA 2022, LNCS 13413, pp. 234–250, 2022.
https://doi.org/10.1007/978-3-031-12053-4_18

around the globe exposed many challenges with diagnosis and treatment. Access to screening strategies and treatment was minimal due to the lack of resources, especially at the start of the pandemic [8].

Polymerase Chain Reaction (PCR) became the gold-standard method for COVID-19 screening. Nevertheless, the limited number of tests and high rate of false negatives (100% false negative on day one of infection and 38% on day 5) gave radiographers grounds to define chest imaging not just as a routine screening standard, but as an integral tool for assessing complications and disease progression [17]. Chest imaging is especially necessary for symptomatic patients that develop pneumonia, which is characterized by an increase in lung density due to inflammation and fluid in the lungs [7]. The Radiological Society of North America (RSNA) developed a standard nomenclature for imaging classification of COVID-19 pneumonia composed by four categories: negative for pneumonia, typical appearance, indeterminate appearance, and atypical appearance of COVID-19 pneumonia [33].

The presence of ground glass opacities (GGOs) and the extent to which they cover lung regions allow radiologists to diagnose COVID-19 pneumonia in chest radiographs. In such manner, the RSNA classifies a case as "typical" if the GGOs are multifocal, round-shaped, present in both lungs, and peripheral with a lower lung-predominant distribution. In an "indeterminate" case, there is an absence of typical findings and the GGOs are unilateral with a predominant distribution in the center or upper sections of the lung. If no GGO is seen and another cause of pneumonia (i.e. pneumothorax, pleural effusion, pulmonary edema, lobar consolidation, solitary lung nodule or mass, diffuse tiny nodules, cavity) is present, the case is categorized as "atypical" [21]. However, the distinction between these classes is a non-trivial task due to the lack of visual cues and the nature of GGOs, as discussed later in this work.

The possibility of using artificial intelligence (AI) to aid in the fight against COVID-19 motivated researchers to turn to deep learning approaches, especially convolutional neural networks (CNNs), for the detection and classification of COVID-19 infections [2]. Many studies have reported high classification performances using chest X-ray radiographies (CXRs) [10,29] and computed tomography (CT) scans [4,19,28] using standard and off-the-shelf CNNs. Despite high reported accuracies by these methods, questions have been raised regarding their clinical usefulness due to the bias of small datasets, poor integration of multistream data, variability of international sources, difficulty of prognosis, and the lack of collaborative work between clinicians and data analysts [31].

In this investigation, we utilize a large, multi-sourced chest X-ray dataset of COVID-19 patients to train deep learning models that have proven effective on computer vision benchmarks. Following this, the models are evaluated and the results are analysed to identify potential weaknesses in the models. The nature of the data and classes are also analysed keeping in mind the clinical needs for the development of such models. Finally, we present an in-depth discussion into the main challenges associated with this task from the machine learning and data perspectives. Our work does not aim to outperform state-of-the-art publications, but rather provide important insights in this challenging problem. The contributions of this work are summarized as follows:

1. Investigating the impact of multi-task learning (classification and segmentation) on the ability of CNNs to differentiate between various appearances of COVID-19 infections in the lung.
2. Employing self-supervised pre-training approaches, namely MoCo and inpaint-ing-CXR, to eliminate the dependence on expensive ground truth annotations for COVID-19 classification.
3. Conducting a critical evaluation of the best performing model to provide insights into the difficulties of fine-grained COVID-19 multi-class classification from chest X-rays.

2   Method

In this work, we trained different deep model architectures to classify each input X-ray image into one of four classes: negative for pneumonia, typical, indeterminate, or atypical appearance of COVID-19. We employed two main elements of the SIIM-FISABIO-RSNA COVID-19 [20] winning solutions, namely pre-training and multi-task learning, and compared them against self-supervised learning approaches to analyze their impact and generalizability on fine-grained COVID-19 multi-class classification.

2.1   Baseline Model

The baseline CNN was chosen from four architectures to explore the performance of lightweight models like MobileNet [14] and EfficientNet [36] against dense models such as ResNet [13] and DenseNet [15]. DenseNet-121 was selected for comparison and evaluation of the different approaches due to its balance between accuracy and training speed, supported by its success with CXRs reported in literature [30].

2.2   Multi-task Learning

Multi-task learning aims to utilize information from multiple tasks in order to improve the performance and generalizability of the model [41]. Inspired by the winning solution of the SIIM-FISABIO-RSNA COVID-19 Detection challenge [24], we employ multi-task learning to improve the classification performance. The first stage of the solution consists of a pre-trained encoder for classification, while the second stage consists of a pre-trained encoder-decoder architecture that is later fine-tuned on the COVID-19 dataset to learn both classification and segmentation tasks. The segmentation was performed using the ground truth bounding boxes converted to opacity masks. A Dice-Weighted Cross Entropy loss is used as the multi-task loss, where W_{CE} and W_{Dice} are the weights for each loss component, and w_c is the weight of each class:

$$L_{DiceWCE} = W_{CE}(-\sum_{c=1}^{C} w_c y^c \log \hat{y}^c) + W_{Dice}(1 - \frac{2\sum_{c=1}^{C}\sum_{i=1}^{N} g_i^c s_i^c}{\sum_{c=1}^{C}\sum_{i=1}^{N} g_i^c + \sum_{c=1}^{C}\sum_{i=1}^{N} s_i^c}) \quad (1)$$

2.3 Self-supervised Pre-training

Self-supervised pre-training has proven effective in numerous medical tasks with a scarcity of labelled training data, e.g. [23,26,34]. Self-supervised deep CNN models have also been employed to classify COVID-19 cases from chest X-ray images and to deal with the problem of class imbalance [11]. We employed MoCo [34] and inpainting [27] as constrastive and generative self-supervised learning (SSL) techniques trained on a large unlabelled dataset, then fine-tuned on the COVID-19 dataset to classify the above-mentioned four classes.

MoCo-CXR. Adding to the work of [34], we introduced further augmentation strategies to the MoCo-CXR architecture: horizontal translation, random scaling, and rotation. We also decreased the InfoNCE loss [25] temperature value, where InfoNCE is defined as

$$L_q = -log(\frac{exp(qk_+/\tau)}{\sum_{i=0}^{k} exp(qk_i/\tau)}) \quad (2)$$

where it measures the cosine distance between a key k_i and query input q and applies scaling to the distance by a temperature parameter τ. We pre-trained DenseNet-121 using the original MoCo-CXR [34], the modified MoCo-CXR approach, and MoCo-V2 [6].

Inpainting-CXR. Based on [27], we also explored the impact of Inpainting-CXR, a focused lung masking inpainting strategy on the model's ability to learn effective representations to identify chest abnormalities. Using this as a pretext task, we applied targeted lung masking by approximating its location for both lungs (Fig. 1). Additionally, center inpainting was also explored, where a center mask is created on the X-ray images, and the model is tasked with reconstructing the original masked region. Figure 2 shows the center mask and Inpainting-CXR (left and right targeted lung mask) with the reconstructed images.

3 Dataset

The primary dataset used for classification in this study is the SIIM-FISABIO-RSNA COVID-19 Detection dataset curated by an international group of 22 radiologists [20]. It includes data from the Valencian Region Medical ImageBank (BIMCV) [16] and the Medical Imaging Data Resource Center (MIDRC) - RSNA International COVID-19 Open Radiology Database (RICORD) [37]. The dataset

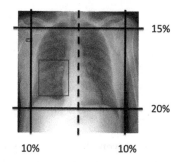

Fig. 1. Mask region constraint for SSL Inpainting-CXR. This is performed by posing the following constraints: 10% from the left and right, 15% from the top, and 20% from the bottom of the chest X-rays.

available for training is composed of 6,054 individual cases (6,334 radiographs), with each case being labelled as negative, typical, indeterminate, or atypical appearance of pneumonia. The dataset also includes radiologists' bounding box annotations that highlight regions of opacities within the chest X-rays.

In addition to the SIIM-FISABIO-RSNA dataset, the CheXpert [18] and RSNA [1] datasets were also used for pre-training. CheXpert is a multilabel dataset composed of 224,316 chest radiographs of 65,240 patients with the presence of 13 chest abnormalities. RSNA is a subset of CheXpert; a pneumonia detection dataset consisting of CXRs from 26,684 patients labelled according to the presence or absence of lung opacities. With such large number of chest radiographs containing various manifestations in the lungs including pneumonia, pleural effusion, consolidation and others, these datasets were chosen for pre-training.

4   Experimental Settings

The baseline DenseNet-121 CNN model was trained with an input size of 224×224 and batch size of 16. A cross-entropy loss function along with ADAM optimizer and learning rate of 0.001 were used. The following augmentations were performed: horizontal flip, rotation up to $\pm 10°$, and scaling up to 20%. For pre-processing, we applied winsorization at 92.5-percentile and normalization between 0 and 1 for the image pixel values.

The multi-task learning encoder-decoder architecture consists of a UNet with a DenseNet-121 backbone. In the first stage, DenseNet-121 was pre-trained for 30 epochs on CheXpert [18], then the weights were transferred to initialize the encoder of UNet in the second stage. The encoder-decoder model was trained for segmentation and classification for 30 epochs on RSNA dataset [1] using a Dice-Cross Entropy compound loss with equal weights. Finally, the pre-trained weights were used to fine-tune the encoder-decoder on the COVID-19 dataset using a Dice-Weighted Cross Entropy loss with a weight of 0.6 and 0.4, respectively. The different classes in Weighted Cross Entropy loss were weighted by 0.2,

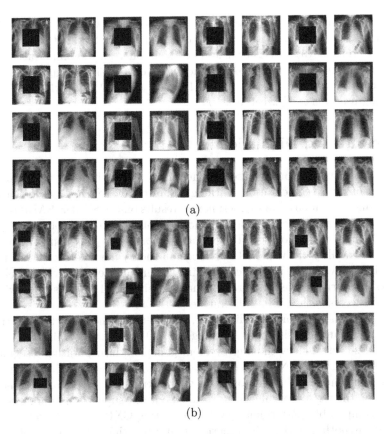

(a)

(b)

Fig. 2. Visualization of inpainting self-supervised pre-training model output, showing image reconstruction from (a) center mask and (b) targeted left and right mask (inpainting-CXR).

0.2, 0.3, and 0.3 for negative, typical, indeterminate, and atypical respectively. The model was optimized with ADAM optimizer using an initial learning rate of 0.0001 and Cosine Annealing LR scheduler.

For self-supervised learning, CheXpert [18] was used without labels for pre-training. DenseNet-121 was chosen as the key and queue encoder for MoCo-CXR, modified MoCo-CXR, and MoCo-V2. For MoCo-V2, the model applied the default augmentations from [34] which included 224×224 pixel crop, random color jittering, random horizontal flip, random gray scale conversion, and image blur. We evaluated MoCo-CXR [6] with the two default augmentations, horizontal flipping and random rotation of $\pm 10°$. We further modified the MoCo-CXR augmentation strategy by increasing the rotation angle to $\pm 20°$, adding horizontal translation 20%, randomly scaling the image in range of $100 - 120\%$, and decreasing the temperature value of the InfoNCE loss from 0.2 to 0.07.

For inpaiting SSL, we substituted the original AlexNet encoder with DenseNet-121. We trained the model using the Mean Squared Error (MSE) loss, and omitted the adversarial loss to focus on transferability rather than fine reconstruction. The targeted left and right lung masking (inpainting-CXR) was used with varying mask sizes from 17×17 up to 32×32, while the center inpainting used mask of size 100×100.

5   Results and Discussion

We first chose an appropriate baseline, then investigated the impact of multi-task classification and segmentation learning, followed by self-supervised learning. Tables 1 and 2 summarize our experimental results on the SIIM-FISABIO-RSNA dataset. Assessing the best performing models from the 80/20% split (Table 1) on the 5-fold cross-validation set (Table 2) allows for better judgment surrounding the generalizability of the model. We focus on the F_1-macro score to ensure fair comparison between the models considering the unbalanced nature of the classes. Our best performing baseline architecture is DenseNet-121, consistent with its reported success with CXRs in literature [30] (Table 3).

Following the baseline establishment, we evaluated the impact of multi-task segmentation and classification learning on COVID-19 fine-grained classification. Tables 1 and 2 show the improvement gain from incorporating a segmentation head and using RSNA pre-training, providing evidence for the effectiveness of including bounding box annotations during training to localize the model's learning on the regions of infection. Notably, our self-supervised approaches also achieve comparable performance, with inpainting-CXR outperforming MoCo-CXR. We hypothesize that the superiority of inpainting-CXR over MoCo-CXR is likely due to its generative nature where the model is forced to learn the distinctive features of the lungs and diseases through reconstruction. While the performance of inpainting-CXR is slightly lower on average than multi-task learning, this method completely avoids the need for expensive bounding box annotations, highlighting an exciting avenue for further exploration particularly in the use of generative self-supervised learning for CXR pathology identification.

Nevertheless, a question remains regarding the deploy-readiness of current models in clinical settings. In the following sections, we provide a critical evaluation of the solutions and demonstrate the challenges and difficulties of COVID-19 fine-grained classification. For further evaluation of the results, we present a thorough analysis with regards to model interpretability.

Table 1. Experimental results for 80–20% train-test split of the SIIM-FISABIO-RSNA dataset.

Approach	F_1 score	Acc. (%)
Baseline: DenseNet-121	0.4205	57.34
Multi-task (MT) without pre-training	0.4300	64.16
MT pre-trained RSNA enc	0.4401	62.23
MT pre-trained RSNA enc. + dec.	**0.4794**	**61.77**
SSL MoCo-CXR	0.4305	58.69
SSL Modified MoCo-CXR	0.4325	59.71
SSL MoCo-V2	0.4583	58.60
SSL Center inpainting	0.4472	59.62
SSL Inpainting-CXR	**0.4706**	**65.22**

Table 2. Experimental results for 5-fold cross-validation on the baseline and top performing solutions of the SIIM-FISABIO-RSNA dataset.

Approach	F_1 score	Acc. (%)
Baseline: DenseNet-121	0.4205 ± 0.0149	57.34 ± 2.79
MT pre-trained RSNA enc. + dec.	**0.4621 ± 0.0099**	**64.07 ± 1.21**
SSL Inpainting-CXR	**0.4599 ± 0.0137**	59.55 ± 1.07

Table 3. Comparison of CNN architectures to define baseline.

Experiments	F_1 score	Acc. (%)
MobileNet	0.3356	57.18
EfficientNet	0.3434	61.47
ResNet-50	0.1617	47.80
DenseNet-121	**0.4345**	58.19

5.1 Lack of Visual Cues in COVID-19 CXRs

CNNs have recorded successes in many medical applications, including in CXRs. Unlike the manifestations of other pathologies such as cardiomegaly (which is characterized by the size of the object of interest) or tuberculosis (which is characterized by the presence of bacteria occurring in colonies), the precise identification of COVID-19 from CXRs presents a particular challenge even to the experienced radiologists [38]. We present the feature maps of tuberculosis and COVID-19 in Figs. 3 and 4 respectively, and show that the learned representations of the latter is much harder than the former. This is likely due to the prevalence of ground-glass opacities in COVID-19 which tend to be more dispersed, fine-to-absent in texture, and typically less concentrated in appearance [3,9,12] – that even on images with more obvious manifestations of COVID-19 (as in Fig. 4), the model is unable to learn proper representations. From a machine learning perspective, the challenge for CNNs stems from the lack of well-defined shapes, sizes, or edges of the infections. CNNs, on the other hand, heavily rely on edge detections, as evidenced by the feature maps shown.

5.2   (Mis)learned Representations

As we have demonstrated the difficulty of COVID-19 detection from CXRs, the question then becomes, what does the model learn? We present the GradCAM [32] outputs of the baseline, MoCo, and inpainting experiments in Fig. 5. Evidently, the model is better able to localize the lung regions when using MoCo and inpainting self-supervised pre-training (Fig. 5; columns 3 and 4), while the decision-making appears to be more sporadic and irregular on the baseline model (Fig. 5; column 2).

A closer inspection of the SSL GradCAMs reveals that the correctly predicted regions (Fig. 5; rows 1–3) are extensive, encompass the majority of the lungs, and have large corresponding regions of infection. We note that the correctly predicted images also belong primarily to the typical class, and that the average areas of infection for the typical class, represented by the bounding box dimensions, is higher than that of the atypical and indeterminate classes (Fig. 6). Conversely, the incorrectly predicted regions (Fig. 5; rows 4–6) are also extensive and highlight the majority of the lungs, but have smaller regions of infection that are often missed by the model. This suggests that the correct predictions of the model may not necessarily be attributed to the true regions of infection within the lungs, but rather to some other non-causal or false positive features of the lung.

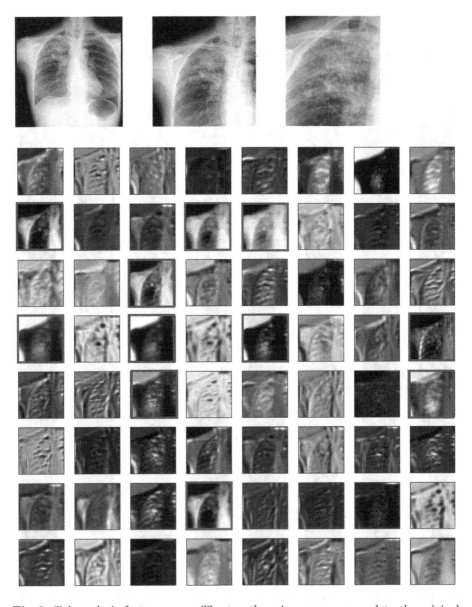

Fig. 3. Tuberculosis feature maps. The top three images correspond to the original CXR (image source [22]), a zoomed-in section nearing the area of infection from which the feature maps are created, and a zoomed-in section directly on the area of infection based on the radiologist's ground truth annotation. We outlined some feature maps that we think may have been pertinent to the model's ability to delineate the features of tuberculosis in the upper lobe of the right lung. The feature maps were created using DenseNet-121 pre-trained on CheXpert and fine-tuned on TBX11K [22].

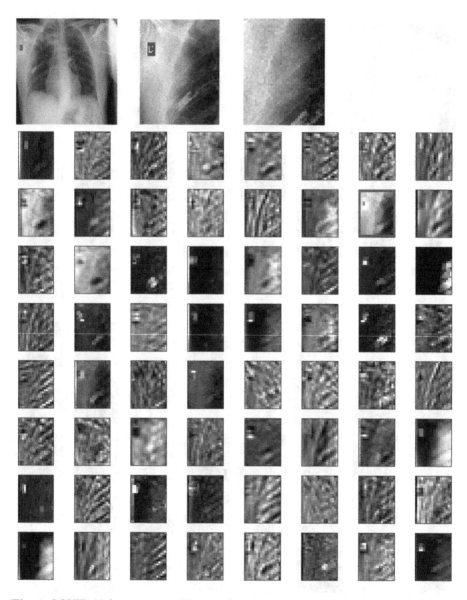

Fig. 4. COVID-19 feature maps. The top three images correspond to the original CXR, a zoomed-in section nearing the area of infection from which the feature maps are created, and a zoomed-in section directly on the area of infection based on the radiologist's ground truth annotation. We outlined the feature map that we think may have been pertinent to the model's ability to delineate the features of COVID-19. Most feature maps were unable to identify the features of infection on the periphery of the left lung. The feature maps were created using DenseNet-121 pre-trained on CheXpert and fine-tuned on SIIM-FISABIO-RSNA COVID-19 [20].

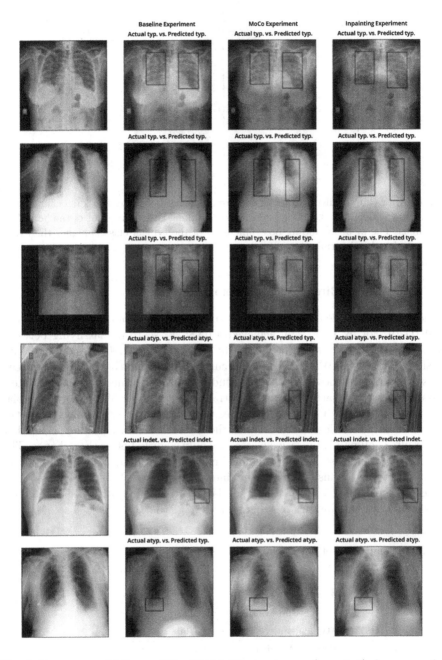

Fig. 5. Successes and failures of GradCAM. The top images (rows 1–3) show examples where the GradCAM outputs correctly localize the regions of infection, while the bottom images (rows 4–6) show examples of incorrect predictions. The bounding boxes display the ground truth radiologists' annotations as provided by the challenge. The heatmap importance increases from red to blue. (Color figure online)

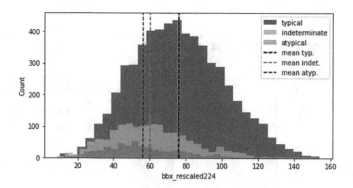

Fig. 6. Approximate distribution of the ground truth bounding box dimensions after re-scaling the CXRs to 224 × 224, generated by taking the square root of the bounding box areas. The mean bounding box dimension of the typical class is higher than that of atypical and indeterminate.

5.3   COVID-19 Binary Classifications

Some studies have demonstrated great successes in the binary classification of COVID-19. For example, [39] achieved a 0.985 F_1-score in classifying between positive and negative cases of COVID-19; [40] reported a 1.00-F_1-score in distinguishing between COVID-19 and tuberculosis. Arguably, the variation between classes is larger in these cases as the studies were performed to separate inter-class differences. We are interested in intraclass differences. We perform an ablation study of each pair of positive classes using DenseNet-121 to investigate the model's ability to differentiate between the COVID-19 cases. Table 4 shows that the results of all pairs of positive classes are only slightly better than chance. The t-SNEs (Fig. 7) also show poorly defined clusters that alludes to the inability of the model to distinguish between the fine-grained COVID-19 classes. However, a clearer separation is evident in the classification of positive-negative cases, consistent with the findings of other studies (e.g., [39]).

Table 4. Comparison of binary classifications for COVID-19 pneumonia appearances.

Binary classes	F_1 score	Acc. (%)
Typical-Indeterminate	0.6177	70.24
Atypical-Indeterminate	0.5760	66.77
Typical-Atypical	0.6252	85.96
Positive-Negative	0.7735	81.98

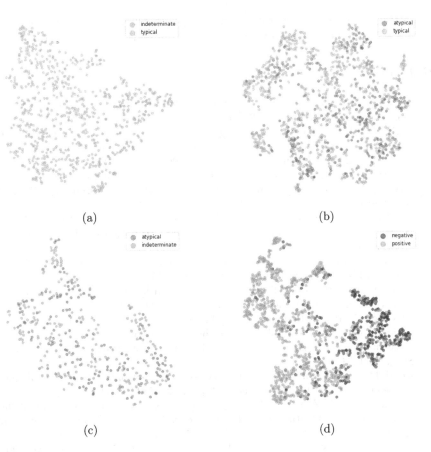

(a)

(b)

(c)

(d)

Fig. 7. t-SNEs of the last DenseNet-121 block of our best-performing model conditioned on the true labels for (a) typical-indeterminate, (b) typical-atypical, (c) atypical-indeterminate, and (d) positive-negative COVID-19 classes.

6   Conclusion

In this work, we have shown the merit of our self-supervised inpainting-CXR method that rivals the performance of multi-task segmentation and classification learning in COVID-19 multi-class classification. We discuss the challenges surrounding the fine-grained distinction of COVID-19 appearances and delve deep into the obstacles hindering the use of current models to develop a clinically viable solution for COVID-19 infections from chest radiographs. We believe among the reasons for the low performance of current models are due to the tendency of CNNs to rely on edge detections and the corresponding lack of visual cues prevalent in COVID-19 CXRs due to the presence of diffused ground-glass opacities. Our work may spark further interest in the community in the use of generative self-supervised learning as a cost-effective method to achieve desirable results without the need for expensive labelled bounding box annotations.

References

1. RSNA pneumonia detection challenge (2018). www.kaggle.com/competitions/rsna-pneumonia-detection-challenge
2. Alghamdi, H.S., Amoudi, G., Elhag, S., Saeedi, K., Nasser, J.: Deep learning approaches for detecting covid-19 from chest x-ray images: a survey. IEEE Access **9**, 20235–20254 (2021). https://doi.org/10.1109/ACCESS.2021.3054484
3. Bai, H., et al.: Performance of radiologists in differentiating covid-19 from viral pneumonia on chest CT. Radiology **296**, 200823 (2020). https://doi.org/10.1148/radiol.2020200823
4. Barstugan, M., Ozkaya, U., Ozturk, S.: Coronavirus (covid-19) classification using CT images by machine learning methods (2020). https://doi.org/10.48550/ARXIV.2003.09424
5. Burki, T.: Outbreak of coronavirus disease 2019. Lancet Infect. Dis. **20**(3), 292–293 (2020). https://doi.org/10.1016/S1473-3099(20)30076-1
6. Chen, X., Fan, H., Girshick, R., He, K.: Improved baselines with momentum contrastive learning (2020). https://doi.org/10.48550/ARXIV.2003.04297
7. Cleverley, J., Piper, J., Jones, M.M.: The role of chest radiography in confirming covid-19 pneumonia. BMJ **370** (2020). https://doi.org/10.1136/BMJ.M2426
8. Coccolini, F., et al.: A pandemic recap: lessons we have learned. World J. Emerg. Surg. **16**(1), 1–8 (2021)
9. Cozzi, D., et al.: Ground-glass opacity (GGO): a review of the differential diagnosis in the era of covid-19. Jpn. J. Radiol. **39**(8), 721–732 (2021)
10. Ji, D., Zhang, Z., Zhao, Y., Zhao, Q.: Research on classification of covid-19 chest x-ray image modal feature fusion based on deep learning. J. Healthcare Eng. **2021** (2021)
11. Gazda, M., Plavka, J., Gazda, J., Drotar, P.: Self-supervised deep convolutional neural network for chest x-ray classification. IEEE Access **9**, 151972–151982 (2021). https://doi.org/10.1109/access.2021.3125324
12. Hansell, D.M., Bankier, A.A., Macmahon, H., McLoud, T.C., Müller, N.L., Remy, J.: Fleischner society: glossary of terms for thoracic imaging. Radiology **246**(3), 697–722 (2008)
13. He, K., Zhang, X., Ren, S., Sun, J.: Deep residual learning for image recognition (2015). https://doi.org/10.48550/ARXIV.1512.03385
14. Howard, A.G., et al.: Mobilenets: Efficient convolutional neural networks for mobile vision applications (2017)
15. Huang, G., Liu, Z., van der Maaten, L., Weinberger, K.Q.: Densely connected convolutional networks (2018)
16. de la Iglesia Vayá, M., et al.: Bimcv covid-19+: a large annotated dataset of RX and CT images from covid-19 patients (2020)
17. Inui, S., et al.: The role of chest imaging in the diagnosis, management, and monitoring of coronavirus disease 2019 (covid-19). Insights Imaging **12**(1), 1–14 (2021)
18. Irvin, J., et al.: Chexpert: a large chest radiograph dataset with uncertainty labels and expert comparison (2019)
19. Jia, G., Lam, H.K., Xu, Y.: Classification of covid-19 chest x-ray and CT images using a type of dynamic CNN modification method. Comput. Biol. Med. **134**, 104425 (2021)

20. Lakhani, P., et al.: The 2021 SIIM-FISABIO-RSNA machine learning covid-19 challenge: Annotation and standard exam classification of covid-19 chest radiographs. (2021). https://doi.org/10.31219/osf.io/532ek
21. Litmanovich, D.E., Chung, M., Kirkbride, R.R., Kicska, G., Kanne, J.P.: Review of chest radiograph findings of covid-19 pneumonia and suggested reporting language. J. Thoracic Imaging **35**(6), 354–360 (2020)
22. Liu, Y., Wu, Y.H., Ban, Y., Wang, H., Cheng, M.M.: Rethinking computer-aided tuberculosis diagnosis. In: Proceedings of the IEEE/CVF Conference on Computer Vision and Pattern Recognition, pp. 2646–2655 (2020)
23. Miller, J.D., Arasu, V.A., Pu, A.X., Margolies, L.R., Sieh, W., Shen, L.: Self-supervised deep learning to enhance breast cancer detection on screening mammography (2022). https://doi.org/10.48550/ARXIV.2203.08812
24. Nguyen, D.B.: 1st place solution for SIIM-FISABIO-RSNA covid-19 detection challenge (2021). https://github.com/dungnb1333/SIIM-COVID19-Detection
25. van den Oord, A., Li, Y., Vinyals, O.: Representation learning with contrastive predictive coding. CoRR abs/1807.03748 (2018)
26. Ouyang, C., Biffi, C., Chen, C., Kart, T., Qiu, H., Rueckert, D.: Self-supervised learning for few-shot medical image segmentation. IEEE Trans. Med. Imaging (2022). https://doi.org/10.1109/TMI.2022.3150682
27. Pathak, D., Krähenbühl, P., Donahue, J., Darrell, T., Efros, A.A.: Context encoders: feature learning by inpainting. CoRR abs/1604.07379 (2016)
28. Pathak, Y., Shukla, P., Tiwari, A., Stalin, S., Singh, S., Shukla, P.: Deep transfer learning based classification model for COVID-19 disease. Innov. Res. BioMedical Eng. (IRBM) **43**(2), 87–92 (2022). https://doi.org/10.1016/j.irbm.2020.05.003
29. Pham, T.D.: Classification of covid-19 chest x-rays with deep learning: new models or fine tuning? Health Inf. Sci. Syst. **9**(1), 1–11 (2021)
30. Rajpurkar, P., et al.: Chexnet: radiologist-level pneumonia detection on chest x-rays with deep learning. CoRR abs/1711.05225 (2017)
31. Roberts, M.: Common pitfalls and recommendations for using machine learning to detect and prognosticate for covid-19 using chest radiographs and ct scans. Nat. Mach. Intell. **3**(3), 199–217 (2021)
32. Selvaraju, R.R., Das, A., Vedantam, R., Cogswell, M., Parikh, D., Batra, D.: Grad-cam: why did you say that? visual explanations from deep networks via gradient-based localization. CoRR abs/1610.02391 (2016)
33. Simpson, S., et al.: Radiological society of North America expert consensus document on reporting chest CT findings related to covid-19: endorsed by the society of thoracic radiology, the American college of radiology, and RSNA. Radiol. Cardiothoracic Imaging **2**(2), e200152 (2020)
34. Sowrirajan, H., Yang, J., Ng, A.Y., Rajpurkar, P.: Moco-cxr: moco pretraining improves representation and transferability of chest x-ray models. In: Proceedings of Machine Learning Research, vol. 143, pp. 727–743 (2021). https://doi.org/10.48550/ARXIV.2010.05352
35. Struyf, T., et al.: Signs and symptoms to determine if a patient presenting in primary care or hospital outpatient settings has covid-19. Cochrane Database Syst. Rev. (2) (2021). https://doi.org/10.1002/14651858.CD013665.pub2
36. Tan, M., Le, Q.V.: Efficientnet: rethinking model scaling for convolutional neural networks (2019). https://doi.org/10.48550/ARXIV.1905.11946
37. Tsai, E.B., et al.: The RSNA international covid-19 open radiology database (RICORD). Radiology **299**(1), E204–E213 (2021)

38. Williams, G.J., et al.: Variability and accuracy in interpretation of consolidation on chest radiography for diagnosing pneumonia in children under 5 years of age. Pediatr. Pulmonol. **48**(12), 1195–1200 (2013)
39. Yang, D., Martinez, C., Visuña, L., Khandhar, H., Bhatt, C., Carretero, J.: Detection and analysis of COVID-19 in medical images using deep learning techniques. Sci. Rep. **11**(1) (2021). https://doi.org/10.1038/s41598-021-99015-3
40. Yoo, S.H., et al.: Deep learning-based decision-tree classifier for COVID-19 diagnosis from chest x-ray imaging. Front. Med. **7** (2020). https://doi.org/10.3389/fmed.2020.00427
41. Zhang, Y., Yang, Q.: A survey on multi-task learning. IEEE Trans. Knowl. Data Eng. (2021). https://doi.org/10.1109/tkde.2021.3070203

Image Segmentation

Ultrasonography Uterus and Fetus Segmentation with Constrained Spatial-Temporal Memory FCN

Bin Kong[1], Xin Wang[1(✉)], Yi Lu[1], Hao-Yu Yang[1], Kunlin Cao[2], Qi Song[2], and Youbing Yin[1(✉)]

[1] Keya Medical, Seattle, WA, USA
{xinw,yin}@keyamedna.com
[2] Keya Medical, Shenzehn, Guangdong, China

Abstract. Automatic segmentation of uterus and fetus from 3D fetal ultrasound images remains a challenging problem due to multiple issues of fetal ultrasound, e.g., the relatively low image quality, intensity variations. In this work, we present a novel framework for the joint segmentation of uterus and fetus. It consists of two main components: a task-specific fully convolutional neural network (FCN) and a bidirectional convolutional LSTM (BiCLSTM). Our framework is inspired by a simple observation: the segmentation task can be decomposed into multiple easier-to-solve subproblems. More specifically, the encoder of the FCN extracts object-relevant features from the ultrasound slices. The BiCLSTM layer is responsible for modeling the inter-slice correlations. The final two branches of the FCN decoder produce the uterus and fetus predictions. In this way, the burden of the whole problem is evenly distributed among different parts of our network, thereby maximally exploiting the capacity of our network. Furthermore, we propose a spatially constrained loss to restrict the spatial positions of the segmented uterus and fetus to boost the performance. Quantitative results demonstrate the effectiveness of the proposed method.

Keywords: Fetal ultrasonography · Uterus and fetus segmentation · Bidirectional convolutional LSTM · Task-specific FCN

1 Introduction

Ultrasound imaging is a dominant technique for prenatal examination and diagnosis due to several important advantages: relatively low-cost, no radiation damage, and real-time imaging capability [5,16,22]. Periodical prenatal ultrasound screenings are strongly recommended in obstetrics for prognosis [1,7,17]. Providing a volumetric view for anatomy inspection and offering potentials for a number of crucial studies (e.g., calculating the fetus volumes), 3D ultrasound is becoming increasingly popular than 2D ultrasound.

Traditionally, ultrasound screening is conducted by manually annotating and interpreting multiple clinically important biometrics. This process requires experienced

© The Author(s), under exclusive license to Springer Nature Switzerland AG 2022
G. Yang et al. (Eds.): MIUA 2022, LNCS 13413, pp. 253–261, 2022.
https://doi.org/10.1007/978-3-031-12053-4_19

obstetricians a significant amount of time and suffers from intra- and inter-variability. Semi-automatic approaches [4,13] have been adopted to alleviate these issues. However, this still requires cumbersome and subjective interactions. In this regard, automatic solutions are highly desirable for fetal ultrasound image analysis. In this work, we focus on the automatic segmentation of uterus and fetus from 3D fetal ultrasound images (Fig. 1). Automatic segmentation of uterus and fetus from 3D fetal ultrasound images remains a challenging problem due to multiple issues of ultrasound images, e.g., the relatively low image quality, various intensity distributions, and different fetal postures and various scanning directions.

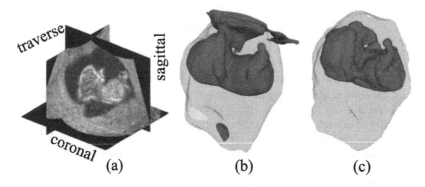

Fig. 1. (a) 3D prenatal utrasound volume with three axes: traverse, coronal and sagittal. (b) Segmentation results of 3D Unet, the fetus body (red) leaks to the outside of the uterus (green). (c) Segmentation results of our spatial constrained model. (Color figure online)

Much effort has been made to address these challenges. For instance, tissue intensity distributions are utilized to segment utero-fetal volume in [2,6]. Lee et al. [10] traced limb boundaries to estimate fetal weight. Random forests are leveraged to segment fetal brain structures and femur in 3D ultrasound [21]. Nevertheless, their performances of these methods are confined by the handcrafted descriptors or their limited capabilities to model objects with highly varying appearances and shapes. Deep neural networks have the potential to overcome these issues. Recently, they have been adopted to segment key anatomic structures from ultrasound images. For example, Looney [12] utilized a 3D FCN model to segment placenta from ultrasound images. Nevertheless, they only focused on the segmentation of a single object. Although Yang et al. [20] dedicated to simultaneously segmenting fetus, gestational sac, and placenta from ultrasound images with 3D FCN, they failed to leverage the spatial correlations of these object. Enforcing structural constraints has been advocated to improve deep learning based frameworks' performance [8,9], but it's not obvious how to directly apply these methods to uterus and fetus segmentation. To this end, one should seek a solution of incorporating the spatial correlations between the objects into the learning procedure (Fig. 1 (b) and (c)). Additionally, performing 3D convolution on highly anisotropic (the spacings for different dimensions are highly variant) 3D medical images introduces two problems, as is pointed out in [3]. First, 3D FCN often requires a significant amount of parameters.

Thus, it is prone to overfitting on a small labeled training dataset, which is often the case in medical imaging. Second, utilizing isotropic convolutional kernels on anisotropic 3D medical images are problematic.

In this work, we present a novel network to address the above limitations. It consists of two main components: a task specific FCN and a bidirectional convolutional LSTM (BiCLSTM) layer [15,18,19]. To be specific, our framework has three phases, encoding, temporal feature learning, and decoding. In the first and third phases, the FCN acts as an encoder and a decoder to learn the spatial patterns of the fetal ultrasound slices, and the BiCLSTM layer learns the temporal information of the slices. The primary contributions of this paper are three-fold. First, we present a BiCLSTM based framework for the joint segmentation of uterus and fetus. Benefited from the ability of BiCLSTM to process sequential data, the proposed method can elegantly address the anisotropic issue. Second, our network is proposed to decompose the two tasks to ease the training. Finally, a spatially constrained loss is designed to address the problem of the ambiguity boundary of both uterus and fetal body. Extensive experimental results demonstrate that the proposed network can handle the fuzzy boundary challenge and give reasonable performance in the uterus and fetal body segmentation.

2   Methodology

2.1   Overview

Our goal is to perform the joint segmentation of uterus and fetus from 3D ultrasound images. The schematic view of the proposed network is illustrated in Fig. 2. The backbone structure of the network is a task-specific FCN. It extracts features from the slices of ultrasound images and generates the final predictions. Another important component of our network, BiCLSTM, helps the FCN to consider the inter-slice correlations.

2.2   Task-Specific FCN

The task-specific FCN consists of two subnets: an encoder and a decoder. The encoder subnet is employed to extract object-relevant (e.g., texture, shapes of uterus and fetus) feature maps for the slices that are invariant to object-irrelevant information (e.g., voxel intensities and noises). In this way, our BiCLSTM layer can focus on learning the inter-slice spatio-temporal correlations to generate the refined feature map. The decoder subnet is responsible for generating the final predictions for uterus and fetus based on the refined feature map. Li et al. [11] demonstrated that a traditional multi-class segmentation network is inferior to a network using multiple prediction branches with each branch generating one object segmentation. The reasonable explanation is that the complex multi-class segmentation problem is decomposed into multiple relatively easier subproblems. Our FCN network follows this approach. It has 2 branches for predicting the uterus and fetus masks. Figure 2 shows the detailed structure of the encoder and decoder. The encoder comprises 4 convolutional layers and the decoder consists of 6 convolutional layers. The kernel size of each convolutional layer is 3×3, which is further followed by a batch normalization and rectified linear unit (ReLU) layer (except for the last two layers denoted by green and red color).

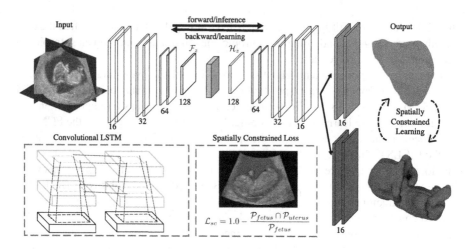

Fig. 2. Schematic view of the proposed constrained spatial-temporal memory FCN network.

2.3 Bidirectional Convolutional LSTM

The task-specific FCN component consider the slices independently. Obviously, FCN componnet is not enough for generating a satisfactory result as it does not consider the inter-slice dependencies. We employ BiCLSTM to obtain the spatial-temporal correlations in the slices. BiCLSTM is extended from covolutional LSTM (CLSTM) [18] and CLSTM is derived from LSTM network. LSTM contains memory blocks which can let it learn and exploit long-range context of input sequences. Nevertheless, the formulation of LSTM is fully-connected and the spatial information is not considered. The CLSTM is proposed by Shi et al. [18] to address this issue. As a standard LSTM, it has three gates to control the information flow, i.e., input gate i_z, forget gate f_z, and output gate o_z. The hidden state $\mathcal{H}_z$ and the memory cell $\mathcal{C}_z$ of unit z can be updated as[1]:

$$i_z = \sigma \left(W_i * \mathcal{F}_z + U_i * \mathcal{H}_{z-1} \right), \tag{1}$$

$$f_z = \sigma \left(W_f * \mathcal{F}_z + U_f * \mathcal{H}_{z-1} \right), \tag{2}$$

$$o_z = \sigma \left(W_o * \mathcal{F}_z + U_o * \mathcal{H}_{z-1} \right), \tag{3}$$

$$\mathcal{M}_z = \tanh \left(W_m * \mathcal{F}_z + U_m * \mathcal{H}_{z-1} \right), \tag{4}$$

$$\mathcal{C}_z = f_z \odot \mathcal{C}_{z-1} + i_z \odot \mathcal{M}_z, \tag{5}$$

$$\mathcal{H}_z = o_z \odot \tanh(\mathcal{C}_z), \tag{6}$$

where $*$ and $\odot$ denote convolutional operation and element-wise multiplication, respectively, $\mathcal{F}_z$ is the input image at the current time step z. W_i, U_i, W_f, U_f, W_o, U_o, W_m, and U_m are the weight matrices for the input, forget, and output gates, and memory cell, respectively. $\mathcal{C}_z$ is the memory cell.

BiCLSTM is a stack of two layers of CLSTM, which are organized in two opposite directions (z^+ and z^-). BiCLSTM layer learns the temporal information of the input

---

[1] We assume zero biases in Eq. (1)–(6) for simplicity.

image along the two directions of the z-axis. The final output of BiCLSTM is a combination of the results of the two CLSTM layers. The detailed procedure is as follows. First, these two CLSTM layers integrate the information from the z^+ and z^- directions, respectively. Then, the final output is generated by summing up the hidden states of both layers for each slice.

2.4 Joint Uterus and Fetus Segmentation

The detailed procedure for joint segmentation of uterus and fetus is as follows. First, We split the input 3D ultrasound volume $\mathcal{I}$ into a sequence of 2D slices $\{\mathcal{X}_1, \mathcal{X}_2, ..., \mathcal{X}_T\}$ along the sagittal axis (z-axis), where T is the number of slices in this volume. The proposed model is composed of two main components: a task-specific FCN composed of an encoder and a decoder, and a BiCLSTM layer. First, the slices go through the encoder, yielding the latent representation $\{\mathcal{F}_1, \mathcal{F}_2, ..., \mathcal{F}_T\}$. Second, the BiCLSTM is utilized to consider spatial-temporal correlations of the consecutive slices, generating $\{\mathcal{H}_1, \mathcal{H}_2, ..., \mathcal{H}_T\}$. Finally, the decoder generates the final predictions.

The motivation of the proposed framework is to decompose the multi-class segmentation problem into multiple easier-to-solve subproblems. More specifically, the encoder extracts and compresses the input slices into object-relevant feature maps. BiCLSTM is only responsible for considering the inter-slice correlations. Additionally, two branches of the decoder produces the fetus and uterus predictions, respectively. In this way, the burden of whole problem is evenly distributed among different parts of our network, thereby maximally exploiting the capacity of our network.

2.5 Learning with Spatial Constrained Loss

Fianlly, our network generates the predictions for uterus $\mathcal{P}_{uterus}$ and fetus $\mathcal{P}_{fetus}$. According to the actual physiological structure, the fetus should be included by uterus. However, in the experiments, we noticed that the fetal body mask is not fully contained in the uterus mask in some of the segmentation results. Obviously, it is not in line with the actual physiological structure. To address this issue, we further propose a spatially constrained loss to penalize the wrong predictions:

$$\mathcal{L}_{sc} = 1.0 - \frac{\mathcal{P}_{fetus} \cap \mathcal{P}_{uterus}}{\mathcal{P}_{fetus}}. \tag{7}$$

If $\mathcal{P}_{fetus}$ is fully contained in $\mathcal{P}_{uterus}$ ($\mathcal{P}_{fetus} \subseteq \mathcal{P}_{uterus}$), the second term of Eq. (7) equals to 1, then $\mathcal{L}_{sc} = 0$. Otherwise, if $\mathcal{P}_{fetus}$ leaks to the outside of $\mathcal{P}_{uterus}$, the second term of Eq. (7) is in the range of $[0, 1)$, then $0 < \mathcal{L}_{sc} \leq 1$. Thus, we have

$$\mathcal{L}_{sc} : \begin{cases} \mathcal{L}_{sc} = 0 & , \mathcal{P}_{fetus} \subseteq \mathcal{P}_{uterus} \\ 0 < \mathcal{L}_{sc} \leq 1, & otherwise. \end{cases} \tag{8}$$

We minimize the averaged sum of dice losses of the predicted uterus and fetus and spatial contrained loss to train the whole network.

3 Experiments

Dataset, Preprocessing and Evaluation Metrics: The dataset used in our experiments consists of 45 3D fetal ultrasound volumes gathered from 20 pregnant women. The fetal gestational age ranges from 11 to 17 weeks. The training and testing set include 17 pregnant women (37 volumes) and 3 pregnant women (8 volumes), respectively. We removed the slices that did not contain the uterus region in all volumes, and the remaining slices were used to evaluate the proposed method. We further resampled all the volumes into the size of 224 × 224 on the x-axis and y-axis. Additionally, the voxel spacing was also adjusted to $1 \times 1 \ mm^2$. The z-axis remains the same. The following evaluation metrics are used for the evaluation: accuracy (Acc), IOU, and dice score.

Implementation Details: Regarding the implementation, all models in the experiments are based on Pytorch. During the training stage, 64 consecutive slices are randomly selected from the training volumes along the z-axis, resulting in a subvolume of size 224 × 224 × 64. Thus, the size of the input feature map for each unit of the BiCLSTM layer is 28 × 28 × 128. The subvolume is further randomly rotated by a 4 multiples of 90° to artificially enlarge the training data. We used the Adam optimizer with the initial learning rate of 1×10^{-4} to train the network. Early-stopping was employed to avoid overfitting.

Main Results: To evaluate the performance of the proposed method, we first compare our framework with [20], the state-of-the-art method for 3D fetal ultrasound segmentation. In this work, the backbone network is a 3D UNet and the encoder has only one branch for multi-class segmentation. As illustrated in Table 1, the proposed method outperforms the 3D UNet based method (3D UNet) for both uterus and fetus in terms of Acc, IOU and Dice. The qualitative comparisions of our method with 3D UNet is also provided in Fig. 3. The uterus and fetus are denoted in red and green color, respectively. The qualitative results also suggest the superior performance of our method. Please refer to the appendix for more qualitative results.

Table 1. Comparison of the proposed method with the state-of-the-art method for fetal ultrasound segmentation (3D UNet [20]), attention augmented 3D UNet (3D attention UNet), multi-branch 3D attention UNet, multi-class version of our network.

Methods	Uterus			Fetus		
	Acc	IOU	Dice	Acc	IOU	Dice
3D UNet [20]	0.931	0.768	0.867	0.949	0.579	0.715
3D attention UNet	0.923	0.614	0.759	0.9643	0.696	0.815
3D attention UNet (multi-branch) [14]	0.953	0.842	0.913	0.969	0.731	0.840
Ours (multi-class)	0.932	0.688	0.812	0.968	0.726	0.840
Ours	**0.958**	**0.865**	**0.927**	**0.970**	**0.747**	**0.854**

Recently, attention has been proven to be beneficial for 3D segmentation [14]. We further compare the proposed method with attention augmented 3D UNet (3D attention

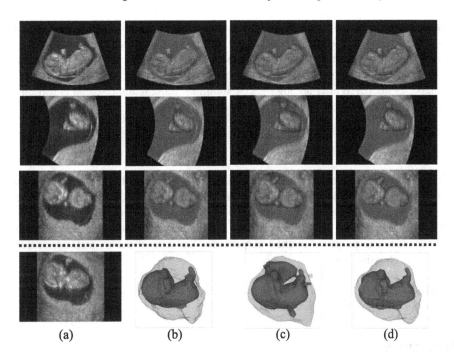

| (a) | (b) | (c) | (d) |

Fig. 3. From left to right: (a) input ultrasound volume, (b) ground truth, segmentation results of (c) 3D UNet and (d) the proposed method. The top three rows shows one slice of the segmentation result. The last row shows the volumetric view of the segmentation results. The uterus and fetus are denoted in red and green color, respectively. (Color figure online)

UNet). The performance significantly improved after adding attention, especially for the IOU and Dice of fetus. Nevertheless, the performance for uterus degraded. We further compare our method with its multi-branch version for multi-class segmentation. The multi-class version is inferior to our framework, especially for the IOU and Dice of uterus. We also compare 3D attention UNet with its multi-branch version (multi-branch 3D attention UNet). Multi-branch 3D attention UNet outperforms 3D attention UNet, demonstrating that decomposing the segmentation task is indeed helpful.

Table 2. Comparison of the proposed method with and without the spatial constrained loss (SCL).

Methods	Uterus			Fetus		
	Acc	IOU	Dice	Acc	IOU	Dice
Ours	95.816	0.865	0.927	96.977	0.747	0.854
Ours w/ SCL	**96.244**	**0.874**	**0.932**	**97.250**	**0.760**	**0.862**

Evaluation of Spatially Constrained Loss: Additional experiment is conducted to evaluate the proposed spatially constrained loss. In this experiment, we compare the proposed network with its final version, with the spatially constrained loss added. Table 2 shows the comparison. According to the results, we can conclude that the performance is improved after adding the constraint, meaning that the spatial constrained loss contributes positively to the proposed network.

4   Conclusion

In this work, we focus on the segmentation of uterus and fetus from 3D prenatal ultrasound images. We divide the problem into multiple easier-to-solve subproblems, which are addressed by different parts of our network. Our prior knowledge regarding the spatial constraint of uterus and fetus is further formulated as a loss function to boost the performance. The proposed method outperforms the state-of-the-art method, demonstrating its effectiveness.

Acknowledgements. This work was supported by Shenzhen Science and Technology Program (Grant No. KQTD2016112809330877).

References

1. Alzubaidi, M., et al.: Towards deep observation: a systematic survey on artificial intelligence techniques to monitor fetus via ultrasound images. arXiv preprint arXiv:2201.07935 (2022)
2. Anquez, J., Angelini, E.D., Grangé, G., Bloch, I.: Automatic segmentation of antenatal 3-d ultrasound images. IEEE Trans. Biomed. Eng. **60**(5), 1388–1400 (2013)
3. Chen, J., Yang, L., Zhang, Y., Alber, M., Chen, D.Z.: Combining fully convolutional and recurrent neural networks for 3d biomedical image segmentation. In: Advances in Neural Information Processing Systems, pp. 3036–3044 (2016)
4. Fiorentino, M.C., Villani, F.P., Di Cosmo, M., Frontoni, E., Moccia, S.: A review on deep-learning algorithms for fetal ultrasound-image analysis. arXiv preprint arXiv:2201.12260 (2022)
5. Gustavo, C., Bogdan, G., Sara, G., Dorin, C.: Detection and measurement of fetal anatomies from ultrasound images using a constrained probabilistic boosting tree. IEEE Trans. Med. Imaging **27**(9), 1342–1355 (2008)
6. Hesse, L.S., et al.: Subcortical segmentation of the fetal brain in 3D ultrasound using deep learning. Neuroimage **254**, 119117 (2022)
7. Kiserud, T., et al.: The world health organization fetal growth charts: a multinational longitudinal study of ultrasound biometric measurements and estimated fetal weight. PLoS Med. **14**(1), e1002220 (2017)
8. Kong, B., Sun, S., Wang, X., Song, Q., Zhang, S.: Invasive cancer detection utilizing compressed convolutional neural network and transfer learning. In: Frangi, A.F., Schnabel, J.A., Davatzikos, C., Alberola-López, C., Fichtinger, G. (eds.) MICCAI 2018. LNCS, vol. 11071, pp. 156–164. Springer, Cham (2018). https://doi.org/10.1007/978-3-030-00934-2_18
9. Kong, B., Wang, X., Li, Z., Song, Q., Zhang, S.: Cancer metastasis detection via spatially structured deep network. In: Niethammer, M., et al. (eds.) IPMI 2017. LNCS, vol. 10265, pp. 236–248. Springer, Cham (2017). https://doi.org/10.1007/978-3-319-59050-9_19

10. Lee, W., Deter, R., Sangi-Haghpeykar, H., Yeo, L., Romero, R.: Prospective validation of fetal weight estimation using fractional limb volume. Ultrasound Obstet. Gynecol. **41**(2), 198–203 (2013)
11. Li, J., Cao, L., Ge, Y., Cheng, W., Bowen, M., Wei, G.: Multi-task deep convolutional neural network for the segmentation of type b aortic dissection. arXiv preprint arXiv:1806.09860 (2018)
12. Looney, P., et al.: Fully automated, real-time 3D ultrasound segmentation to estimate first trimester placental volume using deep learning. JCI Insight **3**(11), e120178 (2018)
13. Meengeonthong, D., Luewan, S., Sirichotiyakul, S., Tongsong, T.: Reference ranges of placental volume measured by virtual organ computer-aided analysis between 10 and 14 weeks of gestation. J. Clin. Ultrasound **45**(4), 185–191 (2017)
14. Oktay, O., Schlemper, J., Folgoc, L.L., Lee, M., Rueckert, D.: Attention u-net: Learning where to look for the pancreas. In: Medical Imaging with Deep Learning (2018)
15. Pătrăucean, V., Handa, A., Cipolla, R.: Spatio-temporal video autoencoder with differentiable memory. In: International Conference on Learning Representations (ICLR) Workshop (2016)
16. Peters, R., et al.: Virtual segmentation of three-dimensional ultrasound images of morphological structures of an ex vivo ectopic pregnancy inside a fallopian tube. J. Clin. Ultrasound **50**, 535–539 (2022)
17. Prieto, J.C., et al.: An automated framework for image classification and segmentation of fetal ultrasound images for gestational age estimation. In: Medical Imaging 2021: Image Processing. vol. 11596, p. 115961N. International Society for Optics and Photonics (2021)
18. Shi, X., Chen, Z., Hao, W., Yeung, D.Y., Wong, W., Woo, W.: Convolutional LSTM network: a machine learning approach for precipitation nowcasting. In: International Conference on Neural Information Processing Systems (2015)
19. Tai, K.S., Socher, R., Manning, C.D.: Improved semantic representations from tree-structured long short-term memory networks. In: International Joint Conference on Natural Language Processing. vol. 1, pp. 1556–1566 (2015)
20. Yang, X., et al.: Towards automated semantic segmentation in prenatal volumetric ultrasound. IEEE Trans. Med. Imaging **38**(1), 180–193 (2019)
21. Yaqub, M., Javaid, M.K., Cooper, C., Noble, J.A.: Investigation of the role of feature selection and weighted voting in random forests for 3-D volumetric segmentation. IEEE Trans. Med. Imaging **33**(2), 258–271 (2014)
22. Zeng, Y., Tsui, P.H., Wu, W., Zhou, Z., Wu, S.: Fetal ultrasound image segmentation for automatic head circumference biometry using deeply supervised attention-gated v-net. J. Digit. Imaging **34**(1), 134–148 (2021)

Thigh and Calf Muscles Segmentation Using Ensemble of Patch-Based Deep Convolutional Neural Network on Whole-Body Water-Fat MRI

Zhendi Gong[1](✉), Rosemary Nicholas[2,3], Susan T. Francis[2,3,4,5], and Xin Chen[1]

[1] Intelligent Modelling and Analysis Group, School of Computer Science,
University of Nottingham, Nottingham, UK
psxzg6@nottingham.ac.uk
[2] Sir Peter Mansfield Imaging Centre, University of Nottingham, Nottingham, UK
[3] Centre for Musculoskeletal Ageing Research, University of Nottingham, Nottingham, UK
[4] NIHR Nottingham Biomedical Research Centre, Nottingham University Hospitals NHS Trust, Nottingham, UK
[5] University of Nottingham, Nottingham, UK

Abstract. Lower limb muscles provide various significant physiological functions, which are the key muscles to support daily activities. Segmentation of these muscles offers quantitative analysis for several clinical applications (e.g., understanding of musculoskeletal diseases). In recent studies on muscle tissues, water-fat quantitative magnetic resonance imaging (MRI) is frequently used as the main image modality due to its capability in distinguishing muscle and fat from their surrounding tissues. However, manual muscle segmentation in MRI is time-consuming and often requires professional knowledge. In this paper, an ensemble framework of combining two patch-based binary-class deep convolutional neural networks with the same architecture is proposed to achieve thigh and calf muscle segmentation from whole-body water-fat (mDIXON) MRIs. We compared our model to a state-of-the-art multi-class 3D U-Net model using a 5-fold cross-validation. A Dice coefficient of 0.9042 was achieved by our method, which was significantly more accurate than the multi-class 3D U-Net method. Additionally, the model deployment costs approximately 13.8 s per case.

Keywords: Lower limb muscle segmentation · Patch-based deep convolutional neural network

1 Introduction

Magnetic resonance imaging (MRI) has emerged as a tool of choice for the development of qualitative and quantitative measurement of muscles. MRI offers high sensitivity to monitor pathological changes in muscle tissues, allowing several musculoskeletal diseases to be studied [1]. In order to extract the imaging biomarkers from specific regions of interest, muscle segmentation is mandatory. Although water-fat MRI provides rich information to study the leg muscles, it is still challenging to segment those muscles

© The Author(s), under exclusive license to Springer Nature Switzerland AG 2022
G. Yang et al. (Eds.): MIUA 2022, LNCS 13413, pp. 262–270, 2022.
https://doi.org/10.1007/978-3-031-12053-4_20

accurately and efficiently due to the similar image intensities of different tissues, the weak boundary information, and the varied shapes of muscles. Thus, manual segmentation of multiple muscles is extremely time-consuming and has high intra and inter observer variations. Hence automated and accurate muscle segmentation is essential.

Recently, deep convolutional neural network (DCNN) has been applied to the automatic muscle segmentation of water and fat images from mDIXON MRI datasets. Due to the large dimensions of whole-body MRI scans in 3D, modern DCNN methods have difficulties in accommodating the whole-body volume due to the limitation of GPU memory. Several methods have used 2D MRI slices as the input to solve this problem. For instance, Ding et al. [2] trained a 2D U-Net [3] to segment four sub muscle classes in the thigh muscle, the fat and water MRI were used as two input channels in their method. Additionally, Amer et al. [4] used a 2D U-Net [3] based method to measure fat infiltration. They focused on muscle region segmentation using U-Net [3] in the first stage of their method and proposed a deep convolutional auto-encoder to perform muscle classification in the second stage. Furthermore, Ahmad et al. [5] compared the performance of FCN-AlexNet [6], FCN-VGGNet (includes FCN-32s, FCN-16s and FCN-8s) [7] and PSPNet [8] to segment the region of interests (ROIs) in MRI thigh scans. The main drawback of these methods is that they used 2D slices independently, ignoring the contextual information along the third dimension. Another similar solution was proposed by Ghosh et al. [9], who used small stacks of 2D MRI slices as input (10 slices). They used a pretrained AlexNet [6] that with principal components analysis output 2D images to represent the 3D structure of the muscles in the input data. However, ten 2D slices were not capable of providing sufficient long-range structural information. Another limitation of the above methods is that they only focused on thigh muscles.

Ni et al. [10] developed a 3D U-Net [11] based framework to segment 35 different lower limb muscles to overcome the above issues. They solved the GPU limitation problem by detecting the muscle bounding boxes obtained from the down-sampled volume of the whole-body 3D MRIs using 3D U-Net [11]. The bounding box region was then cropped from the high-resolution volumes which contain the target muscles. The cropped volumes were used as the input to a second stage 3D U-Net models [11] for muscle segmentation. The main drawback of this method is the model's longer inference time (i.e., 30 to 40 s per pair of left and right muscles) compared to other DCNN-based solutions. Moreover, due to the large size of the thigh and calf muscles, it also restricts the image resolution of the input 3D volume which often needs to be down-sampled. As a result, their method cannot handle large muscles in their original imaging resolutions.

In this paper, we propose a GPU memory-efficient method to overcome the above issues using the ensemble of patch-based DCNN models and a post-processing step for output aggregation and false positive reduction. In our method, two separate binary 3D U-Net models [11] were constructed for each thigh and calf muscle segmentation. These two U-Net models are 3D patch-based and the size of the patch is determined by the memory size of the GPU. The ensemble of the patch-based predicted output is implemented in a bespoke post-processing step, which aims to reduce false-positives. We evaluated our method and compared it to the 3D multi-class U-Net method using 5-fold cross validation.

2 Methodology

As the thigh and calf muscles are located in the bottom half of the body, we firstly use a reference plane that is defined by the proximal end of the two femoral bones to crop the bottom half of the body from the whole-body MRI. This process is a simple and quick process, which is currently performed manually. Then the thigh and calf muscle regions are identified by applying a fixed ratio (lower l_1/L for the calf region and upper l_2/L for thigh region, where L is the height of the cropped volume) to split the volume into two overlapping sub-volumes. Next, two patch-based binary-class 3D U-Net models with the same network architecture are trained for thigh and calf muscle segmentation separately, called 'CalfModel' and 'ThighModel'. During model training, the input volumes for each model were randomly cropped into many overlapping regions and used as the input to train the models. In the model inference process, the input whole-body MRI is pre-processed using the same procedure as the training. The input volume is then divided into non-overlapping 3D patches and input to the corresponding calf or thigh model for muscle segmentation. Finally, a bespoke post-processing method is proposed to combine the predicted outputs of the patches from both models to form a whole-body output and correct any mislabeled areas. Detailed method descriptions are provided in the following subsections.

2.1 Model Architecture and Model Training

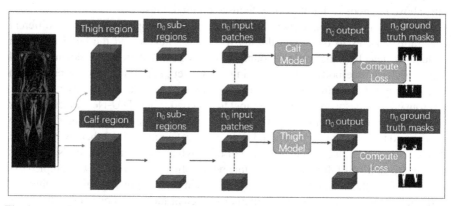

Fig. 1. Workflow of the training process, n0 patches from each subject are the input to the CalfModel and ThighModel. Image shows the fat MRI image.

Each of the CalfModel and ThighModel utilizes a binary-class 3D U-Net [11] to segment the calf and thigh muscles separately to fully use the similarity and symmetry of the left and right muscles. The network architecture for both models is the same, which contains a down-sampling path and an up-sampling path, both include four multi-resolution levels. Specifically, the down-sampling path contains four convolutional blocks, each includes two $3 \times 3 \times 3$ convolutional operators and one $2 \times 2 \times 2$ max-pooling layer.

Additionally, the number of filters is doubled after each max-pooling process. The up-sampling path contains four deconvolutional blocks, each includes two $3 \times 3 \times 3$ convolutional operators and a $2 \times 2 \times 2$ transpose convolutional operator. Additionally, the number of filters is halved for each of the deconvolutional blocks. The input of each "deconvolutional" block is the concatenation of the output of the previous layer and the output of the corresponding layer with the same resolution in the down-sampling path. Furthermore, a batch normalization layer is used before each ReLU activation layer. The last layer is a $1 \times 1 \times 1$ convolutional layer followed by a sigmoid activation.

The whole training process is shown in Fig. 1. The input patches for both models are automatically cropped from the calf and thigh regions. Taking the CalfModel as an example, for each case in the training and validation dataset, the calf region is divided into n0 sub-regions along the foot-head direction, and in each sub-region, a random location is selected to extract a Px × Py × Pz 3D patch. Based on each location, the cropped patch from the whole-body water image and fat image are concatenated to form a 2-channel input volume, and the corresponding left and right calf muscle classes are combined into a single class. Additionally, intensity normalization using min-max method is performed on the input water-fat MRIs. During the model training, the predicted output of each 3D patch is compared with the corresponding binary mask using a binary cross entropy. The training of ThighModel follows the same procedure.

2.2 Model Inference and Post-processing

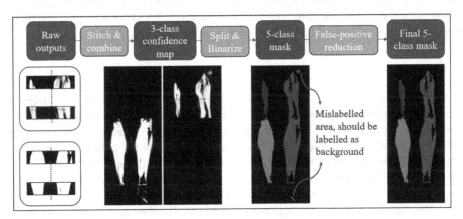

Fig. 2. Workflow of model inference and post-processing.

To deploy the trained CalfModel and ThighModel for muscle segmentation, the same pre-processing steps as described above are applied to the input whole-body water and fat images to obtain the lower limb region. Additionally, a second reference plane is manually defined, with the approximate patella location used to separate the lower limb region into new calf and thigh regions that do not overlap to avoid the wrong prediction in the original overlapping area. The new calf and thigh regions are then divided into non-overlapping Px × Py × Pz 3D patches (with an overlapping patch at the region's boundary). Each of these patches is input to the correspondingly trained CalfModel and ThighModel. The output predictions are then stitched together to form a whole-body prediction map, which contains calf muscle, thigh muscle and background classes. The prediction map is then binarized using argmax. Additionally, the left and right muscles are then determined by finding a sagittal plane with minimal number of positives near the image's vertical central line to split the image into left and right regions, resulting in a five-class mask (including the background class). The next step is to apply connected component analysis to reduce potential false positives by only retaining the largest connected component in each muscle's mask. The whole workflow is shown in Fig. 2.

3 Experiments and Evaluation

3.1 Material

The proposed method was evaluated on local whole-body water-fat mDIXON Quant MRI datasets from 43 subjects collected on the Philips 3T Ingenia at Sir Peter Mansfield Imaging Centre. The mDIXON scans were collected in coronal view using a six-echo 3D gradient echo sequence with a flip angle of $3°$, repetition time (TR) 10 ms, with initial echo time (TE1) of 0.95 ms and echo spacing (ΔTE) of 0.7 ms. Additionally, the coronal scans of each MRI were reconstructed to 3 mm slice thickness with pixel size of either 1.9231×1.9231 mm^2 or 1.7241×1.7241 mm^2 in each coronal slice, resulting in the volume size of either $256 \times 77 \times 839$ or $320 \times 77 \times 917$ respectively. The ground truth masks of left/right of calf/thigh muscles were obtained via a semi-automatic process using an initial rough segmentation, followed by FSL's FAST method [12] and any required manual refinements. The final segmentations were visually inspected.

3.2 Experiments

For model comparison, the multi-class 3D U-Net [11] model, which uses a multi-class version of the same encoder-decoder architecture as our method, was implemented for comparison (denoted as MC-3DUNet). Instead of dividing the volume into 3D patches, MC-3DUNet takes the whole calf and thigh regions obtained from our pre-processing method. The input volume is down-sampled to the same size (Px $\times$ Py $\times$ Pz) as our method using linear interpolation for model training. Thus, each object provides two input volumes, each for calf and thigh muscle respectively. During model deployment of MC-3DUNet, the new calf and thigh regions are located following the same procedure as our method. Additionally, the predicted segmentation images are resized back to the original image size firstly and then combined to form the final 5-class segmentation output. The result is compared with our method in a 5-fold cross validation manner with/without our false-positive reduction method.

For the 5-fold cross validation, 35 volumes and 8 volumes were used for training and testing respectively in each fold. Three random images were chosen from the training set as the validation set in each fold. The model that produced the highest dice coefficient (DC) [13] on the validation set is applied for testing in each fold. For performance evaluation, DC, average symmetric surface distance (ASSD) and a Bland-Altman plot [14] were used. Wilcoxon signed-rank test was applied for statistical test when comparing our method with MC-3DUNet.

3.3 Parameter Settings

To ensure that the size of the calf and thigh regions was the same with some overlapping area, we set $l_1/L = l_2/L = 8/13$ in the pre-processing step. Additionally, the size of the transverse plane of the patch Px $\times$ Py was determined by two rules: (1) each dimension of the image patch should be the power of 2 due to the symmetric U-Net architecture; (2) the plane should contain as much image region of the original transverse plane as possible. Furthermore, based on the first rule above, the size of the third dimension was determined to be a maximum value to fully use the GPU in training the models. Thus, Px $\times$ Py $\times$ Pz was set to $256 \times 64 \times 64$. Additionally, n0 was set to 10 to ensure that the cropped patches had an approximately 50% overlapping area.

The models were trained for a maximum of 80 epochs for both our method and MC-3DUNet, and only the model with the highest DC on the validation set was saved and the training was stopped if the DC remained smaller for another 30 epochs. During training, the Adam optimizer with an initial learning rate of 0.0001 was applied for all models, and the batch size was set to one. Our model used binary cross-entropy, and MC-3DUNet used categorical cross-entropy. All experiments were performed on a single Nvidia 1060 GPU with 6 GB memory.

3.4 Results

Table 1 presents the DC and ASSD measures for all four muscles separately for our method and MC-3DUNet with and without post-processing. It can be seen that our method is significantly better than MC-3DUNet for both DC and ASSD for all muscles (p < 0.001 using Wilcoxon signed-rank test on all test cases). Specifically, the average dice scores of our method are 0.9189, 0.8873, 0.9214, and 0.8893 for left calf, left thigh, right calf, and right thigh respectively. On the other hand, the average dice scores of MC-3DUNet are 0.8374, 0.8571, 0.8308, and 0.8531 for the corresponding muscles. Additionally, the ASSD of our method are 2.9498, 2.7591, 2.9686, 2.6493 for the corresponding muscles, and the ASSD of MC-3DUNet are 4.6543, 4.1774, 5.4972, and 3.7441 for the corresponding muscles. Furthermore, our false-positive reduction method has shown to significantly improve the performance of both our model and MC-3DUNet in terms of the average DC and ASSD values (p < 0.001 in Wilcoxon signed-rank test on all test cases). However, in terms of model inference time including post-processing, the average time of MC-3DUNet is 10.81 s per case, which is faster than our method (13.81 s per case).

We also compared the muscle volume measurement of the segmented result of our method to the manually segmentation result. The Bland-Altman plots of each of the four muscles are shown in Fig. 3. Furthermore, the Pearson's correlation coefficient between the predicted left calf, left thigh, right calf, and right thigh muscle volumes and the corresponding ground truth volumes are 0.8227, 0.7311, 0.8200, and 0.7008 respectively. It can be seen from the results that calf muscles have a better agreement between our method and the ground truth. The Bland-Altman plots indicates that the volumes of thigh muscles are generally larger than the calf muscles, which is a potential reason to make it more difficult to be accurately segmented than the calf muscles. Furthermore, based on error analysis on the cases with larger errors, pose variation is another reason for poorer model performance. If the standing pose inclination was too large, our method in splitting the left and right regions of the output volumes cannot perform robustly.

Table 1. The 5-fold cross-validation results for our proposed method and MC-3DUNet methods. 'A' and 'B' are the results of without post-processing and with post-processing respectively. * indicates our method is better than the MC-3DUNet with statistical significance (measured by Wilcoxon signed-rank test).

Methods	Ours		MC-3DUNet		
Muscles	DC	ASSD	DC	ASSD	
Left calf	*0.9121	*4.1952	0.8197	8.9397	A
Left thigh	*0.8868	*2.7057	0.8487	6.0450	
Right calf	*0.9137	*4.7530	0.8231	7.7666	
Right thigh	*0.8888	*2.5123	0.8445	6.0706	
Average	*0.9004	*3.5416	0.8340	7.2055	
Left calf	*0.9189	*2.9468	0.8347	4.6543	B
Left thigh	*0.8873	*2.7591	0.8571	4.1774	
Right calf	*0.9214	*2.9686	0.8308	5.4972	
Right thigh	*0.8893	*2.6493	0.8531	3.7441	
Average	*0.9042	*2.8309	0.8439	4.5183	

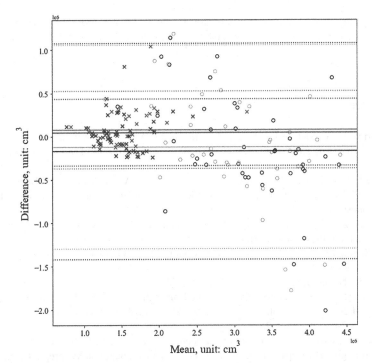

Fig. 3. Bland-Altman plot of the predicted muscle volumes of our method against the manually segmented volumes. Red: left calf muscle; black: left thigh muscle; blue: right calf muscle; green: right thigh muscle. Cross indicates calf muscles and circle indicates thigh muscles. (Color figure online)

4   Conclusions and Discussion

By combining two patch-based binary-class 3D U-Nets and the bespoke post-processing method, we proposed an efficient (approximately 13.8 s per case) muscle segmentation model that can handle any size of muscles if each pair of them shared similarity and symmetry. Moreover, by evaluating the method using a local dataset, our method performed significantly better than the multi-class 3D U-Net model given the same GPU resource. Specifically, we achieved DC of 0.9042 and ASSD of 2.8309 in 5-fold cross-validation. Our method addressed the issue of GPU limitation problem, which can accommodate the original resolution of MRI without image down-sampling. However, the most significant limitation of our method is that it might not work well in dealing with muscles that are joined closely.

For future work, we intend to design a model to automatically detect the region of each muscle from the original whole-body water-fat MRI into approximate calf and thigh regions and extend the method to more muscle and organ types.

Acknowledgement. This research was funded by the NIHR Nottingham Biomedical Research Centre and carried out at/supported by the NIHR Nottingham Clinical Research Facilities. The views expressed are those of the author(s) and not necessarily those of the NHS, the NIHR or the Department of Health and Social Care. Funding was also provided by the Centre for musculoskeletal Ageing Research, University of Nottingham to support the PhD of Rosemary Nicholas.

References

1. Hamrick, M.W., McGee-Lawrence, M.E., Frechette, D.M.: Fatty infiltration of skeletal muscle: mechanisms and comparisons with bone marrow adiposity. Front. Endocrinol. **7**, 69 (2016)
2. Ding, J., Cao, P., Chang, H.C., Gao, Y., Chan, S.H.S., Vardhanabhuti, V.: Deep learning-based thigh muscle segmentation for reproducible fat fraction quantification using fat–water decomposition MRI. Insights Imaging **11**(1), 1–11 (2020)
3. Ronneberger, O., Fischer, P., Brox, T.: U-net: convolutional networks for biomedical image segmentation. In: Navab, N., Hornegger, J., Wells, W.M., Frangi, A.F. (eds.) MICCAI 2015. LNCS, vol. 9351, pp. 234–241. Springer, Cham (2015). https://doi.org/10.1007/978-3-319-24574-4_28
4. Amer, R., Nassar, J., Bendahan, D., Greenspan, H., Ben-Eliezer, N.: Automatic segmentation of muscle tissue and inter-muscular fat in thigh and calf MRI images. In: Shen, D., et al. (eds.) MICCAI 2019. LNCS, vol. 11765, pp. 219–227. Springer, Cham (2019). https://doi.org/10.1007/978-3-030-32245-8_25
5. Ahmad, E., Goyal, M., McPhee, J.S., Degens, H., Yap, M.H.: Semantic segmentation of human thigh quadriceps muscle in magnetic resonance images. arXiv preprint arXiv:1801.00415 (2018)
6. Krizhevsky, A., Sutskever, I., Hinton, G.E.: ImageNet classification with deep convolutional neural networks. In: Advances in Neural Information Processing Systems 25, pp. 1097–1105 (2012)
7. Long, J., Shelhamer, E., Darrell, T.: Fully convolutional networks for semantic segmentation. In Proceedings of the IEEE Conference on Computer Vision and Pattern Recognition, pp. 3431–3440 (2015)
8. Zhao, H., Shi, J., Qi, X., Wang, X., Jia, J.: Pyramid scene parsing network. In: Proceedings of the IEEE Conference on Computer Vision and Pattern Recognition, pp. 2881–2890 (2017)
9. Ghosh, S., Boulanger, P., Acton, S.T., Blemker, S.S., Ray, N.: Automated 3D muscle segmentation from MRI data using convolutional neural network. In: 2017 IEEE International Conference on Image Processing (ICIP), pp. 4437–4441. IEEE, September 2017
10. Ni, R., Meyer, C.H., Blemker, S.S., Hart, J.M., Feng, X.: Automatic segmentation of all lower limb muscles from high-resolution magnetic resonance imaging using a cascaded three-dimensional deep convolutional neural network. J. Med. Imaging **6**(4), 044009 (2019)
11. Çiçek, Ö., Abdulkadir, A., Lienkamp, S.S., Brox, T., Ronneberger, O.: 3D U-net: learning dense volumetric segmentation from sparse annotation. In: Ourselin, S., Joskowicz, L., Sabuncu, M.R., Unal, G., Wells, W. (eds.) MICCAI 2016. LNCS, vol. 9901, pp. 424–432. Springer, Cham (2016). https://doi.org/10.1007/978-3-319-46723-8_49
12. Zhang, Y., Brady, M., Smith, S.: Segmentation of brain MR images through a hidden Markov random field model and the expectation-maximization algorithm. IEEE Trans. Med. Imaging **20**(1), 45–57 (2001)
13. Dice, L.R.: Measures of the amount of ecologic association between species. Ecology **26**(3), 297–302 (1945)
14. Altman, D.G., Bland, J.M.: Measurement in medicine: the analysis of method comparison studies. J. R. Stat. Soc. Ser. D (Stat.) **32**(3), 307–317 (1983)

Fitting Segmentation Networks on Varying Image Resolutions Using Splatting

Mikael Brudfors[1]([✉]), Yaël Balbastre[2], John Ashburner[3], Geraint Rees[4], Parashkev Nachev[5], Sébastien Ourselin[1], and M. Jorge Cardoso[1]

[1] School of Biomedical Engineering and Imaging Sciences, KCL, London, UK
`mikael.brudfors@kcl.ac.uk`
[2] Athinoula A. Martinos Center for Biomedical Imaging, MGH and HMS, Boston, USA
[3] Wellcome Center for Human Neuroimaging, UCL, London, UK
[4] Institute of Cognitive Neuroscience, UCL, London, UK
[5] Institute of Neurology, UCL, London, UK

Abstract. Data used in image segmentation are not always defined on the same grid. This is particularly true for medical images, where the resolution, field-of-view and orientation can differ across channels and subjects. Images and labels are therefore commonly resampled onto the same grid, as a pre-processing step. However, the resampling operation introduces partial volume effects and blurring, thereby changing the effective resolution and reducing the contrast between structures. In this paper we propose a *splat layer*, which automatically handles resolution mismatches in the input data. This layer pushes each image onto a *mean space* where the forward pass is performed. As the splat operator is the adjoint to the resampling operator, the mean-space prediction can be pulled back to the native label space, where the loss function is computed. Thus, the need for explicit resolution adjustment using interpolation is removed. We show on two publicly available datasets, with simulated and real multi-modal magnetic resonance images, that this model improves segmentation results compared to resampling as a pre-processing step.

Keywords: Image segmentation · Splatting · Resampling · Pre-processing · Image resolution

1 Introduction

Automatic semantic segmentation of medical images is widely done using deep-learning-based segmentation networks. To apply these networks, a pre-processing step that resamples all images into the same space is currently performed, as the images can have different orientation, field-of-view and resolution. Choosing the common space can be done in many ways, *e.g.*, based on the median voxel size of the training population [1]. This step is required for stacking channel dimensions

G. Yang et al. (Eds.): MIUA 2022, LNCS 13413, pp. 271–282, 2022.
https://doi.org/10.1007/978-3-031-12053-4_21

when working on multi-modal(channel) data, but also if a batch size larger then one is required. This type of pre-processing is performed in the majority of biomedical challenges, *e.g.*, BRATS [2], Medical Segmentation Decathlon [3] and the WMH Segmentation Challenge [4].

Pre-processing images by resampling to a common space can be seen as a normalisation step, intended to decrease data variance and facilitate both model fitting and generalisability. However, resampling introduces values not present in the original image through interpolation. Furthermore, it has a smoothing effect that, unless coordinates fall exactly at voxel centres, reduces the observed noise variance: let $y = ax_1 + (1 - a)x_2$ be the interpolation of two values $x_1 \sim \mathcal{N}(m_1, v)$ and $x_2 \sim \mathcal{N}(m_2, v)$, with $a \in [0, 1]$; then, $\mathrm{Var}[y] = (1 - 2a(1 - a))v \leq v$. In addition, interpolation algorithms do not embed prior knowledge about the objects being interpolated, resulting in overly smooth images that can bias analyses and cause false positives [5,6]. These limitations can make it challenging to generalise segmentation networks to a wide array of voxel sizes. Furthermore, the networks have no way to know how confident they should be about a particular voxel value, *i.e.*, whether it has been highly interpolated or preserves the raw value. This could be particularly problematic when working with routine clinical MRIs, where thick-sliced (high in-plane, low through-plane resolution), multi-modal acquisitions are the default.

The simplest method for fusing modalities of different image resolution is perhaps to fit separate networks to each modality and then combine their individual predictions. This can be done by integrating multi-modal features from the top layer of each network [7,8], or by fusing their outputs via averaging and majority voting [9]. However, such output-fusion strategies learn only modality-specific features and ignore the complex interactions between modalities. To better account for correlations across modalities, several layer-level fusion methods have been proposed. For example, Hi-Net [10], which learns individual modality features via a modality-specific network and a layer-wise fusion strategy, or HyperDense-Net [11], which employs dense connections across multi-modal streams. However, none of these methods model the fact that the images are defined on different grids in their native spaces. SynthSeg [12], on the other hand, introduced a convolutional neural network (CNN) that learns a mapping between multi-modal scans, defined on different grids, by simulating high-resolution scans from the training data by interpolating the low-resolution scans to 1 mm isotropic. Since the interpolation is simulated from the training data, the network becomes robust to variable image resolutions. The method presented in this paper would avoid interpolation, instead using the proposed splat layers. Finally, CNN-based models exist that take irregularly sampled inputs [13], but they are currently not easily extended to multi-modal data.

In this paper, we propose a method for directly fitting segmentation networks to the raw image data. Our method is based on the splatting operation, which pushes images, across subjects and channels, into a mean space. The network produces its predictions in this space, which are then pulled back into the native space of each input subject where the loss function is computed. If multiple modalities are provided, the loss is computed on the image on which the target segmentation was annotated. The splat layer avoids interpolating the input data, allowing the network to instead infer on the raw voxel values. We validate our proposed method on two semantic segmentation tasks, on publicly available multi-modal brain MR images. Our validation shows that extending a UNet with our proposed splat layers gives improved segmentations, compared to fitting to data that have been pre-processed by resampling. Our implementation uses a PyTorch backend, with custom splatting and resampling layers written in C++/CUDA, publicly available at https://github.com/balbasty/nitorch.

2   Methods

The idea of our method is quite simple; when fitting a segmentation network, instead of resampling the input images as a pre-processing step, we instead add two new layers to the network, one at its head and one at its tail. These two layers are based on the splatting operation [14], which allow the network to learn on the raw voxel data of the images. This avoids interpolation that could introduce partial-volume effects, and for the loss to be computed on the native space data. The idea is that the network implicitly interpolates the data whilst training. To conceptualise the idea of splatting, we next show a simple 1D toy example. The methodology is then extended to D-dimensional input tensors in the subsequent section.

2.1   1D Toy Example

Let's assume we have a training population of M sets of native-space input vectors ($D = 1$), where each set of input vectors represents C channels and can be of different length (*i.e.*, it is not always possible to stack the C vectors of training data). For training a segmentation network, we want to be able to concatenate all input vectors across C and M onto a common grid (*i.e.*, having equal length). Let us define one of these vectors as $\mathbf{f}_{mc} = [10, 11, 12, 13]^{\mathrm{T}}$, with $N_{mc} = 4$ elements and the affine mapping[1] $\mathbf{A}_{mc} = \left(\begin{smallmatrix} 2.5 & 0 \\ 0 & 1 \end{smallmatrix}\right)$. This vector's identity grid is given by $\mathbf{i}_{mc} = [0, 1, 2, 3]^{\mathrm{T}}$. To resize the input vector on a common training grid, we define its length (N_t) and affine mapping (A_t). This could be done in a number of ways, in this paper we use a *mean space*. The mean space is defined later; in this example, for simplicity, we assume $N_t = 8$ and $\mathbf{A}_t = \left(\begin{smallmatrix} 1 & 0 \\ 0 & 1 \end{smallmatrix}\right)$.

There are two ways of resizing the input vector onto the mean-space grid. The standard method is resampling, in which we define an identity grid in the mean space: $\mathbf{i}_t = [0, 1, 2, 3, 4, 5, 6, 7]^{\mathrm{T}}$. We then compose the affine mappings as $\mathbf{A} = \mathbf{A}_{mc}^{-1}\mathbf{A}_t = \left(\begin{smallmatrix} 0.4 & 0 \\ 0 & 1 \end{smallmatrix}\right)$ and transform the identity grid with $\mathbf{A}$ to get the deformation $\boldsymbol{\phi}_t = [0, 0.4, 0.8, 1.2, 1.6, 2, 2.4, 2.8]^{\mathrm{T}}$. Using $\boldsymbol{\phi}_t$ we can then pull values from $\mathbf{f}_{mc}$ onto a grid $\mathbf{f}_t$ using some form of interpolation. With linear

---

[1] For medical images, the affine mapping can be read from the image header. In general, it can be defined from knowledge of orientation, pixel size and field-of-view.

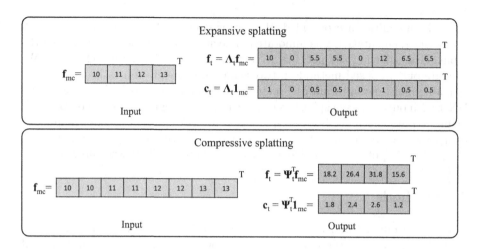

Fig. 1. 1D examples of expansive and compressive splatting.

interpolation we get $\mathbf{f}_t = [10, 10.4, 10.8, 11.2, 11.6, 12, 12.4, 12.8]^T$. This operation can be conceptualised as multiplying $\mathbf{f}_{mc}$ with a sparse matrix $\mathbf{f}_t = \mathbf{\Psi}_t \mathbf{f}_{mc}$, where:

$$\mathbf{\Psi}_t = \begin{bmatrix} 1.0, 0.0, 0.0, 0.0 \\ 0.6, 0.4, 0.0, 0.0 \\ 0.2, 0.8, 0.0, 0.0 \\ 0.0, 0.8, 0.2, 0.0 \\ 0.0, 0.4, 0.6, 0.0 \\ 0.0, 0.0, 1.0, 0.0 \\ 0.0, 0.0, 0.6, 0.4 \\ 0.0, 0.0, 0.2, 0.8 \end{bmatrix}$$

Splatting, on the other hand, does not interpolate the values in $\mathbf{f}_{mc}$. Instead the affine mapping is defined as $\mathbf{A} = \mathbf{A}_t^{-1} \mathbf{A}_{mc} = \left(\begin{smallmatrix} 2.5 & 0 \\ 0 & 1 \end{smallmatrix} \right)$ and the identity grid of the input vector ($\mathbf{i}_{mc}$) transformed as $\boldsymbol{\phi}_{mc} = [0, 2.5, 5, 7.5]^T$. This deformation is then used to push each value in $\mathbf{f}_{mc}$ to a location in the mean-space grid, giving us $\mathbf{f}_t = [10, 0, 5.5, 5.5, 0, 12, 6.5, 6.5]^T$. As multiple values can be pushed to the same location, a count image is also computed $\mathbf{c}_t = [1, 0, 0.5, 0.5, 0, 1, 0.5, 0.5]^T$, which we additionally provide as input to the segmentation network. Note that the splatting is expansive in this example, as there are fewer input voxels than output voxels, so the count image has lots of zeros. Splatting can also be compressive, meaning that multiple values can be pushed onto the same output voxel. As resampling, splatting can be conceptualised as a matrix multiplication $\mathbf{f}_t = \mathbf{\Lambda}_t \mathbf{f}_{mc}$, where:

$$\mathbf{\Lambda}_t = \begin{bmatrix} 1.0, \, 0.0, \, 0.0, \, 0.0, \, 0.0, \, 0.0, \, 0.0, \, 0.0 \\ 0.0, \, 0.0, \, 0.5, \, 0.5, \, 0.0, \, 0.0, \, 0.0, \, 0.0 \\ 0.0, \, 0.0, \, 0.0, \, 0.0, \, 0.0, \, 1.0, \, 0.0, \, 0.0 \\ 0.0, \, 0.0, \, 0.0, \, 0.0, \, 0.0, \, 0.0, \, 0.5, \, 0.5 \end{bmatrix}$$

This matrix is in fact the conjugate transpose of the resampling from the mean space to the input space, that is $\mathbf{\Lambda}_t = \mathbf{\Psi}_{mc}^{\mathrm{T}}$. The expansive and compressive splatting operations are visualised in Fig. 1.

The splatting operation, and its conjugate transpose, are what we add as layers to the head and tail of a segmentation network, respectively. When splatting and its transpose are conceptualised as layers, we now have the first and last layer of the network as adjoint operations, similarly to how convolutions in the encoder and transposed convolutions in the decoder of a UNet are adjoint operations. An additional parallel between splatting (followed by a convolution) and transposed convolutions can be drawn, as they both let the network learn how to optimally invent missing data.

Having the splat operation at the head of the network allows any sized input images to be provided to a network, with multiple channels that may have different sizes or orientations, because the image's voxels will be pushed onto the common training grid. Having the conjugate transpose of the splat operator at the tail of the network allows the loss function (*e.g.*, Dice) to be computed in the image's native space, where the target segmentations were originally drawn. Note that we apply the conjugate transpose to the 'logit' output of the network, and afterwards apply the softmax operation. Furthermore, the splatting operations assume that voxels outside the field-of-view are zero, and the conjugate transposes assume that data outside of the field of view are part of the background class. In the next section we extend the operations to an arbitrary number of dimensions.

2.2   Splatting and Resampling

Let us write as $\mathcal{N} : \mathbb{R}^{N \times C_i} \rightarrow \mathbb{R}^{N \times C_o}$ a CNN that maps N voxels and C_i input channels to N voxels and C_o output channels. Implicitly, each voxel of the grid is associated with a spatial index $\mathbf{x}_n$, which is identical in the input and output images, and in all channels within them. Furthermore, voxel coordinates can be linked to a common coordinate system through the mapping $\mathbf{A} : \mathbf{x}_n \mapsto \mathbf{y}$, which can be encoded in an affine orientation matrix $\mathbf{A} \in \mathbb{R}^{D+1,D+1}$ (D is the dimensionality of the input). These matrices are saved in the headers of most medical imaging file formats. In practice, multiple MR contrasts $\left\{ \mathbf{f}_c \in \mathbb{R}^{N_c} \right\}_{c=1}^{C_i}$ may be defined on different grids, with different coordinate systems $\left\{ \mathbf{A}_c \in \mathbb{R}^{D+1,D+1} \right\}_{c=1}^{C_i}$. Because CNNs require all images to 'live' on the same grid, they are commonly resampled to the same space. For segmentation, this is typically the space in which the manual labels were drawn.

In general, resampling can be written as $\hat{f}_m = \sum_{n=1}^{N} f_n w(\phi(\hat{\mathbf{x}}_m), \mathbf{x}_n)$, where ϕ is a mapping from the new grid ($\hat{\mathbf{x}}$) to the old ($\mathbf{x}$) and w is a weight that depends on the distance between a voxel $\mathbf{x}_m$ and the sampled location $\phi(\mathbf{x}_n)$.

This operation can be conceptualised as a large linear operation $\hat{\mathbf{f}} = \boldsymbol{\Phi}\mathbf{f}$, although in practice, the support of w is small and $\boldsymbol{\Phi}$ is sparse. In this paper, we use trilinear interpolation weights.

Let us write the loss function as $\mathcal{L}$ and the labels as $\mathbf{f}_l$, the forward pass of the CNN should therefore really be written as:

$$\left\{\mathbf{f}_c \in \mathbb{R}^{N_c}, \mathbf{A}_c \in \mathbb{R}^{D+1,D+1}\right\}_{c=1}^{C_i} \mapsto \mathcal{L}\left(\mathcal{N}\left([\boldsymbol{\Phi}_c\mathbf{f}_c]_{c=1}^{C_i}\right), \boldsymbol{\Phi}_l\mathbf{f}_l\right), \qquad (1)$$

although in general the common space is chosen to be that of the labels so that $\boldsymbol{\Phi}_l$ is the identity. When labels have a lower resolution than some of the input images, a different formulation could be to re-slice all images to the higher resolution space (*e.g.*, 1 mm isotropic), and resample the output of the network to the label space:

$$\left\{\mathbf{f}_c \in \mathbb{R}^{N_c}, \mathbf{A}_c \in \mathbb{R}^{D+1,D+1}\right\}_{c=1}^{C_i} \mapsto \mathcal{L}\left(\boldsymbol{\Psi}_l\mathcal{N}\left([\boldsymbol{\Phi}_c\mathbf{f}_c]_{c=1}^{C_i}\right), \mathbf{f}_l\right), \qquad (2)$$

where $\boldsymbol{\Psi}_l$ maps from the common space to the native label space, whereas $\boldsymbol{\Phi}_l$ was used to map from the native label space to the common space (the underlying transformations ψ_l and ϕ_l are inverse of each other). However, this does not solve the issues related to the resampling of the input images raised earlier.

In this paper, we propose to replace the initial resampling with the adjoint operation of its inverse, as part of the forward pass. Since resampling is a linear operation, its adjoint is simply its transpose $\boldsymbol{\Psi}^{\mathrm{T}}\mathbf{f}$. In practice, it means that native data are *splatted* onto the mean space: $\hat{f}_m = \sum_{n=1}^{N} f_n w(\psi(\mathbf{x}_n), \hat{\mathbf{x}}_m)$. Importantly, it means that if the resolution of the common space is higher than that of the native space, the splatted image has many zeros (the data are *not* interpolated). The output of the network is then resampled to the native label space, where the loss is computed:

$$\left\{\mathbf{f}_c \in \mathbb{R}^{N_c}, \mathbf{A}_c \in \mathbb{R}^{D+1,D+1}\right\}_{c=1}^{C_i} \mapsto \mathcal{L}\left(\boldsymbol{\Psi}_l\mathcal{N}\left([\boldsymbol{\Psi}_c^{\mathrm{T}}\mathbf{f}_c, \boldsymbol{\Psi}_c^{\mathrm{T}}\mathbf{1}]_{c=1}^{C_i}\right), \mathbf{f}_l\right), \qquad (3)$$

where we have let the network know which zeros are missing and which are native values, by concatenating splatted images of ones ($\boldsymbol{\Psi}_c^{\mathrm{T}}\mathbf{1}$) to the input. We note that $\boldsymbol{\Psi}_c^{\mathrm{T}}\mathbf{f}_c$ can be seen as the gradient of the resampling operation with respect to its input, while $\boldsymbol{\Psi}_c^{\mathrm{T}}\mathbf{1}$ can be seen as a diagonal approximation of its Hessian.

2.3   The Mean Space

What is the best way of defining the common space, in which the training and inference takes place? Using one of the input images to define this space, for the complete dataset, is not optimal [5]. A more principled solution is to compute a mean space from all input orientation matrices [15,16]. Briefly, this involves (1) extracting all linear components from the input orientation matrices; (2) computing their barycentric mean in an iterative fashion by alternately projecting them to the tangent space of GL(3) about the current barycentre and updating the barycentre by zero-centering the tangent data; (3) finding the closest matrix, in the least square sense, that can be encoded by the product of a rotation matrix (the orientation) and an anisotropic scaling matrix (the voxel size). In this work, we compute the mean space once, from the entire training set, although one mean space per mini-batch could alternatively be used. We constrain the mean-space dimensions to be a power of two or three, to facilitate fitting encoding/decoding architectures. Finally, we use a voxel size of 1 mm isotropic. This could be customised however, *e.g.*, by using larger voxels for a more lightweight model.

3   Experiments and Results

This section investigates whether the splat layer can improve multi-modal MRI brain segmentation in the scenario where, for each subject, we have multiple MR contrasts of differing resolution and the target labels are defined on one of the contrasts. We use a simple baseline network that we fit in two ways: (1) to images that, for each subject, have been resampled to the grid of the target labels; and (2), to native space images, by extending the baseline network with our proposed splat layers. The number of learnable parameters in both networks are the same.

3.1   The Baseline Network

We use a fairly light-weight UNet architecture [17] with (16, 32, 64, 128) channels in the encoder layer and (128, 64, 32, 32) in the decoder layer, where kernel size $3 \times 3 \times 3$ and stride two is used throughout. This is followed by a layer of $3 \times 3 \times 3$ stacked convolutions with (32, 16, 16) channels each, and a stride of one. The last layer then outputs the K segmentations labels, which are passed through a softmax. All layers use ReLU activations and batch normalisation. The final network has about 1 million parameters. This is the baseline network, denoted *UNet*. The UNet is then extended with our proposed splat layers as described in the Methods section. We denote this network *MeanSpaceNet*. The mean-space has dimensions (192, 192, 192) with 1 mm isotropic voxels. Note that the mean-space is defined on only the training data. Both networks are optimised using the Dice loss and the ADAM optimiser ($\text{lr} = 10^{-3}$). During training, we augment with multiplicative smooth intensity non-uniformities and random diffeomorphic deformations. For the mean-space model, any spatial augmentation needs to be defined in the mean-space and then composed to each image's native space using the affine matrices. We train for a fixed number of 100 epochs, with a batch size of one.

3.2   Simulated Data: Brain Tumour Segmentation

TCGA-GBM Dataset. In this experiment, we use the pre-operative, multi-institutional scans of The Cancer Genome Atlas (TCGA) Glioblastoma Multiforme (GBM) collection [18,19], publicly available in The Cancer Imaging

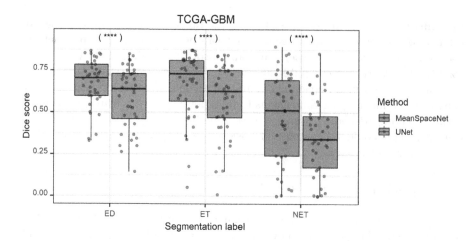

Fig. 2. Pairwise Dice scores computed on the TCGA-GBM test set ($N_{\text{gbm}}^{\text{test}} = 40$), for three tumour labels (ED, ET, NET), and two CNN models (MeanSpaceNet, UNet). On each box, the central mark indicates the median, and the bottom and top edges of the box indicate the 25th and 75th percentiles, respectively. The whiskers extend to the most extreme data points not considered outliers. Asterisks indicate statistical significance of paired Wilcox tests after Holm-Bonferroni correction: 0.05 ($*$), 0.01 ($**$), 0.001 ($* * *$) & 0.0001 ($* * * *$).

Archive [20]. The dataset was acquired from different MRI scanners. Each subject has skull-stripped and co-registered multi-modal (T1w, T1-Gd, T2w, T2-FLAIR) MRIs and segmentation labels of the enhancing part of the tumor core (ET), the non-enhancing part of the tumor core (NET), and the peritumoral edema (ED). All MRIs have been resampled to 1 mm isotropic voxel size and the same dimensions. In this experiment, we use only the subjects with manually-corrected segmentation labels, which gives in total $N_{\text{gbm}} = 97$ subjects, each with four MR modalities and three tumour labels.

Experiment. We simulate two datasets from TCGA-GBM. The first dataset, denoted $\mathcal{D}_{\text{nat}}^{\text{gbm}}$, is created by downsampling the T2-FLAIR image and the segmentation by a factor of three, in a randomly selected dimension. This emulates the situation where manual labels have been drawn on one modality (here the T2-FLAIR), and the other modalities have different voxel size (here the T1w, T1-Gd and T2w). The second dataset, denoted $\mathcal{D}_{\text{res}}^{\text{gbm}}$, is created by trilinearly re-slicing the T1w, T1-Gd and T2w images to the space of the downsampled T2-FLAIR, so that all images have the same dimensions. This in turn emulates the situation where all modalities are resampled to the space of the modality on which the manual labels were drawn. We split the two datasets into equal (train, validation, test) sets as (40, 17, 40). We then fit the UNet to $\mathcal{D}_{\text{res}}^{\text{gbm}}$ and the MeanSpaceNet to $\mathcal{D}_{\text{nat}}^{\text{gbm}}$. Note that it would not be possible to train the UNet model on the $\mathcal{D}_{\text{nat}}^{\text{gbm}}$ dataset, as the subjects' input modalities have different dimensions. After training we apply the two trained networks to their test sets and compute pairwise Dice scores between predicted and target segmentations.

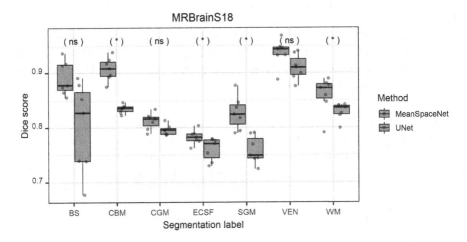

Fig. 3. Pairwise Dice scores computed on the MRBrainS18 datasets from leave-one-out cross-validation ($N = 7$), for seven brain labels (BS, CBM, CGM, ECSF, SGM, VEN, WM), and two CNN models (MeanSpaceNet, UNet).

Results. The experimental results are shown in the boxplot in Fig. 2. The MeanSpaceNet model achieves the best median Dice score over all classes 0.677 vs 0.528; as well as for all individual classes: 0.705 vs 0.639 for ED, 0.731 vs 0.626 for ET and 0.513 vs 0.340 for NET. Paired Wilcoxon tests with Holm-Bonferroni correction shows that the segmentation results are all significant ($p < 0.0001$).

3.3   Real Data: Brain Tissue Segmentation

MRBrains18 Dataset. In this experiment, we use the original scans (before any pre-processing) from the MICCAI MRBrainS18 grand segmentation challenge (https://mrbrains18.isi.uu.nl). The dataset was acquired from the same MRI scanner. Each subject has multi-modal (T1w, T1-IR, T2-FLAIR) MRIs and segmentation labels of ten brain structures: Cortical gray matter (CGM), subcortical gray matter (SGM), white matter (WM), white matter lesions (WML), cerebrospinal fluid in the extracerebral space (ECSF), ventricles (VEN), cerebellum (CBM), brain stem (BS), infarction (INF) and other (OTH). In this experiment, we do not use the INF and OTH labels, and we combine WM and WML into a single label. The images' voxel sizes (mm) are: T1w (1.0, 1.0, 1.0), T1-IR (0.96, 0.96, 3.0) and T2-FLAIR (0.96, 0.96, 3.0). The segmentations were drawn in resampled (0.96, 0.96, 3.0) space. In total, we have $N_{brain} = 7$ subjects, each with three MR modalities and seven brain labels.

Experiment. As in the TCGA-GBM experiment, we construct two datasets. The first dataset, denoted $\mathcal{D}_{\text{nat}}^{\text{brain}}$, is simply the original scans from the MRBrainS18 dataset. The second dataset, denoted $\mathcal{D}_{\text{res}}^{\text{brain}}$, is created by, for each subject in the MRBrainS18 dataset, trilinearly re-slice the T1w image to the space of the segmentation, so that all images have the same dimensions. As the MRBrainS18 dataset has a small number of subjects we perform leave-one-out cross-validation, fitting the UNet on $\mathcal{D}_{\text{res}}^{\text{brain}}$ and the MeanSpaceNet on $\mathcal{D}_{\text{nat}}^{\text{brain}}$, seven times in total, and for each fold computing pairwise Dice scores on the subject held out from training.

Results. The experimental results are shown in Fig. 3. The MeanSpaceNet model achieves the best median Dice score over all classes 0.864 vs 0.813; as well as for all individual classes: 0.878 vs 0.827 for BS, 0.908 vs 0.836 for CBM, 0.816 vs 0.798 for CGM, 0.783 vs 0.770 for ECSF, 0.824 vs 0.749 for SGM, 0.943 vs 0.910 for VEN and 0.871 vs 0.836 for WM. Paired Wilcoxon tests with Holm-Bonferroni correction shows that the segmentation results are significant ($p < 0.05$) for four out of seven segmentation classes.

4   Conclusions

In this paper, we described a splat layer that allows a segmentation network to automatically handle resolution mismatches in input data. The idea is to splat each input channel into a mean-space, without interpolating. The forward pass is then computed in this mean-space and its output prediction pulled back into the original resolution of the target labels. The splat layer therefore removes the need for explicit resolution adjustment. We showed on two multi-modal MRI segmentation tasks that splatting was preferred over resampling. Besides allowing segmentation networks to work on the raw image voxels, and computing the loss function in the space of the original target labels, the splat model could also streamline model deployment as a user does not need to ensure that input images have a specific size. The dimension of the mean-space can additionally be defined to allow optimal application of operations, such as strided convolutions, and/or be made small for faster inference.

Splatting and resampling have the same complexity, which is linear in the number of native voxels. In practice, the loop over native voxels is parallelised (whether running on a CPU or GPU), which makes splatting slightly slower than resampling because multiple native voxels may be pushed to the same output voxel, necessitating the use of atomic assignment (this also makes splatting non-deterministic, as the order in which values are summed-up in an output voxel is architecture-dependent). The cost is therefore somewhat equivalent, compared to resampling all images to the same grid. However, we introduce an additional input channel with the count image, which increases the number of convolution filters in the first layer. However, if the mean space is known a priori, input images can be splatted offline, as a preprocessing step. In this case, only resampling of the prediction to the loss space needs to happen online.

References

1. Isensee, F., Jaeger, P.F., Kohl, S.A., Petersen, J., Maier-Hein, K.H.: nnU-Net: a self-configuring method for deep learning-based biomedical image segmentation. Nat. Methods **18**(2), 203–211 (2021)
2. Menze, B.H., et al.: The multimodal brain tumor image segmentation benchmark (BRATS). IEEE Trans. Med. Imaging **34**(10), 1993–2024 (2014)
3. Antonelli, M., et al.: The medical segmentation decathlon. arXiv preprint arXiv:2106.05735 (2021)
4. Kuijf, H.J., et al.: Standardized assessment of automatic segmentation of white matter hyperintensities and results of the WMH segmentation challenge. IEEE Trans. Med. Imaging **38**(11), 2556–2568 (2019)
5. Yushkevich, P.A., et al.: Bias in estimation of hippocampal atrophy using deformation-based morphometry arises from asymmetric global normalization: an illustration in ADNI 3 T MRI data. Neuroimage **50**(2), 434–445 (2010)
6. Thompson, W.K., Holland, D., Initiative, A.D.N., et al.: Bias in tensor based morphometry Stat-ROI measures may result in unrealistic power estimates. Neuroimage **57**(1), 1–4 (2011)
7. Suk, H.-I., Lee, S.-W., Shen, D., Initiative, A.D.N., et al.: Hierarchical feature representation and multimodal fusion with deep learning for AD/MCI diagnosis. Neuroimage **101**, 569–582 (2014)
8. Nie, D., Wang, L., Gao, Y., Shen, D.: Fully convolutional networks for multi-modality isointense infant brain image segmentation. In: 2016 IEEE 13th International Symposium on Biomedical Imaging (ISBI), pp. 1342–1345. IEEE (2016)
9. Kamnitsas, K., et al.: Ensembles of multiple models and architectures for robust brain tumour segmentation. In: Crimi, A., Bakas, S., Kuijf, H., Menze, B., Reyes, M. (eds.) BrainLes 2017. LNCS, vol. 10670, pp. 450–462. Springer, Cham (2018). https://doi.org/10.1007/978-3-319-75238-9_38
10. Zhou, T., Fu, H., Chen, G., Shen, J., Shao, L.: Hi-net: hybrid-fusion network for multi-modal MR image synthesis. IEEE Trans. Med. Imaging **39**(9), 2772–2781 (2020)
11. Dolz, J., Gopinath, K., Yuan, J., Lombaert, H., Desrosiers, C., Ayed, I.B.: HyperDense-Net: a hyper-densely connected CNN for multi-modal image segmentation. IEEE Trans. Med. Imaging **38**(5), 1116–1126 (2018)
12. Billot, B., et al.: SynthSeg: Domain randomisation for segmentation of brain MRI scans of any contrast and resolution. arXiv preprint arXiv:2107.09559 (2021)
13. Szczotka, A.B., Shakir, D.I., Ravì, D., Clarkson, M.J., Pereira, S.P., Vercauteren, T.: Learning from irregularly sampled data for endomicroscopy super-resolution: a comparative study of sparse and dense approaches. Int. J. Comput. Assist. Radiol. Surg. **15**(7), 1167–1175 (2020). https://doi.org/10.1007/s11548-020-02170-7
14. Westover, L.: Interactive volume rendering. In: Proceedings of the 1989 Chapel Hill workshop on Volume visualization, pp. 9–16 (1989)
15. Ashburner, J., Ridgway, G.R.: Symmetric diffeomorphic modeling of longitudinal structural MRI. Front. Neurosci. **6**, 197 (2013)
16. Pennec, X., Arsigny, V.: Exponential barycenters of the canonical Cartan connection and invariant means on Lie groups. In: Nielsen, F., Bhatia, R. (eds.) Matrix Information Geometry, pp. 123–166. Springer, Heidelberg (2013).https://doi.org/10.1007/978-3-642-30232-9_7

17. Ronneberger, O., Fischer, P., Brox, T.: U-Net: convolutional networks for biomed-ical image segmentation. In: Navab, N., Hornegger, J., Wells, W.M., Frangi, A.F. (eds.) MICCAI 2015. LNCS, vol. 9351, pp. 234–241. Springer, Cham (2015). https://doi.org/10.1007/978-3-319-24574-4_28

18. Bakas, S., et al.: Advancing the cancer genome atlas glioma MRI collections with expert segmentation labels and radiomic features. Sci. Data 4(1), 1–13 (2017)

19. Bakas, S., et al.: Segmentation labels for the pre-operative scans of the TCGA-GBM collection (2017). Data retrieved from the Cancer Imaging Archive, https://doi.org/10.7937/K9/TCIA.2017.KLXWJJ1Q

20. Clark, K., et al.: The Cancer Imaging Archive (TCIA): maintaining and operating a public information repository. J. Digit. Imaging 26(6), 1045–1057 (2013)

Rotation-Equivariant Semantic Instance Segmentation on Biomedical Images

Karl Bengtsson Bernander[✉], Joakim Lindblad, Robin Strand,
and Ingela Nyström

Centre for Image Analysis, Uppsala University, Uppsala, Sweden
{karl.bengtsson_bernander,joakim.lindblad,robin.strand,
ingela.nystrom}@it.uu.se

Abstract. Advances in image segmentation techniques, brought by convolutional neural network (CNN) architectures like U-Net, show promise for tasks such as automated cancer screening. Recently, these methods have been extended to detect different instances of the same class, which could be used to, for example, characterize individual cells in whole-slide images. Still, the amount of data needed and the number of parameters in the network are substantial. To alleviate these problems, we modify a method of semantic instance segmentation to also enforce equivariance to the p4 symmetry group of 90-degree rotations and translations. We perform four experiments on a synthetic dataset of scattered sticks and a subset of the Kaggle 2018 Data Science Bowl, the BBBC038 dataset, consisting of segmented nuclei images. Results indicate that the rotation-equivariant architecture yields similar accuracy as a baseline architecture. Furthermore, we observe that the rotation-equivariant architecture converges faster than the baseline. This is a promising step towards reducing the training time during development of methods based on deep learning.

Keywords: Deep learning · Training · Convergence

1 Introduction

Semantic segmentation and labelling of instances is sometimes said to be one of the most difficult problems in the field of image analysis. Each pixel in the image needs to be classified, and different instances separated from each other. This presents many problems, even for humans, when attempting to isolate objects with similar characteristics close to each other. Consider a pathologist looking in a microscope, trying to diagnose cancer by observing a sample of cells. The cells are numerous, often occluding each other, varying in shape, color and size, and accompanied by waste from the staining process. The diagnostic process can be time-consuming and tedious even for an experienced pathologist. Automation of processes like these, for example, identifying individual malignant cells, is desirable.

© The Author(s), under exclusive license to Springer Nature Switzerland AG 2022
G. Yang et al. (Eds.): MIUA 2022, LNCS 13413, pp. 283–297, 2022.
https://doi.org/10.1007/978-3-031-12053-4_22

In recent years, automated semantic segmentation has made great progress, mainly brought by convolutional neural networks such as U-Net [18] and The One Hundred Layers Tiramisu [15]. However, typically for deep learning, there is a need for a lot of training data. Suitable data can be difficult to find. Also, usually, the more data used in the training, the longer the training takes. One commonly used strategy for reducing the amount of training data is data augmentation, for example, rotating the data while keeping the labels intact, thereby forcing the network to map rotated versions of the input to the same output. However, this is not without problems since rotating the data can introduce interpolation artifacts, and each rotation needs to be learnt separately by the network.

Equivariant neural networks can alleviate these problems. The core idea is to enforce equivariance to transformations such as rotations (R) throughout the network:

$$R(C(x)) = C(R(x)) \tag{1}$$

where C is a convolution operation and x is the input to the corresponding layer. Put simply, rotating the input to a layer yields identical results after convolution as rotating the output of the layer. One way to achieve this is to use G-convolutions [8]. Other methods for achieving rotational equivariance include enforcing it through a loss function in various ways [4,9,16,17]. By using equivariant networks, it has been shown that data augmentation steps can be skipped, while also resulting in less overfitting to training data [3]. While enforcing rotation equivariance for semantic segmentation has seen great progress in the last years [7], the same is not true for semantic instance segmentation, where each instance should be labelled in addition to its class.

In biomedical settings, it is desired to obtain as high accuracy as possible to ensure a correct diagnosis for further treatment. Meanwhile, developing a method based on deep learning for a new problem setting is usually a time-consuming process. While the trained network is usually quite fast, the development phase can take months or years to complete, involving finding capable hardware, software, architectures, data, and fine-tuning of hyperparameters. This involves running many experiments using some kind of prototype model.

Progress in systematizing this exploratory search for optimal settings would be useful for adapting models to new realistic problems. One way to do this is to first optimize a model using a smaller dataset, and then increase the amount of data. This typically moves the model from a low-accuracy region to a high accuracy region. The region in between these regions typically scales with data in a way that can be described using a power law [14]. These results hold for different problem settings. Recent work shows that the exponent of this power law is steeper when using equivariant neural networks [2]. Characterizing such effects is of interest for speeding up the development phase of projects based on deep learning.

In this paper, we combine semantic instance segmentation with rotation-equivariant neural networks. The aims are to match or improve the final accuracy on the test set, and accelerate the training and development of deep learning models. This is performed in four experiments, outlined in Sect. 5.

2   Related Work

Methods based on deep learning for instance segmentation can loosely be grouped into several main categories [11].

The first group is the classification of mask proposals. This typically consists of two stages: first, regions where objects are likely to occur are generated and thereafter these are classified into the corresponding class, along with its bounding box. An example is the R-CNN [10].

The second group is the detection followed by segmentation. This can, very simplified, be seen as an extension of the first group. An important difference is that it further processes the mask proposals into instance masks. An example is the Mask R-CNN [13].

The third group is the labelling of pixels followed by clustering. These methods generally use pixel-wise segmentation architectures such as U-Net to also output an instance representation. This representation is then clustered into separate instances. An example is to use a Discriminative Loss Function [5], which this paper builds upon.

The fourth group is the methods of dense sliding windows. These methods generate object mask proposals or probability masks, which are then compared against the entirety of the image. An example is the Proposal-Free Volumetric Instance Segmentation from Latent Single-Instance Masks [1].

A fifth group consists of those methods related to cellpose method [20]. Here, the instances are labelled using a simulated diffusion process to produce spatial gradients directed to the center of the instance. These flows are then predicted by a neural network, and during test time each pixel is labelled according to the fixed points of the system.

ReDet [12] is a novel method similar to ours, but with some important differences. ReDet provides rotation-invariant instance segmentation on a local scale, by classifying and refining regions of interest. In contrast, our method provides a pixel-wise instance representation over the whole image, and enforces equivariance to rotations in the p4 symmetry group on a global scale. We believe this makes our approach more suited for images with a dense distribution of objects, such as in the analysis of whole-slide images of cell nuclei, where the global orientation under the microscope is irrelevant.

3   Methods

The baseline architecture consists of the U-Net architecture [18] modified to have two output heads [5]. The first head outputs a segmentation mask, while the second head outputs an instance representation. The instance representation associates each pixel with 16 scalar values. This representation can then be postprocessed into instances using a clustering algorithm. The architecture is presented in detail in Fig. 1. Our contribution consists of enforcing equivariance to the p4 group, presented in Sects. 3.2 and 3.3.

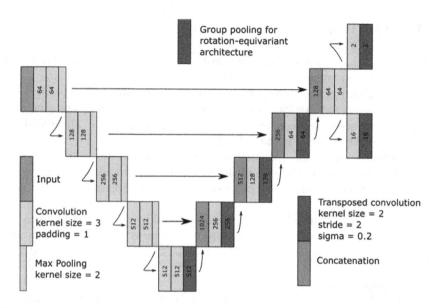

Fig. 1. The modified U-Net architecture, with its two output heads. The upper 2-channel head is the segmentation output, while the lower 16-channel head is the instance representation output. The numbers inside the colored boxes indicate the output number of channels for the corresponding operation. All convolution and pooling parameters are from the default pytorch and E2CNN settings unless otherwise noted.

The instance representation is used for clustering into separate instances using e.g. k-means or mean shift clustering. In this paper, we use the k-means clustering at inference time and set the number of pre-determined clusters to four. We extend an available implementation [21]. The extended code can be found here.

3.1 Loss Function

Pixel-wise segmentation and instance labels are needed for each training example. To train the network, the cross-entropy loss from the semantic segmentation is added to the discriminative loss from the instance segmentation [5]. The loss function enforces separation between the instances in the instance representation:

$$L_{var} = \frac{1}{C} \sum_{c=1}^{C} \frac{1}{N_c} \sum_{i=1}^{N_c} [\|\mu_c - x_i\| - \delta_v]_+^2 \tag{2}$$

$$L_{dist} = \frac{1}{C(C-1)} \sum_{c_A=1}^{C} \sum_{c_B=1}^{C} [2\delta_d - \|\mu_{c_A} - \mu_{c_B}\|]_+^2 (c_A \neq c_B) \tag{3}$$

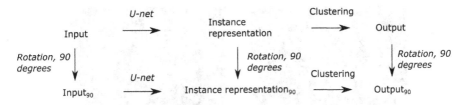

Fig. 2. The full instance segmentation method is equivariant to rotations of multiples of 90°. The input is fed into the rotation-equivariant U-Net, which outputs a binary segmentation mask and 16 additional scalar values per pixel, which form the instance representation. The instance representation is then clustered into instances. Rotations act only on pixel coordinates. No matter where a rotation of 90° is applied, the final output is identical.

$$L_{reg} = \frac{1}{C} \sum_{c=1}^{C} \|\mu_c\| \tag{4}$$

$$L = \alpha \cdot L_{var} + \beta \cdot L_{dist} + \gamma \cdot L_{reg} \tag{5}$$

where we set the constants in the loss function L to $\alpha = 1.0$, $\beta = 1.0$, and $\gamma = 0.001$. L_{var} corresponds to a term that encourages pixels from the same instance to minimize the distance to their center. L_{dist} pushes different clusters apart from each other. L_{reg} prohibits cluster terms from growing too large. The number of clusters is $C = 4$, N_c is the number of elements in cluster c, x_i is an embedding, and μ_c is a cluster center. $\| \cdot \|$ is the L1 or L2 norm, and $[x]_+ = \max(0, x)$. The margins are defined as $\delta_{var} = 0.5$ and $\delta_{dist} = 1.5$.

3.2 Rotation-Equivariance of Architecture

From the selected baseline network, we construct a network that is equivariant to rotations by design, using the E2CNN library [22]. First, the input image is converted from a standard torch tensor to a GeometricTensor. Standard convolutions are replaced with group-equivariant convolutions. The symmetry group is the set of the four discrete 90-degree rotations in a circle in addition to translations, also known as the p4 group. Activations, poolings and normalizations make use of the respective equivariant functions from the E2CNN library.

For the upscaling layers in the up-block (the decoder), the corresponding R2ConvTransposed function is used with a sigma parameter of 0.2. For the skip-connections, where the layers from the down-block and up-block are merged, the direct sum function is used. Finally, group pooling layers are added to the two output representations, and the resulting GeometricTensors are converted back to torch tensors.

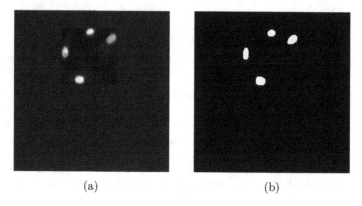

(a)   (b)

Fig. 3. An example from the test partition of the modified BBBC038 dataset. a) The cropped image of nuclei (contrast enhanced for improved visualization) and b) its segmentation mask consisting of four instances.

3.3 Rotation-Equivariance of Clustering

During inference, after a forward pass in the rotation-equivariant network, the instance representation needs to be clustered into separate instances. For the complete method to be equivariant to the p4 group, this clustering step must be shown to be equivariant to rotations as well. Figure 2 illustrates the situation for a generic clustering algorithm.

At the clustering step, the feature map has the same number of pixels as the input. Each pixel is associated with 16 scalar values, which are invariant under rotation of the pixel coordinates. The clustering algorithm operates only in the space spanned by these 16 scalar values, which looks the same regardless of the rotation of the underlying pixels. Therefore, the clustering step is invariant to rotations. This holds for both k-means and the clustering in the discriminative loss, as well as any other clustering algorithm. This also holds for any transformation acting on the pixel coordinates. Hence, in this case, the complete method is equivariant to rotations of multiples of $90°$.

4 Datasets

To evaluate and compare the baseline and rotation-equivariant methods, two datasets were used. Both datasets consists of sets of one input image, one segmentation mask and one image stack with a mask for each instance.

4.1 Synthetic Scattered Sticks

The synthetic scattered sticks consists of a fixed number of rectangular sticks of identical size, but with varying positions and orientations. The sticks are arbitrarily placed in the image and can also occlude each other, meaning that any instance segmentation method must take into account the detailed shape of the objects and cannot only consider adjacent pixels.

The sticks dataset was partitioned into a training set of 512 images and a test partition of 16 images. For both partitions, the data was dynamically generated for each run of the experiment.

4.2 BBBC038

The BBBC038 dataset from the Kaggle 2018 Data Science Bowl [6] consists of a collection of biological images of cell nuclei. The samples have been treated and imaged under highly varied conditions, differing in illumination, magnification, and image modalities. The cells themselves come from different animals and tissues in different states, for example, cell division or genotoxic stress. This dataset offers a highly diverse set of shapes, colors and distribution of objects for semantic segmentation algorithms.

We modified the images in several ways to align them with our experimental setup. First, the dataset is intended for semantic segmentation, while we are interested in semantic instance segmentation. Therefore, we extracted both segmentation and instance masks. Secondly, the clustering methods need the number of clusters as a constant parameter. Since the number of cells in the images vary, the images were cropped to ensure they contained a predetermined number of cells. The image pixels outside the cropped area were padded with the mean intensity of the original image to a fixed size of 256 by 256 pixels. Pixel intensities were converted to greyscale. An example can be seen in Fig. 3.

For the first and second experiments, we use 500 images for the training set and 16 images for the test set. For the third experiment, to increase the amount of test data, we partition 400 images for the training set and 100 images for the test set.

5 Experimental Setup

We performed four experiments. The first tested if the rotation-equivariant architecture would perform similarly as the baseline network in terms of pixelwise classification accuracy. To achieve this, both the baseline and rotation-equivariant networks were trained for 100 epochs. Once during each epoch, instance segmentation Dice scores were calculated. Experiment details such as hyperparameters are outlined in Table 1. For simplicity, dropout or batch normalization were not used. The tests were repeated five times, and averages for each epoch and for all epochs were calculated. After the final epoch, the results on the test set were visually inspected.

The second experiment examined if data augmentation would yield higher accuracy when using data augmentation for the baseline method. Also, it tested if the rotation-equivariant method could match these results without data augmentation. First, 100 images from the BBBC038 training set were selected and rotated by 90, 180 and 270° while keeping their labels intact. Then, both the

Table 1. Hyperparameters and details of the networks.

Parameter	Setting
Loss function	Cross-entropy, discriminative
Weight initialization	He
Optimizer	SGD
Momentum	0.9
Weight decay	0.001
Learning rate	0.001, dynamically decreasing
Number of epochs	100
Activation functions	ReLu

original and the augmented datasets were input to the baseline and rotation-equivariant architectures.

The third experiment tested the effects of varying the amount of training data in terms of Dice scores versus epochs on the test set. The training data was varied from 100 to 400 examples (500 for the sticks dataset) in steps of 100. The fourth experiment tested empirically if the rotation-equivariant architecture is equivariant to rotations. Details for how to perform the rest of the measurements are outlined in the following subsections.

5.1   Evaluation of Segmentation

To evaluate the instance segmentation, a metric that yields a value of 0 when there is no overlap between labels and a value of 1 when there is perfect overlap is desired. To achieve this, we used the Dice score:

$$\frac{2 * TP}{2 * TP + FP + FN} \tag{6}$$

This was performed instance-wise, in addition to the background. Since the instances belong to the same class, there exists a multitude of combinations of possible matches between predicted and ground truth labels. To handle this uncertainty, the first ground truth label was compared pixel-wise with each predicted label, excluding the background. The predicted label with the highest overlap was considered the most likely match. From this, the Dice score for the first instance could be calculated. Then, both the ground truth label and the matching label were removed from the lists of possible matches. This was repeated until all the labels and instances and the background had been processed. Then, the Dice score was calculated by taking the mean of all the instance and background Dice scores. The final Dice score reported is the mean over all the images in the test set. This is similar to a comparable project where a non-global Dice score is used [19].

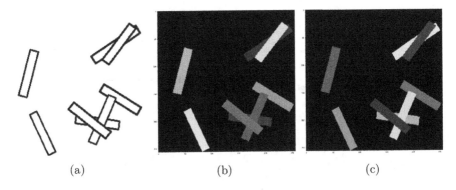

Fig. 4. Example instance segmentations on the scattered sticks dataset. a) Input image, b) an instance segmentation for the baseline architecture, and c) an instance segmentation from the rotation-equivariant architecture.

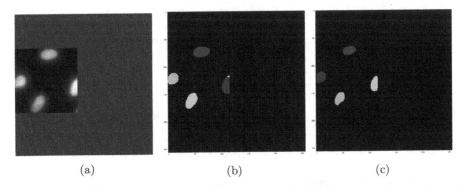

Fig. 5. Example instance segmentations on the modified BBBC038 dataset. a) Input image, b) an instance segmentation from for the baseline architecture, and c) an instance segmentation from the rotation-equivariant architecture.

5.2 Evaluation of Equivariance to Rotations

To evaluate equivariance to rotations, the following procedure was performed. First, one image and a 90-degree rotated copy of the same image were sent through the model, thereby generating output one O_1 and two O_2, respectively. Thereafter, O_2 was rotated by -90 degrees resulting in O_{2rot}.

Finally, O_1 and O_{2rot} were compared pixel-to-pixel, where the final output segmentations were required to overlap exactly to fulfil perfect equivariance to 90-degree rotations.

6   Results

The results for the first three experiments are summarized in Table 2. Figures 4 and 5 show example outputs from the first experiment. The Dice scores for the

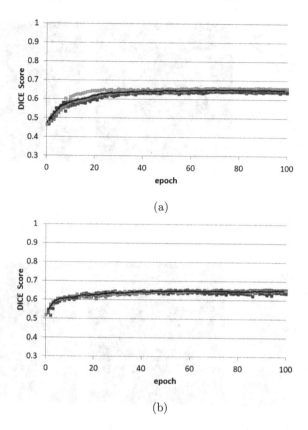

Fig. 6. Dice scores for the BBBC038 dataset during training for a) the baseline network and b) the rotation-equivariant network. Each color represents one experimental run with identical setups, while the black line is the mean of the five experiments. For a), the mean Dice score is 0.626 for all epochs and 0.673 for the last 20 epochs. For b), the mean Dice score is 0.613 for all epochs and 0.638 for the last 20 epochs.

experiments on the modified BBBC038 dataset are shown in Fig. 6. For the third experiments using the rotation-equivariant architecture, the results for the sticks and BBBC038 datasets can be seen in Fig. 7.

The fourth experiment verified the equivariance to rotations empirically, outlined in Sect. 5.2, on the synthetic scattered sticks dataset. Here, on average 167.0625 pixels (that is, 0.25% in the 256×256 size images) differed between the two outputs using the baseline network. The input was the images in the test set. For the rotation-equivariant network the difference was 0 pixels for all images, indicating perfect equivariance.

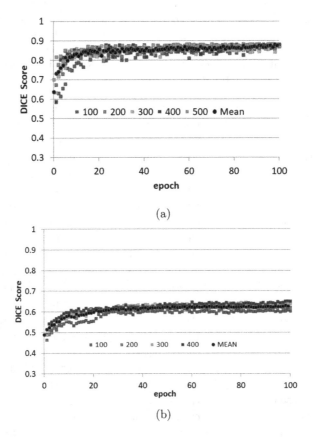

Fig. 7. The Dice scores on a) the sticks test set and b) the BBBC038 test set for different epochs when varying the amount of data. Here, the rotation-equivariant network is used. The learning rate was 0.01 for the sticks dataset, and 0.001 for the BBBC038 dataset.

7   Discussion

From Table 2, it is clear from the first experiment that the baseline and the rotation-equivariant networks are comparable in terms of Dice scores. The Dice score is higher on the scattered sticks dataset compared to the BBBC038 dataset. We believe this is due to BBBC038 being a challenging and highly varied dataset, with cells being adjacent to each other and in different shapes, sizes and colors.

From experiment two it is also clear that augmenting the data for the baseline network increases the accuracy on the test set. The same is not true for the rotation-equivariant network, as expected. However, the rotation-equivariant network yields a slightly lower accuracy than then baseline network with data augmentation. These results are unexpected, and more statistics is needed.

By comparing Figs. 7a and 7b, it is evident that increasing the amount of data is beneficial in terms of accuracy, but the effect is more pronounced on the

Table 2. Experiment results. Initial Dice score is the mean of the first 10 epochs on the test set. Final Dice score is an average for the last epoch on the test set. Data augmentation refers to rotations of 90, 180 and 270°. The number of epochs was 100 except for experiment 2, which used 300 (rows 5–8). CNN refers to the baseline network and GCNN refers to the rotation-equivariant network.

Dataset	No. training data	Network	Augmentation	Initial dice	Final dice
Sticks	500	CNN	None	0.783	0.874
	500	GCNN	None	0.801	0.876
BBBC038	400	CNN	None	0.539	0.649
	400	GCNN	None	0.587	0.649
BBBC038	500	CNN	None	0.439	0.618
	500	CNN	Rotations	0.524	0.656
	500	GCNN	None	0.520	0.632
	500	GCNN	Rotations	0.519	0.620
Sticks	100	CNN	None	0.646	0.865
	200	CNN	None	0.705	0.872
	300	CNN	None	0.736	0.868
	400	CNN	None	0.749	0.877
	500	CNN	None	0.779	0.860
	100	GCNN	None	0.700	0.871
	200	GCNN	None	0.771	0.880
	300	GCNN	None	0.782	0.868
	400	GCNN	None	0.804	0.878
	500	GCNN	None	0.811	0.882
BBBC038	100	CNN	None	0.463	0.610
	200	CNN	None	0.485	0.625
	300	CNN	None	0.500	0.623
	400	CNN	None	0.542	0.648
	100	GCNN	None	0.529	0.605
	200	GCNN	None	0.534	0.624
	300	GCNN	None	0.546	0.637
	400	GCNN	None	0.569	0.62

BBBC038 dataset. This effect was also seen when using the baseline network. We believe the BBBC038 dataset is more representative of data encountered in real applications, meaning that more data is needed to capture the characteristics of the underlying distribution. Furthermore, both the baseline and the rotation-equivariant networks achieve similar accuracy on both datasets.

From the first three experiments, the rotation-equivariant network converges faster than the baseline network. As an example, when training on 200 images, it takes the baseline network ten epochs to reach a Dice score of at least 0.5. For the rotation-equivariant network, reaching this Dice score instead takes three epochs. This corresponds to 707 s versus 384 s, a difference of 323 s, or more than five minutes. One way to quantify this effect is to compare the Dice scores on the test set after a set amount of epochs. In Table 2, we have performed this for the first 10 epochs. It can be seen that the Dice score for the rotation-equivariant network is higher than the baseline network in all cases except when performing data augmentation by rotations on the baseline network.

We have shown that the rotation-equivariant architecture is indeed equivariant to rotations in the p4 group, both by reasoning and by experiment four, including the final clustering step.

8   Conclusions

We have shown how to construct a deep learning architecture for semantic instance segmentation that is equivariant to rotations in the p4 group. To the best of our knowledge, this is the first implementation of a pixel-level rotation-equivariant semantic instance segmentation network. This is a promising step towards reducing overfitting and the need for data augmentation.

In terms of Dice score in the final epoch of training, the rotation-equivariant network performs similar to a baseline network. This hold for both datasets tested, as well as when varying the amount of training data. Furthermore, we have observed that the rotation-equivariant network converges faster than the baseline network. One possible reason for this is that the rotation-equivariant network is able to exploit the underlying symmetries in the data by its design. This faster convergence is similar to what has been found in previous research [2]. However, to our knowledge, this specific effect has not been described before. This could be useful when faster development speed is desired, especially in biomedical image analysis.

The current rotation-equivariant architecture has some limitations and can be extended in useful ways. First, it could use other symmetry groups in the E2CNN library, making it equivariant to the corresponding transformations. Secondly, the clustering methods in the discriminative loss and the post-processing step could be modified to not require a predetermined number of clusters. This would enhance its usability in settings where the number of instances is unknown.

Improving automation in pathology could lead to faster and more efficient diagnosis of medical conditions. However, it could also lead to redundancy for pathologists. What we believe is more likely is that these methods will assist them. Similarly, search engines have not replaced traditional diagnosis.

Acknowledgments. We thank Professor Fred Hamprecht, University of Heidelberg, Germany, for providing guidance on instance segmentation. The project is funded by WASP (Wallenberg, AI, Autonomous Systems and Software Program).

References

1. Bailoni, A., Pape, C., Wolf, S., Kreshuk, A., Hamprecht, F.A.: Proposal-free volumetric instance segmentation from latent single-instance masks. In: Akata, Z., Geiger, A., Sattler, T. (eds.) DAGM GCPR 2020. LNCS, vol. 12544, pp. 331–344. Springer, Cham (2021). https://doi.org/10.1007/978-3-030-71278-5_24

2. Batzner, S., et al.: E(3)-equivariant graph neural networks for data-efficient and accurate interatomic potentials. arXiv (2021)
3. Bernander, K.B., Lindblad, J., Strand, R., Nyström, I.: Replacing data augmentation with rotation-equivariant CNNs in image-based classification of oral cancer. In: Tavares, J.M.R.S., Papa, J.P., González Hidalgo, M. (eds.) CIARP 2021. LNCS, vol. 12702, pp. 24–33. Springer, Cham (2021). https://doi.org/10.1007/978-3-030-93420-0_3
4. Bortsova, G., Dubost, F., Hogeweg, L., Katramados, I., de Bruijne, M.: Semi-supervised medical image segmentation via learning consistency under transformations. In: Shen, D., et al. (eds.) MICCAI 2019. LNCS, vol. 11769, pp. 810–818. Springer, Cham (2019). https://doi.org/10.1007/978-3-030-32226-7_90
5. Brabandere, B.D., Neven, D., Gool, L.V.: Semantic instance segmentation with a discriminative loss function. In: IEEE/CVF Conference on Computer Vision and Pattern Recognition Workshops (CVPRW) (2017)
6. Caicedo, J.C., et al.: Nucleus segmentation across imaging experiments: the: data science bowl. Nature Methods **16**, 1247–1253 (2019)
7. Chidester, B., Ton, T., Tran, M., Ma, J., Do, M.N.: Enhanced rotation-equivariant U-Net for nuclear segmentation. In: IEEE/CVF Conference on Computer Vision and Pattern Recognition Workshops (CVPRW), pp. 1097–1104 (2019). https://doi.org/10.1109/CVPRW.2019.00143
8. Cohen, T.S., Welling, M.: Group equivariant convolutional networks. In: Proceedings of the 33rd International Conference on International Conference on Machine Learning, ICML 2016, pp. 2990–2999. JMLR.org (2016)
9. Feng, Z., Xu, C., Tao, D.: Self-supervised representation learning by rotation feature decoupling. In Proceedings of the IEEE/CVF Conference on Computer Vision and Pattern Recognition (CVPR), June 2019
10. Girshick, R., Donahue, J., Darrell, T., Malik, J.: Rich feature hierarchies for accurate object detection and semantic segmentation. In: IEEE Conference on Computer Vision and Pattern Recognition (CVPR), pp. 580–587 (2014). https://doi.org/10.1109/CVPR.2014.81
11. Hafiz, A.M., Bhat, G.M.: A survey on instance segmentation: state of the art. Int. J. Multimedia Inf. Retrieval **9**(3), 171–189 (2020). https://doi.org/10.1007/s13735-020-00195-x
12. Han, J., Ding, J., Xue, N., Xia, G.-S.: ReDet: a rotation-equivariant detector for aerial object detection. In: IEEE/CVF Conference on Computer Vision and Pattern Recognition (CVPR), pp. 2786–2795 (2021)
13. He, K., Gkioxari, G., Dollár, P., Girshick, R.: Mask R-CNN. In: IEEE International Conference on Computer Vision (ICCV), pp. 2980–2988 (2017). https://doi.org/10.1109/ICCV.2017.322
14. Hestness, J., et al.: Deep learning scaling is predictable, empirically. arXiv (2017)
15. Jégou, S., Drozdzal, M., Vazquez, D., Romero, A., Bengio, Y.: The one hundred layers tiramisu: Fully convolutional densenets for semantic segmentation. In: IEEE Conference on Computer Vision and Pattern Recognition Workshops (CVPRW), pp. 1175–1183 (2017). https://doi.org/10.1109/CVPRW.2017.156
16. Laradji, I., et al.: A weakly supervised consistency-based learning method for covid-19 segmentation in CT images. In: Proceedings of the IEEE/CVF Conference on Computer Vision and Pattern Recognition (CVPR), pp. 2452–2461 (2021). https://doi.org/10.1109/WACV48630.2021.00250

17. Pielawski, N., et al.: CoMIR: contrastive multimodal image representation for registration. In: Advances in Neural Information Processing Systems, vol. 33, pages 18433–18444. Curran Associates Inc (2020). https://proceedings.neurips.cc/paper/2020/file/d6428eecbe0f7dff83fc607c5044b2b9-Paper.pdf
18. Ronneberger, O., Fischer, P., Brox, T.: U-Net: convolutional networks for biomedical image segmentation. In: Navab, N., Hornegger, J., Wells, W.M., Frangi, A.F. (eds.) MICCAI 2015. LNCS, vol. 9351, pp. 234–241. Springer, Cham (2015). https://doi.org/10.1007/978-3-319-24574-4_28
19. Roß, T., et al.: Comparative validation of multi-instance instrument segmentation in endoscopy: Results of the robust-mis: 2019 challenge. Med. Image Anal. **70**, 101920 (2021). https://doi.org/10.1016/j.media.2020.101920
20. Stinger, C., Wang, T., Michaelos, M., Pachitariu, M.: Cellpose: a generalist algorithm for cellular segmentation. Nat. Methods **18**(1), 100–106 (2020)
21. Taniai, H.: pytorch-discriminative-loss (2018). https://github.com/nyoki-mtl/pytorch-discriminative-loss. Accessed 15 Nov 2021
22. Weiler, M., Cesa, G.: General E(2)-equivariant steerable CNNs. In: Advances in Neural Information Processing Systems, vol. 32. Curran Associates Inc (2019). https://proceedings.neurips.cc/paper/2019/file/45d6637b718d0f24a237069fe41b0db4-Paper.pdf

Joint Learning with Local and Global Consistency for Improved Medical Image Segmentation

Md. Atik Ahamed[1]([⊠])[iD] and Abdullah Al Zubaer Imran[2][iD]

[1] Green University of Bangladesh, Dhaka 01207, Bangladesh
atikahamedutso@gmail.com
[2] Stanford University, Stanford, CA 94305, USA
aimran@Stanford.edu

Abstract. Semantic segmentation has been one of the key components in subsequent image-based decision-making across computer vision and biomedical imaging. While a lot of progress has been made with the advent of deep learning, segmentation models rely heavily on large labeled datasets for optimal results. Moreover, with added challenges due to varying imaging conditions, abnormalities, etc., it becomes relatively a harder problem to solve, even by the most sophisticated models. Additionally, segmentation models when employed at small patch-level lose the global context and when employed at the full image-level may lose focus to closely located and small objects-of-interest. In order to resolve such issues and thereby improve the segmentation performance, we propose a novel joint patch- and image-level training framework namely *Image-to-Patch w/ Patch-to-Image (IPPI)* which at the same time preserves the global context and pays attention to local details. Accommodating the joint training, our proposed IPPI technique can be incorporated with any segmentation network for improved performance and local-global consistency. Our experimentation with three different segmentation networks (U-Net, U-Net++, and NodeU-Net) in segmenting cell nuclei and retinal vessel demonstrates the effectiveness of the proposed IPPI method. The segmentation improvements—13.35% over U-Net, 5.56% over U-Net++, and 4.59% over NodeU-Net IoU (Intersection over Union) make it a potentially beneficial tool in challenging segmentation tasks.

Keywords: Semantic segmentation · Deep learning · U-Net · CNN · Biomedical imaging · Computer vision

1 Introduction

Semantic segmentation can be referred to as a process that entails grouping together similar portions of an image that belong to the same class. Semantic segmentation plays a significant role in medical image analysis as a pre-processing

G. Yang et al. (Eds.): MIUA 2022, LNCS 13413, pp. 298–312, 2022.
https://doi.org/10.1007/978-3-031-12053-4_23

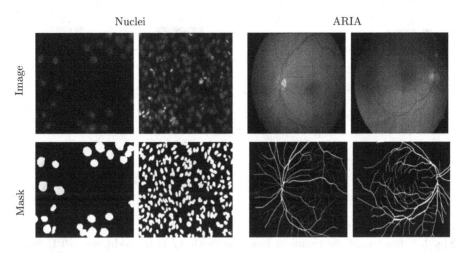

Fig. 1. Sample images from the Nuclei and ARIA datasets: input images and their corresponding ground truth masks are visualized.

step to acquiring valuable quantitative data for medical interpretation. It has allowed for considerable information regarding the anatomy of target structures to be obtainable in a noninvasive manner.

In the current era, digital images consisting of individual pixel values contain a lot of useful information. This leads the researchers to focus on biomedical imaging based on RGB or gray-scaled images. Biomedical images are nowadays passed through a variety of computer-aided processes to make a better diagnosis, such as classification, feature extraction, segmentation, etc. The segmentation process helps improve the performance of the subsequent image-based decision making [13].

Semantic segmentation for cell nucleus is highly important as automated nucleus detection could help unlock cures faster-from rare disorders to the common cold [10]. Moreover, identification of individual cells in a sample can be enabled via identifying their nuclei. Observing how cells respond to various treatments, the underlying biological processes at the action could further be deduced. By automatic this process, a huge amount of time is saved. The development of strong artificial neural networks for semantic segmentation and object detection are mainly focused on accompanying the automation process.

Diabetes and hypertension can be diagnosed by retinal vessels in fundus images [16]. High blood pressure can be a cause of Hypertensive Retinopathy [15]. Therefore, extracting retinal blood vessels from fundus images plays an important role for early diagnosis of several crucial diseases [14].

Deep learning algorithms for computer vision-related tasks is capable of solving a variety of biomedical image diagnosis with increasing level of accuracy. For computer vision tasks, Convolutional Neural Networks (CNNs) have become the go to approach for a number of computer vision and biomedical imaging tasks. For semantic segmentation tasks, mostly the U-Net [22] and its variants are used,

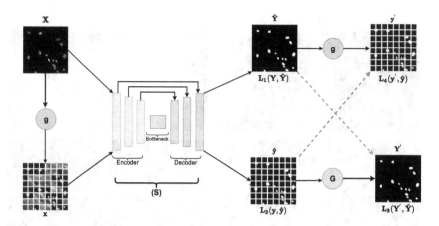

Fig. 2. Schematic of the proposed Image-to-Patch w/ Patch-to-Image (IPPI) framework for medical image segmentation. IPPI jointly learns segmenting full image X and image patch x through the same segmentor S. In addition to the losses for the local and global segmentation predictions $\hat{y}$ and $\hat{Y}$ (L_1 and L_2), consistency losses are calculated from the reconstructed image-level predictions (L_3) and patchified patch-level predictions (L_4).

as these models give highly accurate results [12,30]. Towards segmenting from biomedical image data where attention to local details is required while preserving the global context, we propose the Image-to-Patch w/ Patch-to-Image (IPPI) framework. The main contributions of the present paper can be summarized as follows:

- A novel joint training framework for semantic segmentation deep learning models at patch-level (local) and image-level (global) within the same model
- Consistently improved performance compared to state-of-the-art segmentation models in segmenting nuclei from microscopy images and retinal blood vessels from fundus images

2   Related Work

Not only in biomedical imaging, but semantic segmentation is also crucial across many other fields such as, satellite image processing, autonomous driving, etc. Semantic segmentation in general is performed either at full size images [22,30] or at image patches [23,26]. We review the recent developments in both patch-based and full image-based segmentations as well as specific applications to nuclei segmentation from microscopy images and retinal blood vessel segmentation from fundus images.

Full Image Segmentation: Prior to deep learning, some methodologies such as Support Vector Machine (SVM), Random Decision Forests (RDF) were conducted to perform semantic segmentation [25]. However, breakthrough work by Ronneberger et al. [22] is based on fully convolutional neural network (FCN) [19] with fewer training images. Though the FCN architecture is robust towards unseen data, it consumes more parameters, i.e., more memory than U-Net architecture [3]. Another work Node-UNet architecture proposed by Ahamed et al. [1], combined the baseline U-Net architecture with Neural Ordinary Differential block proposed in [6]. This Node-UNet architecture shows an improvement of 2.2% IoU over the baseline U-Net architecture. In another work, full image segmentation (Patch-free) procedure is proposed by Wang et al. [26]. Another study by Zhu et al. [31] performs full image segmentation of multi-stage caries lesion from oral panoramic X-ray image.

Patch-based Segmentation: Several patch-based methods exist in literature for the semantic segmentation of medical images. A patch-based method is proposed by Jin et al. [16] named as DUNet for retinal vessel segmentation. However, this DUNet method is limited to large memory requirement for training. Even with a batch size of 1, 512×512 images could not be fit with 24GB of GPU memory; hence, this method is not practically applicable. Another work by Sekou et al. [23] demonstrates a two step transfer learning process (patch2image) for semantic segmentation of retinal vessel segmentation. However, this approach lacks the generalization towards unseen data and cannot fully exploit the joint learning scheme. Some other patch-based methods include segmentation of endobronchial ultrasound procedures [18], a combination of supervised and unsupervised patch-based approach for the segmentation of histopathological images [8], and segmentation of haracterize smooth muscle fibers in hematoxylin and eosin stained histopathological images [24].

Cell Nuclei Segmentation: Previous nucleus segmentation work includes an unsupervised segmentation by Bamford and Lovell [2]. A supervised approach for nucleus segmentation is proposed in [28], which uses a CNN architecture for the segmentation task. Several other state-of-the art methodologies such as U-Net++ [30] (A nested U-Net architecture) gained an average IoU of 1.86% over U-Net architecture for cell nucleus segmentation. Another study by Goyzueta et al. [9] also demonstrated cell nucleus segmentation integrating the U-Net [22], ResU-Net [17] and DeepLab [5] architectures.

Retinal Vessel Segmentation: In-case of retinal vessel segmentation, Zana and Klein [29] performed unsupervised segmentation by using mathematical morphology and curvature evaluation. Another popular unsupervised experiment conducted by Hassan et al. [11] where they combined mathematical morphology and k-means clustering to segment blood vessels. Several supervised approaches were conducted to perform retinal vessel segmentation such as a ConvNet-ensemble based framework to process color fundus images and detect blood vessels [20]. Jin et al. [16] proposed a deformable U-Net architecture for segmenting retinal vessel image. However, this method has large memory requirements.

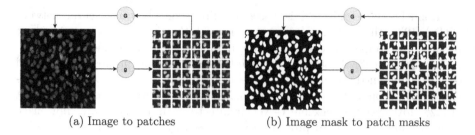

(a) Image to patches   (b) Image mask to patch masks

Fig. 3. Patch Generation and reconstruction: 64×64 patches are extracted from the full image and the segmentation mask.

Deviating from all the existing segmentation methods, we combine full image-based segmentation and patch-based segmentation in a joint learning scheme, for local and global consistency and improved segmentation performance in segmenting the cell nuclei from cell microscopy images and retinal vessel segmentation from fundus images.

3   Image-to-Patch w/Patch-to-Image (IPPI)

Figure 2 illustrates the proposed IPPI framework for biomedical image segmentation. IPPI primarily comprises of three components: g, G, and S. g takes an input image at its original resolution and as a patchifier splits into n number of equi-sized non-overlapping patches. On the other hand, G does the opposite. G takes n number of patches and reconstructs the image at original resolution. S in IPPI is used as a segmentation network or which can perform segmentation of an input image. S is an encoder-decoder network that can be replaced by any general purpose segmentation network. The IPPI model contains two separate branches:

- **Patch segmentation branch**: Generates the segmentation masks at patch resolution from an input image patch x.
- **Image segmentation branch**: Generates the segmentation masks at full image resolution from an input full image X.

Two branches share the same S architecture and its weights to make predictions of patch mask and image mask respectively. Unlike the existing patch2image (P2I) segmentation approach [23], our proposed IPPI approach is more elegant as it can be trained in an end-to-end fashion. The objective of the IPPI model includes a patch segmentation loss at the patch branch and another segmentation loss at the image branch. It also includes consistency losses which are calculated after reconstructing the image mask from the patch segmentation predictions as well as patchifying the predicted full image masks.

Algorithm 1: Model Parameter Optimization for IPPI

Input: Training set of images and segmentation masks $\{X, Y\}$, network architecture M_θ with learnable parameters θ, number of epochs N, threshold λ

1 **for** $i \leftarrow 1$ *to* N **do**
2   **Full Image Segmentation:**
3   Predict full image result, $\hat{\mathbf{Y}} = M_\theta(\mathbf{X})$
4   Image segmentation loss, $L_1 = \tau_\ell(\mathbf{Y}, \hat{\mathbf{Y}})$
5   **Patched Image Segmentation:**
6   Generate patches, $\mathbf{x} = g(X)$
7   Predict patched-image result, $\hat{\mathbf{y}} = M_\theta(\mathbf{x})$
8   Patch segmentation loss, $L_2 = \tau_\ell(\mathbf{y}, \hat{\mathbf{y}})$
9   **Consistency Check:**
10   Reconstruct predicted patches, $\mathbf{Y}' = G(\hat{\mathbf{y}})$
11   Patches from predicted masks, $\mathbf{y}' = g(\hat{\mathbf{Y}})$
12   Image consistency loss, $L_3 = 1 - SSIM(\mathbf{Y}', \hat{\mathbf{Y}})$
13   Patch consistency loss, $L_4 = 1 - SSIM(\mathbf{y}', \hat{\mathbf{y}})$
14   Total training loss $L = (1 - \lambda)(L_1 + L_2) + \lambda(L_3 + L_4)$ according to (1)
15   Update M_θ by backpropagating the loss gradient ∇_L;
16 **end**

Figure 3 illustrates the patch generation and image reconstruction process by g and G respectively. In the proposed IPPI framework, $\mathbf{X} \in X_T$ is first passed through the model M_θ. Here, X is a sample from the training dataset X_T. The loss L_1 is calculated from the reference $Y \in Y_T$ and the prediction $\hat{Y}$ ($\hat{Y} = M_\theta(X)$).

$\mathbf{x} = g(X)$, the patched images are passed within the same model M_θ via the patch segmentation branch. A patched segmentation loss L_2 is calculated from the reference $\mathbf{y}$ obtained via g(Y) and $\hat{y}$ ($\hat{y} = M_\theta(x)$) where $y, Y \in Y_T$.

Once the segmentation predictions are made from the model both at patch-level and image-level, the predicted $\hat{y}$ and $\hat{Y}$ become available. In order to ensure the global consistency at local patch-level, we calculate an image consistency loss $L_3 = 1 - SSIM(Y', \hat{Y})$ based on the structural similarity index (SSIM) [27]. Similarly, to maintain the local detailed segmentation consistency at image-level, we calculate a patch consistency loss $L_4 = 1 - SSIM(y', \hat{y})$. Here, $Y' = G(\hat{y})$ and $y' = g(\hat{Y})$.

3.1 Loss Function

The overall training objective for the IPPI-based segmentation model is therefore,

$$L = (1 - \lambda)(L_1 + L_2) + \lambda(L_3 + L_4). \tag{1}$$

Table 1. Training environment setup

Training Setup	Values
Number of epochs	200
Optimizer	Adam
Initial learning rate	$1e-4$
Batch size	1
Learning rate scheduler	Reduce LR On Plateau
Patience for scheduler	10
Full image size	512×512
Patch image size	64×64

After an ablation experiment, we obtained the best possible segmentation performance at $\lambda = 0.01$. L_1 refers to the image segmentation loss while L_2 is the patch segmentation loss. When the model is trained in regular approach, a segmentation loss only for the full image is used. This loss function combines a binary cross-entropy and a Dice loss. Similar hybrid segmentation loss is applied to the prediction across the pathces. The terms L_3 and L_4 denote image consistency loss and patch consistency loss respectively. We leverage the SSIM loss for the consistency losses.

Algorithm 1 illustrates the training procedure by our proposed IPPI approach.

4   Experiments and Results

4.1   Data

We employed two different datasets for our experiments: The cell nucleus segmentation challenge dataset [4] and Automated Retinal Image Analysis (ARIA) dataset [7].

Nuclei Dataset: The dataset contains images acquired under varying conditions, varying cell type and magnification, and image acquisition methods (brightfield vs fluorescence). We primarily obtained 335 microscopy images from nuclei segmentation dataset. The dataset containing microscopy images and corresponding nucleus masks, is split into train (241) and test (94).

ARIA Dataset: The dataset contains fundoscopy images collected from 2004 to 2006 in the United Kingdom of subjects as adult males/females, and healthy/diseased. The 138 images in the dataset are split into train (121) and test (17).

Figure 1 visualizes example images and their corresponding segmentation ground truth masks from the either datasets. The images and masks are originally of different sizes. We resized them to 512×512. Using the patchifier $g(x)$,

Table 2. Comparison among IPPI-Net approach, regular fully-supervised and P2I based approach for test data of Nuclei Segmentation Dataset

Model	Approach	Full image			Patch image		
		IoU	SSIM	Accuracy	IoU	SSIM	Accuracy
U-Net	Regular	0.496	0.706	0.823	0.125	0.674	0.726
	P2I	0.491	0.701	0.765	0.175	0.690	0.749
	IPPI	**0.630**	**0.728**	**0.851**	**0.200**	**0.696**	**0.851**
U-Net++	Regular	0.505	0.710	0.850	0.137	0.678	0.730
	P2I	0.467	0.695	0.763	0.164	0.689	0.742
	IPPI	**0.561**	**0.795**	**0.851**	**0.187**	**0.693**	**0.744**
NodeU-Net	Regular	0.536	0.710	0.831	0.160	0.686	0.737
	P2I	0.430	0.694	0.758	0.145	0.684	0.736
	IPPI	**0.582**	**0.716**	**0.843**	**0.216**	**0.696**	**0.750**

we obtained 64 patches from each of the 512×512 images. The patch size is set to 64×64. Figure 3 illustrates the patch extraction from input full image and the reconstruction of the full image from the extracted patches. Both the patch generation and image reconstruction are performed *on-the-fly*, making training a segmentation model extremely efficient as there is no need to save a large number of patches unlike patch-based methods. All the images were normalized to 0–1 before passing them to the model.

4.2 Implementation Details

We experimented by incorporating our IPPI training approach with three different state-of-the-art segmentation networks U-Net [22], U-Net++ [30] and NodeU-Net [1]. We use the regular image-level segmentation (w/out IPPI) as the baselines to compare against our proposed IPPI method. Additionally, we used a recently proposed patch2image (P2I) [23] transfer learning scheme as additional baseline by incorporating it into the three segmentation networks. Therefore, for each of the segmentation networks, along with our IPPI-incorporated model, we trained the regular and patch2image (P2I)-based training methods. Table 1 presents the conditions and parameter choices for the training environment. All the models and methods were implemented in Python using the PyTorch [21] framework. For the sake of fair comparison, we consistently used the same environment and parameter choices. All the experiments were conducted with an NVIDIA RTX 3090 GPU in a machine of 32 GB RAM and Intel Core-i9 processor.

4.3 Performance Analysis

Table 2 reports the nuclei segmentation performance in terms of IoU, SSIM, and Accuracy metrics. Experimenting with the state-of-the-art segmentation

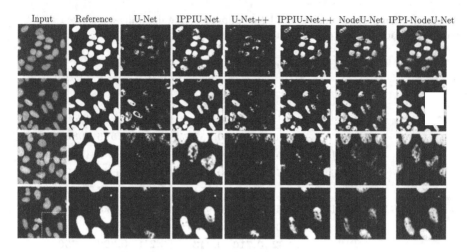

Fig. 4. Visual comparison of full image as well as selected ROIs of nucleus by different models with the regular approach as well as the IPPI approach for the randomly selected test images for nuclei segmentation dataset.

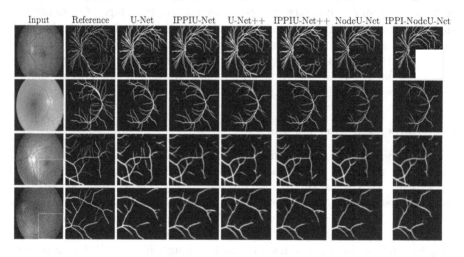

Fig. 5. Visual comparison of full image as well as selected ROIs of retinal vessels by different models with the regular approach as well as the IPPI approach for the randomly selected test images for ARIA dataset.

models (U-Net, U-Net++, and NodeU-Net), we observe improved performance by our proposed IPPI framework over the regular segmentation. For example, the regular U-Net only achieves an IoU of 49.63% wherein by training with IPPI (IPPIU-Net), the same U-Net can achieve 62.98% IoU. This improvement is also consistent across SSIM and accuracy scores. Similarly, we compared the segmentation performance by calculating the metrics at patch level ($\hat{y}$). Like the image-level segmentation, Table 2 reveals the consistently improved

Table 3. Comparison among IPPI-Net approach, regular fully-supervised and P2I based approach for test data of ARIA dataset

Model	Approach	Full Image			Patch Image		
		IoU	SSIM	Acc.	IoU	SSIM	Acc.
U-Net	Regular	0.372	0.764	0.7754	0.164	0.729	0.761
	P2I	0.375	0.765	0.783	0.164	0.747	0.764
	IPPI	**0.379**	**0.765**	**0.800**	**0.220**	**0.784**	**0.764**
U-Net++	Regular	0.374	0.765	0.777	0.129	0.757	**0.766**
	P2I	**0.387**	0.764	0.783	0.176	0.757	0.765
	IPPI	0.372	**0.764**	**0.790**	**0.213**	**0.763**	0.763
NodeU-Net	Regular	0.323	0.766	0.790	0.065	0.720	0.76
	P2I	**0.344**	0.766	0.788	0.119	0.746	0.766
	IPPI	0.334	**0.766**	**0.791**	**0.158**	**0.746**	**0.766**

performance at patch-level with the proposed IPPI across all three segmentation models over the regular segmentation. Moreover, comparison against the two-step patch2image (P2I) segmentation method demonstrates the superiority of IPPI in effectively segmenting the nuclei both at image-level and patch-level (Fig. 6).

We also observe similar improvement trend in retinal vessel segmentation from the ARIA dataset. The segmentation performances are reported in Table 3. In case of U-Net, IPPI consistently outperformed the Regular and P2I across the IoU, SSIM and accuracy metrics when compared both full image and patch segmentations. Again, IPPI predicted segmentations are more accurate with the U-Net++ and NodeU-Net as per SSIM and accuracy. This is further confirmed with the box plots as shown in Fig. 7.

4.4   Visual Prediction

Similar to the quantitative evaluations, the qualitative evaluations also showcase the superior performance by the IPPI-based segmentation over its regular and two-step counterparts. Figure 4 compares the segmentation predictions by the three segmentation networks with and without IPPI approach. As can be seen, the IPPI-based segmentation model provides more improved nuclei segmentation from input microscopy images and vessel segmentation from fundus images. The nuclei and retinal vessels missed by the regular U-Net, U-Net++, and NodeU-Net models were picked up by their IPPI counterparts.

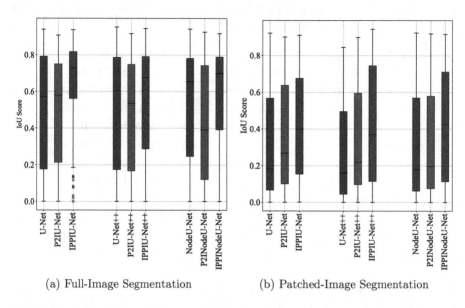

(a) Full-Image Segmentation   (b) Patched-Image Segmentation

Fig. 6. Box-Plots on the IoU score distributions demonstrate consistent improvement for every segmentation network with IPPI compared to the baseline regular and P2I approaches for Nuclei Segmentation dataset

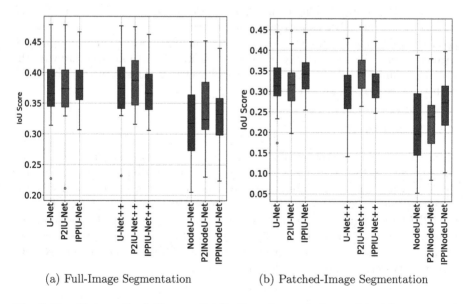

(a) Full-Image Segmentation   (b) Patched-Image Segmentation

Fig. 7. Box-Plots on the IoU score distributions demonstrate consistent improvement for every segmentation network with IPPI compared to the baseline regular and P2I approaches for ARIA dataset.

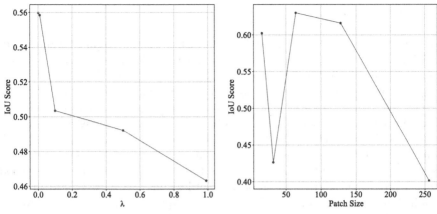

(a) Segmentation IoU against λ values (0.01, 0.1, 0.5, 0.99)

(b) Segmentation IoU against patch sizes ($16\times16, 32\times32, 64\times64, 128\times128, 256\times256$)

Fig. 8. Segmentation performance on different choices of λ parameter and varying resolutions for patch-level segmentation.

Since there are a lot of nucleus cells in each image and from a human perspective, it seems difficult sometimes to understand the critical region segmentation for the cell nuclei. Same goes for retinal vessel segmentation. In some regions there are very thin layer of vessel to segment. To better understand the models' capability, specific cropped and zoomed regions are compared in input images (Fig. 4). Again, the IPPI-based segmentation provides more improved segmentation, making it a potentially beneficial tool to better diagnosis for nuclei related diseases.

4.5   Ablation Experiments

We conducted some ablation study for varying size of patches and λ choices. Figure 8 demonstrates the IoU scores for various λ values and also for different patch size windows. We performed the ablation experiments by taking a small subset of the train set. As demonstrated, the optimal choices for λ is 0.01 and patch size is 64×64. A mix of global and local choice is combined with the λ value. In our training environment fine tuning the λ can enable the segmentation model to capture both global as well as local context for semantic segmentation. The results from Fig. 8 reflects that we should neither only rely on patch based segmentation not on full-image based segmentation. Different patch size results also reflects the same situation. With the increasing patch size the results decrease and with very small patch size the results also decrease. So an optimal patch size needs to be fixed for better segmenting the images.

5 Conclusion

We have presented a novel IPPI framework for training segmentation models in jointly learning at global full image and local patch segmentation predictions from biomedical images. We have validated our proposed IPPI on cell microscopic dataset as well as fundus images in segmenting nuclei and retinal vessel respectively which are crucial for answering many subsequent biological questions. Experimenting with three state-of-the-art biomedical image segmentation models (U-Net, U-Net++, NodeU-Net), we have demonstrated the consistently improved performance by the IPPI-based training. Moreover, IPPI outperforms a recently proposed patch to image transfer learning-based segmentation method, further justifying the true benefit of the joint learning approach. Our future work will include incorporating the IPPI framework applying to image segmentations in more challenging settings as well as other image analysis tasks at scale.

References

1. Ahamed, M.A., Ali Hossain, M., Al Mamun, M.: Semantic segmentation of self-supervised dataset and medical images using combination of u-net and neural ordinary differential equations. In: 2020 IEEE Region 10 Symposium (TENSYMP), pp. 238–241 (2020)
2. Bamford, P., Lovell, B.: Unsupervised cell nucleus segmentation with active contours. Signal Process. **71**(2), 203–213 (1998)
3. Beheshti, N., Johnsson, L.: Squeeze u-net: a memory and energy efficient image segmentation network. In: Proceedings of the IEEE/CVF Conference on Computer Vision and Pattern Recognition Workshops, pp. 364–365 (2020)
4. Caicedo, J.C., et al.: Nucleus segmentation across imaging experiments: the 2018 data science bowl. Nat. Methods **16**(12), 1247–1253 (2019)
5. Chen, L.C., Papandreou, G., Kokkinos, I., Murphy, K., Yuille, A.L.: Deeplab: semantic image segmentation with deep convolutional nets, atrous convolution, and fully connected CRFs. IEEE Trans. Pattern Anal. Mach. Intell. **40**(4), 834–848 (2017)
6. Chen, T.Q., Rubanova, Y., Bettencourt, J., Duvenaud, D.K.: Neural ordinary differential equations. In: Advances in Neural Information Processing Systems, pp. 6571–6583 (2018)
7. Farnell, D.J., Hatfield, F., Knox, P., Reakes, M., Spencer, S., Parry, D., Harding, S.P.: Enhancement of blood vessels in digital fundus photographs via the application of multiscale line operators. J. Franklin Inst. **345**(7), 748–765 (2008)
8. Gerard, G., Piastra, M.: Conditional deep convolutional neural networks for improving the automated screening of histopathological images. arXiv preprint arXiv:2105.14338 (2021)
9. Goyzueta, C.A.R., De la Cruz, J.E.C., Machaca, W.A.M.: Integration of u-net, resu-net and deeplab architectures with intersection over union metric for cells nuclei image segmentation. In: 2021 IEEE Engineering International Research Conference (EIRCON), pp. 1–4. IEEE (2021)
10. Hamilton, B.A.: 2018 data science bowl (2018). https://www.kaggle.com/c/data-science-bowl-2018. Accessed 09 Jan 2022

11. Hassan, G., El-Bendary, N., Hassanien, A.E., Fahmy, A., Snasel, V., et al.: Retinal blood vessel segmentation approach based on mathematical morphology. Procedia Comput. Sci. **65**, 612–622 (2015)

12. Imran, A.A.Z.: From Fully-Supervised, Single-Task to Scarcely-Supervised, Multi-Task Deep Learning for Medical Image Analysis. Ph.D. thesis, UCLA (2020)

13. Imran, A.A.Z., et al.: Fully-automated analysis of scoliosis from spinal x-ray images. In: 2020 IEEE 33rd International Symposium on Computer-Based Medical Systems (CBMS), pp. 114–119 (2020)

14. Imran, A.A.Z., Terzopoulos, D.: Progressive adversarial semantic segmentation. In: 2020 25th International Conference on Pattern Recognition (ICPR), pp. 4910–4917 (2021)

15. Irshad, S., Akram, M.U.: Classification of retinal vessels into arteries and veins for detection of hypertensive retinopathy. In: 2014 Cairo International Biomedical Engineering Conference (CIBEC), pp. 133–136 (2014)

16. Jin, Q., Meng, Z., Pham, T.D., Chen, Q., Wei, L., Su, R.: Dunet: a deformable network for retinal vessel segmentation. Knowl.-Based Syst. **178**, 149–162 (2019)

17. Kulbear: Residual networks (2017). https://github.com/Kulbear/deep-learning-coursera/blob/master/ConvolutionalNeuralNetworks/ResidualNetworks-v1.ipynb. Accessed 19 Aug 2019

18. Lin, C.K., Chang, J., Huang, C.C., Wen, Y.F., Ho, C.C., Cheng, Y.C.: Effectiveness of convolutional neural networks in the interpretation of pulmonary cytologic images in endobronchial ultrasound procedures. Cancer Med. **10**(24), 9047–9057 (2021)

19. Long, J., Shelhamer, E., Darrell, T.: Fully convolutional networks for semantic segmentation. In: Proceedings of the IEEE Conference on Computer Vision and Pattern Recognition, pp. 3431–3440 (2015)

20. Maji, D., Santara, A., Mitra, P., Sheet, D.: Ensemble of deep convolutional neural networks for learning to detect retinal vessels in fundus images. arXiv preprint arXiv:1603.04833 (2016)

21. Paszke, A., et al.: Pytorch: an imperative style, high-performance deep learning library. Adv. Neural. Inf. Process. Syst. **32**, 8026–8037 (2019)

22. Ronneberger, O., Fischer, P., Brox, T.: U-Net: convolutional networks for biomedical image segmentation. In: Navab, N., Hornegger, J., Wells, W.M., Frangi, A.F. (eds.) MICCAI 2015. LNCS, vol. 9351, pp. 234–241. Springer, Cham (2015). https://doi.org/10.1007/978-3-319-24574-4_28

23. Sekou, T.B., Hidane, M., Olivier, J., Cardot, H.: From patch to image segmentation using fully convolutional networks-application to retinal images. arXiv preprint arXiv:1904.03892 (2019)

24. Subramanya, S.K.: Deep Learning Models to Characterize Smooth Muscle Fibers in Hematoxylin and Eosin Stained Histopathological Images of the Urinary Bladder. Ph.D. thesis, Rochester Institute of Technology (2021)

25. Thoma, M.: A survey of semantic segmentation. arXiv preprint arXiv:1602.06541 (2016)

26. Wang, H., et al.: Patch-free 3D medical image segmentation driven by super-resolution technique and self-supervised guidance. In: de Bruijne, M., et al. (eds.) MICCAI 2021. LNCS, vol. 12901, pp. 131–141. Springer, Cham (2021). https://doi.org/10.1007/978-3-030-87193-2_13

27. Wang, Z., Bovik, A.C., Sheikh, H.R., Simoncelli, E.P.: Image quality assessment: from error visibility to structural similarity. IEEE Trans. Image Process. **13**(4), 600–612 (2004)

28. Xing, F., Xie, Y., Yang, L.: An automatic learning-based framework for robust nucleus segmentation. IEEE Trans. Med. Imaging **35**(2), 550–566 (2015)
29. Zana, F., Klein, J.C.: Segmentation of vessel-like patterns using mathematical morphology and curvature evaluation. IEEE Trans. Image Process. **10**(7), 1010–1019 (2001)
30. Zhou, Z., Rahman Siddiquee, M.M., Tajbakhsh, N., Liang, J.: UNet++: a nested u-net architecture for medical image segmentation. In: Stoyanov, D., et al. (eds.) DLMIA/ML-CDS -2018. LNCS, vol. 11045, pp. 3–11. Springer, Cham (2018). https://doi.org/10.1007/978-3-030-00889-5_1
31. Zhu, H., Cao, Z., Lian, L., Ye, G., Gao, H., Wu, J.: Cariesnet: a deep learning approach for segmentation of multi-stage caries lesion from oral panoramic x-ray image. Neural Comput. Appl. 1–9 (2022). https://doi.org/10.1007/s00521-021-06684-2

LKAU-Net: 3D Large-Kernel Attention-Based U-Net for Automatic MRI Brain Tumor Segmentation

Hao Li[1,2], Yang Nan[1], and Guang Yang[1,3]([✉])

[1] National Heart and Lung Institute, Faculty of Medicine, Imperial College London, London, UK
g.yang@imperial.ac.uk
[2] Department of Bioengineering, Faculty of Engineering, Imperial College London, London, UK
[3] Royal Brompton Hospital, London, UK

Abstract. Automatic segmentation of brain tumors from multi-modal magnetic resonance images (MRI) using deep learning methods has emerged in assisting the diagnosis and treatment of brain tumors. However, the diversity in location, shape, and appearance of brain tumors and the dominance of background voxels in MRI images make accurate brain tumor segmentation difficult. In this paper, a novel 3D large-kernel attention-based U-Net (LKAU-Net) is proposed to address these problems for accurate brain tumor segmentation. Advantages of convolution and self-attention are combined in the proposed 3D large-kernel (LK) attention module, including local contextual information, long-range dependence, and channel adaptability simultaneously. The network was trained and evaluated on the multi-modal Brain Tumor Segmentation Challenge (BraTS) 2020 dataset. The effectiveness of the proposed 3D LK attention module has been proved by both five-fold cross-validation and official online evaluation from the organizers. The results show that our LKAU-Net outperformed state-of-the-art performance in delineating all three tumor sub-regions, with average Dice scores of 79.01%, 91.31%, and 85.75%, as well as 95% Hausdorff distances of 26.27, 4.56, and 5.87 for the enhancing tumor, whole tumor, and tumor core, respectively.

Keywords: Brain tumor segmentation · Attention · Deep learning · MRI

1 Introduction

Segmentation on magnetic resonance imaging (MRI) is a critical step in the treatment of brain tumors, allowing clinicians to determine the location, extent, and subtype of the tumor. This aids not just in the diagnosis but also in radiotherapy planning or surgery planning. Further, the segmentation of longitudinal MRI scans can be used to monitor the growth or shrinkage of brain tumors.

© The Author(s), under exclusive license to Springer Nature Switzerland AG 2022
G. Yang et al. (Eds.): MIUA 2022, LNCS 13413, pp. 313–327, 2022.
https://doi.org/10.1007/978-3-031-12053-4_24

Given the significance of this job, the accurate segmentation of tumor regions is typically accomplished manually by experienced radiologists in current clinical practice. This is a time-consuming and laborious process that requires considerable effort and knowledge. Besides, manual labeling results are unreproducible and may involve human bias as they are highly dependent on the radiologists' experience and subjective decision-making. Automatic or computer-assisted segmentation techniques can overcome these problems by reducing the amount of labor required while providing objective and reproducible outcomes for subsequent tumor diagnosis and monitoring.

Image analysis across multiple MRI modalities is important and beneficial for brain tumor identification. A well-known open-source multi-modal MRI dataset is collected by the Brain Tumor Segmentation Challenge (BraTS). The BraTS challenge is an annual international competition for the objective comparison of state-of-the-art brain tumor segmentation methods [1,2,16]. For each patient case, four 3D MRI modalities are provided, including the native T1-weighted (T1), the post-contrast T1-weighted (T1ce), the T2-weighted (T2), and the T2 Fluid Attenuated Inversion Recovery (FLAIR).

Machine learning methods, especially deep learning algorithms, have been intensively investigated for tumor segmentation in the BraTS challenge since 2014 [5,9,10,12,14,17,21,22,27,30]. Due to their automaticity and accuracy, they have been ranked at top of the competition in recent years. Myronenko [17] earned first place in the BraTS 2018 challenge by training an asymmetrical U-Net with a wider encoder and an additional variational decoder branch providing additional regularisation. Jiang et al. [14], the BraTS 2019 winning team, proposed a two-stage cascaded asymmetrical U-Net similar to Myronenko [17]. The first stage was used to generate a coarse prediction, while the second stage employed a larger network to refine the segmentation result. Isensee et al. [10] used a self-configuring framework named nnU-Net [11] won the BraTS 2020, which automatically adapts the conventional U-Net to a specific dataset with only minor modifications. Wang et al. [27] proposed a modality-pairing learning method using a series of layer connections on parallel branches to capture the complex relationships and rich information between different MRI modalities. A Hybrid High-resolution and Non-local Feature Network (H2NF-Net) was developed by Jia et al. [12], which exploited multi-resolution features while maintaining high-resolution feature representation by using parallel multi-scale convolutional blocks. The non-local self-attention mechanism applied therein allows aggregating contextual information across spatial positions and acquiring long-range dependence.

Although a variety of deep learning approaches have been proposed in the BraTS challenge, some common problems need to be addressed. Firstly, brain tumors can appear in any region of the brain and are extremely diverse in size, shape, and appearance [21]. Second, in most cases, the volume of the brain tumor is relatively small compared to the entire MRI scan, resulting in the data being dominated by background [4]. All these issues reduce the accuracy of brain tumor segmentation, as shown in Fig. 1. Applying long-range self-attention to allow the

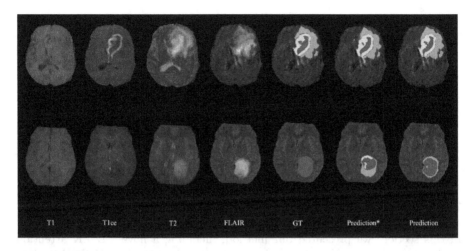

Fig. 1. Representative visual preditions of proposed LKAU-Net on the BraTS 2020 training set. Axial MRI slices in four modalities, ground truth (GT), and predictions are presented from left to right. The labels correspond to the enhancing tumor (yellow), the edema (green), and the necrotic and non-enhancing tumor (red). *: without 3D LK attention module. (Color figure online)

network to selectively learn the truly important tumor-related features is a viable solution [12]. Self-attention originated in Natural Language Processing (NLP) [23]. It is an adaptive selection mechanism based on the input characteristics. Various self-attention mechanisms have been applied in medical image segmentation [3,13,15,19,25,26,29]. Due to their effectiveness in capturing long-range dependencies, they have achieved higher performance compared to conventional Convolutional Neural Networks. However, since self-attention was developed for NLP, it has several drawbacks when it comes to medical image segmentation. First, it interprets images as one-dimensional sequences, omitting the structural information that is necessary for extracting morphological features from medical images. Second, most self-attention studies are based on 2D, since the computational cost with quadratic complexity is prohibitive for 3D scan volumes such as MRI or CT. Third, it ignores channel adaptation, which is crucial in attention mechanisms [7,8,18,24,28].

To address these issues, this paper presents a novel 3D large-kernel attention-based U-Net (LKAU-Net) for automatic segmentation of brain tumors in MRI scans. The 3D LK attention module combines the benefits of self-attention and convolution, such as long-range dependence, spatial adaptability, and local contextual information, while avoiding their drawbacks, including the disregard of channel adaptability. The main contributions of this paper are summarized as follows:

– A novel attention module, dubbed 3D LK attention, is introduced, which balances the advantages of convolution and self-attention, including long-range

dependence, spatial adaptation, and local context, while avoiding their draw-backs, such as high computational cost and neglect of channel adaptation.
– Based on the LK attention, the LKAU-Net is proposed for 3D MRI brain tumor segmentation. LKAU-Net can accurately predict tumor subregions by adaptively increasing the weight of the foreground region while suppressing the weight of the irrelevant background voxels.
– On BraTS 2020 datasets, the LKAU-Net outperformed state-of-the-art methods in delineating all three tumor sub-regions. Besides, the results validated that the new 3D LK attention module can effectively improve the accuracy of automatic MRI brain tumor segmentation.

2   Method

In this section, we presented our method, including a novel 3D LK attention module combining convolution and self-attention, and the LKAU-Net based on it for 3D MRI brain tumor segmentation.

2.1   3D LK Attention

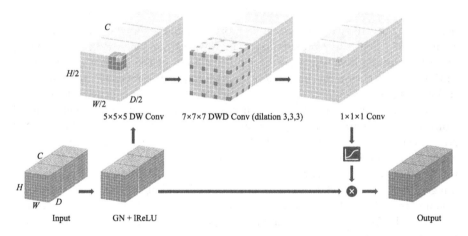

Fig. 2. 3D LK attention module: the feature map after group normalization and leaky ReLU activation is subjected to 3D LK convolution and sigmoid function activation to obtain the attention map, which is multiplied element by element with the feature map before 3D LK convolution to generate the output. The figure illustrates the decomposition of a $21 \times 21 \times 21$ convolution into a $5 \times 5 \times 5$ depth-wise convolution, a $7 \times 7 \times 7$ depth-wise dilated convolution with dilation $(3, 3, 3)$, and a $1 \times 1 \times 1$ convolution. Colored voxels indicate the position of the kernel, and yellow voxels are the kernel centers. (This figure shows only one corner of the feature matrix of the 3D LK convolutional decomposition and ignores the zero-padding)

The attention mechanism is an adaptive selecting process that identifies the discriminative input feature and ignores the background noise. The integration of various attention mechanisms has been shown in many studies to have the potential to improve segmentation performance. The generation of an attention map, which indicates the relative importance of the space, requires the establishment of correlations between different locations. The aforementioned self-attention mechanism can be used to capture long-distance dependence but has several drawbacks outlined. Another strategy is to apply large-kernel convolution to build long-range relationships and create the attention map directly [6,8,18,24,28]. However, this strategy significantly increases the number of parameters and the computational cost.

To address these shortcomings and maximize the benefits of both self-attention and large-kernel convolution, we developed a large-kernel attention module (as shown in Fig. 2). In this module, assuming K as channel number, a $K \times K \times K$ large-kernel convolution was decomposed into a $(2d-1) \times (2d-1) \times (2d-1)$ depth-wise convolution (DW Conv), a $\frac{K}{d} \times \frac{K}{d} \times \frac{K}{d}$ depth-wise dilated convolution (DWD Conv) with dilation (d, d, d) and a $1 \times 1 \times 1$ convolution ($1 \times 1 \times 1$ Conv). Assuming that the input and output have the same dimensions $H \times W \times D \times C$, the number of parameters (N_{PRM}) and floating-point operations (FLOPs) of the original convolution and this decomposition can be computed as follows

$$N_{\mathrm{PRM,O}} = C \times (C \times (K \times K \times K) + 1), \qquad (1)$$
$$\mathrm{FLOPs_O} = C \times (C \times (K \times K \times K) + 1) \times H \times W \times D, \qquad (2)$$

$$N_{\mathrm{PRM,D}} = C \times ((2d-1) \times (2d-1) \times (2d-1) + \frac{K}{d} \times \frac{K}{d} \times \frac{K}{d} + C + 3), \quad (3)$$

$$\mathrm{FLOPs_D} = C \times ((2d-1) \times (2d-1) \times (2d-1) + \frac{K}{d} \times \frac{K}{d} \times \frac{K}{d} + C + 3) \\ \times H \times W \times D, \qquad (4)$$

where the subscripts O and D denote the original convolution and the decomposed convolution, respectively. To find the optimal d for which N_{PRM} is minimal for a specific kernel size K, we let the first-order derivative of Eq. 3 equal 0 and then solved as follows

$$\frac{d}{dd^*}\left(C\left((2d^* - 1)^3 + \left(\frac{K}{d^*}\right)^3 + C + 3\right)\right) = 0, \qquad (5)$$

$$24d^2 - 24d - \frac{3K^3}{d^4} + 6 = 0. \qquad (6)$$

In Eq. 5, the superscript $*$ is used to differentiate dilation d from derivation d. For $K = 21$, solving Eq. 6 using numerical approaches gave an optimum approximation of d of about 3.4159. With the dilation rate of 3, the number of parameters can be remarkably reduced, as detailed in Table 1. We can also

Table 1. Complexity analysis: comparison of the number of parameters N_{PRM} for a $21 \times 21 \times 21$ convolution.

C	$N_{PRM,O}$	$N_{PRM,D}$	$N_{PRM,D}/N_{PRM,O}$
32	9.48 M	16.10 k	0.17%
64	37.94 M	34.24 k	0.09%
128	151.75 M	76.67 k	0.05%
256	606.99 M	186.11 k	0.03%
512	2427.98 M	503.30 k	0.02%

The subscripts O and D denote the original convolution and the proposed decomposed convolution, respectively. C: number of channels.

observe that the decomposition becomes more efficient as the number of channels increases.

The entire 3D LK attention module can be formulated as follows

$$A = \sigma_{\text{sigmoid}}\left(\text{Conv}_{1\times1\times1}\left(\text{Conv}_{DW}\left(\text{Conv}_{DWD}\left(\sigma_{\text{lReLU}}\left(GN\left(Input\right)\right)\right)\right)\right)\right), \quad (7)$$

$$Output = A \otimes \left(\sigma_{\text{lReLU}}\left(GN\left(Input\right)\right)\right), \quad (8)$$

where A is the attention map, and GN denotes the group normalization. σ_{lReLU} and σ_{sigmoid} refer to leaky ReLU activation function and sigmoid activation function, respectively. The output of the 3D LK attention module is obtained by element-wise multiplication ($\otimes$) of the input features and the attention map. Using the 3D LK attention module described above, we can capture long-range relationships in a deep neural network and generate attention maps with minimal computation complexity and parameters.

2.2   3D LK Attention-Based U-Net

The U-Net [20] has been used as the backbone in many research on medical image analysis. Its ability to capture detailed object patterns using skip-architecture is highly beneficial for fine segmentation of lesions. The 3D LKAU-Net architecture, based on the U-Net, consists of an encoding path for semantic feature extraction and a decoding path for segmentation map inference with skip connections, as shown in Fig. 3.

Encoder. The encoder consists of convolution blocks for six resolution levels. Each block has two convolution layers with a filter size of $3 \times 3 \times 3$, a stride of 1, Group Normalization, and leaky ReLU activation (with slope 0.01). The input of size $4 \times 160 \times 192 \times 128$, where four channels corresponding to the four MRI modalities, is convoluted by additional 32 kernels to form initial 32-channel feature maps. Between two resolution levels, a $3 \times 3 \times 3$ convolution with a stride 2 is used for downsampling the feature maps by 2 and doubling the feature channels simultaneously to a maximum of 512. The bottleneck feature map has a size of $512 \times 5 \times 6 \times 4$, which is 1/32 of the original spatial size.

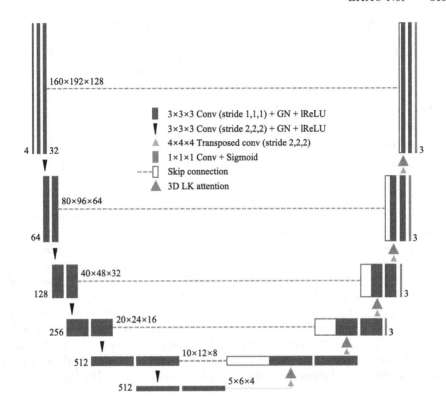

Fig. 3. The network architecture of our proposed LKAU-Net.

3D LK Attention-Based Decoder. The decoder follows the same architecture as the encoder with $4 \times 4 \times 4$ transposed convolution upsampling. The 3D LK attention module is applied to the upsampled feature maps. The output of the 3D LK attention module is then summed back to the feature maps, which are then concatenated with the skip features from of encoder at the same resolution level. The details of the 3D LK attention module at each level are summarized in Table 2. At the final layer of the decoder, a $1 \times 1 \times 1$ convolution is used to compress the feature channels to 3, followed by a sigmoid function to generate prediction probability maps of three overlapping tumor regions: ET, WT, and TC. Additional sigmoid outputs were placed at all resolutions except the two lowest levels to provide deep supervision and increase gradient propagation to previous layers.

3   Experiments

3.1   Data Acquisition

The BraTS 2020 dataset is acquired with different clinical protocols and scanners from multiple institutions. The "ground-truth" segmentation labels are anno-

Table 2. Details of LK attention modules in LKAU-Net

Resolution level	DW Conv		DWD Conv			Equal LK Conv
	Kernel	Padding	Kernel	Dilation	Padding	Kernel
10×12×8	(3, 3, 3)	(1, 1, 1)	(3, 3, 3)	(2, 2, 2)	(2, 2, 2)	(6, 6, 6)
20×24×16	(3, 3, 3)	(1, 1, 1)	(3, 3, 3)	(2, 2, 2)	(2, 2, 2)	(6, 6, 6)
40×48×32	(3, 3, 3)	(1, 1, 1)	(5, 5, 5)	(2, 2, 2)	(4, 4, 4)	(10, 10, 10)
80×96×64	(5, 5, 5)	(2, 2, 2)	(5, 5, 5)	(3, 3, 3)	(6, 6, 6)	(15, 15, 15)
160×192×128	(5, 5, 5)	(2, 2, 2)	(7, 7, 7)	(3, 3, 3)	(9, 9, 9)	(21, 21, 21)

tated by one to four raters and approved by experienced neuro-radiologists, which comprised of the GD-enhancing tumor (ET), the peritumoral edema (ED), and the necrotic and non-enhancing tumor core (NCR and NET). The evaluation of segmentation results is performed on three sub-regions of tumor: GD-enhancing tumor (ET), tumor core (TC = ET + NCR and NET), and whole tumor (WT = ET + NCR and NET + ED)(see Fig. 1). The T1, T1ce, T2, and T2-FLAIR image modalities are co-registered to the same anatomical template with an image size of 240 × 240 × 155, interpolated to the same resolution (1 mm^3), and skull-stripped. Annotations are provided only for the training data (369 cases), while the evaluation of the independent validation dataset (125 cases) should be performed on the online platform (CBICA's IPP[1]).

3.2 Preprocessing and Data Augmentation

Before entering the network, all MRI volumes were cropped to 160 × 192 × 128 to reduce the computation wasted on zero voxels. The input volumes were then preprocessed by intensity normalization. The voxel intensities within each MRI modality were subtracted by the mean and divided by the standard deviation.

To minimize the risk of overfitting and optimize network performance, the following data augmentation techniques have been used: brightness, contrast, Gaussian noise, Gaussian blur, gamma, scaling, rotation, elastic transformation, and mirroring. All augmentations were applied on-the-fly throughout the training process in order to expand the training dataset indefinitely. Moreover, in order to increase the variability of the generated image data, all augmentations were applied randomly based on predetermined probabilities, and most parameters were also drawn randomly from a predetermined range U (detailed in Table 3).

3.3 Training and Optimization

The LKAU-Net was trained on the BraTS 2020 training set (369 cases) with five-fold cross-validation. The objective of the optimization is to minimize the sum of

---

[1] CBICA's Image Processing Portal (https://ipp.cbica.upenn.edu).

Table 3. Summary of details of 3D LK attention modules in LKAU-Net

Methods	Probability	Range
Brightness	30%	$U(0.7, 1.3)$
Contrast	15%	$U(0.6, 1.4)$
Gaussian noise	15%	Variance $\sigma \sim U(0, 1)$
Gaussian blur	20%	Kernal $\sigma \sim U(0.5, 1.5)$
Gamma augmentation	15%	$\gamma \sim U(0.7, 1.5)$
Scaling	30%	$U(0.65, 1.6)$
Rotation	30%	$U(-30, 30)$
Elastic transform	30%	$\alpha \sim U(5, 10), \sigma = 3\alpha$
Flipping	50%	Along all axes

the binary cross-entropy loss and soft Dice loss at both the final full-resolution output and the lower resolution auxiliary outputs. The adaptive moment estimator (Adam) optimizer optimized the network parameters. Each training run lasted 200 epochs with a batch size of 1 and an initial learning rate of 0.0003. All experiments were implemented with Pytorch 1.10.1 on an NVIDIA GeForce RTX 3090 GPU with 24 GB VRAM.

3.4 Postprocessing

Since the network tended to falsely predict the enhancing tumor when the prediction volume is small, the enhancing tumor region was empirically replaced with necrosis in postprocessing when the volume of predicted ET was less than 500 voxels.

3.5 Evaluation Metrics

Dice score and 95% Hausdorff distance were adopted in the BraTS 2020 challenge. Dice score measures spatial overlapping between the segmentation result and the ground truth annotation, while 95% Hausdorff distance (HD95) measures the 95th percentile of maximum distances between two boundaries. We used the Dice score in five-fold cross-validation on the training set (369 cases) and used both the Dice and HD95 scores from the official online platform to evaluate and compare the final performance of LKAU-Net on the independent validation set (125 cases).

4   Results and Discussion

We trained three network configurations of LKAU-Net, with the 3D LK attention module, without the 3D LK attention module, and with the CBAM [28] on the BraTS training set with five-fold cross-validation. This provided us with performance estimates for 369 training cases, allowing us to compare the different network configurations internally and also externally for state-of-the-art approaches, as shown in Table 4. The increase in Dice scores from the 3D LK attention module can be seen by comparing three different network configurations of LKAU-Net. Two segmentation results are also compared visually in Fig. 1, which proves the benefit of the 3D LK attention module. Compared to the best BraTS-specific nnU-Net that was also trained with five-fold cross-validation, LKAU-Net has outperformed all but ET in Dice scores, including the average score.

Table 4. Quantitative results of proposed LKAU-Net on BraTS 2020 training set compared to state-of-the-art methods.

Methods	Dice			
	ET	WT	TC	Mean
nnU-Net baseline	80.83	91.60	87.23	86.55
nnU-Net best	**80.94**	91.60	87.51	86.68
Proposed LKAU-Net*	78.52	92.66	88.74	86.64
Proposed LKAU-Net**	78.15	92.72	88.67	86.66
Proposed LKAU-Net	78.81	**92.81**	**88.99**	**86.87**

Bold numbers: best results. *: without 3D LK attention module. **: with CBAM.

The final segmentation performance of the proposed LKAU-Net was evaluated and compared with state-of-the-art methods on the independent BraTS 2020 validation set (125 cases), with the results shown in Table 5. All segmentation results were evaluated by the Dice score and 95% Hausdorff distance (HD95) and directly obtained from the official online platform (CBICA's IPP).

Table 5. Quantitative results of proposed LKAU-Net on independent BraTS 2020 validation set compared to state-of-the-art methods.

Methods	Dice				HD95			
	ET	WT	TC	Mean	ET	WT	TC	Mean
Myronenko	64.77	84.31	72.61	73.90	41.35	13.85	18.57	24.59
Wang et al.	78.70	90.80	85.60	85.03	35.01	4.71	5.70	15.14
H2NF-Net	78.75	91.29	85.46	85.17	26.58	4.18	**4.97**	**11.91**
nnU-Net baseline	77.67	90.60	84.26	84.18	35.10	4.89	5.91	15.30
nnU-Net best	**79.85**	91.18	85.71	**85.58**	26.41	**3.71**	5.64	11.92
Proposed LKAU-Net*	78.94	91.18	84.99	85.04	29.14	4.77	6.01	13.31
Proposed LKAU-Net	79.01	**91.31**	**85.75**	85.36	**26.27**	4.56	5.87	12.23

Bold numbers: best results. *: without 3D LK attention module.

Quantitative results showed that the proposed LKAU-Net outperformed state-of-the-art methods, including the best nnU-Net model from the BraTS 2020 champion team, in segmenting all three tumor sub-regions. The proposed method achieved the highest Dice score in WT and TC segmentation and the lowest HD95 score in ET segmentation. However, due to the previously mentioned dominance of the best nnU-Net model in ET Dice, our network dropped to second place with a slight difference of 0.22 in the average Dice of the validation set. The LKAU-Net, on the other hand, performed exceptionally well on the HD95 score for ET, which may be attributed to the 3D LK attention module emphasizing the features of the correct tumor region and thus reducing incorrect and scattered ET predictions.

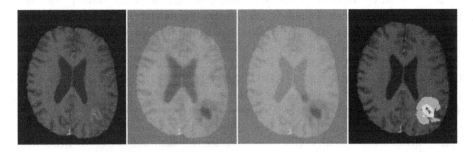

Fig. 4. The representative visual effect of the LK attention module. The first plot is the T1ce input. The second plot shows an upsampled feature map at the finest resolution in the LKAU-Net decoder, while the following plot shows the feature map after applying the 3D LK attention module. The last plot identifies the ground truth labels.

By comparing the evaluation results of LKAU-Nets with and without the 3D LK attention module, the performance improvement due to the presence of the 3D LK attention module can be seen. The performance improvement is more evident for TC and ET, as shown in Table 6. In order to validate the increase of the evaluation metrics, paired t-Tests were done, and the p-values for each category are presented in Table 6. The improvement due to the 3D LK attention module on WT Dice, TC Dice, Mean Dice, WT HD95, and TC HD95 was statistically validated. However, the paired t-Test could not verify the changes on ET due to the high penalty of Dice = 0 and HD95 = 373.13 set by BraTS 2020 for the False Positives of ET. This improvement validated the effectiveness of adaptive feature selection of the 3D LK attention module, which is visualized in Fig. 4.

Table 6. Improvement in quantitative results of LKAU-Net due to the 3D LK attention module.

	Dice				HD95			
	ET	WT	TC	Mean	ET	WT	TC	Mean
Mean results*	78.94	91.18	84.99	85.04	29.14	4.77	6.01	13.31
Mean results	79.01	91.31	85.75	85.36	26.27	4.56	5.87	12.23
Improvement	0.07	0.13	0.76	0.32	−2.87	−0.21	−0.14	−1.07
p-value	0.338	0.017	0.013	0.018	0.159	0.030	0.041	0.130

*: without 3D LK attention module.

In addition to the comparison of numbers of parameters in Table 1, we compared the running times of the original $21 \times 21 \times 21$ convolution and the proposed decomposed LK convolution, as well as the running times of LKAU-Net without and with the 3D LK attention module, respectively, in Table 7. It is worth noting that the LKAU-Net with original LK convolutions was even unable to be implemented on the current GPU of 24 GB VRAM. We recorded the time required to apply different LK convolutions to each batch including the forward and backward propagation. We can observe that the decomposition reduces the time required for the original LK convolution by about 99%, which proved its optimization on complexity. However, even so, the addition of the 3D LK attention module brought an additional training time of nearly 180 s per epoch to LKAU-Net, which is nearly double the original time. Therefore, a lighter architecture can be developed for limited computational resources and research time.

Table 7. Running time comparison: per batch for convolutions and per training epoch for LKAU-Nets.

	Running time (s)
$21 \times 21 \times 21$ Conv	9.566 ± 0.024
$21 \times 21 \times 21$ D Conv	0.088 ± 0.001
LKAU-Net*	199.873 ± 0.597
LKAU-Net	379.243 ± 1.407

The Conv and D Conv denote the original convolution and the proposed decomposed convolution, respectively. *: without 3D LK attention module.

Furthermore, we found another limitation of our approach by analyzing the segmentation results. Figure 1 shows two representative examples of predictions from five-fold cross-validation on the BraTS 2020 training set. In the first case, the network delineated all tumor sub-regions with high accuracy, despite the presence of slight artifacts. In the second case, the WT region was accurately segmented while the TC was not, which might be due to blurring in the T2 volume. This demonstrates the importance of data integrity for the accurate segmentation of medical images. To further improve the network's robustness, these exceptional cases can be covered by more diverse data acquisition or more realistic data augmentation.

5   Conclusion

In this paper, we present a 3D LK attention-based U-Net for MRI brain tumor segmentation that has outperformed state-of-the-art methods on the BraTS 2020 dataset. The 3D LK attention module combines the advantages of convolution and self-attention, exploiting local environment information, long-distance dependence, and spatial and channel adaptation. We integrated this novel attention module into the decoder of U-Net, enabling the network to focus on decisive tumor-related features. The evaluation results on the BraTS 2020 dataset showed that the 3D LK attention module could improve predictions for all three tumor sub-regions, particularly for TC and ET. As shown in Fig. 4, the 3D LK attention module also proved to be effective in adaptively selecting discriminative features and suppressing background noises. Guided by this 3D LK attention, our proposed network achieves state-of-the-art performance, with average Dice scores of 79.01%, 91.31%, 85.75%, and 95% Hausdorff distances of 26.27, 4.56, and 5.87 in segmenting the enhancing tumor, whole tumor, and tumor core, respectively.

References

1. Bakas, S., et al.: Advancing The Cancer Genome Atlas glioma MRI collections with expert segmentation labels and radiomic features. Sci. Data **4**(1), 170117 (2017). https://doi.org/10.1038/sdata.2017.117
2. Bakas, S., Reyes, M., Jakab, A., Menze, B.: Identifying the best machine learning algorithms for brain tumor segmentation, progression assessment, and overall survival prediction in the BRATS Challenge. arXiv:1811.02629 [cs, stat], April 2019
3. Chen, J., et al.: TransUNet: transformers make strong encoders for medical image segmentation. arXiv:2102.04306 [cs], February 2021
4. DSouza, A.M., Chen, L., Wu, Y., Abidin, A.Z., Xu, C.: MRI tumor segmentation with densely connected 3D CNN. In: Angelini, E.D., Landman, B.A. (eds.) Medical Imaging 2018: Image Processing, p. 50. SPIE, Houston, United States, March 2018. https://doi.org/10.1117/12.2293394
5. Guan, X., et al.: 3D AGSE-VNet: an automatic brain tumor MRI data segmentation framework. BMC Med. Imaging **22**(1), 6 (2022). https://doi.org/10.1186/s12880-021-00728-8
6. Guo, M.H., Lu, C.Z., Liu, Z.N., Cheng, M.M., Hu, S.M.: Visual attention network. arXiv:2202.09741 [cs], March 2022
7. Guo, M.H., et al.: Attention mechanisms in computer vision: a survey. Comput. Visual Media (2022). https://doi.org/10.1007/s41095-022-0271-y

8. Hu, J., Shen, L., Albanie, S., Sun, G., Vedaldi, A.: Gather-Excite: exploiting feature context in convolutional neural networks. In: Bengio, S., Wallach, H., Larochelle, H., Grauman, K., Cesa-Bianchi, N., Garnett, R. (eds.) Advances in Neural Information Processing Systems, vol. 31. Curran Associates, Inc. (2018)

9. Huang, H., et al.: A deep multi-task learning framework for brain tumor segmentation. Front. Oncol. **11**, 690244 (2021) https://doi.org/10.3389/fonc.2021.690244. https://www.frontiersin.org/articles/10.3389/fonc.2021.690244/full

10. Isensee, F., Jäger, P.F., Full, P.M., Vollmuth, P., Maier-Hein, K.H.: nnU-Net for brain tumor segmentation. In: Crimi, A., Bakas, S. (eds.) BrainLes 2020. LNCS, vol. 12659, pp. 118–132. Springer, Cham (2021). https://doi.org/10.1007/978-3-030-72087-2_11

11. Isensee, F., Jäger, P.F., Kohl, S.A.A., Petersen, J., Maier-Hein, K.H.: Automated design of deep learning methods for biomedical image segmentation. Nature Methods **18**(2), 203–211 (2021). https://doi.org/10.1038/s41592-020-01008-z, arXiv: 1904.08128

12. Jia, H., Cai, W., Huang, H., Xia, Y.: H^2NF-Net for brain tumor segmentation using multimodal MR imaging: 2nd place solution to BraTS challenge 2020 segmentation task. In: Crimi, A., Bakas, S. (eds.) BrainLes 2020. LNCS, vol. 12659, pp. 58–68. Springer, Cham (2021). https://doi.org/10.1007/978-3-030-72087-2_6

13. Jia, Q., Shu, H.: BiTr-Unet: a CNN-Transformer Combined Network for MRI Brain Tumor Segmentation. arXiv:2109.12271 [cs, eess], December 2021

14. Jiang, Z., Ding, C., Liu, M., Tao, D.: Two-stage cascaded U-Net: 1st place solution to BraTS challenge 2019 segmentation task. In: Crimi, A., Bakas, S. (eds.) BrainLes 2019. LNCS, vol. 11992, pp. 231–241. Springer, Cham (2020). https://doi.org/10.1007/978-3-030-46640-4_22

15. Karimi, D., Vasylechko, S.D., Gholipour, A.: Convolution-free medical image segmentation using transformers. In: de Bruijne, M., Cattin, P.C., Cotin, S., Padoy, N., Speidel, S., Zheng, Y., Essert, C. (eds.) MICCAI 2021. LNCS, vol. 12901, pp. 78–88. Springer, Cham (2021). https://doi.org/10.1007/978-3-030-87193-2_8

16. Menze, B.H., Jakab, A., Bauer, S., Van Leemput, K.: The Multimodal Brain Tumor Image Segmentation Benchmark (BRATS). IEEE Trans. Med. Imaging **34**(10), 1993–2024 (2015). https://doi.org/10.1109/TMI.2014.2377694. http://ieeexplore.ieee.org/document/6975210/

17. Myronenko, A.: 3D MRI brain tumor segmentation using autoencoder regularization. In: Crimi, A., Bakas, S., Kuijf, H., Keyvan, F., Reyes, M., van Walsum, T. (eds.) BrainLes 2018. LNCS, vol. 11384, pp. 311–320. Springer, Cham (2019). https://doi.org/10.1007/978-3-030-11726-9_28

18. Park, J., Woo, S., Lee, J.Y., Kweon, I.S.: BAM: Bottleneck Attention Module. arXiv:1807.06514 [cs], July 2018

19. Peiris, H., Hayat, M., Chen, Z., Egan, G., Harandi, M.: A Volumetric Transformer for Accurate 3D Tumor Segmentation. arXiv:2111.13300 [cs, eess], November 2021

20. Ronneberger, O., Fischer, P., Brox, T.: U-Net: convolutional networks for biomedical image segmentation. In: Navab, N., Hornegger, J., Wells, W.M., Frangi, A.F. (eds.) MICCAI 2015. LNCS, vol. 9351, pp. 234–241. Springer, Cham (2015). https://doi.org/10.1007/978-3-319-24574-4_28

21. Soltaninejad, M., et al.: Automated brain tumour detection and segmentation using superpixel-based extremely randomized trees in FLAIR MRI. Int. J. Comput. Assisted Radiol. Surg. **12**(2), 183–203 (2017) https://doi.org/10.1007/s11548-016-1483-3

22. Soltaninejad, M., et al.: Supervised learning based multimodal MRI brain tumour segmentation using texture features from supervoxels. Comput. Methods Programs Biomed. **157**, 69–84 (2018). https://doi.org/10.1016/j.cmpb.2018.01.003, https://linkinghub.elsevier.com/retrieve/pii/S016926071731355X

23. Vaswani, A., et al.: Attention is All you Need. In: Guyon, I., Luxburg, U.V., Bengio, S., Wallach, H., Fergus, R., Vishwanathan, S., Garnett, R. (eds.) Advances in Neural Information Processing Systems, vol. 30. Curran Associates, Inc. (2017)

24. Wang, F., et al.: Residual attention network for image classification. In: 2017 IEEE Conference on Computer Vision and Pattern Recognition (CVPR), pp. 6450–6458. IEEE, Honolulu, HI, USA, July 2017. https://doi.org/10.1109/CVPR.2017.683. https://ieeexplore.ieee.org/document/8100166/

25. Wang, H., et al.: Mixed Transformer U-Net For Medical Image Segmentation. arXiv:2111.04734 [cs, eess], November 2021

26. Wang, W., Chen, C., Ding, M., Li, J., Yu, H., Zha, S.: TransBTS: multimodal brain tumor segmentation using transformer. arXiv:2103.04430 [cs], June 2021

27. Wang, Y., et al.: Modality-pairing learning for brain tumor segmentation. In: Crimi, A., Bakas, S. (eds.) BrainLes 2020. LNCS, vol. 12658, pp. 230–240. Springer, Cham (2021). https://doi.org/10.1007/978-3-030-72084-1_21

28. Woo, S., Park, J., Lee, J.-Y., Kweon, I.S.: CBAM: convolutional block attention module. In: Ferrari, V., Hebert, M., Sminchisescu, C., Weiss, Y. (eds.) ECCV 2018. LNCS, vol. 11211, pp. 3–19. Springer, Cham (2018). https://doi.org/10.1007/978-3-030-01234-2_1

29. Xie, Y., Zhang, J., Shen, C., Xia, Y.: CoTr: efficiently bridging CNN and transformer for 3D medical image segmentation. arXiv:2103.03024 [cs], March 2021

30. Zhang, W., et al.: ME-Net: multi-encoder net framework for brain tumor segmentation. Int. J. Imaging Syst. Technol. **31**(4), 1834–1848 (2021). https://doi.org/10.1002/ima.22571

Attention-Fused CNN Model Compression with Knowledge Distillation for Brain Tumor Segmentation

Pengcheng Xu[1,2], Kyungsang Kim[2], Huafeng Liu[1,3,4(✉)],
and Quanzheng Li[2(✉)]

[1] College of Optical Science and Engineering, Zhejiang University, Hangzhou, China
liuhf@zju.edu.cn
[2] Radiology Department, Massachusetts General Hospital and Harvard Medical
School, 55 Fruit Street, Boston, MA 02114, USA
Li.Quanzheng@mgh.harvard.edu
[3] Jiaxing Key Laboratory of Photonic Sensing and Intelligent Imaging,
Jiaxing 314000, China
[4] Intelligent Optics and Photonics Research Center, Jiaxing Research Institute,
Zhejiang University, Jiaxing 314000, China

Abstract. 3D brain tumor segmentation is an indispensable part of computer-aided detection systems, which is a very time-consuming and error-prone task. In recent years, many deep learning methods, such as U-net and DeepMedic, have been developed to reduce the burden on physicians and improve segmentation accuracy. Particularly with the transformer, an attention-based approach, the segmentation accuracy has been improved. However, transformer-type methods are computationally heavy and require workstations accelerated with graphic process units for fast inference. In this paper, we fuse attention block and convolutional neural network (CNN) with transformer connection to improve segmentation. Meantime, we compress the model and preserve the accuracy with the knowledge distillation technique. We investigated the knowledge distilling efficiency between different architectures. We found the knowledge from the attention-CNN fused model could improve the accuracy of the compressed U-net model. With the knowledge distillation, the compressed U-net architecture could achieve comparable accuracy with around only 11% parameters of the original U-net architecture. As for the compressed attention-CNN fused model, the knowledge from the feature attention combining the knowledge from soft target work better than soft target only. This work would help researchers to compress their model architecture properly.

Keywords: Knowledge distillation · Transformer connection · Brain tumor segmentation

G. Yang et al. (Eds.): MIUA 2022, LNCS 13413, pp. 328–338, 2022.
https://doi.org/10.1007/978-3-031-12053-4_25

1 Introduction

One-third of all brain tumors are gliomas, which can be less aggressive in a patient with a life expectancy of several years or more aggressive in a patient with a life expectancy of at most two years [5]. Magnetic resonance imaging (MRI) is one of the most common scans used to diagnose brain tumors which could provide detailed images. Brain tumor segmentation from MRI can significantly impact improved diagnostics, growth rate prediction, and treatments planning. While different type of tumors are often diffused, poorly contrasted, and extend tentacle-like structures that make them difficult to segment. Besides, the tumor could appear anywhere with any shape and size in the brain, making segmenting more difficult.

Furthermore, the scale of voxel values in MR images is not standardized, which depends on the type of MR machine used and the acquisition protocol. Brain tumor segmentation aims to identify abnormal areas, namely, activate tumorous tissue, necrotic tissue, and edema compared to normal tissue. Since glioblastomas are infiltrative tumors, their borders are often fuzzy and hard to distinguish from healthy tissues. As a solution, more than one MRI modality, which gives almost a unique signature to each tissue type, is often employed, e.g., T1 (spin-lattice relaxation), T1Gd (post-contrast T1-weighted), T2 (spin-spin relaxation), and fluid attenuation inversion recovery (FLAIR) pulse sequences. In recent years, many deep neural networks have been developed to fully automatically segment brain tumors [5]. Meantime, U-net and its variant becoming the mainstream for medical image segmentation [8,11,12,18]. For example, Chen et al. used a separable 3D U-net to segment the brain tumor and obtained comparable results [3]. To better leverage the multi-modalities and depth information, Xu et al. used an LSTM multi-model U-net to outperform other state-of-the-art methods in BRATS-2015 [16].

Although convolutional neural networks (CNN) methods have excellent representation ability, it is difficult to work with the global features due to the limited receptive fields of the convolution kernel. Inspired by the attention mechanism in natural language processing, this problem has the potential to be solved by fusing the attention mechanism with CNN [14]. Wang et al., for the first time, exploit the transformer in 3D CNN for brain tumor segmentation named TransBTS [15]. Islam et al. adopt 3D U-net architecture and integrate channel, and spatial attention with decoder network for brain tumor segmentation and survival rate prediction with attention [7,15].

However, 3D related work is really time-consuming and computationally expensive, especially the models with attention blocks. Model size may prevent the generalization of clinical applications. Knowledge distillation (KD) is the state-of-the-art method to transfer knowledge from the teacher model to the student model [6]. By transferring the essential knowledge from the teacher model, the student model could achieve higher performance or even comparable performance with teacher models. Furthermore, several attempts have been proposed in medical image segmentation [9,13,17].

In this paper, we proposed a structure of transformer connection to transfer global information in the U-net architecture. Incorporating the knowledge distillation technique, we investigated the efficient way to compress the model for clinical application.

To summarize, our main contributions are as follows:

1) We proposed an attention-based block, named transformer connection, to transfer global information to improve the performance of brain tumor segmentation.
2) We compressed the U-net like architecture models with attention blocks and found an efficient way to distill the knowledge.
3) We studied the high-level hyper-parameter influence when compressing the U-net like architecture models with attention block.

2   Method

2.1   Transformer Connection

The transformer is the first sequence transduction model based entirely on attention, replacing the recurrent layers most commonly used in encoder-decoder architectures with multi-heads self-attention [14]. Vision transformer is simple, scalable, strategy works surprisingly well when coupled with pre-training on the large dataset [4]. Introducing the transformer connection to the U-net architecture could transfer crucial global information, which is hard to archive by the convolutional block, within models.

The transformer connection consists three parts: position encoding, attention block and position decoding.

Position Encoding. To encode the location information, which is vital in the segmentation task, we use the learnable position embeddings for feature embedding as followings [15]:

$$z_0 = f + PE = W \times F + PE \tag{1}$$

where W is the linear projection operation, F is the feature input, z_0 refers to the feature embeddings. And these functions formed the part of position encoding.

Attention Block. The attention block is composed of L transformer layers, each of them has a standard architecture, which consists of a multi-Head self-attention (MSA) block and a multi-layer perceptron (MLP). The output of the l_{th} transformer layer can be calculated by:

$$z_l' = MSA(LN(z_l - 1)) + z_{l-1} \tag{2}$$

$$z_l = MLP(LN(z_l')) + z_l' \tag{3}$$

Position Decoding. We used a position decoding (PDE) layer to map the features into the same shape for the target space to keep the shape consistent. The transformer output will map to the same space as the target with position decoding. The overlapped region was calculated with mean value, the rest of the space was padded with zeros. The output of transformer connection can be write as follows:

$$z_{tc} = PDE(z_l) \tag{4}$$

Our model was based on the backbone of the U-net. The transformer connection was implemented as an extra feature extraction tool to assist the model. As shown in Fig. 1, transformer connection build an additional path connecting the hidden layers, transformer connection of features. The orange dash line shows the application of the transformer connection within the same level features. Besides, We can also build a path to transfer attention map from an early stage to a later stage or transfer features to a different stage level, transformer connection of vertical features. The light blue dash line shows the application of the transformer connection at a different level.

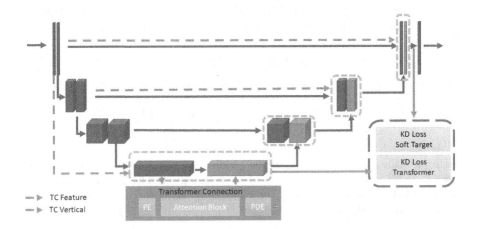

Fig. 1. Framework of experiments, where blue arrow and block build the backbone of U-net, PE means position encoding, PDE means position decoding, TC feature means transformer connection between features, TC vertical means transformer connection between vertical features of the architecture, KD loss soft target means extracted soft target for KD training of the students model, KD loss transformer means the extracted target from the transformer for KD training of the student model (Color figure online)

2.2   Knowledge Distillation

Knowledge distillation is a recently developed deep learning technique to transfer knowledge between models. With the knowledge from the teacher model (original model with high performance), the student model (compressed model sacrificed some accuracy) could obtain competitive performance. In other words, the KD technique could be regarded as a model compression and acceleration method. The KD technique did not get much attention until Hinton et al. proposed the soft target, an excellent knowledge fit to almost all the deep learning frameworks [6]. In this paper, we also utilized the soft target as part of KD, which is the class probability before the last activation function and contains essential features to mimic the outcome from the teacher model. The transfer probability is as follows:

$$q_i = \frac{\exp(c_i/\lambda)}{\sum_j (\exp(c_j/\lambda))} \tag{5}$$

where c_i is the ith class logit output, and the logit output is the neural network output before the softmax layer. Here q_i indicates the probability that the input belongs to the brain tumors. Moreover, the knowledge from transformer connection, the output before PDE, named feature attention here, also implemented to guide the training of the student model.

2.3   Loss Function

The training loss consists of knowledge distilling loss, including knowledge of soft target and knowledge of feature attention, and segmentation loss.

$$L_{student} = L_{kd_T} + L_{kd_S} + L_{seg} \tag{6}$$

where segmentation loss here is derived from categorical dice score as following:

$$L_{seg} = 1 - DSC = 1 - \frac{2}{N_j} \times \sum_j \frac{|p_i \bigcap q_i|}{|p_i| + |q_i|} \tag{7}$$

where p_i is the ground truth, q_i is the prediction, N_j is number of classes. Let $V = \{1, ..., N\}$ be the set of all pixels of the training set. The knowledge distilling loss, knowledge of soft target L_{kd_S} and knowledge of feature attention L_{kd_T}, can be presented as follows:

$$L_{kd_S} = \lambda^2 \cdot \frac{\sum_{v \in V} KL(q_{s,v}, q_{t,v})}{N}, \tag{8}$$

$$L_{kd_T} = \mu^2 \cdot \frac{\sum_{v \in V} KL(z_{s,v}, z_{t,v})}{N}, \tag{9}$$

both of them was evaluated by KL divergence with different weights, λ and μ, respectively. Where q means the soft target, z means the feature attention, the subscript s means the output from student model the and subscript t means the output from teacher model.

2.4   Experimental Setting

Dataset. The dataset implemented in the experiments is provided by the brain tumor segmentation 2020 challenge [1,2,10]. All cases are multi-modal scans with native (T1) post-contrast T1-weighted (T1GD), T2-weighted (T2) and T2 fluid attenuated inversion recovery (T2-FLAIR) volumes. Each modality has volume of $240 \times 240 \times 155$. All imaging datasets have been segmented manually, by one to four raters, following the same annotation protocol, and experienced neuro-radiologists approved their annotations. Annotations comprise the GD-enhancing tumor (ET - label 4), the peritumoral edema (ED-label 2), and the necrotic and no-enhancing tumor core (NCR/NET-label 1). Besides, the same pre-processing was employed as the challenge, including co-registered the same anatomical template, interpolated to the same resolution. BraTs data including a total 369 cases. We split the 300 for training, 30 for validating, and 39 for testing. To fit the memory of GPU, the data was padded to 240×160 and then down-sample to $120 \times 120 \times 80$. A cube of $64 \times 64 \times 64$ random cropped from the volume was used for the training.

Implementation Details. Our framework was based on Tensorflow 2.5, and a NVIDIA GTX1080 GPU was used to train and evaluate the results. Adam optimizer is used in the training with a poly learning rate of initial value of 0.0004 and decays with power 0.9. The training batch size is 1. Model weights of the best performance of the validation set during 8000 epochs was stored and used for evaluating the model with the testing set.

3   Results

3.1   U-Net Architecture Compression

The number of filters is the most important hyper-parameter to determine the training parameters of the U-net like architectures. Reducing the number of filters and depth could simply reduce the size of the model along with the accuracy. Table 1 shows the comparison experiment results when reducing the number of filters. $Dice_1$ is the dice of NCR/NET, $Dice_2$ is the dice of ED, $Dice_3$ is the dice of ET, $Dice_{WT}$ is the dice of whole tumor. Here tf means transformer connection built in the same level feature, also known as TC feature in Fig. 1. tv means transformer connection build in different stages, also known as TC vertical in Fig. 1. Moreover, according to the results in Fig. 2. The gap between models with and without transformer connection increased when reducing the number of filters. Once the number of filters is too small, the model is difficult to catch all the features. For example, the $Unet_4$ can hardly distinguish NCR/NET and ET.

3.2   Transformer Connection Compression

The parameter of transformer connection is highly dependent on four hyper-parameters of attention block: embedded dimension (E), heads of multi-head self-attention (H), number of multi-layer perceptron (M), number of transformer repeated block (L). Table 2 shows the experiments results of a reduced-sized transformer block. According to the results, the transformer connection will lose information if the structure is too simple.

Table 1. Experimental results of model compression, where label 1 is NCR/NET, label 2 is ED, label 3 is ET, $Dice_{WT}$ is dice of the whole tumor

	Model filters	$Dice_1$	$Dice_2$	$Dice_3$	$Dice_{WT}$
U_{tf}	[20, 32, 64, 96]	74.45	83.05	80.46	90.36
U_{tv}	[20, 32, 64, 96]	75.84	82.80	82.06	90.45
U_{tf1}	[4, 7, 9, 12]	64.10	81.51	76.47	88.91
$Unet_1$	[20, 32, 64, 96]	73.86	81.59	79.92	89.95
$Unet_2$	[10, 18, 24, 48]	70.85	79.62	80.28	88.31
$Unet_3$	[4, 7, 9, 12]	65.46	77.42	77.08	84.76
$Unet_4$	[3, 4, 6, 10]	3.71e-4	78.55	7.42e-5	73.30

Table 2. Experimental results of compression of the attention block

	[E, M, H, L]	$Dice_1$	$Dice_2$	$Dice_3$	$Dice_{WT}$
U_{tf1}	[512, 4096, 8, 4]	64.1	81.51	76.47	88.91
U_{tf2}	[512, 2048, 8, 4]	41.33	74.42	73.06	80.53
U_{tf3}	[256, 4096, 8, 2]	2.18e-4	79.64	2.18e-4	70.65
U_{tf4}	[256, 4096, 8, 4]	78.66	80.63	9.33e-4	82.64
U_{tf5}	[512, 4096, 8, 2]	2.01e-3	80.65	77.87	81.81
U_{tf6}	[512, 4096, 4, 4]	66.38	80.3	5.65e-3	80.96
U_{tf7}	[512, 512, 8, 4]	3.84e-3	78.46	1.84e-3	67.78

3.3   Knowledge Distillation Between Models

Knowledge distillation technique was implemented to preserve the accuracy when reduce the model parameters. Table 3 depicted the knowledge distillation results for model with transformer connection. $^{s}U_{tf2}$ describe the model U_{tf2} training with supervision of soft target, $^{st}U_{tf2}$ describe the model U_{tf2} training with supervision of soft target and feature attention. The combined loss work better than soft target only. Table 4 presents the experimental results of training the U-net with the knowledge distillation from U-net and U-net with transformer

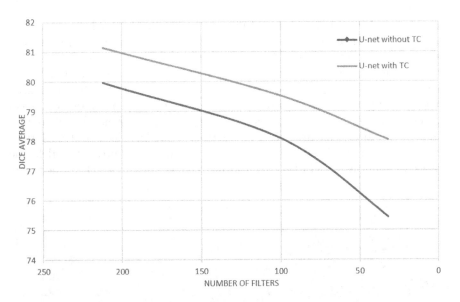

Fig. 2. Model compression with/without transformer connection

connection. The performance of the $Unet_3$ improved significantly with the help of knowledge distillation. And the knowledge from the model with transformer connection could further improved the segmentation. And the performance of $^TUnet_3$ is very close to $Unet_2$ with only 11% parameters. We summarized a typical case of all the model predictions in Fig. 3, where purple region belong to the label NCR/NET, color green belong to label ED, color pink belong to label ET. Comparing the (h) and (i), we could see significant improvement with the knowledge from model with transformer connection, even the improvement in DICE is very small. Comparing the (f) and (g), we could see the knowledge from the model with transformer connection improve the detailed prediction.

Table 3. Experimental results of KD from soft target and feature attention

	IOU_1	IOU_2	IOU_3	$Dice_1$	$Dice_2$	$Dice_3$
U_{tf2}	26.05	59.26	57.56	41.33	74.42	73.06
$^sU_{tf2}$	31.32	65.92	61.84	47.70	79.46	76.42
$^{st}U_{tf2}$	31.87	66.08	62.44	48.34	79.58	76.88

4   Discussion

This paper implemented based on 3D U-net architecture with transformer connection and neglected other advanced architectural features. The main reason is that U-net and its variant were the mainstream for brain tumor segmentation. Moreover, our transformer connection can adapt to multi-level feature fusion or direct connection. The goal of this work is to compress the model with reasonable accuracy. The transformer connection will introduce more parameters into the models. When reducing the model size, the model is less sensitive to the number of multi-layer perceptrons than other hyper-parameters in transformer connection. With the help of knowledge distillation, the compressed model could obtain reasonable performance. According to our results, the knowledge of transformer connection could guide the transformer connection in a compressed model. The knowledge from the model with a transformer connection can also help the model

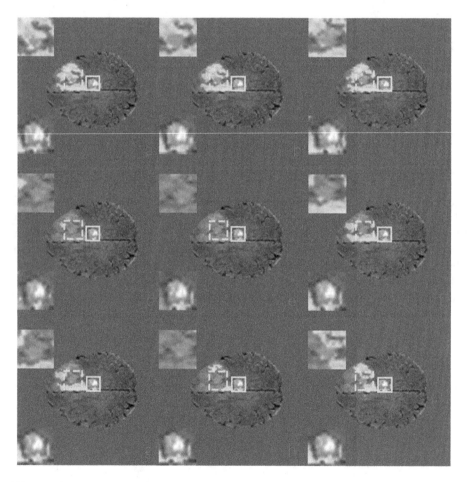

Fig. 3. The comparison of segmentation results from different models. (a) $Unet_1$, (b) U_{tf}, (c) Ground Truth, (d) $Unet_3$, (e) U_{tf2}, (f) $^T Unet_3$, (g) $^U Unet_3$, (h) $^s U_{tf2}$, (i) $^{st} U_{tf2}$ (Color figure online)

Table 4. Experimental results of KD from model w/ and w/o transformer connection

Model	$Dice_1$	$Dice_2$	$Dice_3$	$Dice_{WT}$
$Unet_3$	65.46	77.42	77.08	84.76
$^{U}Unet_3$	67.33	80.09	77.20	87.01
$^{T}Unet_3$	68.71	80.26	77.33	87.19

without a transformer connection. Actually, the inference model without a transformer connection could save many computational resources. Therefore, the best solution is to train the model with a transformer connection while inferring the model without a transformer connection. Fortunately, the transformer connection builds an extra path to transferring feature. The removal of the transformer connection will not change the structure of the model. And then, the loss of the feature information could be distilled from the trained model. To further improve the performance of transformer connection, the model could be pre-trained in a large natural dataset, such as CoCo, ImageNet, and then fine-tuned for brain tumor segmentation. The combination of transfer learning is also our future direction.

5   Conclusion

In this paper, we compress the U-net architecture fused with the transformer connection using knowledge distillation for multi-modality brain tumor segmentation in MRI. Incorporating the transformer connection into the convolution neural network improved the performance of segmentation. The teacher model with transformer connection improved the KD performance of the student U-net.

Acknowledgement. This work was supported in part by the National Key Research and Development Program of China (No: 2020AAA0109502), and by the Talent Program of Zhejiang Province (2021R51004).

References

1. Bakas, S., et al.: Advancing the cancer genome atlas glioma MRI collections with expert segmentation labels and radiomic features. Sci. Data 4(1), 1–13 (2017)
2. Bakas, S., et al.: Identifying the best machine learning algorithms for brain tumor segmentation, progression assessment, and overall survival prediction in the brats challenge. arXiv preprint arXiv:1811.02629 (2018)
3. Chen, W., Liu, B., Peng, S., Sun, J., Qiao, X.: S3D-UNet: separable 3D U-Net for brain tumor segmentation. In: Crimi, A., Bakas, S., Kuijf, H., Keyvan, F., Reyes, M., van Walsum, T. (eds.) BrainLes 2018. LNCS, vol. 11384, pp. 358–368. Springer, Cham (2019). https://doi.org/10.1007/978-3-030-11726-9_32
4. Dosovitskiy, A., et al.: An image is worth 16x16 words: transformers for image recognition at scale. arXiv preprint arXiv:2010.11929 (2020)

5. Havaei, M., et al.: Brain tumor segmentation with deep neural networks. Med. Image Anal. **35**, 18–31 (2017)

6. Hinton, G., Vinyals, O., Dean, J.: Distilling the knowledge in a neural network. arXiv preprint arXiv:1503.02531 (2015)

7. Islam, M., Vibashan, V.S., Jose, V.J.M., Wijethilake, N., Utkarsh, U., Ren, H.: Brain tumor segmentation and survival prediction using 3D attention UNet. In: Crimi, A., Bakas, S. (eds.) BrainLes 2019. LNCS, vol. 11992, pp. 262–272. Springer, Cham (2020). https://doi.org/10.1007/978-3-030-46640-4_25

8. Li, C., Chen, M., Zhang, J., Liu, H.: Cardiac MRI segmentation with focal loss constrained deep residual networks. Phys. Med. Biol. **66**(13), 135012 (2021)

9. Li, K., Yu, L., Wang, S., Heng, P.A.: Towards cross-modality medical image segmentation with online mutual knowledge distillation. In: Proceedings of the AAAI Conference on Artificial Intelligence, vol. 34, pp. 775–783 (2020)

10. Menze, B.H., et al.: The multimodal brain tumor image segmentation benchmark (BRATS). IEEE Trans. Med. Imaging **34**(10), 1993–2024 (2014)

11. Pravitasari, A.A., et al.: Unet-vgg16 with transfer learning for MRI-based brain tumor segmentation. Telkomnika **18**(3), 1310–1318 (2020)

12. Ronneberger, O., Fischer, P., Brox, T.: U-Net: convolutional networks for biomedical image segmentation. In: Navab, N., Hornegger, J., Wells, W.M., Frangi, A.F. (eds.) MICCAI 2015. LNCS, vol. 9351, pp. 234–241. Springer, Cham (2015). https://doi.org/10.1007/978-3-319-24574-4_28

13. Tseng, K.K., Zhang, R., Chen, C.M., Hassan, M.M.: DNetUnet: a semi-supervised CNN of medical image segmentation for super-computing AI service. J. Supercomput. **77**(4), 3594–3615 (2021)

14. Vaswani, A., et al.: Attention is all you need. In: Advances in Neural Information Processing Systems 30 (2017)

15. Wang, W., Chen, C., Ding, M., Yu, H., Zha, S., Li, J.: TransBTS: multimodal brain tumor segmentation using transformer. In: de Bruijne, M., et al. (eds.) MICCAI 2021. LNCS, vol. 12901, pp. 109–119. Springer, Cham (2021). https://doi.org/10.1007/978-3-030-87193-2_11

16. Xu, F., Ma, H., Sun, J., Wu, R., Liu, X., Kong, Y.: LSTM multi-modal UNet for brain tumor segmentation. In: 2019 IEEE 4th International Conference on Image, Vision and Computing (ICIVC), pp. 236–240. IEEE (2019)

17. Xu, P., et al.: Efficient knowledge distillation for liver CT segmentation using growing assistant network. Phys. Med. Biol. **66**(23), 235005 (2021)

18. Zhou, Z., Rahman Siddiquee, M.M., Tajbakhsh, N., Liang, J.: UNet++: a nested U-Net architecture for medical image segmentation. In: Stoyanov, D., et al. (eds.) DLMIA/ML-CDS -2018. LNCS, vol. 11045, pp. 3–11. Springer, Cham (2018). https://doi.org/10.1007/978-3-030-00889-5_1

Lung Segmentation Using ResUnet++ Powered by Variational Auto Encoder-Based Enhancement in Chest X-ray Images

Samar Ibrahim[1,2]([✉]) [ID], Kareem Elgohary[1,2] [ID], Mahmoud Higazy[3],
Thanaa Mohannad[3], Sahar Selim[1,2] [ID], and Mustafa Elattar[1,2,3] [ID]

[1] Medical Imaging and Image Processing Research Group, Center for Informatics Science,
Nile University, Giza, Egypt
S.Ibrahim2144@nu.edu.eg
[2] School of Information Technology and Computer Science, Nile University, Giza, Egypt
[3] Research and Development Division, Intixel Co. S.A.E., Cairo, Egypt

Abstract. X-ray has a huge popularity around the world. This is due to its low cost and easy to access. Most of lung diseases are diagnosed using Chest X-ray (CXR). So, developing computer aided detection (CAD) provided with automatic lung segmentation can improve the efficiency of the detection and support the physicians to make a reliable decision at early stages. But when the input image has image artifacts, then any lung segmentation model will introduce suboptimal lung segmentation results. In this paper, a new approach is proposed to make the lung segmentation model robust and boost the basic models' performance. This is done through two stages: image enhancement and lung segmentation. The first stage aims to enhance the image quality by using the combination of Variational Autoencoder (VAE) and U-Net. The features of VAE and U-Net are concatenated to decode the enhanced output CXR image. The second stage is segmenting the lung using ResUNet++, which can perform well with a few number of images. Moreover, it combines the advantages of residual blocks, squeeze and excitation blocks, Atrous Spatial Pyramidal Pooling (ASPP), and attention blocks. The proposed method is trained on JSRT dataset. The proposed approach achieved Dice score of 0.9848, 0.99 and the Jaccard score of 0.9783, 0.984 on test data of NLM-MC and JSRT datasets, respectively, which outperforms results in other state of the art models.

Keywords: ResUnet++ · Lung segmentation · Variational auto encoder · Chest X-ray enhancement

1 Introduction

CXR is considered a more utilized technique compared to other imaging modalities such as Computed Tomography (CT) scan, and Magnetic Resonance Imaging (MRI) in the world, due to its lower cost and lower amounts of radiation. CXR is a useful tool to study disorders in the thorax area for several diseases including atelectasis, pneumothorax,

© The Author(s), under exclusive license to Springer Nature Switzerland AG 2022
G. Yang et al. (Eds.): MIUA 2022, LNCS 13413, pp. 339–356, 2022.
https://doi.org/10.1007/978-3-031-12053-4_26

pleural and pericardial effusion, cardiac hypertrophy, and hyperinflation. It can be used to identify cancer, infection, or air accumulating around the lung, which can cause the lung to collapse. In addition, it also facilitates tuberculosis (TB) screening for HIV-positive populations in resource-constrained regions. The low cost of CXR makes it affordable especially in areas with little resources [1].

In accordance with the diagnostic imaging dataset statistical report 2022 [2], released by the National Health Services (NAS), England, during the year October 2020 to October 2021, 41.1 million imaging tests were performed. The most dominant technique was X-ray (20.12 million X-rays being performed), followed by Diagnostic Ultrasonography (Ultrasound, 9.6 million), CT scan (6.3 million), and MRI (3.6 million). Based on these statistics, X-ray has a great global impact on medical diagnosis, where it provides significant information about the patients. Hence, developing a Computer-Aided Detection (CAD) system provided by an automatic lung segmentation can support physicians to detect distinct lung diseases at early stages through CXR images. Lung segmentation is a vital component of any clinical decision support system aiming at improved early diagnosis of critical lung disorders such as lung cancer and chronic obstructive pulmonary disease (COPD), etc. [3]. This helps the CAD system to be more efficient by focusing just on the lungs to facilitate and make the detection of the diseases more confident. The entire X-ray usually used for training; however, the presence of unneeded organs might cause noise and false positives (FP) or false negatives (FN). Whereas, segmenting the region of interest (ROI), followed by feature extraction then classification or detection, increases the efficiency of the CAD system. Also, this can result in the false negative and false positive reduction of the CAD system.

Accurate and automatic segmentation of CXRs is a difficult task, due to differences in lung size and edges at the rib cage and clavicle. These variations are a result of the sizes of the different human bodies. Different strategies have been proposed for automatic lung segmentation by multiple researchers in recent years as a result of technology development. These techniques include classical methods such as active shape analysis and deformable models [4, 5] and Deep Learning methods.

In deep learning, the encoder-decoder architecture is widely utilized such as FCNN [6], U-net [7], UNet++ with Efficient Net B4 as the encoder and residual blocks as decoder [1], Patch-based AlexNet, ResNet18 [8],and SegNet [9]. The CNN encoder works as feature extraction, the decoder performs up-sampling operations to obtain final image segmentation results. This saves a lot of effort and time. Nevertheless, image processing techniques must be used to increase the performance of the segmentation models. Furthermore, different augmentation techniques such as standard techniques like rotation, shearing and etc. or advanced techniques like Generative Adversarial Networks (GANs) [10] are greatly required to improve the performance of the models and avoid overfitting.

According to the above literature review, one obvious strategy to increase the different segmentation methods' performance, is to simply improve the quality of the input images and make them usable. Where the clothes of the patients or any fault in the equipment of x-ray imaging could cause some extra/halting structures during CXR image acquisition, resulting in, the origin of artifacts in CXR images [11]. Consequently, much CXR data are publicly available. Most of this data is not usable due to its low quality and deep learning models can't benefit from that huge data. Hence, segmentation models tested on extra/halting structures data could fail to segment the lungs. As their features can be vastly different from features that have been trained on. Also, an accurate lung segmentation model which can deal with small data is highly needed without causing overfitting.

The outline of our research contribution is mentioned below:

- A new method is proposed by training the combination of variational autoencoder (VAE) and U-Net to enhance images instead of using traditional image enhancement techniques for extra/halting structures data. In this work, the VAE is used to do cross-domain mapping between the input and target image domain.
- Due to the lack of annotated data, a synthetic dataset is created to simulate the extra/halting structures and low-quality CXR images by two methods: performing histogram matching and adding blurred mask to the original image to simulate different patterns.
- This simulation dataset is used to train VAE to enhance the CXR images before segmenting the lung, then testing the model on samples of Covid-19 and lung opacity datasets.
- Improved model generalization by using ResUnet++ for lung segmentation. ResUNet++ architecture for image segmentation utilizes residual blocks, squeeze and excitation blocks, Atrous Spatial Pyramidal Pooling (ASPP), and attention blocks.
- The ResUnet++ model was fine-tuned on multiple datasets including NLM-MC.
- Tversky loss function is used with ResUnet++ to give weight to cases in which a region is identified as lung even when no lung is present, and vice versa.

2 Materials and Methods

The Overview of the proposed system for lung segmentation is shown in Fig. 1. It consists of two stages. The first stage targets enhancing CXR images having some artifacts that degrade image quality and may be generated as the result of any fault in the equipment of the x-ray during capturing the CXR images for the patients. These low-quality images make any segmentation model fail to segment the lung. The combination of VAE and U-Net were used to enhance this type of CXR image. The lung is then segmented using ResUNet++ that was trained on JSRT dataset and fine-tuned on NLM-MC dataset to generalize on these two datasets.

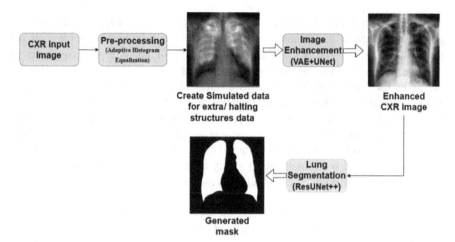

Fig. 1. Proposed methodology for image segmentation

2.1 Dataset

The Japanese Society of Radiological Technology (JSRT) dataset is a lung nodule Chest X-ray dataset from Japan in 2000. It consists of 247 images with and without a lung nodule. In each image, the lung fields have been manually segmented to provide a reference standard [12].

Montgomery (NLM-MC) dataset contains 138 CXR images with right and left lung masks. For this data collection, the tuberculosis control program of Montgomery County's Department of Health and Human Services provided these X-ray images [13].

Simulated Data for Image Enhancement. A lot of low quality CXR images that contain some artifacts are publicly available as shown in Fig. 2, but their corresponding good images are missing and unknown. So due to the lack of annotated data, creating a simulation dataset is critically needed. JSRT is used to simulate real extra/halting structures data. The simulation dataset is originated by two methods: the first by performing histogram matching between JSRT and real extra/halting structures data, the second by adding a blurred mask to the original JSRT image as shown in Fig. 3.

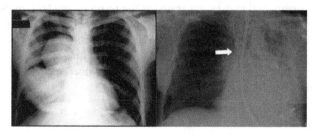

Fig. 2. Example of extra/halting structures data that is publicly available

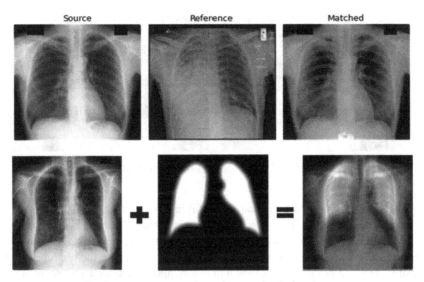

Fig. 3. The technique of creating the simulation dataset.

Covid-19 and Lung Opacity Datasets. These two datasets are available with their lung masks [16]. The lung opacity dataset consists of about 6012 images and masks, while the Covid-19 dataset consists of about 3616 images and masks. These two datasets contain some artifacts and opacity that make any segmentation model introduce suboptimal results.

2.2 Pre-processing

The pre-processing steps are a vital component to make data easier to use and increase the performance of the models. The higher the quality of the images, the more features that can be extracted. Thus, this helps to improve the efficiency of the models. Whereas the dataset used in creating simulation extra/halting structures data and training ResUnet++ for lung segmentation, needs to be high-quality images.

Adaptive Histogram Equalization. Images come in a variety of lighting settings, some of which are a little dark and noisy and difficult to be used in the diagnosis of diseases. So, adaptive histogram equalization was applied to adjust the contrast of the images and avoid stretching noisy areas, then normalized output by dividing on 255 as shown in Fig. 4.

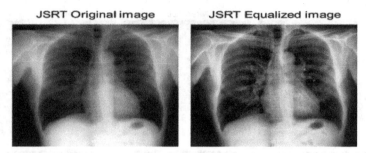

Fig. 4. Example of JSRT after applying adaptive histogram equalization

Image Augmentation. It is a method of modifying existing data in order to generate new data for the model training process. CXR images are obtained from a variety of sources, and hence the contrast of each source will change. Some images may be of high contrast, while others may be of poor contrast. In such cases, the brightness of the original images can be changed as shown in Fig. 5, making the model more resistant to the image quality used in the test data.

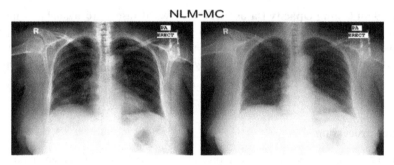

Fig. 5. NLM-MC images after changing the brightness with gamma in the range of 0.9:1.3

2.3 ResUNet++ Architecture

ResUnet++ [14] is an improved medical image segmentation architecture from ResUNet. It works well with a small amount of data, so there is no need for extensive methods of augmentation. Where little data augmentation is enough which consumes less computational power and time and improves generalization. ResU-Net++ is based on the Deep Residual U-Net (ResUNet). This is a model that includes the benefits of deep residual learning and U-Net. ResUnet++ combines 4 advantages of the residual blocks, the squeeze and excitation block, ASPP, and the attention block. All abovementioned is what distinguishes ResUNet++ from ResUNet. ResUNet++ architecture contains Input block followed by three encoder blocks, ASPP, and three decoder blocks as depicted in Fig. 6. The summarized details of each block are shown in Fig. 7 and a brief overview of the advantages of each block is given in the following context. The introduction of Residual blocks alleviated the challenge of training very deep networks, and the ResUNet++ model is built up of these blocks. The skip connections are considered the heart of the residual blocks. These skip connections solve the problem of vanishing gradient. Squeeze and Excitation blocks reduce the computational cost. They act as attention. Their goal is to guide the network to pay attention to related features and ignore unnecessary features. There is a squeeze and excitation block between residual blocks in the encoder. The Atrous Spatial Pyramidal Pooling (ASPP) is based on spatial pyramidal pooling. It's good at resampling features at different scales. Where features are captured at a wide variety of scales. It acts as a bridge between encoder and decoder. Attention block also reduces the computational cost. It determines which parts of the information that neural network must pay attention to. This module is the same as what is used in natural language processing tasks. It is provided in the decoder.

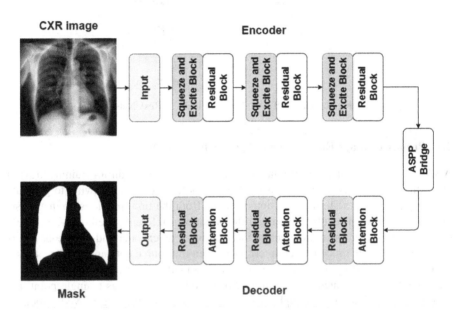

Fig. 6. The overview of ResUNet++ architecture

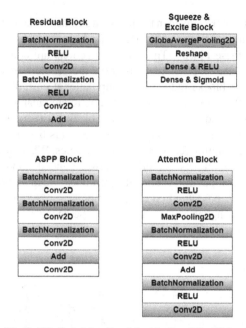

Fig. 7. The brief details of the blocks of ResUNet++

2.4 Proposed Image Enhancement Approach VAEU-Net

A VAE is an autoencoder with regularized encoding distributions during training to avoid overfitting ensure that its latent space has acceptable properties, allowing to generate data. Furthermore, the term "variational" stems from the tight relationship that exists in statistics between regularization and the variational inference method. VAE, like a regular autoencoder, is an architecture that combines an encoder and a decoder and is trained to reduce the reconstruction error between the source data and the target data. However, the encoding-decoding procedure is modified somewhat to incorporate some regularization of the latent space: instead of encoding an input as a single point, it's encoded as a distribution throughout the latent space. The training of VAE model is done as follows. First, the input is represented as a latent space distribution. Second, from that distribution, a point from the latent space is sampled. Third, the reconstruction error can be calculated after the sampled point has been decoded. Finally, the error is backpropagated through the network to do the optimization process.

In this study, the VAE is not used as an autoencoder, but used to perform cross-domain mapping between the input image and target image domains. This model is inspired by [15]. The model is combination of VAE and U-Net. The variational encoder, as shown in Fig. 8, maps input images to a low-dimensional latent space. Samples from the latent space were concatenated to the output of the U-Net encoder, where (Z) is the latent vector and (O) is the output of the U-Net encoder. The decoder is shared by the U-net encoder and the VAE, allowing both to decode the enhanced image together. The U-Net encoder and VAE encoder consist of 4 down-sampling convolution blocks. The shared decoder consists of 4 up-sampling convolution blocks.

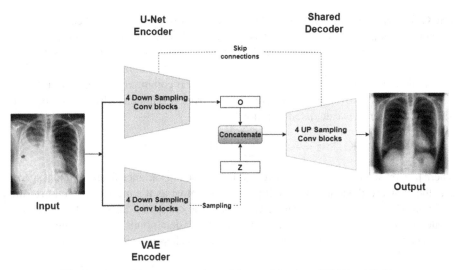

Fig. 8. The architecture overview of the combination of VAE and U-Net

2.5 Loss Functions

Tversky Loss (TL). It is region-based loss. The goal of region-based loss functions is to reduce or maximize the overlap between the ground truth and predicted segmentation zones. The Dice loss is considered the parent of Tversky loss, where Tversky loss is dice loss, but it gives different weights to false negatives (FN) and false positives (FP), as opposed to equal weights for FN and FP in dice loss. The equation of Tversky loss is:

$$TL = 1 - |TP|/(|TP| + \alpha|FN| + \beta|FP|) \tag{1}$$

where TP – the number of pixels that were correctly identified as being in the lung region. TN – the number of pixels in the background that have been accurately detected. FP – the number of pixels that were misidentified as lung region. FN – the number of pixels that were incorrectly assigned to the background.

Dice Loss. The Dice coefficient is a popular pixel segmentation measure that can also be used as a loss function:

$$\text{Dice loss} = 1 - 2 * |X \cap Y|/(|X| + |Y|) \tag{2}$$

where X and Y represent two sets.

Focal Loss (FL). FL can alternatively be thought of as a version of Binary Cross-Entropy. It reduces the importance of easy examples, allowing the model to concentrate more on learning difficult instances. It works best in situations when there are a lot of unequal classes.

The Optimization Objective of a VAEU-Net. The loss function was used for training the combination of VAE and U-Net is hybrid loss of Binary Cross Entropy (BCE) and KL-divergence. The Kullback-Leibler Divergence loss, often known as the KL divergence loss, measures how much one probability distribution differs from another. The KL divergence between two distributions Q and P is commonly expressed as follows: KL(P ∥ Q). Where "divergence" or Ps divergence from Q is indicated by the "∥" operator. The KL-divergence is calculated as follows:

$$\text{KL loss} = -0.5 * \sum (1 + \log(\sigma^2) - \mu^2 - \sigma^2) \tag{3}$$

where μ is the mean from the latent vector. Log is the log variance from the latent space. σ is the standard deviation. It's multiplied by negative as it's needed to minimize the difference between the actual latent vector and the computed latent vector. Also, it's needed to maximize the probability of reassembling data points from the latent space. This means minimizing reconstruction loss. So, BCE loss is used. Hence, the final loss is:

$$\text{Hybrid loss} = \text{BCE loss} + \text{KL loss} \tag{4}$$

This formula of Eq. 3 is called the variational lower bound loss for VAE.

3   Experimental Results

The solution of the lung segmentation problem is mainly based on divide and conquer approach, where it consists of three phases: the first is to train ResUnet++, the second is to train VAEU-Net and the last phase is to combine the 1st and 2nd phases for testing VAEU-Net and ResUnet++ together. The VAEU-Net and ResUnet++ were trained separately. The ResUnet++ was trained on original JSRT and NLM-MC datasets. The VAEU-Net was trained on simulated data. Finally, the two stages: the VAEU-Net and ResUnet++ were tested together on Covid-19 and lung opacity datasets, so that the results of segmentation could be compared before/after enhancement.

3.1   Lung Segmentation Training

The ResUnet++ was trained on JSRT and NLM-MC datasets as shown in Fig. 9. The batch size and learning rate were set to 8 and 0.001 respectively, ResUNet++ was trained to 100 epochs with early stopping. Schedule learning rate was used with Adam optimizer. Input size was $256 \times 256 \times 3$. Cross validation with 5 folds was applied. The training of ResUnet++ was done mainly in two steps as shown in Fig. 10: the first was to train on JSRT with different loss functions, the second was to generalize on NLM-MC using the best loss function was obtained from 1st step and the last step was to compare results with other work in the literature. Table 1 gives the summary of different loss functions used for training ResUnet++ on JSRT. As observed from Table 1, the Tversky loss achieved the highest Dice and Jaccard scores which led us to use Tversky loss in all the following experiments. Table 2 presents different modes that were done to generalize on NLM-MC using Tversky loss: the first mode is fine-tuning to continue training using weights resulting from JSRT and the second mode is to combine the two datasets: JSRT and NLM-MC. The obtained results showed that ResUnet++ achieved the highest scores on NLM-MC in the first mode. Finally, a comparison of testing results with other studies in the literature is shown in Table 3. The comparison in Table 3 proved that the proposed ResUnet++ architecture gives the highest results for the two datasets: JSRT and NLM-MC. The training behavior of ResUnet++ on JSRT with Tversky loss and generalizing on NLM-MC using trained weights on JSRT are illustrated in Fig. 11.

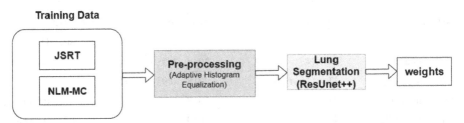

Fig. 9. Training of ResUnet++

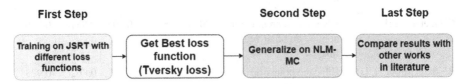

Fig. 10. The different phases of Training ResUnet++

Table 1. Summary of chosen settings for training ResUnet++ on JSRT

Scores/Training method	JSRT			
	Dice loss	Dice + BCE	TL	TL + FL
Dice	0.9791	0.9793	**0.99**	0.9777
Jaccard	0.9607	0.9675	**0.984**	0.9707

Table 2. Results of lung segmentation to generalize on NLM-MC

| Training method | Test | | | |
| | Dice | | Jaccard | |
	JSRT	NLM-MC	JSRT	NLM-MC
1st mode	–	**0.9848**	–	**0.9783**
2nd mode	0.9746	0.9645	0.9704	0.9566

Table 3. A performance comparison of multiple lung segmentation works

| Author | Method | Year | JSRT | | NLM-MC | |
			Jaccard	Dice	Jaccard	Dice
Hooda et al. [6]	FCNN	2018	0.959	–	–	–
Novikov et al. [21]	Deep learning	2018	0.95	0.974	–	–
Dai et al. [23]	SCAN	2018	–	0.973	–	0.966
Souza et al. [8]	Patch-based AlexNet, ResNet18	2019	–	–	0.8807	0.9441
Reamaroon et al. [19]	Total Variation-based Active Contour	2020	–	0.89	–	0.86
Chen et al. [22]	CNN-based architectures applied on binarized images	2020	0.842	0.893	0.831	0.886
Bosdelekidis et al. [18]	Rib cage points-driven region growing	2020	–	–	0.862	0.923
Hamad et al. [20]	GLCM and PNN	2020	–	–	0.915	0.955
Chen et al. [17]	TSCN	2020	–	0.973	–	0.964
Kim et al. [7]	U-Net	2021	0.963	0.968	0.964	0.98
Maity et al. [1]	UNet++	2022	0.968	0.983	0.966	0.981
	ResUNet++ (Proposed method)		**0.984**	**0.99**	**0.9783**	**0.9848**

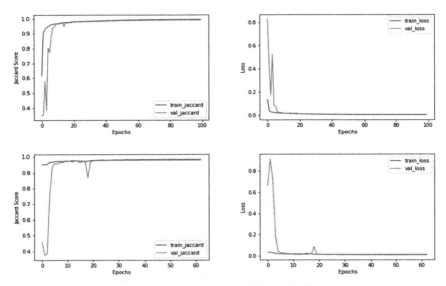

Fig. 11. The Jaccard scores and loss of training and validation respectively.

3.2 The Training of VAEU-Net

The VAEU-Net was trained on simulated extra/halting structures data as shown in Fig. 12. The batch size and learning rate were set to 64 and 0.001 respectively. The dimension of latent space was chosen equal to 8. The model was trained for 100 epochs. Input size was $256 \times 256 \times 1$ and optimizer was Adam. It achieved loss in range 0.89:1.2 as shown in Fig. 13.

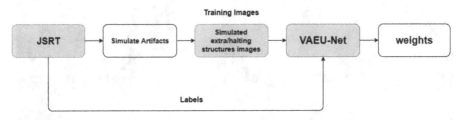

Fig. 12. Training of VAEU-Net

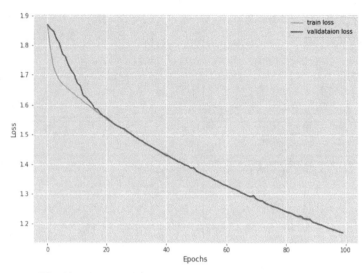

Fig. 13. The loss of VAEU-Net during training and validation

Simulation of Extra/Halting Structures Data. It was created with different patterns to avoid memorizing a specific pattern which leads to the failure of VAEU-Net like the overfitting problem. So, the VAEU-Net was trained on different patterns of simulated data to avoid overfitting problem. Some examples of simulated extra/halting structures data that were produced as depicted in Sect. 2 and used for training VAEU-Net are shown in Fig. 14.

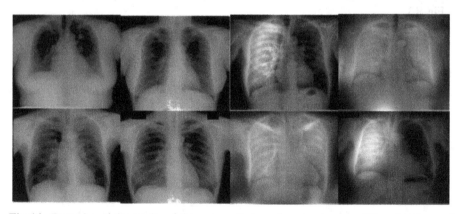

Fig. 14. Examples of the results of the process that are done to simulate different patterns of extra/halting structures data

VAEU-Net to Enhance Simulated Data. The output of training the combination of VAEU-Net to enhance extra/halting structures simulated data is shown in the following Fig. 15.

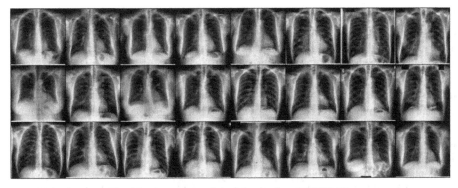

Fig. 15. Some examples of the results of VAEU-Net

3.3 Testing of VAEU-Net and ResUnet++

Finally, the two stages: the VAEU-Net and ResUnet++ were tested together on the two datasets: Covid-19 and lung opacity datasets as shown in Fig. 16 to compare the results of segmentation using ResUnet++ before and after the enhancement using VAEU-Net as shown in Table 4.

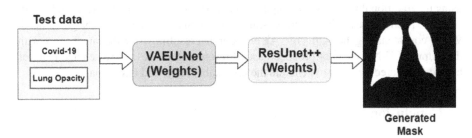

Fig. 16. The testing of two stages together: VAEU-Net and ResUnet++

Table 4. Results of testing ResUnet++ before/after enhancement

Settings	Covid-19 dataset		Lung opacity dataset	
	Dice	Jaccard	Dice	Jaccard
(Baseline) without VAEU-Net	0.8789	0.8198	0.7947	0.7616
After enhancement using VAEU-Net	**0.8954**	**0.8511**	**0.8310**	**0.8069**

4 Discussion

From Table 1, The ResUnet++ was trained with different loss functions such as dice loss, weighted dice cross entropy loss, Tversky loss and combination of Focal and Tversky loss. It is found that the Tversky loss with giving 0.7 weight to FN and 0.3 weight to FP outperforms the resting of the loss functions with a small amount of data. It achieved the highest Dice and Jaccard scores on JSRT and NLM-MC by fine-tuning as depicted in Table 2. It is also observed that the choice of the optimizer, batch size and learning rate has impact on the results. The results of increasing the number of images by combining JSRT and NLM-MC indicate that the advantages of ResUNet++ can deal with a small number of images without needing too extensive data augmentation such as GANS or other advanced techniques to improve the performance. This leads to less computational power and time. Whereas combining the two datasets, NLM-Mc and JSRT as shown in Table 2 to increase the number of images, didn't improve the results of segmentation a lot. And usually, this is contrary to what was expected. On both the NLM-MC and the JSRT datasets, the used ResUNet++ architecture gives the highest results. The segmentation map resulting from ResUNet++ clearly exceeds other architectures in capturing shape information as shown in Table 3. It means that the segmentation mask generated by ResUNet++ is closer to the ground truth than current state-of-the-art models. The attention, Residual, ASPP, Squeeze and Excitation blocks of ResUNet++ could capture information from small data that make model converge faster.

The VAEU-Net to enhance extra/halting structures data produced the promised results as shown in Fig. 15, it could decrease the effect of artifacts and opacity that make any segmentation model fail to segment the lung according to Table 4. Instead of using the traditional image processing techniques that consumes a lot of time and effort. Also, the results of using image processing to deal with this case may not be guaranteed. Where concatenating the output of VAE encoder that resulting from the latent space with the output of U-Net encoder produced useful information. These concatenated features helped the shared decoder to generate the acceptable enhanced CXR image.

5 Conclusion

Most of lung segmentation models can fail when the input CXR image has low contrast and some artifacts, where the boundary of the lung is not clear enough. Hence, in this paper, we present a new method for lung segmentation. Our approach consists of the two stages. The first stage aims to enhance the extra/halting structures data using the combination of U-Net and VAE. The VAE is used to do cross domain mapping. Where the features extracted from U-Net encoder and VAE are concatenated to each other, then the shared decoder uses these concatenated features to form enhanced CXR image. The second stage targets the lung. ResUNet++ is used to segment the lung. ResUNet++ is an improved lung segmentation model which has multiple advantages of the residual blocks, the squeeze and excitation block, ASPP, and the attention block. The proposed method is trained on JSRT dataset and NLM-MC dataset and achieved Dice score of 0.9848, 0.99 and the Jaccard score of 0.9783, 0.984 on test data of NLM-MC and JSRT datasets, respectively, which outperformed other studies in the literature.

References

1. Maity, A., Nair, T.R., Mehta, S., Prakasam, P.: Automatic lung parenchyma segmentation using a deep convolutional neural network from chest X-rays. Biomed. Signal Process. Control **73**, 103398 (2022). https://doi.org/10.1016/J.BSPC.2021.103398
2. Dixon, S.: Diagnostic Imaging Dataset Statistical Release (2022)
3. Bharati, S., Podder, P., Mondal, M.R.H.: Hybrid deep learning for detecting lung diseases from X-ray images. Inform. Med. Unlocked **20**, 100391 (2020). https://doi.org/10.1016/J.IMU.2020.100391
4. Cootes, T.F., Taylor, C.J., Cooper, D.H., Graham, J.: Active shape models-their training and application. Comput. Vis. Image Underst. **61**(1), 38–59 (1995). https://doi.org/10.1006/CVIU.1995.1004
5. Caselles, V., Catté, F., Coll, T., Dibos, F.: A geometric model for active contours in image processing. Numer. Math. **66**(1), 1–31 (1993). https://doi.org/10.1007/BF01385685
6. Hooda, R., Mittal, A., Sofat, S.: An efficient variant of fully-convolutional network for segmenting lung fields from chest radiographs. Wirel. Pers. Commun. **101**(3), 1559–1579 (2018). https://doi.org/10.1007/s11277-018-5777-3
7. Kim, M., Lee, B.D.: Automatic lung segmentation on chest x-rays using self-attention deep neural network. Sensors **21**(2), 369 (2021). https://doi.org/10.3390/S21020369
8. Souza, J.C., Bandeira Diniz, J.O., Ferreira, J.L., França da Silva, G.L., Corrêa Silva, A., de Paiva, A.C.: An automatic method for lung segmentation and reconstruction in chest X-ray using deep neural networks. Comput. Methods Programs Biomed. **177**, 285–296 (2019). https://doi.org/10.1016/J.CMPB.2019.06.005
9. Badrinarayanan, V., Kendall, A., Cipolla, R.: SegNet: a deep convolutional encoder-decoder architecture for image segmentation. IEEE Trans. Pattern Anal. Mach. Intell. **39**(12), 2481–2495 (2017). https://doi.org/10.1109/TPAMI.2016.2644615
10. Chest X-Ray Images Generation Using GAN | College of Science and Engineering. https://cse.umn.edu/datascience/chest-x-ray-images-generation-using-gan
11. Bell, D., Shetty, A.: X-ray artifacts. Radiopaedia.org, January 2014. https://doi.org/10.53347/RID-27307
12. JSRT Database | Japanese Society of Radiological Technology. http://db.jsrt.or.jp/eng.php
13. Tuberculosis Chest X-ray Image Data Sets. - LHNCBC Abstract. https://lhncbc.nlm.nih.gov/LHCpublications/pubs/TuberculosisChestXrayImageDataSets.html
14. Jha, D., et al.: ResUNet++: an advanced architecture for medical image segmentation. In: Proceedings of 2019 IEEE International Symposium on Multimedia, ISM 2019, pp. 225–230, November 2019. https://doi.org/10.48550/arxiv.1911.07067
15. Selvan, R., et al.: Lung Segmentation from Chest X-rays using Variational Data Imputation, May 2020. http://arxiv.org/abs/2005.10052
16. COVID-19 Radiography Database | Kaggle. https://www.kaggle.com/datasets/tawsifurrahman/covid19-radiography-database
17. Chen, B., Zhang, Z., Lin, J., Chen, Y., Lu, G.: Pattern recognition letters two-stream collaborative network for multi-label chest X-ray image classification with lung segmentation (2020)
18. Bosdelekidis, V., Ioakeimidis, N.S.: Lung field segmentation in chest X-rays: a deformation-tolerant procedure based on the approximation of rib cage seed points. Appl. Sci. **10**(18), 6264 (2020). https://doi.org/10.3390/APP10186264
19. Reamaroon, N., et al.: Robust segmentation of lung in chest X-ray: applications in analysis of acute respiratory distress syndrome. BMC Med. Imaging **20**(1), 1–13 (2020). https://doi.org/10.1186/S12880-020-00514-Y/TABLES/6

20. Hamad, Y.A., Simonov, K., Naeem, M.B.: Lung boundary detection and classification in chest X-rays images based on neural network. In: Khalaf, M.I., Al-Jumeily, D., Lisitsa, A. (eds.) ACRIT 2019. CCIS, vol. 1174, pp. 3–16. Springer, Cham (2020). https://doi.org/10.1007/978-3-030-38752-5_1
21. Novikov, A.A., Lenis, D., Major, D., Hladuvka, J., Wimmer, M., Buhler, K.: Fully convolutional architectures for multiclass segmentation in chest radiographs. IEEE Trans. Med. Imaging **37**(8), 1865–1876 (2018). https://doi.org/10.1109/TMI.2018.2806086
22. Chen, H.J., Ruan, S.J., Huang, S.W., Peng, Y.T.: Lung X-ray segmentation using deep convolutional neural networks on contrast-enhanced binarized images. Mathematics **8**(4), 545 (2020). https://doi.org/10.3390/MATH8040545
23. Dai, W., Dong, N., Wang, Z., Liang, X., Zhang, H., Xing, E.P.: SCAN: structure correcting adversarial network for organ segmentation in chest X-rays. In: Stoyanov, D., et al. (eds.) DLMIA/ML-CDS 2018. LNCS, vol. 11045, pp. 263–273. Springer, Cham (2018). https://doi.org/10.1007/978-3-030-00889-5_30

A Neural Architecture Search Based Framework for Segmentation of Epithelium, Nuclei and Oral Epithelial Dysplasia Grading

Neda Azarmehr[1]([⊠]) [ID], Adam Shephard[2], Hanya Mahmood[1], Nasir Rajpoot[2], and Syed Ali Khurram[1]

[1] School of Clinical Dentistry, University of Sheffield, Sheffield, UK
n.azarmehr@sheffield.ac.uk
[2] Department of Computer Science, University of Warwick, Coventry, UK

Abstract. Oral epithelial dysplasia (OED) is a pre-cancerous histopathological diagnosis given to a range of oral lesions. Architectural, cytological and histological features of OED can be modelled through the segmentation of full epithelium, individual nuclei and stroma (connective tissues) to provide significant diagnostic features. In this paper, we explore a customised neural architecture search (NAS) based method for optimisation of an efficient architecture for segmentation of the full epithelium and individual nuclei in pathology whole slide images (WSIs). Our initial experimental results show that the NAS-derived architecture achieves 93.5% F1-score for the full epithelium segmentation and 94.5% for nuclear segmentation outperforming other state-of-the-art models. Accurate nuclear segmentation allows us to perform quantitative statistical and morphometric feature analyses of the segmented nuclei within regions of interest (ROIs) of multi-gigapixel whole-slide images (WSIs). We show that a random forest model using these features can differentiate between low-risk and high-risk OED lesions.

Keywords: Oral epithelial dysplasia · Computational pathology · Neural architecture search · Digital pathology · Deep learning · Machine learning

1 Introduction

Head and neck cancer (HNC) is among the top 10 most widespread cancers globally and accounts for an estimated incidence of 150,000 annually in Europe alone [1]. HNC consists of a large group of cancers; with oral squamous cell carcinoma (OSCC) being one of the most common cancers in this group. In most cases, OSCC is preceded by a potentially malignant state with the proliferation of atypical epithelium known as Oral Epithelial Dysplasia (OED) [2]. Dysplastic regions are much more likely to transform into OSCC and a diagnosis is made following a biopsy and histological assessments using a grading system [3]. OED grading is usually categorised into multiple different categories such as the World Health Organisation (WHO) grading system [4] including

© The Author(s), under exclusive license to Springer Nature Switzerland AG 2022
G. Yang et al. (Eds.): MIUA 2022, LNCS 13413, pp. 357–370, 2022.
https://doi.org/10.1007/978-3-031-12053-4_27

mild, moderate or severe dysplasia, and a Binary system categorising into high-risk versus low-risk lesions [5]. OED is distinguished by architectural and cytological changes of the epithelium reflecting the loss of normal growth and stratification pattern. However, histological assessment of OED and grading is subjective, with significant inter and intra-observer variation [6, 7].

Technical advances in digital pathology have established the digitisation of histology whole-slides images (WSIs) using high-resolution digital scanners and significant growth in computational pathology [8]. Similar advances in new deep learning methods have complemented pathology and radiology leading to the automatic prediction of patient outcomes [9]. In pathology, deep learning has been applied to automatically segment the epithelium within a range of histology images (e.g., prostate, cervical, oral) and further segment the individual nuclei within WSIs [9, 10]. However, there is limited work on head and neck cancer (HNC) [11]. Within OED, previous studies have proposed to segment the epithelium into three layers: a superficial keratin layer, the middle epithelial layer, and the lower basal layer allowing the generation of layer-specific features that could help in OED grading [12–14]. In this study, we focus on segmenting the full epithelium region as a whole without dividing it into sub-layers in addition to simultaneously segmenting the individual nuclei and stroma (connective tissues).

Well-designed established neural network architectures have been developed manually by human experts, which is a time-consuming and error-prone process. Recently, there has been significant interest in automated architecture design. In the past few years, Neural Architecture Search (NAS) has successfully recognised neural networks that outperform human-designed architectures on image classification and segmentation tasks [14–18]. Therefore, the main aims of our study are three-fold: first, to adopt the NAS algorithm particularly Hierarchical Neural Architecture Search to design customised segmentation architecture for segmentation of full epithelium, individual nuclei and stroma to maximise the prediction accuracy. To the best of our knowledge, no other study has applied the NAS technique to the complex problem of epithelium and nuclear segmentation in OED; second, to compare its performance with well-established segmentation architectures (i.e., U-Net, SegNet, DeepLabV3ResNet101); third, to extract nuclear features on the ROIs using the morphometrical and non-morphological features within the full epithelium for automated OED grading (i.e., WHO and binary grading system). Although some studies have examined individual feature correlation to diagnosis and prognostic outcomes, there are very few which have investigated quantitative feature analysis with the application of artificial intelligence (AI). We further assess the importance of features to OED grading, malignant transformation and OED recurrence within the full epithelium, stroma, and a combination of full epithelium and stroma has also been assessed. Figure 1 displays our proposed multi-step NAS-based framework for OED grade prediction.

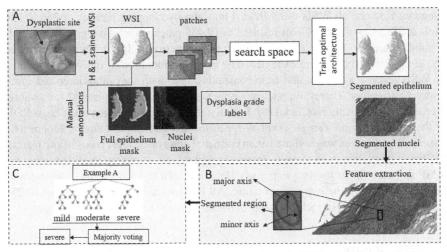

Fig. 1. Proposed NAS-based framework for OED grading. **A. Full epithelium segmentation and nuclear segmentation:** biopsy tissue samples from dysplastic sites are retrieved and Haematoxylin & Eosin (H&E) sections are obtained. These slides are scanned using a digital scanner to obtain WSI. The digitized WSIs are used by an expert to provide several types of manual annotations (i.e., full epithelium boundaries, individual nuclei annotation and dysplasia grades). WSIs divided into patches and one particular NAS technique is used to search for the optimal architectures for the OED dataset. Then, optimal architecture is trained for segmenting the full epithelium. The same stage repeats to segment individual nuclei. **B. Feature extraction:** After nuclear segmentation, architectural and cytological features of the segmented nuclei are extracted within the full epithelium layer using morphological (e.g., size of nuclei, shape of nuclei, etc.) and non-morphological (e.g., entropy, Moran index) features **C. OED grade prediction:** A random forest model is trained using the extracted features to differentiate between OED grades using the WHO and binary grading system.

2   Dataset and Annotations

The study data comprised 43 WSIs from H&E stained sections of oral mucosa/OED collected at the University of Sheffield and scanned at $20 \times$ (0.4952 microns-per-pixel) using an Aperio CS2 scanner. Of these cases, 38 had OED and 5 were healthy controls. To obtain the ground truth, manual annotations were performed by an expert pathologist including labelling for full epithelium, individual nuclei, stroma and dysplasia grades. Initially, OED cases are labelled as either mild (n = 14), moderate (n = 13), or severe (n = 11) according to the WHO 2017 classification system [3] and as low-(n = 20) or high-risk (n = 18) based on the binary grading system [4]. Following dysplasia grades, a contour has been drawn around the boundaries of the epithelium area manually at the WSI level using the Automated Slide Analysis Platform (ASAP) annotation tool (https://computationalpathologygroup.github.io/ASAP/). For each WSI, tissue masks are produced using Otsu thresholding to identify tissue within the WSI and further exclusion of small holes and irrelevant objects. Epithelial masks were generated for each WSI by combining the epithelium annotation with the tissue mask. From the total of 43 WSIs, 60% were selected for training, 20% for validation and the remaining 20% for testing. To avoid redundant features, all WSIs were divided into non-overlapping patches of 256×256 pixels at 20x magnification. This resulted in 19,438 patches for training, 6,473 patches for validation, and 6,473 for testing. During patch extraction, only patches that comprised greater than 10% tissue were extracted. The manual annotation of individual nuclei at the WSIs level is a tedious and time-consuming task with inevitable inter-and intra-observer variability. Therefore, nuclear segmentation was only performed for a subset of cases (n = 20) using NuClick [19]. Initially, the expert pathologist drew large ROIs for these 20 cases and a single point assigned to each nucleus and stroma (connective tissues). Each nucleus was assigned as an epithelial class or stroma class. Following this, NuClick annotations were visually inspected and where necessary modified using the GIMP software (https://www.gimp.org/). Data was split to train/validate and test with the same ratio as epithelium segmentation. All ROIs were divided into patches of 256×256. This led to 1,218 including approximately 50,000 nuclei.

3   Methodology

Proposed by Liu et al. (2019) [20], Auto-DeepLab uses differential NAS to reduce the computational power. Most of the NAS methods usually focus on searching the cell structure and hand-designing an outer network structure. However, Auto-DeepLab will search the network level structure as well as the cell level structure using gradient descent. Auto-Deeplab technique consists of two stages: cell and architecture search and architecture evaluation. As shown in Fig. 2, the horizontal axis indicates the layer index, and the vertical axis indicates the downsampling rate. To reduce the spatial resolution, at the beginning of the network fixed two-layer "stem" structures are added (grey nodes in Fig. 2). Two principles are consistent among the existing network designs. First, after the formal search, the location of each cell can be selected from a variety of cell types: cells from the same spatial resolution of the current cell, or cells twice as large or twice as small as the spatial resolution of the current cell and in this model, it is downsampled by 32. Second, the goal is to find a good path in this trellis. When searching the architecture for resampling a given feature, the *Atrous* Spatial Pyramid Pooling (ASPP) module is put at every layer according to every final spatial dimension factor. A weight β is associated with each grey arrow to run differentiable NAS on this search space and some connections are strengthened, and some get weaker after they are optimised. Following this, the Viterbi algorithm [21] is used to decode the path with the greatest β value products. Next, this network-level architecture is searched in addition to the cell-level one. As shown in Fig. 2-bottom, the output of each cell is combined with the cells of adjacent spatial resolution, and the β value can be identified as the probability of different paths.

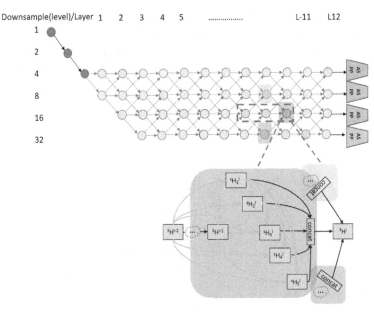

Fig. 2. Top: network-level search space with 12 layers/cells ($L = 12$). Grey nodes represent the fixed "stem" layers. The path along the blue nodes signifies candidate network-level architecture. *Bottom:* During the search, each cell is a densely connected structure. Every yellow arrow is associated with the set of normalised scalars associated with each operator $\alpha_{j\to i}$. The three arrows after "concat" are associated with the scalar β values. (Color figure online)

As shown in the lower half of Fig. 2, a cell is a fully convolutional module consisting of B blocks. The set of possible inputs for a block is the output of the previous two cells (H^{l-2}), and the previous blocks' output (H^{l-1}) in the current cell $(H^l_1, \ldots \ldots . H^l_i)$. Therefore, as more blocks are added in the cell, the next block has more choices as a potential source of input. The output of the cell (H^l) is the concatenation of output from all the blocks. The three cells at the bottom of Fig. 2 with blue, yellow and green respectively, correspond to the three cells on the top figure. As explained earlier, the structure of the network level needs to be searched to find the optimal network which is iteratively calculated and update α and β. The output of each cell will be calculated as shown in Eq. (1) where s is downsample level ($s = 4, 8, 16, 32$) and L is the number of cells/layer ($L = 1, 2\ldots12$). Here β is the set of meta-weights that controls the outer network level, therefore depending on the spatial size and layer index. Each scalar in β governs an entire set of α whereas α specifies the same architecture that does not depend on spatial size or layer index. The calculation method of α is argmax, and the classic Viterbi algorithm [21] is used to calculate β.

$$
\begin{aligned}
s_{H^L} = &\ \beta^l_{\frac{s}{2}\to s}\ Cell\left(\frac{s}{2}_{H^{L-1}}, s_{H^{L-2}}, \alpha\right)\\
&+ \beta^l_{s\to s}\ Cell\left(s_{H^{L-1}}, s_{H^{L-2}}, \alpha\right)\\
&+ \beta^l_{2s\to s}\ Cell\left(2s_{H^{L-1}}, s_{H^{L-2}}, \alpha\right)
\end{aligned}
\tag{1}
$$

The types of candidate branches that will be considered in every block consist of the following 8 operators: 3×3 depthwise-separable conv, 5×5 depthwise-separable conv, 3×3 atrous conv with rate 2, 5×5 atrous conv with rate 2, 3×3 average pooling, 3×3 max pooling, skip connection, and no connection (zero). For the set of possible combination operators, element-wise addition is the only choice.

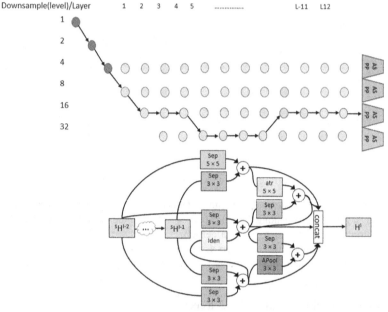

Fig. 3. *Top:* The proposed architecture found by the Hierarchical Neural Architecture Search on the OED dataset. The black arrow displays the best path found in the search space for OED dataset. *Bottom:* The best cell found for the OED dataset. atr: atrous convolution. Sep: depthwise-separable convolution, Iden: skip connection, and APool: average pooling. (Color figure online)

4 Experiment Design and Results

Initially, to search for the optimal architecture, the training data is partitioned into two disjoint sets of training data (50% each) to prevent the architecture from overfitting. For the computationally intensive stage of architecture search, a GPU server equipped with 4 NVIDIA RTX 3090 GPUs with 64 GB is used. Stochastic Gradient Descent (SGD) optimiser with a momentum of 0.9, cosine learning rate that decays from 0.025 to 0.001, and weight decay 0.0003 was used to optimise the weights. The initial values of α, β before softmax are sampled from standard Gaussian times 0.001. They are optimised using Adam optimiser with a learning rate of 0.003 and a weight decay of 0.001. A total $B = 5$ blocks in a cell was used to conduct the search. Every blue node in Fig. 3 has $B \times F \times \frac{s}{4}$ output filters, where B is the block, F is the filter multiplier that controls the model capacity and s is the downsampling rate. During the architecture search, F

= 8 is considered. The search was conducted for a maximum of 60 epochs to find the optimal network. Searching for longer epochs (100) did not reveal any benefit. If α and β are optimised from the beginning when network weights are not well trained, the architecture is likely to fall into local optima. Therefore, α and β optimised after 30 epochs. The ASPP module introduced in [22] has 5 branches such as a 1×1 convolution, three 3×3 convolutions with various *atrous* rates, and pooled image features. However, in this model, ASPP was simplified during the search to have 3 branches by only using one 3×3 convolution with the atrous rate $\frac{96}{s}$. Figure 3 shows the best cell and network obtained after search on the OED dataset.

All patches for all experiments are sized 256×256 pixels, allowing for a fair comparison. All models produce the output with the same spatial size as the input image. All models are trained separately using the annotations provided. The cross-entropy loss is used for all models. For training the automated network, a learning rate of 10^{-4} with a weight decay of 0.0001 and momentum of 0.9, and a maximum number of 100 epochs was used. F1-score, precision, recall and accuracy are employed to evaluate the performance of the models in segmenting the full epithelium and nuclei. The search took ~40 h for the proposed architecture on the OED dataset using Distributed Data-Parallel technique [23]. PyTorch [24] is used to implement the models. All training/prediction of experiments is carried out using identical hardware and software resources. In this study, we also compare the performance of a series of well-known segmentation network architectures (i.e., U-Net, SegNet, DeepLabV3ResNet101) for segmenting the full epithelium and nuclei. Details of these architectures can be found in [25–27]. After nuclei segmentation, the output is post-processed to improve the quality of the segmentation. Then, nuclear features are analysed within the epithelium layer; for this purpose, Auto-Deeplab and other well-established neural networks are used to segment individual nuclei. The segmented nuclei using the model with the highest F1-score are used to extract several morphological (e.g., area of nuclei, nuclei cellularity, nuclei eccentricity, etc.) and non-morphological features (i.e., entropy, Moran index). Following this, a random forest [28] model is trained using these features to classify OED grades using the WHO and binary grading system. In the following, the experimental results for full epithelium segmentation, nuclear segmentation and feature extraction, OED grade prediction and nuclear analysis are explained in detail.

4.1 Full Epithelium Segmentation

The comparative evaluation for epithelium segmentation is shown in Table 1 with the F1-score, precision, recall and accuracy of multiple models. The highest F1-score (0.935) is achieved by the proposed model (Auto-Deeplab) accomplished using the NAS solution and a visual inspection of the automatically segmented epithelium presented in Fig. 4 also confirms this. Also, the DeeplabV3ResNet101 has achieved a comparable F1-score (0.808). While U-Net obtained an F1-score of (0.744) and SegNet showed the lowest performance (0.739) compared to other models due to a simple encoder-decoder architecture without skip connections. In terms of accuracy, the best performance is shown by the Auto-Deeplab (0.930) compared to 0.820 for DeeplabV3ResNet101 and 0.751 and 0.724 for U-Net and SegNet, respectively.

Table 1. Comparison of experimental results for full epithelium segmentation.

Model	F1-score	Precision	Recall	Accuracy
U-Net	0.744	0.740	0.765	0.751
SegNet	0.739	0.731	0.723	0.724
DeeplabV3ResNet101	0.808	0.853	0.786	0.820
Auto-Deeplab	**0.935**	**0.962**	**0.933**	**0.930**

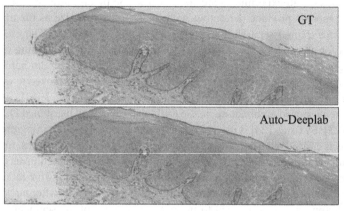

Fig. 4. A visual comparison of the ground-truth (GT) vs the results of the Auto-Deeplab model for full epithelium segmentation.

4.2 Nuclear Segmentation and Feature Extraction

The results for nuclear segmentation for four different network topologies on the OED dataset are included in Table 2. From these results, it can be seen that the proposed NAS-derived model (Auto-Deeplab) provides the overall best segmentation score on all metrics when compared with the prediction of standard architectures. The model achieved using the Auto-Deeplab technique obtains the highest F1-score (0.945) for the segmentation of nuclei. Similarly, DeeplabV3ResNet101 gives an F1-score of 0.895. However, SegNet with an F1-score of 0.660 and U-Net with 0.757 gives the lowest performance, respectively (Fig. 5).

Table 2. Comparative experimental results for intra-epithelial nuclear segmentation.

Model	F1-score	Precision	Recall	Accuracy
U-Net	0.757	0.742	0.740	0.761
SegNet	0.660	0.653	0.652	0.681
DeeplabV3ResNet101	0.895	0.882	0.895	0.910
Auto-Deeplab	**0.945**	**0.944**	**0.945**	**0.952**

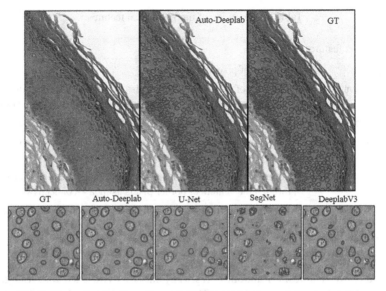

Fig. 5. Example visual results on the OED dataset for nuclei segmentation.

After segmentation of nuclei within the epithelium with the NAS-derived Auto-Deeplab model, eight morphological features are extracted from the segmented nuclei regions. These morphological features include nucleus area, perimeter, nucleus eccentricity, orientation, solidity and nucleus circularity (details in Table 3). In addition, entropy and Moran index were computed as non-morphological features. Entropy measures the intensity levels of an object region and calculates the texture variation of a pixel neighbourhood. In this study, seven sizes of the neighbourhood were utilised based on the study presented in [29]. The Moran-index *(M)* measures the spatial autocorrelation of a pixel in comparison with the average intensity of its region, which is computed as follows:

$$M = \frac{N}{W} + \frac{\sum_i \sum_j W_{ij} Z_i Z_j}{\sum_i Z_i^2} \tag{2}$$

where N is the number of pixels, w_{ij} signifies the neighbourhood of pixel ij, W is the sum of all w_{ij}, and the Z_i and Z_j values denote the deviations of the pixels z_i and z_j in relation to the average z, which can be computed by $Z_k = z_k - z$. For each nucleus (n), 8 features are obtained and aggregated on patch level using the mean.

Table 3. Definition of morphological features.

Morphological features	Definition
Nucleus area	Number of pixels of the region
Nucleus eccentricity	The ratio of the focal distance (distance between focal points) over the major axis length. (1 is a line and 0 is a perfectly round circle)
Nucleus circularity	Circularity was calculated with the $4\pi \times$ area/(perimeter)2
Orientation	Angle between the 0th axis (rows) and the major axis of the ellipse that has the same second moments as the region
Perimeter	Perimeter of object which approximates the contour as a line through the centers of border pixels using a 4-connectivity
Solidity	Ratio of pixels in the region to pixels of the convex hull image

4.3 OED Grade Prediction

Using the above features, a Random Forest [28] classifier is trained for OED grading using WHO and binary grading system. These parameters include the number of trees, minimum criteria for node splitting, minimum node retention criteria, depth of trees and bootstrapping, etc. The model on the test set for the binary grading achieves a higher F1-score (0.787) and higher AUC (0.853) while for the WHO system it achieved an F1-score of 0.627. Further details are provided in Table 4.

Table 4. Comparative experiments for grade prediction (WHO and binary grading system).

Grade system	Grades	F1	Precision	Recall	AUC
WHO	Mild	0.653	0.641	0.665	0.781
	Moderate	0.569	0.557	0.581	0.753
	Severe	0.649	0.705	0.601	0.858
	Average	0.627	0.634	0.615	0.797
Binary	Low	0.857	0.825	0.892	0.856
	High	0.625	0.696	0.567	0.856
	Average	0.787	0.786	0.793	0.853

4.4 Nuclear Analysis

Downstream statistical analyses were performed to analyse the correlation of the morphological and statistical features within the full epithelium, stroma (and combination of full epithelium and stroma) with the OED grades (for the WHO and Binary systems) using one-way analysis of variance (ANOVA) and Student's t-test (assuming equal variances). The SPSS (Statistical Package for the Social Sciences) software, IBM Corporation is used for this analysis. Figure 6-top and bottom provides a results summary of morphological and non-morphological features for the full epithelium, stroma, and combination of full epithelium and stroma with the WHO and binary grading system, respectively. Results with p values < 0.05 are regarded as being potentially statistically significant. The results show potentially statistically significant correlations between the nucleus area and perimeter for either the full epithelium, stroma, or their combination and the two grading systems. However, there was no significant association between nucleus eccentricity and solidity features within stroma in both grading systems. The orientation feature was only significant for the WHO grading system within the stroma and a combination of stroma and full epithelium. There was no statistical correlation between nucleus circularity, for either the full epithelium, stroma, or their combination. Entropy analysis for the full epithelium in OED revealed a significant correlation between full epithelium in both grading systems and stroma in WHO and a combination of epithelium and stroma in the binary system. However, for Moran's analysis, there was no statistical correlation between full epithelium for the WHO grading system.

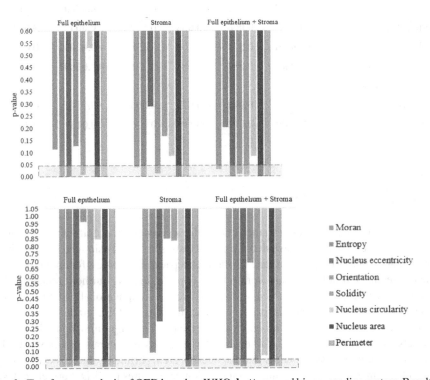

Fig. 6. Top: feature analysis of OED based on WHO, **bottom:** and binary grading system. Results with p values < 0.05 are regarded as statistically significant (green box area). (Color figure online)

Downstream statistical analyses were performed to examine the prognostic correlation of individual morphological and non-morphological nuclear features (either the full epithelium, stroma, or combination of full epithelium and stroma). Table 5 provides a results summary of the analysis. All the features within the full epithelium are shown to be significantly associated with malignant transformation. Similarly, all features within the combination of full epithelium and stroma except the entropy, are strongly associated with malignant transformation as well. Within the full epithelium, there is a prognostic correlation between nucleus area, orientation, entropy, Moran and OED recurrence.

Table 5. Feature analysis of OED based on transformation (Trans) and recurrence (Recurr).

	Full epithelium		Stroma		Full epithelium + Stroma	
	Trans	Recurr	Trans	Recurr	Trans	Recurr
Morphological features						
Nucleus area	<0.00001	0.049	0.566	0.012	<0.00001	0.016
Perimeter	<0.00001	0.067	0.555	0.021	<0.00001	0.013
Nucleus eccentricity	<0.00001	0.510	0.074	0.911	<0.00001	0.019
Orientation	0.003	0.006	0.034	0.149	0.004	0.022
Solidity	<0.00001	0.574	0.700	0.135	<0.00001	0.064
Nucleus circularity	<0.00001	0.264	0.601	0.731	<0.00001	0.501
Non-morphological features						
Entropy	0.002	0.004	0.073	0.006	0.734	0.984
Moran	<0.00001	0.012	0.190	0.276	0.0139	0.237

5   Conclusion and Future Work

We have proposed a NAS based framework for the segmentation of epithelium and intra-epithelial nuclei. We have shown that our initial results achieved using the NAS-derived segmentation model outperform state-of-the-art deep learning models for epithelium and nuclear segmentation tasks. This work reveals opportunities for further efficient architecture search strategies for segmentation in the area of computational pathology. Also, this study highlights the potential role of NAS architectures in OED grade prediction. In future, we will be looking to rigorously validate the proposed algorithm on multi-centric datasets for downstream analysis to ensure that it results in accurate grading of OED. Moreover, our study has indicated that the nucleus area, perimeter, nucleus eccentricity and entropy may be potentially important histological features in OED. Further analysis of these features is required on larger cohorts, with correlation to clinical outcomes, to determine which features are most important in diagnosis.

Acknowledgements. This work was supported by a Cancer Research UK Early Detection Project Grant, as part of the ANTICIPATE study (grant no. C63489/A29674).

References

1. European Cancer Patient Coalition: European Cancer Patient Coalition: Head & Neck Cancers (2018)
2. Barnes, L., Eveson, J.W., Sidransky, D., Reichart, P. (eds.): Pathology and Genetics of Head and Neck Tumors, vol. 9. IARC, Lyon (2005)
3. Wright, A., Shear, M.: Epithelial dysplasia is immediately adjacent to oral squamous cell carcinomas. J. Oral Pathol. Med. **14**(7), 559–564 (1985)
4. Barnes, L., Eveson, J., Reichart, P., Sidransky, D.: World Health Organization classification of tumours: pathology and genetics of head and neck tumours (2005)
5. Kujan, O., Khattab, A., Oliver, R.J., Roberts, S.A., Thakker, N., Sloan, P.: Why oral histopathology suffers inter-observer variability on grading oral epithelial dysplasia: an attempt to understand the sources of variation. Oral Oncol. **43**(3), 224–231 (2007). https://doi.org/10.1016/j.oraloncology.2006.03.009
6. Shubhasini, A.R., Praveen, B.N., Usha Hegde, U.K., Shubha, G., Keerthi, G.: Inter-and intra-observer variability in diagnosis of oral dysplasia. Asian Pac. J. Cancer Prev. APJCP **18**(12), 3251 (2017). https://doi.org/10.22034/APJCP.2017.18.12.3251
7. Krishnan, L., Karpagaselvi, K., Kumarswamy, J., Sudheendra, U.S., Santosh, K.V., Patil, A.: Inter-and intra-observer variability in three grading systems for oral epithelial dysplasia. J. Oral Maxillofac. Pathol. JOMFP **20**(2), 261 (2016). https://doi.org/10.4103/0973-029X.185928
8. Speight, P.M., Khurram, S.A., Kujan, O.: Oral potentially malignant disorders: risk of progression to malignancy. Oral Surg. Oral Med. Oral Pathol. Oral Radiol. **125**(6), 612–627 (2018). https://doi.org/10.1016/j.oooo.2017.12.011
9. Bera, K., Schalper, K.A., Rimm, D.L., Velcheti, V., Madabhushi, A.: Artificial intelligence in digital pathology—new tools for diagnosis and precision oncology. Nat. Rev. Clin. Oncol. **16**(11), 703–715 (2019)
10. Bulten, W., et al.: Epithelium segmentation using deep learning in H&E-stained prostate specimens with immunohistochemistry as reference standard. Sci. Rep. **9**(1), 1–10 (2019). https://doi.org/10.1038/s41598-018-37257-4
11. Mahmood, H., Shaban, M., Rajpoot, N., Khurram, S.A.: Artificial Intelligence-based methods in head and neck cancer diagnosis: an overview. Br. J. Cancer **124**(12), 1934–1940 (2021). https://doi.org/10.1038/s41416-021-01386-x
12. Bashir, R.S., et al.: Automated grade classification of oral epithelial dysplasia using morphometric analysis of histology images. In: Medical Imaging 2020: Digital Pathology, vol. 11320, p. 1132011. International Society for Optics and Photonics, March 2020. https://doi.org/10.1117/12.2549705
13. Shephard, A.J., et al.: Simultaneous nuclear instance and layer segmentation in oral epithelial dysplasia. In: Proceedings of the IEEE/CVF International Conference on Computer Vision, pp. 552–561 (2021)
14. Azarmehr, N., Shephard, A., Rajpoot, N., Khurram, S.A.: An optimal architecture for semantic segmentation in multi-gigapixel images of oral dysplasia. In: 35th Conference on Neural Information Processing Systems (NeurIPS 2021), Sydney, Australia (2021)
15. Zoph, B., Vasudevan, V., Shlens, J., Le, Q.V.: Learning transferable architectures for scalable image recognition. In: Proceedings of the IEEE Conference on Computer Vision and Pattern Recognition, pp. 8697–8710 (2018)
16. Liu, C., et al.: Progressive neural architecture search. In: Ferrari, V., Hebert, M., Sminchisescu, C., Weiss, Y. (eds.) ECCV 2018. LNCS, vol. 11205, pp. 19–35. Springer, Cham (2018). https://doi.org/10.1007/978-3-030-01246-5_2

17. Real, E., Aggarwal, A., Huang, Y., Le, Q.V.: Regularized evolution for image classifier architecture search. In: Proceedings of the AAAI Conference on Artificial Intelligence, vol. 33, no. 01, pp. 4780–4789, July 2019
18. Weng, Y., Zhou, T., Li, Y., Qiu, X.: Nas-unet: Neural architecture search for medical image segmentation. IEEE Access **7**, 44247–44257 (2019)
19. Koohbanani, N.A., Jahanifar, M., Tajadin, N.Z., Rajpoot, N.: NuClick: a deep learning framework for interactive segmentation of microscopic images. Med. Image Anal. **65**, 101771 (2020). https://doi.org/10.1016/j.media.2020.101771
20. Liu, C., et al.: Auto-DeepLab: hierarchical neural architecture search for semantic image segmentation. In: Proceedings of the IEEE/CVF Conference on Computer Vision and Pattern Recognition, pp. 82–92 (2019)
21. Ryan, M.S., Nudd, G.R.: The viterbi algorithm (1993)
22. Chen, L.C., Papandreou, G., Schroff, F., Adam, H.: Rethinking atrous convolution for semantic image segmentation. arXiv preprint arXiv:1706.05587 (2017)
23. Li, S., et al.: PyTorch distributed: experiences on accelerating data parallel training. arXiv preprint arXiv:2006.15704 (2020)
24. Paszke, A., et al.: Automatic differentiation in PyTorch (2017)
25. Ronneberger, O., Fischer, P., Brox, T.: U-net: convolutional networks for biomedical image segmentation. In: Navab, N., Hornegger, J., Wells, W.M., Frangi, A.F. (eds.) MICCAI 2015. LNCS, vol. 9351, pp. 234–241. Springer, Cham (2015). https://doi.org/10.1007/978-3-319-24574-4_28
26. Badrinarayanan, V., Handa, A., Cipolla, R.: SegNet: a deep convolutional encoder-decoder architecture for robust semantic pixel-wise labelling. arXiv preprint arXiv:1505.07293 (2015)
27. He, K., Zhang, X., Ren, S., Sun, J.: Deep residual learning for image recognition. In: Proceedings of the IEEE Conference on Computer Vision and Pattern Recognition, pp. 770–778 (2016)
28. Breiman, L.: Bagging predictors. Mach. Learn. **24**(2), 123–140 (1996)
29. Silva, A.B., et al.: Computational analysis of histological images from hematoxylin and eosin-stained oral epithelial dysplasia tissue sections. Expert Syst. Appl., 116456 (2022). https://doi.org/10.1016/j.eswa.2021.116456

STAMP: A Self-training Student-Teacher Augmentation-Driven Meta Pseudo-Labeling Framework for 3D Cardiac MRI Image Segmentation

S. M. Kamrul Hasan[1(✉)] and Cristian Linte[2]

[1] Center for Imaging Science, Rochester Institute of Technology, Rochester, NY, USA
sh3190@rit.edu
[2] Biomedical Engineering, Rochester Institute of Technology, Rochester, NY, USA

Abstract. Medical image segmentation has significantly benefitted thanks to deep learning architectures. Furthermore, semi-supervised learning (SSL) has led to a significant improvement in overall model performance by leveraging abundant unlabeled data. Nevertheless, one shortcoming of pseudo-labeled based semi-supervised learning is pseudo-labeling bias, whose mitigation is the focus of this work. Here we propose a simple, yet effective SSL framework for image segmentation-*STAMP* (*Student-Teacher A*ugmentation-driven consistency regularization via *M*eta *P*seudo-Labeling). The proposed method uses self-training (through meta pseudo-labeling) in concert with a Teacher network that instructs the Student network by generating pseudo-labels given unlabeled input data. Unlike pseudo-labeling methods, for which the Teacher network remains unchanged, meta pseudo-labeling methods allow the Teacher network to constantly adapt in response to the performance of the Student network on the labeled dataset, hence enabling the Teacher to identify more effective pseudo-labels to instruct the Student. Moreover, to improve generalization and reduce error rate, we apply both strong and weak *data augmentation* policies, to ensure the segmentor outputs a consistent probability distribution regardless of the augmentation level. Our extensive experimentation with varied quantities of labeled data in the training sets demonstrates the effectiveness of our model in segmenting the left atrial cavity from Gadolinium-enhanced magnetic resonance (GE-MR) images. By exploiting unlabeled data with weak and strong augmentation effectively, our proposed model yielded a statistically significant 2.6% improvement ($p < 0.001$) in Dice and a 4.4% improvement ($p < 0.001$) in Jaccard over other state-of-the-art SSL methods using only 10% labeled data for training.

Research reported in this publication was supported by the National Institute of General Medical Sciences Award No. R35GM128877 of the National Institutes of Health, and the Office of Advanced Cyber infrastructure Award No. 1808530 of the National Science Foundation.

G. Yang et al. (Eds.): MIUA 2022, LNCS 13413, pp. 371–386, 2022.
https://doi.org/10.1007/978-3-031-12053-4_28

Keywords: Meta pseudo-label · Cardiac MRI segmentation · Weak and strong augment · Confidence threshold · Student-teacher model

1   Introduction

While deep learning has shown potential for improved performance across a wide variety of medical computer vision tasks, including segmentation [4,5], registration [2], and motion estimation [25], many of these successes are achieved at the cost of a large pool of labeled datasets. Obtaining labeled images, on the other hand, requires substantial domain expertise and manual labor, making large-scale deep learning models challenging to implement in clinical settings. Moreover, when the annotation of medical images requires the assistance of clinical experts, the cost becomes unaffordable. Hence, this ineffectiveness in the low-data domain, in turn, hampers the clinical adoption and use of many medical image segmentation models. Therefore, instead of attempting to improve high-data regime segmentation, this work focuses on data-efficient segmentation training that only uses a few pixel-labeled data and takes advantage of the wide availability of unlabeled data to improve segmentation performance, with the goal of closing the performance gap with supervised models trained with fully pixel-labeled data.

Our work is motivated by the recent progress in image segmentation using semi-supervised learning (SSL), which has shown good results with limited labeled data and large amounts of unlabeled data. Recent research has yielded a variety of semi-supervised learning techniques. Successful examples include MeanTeacher [20], MixMatch [3], and FixMatch [19]. One outstanding key feature of most SSL frameworks is consistency regularization, which encourages the model to produce the same output distribution when its inputs are perturbed [7,16]. As such, pseudo-labeling or self-training is also utilized in conjunction with semi-supervised segmentation to incorporate the model's own predictions into the training [1,11]. As such, to increase training data, models incorporate pseudo-labels of the unlabeled images obtained from the segmentation model trained on the labeled images.

To execute a task, semi-supervised learning (SSL) uses a small number of labeled examples along with unlabeled samples. Most methods follow one or combinations of directions, such as consistency regularization [18,19] or pseudo-labeling [9,11]. Existing methods use conventional data augmentation [10,20] to provide alternative transformations of semantically identical images, or they blend input data to create enhanced training data and labels [8,23]. Liu *et al.* [13] revisit the Semi-Supervised Object Detection and identify the pseudo-labeling bias issue in SS-OD. However, they updated the Teacher network using a non-gradient exponential moving average (EMA), which concentrates on weighting the Student's parameters at each stage of the training process, without explicitly evaluating parameter quality. Sohn *et al.* introduce FixMatch [19], which matches the prediction of the strongly-augmented unlabeled data to the pseudo label of the weakly-augmented counterpart when the model confidence on the weakly-augmented counterpart is high. In contrast to these approaches, here we redesign the pseudo label as well as data augmentations for semantic segmentation utilizing both consistency regularization, as well as pseudo labeling.

A self-training based approach was used by Bai et al. [1] for cardiac MR image segmentation. They use an initial model trained on labeled data to predict the labels on unlabeled data, so that these labels, although less accurate, can be used for training an updated, more powerful model. Recent approaches involve integrating uncertainty map into a mean-Teacher framework to guide the Student network [22] for left atrium segmentation. Zeng et al. [24] propose a Student-Teacher framework for semi-supervised left atrium segmentation. However, they haven't applied any data augmentation and thus omit the idea that a segmentor should output the same probability distribution for an unlabeled pixel even after it has been augmented.

Nevertheless, pseudo-labeling techniques, despite their benefit, suffer from one major flaw: if the pseudo-labels are erroneous, the Student network will learn from inaccurate data, much like the analogy of a Student's performance (i.e., the accuracy of the segmentation labels output by a model) not being able to significantly exceed the Teacher's performance (i.e., the accuracy of the pseudo-labels used for training the model). This flaw is also known as the problem of confirmation bias in pseudo-labeling. To this extent, this paper investigates pseudo-labeling for semi-supervised deep learning from network predictions and shows that in contrast to previous attempts at pseudo-labeling [15,24], simple modifications to correct confirmation bias results in state-of-the-art performance.

To address these issues, we propose a three-stage semi-supervised framework - *STAMP: Student-Teacher Augmentation-Driven Meta Pseudo-Labeling*, inspired by the framework in Noisy-Student [21], a method of training

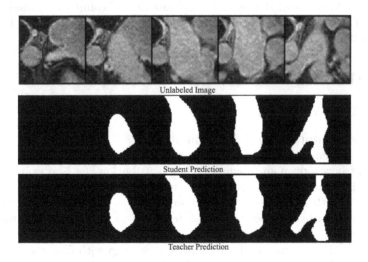

Fig. 1. STAMP model applied to the left atrium dataset, where a large amount of unlabeled data is available. Both the Student and Teacher predictions are shown during a random training iteration.

a Student and a slowly progressing Teacher (Fig. 1) in a mutually advantageous manner. In the first stage, we train a fully convolutional network (FCN) using all labeled data until convergence. In the second stage, the weak data augmentations are applied to each unlabeled image where the Teacher model is trained with unlabeled data and the Student learns from a minibatch of pseudo-labeled data generated by the Teacher. The prediction of strongly-augmented data is then optimized to match its corresponding pseudo-labels with the labeled data pre-trained in the first stage. Later on, the Student progressively updates the Teacher using the response signal in the third stage. Unlike the non-gradient EMA [10] method, this reward signal is utilized to motivate the Teacher during the Student's learning process through a gradient descent algorithm. We evaluate our approach using the Left Atrial Segmentation Challenge dataset by comparing our results to those of existing SSL methods. STAMP achieves a 2.6 fold mean improvement over the state-of-the-art RLSSS [24] method.

Our proposed method presents several key contributions which are summarized as follows: (1) *STAMP* presents simple and effective strategy for dealing with the pseudo-labeling bias problem by adopting a *threshold* where pixels with a confidence score higher than 0.5 will be used as pseudo labels, while the remaining are treated as ignored regions. Additionally, since a large pool of labeled data is not available, the proposed method inherently mitigates the over-fitting problem; (2) The different strong and weak *data augmentation* policies improve the generalization performance and reduce the error rate significantly. Our observation shows that when replacing weak augmentation with no augmentation, the model overfits the predicted unlabeled labels; (3) The use of pseudo-labels enables a *gradient descent* response loop from the Student network to the Teacher network that improves the teaching of the Teacher network and minimizes the prediction bias; and (4) Extensive experimental studies on the MICCAI STACOM 2018 *Atrial segmentation* challenge dataset and comparative analyses are conducted to validate the effectiveness of this method at not only the low-data regime, but also the high-data regime.

2   Methodology

2.1   STAMP Model Framework

2.1.1   Segmentation Model Formulation

We define the semi-supervised image segmentation problem in a semi-supervised setting as follows: given an (unknown) data distribution $p(x,y)$ over images and segmentation masks, we have a source domain having a training set, $\mathcal{D}_{\mathcal{L}} = \{(x_i^l, y_i^l)\}_{i=1}^{n_l}$ with n_l labaled examples and $\mathcal{D}_{\mathcal{UL}} = \{(x_j^{ul})\}_{j=1}^{n_{ul}}$ with n_{ul} unlabaled examples which are sampled i.i.d. from $p(x,y)$ and $p(x)$ distribution and $n_l \ll n_{ul}$, where x_i^l is the i-th labeled image with spatial dimensions $H \times W$, $y_i^l \in \{0,1\}^{C \times H \times W}$ is its corresponding pixelwise label map with C as the number of categories, and x_j^{ul} is the j-th unlabeled image. Empirically, we want to minimize the target risk $\phi_t(\theta^S, \theta^T) = min_{\theta^S, \theta^T} \ \mathcal{L}_{\mathcal{L}}(\mathcal{D}_{\mathcal{L}}, (\theta^S, \theta^T)) + \gamma \mathcal{L}_{\mathcal{UL}}(\mathcal{D}_{\mathcal{UL}}, (\theta^S, \theta^T))$,

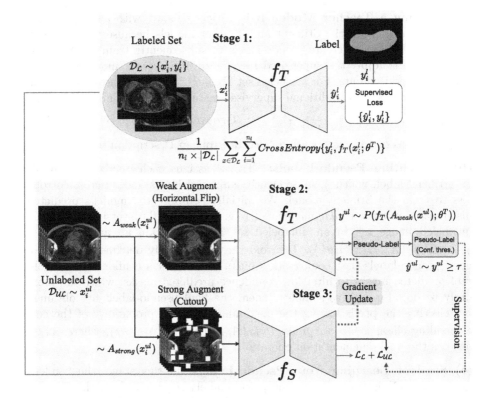

Fig. 2. Schematic of *STAMP* model: The Teacher model is trained using all labeled data until convergence. Weak data augmentations are applied to each unlabeled image, such that the Teacher model is trained with unlabeled data and the Student learns from a mini-batch of pseudo-labeled data generated by the Teacher. In turn, the Teacher's parameters θ_T are updated based on the response signal from the Student's parameters θ_S via gradient-descent in the later stage.

where $\mathcal{L}_\mathcal{L}$ is the supervised loss for segmentation, $\mathcal{L}_{\mathcal{UL}}$ is unsupervised loss defined on unlabeled images and θ^S, θ^T denotes the learnable parameters of the overall network.

2.1.2 Model Architecture and Components

We propose **STAMP** – a simple yet effective **S**tudent-**T**eacher SSL framework for image segmentation based on **A**ugmentation driven Consistency regularization and Self-Training (through **M**eta **P**seudo-labeling), as illustrated in Fig. 2. The overall model entails three stages of training, where we train a Teacher model using all available labeled data in the first stage as a pre-trained initializer, while in the second stage, we train STAMP using both labeled and unlabeled data. We manage the quality of pseudo labels constituted of segmentation masks using a high confidence-based threshold value inspired by FixMatch [19]. The training steps for STAMP are summarized in the subsequent sections.

(a) **Training a Teacher Model:** It is critical to start with an appropriate initialization for both the Student and Teacher models because we'll be relying on the Teacher to create pseudo-labels to subsequently train the Student. Hence, we first apply the supervised loss $\mathcal{L}_{\mathcal{L}}$ to improve our model using the existing supervised data. For a labeled set $\mathcal{D}_{\mathcal{L}} = \{(x_i^l, y_i^l)\}_{i=1}^{n_l}$, the segmentation network is trained in a traditional supervised manner which minimizes the cross-entropy (CE) loss, $\mathcal{L}_{\mathcal{L}} = \frac{1}{n_l \times |\mathcal{D}_{\mathcal{L}}|} \sum_{x \in \mathcal{D}_{\mathcal{L}}} \sum_{i=1}^{n_l} CrossEntropy\{y_i^l, f_T(x_i^l; \theta^T)\}$, where the definitions of parameters are defined in Problem Description section.

(b) **Generating Pseudo-Labels:** STAMP assigns each unlabeled example an artificial label, which is subsequently employed in a standard cross-entropy loss to train the Student model. We initially compute the model's predicted distribution using a *weakly-augmented* (e.g. horizontal flip) version of a given unlabeled image x_j^{ul} in an unlabeled set $\mathcal{D}_{\mathcal{UL}}$ to obtain an artificial label, $y^{ul} \sim P(f_T(A_{weak}(x^{ul}); \theta^T))$. To avoid the cumulatively detrimental effect of noisy pseudo-labels (i.e., confirmation bias), we first set a confidence threshold τ of predicted masks to filter low-confidence predicted masks, which are more likely to be false-positive samples. Then, the final pseudo-labels are obtained by selecting the pixels having the maximum predicted probability of the corresponding class, $\hat{y}^{ul} = (argmax(P(f_T(A_{weak}(x^{ul})); \theta^T)) \geq \tau)$, where A_{weak} denotes the weak-augmentation operation.

(c) **Student Learning from Pseudo-Labels:** In this stage, the Student model $f_S(., \theta^S)$ is trained with the pseudo-labels generated from the Teacher model, where we use both the labeled and unlabeled datasets $\mathcal{D}_{\mathcal{L}}, \mathcal{D}_{\mathcal{UL}}$. We enforce the cross-entropy loss against the Student model's output for the *strong-augmentation* of the unlabeled images having the idea that the Student model would output the same probability distribution for an unlabeled pixel even after it has been augmented. Additionally, we utilize a consistency regularizer function to enforce consistency between the generated pseudo masks and the masks predicted by the Student model itself (Eq'n 1).

$$\frac{1}{n_{ul} \times |\mathcal{D}_{\mathcal{UL}}|} \sum_{x \in \mathcal{D}_{\mathcal{UL}}} \sum_{j=1}^{n_{ul}} CrossEntropy\{\hat{y}_i^{ul}, f_S(A_{strong}(x_j^{ul}); \theta^S)\} +,$$

$$\underbrace{\sum_{x_i \in \mathcal{D}} ||(\hat{y^{ul}}) - (f_S(A_{strong}(x_j^{ul}); \theta^S))||^2}_{\textbf{Regularizer}} \tag{1}$$

where A_{strong} denotes the strong-augmentation (Cutout, Gaussian blur, Shift-ScaleRotate) operation. Since the Student parameters always depend on the Teacher parameters via the pseudo labels, we need to compute the Jacobian, as shown in Eq'n (2) (Algorithm 1).

Algorithm 1. STAMP's main learning algorithm

Input:

Training set of labeled data x^l, y^l ϵ $\mathcal{D}_\mathcal{L}$, and unlabeled data x^{ul} ϵ $\mathcal{D}_{\mathcal{UL}}$

Require: Learned parameters: (θ^T, θ^S), number of pre-train epoch, number of main-train epoch, confidence threshold, τ

for *each epoch* **do**

  if *epoch $<$ main$_{train}$* **then**

    Sample mini-batch from $x^l_i; x^l_1, \ldots, x^l_{n_l}$;

    $\theta^T \leftarrow \theta^T + \gamma \frac{\partial L_{sup}}{\partial \theta^T}$ {Train the Teacher network with all the labeled data}

  else

    Teacher UPDATE STAGE:

    Sample mini-batch from $x^l_i; x^l_1, \ldots, x^l_{n_l}$; and $x^{ul}_j; x^{ul}_1, \ldots, x^{ul}_{n_{ul}}$;

    Apply weak data augmentation to $x^{ul}, x^{ul} = A_{weak}(x^{ul})$ to train the Teacher model

    Apply strong data augmentation to $x^{ul}, x^{ul} = A_{strong}(x^{ul})$ to train the Student model

    Sample a pseudo label $y^{ul} \sim P(f_T(A_{weak}(x^{ul}); \theta^T))$

    Use a confidence threshold, τ

    if $P(f_T(A_{weak}(x^{ul}); \theta^T)) \geq \tau$ **then**

      pseudo-mask, $\hat{y^{ul}} = argmax(y^{ul})$

    end if

    Update the Student using the pseudo label $\hat{y^{ul}}$:

$$\theta^S_{(t+1)} = \theta^S_{(t)} - \eta S \nabla_{\theta^S} CE(\hat{y^{ul}}, f_S((A_{weak}(x^{ul}); \theta^S))|_{\theta^S = \theta^S_{(t)}} \quad (2)$$

    Compute the Teacher's response coefficient

$$h = \eta S. \left((\nabla_{\theta'^S} CE(y^l, f_S(x^l; \theta^S_{(t+1)})))^\top . \right.$$

$$\left. \nabla_{\theta^S} CE(\hat{y^{ul}}, f_S(A_{weak}(x^{ul}); \theta^S)) \right) \quad (3)$$

    Compute the Teacher's gradient from the Student's response signal:

$$g^T_{(t)} = h. \nabla_{\theta^T} CE(\hat{y^{ul}}, f_T(A(x^{ul}); \theta^T))|_{\theta^T = \theta^T_{(t)}} \quad (4)$$

    Compute the Teacher's gradient on labeled data:

$$g^{T,Sup}_{(t)} = \nabla_{\theta^T} CE(y^l, f_T(x^l; \theta^T)) \quad (5)$$

    Update the Teacher:

$$\theta^T_{(t+1)} = \theta^T_{(t)} - \eta T. \left(g^T_{(t)} + g^{T,Sup}_{(t)} \right) \quad (6)$$

  end if

end for

(d) Updating the Teacher Model: To obtain more stable meta pseudo-labels, we use the response signal from the Student to gradually update the Teacher model. Unlike the non-gradient EMA [10] method, this reward signal is

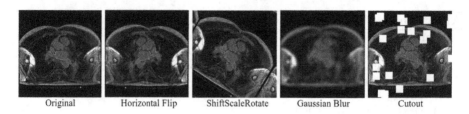

| Original | Horizontal Flip | ShiftScaleRotate | Gaussian Blur | Cutout |

Fig. 3. Visualization of different types of augmentation strategies. Original image, Horizontal Flip, ShiftScaleRotate, Gaussian Blur, and Cutout (left to right).

utilized to motivate the Teacher during the Student's learning process through the gradient descent algorithm as described in [17] (Eq'n 3–6).

2.2 Data Augmentation Strategies

A robust data augmentation is a vital aspect in the success of SSL approaches like MixMatch [3], FixMatch [19] etc. We leverage the Cutout augmentation [6] (strong augmentation) with a rectangle of 50×50 pixels because of its consistent results. We investigate various transformation techniques including Horizontal Flip (weak augmentation), Gaussian Blur, ShiftScaleRotate colorJitter, etc. Each operation has a magnitude that determines the degree of strength augmentation. We visualize transformed images with the aforementioned augmentation strategies in Fig. 3.

2.3 Experiments

Data: The model was trained and tested on the MICCAI STACOM 2018 Atrial Segmentation Challenge datasets featuring 100 3D gadolinium-enhanced MR imaging scans (GE-MRIs) and LA segmentation masks, with an isotropic resolution of $0.625 \times 0.625 \times 0.625 \, \text{mm}^3$. The dimensions of the MR images vary depending on each patient, however, all MR images contain exactly 88 slices in the z axis. All the images were normalized and resized to $112 \times 112 \times 80$ before feeding them to the models. We split the dataset into 80 scans for training and 20 scans for validation, and apply the same pre-processing methods.

Baselines Architecture: For a fair comparison, we use V-Net [14] as the backbone for both the Teacher and the Student models in our semi-supervised segmentation experiments.

Training: The performance of semi-supervised models trained for image segmentation can significantly be enhanced by the selection of the regularizer, optimizer, and hyperparameters. We implement our method using the *PyTorch* framework and set the batch size to 4. In self-training, a batch of 4 images is composed of 2 labeled images and 2 unlabeled images. Both the Teacher and the Student models are trained for 6000 iterations, with an initial learning rate 0.01, decayed by 0.1 every 2500 iterations. We train the network on varying proportions of labeled data – 10%, 20%, 30%, 50%, and 100% – while enforcing that $|\mathcal{D}_\mathcal{L}| \leq |\mathcal{D}_{\mathcal{UL}}|$. We include an ablation study to elucidate and investigate the effects of the different components and hyperparameters of our model. All experiments were conducted on a workstation equipped with two NVIDIA RTX 2080 Ti GPUs (each 11GB memory). The detailed training procedure is presented in Algorithm 1.

2.4 Evaluation

To evaluate the performance of semantic segmentation of cardiac structures, we use several standard metrics, including Dice score (Dice), Jaccard index, Hausdorff distance (HD), Precision, and Recall. We compare the segmentation results achieved using our proposed *STAMP* architecture with those achieved using five other frameworks: V-Net, MT, UA-MT, SASSNet, and RLSSS.

To justify the choice of these frameworks as benchmarks, here we briefly highlight their features. The UA-MT [22] model is based on the uncertainty-aware mean Teacher framework, in which the Student model learns from meaningful targets over time by leveraging the Teacher model's uncertainty information. The Teacher model not only generates the target outputs, but it also uses Monte Carlo sampling to quantify the uncertainty of each target prediction. When computing the consistency loss, they use the estimated uncertainty to filter out the faulty predictions and keep only the dependable ones (low uncertainty).

Similarly, to take advantage of the unlabeled data and enforce a geometric form constraint on the segmentation output, SASSNet [12] offered a shape-aware semi-supervised segmentation technique. Meanwhile, in semi-supervised image segmentation, self-ensembling approaches, particularly the mean Teacher (MT) model [20], have received a lot of attention. The mean Teacher (MT) structure guarantees consistency of predictions with inputs under varied perturbations between the Student and Teacher models, boosting model performance even more. In RLSSS [24], the Teacher updates its parameters autonomously according to the reciprocal feedback signal of how well Student performs on the labeled set.

3 Results and Discussion

3.1 Image Segmentation Evaluation

We first evaluate our proposed framework on Left Atrium MRI dataset. The quantitative comparison of various approaches in terms of Dice score (Dice), Jaccard index, Hausdorff distance (HD), Precision, and Recall is shown in Table 1. A better segmentation yields a higher Dice, Jaccard, Precision and Recall values and lower values for the other metrics. All semi-supervised approaches that take advantage of un-annotated images enhance segmentation performance significantly when compared to fully-supervised V-Net trained with only 8 (10%) annotated images.

Table 1. Quantitative comparison of left atrium segmentation across several frameworks. Mean (standard deviation) values are reported for $Dice(\%), Jaccard(\%), 95HD(\%), ASD(\%), Precision(\%)$, and $Recall(\%)$ from all networks against our proposed STAMP. The statistical significance of the STAMP results compared to those achieved by the other top performing models, including RLSSS, for 10% and 20% labeled data are represented by $*$ and $**$ for p−values 0.1 and 0.001, respectively. The best performance metric is indicated in **bold** text.

METHODS	SCANS USED		METRICS		
	Labeled	Unlabeled	Dice(%) ↑	Jaccard(%)↑	HD95(mm) ↓
V-Net [14]	10%	0	79.98 ±1.88	68.14±2.01	21.12±15.19
MT [20]	10%	90%	83.76±1.03	73.01±1.56	14.56±14.03
UA-MT [22]	10%	90%	84.25±1.61	73.48±1.73	13.84±13.15
SASSNet [12]	10%	90%	87.32±1.39	77.72±1.49	12.56±11.30
RLSSS [24]	10%	90%	88.13±1.68	79.20±1.78	11.59±9.28
STAMP (Proposed)	10%	90%	****90.43±0.75**	****82.67±.82**	****6.22±4.55**
V-Net [14]	20%	0	85.64±1.73	75.40±1.84	16.96±14.37
MT [20]	20%	80%	88.23±1.01	79.29±1.80	10.64±9.32
UA-MT [22]	20%	80%	88.88±0.73	80.20±0.82	8.13±6.78
SASSNet [12]	20%	80%	89.54±0.66	81.24±0.75	8.24±6.58
RLSSS [24]	20%	80%	90.07±0.76	82.03±0.84	**6.67±3.54**
STAMP (Proposed)	20%	80%	***91.90±0.64**	****84.38±0.83**	7.15±4.74

METHODS	SCANS USED		METRICS		
	Labeled	Unlabeled	ASD(mm)↓	Precision(%) ↑	Recall(%)↑
V-Net [14]	10%	0	5.47±1.92	83.67±1.79	74.55±1.90
MT [20]	10%	90%	4.43±1.08	87.23±1.06	76.31±1.88
UA-MT [22]	10%	90%	3.36±1.58	87.57±1.53	77.85±1.65
SASSNet [12]	10%	90%	2.55±1.86	87.66±1.38	87.22±1.37
RLSSS [24]	10%	90%	2.91±0.59	90.33±1.66	87.08±1.70
STAMP (Proposed)	10%	90%	***1.82±0.40**	**90.96±0.74**	****90.30±0.75**
V-Net [14]	20%	0	4.03±1.53	88.78±1.70	83.79±1.51
MT [20]	20%	80%	2.66±1.26	89.89±0.92	87.54±0.66
UA-MT [22]	20%	80%	2.35±1.16	89.57±0.73	88.82±0.72
SASSNet [12]	20%	80%	2.27±0.81	89.86±0.65	90.42±0.66
RLSSS [24]	20%	80%	2.11±4.67	90.16±**0.77**	89.97±**0.76**
STAMP (Proposed)	20%	80%	**2.04±0.34**	**90.92±0.93**	***91.43±0.92**

Our proposed model outperformed the fully supervised method according to all metrics, achieving a 90.4% Dice and 82.7% Jaccard scores, which represent a 13% and 21.3% improvement, respectively. Moreover, in comparison to other methods, our proposed framework more efficiently utilized the limited labeled data by employing a Teacher-Student mutual learning strategy, which allowed the Teacher model to update its parameters autonomously and generate more reliable annotations for unlabeled data.

The paired statistical test reported in Table 1 shows that our proposed model significantly improved the segmentation performance compared to the semi-supervised, fully-supervised, models in terms of the Dice, Jaccard, 95% Hausdorff Distance (95HD), average surface distance (ASD), Precision, and Recall. In addition, by effectively exploiting unlabeled data with weak and strong augmentation, our proposed model yielded a statistically significant 2.6%improvement ($p < 0.05$) in Dice and 4.4% Jaccard ($p < 0.05$) over the RLSSS framework, while using *only* 10% labeled data for training.

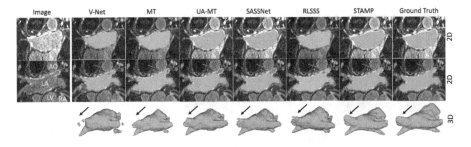

Fig. 4. Qualitative comparison result in 2D as well as 3D of the MICCAI STACOM 2018 Atrial Segmentation challenge dataset yielded by six different frameworks (V-Net, MT, UA-MT, SASSNet, RLSSS, and STAMP). The comparison of segmentation results between the proposed method and five typical deep learning networks indicates that the performance of our proposed network is superior. The black arrows indicate the locations where the segmentation masks yielded by the other networks used as benchmarks fail to correctly capture the aorta (AO) in 3D.

Figure 4 shows the results obtained by V-Net [14], MT [20], UA-MT [22], SASSNet [12], RLSSS [24], our proposed STAMP framework, and the corresponding ground truth on the MICCAI STACOM 2018 Atrial Segmentation Challenge. Figure 4 (bottom row) also shows that all frameworks but STAMP yield segmentation masks that miss portions of the aortic (AO) region (indicated by the red arrows in 2D and black arrows in 3D). On the other hand, the STAMP framework yields a complete segmentation of the left atrium that closely matches the ground truth segmentation mask, preserves more details, and yields fewer false positive results, overall demonstrating the increased efficacy of the proposed learning strategy.

Figure 5(a) shows the best segmentation contours yielded by the STAMP framework (green) and the corresponding ground truth contours (red). We trained our model on varying proportions of labeled data – 10%, 20%, 30%, 50%, and 100% – while enforcing that $|\mathcal{D}_\mathcal{L}| \leq |\mathcal{D}_{\mathcal{UL}}|$. Figure 5(b) shows that STAMP accuracy further increases with increasing proportions of labeled data for training. The mean Dice score (%) increases from 90% with only 10% labeled data to 93% with 100% labeled data. This experiment clearly emphasizes the robustness and high performance of STAMP using mostly (90%) unlabeled data, and its *only incremental improvement* with the addition of large quantities of labeled data.

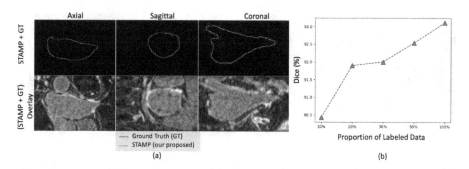

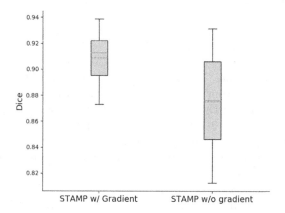

Fig. 5. (a) Axial, coronal and sagittal views of the of the STAMP (green) and ground truth (red) left atrium segmentation contours; (b) robust and high performance (90% Dice score) STAMP segmentation with 10%: 90% labeled: unlabeled data and consistent steady performance increase (up to 93% Dice score) with additional labeled data. (Color figure online)

Fig. 6. Ablation study designed to investigate the effect of gradient-based teacher training (GTT) on Dice score for left atrial segmentation using only 20% labeled data with and without GTT.

3.2   Ablation Study

We also conducted ablation studies to demonstrate the effectiveness of incorporating a response signal loop by *gradient descent* step from the Student network to the Teacher network to improve the teaching of the Teacher network and minimize the prediction bias in a semi-supervised setting, as well as study the benefit of different forms of augmentation.

3.2.1   Effect of the Gradient-based Teacher Training

To illustrate the impact of *Gradient-based Teacher training (GTT)*, we compared our model performance with and without GTT. Figure 6 shows that the incorporation of GTT significantly improves segmentation performance, as quantified by the Dice score. This significant improvement can be explained by the fact that while conventional training (without GTT) often generates imbalanced pseudo-labels, where most pixel category instances in the pseudo-labels vanish, leaving just instances of specific pixel categories, GTT constrains the generation of imbalanced pseudo-labels, leading to improved performance.

3.2.2 Effect of Pre-Training Stage

For both the Student and Teacher models, a proper initialization is critical. Figure 7 shows the effects of using a pre-training stage. We observe that using the *pre-training step*, the model may generate more accurate pseudo-labels early in the training process. As a result, the model can attain lower loss in the training process, as well as better performance once the model converges.

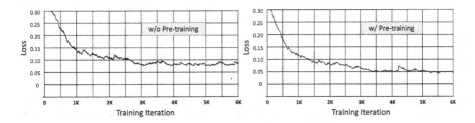

Fig. 7. Experiment conducted on a left atrial image datasets consisting of only 20% labeled data showing the benefits of using a pre-training stage (right) in concert with *STAMP*, which leads to lower loss compared with no pre-training stage (left).

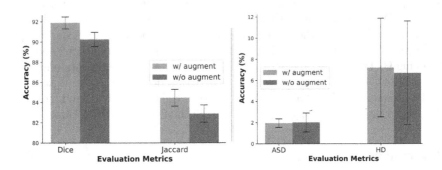

Fig. 8. Experiment conducted on a left atrial image datasets consisting of only 20% labeled data showing the benefits of using data augmentation (orange) in concert with STAMP, which leads to higher accuracy (Dice and Jaccard) compared with no data augmentation (purple). (Color figure online)

3.2.3   Effect of Data Augmentation

To improve generalization and significantly reduce error rate, we applied different strong and weak *data augmentation* strategies. Figure 8 shows a comparison of the model with and without the augmentation strategies. Our observation shows that when replacing weak augmentation with no augmentation, the model overfits the predicted unlabeled labels. The statistical significance of the *Dice and **Jaccard for STAMP model *with* and *without* data augmentation for 20% labeled data are represented by * and ** for $p-$values 0.1 and 0.001, respectively.

4   Conclusion

In this paper, we propose an effective Student-Teacher Augmentation-driven Meta pseudo-labeling (STAMP) model for 3D cardiac MRI image segmentation. The proposed framework mitigates the pseudo-labeling bias problem arising due to class imbalance by adopting a *threshold* where pixels with a confidence score higher than 0.5 will be used as pseudo labels, while the remaining are treated as ignored regions. Additionally, the proposed model also mitigates the overfitting challenge induced by the lack of a large pool of labeled data. The meta pseudo-labeling approach generates pseudo labels by a Teacher-Student mutual learning process where the Teacher learns from the Student's reward signal, which, in turn, best helps the Student's learning. Unlike the non-gradient exponential moving average (EMA) method, this reward signal is utilized to motivate the Teacher during the Student's learning process through the gradient descent algorithm. Moreover, the application of different strong and weak *data augmentation* strategies improve the generalization performance and reduce the error rate significantly. We evaluated our proposed framework within the SSL setting by comparing the segmentation results with those yielded by several existing methods. When using only 10% labeled data, STAMP achieves a 2.6 fold mean Dice improvement over the state-of-the-art RLSSS model. In addition, our proposed model outperforms existing methods in terms of both Jaccard and Dice, achieving 90.4% Dice and 82.7% Jaccard with only 10% labeled data and 91.9% Dice and 84.4% Jaccard with only 20% labeled data for atrial segmentation, both of which showed at least 2.6% improvement over the best methods and more than 11% improvement over fully-supervised traditional V-Net architecture.

References

1. Bai, W., et al.: Semi-supervised learning for network-based cardiac MR image segmentation. In: Descoteaux, M., Maier-Hein, L., Franz, A., Jannin, P., Collins, D.L., Duchesne, S. (eds.) MICCAI 2017. LNCS, vol. 10434, pp. 253–260. Springer, Cham (2017). https://doi.org/10.1007/978-3-319-66185-8_29
2. Balakrishnan, G., et al.: VoxelMorph: a learning framework for deformable medical image registration. IEEE Trans. Med. Imaging **38**(8), 1788–1800 (2019)
3. Berthelot, D., et al.: Mixmatch: a holistic approach to semi-supervised learning. In: Advances in Neural Information Processing Systems 32 (2019)

4. Chaitanya, K., et al.: Contrastive learning of global and local features for medical image segmentation with limited annotations. Adv. Neural. Inf. Process. Syst. **33**, 12546–12558 (2020)
5. Chen, L.C., et al.: DeepLab: semantic image segmentation with deep convolutional nets, atrous convolution, and fully connected CRFS. IEEE Trans. Pattern Anal. Mach. Intell. **40**(4), 834–848 (2017)
6. DeVries, T., et al.: Improved regularization of convolutional neural networks with cutout. arXiv preprint arXiv:1708.04552 (2017)
7. French, G., et al.: Semi-supervised semantic segmentation needs strong, high-dimensional perturbations (2019)
8. Guo, H., et al.: Mixup as locally linear out-of-manifold regularization. In: Proceedings of the AAAI Conference on Artificial Intelligence, vol. 33, pp. 3714–3722 (2019)
9. Iscen, A., et al.: Label propagation for deep semi-supervised learning. In: Proceedings of the IEEE/CVF Conference on Computer Vision and Pattern Recognition, pp. 5070–5079 (2019)
10. Laine, S., et al.: Temporal ensembling for semi-supervised learning. arXiv preprint arXiv:1610.02242 (2016)
11. Lee, D.H., et al.: Pseudo-label: the simple and efficient semi-supervised learning method for deep neural networks. In: Workshop on Challenges in Representation Learning, ICML, vol. 3, p. 896 (2013)
12. Li, S., Zhang, C., He, X.: Shape-aware semi-supervised 3d semantic segmentation for medical images. In: Martel, A.L., Abolmaesumi, P., Stoyanov, D., Mateus, D., Zuluaga, M.A., Zhou, S.K., Racoceanu, D., Joskowicz, L. (eds.) MICCAI 2020. LNCS, vol. 12261, pp. 552–561. Springer, Cham (2020). https://doi.org/10.1007/978-3-030-59710-8_54
13. Liu, Y.C., et al.: Unbiased teacher for semi-supervised object detection. arXiv preprint arXiv:2102.09480 (2021)
14. Milletari, F., et al.: V-net: fully convolutional neural networks for volumetric medical image segmentation. In: 2016 Fourth International Conference on 3D Vision (3DV), pp. 565–571. IEEE (2016)
15. Oliver, A., et al.: Realistic evaluation of deep semi-supervised learning algorithms. In: Advances in Neural Information Processing Systems 31 (2018)
16. Ouali, Y., et al.: Semi-supervised semantic segmentation with cross-consistency training. In: Proceedings of the IEEE/CVF Conference on Computer Vision and Pattern Recognition, pp. 12674–12684 (2020)
17. Pham, H., et al.: Meta pseudo labels. In: Proceedings of the IEEE/CVF Conference on Computer Vision and Pattern Recognition, pp. 11557–11568 (2021)
18. Sajjadi, M., et al.: Regularization with stochastic transformations and perturbations for deep semi-supervised learning. In: Advances in Neural Information Processing Systems 29 (2016)
19. Sohn, K., et al.: FixMatch: simplifying semi-supervised learning with consistency and confidence. Adv. Neural. Inf. Process. Syst. **33**, 596–608 (2020)
20. Tarvainen, A., et al.: Mean teachers are better role models: weight-averaged consistency targets improve semi-supervised deep learning results. In: Advances in Neural Information Processing Systems 30 (2017)
21. Xie, Q., et al.: Self-training with noisy student improves imagenet classification. In: Proceedings of the IEEE/CVF Conference on Computer Vision and Pattern Recognition, pp. 10687–10698 (2020)

22. Yu, L., Wang, S., Li, X., Fu, C.-W., Heng, P.-A.: Uncertainty-aware self-ensembling model for semi-supervised 3D left atrium segmentation. In: Shen, D., Liu, T., Peters, T.M., Staib, L.H., Essert, C., Zhou, S., Yap, P.-T., Khan, A. (eds.) MICCAI 2019. LNCS, vol. 11765, pp. 605–613. Springer, Cham (2019). https://doi.org/10.1007/978-3-030-32245-8_67

23. Yun, S., et al.: CutMix: regularization strategy to train strong classifiers with localizable features. In: Proceedings of the IEEE/CVF International Conference on Computer Vision, pp. 6023–6032 (2019)

24. Zeng, X., et al.: Reciprocal learning for semi-supervised segmentation. In: de Bruijne, M., et al. (eds.) MICCAI 2021. LNCS, vol. 12902, pp. 352–361. Springer, Cham (2021). https://doi.org/10.1007/978-3-030-87196-3_33

25. Zheng, Q., et al.: Explainable cardiac pathology classification on cine MRI with motion characterization by semi-supervised learning of apparent flow. Med. Image Anal. 56, 80–95 (2019)

Implicit U-Net for Volumetric Medical Image Segmentation

Sergio Naval Marimont[1]([✉]) [iD] and Giacomo Tarroni[1,2] [iD]

[1] CitAI Research Centre, City, University of London, London, UK
{sergio.naval-marimont,giacomo.tarroni}@city.ac.uk
[2] BioMedIA, Imperial College, London, UK

Abstract. U-Net has been the go-to architecture for medical image segmentation tasks, however computational challenges arise when extending the U-Net architecture to 3D images. We propose the Implicit U-Net architecture that adapts the efficient Implicit Representation paradigm to supervised image segmentation tasks. By combining a convolutional feature extractor with an implicit localization network, our implicit U-Net has 40% less parameters than the equivalent U-Net. Moreover, we propose training and inference procedures to capitalize sparse predictions. When comparing to an equivalent fully convolutional U-Net, Implicit U-Net reduces by approximately 30% inference and training time as well as training memory footprint while achieving comparable results in our experiments with two different abdominal CT scan datasets.

Keywords: Efficient segmentation · Supervised learning · Volumetric segmentation · CT

1 Introduction

U-Net [18] is the go-to architecture for medical image segmentation tasks [10]. A U-Net consists of two convolutional networks an encoder or feature extraction network and a decoder or localization network. U-Net incorporates *skip connections* that share feature maps directly from encoder to decoder layers with the same spatial resolution.

Different approaches have been proposed to extend U-Nets to volumetric images. 3D convolutions, as used in V-Net [13], are very computationally challenging at training and inference time [6]. Despite this limitation, U-Nets with fully 3D convolutional architectures have been the building block of general purpose segmentation techniques such as [7,8] that have been state-of-the art until recently. Lately substantial changes to the network design have been made: e.g. Cotr [22] and UNETR [5] improve U-Net performance by replacing some of the convolutions with Transformers in the architecture.

In a related research direction, there is a growing interest in reducing computational requirements towards improved practical application of deep learning in medical image analysis. Lighter and faster models lead to faster experiments

G. Yang et al. (Eds.): MIUA 2022, LNCS 13413, pp. 387–397, 2022.
https://doi.org/10.1007/978-3-031-12053-4_29

to test achievable segmentation performance, faster hyper-parameter tuning; faster inference time is highly beneficial when processing large medical datasets [20]; smaller memory footprint translates to better model portability and lower hardware requirements for hospitals and companies running actual segmentation tasks. [23] won the MICCAI FLARE 2021[1] challenge with a U-Net architecture in which 3D decoder convolutions were replaced by anisotropic convolutions and a two step, coarse-to-fine segmentation framework. A different strategy to improve efficiency is to integrate features extracted with 2D convolutions from three orthogonal views of a volumetric image. This strategy is generally referred to as 2.5D convolution and it has been widely explored in segmentation methods [14,17,19]. However, 2.5D approaches are lagging behind in performance and they do not leverage the availability of volumetric data [6]. [4] proposes to improve efficiency by training a 3D encoder network to predict the transformations required to compare the volume against an atlas and thus associate a segmentation mask. This approach is largely efficient given that it removes most of the computation associated with the 3D decoder branch, however it requires additional validation in image modalities with high inter-subject variance such as abdominal CT scans. [1] proposed to use depth-wise separable convolutions in the encoder network to improve the overall efficiency.

Implicit Representation: Implicit Field learning (or occupancy networks) has been recently proposed for 3D shape representation. Implicit networks can reconstruct 3D shapes using their implicit surface representation [3,11]. Instead of using convolutional architectures to generate dense voxel outputs, a linear neural network learns to classify as background or object the spatial coordinates [3,11]. In a related approach, [16] learns the signed distance function with respect to the object surface instead of performing object/background classification.

Implicit approaches can be more efficient than voxel representations in 3D images because they can generate sparse outputs (i.e. for only a subset of points), while in voxel representations, number of parameters and computation grow with a cubic function of the image size. Some recent research has proposed to leverage Implicit Fields in medical image analysis, including unsupervised anomaly detection [15] and super resolution [21].

Contributions: The Implicit Field formalism has allowed to avoid the use of convolutional layers and still produce smooth(er) outputs for shape reconstruction. Following the previously described research direction of making changes to the UNet architecture, we explored what could be achieved by removing the Decoding branch of the UNet, aiming for a more lightweight and faster to train design, without sacrificing accuracy.

We propose a new architecture, named Implicit U-Net, that adapts the principles of the efficient implicit representation paradigm to supervised volumetric

---

[1] Fast and Low GPU memory Abdominal oRgan sEgmentation https://flare.grand-challenge.org/FLARE21/.

medical image segmentation. Given that the Implicit decoder enables prediction of only a subset of points, we evaluate mechanisms to leverage this feature to improve the efficiency of both training and inference. Our main contributions are the following:

- We propose an adaptation of the implicit architecture for segmentation tasks whereby the Implicit decoder receives features from multiple spatial resolutions, replicating the function of skip-connections in a standard U-Net;
- We introduce training and inference procedures that leverage sparse predictions as a strategy to improve training and inference efficiency, obtaining important reductions in time and memory footprint;
- We tested this approach in two datasets from the Medical Segmentation Decathlon [2] and achieved accuracy comparable to the standard U-Net while reducing the inference and training time as well as memory footprint by approximately 30%.

2   Methods

Implicit Field Representation: 3D images are commonly represented as a dense set of voxels. Implicit field networks represent images by learning a continuous mapping f between spatial coordinates $\mathbf{p} = (x, y, z) \in \mathbb{R}^3$ and a target variable T. Therefore, implicit networks receive as inputs and make predictions for a sparse set of points. We leverage this feature to reduce computation during training and inference time.

In addition to spatial coordinates, features $\mathbf{z} \in \mathbb{R}^D$ describing the image are also received as inputs by the Implicit decoder network:

$$f : \mathbb{R}^3 \times \mathbb{R}^D \to T \tag{1}$$

In a segmentation task f learns the posterior probability over C objective classes for continuous spatial coordinates $\mathbf{p}$ and latent features $\mathbf{z}$. In binary segmentation, we model the posterior probability using the logistic sigmoid activation function. Training an implicit network generally implies minimizing the training loss $\mathcal{L}$ over a set of k points which are randomly sampled from N images. For an implicit network parametrized by θ, Eq. 2 describes the training objective:

$$\arg\min_{\theta} \sum_{i=1}^{N} \left(\sum_{j=1}^{K} \mathcal{L}\left(f_\theta\left(\mathbf{z}_i, \mathbf{p}_{i,j}\right), t_{i,j}\right) \right) \tag{2}$$

In our implicit decoder we used the architecture proposed in [16]. The decoder is a feed-forward network composed of 8 fully-connected layers with all hidden layers with 512 units, ReLU as activation, weight normalization and dropout 0.2 in all layers. Prior to feeding coordinates (x, y, z) to the decoder, the coordinates are normalized to the range $[-1, 1]$ and then encoded using function described in [12] (we used $L = 10$ in our experiments).

Implicit U-Net Architecture: We propose to use a standard 3D convolutional neural network (CNN) to generate features $\mathbf{z}$ that are typically passed to the decoder. In a standard CNN encoder, spatial dimensions of feature maps are contracted progressively. In our implementation we use 2- for pooling. Consequently, given an image with dimensions (W, H, D), the feature map dimensions in the downward block (identified with index $b = \{0, 1, ...n\}$) are $(W//2^b, H//2^b, D//2^b)$, $//$ being the floor division operation.

In the original implicit network implementations, it is proposed to obtain features only from the deepest CNN encoder layer, which is expected to contain global features. However, for segmentation tasks we hypothesized that both global and local features are required to make voxel-wise predictions. Consequently, we propose an architecture that extracts features from multiple spatial resolutions at the same time. In order to achieve this, we concatenate features at each resolution in the encoder network. Specifically, for a point $\mathbf{p}$ with spatial coordinates (x, y, z), we concatenate the vectors with coordinates $(x//2^b, y//2^b, z//2^b)$ from the b feature maps in the CNN encoder. Intuitively, we gather the feature vector in the same relative position as the point in the original image (see Fig. 1). With this approach we intend to not only give the decoder access to local features but to provide signal directly at multiple depths in the CNN, similarly to how *deep supervision* [9] in standard U-Nets operate.

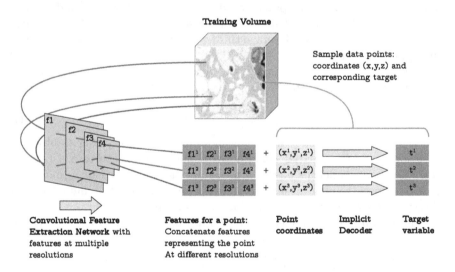

Fig. 1. Diagram of the gather feature vector operation. For example, for $\mathbf{p}$ with coordinates (8, 16), in the 2nd feature map get (4, 8), in 3rd feature map get (2, 4), etc. Features extracted at different resolutions are concatenated with the spatial coordinates and passed to the Implicit decoder.

We adapted the encoder architecture from [7], using in all our experiments 2 blocks of 2 convolutions followed by 2 blocks of 4 convolutions. We also evaluated the original architecture of 5 blocks of 2 convolutions but found that it

produced *patchy* artefacts. We hypothesised that the sharp edges in the artefacts are related to the gather feature vectors operation and that the sharp
straight edges are produced in the image areas where there is a transition from
one deep latent vector to the next. We therefore use a fewer number of blocks
but with more convolutions per block to effectively increase the receptive field
of the 4th block. This subtle change in the encoder architecture reduced the
artefacts because each of the deepest feature vectors is used in the predictions of
smaller areas ($16 \times 16 \times 16$ voxels) compared to the architecture with 5 blocks
($32 \times 32 \times 32$ voxels) (Fig. 2).

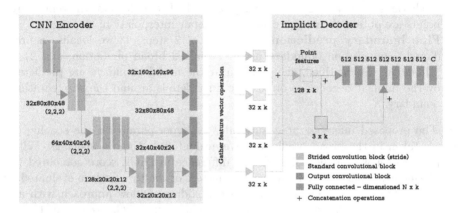

Fig. 2. Implicit U-Net architecture with CNN encoder and Implicit decoder blocks.
Gather feature vector operation selects the feature vectors at the relative position of
the point with respect the original image.

Training Procedure: The CNN encoder and Implicit decoder networks are
trained simultaneously end-to-end. The training consist of 1) CNN encoder forward pass, 2) random sampling of k points from the image, 3) gather feature
vector operation for the sampled points, 4) Implicit decoder forward pass with
feature vectors and point coordinates and 5) backward pass.

In reference to step 2, we hypothesized that model training and final accuracy could be improved by oversampling points near label boundaries. We implemented this strategy with two hyper-parameters. $\alpha = [0, 1]$ specifies the proportion of points that are sampled from the label boundary, with $(1 - \alpha)$ being the
proportion of points being sampled uniformly from the full image. Secondly, σ
is used to control the distance from the boundary of the $k \times \alpha$ sampled points.
The final points are obtained by adding displacement sampled from $N(0, \sigma)$ to
the $k \times \alpha$ points sampled from the boundary. We performed hyper-parameter
tuning for k, α and σ (see results on Fig. 3 for the Lungs dataset). The final
experiments were run with $k = 30,000$, $\alpha = 0.5$ and $\sigma = 5$.

In our experiments we used a patch-based training pipeline, with the spatial coordinate system defined for each patch as opposed to the full image.

We sampled patches using 1 to 2 positive to negative ratio. Patch-sizes are described in the Experiments section.

Inference Procedure: With the objective of improving inference efficiency, we capitalize the feature of Implicit Fields that allows to make predictions for sparse points and propose a three-stage inference process:

- **Broad prediction**: this stage makes predictions for a subset of points in the image forming a broad mesh. In our final implementation the broad mesh was created selecting one in every 4 voxels across all dimensions, thus extracting predictions for $1/4^3 = 1/64$ of the input voxels. Predictions for the remaining points are obtained through nearest neighbour interpolation;
- **Fine boundary prediction**: it consists of 2 steps: 1) we localise a predicted segmentation boundary using the initial broad prediction; and 2) If a boundary is identified, the points near the broad boundary are predicted by the Implicit decoder to obtain the finer details around the segmentation boundary.

The proposed inference procedure adds as hyper-parameter the spacing of voxels taken in the broad prediction. We evaluated 2, 4 and 8 spacings. With a spacing of 4 we did not observe any difference in DICE score compared to predicting every single voxel and was the fastest of the three values evaluated.

Also inference is patch-based and uses a sliding-window approach with an overlap of 0.3. Patch predictions are consolidated using Gaussian weighting. Predictions are finally smoothed using a 3D average pooling filter with a kernel of size 3.

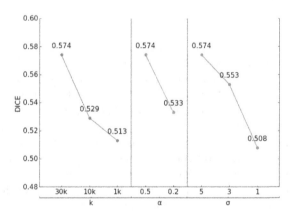

Fig. 3. Mean DICE score in Lungs dataset for different sets of hyper-parameters, starting from the baseline $k = 30,000$, $\alpha = 0.5$ and $\sigma = 5$. Results are from preliminary experiments with a batch-size 3 and 1,200 epochs.

3   Experiments and Results

3.1   Experimental Set-Up

We evaluated our Implicit-U-Net on two datasets from the Medical Segmentation Decathlon [2], specifically Pancreas and Lung CT scans:

- **Task06 Lung dataset**: 64 abdominal CT scans. The task is to identify the lung tumor mass. Images were resampled to a common 1.25 mm resolution along the the z-axis.
- **Task07 Pancreas dataset**: 282 contrast-enhanced, abdominal CT scans. The task is to identify pancreas (label 1) and pancreatic tumor mass (label 2). Images were resampled to a common 2.5 mm resolution along the z-axis.

Image intensities were capped at the 95th percentile dataset-wise. Subsequently we applied z-score intensity normalization. Training and evaluation were both performed patch-wise with $160 \times 160 \times 96$ patches in both abdominal CT datasets. Training augmentations included elastic transforms, scaling, rotations, axis flip, gaussian noise and random contrast.

We compared our model with an equivalent standard 3D U-Net architecture as implemented in [7]. Both standard U-Net and ours were trained using a combined DICE and Cross-Entropy loss, and AdamW optimizer with a learning rate of 10^{-4} and a batch-size of 6 for a fixed number of epochs (2,000 in Lungs and 800 in Pancreas).

5-fold cross validation was used in the two datasets. The reported results show the mean validation set performance for the best performing models fold-wise.

Network implementation, training and testing procedures are made publicly available in[2]. Experiments were run across multiple hardware, including Nvidia 2 x RTX2080Ti, TITAN RTX and A100.

3.2   Results and Discussion

Table 1 contains quantitative results for the experiments in the two datasets. Mean DICE score for each label and standard deviation across subjects are reported as performance metrics. Additionally, mean inference time, training time and peak GPU memory usage for 100 training steps are reported.

Figure 4 shows qualitative comparisons in both dataset between segmentation outputs obtained with the the proposed Implicit U-Net (im-UNet) and the standard U-Net.

Implicit U-Net achieves comparable performance to U-Net in both datasets. Our technique seems to outperform the U-Net in the Lungs dataset while underperforming in tumor segmentation in the Pancreas dataset, however in all datasets performance differences are well below one standard deviation. Of note, the relatively low DICE scores and high standard deviations (e.g. in the Lungs dataset) reflect the difficulty of performing the required segmentation task. These

---

[2] https://github.com/snavalm/imunet_miua22.

Table 1. Quantitative results on segmentation Decathlon datasets.

Lung				
Method	DICE	Inf t[a]	Tr t[b]	Tr Mem[b]
UNet[c]	64.1 ± 27.3	36.7	58.2	16,060
im-UNet	**65.7 ± 23.3**	**25.2**	**41.7**	**11,728**

Pancreas					
Method	DICE 1	DICE 2	Inf t[a]	Tr t[b]	Tr Mem[c]
UNet [3]	**75.8 ± 9.1**	**35.5 ± 29.6**	9.2	59.7	16,151
im-UNet	**75.8 ± 9.1**	33.3 ± 29.2	**6.7**	**44.4**	**11,459**

[a] Mean inference time for N = 10 images in seconds using sliding window.
[b] GPU time in seconds and peak memory usage for 100 training steps on
2xRTX2080Ti using mixed-precision.
[c] 3D UNet architecture with deep-supervision as in [7].

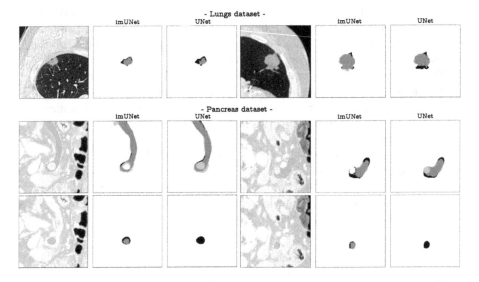

Fig. 4. Qualitative comparison of Implicit U-Net and standard U-Net in 2 different lungs images and pancreas image. For each image, columns show image and ground truth, Implicit U-Net prediction vs ground truth and U-Net prediction and ground truth. In Pancreas, first row correspond to the label 0 (Pancreas) and second row to label 1 (Tumor).

datasets where in fact selected to provide a good testbed for our comparisons. Differently from DICE scores, inference, training time and training memory show instead a clear advantage of the Implicit U-Net over the standard U-Net, with reductions in the range of 30–35%. It is important to note that inference time in implicit U-Net depends on the characteristics of the lesion because of the number of fine-boundary prediction steps required at inference.

With regards to the hyper-parameters added by the model, k, α and σ for training and the broad-mesh scale for inference, we found that the final parameters proposed appeared optimal in the two Abdominal CT scan datasets evaluated. Further evaluation would be required in very different image modalities or targets.

4 Conclusion

We introduced a new strategy to improve efficiency of deep learning architectures in 3D segmentation tasks, which consists in leveraging sparse predictions in an Implicit network that replaces the standard convolutional decoder network. Our experiments show that our method achieves competitive results when compared to the reference architecture for this task (i.e. the 3D U-Net) while improving training and inference times by 30%. Training time and memory advantages lead to faster research iterations and hyper-parameter tuning. Faster inference makes Implicit U-Net relevant in the current practice dealing with larger datasets, larger image sizes and for hospitals and companies running actual segmentation tasks.

We propose Implicit U-Net in the context of growing research interest to improve U-Net architecture replacing some of the computationally expensive 3D convolutions and we believe that is complementary to other methods such as UNETR that focuses on the encoder architecture.

Future research will focus on further uncovering the power of the implicit field representations and testing the proposed approach on other datasets/settings. We will also exploring combinations of implicit decoders with transformer encoders, potentially speeding up and improving the model footprint of high-parameter architectures like UNETR.

References

1. Alalwan, N., Abozeid, A., ElHabshy, A.A.A., Alzahrani, A.: Efficient 3D deep learning model for medical image semantic segmentation. Alex. Eng. J. **60**, 1231–1239 (2021)
2. Antonelli, M., et al.: The medical segmentation decathlon. arXiv preprint arXiv:2106.05735 (2021)
3. Chen, Z., Zhang, H.: Learning implicit fields for generative shape modeling. In: Proceedings of the IEEE/CVF Conference on Computer Vision and Pattern Recognition, pp. 5939–5948 (2019)
4. Dong, S., et al.: Deep atlas network for efficient 3D left ventricle segmentation on echocardiography. Med. Image Anal. **61**, 101638 (2020)
5. Hatamizadeh, A., et al.: UNETR: transformers for 3D medical image segmentation. In: Proceedings of the IEEE/CVF Winter Conference on Applications of Computer Vision, pp. 574–584 (2022)
6. Hesamian, M.H., Jia, W., He, X., Kennedy, P.: Deep learning techniques for medical image segmentation: achievements and challenges. J. Digit. Imaging **32**(4), 582–596 (2019). https://doi.org/10.1007/s10278-019-00227-x

7. Isensee, F., Jaeger, P.F., Kohl, S.A.A., Petersen, J., Maier-Hein, K.H.: nnU-Net: a self-configuring method for deep learning-based biomedical image segmentation. Nat. Methods **18**, 203–211 (2021)

8. Jin, Q., Meng, Z., Sun, C., Cui, H., Su, R.: RA-UNet: a hybrid deep attention-aware network to extract liver and tumor in CT scans. Front. Bioeng. Biotechnol. **8**, 101638 (2020)

9. Lee, C.Y., Xie, S., Gallagher, P., Zhang, Z., Tu, Z.: Deeply-supervised nets. In: Artificial Intelligence and Statistics, pp. 562–570. PMLR (2015)

10. Litjens, G., et al.: A survey on deep learning in medical image analysis. Med. Image Anal. **42**, 60–88 (2017)

11. Mescheder, L., Oechsle, M., Niemeyer, M., Nowozin, S., Geiger, A.: Occupancy networks: learning 3D reconstruction in function space. In: Proceedings of the IEEE/CVF Conference on Computer Vision and Pattern Recognition, pp. 4460–4470 (2019)

12. Mildenhall, B., Srinivasan, P.P., Tancik, M., Barron, J.T., Ramamoorthi, R., Ng, R.: NeRF: representing scenes as neural radiance fields for view synthesis. In: Vedaldi, A., Bischof, H., Brox, T., Frahm, J.-M. (eds.) ECCV 2020, Part I. LNCS, vol. 12346, pp. 405–421. Springer, Cham (2020). https://doi.org/10.1007/978-3-030-58452-8_24

13. Milletari, F., Navab, N., Ahmadi, S.A.: V-Net: fully convolutional neural networks for volumetric medical image segmentation. In: 2016 Fourth International Conference on 3D Vision (3DV), pp. 565–571. IEEE (2016)

14. Moeskops, P., et al.: Deep learning for multi-task medical image segmentation in multiple modalities. In: Ourselin, S., Joskowicz, L., Sabuncu, M.R., Unal, G., Wells, W. (eds.) MICCAI 2016, Part II. LNCS, vol. 9901, pp. 478–486. Springer, Cham (2016). https://doi.org/10.1007/978-3-319-46723-8_55

15. Naval Marimont, S., Tarroni, G.: Implicit field learning for unsupervised anomaly detection in medical images. In: de Bruijne, M., et al. (eds.) MICCAI 2021, Part II. LNCS, vol. 12902, pp. 189–198. Springer, Cham (2021). https://doi.org/10.1007/978-3-030-87196-3_18

16. Park, J.J., Florence, P., Straub, J., Newcombe, R., Lovegrove, S.: DeepSDF: learning continuous signed distance functions for shape representation. In: Proceedings of the IEEE/CVF Conference on Computer Vision and Pattern Recognition, pp. 165–174 (2019)

17. Prasoon, A., Petersen, K., Igel, C., Lauze, F., Dam, E., Nielsen, M.: Deep feature learning for knee cartilage segmentation using a triplanar convolutional neural network. In: Mori, K., Sakuma, I., Sato, Y., Barillot, C., Navab, N. (eds.) MICCAI 2013, Part II. LNCS, vol. 8150, pp. 246–253. Springer, Heidelberg (2013). https://doi.org/10.1007/978-3-642-40763-5_31

18. Ronneberger, O., Fischer, P., Brox, T.: U-Net: convolutional networks for biomedical image segmentation. In: Navab, N., Hornegger, J., Wells, W.M., Frangi, A.F. (eds.) MICCAI 2015, Part III. LNCS, vol. 9351, pp. 234–241. Springer, Cham (2015). https://doi.org/10.1007/978-3-319-24574-4_28

19. Roth, H.R., et al.: Spatial aggregation of holistically-nested convolutional neural networks for automated pancreas localization and segmentation. Med. Image Anal. **45**, 94–107 (2018)

20. Sudlow, C., et al.: UK biobank: an open access resource for identifying the causes of a wide range of complex diseases of middle and old age. PLoS Med. **12**(3), e1001779 (2015)

21. Wu, Q., et al.: IREM: high-resolution magnetic resonance image reconstruction via implicit neural representation. In: de Bruijne, M., et al. (eds.) MICCAI 2021, Part VI. LNCS, vol. 12906, pp. 65–74. Springer, Cham (2021). https://doi.org/10.1007/978-3-030-87231-1_7

22. Xie, Y., Zhang, J., Shen, C., Xia, Y.: CoTr: efficiently bridging CNN and transformer for 3D medical image segmentation. In: de Bruijne, M., et al. (eds.) MICCAI 2021, Part III. LNCS, vol. 12903, pp. 171–180. Springer, Cham (2021). https://doi.org/10.1007/978-3-030-87199-4_16

23. Zhang, F., Wang, Y., Yang, H.: Efficient context-aware network for abdominal multi-organ segmentation. arXiv preprint arXiv:2109.10601 (2021)

A Deep-Learning Lesion Segmentation Model that Addresses Class Imbalance and Expected Low Probability Tissue Abnormalities in Pre and Postoperative Liver MRI

Nora Vogt, Zobair Arya$^{(\boxtimes)}$, Luis Núñez, Kezia Hobson, John Connell, Sir Michael Brady, and Paul Aljabar

Perspectum Ltd., Oxford, UK
zobair.arya@perspctum.com

Abstract. Class imbalance in various forms is a common challenge in machine learning (ML) applied to medical imaging. One of these forms is the presence of low probability, but unsurprising, tissue abnormalities as a result of e.g. implants and surgery. Assessments from automated methods can be impeded if the ML system cannot address these abnormalities. A context where this issue arises is segmentation of lesions within the liver when postoperative scans are possible inputs to the model, since surgical clips and postoperative seromas can distort measures such as future liver remnant volume if they are not correctly identified. To this end, we developed a deep learning segmentation model with classes that expliciltly include surgery-related structures: liver parenchyma, lesions, surgical clips, and postoperative seromas. Given a heavy class imbalance in this task, we deployed an asymmetric focal loss function and hysteresis thresholding post-processing. We applied our model to T1-weighted MRI data, reporting average Dice scores of 0.96, 0.57, 0.71, and 0.84 for the four classes, respectively. Finally, we tested the model's potential in a semi-automatic workflow, finding a user-interaction speedup and an increased inter-rater agreement compared to fully manual delineations. To our knowledge, this is the first study to investigate an automated lesion segmentation model for postoperative MRI with both surgical clips and seromas as explicit classes, and the first work to explore an asymmetric focal loss function for segmentation in liver cancer.

Keywords: Liver cancer · Deep learning segmentation · Hepatectomy · Asymmetric focal loss · Hysteresis thresholding · Semi-automatic workflows

Supplementary Information The online version contains supplementary material available at https://doi.org/10.1007/978-3-031-12053-4_30.

G. Yang et al. (Eds.): MIUA 2022, LNCS 13413, pp. 398–411, 2022.
https://doi.org/10.1007/978-3-031-12053-4_30

1   Introduction

It can be common for medical images to contain infrequently occurring objects, such as implants, that are not always present in the population of interest [4,9]. Although they may be infrequently occuring, they are still unsurprising if they do occur, which means clinicians are typically trained in their indentification. Therefore, it is important for automated methods that process such images to recognise these low probability, but unsurprising, objects for what they are and label them correctly. Otherwise, automated methods may be impeded, which can in turn reduce the trust in the automated system. One context where this is an isssue is segmentation of lesions within the liver in pre and postoperative scans.

Liver surgery plays an important role in the treatment of primary and secondary liver cancer and careful risk assessments are essential to predict whether a patient's liver will recover after surgery [1,16]. Metrics such as the tumour burden and the future liver remnant (FLR) volume [15] are computed from routine preoperative magnetic resonance imaging (MRI) or computed tomography (CT) imaging and require accurate lesion and liver masks. As manual delineations are time-consuming and prone to variability, deep learning-based segmentation methods have gained greater acceptance for supporting clinical workflows.

While very accurate automated masks can be achieved for the liver parenchyma, the segmentation of liver lesions remains a challenging task due to high heterogeneity in appearance and limited access to data [2]. As discussed previously, a further challenge for automated methods in the context of surgical planning is the presence of surgery-related tissue abnormalities. Many hepatectomy candidates have had surgery for a previous tumour and can show tissue abnormalities such as postoperative seromas (fluid accumulation within the liver) and surgical clips (used to control the bleeding from nearby blood vessels during the procedure). If these types of abnormalities are not identified correctly, assessments such as FLR may be impeded. Only a limited number of studies have explored the segmentation of post-treatment scans and the handling of imaging features that impede the detection and delineation of the liver and lesions. Early work [5,17] proposed lesion segmentation methods that used pre-treatment priors to guide the segmentation of follow-up contrast-enhanced CT scans but did not comment on the treatment applied or the tissue changes observed. More recently, Goehler et al. [7] automatically detected liver metastases and assessed tumour volume changes in longitudinal contrast-enhanced MRI, while explicitly excluding patients who had ablative therapy or surgery between baseline and follow-up examination, which does not directly address the issue. To our knowledge, this is the first study to develop a model to explicitly segment surgical clips and seromas, in addition to lesions, in postoperative MRI.

As discussed above, surgery-related tissue abnormalities may occur relatively infrequently in a given scan. In addition, lesions, surgical clips and postoperative seromas encompass many fewer voxels in an MRI image compared to the background and liver parenchyma. These two characteristics lead to a strong class imbalance. Unbalanced class distributions can negatively affect network training for segmentation tasks and numerous studies have investigated strategies to increase the robustness of learnt representations [18]. Popular strategies include the over-sampling of under-represented class samples, the re-weighting of class-related loss terms, or the design of loss functions aiming to control network sensitivity and precision for rarer classes [8]. Ma et al. [12] recently published a systematic review analysing twenty loss functions for the evaluation on four different unbalanced datasets. For the lesion segmentation task of the LiTS challenge dataset, a compound loss of soft Dice and Hausdorff Distance achieved the best Dice scores, while weighted cross-entropy and focal loss performed comparably worse. This observation is in line with the work of Li et al. [10] who demonstrated that previously proposed solutions that assign higher weights for under-represented samples might even increase overfitting effects. They showed that overfitting with unbalanced classes introduces a shift of classification layer activation distributions at test time that results in false-negative predictions for the rare classes and they proposed 'asymmetric' loss functions to shift the decision boundary away from the dominant class(es). This motivates an exploration of an asymmetric focal loss function for segmentation tasks in liver cancer since lesions and surgical tissue abnormalities are typically under-represented.

Taking the above points into consideration, the purpose of this work is as follows:

1. Develop and validate a 3D U-Net model for automated delineation of the liver, lesions, surgical clips, and postoperative seromas in pre and postoperative MRI images.
2. Investigate the use of a previously reported asymmetric focal loss function for improving the accuracy for under-represented classes and compare this to a U-Net trained with a conventional loss function.
3. The asymmetric focal loss function produces smoother output distributions that enable more flexible control for under- and over-segmentation effects in the network outputs. To this end, evaluate and compare the performance of a network that uses hysteresis thresholding in a post-processing step.
4. Evaluate the added benefit of a semi-automatic workflow incorporating the model compared to a fully manual one.

2   Methodology

2.1   Data and Pre-processing

We analysed image data for 180 liver cancer patients from three different clinical trials: HepaT1ca, Precision1, and NCCS (ClinicalTrials.gov NCT03213314, NCT0459-7710, and NCT04451603 respectively). The majority of patients were scanned as part of the HepaT1ca trial evaluating the clinical utility of multiparametric MRI in quantifying liver health prior to liver resection [13,14]. A more detailed study breakdown is provided in Table 1. The patients gave consent for their data to be used for future research purposes at the time of signing up to the trials. Detailed inclusion and exclusion criteria for the trials can be found on

Table 1. A breakdown of the dataset used in this study. The number of subjects from each trial and field strength is shown, with the total number of scans (some subjects were scanned at multiple timepoints) shown in parentheses.

	1.5 T	3 T	Total
HepaT1ca	89 (146)	41 (70)	130 (216)
NCCS	21 (66)	–	21 (66)
Precision1	29 (29)	–	29 (29)

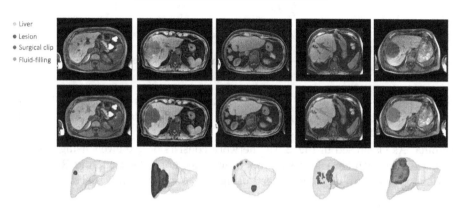

Fig. 1. Examples of pre and postoperative T1 VIBE images for five cases along with their manual segmentations.

their ClinicalTrials.gov entries. For each subject, we included one pre-treatment (potentially with treatment history) and up to two post-treatment 3D T1 VIBE MRI images, resulting in a total number of 311 scans. The most frequently observed lesion types were colorectal metastases and hepatocellular carcinoma, while the most frequently applied treatment was surgical resection. We randomly assigned patients to the training, validation, and test set with 141, 19, and 20 subjects (corresponding to 243, 34, and 34 scans), respectively. Figure 1 shows examples representing the four target labels: the liver parenchyma (including vessels), lesions (including primary cancer and metastases), surgical clips, and postoperative seromas.

Image pre-processing included clamping of the upper intensities to the 99th percentile intensity value, normalising the values to the range [0, 1] and resampling the image to a 1.5 × 1.5 × 3.0 mm resolution using linear interpolation.

2.2   The Network Architecture

The 3D U-Net network for the semantic segmentation of the four target classes is shown in Fig. 2 and based on the work by Arya et al. [3]. As background regions in large abdominal scans can impede training, the proposed pipeline uses a cascaded approach, initially identifying the liver bounding box as a region of interest. In a second stage, the lesion segmentation network is applied to the cropped

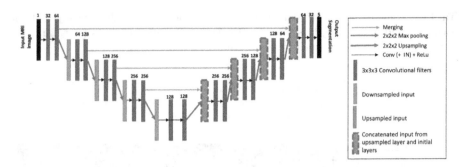

Fig. 2. The U-Net architecture we use in this study.

liver region in a patch-based manner (extracting patches of size $176 \times 176 \times 80$ voxels) and produces a softmax output with five channels corresponding to the class labels: 0-background, 1-liver, 2-lesion, 3-surgical clip, and 4-postoperative seroma. As visualised in Fig. 2, the network consists of five levels using convolutional blocks with kernel sizes $3 \times 3 \times 3$, instance normalisation, and ReLU activations. Downsampling is performed using max-pooling with kernel size $2 \times 2 \times 2$.

2.3   Asymmetric Focal Loss

Networks trained on datasets with imbalanced class distributions can overfit to samples of under-represented classes, leading to a poor generalisability for unseen test cases [10]. In our case, class imbalance occurs due to the lesion, surgical clips and postoperative seromas classes being under-represented compared to the background and liver classes. Li et al. [10] observed that models trained on data with strong class imbalance show a different distribution of classification layer activations (logits) at training and test time. The more strongly a model memorises the appearance of under-represented training samples during training, the more it tends to project unseen samples of the under-represented classes closer to the dominant class decision boundary. As the activation distribution for test samples of over-represented classes appears unaffected, this biased logit shift leads to under-segmentation of under-represented classes. Asymmetric loss functions can encourage increased sensitivity for rare classes by shifting the decision boundary away from the dominant class(es). Following the work of Li et al., we investigate the use of an asymmetric focal loss for our segmentation task.

The ('symmetric') focal loss was designed to improve the cross-entropy loss by reducing the contribution of well-classified, 'easy' samples while assigning greater weights to misclassified, 'hard' samples [11]. It is defined as:

$$L_{FocalCE}(x_i, y_i) = -\sum_j (1 - p_{i,j})^\gamma y_{i,j} \log(p_{i,j}) \tag{1}$$

where $0 \leq i \leq N-1$ indexes pixels and $0 \leq j \leq C-1$ indexes the class, $\mathbf{x} \in \mathbb{R}^N$ is the flattened image representation, $\mathbf{y} \in \mathbb{R}^{N \times C}$ is the one-hot representation of the target label, $\mathbf{p} \in \mathbb{R}^{N \times C}$ is the softmax output of the network. The hyper-parameter γ controls the value of $p_{i,j}$ for which a sample is considered well-classified and requires a reduced contribution to the loss. While a model trained with standard cross-entropy ($\gamma = 0$) pushes predicted target class scores to approach 1, a model trained with focal loss ($\gamma > 0$) focuses the loss function on samples with small predicted $p_{i,j}$.

Lin et al. [11] argue that preventing the scores from becoming large makes samples stay closer to the decision boundary, thus causing unseen foreground samples to more easily shift across the decision boundary due to the aforementioned logit shift. To increase the distance between the rare foreground classes and the background (or dominating class) decision boundary, they propose an asymmetric focal loss formulation that introduces γ only for the over-represented classes. Their asymmetric focal loss is defined as:

$$L_{AsymFocalCE}(x_i, y_i) = -\sum_j y_{i,j} \left[r_j \log(p_{i,j}) + (1 - r_j)(1 - p_{i,j})^\gamma \log(p_{i,j}) \right]$$

(2)

with $\mathbf{r} \in \mathbb{R}^C$ a binary vector that determines the classes for which a focus is applied. In this work, we consider the background and the liver class as over-represented classes and choose $r = [0, 0, 1, 1, 1]$ and $\gamma = 2$.

Similarly, Lin et al. introduce an asymmetric soft Dice-like loss, which is derived from the fact that $1 - DSC = (FP + FN)/(2TP + FP + FN)$ (where $DSC, TP, FP,$ and FN represent Dice, true positives, false positives, and false negatives respectively):

$$L_{AsymFocalDSC}(x_i, y_i) = \sum_j \left[\frac{(1 - y_{i,j})p_{i,j} + r_j y_{i,j}(1 - p_{i,j})}{2y_i p_{i,j} + (1 - y_{i,j})p_{i,j} + y_{i,j}(1 - p_{i,j})} \right.$$
$$\left. + \frac{(1 - y_{i,j})p_{i,j} + (1 - r_j)(1 - p_{i,j})^\gamma y_{i,j}(1 - p_{i,j})}{2y_{i,j}p_{i,j} + (1 - y_{i,j})p_{i,j} + y_{i,j}(1 - p_{i,j})} \right]$$

(3)

In this work, we will compare the performance of models with two different loss functions for training. The first model, denoted by '$model_{CE+DSC}$', will be trained using a combined loss of standard cross-entropy and soft Dice:

$$L_{CE+DSC}(x_i, y_i) = L_{CE}(x_i, y_i) + L_{DSC}(x_i, y_i)$$

(4)

For the training of the second model, denoted by '$model_{AsymFocal}$', we consider a combined loss function of asymmetric cross-entropy and asymmetric soft Dice:

$$L_{AsymFocal}(x_i, y_i) = L_{AsymFocalCE}(x_i, y_i) + L_{AsymFocalDSC}(x_i, y_i)$$

(5)

2.4 Training and Evaluation

The network was trained on an Nvidia Titan RTX GPU using TensorFlow 2.3.0 along with the Adam optimiser, setting an initial learning rate of 5×10^{-5}, and using a batch size of one. Random data augmentation was applied on-the-fly,

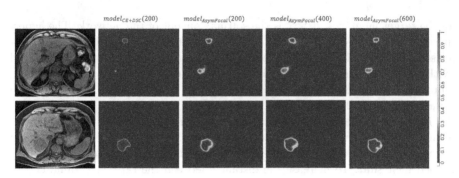

Fig. 3. Examples of lesion class softmax outputs for $model_{CE+DSC}$ and $model_{AsymFocal}$ at epochs 200, 400 and 600. While $model_{CE+DSC}$ produces nearly binary outputs, $model_{AsymFocal}$ shows region of 'uncertainty'.

consisting of random translations along each axis in the range $[-5\%, +5\%]$ of each axis's size, rotation around the z axis in the range $[-10°, +10°]$ and scaling by a factor in the range $[0.9, 1.1]$. Models were trained until convergence of the validation loss. The number of required epochs for the $model_{CE+DSC}$ and $model_{AsymFocal}$ models were approximately 200 and 400 respectively. We evaluated model performance based on Dice scores computed between the predicted segmentation maps and manually created target annotations. Note that if both the predicted and the target masks were empty for a given class, then a Dice score of 1 was assigned for that class and sample.

2.5   Hysteresis Thresholding

We observed that $model_{CE+DSC}$ produced very 'confident' softmax outputs (with values approaching either 0 or 1), while $model_{AsymFocal}$ generated smoother output distributions with a broader range of values in $[0, 1]$ (see Fig. 3 for an example of softmax outputs for both models). Consequently, the categorical output segmentations of $model_{AsymFocal}$ are strongly affected by the subsequent definition of thresholds for class assignment. Hysteresis thresholding [6] aims at expanding predictions of high-confidence areas to areas of lower certainty while excluding noisy, unconnected predictions to reduce the number of false-positive predictions. Specifically, areas above some low threshold t_{low} are considered part of the output segmentation if they are also connected to areas above a higher, more rigorous, threshold t_{high}.

Given our multi-class segmentation task, we apply hysteresis thresholding to all softmax output channels, $j \in 1, 2, 3, 4$ to yield a binary segmentation map y^j_{hyst} for each of the foreground classes. The binary segmentations in y^j_{hyst} may contain foreground voxels that overlap across different classes. When a voxel has more than one associated label, we assign the final label for that voxel based on the following priority: 2, 4, 3, 1, i.e., prioritising the lesion class. In the following, we will denote the asymmetric focal loss model using hysteresis thresholding in a post-processing step as $model_{AsymFocal} + HT$. The hyperparameter choices for thresholds t_{low} and t_{high} will be discussed later.

2.6 Post-processing

All three models ($model_{CE+DSC}$, $model_{AsymFocal}$ and $model_{AsymFocal} + HT$) apply a simple post-processing step, in which predictions for the liver, lesion, surgical clips and postoperative seroma classes that do not belong to the largest connected component after calculating the union over these classes are set to the background.

2.7 Manual Editing

The proposed methods were assessed as part of a semi-automatic pipeline in which operators review and manually edit predicted segmentation maps in ITK-SNAP [19], where necessary. To assess user interaction times and the repeatability of the pipeline, we arranged for two operators (Op1 and Op2) to edit the network outputs, and compared this to the case when the same operators segment the images from scratch in a fully manual manner. Note that the liver class was discarded during the editing and from-scratch delineation processes as it was not the main focus of this study.

2.8 Statistical Analysis

A one-sided Wilcoxon signed-rank significance test was performed to compare any improvement of $model_{AsymFocal} + HT$ over $model_{CE+DSC}$. The same test was also used to compare the agreement between the two operators, represented by the Dice score, for the semi-automatic and the fully manual setup. Significance was set at $P = 0.05$.

3 Results

3.1 Hyper-parameter Tuning on the Validation Set

While a high sensitivity is a desirable model property for tumour detection, we observed that assigning the class with maximum softmax score led to numerous false-positive foreground class predictions in the categorical output segmentation of $model_{AsymFocal}$ for the validation set. Applying hysteresis thresholding proved promising in eliminating outlier predictions while ensuring accurate coverage of abnormality regions. A grid search for the choice of thresholds t_{low} and t_{high} suggested that a relatively high upper threshold ($t_{high} \geq 0.9$) was associated with best validation set performances (see Figure S1 in the supplementary material). Also incorporating qualitative assessments of under- and over-segmentation effects, our final threshold choice was $t_{low} = 0.5, 0.5, 0.5, 0.3$ and $t_{high} = 0.99, 0.99, 0.95, 0.99$ for the classes $c = 1, 2, 3, 4$, respectively. Note that the hyperparameters were tuned on the validation set only and fixed for the test set.

Table 2. Mean values and standard deviations (in parentheses) of Dice scores obtained for the validation set.

Proposed method	Liver	Lesion	Surgical clip	Postoperative seroma
$model_{CE+DSC}$	0.956 ($\pm$ 0.022)	0.544 ($\pm$ 0.372)	0.720 ($\pm$ 0.352)	0.869 ($\pm$ 0.327)
$model_{AsymFocal}$	0.957 ($\pm$ 0.024)	0.591 ($\pm$ 0.323)	0.524 ($\pm$ 0.411)	0.642 ($\pm$ 0.470)
$model_{AsymFocal} + HT$	**0.958** ($\pm$ 0.024)	**0.639** ($\pm$ 0.324)	**0.795** ($\pm$ 0.293)	**0.904** ($\pm$ 0.285)

3.2   Validation Set Performance

As shown in Table 2, the proposed $model_{AsymFocal} + HT$ outperformed the baseline $model_{CE+DSC}$ across all target classes. Figure 4 shows two representative cases for which accurate lesion segmentations were achieved for all models (3D visualisations can be found in Figure S2 of the supplementary material). Overall, we observed that the asymmetric focal loss increased the model's sensitivity for the classes 2 to 4, reporting sensitivities of 0.492 ± 0.374, 0.694 ± 0.374, and 0.864 ± 0.333 for $model_{CE+DSC}$ and sensitivities of 0.604 ± 0.349, 0.762 ± 0.332, and 0.902 ± 0.287 for $model_{AsymFocal} + HT$. One example for which the focal loss showed reduced under-segmentation compared to $model_{CE+DSC}$ is shown in the bottom row of Fig. 4. Applying hysteresis thresholding in a post-processing step can markedly boost the Dice score performances of the asymmetric focal loss, which can be partly explained by the elimination of false-positive predictions observed in $model_{AsymFocal}$. A small lesion outlier of $model_{AsymFocal}$ that was eliminated in $model_{AsymFocal} + HT$ is shown in the top row of Fig. 5. Despite a small missed postoperative seroma region at the liver boundary, this example shows promising delineations of both surgical clips and postoperative seroma objects. The bottom row of Fig. 5 highlights the difficulty of distinguishing lesions and surgery-related fluid accumulations, showing a lesion that all models partly mislabelled as postoperative seroma (possibly due to an unusual hypointense appearance). There remained a few cases in which outlier predictions propagated to the output of the hysteresis thresholding. One example where a hypointense liver parenchyma region caused a large false-positive lesion prediction is shown in the top row of Fig. 6. There were also a few lesions that were entirely missed by the networks, with one example being shown at the bottom of Fig. 6. In this case, one false-negative prediction for a unifocal, small lesion caused an overall lesion Dice score of 0.

3.3   Test Set Performance

Table 3 and Fig. 7 report the test set performances for the proposed models, manually edited segmentations of $model_{AsymFocal} + HT$, and fully manual delineations. For brevity the Dice scores for the liver parenchyma class are not included in the table, but for reference they were 0.957 ± 0.019, 0.960 ± 0.016 and 0.961 ± 0.016 for $model_{CE+DSC}$, $model_{AsymFocal}$ and $model_{AsymFocal} + HT$, respectively. The average Dice scores for the fully automated predictions of $model_{AsymFocal} + HT$ were 0.57, 0.71, and 0.84 for the

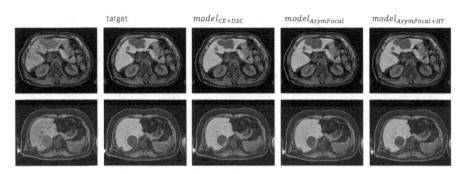

Fig. 4. Examples of accurate validation set predictions with similar lesion segmentation performances across models. Bottom: a case with slightly higher lesion sensitivity of $model_{AsymFocal} + HT$ compared to $model_{CE+DSC}$ resulting in reduced undersegmentation (with lesion Dice scores of 0.90 and 0.83)

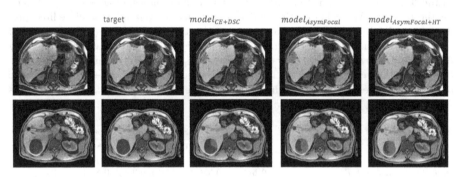

Fig. 5. Less accurate prediction examples with top: better postoperative seroma coverage of $model_{AsymFocal} + HT$ compared to $model_{CE+DSC}$ (with class 4 Dice scores of 0.74 and 0.54) and bottom: severe lesion and fluid seroma class mislabelling.

lesion, surgical clip and postoperative seroma classes, respectively (outperforming $model_{CE+DSC}$ for the lesion and postoperative seroma class, although these improvements did not pass statistical testing given the relatively small sample size). The reported performances suggest that there was no significant performance difference between the editing of segmentations ($model_{AsymFocal} + HT + Edit_{Op1}$, $model_{AsymFocal} + HT + Edit_{Op2}$) and the fully manual delineations ($FromScratch_{Op1}$, $FromScratch_{Op2}$), while there was a reduction in operator time as summarised in Fig. 7. On average, the operators required 03:03 and 02:34 (mm:ss) for the editing and 03:39 and 04:09 for the segmentation from scratch. The increase in inter-observer agreement, as measured by the Dice score, was statistically significant for the lesion class.

| target | $model_{CE+DSC}$ | $model_{AsymFocal}$ | $model_{AsymFocal+HT}$ |

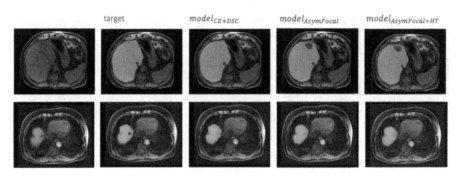

Fig. 6. Example cases presenting very poor lesion class Dice scores due to (top): false-positive prediction of $model_{AsymFocal} + HT$ and (bottom): a missed lesion that caused a lesion Dice scores of 0 for all models.

Table 3. Mean values and standard deviations (in parentheses) of Dice scores obtained for the test set. We evaluated the model predictions, as well as manually edited predictions and fully manual delineations from the two operators against the ground truth. Also included are Dice scores between the two operators when segmenting from scratch ($FromScratch_{Op1}$ vs $FromScratch_{Op2}$) and editing model predictions ($Edit_{Op1}$ vs $Edit_{Op2}$). Finally, the last row shows the output of a one-sided significance test for inter-observer agreement, inspecting whether $Edit_{Op1}$ vs $Edit_{Op2}$ outperforms $FromScratch_{Op1}$ vs $FromScratch_{Op2}$.

Proposed method	Lesion	Surgical clip	Postoperative seroma
$model_{CE+DSC}$	0.528 ($\pm$ 0.326)	**0.710** ($\pm$ 0.366)	0.800 ($\pm$ 0.394)
$model_{AsymFocal}$	0.536 ($\pm$ 0.301)	0.449 ($\pm$ 0.416)	0.671 ($\pm$ 0.446)
$model_{AsymFocal} + HT$	**0.568** ($\pm$ 0.326)	0.707 ($\pm$ 0.368)	**0.843** ($\pm$ 0.342)
P-value $_{(AsymFocal+HT\ vs\ CE+DSC)}$	0.187	0.535	0.072
$model_{AsymFocal} + HT + Edit_{Op1}$	0.743 ($\pm$ 0.237)	0.816($\pm$ 0.280)	0.894 ($\pm$ 0.285)
$model_{AsymFocal} + HT + Edit_{Op2}$	0.760 ($\pm$ 0.225)	0.730 ($\pm$ 0.355)	0.834 ($\pm$ 0.352)
$FromScratch_{Op1}$	0.740 ($\pm$ 0.246)	0.814 ($\pm$ 0.275)	0.895 ($\pm$ 0.285)
$FromScratch_{Op2}$	0.759 ($\pm$ 0.206)	0.817 ($\pm$ 0.284)	0.837 ($\pm$ 0.353)
$FromScratch_{Op1}$ vs $FromScratch_{Op2}$	0.776 ($\pm$ 0.213)	0.783 ($\pm$ 0.303)	0.891($\pm$ 0.284)
$Edit_{Op1}$ vs $Edit_{Op2}$	0.817 ($\pm$ 0.253)	0.841 ($\pm$ 0.298)	0.928 ($\pm$ 0.235)
P-value	0.003*	0.078	0.087

4   Discussion

In this study we have attempted to develop a segmentation model for liver cancer that, in addition to identifying lesions, can identify postoperative surgical clips and seromas. We observed that the asymmetric focal loss achieved higher sensitivities than the compound loss L_{CE+DSC}, with hysteresis thresholding as an important post-processing step. However, we observed that the upper bound of the hysteresis thresholding produced many false-negative surgical clip predictions, whereas lowering the bound led to an overall Dice score decrease for this class. Similarly, some smaller, missed lesions achieved output activations that did not exceed the upper lesion class threshold. This means that there is potential for more advanced thresholding approaches to further improve the

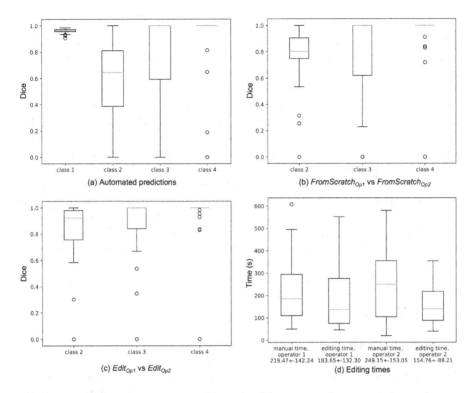

Fig. 7. Test set Dice scores computed between (a) automated segmentation and target annotations, (b) from-scratch delineations, and (c) edited segmentations. Finally, (d) compares times spent on manual from scratch delineations and segmentation mask editing for the two operators.

detection rate. One option we aim to explore in future work are (user-interactive) post-processing tools with adaptive thresholding for individual lesion candidates, in addition to boundary-aware segmentation refinements.

We believe that semi-automatic pipelines can reduce the need for user interactions and speed up manual workflows. We found that while the highest speed-up was observed for the delineations of particularly large lesions, the model also showed potential for accurate delineation of smaller objects. However, there were also cases with an editing increase. Our experiment enforced the correction of automated masks but allowing for a fully manual delineation for cases with very inaccurate predictions could be more beneficial in the semi-automatic workflow, and this would need to be assessed.

The high intra- and inter-observer variabilities observed between the manual delineations of the two operators demonstrate the difficulty of delineating lesions in (postoperative) non-contrast MRI data. As postoperative seromas are usually located next to surgical clips, incorporating such prior knowledge could further guide network training or post-processing tools to reduce confusion between predictions for the lesion and postoperative seroma classes.

One limitation of this study was the distribution and quantity of data. Not only would more data allow for a more accurate trained model, but it would also allow for more statistical power to test the significance of the differences in performance across the different U-Net models. In addition, all of the data in this study came from one scanner manufacturer. Data from multiple scanner manufacturers would allow for a more thorough examination of real-world generalisability of the models. Another limitation related to the data is the fact that we only applied our model to non-contrast T1-weighted scans. Other types of scans, including contrast-agent-enhanced data and diffusion weighted scans are acquired in clinical imaging sessions and can provide better lesion-to-parenchyma contrast. Applying the methodology reported in this study to postoperative scans with these types of acquisitions could be explored as further work. The use of non-contrast T1-weighted data is also the reason for the low average lesion dice scores across models compared to studies that have reported lesion segmentation dice scores on contrast enhanced data. Finally, in the experiment where we compared a semi-automatic workflow to a manual one, the editing was performed before the fully manual delineations, meaning that the speed-up provided by the segmentation model was likely underestimated as the operators already had some experience in working with the data.

5   Conclusion

We proposed a deep learning segmentation model to aid clinical delineation workflows for treatment planning and surveillance. The model showed promising lesion segmentation performances in pre- and post-treatment MRI and supports the delineation of surgical clips and postoperative seromas. Given an imbalanced class distribution, we found that an asymmetric focal loss outperformed a combination of cross-entropy and soft Dice when followed by hysteresis thresholding in a post-processing step. Finally, we demonstrated the model's potential for a semi-automatic workflow in which operators manually edited the network outputs, showing a speedup in user-interaction times and an increased inter-observer agreement compared to fully manual delineations.

References

1. Adam, R., Kitano, Y.: Multidisciplinary approach of liver metastases from colorectal cancer. Annal. Gastroenterological Surg. **3**(1), 50–56 (2019). https://doi.org/10.1002/ags3.12227
2. Antonelli, M., et al.: The Medical Segmentation Decathlon, June 2021
3. Arya, Z., Ridgway, G., Jandor, A., Aljabar, P.: Deep learning-based landmark localisation in the liver for couinaud segmentation. In: Papież, B.W., Yaqub, M., Jiao, J., Namburete, A.I.L., Noble, J.A. (eds.) MIUA 2021. LNCS, vol. 12722, pp. 227–237. Springer, Cham (2021). https://doi.org/10.1007/978-3-030-80432-9_18
4. Beichel, R., Bischof, H., Leberl, F., Sonka, M.: Robust active appearance models and their application to medical image analysis. IEEE Tran. Med. Imaging **24**(9), 1151–1169 (2005). https://doi.org/10.1109/TMI.2005.853237. https://pubmed.ncbi.nlm.nih.gov/16156353/

5. Ben Cohen, A., Diamant, I., Klang, E., Amitai, M., Greenspan, H.: Automatic detection and segmentation of liver metastatic lesions on serial CT examinations, p. 903519, March 2014. https://doi.org/10.1117/12.2043718
6. Canny, J.: A computational approach to edge detection. IEEE Trans. Pattern Anal. Mach. Intell. **PAMI-8**(6), 679–698 (1986). https://doi.org/10.1109/TPAMI.1986. 4767851
7. Goehler, A., et al.: Three-dimensional neural network to automatically assess liver tumor burden change on consecutive liver MRIs. J. Am. College Radiol. **17**(11), 1475–1484 (2020). https://doi.org/10.1016/j.jacr.2020.06.033
8. Hashemi, S.R., Mohseni Salehi, S.S., Erdogmus, D., Prabhu, S.P., Warfield, S.K., Gholipour, A.: Asymmetric loss functions and deep densely-connected networks for highly-imbalanced medical image segmentation: application to multiple sclerosis lesion detection. IEEE Access **7**, 1721–1735 (2018). https://doi.org/10.1109/ ACCESS.2018.2886371
9. Juanpere, S., Perez, E., Huc, O., Motos, N., Pont, J., Pedraza, S.: Imaging of breast implants-a pictorial review. Insights Imaging **2**(6), 653 (2011). https://doi.org/10.1007/S13244-011-0122-3, /pmc/articles/PMC3259319/ /pmc/ articles/PMC3259319/?report=abstract https://www.ncbi.nlm.nih.gov/pmc/ articles/PMC3259319/
10. Li, Z., Kamnitsas, K., Glocker, B.: Analyzing overfitting under class imbalance in neural networks for image segmentation. IEEE Trans. Med. Imaging **40**(3), 1065–1077 (2020). https://doi.org/10.1109/TMI.2020.3046692
11. Lin, T.Y., Goyal, P., Girshick, R., He, K., Dollár, P.: Focal Loss for Dense Object Detection, August 2017
12. Ma, J., Chen, J., Ng, M., Huang, R., Li, Y., Li, C., Yang, X., Martel, A.L.: Loss odyssey in medical image segmentation. Med. Image Anal. **71**, 102035 (2021). https://doi.org/10.1016/j.media.2021.102035
13. Mole, D.J., et al.: Study protocol: HepaT1ca - an observational clinical cohort study to quantify liver health in surgical candidates for liver malignancies. BMC Cancer **18**(1), 890 (2018). https://doi.org/10.1186/s12885-018-4737-3
14. Mole, D.J., et al.: Quantitative magnetic resonance imaging predicts individual future liver performance after liver resection for cancer. PLOS ONE **15**(12), e0238568 (2020). https://doi.org/10.1371/journal.pone.0238568
15. Suzuki, K., et al.: Quantitative radiology: automated CT liver volumetry compared with interactive volumetry and manual volumetry. Am. J. Roentgenol. **197**(4), W706–W712 (oct 2011). https://doi.org/10.2214/AJR.10.5958
16. Villanueva, A.: Hepatocellular Carcinoma. New England J. Med. **380**(15), 1450–1462 (2019). https://doi.org/10.1056/NEJMra1713263
17. Vivanti, R., Joskowicz, L., Lev-Cohain, N., Ephrat, A., Sosna, J.: Patient-specific and global convolutional neural networks for robust automatic liver tumor delineation in follow-up CT studies. Med. Biol. Eng. Comput. **56**(9), 1699–1713 (2018). https://doi.org/10.1007/s11517-018-1803-6
18. Wang, S., Liu, W., Wu, J., Cao, L., Meng, Q., Kennedy, P.J.: Training deep neural networks on imbalanced data sets. In: 2016 International Joint Conference on Neural Networks (IJCNN), pp. 4368–4374. IEEE, July 2016. https://doi.org/10. 1109/IJCNN.2016.7727770
19. Yushkevich, P.A., et al.: User-guided 3D active contour segmentation of anatomical structures: significantly improved efficiency and reliability. NeuroImage **31**(3), 1116–1128 (2006). https://doi.org/10.1016/j.neuroimage.2006.01.015

Utility of Equivariant Message Passing in Cortical Mesh Segmentation

Dániel Unyi[1]($\boxtimes$), Ferdinando Insalata[2], Petar Veličković[3],
and Bálint Gyires-Tóth[1]

[1] Department of Telecommunications and Media Informatics, Budapest University
of Technology and Economics, Műegyetem rkp. 3., 1111 Budapest, Hungary
{unyi.daniel,toth.b}@tmit.bme.hu

[2] Department of Mathematics, Imperial College London, London SW7 2AZ, UK
f.insalata17@imperial.ac.uk

[3] DeepMind, London, UK
petarv@deepmind.com

Abstract. The automated segmentation of cortical areas has been a long-standing challenge in medical image analysis. The complex geometry of the cortex is commonly represented as a polygon mesh, whose segmentation can be addressed by graph-based learning methods. When cortical meshes are misaligned across subjects, current methods produce significantly worse segmentation results, limiting their ability to handle multi-domain data. In this paper, we investigate the utility of E(n)-equivariant graph neural networks (EGNNs), comparing their performance against plain graph neural networks (GNNs). Our evaluation shows that GNNs outperform EGNNs on aligned meshes, due to their ability to leverage the presence of a global coordinate system. On misaligned meshes, the performance of plain GNNs drop considerably, while E(n)-equivariant message passing maintains the same segmentation results. The best results can also be obtained by using plain GNNs on realigned data (co-registered meshes in a global coordinate system).

Keywords: Mesh segmentation · Graph neural networks · Equivariance · Point cloud registration · fMRI

1 Introduction

It has long been recognized that machine learning is an important technique in medical data analysis. With advances in deep learning, state-of-the-art solutions are even able to outperform medical professionals on certain datasets [1]. fMRI allows the non-invasive and non-radioactive examination of the brain, and there has been much interest in the application of deep learning to fMRI scans [2–4]. An important area of scan analysis focuses on segmentation, i.e. classifying unstructured 2-, 3-, and 4-dimensional scans by comparing certain statistical properties.

P. Veličković and B. Gyires-Tóth—Equal contribution

G. Yang et al. (Eds.): MIUA 2022, LNCS 13413, pp. 412–424, 2022.
https://doi.org/10.1007/978-3-031-12053-4_31

Manual segmentation is a labor-intensive process that requires highly-trained experts, hence the interest in automating it. Automatic segmentation assists doctors to identify normal and abnormal regions. The difficulty stems from the variable nature of human brains, scanning methods, and environmental conditions. The scans can be segmented in 2-dimensions as images, in 3-dimensions as meshes (or point clouds), and in 4-dimensions that also includes temporal information.

Historically, the main approach in automatic segmentation was to apply computer vision techniques. Within deep learning, mainly convolutional neural networks (CNNs) were applied [3,4]. 3D CNNs are able to work on volumetric data, and were successfully utilized for segmentation tasks in the U-Net structure [5,6]. Lately, with the rise of the transformer architecture [7], such methods were also applied for segmentation tasks separately or combined with CNNs [8–10].

With the marching cubes algorithm, the brain can be reconstructed as a 3D mesh by combining multiple MRI scans taken from the parallel brain slices of a patient [11]. Reconstruction methods involve several preprocessing steps (e.g. thresholds are set based on the data, sometimes subjectively) that introduce minor or major distortions to the resulting mesh. Reconstruction quality is also heavily influenced by the resolution of MRI scans. When machine learning techniques are applied to 3D meshes – which are reconstructed from 2D images – these constraints create an irreducible error barrier. In spite of these constraints, reconstructing 3D meshes can still provide a greater amount of spatial information than analyzing 2D images separately.

The cerebral cortex is a sheet of neural tissue located on the outer surface of the brain. A large number of neurons live within its folds and grooves (up to 16 billion neurons in humans), which facilitate the processing of large amounts of information. Cortical meshes have emerged as a popular way of representing its complex geometry, being a valuable tool for studying patterns in healthy brains as well as the structural and functional abnormalities that accompany pathological conditions. Complex cognitive processes, including sensory, motory and association, involve distinct areas of the cortex. The task of segmenting these areas is therefore of great scientific and medical interest.

In this work, we investigate the segmentation performance of neural network architectures, that (i) processes each node of the cortical meshes separately with a multilayer perceptron (ii) considers the underlying geometry, i.e. the edge structure of the cortical meshes with a graph neural network [12], (iii) considers the underlying geometry, and is equivariant to isometric transformations with E(n)-equivariant graph neural networks [13].

The main contributions of this paper are the following:

- We are the first to investigate the utility of E(n)-equivariant graph neural networks (EGNNs) in cortical mesh segmentation.
- We evaluate the segmentation performance of EGNNs against plain graph neural networks (GNNs), both on aligned and misaligned cortical meshes.

- We explain why GNNs are better choice for segmentation than EGNNs when the cortical meshes are aligned or can be realigned in a global coordinate system.

2 Background

2.1 Graph Neural Networks

Graph Neural Networks (GNNs) are neural networks which operate on graph-structured data [14–17]. Let $\mathcal{G} = (\mathcal{V}, \mathcal{E})$ be a graph with N nodes, adjacency matrix $\mathbf{A} \in \mathbb{R}^{N \times N}$ and node embedding matrix $\mathbf{H} = (\mathbf{h}_0, \mathbf{h}_1, ... \mathbf{h}_N) \in \mathbb{R}^{N \times D}$. Since nodes can be re-indexed arbitrarily, a common property of GNN layers is permutation equivariance:

$$f(\mathbf{PH}, \mathbf{PAP}^T) = \mathbf{P}(f(\mathbf{H}, \mathbf{A}))$$

where f is a GNN layer and $\mathbf{P} \in \mathbb{R}^{N \times N}$ is an arbitrary permutation matrix. Such functions can be constructed in numerous ways, and GNN layer design is a remarkably active research area [18,19]. One of the most expressive GNN layer is the message passing layer, proposed by Gilmer et al. for quantum chemical applications [12]. The l-th layer is constructed as follows:

1. Concatenate the node embeddings along the edges, and transform the resulting edge embeddings using a small MLP ϕ_e:

$$\mathbf{m}_{ij}^l = \phi_e(\mathbf{h}_i^l, \mathbf{h}_j^l)$$

2. Sum up the edge embeddings in each neighbourhood:

$$\mathbf{m}_i^l = \sum_{j \in \mathcal{N}(i)} \mathbf{m}_{ij}^l$$

3. Concatenate the updated node embeddings to the original ones, and transform the resulting node embeddings using a small MLP ϕ_h:

$$\mathbf{h}_i^{l+1} = \phi_h(\mathbf{h}_i^l, \mathbf{m}_i^l)$$

2.2 E(n) Equivariance

In MRI-based mesh segmentation and many other applications (e.g. point clouds [20], 3D molecular structures [21], or N-body simulations [22]), graphs are embedded into 3D Euclidean space. It means that beyond node features $\mathbf{F} = (\mathbf{f}_0, \mathbf{f}_1, ... \mathbf{f}_N) \in \mathbb{R}^{N \times F}$, the node coordinates $\mathbf{X} = (\mathbf{x}_0, \mathbf{x}_1, ..., \mathbf{x}_N) \in \mathbb{R}^{N \times 3}$ are also available. Now one can not only choose the arbitrary permutation of node indices, but also an arbitrary basis which the node coordinates are represented on. E(n)-equivariant GNNs turned out to be more effective in these applications [19,23,24], and recently, Satorras et al. proposed a very simple and effective E(n)-equivariant GNN (EGNN) based on message passing [13]. The l-th layer is constructed as follows:

1. Concatenate the node embeddings along the edges as well as the node distances, and transform the resulting edge embeddings using a small MLP ϕ_e:

$$\mathbf{m}_{ij}^l = \phi_e(\mathbf{h}_i^l, \mathbf{h}_j^l, ||\mathbf{x}_i^l - \mathbf{x}_j^l||)$$

2. Sum up the edge embeddings in each neighbourhood:

$$\mathbf{m}_i^l = \sum_{j \in \mathcal{N}(i)} \mathbf{m}_{ij}^l$$

3. Concatenate the updated node embeddings to the original ones, and transform the resulting node embeddings using a small MLP ϕ_h:

$$\mathbf{h}_i^{l+1} = \phi_h(\mathbf{h}_i^l, \mathbf{m}_i^l)$$

4. Update the node coordinates, using a small MLP ϕ_x:

$$\mathbf{x}_i^{l+1} = \mathbf{x}_i^l + \frac{1}{|\mathcal{N}(i)|} \sum_{j \in \mathcal{N}(i)} \phi_x(\mathbf{m}_{ij})(\mathbf{x}_i^l - \mathbf{x}_j^l)$$

The elements of the E(n) group are orthogonal transformations (i.e. rotations and reflections) and translations, collectively called isometric transformations as they preserve the length of the transformed vectors. Let $\mathbf{O}$ be an orthogonal matrix, $\mathbf{t}$ a translation vector, and f an EGNN layer. Since node embeddings depend only on the distances between nodes, their transformation rule is E(n)-invariant:

$$f(\mathbf{OH} + \mathbf{t}, \mathbf{A}) = f(\mathbf{H}, \mathbf{A})$$

Node coordinates are also updated in each layer, such that their transformation rule is E(n)-equivariant:

$$f(\mathbf{OX} + \mathbf{t}, \mathbf{A}) = \mathbf{O}f(\mathbf{X}, \mathbf{A}) + \mathbf{t}$$

2.3 Point Cloud Registration

Assume we measure two point clouds $\mathbf{X} \in \mathbb{R}^{N \times 3}$ and $\mathbf{X}' \in \mathbb{R}^{N \times 3}$ which are identical up to an isometric transformation. The goal is to estimate the isometric transformation, by minimizing the error function

$$\sum_{i=1}^{N} ||\mathbf{x}_i' - (\mathbf{Ox}_i + \mathbf{t})||^2$$

According to Arun et al. [25], this problem can be solved exactly:

1. Compute the centre of mass of each point cloud:

$$\mu = \frac{1}{N} \sum_{i=1}^{N} \mathbf{x}_i \quad \text{and} \quad \mu' = \frac{1}{N} \sum_{i=1}^{N} \mathbf{x}_i'$$

2. Compute the point cloud matrix $\mathbf{W}$ and its singular value decomposition:

$$\mathbf{W} = \sum_{i=1}^{N} (\mathbf{x}_i - \mu)(\mathbf{x}_i' - \mu')^T = \mathbf{U}\mathbf{\Sigma}\mathbf{V}^T$$

3. Express the isometric transformation as the following orthogonal matrix and translation vector:

$$\mathbf{O} = \mathbf{U}\mathbf{V}^T \quad \text{and} \quad \mathbf{t} = \mu' - \mathbf{O}\mu$$

2.4   Related Work

Deep learning methods have been used in several previous studies to segment cortical areas, including MLPs [26], CNNs [27,28], spherical CNNs [29,30], mesh CNNs [31], and GNNs [31–33]. MRI scans are very often transformed into meshes before segmentation; and in many cases, meshes are further simplified by mapping their surfaces to planes (for CNNs) or spheres (for spherical CNNs), which may lead to the loss of potentially important information. Mesh-based representations clearly have the advantage of carrying lots of information about the local and global geometric relationships of the cortical surface. Due to their immediate applicability on these irregular surfaces, mesh CNNs and GNNs are more successful in this task.

Cucurull et al. were the first to apply GNNs to cortical mesh segmentation, focusing on Broca's area [33]. They demonstrated that by incorporating the edge structure of the meshes, GNNs [15–17] significantly improve on previous state-of-the-art methods. The node coordinates were also concatenated to the node features, which further improved the segmentation accuracy.

Rotational equivariance was studied in a recent work by Fawaz et al. [31]. They mapped the cortical surfaces to a sphere, and tested various geometric deep learning methods in two tasks: cortical segmentation and neurodevelopmental phenotype prediction. They found that rotational equivariance is less important than filter expressivity or the method of pooling, provided the whole dataset was pre-aligned. Non-equivariant filters showed deteriorated performance when the test data was rotated.

The importance of cortical mesh alignment was also recognized by Gopinath et al. [34]. Using adversarial training, they trained two models: a segmentator GNN and a discriminator GNN. The segmentator GNN was trained to segment both aligned and unaligned meshes, and the discriminator GNN was trained to predict whether the segmentation result comes from an aligned or an unaligned mesh. The discriminator loss was minimized while the discriminator parameters were updated, but maximized while the segmentator parameters were updated, hence the segmentator was forced to segment the aligned and the unaligned meshes similarly. In this case, instead of the structure of the network, the network parameters carry the alignment invariance.

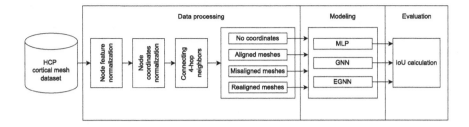

Fig. 1. Main steps of the proposed methodology.

3   Methodology

The goal of the proposed work is to investigate whether and how co-registering in a global coordinate system (GCS) supports the segmentation of cortical meshes. For this purpose, we evaluate the performance of the E(n)-equivariant graph neural network [13] against its non-equivariant version [12] in a series of experiments, in which:

1. We use the GCS defined by the initially co-registered meshes;
2. We drop this GCS by applying random isometric transformations to each of the meshes;
3. We define another GCS by estimating the isometric transformations between the meshes and an arbitrarily chosen reference mesh.

In all cases, we provide brief explanations to clarify the results achieved by the networks. Code to reproduce the results is available on GitHub[1].

We show the main steps of our methodology in Fig. 1. The first step was data preprocessing, introduced in Subsect. 3.1, and the four approaches for node coordinate representations in Subsect. 3.3. As the next step, modeling was performed with three distinct neural network architectures: a multilayer perceptron (MLP), a plain graph neural network (GNN) and an E(n)-equivariant graph neural network (EGNN). As the final step, evaluation was performed.

3.1   Dataset and Preprocessing

The data we used comes from the Human Connectome Project (HCP). The dataset consists of 100 cortical meshes, one for each of 100 human subjects. The meshes share the same edge structure, so they are represented by the same adjacency matrix. Each mesh has 1195 nodes, and each node has 6 structural features (cortical thickness, myelin, curvature, sulcal depth, folding corrected cortical thickness and bias-corrected myelin), 3 functional features (rsfMRI correlation with anterior temporal and two parietal regions of interest [35]), and

---

[1] https://github.com/daniel-unyi-42/Equivariant-Cortical-Mesh-Segmentation.

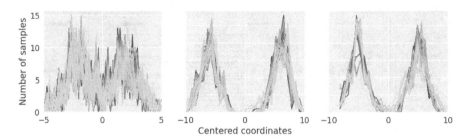

Fig. 2. Histograms of the distribution (across all 100 meshes) of node coordinate pairs which lie at a distance that is close to the typical size of the meshes, along each axis. For all pairs, two peaks are distinguishable, as the variability of node coordinates across meshes is much smaller than the node distances. Hence a node can be identified from its position. We plotted the pairs that lie at a distance between 0.98 and 1.02 of the typical size of the meshes, along each axis (calculated as the minimum standard deviation of the given coordinate).

the 3-dimensional Cartesian coordinates of the node. Same nodes have approximately the same coordinates across the 100 meshes, as shown in Fig. 2. Furthermore, each node has a single, manually-assigned label according to the region of the cerebral cortex it belongs to: Brodmann area 44 (BA44), Brodmann area 45 (BA45), both parts of the Broca's area on the left hemisphere of the cerebral cortex, or neither (background) [36]. The segmentation of this area is particularly challenging as it shows high variability across subjects [35].

Data preprocessing involved three steps. First, we normalized the node features to sum-up to one. Second, we centered and normalized the node coordinates to the interval $[-1, 1]$. Third, we connected the nodes with all other nodes within their 4-hop neighbourhood as it consistently improved the IoU score of GNN and EGNN.

3.2 Models, Training and Evaluation

We applied the following models in our work:

Multi-Layer Perceptron (MLP): this model is a stack of 6 linear layers, with 32 units in each hidden layer, resulting 5k learnable parameters. We applied ReLU activation and batch normalization after each layer, except the last one where we applied softmax to output label probabilities.

Graph Neural Network (GNN): this model has an encoder of one linear layer, 4 hidden message passing layers, and a decoder of one linear layer. The edge and node MLPs have 2 layers, with 32 units in each layer, resulting 26k learnable parameters. We applied Swish activation [40] after each layer, except the last one where we applied softmax to output label probabilities.

E(n)-equivariant GNN (EGNN): this model has the same architecture as GNN, except it has coordinate MLPs beyond the edge and node MLPs. The coordinate MLPs have 2 layers, with 32 units in each layer, resulting a total of 30k learnable parameters.

We trained the models in two stages, using the class-averaged dice loss (Dice $= 1 - 2 \cdot$ IoU) as loss function [37]. In the first stage, we used the Adam optimizer [38] with learning rate 0.001. The first stage was halted when the validation loss did not decrease in the last 200 epochs, and we restored the parameters of the best performing model. In the second stage, we trained the restored model further with SGD + momentum [39], where the learning rate and momentum were set to 0.001 and 0.9, respectively. The second stage was halted after 200 epochs, and once again, we restored the parameters of the best performing model. The batch size was set to 10.

All results were obtained by the 10-fold cross validation of the models. We split the data such that we used eight folds for training, one for validation, and the remaining one for testing. We repeated this process 10 times, each time with a different test fold, and report the means and standard deviations of results across the different test folds. Results are reported in terms of Intersection over Union (IoU, also referred to as Jaccard index) of the two classes of interest (BA44 and BA45):

$$\text{IoU} = \frac{y\hat{y}}{y + \hat{y}}$$

where y are the ground-truth labels (one-hot encoded), and $\hat{y}$ are the label probabilities predicted by the network.

3.3   Experiments

Segmentation Using Node Adjacencies. In our first experiment, we measured the performance of MLP and GNN without using the node coordinates (the column *without coord.* in Table 1). Since MLP cannot exploit node adjacencies, it relies solely on node features, not using any kind of positional information. As a result, its IoU score is well below the IoU score of rule-based methods reported in previous papers [33,35]. On the contrary, GNN is able to exploit node adjacencies and outperforms the aforementioned rule-based methods, as explored by Cucurull et al. [33].

Segmentation Using Node Coordinates. Next we investigated whether and how using node coordinates helps our models to achieve better results. In MLP and GNN, we simply concatenated the node coordinates to the node features. We also considered the E(n)-equivariant GNN (EGNN) model. In EGNN, we applied the node distances as edge features, and transformed the node coordinates separately (see the Background section for the details).

Based on the results (the column *aligned meshes* in Table 1), we can safely conclude that MLP and GNN perform better than EGNN. The reason is that EGNN is a coordinate-free method: on one hand, its output does not depend on the arbitrary choice of coordinates; but on the other hand, it cannot exploit that our cortical meshes are co-registered in a global coordinate system. In opposition, the output of MLP and GNN depend on the choice of coordinates, and so they can assign a label probability to each coordinate in 3D space.

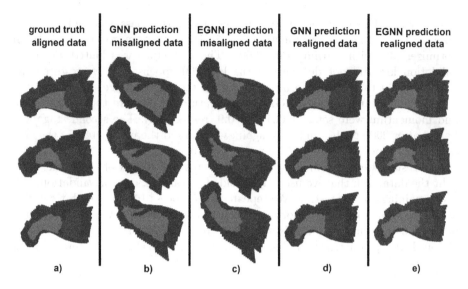

| ground truth aligned data | GNN prediction misaligned data | EGNN prediction misaligned data | GNN prediction realigned data | EGNN prediction realigned data |

a)   b)   c)   d)   e)

Fig. 3. Segmentation results when the test set is misaligned by a rotoreflection. The segmented areas are colour-coded: BA44 by red, BA45 by green, and background by blue. EGNN is unaffected by isometric transformations, producing the same segmentation results for misaligned and realigned meshes (c and e). GNN completely mispredicts the two areas when meshes are misaligned (b), but provides better results than EGNN following realignment (d). (Color figure online)

Segmentation Following Misalignment. To emphasize the importance of alignment, we generated 100 random isometric transformations, one for each of the cortical meshes. An isometric transformation consists of an orthogonal matrix and a translation vector. Both were generated according to a uniform distribution, and the 3 components of the translation vector were bounded by $[-1, 1]$. After transforming the meshes, we re-evaluated the performance of the networks. Regarding real-world implications, such misalignment may occur due to the different co-registration protocols, for instance when the data is coming from multiple sources, or a pre-trained model is being used.

The results are in agreement with our previous interpretation (the column *misaligned meshes* in Table 1). Once we misalign the meshes, the performance of MLP and GNN decreases by a significant amount. EGNN performs better than MLP and GNN, producing approximately the same IoU score as in the case of aligned meshes. Because GNN can still rely on the positional information conveyed by node adjacencies, it is considerably more robust to misalignment than MLP.

To further illustrate the importance of alignment, we generated two different isometric transformations, one for the train set and one for the test set. Such transformations severely fool MLPs and GNNs: they need to be evaluated in the same coordinate system they were trained in, otherwise they produce worse

Table 1. Segmentation results on cortical meshes coming from the HCP Dataset, reported in terms of per-class and average IoU across test folds (mean ± standard deviation).

Model	Brodmann area	Without coord.	Aligned meshes	Misaligned meshes	Realigned meshes
MLP	BA44	46.9±3.6	60.5±3.4	42.6±4.7	60.8±3.4
	BA45	27.7±5.3	52.8±7.1	22.2±4.7	53.2±7.0
	Average	37.3±3.3	56.6±4.4	32.4±3.7	57.0±4.4
GNN	BA44	**59.3±3.7**	**61.4±3.1**	54.3±3.1	**61.6±3.6**
	BA45	**51.8±7.9**	**53.5±6.9**	49.1±6.4	**53.4±6.8**
	Average	**55.6±4.5**	**57.4±3.8**	51.7±3.7	**57.5±4.2**
EGNN	BA44	–	60.4±5.3	**60.5±4.3**	59.8±3.9
	BA45	–	51.7±6.2	**51.9±6.0**	52.1±8.2
	Average	–	56.1±4.2	**56.2±3.5**	56.0±4.5

test IoU than a randomly generated one. EGNN is free from such constraints: it produced consistent test results as before (illustrated in Fig. 3).

Segmentation Following Realignment. As our final experiment, we tried to recover the performance of MLP and GNN by realigning the misaligned cortical meshes. We selected an arbitrary reference mesh (the first sample of the shuffled training set), and estimated the isometric transformation between the reference and the other meshes. Since coordinates that belong to the same node are somewhat different across meshes, we applied the point cloud registration algorithm by Arun et al. [25] in an iterative manner (20 iterations).

We obtained almost the same result as for the original meshes (the column *realigned meshes* in Table 1). It shows that we successfully co-registered the meshes in a global coordinate system, in which case MLP and GNN can perform better than EGNN. We conclude that the co-registration of meshes (or point clouds) in a global coordinate system and using coordinate dependent methods altogether works better than using coordinate independent methods.

4   Conclusion

In this work, we segmented the cortical mesh of 100 human subjects using graph neural networks (GNNs). We demonstrated that co-registering the meshes in a global coordinate system allows GNN to perform better than the isometry-equivariant EGNN. It happens because GNN can exploit the alignment of meshes and assign a label probability to each coordinate in 3D space. We also showed that once we ruin this alignment – a situation we reproduce via random isometric transformations – EGNN is unaffected and superior to GNN. These findings are relevant to situations in which training data is not co-registered with test data. For instance, when the data is coming from multiple sources, or a pre-trained model is being used. Co-registration, if possible, eliminates the requirement of E(n)-equivariance in this application domain. Regarding future research, we are planning to focus on intrinsic mesh CNNs [19], whose prediction depends only on the intrinsic shape of the 2D mesh, and not on its embedding in 3D space.

Acknowledgement. The authors are especially grateful to Konrad Wagstyl for his valuable insights into the data. The research reported in this paper has been partly supported by the Hungarian National Laboratory of Artificial Intelligence funded by the NRDIO under the auspices of the Hungarian Ministry for Innovation and Technology. We thank for the usage of the ELKH Cloud GPU infrastructure (https://science-cloud.hu/) that significantly helped us achieve the results published in this paper. We gratefully acknowledge the support of NVIDIA Corporation with the donation of the NVIDIA GPU also used for this research. The publication of the work reported herein has been supported by ETDB at BME.

References

1. Liu, X., et al.: A comparison of deep learning performance against health-care professionals in detecting diseases from medical imaging: a systematic review and meta-analysis. Lancet Digital Health **1**(6), e271–e297 (2019)
2. Wen, D., Wei, Z., Zhou, Y., Li, G., Zhang, X., Han, W.: Deep learning methods to process fMRI data and their application in the diagnosis of cognitive impairment: a brief overview and our opinion. Front. Neuroinform. **12**, 23 (2018)
3. Tahmassebi, A., Gandomi, A.H., McCann, I., Schulte, M.H., Goudriaan, A.E., Meyer-Baese, A.: Deep learning in medical imaging: fMRI big data analysis via convolutional neural networks. In: Proceedings of the Practice and Experience on Advanced Research Computing, pp. 1–4 (2018)
4. Cai, L., Gao, J., Zhao, D.: A review of the application of deep learning in medical image classification and segmentation. Annal. Transl. Med. **8**(11) (2020)
5. Ronneberger, O., Fischer, P., Brox, T.: U-Net: convolutional networks for biomedical image segmentation. In: Navab, N., Hornegger, J., Wells, W.M., Frangi, A.F. (eds.) MICCAI 2015. LNCS, vol. 9351, pp. 234–241. Springer, Cham (2015). https://doi.org/10.1007/978-3-319-24574-4_28
6. Chen, W., Liu, B., Peng, S., Sun, J., Qiao, X.: S3D-UNet: separable 3D U-Net for brain tumor segmentation. In: Crimi, A., Bakas, S., Kuijf, H., Keyvan, F., Reyes, M., van Walsum, T. (eds.) BrainLes 2018. LNCS, vol. 11384, pp. 358–368. Springer, Cham (2019). https://doi.org/10.1007/978-3-030-11726-9_32
7. Vaswani, A., et al.: Attention is all you need. In: Advances in Neural Information Processing Systems, 30 (2017)
8. Chen, J., et al.: TransUNet: Transformers make strong encoders for medical image segmentation. arXiv preprint arXiv:2102.04306 (2021)
9. Cao, H., et al.: Swin-Unet: Unet-like pure transformer for medical image segmentation. arXiv preprint arXiv:2105.05537 (2021)
10. Zhang, Y., Liu, H., Hu, Q.: TransFuse: fusing transformers and CNNs for medical image segmentation. In: de Bruijne, M., Cattin, P.C., Cotin, S., Padoy, N., Speidel, S., Zheng, Y., Essert, C. (eds.) MICCAI 2021. LNCS, vol. 12901, pp. 14–24. Springer, Cham (2021). https://doi.org/10.1007/978-3-030-87193-2_2
11. Lorensen, W., Cline, H.: Marching cubes: a high resolution 3D surface construction algorithm. Comput. Graph. **21**(4), 163–169 (1987)
12. Gilmer, J., Schoenholz, S. S., Riley, P. F., Vinyals, O., Dahl, G.E.: Neural message passing for quantum chemistry. In: International Conference on Machine Learning, pp. 1263–1272. PMLR, July 2017

13. Satorras, V.G., Hoogeboom, E., Welling, M.: E(n) equivariant graph neural networks. In: International Conference on Machine Learning, pp. 9323–9332. PMLR, July 2021

14. Bruna, J., Zaremba, W., Szlam, A., LeCun, Y.: Spectral networks and locally connected networks on graphs. arXiv preprint arXiv:1312.6203 (2013)

15. Defferrard, M., Bresson, X., Vandergheynst, P.: Convolutional neural networks on graphs with fast localized spectral filtering. In: Advances in Neural Information Processing Systems, 29 (2016)

16. Kipf, T.N., Welling, M.: Semi-supervised classification with graph convolutional networks. arXiv preprint arXiv:1609.02907 (2016)

17. Veličković, P., Cucurull, G., Casanova, A., Romero, A., Lio, P., Bengio, Y.: Graph attention networks. arXiv preprint arXiv:1710.10903 (2017)

18. Wu, Z., Pan, S., Chen, F., Long, G., Zhang, C., Philip, S.Y.: A comprehensive survey on graph neural networks. IEEE Trans. Neural Networks Learn. Syst. 32(1), 4–24 (2020)

19. Bronstein, M.M., Bruna, J., Cohen, T., Veličković, P.: Geometric deep learning: Grids, groups, graphs, geodesics, and gauges. arXiv preprint arXiv:2104.13478 (2021)

20. Uy, M.A., Pham, Q.H., Hua, B.S., Nguyen, T., Yeung, S.K.: Revisiting point cloud classification: A new benchmark dataset and classification model on real-world data. In: Proceedings of the IEEE/CVF International Conference on Computer Vision, pp. 1588–1597 (2019)

21. Ramakrishnan, R., Dral, P.O., Rupp, M., Von Lilienfeld, O.A.: Quantum chemistry structures and properties of 134 kilo molecules. Sci. Data 1(1), 1–7 (2014)

22. Kipf, T., Fetaya, E., Wang, K.C., Welling, M., Zemel, R.: Neural relational inference for interacting systems. In: International Conference on Machine Learning, pp. 2688–2697. PMLR, July 2018

23. Köhler, J., Klein, L., & Noé, F.: Equivariant Flows: sampling configurations for multi-body systems with symmetric energies. arXiv preprint arXiv:1910.00753 (2019)

24. Thomas, N., Smidt, T., Kearnes, S., Yang, L., Li, L., Kohlhoff, K., Riley, P.: Tensor field networks: Rotation-and translation-equivariant neural networks for 3D point clouds. arXiv preprint arXiv:1802.08219 (2018)

25. Arun, K.S., Huang, T.S., Blostein, S.D.: Least-squares fitting of two 3-D point sets. IEEE Trans. Pattern Anal. Mach. Intell. 5, 698–700 (1987)

26. Glasser, M.F., et al.: A multi-modal parcellation of human cerebral cortex. Nature 536(7615), 171–178 (2016)

27. Cheng, J., Dalca, A.V., Fischl, B., Zöllei, L., Initiative, A.D.N.: Cortical surface registration using unsupervised learning. Neuroimage 221, 117161 (2020)

28. Seong, S.B., Pae, C., Park, H.J.: Geometric convolutional neural network for analyzing surface-based neuroimaging data. Front. Neuroinform. 12, 42 (2018)

29. Zhao, F., Xia, S., Wu, Z., Duan, D., Wang, L., Lin, W., Gilmore, J.H., Shen, D., Li, G.: Spherical U-Net on cortical surfaces: methods and applications. In: Chung, A.C.S., Gee, J.C., Yushkevich, P.A., Bao, S. (eds.) IPMI 2019. LNCS, vol. 11492, pp. 855–866. Springer, Cham (2019). https://doi.org/10.1007/978-3-030-20351-1_67

30. Zhao, F., et al.: Spherical deformable U-Net: application to cortical surface parcellation and development prediction. IEEE Trans. Med. Imaging 40(4), 1217–1228 (2021)

31. Fawaz, A., et al.: Benchmarking geometric deep learning for cortical segmentation and neurodevelopmental phenotype prediction. bioRxiv, 2021.12.01.470730 (2021)

32. Gopinath, K., Desrosiers, C., Lombaert, H.: Graph convolutions on spectral embeddings for cortical surface parcellation. Med. Image Anal. **54**, 297–305 (2019)
33. Cucurull, G., et al.: Convolutional neural networks for mesh-based parcellation of the cerebral cortex. In: International Conference on Medical Imaging with Deep Learning (2018)
34. Gopinath, K., Desrosiers, C., Lombaert, H.: Graph domain adaptation for alignment-invariant brain surface segmentation. In: Sudre, C.H., Fehri, H., Arbel, T., Baumgartner, C.F., Dalca, A., Tanno, R., Van Leemput, K., Wells, W.M., Sotiras, A., Papiez, B., Ferrante, E., Parisot, S. (eds.) UNSURE/GRAIL -2020. LNCS, vol. 12443, pp. 152–163. Springer, Cham (2020). https://doi.org/10.1007/978-3-030-60365-6_15
35. Jakobsen, E., Liem, F., Klados, M.A., Bayrak, Ş, Petrides, M., Margulies, D.S.: Automated individual-level parcellation of Broca's region based on functional connectivity. Neuroimage **170**, 41–53 (2018)
36. Jakobsen, E., Böttger, J., Bellec, P., Geyer, S., Rübsamen, R., Petrides, M., Margulies, D.S.: Subdivision of Broca's region based on individual-level functional connectivity. Eur. J. Neurosci. **43**(4), 561–571 (2016)
37. Sudre, C.H., Li, W., Vercauteren, T., Ourselin, S., Jorge Cardoso, M.: Generalised dice overlap as a deep learning loss function for highly unbalanced segmentations. In: Cardoso, M.J., Arbel, T., Carneiro, G., Syeda-Mahmood, T., Tavares, J.M.R.S., Moradi, M., Bradley, A., Greenspan, H., Papa, J.P., Madabhushi, A., Nascimento, J.C., Cardoso, J.S., Belagiannis, V., Lu, Z. (eds.) DLMIA/ML-CDS -2017. LNCS, vol. 10553, pp. 240–248. Springer, Cham (2017). https://doi.org/10.1007/978-3-319-67558-9_28
38. Kingma, D.P., Ba, J.: Adam: a method for stochastic optimization. arXiv preprint arXiv:1412.6980 (2014)
39. Rumelhart, D.E., Hinton, G.E., Williams, R.J.: Learning representations by back-propagating errors. Nature **323**(6088), 533–536 (1986)
40. Hendrycks, D., Gimpel, K.: Gaussian error linear units (GELUs). arXiv preprint arXiv:1606.08415 (2016)

A Novel Framework for Coarse-Grained Semantic Segmentation of Whole-Slide Images

Raja Muhammad Saad Bashir[1]($\boxtimes$)[iD], Muhammad Shaban[2][iD],
Shan E. Ahmed Raza[1][iD], Syed Ali Khurram[3][iD], and Nasir Rajpoot[1][iD]

[1] Tissue Image Analytics Centre, University of Warwick, Coventry, UK
{saad.bashir,shan.raza,n.m.rajpoot}@warwick.ac.uk
[2] Department of Pathology, Harvard Medical School,
Brigham and Women's Hospital, Boston, MA, USA
mshaban@bwh.harvard.edu
[3] School of Clinical Dentistry, University of Sheffield, Sheffield, UK
s.a.khurram@sheffield.ac.uk

Abstract. Semantic segmentation of multi-gigapixel whole-slide images (WSI) is fundamental to computational pathology, as segmentation of different tissue types and layers is a prerequisite for several downstream histology image analysis, such as morphometric analysis, cancer grading, and survival. Both patch-based classification and pixel-wise segmentation have been used for these tasks, where patch-based classification outputs only one label per patch while pixel-wise segmentation is more accurate and precise but it requires a large number of pixel-wise precise annotated ground truth. In this paper, we propose coarse segmentation as a new middle ground to both techniques for leveraging more context without requiring pixel-level annotations. Our proposed coarse segmentation network is a convolutional neural network (CNN) with skip connections but does not contain any decoder and utilizes sparsely annotated images during training. It takes an input patch of size $M \times N$ and outputs a dense prediction map of size $m \times n$, which is coarser than pixel-wise segmentation methods but denser than patch-based classification methods. We compare our proposed method with its counterparts and demonstrate its superior performance for both pixel-based segmentation and patch-based classification tasks. In addition, we also compared the impact on performance of coarse-grained and pixel-wise semantic segmentation in downstream analysis tasks and showed coarse-grained semantic segmentation has no/marginal impact on the final results.

1 Introduction

Semantic segmentation of various tissue components such as glands, nerves, and vessels is an important prerequisite for downstream analysis tasks in computational pathology pipelines. For instance morphological analysis [1,3] of different

G. Yang et al. (Eds.): MIUA 2022, LNCS 13413, pp. 425–439, 2022.
https://doi.org/10.1007/978-3-031-12053-4_32

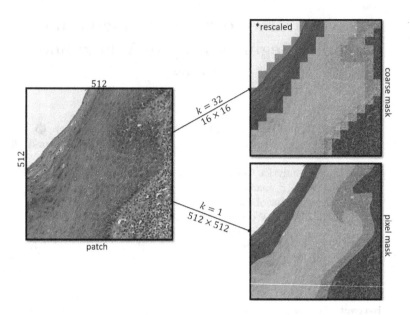

Fig. 1. Coarse and pixel-wise masks: (*Left*) a visual field of 512 × 512 pixels showing the epithelium in oral tissue on left and its corresponding coarse and pixel-wise masks (*Right*). Coarse mask is generated using on mini-patch window of $k = 32$ pixels resulting in coarse mask of 16 × 16 pixels.

tissue structures (i.e., nuclei [8,14], glands [7], and other tissue regions [4]) is used for quantitative analysis of the malignancy in various cancer types. Several pixel-based segmentation methods have been proposed in this regard that require precise segmentation, such as glands and nuclei segmentation. In contrast, patch-based classification is commonly used as an alternative to pixel-wise segmentation of tissue regions e.g., in tumor segmentation, where an estimation of the tumor area is required for further downstream analysis. In patch-based classification, a single label is assigned to a patch instead of a pixel, where patch size of 256 × 256 pixels is normally used but that may vary depending on the application. Often patch-based classification suffices for downstream analysis, e.g., in survival analysis [16,17] and mutation prediction [12]. However, patch-based classification comes with a context-accuracy tradeoff i.e., if higher localization accuracy is required, a smaller patch size should be used where it loses context, while for wider context a bigger patch size should be used which compromises the localization accuracy [21]. Moreover, a single patch may contain different regions of the tissue, e.g., tumor, stroma and assigning a single label to a patch may introduce noise, affecting the overall accuracy of segmentation.

On the other hand, pixel-based segmentation can produce high quality segmentation maps, but it also requires high quality ground truth annotation which can be time consuming and needs expert knowledge to obtain well annotated histology images. Further, training such networks may be computationally demanding at both training and inference stages which may slow down the analysis workflow.

In this paper, we propose a coarse segmentation method addressing the challenges associated with context, accuracy, labeling and complexity. Unlike patch-based classification, it outputs a denser prediction map but coarser than pixel-based segmentation. The proposed coarse segmentation network (CSNet) takes an input patch of size $M \times N$ and outputs the prediction map of size $m \times n$ where the prediction map size is k^2 times smaller than the original patch size as seen in Fig. 1. Choice of k depends on how much accuracy and context is needed i.e. if $k = M$ then it is equivalent to patch-based classification whereas $k = 1$ is the same as pixel-wise segmentation. The ability of CSNet to make dense predictions also enables it to take patches at lower resolutions e.g., $20\times$ or $10\times$ where more context can be incorporated without introducing much noise or false positives. Moreover, it only requires sparsely annotated coarse segmentation masks of mini-patches of size $k \times k$ pixels, reducing the time and cost of annotation.

Coarse segmentation is more appropriate where instead of accurate estimation of tissue components, a rough estimation would also suffice, e.g., in survival analysis, and cancer grading, etc., because aggregation methods can smooth out small artifacts or noises in segmentation map in the downstream analysis. We evaluate our proposed approach on two different datasets for two different tasks, i.e., survival analysis in head and neck squamous cell carcinoma (HNSCC) and binary grade prediction in oral epithelial dysplasia (OED). To summarize the contributions in this paper:

– We propose a coarse segmentation method with feed forward convolutional network only that can be trained on sparsely annotated data, incorporate more context than patch-based classification method unlike typical segmentation networks with encoder-decoder architecture and is also faster than pixel-based segmentation;
– We conduct extensive experiments to compare the efficacy of the proposed approach with both patch-based classification and pixel-based segmentation methods in terms of accuracy and run time;
– We validate CSNet performance on two different datasets using two different downstream tasks i.e., binary grading of OED and survival analysis HNSCC.

2   The Proposed Method

The proposed framework takes a whole-slide image (WSI) as an input and processes it in a tessellated manner through CSNet to generate a WSI-level segmentation masks. In training phase, CSNet model only requires sparsely annotated coarse segmentation masks with their respective image patches as shown in Fig. 2. The following sections will explain network input, architecture, and training in detail.

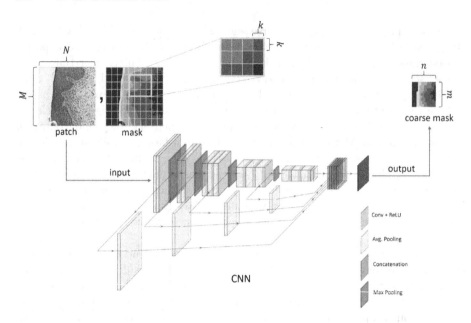

Fig. 2. The architecture of the proposed method where input of size $M \times N$ is fed into the coarse segmentation network outputting coarse segmentation mask of size $m \times n$ and size of output depends on size of mini-patch k.

2.1   Network Input

The input to our proposed framework is a patch (x_i) from a dataset, $D = \{x_i, y_i; i = 1, \ldots L\}$, containing L patches extracted from WSIs with corresponding coarse level segmentation masks. Each patch x_i is of size $M \times N$ and its corresponding coarse mask y_i is of size $m \times n$ where each pixel in y_i represents class label for mini-patch of size of $k \times k$ in x_i. In case of pixel-level ground truth, coarse mask can be generated using majority voting of the pixel-level labels in mini-patch. The coarse mask is m times smaller than the original mask where $m = \frac{M}{k}$, e.g., a patch x_i of size 512×512 and mini-patch of size $k = 32$ is selected then the coarse segmentation mask y_i will be of size 16×16 where each pixel represents 32×32 pixels in original mask.

2.2   Network Architecture

Any standard convolutional neural network (CNN) can be used as a coarse segmentation network with small modifications in the network architecture, where instead of using the fully connected (FC) layers at the end a resize layer of size of $m \times n$ is used followed by 1×1 convolution to output the coarse prediction map unlike fully convolutional network (FCN) [13] where the output is resized $M \times N$. In this paper, we used DenseNet [11] based CSNet where we replaced the last average pooling layer of DenseNet with 1×1 convolution. To further improve the accuracy of the prediction, we introduced additional skip connections (SC) in the network from each dense block concatenated at the end of the network as shown in Fig. 2. These skip connections help the model to improve the spatial context in the final prediction map as with the use of pooling layers the spatial context is lost in the final layers. Although the CSNet output is a segmentation mask, there is no encoder-decoder involved in our network design as it is a simple CNN with final classification layers replaced with convolutional layers.

2.3   Weighted Sparse Loss

To train CSNet, instead of trivial cross entropy (CE) loss function, a sparsely weighted cross-entropy loss function is used to handle the sparsely annotated data. As annotating the entire WSI is a tedious and laborious task, a WSI is often annotated sparsely where there are some un-annotated regions that can act as noise if being treated as background during training. Also this can sometimes help in the decision where there is ambiguity for annotators due to inter- and intra- observer variability to let the model decide the labels during training without incorporating the loss of these un-annotated regions. As this incorporates the loss from the annotated parts only, therefore, it can introduce a high class imbalance, which is catered using the weights for each class calculated during training epochs. Higher weight is assigned to the class with less number of pixels and less weight is assigned to the class with more pixels using the count per class as given below.

$$E = \frac{\sum_{i=1}^{C} r_i}{C'} \tag{1}$$

where E is the expected count and r_i is the annotated region for i^{th} class, C is the total number of classes in the dataset and C' is the number of classes with regions annotated. Final weights W_i are calculated from expected count E as follows.

$$W_i = \frac{E}{r_i} \tag{2}$$

where W_i is the weight for r_i and it will be greater than 1 if the number of pixel in r_i region is less than the expected count and vice versa. Finally, the weighted sparse cross entropy (WSCE) loss is calculated as.

$$L_{WSCE} = -\sum_{x \in X} p(x) \log q(x) \odot W \tag{3}$$

2.4   Model Training

Input patches were pre-processed using standard pre-processing steps of normalization and augmentation (i.e., random rotation [0, 90, 180, and 270°], random clipping [horizontal, vertical], random jittering [0–128] pixels and random color perturbation), and then the model is trained using RMSProp optimizer with an adaptive learning rate starting from 0.001 for a minimum of 100 epochs. The experiments were performed on system where specifications are core i9 machine with 128 giga bite of ram and 2 Nvidia Titan X GPUs. Python language with Tensorflow deep learning framework was used to develop this framework.

3   Experiments with Downstream Analysis Tasks

Once the model is trained, the results of the coarse segmentation are further used in downstream analysis for OED grading and HNSCC survival prediction.

3.1   OED Grading

For OED grading, the epithelium layer is segmented into three sub-layers namely, keratin, epithelium, and basal using the coarse segmented model trained for OED layer segmentation. These sub-layers can help in many aspects one of which is grade prediction using layer-wise nuclear feature analysis. There are a number of cytological and architectural features that can be used to assess the WSI for grading e.g., varying shape and size of nuclei, nuclear to cytoplasmic ratio etc. In lower OED grades, these changes are limited to the bottom third of the epithelium which is the basal layer, the OED grade progresses upwards as the grade worsens to the middle (epithelium) and top (keratin) layer [20]. Using these indicators, we explored the architectural and cytological characteristics of the nuclei in each layer. To segment the nuclei in the epithelium, we use pre-trained Hover-Net [8] on the PanNuke dataset [6] where Hover-Net is a deep CNN for simultaneous instance segmentation and classification of nuclei using the horizontal and vertical distance of nuclei for accurate estimation of boundary. A range of statistical and spatial features are extracted from each nucleus as these features may unravel some underlying correlations between nuclei and grading. Once features are extracted, gradient boosted trees are trained with hyperparameter optimization of different tree parameters, e.g., number of trees, minimum criteria for node splitting, minimum node retention criteria, depth of trees etc.

3.2   HNSCC Survival Analysis

To further illustrate the usefulness of the proposed method in downstream analysis tasks, we also use the proposed coarse segmentation method as an intermediate step (segmentation of WSIs into different classes) for survival analysis [19]. We segment the tumor, tumor-associated stroma, and lymphocyte regions in Head and Neck Squamous Cell Carcinoma WSIs. The resultant segmentation map of each WSI is then used to calculate tumor-associated stroma infiltrating lymphocytes, termed as the $TASIL_{score}$. The $TASIL_{score}$ is calculated as follows:

$$TASIL_{score} = SL/(SS + SL + ST) \tag{4}$$

where SL, SS, and ST represent the number of times tumor-associated stroma regions appear adjacent to lymphocyte, tumor-associated stroma, and tumor regions, respectively. The TASIL score is then used to split the HNSCC patients into two groups of long (low risk) and short (high risk) disease-specific survival. The Kaplan-Meier estimator is used to show the difference between low and high-risk patient groups, where log-rank test based p-value is calculated for statistical significance analysis.

4   Datasets and Experiments

4.1   Datasets

Two different datasets were used for the evaluation of the proposed coarse segmentation method. First dataset contains Haematoxylin and Eosin (H&E) stained 43 WSIs of OED cases from University of Sheffield whereas second dataset consists of 440 H&E stained WSIs of HNSCC cases collected from two different sources, 340 from TCGA-HC cohort and remaining 100 from University of Sheffield. For the training of coarse segmentation network WSIs were manually annotated by an expert oral and maxillofacial pathologist SAK. From 43 OED WSIs, the pathologist annotated pixel-level ROIs, 16282 training, 3617 validation, and 3710 for test of size 512×512 at $10\times$ magnification. The coarse mask for each ROI was generated by aggregating the pixel-level annotation of $k \times k$ mini-patches. From HNSCC dataset, 24 WSIs (12 from TCGA-HN, and 12 from inhouse dataset) were annotated at mini-patch ($k = 32$) level which resulted in 141541 training and 38893 test ROIs at $10\times$ magnification. Survival information for HNSCC dataset were also available which were used for survival analysis.

4.2   Experiments

To compare and validate the proposed coarse segmentation approach, we conducted the following experiments and used F1-score for evaluation purposes.

- To compare pixel-wise and coarse segmentation, different pixel-wise segmentation algorithms e.g., FCN [13], SegNet [2], UNet [15] and DeepLab-v3 can be used but we picked DeepLab-v3 as it has better performance. DeepLab-v3 was trained for pixel-wise as well as for coarse segmentation. The OED dataset for layer segmentation task was selected for this task as pixel-wise annotations were only available for this dataset and were not available for the HNSCC dataset.
- To compare patch-based classification and coarse segmentation, various standard CNNs were trained for patch-based classification. HNSCC dataset for tissue classification was selected for patch-based classification because of two reasons patch based was not feasible for layer segmentation in OED with bigger patch sizes and lack of pixel-wise annotation for HNSCC dataset.
- To compare the inference time of patch-based classification and pixel-wise segmentation with coarse segmentation, one standard WSI was processed with all methods and the final time was reported.

– Downstream analysis on two different datasets for verification and validation of using coarse segmentation as a prior step in the two different pipelines was performed.

5 Results

5.1 Pixel-wise vs Coarse Segmentation

Table 1 compares the results of coarse segmentation and pixel-wise segmentation methods using DeepLab-v3 and CSNet on various mini-patch sizes k. For a fair comparison, we compared the methods with the same mini-patch e.g., it can be seen that our method with mini-patch size of 16 and 32 performed superior to DeepLab-v3, which shows that for coarse segmentation we can use CSNet like methods rather than using the pixel-wise segmentation approaches. WSI level masks were generated using the sliding window approach with an overlap of 80% and resizing the output size to input using linear interpolation as its already a coarse output. The result is showed in Fig. 4 where it shows the prediction of our proposed CSNet with and mini-patch of $k = 32$.

Table 1. F1-score for pixel-wise and coarse segmentation in OED layer segmentation for patch size of 512×512

Method	Mini-patch k	F1-score
DeepLab-v3	$k = 1$	78.82
DeepLab-v3	$k = 16$	80.57
CSNet	$k = 16$	**81.24**
DeepLab-v3	$k = 32$	78.32
CSNet	$k = 32$	**80.54**

5.2 Patch-Based Classification vs Coarse Segmentation

Table 2 compares the results of patch-based classification and coarse segmentation where for patch-based classification simple standard CNNs (i.e., ResNet [9], MobileNet [10] and DenseNet [11]) were used. To make the CNN's output comparable with coarse segmentation results, the stride was set to 32 and only 32×32 region was assigned a label from the CNN's output, as shown in Fig. 3, because assigning a single label to 256×256 will result in very low accuracy. It can be seen that CSNet performs superior by 5–10% as compared to standard CNNs due to the additional skip connection added to it. Moreover, if we lower the patch size of standard CNN, the accuracy further drops below the current one due to the lack of context in that patch as we experimented with smaller patch size of 128×128 and the F1-score achieved was 66.10 which is lower than the previous one. Figure 5 shows the prediction of our proposed method, where it can be seen that the CSNet model performs better in most of the tissue regions except for some highlighted in black circles.

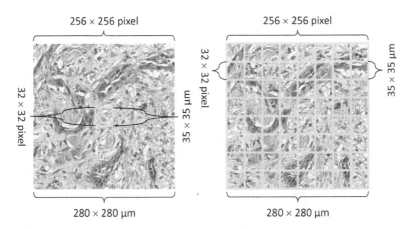

Fig. 3. Yellow boxes show the region to which label is assigned in a 32 × 32 window, where the left one shows the output label to be assigned using standard CNN while the right one shows the output to be assigned from coarse segmentation. (Color figure online)

Table 2. F1-score for patch-based classification and Coarse segmentation in HNSCC for patch size of 256 × 256

Method	k	Stride	F1-score
ResNet-50	$k = 32$	32	73.23
MobileNet	$k = 32$	32	74.78
DensetNet	$k = 32$	32	78.76
CSNet	$k = 32$	256	**83.11**

5.3   Inference Time Comparison

Simple performance based comparisons are not enough to show that our proposed CSNet is much better than the simple patch-based classification and pixel-wise segmentation until we compare the inference time for these methods. To compare the inference time for these approaches, we processed an entire WSI and calculated the total time in minutes as shown in Table 3. It can be seen that the simple CNN architecture DenseNet took 20 h to process a WSI because it has to assign a single label to 32 × 32 each windows which increases the time required to complete the WSI as compared to pixel-wise and the proposed CSNet where it took only 21 min and is 60× faster than the normal patch-based classification and 1.35× faster than the pixel-wise segmentation.

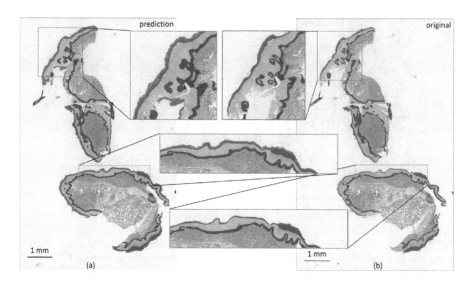

Fig. 4. a) shows the prediction overlay of coarse segmentation using our proposed CSNet model with mini-patch of size $k = 32$ as compared to **b)** which is pixel-wise ground truth overlaid on WSI. Red boxes shows some of the areas of false predictions while the green boxes shows some of the true predictions areas in the WSI (Color figure online)

Table 3. Inference time comparisons for different segmentation methods for processing one WSI

Method	Patch size	k	Stride	Prediction	Time (min)
DenseNet	256×256	256	32	1×1	1208.28
DeepLab-v3	512×512	1	512	512×512	27.47
CSNet	256×256	8	256	32×32	**20.98**

5.4   Downstream Tasks

Furthermore, the importance of coarse segmentation is incomplete without its applicability in real world problems. To elaborate, we performed two downstream analysis tasks, where precise segmentation for morphological or structural analysis is not required and an estimation of the tissue region should suffice.

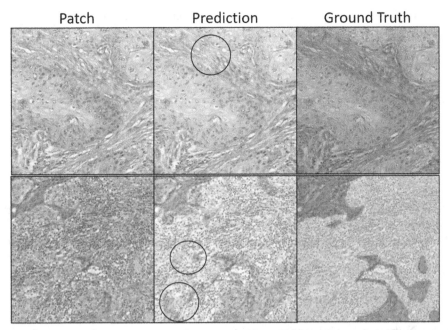

| Patch | Prediction | Ground Truth |

Red: Tumor | **Green**: Lymphocyte | **Blue**: Tumor-associated stroma

Fig. 5. Overlay of two visual fields from HNSCC internal data for coarse segmentation where ground truth is smoothed before overlaying for display. It can be seen that most of the tissue regions are being segmented correctly with some false predictions highlighted in black circles. (Color figure online)

OED Grading. In binary grading of OED, it is graded into high risk or low risk based on different architectural and cytological changes found in the oral epithelium [5]. For this purpose, we utilized the pixel-wise layer ground truth, DeepLab-v3 trained with pixel-wise and coarse segmentation and our proposed method predictions for epithelial layer segmentation. Hover-Net is used to segment nuclei from these layers and different morphological and spatial features were extracted to train a machine learning model on the extracted features. As can be seen in Table 4, comparable results were achieved using the coarse segmentation giving the F1-score of 67%, almost equal to that using the ground truth for OED grading with layer-wise nuclear features.

HNSCC Survival Analysis. We investigated the prognostic significance of the coarse segmentation based $TASIL_{score}$ [18] for disease specific survival analysis of HNSCC patients. Patients in the TCGA-HN cohort were divided into two groups based on the $TASIL_{score}$ using an optimal threshold value obtained from the analysis of the internal cohort. We found that the patient group with the higher $TASIL_{score}$ shows significantly longer disease specific survival (p = 0.00239, hazard ratio = 0.49, 95% confidence interval 0.30–0.78) in

Table 4. F1-score for OED grading using different segmentation methods

Method	Mini-patch k	F1-score
GT	-	68.0
DeepLab-v3	$k = 1$	**68.0**
DeepLab-v3	$k = 16$	68.0
DeepLab-v3	$k = 32$	67.0
CSNet	$k = 16$	66.0
CSNet	$k = 32$	67.0

the TCGA-HN cohort. The Kaplan-Meier curves along with the corresponding log-rank test based p-values are presented in Fig. 6. These curves show a clear separation between low- and high-risk patient groups when stratified using the $TASIL_{score}$.

6   Ablation Studies

6.1   Network Variations

Table 5 shows our network variations and their performance on patch-based classification of HNSCC dataset, as we have used DenseNet-121 for baseline of coarse segmentation network, which is further modified with additional skip connections between the dense blocks. The intuition was to increase the spatial context in the final output maps, which in return increases the overall accuracy of the network. As it can be seen that with the additional skip connections (SC) the F1-score of the model was improved by almost 4 points margin and to further justify the addition of SC, the network size was reduced to half as DenseNet-61 was used as baseline with skip connections and it can be seen that the smaller model still performs better than the larger DenseNet-121 by a margin of one point.

Table 5. Performance comparison of different network variants for coarse segmentation

Network	Variation	F1-score
CSNet-121	Standard	79.28
CSNet-121	Skip connections	**83.11**
CSNet-61	Skip connections	80.56

6.2   Mini-Patch Variation

Table 1 shows the variations in mini-patch k in our proposed CSNet where it can be seen that using bigger k doesn't affect the performance drastically as the

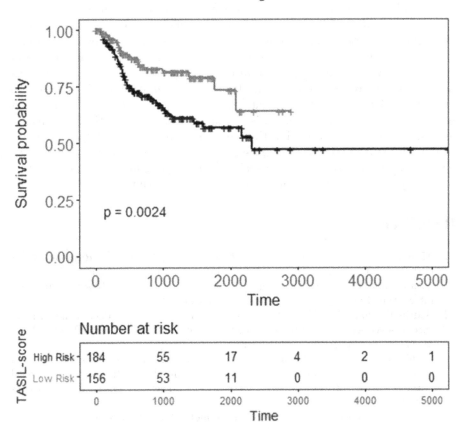

Fig. 6. TCGA HNSCC survival analysis using coarse segmentation based $TASIL_{score}$

difference is only of 1 point. Also, using a smaller mini-patch increases the performance due to the fact that there is less noise and more precise ground truth. Where as in pixel-wise segmentation model DeepLab-v3 the accuracy dropped by 2 points in using bigger mini-patch as compared to CSNet segmentation which shows that pixel-wise methods are not suitable for this coarse segmentation methods.

7   Conclusions

In this paper, we proposed a coarse segmentation method which offers a trade-off between context and accuracy in patch-based classification, and annotation and training time in pixel-wise segmentation. The proposed method, can employ simple CNN with additional skip connections where it leverages the skip connections to improve the spatial segmentation in the final prediction as compared to simple CNNs. The use of sparse loss further improves the training process by ignoring the non-annotated parts in the training images. Coarse segmentation takes an input of size $M \times N$ and outputs the prediction map of size $M/k \times N/k$. Our proposed method achieves superior performance in patch-based classification for HNSCC and as compared to pixel-wise segmentation in OED dataset as compared to its counterparts. To further prove the point of using coarse segmentation, we have used the output of coarse segmentation in two downstream analysis. In OED grading using nuclear features, we have found that CSNet worked comparable to the pixel-wise segmentation where in HNSCC survival analysis tasks, CSNet based TASIL-score shows prognostic significance for disease specific survival. In future, a possible direction is to extend the technique by using super-pixels instead of using simple $k \times k$ windows for coarse segmentation which may result in further improved segmentation results.

References

1. Alsubaie, N., Sirinukunwattana, K., Raza, S.E.A., Snead, D., Rajpoot, N.: A bottom-up approach for tumour differentiation in whole slide images of lung adenocarcinoma. In: Medical Imaging 2018: Digital Pathology, vol. 10581, p. 105810E. International Society for Optics and Photonics (2018)
2. Badrinarayanan, V., Kendall, A., Cipolla, R.: SegNet: a deep convolutional encoder-decoder architecture for image segmentation. IEEE Trans. Pattern Anal. Mach. Intell. **39**(12), 2481–2495 (2017)
3. Bashir, R.S., et al.: Automated grade classification of oral epithelial dysplasia using morphometric analysis of histology images. In: Medical Imaging 2020: Digital Pathology, vol. 11320, p. 1132011. International Society for Optics and Photonics (2020)
4. Chan, L., Hosseini, M.S., Rowsell, C., Plataniotis, K.N., Damaskinos, S.: HistosegNet: semantic segmentation of histological tissue type in whole slide images. In: Proceedings of the IEEE/CVF International Conference on Computer Vision, pp. 10662–10671 (2019)
5. El-Naggar, A.K., Chan, J.K.C., Grandis, J.R., Takata, T., Slootweg, P.J.: WHO classification of head and neck tumours. In: International Agency for Research on Cancer, January 2017. Google-Books-ID: EDo5MQAACAAJ
6. Gamper, J., Alemi Koohbanani, N., Benet, K., Khuram, A., Rajpoot, N.: PanNuke: an open pan-cancer histology dataset for nuclei instance segmentation and classification. In: Reyes-Aldasoro, C.C., Janowczyk, A., Veta, M., Bankhead, P., Sirinukunwattana, K. (eds.) ECDP 2019. LNCS, vol. 11435, pp. 11–19. Springer, Cham (2019). https://doi.org/10.1007/978-3-030-23937-4_2
7. Graham, S., et al.: Mild-net: minimal information loss dilated network for gland instance segmentation in colon histology images. Med. Image Anal. **52**, 199–211 (2019)
8. Graham, S., et al.: Hover-net: simultaneous segmentation and classification of nuclei in multi-tissue histology images. Med. Image Anal. **58**, 101563 (2019)
9. He, K., Zhang, X., Ren, S., Sun, J.: Deep residual learning for image recognition. In: Proceedings of the IEEE Conference on Computer Vision and Pattern Recognition, pp. 770–778 (2016)

10. Howard, A.G., et al.: MobileNets: efficient convolutional neural networks for mobile vision applications. arXiv preprint arXiv:1704.04861 (2017)
11. Huang, G., Liu, Z., Van Der Maaten, L., Weinberger, K.Q.: Densely connected convolutional networks. In: Proceedings of the IEEE Conference on Computer Vision and Pattern Recognition, pp. 4700–4708 (2017)
12. Kather, J.N., et al.: Deep learning can predict microsatellite instability directly from histology in gastrointestinal cancer. Nat. Med. **25**(7), 1054–1056 (2019)
13. Long, J., Shelhamer, E., Darrell, T.: Fully convolutional networks for semantic segmentation. In: Proceedings of the IEEE Conference on Computer Vision and Pattern Recognition, pp. 3431–3440 (2015)
14. Raza, S.E.A., et al.: Micro-net: a unified model for segmentation of various objects in microscopy images. Med. Image Anal. **52**, 160–173 (2019)
15. Ronneberger, O., Fischer, P., Brox, T.: U-net: convolutional networks for biomedical image segmentation. In: Navab, N., Hornegger, J., Wells, W.M., Frangi, A.F. (eds.) MICCAI 2015. LNCS, vol. 9351, pp. 234–241. Springer, Cham (2015). https://doi.org/10.1007/978-3-319-24574-4_28
16. Saltz, J., et al.: Spatial organization and molecular correlation of tumor-infiltrating lymphocytes using deep learning on pathology images. Cell Rep. **23**(1), 181–193 (2018)
17. Shaban, M., et al.: A novel digital score for abundance of tumour infiltrating lymphocytes predicts disease free survival in oral squamous cell carcinoma. Sci. Rep. **9**(1), 1–13 (2019)
18. Shaban, M., et al.: A digital score of tumour-associated stroma infiltrating lymphocytes predicts survival in head and neck squamous cell carcinoma. J. Pathol. **256**(2), 174–185 (2022). https://doi.org/10.1002/path.5819, https://onlinelibrary.wiley.com/doi/abs/10.1002/path.5819
19. Shaban, M., et al.: A digital score of tumour-associated stroma infiltrating lymphocytes predicts survival in head and neck squamous cell carcinoma. J. Pathol. **256**(2), 174–185 (2022)
20. Warnakulasuriya, S., Reibel, J., Bouquot, J., Dabelsteen, E.: Oral epithelial dysplasia classification systems: predictive value, utility, weaknesses and scope for improvement. J. Oral Pathol. Med. **37**(3), 127–133 (2008). https://doi.org/10.1111/j.1600-0714.2007.00584.x
21. Wilson, R., Knutsson, H.: Uncertainty and inference in the visual system. IEEE Trans. Syst. Man Cybern. **18**(2), 305–312 (1988)

Generative Adversarial Network, Transformer and New Models

How Effective is Adversarial Training of CNNs in Medical Image Analysis?

Yiming Xie[1] and Ahmed E. Fetit[1,2(✉)]

[1] Department of Computing, Imperial College London, London, UK
`a.fetit@imperial.ac.uk`
[2] UKRI Centre for Doctoral Training in Artificial Intelligence for Healthcare,
Imperial College London, London, UK

Abstract. Adversarial attacks are carefully crafted inputs that can deceive machine learning models into giving wrong results with seemingly high confidence. One approach that is commonly used in the image analysis literature to defend against such attacks is the introduction of adversarial images during training time, i.e. adversarial training. However, the effectiveness of adversarial training remains unclear in the healthcare domain, where the use of complex medical scans is crucial for a wide range of clinical workflows. In this paper, we carried out an empirical investigation into the effectiveness of adversarial training as a defence technique in the context of medical images. We demonstrated that adversarial training is, in principle, a transferable defence on medical imaging data, and that it can potentially be used on attacks previously unseen by the model. We also empirically showed that the strength of the attack, determined by the parameter ϵ, and the percentage of adversarial images included during training, have key influence over the level of success of the defence. Our analysis was carried out using 58,954 images from the publicly available MedNIST benchmarking dataset.

Keywords: Adversarial training · Robustness · CNNs · Medical image analysis

1 Introduction

Deep learning, a sub-domain of artificial intelligence (AI), has attracted much attention over the past few years. Several studies reported success in a range of medical imaging applications [19], e.g. in radiology [10,14,22], dermatology [6], ophthalmology [4] and pathology [3]. This led to the question of whether machines may be able to take partial responsibility in image characterisation workflows, and in the wider healthcare sector in general. However, the phenomenon of *adversarial attacks* has exposed some potential problems with state-of-the-art deep neural networks [9]. Adversarial attacks are carefully crafted inputs that can be used to deceive deep networks into giving wrong results with seemingly high confidence. The existence of such attacks highlights the fact that

© The Author(s), under exclusive license to Springer Nature Switzerland AG 2022
G. Yang et al. (Eds.): MIUA 2022, LNCS 13413, pp. 443–457, 2022.
https://doi.org/10.1007/978-3-031-12053-4_33

deep learning models tend to rely on brittle and easily perturbed features to make predictions; a by-product of optimisation mechanisms used in neural networks. This, in turn, raises serious safety concerns about deploying deep learning models into applications that require high levels of safety, such as healthcare. Recent work showed that adversarial attacks are able to manipulate deep learning models used in medical applications; for instance, it was shown by Ma et al. [20] that medical images are easier targets than natural images due to their complex biological textures and the inner workings of convolutional neural networks (CNNs).

According to the NHS Counter Fraud Authority, £17.3 m worth of fraud were detected only in 2019–2020 [24]. AI algorithms may eventually be used by healthcare systems around the world to help automate all types of workflows, from diagnosis to medical reimbursement and pharmaceutical approvals, which could present new windows of vulnerabilities for attackers to imperceptibly earn illegal profits or cause societal harm [9]. Crucially, implementing deep learning-based AI models without well established defences and safeguards can also leave patients exposed to hazardous situations, such as incorrect disease characterisation [17], e.g. by selectively perturbing borderline cases that are not easy to review [8]. Noteworthy, the algorithmic challenges presented by adversarial attacks are compounded in healthcare settings, such as medical imaging workflows. For instance, health information systems across the world are difficult to update [8], so new safeguards can be challenging to roll out swiftly when an attack is suspected. Therefore, we argue that a robust defense strategy needs to already be in place before AI models can be safely deployed in routine clinical practice. In this regard, it is crucial for the medical image analysis community to be aware of the potential vulnerabilities of deep learning models and to develop suitable safeguards against adversarial attacks.

In this paper, we take a step towards understanding how to build an effective algorithmic defence to mitigate against adversarial attacks in medical settings, and study the effectiveness of adversarial training as a suitable defence for medical imaging CNNs. Specifically, our main contributions are:

i) We show that adversarial training is a transferable technique that can mitigate against attacks not previously seen by the model. To the best of our knowledge, the transferability of adversarial training has not been previously studied in the medical image analysis literature.

ii) We investigate ϵ, the parameter that determines the level of perturbation in an attack, and show that the effectiveness of a defence against an attack's ϵ at test time is directly related to the ϵ used during adversarial training. The relationship between the training and attacking ϵ's is an important empirical question as it determines the robustness of adversarial training as a reliable defence on medical data.

iii) Finally, we explore the extent to which the percentage of adversarial perturbed images in the training set can affect the performance at test time.

2   Related Work

In 2014, early work by Szegedy et al. [27] investigated the effects of introducing small perturbations to the input data of a deep learning model, i.e. adversarial attacks. Several experiments were carried out on non-medical datasets such as MNIST [15] and ImageNet [5], and the paper concluded that adversarial samples were possible to generate for any of the samples that were chosen. Additionally, the paper showed that adversarial samples were able to deceive the original networks to result in an incorrect classification; this happened regardless of the chosen hyper-parameters, network architectures or initial weights. Moreover, even when trained with disjoint training sets, the attacks still resulted in models misclassifying the adversarial examples.

Another interesting line of research looks into directly applying attacks on physical objects. In 2017, Eykholt et al. [7] introduced Robust Physical Perturbations, which if placed on real-world road traffic signs can consistently deceive deep learning-based classifiers. The underlying algorithm takes in a target input, models the physical dynamics (viewing distances and angles), and then generates noise in the form of object-constrained poster attacks or graffiti-shaped perturbations. This algorithm was applied on two datasets: LISA, a US traffic sign dataset [23] as well as the German Traffic Sign Recognition Benchmark (GTSRB) dataset [26] and was highly effective in generating physical perturbations.

In the medical image analysis literature, Paschali et al. [25] were amongst the first to study the adversarial attacks phenomenon. Their work investigated skin lesion classification and brain segmentation tasks with deep neural networks such as Inception and UNet, and showed that models that achieve comparable generalisability performance may have significant variations in the underlying data manifold, leading to an extensive performance gap in their robustness. Other research in the medical image analysis community looked into detecting the presence of adversarial attacks on medical scans. For instance, Li et al. [17] proposed an unsupervised learning approach that is capable of detecting a wide range of adversarial attacks in chest X-rays without sacrificing performance.

With regards to exploring defence techniques, a study by Li et al. [18] looked into the impact of adversarial perturbations in the specific problem of predicting an individual's age based on a 3D brain MRI scan. The authors investigated two models: a standard deep neural network, and a hybrid deep learning model which additionally uses features informed by anatomical context. The results highlighted the weakness of conventional neural networks against adversarial attacks, and suggested that hybrid models informed by context can be more robust to adversarial perturbations than conventional networks. Other ways to defend against adversarial attacks in medical images include the work by Taghanaki et al., [28] which proposed the use of radial basis mapping kernels to transform features onto a manifold where the effects of perturbations can be alleviated.

More relevant to this paper is the area of adversarial training [21]. Compared to the standard training set-up where the classifier aims to minimise the loss on 'clean' data, adversarial training essentially introduces the worst-case scenario around the original data distribution at the training stage [11]. This can be achieved by simply using both clean and adversarial samples in the training stage. However, despite the differences between natural images and medical scans, the effectiveness of adversarial training and the factors of a successful defence are understudied in the medical context, which inspired this paper. Recently, Li et al. [16] proposed a framework that makes use of semi-supervised adversarial training, and tested it on a large, publicly available retinal imaging dataset. The reported results are encouraging as they showed that a model's adversarial robustness can be improved without compromising performance.

3   Materials and Methods

3.1   Dataset

The dataset used is the large, publicly available benchmarking MedNIST [1], which contains 6 classes: 10,000 Abdomen CT, 8,954 Breast MRI, 10,000 Chest X-Ray, 10,000 Chest CT, 10,000 Hand and 10,000 Head CT images. The dataset was randomly split into 3 parts: 46,946 (80%) images for training, 6,022 (10%) for validation and 5,986 (10%) images for testing. Augmentation was carried out on the training data (random rotation, random flip and random zoom) to amplify the variation within the dataset.

3.2   CNN Model and Adversarial Attacks

In terms of architecture, we used a CNN model based on the DenseNet-121 implementation available from the MONAI library [2]. It consists of four dense blocks, each containing different numbers of 1×1 and 3×3 convolution layers. DenseNet was chosen as it can help reduce the effects of vanishing gradient problems; it also has relatively few parameters and hence little training time is required [12]. Given that the classes in the dataset are very well balanced, classification accuracy was used as the evaluation metric. Throughout this paper, we made use of commonly studied attacks: Fast Gradient Sign Method (FGSM) [11] and Projected Gradient Descent (PGD) [21]. To facilitate reproducibility, we made the code publicly available via Github.

3.3   Experiments

When implementing adversarial attacks, an important parameter, ϵ, which indicates the extent to which the images are perturbed, is defined. Intuitively, the higher the value, the more noise will be allowed in the input, and the worse the performance of the model will be (e.g. Fig. 1). We carried out a series of experiments to investigate the effectiveness of adversarial training on medical images, see the extent to which it is a transferable defence technique, and identify the role of training ϵ and percentage of adversarial examples in the training set.

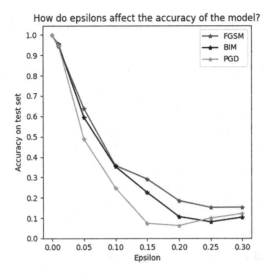

Fig. 1. Accuracy of a standard model against perturbed test sets (varying ϵ). Three attacks were used here to generate the perturbations: Fast Gradient Sign Method (FGSM) [11], Projected Gradient Descent (PGD) [21], and Basic Iterative Method (BIM) [13]

(a) Transferability of adversarial training. We carried out an initial test to evaluate the performances of an adversarially trained model and the standard model against the same FGSM-perturbed test set. We then tested the transferability of adversarial training as a defence technique. In [27], Szegedy et al. demonstrated that adversarial samples can be transferable, in the sense that if a sample can deceive one model, it can probably deceive a similar model that is performing the same task. This led us to the question of whether adversarial training is a transferable defence technique in medical imaging settings. In other words, if a model is trained using only one type of attack, would that be sufficient against a test set perturbed with other attacks? If training using one attack can improve the robustness of the model against previously unseen attacks, this would be useful in practical settings when the exact type of attacks are unknown or difficult to predict. In this regard, two subsequent tests were designed:

- Testing an FGSM-trained model against a PGD-perturbed test set.
- Testing a PGD-trained model against an FGSM perturbed test set.

(b) The role of ϵ when carrying out adversarial training. An important component of adversarial attacks is the value of ϵ used on the test set, which determines the severity of perturbation on the images. In this experiment, we investigate the relationship between the attack's ϵ at test time and the training ϵ, i.e. the value used when carrying out adversarial training. Intuitively, when adversarial training is used as a defence, the model **trained** with a higher ϵ may demonstrate a higher level of robustness because it has seen and adjusted to the 'most serious' attacks; but is this the case? Or is any **training** ϵ acceptable as long as some adversarial samples are present in the training set? To investigate how the ϵ in the training stage can affect the robustness against adversarial attacks, four further tests were designed and implemented as follows:

- FGSM-trained model against FGSM-perturbed test set.
- FGSM-trained model against PGD-perturbed test set.
- PGD-trained model against PGD-perturbed test set.
- PGD-trained model against FGSM-perturbed test set.

For each test, we trained a total of 7 models using the attack with $\epsilon = \{0, 0.05, 0.1, 0.15, 0.2, 0.25, 0.3\}$. These 7 models were tested against 7 test sets, each is perturbed with the same set of ϵ as above. The best performing ϵ from the perspective of the test set was selected, and the relationship between training and testing ϵ was investigated.

(c) Percentage of adversarial samples in training. The work of Christian et al. [27] suggested that mixing adversarial examples with clean images in the training set can improve the robustness of the model against attacks. However, it was not clear what percentage of adversarial samples is sufficient for a good defence. After finding the best training ϵ under each setting, we looked into the extent to which percentage matters in medical imaging settings.

In this experiment, the training and testing attacks were fixed to FGSM, and the ϵ values that resulted the best in the experiment above were picked and listed below. For each test, 10 models were trained, each with 0% to 100% of images perturbed in the training set. The following ϵ values were used:

- ϵ of 0.1 for training and 0.05 for testing.
- ϵ of 0.15 for training and 0.1 for testing.
- ϵ of 0.2 for training and 0.15 for testing.
- ϵ of 0.2 for training and 0.2 for testing.
- ϵ of 0.25 for training and 0.25 for testing.
- ϵ of 0.3 for training and 0.3 for testing.

4   Results and Discussion

(a) Transferability of adversarial training. Figure 2 show that the initial adversarially trained models were, in principle, more robust than standard models when facing attacks (e.g. overall accuracy was boosted from 35.75% to 94.05%). From the results, the FGSM-trained model achieved an accuracy of 79.3% while facing a PGD-perturbed test set, which shows that it did reasonably well (Table 1). This suggests that it was able to deal with the PGD-perturbed test set even though no PGD-related noise was involved in the training phase. Similarly, the findings also apply the other way around as the PGD-trained model could successfully classify images perturbed by FGSM, achieving an 86% accuracy. We further compared the results between four different permutations

(Fig. 3). When the training method and testing method were the same, the overall performances across all metrics were better than the ones with different methods. With the cross methods set-up, the model trained with FGSM was performing slightly worse than the one trained with PGD. One possible reason for this is that PGD is a stronger attack compared to FGSM, and the model only managed to find an optimal parameter for the weaker attack. However, both cross method set-ups were doing reasonably well, showing that a good level of transferability did indeed exist. This may have been facilitated by the fact that both FGSM and PGD are first-order attacks, and that they are relying on the same basic idea of gradient perturbation.

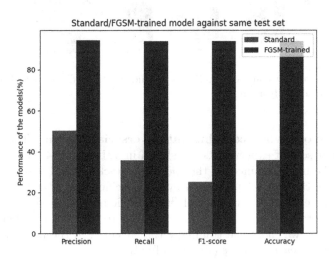

Fig. 2. Performance of a standard model & an FGSM-trained model ($\epsilon = 0.1$) on an FGSM-perturbed test set ($\epsilon = 0.1$).

Table 1. Performance (in percentages) of a FGSM-trained model on a PGD-attacked test set.

	Precision	Recall	F1-score	Accuracy
Abdomen CT	99.32	56.59	72.10	
Breast MRI	68.88	76.37	72.43	
Chest X-Ray	98.30	93.72	95.95	79.30
Chest CT	61.10	96.71	74.89	
Hand	80.82	97.62	88.43	
Head CT	92.98	56.76	70.49	

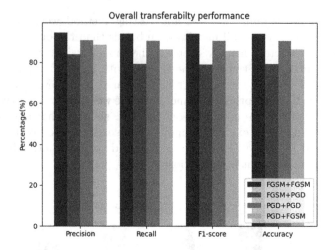

Fig. 3. Transferability comparison. Figure legend corresponds to 'attack used when training' + 'attack at test time'.

(b) The role of ϵ when carrying out adversarial training. The accuracies from the four sets of experiments are shown in Tables 2, 3, 4 and 5. Each row represents the model trained by the specified attack method and ϵ, while each column shows the test set perturbed by the specified attack and ϵ. The values within the table show the accuracy of that specific model's performance against the attack represented by the column. In order to find the best performing ϵ against attacks, we chose the training ϵ that resulted in the best classification accuracy against each attack ϵ (shown in bold).

Table 2. Classification accuracy values (in percentages) obtained when FGSM is used for both training and testing.

		FGSM test ϵ						
		0.0	0.05	0.10	0.15	0.20	0.25	0.3
FGSM training ϵ	0.0	**99.87**	67.56	41.00	24.71	22.35	22.65	21.63
	0.05	99.68	96.21	76.98	51.22	37.99	21.90	19.23
	0.10	97.79	**98.18**	92.15	70.01	51.24	36.62	26.53
	0.15	84.96	80.82	**98.38**	95.62	81.16	63.45	45.11
	0.20	73.99	55.78	82.49	**96.86**	**94.00**	81.82	68.11
	0.25	62.55	52.77	58.62	91.78	85.60	**90.61**	78.22
	0.30	54.94	38.99	51.75	63.85	87.05	80.59	**80.76**

We also visualised the patterns of how models trained with different ϵ values responded to attacks with different levels of ϵ in the test set when using FGSM

Table 3. Classification accuracy values (in percentages) obtained when FGSM is used for training and PGD is used for testing.

		PGD test ϵ						
		0.0	0.05	0.10	0.15	0.20	0.25	0.3
	0.0	**99.82**	55.76	23.92	17.12	14.57	03.81	00.50
	0.05	99.67	94.75	62.63	43.55	26.33	18.04	17.27
FGSM training ϵ	0.10	94.42	**97.03**	89.53	53.79	44.62	30.09	20.35
	0.15	82.81	78.75	**90.13**	57.55	45.69	39.36	25.81
	0.20	72.65	51.10	79.97	71.45	40.96	27.71	27.18
	0.25	60.91	40.56	45.91	**82.59**	64.15	43.34	29.20
	0.30	60.57	41.06	38.72	48.55	**78.57**	**56.36**	**33.88**

Table 4. Classification accuracy values (in percentages) obtained when PGD is used for both training and testing.

		PGD test ϵ						
		0.0	0.05	0.10	0.15	0.20	0.25	0.3
	0.0	**99.85**	55.21	22.59	17.02	07.62	00.57	02.86
	0.05	99.26	**94.52**	68.88	44.20	26.18	18.93	17.27
PGD training ϵ	0.10	97.74	93.59	88.67	73.05	54.61	43.87	33.29
	0.15	97.73	94.37	**89.51**	81.31	70.95	54.16	36.10
	0.20	95.56	91.45	87.24	82.28	76.04	68.11	52.12
	0.25	92.08	89.01	85.98	83.36	**80.34**	**75.94**	**68.08**
	0.30	92.62	89.63	87.17	**83.93**	79.52	74.27	66.78

(Fig. 4; both of the attack methods used when training and testing were FGSM). The x-axis shows the training ϵ while the y-axis shows the accuracy obtained against a particular test set, specified in the title of the corresponding sub-plot. To illustrate, in the first sub-plot, 7 models trained with $\epsilon = \{$ 0.0, 0.05, 0.1, 0.15, 0.2, 0.25, 0.3$\}$ are tested against the test set perturbed by 0.05. The best performing model is highlighted by the dot, in this case, the model trained with $\epsilon = 0.1$ performed best when facing an $\epsilon = 0.05$ in the test set.

It is clear from the results that the choice of ϵ at training is crucial. The best performing models were usually trained using ϵ that was greater than or equal to the attack's ϵ, and the differences between them were in the range of 0 to 0.1, which suggests the training ϵ ought to be close to attack's ϵ at test time. This observation applies to both FGSM and PGD perturbed test sets, thanks to the transferability shown in the previous experiment.

The models trained using PGD showed a slightly different behaviour. The best performing training ϵ's were still mostly within the range of 0 to 0.1 from the attacking ϵ, except for one case where the PGD-trained model with $\epsilon = 0.3$ performed the best against the PGD-0.15-perturbed test set. However, what

Table 5. Classification accuracy values (in percentages) obtained when PGD is used for training and FGSM is used for testing.

		FGSM test ϵ						
		0.0	0.05	0.10	0.15	0.20	0.25	0.3
	0.0	**99.45**	55.18	33.43	23.55	22.10	24.31	24.74
	0.05	99.30	94.24	74.06	56.10	34.75	21.17	18.24
PGD training ϵ	0.10	98.56	96.07	92.00	85.32	72.90	61.83	51.52
	0.15	98.53	**96.44**	94.05	90.21	84.03	71.47	56.05
	0.20	98.18	95.74	**95.26**	**94.15**	**92.38**	**88.01**	**80.04**
	0.25	57.78	50.52	49.01	71.65	76.68	74.69	68.48
	0.30	54.36	47.49	46.41	49.01	64.97	64.88	59.89

is different from the FGSM models was that with PGD-trained models, it was possible to have the training ϵ at a lower value than the attack ϵ and still perform well, e.g. the case where $\epsilon = 0.2$ was used for training and $\epsilon = 0.3$ was used in the attack. In addition, when the attack ϵ is greater or equal to 0.15, the best training ϵ were almost fixed to 0.25 and 0.2 respectively.

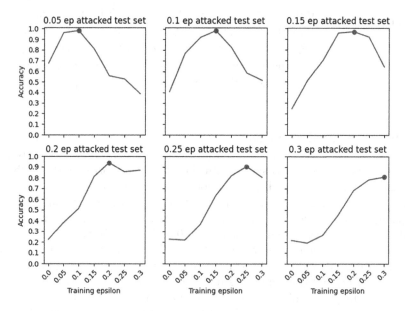

Fig. 4. The performance of models trained with different values of ϵ when tested on test sets perturbed with different levels of severity. FGSM attacks were used when training and testing.

Figure 5 illustrates the relationships between the test time ϵ and the best performing training ϵ across all four permutations. The overall trend is that the higher the test time ϵ, the higher the training ϵ needed for optimal defence. In other words, the stronger the attack at test time, the higher the training ϵ needs to be to better defend against the attacks, regardless of the attack. In summary, training ϵ matters a lot while defending against adversarial attacks, and it is strongly related to the test time ϵ, with optimal defence achieved within 0–0.1 of the attack.

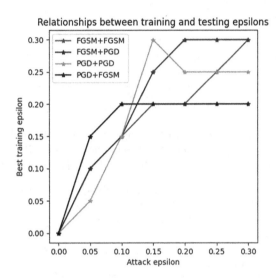

Fig. 5. The relationships between the attack's ϵ at test time and the best performing training ϵ. The legend corresponds to 'training method + attack method'.

(c) Percentage of adversarial samples in training: Accuracies from all the settings are summarised in Fig. 6. When the test set was perturbed by ϵ 0.05 (blue line), any percentages above 30% gave excellent results (above 90% accuracy). However, when higher ϵ (stronger attacks) were applied, we observed an interesting behaviour. For the model trained with ϵ of 0.15, the performance fluctuated a lot around 60% accuracy, when the number of adversarial images in the training set was lower than 100%. Similarly, all the other models achieved around 40% accuracy when the percentages of adversarial images in the training set were below 100%. However, the performance boosted to over 90% accuracy, by increasing the adversarial sample numbers to 100% of the training set. This was a common pattern across 5 of the 6 models; when the entire training set was perturbed (i.e. 100% on the x-axis), the observed accuracy showed a sharp increase (Fig. 6).

It may be argued that the cause of this boost in performance was the fact that the **test set** was also 100% perturbed, leading to the training and test

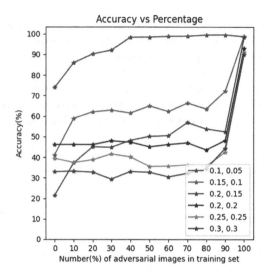

Fig. 6. The relationships between the percentage of adversarial samples in the training set and the classification accuracy on the test set. The test set is 100% perturbed. The figure legend corresponds to 'training ϵ, attack ϵ'. (Color figure online)

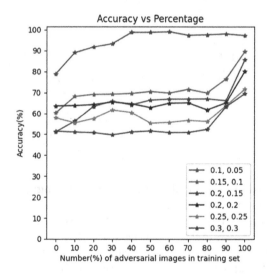

Fig. 7. The relationships between the percentage of adversarial samples in the training set and the classification accuracy on the test set, but the test set is only 50% perturbed. The figure legend corresponds to 'training ϵ, attack ϵ'. (Color figure online)

distributions being highly similar. Hence, we extended the experiment with only 50% of the test set perturbed to see if the test result changed. Interestingly, when the test set was only perturbed by 50%, the same pattern emerged (Fig. 7). When the attack was light (i.e. $\epsilon = 0.05$), all percentages above 10% showed excellent performance (blue line). This time it seemed that perturbing 40% to 60% of the training set actually gives the best performance instead of 100%, but the differences were fairly subtle. All the other models fluctuated between approx. 50–60% accuracy when the adversarial sample percentages were below 90%, then experienced a sharp increase after more than 90% of the samples in the training set were perturbed. Finally, all models apart from the weakest attack setting (blue line) achieved the best performance when the training set was 100% perturbed with adversarial samples.

5 Conclusion

In this paper, we explored a number of ways in which adversarial attacks can interact with deep learning models in the medical imaging domain, with focus on setting up a defence to make CNNs more robust. One of the most popular defence strategies, adversarial training, was explored in depth. We demonstrated its effectiveness on the publicly available MedNIST dataset, and used it to set up a fairly robust initial model. We also demonstrated that there is clear transferability across attacks, where a model that was trained on data perturbed using one method was successfully applied against other unseen attacks.

A key, novel finding of this paper is on the relationship between training and attacking ϵ, where we empirically showed that the training ϵ needs to be within 0.1 of the attack's ϵ for optimal robustness. Additionally, the question of whether the percentage of adversarial samples in the training set matters for the accuracy was explored, and the result suggested that it was indeed important; in most cases the completely perturbed training set resulted in the best performances.

Nevertheless, the generalisation of our observations ought to be further investigated with different test settings, including different model architectures and more sophisticated attacks. The use of the public MedNIST dataset in this paper establishes an empirical proof of principle using a fairly large number of samples (58,954), but the effectiveness of adversarial training remains unexplored on realistic data or practical clinical settings (e.g. diagnosing pathologies or rare diseases), as opposed to classifying the imaging modality. Moreover, the performance on other medical imaging paradigms like histopathology remains an open question. Importantly, even though adversarial training was shown to be effective, adversarial attacks are constantly and rapidly evolving in complexity and capability, and current successful defences are likely to be broken by future methods. Hence, it is important for the medical image analysis community to be aware of this vulnerability when designing AI models for healthcare applications.

Acknowledgment. The work of Dr Ahmed E. Fetit was supported by the UK Research and Innovation Centre for Doctoral Training in Artificial Intelligence for Healthcare under Grant EP/S023283/1.

References

1. Medical Image Classification Using the MedNIST Dataset. https://colab.research. google.com/github/abhaysrivastav/Pytorch/blob/master/MedNIST.ipynb

2. MONAI: Medical Open Network for AI. https://monai.io/
3. Bar, Y., Diamant, I., Wolf, L., Lieberman, S., Konen, E., Greenspan, H.: Chest pathology detection using deep learning with non-medical training. In: 2015 IEEE 12th International Symposium on Biomedical Imaging, ISBI, pp. 294–297 (2015)
4. De Fauw, J., et al.: Clinically applicable deep learning for diagnosis and referral in retinal disease. Nat. Med. **24**(9), 1342–1350 (2018)
5. Deng, J., Dong, W., Socher, R., Li, L.J., Li, K., Fei-Fei, L.: ImageNet: a large-scale hierarchical image database. In: 2009 IEEE Conference on Computer Vision and Pattern Recognition, pp. 248–255. IEEE (2009)
6. Esteva, A., Kuprel, B., Novoa, R.A., Ko, J., Swetter, S.M., Blau, H.M., Thrun, S.: Dermatologist-level classification of skin cancer with deep neural networks. Nature **542**(7639), 115–118 (2017)
7. Eykholt, K., et al.: Robust physical-world attacks on deep learning visual classification. In: Proceedings of the IEEE Conference on Computer Vision and Pattern Recognition, pp. 1625–1634 (2018)
8. Finlayson, S.G., Bowers, J.D., Ito, J., Zittrain, J.L., Beam, A.L., Kohane, I.S.: Adversarial attacks on medical machine learning. Science **363**(6433), 1287–1289 (2019)
9. Finlayson, S.G., Chung, H.W., Kohane, I.S., Beam, A.L.: Adversarial attacks against medical deep learning systems. arXiv preprint arXiv:1804.05296 (2018)
10. Gale, W., Oakden-Rayner, L., Carneiro, G., Bradley, A.P., Palmer, L.J.: Detecting hip fractures with radiologist-level performance using deep neural networks. arXiv preprint arXiv:1711.06504 (2017)
11. Goodfellow, I., Shlens, J., Szegedy, C.: Explaining and harnessing adversarial examples. In: International Conference on Learning Representations (2015)
12. Huang, G., Liu, Z., van der Maaten, L., Weinberger, K.Q.: Densely connected convolutional networks. In: Proceedings of the IEEE Conference on Computer Vision and Pattern Recognition, CVPR (2017)
13. Kurakin, A., Goodfellow, I.J., Bengio, S.: Adversarial examples in the physical world. In: Artificial Intelligence Safety and Security, pp. 99–112. Chapman and Hall/CRC (2018)
14. Lakhani, P., Sundaram, B.: Deep learning at chest radiography: automated classification of pulmonary tuberculosis by using convolutional neural networks. Radiology **284**(2), 574–582 (2017)
15. LeCun, Y., Cortes, C., Burges, C.: The MNIST database of handwritten digits. http://yann.lecun.com/exdb/mnist/
16. Li, X., Pan, D., Zhu, D.: Defending against adversarial attacks on medical imaging AI system, classification or detection? In: 2021 IEEE 18th International Symposium on Biomedical Imaging, ISBI, pp. 1677–1681. IEEE (2021)
17. Li, X., Zhu, D.: Robust detection of adversarial attacks on medical images. In: 2020 IEEE 17th International Symposium on Biomedical Imaging, ISBI, pp. 1154–1158. IEEE (2020)
18. Li, Y., Zhang, H., Bermudez, C., Chen, Y., Landman, B.A., Vorobeychik, Y.: Anatomical context protects deep learning from adversarial perturbations in medical imaging. Neurocomputing **379**, 370–378 (2020)
19. Liu, X., et al.: A comparison of deep learning performance against health-care professionals in detecting diseases from medical imaging: a systematic review and meta-analysis. Lancet Dig. Health **1**(6), e271–e297 (2019)
20. Ma, X.: Understanding adversarial attacks on deep learning based medical image analysis systems. Pattern Recogn. **110**, 107332 (2021)

21. Madry, A., Makelov, A., Schmidt, L., Tsipras, D., Vladu, A.: Towards deep learning models resistant to adversarial attacks. In: International Conference on Learning Representations, ICLR (2018)
22. McKinney, S.M., et al.: International evaluation of an AI system for breast cancer screening. Nature **577**(7788), 89–94 (2020)
23. Møgelmose, A., Trivedi, M.M., Moeslund, T.B.: Vision-based traffic sign detection and analysis for intelligent driver assistance systems: perspectives and survey. IEEE Trans. Intell. Transp. Syst. **13**(4), 1484–1497 (2012)
24. NHS Counter Fraud Authority: NHS Counter Fraud Authority Annual Report & Accounts 19–20. https://www.gov.uk/government/publications/nhs-counter-fraud-authority-annual-report-and-accounts-2019-to-2020
25. Paschali, M., Conjeti, S., Navarro, F., Navab, N.: Generalizability *vs.* robustness: investigating medical imaging networks using adversarial examples. In: Frangi, A.F., Schnabel, J.A., Davatzikos, C., Alberola-López, C., Fichtinger, G. (eds.) MICCAI 2018. LNCS, vol. 11070, pp. 493–501. Springer, Cham (2018). https://doi.org/10.1007/978-3-030-00928-1_56
26. Stallkamp, J., Schlipsing, M., Salmen, J., Igel, C.: Man vs. computer: benchmarking machine learning algorithms for traffic sign recognition. Neural Netw. **32**, 323–332 (2012)
27. Szegedy, C., et al.: Intriguing properties of neural networks. In: 2nd International Conference on Learning Representations, ICLR (2014)
28. Taghanaki, S.A., Abhishek, K., Azizi, S., Hamarneh, G.: A kernelized manifold mapping to diminish the effect of adversarial perturbations. In: Proceedings of the IEEE/CVF Conference on Computer Vision and Pattern Recognition, CVPR, pp. 11340–11349 (2019)

A U-Net Based Progressive GAN for Microscopic Image Augmentation

Qifan Zhou[ID] and Hujun Yin[(✉)][ID]

The University of Manchester, Manchester M13 9PL, UK
qifan.zhou@postgrad.manchester.ac.uk, hujun.yin@manchester.ac.uk

Abstract. Dealing with limited medical imagery data by deep neural networks is of a great concern. Obtaining large-scale labelled images requires expertise, is laborious and time consuming, and remains a challenge in medical applications. In this paper, we present a data augmentation method to cope with scarcely available medical imagery data. We propose a U-Net based generative adversarial network to synthesise microscopic images. We adopt a progressive training strategy to guide the synthesising process at multiple resolutions. This also stabilises the training process. The proposed model has been tested on three public datasets and quantitatively evaluated in terms of classification, detection and segmentation performances. Results suggest that training with the proposed augmentation method can provide significant improvements on limited and imbalanced datasets.

Keywords: Data augmentation · Generative adversarial network · Microscopy

1 Introduction

In modern medicine, measurement and diagnostic data is being generated in massive quantities and has become more prevalent than ever [28]. One of the greatest challenges accompanied is how to cope with limited and imbalanced datasets when employing deep learning techniques [5,17,20]. Usually, for supervised learning, a well-performed model requires ample annotated samples from various different classes. Yet in most medical imaging tasks, it is hard if not impossible to collect a large and balanced dataset due to rare presence of certain disease phenotype and patient privacy. To acquire annotated data is another issue that requires expert knowledge or trained physicians. While there are some public datasets available, the majority of them are inadequate and inter-class imbalanced. More severely, those datasets are specific to the targeted problems and have poor transferability even if fine-tuning is considered [2].

To overcome these challenges, researchers have attempted to take advantage of data augmentation, a widely used technique in machine learning. Imagery data augmentation has been proved effective to improve the performance of deep networks for computer vision tasks. After a series of random changes to

G. Yang et al. (Eds.): MIUA 2022, LNCS 13413, pp. 458–468, 2022.
https://doi.org/10.1007/978-3-031-12053-4_34

images, training set is expanded. Such operations allow deep models to be less reliant on certain attributes, hence avoiding over-fitting problems. Basic augmentation algorithms include geometric transformation, changing image colours, mosaic and mixing images. However, these traditional methods do not perform image synthesis, which is increasingly achieved by generative adversarial networks (GANs) [8], especially when there are insufficient samples available [26]. GANs benefit from the adversarial learning strategy, thereby producing natural and realistic images that can be hardly distinguishable from real images. Using GANs for image augmentation has become a popular means in medical image analysis.

In this paper, we propose a U-Net [25] based GAN architecture for image synthesis. We aim to tackle issues of limited and imbalanced datasets. Our generator follows the structure of U-Net, hence the generated images are guided to be similar to the input images with the help of the discriminator. We adopt a progressive growing approach [12] to generate high-quality images at multiple resolutions. We test and evaluate the proposed method on three different microscopic image datasets on their performance in image synthesis, classification, detection and segmentation.

2   Related Work

2.1   GANs for Image Synthesis

GAN leverages the power of discriminative models, e.g. classifiers and regressors, to obtain good generative models. The groundbreaking work of GAN is credited to Goodfellow [8]. Controlled by the discriminative model, the generative model takes random vectors and outputs synthetic data which resembles the distribution of the training data. The discriminative model, i.e. a discriminator, uses fully connected layers to decide whether the synthetic data is real or fake. Deep Convolutional GAN (DCGAN) [24] replaced the fully connected layers with deeper architectures which are composed of convolution and transposed convolution layers to achieve better performance. Since then such deep architectures have been commonly used in many GANs. However, in the original GAN, one cannot control what to be generated since the input is random noise. Conditional GAN (cGAN) [23] was proposed to add a condition to the input random noise so that the output could be defined. Usually, the condition can be a class of images, as a result of this, one-to-one mappings from input to output can be guided by these conditional images. VAE-GAN [16] is another clever GAN architecture which achieves one-to-one mappings between input and output images. It combines the variational auto-encoder (VAE) whose decoder acts as a generator with a discriminator. By converting the input into a latent code, and then reconstructing it, a loss between the original input and the reconstructed output makes the mapping possible. This kind of architecture can also alleviate the model collapse problem [8], from which GANs usually suffer.

Apart from those basic GANs, Progressive GAN [12] is worth mentioning. To obtain high resolution images, Progressive GAN begins with training a 4×4

generator and discriminator, and eventually ends at the resolution of 1024×1024. This gradual approach allows the model to learn in a coarse-to-fine way and stabilises the training to obtain more reliable images. On this basis, StyleGAN [14] adopts the progressive learning strategy to enrich details for high resolution images. StyleGAN generates new images with weighted styles from the original images. The synthetic images are perceptually similar to the real ones.

2.2   Medical Image Augmentation

Deep learning in medical image analysis and classification often encounters the problem that medical image datasets are typically limited. For classification tasks, scarce and imbalanced data can lead to poor generalisation of a developed model and unsuitable for application. For detection and segmentation tasks, the limitation mainly reflects in scarce annotations where only limited annotated data is available for training [27]. Labeling medical images is a time-consuming work and requires expert knowledge and experience. Data augmentation is one of the effective techniques to alleviate these problems.

Mikołajczyk et al. [22] surveyed traditional augmentation methods such as affine transformations and colour transformations on skin lesion images. Such methods are easy to implement, but do not bring any new attributes or samples to the datasets. They also analysed deep learning methods such as style transfer and GANs. Despite high computation costs, GANs can give satisfying results by increasing the training data size. Frid-Adar et al. [7] modified DCGAN [24] and applied such a scheme to synthesise lesion images. Their augmentation method increased sensitivity by 7.1% and specificity by 4.0% for lesion classification. Zhao et al. [32] used the U-Net architecture to learn the transform models between labeled and unlabeled magnetic resonance imaging (MRI) images. They employed this model to synthesise new labeled images, resulting in higher Dice score [3] on testsets. The Nvidia Labs [13] proposed an adaptive discriminator augmentation mechanism with their latest StyleGAN2 [15]. They improved Fréchet inception distance (FID) [10] score with limited data. However, all these methods share the same problem: one-to-one mapping, i.e. one cannot control what to generate due to random vectors as inputs. Although GANs are capable of fitting the distribution of training data, new data that has been generated may not be what we want, and this, from a medical application perspective, is undesirable.

3   U-Net Based Progressive GAN

We take advantage of an encoder-decoder structure to guide the training process. Our inputs are now source images from the dataset instead of random vectors. In this way, the synthetic images would be perceptually similar to the inputs rather than random projections from uncertain vectors. In general, we use U-Net as the generator. The discriminator is a classifier to tell if images created by the generator are real or fake. Figure 1 illustrates the architecture of the proposed model. For convenience, here we refer the downsampling block in U-Net as the encoder, and the upsampling block as the decoder.

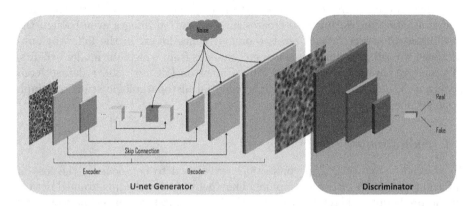

Fig. 1. Architecture of proposed network. The network takes input images at the resolution of 32×32, which are downsampled to 4×4 by the decoder and then resolved to any higher resolutions due to progressive training strategy. Empirically, magnification within four times is acceptable. For alternative inputs, we can modify our networks by removing same number of layers respectively in the encoder, decoder and discriminator. We apply skip connection and further introduce noise injection where the feature maps are convolved with random noise. The discriminator learns gradually to distinguish real and fake images.

Inspired by the Progressive GAN [12] and StyleGAN [13], we adopt progressive training to synthesise high quality images since details are crucial to medical images. In practice, only the decoder part of U-Net participates in the progressive learning. The encoder's role is to project the input into a latent code and to preserve it for the decoder to reconstruct. The progressive growing decoder allows for flexible choices of images at multiple resolutions, say 4×4, 8×8 to higher resolutions like 256×256 and 512×512. Our progressive GAN refines itself during each training step; as a result, uncertainty caused by the span from low dimension to high dimension can be reduced.

To generate images that are similar to the ground-truth, we combine the adversarial loss with R1 loss, a norm-based regularisation term which was first proposed in Pix2Pix [11]. Specifically, our adversarial loss is non-saturating loss that drives the generator to approach maximum probability of images being real rather than minimum probability of images being fake, which helps avoid mode collapse as suggested in [18]. The adversarial loss for generator is defined as:

$$L_G = -\mathbb{E}[\log(D(G(x)))] \tag{1}$$

The adversarial loss for discriminator is defined as:

$$L_D = -\mathbb{E}[\log(D(x))] - \mathbb{E}[\log(1 - D(G(x)))] + \frac{\gamma}{2}\mathbb{E}[\|\nabla_x D(x)\|^2] \tag{2}$$

where γ is a parameter to weigh the regularisation term and normally set to 10. More details about R1 and non-saturating loss can be referred to the supplementary material in [21].

Our proposed GAN not only keeps the perceptual consistency between source and synthetic images, but also creates high-resolution images even though the resolutions of source images are two or four times lower. In the following subsections, we will introduce some key mechanisms from which our model benefits. We conduct these mechanisms on PatchCamelyon (PCam) [30], a dataset consisting of 327680 colour images extracted from histopathologic scans of lymph node sections.

3.1 Skip Connections

In original U-Net [25], skip connections were used to compensate the loss of information caused by downsampling. They help recover the fine-grained details in the prediction. Therefore, We keep the skip connections in our network and investigate its effect on synthetic images, as shown in Fig. 2. We observe that skip connections make our network easier to converge. As a result, synthetic images are perceptually consistent to source images. By reusing feature maps, skip connections bring high-level details to resolved images.

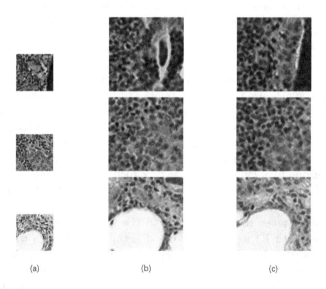

(a)   (b)   (c)

Fig. 2. Skip connection. (a) Source images at the resolution of 64 × 64. (b) Synthetic images at the resolution of 128 × 128 without skip connection. (c) Synthetic images at the resolution of 128 × 128 with skip connection.

3.2   Noise Injection

The idea of noise injection was first applied by Bishop [1] as regularisation to tackle overfitting problems in neural networks. This effective idea has been widely used in deep learning. Recently, noise injection has attracted more and more attention in GANs. Especially in StyleGAN [14,15], it exhibits astonishing capability of helping synthesise high-fidelity images. Following SytleGAN, we introduce the same way of noise injection in our network, in a form of linear transformation as:

$$f^k \leftarrow f^k + \alpha\varepsilon, \varepsilon \sim \mathcal{N}(0,1) \tag{3}$$

where f^k is the k-th channel of feature maps, α is a learnable scalar parameter for scaling the noise, ε stands for Gaussian noise. In implementation, we convolve random noise with the features and concatenate the results to those feature maps from skip connections, as illustrated in Fig. 1. Noise injection regularises the network, thereby stabilising the training process in GAN [6], which has been proven while training our GAN. Figure 3 shows the effect of noise injection. Thanks to the random condition, every time we run the generator, we obtain different but visually similar images. Therefore, we exploit this advantage as an augmentation method for generating images.

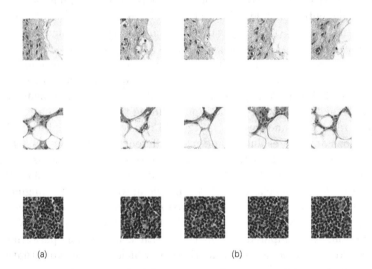

(a)   (b)

Fig. 3. Noise injection. (a) Source images at the resolution of 64 × 64. (b) Synthetic images at the resolution of 64 × 64 after random noise injection. In each column of (b) list the resulting images under the same random seed.

4   Experiments

We conducted experiments on several public datasets including PCam [30], HAM10000 [29] and LIVECell [4]. The synthesis performances on PCam have already been shown in Fig. 2 and Fig. 3. In this section, we quantitatively evaluate performance of the proposed augmentation method on HAM10000 for classification, and on LIVECell for detection and segmentation.

4.1   Datasets and Implementation Details

PCam. The size of PCam images is of 96×96 pixels. To fit to our network, we resized the images to 32×32 as the input. During the training phase, we began with 4×4 resolution and ended at 128×128. We ran 300k iterations at each resolution and used different mini-batches {4: 128, 8: 64, 16: 32, 32: 16, 64: 8, 128: 4}. For the loss function, $\gamma = 10$ in Eq. (2). We used Adam Optimiser with $\beta_1 = 0.00, \beta_2 = 0.99$ and learning rate $lr = 0.01$. For noise injection, we used Gaussian noise and $\alpha = 10^{-8}$ in Eq. (3). It took about 1 day to complete the training on 2 Nvidia v100 GPUs.

HAM10000. HAM10000 consists of 10015 dermatoscopic images with 7 categories of pigmented skin lesions: Actinic keratoses and intraepithelial carcinoma/Bowen's disease (*akiec*), basal cell carcinoma (*bcc*), benign keratosis-like lesions (solar lentigines/seborrheic keratosis and lichen-planus like keratoses, *bkl*), dermatofibroma (*df*), melanoma (*mel*), melanocytic nevi (*nv*) and vascular lesions (angiomas, angiokeratomas, pyogenic granulomas and hemorrhage, *vasc*).

The size of HAM10000 images is of 600×450 pixels. For augmentation, We resized the images to 64×64 as the input. During the training phase, we began with 8×8 resolution and ended at 512×512 only for augmentation. We ran 600k iterations at each resolution and used different mini-batches {8: 64, 16: 32, 32: 16, 64: 8, 128\256\512: 4}. Other parameters were the same as in training the PCam images. It took about 3 day to complete on 2 Nvidia v100 GPUs.

Since HAM10000 has class-imbalance problem, we applied our augmentation method to each class to make it more balanced. Synthesised images can be referred in Fig. 4. The classification model used was the baseline ResNet-50 [9]. For evaluation, we compared our method with classification performance on the original dataset and a simple method in which imbalanced situation was eliminated by randomly duplicating samples in the same class.

LIVECell. LIVECell is a large-scale dataset for label-free live cell segmentation. It contains more than 1.6 million annotated cells. These cells of eight types are distinct in morphology during which they grew from early seeding to full confluence. In the experiment, we took 2%, 4% and 25% of the dataset with cell type *A172* since augmentation is not necessary if data is sufficient.

For augmentation, we picked out the annotated cells (in bounding boxes) at different morphological phases. We resized these images uniformly to 32×32 as

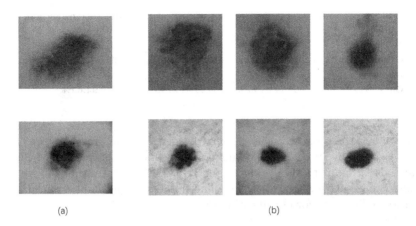

(a)   (b)

Fig. 4. Synthetic HAM10000 Images. First row includes images in *nv*. Second row includes images in *mel*. (a) Source images. (b) Synthetic images.

inputs. During the training phase, we started with 4×4 resolution and finished at 64×64. 300k iterations were run at each resolution with different mini-batches {4: 32, 8: 16, 16: 4, 32: 4, 64: 4}. Other parameters were set the same as in training PCam images. It took about 15 h to train on 2 Nvidia v100 GPUs.

(a)   (b)

Fig. 5. Augmentation method for LIVECell *A172*. (a) Original training image in the initial phase. (b) Corresponding augmented image.

We synthesised certain amounts of *A172* cells and placed them in the blank field of original images, as shown in Fig. 5. For evaluation, we tested the detection and segmentation performances with ResNeSt [31].

4.2   Evaluation

Classification Performance. To objectively evaluate our augmentation method, we used k-fold ($k = 5$) cross-validation.

Table 1. Classification performance with different augmentation methods.

Methods	Fold 0	Fold 1	Fold 2	Fold 3	Fold 4	Average accuracy
Original imbalanced	76.90%	76.65%	75.85%	72.60%	75.12%	75.43%
Randomly duplicated	89.91%	86.96%	88.71%	86.74%	86.57%	87.78%
Our method	95.29%	90.83%	96.40%	94.15%	96.42%	**94.62%**

In Table 1, the proposed method achieved significant improvement in classification accuracy by 19% over the original dataset, and also outperformed the simple augmentation method by a marked margin. This indicates that the proposed method can effectively cope with imbalanced datasets and improve accuracy to a considerable extent for classification tasks.

Detection and Segmentation Performance. For evaluating detection and segmentation performance, we referred to Microsoft COCO evaluation standard [19]. We report the overall average precision (mAP), which is measured over IoU thresholds in [0.5:0.05:0.95].

Table 2. Detection and segmentation performance over different data sizes.

Data size	Detection mAP	Augmentation with our method	Segmentation mAP	Augmentation with our method
2%	31.15%	**32.73%**	31.85%	**33.48%**
4%	31.26%	**32.44%**	32.42%	**33.55%**
25%	34.30%	34.24%	35.43%	35.51%
100%	36.37%	/	38.02%	/

* 2% contains 24197 instances, 4% contains 45308 instances and 25% contains 254693 instances. Our method augments 1138 instances. We include benchmark with 100% data size for reference.

As shown in Table 2, our method achieved slightly improved performances on 2% and 4% of the LIVEcell dataset, respectively. It outperformed the baseline by small margins of 1.58%/1.63% for box/mask performance with 2% of the dataset and 1.18%/1.13% with 4% of the dataset. The small improvements may be due to that even 2% or 4% of the dataset is already large enough. It suggests that our augmentation method can still improve the condition of datasets when they are already large and sufficient. In such cases further data augmentation may not be necessary.

5   Conclusion

In this paper, a U-Net based GAN architecture is proposed for microscopic image augmentation. The model generates realistic images that are semantically consistent to source images. Using progressive training, we have flexible choices for image sizes. The noise injection mechanism allows diverse and quantity of various synthesised images. With our image augmentation approach, we can make full use of limited, imbalanced dataset and boost classification and detection performances. We believe that such an architecture can be used in other medical image tasks.

References

1. Bishop, C.M.: Training with noise is equivalent to Tikhonov regularization. Neural Comput. **7**(1), 108–116 (1995)
2. Cheplygina, V., de Bruijne, M., Pluim, J.P.: Not-so-supervised: a survey of semi-supervised, multi-instance, and transfer learning in medical image analysis. Med. Image Anal. **54**, 280–296 (2019)
3. Dice, L.R.: Measures of the amount of ecologic association between species. Ecology **26**(3), 297–302 (1945)
4. Edlund, C., et al.: Livecell-a large-scale dataset for label-free live cell segmentation. Nat. Methods **18**(9), 1038–1045 (2021)
5. Esteva, A., et al.: A guide to deep learning in healthcare. Nat. Med. **25**(1), 24–29 (2019)
6. Feng, R., Zhao, D., Zha, Z.J.: Understanding noise injection in GANs. In: International Conference on Machine Learning, pp. 3284–3293. PMLR (2021)
7. Frid-Adar, M., Diamant, I., Klang, E., Amitai, M., Goldberger, J., Greenspan, H.: Gan-based synthetic medical image augmentation for increased CNN performance in liver lesion classification. Neurocomputing **321**, 321–331 (2018)
8. Goodfellow, I., et al.: Generative adversarial nets. Adv. Neural Inf. Process. Syst. **27** (2014)
9. He, K., Zhang, X., Ren, S., Sun, J.: Deep residual learning for image recognition. In: Proceedings of the IEEE Conference on Computer Vision and Pattern Recognition, pp. 770–778 (2016)
10. Heusel, M., et al.: GANs trained by a two time-scale update rule converge to a local Nash equilibrium. Adv. Neural Inf. Process. Syst. **30** (2017)
11. Isola, P., Zhu, J.Y., Zhou, T., Efros, A.A.: Image-to-image translation with conditional adversarial networks. In: Proceedings of the IEEE Conference on Computer Vision and Pattern Recognition, pp. 1125–1134 (2017)
12. Karras, T., Aila, T., Laine, S., Lehtinen, J.: Progressive growing of GANs for improved quality, stability, and variation. arXiv preprint arXiv:1710.10196 (2017)
13. Karras, T., Aittala, M., Hellsten, J., Laine, S., Lehtinen, J., Aila, T.: Training generative adversarial networks with limited data. Adv. Neural. Inf. Process. Syst. **33**, 12104–12114 (2020)
14. Karras, T., Laine, S., Aila, T.: A style-based generator architecture for generative adversarial networks. In: Proceedings of the IEEE/CVF Conference on Computer Vision and Pattern Recognition, pp. 4401–4410 (2019)
15. Karras, T., Laine, S., Aittala, M., Hellsten, J., Lehtinen, J., Aila, T.: Analyzing and improving the image quality of StyleGAN. In: Proceedings of the IEEE/CVF Conference on Computer Vision and Pattern Recognition, pp. 8110–8119 (2020)
16. Larsen, A.B.L., Sønderby, S.K., Larochelle, H., Winther, O.: Autoencoding beyond pixels using a learned similarity metric. In: International Conference on Machine Learning, pp. 1558–1566. PMLR (2016)

17. Leevy, J.L., Khoshgoftaar, T.M., Bauder, R.A., Seliya, N.: A survey on addressing high-class imbalance in big data. J. Big Data **5**(1), 1–30 (2018). https://doi.org/10.1186/s40537-018-0151-6
18. Li, K., Malik, J.: Implicit maximum likelihood estimation. arXiv preprint arXiv:1809.09087 (2018)
19. Lin, T.Y., et al.: Microsoft COCO: common objects in context. In: European Conference on Computer Vision, pp. 740–755. Springer (2014). https://doi.org/10.1007/978-3-319-10602-1_48
20. Litjens, G., et al.: A survey on deep learning in medical image analysis. Med. Image Anal. **42**, 60–88 (2017)
21. Mescheder, L., Geiger, A., Nowozin, S.: Which training methods for GANs do actually converge? In: International Conference on Machine Learning, pp. 3481–3490. PMLR (2018)
22. Mikołajczyk, A., Grochowski, M.: Data augmentation for improving deep learning in image classification problem. In: 2018 International Interdisciplinary PhD Workshop (IIPhDW), pp. 117–122. IEEE (2018)
23. Mirza, M., Osindero, S.: Conditional generative adversarial nets. arXiv preprint arXiv:1411.1784 (2014)
24. Radford, A., Metz, L., Chintala, S.: Unsupervised representation learning with deep convolutional generative adversarial networks. arXiv preprint arXiv:1511.06434 (2015)
25. Ronneberger, O., Fischer, P., Brox, T.: U-Net: Convolutional Networks for Biomedical Image Segmentation. In: Navab, N., Hornegger, J., Wells, W.M., Frangi, A.F. (eds.) MICCAI 2015. LNCS, vol. 9351, pp. 234–241. Springer, Cham (2015). https://doi.org/10.1007/978-3-319-24574-4_28
26. Shorten, C., Khoshgoftaar, T.M.: A survey on image data augmentation for deep learning. J. Big Data **6**(1), 1–48 (2019)
27. Tajbakhsh, N., Jeyaseelan, L., Li, Q., Chiang, J.N., Wu, Z., Ding, X.: Embracing imperfect datasets: a review of deep learning solutions for medical image segmentation. Med. Image Anal. **63**, 101693 (2020)
28. Topol, E.J.: High-performance medicine: the convergence of human and artificial intelligence. Nat. Med. **25**(1), 44–56 (2019)
29. Tschandl, P., Rosendahl, C., Kittler, H.: The ham10000 dataset, a large collection of multi-source dermatoscopic images of common pigmented skin lesions. Sci. Data **5**(1), 1–9 (2018)
30. Veeling, B.S., Linmans, J., Winkens, J., Cohen, T., Welling, M.: Rotation equivariant CNNs for digital pathology. In: Frangi, A.F., Schnabel, J.A., Davatzikos, C., Alberola-López, C., Fichtinger, G. (eds.) MICCAI 2018. LNCS, vol. 11071, pp. 210–218. Springer, Cham (2018). https://doi.org/10.1007/978-3-030-00934-2_24
31. Zhang, H., et al.: ResNeSt: split-attention networks. arXiv preprint arXiv:2004.08955 (2020)
32. Zhao, A., Balakrishnan, G., Durand, F., Guttag, J.V., Dalca, A.V.: Data augmentation using learned transformations for one-shot medical image segmentation. In: Proceedings of the IEEE/CVF Conference on Computer Vision and Pattern Recognition, pp. 8543–8553 (2019)

A Deep Generative Model of Neonatal Cortical Surface Development

Abdulah Fawaz[1]($\boxtimes$), Logan Z. J. Williams[1,2], A. David Edwards[2,3,4], and Emma C. Robinson[1,2]

[1] Department of Biomedical Engineering, School of Biomedical Engineering and Imaging Sciences, King's College London, London, UK
abdulah.fawaz@kcl.ac.uk
[2] Centre for the Developing Brain, School of Biomedical Engineering and Imaging Sciences, King's College London, London, UK
[3] Department for Forensic and Neurodevelopmental Sciences, Institute of Psychiatry, Psychology and Neuroscience, King's College London, London SE5 8AF, UK
[4] MRC Centre for Neurodevelopmental Disorders, King's College London, London SE1 1UL, UK

Abstract. The neonatal cortical surface is known to be affected by preterm birth, and the subsequent changes to cortical organisation have been associated with poorer neurodevelopmental outcomes. Deep Generative models have the potential to lead to clinically interpretable models of disease, but developing these on the cortical surface is challenging since established techniques for learning convolutional filters are inappropriate on non-flat topologies. To close this gap, we implement a surface-based CycleGAN using mixture model CNNs (MoNet) to translate sphericalised neonatal cortical surface features (curvature and T1w/T2w cortical myelin) between different stages of cortical maturity. Results show our method is able to reliably predict changes in individual patterns of cortical organisation at later stages of gestation, validated by comparison to longitudinal data; and translate appearance between preterm and term gestation (>37 weeks gestation), validated through comparison with a trained term/preterm classifier. Simulated differences in cortical maturation are consistent with observations in the literature.

Keywords: Geometric deep learning · Cortical surfaces · Neurodevelopment

1 Introduction

Deep Generative modelling presents enormous opportunities for medical imaging analysis: from image segmentation [8,9,13,40], registration [39], motion correction and denoising [1,23,30,42], to anomaly detection [4,14,45] and the development of clinically interpretable models of disease progression [2,3,25]. Image-to-image translation is a type of generative modelling problem where images

G. Yang et al. (Eds.): MIUA 2022, LNCS 13413, pp. 469–481, 2022.
https://doi.org/10.1007/978-3-031-12053-4_35

are transformed across domains, in a way that preserves their content. Common image-to-image translation tasks include transforming between imaging modalities [15,36,41] and to increase image resolution [11,17,44], though the methods used are general to any sets of imaging domains or classes, and can be applied to both 2D and 3D imaging data (see [43] for a full review of GANs in medical imaging).

The application of deep learning on surfaces, including medical surfaces, has been hindered by the mathematical incompatibility of data structures with non-flat topologies to conventional approaches for convolutional filtering. In response, the field of geometric deep learning (gDL) has emerged to extend deep learning to domains such as graphs, surfaces and meshes [7]. gDL is yet to produce a singular approach and numerous, often competing, tools and methods have been developed.

In this paper, we aim to develop surface-to-surface translation models of the developing cortex sensitive to individual changes in cortical maturation. Such difference maps could act as imaging biomarkers of interest to clinicians, since the negative impact of preterm birth on neurodevelopmental outcome remains an area of active research [5,29]. This task is too challenging for traditional imaging analysis methods due to the significant variation in functional and structural organisation of human cortices, even amongst healthy populations. The heterogeneity is present in neonatal cortical surface patterns from an early stage, which then undergo rapid and complex cortical maturation during development, which are further obfuscated by the impact of preterm birth. These factors make this task a fitting domain for the use of gDL, and gDL models have already been shown to achieve state of the art performance for neurodevelopmental phenotype regression and on cortical segmentation, when benchmarked against classical methods [10,12,35,37,46]. To achieve this, we adapt the CycleGAN framework [47] with methods from gDL for use on surfaces.

2   Methods

The CycleGAN framework [47] is a well-established method for unsupervised bidirectional image-to-image translation across two domains. This is achieved with a pair of generators that learn mappings from a source domain to a target domain, trained adversarially to a corresponding pair of discriminators that differentiate between real and synthetic images. Traditionally, these generators and discriminators are Euclidean CNNs but in this work, we retain the architecture but replace the convolutions with a surface-compatible convolution operation from the MoNet model [28]. CycleGANs produce realistic images and do not require paired examples, which can be practically difficult to acquire in medical imaging. These fit in with our overall aim of generating realistic, subject-specific cross-domain difference maps that can identify individual deviations from normal morphological development.

2.1   Model Architecture

The following adaptions were made to the original CycleGAN [47] to facilitate application on surfaces:

Geometric Convolutions: All surface convolutions are implemented using MoNet Gaussian Mixture Model convolutions (GMMConv) [28]:

$$(f \star g)(x) = \sum_{j=1}^{J} g_j D_j(x) f$$
$$D_j(x) f = \sum_{y \in \mathcal{N}(x)} w_j(\mathbf{u}(x, y)) f(y), \quad j = 1, \ldots, J$$

(1)

where f, g are the input and filter respectively, $D(x)f$ is a parameterisable patch operator that determines how the data is extracted from the surface before being weighted by the filter. Its general form is given in equation (1), with x a point on the surface, y a point in the defined neighbourhood of x, and w a kernel applied to the pseudo-coordinates $u(x, y)$ that define how the neighbourhood of an individual point is weighted relative to its neighbours on the surface. In MoNet, the weighting function w takes a Gaussian form:

$$w_j(\mathbf{u}) = \exp(-\frac{1}{2}(\mathbf{u} - \mu_j)^T \Sigma_j^{-1}(\mathbf{u} - \mu_j))$$

(2)

where Σ_j and μ_j are learnable $d \times d$ and $d \times 1$ covariance matrix and mean vector of a Gaussian kernel, respectively. The covariances are further restricted to diagonal form. In this paper, Gaussian kernels are defined using a two dimensional $(J = 2)$ local pseudo-coordinate system defined as the vector difference between neighbouring points on the surface in polar coordinates. This is pre-computed.

Icospheric Pooling: Since GMMConv has no transposed convolution, and does not reduce the dimensionality of the data, we require pooling and unpooling layers adapted for the surface. This can be challenging for general surfaces, but icospheres of different resolutions may be generated from each other by iterative barycentric interpolation (Fig. 1). This allows us to define a native down/upsampling method on the icosphere; the former as a direct downsample of the data by including only points of the lower icosphere (e.g. the red points in Fig. 1), and the latter as a mean-unpool operation where the new points are the average of their direct neighbours during the upsampling process. Skip connections are also added to make the generator a U-net.

Training: The network is optimised following the protocol of a standard Cycle-GAN [47], which learns mappings $G_X : X \to Y$ and $G_Y : Y \to X$, through adversarial training. Unpaired images $\{x, y\}$ are input through each of the Generators, G, to produce synthetic images $\{\hat{x}_X, \hat{y}_X\}$ and $\{\hat{x}_Y, \hat{y}_Y\}$ from generators

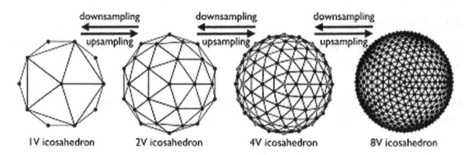

Fig. 1. Icosahedrons can be efficiently up and downsampled to different resolutions. New points are generated by barycentric interpolation of existing points. Our downsampling process simply keeps the points of the lower resolution icosphere while discarding the rest (e.g. to downsample from 4 V to 2 V, keep the points shown in red). Our upsampling procedure mimics the upsampling of the icospheres but with the new points added as an average of the existing points within its neighbourhood. (Color figure online)

G_X and G_Y respectively. The identity loss penalises each generator for changing an image already in its domain i.e. it forces $\hat{x}_X \approx x$, and $\hat{y}_Y \approx y$. The discriminators D_x and D_Y attempt to classify the true from synthetic images of their respective classes. Finally, the synthetic output of one generator is fed into the other $X \to Y \to X$ in order to generate a recovered image. The cycle loss penalises each generator for failing to reproduce the original image during this cycle.

We use an L1 loss for the cycle and identity losses, and an MSE loss for the adversarial loss. All networks are trained with an Adam optimizer with learning rate $= 0.002$, betas $= [0.9, 0.99]$. We set the real and false labels to 0.9 and 0.1 to help avoid discriminator overfitting. Networks were trained for 250 epochs.

The data is augmented with non-linear warps to represent realistic variations. These were generated offline by creating surface meshes warped by very small random displacements in the vertices, and resampling the original data onto these warped surface meshes by barycentric interpolation [12]. 100 warped counterparts are created for each image in our dataset. Each imaging modality was normalised to between 0 and 1 across the dataset.

3   Experimental Methods and Results

3.1   Data

All of the data used are part of the third release of the publically available Developing Human Connection Project (dHCP) dataset, consisting of cortical surface meshes and metrics, derived from T1-weighted and T2-weighted MRI images, processed and registered as described in [27] and references therein [16,20,21,33]. We utilise left cortical hemispheres scanned between 25 and 45 weeks post-menstrual age (PMA) with myelination and cortical curvature metrics initially registered to a 32k-vertex sphere using Multimodal Surface Matching (MSM) [31,32] and upsampled to a regular icosphere. The data set contains 419 neonates born at term (>=37 weeks gestational age (GA)) and 161 born preterm (<37 weeks gestational age), where 45 preterm subjects were scanned twice, once at birth and once at term-equivalent age (TEA), giving a total of 625 scans.

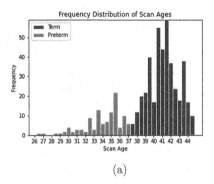 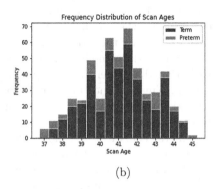

(a)   (b)

Fig. 2. A bar chart showing the distribution of subjects' PMA at Scan in weeks for (a) Experiment 1 and (b) Experiment 2.

3.2 Experiment 1: Cortical Maturity

In this experiment, the objective was to simulate healthy cortical maturation; thus the two domains to be translated between were: A) preterm infants' first scans (PMA <37 weeks); and B) healthy term controls. We exclude the later scans of preterm subjects to avoid modelling atypical cortical maturation, giving a total of 530 subjects: 419 term/111 preterm (as shown in Fig. 2a).

A spatio-temporal atlas of cortical maturation maps is available for the dHCP data [6], and shows a general increase in myelination around the brain, but especially strongly along the central sulcus (somatosensory cortex), the posterior portion of the lateral fissure (auditory cortex), and at higher scan ages, around the calcarine sulcus (visual cortex). By 28 weeks, all the primary sulci are formed and there are already heterogeneities in cortical structure. These sulci are initially smooth but become significantly more folded during development, and the cortical surface further increases in complexity by the emergence of tertiary sulci. Our model must be able to preserve and extend the existing folding patterns of an immature brain in its predictions.

The presence of longitudinal data in the form of preterm subjects' second scans allows us to quantitatively evaluate our model's predictions by comparing the actual appearance of a preterm subject's later scan to the model's matured prediction based on the same subjects first scan. We analyse these both quantitatively, via the image similarity metric Peak Signal to Noise Ratio (PSNR), and qualitatively by visual comparison. We compare the images as a whole and by individual modality (myelination/curvature). If the model represents cortical maturation, the model's synthetic predictions would be expected to be more similar to the later second scans than the original first scans. However, we would expect some differences due to variation around the age at scan and the impact of preterm birth on cortical development.

Figures 3a and b show the predicted surface to surface translation for low-to-high PMA of two different subjects' myelination and curvature respectively, displaying only the lateral view for clarity. The first, second and third columns show, in order, the original first scans, the true second scans and the synthetic scans produced by the model. The final column is a difference map between the model input and the model output. Each row shows a different subject and it can be seen that the model correctly predicts the broad structural changes expected in both myelination and curvature for both subjects. The relative homogeneity of myelination makes it easy to see that the model has correctly learned to simulate subject development.

Changes in curvature are more subtle and display greater heterogeneity across subjects and so are the better benchmark of performance. The preservation of cortical folding patterns is a key factor required for proper modelling of curvature and we see that our model does this well for both subjects despite significant topological differences between the two. Further, we observe that the model has added significant branching to most sulci, particularly the superior temporal sulcus which increases greatly in folding. The model has created new smaller folds in the temporal lobe, the parietal lobe and the frontal lobe and, extended existing sulci throughout. In the second row, the model even correctly predicts a change in the topology of a sulcus in the frontal lobe, which is split by a gyrus as a it develops (shown by the red circle).

Figure 4a is a scatterplot showing the quantified similarity between the second scans, which acts as a fuzzy 'ground truth', and the model's synthetic aged scans as compared to the first original scan, plotted against PMA at second scan. The results show that, in almost every case, the model predictions demonstrate a significant increase in similarity to the second scan compared to the original. The exceptions are mostly confined to subjects with second scans at low PMA. The results are summarised in the boxplots in Fig. 4b, where the synthetic images are of greater similarity than the originals over both modalities individually and combined. We observe that, whilst synthetically generated curvature is consistently improved, there is a greater variation in myelination with a tail of synthetic images with low image similarity to the second scans. Visual inspection reveals that this discrepancy is responsible for the reduction in image similarity of synthetic images for low PMA second scans due to the model's predictions being significantly more mature than both the first and second scans in these cases, as seen in Fig. 3c where the predicted myelination is significantly greater than found in the second scan, but still consistent with expected development. This discrepancy is a consequence of the discontinuous nature of cycleGAN translations.

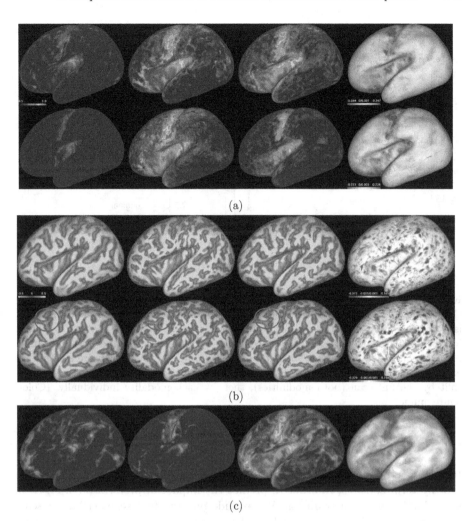

Fig. 3. Low to high PMA translation for the (a) myelination and (b) curvature modalities of two different subjects. The synthetic aged model predictions (column 3) are closer to the later second scans (column 2) than the original first scans (column 1). The fourth column gives the difference map between model input and model output. The red circles indicate a region of folding where the model correctly predicted a change in topology as the sulcus was split into two during development. (c) Myelination prediction for a subject with low PMA (39 weeks) at second scan showing the relative immaturity of the second scan myelination compared to the model prediction, resulting in a higher image similarity to the original first scan than to the model prediction. (Color figure online)

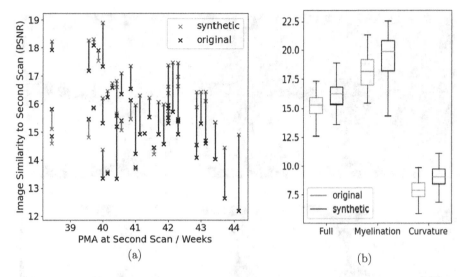

Fig. 4. (a) Image similarity of original first scans vs synthetic aged images compared to the same subject's second scans, given by Peak Signal-to-Noise Ratio (PSNR). PSNR is plotted against PMA at second scan in weeks. Green lines indicate that the synthetic images are closer to the second scan than original first scans, and red lines indicate a reduction in image similarity. (b) Box plots comparing the range of image similarities as measured by PSNR of original first scans and synthetic aged scans to second scans, split by the full scan (both modalities), then by each modality individually. (Color figure online)

3.3   Experiment 2: Prematurity

In this experiment, the aim is to translate between preterms' second scan and healthy term controls, in order to predict the impact of preterm birth on each individual's cortical maturation. We exclude preterm first scans (PMA at scan <37 weeks) to only model the effect of preterm birth at term equivalent ages (TEA), leaving a total of 514 neonatal subjects (419 term/95 preterm). A plot of the cohort used is shown in Fig. 2b.

In this case, there can be no ground truth examples scanned at multiple birth ages, so to validate we train a classifier with same architecture as the discriminator to predict prematurity and apply it to our model's predictions. Our classifier obtained an accuracy of 94% on the raw dataset, but our cycleGAN model's synthetic images had an overall 78% success rate in fooling the classifier, and in the other 22% of cases reduced the classifiers confidence by a significant margin.

Figure 5 shows a subject (true GA at birth 40 weeks, PMA at scan 44 weeks) (column 1) that has been translated from term age to a synthetic preterm age (column 2). The image fools our classifier which predicts prematurity with $p = 0.96$ for the synthetic preterm and $p = 0.22$ for the original term subject. The difference map (column 3) shows that myelination is decreased overall but remains broadly unchanged in structure. The folding patterns are completely unchanged but there is a noticeable increase in overall curvature, and it can be seen from the difference map that increases in curvature are more pronounced along the gyri (folds), not the sulci. Comparing these observations to existing work, we note that increased overall cortical curvature has previously been associated with preterm birth when compared to age-equivalent fetuses [24], and when compared with normal term infants [26], with curvature especially high across a number of gyri. Increased curvature has also been implicated as a prognostic biomarker of adverse neurodevelopment [19]. Shimony et al. [34] also found increased overall curvature in preterm neonates compared to term neonates, with increased localised curvature around the gyri, but could not positively determine that the metric was predictive of preterm birth due to the differences in folding patterns between subjects obfuscating the measure - an issue circumvented here as we compare like-for-like subjects through our cycleGAN.

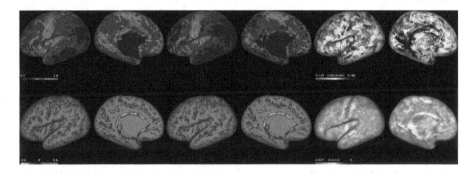

Fig. 5. Original term (columns 1–2) to synthetic premature (columns 3–4) image translation with difference map (columns 5–6). Subject's true GA at birth is 40 weeks and was scanned at 44 weeks PMA. Classifier predicts $P_{prem} = 0.22$ for the original term image and $P_{prem} = 0.96$ for the synthetic premature image.

4   Conclusion

By integrating MoNet into a CycleGAN model, we developed a generative surface-to-surface translation model of cortical maturation that shows accurate, realistic, subject-specific predictions of future myelination and curvature, validated on longitudinal ground truth data. We also developed a model that transformed surfaces between term/preterm classes, producing outputs that fooled a pretrained classifier and showed structural differences in line with what has been observed in the literature. The primary issue with our models was that the Cycle-GAN architecture is limited to transformation between discrete classes when this is a fundamentally a problem of continuous interpolation. There are a number of different generative models that do allow continuous representation that would be able to interpolate smoothly between scan ages, with which gDL could be adapted. One class of methods utilise variational encodings such as variational autoencoders (VAEs) [18], and VAE-GANs [22], although the authors found that attempts to adapt these methods to surface domains were unsuccessful, with models unable to capture individual cortical folding variation and collapsing to group averages. A more powerful example of this applied to volumetric cortical data is the iCAM architecture [3], which encodes separate variational disentangled spaces for content and age, which may be more amenable to adaptation with gDL. There are further alternatives that utilise direct conditioning on latent variables such as conditional VAEs and conditional GANs, but these too are more commonly associated with conditioning on classes, not continuous variables. Again more complex variations of these models have been successfully applied to the volumetric brain [38] that may be successfully adapted to the surface.

References

1. Armanious, K., Gatidis, S., Nikolaou, K., Yang, B., Kustner, T.: Retrospective correction of rigid and non-rigid MR motion artifacts using GANs. In: 2019 IEEE 16th International Symposium on Biomedical Imaging (ISBI 2019), pp. 1550–1554. IEEE (2019)
2. Bass, C., da Silva, M., Sudre, C., Tudosiu, P.D., Smith, S., Robinson, E.: ICAM: interpretable classification via disentangled representations and feature attribution mapping. arXiv preprint arXiv:2006.08287 (2020)
3. Bass, C., et al.: ICAM-REG: interpretable classification and regression with feature attribution for mapping neurological phenotypes in individual scans. arXiv preprint arXiv:2103.02561 (2021)
4. Benson, S., Beets-Tan, R.: GAN-based anomaly detection in multi-modal MRI images. bioRxiv (2020)
5. Boardman, J.P., Counsell, S.J.: Invited review: factors associated with atypical brain development in preterm infants: insights from magnetic resonance imaging. Neuropathol. Appl. Neurobiol. **46**(5), 413–421 (2020)
6. Bozek, J., et al.: Construction of a neonatal cortical surface atlas using multimodal surface matching in the developing human connectome project. Neuroimage **179**, 11–29 (2018)
7. Bronstein, M.M., Bruna, J., LeCun, Y., Szlam, A., Vandergheynst, P.: Geometric deep learning: going beyond Euclidean data. IEEE Sig. Process. Mag. **34**(4), 18–42 (2017). https://doi.org/10.1109/MSP.2017.2693418
8. Cirillo, M.D., Abramian, D., Eklund, A.: Vox2Vox: 3D-GAN for brain tumour segmentation. In: Crimi, A., Bakas, S. (eds.) BrainLes 2020. LNCS, vol. 12658, pp. 274–284. Springer, Cham (2021). https://doi.org/10.1007/978-3-030-72084-1_25
9. Costa, P., et al.: End-to-end adversarial retinal image synthesis. IEEE Trans. Med. Imaging **37**(3), 781–791 (2017)

10. Dahan, S., Williams, L.Z.J., Rueckert, D., Robinson, E.C.: Improving phenotype prediction using long-range spatio-temporal dynamics of functional connectivity (2021)
11. Do, H., Helbert, D., Bourdon, P., Naudin, M., Guillevin, C., Guillevin, R.: MRI super-resolution using 3D cycle-consistent generative adversarial network. In: 2021 Sixth International Conference on Advances in Biomedical Engineering (ICABME), pp. 85–88. IEEE (2021)
12. Fawaz, A., et al.: Benchmarking geometric deep learning for cortical segmentation and neurodevelopmental phenotype prediction. bioRxiv (2021). https://doi.org/10.1101/2021.12.01.470730, https://www.biorxiv.org/content/early/2021/12/02/2021.12.01.470730
13. Gadermayr, M., et al.: Image-to-image translation for simplified MRI muscle segmentation. Front. Radiol. 1 (2021). https://doi.org/10.3389/fradi.2021.664444, https://www.frontiersin.org/article/10.3389/fradi.2021.664444
14. Han, C., et al.: MadGAN: unsupervised medical anomaly detection GAN using multiple adjacent brain MRI slice reconstruction. BMC Bioinformatics 22(2), 1–20 (2021)
15. Hiasa, Y., et al.: Cross-modality image synthesis from unpaired data using Cycle-GAN. In: Gooya, A., Goksel, O., Oguz, I., Burgos, N. (eds.) SASHIMI 2018. LNCS, vol. 11037, pp. 31–41. Springer, Cham (2018). https://doi.org/10.1007/978-3-030-00536-8_4
16. Hughes, E.J., et al.: A dedicated neonatal brain imaging system. Magn. Reson. Med. 78(2), 794–804 (2017)
17. Jiang, M., et al.: Fa-GAN: fused attentive generative adversarial networks for MRI image super-resolution. Comput. Med. Imaging Graph. 92, 101969 (2021)
18. Kingma, D.P., Welling, M.: Auto-encoding variational Bayes. arXiv preprint arXiv:1312.6114 (2013)
19. Kline, J.E., Illapani, V.S.P., He, L., Altaye, M., Logan, J.W., Parikh, N.A.: Early cortical maturation predicts neurodevelopment in very preterm infants. Arch. Dis. Child Fetal Neonatal. Ed. 105(5), 460–465 (2020)
20. Kuklisova-Murgasova, M., et al.: A dynamic 4D probabilistic atlas of the developing brain. Neuroimage 54(4), 2750–2763 (2011)
21. Kuklisova-Murgasova, M., Quaghebeur, G., Rutherford, M.A., Hajnal, J.V., Schnabel, J.A.: Reconstruction of fetal brain MRI with intensity matching and complete outlier removal. Med. Image Anal. 16(8), 1550–1564 (2012)
22. Larsen, A.B.L., Sønderby, S.K., Larochelle, H., Winther, O.: Autoencoding beyond pixels using a learned similarity metric. In: International Conference on Machine Learning, pp. 1558–1566. PMLR (2016)
23. Latif, S., Asim, M., Usman, M., Qadir, J., Rana, R.: Automating motion correction in multishot MRI using generative adversarial networks. arXiv preprint arXiv:1811.09750 (2018)
24. Lefèvre, J., et al.: Are developmental trajectories of cortical folding comparable between cross-sectional datasets of fetuses and preterm newborns? Cereb. Cortex 26(7), 3023–3035 (2015)
25. Li, M., Tang, H., Chan, M.D., Zhou, X., Qian, X.: DC-AL GAN: pseudoprogression and true tumor progression of glioblastoma multiform image classification based on DCGAN and AlexNet. Med. Phys. 47(3), 1139–1150 (2020)
26. Makropoulos, A., et al.: Regional growth and atlasing of the developing human brain. Neuroimage 125, 456–478 (2016)

27. Makropoulos, A., et al.: The developing human connectome project: a minimal processing pipeline for neonatal cortical surface reconstruction. Neuroimage **173**, 88–112 (2018)

28. Monti, F., Boscaini, D., Masci, J., Rodola, E., Svoboda, J., Bronstein, M.M.: Geometric deep learning on graphs and manifolds using mixture model CNNs. In: Proceedings of the IEEE Conference on Computer Vision and Pattern Recognition (CVPR), July 2017

29. Morel, B., et al.: Automated brain MRI metrics in the Epirmex cohort of preterm newborns: Correlation with the neurodevelopmental outcome at 2 years. Diagn. Interv. Imaging **102**(4), 225–232 (2021)

30. Ran, M., et al.: Denoising of 3D magnetic resonance images using a residual encoder-decoder Wasserstein generative adversarial network. Med. Image Anal. **55**, 165–180 (2019)

31. Robinson, E.C., et al.: Multimodal surface matching with higher-order smoothness constraints. Neuroimage **167**, 453–465 (2018)

32. Robinson, E.C., et al.: MSM: a new flexible framework for multimodal surface matching. Neuroimage **100**, 414–426 (2014)

33. Schuh, A., et al.: A deformable model for the reconstruction of the neonatal cortex. In: 2017 IEEE 14th International Symposium on Biomedical Imaging (ISBI 2017), pp. 800–803. IEEE (2017)

34. Shimony, J.S., et al.: Comparison of cortical folding measures for evaluation of developing human brain. Neuroimage **125**, 780–790 (2016)

35. Vosylius, V., et al.: Geometric deep learning for post-menstrual age prediction based on the neonatal white matter cortical surface. In: Sudre, C.H., et al. (eds.) UNSURE/GRAIL -2020. LNCS, vol. 12443, pp. 174–186. Springer, Cham (2020). https://doi.org/10.1007/978-3-030-60365-6_17

36. Welander, P., Karlsson, S., Eklund, A.: Generative adversarial networks for image-to-image translation on multi-contrast MR images-a comparison of CycleGAN and unit. arXiv preprint arXiv:1806.07777 (2018)

37. Williams, L.Z., Fawaz, A., Glasser, M.F., Edwards, D., Robinson, E.C.: Geometric deep learning of the human connectome project multimodal cortical parcellation. bioRxiv (2021)

38. Xia, T., Chartsias, A., Wang, C., Tsaftaris, S.A., Initiative, A.D.N., et al.: Learning to synthesise the ageing brain without longitudinal data. Med. Image Anal. **73**, 102169 (2021)

39. Yan, P., Xu, S., Rastinehad, A.R., Wood, B.J.: Adversarial image registration with application for MR and TRUS image fusion. In: Shi, Y., Suk, H.-I., Liu, M. (eds.) MLMI 2018. LNCS, vol. 11046, pp. 197–204. Springer, Cham (2018). https://doi.org/10.1007/978-3-030-00919-9_23

40. Yan, W., et al.: The domain shift problem of medical image segmentation and vendor-adaptation by Unet-GAN. In: Shen, D., et al. (eds.) MICCAI 2019. LNCS, vol. 11765, pp. 623–631. Springer, Cham (2019). https://doi.org/10.1007/978-3-030-32245-8_69

41. Yang, H., et al.: Unpaired brain MR-to-CT synthesis using a structure-constrained CycleGAN. In: Stoyanov, D., et al. (eds.) DLMIA/ML-CDS -2018. LNCS, vol. 11045, pp. 174–182. Springer, Cham (2018). https://doi.org/10.1007/978-3-030-00889-5_20

42. Yang, Q., et al.: Low-dose CT image denoising using a generative adversarial network with Wasserstein distance and perceptual loss. IEEE Trans. Med. Imaging **37**(6), 1348–1357 (2018)

43. Yi, X., Walia, E., Babyn, P.: Generative adversarial network in medical imaging: a review. Med. Image Anal. **58**, 101552 (2019)

44. You, C., et al.: Ct super-resolution GAN constrained by the identical, residual, and cycle learning ensemble (GAN-circle). IEEE Trans. Med. Imaging **39**(1), 188–203 (2019)

45. Zenati, H., Foo, C.S., Lecouat, B., Manek, G., Chandrasekhar, V.R.: Efficient GAN-based anomaly detection. arXiv preprint arXiv:1802.06222 (2018)

46. Zhao, F., et al.: Spherical U-net on cortical surfaces: methods and applications. CoRR abs/1904.00906 (2019). http://arxiv.org/abs/1904.00906

47. Zhu, J.Y., Park, T., Isola, P., Efros, A.A.: Unpaired image-to-image translation using cycle-consistent adversarial networks. In: Proceedings of the IEEE International Conference on Computer Vision, pp. 2223–2232 (2017)

A Generative Framework for Predicting Myocardial Strain from Cine-Cardiac Magnetic Resonance Imaging

Nina Cheng[1], Rodrigo Bonazzola[1], Nishant Ravikumar[1(✉)],
and Alejandro F. Frangi[1,2]

[1] CISTIB, Centre for Computational Imaging and Simulation Technologies in Biomedicine,
School of Computing and LICAMM, School of Medicine, University of Leeds, Leeds, UK
N.Ravikumar@leeds.ac.uk
[2] Department of Cardiovascular Sciences, and Department of Electrical Engineering,
KU Leuven, Leuven, Belgium

Abstract. Myocardial strain is an important measure of cardiac performance, which can be altered when ejection fraction (EF) and other ventricular volumetric indices remain normal, providing an additional indicator for early detection of cardiac dysfunction. Cardiac tagging MRI is the gold standard for myocardial strain quantification but requires additional sequence acquisition and relatively complex post-processing procedures, which limit its clinical application. In this paper, we propose a framework for learning a joint latent representation of cine MRI and tagging MRI, such that tagging MRI can be synthesised and used to derive myocardial strain, given just cine MRI as inputs. Specifically, we use a multi-channel variational autoencoder to simultaneously learn features from tagging MRI and cine MRI, and project the information from these distinct channels into a common latent space to jointly analyse the multi-sequence data information. The inference process generates tagging MRI using only cine MRI as input, by conditionally sampling from the learned latent representation. Finally, automated tag tracking was performed using a cardiac motion tag tracking network on the generated tagging MRI, and myocardial strain was estimated. Experiments on the UK Biobank dataset show that our proposed framework can generate tagging images from cine images alone, and in turn, can be used to estimate myocardial strain effectively.

Keywords: Cardiac tagging MRI · Cardiac cine MRI · Myocardial strain estimation · Convolutional neural network · Machine learning

1 Introduction

Myocardial strain is used to quantitatively assess local myocardial deformation and is an important indicator regional cardiac function. Cardiac magnetic resonance tagging

---

N. Ravikumar and A. F. Frangi—Joint last authors.

G. Yang et al. (Eds.): MIUA 2022, LNCS 13413, pp. 482–493, 2022.
https://doi.org/10.1007/978-3-031-12053-4_36

(CMR-tagging) is a non-invasive imaging technique, and the current gold standard for quantification of local measures of myocardial motion/deformation such as strain and strain rate [1]. Strain reflects the rate of change in the length of the myocardium (typically along the circumferential or radial directions) across the cardiac cycle. Strain rate refers to the strain per unit time [2]. CMR-tagging sequences use selective radiofrequency pulses (e.g. SPAMM, DANTE) to superimpose the myocardium with tags or grids of tags that are subsequently tracked as the heart deforms across the cardiac cycle. The clinical application of tagging MRI, however, has been hindered by the need for acquiring additional sequences which increases scan time, cumbersome manual/semi-automatic post-processing steps required to derive regional strain measurements, and limited validation. Consequently, CMR-tagging has not been widely adopted in clinical settings due to the lack of rapid analysis techniques. Although several methods for tag-tracking have been proposed previously [3–6], most approaches rely on manual/semi-automatic landmark localisation and/or segmentation to derive strain measures by tracking superimposed tags across the cardiac cycle. We propose to synthesise tagged-CMR from cine-CMR images and use the synthesised images to quantify strain. This will help reduce scan time and facilitate myocardial strain quantification directly from routinely acquired cine-CMR images.

Recently, machine learning methods, especially convolutional neural networks (CNN) in deep learning [7], have shown promise in the field of medical image analysis and understanding, including automated cine-CMR image analysis, enabling detection and diagnosis of cardiovascular diseases, extraction of quantitative clinical indices and biomarkers, among others. Deep learning-based generative models such as generative adversarial networks (GANs) and variational autoencoders (VAEs) [8] have been explored extensively for image synthesis applications. We propose to tackle the limitations inhibiting wider clinical adoption of CMR-tagging imaging for strain quantification by learning to synthesise tagged-CMR images from cine-CMR images, in a patient-specific manner. We formulate this image synthesis problem in a probabilistic manner, as one of learning a joint latent representation across both types of images for subjects within a population. To this end, we utilise a Bayesian approach, namely, a multi-channel sparse variational autoencoder (mcVAE) [9] to learn a joint latent space given both channels of information for each subject in a population, i.e. their respective tagged-CMR and cine-CMR images. The latent representation learned using mcVAE subsequently enables generation of a tagged-CMR image for new/unseen subjects during inference, given just their cine-CMR image as input.

To the best of our knowledge this is the first study to investigate synthesis of tagged-CMR images from cine-CMR images. Only one other study has investigated tagged-MR image to cine-MR synthesis [10], for images of the throat. In Liu, et al. the authors proposed a dual-cycle constrained bijective VAE-GAN to synthesise cine-MR images from their paired tagged-MR images for each subject. Additionally, we go beyond just image synthesis to demonstrate that the tagged-CMR images synthesised from cine-CMR images can be used to quantify myocardial strain. The synthesised tagged-CMR images are used to quantify circumferential and radial strain across the cardiac cycle using a cardiac motion tracking network proposed in [11]. The proposed approach was trained and validated on data from the UK Biobank population imaging database.

2   Dataset and Pre-processing

2.1   Dataset

We utilised data from the UK Biobank [12] throughout this study, including two cardiac MR sequences for each subject, namely, cine-CMR and tagged-CMR. Participants were recruited to the initial assessment visit from 2006 to 2010, the first repeat assessment visit from 2012 to 2013, and the first imaging visit in 2014. The rationale and protocol for cardiac MRI examinations are described in [13], and this study was reviewed and approved by the Northwestern Research Ethics Committee (REC reference number: 06/MRE08/65). Scans were acquired using a 1.5 T scanner to obtain steady-state short-axis free precession cine-CMR and tagged-CMR sequences. All participants gave written informed consent.

2.2   Data Preprocessing

For cine-CMR images, we used a CNN model [14] to identify and crop regions of interest (ROI) around the heart. The purpose of cropping is to reduce the computational time and resources required to train our model. As the number of short-axis slices in the CMR data from the UK Biobank generally varies between 7 and 14 slices, the short-axis image stack was resampled to volume of 15 slices using cubic B-spline interpolation, with an isotropic resolution of 1 mm^3, then adjusted each slice of data at a common resolution of 128×128 pixels. Finally, we normalise the intensities in each image to a range of 0 to 1.

For the tagged-CMR images, we transformed the ROI coordinates obtained in the cine-CMR image space and cropped them. Coordinate transformation converts 2D image coordinates and 3D patient space coordinates, i.e. converts ROI coordinates to 3D world coordinates using the cine image, and then converts back to 2D coordinates using the tagging image. Following cropping, the tagged-CMR images were pre-processed in the same way as the cine-CMR images, including spatial resampling and intensity normalisation.

The coordinate transformation process is shown in Fig. 1. The key to determining the ROI in the tagging image is that the 3D spatial coordinates of the two sequence images are the same, and the process performs coordinate transformation on all samples in the experiment.

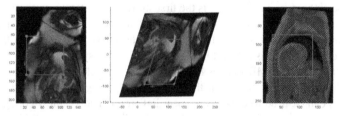

Fig. 1. Left: 2D cine image ROI; Intermediate: 3D cine image ROI; Right: 2D tagging image ROI. The CMR images were reproduced with permission from UK Biobank.

3 Methodology

3.1 System Overview

The deep learning framework in this paper consists of the following steps: (a) After multi-sequence image pre-processing, the mcVAE is trained using cine-CMR and tagged-CMR images to learn a joined latent space and to reconstruct each channel of information (i.e. each CMR sequence); (b) during inference, the trained mcVAE model is used to synthesise tagged-CMR images from unseen (test) cine-CMR images; (c) using the synthesised tagged-CMR images from (b), cardiac motion is tracked using a ResNet CNN model pre-trained on synthetic data [15]. Finally strain analysis is performed using the predicted motion trajectories, and radial and circumferential strains are estimated (Fig. 2.).

The neural network is trained using a large amount of synthetic data generated from natural images and verified by a cardiac phantom model with known strain. The procedure pre-trains it with the landmarks defined at the first time point (ED), then predicts the landmark at subsequent time points and uses it to compute the motion trajectory and the resulting deformation field. The network outputs the predicted motion path and finally calculates the strain from the deformation field.

3.2 Multi-channel Variational Autoencoder

Our method is based on a multi-channel sparse variational autoencoder [9], where two encoder/decoder network pairs are trained simultaneously, using on one of the two sequences (i.e. cine-CMR and tagged-CMR) as input channels to each pair. The two encoder-decoder network pairs share a latent space enabling a joint latent representation to be learned for the input channels/sequences. The network architecture is shown in Table 1.

In our mcVAE network, each subject's data x includes two information channels from the two CMR sequences, and the latent space s is represented by an l-dimensional vector shared between each data point x. The generative process for the observed channels of information can be described by,

$$s \sim p(s),$$

$$x_c \sim p(x_c|s, \theta_c), \quad c \, in \, 1, \ldots, C, \tag{1}$$

where, $p(s)$ is the prior distribution, and $x_c \sim p(x_c|s, \theta_c)$ represents the likelihood distribution of the observation. Each likelihood function belongs to distribution family $\mathcal{P}$, which is parameterised by parameter set $\theta = \{\theta_1, \ldots, \theta_c\}$.

The inference process can determine the common latent space, and each channel generate the observation data from this latent space. $p(s|x_c, \phi_c)$ represents the posterior distribution of the problem, and variational inference is often used to calculate the approximate posterior. Each channel contributes information about the distribution of latent variables, and the posterior distribution $q(s|x_c, \phi_c)$ is approximated by a single

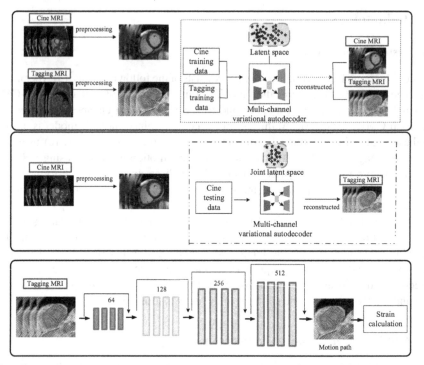

Fig. 2. Overview of machine learning framework that joint cine MRI and tagging MRI to estimate tagging MRI and myocardial strain using cine MRI alone.

channel and parameter c. Since each channel provides different approximations, constraints are imposed to force each q $(s|\boldsymbol{x}_c, \phi_c)$ to be as close as possible to the target posterior distribution. The distribution is measured using Kullback-Leibler (KL) divergence, specified as follows:

$$arg \min_{q \in Q} \mathbb{E}_c[D_{KL}(q(s|\boldsymbol{x}_c, \phi_c||p(s|\boldsymbol{x}_1, \boldsymbol{x}_2, \dots, \boldsymbol{x}_c, \theta))], \tag{2}$$

where the $q(s|\boldsymbol{x}_c, \phi_c)$ belong to a distribution family Q parametrized by the parameters $\phi = \{\phi_1, \phi_2, \dots, \phi_c\}$. The quantity $\mathbb{E}_c$ is the average over all channels. Minimising Eq. (3.2) is equivalent to the optimization of the following formula:

$$\mathcal{L}(\theta, \phi, \boldsymbol{x}) = \mathbb{E}_c[L_c - \mathcal{D}_{KL}(q(s|\boldsymbol{x}_c, \phi_c)||p(s))], \tag{3}$$

where, $L_c = \mathbb{E}_{q(s|\mathbf{x}_c, \phi_c)} \sum_{i=1}^{C} \ln p(\boldsymbol{x}_i|s, \theta_i)$ is the expected log-likelihood of decoding each channel from the latent representation. After learning the joint latent space, L_c can reconstruct multi-channel information only from one single channel, that is, only use the coding information of a single channel to reconstruct other channels, or both channels.

In our study, once trained, the mcVAE network was used to reconstruct tagged-CMR images given only cine-CMR images as inputs. The synthesised tagged-CMR images were subsequently used to calculate myocardial strain.

Table 1. Network architecture for each channel of a multi-channel variational autoencoder.

Channel	Encoder	Decoder
Tagging	Input 128 * 128 * 25	Latent variables, FC, Reshape
	Five times: 3 * 3 conv, ReLU, Dropout 0.15	Five times: 3 * 3 ConvTranspose2d, LeakyReLU (alpha 0.2), Dropout 0.15
	FC output layer, Latent variables	Tanh activation, Reconstructed tagging images
Cine	Input 128 * 128 * 10	Latent variables, FC, Reshape
	Five times: 3 * 3 conv, ReLU, Dropout 0.15	Five times: 3 * 3 ConvTranspose2d, LeakyReLU (alpha 0.2), Dropout 0.15
	FC output layer, Latent variables	Tanh activation, Reconstructed Cine images

3.3 Cardiac Motion Tag Tracking

We use a CNN-based approach [15] to track cardiac motion in synthesised tagged-CMR images. First, we created a synthetic training set comprising 1 million patches and trained a ResNet (ResNet-18) model on the same to learn to predict spatial position vectors of the estimated motion path, enabling tag tracking automatically.

Synthetic images for the training process were randomly sampled from ImageNet [16], and the process for creating the synthetic training set is the same as that proposed in [15]. The tag tracking network uses a modified version of ResNet (ResNet-18), with spatiotemporal (2 + 1)D convolutional layers [17] and CoordConv channels [18] for each convolutional block. The last layer of the network is a fully connected layer with linear activations, which outputs the spatial position vector of the estimated motion path. The optimization process uses stochastic gradient descent, the learning rate is adjusted using cosine annealing methods [19], 90% of the data is used for model training and 10% is used for model inference, and 10 patches are randomly selected per image in the synthetic image, so the training contains 1 million patches. The error between the predicted motion path and the real motion path is measured using the mean squared error (MSE) loss function.

Strain analysis needs to manually mark the intersection points in the end diastole (ED) time point. The model predicts and obtains the motion paths of other time points in all time ranges, essentially predicting the landmark displacement at subsequent time points, and calculates the strain through these paths of all points. Calculate strain by first fitting the deformation map using a Gaussian radial basis function (RBF) [19] with the shape parameter is twice of the tracking points spacing, then solving for the analytical derivative of the RBF in order to calculate the Green-Lagrange strain tensor, the formula for the Green-Lagrange strain is as follows:

$$\epsilon(t) = \frac{1}{2}(\frac{L_t^2 - L_0^2}{L_0^2}) \tag{4}$$

where L_t represents the segment length at any frame t, and L_0 represents the initial length.

4 Experiments and Results

In this study, we trained a mcVAE for jointly learning cine MRI and tagging MRI, which can generate tagging MRI from cine MRI, and realize the estimation of myocardial strain in the inference stage.

4.1 Experimental Setup

We use total of 535 subjects' (13375 slice pairs) images in our experiments, 60% of which were selected for training, 20% for validation, and 20% for evaluation. Cardiac cine and tagging MRI images from the UK Biobank database were used in our experiments, and we resized these images to 128×128 for a fair comparison. Our learning framework is implemented using the PyTorch deep learning toolbox [20], and the training takes about 9 h on NVIDIA V100 GPUs. After obtaining the generated tagging images, the tag points are obtained using a pretrained tag tracking network, and the radial and circumferential strains are calculated based on the displacement of the tag points, which takes about 0.1 s. Specifically, we use the Adam optimizer for training. The learning rate is set to $5e-4$ and the weight decay is set to $1e-5$.

4.2 Qualitative Evaluations

Figure 3 shows the generated results of the multi-channel VAE, which shows that the proposed framework successfully generates tagging MRI images from only cine MRI images, which is consistent with the target original tagging MR images. The generated images achieve visually pleasing results with good structural consistency with respect to the original images. For quantitative evaluation, we employed evaluation metrics widely used in images: root mean square error (RMSE) [21], structural similarity index measure (SSIM) [22], and peak signal-to-noise ratio (PSNR) [23]. Table 2 lists the numerical comparisons of the test dataset results of simultaneously inputting cine and tagging images to generate cine and tagging images, as well as reconstructing tagging images using only cine images, and reconstructing cine images using only tagging images. We note that the generation results with a single channel are inferior to the two channels generation results, which is to be expected.

Table 2. Quantitative numerical comparisons of generated results.

	RMSE	SSIM	PSNR
Tagging	0.14 ± 0.01	0.84 ± 0.21	28.13 ± 4.85
Cine	0.21 ± 0.04	0.69 ± 0.27	23.91 ± 6.68
Only cine to tagging	0.17 ± 0.02	0.72 ± 0.24	24.57 ± 5.84
Only tagging to cine	0.31 ± 0.10	0.65 ± 0.29	20.44 ± 7.51

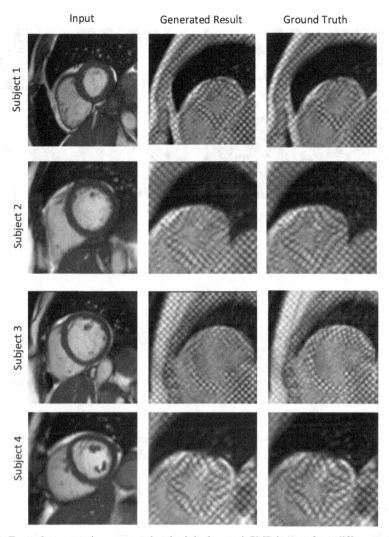

Fig. 3. Examples comparing generated and original tagged-CMR images from different subjects. The CMR images were reproduced with permission from UK Biobank.

4.3 Tag Tracking

Our tag tracking method uses a Resnet-18 neural network trained on a synthetic dataset of tagged images. This approach has been shown to accurately track tag intersections when applied to in vivo data. The points to be tracked are first selected in the ED time frame of the tagging images and fed into the neural network. The network outputs the Lagrangian displacement vector of the tracking point at each time point, and the network can track any point in the image, not just along the tagged line or the intersection of

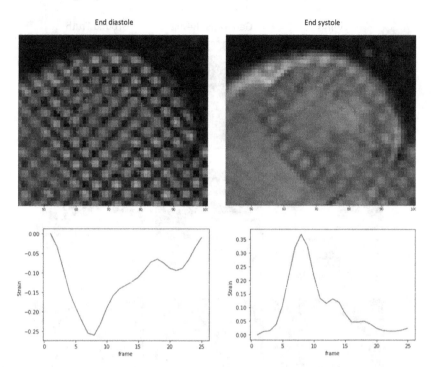

Fig. 4. Examples of tag tracking estimated during end-diastole (ED) and end-systole (ES) (top row) and strain calculations for the entire cine; circumferential strain (bottom left) and radial strain (bottom right).

the tagged lines. Figure 4 shows an example of tag detection and tracking produced at ED and ES from the generated images, along with strain estimates (circumferential and radial) at all time frames.

4.4 Strain Analysis

To validate the generative model, we performed strain analysis on the original tagging images and those generated from cine images, calculating circumferential and radial strains. Bland-Altman analysis [24] was used to quantify the agreement of two measurements, the result is shown in Fig. 5. These results show that the mean difference between circumferential strain and radial strain is close to zero, and most cases are within 95% agreement. Some outliers indicate cases of large error, which require further investigation that we will undertake in future work. The results obtained for radial strain were worse than circumferential strain, which is consistent with previous studies showing reduced accuracy in calculating radial strain using tagging MRI [25].

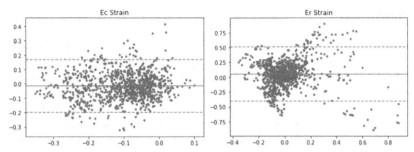

Fig. 5. Bland-Altman plot of end-systolic strain. The strain values obtained from the generated tagging images are compared with the strain values of the original images. Left plot shows mean circumferential strain, right plot shows mean radial strain, solid line indicates mean difference; dashed line indicates 95% concordance limit (mean ± 1.96 * Standard Deviation [SD]).

In addition to this, we randomly select the original and generated images of ten test results, and using the semi-automatic approach described previously for tag tracking on the original and generated images, calculated the strain, and plotted the errorbars for the estimated strains across the cardiac cycle. The results are shown in Fig. 6, and the circumferential and radial strains of the original and generated images are consistent.

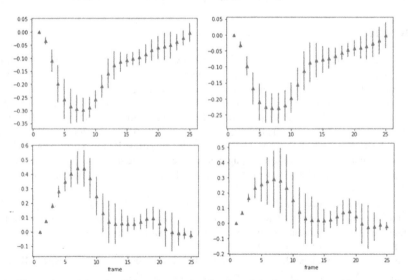

Fig. 6. Circumferential and radial strain errorbar for the original and generated images of the ten test results, top left: original images circumferential strain; top right: synthetic images circumferential strain; bottom left: original images radial strain; bottom right: synthetic images radial strain.

5 Conclusion

We propose a novel deep learning framework to jointly learn tagging MRI and cine MRI to generate tagging MRI and estimate myocardial strain using cine MRI alone. The generative process uses a multi-channel variational autoencoder to project data from different sequences into a common latent space data, which enables the reconstruction of one channel's information using only the encoded information from the other channel, i.e. of tagging-MRI from cine-MRI. After obtaining the resulting tagging MR images, automatic tag tracking was performed using a cardiac motion tag tracking neural network, and radial and circumferential strain was estimated across the full cardiac cycle, achieving comparable results to strains quantified using the original tagging MR images. Estimating myocardial strain from tagging images is a challenging problem, and our designed framework facilitates strain quantification using just cine-MR images as input. To the best of our knowledge, this proof-of-concept study is the first of its kind and opens up new avenues for research in myocardial strain quantification.

Acknowledgements. This research was conducted using data from the UK Biobank under access application 11350. AFF is funded by the Royal Academy of Engineering (INSILEX CiET1819\19), Engineering and Physical Sciences Research Council (EPSRC) programs TUSCA EP/V04799X/1, and the Royal Society Exchange Programme CROSSLINK IES\NSFC\201380, and was supported partly by China Scholarship Council Studentship with the University of Leeds.

References

1. Ibrahim, E.-S.H.: Myocardial tagging by cardiovascular magnetic resonance: evolution of techniques–pulse sequences, analysis algorithms, and applications. J. Cardiovasc. Magn. Reson. **13**(1), 1–40 (2011). https://doi.org/10.1186/1532-429X-13-36
2. Sutherland, G.R., Di Salvo, G., Claus, P., D'hooge, J., Bijnens, B.: Strain and strain rate imaging: a new clinical approach to quantifying regional myocardial function. J. Am. Soc. Echocardiogr. **17**(7), 788–802 (2004). https://doi.org/10.1016/j.echo.2004.03.027
3. Wu, L., Germans, T., Güçlü, A., Heymans, M.W., Allaart, C.P., van Rossum, A.C.: Feature tracking compared with tissue tagging measurements of segmental strain by cardiovascular magnetic resonance. J. Cardiovasc. Magn. Reson. **16**(1), 1–11 (2014). https://doi.org/10.1186/1532-429X-16-10
4. Götte, M.J., Germans, T., Rüssel, I.K., Zwanenburg, J.J., Marcus, J.T., van Rossum, A.C., et al.: Myocardial strain and torsion quantified by cardiovascular magnetic resonance tissue tagging: studies in normal and impaired left ventricular function **48**(10), 2002–2011 (2006). https://doi.org/10.1016/j.jacc.2006.07.048
5. Guttman, M.A., Prince, J.L., McVeigh, E.R.: Tag and contour detection in tagged MR images of the left ventricle **13**(1), 74–88 (1994). https://doi.org/10.1109/42.276146
6. Young, A.A., Kraitchman, D.L., Dougherty, L., Axel, L.: Tracking and finite element analysis of stripe deformation in magnetic resonance tagging. IEEE Trans. Med. Imaging **14**(3), 413–421 (1995). https://doi.org/10.1109/42.414605
7. O'Shea, K., Nash, R.: An introduction to convolutional neural networks. arXiv preprint arXiv: 1511.08458 (2015)
8. Pu, Y., Gan, Z., Henao, R., Yuan, X., Li, C., Stevens, A., et al.: Variational autoencoder for deep learning of images, labels and captions. In: 29th Conference on Neural Information Processing Systems (NIPS 2016), Barcelona, Spain, p. 29 (2016). https://doi.org/10.48550/arXiv.1609.08976

9. Antelmi, L., Ayache, N., Robert, P., Lorenzi, M.: Sparse multi-channel variational autoencoder for the joint analysis of heterogeneous data. In: International Conference on Machine Learning, Long Beach, California (2019)

10. Liu, X., Xing, F., Prince, J.L., Carass, A., Stone, M., El Fakhri, G., et al.: Dual-cycle constrained bijective VAE-GAN for tagged-to-cine magnetic resonance image synthesis. In: 2021 IEEE 18th International Symposium on Biomedical Imaging (ISBI), IEEE, France (2021). https://doi.org/10.1109/ISBI48211.2021.9433852

11. Loecher, M., Hannum, A.J., Perotti, L.E., Ennis, D.B.: Arbitrary point tracking with machine learning to measure cardiac strains in tagged MRI. In: Ennis, D.B., Perotti, L.E., Wang, V.Y. (eds.) FIMH 2021. LNCS, vol. 12738, pp. 213–222. Springer, Cham (2021). https://doi.org/10.1007/978-3-030-78710-3_21

12. Biobank U: About uk biobank (2014)

13. Petersen, S.E., Matthews, P.M., Bamberg, F., Bluemke, D.A., Francis, J.M., Friedrich, M.G., et al.: Imaging in population science: cardiovascular magnetic resonance in 100,000 participants of UK Biobank-rationale, challenges and approaches 15(1), 1–10 (2013). https://doi.org/10.1186/1532-429X-15-46

14. Zheng, Q., Delingette, H., Duchateau, N., Ayache, N.: 3-D consistent and robust segmentation of cardiac images by deep learning with spatial propagation. IEEE Trans. Med. Imaging 37(9), 2137–48 (2018). https://doi.org/10.48550/arXiv.1804.09400

15. Loecher, M., Perotti, L.E., Ennis, D.B.: Using synthetic data generation to train a cardiac motion tag tracking neural network. Med. Image Anal. 74,1022–1023 (2021). https://doi.org/10.1016/j.media.2021.102223

16. Deng, J., Dong, W., Socher, R., Li, L.-J., Li, K., Fei-Fei, L.: ImageNet: a large-scale hierarchical image database. In: 2009 IEEE Conference on Computer Vision and Pattern Recognition, Miami. IEEE (2009). https://doi.org/10.1109/CVPR.2009.5206848

17. Tran, D., Wang, H., Torresani, L., Ray, J., LeCun, Y., Paluri, M.: A closer look at spatiotemporal convolutions for action recognition. In: Proceedings of the IEEE Conference on Computer Vision and Pattern Recognition, USA, pp. 6450–6459 (2018)

18. Liu, R., Lehman, J., Molino, P., Petroski Such, F., Frank, E., Sergeev, A., et al.: An intriguing failing of convolutional neural networks and the coordconv solution, 31 (2018)

19. Loshchilov, I., Hutter, F.: SGDR: stochastic gradient descent with warm restarts. In: 5th International Conference on Learning Representations (ICLR 2016), Toulon, France (2016)

20. Prakash, K.B., Kanagachidambaresan, G.R. (eds.): Programming with TensorFlow. EICC, Springer, Cham (2021). https://doi.org/10.1007/978-3-030-57077-4

21. Wang, W., Lu, Y.: Analysis of the mean absolute error (MAE) and the root mean square error (RMSE) in assessing rounding model. In: IOP Conference Series: Materials Science and Engineering. IOP Publishing, (2018). https://doi.org/10.1088/1757-899X/324/1/012049

22. Dosselmann, R., Yang, X.D.: A comprehensive assessment of the structural similarity index. Signal Image Video Process. 5(1), 81–91 (2011). https://doi.org/10.1007/s11760-009-0144-1

23. Poobathy, D., Chezian, R.M.: Edge detection operators: peak signal to noise ratio based comparison. IJ Image Graph. Signal Process. 10, 55–61 (2014). https://doi.org/10.5815/ijigsp.2014.10.07

24. Bunce, C.: Correlation, agreement, and Bland–Altman analysis: statistical analysis of method comparison studies. Am. J. Ophthalmol. 148(1), 4–6 (2009). https://doi.org/10.1016/j.ajo.2008.09.032

25. Young, A.A., Li, B., Kirton, R.S., Cowan, B.R.: Generalized spatiotemporal myocardial strain analysis for DENSE and SPAMM imaging. Magn. Reson. Med. 67(6), 1590–159 (2012). https://doi.org/10.1002/mrm.23142

An Uncertainty-Aware Transformer for MRI Cardiac Semantic Segmentation via Mean Teachers

Ziyang Wang[1]([✉]), Jian-Qing Zheng[2], and Irina Voiculescu[1]

[1] Department of Computer Science, University of Oxford, Oxford, UK
`ziyang.wang@cs.ox.ac.uk`
[2] The Kennedy Institute of Rheumatology, University of Oxford, Oxford, UK

Abstract. Deep learning methods have shown promising performance in medical image semantic segmentation. The cost of high-quality annotations, however, is still high and hard to access as clinicians are pressed for time. In this paper, we propose to utilize the power of Vision Transformer (ViT) with a semi-supervised framework for medical image semantic segmentation. The framework consists of a student model and a teacher model, where the student model learns from image feature information and helps teacher model to update parameters. The consistency of the inference of unlabeled data between the student model and teacher model is studied, so the whole framework is set to minimize segmentation supervision loss and consistency semi-supervision loss. To improve the semi-supervised performance, an uncertainty estimation scheme is introduced to enable the student model to learn from only reliable inference data during consistency loss calculation. The approach of filtering inconclusive images via an uncertainty value and the weighted sum of two losses in the training process is further studied. In addition, ViT is selected and properly developed as a backbone for the semi-supervised framework under the concern of long-range dependencies modeling. Our proposed method is tested with a variety of evaluation methods on a public benchmarking MRI dataset. The results of the proposed method demonstrate competitive performance against other state-of-the-art semi-supervised algorithms as well as several segmentation backbones.

Keywords: Semi-supervised learning · Image semantic segmentation · Vision transformer

1 Introduction

Medical image semantic segmentation is an essential computer vision task with a wide range of applications including robotic surgery, clinical diagnosis, and image alignment. The goal of image semantic segmentation is to classify each pixel of an input image as to whether or not it is part of a Region Of Interest

© The Author(s), under exclusive license to Springer Nature Switzerland AG 2022
G. Yang et al. (Eds.): MIUA 2022, LNCS 13413, pp. 494–507, 2022.
https://doi.org/10.1007/978-3-031-12053-4_37

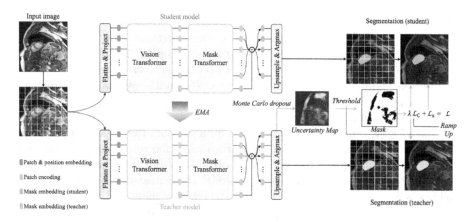

Fig. 1. The framework of semi-supervised uncertainty-aware mean teacher transformer network for medical image segmentation

(ROI) or background. Various deep-learning-based methods haven been widely studied in medical imaging community. The Encoder-Decoder style of Convolutional Neural Network (CNN) is one of the most commonly used segmentation techniques i.e. U-Net [14], and many researchers have studied 3D convolution, atrous convolution, residual learning, attention mechanism with U-Net for a wide range of medical imaging tasks which results in a family of U-Net such as 3D UNet, ResUNet, DenseUNet, Attention-UNet for MRI, ultrasound, CT segmentation [3,5,11,20,21]. There are three main concerns are yet to be further studied: a) the success of deep learning methods relies on a large amount of high-quality annotation data, which is high-cost, time consuming, and difficult to access especially in the clinical domain, b) the semantic feature information cannot be sufficiently condensed and transferred through traditional deep CNN layers or down/up-sampling operations, c) the limitation of the receptive fields in CNNs is not able to model long-range feature information. On order to tacke this challenge, Transformers [18] which use a pure self-attention architecture to model long-range dependencies in natural language processing without CNN are currently studied in the computer vision community. In a similar vein, we propose a ViT network in a semi-supervised manner with uncertainty estimation scheme for medical image semantic segmentation.

We first present a semi-supervised framework that effectively leverages the unlabeled data by encouraging consistent predictions of the same input under different perturbations. Following the Mean Teacher [17] to overcome limitation of Temporal Ensembling [7], the framework consists of the student model and the teacher model where the student model is able to update parameters with gradient descent, and teacher model is updated as an exponential moving average of the student weights. The whole training process is to minimize the segmentation supervision loss between student's machine segmentation (MS) and ground truth (GT), and consistency semi-supervision loss between the teacher's MS and the student's MS. Secondly, inspired by uncertainty estimation [6,23], we utilized Monte Carlo Dropout [6] to estimate the uncertainty with cross-entropy, thus enable student-teacher gradually learn from properly filtering reliable and valuable feature information. And then, to tackle the lack of semantic feature information being transferred through the CNN multi-layers and pooling, we introduce a pure self-attention-based ViT [4] as the semantic segmentation backbone. The segmentation performance benefits from a context model from Natural Language Processing [18], which is also helpful in computer vision especially in pixel-level classification tasks [8]. Finally, the evaluation results demonstrate our method's promising performance against other state-of-the-art semi-supervised methods. Ablation studies include proposed ViT against different CNN-based backbones, several approaches of filtering uncertainty map, and the assumption of different ratio of labeled data provided for training are also explored.

2   Methodology

In the task of semi-supervised learning, $\mathbf{L}$, $\mathbf{U}$, $\mathbf{T}$ normally denote labeled training dataset, unlabeled training dataset, and testing set. We denote a batch of labeled data as $(\boldsymbol{X}, \boldsymbol{Y}_{gt}) \in \mathbf{L}, (\boldsymbol{X}, \boldsymbol{Y}_{gt}) \in \mathbf{T}$, and a batch of only raw data as $(\boldsymbol{X}) \in \mathbf{U}$ in unlabeled dataset, where $\boldsymbol{X} \in \mathbb{R}^{h \times w}$ representing a 2D image. $\boldsymbol{Y}_t, \boldsymbol{Y}_s$ are the dense map predicted by the teacher ViT $f_t : \boldsymbol{X} \mapsto \boldsymbol{Y}_t$, and student ViT $f_s : \boldsymbol{X} \mapsto \boldsymbol{Y}_s$, respectively. $\mathcal{L}_s : (\boldsymbol{Y}_s, \boldsymbol{Y}_{gt}) \mapsto \mathbb{R}, \mathcal{L}_c : (\boldsymbol{Y}_s, \boldsymbol{Y}_t) \mapsto \mathbb{R}$ represent supervised segmentation loss, and semi-supervised consistency loss. In general, the training is to update the parameter of student ViT f_s aiming to minimize the combined loss $\mathcal{L}$, which is detailed in Eq. 1. Exponential Moving Average (EMA) [17] is utilized to update parameters of teacher ViT f_t from student ViT f_s in each training iteration. Uncertainty estimation scheme is applied in $\mathcal{L}_c$ that enable f_t to properly guide the training of f_s with the certain part of inference. The proposed framework is sketched in Fig. 1. Details of the framework including semi-supervised mean teacher with uncertainty estimation scheme, and segmentation ViT, are discussed in Sects. 2.1 and 2.2.

2.1   Semi-supervised Learning Framework

Inspired by temporal ensembling [7], mean teachers [17], and uncertainty-aware self-ensembling [23], we propose a semi-supervised mean teacher framework with uncertainty estimation scheme for medical image semantic segmentation. The framework is designed to effectively leverage the unlabeled data by encouraging consistent predictions from different perturbations. In each training iteration, the student ViT f_s is updated with gradient decent to minimize the combined loss $\mathcal{L}_s + \lambda \mathcal{L}_c = \mathcal{L}$, which is detailed in Eq. 1. λ for $\mathcal{L}_c$ is calculated based on consistency ramp-up method, because it can enable both f_s, f_t can properly make a consistency prediction, and also allow whole framework is able to put more focus on unlabeled data [7] during training process. In the end of each training iteration, EMA is utilized to update parameters of f_t, and the prediction of f_t is more likely to be correct than f_s after a series of study [17].

To further improve semi-supervised performance by enabling f_t guide f_s to learn feature information via semi-supervised consistency loss $\mathcal{L}_c$, i.e. study on the region where with confident and reliable inference should be utilized to calculate for $\mathcal{L}_c$. We hereby propose uncertainty-aware scheme to enable f_s is optimized with $\mathcal{L}_c$ only on confident and reliable inference images. Uncertainty estimation of inference of each pixel, and the approach of filtering the certain/uncertain inference are hereby introduced. Uncertainty estimation is mainly based on the Monte Carlo Dropout [6] on f_t, where 8 times stochastic forward passes with dropout and input Gaussian noise. In semantic segmentation task, each pixel is classified with the probability p of ROI, and it is calculated as $p = \frac{1}{T}\sum_t p'_t$ as dropout is utilized, where p' is the probability before dropout. The cross-entropy of predictive U is selected as the metric to estimate the uncertainty of targets [23], and it is calculated as $U = -\sum p \log p$. Therefore, only the region of reliable targets provided by f_t (including both ROI and background) are filtered by a threshold τ for f_s to be trained with consistency semi-supervision loss $\mathcal{L}_c$, which is detailed in Eq. 2. The supervision segmentation loss $\mathcal{L}_s$ is detailed in Eq. 3.

$$\mathcal{L} = \alpha\mathcal{L}_s(f_s(X), Y_{gt}) + \lambda\mathcal{L}_c(f_t(X), f_s(X)) \tag{1}$$

$$\mathcal{L}_c(f_t(X), f_s(X)) = \frac{\|\mathcal{I}(U < \tau) \odot (f_t(X) - f_s(X))^2\|_1}{2\|\mathcal{I}(U < \tau)\|_1 + \epsilon} \tag{2}$$

$$\mathcal{L}_s(f_s(X), Y_{gt}) = \frac{1}{2}(\text{CrossEntropy}(f_s(X), Y_{gt}) + \text{Dice}(f_s(X), Y_{gt})) \tag{3}$$

where $\epsilon = 10^{-6}$, τ is the threshold which is modified in each training iteration based on ramp-up approach. In this way, less data will be removed in training process that enable student model to gradually learn from certain to less certain feature information. λ is a factor for $\mathcal{L}_c$ which is also modified in each training iteration which make the whole framework move focus on minimizing the $\mathcal{L}_s$ to $\mathcal{L}_c$ of training process [23].

2.2   Segmentation Transformer

Semantic feature information is essential in semantic segmentation. The image feature, however, is going to be blurred after multiple layers of CNN encoding. In U-Net, copy and crop are utilized between encoder and decoder to make sufficient semantic feature information been transferred through CNN which results in dominant position in segmentation [14]. The boundary of ROI, especially the information of edge response, can be lost after CNN layers and pooling layers which is harmful for performance [25]. In this section, we introduce a pure self-attention-based vision transformer without CNN for semantic segmentation aiming to achieve sufficient global image context modeling. The model is inspired by Transformer [18], Vision Transformer [4], DETR [2], and Segmentor [16]. The setting of ViT encoder and ViT mask decoder are discussed in this section, and the technical hyper-parameters setting details was introduced in Sect. 3.2.

As shown in Fig. 1, a sequence of patches $X' = [x'_1 \cdots x'_N]^\top \in \mathbb{R}^{N \times P^2}$ is processed from an medical image $X \in \mathbb{R}^{h \times w}$, where P is the patch size, and $N = \frac{h \times w}{P^2}$ is the number of patch from each input image. Each patch is then flatten into a 1D vector and been projected with patch embedding $X_0 = [E_1 \cdots E_N]^\top, E_{1 \dots N} \in \mathbb{R}^{D \times P^2}$. The positional embeddings to collect positional information $pos = [pos_1 \cdots pos_N]^\top \in \mathbb{R}^{N \times D}$ are added, and the final input sequence of tokens for encoder is $Z_0 = X_0 + pos$. The transformer encoder consists of a multi-headed self-attention (MSA) block followed by a point-wise MLP block of two layers. Residual connections and layer normalization (LN) are both applied in each block. The details of MSA and MLP block for feature learning are demonstrated in Eq. 4, 5, where $i \in 1 \cdots L$, and L is the number of layers in encoder. The self-attention mechanism is composed of three point-wise linear layers mapping tokens to intermediate representations: quires Q, keys K, and values V, which is introduced in Eq. 6. In this way, the transformer encoder maps input sequence $Z_0 = [z_{0,1} \cdots z_{0,N}]$ with position to $Z_L = [z_{L,1}, ..., z_{L,N}]$. All these settings are following by [4]. In this way, the much richer sufficient semantic feature information are fully used in the encoder.

$$A_{i-1} = \text{MSA}(\text{LN}(Z_{i-1})) + Z_{i-1} \tag{4}$$

$$Z_i = \text{MLP}(\text{LN}(A_{i-1})) + A_{i-1} \tag{5}$$

where MSA is calculated by:

$$\text{MSA}(Z') = \text{softmax}(\frac{QK}{\sqrt{D}})V, \tag{6}$$

and the Q, K, V are given by:

$$Q = \text{Linear}_\text{Q}(Z'), K = \text{Linear}_\text{K}(Z'), V = \text{Linear}_\text{V}(Z') \tag{7}$$

The sequence of Z_L is then decoded to dense map $S \in \mathbb{R}^{h \times w \times k}$ as segmentation results via a transformer mask decoder, where k is the number of classes. The decoder acts as mapping patch from encoder and unsample to pixel-level probability of dense map [16]. The learnable class embedding cls is processed with Z_L in mask decoder same with transformer encoder with M layers. The output patch sequence is then reshaped to a 2D mask and been bilinearly upsampled to the original image size as prediction results. In transformer mask decoder, both class embedding and patch sequence are jointly processed, and semantic segmentation mask is finally inferenced.

3   Experiments

3.1   Datasets

In this experiment, a MRI cardiac segmentation dataset is selected from the automated cardiac diagnosis MICCAI Challenge 2017 [1]. It consists of 100 different patients divided into 5 evenly distributed subgroups including normal, myocardial infarction, dilated cardiomyopathy, hypertrophic cardiomyopathy, and abnormal right ventricle. We use 44,025 232×256 images from 100 patients. All images are resize to 256×256. 20% of images are selected as testing set, and the rest of dataset is for training. The ratio of assumed labeled data/training set is 10% for direct comparison experiment with similarity measures and difference measures against other semi-supervised methods, other segmentation backbones, and ablation studies, 1%, 2%, 3%, 5%, 10%, 15% and 20% for direct comparison with IOU against other semi-supervised methods.

3.2 Training Details

Our code has been developed under Ubuntu 20.04 in Python 3.8.8 using Pytorch 1.10 [12] and CUDA 11.3 using four Nvidia GeForce RTX 3090 GPU with 24 GB memory, and Intel (R) Intel Core i9-10900K. All the baseline algorithms are directly utilized from [10], and the ViT for segmentation purpose is based on [16] from [15] and TIMM library [22]. The runtime averaged around 3.5 h, including the data transfer, model training, inference and evaluation. All semi-supervised methods are trained with same settings, i.e. training for 30,000 iterations then been tested directly, batch size is set to 24, optimizer is SGD, and learning rate is initially set to 0.01, momentum is 0.9, and weight decay is 0.0001. After multi-times experiments, we finally come up with a proper hyper parameters setting for segmentation ViT which achieve the best results with limited computation resources(6 GB in GPU memory costs): The patch size is 16×16, the number of multi-attention heads is 6, the number of layers L of encoder is 12, normalization method is same with Transformer [18], and the number of layers M of decoder is 2.

3.3 Evaluation

Our proposed semi-supervised method is compared with mean teachers [17], deep adversarial network [24], adversarial entropy minimization for domain adaptation [19], uncertainty-aware self-ensembling model [23], and deep co-training [13] as semi-supervised baseline methods with U-Net [14] as backbone. The direct comparison experiments are conducted with a variety of evaluation metrics including similarity measures: Dice, IOU, Accuracy, Precision, Recall/Sensitivity, Specificity, which are the higher the better. We also investigate difference measures: Relative Volume Difference (RVD), Hausdorff Distance (HD), Average Symmetric Surface Distance (ASSD), which are the lower the better.

3.4 Results

Figure 2 illustrates some examples of raw images, and MS against GT where Yellow, Red, Green and Black represent as True Positive, False Positive, False Negative and True Negative pixel, respectively. Example raw images with uncertainty map, and mask of certain image in three different training stages are illustrated in Appendix. The best result was in **Bold**, and quantitative results are

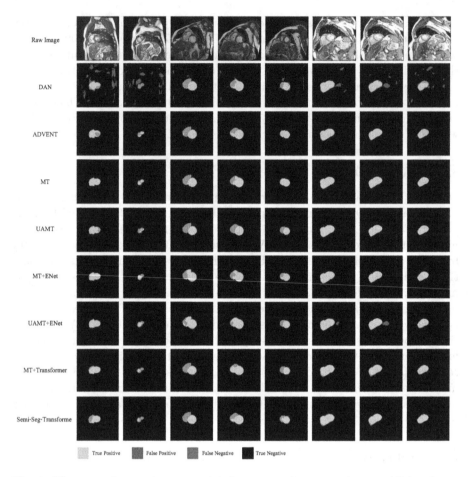

Fig. 2. The example raw images and inference results on testing set (Color figure online)

detailed in Table 1 and Table 2. The evaluation results demonstrate that proposed method promising performance against other semi-supervised methods. Figure 3 gives a systematic review of how the IOU varies when 1%, 2%, 3%, 5%, 10%, 15% and 20% of the training set is labeled. More details of quantitative analysis for different assumed ratio of labeled data given is illustrated in Appendix.

3.5   Ablation Study

In order to analyze the effects of each of the proposed contributions and their combinations, extensive ablation experiments have been conducted. Table 3 annotates with ✓ the use of the mandatory mean teacher for semi-supervise purpose, demonstrating how the removal of uncertainty estimation compromises the overall performance. The model is selected and tested with U-Net [14],

Table 1. Direct comparison with similarity measures on cardiac MRI testing set (the higher, the better)

Model	Dice	IOU	Acc	Pre	Rec/Sen	Spe
[17]	0.8567	0.7494	0.9895	0.7903	0.7903	**0.9977**
[24]	0.5395	0.3694	0.9480	0.4172	0.7631	0.9557
[19]	0.8612	0.7563	0.9896	0.9258	0.8051	0.9973
[23]	0.8347	0.7164	0.9873	0.8683	0.8037	0.9949
[13]	0.8787	0.7836	0.9908	0.9248	0.8370	0.9972
Ours	**0.8821**	**0.7891**	**0.9910**	**0.9288**	**0.8398**	0.9973

Table 2. Direct comparison with difference measures on cardiac MRI testing set (the lower, the better)

Model	RVD	HD	ASSD
[17]	0.3715	28.5797	6.4947
[24]	2.2593	145.4982	49.5673
[19]	0.2669	20.3860	4.7762
[23]	0.3925	27.2209	6.4702
[13]	**0.2630**	21.0363	4.3865
Ours	0.2732	**13.1815**	**3.7085**

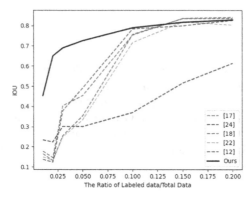

Fig. 3. The IOU performance on test set with different ratio of labeled/total training set

E-Net [12], and proposed segmentation ViT. Further experiments under the assumption of fully supervised learning are also conducted annotated with full ✗ in Table 3. Our proposed ViT with uncertainty estimation scheme shows promising performance especially in IOU and sensitivity in both semi-supervised and fully-supervised manner, respectively. The extended experiments of threshold setting of τ and weight λ of $\mathcal{L}_s$ in training process is illustrated in Appendix.

Table 3. Ablation studies on contributions of architecture and modules (the higher, the better)

Mean teacher	Uncertainty aware	Model	IOU	Sen	Spe
✓		UNet	0.7494	0.7903	**0.9977**
✓	✓	UNet	0.7164	0.8037	0.9949
✓		ENet	0.7549	0.8314	0.9958
✓	✓	ENet	0.7460	0.8529	0.9941
✓		Ours	0.7840	0.8405	0.9970
✓	✓	**Ours**	**0.7891**	**0.8398**	0.9973
✗	✗	UNet	0.7924	0.8409	**0.9975**
✗	✗	ENet	0.7549	0.8696	0.9937
✗	✗	**Ours**	**0.8173**	**0.9137**	0.9951

4 Conclusion

Our semi-supervised uncertainty-aware segmentation is successful in using ViT for medical image semantic segmentation via a mean teacher framework. Experimental results on the public MRI dataset demonstrate our method's promising performance compared against both supervised and semi-supervised existing methods. In the future, multi-task learning and multi-view learning which potentially improve semi-supervised learning performance will be further studied.

A Appendix

Table 4 gives detailed systematic IOU results under different assumptions of the ratio of labeled to total data, on the MRI Cardiac test set. It is pleasantly remarkable to see serviceable results being obtained with a proportion of labelled data as small as 1%, 2%, or 3% of the total. Given the small set of type-specific annotations that exist, they can now be put to good use by pairing them with large amounts of unlabeled data and making them available through our proposed method.

Table 4. The IOU results under different assumption of ratio of label/total data on MRI cardiac test set (the higher, the better)

	1%	2%	3%	5%	10%	15%	20%
[17]	0.1776	0.1457	0.4034	0.4536	0.7533	**0.8354**	**0.8411**
[24]	0.2331	0.2230	0.3010	0.3007	0.3694	0.5155	0.6130
[19]	0.1649	0.1309	0.2543	0.3538	0.7563	0.8345	0.8356
[23]	0.1486	0.1334	0.2480	0.3341	0.7163	0.8180	0.8029
[13]	0.1372	0.1232	0.3790	0.4912	0.7836	0.7990	0.8265
Ours	**0.4531**	**0.6500**	**0.6900**	**0.7256**	**0.7891**	0.8165	0.8282

Table 5 and Table 6 reports the different approaches to modify the threshold τ of filtering certain or uncertain pixels with uncertainty estimation scheme, and the weight λ of loss $\mathcal{L}_c$ in each training iteration. We explore the fixed value, exponential ramp up [7], linear ramp up, cosine ramp down [9] and variants of them. Details of exponential ramp up, linear ramp up and cosine ramp down is illustrated in the following Eq. 8, 9, 10, respectively. Each experiment is conducted with different approaches under the other one either τ or λ is fixed with exponential ramp up. The results illustrates different approaches of updating τ, λ in each training iteration cannot significantly improve the performance of proposed method, and all other experiments for τ, λ is with exponential ramp up.

$$\tau\, or\, \lambda = e^{-5 \times (1 - t_{\text{iteration}}/t_{\text{maxiteration}})^2} \tag{8}$$

$$\tau\, or\, \lambda = t_{\text{iteration}}/t_{\text{maxiteration}}) \tag{9}$$

$$\tau\, or\, \lambda = 0.5 \times (cosine(\pi \times t_{\text{iteration}}/t_{\text{maxiteration}}) + 1) \tag{10}$$

Table 5. Ablation studies on the threshold setting of uncertainty in training process (the higher, the better)

Threshold	Model	IOU	Acc	Pre	Sen	Spe
Threshold 0.2	UNet	0.7465	0.9889	0.8895	0.8229	0.9958
Threshold 0.5	UNet	0.7480	0.9891	0.9048	0.8119	0.9965
Threshold 0.8	UNet	0.7042	0.9862	0.8299	0.8231	0.9930
Exponential Ramp Up	UNet	0.7543	0.9892	0.8895	0.8324	0.9957
Linear Ramp Up	UNet	0.7179	0.9866	0.8189	0.8534	0.9922
Cosine Ramp Down	UNet	0.7046	0.9861	0.8230	0.8305	0.9926
0.6 * Exponential Ramp Up	UNet	0.7321	0.9879	0.8588	0.8324	0.9943
0.6 * Linear Ramp Up	UNet	0.7354	0.9883	0.8852	0.8130	0.9956
0.6 * Cosine Ramp Down	UNet	0.8552	0.9889	0.8931	0.8205	0.9959
0.8 * Exponential Ramp Up	UNet	0.7240	0.9874	0.8528	0.8275	0.9941
0.8 * Linear Ramp Up	UNet	0.7326	0.9882	0.8836	0.8109	0.9956
0.8 * Cosine Ramp Down	UNet	0.7674	0.9899	0.9017	0.8374	0.9962
1.2 * Exponential Ramp Up	UNet	0.7326	0.9882	0.8834	0.8109	0.9956
1.2 * Linear Ramp Up	UNet	0.7304	0.9876	0.8458	0.8426	0.9936
1.2 * Cosine Ramp Down	UNet	0.7493	0.9889	0.8807	0.8340	0.9953
1.4 * Exponential Ramp Up	UNet	0.8359	0.9874	0.8724	0.8024	0.9951
1.4 * Linear Ramp Up	UNet	0.8167	0.9856	0.8305	0.8034	0.9932
1.4 * Cosine Ramp Down	UNet	0.7427	0.9884	0.8638	0.8412	0.9945

Table 6. Ablation studies on the weight setting of consistency loss in training process (the higher, the better)

Weight	Model	IOU	Acc	Pre	Sen	Spe
Threshold 0.2	UNet	0.5243	0.9723	0.6238	0.7667	0.9808
Threshold 0.5	UNet	0.3956	0.9567	0.4719	0.7101	0.9670
Threshold 0.8	UNet	0.4052	0.9703	0.6667	0.5082	0.9894
Exponential Ramp Up	UNet	0.7105	0.9870	0.8613	0.8023	0.9946
Linear Ramp Up	UNet	0.7149	0.9868	0.8357	0.8319	0.9932
Cosine Ramp Down	UNet	0.7547	0.9894	0.9044	0.8201	0.9964
0.6 * Exponential Ramp Up	UNet	0.7723	0.9900	0.8978	0.8467	0.9960
0.6 * Linear Ramp Up	UNet	0.7586	0.9896	0.9069	0.8227	0.9965
0.6 * Cosine Ramp Down	UNet	0.7742	0.9900	0.8908	0.8554	0.9956
0.8 * Exponential Ramp Up	UNet	0.7110	0.9864	0.8216	0.8408	0.9924
0.8 * Linear Ramp Up	UNet	0.7248	0.9875	0.8559	0.8256	0.9942
0.8 * Cosine Ramp Down	UNet	0.7178	0.9869	0.8376	0.8338	0.9933
1.2 * Exponential Ramp Up	UNet	0.7432	0.9887	0.8854	0.8223	0.9956
1.2 * Linear Ramp Up	UNet	0.5596	0.9742	0.6363	0.8227	0.9805
1.2 * Cosine Ramp Down	UNet	0.7509	0.9891	0.8955	0.8230	0.9960
1.4 * Exponential Ramp Up	UNet	0.6968	0.9864	0.8621	0.7482	0.9948
1.4 * Linear Ramp Up	UNet	0.6557	0.9832	0.7807	0.8037	0.9906
1.4 * Cosine Ramp Down	UNet	0.7550	0.9893	0.8979	0.8259	0.9961

Figure 4 sketches randomly selected raw images with their corresponding uncertainty maps, and masks generated by proposed method at three different stages (from the beginning to the end) of the training process. In uncertainty maps, yellow represents the teacher ViT f_t is uncertain of prediction with the given pixels, and blue represents the teacher ViT f_t is certain of prediction with the given pixels. The uncertainty map is gradually moving from yellow to green in the training process as shown in Fig. 4. The threshold of certainty estimation is then applied with uncertainty map which results in masks, where the white represents that the prediction by teacher ViT f_t is certain enough to guide the student ViT f_s i.e. for calculation the consistency loss $\mathcal{L}_s$, and the black represents that the pixels with uncertainty is temporally unavailable to be considered in consistency semi-supervision loss calculation. Please remind that both the background and ROI can be certain with the white simultaneously. Some typical example masks illustrates that model is only uncertain with the boundary of ROI as shown in Fig. 4, and finally the framework is very likely to be certain with the whole image with a proper threshold setting, that the uncertainty map is going to be blue, mask is going to be white in the end of training process.

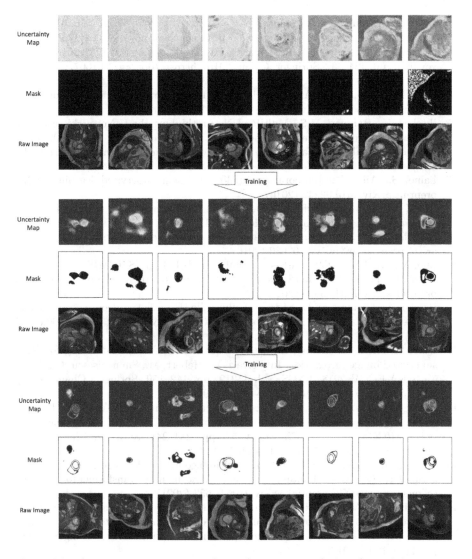

Fig. 4. Sample uncertainty maps, masks, and raw images during the training process (Color figure online)

References

1. Bernard, O., et al.: Deep learning techniques for automatic MRI cardiac multi-structures segmentation and diagnosis: is the problem solved? IEEE Trans. Med. Imaging **37**(11), 2514–2525 (2018)
2. Carion, N., Massa, F., Synnaeve, G., Usunier, N., Kirillov, A., Zagoruyko, S.: End-to-end object detection with transformers. In: Vedaldi, A., Bischof, H., Brox, T., Frahm, J.-M. (eds.) ECCV 2020. LNCS, vol. 12346, pp. 213–229. Springer, Cham (2020). https://doi.org/10.1007/978-3-030-58452-8_13

3. Çiçek, Ö., Abdulkadir, A., Lienkamp, S.S., Brox, T., Ronneberger, O.: 3D U-Net: learning dense volumetric segmentation from sparse annotation. In: Ourselin, S., Joskowicz, L., Sabuncu, M.R., Unal, G., Wells, W. (eds.) MICCAI 2016. LNCS, vol. 9901, pp. 424–432. Springer, Cham (2016). https://doi.org/10.1007/978-3-319-46723-8_49

4. Dosovitskiy, A., et al.: An image is worth 16x16 words: transformers for image recognition at scale. arXiv preprint arXiv:2010.11929 (2020)

5. Ibtehaz, N., Rahman, M.S.: MultiResUNet: rethinking the U-Net architecture for multimodal biomedical image segmentation. Neural Netw. **121**, 74–87 (2020)

6. Kendall, A., Gal, Y.: What uncertainties do we need in Bayesian deep learning for computer vision? Adv. Neural. Inf. Process. Syst. **30**, 5574–5584 (2017)

7. Laine, S., Aila, T.: Temporal ensembling for semi-supervised learning. arXiv preprint arXiv:1610.02242 (2016)

8. Liu, Z., et al.: Swin transformer: hierarchical vision transformer using shifted windows. arXiv preprint arXiv:2103.14030 (2021)

9. Loshchilov, I., Hutter, F.: SGDR: stochastic gradient descent with warm restarts. arXiv preprint arXiv:1608.03983 (2016)

10. Luo, X.: SSL4MIS (2020). https://github.com/HiLab-git/SSL4MIS

11. Oktay, O., et al.: Attention U-Net: learning where to look for the pancreas. arXiv preprint arXiv:1804.03999 (2018)

12. Paszke, A., Chaurasia, A., Kim, S., Culurciello, E.: ENet: a deep neural network architecture for real-time semantic segmentation. arXiv preprint arXiv:1606.02147 (2016)

13. Qiao, S., Shen, W., Zhang, Z., Wang, B., Yuille, A.: Deep co-training for semi-supervised image recognition. In: Ferrari, V., Hebert, M., Sminchisescu, C., Weiss, Y. (eds.) ECCV 2018. LNCS, vol. 11219, pp. 142–159. Springer, Cham (2018). https://doi.org/10.1007/978-3-030-01267-0_9

14. Ronneberger, O., Fischer, P., Brox, T.: U-Net: convolutional networks for biomedical image segmentation. In: Navab, N., Hornegger, J., Wells, W.M., Frangi, A.F. (eds.) MICCAI 2015. LNCS, vol. 9351, pp. 234–241. Springer, Cham (2015). https://doi.org/10.1007/978-3-319-24574-4_28

15. Strudel, R.: Segmenter (2021). https://github.com/rstrudel/segmenter

16. Strudel, R., Garcia, R., Laptev, I., Schmid, C.: Segmenter: transformer for semantic segmentation. arXiv preprint arXiv:2105.05633 (2021)

17. Tarvainen, A., Valpola, H.: Mean teachers are better role models: weight-averaged consistency targets improve semi-supervised deep learning results. In: Proceedings of the 31st International Conference on Neural Information Processing Systems, pp. 1195–1204 (2017)

18. Vaswani, A., et al.: Attention is all you need. In: Advances in Neural Information Processing Systems, pp. 5998–6008 (2017)

19. Vu, T.H., Jain, H., Bucher, M., Cord, M., Pérez, P.: ADVENT: adversarial entropy minimization for domain adaptation in semantic segmentation. In: Proceedings of the IEEE/CVF Conference on Computer Vision and Pattern Recognition, pp. 2517–2526 (2019)

20. Wang, Z., Voiculescu, I.: Quadruple augmented pyramid network for multi-class COVID-19 segmentation via CT. In: 2021 43rd Annual International Conference of the IEEE Engineering in Medicine Biology Society (EMBC) (2021)

21. Wang, Z., Zhang, Z., Voiculescu, I.: RAR-U-Net: a residual encoder to attention decoder by residual connections framework for spine segmentation under noisy labels. In: 2021 IEEE International Conference on Image Processing (ICIP), pp. 21–25. IEEE (2021)

22. Wightman, R.: Pytorch image models (2019). https://github.com/rwightman/pytorch-image-models. https://doi.org/10.5281/zenodo.4414861
23. Yu, L., Wang, S., Li, X., Fu, C.-W., Heng, P.-A.: Uncertainty-aware self-ensembling model for semi-supervised 3D left atrium segmentation. In: Shen, D., et al. (eds.) MICCAI 2019. LNCS, vol. 11765, pp. 605–613. Springer, Cham (2019). https://doi.org/10.1007/978-3-030-32245-8_67
24. Zhang, Y., Yang, L., Chen, J., Fredericksen, M., Hughes, D.P., Chen, D.Z.: Deep adversarial networks for biomedical image segmentation utilizing unannotated images. In: Descoteaux, M., Maier-Hein, L., Franz, A., Jannin, P., Collins, D.L., Duchesne, S. (eds.) MICCAI 2017. LNCS, vol. 10435, pp. 408–416. Springer, Cham (2017). https://doi.org/10.1007/978-3-319-66179-7_47
25. Zhang, Z., Li, S., Wang, Z., Lu, Y.: A novel and efficient tumor detection framework for pancreatic cancer via CT images. In: 2020 42nd Annual International Conference of the IEEE Engineering in Medicine & Biology Society (EMBC), pp. 1160–1164. IEEE (2020)

SF-SegFormer: Stepped-Fusion Segmentation Transformer for Brain Tissue Image via Inter-Group Correlation and Enhanced Multi-layer Perceptron

Jinjing Zhang[1]([✉])[iD], Lijun Zhao[2][iD], Jianchao Zeng[1]([✉])[iD], and Pinle Qin[1]

[1] North University of China, No. 3 Xueyuan Road,
Jiancaoping Disctrict, Taiyuan, China
B1707007@st.nuc.edu.cn, 1595928799@qq.com
[2] Taiyuan University of Science and Technology, No. 66, Waliu Road,
Wanbailin District, Taiyuan, China
leejun@tyust.edu.cn

Abstract. Many brain tissue segmentation methods generally utilize one-level fusion to explore complementary discrepancies among different modalities. However, this one-level fusion manner cannot fully explore potential characteristics of multi-modality images. To this end, we propose a multi-level fusion segmentation transformer framework (dubbed SF-SeFormer) for brain tissue segmentation. Specifically, the proposed SF-SegFormer consists of three parts: Double Paired-modality Encoding (DPE) network, Cross Feature Decoding (CFD) network and Semantical Double Boundary Generation (SDBG) branch. Firstly, our DPE network is introduced to extract features from two pairs of dual-modality for the first-level fusion. Secondly, we design CFD network for the second-level and the third-level fusion by using cross-feature updating block and Cross Feature Fusion (CFF) block. Thirdly, we propose multi-stage channel aggregation-based multi-layer perceptron to enrich channel-aggregation diversity for efficient feature representation. Besides, semantical double boundaries can help to distinguish brain tissues, so we design SDBG branch to predict boundary of each target region, which can regularize multi-resolution CFF features. A large number of experiments have shown that proposed method outperforms many state-of-the-art segmentation methods, when evaluating on BrainWeb dataset.

Keywords: Brain tissues · Image segmentation · Deep neural network · Transformer layer · Feature fusion · Double boundary prediction

1 Introduction

Deep Neural Network (DNN) based brain tissue segmentation methods develop rapidly since these methods predict brain tissues accurately and efficiently in

G. Yang et al. (Eds.): MIUA 2022, LNCS 13413, pp. 508–518, 2022.
https://doi.org/10.1007/978-3-031-12053-4_38

an automatic manner, which saves much time and energy of doctors to annotate brain tissues. However, convolutional kernels with limited receptive fields
are difficult to learn global information of MR images, which inevitably lead to
weak recognition of large regions with varied shapes. To overcome this problem, transformer methods are widely adopted to capture global information.
Although transformers efficiently capture contextual information for brain tissue segmentation, they have not considered the problem of early multi-modality
fusion.

In general, many DNN based segmentation methods fuse all the MR modalities at once in the input convolutional layer [1–5], which is named one-level
convolutional fusion manner. This fusion manner uses a convolutional kernel to
linearly combine MR modalities by sliding kernels on the spatial space of MR
images. Therefore, the convolution-based fusion manner shares fusion weights at
spatial dimension of MR images. However, the intensity contrast of MR modalities at spatial dimension is inconsistent, so it inevitably leads to details counteracting for convolutional fusion manner. To resolve this problem, we propose
to fuse multiple MR modalities in a step-wise manner. Specifically, two of three
MR modalities are fused in each encoding path firstly, and then feature maps
from fused MR modality are combined in decoding path.

Brain tissues such as white matter, gray matter and cerebrospinal are inter-
twined, and each region is neighbor to other regions, so some pixels along their
boundaries are easy to be predicted wrongly. To alleviate the problem of inaccurate prediction on boundary, the semantic boundary is proposed to regularize
prediction of brain tissue boundary [6]. However, it is hard to discriminate the
true boundary for different segmentation classes, as shown in Fig. 1(b). To solve
the ambiguity problem of boundary prediction task, we propose semantic double-
boundary for brain tissue segmentation, as shown in Fig. 1(c).

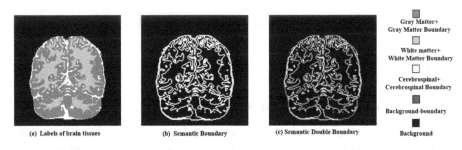

Fig. 1. The difference between semantic boundaries (Ambiguity) and semantic double
boundaries (Clarity).

In transformer layers, after window-based attention, the multi-perceptron
(MLP) layer correlates feature maps by capturing information along channel
dimension. In general, MLP consisting of linear layer, activation layer and
dropout layer fuse all the feature maps at once, which easily leads to feature

counteracting. In this paper, to resolve the problem of early fusion in brain tissue segmentation, and to remain details as more as possible for fusion, we propose Multi-stage Channel Aggregation (MCA)-based MLP to capture local and global channel distribution simultaneously. Our contributions can be summarized as follows:

1) We propose a double paired-modality encoding network to fuse MR three-modality features (T_1, T_2, Pd) in a step-wise way. Firstly, we construct two encoders to extract features from two of three MR modalities respectively. Since T1 weighted MR image shows brain tissue clearly, we divide T_1, T_2, Pd into (T_1, T_2) and (T_1, Pd) as the inputs of two encoders.
2) We propose a cross-feature decoding network to fuse feature maps of these two encoders, since features of two encoders are obtained from different modalities.
3) We propose semantical double-boundary generation branch to generate double brain tissue boundaries as ground-truth to regularize brain tissue boundary prediction task, which can assist brain tissue segmentation.
4) We propose MCA-based MLP to alleviate detail-feature losing problem (Fig. 2).

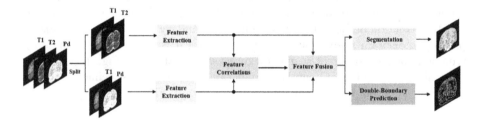

Fig. 2. The pipeline of the proposed method.

2   Related Works

2.1   Transformer-Layer Based Segmentation Method

Transformer-layer based segmentation methods appeal many attentions due to its ability of contextual capturing [7–10]. Transformer is firstly proposed in nature language processing [11], which achieves effective long range dependence in language processing outperforming other memory-based networks such as recurrent neural network and long-short term memory. In computer vision task, transformer is achieved by using self-attention mechanism [8]. However, as we all know that self-attention costs a lot of computation and memory, so transformer layer divides feature maps into non-overlapping patches and do self-attention for each patch, which saves much memory and reduces computation cost. In medical image segmentation, transformer is applied to capture global context information, which improves segmentation accuracy efficiently [7,9,10]. However, these methods have not considered the influence of MR modality fusion manner on the segmentation performance. To enhance recognition ability along region boundaries during segmentation, many semantic boundary recognition methods are proposed [6]. However, these boundaries have not considered boundary ambiguity problem among neighbored regions.

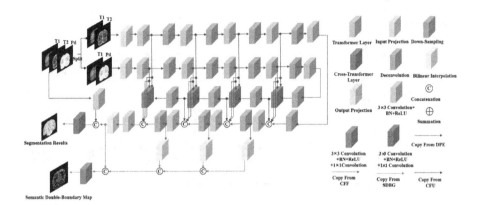

Fig. 3. The network structure of SF-SegFormer

3 The Proposed Method

As shown in Fig. 3, the proposed SF-SegFormer consists of Double Paired-modality Encoding (DPE) network, Cross-Feature Decoding (CFD) network and Semantical Double-Boundary Generation (SDBG) branch. We will elaborate the structure of each part in the following subsections.

3.1 Double Paired-modality Encoding (DPE) Network

To resolve the detail loss problem led by one-time multi-modality fusion manner, we propose DPE network, where the inputs of each encoder are two of three MR modalities, as shown in Fig. 3. Since T_1 weighted MR image can clearly show anatomical structure of brain tissues, which can provide complementary information for T_2 and Pd, we share T_1 MR image between two encoders. Two encoder structures are same, so we just introduce one encoder structure.

Our DPE network consists of transformer layers and down-sampling layers to capture global information of feature maps. The input projection layer uses convolutional layers followed by Leaky ReLU to generate feature maps, then it reshapes 2D feature maps into 1D versions for subsequent transformer layers. The transformer layers mainly use patch based self-attention and MLP to capture

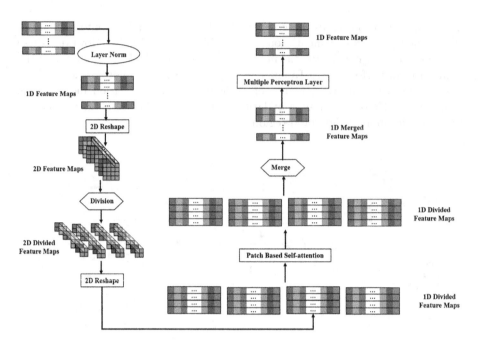

Fig. 4. The diagram of transformer layer

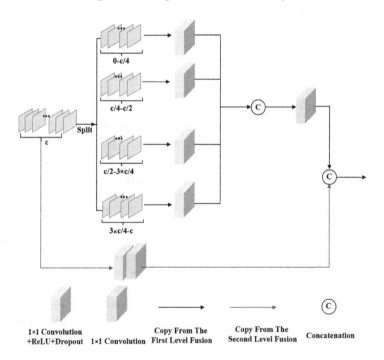

Fig. 5. The structure of Multi-level Channel Aggregation (MCA)-based MLP

global context. The structure of transformer layer in the proposed SF-SegFormer method is shown in Fig. 4.

In the transformer layer and cross transformer layer, the MLP aims to capture features along channel dimension by 1×1 convolution. To capture accurate distribution along channel dimension of feature maps, we use MCA-based MLP method to fuse these features. The structure of MCA-based MLP is shown in Fig. 5. In the first stage, we divided features into four groups. Each group of features are fused by 1×1 convolutions to obtain group channel distribution. Then, we fuse these four groups of channel distribution by 1×1 convolutions. In the second stage, the 1×1 convolutions fuse all the input features to capture channel distributions for new feature-maps generation. The features from the first and the second stages are fused at the final layer.

3.2 Cross-Feature Decoding (CFD) Network

In the CFD network, the Cross-Feature Updating (CFU) block assists Cross-Feature Fusion (CFF) block to achieve feature fusion. The CFU block is introduced for features correlation of two encoding paths by matrix multiplication of cross transformer layers to generate correlation maps. Besides, the CFF block fuses two encoding features and their correlation maps by convolutions.

In CFU block, the features extracted from two encoding paths are different. The features extracted from T_1 and Pd are associated with features extracted from T_1 and T_2 in a manner of matrix multiplication. The multi-head attention of cross transformer layer assigns different features to Q, K and V, which are combined according to the following equation:

$$Y = softmax(\frac{Q \times K^\top}{\sqrt{d_k}}) \times V \tag{1}$$

where, d_k is scaling factor. The Y remains significant features from V, and it is updated by features from Q and K. Q denotes features extracted from T_1 and T_2 MR images. Besides, K and V denote features extracted from T_1 and Pd.

In the CFF block, the discriminative fused-features are obtained by transformer layers, as shown in Fig. 3. Although the transformer layers can capture global features of the image, they cannot well capture local features. Therefore, at the end of decoder network, the low-level features are extracted to compensate the detail features for brain tissues segmentation.

3.3 Semantical Double-Boundary Generation (SDBG) Branch

To solve the ambiguity of semantic boundary, we propose SDBG branch to predict brain tissue boundaries. In SDBG branch, multi-resolution features from CFF block of CFD network are resized into the same resolution, and then the resized features are fed into convolution layers to predict the double-boundary of brain tissues, as shown in Fig. 3.

3.4   Segmentation Loss

During training, the proposed SF-SegFormer is optimized according to the summation of two losses, which can be written as:

$$\mathcal{L}_{Total}(\mathcal{I}, \omega) = \alpha \mathcal{L}_{Seg}(\mathcal{I}, \omega) + \beta \mathcal{L}_{Boundary}(\mathcal{I}, \omega) \tag{2}$$

where $\mathcal{I}$ and ω are input image and DNN parameters respectively. $\mathcal{L}_{Seg}(I, \omega)$ is semantic segmentation loss, and $\mathcal{L}_{Boundary}(I, \omega)$ is the brain tissue boundary prediction loss, both of which use cross-entropy loss. Here, α and β trade-off the contributions of different tasks. Specifically, since the brain tissues are divided into three classes: white matter, gray matter and cerebrospinal fluid, the semantic segmentation loss is a three-class based cross-entropy loss, which can be written as:

$$\mathcal{L}_{Seg}(\mathcal{I}, \omega) = \frac{1}{N} \sum_{i=1}^{N} \left(\sum_{k=1}^{3} (l_i^k ln p_i^k(\mathcal{I}, \omega)) \right) \tag{3}$$

Besides, there are four classes, that is, white matter boundary, gray matter boundary, cerebrospinal fluid boundary and non-boundary in brain tissue boundary prediction task, so the brain tissue boundary prediction loss is a four-class based cross-entropy loss that can be written as:

$$\mathcal{L}_{Boundary}(\mathcal{I}, \omega) = \frac{1}{N} \sum_{i=1}^{N} \sum_{k=1}^{4} (l_i^k ln p_i^k(\mathcal{I}, \omega)) \tag{4}$$

4   Experimental Results and Analysis

4.1   Implementation Details

The proposed SF-SegFormer is implemented by PyTorch [12], which runs on the NVIDIA TITAN RTX GPU. At the beginning of training, the proposed network is initialized by Kaiming uniform initialization method and is optimized by Adam optimizer. 40,000 total updates are used for training SF-SegFormer. Note that, before training and testing, the intensity of multi-modality images on BrainWeb is normalized into range of $[0, 1]$, which can be written as:

$$\widetilde{\mathcal{I}} = \frac{\mathcal{I} - Min(\mathcal{I})}{Max(\mathcal{I}) - Min(\mathcal{I})}, \tag{5}$$

where $\widetilde{\mathcal{I}}$ and $\mathcal{I}$ are the preprocessed MR images and original MR images.

We use dice and Pixel Accuracy (PA) to evaluate the performance of the proposed method. The calculation of these two evaluation indexes can be written as:

$$dice = \frac{2 \times \mathcal{TP}}{2 \times \mathcal{TP} + \mathcal{FP} + \mathcal{FN}}, \tag{6}$$

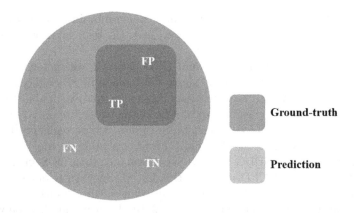

Fig. 6. The diagram of four regions generated by ground-truth and prediction regions.

$$PA = \frac{\mathcal{TP} + \mathcal{TN}}{\mathcal{TP} + \mathcal{FP} + \mathcal{TN} + \mathcal{FN}}, \tag{7}$$

where regions of $\mathcal{TP}$, $\mathcal{TN}$, $\mathcal{FP}$ and $\mathcal{FN}$ represent true positive, true negative, false positive and false negative respectively, as shown in Fig. 6.

4.2 Ablation Study

To clearly observe the influence of loss proportions on SF-SegFormer performance, we assign α and β with different values to get different the loss proportions. The segmentation results are shown in Table 1. From this table, it can be

Table 1. The ablation study on different loss proportions for SF-SegFormer. (Numbers in bold font are the best score at the column.)

Loss proportion		Dice	PA
α	β		
1	0.1	0.9950	0.9976
1	0.2	**0.9952**	**0.9977**
1	0.3	0.9949	0.9975
1	0.4	0.9947	0.9974
1	0.5	0.9948	0.9975
1	0.6	0.9944	0.9973
1	0.7	0.9947	0.9975
1	0.8	0.9945	0.9973
1	0.9	0.9947	0.9974
1	1	0.9944	0.9973
0.1	1	0.9944	0.9973
0.2	1	0.9942	0.9972

seen that these two losses have different influences on brain tissue segmentation. Meanwhile, when α is set as 0.2 and β is set as 1, the segmentation performance of SF-SegFormer is the best.

To validate efficiency of SDBG and CFD network, we remove SDBG network and replace CFD network by single CFF block in SF-SegFormer to segment brain tissues, whose segmentation results are shown in the first row of Table 2. To clearly see the significance of SDBG network, we only remove CFD network of SF-SegFormer to segment brain tissues, whose segmentation results are shown in the second row of Table 2. From this table, it can seen that the SF-SegFormer without SDBG has better performance than SF-SegFormer without SDBG branch and CFD network. Besides, SF-SegFormer outperforms SF-SegFormer without SDBG branch 0.01% in terms of dice and PA. From these results, it can be found that the proposed SDBG branch and CFD network are indispensable for accurate image segmentation.

Table 2. The ablation studies on SDBG branch and CFD network in SF-SegFormer.

Method	Dice	PA
SF-SegFormer w/o (SDBG and CFD)	0.9944	0.9972
SF-SegFormer w/o SDBG	0.9950	0.99976
SF-SegFormer	**0.9952**	**0.9977**

4.3 Performance Comparisons

The segmentation results of the comparative methods are shown in Table 3. From this table, it can be found that SF-SegFomer is at least 0.13% and 0.24% higher than VGG backbone methods in terms of PA and dice respectively. Meanwhile, it also improves PA and dice of ResNet50 backbone methods at least 0.17% and 0.31%. Moreover, the proposed method has 0.1% and 0.17% higher PA and dice scores than UNet-backbone methods. Although KiUNet [3] has fewer parameter numbers than the proposed method, it has 0.03% and 0.05% lower PA and dice scores than the proposed method. Additionally, FCDenseNet [2] and R-Seg [13] have inferior performance than the proposed method, and their parameter numbers are larger than that of the proposed method.

Table 3. Performance comparisons of the state-of-the-art medical image segmentation methods in terms of dice, PA and parameter number on BrainWeb dataset. (The numbers in brackets represent the ranks of different methods in the first column. In last column, we calculate mean rank of each method in each row. $M = 1.0E + 6$)

Methods	PA	Dice	Parameters	Ranks
FCN	0.9575(14)	0.9142(13)	50.42M(14)	31.67
SegNet	0.9834(11)	0.9679(10)	29.45M(12)	11.00
VGGUNet	0.9962(7)	0.9923(6)	25.86M(11)	8.00
VGGCRDN	0.9964(6)	0.9927(5)	14.91M(9)	6.67
ResNet50FCN	0.9554(9)	0.9115(14)	115.84M(16)	13.00
ResNet50UNet	0.9954(9)	0.9909(8)	71.87M(15)	10.67
ResNet50CRDN	0.9960(8)	0.9920(7)	23.66M(10)	8.33
UNetFCN	0.9579(13)	0.9176(12)	1.24M(4)	9.67
UNetSegNet	0.9715(12)	0.9455(11)	2.36M(6)	9.67
U-Net	0.9945(10)	0.9892(9)	1.94M(5)	8.00
CRDN	0.9967(5)	0.9934(4)	1.23M(3)	4.00
IVDNet	0.9974(3)	0.9946(2)	13.61M(8)	4.33
FCDenseNet	0.9975(2)	0.9946(2)	3.46M(7)	3.67
KiUNet	0.9974(3)	0.9946(2)	**0.29M(1)**	2.00
R-Seg	0.9972(4)	0.9944(3)	38.76M(13)	6.67
Our SF-SegFormer	**0.9977(1)**	**0.9952(1)**	1M(2)	**1.33**

5 Conclusion

In this paper, we propose a SF-SegFormer method for brain tissue segmentation. In SF-SegFormer method, the DPE network extracts features from two pairs of dual-modality for the first-level fusion. Then, the CFD network achieves the second-level and the third-level fusion by CFU block and CFF block respectively. Meanwhile, MCA-based MLP is introduced to enrich channel-aggregation diversity for feature representation. Besides, the SDBG branch predicts brain tissue boundaries to improve segmentation accuracy. Experimental results have shown that proposed method has better performances than existing brain tissue segmentation methods. Our future work will study simultaneous brain tissue and tumor segmentation, since brain tissue and tumor show different characteristics, which provide more clues to discriminate them.

Acknowledge. This work is supported by Fundamental Research Program of Shanxi Province (No. 202103021223284) and Taiyuan University of Science and Technology Scientific Research Initial Funding (No. 20192023 and No. 20192055). This study is also support by Scientific and Technological Innovation Programs of Higher Education Institutions in Shanxi, China (Grant No. 2019L0580).

References

1. Wen, Y., Xie, K., He, L.: Segmenting medical MRI via recurrent decoding cell, pp. 12452–12459. AAAI Press (2020)
2. Jégou, S., Drozdzal, M., Vázquez, D., Romero, A., Bengio, Y.: The one hundred layers tiramisu: fully convolutional DenseNets for semantic segmentation. In: 2017 IEEE Conference on Computer Vision and Pattern Recognition Workshops, CVPR Workshops 2017, Honolulu, HI, USA, 21–26 July 2017, pp. 1175–1183. IEEE Computer Society (2017)
3. Valanarasu, J.M.J., Sindagi, V.A., Hacihaliloglu, I., Patel, V.M.: KiU-Net: towards accurate segmentation of biomedical images using over-complete representations. In: Martel, A.L. (ed.) Medical Image Computing and Computer Assisted Intervention - MICCAI 2020 - 23rd International Conference, Lima, Peru, 4–8 October 2020, Proceedings, Part IV, vol. 12264 of Lecture Notes in Computer Science, pp. 363–373. Springer (2020). https://doi.org/10.1007/978-3-030-59719-1_36
4. Badrinarayanan, V., Kendall, A., Cipolla, R.: SegNet: a deep convolutional encoder-decoder architecture for image segmentation. IEEE Trans. Pattern Anal. Mach. Intell. **39**(12), 2481–2495 (2017)
5. Dolz, J., Desrosiers, C., Ben Ayed, I.: IVD-Net: intervertebral disc localization and segmentation in MRI with a multi-modal UNet. In: Zheng, G., Belavy, D., Cai, Y., Li, S. (eds.) CSI 2018. LNCS, vol. 11397, pp. 130–143. Springer, Cham (2019). https://doi.org/10.1007/978-3-030-13736-6_11
6. Liu, Y., Cheng, M.-M., Fan, D.-P., Zhang, L., Bian, J.-W., Tao, D.: Semantic edge detection with diverse deep supervision. Int. J. Comput. Vis. **130**(1), 179–198 (2022)
7. Chen, J., et al.: TransUNet: transformers make strong encoders for medical image segmentation. CoRR, abs/2102.04306 (2021)
8. Liu, Z., et al.: Swin transformer: hierarchical vision transformer using shifted windows. CoRR, abs/2103.14030 (2021)
9. Lin, A., Chen, B., Xu, J., Zhang, Z., Lu, G.: DS-TransUNet: dual swin transformer U-Net for medical image segmentation. CoRR, abs/2106.06716 (2021)
10. Wang, Z., Cun, X., Bao, J., Liu, J.: Uformer: a general U-shaped transformer for image restoration. CoRR, abs/2106.03106 (2021)
11. Vaswani, A., et al.: Attention is all you need. Adv. Neural Inf. Process. Syst. **30** (2017)
12. Paszke, A., et al.: PyTorch: an imperative style, high-performance deep learning library. In: Wallach, H.M., Larochelle, H., Beygelzimer, A., d'Alché-Buc, F., Fox, E.B., Garnett, R. (eds.) Advances in Neural Information Processing Systems 32: Annual Conference on Neural Information Processing Systems 2019, NeurIPS 2019, 8–14 December 2019, Vancouver, BC, Canada, pp. 8024–8035 (2019)
13. Pereira, S., Pinto, A., Amorim, J., Ribeiro, A., Alves, V., Silva, C.A.: Adaptive feature recombination and recalibration for semantic segmentation with fully convolutional networks. IEEE Trans. Medical Imaging **38**(12), 2914–2925 (2019)

Polyp2Seg: Improved Polyp Segmentation with Vision Transformer

Vittorino Mandujano-Cornejo[1(✉)] and Javier A. Montoya-Zegarra[1,2]

[1] Department of Computer Science, Universidad Católica San Pablo (UCSP),
Arequipa, Peru
`vittorino.mandujano@ucsp.edu.pe`
[2] Lucerne University of Applied Sciences and Arts (HSLU), Lucerne, Switzerland
`javier.montoya@hslu.ch`

Abstract. Colorectal cancer (CRC) is the third most common type of cancer worldwide. It can be prevented by screening the colon and detecting polyps which might become malign. Therefore, an accurate detection/segmentation of polyps in colonoscopy images is crucial for CRC prevention. In this paper, we propose a novel transformer-based architecture for polyp image segmentation named Polyp2Seg. The model adopts a transformer architecture as its encoder to extract multi-hierarchical features. Additionally, a novel Feature Aggregation Module (FAM) merges progressively the multi-level features from the encoder to better localise polyps by adding semantic information. Next, a Multi-Context Attention Module (MCAM) removes noise and other artifacts, while incorporating a multi-scale attention mechanism to further improve polyp detections. Quantitative and qualitative experiments on five challenging datasets and over 5 different SOTAs demonstrate that our method significantly improves the segmentation accuracy of Polyps under different evaluation metrics. Our model achieves a new state-of-the-art over most of the datasets.

Keywords: Colorectal cancer · Colonoscopy · Automatic polyp segmentation

1 Introduction

Colorectal cancer (CRC) is the third most common type of cancer worldwide [40]. In 2018, nearly 1 Million of new CRC cases were detected and caused around 551′000 of demises [1]. Therefore, early detection (cancer screening) plays an important role for reducing human mortality. One of the most common CRC screening methods is based on colonoscopy, which relies on the visual inspection of polyps. Polyps are usually benignant, however, it is necessary to monitor them as they can become malignant. Some adenomatus polyps are though hard to see and might be overlooked. In addition, polyps vary in size, shape, and texture, which combined together with different image acquisition conditions (e.g. illumination or low contrast), make the visual inspection of polyps a difficult

G. Yang et al. (Eds.): MIUA 2022, LNCS 13413, pp. 519–534, 2022.
https://doi.org/10.1007/978-3-031-12053-4_39

task even for an expert doctor. Because of these aspects, there is a need for robust Computer-Aided Detection (CAD) systems targeting the automatic triage of colorectal cancer.

Nowadays, the core functionalities of CAD systems are based on deep learning models due to their improved performance. Nonetheless, the scarcity of data together with subjective annotations make this task challenging. To improve polyp segmentation, different neural architectures were proposed, starting with generic CNN architectures, such as the UNet [38] or UNet++ [57]. More recently, specific neural networks targeting polyp segmentation were designed, such as SANet [50] or DCRNet [53], which use ResNets [20] on their backbones. Furthermore, given the recent success of transformers [7,11], the literature has shown promising efforts in hybrid architectures that combine transformers (usually in the encoder) and CNNs (in the decoder). Recent examples include Unet-Trans [37], UNeTR [19], or more specialised models for polyp-segmentation tasks such as the PolypPVT [9]. Following these recent successes we present a novel hybrid architecture named Polyp2Seg, which relies on the strong capabilities of transformers [11] for modelling long-range interactions, whilst covering spatial interactions among local structures. Combined with two novel CNN-based blocks, our proposed model outperforms most of the SOTAs for polyp segmentation on five challenging public datasets, namely, KvasirSEG [24], CVC-Clinic-DB [4], CVC-ColonDB [43], ETIS-LaribPolypDB [41], and EndoScene [46].

Our main contributions are summarised as follows: (*i*) we introduce a novel approach for polyp segmentation, named Polyp2Seg. Our model comprises a novel feature aggregation module (FAM), which extracts and aggregates multi-content hierarchical feature representations at local and regional level. Furthermore, by using a multi-context attention mechanism (MCAM), our model uses attention mechanisms to characterise relevant polyps' low-level cues, which are useful for improving the polyps segmentation accuracies, (*ii*) we conduct extensive experiments on five challenging polyp segmentation datasets. We compare our results with different state-of-the-art techniques and report improved results on almost all datasets defining, thus, a new state-of-the-art for polyp segmentation.

2   Related Work

2.1   Hand-Crafted Approaches

Initial polyp image segmentation approaches were developed by extracting predefined patterns from hand-crafted features. The extracted features were mainly based on color and texture cues [26,39]. More recent approaches in this direction also use shape and contour information as in [17]. In [31], the authors further incorporated super-pixel information for improving polyp detections by giving support to local object regions. Despite their promising results back then, such techniques lack of generalization and might generate different false-positives.

2.2 Deep Learning-Based Approaches

CNN-Based Segmentation. One of the seminal approaches targeting polyp segmentation based on CNNs is the method of [2]. In their work, the authors applied a Fully Convolutional Network (FCN) [29] for detecting polyps in video sequences. Different experimental results showed that their model outperformed other approaches based on hand-crafted features.

In [38] the authors proposed an encoder-decoder architecture named UNet, which has been successfully applied to different medical problems. More recently, the literature has shown different efforts to improve UNets based on some model variations, such as: UNet++ [57], ResUNet++ [23], MobileUNet [25], EfficientUNet [3], to cite some. The encoder-decoder structure of UNets served as inspiration to other architectures as well.

On the other hand, the literature has presented recent CNN-based architectures targeting polyp image segmentation. In [42], the authors proposed an encoder-decoder architecture, in which dilated convolutions were introduced in the encoder-part. The feature maps from the decoder are further upsampled and aggregated together to obtain a more robust segmentation mask. Other successful approaches include PraNet [15], which uses an inverse attention block to better detect polyps by incorporating boundary information of the lesions. The model further combines high- and low-features to obtain the final polyp predictions. Another encoder-decoder architecture intended for real-time polyp identification is HarDNet-MSEG [21]. It relies on the lightweight encoder named HardNet [6]. The decoder was inspired by a Cascaded Partial Decoder [51], which is know to be a reliable and fast module for accurate object saliency detection. Combining those two light-weight modules, the authors achieved promising real-time results.

In DCRNet [53], the authors exploit contextual pixel-wise relationships to improve the segmentation of polyps using attention mechanisms. Therefore, two blocks are attached onto the model's bottleneck to capture pixel-wise contextual information at image-level and at cross-image-level. Finally, in EUNet [36] the authors proposed an encoder-decoder architecture that incorporates attention mechanisms. First to tackle the size variability in polyps, multi-scale non-local attention blocks are used. Second, account for noise in the images, the author use a spatial cross attention applied onto the decoder layers.

Transformer-Based Segmentation. Visual transformers are starting to gain momentum because of their promising results in different tasks [7,27,55]. Originally, transformers were proposed for machine translation tasks [45]. However, because of their high performance, transformers have been extended to the visual domain. One seminal work is called ViT [10]. The ViT model divides the input image into a set of non-overlapping patches that are sequentially fed onto a transformer module. Visual Transformers like HVT [35] and PVT [49] are further new approaches that focus on extracting multi-scale robust feature representations. Examples of transformers for segmentation tasks include SwingUnet [5] or the UnetTransformer [37]. Transformers have been also recently adapted for polyp segmentation tasks [9]. The so-called Poly-PVT model combines multi-scale features extracted from the PVTv2 transformer [48] and uses a CNN-based decoder to obtain precise polyp segmentations. This model represents the current SOTA for polyp segmentation tasks.

3   Method

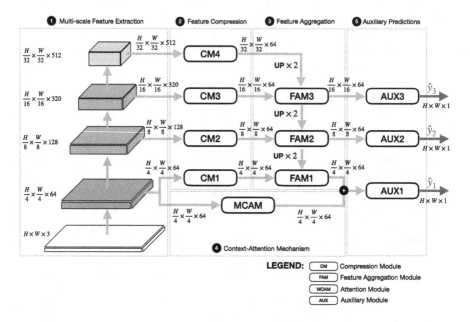

Fig. 1. Overview of our Polyp2Seg network. A set of multi-scale features are extracted from our encoder, which is based on the recent Pyramid Vision Transformer (PVTv2) [47]. Next, the extracted multi-scale features are further compressed {CM$_1$~CM$_4$} and fed into a set of feature aggregation modules {FAM$_1$~FAM$_3$} to directly combine lower-level with higher-level local features. A Multi-Context Attention Module (MCAM) is applied on the lowest-level feature maps to characterise low-level polyp cues such as texture and color. Finally, a set of auxiliary side-outputs are used to predict the final polyp segmentation masks.

The overall architecture of our proposed model is shown in Fig. 1. Our architecture is based on bottom-up/top-down strategies to extract meaningful hierarchical features. Poyp2Seg is composed of five main modules: (*i*) a transformer-based encoder which extracts multi-scale pixel-level features given an input image, (*ii*) a Feature Compression Module (CM), which reduces the side-output features of the encoder to an identical, smaller number, of feature channels to reduce the model's complexity, *(iii)* a Feature Aggregation Module (FAM), which progressively aggregates high-level features to better localize polyps and also adds semantic information, *(iv)* a Multi-Context Attention Module (MCAM), which is designed to remove noise and artifacts, whilst also incorporating a multi-scale attention mechanism to further enhance the polyp detections, and *(v)* a set of Auxiliary side outputs $\hat{y}_i$ activated during training to effectively compensate the diverse size and shape of polyps. During training, we optimise a $\mathcal{L}_{\mathrm{main}}$ main loss function together with a set of auxiliary losses $\mathcal{L}_{\mathrm{aux}}$ by upsampling and comparing the side outputs with the ground-truth. During evaluation, we use only the prediction with highest resolution $\hat{y}_1$. All in all, our versatile and lightweight Poyp2Seg model combines rich low-level and high-level features while transmitting relevant information across the whole model to aggregate pixel-level to object-level polyp information. Next, we describe each of the model's components.

3.1   Multi-scale Feature Representation

Our model relies on transformer-based approaches [11] to extract multi-scale features. Transformers have shown to be robust and to outperform CNNs in different tasks, ranging from: supervised-, adversarial-, contrastive-, to transfer-learning [7]. In our approach, we adopt the recent Pyramid Vision Transformer (PVTv2) [47] as encoder since it has proven to be a lightweight yet accurate backbone for various dense prediction tasks, where multi-scale hierarchical representations are relevant. In the case of polyps this is relevant, as polyps can present different sizes, shapes, and appearances. Thus an effective multi-scale representation is needed.

More formally, given the input image $\mathcal{I} \in \mathcal{R}^{H \times W \times 3}$, we extract a set of multi-scale features of the form $\mathcal{X}_i \in \mathcal{R}^{\frac{H}{2^{i+1}} \times \frac{W}{2^{i+1}} \times C_i}$, for each scale $i \in \{1, 2, 3, 4\}$ and channel $C_i \in \{64, 128, 320, 512\}$. Each of the $\mathcal{X}_i$ generated features provides different high-level semantic cues. Roughly speaking, the feature maps in $\mathcal{X}_1$ account for general appearance cues of polyps, whilst the feature maps $\{\mathcal{X}_2 \sim \mathcal{X}_4\}$ provide mid-level to high-level features.

Next, each of the hierarchical feature maps are fed onto a corresponding Feature Compression Module $\{\mathrm{CM}_1 \sim \mathrm{CM}_4\}$ to further reduce the number of side-output feature channels to 64. The feature compression function $\mathcal{F}_c(\cdot)$ comprises: *(i)* a convolutional layer with a kernel size of 3×3 with padding and stride values set to 1, *(ii)* a batch normalisation [22] layer, followed by a *(iii)* ReLU [18] non-linearity. The $\mathcal{F}_c(\cdot)$ function is used for three main reasons. First, to reduce the model's memory and computational complexity. Second, by compressing the number of feature channels we are also forcing the model to avoid learning duplicate/similar filters, and thus it helps to improve the model generalisation capabilities. Lastly, it homogenises and simplifies the successive element-wise operations in the following layers.

3.2 Feature Aggregation Module (FAM)

As seen in Fig. 1, the different hierarchical compressed feature maps from $\{CM_1 \sim CM_4\}$ are fed onto a set of Feature Aggregation Modules (FAMs) $\{FAM_1 \sim FAM_3\}$, which receive as input both the current compressed feature map f^{cm_i} and the compressed feature map from the previous direct level $f^{cm_{i+1}}$. The goal of the FAM is to combine lower-level with higher-level local features. The combination of local context information from low-level features together with rich global context information from high-level features contribute to obtain more refined object segmentations. Specifically, given a pair of compressed feature maps $(\{f^{cm_i}, f^{cm_{i+1}}\}, i \in \{1, 2, 3\})$, a FAM is defined as a compositional function $\mathcal{F}_{fam}(\{f^{cm_i}, f^{cm_{i+1}}\})$ of the form:

$$\mathcal{F}_{fam}(\cdot) = \text{SiLU}\left(\mathcal{H}_{CB}\left(\mathcal{F}_{sil}(\{f^{cm_i}, f^{cm_{i+1}}\})\right) \oplus f^{cm_i}\right) \tag{1}$$

where the SiLU [12] activation function is applied over the element-wise addition $\oplus$ between the compressed feature map f^{cm_i} and the $\mathcal{H}_{CB}(\cdot)$ block. The $\mathcal{H}_{CB}(\cdot)$ block consists of a convolutional layer with a 1×1 kernel that recovers the original channel dimension followed by a batch normalisation layer. Furthermore, the input to the $\mathcal{H}_{CB}(\cdot)$ block consists of a SiLU-based compositional function $\mathcal{F}_{sil}(\cdot)$ given by:

$$\mathcal{F}_{sil}(\cdot) = \mathcal{H}_{DCSil}\left(\mathcal{H}_{CSil}(f^{cm_i}) \otimes \mathcal{H}_{CSil}(\mathcal{F}_{UP}(f^{cm_{i+1}}))\right) \tag{2}$$

where $\otimes$ denote the element-wise multiplication operator. In addition, the $\mathcal{H}_{DCSil}(\cdot)$ block consists of a depth-wise convolutional layer with a 3×3 kernel to reduce the channel dimension followed by batch normalisation layer and a SiLU layer. By using a depth-wise convolutional layer, the $\mathcal{H}_{DCSil}(\cdot)$ block allows us to further reduce the number of model parameters.

Furthermore, the $\mathcal{F}_{sil}(\cdot)$ compositional function also relies on the pairwise multiplication $\otimes$ of two $\mathcal{H}_{CSil}(\cdot)$ blocks, each of which is applied over a pair of compressed feature maps $\{f^{cm_i}, \mathcal{F}_{UP}(f^{cm_{i+1}})\}$ and allows us to respectively combine low-level with higher-level local features. Note that the $\mathcal{F}_{UP}(\cdot)$ operator represents a bilinear upsampling layer. A $\mathcal{H}_{CSil}(\cdot)$ block consists of a convolutional layer with 1×1 kernel size to reduce the channel dimensions, followed by a batch normalisation layer and a SiLU non-linearity. An illustration of the novel FAM block is presented in Fig. 2.

3.3 Multi-context Attention Module (MCAM)

It is known that especially in polyp segmentation low-level cues such as texture and color play an important role [15,50]. In this sense, we extract discriminative low-level features using the proposed Multi-Context Attention Module (MCAM), which is applied only on the low-level feature map $\mathcal{X}_1$ and also integrates attention information. More formally, the MCAM is represented as a compositional function $\mathcal{F}_{mcam}(\mathcal{X}_1)$ which is first built upon feature normalisation strategies:

$$\mathcal{X}_{cat} = \mathcal{F}_{CAT}\left(\mathcal{R}_{max}(\mathcal{X}_1), \mathcal{R}_{avg}(\mathcal{X}_1)\right) \tag{3}$$

FEATURE AGGREGATION MODULE (FAM)

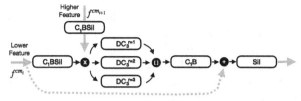

Fig. 2. Feature Aggregation Module (FAM): The FAM block merges progressively the multi-level features from the encoder to better localise polyps by adding semantic information.

where the $\mathcal{F}_{\text{CAT}}(\cdot)$ operator represents the concatenation operation along the feature channel dimension, whilst $\mathcal{R}_{\max}(\cdot)$ and $\mathcal{R}_{\text{avg}}(\cdot)$ denote respectively the maximum and average feature map values along the channel dimension as well. A particular note on the $\mathcal{R}_{\max}(\cdot)$ and $\mathcal{R}_{\text{avg}}(\cdot)$ functions is that they both help respectively to intrinsically remove noisy artifacts, while looking for dominant features related to the foreground objects. Next, the $\mathcal{F}_{\text{mcam}}(\mathcal{X}_1)$ compositional function can be defined as:

$$\mathcal{F}_{\text{mcam}}(\cdot) = \mathcal{F}_{\text{CAT}}\left(\mathcal{X}_1 \otimes \prod_{k=\{3,5,7\}} \mathcal{H}_{DSA_{k \times k}}(\mathcal{X}_{\text{CAT}})\right) \tag{4}$$

where the application of the $\mathcal{H}_{DSA}\, k \times k(\cdot)$ attention block generates three different parallel branches $\{b_k, k = \{3, 5, 7\}\}$, each of them consisting of a sequence of convolutional and depth-wise dilated convolutional operators with kernels of size $k \times k$. The last convolutional layer of each $\mathcal{H}_{DSA}(\cdot)$ is formed by a Sigmoid so as to obtain a probabilistic interpretation of the feature maps. Finally, all parallel $\mathcal{H}_{DSA}(\cdot)$ branches are concatenated together using the $\mathcal{F}_{\text{CAT}}(\cdot)$ operator. Note that the MCAM allows us to account for local semantic cues by imposing rich context local information combined with attention information. An illustration of the MCAM module is depicted in Fig. 3.

MULTI-CONTEXT ATTENTION MODULE (MCAM)

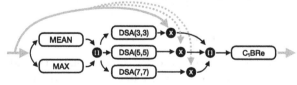

Fig. 3. Multi-Context Attention Module (MCAM): The MCAM block helps to compensante for noise and other artifacts, while incorporating a multi-scale attention mechanism to further improve polyp detections.

3.4 Loss Function

Our overall loss function is composed of two losses, namely a main loss $\mathcal{L}_{\text{main}}$ and auxiliary losses $\mathcal{L}_{\text{aux}}$. Given the ground-truth $\mathcal{Y}$ and the prediction $\hat{y}$, the total loss function $\mathcal{L}_{\text{total}}$ is given by: $\mathcal{L}_{\text{total}} = \mathcal{L}_{\text{main}}(\mathcal{Y}, \hat{y}_1) + \lambda \sum_{k=3}^{5} \mathcal{L}_{\text{aux}}(\mathcal{Y}, \hat{y}_k)$ where each loss term $\mathcal{L}$ is defined as: $\mathcal{L} = \mathcal{L}_{\text{dice}}^{w} + \mathcal{L}_{\text{iou}}^{w}$ and where $\mathcal{L}_{\text{dice}}^{w}$ and $\mathcal{L}_{\text{iou}}^{w}$ represent respectively the weighted Dice and IoU losses. Note that the λ parameter was set experimentally to $\lambda = 1$.

The auxiliary losses are computed over the different side outputs of our model $\{\hat{y}_1 \sim \hat{y}_3\}$, which are obtained from the Auxiliary Blocks $\{\text{AUX}_1 \sim \text{AUX}_3\}$. Each Auxiliary Block consists of an Upsampling step followed by a 3×3 convolutional layer together a Sigmoid function.

4 Experimental Results

4.1 Datasets

We report results on five challenging polyp segmentation datasets, namely the Kvasir-SEG [24], the CVC-Clinic [4], ETIS [41], CVC-ColonDB [43], and EndoScene [46] datasets. In our experiments, we adopt the same training protocol as originally proposed in [15]. We perform different quantitative and qualitative experiments and compare our proposed model against six SOTA medical image segmentation methods, namely: PraNet [15], DCRNet [53], SANet [50], MSNet [56], and Polyp-PVT [9], and also with other standard segmentation models, such as: the U-Net [38], U-Net++ [58], SFA(MICCAI'19) [16]

4.2 Evaluation Metrics

To evaluate the different models, we use six different widely-adopted evaluation metrics for medical image segmentation tasks, namely: Dice [33], Intersection-over-Union (IoU), mean absolute error (MAE), weighted F-measure (F_{β}^{w}) [32], S-measure (S_{α}) [13], and E-measure (E_{ξ}) [14]. Whilst the lower value is better for the MAE, the higher values are better for the other metrics. For a fair comparison, all the models have been trained on the same training, validation, and test splits. Furthermore, whenever available, we used the authors' source code together with pre-trained backbones on the Imagenet dataset [8].

4.3 Implementation Details

Our model is implemented using the PyTorch framework and trained on a TitanXP GPU for 75 epochs with a mini-batch size of 8. All images are resized to 352×352 px. and we employ the multi-scale training strategy as in PraNet [15]. To optimise our model parameters, we rely on the AdamW [30] optimiser and set both the learning rate and the weight decay to $1e - 4$. Warm-up and linear decay strategies are used to adjust the learning rate. The total training time of the model is of nearly 3.5 h on average. To avoid overfitting, we perform different image transformations on-the-fly, including: horizontal flipping, vertical flipping, and random rotation between $[-20, 20]$ degrees, and color-jittering. During evaluation, we resize the images to 352×352 and do not perform any post-processing optimisation tasks.

4.4   Quantitative Analysis

Table 1 compares the performance of different SOTAs in terms of 7 different metrics. Based on the overall performances, we can notice that our model outperforms its counterparts in almost all the metrics. A larger improvement can be seen on the Kvasir and ETIS datasets. On the Kvasir dataset, our model improves the mDice score by a margin of 1.3% and 2.4% when compared respectively to the second-, and third-best models, namely PolypPVT [9] and MSNet [56] models. On the ETIS dataset, our proposed model achieves an important improvement in the mDice score of 4.2% over the second best method, PolypPVT [9], and of 14.0% compared to the third-best method named MSNet [56].

Furthermore, we compare in Table 2 the different baselines by their number of parameters against their corresponding mean Dice score. We illustrate results on 4 datasets: Kvasir [24], ETIS [41], ClinicDB [4], and ColonDB [43]. Our model shows a good balance between performance and number of parameters.

In addition, we report in Table 3 the number of parameters in Millions for each evaluated baseline.

Ablation Studies. As part of our ablation studies, we conduct different experiments to evaluate key components of the proposed architecture, namely the impact of the backbone and the proposed modules. We use PVTv2 [48] as our baseline and compare in Table 4 the overall performance improvement of the model when trained with transformers and with the different proposed modules (FAM and CAM). More specifically, the mDic score increases by 3.7% in Kvasir-SEG [24], 4.1% in Clinic DB [4], 6.5% in ColonDB [43], and 7.0% in ETIS [41] when the PVTv2 [48] backbone is preferred over traditional CNN backbones such as the EfficientNet [52] on the evaluated datasets.

Effectiveness of FAM: We investigate the contribution of the FAM module. We replace the FAM module by a simple concatenation and weighted 3×3 convolution block. The use of FAM increases the mDice by 0.3% in Kvasir [24] and ClinicDB [4] and by 1.1% in ColonDB [43] with less than 153k parameters.

Effectiveness of MCAM: The MCAM block was designed to capture camouflage patterns in Polyps. As it is shown in Table 4 the MCAM block helps to improve the performance by 1% in Kvasir [24] and by 0.5% in ColonDB [43].

4.5   Qualitative Analysis

In Table 5 we compare the results of our model (Ours) against the corresponding ground-truths (GTs) and the results from the SOTA. Among the different SOTAs,

Table 1. Quantitative results on the different evaluated datasets. ↑ and ↓ denote respectively that the larger and smaller scores are better. The highest and second highest scores are shown in **red** and **blue** respectively.

	Model	mDic ↑	mIoU ↑	F_β^w ↑	S_α ↑	mE_ϵ ↑	$maxE_\epsilon$ ↑	MAE ↓
Kvasir	FCN8s (CVPR'15) [29]	0.877	0.813	0.855	0.891	0.933	0.938	0.041
	U-Net (MICCAI'15) [38]	0.821	0.756	0.794	0.858	na	0.901	0.055
	AttUNet (MIDL'18) [34]	0.802	0.718	0.768	0.834	0.877	0.884	0.067
	U-Net++ (TMI'19) [58]	0.824	0.753	0.808	0.862	na	0.907	0.048
	SFA (MICCAI'19) [16]	0.725	0.619	0.670	0.782	na	0.828	0.075
	PraNet (MICCAI'20) [15]	0.898	0.840	0.885	0.915	0.944	0.948	0.030
	DCRNet (arXiv'21) [53]	0.886	0.825	0.868	0.911	0.933	0.941	0.035
	SANet (MICCAI'21) [50]	0.904	0.847	0.892	0.915	0.949	0.953	0.028
	MSNet (MICCAI'21) [56]	0.907	0.862	0.893	0.922	na	0.944	0.028
	Polyp-PVT (arXiv'21) [9]	0.917	0.864	0.911	0.925	0.956	0.962	0.023
	Polyp2Seg (Ours)	0.929	0.882	0.925	0.937	0.969	0.973	0.018
ClinicDB	FCN8s(CVPR'15) [29]	0.885	0.819	0.885	0.914	0.954	0.964	0.018
	U-Net (MICCAI'15) [38]	0.824	0.767	0.811	0.889	na	0.917	0.019
	AttUNet (MIDL'18) [34]	0.753	0.672	0.735	0.834	0.882	0.892	0.032
	U-Net++ (TMI'19) [58]	0.797	0.741	0.785	0.872	na	0.898	0.022
	SFA (MICCAI'19) [16]	0.698	0.615	0.647	0.793	na	0.816	0.042
	PraNet (MICCAI'20) [15]	0.899	0.849	0.896	0.936	0.963	0.979	0.009
	DCRNet (arXiv'21) [53]	0.896	0.844	0.890	0.933	0.964	0.978	0.010
	SANet (MICCAI'21) [50]	0.916	0.859	0.909	0.939	0.971	0.976	0.012
	MSNet (MICCAI'21) [56]	0.921	0.879	0.914	0.941	na	0.972	0.008
	Polyp-PVT (arXiv'21) [9]	0.937	0.889	0.936	0.949	0.985	0.989	0.006
	Polyp2Seg (Ours)	0.929	0.881	0.926	0.946	0.978	0.981	0.007
CVC-300	FCN8s(CVPR'15) [29]	0.861	0.778	0.835	0.906	0.948	0.954	0.010
	U-Net (MICCAI'15) [38]	0.717	0.639	0.684	0.842	na	0.867	0.022
	AttUNet (MIDL'18) [34]	0.778	0.700	0.753	0.862	0.894	0.916	0.013
	U-Net++ (TMI'19) [58]	0.714	0.636	0.687	0.838	na	0.884	0.018
	SFA (MICCAI'19) [16]	0.465	0.332	0.341	0.640	na	0.604	0.065
	PraNet (MICCAI'20) [15]	0.871	0.797	0.843	0.925	0.95	0.972	0.010
	DCRNet (arXiv'21) [53]	0.856	0.788	0.830	0.921	0.943	0.960	0.010
	SANet (MICCAI'21) [50]	0.888	0.815	0.859	0.928	0.962	0.972	0.008
	MSNet (MICCAI'21) [56]	0.869	0.807	0.849	0.925	na	0.943	0.010
	Polyp-PVT (arXiv'21) [9]	0.900	0.833	0.884	0.935	0.973	0.981	0.007
	Polyp2Seg (Ours)	0.890	0.818	0.865	0.931	0.962	0.975	0.007
ColonDB	FCN8s(CVPR'15) [29]	0.681	0.601	0.666	0.794	0.815	0.840	0.046
	U-Net (MICCAI'15) [38]	0.519	0.449	0.498	0.711	na	0.763	0.061
	AttUNet (MIDL'18) [34]	0.650	0.560	0.624	0.774	0.804	0.832	0.046
	U-Net++ (TMI'19) [58]	0.490	0.413	0.467	0.691	na	0.762	0.064
	SFA (MICCAI'19) [16]	0.467	0.351	0.379	0.634	na	0.648	0.094
	PraNet (MICCAI'20) [15]	0.712	0.640	0.699	0.820	0.847	0.872	0.043
	DCRNet (arXiv'21) [53]	0.704	0.631	0.684	0.821	0.84	0.848	0.052
	SANet (MICCAI'21) [50]	0.753	0.670	0.726	0.837	0.869	0.878	0.043
	MSNet (MICCAI'21) [56]	0.755	0.678	0.737	0.836	na	0.883	0.041
	Polyp-PVT (arXiv'21) [9]	0.808	0.727	0.795	0.865	0.913	0.919	0.031
	Polyp2Seg (Ours)	0.808	0.727	0.787	0.866	0.902	0.907	0.031
ETIS	FCN8s(CVPR'15) [29]	0.696	0.605	0.647	0.810	0.841	0.848	0.021
	U-Net (MICCAI'15) [38]	0.406	0.343	0.366	0.682	na	0.645	0.036
	AttUNet (MIDL'18) [34]	0.485	0.400	0.429	0.699	0.713	0.720	0.034
	U-Net++ (TMI'19) [58]	0.413	0.342	0.390	0.681	na	0.704	0.035
	SFA (MICCAI'19) [16]	0.297	0.219	0.231	0.557	na	0.515	0.109
	PraNet (MICCAI'20) [15]	0.628	0.567	0.600	0.794	0.808	0.841	0.031
	DCRNet (arXiv'21) [53]	0.556	0.496	0.506	0.736	0.742	0.773	0.096
	SANet (MICCAI'21) [50]	0.750	0.654	0.685	0.849	0.881	0.897	0.015
	MSNet (MICCAI'21) [56]	0.719	0.664	0.678	0.840	na	0.830	0.020
	Polyp-PVT (arXiv'21) [9]	0.787	0.706	0.750	0.871	0.906	0.910	0.013
	Polyp2Seg (Ours)	0.820	0.738	0.779	0.890	0.916	0.928	0.015

we selected the top 4 performing models, namely the MSNet [56], SANet [50], PraNet [15], and PolypPVT [9]. The visual inspection of the results over the different datasets demonstrate that our model can accurately localise different types of polyps, which vary in size, shape, and photommetrical properties. These visualisations cover challenging situations, which include: (i) small polyps, (ii) artifacts from image acquisition conditions, (iii) partial occlusions, and (iv) complex backgrounds.

Table 2. Model parameters: for each model we compare its total number of parameters (x-axis) against the mean Dice score (y-axis) in four different datasets.

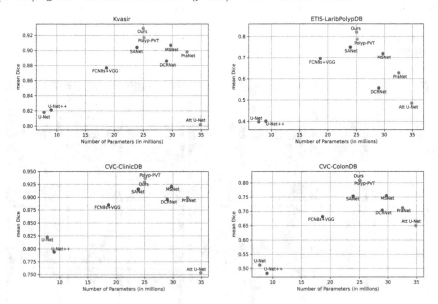

Table 3. Model parameters: number of parameters of the compared models counted in millions.

Model	Params ↓ (M)
AttUNet (MIDL'18) [34]	34.88
PraNet (MICCAI'20) [15]	32.55
MSNet (MICCAI'21) [56]	29.74
DCRNet (arXiv'21) [53]	29.0
Polyp-PVT (arXiv'21) [9]	25.11
Polyp2Seg (Ours)	25.0
SANet (MICCAI'21) [50]	23.9
FCN8s (CVPR'15) [29]	18.64
U-Net++ (TMI'19) [58]	9.0
U-Net (MICCAI'15) [38]	7.76

Table 4. Quantitative results for ablation studies on the evaluated datasets considering mDice and mIoU. The different rows denote the impact on using different configurations.

Ablation		Kvasir		Clinic		CVC-300		ColonDB		ETIS	
Backbones	Modules	mDic ↑	mIoU ↑	mDic ↑	mIoU ↑	mDic ↑	mIoU ↑	mDic ↑	mIoU ↑	mDic ↑	mIoU ↑
EfficientNetB6 [44]	–	0.896	0.837	0.892	0.830	0.898	0.831	0.759	0.675	0.766	0.689
ConvNeXt [28]	–	0.922	0.873	0.914	0.864	0.905	0.840	0.775	0.696	0.798	0.711
PoolFormer [54]	–	0.904	0.847	0.905	0.848	0.868	0.802	0.767	0.684	0.782	0.706
PVTv2 [47]	w/o FAM	0.926	0.876	0.926	0.877	0.902	0.836	0.799	0.718	0.836	0.761
	w/o MCAM	0.920	0.870	0.928	0.879	0.899	0.833	0.804	0.723	0.823	0.743
	Final	0.929	0.882	0.929	0.881	0.890	0.818	0.808	0.727	0.820	0.738

Table 5. Qualitative visual comparison of the proposed model (Ours) against 4 top-performing SOTAs in the Kvasir [24], ClinicDB [4], ColonDB [43], and ETIS [41] datasets. Correct polyps (true positives) are displayed in yellow. Missed polyps (false negatives) are displayed in blue. Wrong detected polyps are displayed in red (false positives).

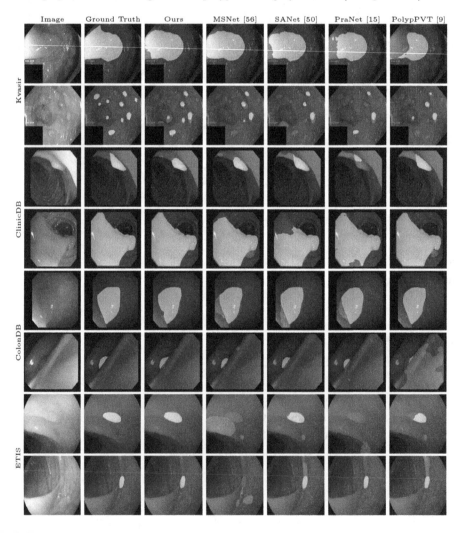

Table 6. Internal representations: visual inspection of the learned features in the $MCAM$ block, focused on camouflage, and in the $FAM_{1,2,3}$ blocks focused on scale-representation.

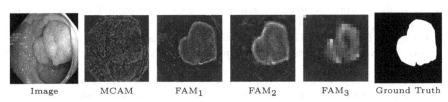

| Image | MCAM | FAM_1 | FAM_2 | FAM_3 | Ground Truth |

Furthermore, to visually inspect the feature representations learned by the MCAM and FAM blocks, we depict in Table 6 some examples of learned features.

5 Conclusions

In this work, we have presented a new model for the automatic segmentation of polyps, which can exhibit large variations in size, shape and might be indistinguishable from background noise. To overcome these issues, our approach relies on different novel modular blocks, such as the Feature Aggregation Module (FAM) (See Sect. 3.2) and the Multi-Context Attention Module (MCAM) (See Sect. 3.3), in order to extract local-level and global-level cues for discriminative polyp characterisation. Quantitative and qualitative evaluations, combined with additional comprehensive ablation studies, on five challenging datasets demonstrate the superiority of the proposed model over the state-of-the-art. In the future, we would like to incorporate geometrical cues onto our model, such as contour information to better localise polyps and to compensate their variations in size and shape.

References

1. Erratum: Global cancer statistics 2018: GLOBOCAN estimates of incidence and mortality worldwide for 36 cancers in 185 countries. CA: A Cancer J. Clinicians **70**(4), 313–313 (2020). https://doi.org/10.3322/caac.21609. https://doi.org/10.3322/caac.21609
2. Akbari, M., et al.: Polyp segmentation in colonoscopy images using fully convolutional network (2018)
3. Baheti, B., Innani, S., Gajre, S., Talbar, S.: Eff-unet: a novel architecture for semantic segmentation in unstructured environment, pp. 1473–1481, June 2020. https://doi.org/10.1109/CVPRW50498.2020.00187
4. Bernal, J., Sánchez, F.J., Fernández-Esparrach, G., Gil, D., Rodríguez, C., Vilariño, F.: Wm-dova maps for accurate polyp highlighting in colonoscopy: validation vs. saliency maps from physicians. Comput. Med. Imaging Graph. Official J. Comput. Med. Imaging Soc. **43**, 99–111 (2015). https://doi.org/10.1016/j.compmedimag.2015.02.007. https://doi.org/10.1016/j.compmedimag.2015.02.007

5. Cao, H., et al.: Swin-unet: Unet-like pure transformer for medical image segmentation (2021)
6. Chao, P., Kao, C.Y., Ruan, Y.S., Huang, C.H., Lin, Y.L.: Hardnet: a low memory traffic network. In: International Conference on Computer Vision (ICCV), pp. 3552–3561, October 2019
7. Chen, X., Hsieh, C.J., Gong, B.: When vision transformers outperform resnets without pretraining or strong data augmentations. arXiv preprint arXiv:2106.01548 (2021)
8. Deng, J., Dong, W., Socher, R., Li, L.J., Li, K., Fei-Fei, L.: Imagenet: a large-scale hierarchical image database. In: Conference on Computer Vision and Pattern Recognition (CVPR), pp. 248–255 (2009)
9. Dong, B., Wang, W., Fan, D., Li, J., Fu, H., Shao, L.: Polyp-pvt: polyp segmentation with pyramid vision transformers. CoRR abs/2108.06932 (2021). https://arxiv.org/abs/2108.06932
10. Dosovitskiy, A., et al.: An image is worth 16x16 words: Transformers for image recognition at scale. CoRR abs/2010.11929 (2020). https://arxiv.org/abs/2010.11929
11. Dosovitskiy, A., et al.: An image is worth 16x16 words: Transformers for image recognition at scale (2021)
12. Elfwing, S., Uchibe, E., Doya, K.: Sigmoid-weighted linear units for neural network function approximation in reinforcement learning. Neural Networks official J. Int. Neural Network Soc. **107**, 3–11 (2018)
13. Fan, D., Cheng, M., Liu, Y., Li, T., Borji, A.: Structure-measure: a new way to evaluate foreground maps. In: International Conference on Computer Vision (ICCV), pp. 4558–4567 (2017)
14. Fan, D.P., Gong, C., Cao, Y., Ren, B., Cheng, M.M., Borji, A.: Enhanced-alignment measure for binary foreground map evaluation. In: International Joint Conference on Artificial Intelligence IJCAI, pp. 698–704, June 2018
15. Fan, D.P., et al.: Pranet: parallel reverse attention network for polyp segmentation (2020)
16. Fang, Y., Chen, C., Yuan, Y., Tong, K.: Selective feature aggregation network with area-boundary constraints for polyp segmentation. In: Shen, D., Liu, T., Peters, T.M., Staib, L.H., Essert, C., Zhou, S., Yap, P.-T., Khan, A. (eds.) MICCAI 2019. LNCS, vol. 11764, pp. 302–310. Springer, Cham (2019). https://doi.org/10.1007/978-3-030-32239-7_34
17. Ganz, M., Yang, X., Slabaugh, G.: Automatic segmentation of polyps in colonoscopic narrow-band imaging data. IEEE Trans. Biomed. Eng. **59**(8), 2144–2151 (2012). https://doi.org/10.1109/TBME.2012.2195314
18. Glorot, X., Bordes, A., Bengio, Y.: Deep sparse rectifier neural networks. In: International Conference on Artificial Intelligence and Statistics. Proceedings of Machine Learning Research, vol. 15, pp. 315–323 (2011)
19. Hatamizadeh, A., et al.: Unetr: transformers for 3d medical image segmentation (2021)
20. He, K., Zhang, X., Ren, S., Sun, J.: Deep residual learning for image recognition. CoRR abs/1512.03385 (2015). http://arxiv.org/abs/1512.03385
21. Huang, C., Wu, H., Lin, Y.: Hardnet-mseg: a simple encoder-decoder polyp segmentation neural network that achieves over 0.9 mean dice and 86 FPS. CoRR abs/2101.07172 (2021). https://arxiv.org/abs/2101.07172
22. Ioffe, S., Szegedy, C.: Batch normalization: Accelerating deep network training by reducing internal covariate shift. In: International Conference on Machine Learning (ICML). Proceedings of Machine Learning Research, vol. 37, pp. 448–456 (2015)

23. Jha, D., et al.: Simulamet: Resunet++: an advanced architecture for medical image segmentation, December 2019. https://doi.org/10.1109/ISM46123.2019.00049
24. Jha, D., Smedsrud, P.H., Riegler, M.A., Halvorsen, P., de Lange, T., Johansen, D., Johansen, H.D.: Kvasir-SEG: a segmented polyp dataset. In: Ro, Y.M., Cheng, W.-H., Kim, J., Chu, W.-T., Cui, P., Choi, J.-W., Hu, M.-C., De Neve, W. (eds.) MMM 2020. LNCS, vol. 11962, pp. 451–462. Springer, Cham (2020). https://doi.org/10.1007/978-3-030-37734-2_37
25. Jing, J., Wang, Z., Rätsch, M., Zhang, H.: Mobile-unet: an efficient convolutional neural network for fabric defect detection. Textile Res. J. 004051752092860, May 2020. https://doi.org/10.1177/0040517520928604
26. Jorge Bernal, J.S., Vilario, F.: Towards automatic polyp detection with a polyp appearance model (2012)
27. Liu, Z., et al.: Swin transformer: hierarchical vision transformer using shifted windows. In: International Conference on Computer Vision (ICCV), pp. 10012–10022, October 2021
28. Liu, Z., Mao, H., Wu, C.Y., Feichtenhofer, C., Darrell, T., Xie, S.: A convnet for the 2020s. arXiv preprint arXiv:2201.03545 (2022)
29. Long, J., Shelhamer, E., Darrell, T.: Fully convolutional networks for semantic segmentation. CoRR abs/1411.4038 (2014). http://arxiv.org/abs/1411.4038
30. Loshchilov, I., Hutter, F.: Decoupled weight decay regularization. In: International Conference on Learning Representations (ICLR) (2019)
31. Maghsoudi, O.: Superpixel based segmentation and classification of polyps in wireless capsule endoscopy, pp. 1–4, December 2017. https://doi.org/10.1109/SPMB.2017.8257027
32. Margolin, R., Zelnik-Manor, L., Tal, A.: How to evaluate foreground maps? In: Conference on Computer Vision and Pattern Recognition (CVPR), pp. 248–255, June 2014
33. Milletari, F., Navab, N., Ahmadi, S.: V-net: fully convolutional neural networks for volumetric medical image segmentation. In: International Conference on 3D Vision, pp. 565–571 (2016)
34. Oktay, O., et al.: Attention u-net: learning where to look for the pancreas, April 2018
35. Pan, Z., Zhuang, B., Liu, J., He, H., Cai, J.: Scalable visual transformers with hierarchical pooling. CoRR abs/2103.10619 (2021), https://arxiv.org/abs/2103.10619
36. Patel, K., Bur, A.M., Wang, G.: Enhanced u-net: a feature enhancement network for polyp segmentation (2021)
37. Petit, O., Thome, N., Rambour, C., Soler, L.: U-net transformer: self and cross attention for medical image segmentation (2021)
38. Ronneberger, O., Fischer, P., Brox, T.: U-net: convolutional networks for biomedical image segmentation. CoRR abs/1505.04597 (2015). http://arxiv.org/abs/1505.04597
39. Gross, S.: Manuel Kennel. Springer, Berlin, Heidelberg, T.S.J.W.J.T.C.T.T.A. (2009)
40. Silva, J., Histace, A., Romain, O., Dray, X., Granado, B.: Toward embedded detection of polyps in WCE images for early diagnosis of colorectal cancer. Int. J. Comput. Assisted Radiol. Surg. 9(2), 283–293 (2013). https://doi.org/10.1007/s11548-013-0926-3, https://doi.org/10.1007/s11548-013-0926-3
41. Silva, J.S., Histace, A., Romain, O., Dray, X., Granado, B.: Towards embedded detection of polyps in WCE images for early diagnosis of colorectal cancer. Int. J. Comput. Assisted Radiol. Surg. 9(2), 283–293 (2014). https://doi.org/10.1007/s11548-013-0926-3. https://hal.archives-ouvertes.fr/hal-00843459

42. Sun, X., Zhang, P., Wang, D., Cao, Y., Liu, B.: Colorectal polyp segmentation by u-net with dilation convolution (2019)

43. Tajbakhsh, N., Gurudu, S., Liang, J.: Automated polyp detection in colonoscopy videos using shape and context information. IEEE Trans. Med. Imaging **35**(2), 630–644 (2016). https://doi.org/10.1109/TMI.2015.2487997, publisher Copyright: 2015 IEEE

44. Tan, M., Le, Q.V.: Efficientnet: rethinking model scaling for convolutional neural networks. CoRR abs/1905.11946 (2019), http://arxiv.org/abs/1905.11946

45. Vaswani, A., et al.: Attention is all you need. CoRR abs/1706.03762 (2017). http://arxiv.org/abs/1706.03762

46. Vázquez, D., et al.: A benchmark for endoluminal scene segmentation of colonoscopy images. J. Healthc. Eng. **2017** (2017)

47. Wang, W., et al.: Pyramid vision transformer: a versatile backbone for dense prediction without convolutions. In: International Conference on Computer Vision (ICCV), pp. 568–578

48. Wang, W., et al.: Pvtv 2: improved baselines with pyramid vision transformer. CoRR abs/2106.13797 (2021). https://arxiv.org/abs/2106.13797

49. Wang, W., et al.: Pyramid vision transformer: a versatile backbone for dense prediction without convolutions. CoRR abs/2102.12122 (2021). https://arxiv.org/abs/2102.12122

50. Wei, J., Hu, Y., Zhang, R., Li, Z., Zhou, S.K., Cui, S.: Shallow attention network for polyp segmentation. CoRR abs/2108.00882 (2021). https://arxiv.org/abs/2108.00882

51. Wu, Z., Su, L., Huang, Q.: Cascaded partial decoder for fast and accurate salient object detection. In: The IEEE Conference on Computer Vision and Pattern Recognition (CVPR), June 2019

52. Xie, S., Girshick, R.B., Dollár, P., Tu, Z., He, K.: Aggregated residual transformations for deep neural networks. CoRR abs/1611.05431 (2016). http://arxiv.org/abs/1611.05431

53. Yin, Z., Liang, K., Ma, Z., Guo, J.: Duplex contextual relation network for polyp segmentation. CoRR abs/2103.06725 (2021). https://arxiv.org/abs/2103.06725

54. Yu, W., et al.: Metaformer is actually what you need for vision. arXiv preprint arXiv:2111.11418 (2021)

55. Zhang, P., et al.: Multi-scale vision longformer: a new vision transformer for high-resolution image encoding. In: International Conference on Computer Vision (ICCV), pp. 2998–3008, October 2021

56. Zhao, X., Zhang, L., Lu, H.: Automatic polyp segmentation via multi-scale subtraction network. CoRR abs/2108.05082 (2021). https://arxiv.org/abs/2108.05082

57. Zhou, Z., Siddiquee, M.M.R., Tajbakhsh, N., Liang, J.: Unet++: a nested u-net architecture for medical image segmentation. CoRR abs/1807.10165 (2018). http://arxiv.org/abs/1807.10165

58. Zhou, Z., Rahman Siddiquee, M.M., Tajbakhsh, N., Liang, J.: UNet++: a nested U-Net architecture for medical image segmentation. In: Stoyanov, D., Taylor, Z., Carneiro, G., Syeda-Mahmood, T., Martel, A., Maier-Hein, L., Tavares, J.M.R.S., Bradley, A., Papa, J.P., Belagiannis, V., Nascimento, J.C., Lu, Z., Conjeti, S., Moradi, M., Greenspan, H., Madabhushi, A. (eds.) DLMIA/ML-CDS -2018. LNCS, vol. 11045, pp. 3–11. Springer, Cham (2018). https://doi.org/10.1007/978-3-030-00889-5_1

Multi-resolution Fine-Tuning of Vision Transformers

Kerr Fitzgerald[1]([✉]), Meng Law[2], Jarrel Seah[2], Jennifer Tang[3],
and Bogdan Matuszewski[1]

[1] University of Central Lancashire, Preston, UK
kffitzgerald@uclan.ac.uk
[2] Department of Radiology, Alfred Health, Melbourne, Australia
[3] St. Vincent's Hospital, Melbourne, Australia

Abstract. For computer vision systems based on artificial neural networks, increasing the resolution of images typically improves the performance of the network. However, ImageNet pre-trained Vision Transformer (ViT) models are typically only openly available for 224^2 and 384^2 image resolutions. To determine the impact of using higher resolution images with ViT systems the performance differences between ViT-B/16 models (designed for 384^2 and 544^2 image resolutions) were evaluated. The multi-label classification RANZCR CLiP challenge dataset, which contains over 30,000 high resolution labelled chest X-ray images, was used throughout this investigation. The performance of the ViT 384^2 and ViT 544^2 models with no ImageNet pre-training (i.e. models were only trained using RANZCR data) was firstly compared to see if using higher resolution images increases performance. After this, a multi-resolution fine-tuning approach was investigated for transfer learning. This approach was achieved by transferring learned parameters from ImageNet pre-trained ViT 384^2 models, which had undergone further training on the 384^2 RANZCR data, to ViT 544^2 models which were then trained on the 544^2 RANZCR data. Learned parameters were transferred via a tensor slice copying technique. The results obtained provide evidence that using larger image resolutions positively impacts ViT network performance and that multi-resolution fine-tuning can lead to performance gains. The multi-resolution fine-tuning approach used in this investigation could potentially improve the performance of other computer vision systems which use ViT based networks. The results of this investigation may also warrant the development of new ViT variants optimized to work with high resolution image datasets.

Keywords: Computer vision · Vision transformer · ViT · Fine-tuning · Transfer learning · Medical data · RANZCR CLiP

1 Introduction

When developing artificial neural networks for computer vision tasks, increasing the resolution of images used for training and inference often improves the performance of the network. Intuitively, this is because higher resolution images contain more information that can be used by the network. However, once a certain image size is reached the

G. Yang et al. (Eds.): MIUA 2022, LNCS 13413, pp. 535–546, 2022.
https://doi.org/10.1007/978-3-031-12053-4_40

performance gained from increasing image resolution will plateau. For EfficientNet [1] and EfficientNetV2 [2], models pre-trained on ImageNet are available that can use 224^2 image resolutions (B0 model variants) to 600^2 image resolutions (B7 model variants). These Convolutional Neural Networks (CNNs) provide good examples of increased classification accuracy on the ImageNet benchmark [3] when using higher image resolutions and also how accuracy begins to plateau once a given image resolution (600^2) is reached. It should be noted that the image resolution at which performance begins to plateaus will likely be different depending on the dataset.

Image resolution has also been shown to have an important effect on CNNs when evaluating their performance on test datasets and for transfer learning applications. Touvron et al. [4] used a light-weight parameter adaptation of a CNN to allow larger image resolutions to be used while testing the network (the main aim was to fix the resolution discrepancy seen by CNNs between training and testing). Touvron et al. showed that test performance increased when using higher resolution images (up to a plateau value) than those the CNN was trained on. Kolesnikov et al. [5] investigated methods to improve the generalization of CNNs for transfer learning tasks by altering network architecture (e.g. replacing Batch Normalization with Group Normalization). They also showed that fine-tuning CNNs to the test dataset resolution can improve transfer learning performance.

In the original Vision Transformer (ViT) paper [6] the authors fine-tuned the ViT network at higher resolution (384^2) than that used in pre-training (224^2) and attained higher accuracies on popular image classification benchmarks (including ImageNet) when using 384^2 ViT models when compared to 224^2 ViT models. This was achieved by keeping the image patch size the same, which results in the ViT network having a larger sequence of patches. However, ViT networks for image resolutions larger than 384^2 were not created and trained/fine-tuned in the original paper.

More recently, the rules determining how ViT models scale have been investigated by scaling ViT models and characterizing the relationships between error rate, data requirements and computing power [7]. This resulted in the creation of the ViT-G/14 model variant [7] which was trained on extremely large proprietary datasets (e.g. JFT-300M) using 224^2 image resolutions before being fine-tuned using the same extremely large proprietary datasets with 518^2 image resolutions. The ViT-G/14 model, which contains approximately two billion parameters, attained previous state-of-the-art on ImageNet with 90.45% top-1 accuracy (top-1 accuracy relates to where the highest class prediction probability is the same as the target label). However, for many users the current hardware requirements needed to train the ViT-G/14 network or use it for transfer learning tasks would be prohibitively expensive. It would be even more challenging to use ViT-G/14 as an encoder for dense prediction (e.g. segmentation or monocular depth estimation) tasks due to even more parameters being needed within the models.

The work presented in this paper details the results of an investigation to take a multi-resolution fine-tuning approach (whereby networks are trained through transfer learning, initially on low resolution images before being fine-tuned on higher resolutions versions of these images) and apply this directly to transfer learning applications relating to medical image analysis using ViT systems. To the best of the authors knowledge, this is the first time that multi-resolution fine-tuning has been applied directly to medical imaging for ViT systems. The medical image dataset used in this investigation consists of over 30,000 chest X-rays (taken to evaluate the positioning of multiple catheters) and allows the multi-label classification performance of ViT models to be evaluated. Firstly, a performance comparison between ViT 384^2 and ViT 544^2 networks with no prior training (i.e. models were only trained using RANZCR CLiP data) was conducted. After the initial performance comparison showed that using larger image sizes is beneficial, a multi-resolution fine-tuning approach was applied directly to the RANZCR CLiP transfer learning task. This was achieved by transferring learned network parameters (via a tensor slice copying technique) from ImageNet pre-trained ViT 384^2 models, which had undergone further training on the 384^2 RANZCR CLiP data, to newly initialized ViT 544^2 models which were further trained on the 544^2 RANZCR CLiP data. Results provide strong evidence that this approach increases multi-label classification accuracy and that using higher image resolution can improve network performance.

2   Method

2.1   Image Dataset Selection

The Royal Australian and New Zealand College of Radiologists (RANZCR) Catheter and Line Position (CLiP) challenge dataset consists of over 30,000 high resolution (typically greater than 2000^2) labelled chest X-ray images [8]. The aim of the original dataset challenge [9] was to detect the presence and position of different catheters and lines within chest X-ray images. The positions of the inserted catheters/lines are important since if they are poorly placed, they can worsen the patient's condition. There are four types of catheters/lines: Endotracheal Tube (ETT), NasoGastric Tube (NGT), Central Venous Catheter (CVC) and Swan-Ganz Catheter (SGC). The ETT, NGT and CVC can be categorized as 'Normal', 'Borderline' or 'Abnormal' and the SGC is either 'Present' or 'Not Present' hence making this a multi-label classification problem with 11 classes. The metric used to evaluate the multi-label classification performance in the original challenge was the 'One vs Rest Area Under Curve Receiver Operator Characteristic' (AUC-ROC) and this metric is used to evaluate performance of models within this investigation. The RANZCR CLiP dataset was selected for this transfer learning investigation due to the high resolution of the images and because classifying the placement of catheters/lines likely requires analysis of fine detail within the images (Fig. 1).

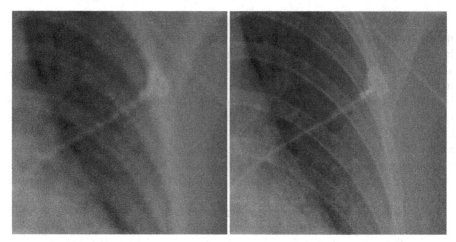

Fig. 1. Example of a cropped X-ray image region (from the RANZCR CLiP database) [8] generated using two different original image resolutions. This demonstrates potential information loss as the image size decreases.

2.2 Multi-resolution Fine-Tuning for Transfer Learning

When using the PyTorch deep learning framework for transfer learning, it is necessary to load weights from pre-trained models into your current model. This commonly requires that the tensors containing the parameters of the models match in name, shape, and size. Therefore, using larger image sizes as input into a ViT model which has been trained on smaller sized images would not be immediately possible. To overcome this limitation, it is possible to copy parameters (in the form of tensor slices) from pre-trained ViT models and insert these into the tensors (which are either the same size or are larger) of a new ViT model capable of processing higher resolution images. This tensor slice copying technique also allows other network design features of the new ViT model to be changed whilst still making use of the original pre-trained ViT model parameters. Examples of such network design features include: fully connected layer ratio, image embedding size, network depth and number of attention heads.

As an example, comparing a standard (i.e. ViT-B/16) ViT 544^2 model to a standard pre-trained ViT 384^2 model shows that only the size and shape of the Layer 2 tensor changes, while for all other layers the size and shape of tensors is identical. Therefore, the learned ViT 384^2 model parameters can be transferred via tensor slice copying to every layer of the 544^2 ViT model. Specifically, for Layer 2 it is possible to either: (1) ignore the ViT 384^2 Layer 2 tensor learned parameters and leave the Layer 2 tensor of the ViT 544^2 with its original initialization state; or (2) transfer the ViT 384^2 Layer 2 tensor learned parameters to the Layer 2 tensor of the ViT 544^2 which only partially fills the tensor.

In this investigation parameters from ImageNet pre-trained ViT-B/16 384^2 models [6, 10] were inserted via the tensor slice copying technique into a newly created ViT 544^2 ViT-B/16 models which had an increased fully connected layer ratio (4.25 compared to 4 in the original ViT 384^2 model). All possible parameters were transferred meaning that some ViT 544^2 layer tensors would have been only partially filled (i.e. option (2) from the previous paragraph) (Table 1).

Table 1. Comparison of the first four layers of a ViT 544^2 network and ViT 384^2 ViT network. Only the size of Layer 2 changes between the models, all other layer sizes match.

Image input size	(384^2)	(544^2)
No. parameters	86,094,341	86,539,781
Layer 1 size	[1, 1, 768]	[1, 1, 768]
Layer 2 size	[1, 577, 768]	[1, 1157, 768]
Layer 3 size	[768, 3, 16, 16]	[768, 3, 16, 16]
Layer 4 size	[768]	[768]

2.3 Fold Selection and PyTorch Model Training

The RANZCR CLiP data was split into twenty folds (using a typical K-Fold random stratified sampling approach) with care also being taken to ensure that no data leakage occurred (e.g. data from a given patient was always contained in the same fold). Due to hardware limitations (all training and validation was run on a single Nvidia 3090 GPU) and the need for repeat runs using different random number seeds, it was not possible to use all twenty folds for cross validation in the transfer learning investigation. Instead six folds consisting of the three highest scoring and three lowest scoring AUC ROC validation scores were selected after the twenty-fold cross validation study was conducted using an ImageNet pre-trained ViT 384^2 network [6, 10] which underwent additional training on the RANZCR CLiP data. This found that the highest scoring validation folds were 14, 8 and 10, with the lowest scoring validation folds being 2, 20 and 12. After six epochs of training overfitting began to occur. The results of the twenty-fold cross validation study are displayed in Fig. 2. No data augmentation or image pre-processing was conducted (Fig. 2).

Before conducting the transfer learning investigation, a performance comparison between ViT 384^2 and ViT 544^2 models with no prior ImageNet training was conducted (i.e. only RANZCR CLiP data was used for training and validation) for each of the six folds selected.

For the investigation into the multi-resolution fine-tuning approach which can be directly applied to transfer learning, the model states of ImageNet pre-trained ViT 384^2 models which underwent additional training on the RANZCR CLiP data were saved for each of the six folds investigated. The saved ViT 384^2 model states after epoch three of training were then transferred to the corresponding ViT 544^2 networks using the tensor slice copying technique. ViT 544^2 networks were then trained on the RANZCR CLiP data, hence allowing for a multi-resolution fine-tuning approach. For each fold, six ViT 544^2 model runs were then conducted using different random number generation seeds. An additional six ViT 384^2 model runs were conducted using different random

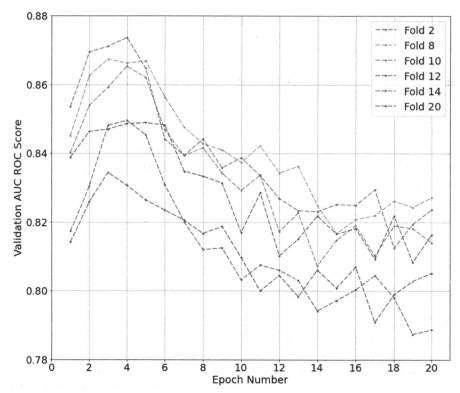

Fig. 2. Comparison of the three highest scoring and three lowest scoring AUC ROC validation scores from the twenty-fold cross validation scoping study conducted using a pre-trained ViT 384^2 network which underwent additional training on the RANZCR CLiP data. Overfitting begins to occur after approximately six epochs.

number generation seeds. These repeat runs were conducted to give confidence that improvements in performance are not down to the small random variability of network predictions. The different random number generation seeds impact the order of how image batches are loaded. In order to focus on the effects of image resolution, the PyTorch training settings and hyperparameters were kept the same between runs. However, it is likely that the training process followed in the original ViT paper [6] is heavily optimized compared to that used this investigation (Table 2).

Table 2. PyTorch training settings and parameters used in this investigation.

PyTorch training option	Selected setting
Optimizer	Adam
Loss function	BCEWithLogitsLoss
Learning rate	1.00e-05
Learning rate decay factor	0.95
Image batch size	4
MLP dropout rate	0.1
Residual path dropout rate	0.1
Attention dropout rate	0.1

3 Results

3.1 ViT 384^2 vs ViT 544^2 Model Comparison with no Prior Training

The results of the performance comparison between the ViT 384^2 and ViT 544^2 networks which had no pre-training for the six folds investigated (i.e. only trained using RANZCR CLiP data) are presented in Fig. 3. It can be seen that the average, maximum and minimum (shown with error bar range) AUC ROC validation scores of the six folds investigated are higher for the ViT 544^2 network (after eight training epochs) when compared to the 384^2 ViT network. Numerical values of the maximum achieved AUC ROC validation scores for each fold investigated are presented in Table 3.

These results provide further evidence of how increasing image resolution can increase the performance of deep learning image classification systems and that this relationship is valid for ViT systems. However, the maximum achieved AUC ROC validation scores for each fold are significantly lower for the ViT 544^2 network with no pre-training compared to those of the ImageNet pre-trained ViT 384^2 network shown in Fig. 2. This necessitates the need for multi-resolution fine-tuning which can be directly applied to transfer learning tasks (Fig. 3 and Table 3).

3.2 Multi-resolution Fine Tuning

The results of the multi-resolution fine-tuning approach directly applied to the transfer learning task of medical image multi-label classification are visualized for each fold using box plots (showing the minimum, maximum, quartiles and median validation AUC ROC scores) in Fig. 4. Apart from for fold 14, the maximum and median AUC ROC scores achieved using the ViT 544^2 network are higher than those obtained using the ViT 384^2 network. However, even though the maximum achieved accuracies are significantly higher when pre-training is used, the magnitude of the performance increase between ViT 544^2 networks and ViT 384^2 networks is smaller compared to when no pre-training was used.

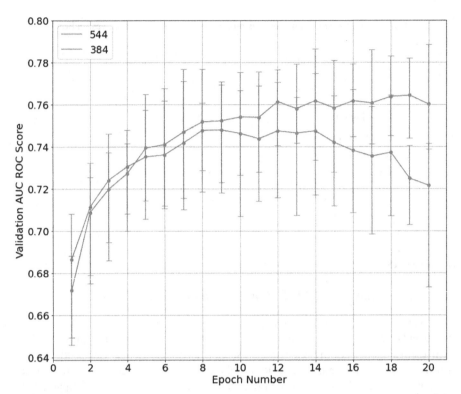

Fig. 3. Comparison of the average, maximum and minimum AUC ROC validation scores of the six folds investigated for the ViT 384^2 and ViT 544^2 networks.

Table 3. ViT 384^2 and ViT 544^2 maximum achieved AUC ROC validation scores for each fold when no pre-training is used.

Fold	384^2	544^2	Difference
14	0.7666	0.7812	0.0146
8	0.7749	0.7885	0.0136
10	0.7571	0.7651	0.0080
2	0.7506	0.7747	0.0241
20	0.7561	0.7602	0.0042
12	0.7185	0.7488	0.0303

These results provide further evidence that multi-resolution fine-tuning can improve network performance and that, importantly, this approach can be directly applied to transfer learning tasks using ViT systems (Fig. 4 and Table 4).

Table 4. Maximum achieved AUC ROC validation scores for each fold for ViT 384^2 pretrained networks and ViT 544^2 networks using the multi-resolution fine-tuning approach.

Fold	384^2	544^2	Difference
14	0.8756	0.8725	−0.0031
8	0.8763	0.8830	0.0067
10	0.8653	0.8689	0.0036
2	0.8496	0.8559	0.0063
20	0.8496	0.8615	0.0119
12	0.8439	0.8519	0.0080

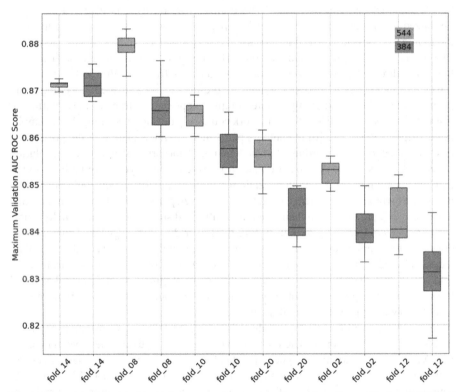

Fig. 4. Box plots showing the minimum, maximum, quartiles and median validation AUC ROC scores of the repeat runs of the six folds investigated for the ViT 384^2 (red) and ViT 544^2 (blue) networks. (Color figure online)

4 Discussion

The performance comparison between the ViT 384^2 and ViT 544^2 networks which had no pre-training strongly demonstrate how using larger image resolutions positively impacts

ViT network performance. This is further supported by the results of the multi-resolution fine-tuning approach which found that the ViT 544^2 network slightly outperformed the ViT 384^2 network for five out of the six folds tested.

The multi-resolution fine-tuning approach could potentially impact the performance of other computer vision systems designed for dense prediction tasks (e.g. monocular depth estimation) which use pre-trained ViT models as encoders. An example of such a system would be the Dense Prediction Transformer (DPT) [11] which previously held state-of-art performance on certain monocular depth challenges (such as NYU-Depth V2 [12]). The DPT used the original ViT 384^2 ImageNet pretrained network as the encoder starting point. In addition, the multi-resolution fine-tuning approach for direct transfer learning may also be applicable to new ViT systems (such as the Vision Longformer [13]) being developed.

It is likely that further improvements could be made to the multi-resolution fine-tuning approach used in this study. The training method used is likely to not be as optimized as that used in the original ViT paper [6] and any improvements made to the training process could further increase the performance of the ViT 544^2 networks. The tensor slice copying technique could also be improved as the approach used in this study directly copied Layer 2 learned parameters from the ViT 384^2 network to Layer 2 of the ViT 544^2 network. Layer 2 represents learned image embeddings with positional encodings and using a more complex approach to transfer these particular learned parameters to the ViT 544^2 network could help during fine-tuning. For example, in the original ViT paper [6] the authors performed 2D interpolation of the pre-trained position embeddings, according to their location in the original image, for resolution adjustment. This would also ensure that all parameters in Layer 2 are updated rather than some parameters keeping their randomly initialized value which could potentially be adversely impacting gradient calculations. However, preliminary investigations which left all Layer 2 parameters in their randomly initialized state had only marginally worse performance compared to partially filling the Layer 2 tensor, suggesting that adverse effects on the gradient calculations are minimal. Examining all twenty folds rather than the six selected folds would also reduce possible bias and conducting more runs for each fold would give even higher confidence in the results obtained. Applying the developed transfer learning approach to other imaging problems and investigating performance would allow external validation of the methods used.

Since the performance gains of the ViT 544^2 networks were essentially attained by changing the number of patches used, this might also justify the development of new ViT network variants designed specifically to work with larger image sizes but with network design parameters which are not as extreme as the ViT-G/14 variant (i.e. significantly reduced network depth and total parameter number). Pre-training and fine-tuning of these ViT networks with higher image resolutions (e.g. $>500^2$) than those used in the original ViT paper (224^2 and 384^2) using large image databases (e.g. ImageNet dataset variants) could lead to significant performance increases. Such models would likely have hardware requirements that would make them accessible to a large number of users/developers and also make them suitable for use in encoder-decoder style systems for dense prediction tasks.

5 Conclusion

The impact of using ViT networks with higher resolution images (compared to those typically used for training on ImageNet dataset variants) on a multi-label classification problem has been evaluated. The dataset used in this investigation was the RANZCR CLiP challenge dataset which consists of over 30,000 high resolution labelled chest X-ray images [8].

A performance comparison between two ViT-B/16 networks [6, 10], which had no pre-training, designed to work with 384^2 and 544^2 image resolutions has been conducted on the RANZCR CLiP medical image multi-label classification task. The ViT 544^2 network outperforms the ViT 384^2 network for all six of the data folds that were tested.

A multi-resolution fine-tuning approach was applied to ViT 544^2 networks directly for the RANZCR CLiP medical image multi-label classification task. To achieve this, ImageNet pre-trained ViT 384^2 model states, after three epochs of additional training on the RANZCR CLiP dataset, were saved. The ViT 384^2 model states were then transferred to ViT 544^2 models using a tensor slice copying technique and the 544^2 models were then trained on the RANZCR CLiP dataset. The results of this approach show that the ViT 544^2 network outperformed the ViT 384^2 network for five out of the six data folds that were tested.

The results obtained provide strong evidence that using larger image resolutions positively impacts ViT network performance. This may justify the development of new ViT network variants (with significantly less computational requirements than the current state-of-the-art ViT-G/14 variant) designed to work with higher image resolutions (i.e. greater than 384^2). Such variants would likely be more accessible to a larger number of users and may also be suitable for use in encoder-decoder systems for dense prediction tasks. The performance of existing encoder-decoder systems for dense prediction tasks, which use ViT based systems as encoders, may also receive transfer learning performance increases by using multi-resolution fine-tuning approaches similar to that used in this investigation.

References

1. Tan, M., Le, Q.: EfficientNet: rethinking model scaling for convolutional neural networks. In: International Conference on Machine Learning (ICML), Long Beach (2019)
2. Tan, M., Le, Q.: EfficientNetV2: smaller models and faster training. In: International Conference on Machine Learning (ICML), Virtual (2021)
3. Deng, J., Dong, W., Socher, R., Li, L., Li, K., Fei-Fei, L.: ImageNet: a large-scale hierarchical image database. In: IEEE Conference on Computer Vision and Pattern Recognition, Miami (2009)
4. Touvron, H., Vedaldi, A., Douze, M., Jegou, H.: Fixing the train-test resolution discrepancy. In: Advances in Neural Information Processing Systems (2019)
5. Kolesnikov, A., et al.: Big transfer (BiT): general visual representation learning. In: Vedaldi, A., Bischof, H., Brox, T., Frahm, J.-M. (eds.) ECCV 2020. LNCS, vol. 12350, pp. 491–507. Springer, Cham (2020). https://doi.org/10.1007/978-3-030-58558-7_29
6. Dosovitskiy, A., et al.: An image is worth 16x16 words: transformers for image recognition at scale. In: International Conference on Learning Representations (ICLR), Virtual (2021)

7. Zhai, X., Kolesnikov, A., Houlsby, N., Beyer, L.: Scaling vision transformers. arXiv (2021)
8. Tang, J., et al.: CLiP, catheter and line position dataset. Sci. Data **8**, 1–7 (2021)
9. Law, M., et al.: RANZCR CLiP - catheter and line position challenge. Kaggle, 8 March 2021. https://www.kaggle.com/competitions/ranzcr-clip-catheter-line-classification/ overview. Accessed June 2021
10. Wightman, R.: PyTorch image models. GitHub Repository (2019)
11. Ranftl, R., Bochkovskiy, A., Koltun, V.: Vision transformers for dense prediction. In: International Conference on Computer Vision (ICCV), Montreal (2021)
12. Silberman, N., Hoiem, D., Kohli, P., Fergus, R.: Indoor segmentation and support inference from RGBD images. In: Fitzgibbon, A., Lazebnik, S., Perona, P., Sato, Y., Schmid, C. (eds.) ECCV 2012. LNCS, vol. 7576, pp. 746–760. Springer, Heidelberg (2012). https://doi.org/10. 1007/978-3-642-33715-4_54
13. Zhang, P., et al.: Multi-scale vision longformer: a new vision transformer for high-resolution image encoding. In: International Conference on Computer Vision (ICCV), Virtual (2021)

From Astronomy to Histology: Adapting the FellWalker Algorithm to Deep Nuclear Instance Segmentation

Michael Yeung[1,2]([✉]) [ID], Todd Watts[3] [ID], and Guang Yang[2] [ID]

[1] School of Clinical Medicine, University of Cambridge, Cambridge, UK
[2] National Heart and Lung Institute, Imperial College London, London, UK
michael.yeung21@imperial.ac.uk
[3] Department of Medical Genetics, University of Cambridge, Cambridge, UK

Abstract. Accurate cell nuclei segmentation is necessary for subsequent histopathology image analysis, including tumour classification, grading and prognosis. Manually identifying cell nuclei is both difficult and time-consuming, with cell nuclei exhibiting dramatic differences in morphology and staining characteristics. Recently, significant advancements in automatic cell nuclei segmentation have been achieved using deep learning, with methods particularly successful in identifying cell nuclei from background tissue. However, delineating individual cell nuclei remains challenging, with often unclear boundaries between neighbouring nuclei. In this paper, we incorporate the FellWalker algorithm, originally developed for analysing molecular clouds, into a deep learning-based pipeline to perform instance cell nuclei segmentation. We evaluate our proposed method on the Lizard dataset, the largest publicly available nuclear segmentation dataset in digital pathology, and compare it against popular methods such as U-Net with Watershed and Mask R-CNN. Our proposed method consistently outperforms the other methods across dataset sizes, achieving an object Dice of 0.7876, F1 score of 0.8245 and Aggregated Jaccard Index of 0.6526. The flexible nature of our pipeline incorporating the FellWalker algorithm has the potential for broader application in biomedical image instance segmentation tasks.

Keywords: Digital pathology · Deep learning · Image processing · Instance segmentation

1 Introduction

Histopathology examination remains the gold standard for determining cancer diagnosis and prognosis. While the demand for biopsy sample analysis continues to increase, the number of pathologists remain in short supply [34]. Digital pathology is an important advancement that involves automating the process of analysing histopathology slides [18], with comparable performance to humans for detecting tumours [2,25,27]. To localise, quantify and characterise cells for diagnosis, accurate cell nuclei segmentation is required.

© The Author(s), under exclusive license to Springer Nature Switzerland AG 2022
G. Yang et al. (Eds.): MIUA 2022, LNCS 13413, pp. 547–561, 2022.
https://doi.org/10.1007/978-3-031-12053-4_41

Classical approaches to automating cell nuclei segmentation include Otsu thresholding [32], clustering [20], graph-based [41], and active contour techniques [8]. However, the reliance of these methods on clear pixel intensity differences limits their use in identifying cell nuclei, which exhibit significant variation in morphology and staining on histology slides. Furthermore, these methods are unable to distinguish between overlapping nuclei, and often depend on first applying a distance transform to the segmentation mask [1], followed by processing using a watershed algorithm [33,43,45]. This task is known as instance segmentation, which is more challenging than the pixel-level classification seen in semantic segmentation, because an additional object detection stage is required.

Later approaches focused on applying traditional machine learning techniques [3], and in recent years, significant improvements have been achieved by adopting deep learning methods [16]. Deep neural networks learn complex representations combining shape, colour and texture information, and with the introduction of Fully Convolutional Networks (FCN), enabled Convolutional Neural Network (CNN) architectures to handle semantic image segmentation tasks [26]. Current state-of-the-art approaches for nuclear segmentation are largely based on the U-Net, a modified FCN architecture comprised of symmetrical encoder-decoder subnetworks with skip connections [35].

The simplest method to adapt the U-Net for instance segmentation involves directly learning ternary maps, training the model to predict separate labels for the nucleus, background and boundary pixels [7,23]. More complicated segmentation pipelines such as Cellpose [39] and Stardist [36], use a U-Net variant to indirectly predict auxillary representations of segmentation masks, in these cases gradient vector fields and star-convex polygons respectively.

Mask R-CNN [14] is another CNN-based innovation originally developed for natural image segmentation, but has also been applied to nuclear segmentation by frameworks such as nucleAIzer [17]. Here, Mask R-CNN uses a regional proposal network to first identify possible cell nuclei regions, which are then processed as a binary segmentation task to identify individual nuclei. Newer methods have combined Mask-RCNN with the U-Net, either in series [19], as an ensemble [42], or through merging the two methods by integrating the regional proposal network into the U-Net architecture [44].

Recent approaches have also focused on integrating deep learning with traditional methods, leveraging the representational power of CNNs with the simplicity of traditional methods to reduce inference times. Separate U-Nets have been used to output the segmentation mask and distance transform map, which were then processed using a watershed algorithm [29]. This has also been accomplished using a single modified U-Net which outputs both the segmentation mask and distance transform map, which is not only more parameter efficient, but may also offer additional performance benefits through regularisation [28].

Despite significant performance gains observed when combining deep learning with watershed, the segmentation accuracy is limited by the reliance of the watershed algorithm on clear pixel intensity differences at nuclei borders. The FellWalker algorithm is related to watershed methods, but its use has been

largely restricted to analysing molecular clouds in astronomy [4]. Coinciden-
tally, radio observations of molecular clouds resemble distance transform maps
in appearance, and applying the FellWalker algorithm on this auxiliary representation of the segmentation mask avoids relying on the original image to identify
boundaries.

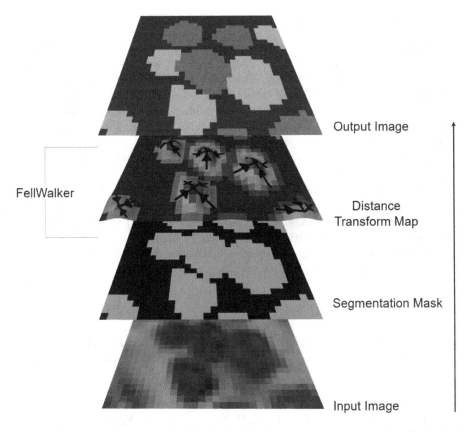

FellWalker

Output Image

Distance
Transform Map

Segmentation Mask

Input Image

Fig. 1. The FellWalker algorithm applied to nuclear instance segmentation. Each pixel
identified as a cell nuclei in the segmentation mask is used as a starting point for a walk
on the distance transform map, which follows an uphill path (arrows) by moving to the
neighbourhood pixel with the highest intensity as the next step in the walk. Pixels are
clustered together if they converge onto the same peak, producing the output image.

The main contributions of this work are summarised as follows:

1. We adapt the FellWalker algorithm from analysing molecular clouds in astronomy, to instance segmentation of cell nuclei in histology.
2. We evaluate our method on the Lizard dataset against the U-Net with Watershed and Mask R-CNN methods.

3. We demonstrate further performance gains by evaluating several other deep learning architectures used to generate the segmentation mask and distance transform map.

2   Materials and Methods

2.1   Dataset Description and Evaluation Metrics

For our experiments, we use the Lizard dataset [12], which combines data from 6 separate data sources and is the largest instance segmentation and classification dataset in digital pathology. This dataset consists of whole slide images at 20x objective magnification of colonic tissue stained with Haematoxylin and Eosin. In total, 495,179 nuclei with manually refined labels are provided, classified as either: epithelial cell, lymphocyte, plasma cell, neutrophil, eosinophil or connective tissue.

For evaluation, we use three metrics from the MICCAI 2015 Gland Segmentation in Colon Histology Images Challenge Contest (GlaS) and MICCAI 2018 Multi-Organ Nucleus Segmentation Challenge (MoNuSeg): the object-level Dice index (Dice_{obj}) for segmentation accuracy, the F1 score metric (F1) for detection accuracy, and the average Aggregated Jaccard Index (AJI) which incorporates both segmentation and detection accuracy [23,24,37,38].

The Dice index is a common overlap metric for evaluating pixel-level segmentation accuracy [11], defined as:

$$\text{Dice} = \frac{2|X \cap Y|}{|X| + |Y|}, \tag{1}$$

where X and Y represent the set of pixels labelled by the prediction mask and ground truth respectively. To account for the segmentation quality of individual objects, the Dice_{obj} is computed as:

$$\text{Dice}_{\text{obj}} = \frac{1}{2} \left[\sum_{i=1}^{n_Y} w_i Dice\left(Y_i, X_*\left(Y_i\right)\right) + \sum_{j=1}^{n_X} \tilde{w}_j Dice\left(Y_*\left(X_j\right), X_j\right) \right], \tag{2}$$

$$w_i = |Y_i| \Big/ \sum_{p=1}^{n_Y} |Y_p|, \quad \tilde{w}_j = |X_j| \Big/ \sum_{q=1}^{n_X} |X_q|, \tag{3}$$

where n_X and n_Y refer to the number of predicted and ground truth objects respectively, $X_*(Y_i)$ and $Y_*(X_j)$ refer to the ground truth object with maximum overlap with predicted object i, and predicted object with maximum overlap with ground truth object j, respectively, and w_i and $\tilde{w}_i$ are weights used to more heavily penalise the prediction of larger ground truth objects.

The F1 score measures the detection accuracy, with a predicted object that has at least 50% overlap with a ground truth object assigned as a true positive (TP), and a false positive (FP) otherwise. The number of false negative (FN) predictions is given by subtracting the number of true positives from number of ground truth objects. The F1 score is defined as:

$$F1 = \frac{2TP}{2TP + FP + FN}.$$ (4)

Finally, the AJI encompasses both segmentation and detection accuracy, and involves matching every ground truth object with a detected object that has maximal overlap. The AJI is computed as the ratio of the sum of the cardinals of intersection and union of these matched objects, with the remaining detected objects added to the denominator.

The value of all three metrics range from 0 to 1, with a higher value indicating better performance.

2.2 FellWalker Algorithm

The FellWalker algorithm was originally developed for clustering radio observations of molecular clouds [4]. The algorithm belongs to a larger class of watershed algorithms, which consider grayscale images as topographic maps, where height is represented by pixel intensity, to separate the image into regions based on local minima [22]. However, the FellWalker algorithm differs from other watershed algorithms by instead using gradient information and local maxima to segment image regions. The key method is summarised in Algorithm 1.

Following the fell-walking metaphor, which refers to the pastime of hill walking, the algorithm involves iteratively taking uphill walks from various pixel starting locations, and following the direction of steepest ascent by querying immediate neighbouring pixels. Therefore, low-intensity pixels follow paths towards a peak, which represents the highest pixel intensity within its broader neighbouring region. Any pixels encountered on a walk towards the same peak are assigned to the same image region (Fig. 1).

2.3 Deep Learning-Based Nuclear Segmentation

The overview of the pipeline is shown in Fig. 2.

The image is first processed by a deep neural network based on the U-Net architecture [35], but with two separate decoder pathways which are trained to produce either the segmentation mask or the distance transform map. The distance transform map is computed using the Euclidean distance and normalised in the range [0, 1]. Both decoder pathways end with a final sigmoid activation function.

Prior to applying the FellWalker algorithm, the segmentation mask is used to mask out the background pixels in the distance transform map.

2.4   Implementation Details

Our experiments were carried out on Google Colab using Tesla P100 GPUs. We used image patches of the Lizard dataset provided by the CoNIC challenge

---

Algorithm 1: FellWalker algorithm

Input   : 2D array of data D, mask M and threshold T
Output: 2D array of assigned clusters C

1 Initialise output array C ← array of zeros with same shape as D;
2 Initialise path list P ← [];
3 Initialise cluster value N ← 1;
4 **for** *pixel in D* **do**
5   **if** *pixel in M and pixel value > T and pixel not in P* **then**
6   path = [];
7   **while** *True* **do**
8   append pixel to path;
9   **if** *pixel value higher than immediate neighbourhood pixel values* **then**
10   **if** *pixel value higher than broader neighbourhood pixel values* **then**
11   append path to P;
12   break;
13   **end**
14   **end**
15   **else**
16   **if** *highest immediate neighbourhood pixel value in P* **then**
17   append path to same list as immediate neighbourhood pixel in P;
18   break;
19   **end**
20   **else**
21   pixel ← highest immediate neighbourhood pixel value;
22   **end**
23   **end**
24   **end**
25   **end**
26 **end**
27 **for** *path in P* **do**
28   **for** *pixel in path* **do**
29   pixel in C ← N
30   **end**
31    $N ← N + 1$;
32 **end**

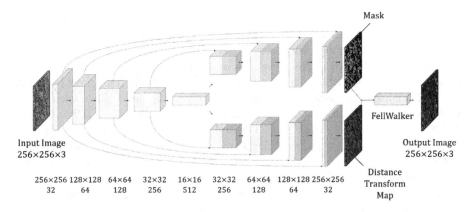

Fig. 2. Overview of our proposed method. The modified U-Net processes an input image through two decoder pathways in parallel to learn a segmentation mask and distance transform map. The segmentation mask is used to mask background pixels in the distance transform map prior to input into the FellWalker algorithm to produce the final instance segmentation output image.

2022, which consists of 4981 non-overlapping image patches of size 256×256 [13]. We randomly partitioned the dataset into 80% development set and 20% test set, and further partitioned the development set into 80% training and 20% validation set. We trained models on different subsets of the development set used as shown in Table 1.

Table 1. Number of image patches used for training, validation and testing. The same test patches are used for each dataset proportion.

% Data	#Train	#Validation	#Test
1	30	8	969
10	309	78	969
25	774	194	969
50	1549	387	969
100	3098	774	969

Image patches were normalised to [0, 1], and we applied the following on-the-fly data augmentation using the Albumentations library [6], with $p = 0.2$: crop, flip (horizontal and vertical), rotation ($90°, 180°, 270°$), CLAHE, gamma, brightness, contrast and blur.

We used OpenCV's implementation of the Meyer's flooding algorithm (referred to as Watershed) [30], and CUPID's implementation of the FellWalker algorithm [5]. For fair comparison, we applied these algorithms on the same binary segmentation masks and distance transform maps produced by the deep neural networks.

To evaluate the performance of the FellWalker algorithm using different deep neural networks, we used a range of modified state-of-the-art neural networks with ResNet-50 pretrained encoders: U-Net [35], LinkNet [9], DeepLabv3+ [10] and U-Net++ [47]. All neural networks were implemented in PyTorch, except for the Mask R-CNN which was implemented in Keras with Tensorflow backend.

We initialised the models using He initialisation [15], and trained each model with Batch normalisation, using the Adam optimiser with $\beta_1 = 0.9$ and $\beta_2 = 0.999$ [21]. We used a batch size of 8 and initial learning rate of 0.001. For convergence criteria, we reduced the learning rate by 0.1 if the validation loss did not improve after 5 epochs, and terminated training if the validation loss did not improve after 15 epochs.

To train the neural networks, we used the Dice loss ($\mathcal{L}_{\text{Dice}}$) and binary cross entropy loss ($\mathcal{L}_{\text{BCE}}$) for binary segmentation [40, 46], and the mean squared error ($\mathcal{L}_{\text{MSE}}$) for the distance transform map regression:

$$\mathcal{L}_{\text{Total}} = \mathcal{L}_{\text{Dice}} + \mathcal{L}_{\text{BCE}} + \lambda \mathcal{L}_{\text{MSE}}, \tag{5}$$

where

$$\mathcal{L}_{\text{Dice}} = 1 - \frac{1}{n} \sum_{i=1}^{n} \text{Dice}(X_i, Y_i), \tag{6}$$

$$\mathcal{L}_{\text{BCE}} = -\frac{1}{n} \sum_{i=1}^{n} (Y_i \log(X_i) + (1 - Y_i) \log(1 - X_i), \tag{7}$$

$$\mathcal{L}_{\text{MSE}} = \frac{1}{n} \sum_{i=1}^{n} (Y_i - X_i)^2. \tag{8}$$

Here, λ control the relative contribution of the losses and is set as 10 to maintain a significant contribution from the regression loss.

To test for statistical significance, we used the Wilcoxon rank sum test. A statistically significant difference was defined as $p < 0.05$.

3   Results

In this section, we first describe the results comparing three different algorithms across a range of dataset sizes, followed by a comparison of five state-of-the-art deep neural networks and the effect on the FellWalker algorithm performance.

3.1   Algorithm Performances Across Different Dataset Sizes

The results for the performance of the Watershed, Mask R-CNN and Fell-Walker algorithms on various dataset sizes of the Lizard dataset are shown in Table 2, and visualised in Fig. 3. Across all dataset sizes, the best performance was consistently observed with the FellWalker algorithm, achieving a Dice_{obj} of 0.7876 ± 0.0041, F1 score of 0.8245 ± 0.0053 and AJI of 0.6526 ± 0.0052 using 100% of the data. Moreover, the FellWalker algorithm trained on 10%

of the data outperformed the Watershed and Mask R-CNN trained on 100% of the data. The Watershed was the lowest performing algorithm across the dataset sizes. All algorithms demonstrated better performance with larger training data, but only limited performance gains were observed when using over 10% of the data. For qualitative comparison, example segmentations are shown in Fig. 4.

Table 2. Performance comparisons using the Watershed, Mask R-CNN and FellWalker algorithms on different proportions of the Lizard dataset. The highest values for each dataset size is indicated in bold. The 95% confidence intervals are displayed in brackets. *Statistically significant difference (p < 0.05).

%Data	Algorithm	$Dice_{obj}$ (↑)	F1 (↑)	AJI (↑)
1	Watershed	0.3716 (0.0091)	0.3523 (0.0137)	0.2506 (0.0088)
	Mask R-CNN	0.5170 (0.0081)	**0.5912* (0.0108)**	0.3487 (0.0078)
	FellWalker	**0.5332* (0.0074)**	0.5674 (0.0120)	**0.3786* (0.0069)**
10	Watershed	0.4957 (0.0056)	0.4598 (0.0089)	0.4138 (0.0042)
	Mask R-CNN	0.6299 (0.0057)	0.7140 (0.0079)	0.4681 (0.0060)
	FellWalker	**0.7252* (0.0044)**	**0.7516* (0.0066)**	**0.5708* (0.0055)**
25	Watershed	0.5243 (0.0054)	0.5035 (0.0086)	0.4359 (0.0040)
	Mask R-CNN	0.6650 (0.0054)	0.7404 (0.0072)	0.5034 (0.0059)
	FellWalker	**0.7541* (0.0041)**	**0.7868* (0.0058)**	**0.6077* (0.0052)**
50	Watershed	0.5417 (0.0052)	0.5309 (0.0082)	0.4509 (0.0040)
	Mask R-CNN	0.6978 (0.0047)	0.7713 (0.0060)	0.5275 (0.0059)
	FellWalker	**0.7777* (0.0041)**	**0.8126* (0.0055)**	**0.6389* (0.0051)**
100	Watershed	0.5498 (0.0051)	0.5432 (0.0081)	0.4578 (0.0038)
	Mask R-CNN	0.7219 (0.0045)	0.7896 (0.0061)	0.5630 (0.0056)
	FellWalker	**0.7876* (0.0041)**	**0.8245* (0.0053)**	**0.6526* (0.0052)**

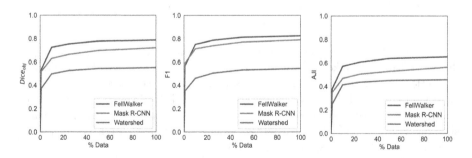

Fig. 3. Graphical representation of the performances of the Watershed, Mask R-CNN and FellWalker algorithms trained on different proportions of the Lizard dataset.

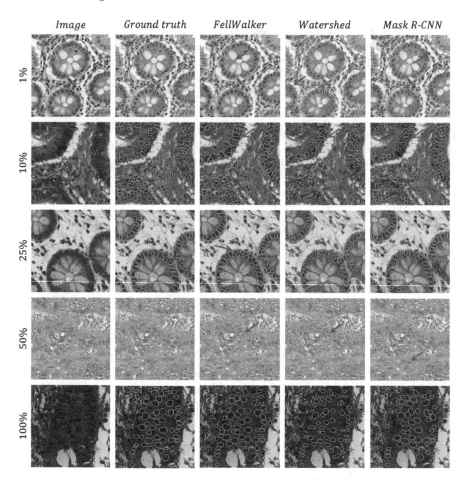

Fig. 4. Example segmentations for each algorithm on each dataset proportion. The image and ground truth are provided for reference. The red arrows highlight example areas where segmentation quality differs. (Color figure online)

Across dataset sizes, the highest quality segmentations were generally produced by the FellWalker algorithm, although a higher number of false positive predictions are visible at smaller dataset sizes when compared to Watershed algorithm and Mask R-CNN. In contrast, the Mask R-CNN appears to exhibit a lower true positive rate and tendency to undersegment the nuclei. The Watershed algorithm appears to consistently undersegment the cell nuclei irrespective of dataset size, producing irregular borders.

The inference times for the three algorithms are shown in Table 3. The Watershed algorithm performed the fastest inference, followed by the FellWalker algorithm and Mask R-CNN.

Table 3. Inference time for the Watershed, Mask R-CNN and FellWalker algorithms. The highest value is indicated in bold. The 95% confidence intervals are displayed in brackets. *Statistically significant difference ($p < 0.05$).

Algorithm	Inference time (s) ($\downarrow$)
Watershed	**0.013* (0.006)**
Mask R-CNN	0.450 (0.012)
FellWalker	0.190 (0.011)

3.2 FellWalker Performance with Different Segmentation Models

The results of applying the FellWalker algorithm to outputs from various state-of-the-art deep neural networks on 1% of the Lizard dataset are shown in Table 4, and visualised in Fig. 5. Generally, larger networks performed better, with the U-Net++ achieving the highest $Dice_{obj}$ of 0.6553 ± 0.0053, F1 score of 0.7080 ± 0.0085 and AJI of 0.4932 ± 0.0059.

Table 4. Performance comparisons of different deep neural networks with the Fell-Walker algorithm on 1% of the Lizard dataset. The highest value is indicated in bold. The 95% confidence intervals are displayed in brackets. *Statistically significant difference ($p < 0.05$).

Model	Backbone	#Params (10^6)	$Dice_{obj}$ ($\uparrow$)	F1 ($\uparrow$)	AJI ($\uparrow$)
U-Net [35]	-	10.8	0.5332 (0.0074)	0.5674 (0.0120)	0.3786 (0.0069)
DeepLabv3+ [10]	ResNet-50	26.8	0.5710 (0.0057)	0.6349 (0.0092)	0.4205 (0.0054)
LinkNet [9]	ResNet-50	38.8	0.6318 (0.0055)	0.6751 (0.0085)	0.4718 (0.0058)
U-Net [35]	ResNet-50	64.3	0.6458 (0.0061)	0.6723 (0.0092)	0.4886 (0.0064)
U-Net++ [47]	ResNet-50	99.1	**0.6553* (0.0053)**	**0.7080* (0.0085)**	**0.4932* (0.0059)**

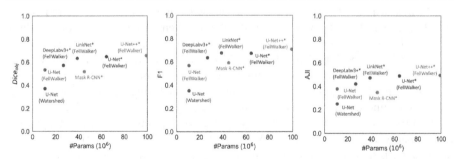

Fig. 5. Graphical representation of the performances of different neural networks with the FellWalker on 1% of the Lizard dataset. The performances of the Watershed and Mask R-CNN algorithms are shown for reference. *models with ResNet-50 pretrained encoders.

4   Discussion and Conclusions

In this work, we incorporated the FellWalker algorithm as part of a deep learning-based pipeline to perform automatic instance segmentation of cell nuclei on histology slides. We observed significantly improved performance using the Fell-Walker algorithm compared to the Watershed and Mask R-CNN algorithms, consistent across training data subsets of different sizes, from 1% to 100% of the Lizard dataset. Moreover, we compared the performance of the FellWalker algorithm using different deep neural network outputs, and demonstrated significant performance improvements with pretrained encoders and more complex networks.

Two reasons explain the performance improvements observed when using the FellWalker algorithm over the Watershed algorithm. Firstly, the FellWalker algorithm relies heavily on the segmentation mask to select the pixels used for clustering. Identifying cell nuclei among background tissue is a relatively easy task for deep neural networks to handle, and therefore serves as a useful prior for the FellWalker algorithm to exploit. In contrast, the Watershed algorithm uses the segmentation mask to establish the background tissue, but does not guarantee that identified cell nuclei regions will be retained, causing it to under-segment across dataset sizes (Fig. 4). Secondly, the FellWalker algorithm is a gradient-tracing method and is therefore data-efficient with respect to the distance transform map. This differs from the Watershed algorithm, which thresholds the distance transform map to establish markers, resulting in the loss of gradient information. This gradient information is particularly useful where pixel intensities from the image are less informative, which is often the case with histology slides where heterogeneous staining is a significant issue.

The watershed algorithm offers two advantages over the FellWalker algorithm, despite its lower segmentation accuracy. Firstly, the reliance of the Fell-Walker algorithm on the segmentation mask reduces robustness to error from the segmentation network. This is apparent with more false positive predictions visible compared to the Watershed algorithm when trained on 1% of the data (Fig. 4). However, the robustness of the FellWalker algorithm to segmentation noise can be tuned with the threshold hyperparameter. Secondly, the Watershed algorithm is significantly faster than the FellWalker algorithm (Table 3). Although this is less relevant in the context of analysing histopathology slides where real-time inference is not required and performance is more important.

In future work, we will further investigate different deep neural network architectures as input to the FellWalker algorithm. We used entirely separate decoder pathways for the segmentation mask and distance transform map, but other variants such as multi-head and reconstruction branches are possible [28]. Furthermore, it would be useful to incorporate other image features such as edge information to improve the performance of the FellWalker algorithm [31]. Finally, implementation of the FellWalker algorithm for 3D data is available [5], and therefore suggests the potential for wider application in biomedical image instance segmentation tasks.

Acknowledgements. This work was funded in part by the UK Research and Innovation Future Leaders Fellowship [MR/V023799/1], in part by the Medical Research Council [MC/PC/21013], in part by the European Research Council Innovative Medicines Initiative [DRAGON, H2020-JTI-IMI2 101005122], and in part by the AI for Health Imaging Award [CHAIMELEON, H2020-SC1-FA-DTS2019-1 952172]. The views expressed are those of the authors and not necessarily those of the NHS, the NIHR, or the Department of Health and Social Care.

References

1. Abdolhoseini, M., Kluge, M.G., Walker, F.R., Johnson, S.J.: Segmentation of heavily clustered nuclei from histopathological images. Sci. Rep. **9**(1), 1–13 (2019)
2. Alsubaie, N., Sirinukunwattana, K., Raza, S.E.A., Snead, D., Rajpoot, N.: A bottom-up approach for tumour differentiation in whole slide images of lung adenocarcinoma. In: Medical Imaging 2018: Digital Pathology, vol. 10581, p. 105810E. International Society for Optics and Photonics (2018)
3. Berg, S., et al.: Ilastik: interactive machine learning for (bio) image analysis. Nat. Methods **16**(12), 1226–1232 (2019)
4. Berry, D.S.: Fellwalker - a clump identification algorithm. Astron. Comput. **10**, 22–31 (2015)
5. Berry, D., Reinhold, K., Jenness, T., Economou, F.: Cupid: a clump identification and analysis package. In: Astronomical Data Analysis Software and Systems XVI, vol. 376, p. 425 (2007)
6. Buslaev, A., Iglovikov, V.I., Khvedchenya, E., Parinov, A., Druzhinin, M., Kalinin, A.A.: Albumentations: fast and flexible image augmentations. Information **11**(2), 125 (2020)
7. Caicedo, J.C., et al.: Evaluation of deep learning strategies for nucleus segmentation in fluorescence images. Cytometry A **95**(9), 952–965 (2019)
8. Chan, T.F., Vese, L.A.: Active contours without edges. IEEE Trans. Image Process. **10**(2), 266–277 (2001)
9. Chaurasia, A., Culurciello, E.: Linknet: Exploiting encoder representations for efficient semantic segmentation. In: 2017 IEEE Visual Communications and Image Processing (VCIP), pp. 1–4. IEEE (2017)
10. Chen, L.C., Zhu, Y., Papandreou, G., Schroff, F., Adam, H.: Encoder-decoder with atrous separable convolution for semantic image segmentation. In: Proceedings of the European Conference on Computer Vision (ECCV), pp. 801–818 (2018)
11. Dice, L.R.: Measures of the amount of ecologic association between species. Ecology **26**(3), 297–302 (1945)
12. Graham, S., et al.: Lizard: a large-scale dataset for colonic nuclear instance segmentation and classification. In: Proceedings of the IEEE/CVF International Conference on Computer Vision, pp. 684–693 (2021)
13. Graham, S., et al.: Conic: Colon nuclei identification and counting challenge 2022. arXiv preprint arXiv:2111.14485 (2021)
14. He, K., Gkioxari, G., Dollár, P., Girshick, R.: Mask R-CNN. In: Proceedings of the IEEE International Conference on Computer Vision, pp. 2961–2969 (2017)
15. He, K., Zhang, X., Ren, S., Sun, J.: Delving deep into rectifiers: surpassing human-level performance on imagenet classification. In: Proceedings of the IEEE International Conference on Computer Vision, pp. 1026–1034 (2015)
16. Hollandi, R., Moshkov, N., Paavolainen, L., Tasnadi, E., Piccinini, F., Horvath, P.: Nucleus segmentation: towards automated solutions. Trends Cell Biol. (2022)

17. Hollandi, R., et al.: Nucleaizer: a parameter-free deep learning framework for nucleus segmentation using image style transfer. Cell Syst. **10**(5), 453–458 (2020)

18. Irshad, H., Veillard, A., Roux, L., Racoceanu, D.: Methods for nuclei detection, segmentation, and classification in digital histopathology: a review-current status and future potential. IEEE Rev. Biomed. Eng. **7**, 97–114 (2013)

19. Jung, H., Lodhi, B., Kang, J.: An automatic nuclei segmentation method based on deep convolutional neural networks for histopathology images. BMC Biomed. Eng. **1**(1), 1–12 (2019)

20. Kanungo, T., Mount, D.M., Netanyahu, N.S., Piatko, C.D., Silverman, R., Wu, A.Y.: An efficient k-means clustering algorithm: analysis and implementation. IEEE Trans. Pattern Anal. Mach. Intell. **24**(7), 881–892 (2002)

21. Kingma, D.P., Ba, J.: Adam: a method for stochastic optimization. arXiv preprint arXiv:1412.6980 (2014)

22. Kornilov, A.S., Safonov, I.V.: An overview of watershed algorithm implementations in open source libraries. J. Imaging **4**(10), 123 (2018)

23. Kumar, N., et al.: A multi-organ nucleus segmentation challenge. IEEE Trans. Med. Imaging **39**(5), 1380–1391 (2019)

24. Kumar, N., Verma, R., Sharma, S., Bhargava, S., Vahadane, A., Sethi, A.: A dataset and a technique for generalized nuclear segmentation for computational pathology. IEEE Trans. Med. Imaging **36**(7), 1550–1560 (2017)

25. Liu, Y., et al.: Detecting cancer metastases on gigapixel pathology images. arXiv preprint arXiv:1703.02442 (2017)

26. Long, J., Shelhamer, E., Darrell, T.: Fully convolutional networks for semantic segmentation. In: Proceedings of IEEE/CVF Conference on Computer Vision and Pattern Recognition (CVPR), pp. 3431–3440 (2015)

27. Lu, C., et al.: A prognostic model for overall survival of patients with early-stage non-small cell lung cancer: a multicentre, retrospective study. Lancet Digit. Health **2**(11), e594–e606 (2020)

28. Ma, J., et al.: How distance transform maps boost segmentation CNNs: an empirical study. In: Medical Imaging with Deep Learning, pp. 479–492. PMLR (2020)

29. Mahbod, A., Schaefer, G., Ellinger, I., Ecker, R., Smedby, Ö., Wang, C.: A two-stage U-net algorithm for segmentation of nuclei in H&E-stained tissues. In: Reyes-Aldasoro, C.C., Janowczyk, A., Veta, M., Bankhead, P., Sirinukunwattana, K. (eds.) ECDP 2019. LNCS, vol. 11435, pp. 75–82. Springer, Cham (2019). https://doi.org/10.1007/978-3-030-23937-4_9

30. Meyer, F., Maragos, P.: Multiscale morphological segmentations based on watershed, flooding, and Eikonal PDE. In: Nielsen, M., Johansen, P., Olsen, O.F., Weickert, J. (eds.) Scale-Space 1999. LNCS, vol. 1682, pp. 351–362. Springer, Heidelberg (1999). https://doi.org/10.1007/3-540-48236-9_31

31. Murugesan, B., Sarveswaran, K., Shankaranarayana, S.M., Ram, K., Joseph, J., Sivaprakasam, M.: PSI-net: shape and boundary aware joint multi-task deep network for medical image segmentation. In: 2019 41st Annual International Conference of the IEEE Engineering in Medicine and Biology Society (EMBC), pp. 7223–7226. IEEE (2019)

32. Otsu, N.: A threshold selection method from gray-level histograms. IEEE Trans. Syst. Man Cybern. **9**(1), 62–66 (1979)

33. Plissiti, M.E., Nikou, C., Charchanti, A.: Watershed-based segmentation of cell nuclei boundaries in pap smear images. In: Proceedings of the 10th IEEE International Conference on Information Technology and Applications in Biomedicine, pp. 1–4. IEEE (2010)

34. Robboy, S.J., et al.: Pathologist workforce in the united states: I. Development of a predictive model to examine factors influencing supply. Arch. Pathol. Lab. Med. **137**(12), 1723–1732 (2013)
35. Ronneberger, O., Fischer, P., Brox, T.: U-net: convolutional networks for biomedical image segmentation. In: Navab, N., Hornegger, J., Wells, W.M., Frangi, A.F. (eds.) MICCAI 2015. LNCS, vol. 9351, pp. 234–241. Springer, Cham (2015). https://doi.org/10.1007/978-3-319-24574-4_28
36. Schmidt, U., Weigert, M., Broaddus, C., Myers, G.: Cell detection with star-convex polygons. In: Frangi, A.F., Schnabel, J.A., Davatzikos, C., Alberola-López, C., Fichtinger, G. (eds.) MICCAI 2018. LNCS, vol. 11071, pp. 265–273. Springer, Cham (2018). https://doi.org/10.1007/978-3-030-00934-2_30
37. Sirinukunwattana, K., et al.: Gland segmentation in colon histology images: the GLAS challenge contest. Med. Image Anal. **35**, 489–502 (2017)
38. Sirinukunwattana, K., Snead, D.R., Rajpoot, N.M.: A stochastic polygons model for glandular structures in colon histology images. IEEE Trans. Med. Imaging **34**(11), 2366–2378 (2015)
39. Stringer, C., Wang, T., Michaelos, M., Pachitariu, M.: Cellpose: a generalist algorithm for cellular segmentation. Nat. Methods **18**(1), 100–106 (2021)
40. Taghanaki, S.A., et al.: Combo loss: handling input and output imbalance in multi-organ segmentation. Comput. Med. Imaging Graph. **75**, 24–33 (2019). https://doi.org/10.1016/j.compmedimag.2019.04.005
41. Vicente, S., Kolmogorov, V., Rother, C.: Graph cut based image segmentation with connectivity priors. In: 2008 IEEE Conference on Computer Vision and Pattern Recognition, pp. 1–8. IEEE (2008)
42. Vuola, A.O., Akram, S.U., Kannala, J.: Mask-RCNN and U-net ensembled for nuclei segmentation. In: 2019 IEEE 16th International Symposium on Biomedical Imaging (ISBI 2019), pp. 208–212. IEEE (2019)
43. Wählby, C., Sintorn, I.M., Erlandsson, F., Borgefors, G., Bengtsson, E.: Combining intensity, edge and shape information for 2D and 3D segmentation of cell nuclei in tissue sections. J. Microsc. **215**(1), 67–76 (2004)
44. Yang, L., et al.: NuSet: a deep learning tool for reliably separating and analyzing crowded cells. PLoS Comput. Biol. **16**(9), e1008193 (2020)
45. Yang, X., Li, H., Zhou, X.: Nuclei segmentation using marker-controlled watershed, tracking using mean-shift, and Kalman filter in time-lapse microscopy. IEEE Trans. Circuits Syst. I Regul. Pap. **53**(11), 2405–2414 (2006)
46. Yeung, M., Sala, E., Schönlieb, C.B., Rundo, L.: Unified Focal loss: generalising Dice and cross entropy-based losses to handle class imbalanced medical image segmentation. Comput. Med. Imaging Graph. **95**, 102026 (2022)
47. Zhou, Z., Rahman Siddiquee, M.M., Tajbakhsh, N., Liang, J.: UNet++: a nested U-net architecture for medical image segmentation. In: Stoyanov, D., et al. (eds.) DLMIA/ML-CDS -2018. LNCS, vol. 11045, pp. 3–11. Springer, Cham (2018). https://doi.org/10.1007/978-3-030-00889-5_1

Image Classification

Leveraging Uncertainty in Deep Learning for Pancreatic Adenocarcinoma Grading

Biraja Ghoshal[1]([✉]), Bhargab Ghoshal[2], and Allan Tucker[1]

[1] Department of Computer Science, Brunel University, London, UK
Biraja.Ghoshal@brunel.ac.uk
[2] Faculty of Medical Sciences, University College London, London, UK

Abstract. Pancreatic cancers have one of the worst prognoses compared to other cancers, as they are diagnosed when cancer has progressed towards its latter stages. The current manual histological grading for diagnosing pancreatic adenocarcinomas is time-consuming and often results in misdiagnosis. In digital pathology, AI-based cancer grading must be extremely accurate in prediction and uncertainty quantification to improve reliability and explainability and are essential for gaining clinicians' trust in the technology. We present Bayesian Convolutional Neural Networks for automated pancreatic cancer grading from MGG and H&E stained images to estimate uncertainty in model prediction. We show that the estimated uncertainty correlates with prediction error. Specifically, it is useful in setting the acceptance threshold using a metric that weighs classification accuracy-reject trade-off and misclassification cost controlled by hyperparameters and can be employed in clinical settings.

Keywords: Bayesian Deep Learning · Uncertainty estimation · Cancer grading · Pancreatic adenocarcinoma

1 Introduction

Pancreatic adenocarcinoma has one of the worst prognoses compared to other cancers, with a 10% 5 year survival rate, and it is projected to become the second-leading cause of cancer-related mortality by 2030 [31]. Early diagnosis is important to improving the likelihood of survival, which is reflected in the survival rates of 39.4% in patients whose tumours have not metastasised [22]. Intraepithelial neoplasms develop into adenocarcinomas and these are stratified into three progressive categories: Grade I, II and III. Grade I neoplasia comprises of well-differentiated tissue, which do not divide rapidly and so do not respond very well to chemotherapy. Grade II neoplasia represents moderately differentiated tissue, whilst Grade III represents poorly differentiated tissue, which is rapidly proliferating. The grading of neoplasia can be performed using histological samples stained using Hematoxylin and Eosin (H&E) and May-Grunwald-Giemsa stain (MGG). H&E stains nuclear components blue-purple and cytoplasmic components pink, whilst MGG stains help to ascertain the morphology of cells.

© The Author(s), under exclusive license to Springer Nature Switzerland AG 2022
G. Yang et al. (Eds.): MIUA 2022, LNCS 13413, pp. 565–577, 2022.
https://doi.org/10.1007/978-3-031-12053-4_42

Pancreatic cancers are usually detected towards their latter stages in locally advanced (30%–35%) or metastatic (50%–55%) stage as most patients are asymptomatic in the early stages [19]. As a result, pancreatic tumour diagnosis requires urgent action and a definite surgical plan. Pancreatic cancer detection and classification has either focused only on distinguishing benign tumor from malignant ones or tumor presence on radiology images [29]. The diagnostic performance by means of manual examination of pancreatic cancer grading is very tedious, time consuming, depends on clinicians' experience, and often results in misdiagnosis and thus incorrect treatment. There is an urgent need for novel methods to supplement radiologist interpretations in improving the sensitivity of pancreatic cancer detection from histopathology images.

Several methods use deep learning in cancer detection and diagnosis such as the Gleason grading of prostate cancer, colon cancer grading, and breast cancer detection [1,7,27,32]. However, it is critical to estimate uncertainty in medical image analysis as an additional insight to point predictions to improve the reliability in making decisions. Our objective is not to achieve state-of-the-art performance, but rather to evaluate the usefulness of estimating uncertainty approximating Bayesian Convolutional Neural Networks (BCNN) with Dropweights to improve the diagnosis.

In digital pathology, multi-gigapixel Whole Slide digitised histopathology Images (WSI) are divided into small patches because (i) different chemical preparations typically render different slides for the same piece of tissue, (ii) they are generated by different digitisation devices, (iii) the device settings may produce different images from the same slide and (iv) size limitations for CNN image inputs [6].

It is crucial to accurately grade pancreatic cancer in patients where the cost of an error is very high. In order to avoid misdiagnoses, it is necessary to estimate uncertainty in a model's predictions for automatically handling clear-cut diagnoses, whilst elevating difficult decisions to medical professionals, who can request further scans, recognizing the uncertainty and seek assistance.

There are many methods proposed for quantifying uncertainty or confidence estimates in deep learning such as Hamiltonian Monte Carlo, Stochastic Gradient Langevin Dynamic (SGLD), Laplace approximation, Bayes by backprop, Deep ensembles, Monte Carlo (MC) dropout, MC-dropweight and MC-batch normalization [4,10,14,17,21,24,28,30]. There are also many measures to estimate uncertainty such as softmax variance, predictive entropy, mutual information, BALD [20], Uncertainty measure proposed by Leibig [26] and Feinman [8] and averaging predictions over multiple models, which are mostly focused on rejection accuracy and log-likelihood without assessing the quality of predictive uncertainty with calibrated expectations.

In this paper, we propose Bayesian Convolutional Neural Networks (BCNN) approach to predict pancreatic cancer grading from two different May-Grunwald-Giemsa (MGG) and Haematoxylin and Eosin (H&E) stained images and show that the estimated uncertainty in prediction has a strong correlation with classification accuracy, thus enabling the identification of false predictions or unknown cases. We present the first approach (to the best of our knowledge) in leveraging uncertainty in automated grading of pancreatic cancer based on histopathology images. The proposed Bayesian deep learning model can be very useful to clinicians in diagonising cancer grading system, which can address the problems in manual grading. We believe that the availability of uncertainty-aware deep learning solution will enable a wider adoption of Artificial Intelligence (AI) in a clinical setting.

2   Proposed Method

2.1   Dataset

Our approach was based on the patch-level prediction to include all tumor histological subtypes, ensuring that the selected patches were widely representative for practical diagnosis in order to be adaptable to meet the input size of most neural networks training and derive the likelihood of neoplasia at patch-level. The patches of approximately 200×200 pixels of non-overlapping regions in a WSI were firstly extracted from 138 high-resolution tissue-samples stained with MGG and H&E [33] with varying dimensions annotated with Normal, Grade-I, Grade-II and Grade-III. Overall, 49.5% (3201) of the patches were selected after discarding patches with non-tissue information. The flow chart is shown in Fig. 1. An imbalanced number of patch images in each class i.e. bias towards the majority proportions of cancer cells is reduced by class weight to regularise the loss function.

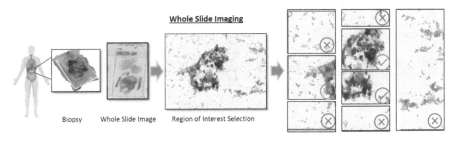

Fig. 1. Whole Slide Image (WSI) processing and selection of tissue patches. Whole slide image was considered by dividing the slide into patches of 200×200 pixels. Each patch was then selected based on tissue presence.

2.2   Approximate Bayesian Neural Networks (BCNN) and Model Uncertainty

During the training phase, histological pancreatic cancer image dataset $X = \{x_1, x_2 \ldots x_N\}$ and the corresponding grade $Y = \{y_1, y_2 \ldots y_N\}$ where $X \in R^d$ is a d-dimensional input vector and $Y \in \{1 \ldots C\}$ with $y_i \in \{1 \ldots C\}$, given C class labels (here four: Normal, Grade I, Grade II and Grade III), a set of independent and identically distributed (i.i.d.) training samples size $N\{x_i, y_i\}$ for $i = 1$ to N, are used to learn the weights of the neural networks. Uncertainty of the model prediction was captured by placing a prior distribution over weights W. The principled predictive distribution of an unknown grading of cancer prediction label $\hat{y}$ of a test input data $\hat{x}$ by marginalizing the parameters:

$$p(\hat{y}|\hat{x}, X, Y) = \int P(\hat{y}|\hat{x}, w) P(w|X, Y, \hat{x}) dw \tag{1}$$

Unfortunately, finding the posterior distribution $p(w|X, Y)$ is often computationally intractable. Following Gal, Ghoshal et al. showed that neural networks with dropweights with the cross-entropy loss of the network, is equivalent to a variational approximation by minimising the Kullback-Leibler (KL) divergence on a Bayesian neural network. At test time, the unseen images are passed through the network, the posterior $P(W|X, Y, \hat{x})$ was approximated by averaging stochastic feed forward Monte Carlo (MC) sampling to estimate uncertainty.

Practically, the expectation of $\hat{y}$ is called the predictive mean of the model. The estimate of the vector of Softmax probabilities i.e., the predictive mean μ_{pred} over the MC iterations is then used as the final prediction on the test sample:

$$\mu_{pred} \approx \frac{1}{T} \sum_{t=1}^{T} p\left(\hat{y} = c|\hat{x}, \hat{\omega}_t\right); \quad c \in \{1, \ldots, C\} \tag{2}$$

For each test sample $\hat{x}$, the class with the largest predictive mean μ_{pred} is selected as the output prediction. We present a novel approximation of predictive model uncertainty as below:

$$\sigma_{uncertainty} = \frac{1}{C} \sum_{i=1}^{C} \sqrt{\frac{1}{T} \sum_{t=1}^{T} \left[p\left(\hat{y}_t = c|\hat{x}, \hat{\omega}_t\right) - \hat{\mu}_{pred}\right]^2} \tag{3}$$

$$\text{where } \hat{y}_t = y\left(\hat{\omega}_t\right) = \text{Softmax}\left\{f^{\hat{\omega}_t}(\hat{x})\right\} \tag{4}$$

In our approximated uncertainty measure in model prediction (i.e. Eq. 3), we take into account the uncertainty associated with every class in the predictive mean μ_{pred}. Furthermore in the approximation, we take the mean of the standard deviations of the class probabilities, instead of the variance. It assigns the highest average uncertainty to the most frequently mislabelled class.

2.3   Uncertainty Metrics in Deep Learning

We can compute an uncertainty metric from the multiple predictions per input image captured during test time. In this work we compared four well established metrics: predictive entropy; mutual information [9,20], Feinman uncertainty, which measures of uncertainty for each observation by averaging the mean squared prediction error of each class [8]; Leibig uncertainty, which returns the empirical standard deviation as a proxy for predictive uncertainty [26]; and moment based aleatoric and epistemic uncertainty metrics by Kwon [23]. In addition, we introduce a novel approximation of predictive model uncertainty which averages the standard deviations of the predictions in the predictive mean vector of class probabilities [11,16].

2.4 Experiment

Instead of training a very deep model from scratch on a small dataset, we decided to run this experiment in a transfer learning setting, where we used a pretrained DenseNet-201, VGG-19 and ResNet-152V2 model [18] and acquired data only to fine-tune the original model. We split the whole dataset into 60%–20%–20% between training, validation and test sets respectively. This is suitable when the data is abound for an auxiliary domain, but very limited labelled data is available for the domain of experiment. We introduced fully connected layers on top of the pre-trained convolutional base. Dropweights followed by a softmax activated layer is applied to the network as an approximation to the Gaussian Process (GP) and cast as an approximate Bayesian inference in the fully connected layer to estimate meaningful model uncertainty [15]. The softmax layer outputs the probability distribution over each possible class label. We resized all images to 224×224 pixels (using a bicubic interpolation over 4×4 pixel neighbourhood). The images [33] were then standardised using the mean and standard deviation values of the MGG and H&E dataset.

Real-time data augmentation was also applied, leveraging Keras ImageData-Generator during training, to prevent overfitting and enhance the learning capability of the model. Training images were rotated 90 °C, randomly flipped horizontally and vertically, scaled outward and inward, shifted, and sheared. The Adam optimiser was used with default initial learning rate of $\alpha = 0.01$ and moment decay rate of $\beta1 = 0.9$ and $\beta1 = 0.999$. All our experiments were run for 100 epochs and batch size was set to 64. Dropweights with rates of 0.5 were added to the fully-connected layer. We monitored the validation accuracy after every epoch and saved the model with the best accuracy on the validation dataset. During test time, Dropweights were active and Monte Carlo sampling was performed by feeding the input image with MC-samples 50 through the Bayesian Deep Convolutional Neural Networks (Fig. 2).

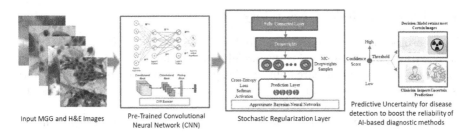

Fig. 2. Overview of the proposed Bayesian Convolutional Neural Network (BCNN) framework.

3   Model Performance

On average, Bayesian DenseNet-201 model based inference improves the detection accuracy of the ResNet-152V2 and VGG-19 model in our sample dataset. Table 1 summarizes the Precision, Recall, F1-Score and prediction accuracy of our implemented models.

Table 1. Summarizes the precision, recall, F1-score and prediction accuracy of our implemented models

Dataset	VGG-19				ResNet-152V2				DenseNet-201			
May Grunwald-Giemsa (MGG)	Precision	Recall	F1-score	Accuracy	Precision	Recall	F1-score	Accuracy	Precision	Recall	F1-score	Accuracy
Normal	79.60%	78.80%	79.00%		80.20%	81.40%	80.60%		85.20%	83.40%	84.00%	
Grade I	53.00%	22.00%	31.50%		65.40%	40.80%	50.80%		72.20%	45.60%	55.40%	
Grade II	66.00%	82.40%	73.20%		75.80%	80.60%	78.20%		78.20%	84.20%	81.20%	
Grade III	50.20%	30.00%	38.00%		65.60%	58.60%	61.20%		72.20%	66.00%	68.80%	
Average score	62.89%	66.69%	63.66%	66.69%	74.14%	74.12%	73.77%	74.23%	78.19%	78.19%	77.86%	85.53%
Haematoxylin and Eosin (H&E)												
Normal	87.60%	83.40%	85.20%		90.00%	87.80%	88.80%		90.00%	90.00%	90.00%	
Grade I	84.40%	79.60%	81.80%		85.40%	86.80%	86.20%		88.20%	88.40%	88.20%	
Grade II	62.40%	77.40%	68.80%		79.60%	79.60%	79.80%		81.00%	81.40%	81.20%	
Grade III	76.80%	65.80%	70.80%		79.80%	78.60%	79.80%		83.20%	82.60%	82.80%	
Average score	78.02%	76.51%	76.79%	76.52%	83.34%	83.48%	83.62%	83.60%	85.65%	85.71%	85.61%	**85.60%**
Mixed (H&E and MGG)												
Normal	66.40%	57.00%	59.00%		79.00%	82.60%	80.60%		82.20%	86.20%	84.20%	
Grade I	79.60%	66.80%	72.60%		84.00%	80.00%	81.80%		85.80%	78.60%	82.00%	
Grade II	57.60%	83.00%	63.80%		75.00%	80.40%	77.80%		76.80%	81.80%	79.20%	
Grade III	40.80%	37.00%	54.50%		72.60%	63.20%	67.60%		75.00%	69.60%	71.80%	
Average score	60.55%	59.81%	55.12%	59.75%	77.19%	77.16%	77.08%	77.16%	79.35%	79.33%	79.15%	79.29%

All models trained with the H&E stained images achieved the highest accuracy and F1-score compared to MGG and mixed. VGG-19 model trained with the mixed dataset performed the lowest compared to H&E and MGG which indicates H&E stained images are easier to learn and achieve better prediction than MGG. All models achieved an exceptional performance in identifying normal tissue from H&E stained images, which could be due to the distinct differences between neoplastic and non-neoplastic tissue. We also observed that all models performed the weakest in Grade-III class prediction compared other grades.

4   Prediction Error vs Uncertainty

4.1   Bayesian Model Uncertainty

We measured the uncertainty associated with the predictive probabilities of the deep learning model by keeping dropweights on during test time. Figure 3 shows that the pancreatic adenocarcinoma grade-specific approximations of uncertainty is consistent with the confusion matrix. Higher uncertainty seems to be associated with slides that tend to be misclassified.

Figure 4 shows the boxplots of estimated uncertainty in deep learning model for pancreatic adenocarcinoma grading.

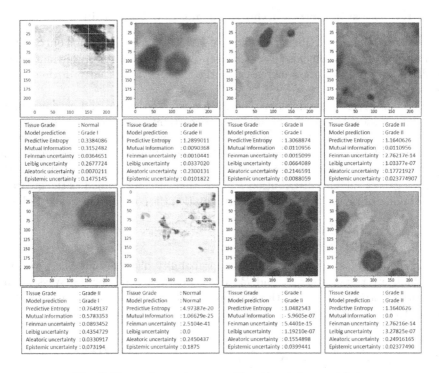

Fig. 3. Example test images with estimated uncertainty

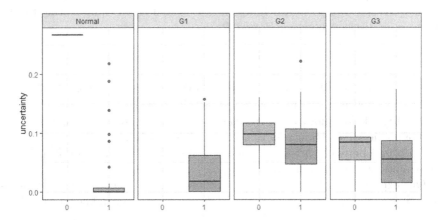

Fig. 4. The red box indicates the uncertainty of incorrectly graded images. The green box corresponds to correctly classified images. Our model assigns the highest average uncertainty to the mislabelled grades and less contribution to high uncertainty values by correctly classified images. Therefore, uncertainty information provides as an additional insight to point prediction to refer the uncertain images to radiologists for further investigation, which improves the overall prediction performance. (Color figure online)

4.2   Relationship Between the Accuracy and Uncertainty

Trustworthy clinical Artificial Intelligence (AI) systems should not only return accurate predictions, but also a credible representation of their uncertainty. The model's expected accuracy increases as the model's uncertainty in prediction decreases [12].

The true error is the difference between estimated values and actual values. In order to assess the quality of predictive uncertainty, we leveraged Spearman's correlation coefficient. We quantified the predictive accuracy by 1-Wasserstein distance (WD) to measure how much the estimated uncertainty correlates with the true errors [2,25]. The Wasserstein distance for the real data distribution P_r and the generated data distribution P_g is mathematically defined as the greatest lower bound (infimum) for any transport plan (i.e. the cost for the cheapest plan):

$$W(P_r, P_g) = \inf_{\gamma \sim \Pi(P_r, P_g)} \mathbb{E}_{(x,y) \sim \gamma}[\|x - y\|] \tag{5}$$

$\Pi(P_r, P_g)$ is the set of all possible joint probability distributions $\gamma(x, y)$ whose marginals are respectively P_r and P_g. However, the Eq. (5) for the Wasserstein distance is intractable. Using the Kantorovich-Rubinstein duality it can be simplified to

$$W(P_r, P_g) = \frac{1}{K} \sup_{\|f\|_L \leq K} \mathbb{E}_{x \sim P_r}[f(x)] - \mathbb{E}_{x \sim P_g}[f(x)] \tag{6}$$

where sup (supremum) is the least upper bound and f is a 1-Lipschitz continuous functions $\{f_w\}_{w \in W}$, parameterized by w and the K-Lipschitz constraint $|f(x_1) - f(x_2)| \leq K|x_1 - x_2|$. The error function can be configured as measuring the 1 - Wasserstein distance between P_r and P_g.

$$E(P_r, P_g) = W(P_r, P_g) = \max_{w \in W} \mathbb{E}_{x \sim P_r}[f_w(x)] - \mathbb{E}_{z \sim P_r(z)}[f_w(g_\theta(z))] \tag{7}$$

The advantage of Wasserstein distance (WD) is that it can reflect the distance of two non-overlapping or little overlapping distributions.

The Fig. 5 below shows the correlation between estimated uncertainty and the error of prediction and Spearman correlation. The results show strong correlation with $\rho > 0.95$ between entropy of the probabilities as a measure of the epistemic uncertainty and prediction errors.

Our experiments show that the prediction uncertainty correlates with accuracy, thus enabling the identification of false predictions or unknown cases.

4.3   Performance Improvement via Uncertainty-Aware Cancer Grading Classification

We performed predictions for all test images and sorted the predictions by their associated predictive uncertainty. We then referred predictions based on the various levels of uncertainty for further diagnosis and measured the accuracy of the predictions for the remaining cases. We observed in Fig. 6, uncertainty

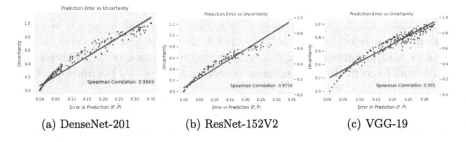

(a) DenseNet-201   (b) ResNet-152V2   (c) VGG-19

Fig. 5. Correlation between estimated predictive entropy as a measure of Uncertainty and Accuracy in prediction

estimation can usually be used in every image classifier to improve prediction accuracy of man-machine combination via uncertainty-aware referral with the additional computational load cost of performing multiple forward passes.

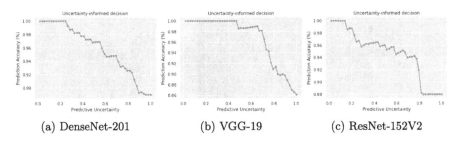

(a) DenseNet-201   (b) VGG-19   (c) ResNet-152V2

Fig. 6. The classification accuracy as a function of the tolerated normalized model uncertainty

5   Leveraging Uncertainty in Classification Error and Reject Tradeoff

In safety critical decision making scenarios, the goal of a deep learning model is that the algorithm abstains from making a prediction on the most uncertain images rather than making an incorrect prediction, where the risk of making a incorrect prediction is too large i.e. allowing the model to say "I don't know".

A low model uncertainty ascertained when the probability of predicting into the most possible category has much greater margin over the 2nd most likely category [13]. In rejection, the prediction was ambiguous among all categories because the model failed to reach a definitive conclusion between all the grades.

For example, if the model was presented with a out-of-distribution or non-domain image, it would still classify the image into one of the 4 grades albeit with a high estimated uncertainty measure, which is not an expected outcome.

Instead, the model should be able to reject predicting the grade for the test images where the uncertainty is too high. Such abstention is known as classification with a reject option. In the context of the clinical diagnostic process, accuracy is of paramount importance. The overall decision is the following: the model would accept if the acceptance criteria defined as $\Lambda(x)$ defined as [3,5]:

$$\Lambda(x) := |P(\mathbf{x}^{(i)})_1 - P(\mathbf{x}^{(i)})_2| \geq \epsilon * [\sigma_{uncertainty}(\mathbf{x}^{(i)})_1] \tag{8}$$

where $P(\mathbf{x}^{(i)})$ is the predictive probability for input image $\mathbf{x}^{(i)}$ with $P(\mathbf{x}^{(i)})_j$ being defined as the probability of the j_{th} most likely class, and $U(\mathbf{x}^{(i)})_1$ is the estimated uncertainty of the most likely class returned by the model for input $\mathbf{x}^{(i)}$. Note that the ϵ probability threshold parameter defines a trade-off between the number of classified examples at the number of examples that would have been incorrectly classified but were accepted instead.

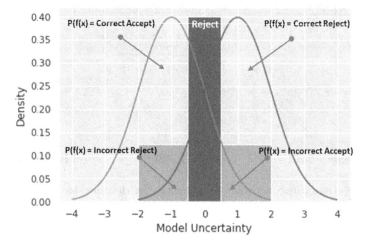

Fig. 7. Distribution of predictive uncertainty values grouped by correct and erroneous predictions

Figure 7 illustrates two class-conditional distribution of predictive uncertainty for the discriminant. The conditional accept or reject with estimated uncertainty depends on uncertainty thresholds.

5.1   Evaluation Metric - Accuracy-Rejection Quotient (ARQ)

The standard metric for evaluating a model f on a classification task is the accuracy:

$$\text{Accuracy} = \frac{1}{N} \sum_{i=1}^{N} \mathbb{1}(P(\mathbf{x}^{(i)}) = y^{(i)}) \tag{9}$$

where N is the number of test data points and $(\mathbf{x}^{(i)}, y^{(i)})$ is the ith test point. Note that the accuracy does not take into account the uncertainty with which a model makes the prediction and only rewards correctly classified examples.

The metric Accuracy-Rejection Quotient (ARQ) for classification with a accuracy-reject trade-off by assigning a cost α to misclassification, and a cost β to the acceptance option $\Lambda(x)$ is defined as [3,5]:

$$\text{ARQ}_{\alpha,\beta} = \frac{1}{N} \sum_{i=1}^{N} \mathbb{1}(P(\mathbf{x}^{(i)}) = y^{(i)}) - \alpha\mathbb{1}(P(\mathbf{x}^{(i)}) \neq y^{(i)}) - \beta\mathbb{1}(P(\mathbf{x}^{(i)}) \neq \Lambda(\mathbf{x}^{(i)}))$$

$$(10)$$

Here, α and β are hyperparameters. A large value for α corresponds to cases where cost of misclassification is extremely high such as in medical diagnosis. The β intuitively is a trade-off indicator - higher β will decrease the cost of the accept option.

The Fig. 8 shows the trade-off between the number of misclassified but accepted images and the number of correctly classified but rejected images.

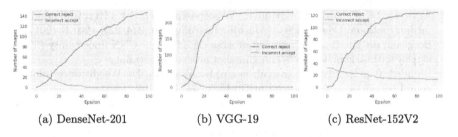

(a) DenseNet-201   (b) VGG-19   (c) ResNet-152V2

Fig. 8. Accuracy-Rejection Quotient (ARQ) obtained using varying ϵ and α but setting $\beta = 0$. For $\alpha > 0$ there seems to be an optimal value of ϵ around 17 in case of DenseNet-201.

6   Conclusion and Future Work

Clinical AI systems are now regularly being used in medical settings although regulatory oversight is inconsistent and undeveloped. Computer based medical systems in clinical setting requires informed users, who are generally responsible for identifying and reporting emerging problems [32]. Understanding the confidence of predictions made by a deep learning model can aide clinicians identify when AI systems fail is essential for gaining clinicians' trust in the technology. In this work, Bayesian Deep Learning classifier has been trained using transfer learning method on pancreatic cancer grade from histopathology images to estimate model uncertainty. The evaluation shows that the Bayesian DenseNet-201 model trained by H&E stained image dataset achieved the best performance compared to the other models and dataset. Our experiment has shown a strong correlation between model uncertainty and error in prediction. We have also shown how to leverage estimated uncertainty in prediction as rejection threshold in classifying images by user-defined hyperparameters for a given cost of misclassification and rejection cost to control the accuracy-acceptance rate of the model. The estimated uncertainty in deep learning yields more reliable predictions; protects against model limitations from possible scenarios in training dataset such as minority class, dismissal, automation bias or out-of-distribution test dataset, which can alert radiologists on false predictions, increasing the acceptance of deep learning into clinical practice in disease detection. With this Bayesian Deep Learning based classification, studies correlating with multi "omics" datasets (pathology with radiological, genomic, and proteomic) and treatment responses could further reveal insights about imaging markers and findings towards improved diagnosis and treatment for pancreatic adenocarcinomas.

References

1. Anaya-Isaza, A., Mera-Jiménez, L., Zequera-Diaz, M.: An overview of deep learning in medical imaging. Inform. Med. Unlocked **26**, 100723 (2021)
2. Arjovsky, M., Chintala, S., Bottou, L.: Wasserstein generative adversarial networks. In: International Conference on Machine Learning, pp. 214–223. PMLR (2017)
3. Borgeaud dit Avocat, S.: Gaussian process classifiers for CNN uncertainty (2018). https://github.com/seb5666/cnn_gaussian_process_uncertainty
4. Blundell, C., Cornebise, J., Kavukcuoglu, K., Wierstra, D.: Weight uncertainty in neural networks. arXiv preprint arXiv:1505.05424 (2015)
5. Chow, C.: On optimum recognition error and reject tradeoff. IEEE Trans. Inf. Theory **16**(1), 41–46 (1970)
6. Esteva, A., et al.: Deep learning-enabled medical computer vision. NPJ Digit. Med. **4**(1), 1–9 (2021)
7. Esteva, A., et al.: A guide to deep learning in healthcare. Nat. Med. **25**(1), 24–29 (2019)
8. Feinman, R., Curtin, R.R., Shintre, S., Gardner, A.B.: Detecting adversarial samples from artifacts. arXiv preprint arXiv:1703.00410 (2017)
9. Gal, Y., Ghahramani, Z.: Dropout as a Bayesian approximation: representing model uncertainty in deep learning. In: 33rd International Conference on Machine Learning, ICML 2016, vol. 3, pp. 1651–1660 (2016)
10. Gal, Y.: Uncertainty in deep learning. Ph.D. thesis, University of Cambridge (2016)
11. Ghoshal, B., Tucker, A.: On calibrated model uncertainty in deep learning. In: The European Conference on Machine Learning (ECML PKDD 2020) Workshop on Uncertainty in Machine Learning (2020)
12. Ghoshal, B., Ghoshal, B., Swift, S., Tucker, A.: Uncertainty estimation in SARS-CoV-2 B-cell epitope prediction for vaccine development. In: Tucker, A., Henriques Abreu, P., Cardoso, J., Pereira Rodrigues, P., Riaño, D. (eds.) AIME 2021. LNCS (LNAI), vol. 12721, pp. 361–366. Springer, Cham (2021). https://doi.org/10.1007/978-3-030-77211-6_41
13. Ghoshal, B., Hikmet, F., Pineau, C., Tucker, A., Lindskog, C.: DeepHistoClass: a novel strategy for confident classification of immunohistochemistry images using deep learning. Mol. Cell. Proteomics **20**, 100140 (2021)

14. Ghoshal, B., Swift, S., Tucker, A.: Bayesian deep active learning for medical image analysis. In: Tucker, A., Henriques Abreu, P., Cardoso, J., Pereira Rodrigues, P., Riaño, D. (eds.) AIME 2021. LNCS (LNAI), vol. 12721, pp. 36–42. Springer, Cham (2021). https://doi.org/10.1007/978-3-030-77211-6_4

15. Ghoshal, B., Tucker, A.: Estimating uncertainty and interpretability in deep learning for coronavirus (COVID-19) detection. arXiv preprint arXiv:2003.10769 (2020)

16. Ghoshal, B., Tucker, A.: On cost-sensitive calibrated uncertainty in deep learning: An application on COVID-19 detection. In: 2021 IEEE 34th International Symposium on Computer-Based Medical Systems (CBMS), pp. 503–509. IEEE (2021)

17. Ghoshal, B., Tucker, A., Sanghera, B., Lup Wong, W.: Estimating uncertainty in deep learning for reporting confidence to clinicians in medical image segmentation and diseases detection. Comput. Intell. 37(2), 701–734 (2021)

18. Goodfellow, I., Bengio, Y., Courville, A.: Deep Learning. MIT Press, Cambridge (2016). 1

19. Hidalgo, M.: Pancreatic cancer. N. Engl. J. Med. 362(17), 1605–1617 (2010)

20. Houlsby, N., Huszár, F., Ghahramani, Z., Lengyel, M.: Bayesian active learning for classification and preference learning. arXiv preprint arXiv:1112.5745 (2011)

21. Kendall, A., Gal, Y.: What uncertainties do we need in Bayesian deep learning for computer vision? In: Advances in Neural Information Processing Systems, pp. 5580–5590 (2017)

22. Kenner, B., et al.: Artificial intelligence and early detection of pancreatic cancer: 2020 summative review. Pancreas 50(3), 251 (2021)

23. Kwon, Y., Won, J.H., Kim, B.J., Paik, M.C.: Uncertainty quantification using Bayesian neural networks in classification: application to ischemic stroke lesion segmentation. In: Medical Imaging with Deep Learning Conference (2018)

24. Lakshminarayanan, B., Pritzel, A., Blundell, C.: Simple and scalable predictive uncertainty estimation using deep ensembles. In: Advances in Neural Information Processing Systems 30 (2017)

25. Laves, M.H., Ihler, S., Ortmaier, T., Kahrs, L.A.: Quantifying the uncertainty of deep learning-based computer-aided diagnosis for patient safety. Curr. Dir. Biomed. Eng. 5(1), 223–226 (2019)

26. Leibig, C., Allken, V., Ayhan, M.S., Berens, P., Wahl, S.: Leveraging uncertainty information from deep neural networks for disease detection. Sci. Rep. 7(1), 1–14 (2017)

27. Litjens, G., et al.: A survey on deep learning in medical image analysis. Med. Image Anal. 42, 60–88 (2017)

28. MacKay, D.J.: A practical Bayesian framework for backpropagation networks. Neural Comput. 4(3), 448–472 (1992)

29. Naito, Y.: A deep learning model to detect pancreatic ductal adenocarcinoma on endoscopic ultrasound-guided fine-needle biopsy. Sci. Rep. 11(1), 1–8 (2021)

30. Neal, R.M.: Bayesian learning via stochastic dynamics. In: Advances in Neural Information Processing Systems, pp. 475–482 (1993)

31. Park, W., Chawla, A., O'Reilly, E.M.: Pancreatic cancer: a review. Jama 326(9), 851–862 (2021)

32. Rajpurkar, P., Chen, E., Banerjee, O., Topol, E.J.: AI in health and medicine. Nat. Med. 28, 31–38 (2022)

33. Sehmi, M.N.M., Fauzi, M.F.A., Ahmad, W.S.H.M.W., Chan, E.W.L.: Pancreatic cancer grading in pathological images using deep learning convolutional neural networks. F1000Research 10(1057), 1057 (2021)

A Novel Bi-level Lung Cancer Classification System on CT Scans

Shubham Dodia[1]([⊠]) [iD], B. Annappa[1] [iD], and Mahesh A. Padukudru[2] [iD]

[1] Department of Computer Science and Engineering,
National Institute of Technology Karnataka, Surathkal, India
shubham.dodia8@gmail.com, annappa@ieee.org
[2] Department of Respiratory Medicine, JSS Medical College, JSS Academy of Higher Education and Research, Mysuru, Karnataka, India

Abstract. Purpose: Lung cancer is a life-threatening disease that affects both men and women . Accurate identification of lung cancer has been a challenging task for decades. The aim of this work is to perform a bi-level classification of lung cancer nodules. In Level-1, candidates are classified into nodules and non-nodules, and in Level-2, the detected nodules are further classified into benign and malignant.

Methods: A new preprocessing method, named, Boosted Bilateral Histogram Equalization (BBHE) is applied to the input scans prior to feeding the input to the neural networks. A novel Cauchy Black Widow Optimization-based Convolutional Neural Network (CBWO-CNN) is introduced for Level-1 classification. The weight updation in the CBWO-CNN is performed using Cauchy mutation, and the error rate is minimized, which in turn improved the accuracy with less computation time. A novel hybrid Convolutional Neural Network (CNN) model with shared parameters is introduced for performing Level-2 classification. The second model proposed in this work is a fusion of Squeeze-and-Excitation Network (SE-Net) and Xception, abbreviated as "SE-Xception". The weight parameters are shared for the SE-Xception model trained from CBWO-CNN, i.e., a knowledge transfer approach is adapted.

Results: The recognition accuracy obtained from CBWO-CNN for Level-1 classification is 96.37% with a reduced False Positive Rate (FPR) of 0.033. SE-Xception model achieved a sensitivity of 96.14%, an accuracy of 94.75%, and a specificity of 92.83%, respectively, for Level-2 classification.

Conclusion: The proposed method's performance is better than existing deep learning architectures and outperformed individual SE-Net and Xception with fewer parameters.

Keywords: Lung cancer · Cauchy Black Widow Optimization based Convolutional Neural Network (CBWO-CNN) · Shared network parameters · SE-Xception

© The Author(s), under exclusive license to Springer Nature Switzerland AG 2022
G. Yang et al. (Eds.): MIUA 2022, LNCS 13413, pp. 578–593, 2022.
https://doi.org/10.1007/978-3-031-12053-4_43

1   Introduction

Cancer is one of the world's deadliest illnesses, with a high death rate in men and women. Cancer is formed by abnormal cell growth in any tissue, which leads to the formation of tissue lumps, masses, or nodules. Lung cancer is one of the most life-threatening cancers, accounting for the majority of cancer-related deaths. There has been increasing interest in research in the early identification of lung cancer by investigating lung nodules. Some Computer-Aided Diagnosis (CAD) systems have been previously developed, but there is still no accurate CAD system designed to identify and classify lung nodules. As most patients get lung cancer diagnosed in the middle or advanced stages, CAD systems will help in providing a second opinion for radiologists to proceed with further invasive tests [19]. Nodules in lung cancer may be characterized into two categories, namely, cancerous and non-cancerous. Malignant nodules are cancerous, while benign nodules are not.

The vital information is captured using images. These images can be acquired in different forms, such as Magnetic Resonance Imaging (MRI), Computed Tomography (CT) scans, radiographs (X-rays), Positron Emission Tomography (PET) scans, etc. CT scans proved to be more effective than other techniques and is preferable to the image mentioned above acquisition techniques. CT scanning can be used to identify lung mass tissue as it can detect minor irregularities that suggest lung cancer [1]. A bi-level lung cancer classification with shared network parameters is performed in this work. A novel Cauchy Black Widow based Convolutional Neural Network (CBWO-CNN) is used to classify nodules and non-nodules. A second model, which is a hybrid of SE-Net and Xception, is developed in this work. These two architectures have not been proposed as far as our knowledge is concerned. A knowledge transfer approach is used to train the SE-Xception model. The proposed method outperformed most state-of-the-art deep learning architectures in terms of performance.

1.1   Contribution of the Work

- A novel preprocessing technique named Boosted Bilateral Histogram Equalization (BBHE) is adapted in this work to improve the quality of CT scans.
- Level-1 classification is performed using the novel CBWO-CNN, in which Cauchy mutation is used to choose the best weights.
- A novel SE-Xception CNN model with shared network parameters is proposed for performing Level-2 classification of lung cancer in CT scans.
- The results obtained from the models are verified and recommended for deploying in real-time analysis from an expert pulmonologist.

The rest of the paper is organized as follows: The details of existing CAD systems are presented in Sect. 2. The dataset used in the proposed work is discussed in detail in Sect. 3. Section 4 provides detailed information on the proposed methodology. Section 5 presents a discussion of current architectures as well as the findings of the proposed approach. Section 6 provides the conclusion of the work done in this paper.

1.2   Related Work

In recent research, deep learning has captured many researchers' attention in developing CAD systems for detecting and classifying nodules in lung cancer. An enhanced CNN was used to classify nodule and non-nodule on CT scans [9]. Deep Neural Networks (DNNs) usually are computationally expensive as they consist of many layers. In contrast to this, there are light-weight CNNs that provide comparatively accurate results close to the results of a DNN. A multi-section light-weight CNN for classification of nodules was proposed in [14]. Two such architectures, namely AlexNet and LeNet, were used in [21]. An optimal DNN was trained using a modified gravitational search algorithm used in [10], where these features were provided to Linear Discriminant Analysis (LDA) classifier. A deep convolutional network for lung nodule detection and classification was proposed in [12]. A combination of dense convolution network and a binary tree network, DenseBTNet, was proposed in [11]. A CNN architecture was proposed in [20] to perform lung cancer classification. Three different deep learning architectures were used in their work, namely CNN, DNN, and Stacked AutoEncoder. To classify lung cancer nodules, authors from [17] suggested a multi-scale CNN model. Hence, DNN usage can improve the CAD system's performance.

2   Dataset

The dataset utilized for performing lung cancer nodules classification is LUng Nodule Analysis (LUNA), released in the year 2016. The LUNA16 challenge is an open challenge, where the reference standards and the images are made publicly available. LUNA16 dataset is a curated version of the LIDC-IDRI dataset [2], which is also a public-access dataset. Four expert radiologists have provided the annotations [15]. The main aim of the challenge was to develop large-scale automated nodule detection algorithms for the LIDC-IDRI dataset. Details related to the LUNA dataset are provided in Table 1.

Table 1. Details of LUNA16 dataset

Parameters	Details	Parameters	Details
Dataset	LUNA16 [15]	Image modality	CT
Date of release	2016	Image dimension	512×512
Dataset size (GB)	116	Image format	DICOM
Number of samples	888	Ground truth available	Yes

3   Proposed Methodology

3.1   Overview

The proposed method is divided into four main stages: data preparation, Level-1 classification, transfer-learned knowledge, and Level-2 classification. The block diagram of the proposed methodology is shown in Fig. 1.

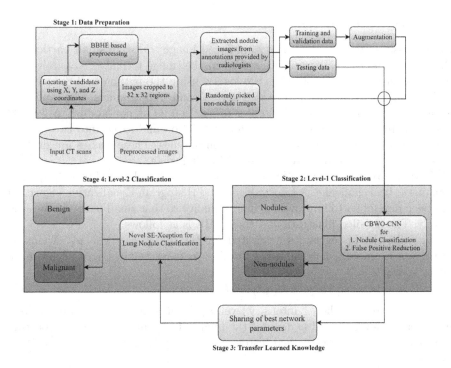

Fig. 1. Block diagram of the proposed approach

In the first stage, data preparation involves the preprocessing of input CT scans. The input CT needs to be preprocessed before providing the image data for the Level-1 classification task. BBHE filtering technique is used to preprocess input CT scans. The second stage is to differentiate between nodules and non-nodules. The dataset consists of very few positive nodules as compared to non-nodules. To mitigate this issue, positive lung nodule data is augmented only for training and validation dataset splits. This process is described in the data augmentation section. The level-1 classification task is performed using the proposed CBWO-CNN. The third stage is the transferring of learned knowledge from the CBWO-CNN model to the proposed SE-Xception model. The reason for adapting the transfer learning approach is that the size of the data used for classifying benign and malignant nodules is significantly less. Deep learning models perform well on large datasets. Therefore, to address this issue, a weight-sharing scheme is adapted in this work. The best pre-trained weights obtained from the trained CBWO-CNN model for nodule and non-nodule images are used as initialization weights for training the SE-Xception model for benign and malignant nodules. The classification of lung nodules into benign and malignant nodules is the fourth stage of the proposed method. A novel architecture named "SE-Xception" is proposed in this work. A detailed description of all the methods is provided in the below sections.

3.2   Image Preprocessing

Preprocessing provides the quality enhanced image to locate small particles in the scanned image. CT scans are stored in the image format of the 'raw' and 'mhd' extension. These CT scans are loaded using the python tool SimpleITK. The location of candidates is provided in X, Y, and Z coordinates. The candidate location is chosen based on the center of the nodule or non-nodule. A 32×32 region is cropped out from each candidate location and saved into two classes, positive and negative, i.e., nodules and non-nodules. These classes are decided based on the annotations provided by the radiologists.

Various preprocessing methodologies have been developed, but still, quality remains to be a challenge. A Boosted Bilateral Histogram Equalization algorithm has been developed to improve the image quality so that small parts can be seen clearly. The detailed illustration of the BBHE is as follows:

Initially, the histogram is generated for the image $\hbar(\chi_j) = n_j^p$. Then the histogram is smoothed by bilateral filtering to preserve the edges in an image given by Eq. 1.

$$\hbar_\chi(\chi_j) = \hbar(\chi_j) * \psi \tag{1}$$

where, χ_j represents the jth intensity level, n_j^p denotes the numbers of pixels having intensity level χ_j and ψ denotes the bilateral filtering. Thereafter, boosting is applied on the edge preserved histogram given by Eq. 2.

$$\hbar_B(\chi_j) = \begin{cases} \frac{\hbar_\chi(\chi_j) - P_{min}}{(P_{max} - P_{min})}(m(K) - P_{min})\alpha + P_{min}, & if \hbar_B(\chi_j) > P_{min} \\ \hbar_\psi(\chi_j), & otherwise \end{cases} \tag{2}$$

where, $m(k)$ denotes the peak histogram's smoothed value, P_{min} and P_{max} denotes the local minimum and maximum pixel values, α boosts the minor regions which is given by $\alpha = log(P_{max} - P_{min})/log(m(k) - P_{min})$. Now, mapping is done using HE and the contrast enhance image is obtained (χ'). δ is multiplied by the gain (Γ_g) and noise reduction (Γ_n) functions to improve detail. The detail gain function is given as Eq. 3.

$$\Gamma_{detail(i,j)} = \lfloor \Gamma_g(i,j) . \Gamma_n(i,j) \rfloor * B(i,j) \tag{3}$$

where, $\Gamma_g(i,j) = 1/\{\mathbb{R}. [\chi_s(i,j) + 1.0]^p\}$ and where $\Gamma_n(i,j) = N_{offset} + \{N_{band}/[1 + e^{-\delta(i,j) - E}]\}$.

Finally, by multiplying the details with the detail function (Γ_{detail}) using Eq. 4, the improved detail image δ' is obtained.

$$\delta'(i,j) = \sum \Gamma_{detail} . \delta(i,j) \tag{4}$$

Equation 5 is used to integrate the χ' and δ' in the final step.

$$\chi''(i,j) = w \times \chi_s(i,j) + (1 - w) \times \delta'(i,j) \tag{5}$$

where, the final enhanced image is $\chi''(i,j)$, and w is a weighted function. The value of w can be anywhere between 0.0 and 1.0.

An illustration of nodules, non-nodules, benign and malignant nodules is shown in Fig. 2. There is a considerable difference in number of nodules and non-nodules in this dataset. To avoid the above-mentioned skewness in the data, the non-nodule data images are sub-sampled, i.e., the images are randomly selected from all the subsets of the dataset. Nodules must be further classified into benign and malignant nodules after the nodule, and non-nodule categories have been established.

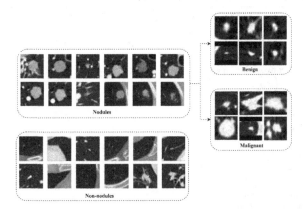

Fig. 2. Illustration of nodule, non-nodule, benign, and malignant images after preprocessing of CT scans

3.3   Data Augmentation

In the above step, there is a clear data imbalance in the data of the two classes. To overcome this problem, the augmentation of positive nodules is performed. The images are augmented by performing some image operations such as modifying brightness, contrast, random rotation of the image to 90°, transposing, scaling the images, and flipping the images horizontally and vertically. Figure 3 illustrates some of the augmented images of a nodules' CT scan. The augmentation images shown in the figure are taken only from one CT scan.

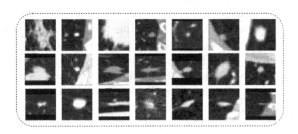

Fig. 3. Illustration of augmented images of a nodule CT scan

3.4 Level-1 Classification: CBWO-CNN

Classifying candidates in a lung CT scan into nodules and non-nodules is critical because some nodules resemble tissues or organs in that area, making it difficult to classify the nodule properly. The training should be done properly to avoid high bias and low variance as well as low bias and high variance.

Algorithm 1 : Proposed Algorithm: CBWO-CNN

1: **Input:** Extracted features $F'_{EXT} = \left\lfloor \xi_1^+, \xi_2^+, \xi_3^+, \xi_4^+, ..., \xi_N^+ \right\rfloor$

2: **Output:** Lung cancer nodule detection

3: Initialize the kernel ($K_{(x,y)}$), bias φ_b, pooling layers (l_{layers}^{PL}), weights

4: **for** i pixels in image $\xi_{x,y}^+$ **do**

5:    Evaluate the convolution operation using

6:    $\wp_2^{conv} = L_{relu}\left(\varphi_B + \Sigma_{x=0}^2 + \Sigma_{y=0}^2 w_{i,j}\xi_{x,y}^+\right)$

7:    Evaluate the pooling layer using

8:    $\wp_3^{pooling} = l_{layers}^{PL}\left(\left|\xi_{x,y}^+\right|\right)$

9:    Generate flattened feature vectors

10:    $\wp_3^{pooling}(\zeta_{flatten}) = \left\lfloor \xi_1^+, \xi_2^+, \xi_3^+, \xi_4^+, ..., \xi_n^+ \right\rfloor.$

11:    Evaluate the fully connected layer using

12:    $\wp_4^{FC} = \gamma\left(\sum_{i=1}^n w_i\zeta_{flatten} + \varphi_b\right)$

13:    **if** $\sum\left(\xi_{x,y}^+ - \bar{\xi}_{x,y}^+\right)=0$ **then**

14: Lung cancer nodule is detected

15:    **else**Update weights using

16: $\partial_{fitness} = f\left(W_k^+\right) = f\left\{w_1^+, w_2^+, w_3^+, w_4^+, ...w_n^+\right\}$

17: $\begin{aligned} w_1 &= \alpha \times w_1^+ + (1-\alpha) \times w_2^+ \\ w_2 &= \alpha \times w_2^+ + (1-\alpha) \times w_1^+ \end{aligned}$

18: Based on cannibalism the strong solution is preserved and then

19: Cauchy mutation is performed for better accuracy rate

20: $v_w^{k+1} = (1-\alpha)\,w_k^+ v_w^k + \alpha\,(\eta_i.N\,(0,\sigma)) + \mu_1\mu_2\left(p_k - w_k^+\right)$

21:    **end if**

22: **end for**

23: **for** $\bar{\xi}_{x,y}^+ ->$ Malignant nodule **do**

24:    **if** malignancy rate> 3 and malignancy rate $<= 5$ **then**

25: Nodule is malignant

26:    **else**Nodule is benign

27:    **end if**

28: **end for**

The first step in the algorithm is feature extraction F'_{EXT} from the input images. These features are fed convolutional layers $\wp_2^{conv}$. The input image is filtered, and the convolution operation learns the same feature across the image. The pooling layer is responsible for reducing the Convolved Feature's spatial size $\wp_3^{pooling}$. This is to reduce the computing power needed by dimensionality reduction to process the data. The convolutional layer and the pooling layer form the ith layer of a convolutional neural network together. The number of such layers can be increased to capture low-level information much more depending on the complexity of the images. Thus, the output from the convolutional layer is flattened $\wp_3^{pooling}(\zeta_{flatten})$. The output of the convolutional layer is distorted and fed to the fully connected layer as the input to the fully connected layer $\wp_4^{FC}$. In order to minimize the loss Back Propagation is done which minimize the loss between the observed output and actual output. CBWO provides with selecting the best weights that is $W_K^+ = \{w_1^+, w_2^+, w_3^+, w_4^+, ...w_n^+\}$ and improving the accuracy within less computation time. The outline of the proposed technique that is CBWO-CNN, is elaborated in the form of pseudo-code in Algorithm 1.

3.5   Level-2 Classification: SE-Xception

Lung cancer nodule classification is a challenging task. A novel CNN, SE-Xception, a combination of two best performing and popular deep learning architectures, SE-Net, and Xception is introduced in this work. SE-Net architecture consists of a block named as Squeeze-and-Excitation (SE) block. In this block, the channel-wise feature responses are adaptively recalibrated using modeling channel inter-dependency explicitly. The SE block illustration can be shown in Fig. 4(a).

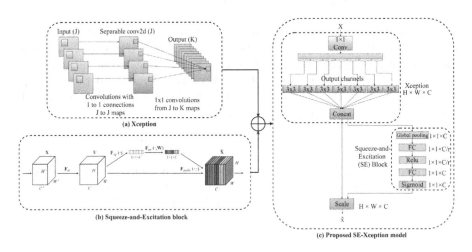

Fig. 4. Diagrammatic representation of: (a) Xception network, (b) Squeeze-and-Excitation block, and (c) Proposed SE-Xception model

In the SE block diagram, F_{tr} represents a convolution operation where the input X is transformed to U. The F_{tr} in the proposed work is an Xception block. In previous works, inception and residual blocks are used as convolution operations. F_{tr} is represented in Eq. 6.

$$F_{tr} : X \rightarrow U, X \epsilon \mathbb{R}^{H'xW'xC'}, U \epsilon \mathbb{R}^{HxWxC} \tag{6}$$

The notation $V = [v_1, v_2, ..., v_C]$ is used to illustrate a set of learned filter kernels, where v_C denotes the parameters of filter kernel. The outputs can be written as $U = [u_1, u_2, ..., u_C]$, where u_C is given in Eq. 7.

$$u_c = v_c * X = \sum_{s=1}^{C'} v_c^s X x^s \tag{7}$$

The features that are obtained after performing F_{tr} are U. The first operation that is carried out in the network is the passing of features through the squeeze operation (F_{sq}). A channel descriptor is produced from the feature maps when passed through the squeeze operation. The feature maps are aggregated across the spatial dimensions (H x W). An embedding of the global distribution of feature responses is generated channel-wise from this descriptor. It makes the information from the network's global receptive area that all its layers are to use. The squeeze operation can be shown in Eq. 8. By shrinking U by its spatial dimensions H x W, a statistic $z \epsilon R$ is generated such that c^{th} is calculated.

$$z_c = F_{sq}(u_c) = \frac{1}{HxW} \sum_{i=1}^{H} \sum_{j=1}^{W} u_c(i,j) \tag{8}$$

Followed by the squeeze operation, to capture the aggregated information of the channel descriptors, an excitation operation is performed. This operation fully captures the channel-wise dependencies, where it learns the non-linear and non-mutually-exclusive relationship of the channels. This operation is represented in Eq. 9, where Rectified Linear Unit (ReLU) activation function is denoted using δ notation, $W_1 = \mathbb{R}^{\frac{C}{r} X C}$, and $W_2 = \mathbb{R}^{\frac{C}{r} X C}$.

$$s = F_{ex}(z, W) = \sigma(g(z, W)) = \sigma(W_2 \delta(W_1 z)) \tag{9}$$

Using a reduction ratio r, a bottleneck with two completely connected (FC) layers is created with dimensionality reduction. This block's final output is given by rescaling U with s activations, which can be expressed in Eq. 10.

$$\widetilde{x}_c = F_{scale}(u_c, s_c) = s_c u_c \tag{10}$$

where $X_c = x_1, x_2, ..., x_c$, $F_{scale}(u_c, s_c)$ represents channel-wise multiplication of scalar s_c and the feature map $u_c \epsilon \mathbb{R}^{(HxW)}$.

Xception network architecture is completely based on depth-wise separable convolution blocks. The working of the Xception model is illustrated in Fig. 4(b). The hypothesis includes calculating spatial correlations, so it is possible to decouple cross-channel correlations in the CNN feature maps fully. The name Xception means "Extreme Inception". It is named Xception because it has a more robust hypothesis than the underlying architecture of InceptionV3 [3]. Xception architecture consists of 36 convolution layers. These convolution layers are organized into 14 different modules. Every module consists of linear residual connections except for the first and last layers. In brief, the Xception network can be said as the stacking of depth-wise separable convolution layers in a linear fashion, which consists of residual connections. The input is data is mapped to spatial correlations for each output channel separately, and then 1×1 depthwise convolution operation is performed. This operation captures the cross-channel correlation.

These correlations can be pictured as a 2D+1D mapping instead of a 3D mapping. Here, the 2D space correlations are performed first, and then 1D space correlation is performed. Xception proved to provide slightly better results as compared to InceptionV3 on the LUNA16 dataset.

The proposed SE-Xception model is a combination of SE-Net and Xception. SE-Net consists of a squeeze-and-excitation block, which performs operations mentioned in the above sections. The addition of these modules in the Xception reduces the parameters of the model. Figure 4(c) shows the graphical representation of the proposed methodology. The figure represents the operations performed in the SE-Xception model. Only one module operation is illustrated. Input X is first passed to an Xception module. The input is given to a convolution filter with a filter size of 1, and then it is passed to a convolution filter with a filter size of 3. These two operations are concatenated, which is known as depth-wise separable convolution. This operation is followed by a SE-block where the squeeze and excitation operation is performed. Initially, to generate a channel descriptor, a global pooling operation is performed on the Xception module's output. The pooling operation is followed by a Fully Connected (FC) layer with the ReLU as the activation function. The sigmoid activation function acts as a simple gating mechanism. This operation is known as the excitation operation. Once this step is completed, the output is scaled, represented as $\widetilde{X}$.

4   Results and Discussion

4.1   Level-1 Classification

This section describes the performance of the proposed models. As the data is skewed, the non-nodules are selected by performing sub-sampling, where a set of non-nodule images are chosen from each subset to balance the data. The data imbalance may be the reason for overfitting the model, which affects the model's performance. The model is validated on 10% of the total data and tested on 20% of the data. Adam optimizer used in both the networks. The loss function used is binary cross-entropy. The total number of epochs are set to 200. An early-stopping criterion is used while training, in which if no improvement is found in the validation loss after 20 epochs, the training is terminated. CBWO-CNN model is initially evaluated on four different activation functions namely, Exponential Linear Unit (ELU) [4], Tanh [13], LeakyReLU [5], and Rectified Linear Unit (ReLU) [8]. The model performance of various activation functions on the CBWO-CNN model is demonstrated in Fig. 5.

Considering ELU as an activation function in the networks, its convergence is faster than other activation functions. The difference between tanh and sigmoid lies in the range of the output value it returns. Tanh output value ranges from -1 to 1, whereas the sigmoid output value ranges from 0 to 1. However, the tanh function's performance in the models' hidden layers is relatively poor compared to other activation functions. LeakyReLU activation function is an extension of ReLU. The alpha value is added to the function to solve the issue of "dying ReLU" in this activation function. The results obtained from the LeakyReLU

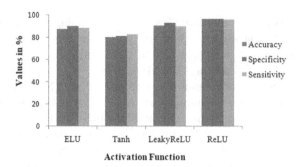

Fig. 5. CBWO-CNN model evaluated on various activation functions on testing data

activation function in the hidden layer are second-best among the other activation functions used to evaluate the model. ReLU provide faster and more accurate results as it removes the negative values to pass to the next layer. The model performed best with the ReLU activation function in the hidden layer.

The performance metrics used to evaluate the CBWO-CNN model are accuracy, specificity, sensitivity, precision, recall, F1-score, and FPR. The corresponding results achieved from these confusion matrices are illustrated in Table 2. Average results obtained from the 5-fold validation of the model are depicted in the table. The table represents the performance measures stated above with their corresponding results.

Table 2. Performance evaluation of the proposed CBWO-CNN model for Level-1 classification assessed using 5-fold cross-validation

Performance measures	Fold 1	Fold 2	Fold 3	Fold 4	Fold 5	Average
Accuracy	95.21%	94.04%	96.18%	95.77%	97.63%	96.37%
Sensitivity	96.16%	96.81%	95.23%	94.57%	97.73%	96.10%
Specificity	94.29%	97.26%	97.110%	96.94%	97.54%	96.63%
Precision	94.26%	97.18%	96.98%	96.79%	97.48%	96.53%
F1-score	95.21%	97.00%	96.10%	95.67%	97.61%	96.32%
FPR	0.057	0.027	0.028	0.030	0.024	0.033

Several popular deep learning architectures are used to evaluate the lung cancer classification system. The architectures chosen for the evaluation of the Level-1 classification system are CNN, VGG-19, Inception-V3, Deep Belief Network, ResNet, Recurrent Neural Network, and proposed CBWO-CNN. Accuracy, sensitivity, and specificity are the performance metrics that are evaluated. The results obtained are presented in Table 3. Hence, it can be noted that the proposed CBWO-CNN model performed better for Level-1 classification.

Table 3. Evaluation of proposed CBWO-CNN in comparison with existing deep models

Models	Accuracy	Sensitivity	Specificity
CNN	84.65%	82.88%	83.47%
VGG-19	87.89%	86.77%	86.56%
Inception-V3	86.51%	85.98%	87.40%
Deep Belief Network	89.95%	87.21%	88.68%
ResNet	94.65%	92.80%	93.91%
Recurrent Neural Network	95.83%	94.41%	95.03%
Proposed CBWO-CNN	**96.37%**	**96.10%**	**96.63%**

4.2   Level-2 Classification

The task of classifying positive lung nodules into benign and malignant nodules is known as lung nodule classification. In this work, the lung cancer nodule classification is performed using the proposed SE-Xception model with shared parameters from the CBWO-CNN model trained in Level-1 classification. To get the best performing model, the proposed model is evaluated on four activation functions in the model's hidden layer. The activation functions used are ELU, Tanh, LeakyReLU, and ReLU. The network proved to provide better performance for the ReLU activation function. The four activation functions' performance has been assessed for three models, SE-Net, Xception, and proposed SE-Xception is demonstrated in Fig. 6.

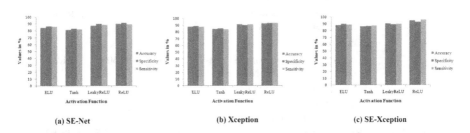

Fig. 6. (a) SE-Net, (b) Xception and (c) Proposed SE-Xception evaluated on various activation functions on testing data for Level-2 classification

The proposed SE-Xception is evaluated with performance metrics such as accuracy, sensitivity, specificity, precision, F1-score, and FPR. The results achieved are presented in Table 4. The results are presented without shared network parameters and with shared network parameters for the SE-Xception model. The model trained without shared parameters resulted in overfitting of the model due to fewer training images. The accuracy achieved for the proposed SE-Xception is 82.29%. The improvement in the result is performed using pre-trained weights from Level-1 classification. This improved accuracy by almost 12%. The accuracy achieved for the proposed SE-Xception was 94.76%.

The proposed SE-Xception model is compared with the previous works performing lung cancer nodule classification. The results achieved from the proposed model outperformed the previous works. Performance comparison of the previous works is illustrated in Table 5.

Table 4. Performance evaluation of the proposed model assessed without shared network parameters and with shared network parameters

Performance measures	Without shared parameters	With shared parameters
Accuracy	82.29%	94.75%
Sensitivity	85.85%	96.14%
Specificity	78.49%	92.83%
Precision	80.95%	94.89%
F1 score	83.33%	95.52%
False positive rate	0.21	0.07

Table 5. Comparison of previous works with proposed model for nodule classification

Reference	Methods used	Accuracy	Sensitivity	Specificity
[7]	Super-Resolution CNN, SVM	85.70%	–	–
[17]	Multi-scale CNN, Random forest	86.84%	–	–
[18]	Taxonomic indexes and phylogenetic trees, SVM	88%	82%	94%
[20]	CNN, DNN, SAE	84.15%	–	–
[16]	Intensity, shape, texture features and Artificial Neural Network	93.70%	95.50%	94.28%
[6]	3D tensor filtering, 3D level set segmentation, correlation feature selection, and random forest	–	84.62%	–
Proposed work	**SE-Xception**	**94.75%**	**96.14%**	**92.83%**

The effect of the proposed SE-Xception method is visually demonstrated in Fig. 7. The images given in the green box are malignant nodules correctly classified as malignant nodules, and the images presented in the red box are benign nodules misclassified as malignant nodules. The reason for some of this misclassification is the indistinguishable similarity in the anatomical structure of the nodules. Even though the FPR of the proposed method is significantly less, the method still has the scope of improvement, as minimal misclassification is also not acceptable in medical applications.

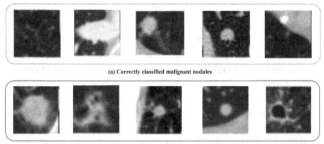

(a) Correctly classified malignant nodules

(b) Misclassification of benign nodules into malignant nodules

Fig. 7. Visual depiction of correctly and misclassified nodules for Level-2 classification (Color figure online)

5 Conclusion

Lung cancer classification has been in the interest of researchers for three decades. Several traditional and deep learning methods have been proposed for classifying and detecting lung cancer nodules. In this work, a bi-level classification model is proposed for the classification of the lung cancer nodules. To enhance the CT scan images, a novel BBHE technique is used. Level-1 classification performs bifurcation among nodules and non-nodules found in the candidates based on the locations provided by the radiologists. Level-2 classification performs classification of benign and malignant lung cancer nodules from the nodules identified in the Level-1 classification.

A novel deep learning architecture, CBWO-CNN, is introduced to perform Level-1 classification and a novel SE-Xception network is introduced to perform Level-2 classification. The proposed SE-Xception model uses the shared network parameters from the CBWO-CNN model used for training nodules and non-nodules. This hybrid network is designed and developed using recently proposed and best performing models, namely, SE-Net and Xception. SE-Net is made use to obtain a lesser number of parameters. The Xception network is an extreme version of the InceptionV3 network. CBWO-CNN and SE-Xception models are the contributions of this paper. The proposed network's performance outperformed recently introduced deep learning models. In the future, a 3D model can be built and trained using 3D image input, where the model can learn volumetric information.

References

1. Aggarwal, T., Furqan, A., Kalra, K.: Feature extraction and LDA based classification of lung nodules in chest CT scan images. In: 2015 International Conference on Advances in Computing, Communications and Informatics (ICACCI), pp. 1189–1193. IEEE (2015)

2. Armato III, S., et al.: The Lung Image Database Consortium (LIDC) and Image Database Resource Initiative (IDRI): a completed reference database of lung nodules on CT scans. Med. Phys. **38**, 915–931 (2011)
3. Chollet, F.: Xception: deep learning with depthwise separable convolutions. In: Proceedings of the IEEE Conference on Computer Vision and Pattern Recognition, pp. 1251–1258 (2017)
4. Clevert, D.A., Unterthiner, T., Hochreiter, S.: Fast and accurate deep network learning by exponential linear units (ELUS). arXiv preprint arXiv:1511.07289 (2015)
5. Glorot, X., Bordes, A., Bengio, Y.: Deep sparse rectifier neural networks. In: Proceedings of the Fourteenth International Conference on Artificial Intelligence and Statistics, pp. 315–323 (2011)
6. Gong, J., Liu, J.Y., Wang, L.J., Sun, X.W., Zheng, B., Nie, S.D.: Automatic detection of pulmonary nodules in CT images by incorporating 3d tensor filtering with local image feature analysis. Physica Medica **46**, 124–133 (2018)
7. Gupta, A., Das, S., Khurana, T., Suri, K.: Prediction of lung cancer from low-resolution nodules in CT-scan images by using deep features. In: International Conference on Advances in Computing, Communications and Informatics (ICACCI), pp. 531–537 (2018)
8. He, K., Zhang, X., Ren, S., Sun, J.: Delving deep into rectifiers: surpassing human-level performance on ImageNet classification. In: Proceedings of the IEEE International Conference on Computer Vision, pp. 1026–1034 (2015)
9. Kasinathan, G., Jayakumar, S., Gandomi, A.H., Ramachandran, S.J., Patan, R.: Automated 3-D lung tumor detection and classification by an active contour model and CNN classifier. Expert Syst. Appl. **134**, 112–119 (2019)
10. Lakshmanaprabu, S., Mohanty, S.N., Shankar, K., Arunkumar, N., Ramirez, G.: Optimal deep learning model for classification of lung cancer on CT images. Futur. Gener. Comput. Syst. **92**, 374–382 (2019)
11. Liu, Y., Hao, P., Zhang, P., Xu, X., Wu, J., Chen, W.: Dense convolutional binary-tree networks for lung nodule classification. IEEE Access **6**, 49080–49088 (2018)
12. Mendoza, J., Pedrini, H.: Detection and classification of lung nodules in chest x-ray images using deep convolutional neural networks. Comput. Intell. **36**(2), 370–401 (2020)
13. Nwankpa, C., Ijomah, W., Gachagan, A., Marshall, S.: Activation functions: Comparison of trends in practice and research for deep learning. arXiv preprint arXiv:1811.03378 (2018)
14. Sahu, P., Yu, D., Dasari, M., Hou, F., Qin, H.: A lightweight multi-section CNN for lung nodule classification and malignancy estimation. IEEE J. Biomed. Health Inform. **23**(3), 960–968 (2018)
15. Setio, A.A.A., et al.: Validation, comparison, and combination of algorithms for automatic detection of pulmonary nodules in computed tomography images: the LUNA16 challenge. Med. Image Anal. **42**, 1–13 (2017)
16. Shaukat, F., Raja, G., Ashraf, R., Khalid, S., Ahmad, M., Ali, A.: Artificial neural network based classification of lung nodules in CT images using intensity, shape and texture features. J. Ambient. Intell. Humaniz. Comput. **10**(10), 4135–4149 (2019)
17. Shen, W., Zhou, M., Yang, F., Yang, C., Tian, J.: Multi-scale convolutional neural networks for lung nodule classification. In: Ourselin, S., Alexander, D.C., Westin, C.-F., Cardoso, M.J. (eds.) IPMI 2015. LNCS, vol. 9123, pp. 588–599. Springer, Cham (2015). https://doi.org/10.1007/978-3-319-19992-4_46

18. Silva, G.L.F.D., Filho, A.O.D.C., Silva, A.C., Paiva, A.C.D., Gattass, M.: Taxonomic indexes for differentiating malignancy of lung nodules on CT images. Res. Biomed. Eng. **32**(3), 263–272 (2016)
19. Sinha, T.: Tumors: benign and malignant. Cancer Therapy Oncol. Int. J. **10**(3), 555790 (2018)
20. Song, Q., Zhao, et al.: Using deep learning for classification of lung nodules on computed tomography images. J. Healthc. Eng. 1–7 (2017)
21. Zhao, X., Liu, L., Qi, S., Teng, Y., Li, J., Qian, W.: Agile convolutional neural network for pulmonary nodule classification using CT images. Int. J. Comput. Assist. Radiol. Surg. **13**(4), 585–595 (2018). https://doi.org/10.1007/s11548-017-1696-0

Jointly Boosting Saliency Prediction and Disease Classification on Chest X-ray Images with Multi-task UNet

Hongzhi Zhu[1(✉)], Robert Rohling[1,2,3], and Septimiu Salcudean[1,2]

[1] School of Biomedical Engineering, University of British Columbia,
Vancouver, Canada
{hzhu,rohling,tims}@ece.ubc.ca
[2] Department of Electrical and Computer Engineering,
University of British Columbia, Vancouver, Canada
[3] Department of Mechanical Engineering, University of British Columbia,
Vancouver, Canada

Abstract. Human visual attention has recently shown its distinct capability in boosting machine learning models. However, studies that aim to facilitate medical tasks with human visual attention are still scarce. To support the use of visual attention, this paper describes a novel deep learning model for visual saliency prediction on chest X-ray (CXR) images. To cope with data deficiency, we exploit the multi-task learning method and tackle disease classification on CXR simultaneously. For a more robust training process, we propose a further optimized multi-task learning scheme to better handle model overfitting. Experiments show our proposed deep learning model with our new learning scheme can outperform existing methods dedicated either for saliency prediction or image classification. The code used in this paper is available at [webpage, concealed for double-blind review].

Keywords: Saliency prediction · Disease classification · X-ray imaging · Deep learning · Multi-task learning

1 Introduction

Recent work in machine learning and computer vision have demonstrated advantages of integrating human attention with artificial neural network models, as studies show that many machine vision tasks, i.e., image segmentation, image captioning, object recognition, etc., can benefit from adding human visual attention [36].

Visual attention is the ability inherited in biological visual systems to selectively recognize regions or features on scenes relevant to a specific task [3], where "bottom-up" attention (also called exogenous attention) focuses on physical properties in the visual input that are salient and distinguishable, and "top-down" attention (also called endogenous attention) generally refers to mental

G. Yang et al. (Eds.): MIUA 2022, LNCS 13413, pp. 594–608, 2022.
https://doi.org/10.1007/978-3-031-12053-4_44

strategies adopted by the visual systems to accomplish the intended visual tasks [44]. Early research on saliency prediction aims to understand attentions triggered by visual features and patterns, and thus "bottom-up" attention is the research focus [3]. More recent attempts, empowered by interdisciplinary efforts, start to study both "bottom-up" and "top-down" attentions, and therefore the terms, saliency prediction and visual attention prediction, are used interchangeably [53]. In this paper, we use the term saliency prediction as the prediction of human visual attentions allocations when viewing 2D images, containing both "bottom-up" and "top-down" attentions. 2D heatmap is usually used to represent human visual attention distribution. Note that saliency prediction studied in this paper is different from neural network's saliency/attention which can be visualized through class activation mapping (CAM) by [63] and other methods [15,48,51]. With the establishment of several benchmark datasets, data driven approaches demonstrated major advancements in saliency prediction (review in [2] and [60]). However, saliency prediction for natural scenes is the primary focus, and more needs to be done in the medical domain. Hence, we intend to study the saliency prediction for examining chest X-ray (CXR) images, one of the most common radiology tasks worldwide.

CXR imaging is commonly used for the diagnosis of cardio and/or respiratory abnormalities; it is capable of identifying multiple conditions through a single shot, i.e., COVID-19, pneumonia, heart enlargement, etc. [6]. There exists multiple public CXR datasets [20,61]. However, the creation of large comprehensive medical datasets is labour intensive, and requires significant medical resources which are usually scarce [9]. Consequently, medical datasets are rarely as abundant as those for non-medical fields. Thus, machine learning approaches applied on medical datasets need to address the problem of data scarcity. In this paper, we exploit the multi-task learning for a solution.

Multi-task learning is known for its inductive transfer characteristics that can drive strong representation learning and generalization of each component task [8]. Therefore, multi-task learning methods partially alleviates some of the major shortcomings in deep learning, i.e., high demands for data sufficiency and heavy computation loads [11]. However, to apply multi-task learning methods successfully, challenges still exist, which can be the proper selection of component tasks, the architecture of the network, the optimization of the training schemes and many others [11,62]. This paper investigates the proper configuration of a multi-task learning model that can tackle visual saliency prediction and image classification simultaneously.

The main contributions of this paper are: 1) development of a new deep convolutional neural network (DCNN) architecture for CXR image saliency prediction and classification based on UNet [47], and 2) proposal of an optimized multi-task learning scheme that handles overfitting. Our method aims to outperform the state-of-the-art networks dedicated either for saliency prediction or image classification.

2   Background

2.1   Saliency Prediction with Deep Learning

DCNN is the leading machine learning method applied to saliency prediction [22,30,31,43]. Besides, transfer learning with pre-trained networks was observed to boost the performance of saliency prediction [31,41,42]. A majority of DCNN approaches are for natural scene saliency prediction, and so far, only a few studied the saliency prediction for medical images. By [5], the generative adversarial network is used to predict expert sonographer's saliency when performing standard fetal head plane detection on ultrasound (US) images. However, the saliency prediction is used as a secondary task to assist the primary detection task, and thus, the saliency prediction performance failed to outperform benchmark prediction methods in several key metrics. Similarly, by [25], as a proof-of-concept study, the gaze data is used as an auxiliary task for CXR image classification, and the performance of saliency prediction is not reported in the study.

2.2   CXR Image Classification with Deep Learning

Public datasets for CXR images enabled data driven approaches for automatic image analysis and diagnosis [33,50]. Advancements in standardized image classification networks, i.e., ResNet [18], DenseNet [19], and EfficientNet [55], facilitate CXR image classification. Yet, CXR image classification remains challenging, as CXR images are noisy, and may contain subtle features that are difficult to recognize even by experts [6,28].

3   Multi-task Learning Method

As stated in Sect. 1, component task selection, network architecture design, and training scheme are key factors for multi-task learning. We select the classification task together with the saliency prediction based on the fact that attention patterns are task specific [26]. Radiologists are likely to exhibit distinguishable visual behaviors when different patient conditions are shown on CXR images [38]. This section introduces our multi-task UNet (MT-UNet) architecture, and derives a better multi-task training scheme for saliency prediction and image classification.

3.1   Multi-task UNet

Figure 1 shows the architecture of the proposed MT-UNet. The network takes CXR images, $x \in \mathbf{R}^{1 \times H \times W}$, where H and W are image dimensions, as input, and produces two outputs, predicted saliency $y_s \in \mathbf{R}^{1 \times H \times W}$, and predicted classification $y_c \in \mathbf{R}^C$, where C is the number of classes. As the ground truth for y_s is human visual attention distribution, represented as a 2D matrix whose elements are non-negative and sum to 1, y_s is normalized by Softmax before

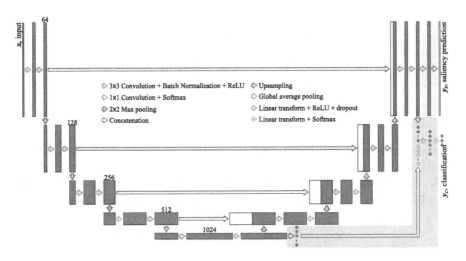

Fig. 1. MT-UNet architecture. The solid blocks represent 3D tensors, $\mathbf{R}^{F \times H \times W}$, where F, H, and W denote feature (channel), height and width dimensions, respectively. The solid circles represent 1D tensors. Arrows denote operations to the tensors. Numbers above some of the solid blocks stand for the number features in tensors.

output from MT-UNet. Softmax is also applied to $\boldsymbol{y}_c$ before output so that the classification outcome can be interpreted as class probability. For the simplicity of notation, batch dimensions are neglected.

The proposed MT-UNet is derived from standard UNet architecture [47]. As a well-known image-to-image deep learning model, the UNet structure has been adopted for various tasks. For example, the UNet is appended with additional structures for visual scene understanding [21], the features from the bottleneck (middle of the UNet) are extracted for image classification tasks [25], and by combining UNet with Pyramid Net [35], features at different depth are aggregated for enhanced segmentation [40]. What's more, the encoder-decoder structure of UNet is utilized for multi-task learning, where the encoder structure is used to learn representative features, along with designated decoder structures or classification heads for image reconstruction, segmentation, and/or classification [1,64]. In our design, we apply classification heads (shaded in light green in Fig. 1), which are added not only to the bottleneck but also the ending part of the UNet architecture. This additional classification specific structure aggregates middle and higher-level features for classification, exploiting features learnt at different depths. The attention heads perform global average pooling operations to the 4D tensors, followed by concatenation, and two linear transforms (dense layers) with dropout (rate = 25%) in the middle to produce classification outcomes. The MT-UNet belongs to the hard parameter sharing structure in multi-task learning, where different tasks share the same trainable parameters before branched out to each tasks' specific parameters [58]. Having more trainable parameters in task specific structures may improve the performance for that task at the cost of introducing additional parameters and increasing computational load [11,58]. In our design, we wish to avoid heavy structures with lots of task specific parameters, and therefore, task specific structures are minimized. In Fig. 1, we use yellow and green shades to denote network structures dedicated for saliency prediction and classification, respectively.

3.2   Multi-task Training Scheme

Balancing the losses between tasks in a multi-task training process has a direct impact on the training outcome [58]. There exist multi-task training schemes [10, 16,27,49], and among which, we adopt the uncertainty based balancing scheme [27] with the modification used in [34,65]. Hence, the loss function is:

$$\mathcal{L} = \frac{1}{\sigma_s^2} L_s + \frac{1}{\sigma_c^2} L_c + \ln(\sigma_s + 1) + \ln(\sigma_c + 1) \qquad (1)$$

where L_s and L_c are loss values for $\boldsymbol{y}_s$ and $\boldsymbol{y}_c$, respectively; $\sigma_s > 0$ and $\sigma_c > 0$ are trainable scalars estimating the uncertainty of L_s and L_c, respectively; σ_s and σ_c are initialized to 1; $\ln(\sigma_s + 1)$ and $\ln(\sigma_c + 1)$ are regularizing terms to avoid arbitrary decrease of σ_s and σ_c. With Eq. 1, we know that σ values can dynamically weigh losses of different amplitudes during training, and loss with low uncertainty (small σ value) is prioritized in the training process. $\mathcal{L} > 0$. Given $\boldsymbol{y}_s$ and $\boldsymbol{y}_c$ with their ground truth $\bar{\boldsymbol{y}}_s$ and $\bar{\boldsymbol{y}}_c$, respectively, the loss functions are:

$$L_s = H(\bar{\boldsymbol{y}}_s, \boldsymbol{y}_s) - H(\bar{\boldsymbol{y}}_s), \qquad (2)$$

$$L_c = H(\bar{\boldsymbol{y}}_c, \boldsymbol{y}_c) \qquad (3)$$

where $H(Q, R) = -\Sigma_i^n Q_i \ln(R_i)$ stands for cross entropy of two discrete distributions Q and R, both with n elements; $H(Q) = H(Q, Q)$ stands for the entropy, or self cross entropy, of discrete distribution Q. L_s is the Kullback-Leibler divergence (KLD) loss, and L_c is the cross-entropy loss. By observing Eq. 2 and Eq. 3, we know that only the cross entropy terms, $H(\cdot, \cdot)$, generate gradient when updating network parameters, as the term $-H(\bar{\boldsymbol{y}}_s)$ in L_s is a constant and has zero gradient. Therefore, we extend the method in [27], and use $\frac{1}{\sigma^2}$ to scale a KLD loss (L_s) as that for a cross-entropy loss (L_c).

Although the training scheme in Eq. 1 yields many successful applications, overfitting for multi-task networks still can jeopardize the training process, especially for small datasets [59]. Multiple factors can cause overfitting, among which, learning rate, $r > 0$, shows the most significant impact [32]. Also, r generally has significant influences on the training outcome [52], making it one of the most important hyper-parameters for a training process. When training MT-UNet, r is moderated by several factors. The first factor is the use of an optimizer. Many optimizers, i.e., Adam [29] and RMSProp [57], deploy the momentum mechanism or its variants, which can adaptively adjust the effective learning rate, r_e, during training. As a learning rate scheduler is often used for more efficient training, it is the second factor to influence r. The influence of r from a learning rate

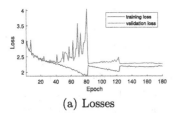

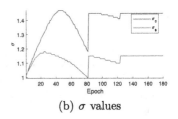

(a) Losses   (b) σ values

Fig. 2. Training process visualization with Eq. 1

scheduler can be adaptive, i.e., reduce learning rate on plateau (RLRP), or more arbitrary, i.e., cosine annealing with warm restarts [37]. By observing Eq. 1, we know that an uncertainty estimator σ for a loss L also serves as a learning rate adaptor for L, which is the third factor. More specifically, given a loss value L with learning rate r, the effective learning rate for parameters with a scaled loss value $\frac{L}{\sigma^2}$ is $\frac{r}{\sigma^2}$.

Decreasing r upon overfitting can alleviate its effects [12,52], but Eq. 1 leads to increased learning rate upon overfitting, further worsening the training process. This happens because training loss decreases when overfitting occurs, reducing its variance at the same time. Thus, σ decreases accordingly, which increases the effective learning rate, thus creating a vicious circle of overfitting. This phenomenon can be observed in Fig. 2, where changes of losses and σ values during a training process following Eq. 1 are presented. We can see from Fig. 2(a), at epoch 40, after an initial decrease in both the training and validation losses, the training loss start to decrease acceleratedly while the validation loss start to amplify, which is a vicious circle of overfitting. A RLRP scheduler can halt the vicious circle by resetting the model parameters to a former epoch and reducing r. Yet, even with reduced r, a vicious circle of overfitting can remerge in later epochs. The mathematical proof of the aforementioned vicious circle of overfitting is presented in Appendix A.

To alleviate overfitting, we propose the use of the following equations to replace Eq. 1:

$$\mathcal{L} = \frac{1}{\sigma_s^2} L_s + L_c + \ln(\sigma_s + 1), \tag{4}$$

$$\mathcal{L} = L_s + \frac{1}{\sigma_c^2} L_c + \ln(\sigma_c + 1). \tag{5}$$

The essence of Eqs. 4 and 5 is to fix the uncertainty term for one loss in Eq. 1 to 1, so that the flexibility in changing effective learning rate is reduced. With the uncertainty term fixed for one component loss, Eqs. 4 and 5 demonstrate the ability to alleviate overfitting and stabilize the training process. It is worth noting that Eqs. 4 and 5 cannot be used interchangeably. We need to test both equations to check which can achieve better performances, as depending on the dataset and training process, overfitting can occur of different severity in all component tasks. In this study, the training process with Eq. 5 achieves the best performance. Ablation study of this method is presented in Sect. 5.

4   Dataset and Evaluation Methods

We use the "chest X-ray dataset with eye-tracking and report dictation" [25] shared via PhysioNet [39] in this study. The dataset was derived from the MIMIC-CXR dataset [23, 24] with additional gaze tracking and dictation from an expert radiologist. 1083 CXR images are included in the dataset, and accompanying each image, there are tracked gaze data; a diagnostic label (either normal, pneumonia, or enlarged heart); segmentation of lungs, mediastinum, and aortic knob; and radiologist's audio with dictation. The CXR images in the dataset are in resolutions of various sizes, i.e., 3056×2044, and we down sample and/or pad each image to 640×416. A GP3 gaze tracker by Gazepoint (Vancouver, Canada) was used for the collection of gaze data. The tracker has an accuracy of around $1°$ of visual angle, and has a 60 Hz sampling rate [66].

Several metrics have been used for the evaluation of saliency prediction performances, and they can be classified into location-based metrics and distribution-based metrics [4]. Due to the tracking inaccuracy of the GP3 gaze tracker, location-based metrics are not suited for this study. Therefore, in this paper, we follow suggestions in [4] and use KLD for performance evaluation. We also include histogram similarity (HS), and Pearson's correlation coefficient (PCC) for reference purposes. For the evaluation of classification performances, we use the area under curve (AUC) metrics for multi-class classifications [14, 17], and the classification accuracy (ACC) metrics. We also include the AUC metrics for each class: normal, enlarged heart, and pneumonia, denoted as AUC-Y1, AUC-Y2, and AUC-Y3, respectively. In this paper, all metrics values are presented as median statistics followed by standard deviations behind the $\pm$ sign. Metrics with up-pointing arrow ↑ indicates greater values reflect better performances, and vice versa. Best metrics are emboldened.

5   Experiments and Result

5.1   Benchmark Comparison

In this subsection, we compare the performance of MT-UNet, with benchmark networks for CXR image classification and saliency prediction. Detailed training settings are presented in Appendix B.

For CXR image classification, the benchmark networks are chosen from the top performing networks for CXR image classification examined in [13], which are ResNet50 [18] and Inception-ResNet v2 (abbreviated as IRNetV2 in this paper) [54]. Following [25], we also include a state-of-the-art general purpose classification network: EfficientNetV2-S (abbreviated as EffNetV2-S) [56] for comparison. For completeness, classification using standard UNet with additional classification head (denoted as UNetC) is included. Results are presented in Table 1, and We can see that MT-UNet outperforms the other classification networks.

For CXR image saliency prediction, comparison was conducted with 3 state-of-the-art saliency prediction models, which are SimpleNet [46], MSINet [30] and VGGSSM [7]. Saliency prediction using standard UNet (denoted as UNetS) is

Table 1. Performance comparison between classification models.

Metrics	MT-UNet	UNetC	EffNetv2-S	IRNetv2	ResNet50
ACC ↑	**0.670** ± 0.018	0.593 ± 0.009	0.640 ± 0.037	0.640 ± 0.017	0.613 ± 0.013
AUC ↑	**0.843** ± 0.012	0.780 ± 0.006	0.826 ± 0.015	0.824 ± 0.014	0.816 ± 0.010
AUC-Y1 ↑	**0.864** ± 0.014	0.841 ± 0.007	0.852 ± 0.013	0.862 ± 0.016	0.845 ± 0.015
AUC-Y2 ↑	**0.912** ± 0.008	0.840 ± 0.003	0.901 ± 0.015	0.897 ± 0.011	0.896 ± 0.015
AUC-Y3 ↑	**0.711** ± 0.027	0.597 ± 0.018	0.653 ± 0.017	0.633 ± 0.036	0.622 ± 0.022

Table 2. Performance comparison between saliency prediction models.

Metrics	MT-UNet	UNetS	SimpleNet	MSINet	VGGSSM
KLD ↓	**0.726** ± 0.004	0.750 ± 0.002	0.758 ± 0.009	0.748 ± 0.003	0.743 ± 0.007
PCC ↑	**0.569** ± 0.004	0.552 ± 0.002	0.545 ± 0.008	0.557 ± 0.002	0.561 ± 0.005
HS ↑	**0.548** ± 0.001	0.540 ± 0.001	0.541 ± 0.002	0.545 ± 0.001	0.545 ± 0.003

also included for reference. Table 2 shows the result, where MT-UNet outperforms the rest. Visual comparisons for saliency prediction results are presented through Table 4 in Appendix C.

5.2 Ablation Study

To validate the modified multi-task learning scheme, ablation study is performed. The multi-task learning schemes following Eqs. 1, 4, and 5 are compared, and they are denoted as MTLS1, MTLS2, and MTLS3, respectively. Please note that the best-performing MTLS3 is used for benchmark comparison in Sect. 5.1. Figure 3 shows the training process for MTLS2 and MTLS3. With Figs. 2 and 3, we can see that overfitting occurs both for MTLS1 and MTLS2, but the overfitting is reduced in MTLS3. The training processes shown in Figs. 2 and 3 are with optimized hyper-parameters. The resulting performances are compared in Table 3. We can see that MTLS3 outperforms the rest learning schemes both in classification and in saliency prediction.

To validate the effects of using classification head that aggregates features from different depths, we create ablated versions of MT-UNet that use features from either the bottleneck or the top layer of the MT-UNet for classification, denoted as MT-UNetB and MT-UNetT, respectively. Results are presented in Table 3. We can see that MT-UNet generally performs better than MT-UNetT and MT-UNetB.

Table 3. Ablation study performance comparison.

Metrics	MTLS1	MTLS2	MTLS3	MT-UNetB	MT-UNetT
KLD ↓	0.730 ± 0.007	0.738 ± 0.006	**0.726** ± 0.004	0.730 ± 0.003	0.734 ± 0.007
CC ↑	0.566 ± 0.005	0.563 ± 0.005	**0.569** ± 0.004	0.568 ± 0.003	0.561 ± 0.007
HS ↑	0.547 ± 0.002	0.545 ± 0.002	**0.548** ± 0.001	**0.548** ± 0.001	0.544 ± 0.003
ACC ↑	0.649 ± 0.041	0.638 ± 0.019	**0.670** ± 0.018	0.653 ± 0.013	0.649 ± 0.011
AUC ↑	0.832 ± 0.019	0.832 ± 0.010	0.843 ± 0.012	0.836 ± 0.009	**0.847** ± 0.008
AUC-Y1 ↑	0.859 ± 0.014	0.861 ± 0.015	0.864 ± 0.014	0.859 ± 0.007	**0.883** ± 0.005
AUC-Y2 ↑	0.906 ± 0.016	0.913 ± 0.005	**0.912** ± 0.008	0.907 ± 0.011	0.910 ± 0.006
AUC-Y3 ↑	0.682 ± 0.035	0.672 ± 0.010	**0.711** ± 0.027	0.694 ± 0.023	0.695 ± 0.025

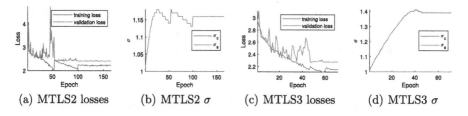

(a) MTLS2 losses   (b) MTLS2 σ (c) MTLS3 losses   (d) MTLS3 σ

Fig. 3. Multi-task learning schemes comparison

6   Discussion

In this paper, we build the MT-UNet model and propose a further optimized multi-tasking learning scheme for saliency prediction and disease classification with CXR images. While a multi-task learning model has the potential of enhancing the performances for all component tasks, a proper training scheme is one of the key factors to fully unveil its potentiality. As shown in Table 3, MT-UNet with the standard multi-task learning scheme may barely outperform existing models for saliency prediction or image classification.

Several future work could be done to improve this study. The first would be the expansion of the gaze tracking dataset for medical images. So far, only 1083 CXR images are publicly available with radiologist's gaze behavior, limiting extensive studies of gaze-tracking assisted machine learning methods in the medical field. Also, more dedicated studies on multi-task learning methods, especially for small datasets, can be helpful for medical machine learning tasks. Overfitting and data deficiency are the lingering challenges encountered by many studies. A better multi-task learning method may handle these challenges more easily.

A   Mathematical Derivation of Vicious Circle for Overfitting

Let $L \geq 0$ be the loss for a task, $\mathcal{T}$, and $\sigma > 0$ be the variance estimator for L used in Eq. 1. Therefore, the loss for $\mathcal{T}$ following Eq. 1 can be expressed as:

$$\mathcal{L} = \frac{L}{\sigma^2} + \ln(\sigma + 1). \tag{6}$$

The partial derivative of $\mathcal{L}$ with respect to σ is:

$$\frac{\partial \mathcal{L}}{\partial \sigma} = -\frac{2L}{\sigma^3} + \frac{1}{\sigma + 1}. \tag{7}$$

During a gradient based optimization process, to minimize $\mathcal{L}$, σ converges to the equilibrium value (σ remains unchanged after gradient descend) which is achieved when $\frac{\partial \mathcal{L}}{\partial \sigma} = 0$. Therefore, the following equation holds when σ is at its equilibrium value, denoted as $\tilde{\sigma}$:

$$L = \frac{\tilde{\sigma}^3}{2\tilde{\sigma} + 2} \tag{8}$$

which is calculated by letting $\frac{\partial \mathcal{L}}{\partial \sigma} = 0$. Let $f(\tilde{\sigma}) = L$, $\tilde{\sigma} > 0$, we can calculate that:

$$\frac{df(\tilde{\sigma})}{d\tilde{\sigma}} = \frac{\tilde{\sigma}^2(2\tilde{\sigma} + 3)}{2(\tilde{\sigma} + 1)^2} > 0, \quad \forall \tilde{\sigma} > 0. \tag{9}$$

Therefore, we know that $f(\tilde{\sigma})$ is strictly monotonically increasing with respect to $\tilde{\sigma}$, and hence the inverse function of $f(\tilde{\sigma})$, $f^{-1}(\cdot)$, exists. More specifically, we have:

$$\tilde{\sigma} = f^{-1}(L). \tag{10}$$

As a pair of inverse functions share the same monotonicity, we know that $\tilde{\sigma} = f^{-1}(L)$ is also strictly monotonically increasing. Thus, when L decreases due to overfitting, we know that $\tilde{\sigma}$ will decrease accordingly, forcing σ to decrease. The decreased σ leads to an increase in the effective learning rate for $\mathcal{T}$, forming a vicious circle of overfitting.

B   Training Settings

We use the Adam optimizer with default parameters [29] and the RLRP scheduler for all the training processes. The RLRP scheduler reduces 90% of the learning rate when validation loss stops improving for P consecutive epochs, and reset model parameters to an earlier epoch when the network achieves the best validation loss. All training and testing are performed with the PyTorch framework [45]. Hyper-parameters for optimizations are learning rate r, and P in RLRP scheduler. The dataset is randomly partitioned into 70%, 10% and 20% subsections for training, validation and testing, respectively. The random data partitioning process preserves the balanced dataset characteristic, and all classes have equal share in all sub-datasets. All the results presented in this paper are based on at least 5 independent training with the same hyper-parameters. NVIDIA V100 and A100 GPUs (Santa Clara, USA) were used.

C   Saliency Map visualization

Table 4. Visualization of predicted saliency distributions. The ground truth and predicted saliency distributions are overlaid over CXR images. Jet colormap is used for saliency distributions where warmer (red and yellow) colors indicate higher concentration of saliency and colder (green and blue) colors indicate lower concentration of saliency.

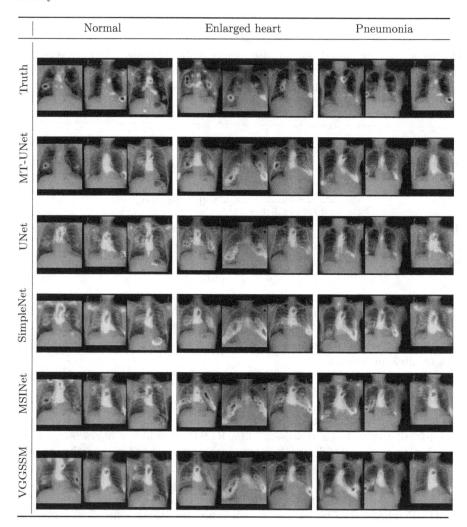

References

1. Amyar, A., Modzelewski, R., Li, H., Ruan, S.: Multi-task deep learning based CT imaging analysis for COVID-19 pneumonia: classification and segmentation. Comput. Biol. Med. **126**, 104037 (2020)
2. Borji, A.: Saliency prediction in the deep learning era: successes and limitations. IEEE Trans. Patt. Anal. Mach. Intell. **43**, 679–700 (2019)
3. Borji, A., Sihite, D.N., Itti, L.: Quantitative analysis of human-model agreement in visual saliency modeling: a comparative study. IEEE Trans. Image Process. **22**(1), 55–69 (2012)
4. Bylinskii, Z., Judd, T., Oliva, A., Torralba, A., Durand, F.: What do different evaluation metrics tell us about saliency models? IEEE Trans. Pattern Anal. Mach. Intell. **41**(3), 740–757 (2018)
5. Cai, Y., Sharma, H., Chatelain, P., Noble, J.A.: Multi-task SonoEyeNet: detection of fetal standardized planes assisted by generated sonographer attention maps. In: International Conference on Medical Image Computing and Computer-Assisted Intervention, pp. 871–879. Springer (2018). https://doi.org/10.1007/978-3-030-00928-1_98
6. Çallı, E., Sogancioglu, E., van Ginneken, B., van Leeuwen, K.G., Murphy, K.: Deep learning for chest x-ray analysis: a survey. Med. Image Anal. **72**, 102125 (2021)
7. Cao, G., Tang, Q., Jo, K.: Aggregated deep saliency prediction by self-attention network. In: Huang, D.-S., Premaratne, P. (eds.) ICIC 2020. LNCS (LNAI), vol. 12465, pp. 87–97. Springer, Cham (2020). https://doi.org/10.1007/978-3-030-60796-8_8
8. Caruana, R.: Multitask learning. Mach. Learn. **28**(1), 41–75 (1997)
9. Castro, D.C., Walker, I., Glocker, B.: Causality matters in medical imaging. Nat. Commun. **11**(1), 1–10 (2020)
10. Chen, Z., Badrinarayanan, V., Lee, C.Y., Rabinovich, A.: GradNorm: gradient normalization for adaptive loss balancing in deep multitask networks. In: International Conference on Machine Learning, pp. 794–803. PMLR (2018)
11. Crawshaw, M.: Multi-task learning with deep neural networks: a survey. arXiv preprint arXiv:2009.09796 (2020)
12. Duffner, S., Garcia, C.: An online backpropagation algorithm with validation error-based adaptive learning rate. In: de Sá, J.M., Alexandre, L.A., Duch, W., Mandic, D. (eds.) ICANN 2007. LNCS, vol. 4668, pp. 249–258. Springer, Heidelberg (2007). https://doi.org/10.1007/978-3-540-74690-4_26
13. El Asnaoui, K., Chawki, Y., Idri, A.: Automated methods for detection and classification pneumonia based on X-Ray images using deep learning. In: Maleh, Y., Baddi, Y., Alazab, M., Tawalbeh, L., Romdhani, I. (eds.) Artificial Intelligence and Blockchain for Future Cybersecurity Applications. SBD, vol. 90, pp. 257–284. Springer, Cham (2021). https://doi.org/10.1007/978-3-030-74575-2_14
14. Fawcett, T.: An introduction to roc analysis. Pattern Recogn. Lett. **27**(8), 861–874 (2006)
15. Fu, K., Dai, W., Zhang, Y., Wang, Z., Yan, M., Sun, X.: MultiCAM: multiple class activation mapping for aircraft recognition in remote sensing images. Remote Sens. **11**(5), 544 (2019)
16. Guo, M., Haque, A., Huang, D.A., Yeung, S., Fei-Fei, L.: Dynamic task prioritization for multitask learning. In: Proceedings of the European Conference on Computer Vision (ECCV), pp. 270–287 (2018)

17. Hand, D.J., Till, R.J.: A simple generalisation of the area under the ROC curve for multiple class classification problems. Mach. Learn. **45**(2), 171–186 (2001)
18. He, K., Zhang, X., Ren, S., Sun, J.: Deep residual learning for image recognition. In: Proceedings of the IEEE Conference on Computer Vision and Pattern Recognition, pp. 770–778 (2016)
19. Huang, G., Liu, Z., Van Der Maaten, L., Weinberger, K.Q.: Densely connected convolutional networks. In: Proceedings of the IEEE Conference on Computer Vision and Pattern Recognition, pp. 4700–4708 (2017)
20. Irvin, J., et al.: CheXpert: a large chest radiograph dataset with uncertainty labels and expert comparison. In: Proceedings of the AAAI Conference on Artificial Intelligence, vol. 33, pp. 590–597 (2019)
21. Jha, A., Kumar, A., Pande, S., Banerjee, B., Chaudhuri, S.: MT-UNET: a novel U-Net based multi-task architecture for visual scene understanding. In: 2020 IEEE International Conference on Image Processing (ICIP), pp. 2191–2195. IEEE (2020)
22. Jia, S., Bruce, N.D.: EML-NET: an expandable multi-layer network for saliency prediction. Image Vis. Comput. **95**, 103887 (2020)
23. Johnson, A.E., et al.: MIMIC-CXR, a de-identified publicly available database of chest radiographs with free-text reports. Sci. Data **6**(1), 1–8 (2019)
24. Johnson, A.E., et al.: MIMIC-CXR-JPG, a large publicly available database of labeled chest radiographs. arXiv preprint arXiv:1901.07042 (2019)
25. Karargyris, A., et al.: Creation and validation of a chest x-ray dataset with eye-tracking and report dictation for AI development. Sci. Data **8**(1), 1–18 (2021)
26. Karessli, N., Akata, Z., Schiele, B., Bulling, A.: Gaze embeddings for zero-shot image classification. In: Proceedings of the IEEE Conference on Computer Vision and Pattern Recognition, pp. 4525–4534 (2017)
27. Kendall, A., Gal, Y., Cipolla, R.: Multi-task learning using uncertainty to weigh losses for scene geometry and semantics. In: Proceedings of the IEEE Conference on Computer Vision and Pattern Recognition, pp. 7482–7491 (2018)
28. Khan, W., Zaki, N., Ali, L.: Intelligent pneumonia identification from chest x-rays: a systematic literature review. IEEE Access **9**, 51747–51771 (2021)
29. Kingma, D.P., Ba, J.: Adam: a method for stochastic optimization. arXiv preprint arXiv:1412.6980 (2014)
30. Kroner, A., Senden, M., Driessens, K., Goebel, R.: Contextual encoder-decoder network for visual saliency prediction. Neural Netw. **129**, 261–270 (2020)
31. Kümmerer, M., Wallis, T.S., Bethge, M.: DeepGaze II: reading fixations from deep features trained on object recognition. arXiv preprint arXiv:1610.01563 (2016)
32. Li, H., Li, J., Guan, X., Liang, B., Lai, Y., Luo, X.: Research on overfitting of deep learning. In: 2019 15th International Conference on Computational Intelligence and Security (CIS), pp. 78–81. IEEE (2019)
33. Li, Y., Zhang, Z., Dai, C., Dong, Q., Badrigilan, S.: Accuracy of deep learning for automated detection of pneumonia using chest x-ray images: a systematic review and meta-analysis. Comput. Biol. Med. **123**, 103898 (2020)
34. Liebel, L., Körner, M.: Auxiliary tasks in multi-task learning. arXiv preprint arXiv:1805.06334 (2018)
35. Lin, T.Y., Dollár, P., Girshick, R., He, K., Hariharan, B., Belongie, S.: Feature pyramid networks for object detection. In: Proceedings of the IEEE Conference on Computer Vision and Pattern Recognition, pp. 2117–2125 (2017)
36. Liu, X., Milanova, M.: Visual attention in deep learning: a review. Int. Rob. Auto J. **4**(3), 154–155 (2018)
37. Loshchilov, I., Hutter, F.: SGDR: stochastic gradient descent with warm restarts. arXiv preprint arXiv:1608.03983 (2016)

38. McLaughlin, L., Bond, R., Hughes, C., McConnell, J., McFadden, S.: Computing eye gaze metrics for the automatic assessment of radiographer performance during x-ray image interpretation. Int. J. Med. Inform. **105**, 11–21 (2017)
39. Moody, G., Mark, R., Goldberger, A.: PhysioNet: a research resource for studies of complex physiologic and biomedical signals. In: Computers in Cardiology 2000, vol. 27 (Cat. 00CH37163), pp. 179–182. IEEE (2000)
40. Moradi, S., et al.: MFP-Unet: a novel deep learning based approach for left ventricle segmentation in echocardiography. Physica Med. **67**, 58–69 (2019)
41. Oyama, T., Yamanaka, T.: Fully convolutional DenseNet for saliency-map prediction. In: 2017 4th IAPR Asian Conference on Pattern Recognition (ACPR), pp. 334–339. IEEE (2017)
42. Oyama, T., Yamanaka, T.: Influence of image classification accuracy on saliency map estimation. CAAI Trans. Intell. Technol. **3**(3), 140–152 (2018)
43. Pan, J., Sayrol, E., Giro-i Nieto, X., McGuinness, K., O'Connor, N.E.: Shallow and deep convolutional networks for saliency prediction. In: Proceedings of the IEEE Conference on Computer Vision and Pattern Recognition, pp. 598–606 (2016)
44. Paneri, S., Gregoriou, G.G.: Top-down control of visual attention by the prefrontal cortex. functional specialization and long-range interactions. Front. Neurosci. **11**, 545 (2017)
45. Paszke, A., et al.: PyTorch: an imperative style, high-performance deep learning library. Adv. Neural. Inf. Process. Syst. **32**, 8026–8037 (2019)
46. Reddy, N., Jain, S., Yarlagadda, P., Gandhi, V.: Tidying deep saliency prediction architectures. In: 2020 IEEE/RSJ International Conference on Intelligent Robots and Systems (IROS), pp. 10241–10247. IEEE (2020)
47. Ronneberger, O., Fischer, P., Brox, T.: U-net: convolutional networks for biomedical image segmentation. In: International Conference on Medical Image Computing and Computer-Assisted Intervention, pp. 234–241. Springer (2015). https://doi.org/10.1007/978-3-319-24574-4_28
48. Selvaraju, R.R., Das, A., Vedantam, R., Cogswell, M., Parikh, D., Batra, D.: Grad-cam: why did you say that? arXiv preprint arXiv:1611.07450 (2016)
49. Sener, O., Koltun, V.: Multi-task learning as multi-objective optimization. arXiv preprint arXiv:1810.04650 (2018)
50. Serte, S., Serener, A., Al-Turjman, F.: Deep learning in medical imaging: a brief review. Trans. Emerg. Telecommun. Technol. 14 (2020)
51. Simonyan, K., Vedaldi, A., Zisserman, A.: Deep inside convolutional networks: visualising image classification models and saliency maps. arXiv preprint arXiv:1312.6034 (2013)
52. Smith, L.N.: A disciplined approach to neural network hyper-parameters: part 1-learning rate, batch size, momentum, and weight decay. arXiv preprint arXiv:1803.09820 (2018)
53. Sun, Y., Zhao, M., Hu, K., Fan, S.: Visual saliency prediction using multi-scale attention gated network. Multimedia Syst. **28**(1), 131–139 (2021). https://doi.org/10.1007/s00530-021-00796-4
54. Szegedy, C., Ioffe, S., Vanhoucke, V., Alemi, A.A.: Inception-v4, inception-resnet and the impact of residual connections on learning. In: Thirty-first AAAI Conference on Artificial Intelligence (2017)
55. Tan, M., Le, Q.: EfficientNet: rethinking model scaling for convolutional neural networks. In: International Conference on Machine Learning, pp. 6105–6114. PMLR (2019)
56. Tan, M., Le, Q.V.: Efficientnetv2: smaller models and faster training. arXiv preprint arXiv:2104.00298 (2021)

57. Tieleman, T., Hinton, G., et al.: Lecture 6.5-rmsprop: divide the gradient by a running average of its recent magnitude. COURSERA: Neural Netw. Mach. Learn. **4**(2), 26–31 (2012)

58. Vandenhende, S., Georgoulis, S., Van Gansbeke, W., Proesmans, M., Dai, D., Van Gool, L.: Multi-task learning for dense prediction tasks: a survey. IEEE Trans. Patt. Anal. Mach. Intell. **44**(7) (2021)

59. Wang, W., Tran, D., Feiszli, M.: What makes training multi-modal classification networks hard? In: Proceedings of the IEEE/CVF Conference on Computer Vision and Pattern Recognition, pp. 12695–12705 (2020)

60. Wang, W., Shen, J., Xie, J., Cheng, M.M., Ling, H., Borji, A.: Revisiting video saliency prediction in the deep learning era. IEEE Trans. Pattern Anal. Mach. Intell. **43**(1), 220–237 (2019)

61. Wang, X., Peng, Y., Lu, L., Lu, Z., Bagheri, M., Summers, R.M.: ChestX-ray8: hospital-scale chest x-ray database and benchmarks on weakly-supervised classification and localization of common thorax diseases. In: Proceedings of the IEEE Conference on Computer Vision and Pattern Recognition, pp. 2097–2106 (2017)

62. Zhang, Y., Yang, Q.: A survey on multi-task learning. In: IEEE Transactions on Knowledge and Data Engineering (2021). https://doi.org/10.1109/TKDE.2021.3070203

63. Zhou, B., Khosla, A., Lapedriza, A., Oliva, A., Torralba, A.: Learning deep features for discriminative localization. In: Proceedings of the IEEE Conference on Computer Vision and Pattern Recognition, pp. 2921–2929 (2016)

64. Zhou, Y., et al.: Multi-task learning for segmentation and classification of tumors in 3D automated breast ultrasound images. Med. Image Anal. **70**, 101918 (2021)

65. Zhu, H., Salcudean, S., Rohling, R.: Gaze-guided class activation mapping: leveraging human attention for network attention in chest x-rays classification. arXiv preprint arXiv:2202.07107 (2022)

66. Zhu, H., Salcudean, S.E., Rohling, R.N.: A novel gaze-supported multimodal human-computer interaction for ultrasound machines. Int. J. Comput. Assist. Radiol. Surg. **14**(7), 1107–1115 (2019)

Deep Bayesian Active-Learning-to-Rank for Endoscopic Image Data

Takeaki Kadota[1](✉), Hideaki Hayashi[1], Ryoma Bise[1,2], Kiyohito Tanaka[3], and Seiichi Uchida[1,2]

[1] Kyushu University, Fukuoka, Japan
takeaki.kadota@human.ait.kyushu-u.ac.jp
[2] National Institute of Informatics, Tokyo, Japan
[3] Kyoto Second Red Cross Hospital, Kyoto, Japan

Abstract. Automatic image-based disease severity estimation generally uses discrete (i.e., quantized) severity labels. Annotating discrete labels is often difficult due to the images with ambiguous severity. An easier alternative is to use relative annotation, which compares the severity level between image pairs. By using a learning-to-rank framework with relative annotation, we can train a neural network that estimates rank scores that are relative to severity levels. However, the relative annotation for all possible pairs is prohibitive, and therefore, appropriate sample pair selection is mandatory. This paper proposes a *deep Bayesian active-learning-to-rank*, which trains a Bayesian convolutional neural network while automatically selecting appropriate pairs for relative annotation. We confirmed the efficiency of the proposed method through experiments on endoscopic images of ulcerative colitis. In addition, we confirmed that our method is useful even with the severe class imbalance because of its ability to select samples from minor classes automatically.

Keywords: Computer-aided diagnosis · Learning to rank · Active learning · Relative annotation · Endoscopic image dataset

1 Introduction

For image-based estimation of disease severity, it is common to prepare training samples with severity labels annotated by medical experts. Standard annotation (hereafter called *absolute annotation*) assumes discretized severity labels. However, absolute annotation is often difficult to even for medical experts. This is because disease severity is not discrete in nature, and thus there are many ambiguous cases. For example, when annotating medical images with four discrete labels (0, 1, 2, and 3), they will frequently encounter medical images with a severity of 1.5.

A promising alternative annotation approach is *Relative annotation*, which compares two images for their severity and attaches a relative label that indicates the comparison result. Figure 1 shows the characteristics of absolute and relative

G. Yang et al. (Eds.): MIUA 2022, LNCS 13413, pp. 609–622, 2022.
https://doi.org/10.1007/978-3-031-12053-4_45

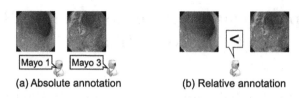

(a) Absolute annotation   (b) Relative annotation

Fig. 1. Characteristics of absolute and relative annotations

annotations to endoscopic images of ulcerative colitis (UC). Relative annotation is far easier than absolute annotation and is expected to be stable even for real-valued targets [8].

Using image pairs with relative annotation, it is possible to train a *ranking function* $f(x)$ that satisfies $f(x_i) > f(x_j)$ for a pair (x_i, x_j) where x_i shows a higher severity than x_j. By training $f(x)$ with many image pairs, it will give larger rank scores for severer images; in other words, the rank score $f(x)$ can be used as the severity level of x. As discussed later, the training process of $f(x)$ can be combined with representation learning to have a feature representation for better ranking. A convolutional neural network (CNN) is, therefore, a natural choice to realize $f(x)$.

A practically important issue in the above learning-to-rank framework with relative annotations is that we must select appropriate image pairs to annotate from all possible pairs. This is because we have $N(N-1)/2$ possible pairs for N image samples. Even if individual relative annotations are easy, it is intractable to annotate all of them. In other words, careful selection of image pairs to be annotated is essential to fully demonstrate the efficiency of relative annotation. A naive selection strategy is a random selection; however, it easily overlooks minor but important samples, which often appear in medical applications.

In this paper, we propose a deep Bayesian active-learning-to-rank that fully maximizes the efficiency of relative annotation for efficient image-based severity estimation. The technical novelty of the proposed method is to introduce an *active learning* technique into the learning-to-rank framework for selecting a less number of effective sample pairs. Active learning has been studied [2] and generally takes the following steps. Firstly, a neural network is trained with a small amount of annotated samples. The trained network then suggests other samples to be annotated. These steps are repeated to have enough amount of the annotated training samples.

For suggesting important samples to be annotated, we employ an *uncertainty* of the samples. If we find two samples with high uncertainty about their rank score, a new relative annotation between them will be useful to boost the ranking performance. For this purpose, we employ Bayesian CNN [4] to realize a ranking function because it can give an uncertainty of each sample. In summary, our deep Bayesian active-learning-to-rank uses Bayesian CNN for ranking with representation learning and uncertainty-based active learning.

As an experimental validation of the efficiency of the proposed method, we perform UC severity estimation using approximately 10,000 endoscopic images collected from the Kyoto Second Red Cross Hospital. Quantitative and qualitative evaluations clearly show the efficiency of the proposed framework. Especially, we reveal that the proposed method automatically selects minor but important samples.

The main contributions of this paper are summarized as follows:

- We propose a deep Bayesian active-learning-to-rank that can rank the image samples according to their severity level. The proposed method can automatically select important image pairs for relative annotation, resulting in learning with a less number of relative annotations.
- Through UC severity estimation experiments, we demonstrated that the proposed method could suppress the number of relative annotations while keeping ranking performance.
- We also experimentally confirmed that the proposed method shows robustness to class imbalance by its ability to select minor but important samples.

2 Related Work

The application of deep learning to UC severity estimation has been studied [11, 12]. UC is a chronic inflammatory bowel disease with recurrent inflammation and ulcer recurrence in the colon. Accurate evaluation of treatment effects is important because the type and dosage of treatment medicines are adjusted in accordance with the condition of the patient with UC. Recently, Schwab et al. [10] proposed an automatic UC severity estimation method for treatment effectiveness evaluation. Their method assumes a weakly supervised learning scenario because full annotation of all captured images is too costly. Since it uses absolute annotation, it will suffer from ambiguous labels, as noted above.

Active learning has been widely applied to medical image analysis [14,16]. Active learning selects the samples whose annotations are most effective for further learning from the unlabeled samples. Many uncertainty-based sampling techniques have been proposed to select highly uncertain samples as informative samples. Nair et al. [7] proposed a method using active learning for medical image analysis with uncertainty obtained from a Bayesian CNN. This method deals with an orthodox classification task with absolute annotation and thus does not assume any relative annotation and learning-to-rank.

In the natural language process (NLP) field, Wang et al. [13] recently introduced deep Bayesian active learning to learning-to-rank. Although their method sounds similar to ours, its aim and structure, as well as application, are totally different from ours. Specifically, it aims to rank sentences (called answers) to a fixed sentence (called a query) according to their relevance. For this aim, its network always takes two inputs (like $f(x_i, x_j)$) whereas ours takes a single input (like $f(x_i)$). From these differences, it is impossible to use it for the active annotation task and thus even to compare ours with it.

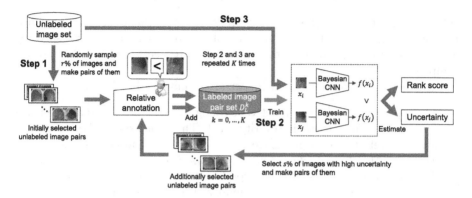

Fig. 2. Overall structure of proposed deep Bayesian active learning-to-rank for severity estimation of medical image data.

3   Deep Bayesian Active-Learning-to-Rank

3.1   Overview

Figure 2 shows an overall structure of the proposed deep Bayesian active-learning-to-rank. The proposed method is organized in an active learning framework using Bayesian learning and learning-to-rank for severity estimation of medical image data; experts progressively add relative annotations to image pairs selected based on the uncertainty provided by a Bayesian CNN while training the Bayesian CNN based on the learning-to-rank algorithm.

The deep Bayesian active-learning-to-rank consists of three steps. In Step 1, for initial training, a small number of image pairs are randomly sampled from the unlabeled image set and then annotated by medical experts. In Step 2, a Bayesian CNN is trained with the labeled image pairs for estimating rank scores and the uncertainties of individual training samples. In Step 3, images to be additionally labeled are selected on the basis of estimated uncertainties, having the medical experts annotate the additionally selected images via relative annotation. Steps 2 to 3 are repeated K times to train the Bayesian CNN while progressively increasing the number of labeled image pairs.

3.2   Details

More details of each step are explained as follows.

Step 1: Preparing a Small Number of Image Pairs for Initial Training.
A set with a small number of annotated image pairs $\mathcal{D}_L^0$ is prepared for initial training as follows. First, given an unlabeled image set comprising N unlabeled images, we randomly sample $r\%$ of them (i.e., $R = rN/100$ image samples). Then, to form a set of R pairs (instead of all possible $R(R-1)/2$ pairs), one of

the $R-1$ samples is randomly paired for each of the R samples[1]. Relative labels are attached to these image pairs by medical experts. For an image pair (x_i, x_j), a relative label $C_{i,j}$ is defined as follows:

$$C_{i,j} = \begin{cases} 1, & \text{if } x_i \text{ has a higher level than } x_j, \\ 0.5, & \text{else if } x_i \text{ and } x_j \text{ have the same level,} \\ 0, & \text{otherwise.} \end{cases} \quad (1)$$

After this step, we have the annotated image pair set $\mathcal{D}_L^0 = \{(x_i, x_j, C_{i,j})\}$ and $|\mathcal{D}_L^0| = R$.

Step 2: Training a Bayesian CNN. A Bayesian CNN is trained as a ranking function with the labeled image pair set $\mathcal{D}_L^0$. The CNN outputs a rank score that predicts the severity of the input image along with the uncertainty of the prediction. In training, we employ a probabilistic ranking cost function [1] to conduct learning-to-rank with a neural network and Monte Carlo (MC) dropout [3,4] for approximate Bayesian inference.

Let $f(\cdot)$ be a ranking function by a CNN with L weighted layers. Given an image x, the CNN outputs a scalar value $f(x)$ as the rank score of x. We denote by $\mathbf{W}_l$ the l-th weight tensor of the CNN. For a minibatch $\mathcal{M}$ sampled from $\mathcal{D}_L^0$, the Bayesian CNN is trained while conducting dropout with the loss function $\mathcal{L}_\mathcal{M}$ defined as follows:

$$\mathcal{L}_\mathcal{M} = - \sum_{(i,j)\in\mathcal{I}_\mathcal{M}} \{C_{i,j} \log P_{i,j} + (1 - C_{i,j}) \log(1 - P_{i,j})\} + \lambda \sum_{l=1}^{L} \|\mathbf{W}_l\|_F^2, \quad (2)$$

where $\mathcal{I}_\mathcal{M}$ is a set of index pairs of the elements in $\mathcal{M}$, $P_{i,j} = \text{sigmoid}(f(x_i) - f(x_j))$, λ is a constant value for weight decay, and $\|\cdot\|_F$ represents a Frobenius norm. In Eq. (2), the first term is a probabilistic ranking cost function [1], which allows the CNN to train rank scores, and the second term is a weight regularization term that can be derived from the Kullback-Leibler divergence between the approximate posterior and the posterior of the CNN weights [3]. The CNN is trained by minimizing the loss function $\mathcal{L}_\mathcal{M}$ for every minibatch while conducting dropout; a binary random variable that takes one with a probability of p_{dropout} is sampled for every unit in the CNN at each forward calculation, and the output of the unit is set to zero if the corresponding binary variable takes zero.

The rank score for an unlabeled image x^* is predicted by averaging over the output of the trained Bayesian CNN with MC dropout as $y^* = \frac{1}{T}\sum_{t=1}^{T} f(x^*; \omega_t)$, where T is the number of MC dropout trials, ω_t is the t-th realization of a set of the CNN weights obtained by MC dropout, and $f(\cdot; \omega_t)$ is the output of $f(\cdot)$ given a weight set ω_t.

---

[1] The strategy of making pairs is arbitrary. Here, we want to annotate all of the R samples at least one time while avoiding $O(R^2)$ annotations and thus take this strategy.

The uncertainty of the prediction is defined as the variance of the posterior distribution of y^*. This uncertainty is used to select images to be annotated in the next step, playing an important role in achieving active learning. The variance of the posterior distribution, $\mathrm{Var}_{q(y^*|x^*)}[y^*]$, is approximately calculated using MC dropout as follows:

$$\mathrm{Var}_{q(y^*|x^*)}[y^*] = \mathbb{E}_{q(y^*|x^*)}[(y^*)^2] - \left(\mathbb{E}_{q(y^*|x^*)}[y^*]\right)^2$$
$$\approx \frac{1}{T}\sum_{t=1}^{T}(f(x^*;\omega_t))^2 - \left(\frac{1}{T}\sum_{t=1}^{T}f(x^*;\omega_t)\right)^2 + \mathrm{const.}, \quad (3)$$

where $q(y^*|x^*)$ is the posterior distribution estimated by the model. The constant term can be ignored because the absolute value of uncertainty is not required in the following step.

Step 3: Uncertainty-Based Sample Selection. A new set of annotated image pairs is provided based on the estimated uncertainty and relative annotation. We estimate the rank scores and the related uncertainties for the unlabeled images, using the trained Bayesian CNN and select $s\%$ of images with high uncertainty. Image pairs are made by pairing the selected images in the same manner as Step 1, and medical experts attach relative annotations to the image pairs. The newly annotated image pairs are added to the current annotated image pair set $\mathcal{D}_L^0$. The Bayesian CNN is retrained with the updated $\mathcal{D}_L^1$. Steps 2 and 3 are repeated K times while increasing the size of the annotated set $\mathcal{D}_L^k$ $(k = 0, \ldots, K)$.

4   Experiments and Results

To evaluate the efficiency of our active-learning-to-rank, we conducted experiments on a task for estimating rank scores of ulcerative colitis (UC) severity. In the experiments, we quantitatively compared our method with baseline methods in terms of the accuracy of relative label estimation, that is, the correctness of identifying the higher severity image in a given pair of two endoscopic images. We also evaluated the relationship between the human-annotated absolute labels and the estimated rank scores.

In addition, we analyzed the reason why our method successfully improved the performance of relative label estimation. Especially, we analyze the relationship between the uncertainty and class prior and show that our uncertainty-based sample selection could mitigate the class imbalance problem and then finally improve the performance.

4.1   Dataset

In order to analyze the relationship between the absolute severity and the estimated severity scores, we used a dataset that has absolute severity labels (called

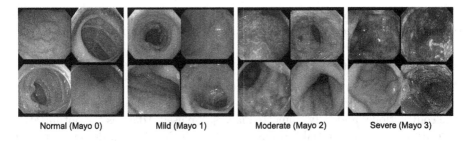

Normal (Mayo 0)   Mild (Mayo 1)   Moderate (Mayo 2)   Severe (Mayo 3)

Fig. 3. Examples of endoscopic images of ulcerative colitis at each Mayo (severity).

Mayo score) for UC. A Mayo score was annotated for each image on a four-level scale (Mayo 0–3) by multiple medical experts carefully[2]. Figure 3 shows examples of Mayo scores in the dataset. According to Schroeder et al. [9], Mayo 0 is normal or endoscopic remission. Mayo 1 is a mild level that shows erythema, decreased vascular pattern, and mild friability. Mayo 2 is a moderate level that shows marked erythema, absent vascular pattern, friability, and erosions. Mayo 3 is a severe level with spontaneous bleeding and ulceration. The dataset consists of 10, 265 endoscopic images from 388 patients captured in the Kyoto Second Red Cross Hospital[3]. It should be noted that the dataset has imbalanced class priors, which is a typical condition in medical image analysis. Specifically, it contains 6,678, 1,995, 1,395, and 197 samples for Mayo 0, 1, 2, and 3, respectively.

To evaluate relative label-based methods, we made a set of pairs of two images and gave relative labels for each pair based on the Mayo labels. For N training samples, the number of possible pairs is too large ($O(N^2)$) to train the network with various settings; we, therefore, made a limited number of pairs for training data by random sampling. Specifically, we used N pairs (instead of $O(N^2)$ pairs) by selecting one of the $N - 1$ samples for each of the N samples. (In Sect. 3.2, R samples of the initial set are also selected from these pairs.) We consider this setting reasonable since it used all the original samples, and we could conduct the experiments in a realistic running time. Also, note that this setting is typical for evaluating learning-to-rank [6, 15, 17].

Five-fold cross-validation was conducted for all comparative methods. The data were divided into training (60%), validation (20%), and test (20%) sets by patient-based sampling (that is, each data did not contain an image from the same patient). Note that the above pair image preparation was done after dividing the training, validation, and test sets for a fair evaluation. It indicates that each set did not contain the same image. As the performance metrics, we

---

[2] During this absolute annotation process, medical experts might encounter ambiguous cases due to the discretized severity, as noted in Sect. 1. However, this ambiguity was minimized through careful observation by multiple experts. In other words, reliable absolute annotation is very costly, and this fact is the motivation of this work.

[3] This study was approved by the Ethics Committee of the Kyoto Second Red Cross Hospital.

used the accuracy of estimated relative labels, which is defined as the ratio of the number of correctly estimated relative labels over all the pairs.

4.2   Implementation Details

We used DenseNet-169 [5] as the backbone of the Bayesian CNN. The model was trained with dropout ($p_{\mathrm{dropout}} = 0.2$) and weight decay ($\lambda = 1{\times}10^{-4}$) in the convolutional and fully connected layers. We used Adam as the optimization algorithm and set the initial learning rate to $1{\times}10^{-5}$. All image data were resized to 224×224 pixels and normalized between 0 and 255.

In all experiments, our method incrementally increased the training data during $K = 6$ iterations by selecting effective samples ($s = 5\%$ of training data) and adding them to the initial training data ($r = 20\%$ of all training images). In total (after six iterations), the ratio of the labeled data used for training was 50% ($r + sK = 20 + 5 \times 6$). The number of estimations for uncertainty estimation was set to $T = 30$.

4.3   Baselines

To demonstrate the effectiveness of our method, we compared our method with three baseline methods: 1) Baseline, which trained by randomly sampled ($r + sK =$) 50% pairs of training data, which indicates that the same number of pairs were used in the proposed method; 2) Baseline (all data), which uses all N training pairs (i.e., 100%), which indicates the number of training data was as twice as that of the proposed method; 3) Proposed w/o uncertainty-based sampling (UBS), which also incrementally increased the training data during K iterations but the additional training data was selected by random sampling (without using uncertainty-based sampling); For a fair comparison, we used the same backbone (DenseNet-169 based Bayesian CNN) for all the methods. Given an input image, all methods used the mean of rank scores of $T = 30$ times estimation as the rank score.

4.4   Evaluation of Relative Severity Estimation

As the accuracy evaluation, we measured the correctness of the estimated rank scores in a relative manner. Specifically, given a pair of images (x_i, x_j) where x_i shows a higher severity, the estimation is counted as "correct" if $f(x_i) > f(x_j)$.

For the test data, we prepared two types of pairs.

"Overall": The pairs were randomly made among all Mayo. Specifically, we selected images in test images so that the number of samples in each Mayo score was the same and then randomly made the pairs among the selected images. Using this test dataset, we evaluated the overall performances of the comparative methods. However, this test data may contain many easy pairs, that is, a pair of Mayo 0 (a normal image) and Mayo 3 (a high severity image), whose image features are very different, as shown in Fig. 3. Thus it is easy to identify the relative label.

Table 1. Quantitative performance evaluation in terms of accuracy of estimated relative labels. '*' denotes a statistically significant difference between the proposed method and each comparison method ($p < 0.05$ in McNemar's test.).

Method	Labeling ratio	Overall	Neighboring			
			0–1	1–2	2–3	Mean
Baseline	50%	0.861*	0.827	0.837	0.628	0.763*
Baseline (all data)	100%	0.875	**0.855**	0.870	0.635	0.785*
Proposed w/o UBS	50%	0.856*	0.818	0.842	0.634	0.763*
Proposed	50%	**0.880**	0.787	**0.871**	**0.736**	**0.797**

"Neighboring": We prepared the neighboring pairs that contain the images of neighboring-level Mayo, such as Mayo 0–1, Mayo 1–2, and Mayo 2–3 pairs. It is important for clinical applications to compare the severity of difficult cases. This estimation is more difficult since the severity gradually changes in neighboring Mayo, and these image features are similar. Using this test dataset, we evaluated the performance of methods in difficult cases.

Table 1 shows the mean of the accuracy of estimated rank scores for each method in five-fold cross-validation. A labeling ratio denotes the ratio of the number of labeled images that were used for training, and '*' indicates that there were significant differences at $p < 0.05$ by multiple statistical comparisons using McNemar's tests.

In the results of "Overall," the accuracy of Baseline and Proposed w/o UBS were comparable because these methods used the same number of training pairs. Baseline (all data) improved the accuracy compared to these two methods by using the larger size (twice) of training data. Surprisingly, our method was better than Baseline (all data), although the training data of ours is half of that of Baseline (all data) with the same settings, that is, the network structure and the loss. As analyzed in the later Sect. 4.5, this difference comes from class imbalance. Since this dataset has a severe class imbalance, that is, the samples in Mayo 0 were 33 times of those in Mayo 3, it was difficult to learn the image features of highly severe images. In such severe imbalance cases, even if the number of training data decreases, appropriate sampling could mitigate the class imbalance and improve the accuracy.

In the results of "Neighboring" (difficult cases), the proposed method was also better than all the comparative methods in the mean accuracy of the neighboring pairs. In particular, the proposed method improved the accuracy in the case "Mayo 2–3" over 10%. Since the accuracy of image comparisons at high severity is important for evaluating treatment effects, the proposed method is considered superior to the other methods in clinical practice. In the case "Mayo 0–1", the accuracy of the proposed method was lower than that of the comparison methods because the number of labeled samples for Mayo 0 and 1 was reduced due to the mitigation of class imbalance.

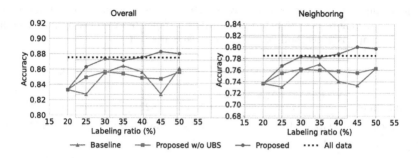

Fig. 4. Accuracy of estimated relative labels of Baseline (blue), Proposed w/o UBS (green), and Proposed (red) at each labeling ratio. The black dotted line indicates the results of Baseline (all data). (Color figure online)

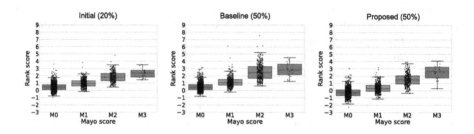

Fig. 5. Box plots of estimated rank scores at each Mayo. Initial was measured under the initial condition at the labeling ratio of 20%. Performance of Baseline and Proposed were measured at the labeling ratio of 50%. If the distributions of each Mayo score have less overlap, the estimation can be considered reasonable.

Figure 4 shows the changes of the accuracy at each iteration in both test datasets "Overall" and "Neighboring." The horizontal axis indicates the labeling ratio, the vertical axis indicates the mean accuracy in cross-validation, and the black dot line indicates the results of Baseline (all data), which used the 100% of the training data. This result shows the effectiveness of our uncertainty-based active learning. Our method (red) increased the accuracy with the number of training data, and the improvement was larger than the other methods. In contrast, for Baseline (blue) and Proposed w/o UBS (green), it was not always true to increase the accuracy by increasing the training data. As a result, the improvements from the initial training data were limited for them.

Figure 5 shows box plots of the estimated rank scores of three methods at each Mayo score. Here, the vertical axis indicates the estimated rank score, and "Initial" indicates the method that trained the network using only the initial training data without iterations (20% of training data). In this plot, if the distributions of each Mayo score have less overlap, the estimation can be considered reasonable. In Initial and "Baseline," the score distributions in Mayo 2 and 3 significantly overlapped. In contrast, our method improved the overlap distributions. This indicates that the estimated rank scores were more correlated to the Mayo scores.

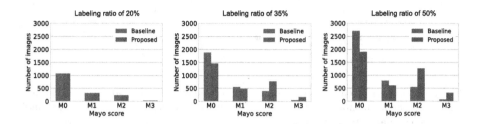

Fig. 6. Class proportion of the accumulated sampled images at iteration $K = 0$ (labeling ratio is 20%), 3 (35%), and 6 (50%). When the labeling ratio was 20%, the class proportion was the same between Baseline and Proposed. The proposed method selected many samples of minor classes (Mayo 2 and 3) and mitigated the class imbalance problem.

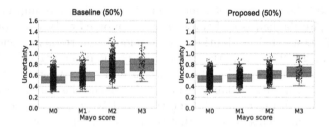

Fig. 7. Box plots of model uncertainty in each class. Performance of Baseline and Proposed were measured at the labeling ratio of 50%. In Baseline, the uncertainty of minor classes (Mayo 2 and 3) was higher than that of major classes. In Proposed, the uncertainty of Mayo 2 and 3 decreases since the class imbalance was mitigated.

4.5   Relationship Between Uncertainty and Class Imbalance

As described in Sect. 4.4, we considered that improvement by our method is because our uncertainty-based sampling mitigated the class imbalance. Therefore, we investigated the relationship between the uncertainty and the number of the Mayo labels of the sampled images from the training data during iterations.

Figure 6 shows the number of sampled images by uncertainty-based sampling at each class when the labeling ratio was 20% ($k = 0$), 35% ($k = 3$), and 50% ($k = K = 6$), where the vertical axis indicates the average numbers of five-fold cross-validation. The initial training data ($k = 0$) has a class imbalance in accordance with that in all the training data due to random sampling. In 35% and 50%, the sampled images by Baseline have a similar class imbalance to that in the initial

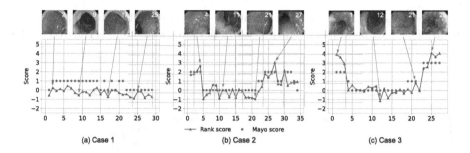

Fig. 8. Examples of changes in the rank score along with the capturing order in a sequence. The horizontal axis indicates the capturing order, and the vertical axis indicates the estimated rank score (red) and the Mayo score (blue). (Color figure online)

training data. This class imbalance affected the performance improvements even though the number of training images increased, and thus the improvement was limited. In contrast, our uncertainty-based sampling selected many samples of the minor Mayo level; that is, the samples of Mayo 2 and 3 increased with iteration; therefore, the class imbalance was gradually mitigated with iteration. Consequently, the accuracy of relative label estimation was improved by our method despite the half size of training data compared to Baseline (all data).

Figure 7 shows the distributions of the model uncertainty of each class in training data. In "Baseline," the uncertainty of the minor classes (Mayo 2 and 3) was higher than the major classes (Mayo 0 and 1). After six iterations of active learning (that is, the labeling ratio is 50%), the class imbalance was mitigated, as shown in Fig. 6, and the uncertainty of Mayo 2 and 3 was lower than those of "Baseline." This indicates that the uncertainty is correlated to the class imbalance; the fewer samples of a class are, the higher uncertainty is. Therefore, our uncertainty-based active learning, which selects the higher uncertainty samples as additional training data, can select many samples of the minor classes and consequently mitigate the class imbalance problem. This knowledge is useful for learning-to-rank tasks in medical image analysis since severe class imbalance problems often occur in medical images.

4.6 Application Using the Estimated Rank Score

This section shows an example of the clinical applications of the proposed method. In UC severity diagnosis, endoscopic images are acquired in sequence while the endoscope is moved through the colon. In clinical, a doctor checks all the images and finds the most severe images, and diagnoses the severity of the UC. To facilitate this diagnosis process, it is useful to show the estimated severity score along with the capturing order. Figure 8 shows three examples of the changes in the rank score (severity), where the horizontal axis indicates the capturing order in a sequence, and the vertical axis indicates the estimated rank score. These sequences were taken from different patients and were not used in the training data. In these results, the estimated rank scores (red) were similar to the Mayo scores (blue) that were annotated by medical doctors. Case 1 was a sequence of a patient with a mild disease level. The severity was low in the entire region. Case 2 and 3 were sequences of patients with moderate and severe disease levels. In these examples, we can observe that the severe areas were biased in the order of the sequence; the severity was high at the beginning and the end of the sequence, but it was low in the middle of the sequence. Using this graph, medical doctors can easily check if the disease is severe or not and find the severe areas and check them. In addition, it is also easy to show both cases before and after treatment and diagnose the recovery of the disease.

5 Conclusion

In this paper, we proposed a deep Bayesian active-learning-to-rank for efficient relative annotation. The proposed method actively determines effective sample pairs for additional relative annotations by estimating the uncertainty using a Bayesian CNN. We first evaluated the accuracy and the efficiency of the proposed method with an experiment about the correctness of the relative severity between a pair of images. The results indicate the usefulness of uncertainty-based active learning for selecting samples for better ranking. We also revealed that the proposed method selects minor but important samples and thus shows the robustness to class imbalance.

The limitation of the proposed method is that it provides rank scores instead of Mayo scores that medical experts are familiar with. If an application needs Mayo score-like rank scores, an additional calibration process is necessary. The proposed method is very general and applicable to other severity-level estimation tasks—this means more experiments on different image datasets are important for future tasks.

Acknowledgments. This work was supported by JSPS KAKENHI Grant Number JP20H04211 and AMED Grant Number JP20lk1010036h0002.

References

1. Burges, C., et al.: Learning to rank using gradient descent. In: Proceedings of the 22nd International Conference on Machine Learning (ICML), pp. 89–96 (2005)
2. Cohn, D.A., et al.: Active learning with statistical models. J. Artif. Intell. Res. **4**, 129–145 (1996)
3. Gal, Y., Ghahramani, Z.: Dropout as a bayesian approximation: representing model uncertainty in deep learning. In: Proceedings of the 33rd International Conference on Machine Learning (ICML), pp. 1050–1059 (2016)
4. Gal, Y., et al.: Deep Bayesian active learning with image data. In: Proceedings of the 34th International Conference on Machine Learning (ICML), pp. 1183–1192 (2017)
5. Huang, G., et al.: Densely connected convolutional networks. In: 2017 IEEE Conference on Computer Vision and Pattern Recognition (CVPR), pp. 2261–2269 (2017)

6. Kadota, T., et al.: Automatic estimation of ulcerative colitis severity by learning to rank with calibration. IEEE Access **10**, 25688–25695 (2022)

7. Nair, T., et al.: Exploring uncertainty measures in deep networks for Multiple sclerosis lesion detection and segmentation. Med. Image Anal. **59**, 101557 (2020)

8. Parikh, D., Grauman, K.: Relative attributes. In: Proceedings of the 2011 International Conference on Computer Vision (ICCV), pp. 503–510 (2011)

9. Schroeder, K.W., et al.: Coated oral 5-aminosalicylic acid therapy for mildly to moderately active ulcerative colitis. New Engl. J. Med. **317**(26), 1625–1629 (1987)

10. Schwab, E., et al.: Automatic estimation of ulcerative colitis severity from endoscopy videos using ordinal multi-instance learning. In: Computer Methods in Biomechanics and Biomedical Engineering: Imaging & Visualization, pp. 1–9 (2021)

11. Stidham, R.W., et al.: Performance of a deep learning model vs human reviewers in grading endoscopic disease severity of patients with ulcerative colitis. JAMA Netw. Open **2**(5), e193963 (2019)

12. Takenaka, K., et al.: Development and validation of a deep neural network for accurate evaluation of endoscopic images from patients with ulcerative colitis. Gastroenterology **158**(8), 2150–2157 (2020)

13. Wang, Q., et al.: Deep bayesian active learning for learning to rank: a case study in answer selection. IEEE Trans. Knowl. Data Eng. (2021)

14. Wen, S., et al.: Comparison of different classifiers with active learning to support quality control in nucleus segmentation in pathology images. In: AMIA Joint Summits on Translational Science Proceedings. AMIA Joint Summits on Translational Science 2017, pp. 227–236 (2018)

15. Xu, Q., et al.: Deep partial rank aggregation for personalized attributes. In: Proceedings of the AAAI Conference on Artificial Intelligence, pp. 678–688 (2021)

16. Yang, L., et al.: Suggestive annotation: a deep active learning framework for biomedical image segmentation. In: Descoteaux, M., Maier-Hein, L., Franz, A., Jannin, P., Collins, D.L., Duchesne, S. (eds.) MICCAI 2017. LNCS, vol. 10435, pp. 399–407. Springer, Cham (2017). https://doi.org/10.1007/978-3-319-66179-7_46

17. You, Y., et al.: Relative CNN-RNN: learning relative atmospheric visibility from images. IEEE Trans. Image Process. **28**(1), 45–55 (2019)

Improving Image Representations via MoCo Pre-training for Multimodal CXR Classification

Francesco Dalla Serra[1,2(✉)], Grzegorz Jacenków[3], Fani Deligianni[2], Jeff Dalton[2], and Alison Q. O'Neil[1,3]

[1] Canon Medical Research Europe, Edinburgh, UK
`francesco.dallaserra@mre.medical.canon`
[2] University of Glasgow, Glasgow, UK
[3] University of Edinburgh, Edinburgh, UK

Abstract. Multimodal learning, here defined as learning from multiple input data types, has exciting potential for healthcare. However, current techniques rely on large multimodal datasets being available, which is rarely the case in the medical domain. In this work, we focus on improving the extracted image features which are fed into multimodal image-text Transformer architectures, evaluating on a medical multimodal classification task with dual inputs of chest X-ray images (CXRs) and the indication text passages in the corresponding radiology reports. We demonstrate that self-supervised Momentum Contrast (MoCo) pre-training of the image representation model on a large set of unlabelled CXR images improves multimodal performance compared to supervised ImageNet pre-training. MoCo shows a 0.6% absolute improvement in AUROC-macro, when considering the full MIMIC-CXR training set, and 5.1% improvement when limiting to 10% of the training data.

To the best of our knowledge, this is the first demonstration of MoCo image pre-training for multimodal learning in medical imaging.

Keywords: Multimodal learning · multimodal BERT · Image representation · Self-supervised image pre-training · CXR classification

1 Introduction

Multimodal learning has recently gained attention for healthcare applications [1], due to the rich patient representation enabled by combination of different data sources *e.g.* images, reports, and clinical data. Recent works in multimodal learning have mainly focused on Transformer [2] architectures, with similar approaches adopted in the medical domain [3]. Whilst the role of the joint pre-training process has been widely explored [4], fewer works have focused on the single modality components of the models. In particular, the role of the image representation is frequently neglected. However, the task of multimodal representation learning is complex and one of the main challenges in the medical domain is the lack of large-scale, labeled datasets, compared to the millions

G. Yang et al. (Eds.): MIUA 2022, LNCS 13413, pp. 623–635, 2022.
https://doi.org/10.1007/978-3-031-12053-4_46

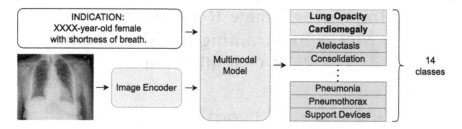

Fig. 1. Illustration of the multimodal CXR multi-label classification pipeline. The indication field and CXR image are dual input modalities, and the output is a set of positive (green) or negative (red) predictions for 14 radiographic findings labels, as annotated in the MIMIC-CXR dataset [13–15]. In this data, taken from the IU-Xray dataset [16], ages (and other patient-identifiable information) is replaced by a placeholder, here indicated by XXXX. The **image encoder** is the component that we investigate in this paper, to discover a strategy for learning a good image representation. (Color figure online)

of images available in computer vision tasks in the general domain. Therefore, we seek to mitigate the complexity of multimodal learning by providing robust image representation as input.

In the general multimodal domain, the "bottom-up top-down" [5] approach is a popular image representation paradigm for multimodal Transformer architectures such as VisualBERT [6] and ViLBERT [7]. These models use Region of Interest (RoI) feature maps extracted from Faster R-CNN [8], which is pretrained on large object detection datasets (*e.g.* VisualGenome [9]). Faster R-CNN requires large scale datasets with bounding box annotations. The image encoder is then frozen during fine-tuning of the Transformer model, based on the strong assumption that pre-trained detectors extract representative features for the downstream task. Other image representation strategies have been proposed. In Pixel-BERT [10], the image representation is defined as the feature map of the last convolutional layer of a convolutional neural network (CNN). Similarly, the discrete latent space of a variational autoencoder (VAE) has been adopted in DALL-E [11]. Alternatively, the Vision Transformer (ViT) [12] consists of directly feeding raw pixel patches as the input for Transformer architectures.

In this paper, we are interested in multimodal CXR multi-label classification of medical images supported by the medical history of the patient which is available in free-text radiology reports (indication field), as shown in Fig. 1. We use MIMIC-CXR [13–15], which is the largest open access multimodal medical dataset, to evaluate our proposed methodology, for the task of Chest X-Ray classification of 14 radiographic findings classes. In MIMIC-CXR, bounding boxes are not available, making the "bottom-up top-down" [5] approach unsuitable for this task. To the best of our knowledge, there are two works performing multimodal classification of CXR using the text indication section as an additional inference-time input: ChestBERT [3] and what we denote as "Attentive" [17]. Following ChestBERT [3], the state-of-the-art for this task, we adopt the

Table 1. Summary of the considered image pre-training strategies suited to CXR image classification.

Method	Ease of training	Medical image suitability
Supervised ImageNet *Supervised training on 1000 ImageNet classes*	No training required. Pre-trained weights available for standard CNN architectures	Weak – trained on natural images
Autoencoder *Encoder-decoder architecture trained on reconstruction loss*	Easy – does not require large batches	Flexible - can train on relevant medical image data (no labels required)
SimCLR *Contrastive learning approach*	Hard – requires high compute power to handle the large batches ($>10^3$ images)	
MoCo *Contrastive learning approach*	Moderate – designed to work with a small batch size ($\sim10^2$ images) & uses efficient updating of the large dynamic dictionary	

multimodal bitransformer model (MMBT), which has a similar image representation to Pixel-BERT. Differently to the previously described multimodal BERT models, MMBT does not include a joint pre-training step. More recently, Liao et al. [18] have shown a method of joint modality pre-training to be effective by maximising the mutual information between the encoded representations of images and their corresponding reports. At inference time, the image only is used for classification. However, we consider the situation where we may have limited task-specific labelled multimodal (paired image and text) training data, but ample unlabelled unimodal (imaging) data available for pre-training and therefore we investigate image-only pre-training techniques.

For learning good visual representations, many self-supervised contrastive learning strategies have shown promising results in the medical domain (Table 1), for instance Momentum Contrast (MoCo) contrastive training [19,20] and Multi-Instance Contrastive Learning (MICLe) [21] – an application of SimCLR [22] to medical imaging. In particular, MoCo pre-training has shown superior results in a similar chest X-Ray imaging classification task, outperforming other methods using standard supervised pre-training on ImageNet [20]. Similarly, MedAug [23] has extended the work of Sowrirajan et al. [20], by considering different criteria to select positive pairs for MoCo. However, the best approach in [23] (which targets mixed-view classification) is to create pairs from lateral and frontal views of CXR, while we focus our work on frontal views only, making this method unsuitable for our task. MoCo works by minimising the embedding distance between positive pairs – generated by applying different data augmentations to an image – and maximising the distance to all other augmented images in the dataset [19]. MoCo maintains a large dynamic dictionary of negative samples as a queue with fixed length (set as a hyperparameter) which is updated every step by adding the newest batch of samples and removing the oldest. This allows the model to have a large number of negative samples without the need for very large batches, unlike other contrastive learning approaches (*e.g.* SimCLR [22]), making MoCo a sensible choice when training on fewer GPUs[1]. In this work, for the imaging component of MMBT we experiment with two strategies for training a CNN image encoding: a) MoCo and b) a classic autoencoder (AE) strategy (as in DALL-E [11], although the VAE is not required for our task).

In summary, our contributions are to:

1. Compare how different pre-training strategies of the image encoder perform in the multimodal setup: autoencoder (AE), MoCo, and standard (supervised) ImageNet pre-trained weights; finding MoCo to perform best.
2. Explore how these strategies degrade when the multimodal transformer is fine-tuned on a smaller subset of the training set, finding MoCo pre-trained weights to perform better in a limited data scenario.
3. Extend the work of [20] – which demonstrates the effectiveness of MoCo pre-training for image-only pleural-effusion classification – to a multimodal multi-label classification problem.
4. Apply Gradient-weighted Class Activation Mapping (Grad-CAM) [24] to evaluate the impact of the pre-training strategy on the image features that activate the model, and report quantitative results on a small subset of the ChestX-ray8 test set with annotated bounding boxes [25].

2 Method

Our proposed three step pipeline is shown in Fig. 2. In particular, in this work, we explore the effectiveness of different image representations for the model by considering different pre-training strategies.

2.1 Model

The overall architecture for this work is based on the multimodal bitransformer model (MMBT) [26] as shown in Fig. 2c. This builds on the BERT architecture [27], adapting it for multimodal data by introducing an additional visual input. Both the textual and the visual input are projected into the input embedding space and summed with the related positional and segment embedding; the segment embedding is then available to the model to discriminate between textual and visual inputs. The image embedding corresponds to the feature map outputted from the last convolutional layer of ResNet-50. This is flattened to obtain $N = 49$ embedding and projected by a single fully connected layer, indicated as $I = \{I_1 \ldots I_N\}$. The textual input is tokenised into M BERT subword tokens,

---

[1] Due to the limited computing power, we decided to neglect the contrastive learning approach proposed by [21], trained on 16–64 Cloud TPU cores.

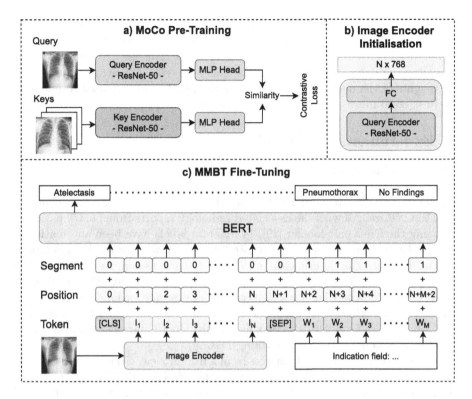

Fig. 2. Illustration of the proposed three step pipeline: a) MoCo pre-training of ResNet-50; b) initialisation of ResNet-50 using the query-encoder weights; and c) fine-tuning of MMBT on the 14 classes in MIMIC-CXR.

indicated as $W = \{W_1 \ldots W_M\}$. A $[CLS]$ token is used at the beginning of the input sequence, and its final hidden vector is used as the multimodal sequence representation for classification. The $[SEP]$ token is used to separate the two input modalities.

2.2   Self-supervised Image Pre-training

We experiment with two self-supervised strategies: an Autoencoder (AE) and Momentum Contrast (MoCo).

The **AE** consists of a ResNet-50 encoder and decoder. The model is trained by minimising the reconstruction loss, defined as the mean squared error between the input and the reconstructed image. Following pre-training, the decoder is discarded and the ResNet-50 encoder weights are used as initialization for the MMBT image encoder.

As shown in Fig. 2a, **MoCo** employs two ResNet-50 models – a query encoder and a key encoder – each followed by a MultiLayer Perceptron (MLP) projection head composed by two fully connected layers. The model is then trained by optimising the Info Noise Contrastive Estimation (InfoNCE) loss function [28]. Due to the large dictionary, training of the key encoder through backpropagation is computationally intractable; instead, network parameters are updated using momentum updates in tandem with the query encoder. Following pre-training, the weights of the query encoder (without the MLP head) are used to initialise the ResNet-50 image encoder, shown in Fig. 2b.

3   Experiments and Results

3.1   Experimental Setup

Dataset: We evaluated our method on MIMIC-CXR [13–15], which contains 377,110 CXR images with the associated radiology reports from 65,379 patients.

Using the CheXpert labeler [29], 14 different labels have been automatically extracted from the radiology report: *Atelectasis, Cardiomegaly, Consolidation, Edema, Enlarged Cardiomediastinum, Fracture, Lung Lesion, Lung Opacity, No Finding, Pleural Effusion, Pleural Other, Pneumonia, Pneumothorax, Support Devices*. The CheXpert labeler assigns a value of whether the label has a *positive, negative,* or *uncertain* mention in the report, or is not discussed (*missing*). For each label, we re-formulate the task as a multi-label binary classification task: *positive* vs. *others* (*negative, uncertain, missing*).

In this study, we select only images from a frontal view, either anteroposterior (AP) and posteroanterior (PA). Following the official MIMIC-CXR split, this yields 208,794 training pairs, 1,695 validation pairs and 2,920 test report/image pairs. As presented in [3], the text modality corresponds to the indication field (*i.e.* scan request text) extracted from the radiology reports. This is the part that would be available at imaging time and describes relevant medical history.

The self-supervised pre-training of the image encoder is performed on the CheXpert dataset [29] which consists of 224,316 CXR images from 65,240 patients; we ignore the available annotations and treat this dataset as a large unlabelled dataset. Input images are resized by matching the smaller edge to 224 pixels and maintaining the original aspect ratio.

Model Implementation & Training: For the self-supervised pre-training, we adopt the AE and MoCo implementations available from the PyTorch Lightning library[2]. During pre-training, the input images are resized by matching the smaller edge to 224 pixels and maintaining the original aspect ratio. Similar to Sowrirajan et al. [20], we employ the following data augmentation techniques: random rotation ($-10° \leq \theta \leq 10°$), random horizontal flipping; and random crop of 224×224 pixels. The same data augmentations are also applied during the fine-tuning step.

At the fine-tuning stage, we adopt the MMBT implementation made available by the authors of ChestBERT [3][3], which uses the MultiModal Framework

---

[2] https://pytorch-lightning-bolts.readthedocs.io/en/latest/self_supervised_models.html.

[3] https://github.com/jacenkow/mmbt.

(MMF) [30]. We use the same training parameters as [3]: models are trained using a batch size of 128 and Adam optimiser with weight decay, with the learning rate set to 5×10^{-5}, and a linear warm-up schedule for the first 2000 steps, and micro F1 score computed on the validation set was used as the early stopping criterion and a patience of 4000 steps, up to a maximum of 14 epochs. Each experiment was repeated 5 times using different random seeds to initialise the model weights and randomise batch shuffling.

Baselines: The chosen method is compared with two unimodal baselines, to verify the improvement brought by inputting both visual and textual modalities at once. Moreover, we compare MMBT with another multimodal approach which we denote "Attentive" [17], to justify the architecture design chosen for our multimodal experiments.

- **BERT** [27] - using a BERT model only (similar to the backbone of MMBT) a unimodal text classifier is trained, without the CXR image.
- **ResNet-50** [31] - using ResNet-50 only (similar to the network used for the image representation in MMBT) a unimodal image classifier is trained, without text information.
- **Attentive** [17] - this model follows a two stream approach where a) the CXR image is processed by a ResNet-50 model and b) the indication field is encoded by BioWordVec embeddings [32] followed by two sequential bidirectional Gated Recurrent Units (GRUs) [33]. The visual and textual feature representations are then fused using two multimodal attention layers.

Metrics and Experiments: We report the F1 score and the Area Under the Receiver Operating Characteristic (AUROC), multiplying all metrics by 100 for ease of reading. To assess whether a pre-training strategy helps in a limited training data scenario, the same experiments are conducted using only a 10% random sample of the original training set.

3.2 Comparison of Self-supervised Pre-training Strategies

Here we compare MMBT with the baselines, adopting different pre-training strategies for the image encoder, as described in Sect. 2.2. The AE and MoCo pre-trained ResNet-50 are compared against: (1) random initialization – to verify the benefit of starting from pre-trained weights; (2) ImageNet initialization – widely adopted in computer vision.

Results: As shown in Table 2 (top), both unimodal baselines (text-only BERT and image-only ResNet-50) obtain lower classification scores compared to the multimodal approaches (Attentive and MMBT); with MMBT achieving the best results, as previously reported in [3]. However, in the limited data scenario (Table 2 (bottom)), the gap between unimodal and multimodal approaches is reduced when considering the standard ImageNet initialization. This suggests

Table 2. Results on the MIMIC-CXR test set, comparing different ResNet-50 pre-training strategies. The models are fine-tuned on the full training set (top) and on 10% of the training set (bottom).

100% training set						
Model	Image Pre-Training		F1		AUROC	
	Method	Dataset	Macro	Micro	Macro	Micro
BERT	-		$24.4_{\pm1.0}$	$40.2_{\pm0.5}$	$71.5_{\pm0.3}$	$82.1_{\pm0.4}$
ResNet-50	Supervised	ImageNet	$27.2_{\pm0.6}$	$48.4_{\pm0.9}$	$75.8_{\pm1.2}$	$85.3_{\pm0.8}$
ResNet-50	MoCo	CheXpert	$\mathbf{28.5_{\pm0.7}}$	$\mathbf{49.5_{\pm0.6}}$	$\mathbf{76.3_{\pm0.3}}$	$\mathbf{85.5_{\pm0.1}}$
Attentive	Supervised	ImageNet	$29.3_{\pm0.5}$	$51.1_{\pm0.6}$	$76.3_{\pm0.5}$	$85.9_{\pm0.5}$
Attentive	MoCo	CheXpert	$\mathbf{31.9_{\pm0.3}}$	$\mathbf{53.2_{\pm0.5}}$	$\mathbf{77.8_{\pm0.6}}$	$\mathbf{86.4_{\pm0.4}}$
MMBT	*Random Initialization*		$32.0_{\pm1.2}$	$49.7_{\pm0.7}$	$76.1_{\pm0.3}$	$85.2_{\pm0.3}$
MMBT	Supervised	ImageNet	$34.3_{\pm2.1}$	$54.7_{\pm0.7}$	$79.8_{\pm1.1}$	$87.4_{\pm0.8}$
MMBT	AE	CheXpert	$34.5_{\pm1.2}$	$52.4_{\pm0.3}$	$77.9_{\pm0.4}$	$86.3_{\pm0.4}$
MMBT	MoCo	CheXpert	$\mathbf{36.7_{\pm1.4}}$	$\mathbf{55.3_{\pm0.6}}$	$\mathbf{80.4_{\pm0.3}}$	$\mathbf{87.6_{\pm0.4}}$
10% training set						
Model	Image Pre-Training		F1		AUROC	
	Method	Dataset	Macro	Micro	Macro	Micro
BERT	-		$21.3_{\pm2.7}$	$36.6_{\pm1.7}$	$67.4_{\pm0.4}$	$79.7_{\pm1.3}$
ResNet-50	Supervised	ImageNet	$22.1_{\pm0.9}$	$42.1_{\pm0.7}$	$68.0_{\pm1.9}$	$79.7_{\pm3.4}$
ResNet-50	MoCo	CheXpert	$\mathbf{23.6_{\pm1.1}}$	$\mathbf{43.8_{\pm1.8}}$	$\mathbf{70.8_{\pm0.9}}$	$\mathbf{81.3_{\pm0.9}}$
Attentive	Supervised	ImageNet	$21.7_{\pm0.9}$	$42.1_{\pm1.4}$	$65.1_{\pm1.1}$	$78.9_{\pm0.6}$
Attentive	MoCo	CheXpert	$\mathbf{22.8_{\pm1.0}}$	$\mathbf{44.3_{\pm1.9}}$	$\mathbf{70.2_{\pm0.5}}$	$\mathbf{82.7_{\pm0.4}}$
MMBT	*Random Initialization*		$25.1_{\pm2.1}$	$40.7_{\pm3.0}$	$69.6_{\pm0.7}$	$81.6_{\pm0.6}$
MMBT	Supervised	ImageNet	$26.4_{\pm2.1}$	$44.3_{\pm1.5}$	$69.0_{\pm0.4}$	$79.3_{\pm1.8}$
MMBT	AE	CheXpert	$27.6_{\pm1.2}$	$44.2_{\pm1.1}$	$70.5_{\pm0.4}$	$82.1_{\pm0.3}$
MMBT	MoCo	CheXpert	$\mathbf{28.5_{\pm2.4}}$	$\mathbf{48.8_{\pm1.1}}$	$\mathbf{74.1_{\pm0.7}}$	$\mathbf{84.5_{\pm0.9}}$

that the image modality is not processed effectively by the multimodal architectures, which motivates us to investigate how to improve the image representations to maintain the benefit of using both modalities with limited data.

Table 2 shows a consistent improvement from adopting MoCo initialization of the image encoder (ResNet-50), which demonstrates that MMBT benefits from such domain-specific image pre-training strategy. The margin of improvement from ImageNet increases with a limited training set, aligned with the results in [20]. Compared to Sowrirajan et al. [20]—who showed the benefit of MoCo pre-training only on pleural effusion classification, using an image-only CNN – we broaden the paradigm to multimodal classification of 14 different classes. Furthermore, we report the AUROC scores for each class in Table 4. This shows that MoCo pre-trained MMBT yields the highest scores for most classes, when

Table 3. IoU results computed on the ChestX-ray8 test set, containing bounding box annotations. We evaluate only on the five classes that overlap with MIMIC-CXR.

Image pre-training		IoU				
Method	Dataset	Atelectasis	Cardiomegaly	Effusion	Pneumonia	Pneumothorax
Supervised	ImageNet	1.3	3.8	5.9	0.0	0.1
MoCo	CheXpert	**2.6**	**16.0**	**11.9**	**1.8**	**2.7**

fine-tuned on the full MIMIC-CXR training set, and more obviously when fine-tuned on a 10% random subset of the training set.

On the contrary, AE seems to be a less effective pre-training strategy. This might be attributed to the reconstruction loss, which encourages the model to focus on the intensity variation of CXRs rather than other meaningful features (*e.g.* shapes and textures) to discriminate between different classes.

Table 2 shows a consistent improvement achieved by adopting MoCo pre-trained weights also for the image encoder of the Attentive model and the image-only ResNet-50. This confirms that both unimodal and multimodal models benefit from the MoCo pre-training of the image encoder.

3.3 Model Explainability

To investigate the impact of pre-training on the learned features, we visually assess the quality of the activation maps obtained by two of the pre-training strategies: supervised ImageNet pre-training and MoCo pre-training on CheXpert. First, we fine-tune the fully connected layer of the ResNet-50 architecture on the full training set of MIMIC-CXR, while freezing the remaining pre-trained weights. Second, we apply Grad-CAM [24] to the final 7×7 activation map, computed before the fully connected layer. Finally, we assess if the generated maps highlight the correct anatomical location of the pathology, by computing the Intersection over Union (IoU) between the bounding boxes – annotated in the ChestX-ray8 dataset [25] – and the regions in the activation map that contribute positively to the classification of a target label. In this final step, we only consider the subset of ChestX-ray8 labels overlapping with those in MIMIC-CXR: *Atelectasis, Cardiomegaly, Pleural Effusion, Pneumonia, Pneumothorax*.

The mean IoU scores for each class are reported in Table 3. Although the overlap between the positive areas of the activation maps and the bounding boxes is low for both pre-training strategies, it can be observed that MoCo pre-training outperforms ImageNet for each class. This suggests that, when adopting MoCo pre-training, the CNN learns more meaningful features of CXRs that can be effectively exploited by the model for the downstream classification task. This is shown visually in Fig. 3, where MoCo pre-trained ResNet-50 focuses more accurately to the areas matching with the bounding boxes. However, both pre-training strategies frequently focus on incorrect areas in the images.

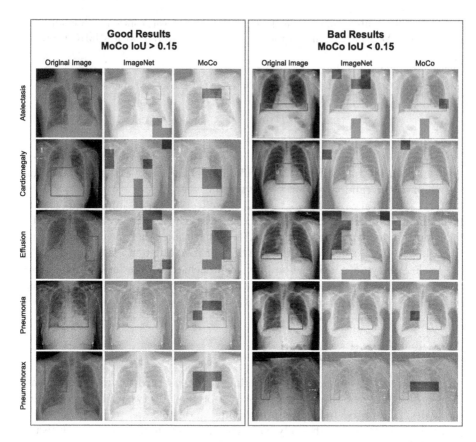

Fig. 3. Examples of CXRs taken from ChestX-ray8 dataset with the corresponding bounding box annotations highlighted in red. Grad-CAM is computed on the last 7×7 activation map, before the fully connected layer of ResNet-50, for both ImageNet and MoCo pre-training. The green regions show the activations thresholded at 0 i.e. all positive activations (activations can also be negative). The left side images are selected having an IoU score greater than 0.15 between the bounding box and the positive regions, using MoCo pre-trained weights; the right side images are selected with an IoU score lower than 0.15. (Color figure online)

4   Conclusion

In this work we have demonstrated the benefit of domain-specific self-supervised MoCo pre-training of the MMBT image encoder for multimodal multi-label CXR classification. To the best of our knowledge, this is the first study to compare how different self-supervised pre-training strategies affect multimodal performance in the medical domain. Our results show that the choice of image encoder plays a substantial role, especially with limited annotated data, where ResNet pre-trained using MoCo achieves the best performances. In future research, it would be interesting to combine unsupervised unimodal pre-training, as demonstrated in this paper, followed by an unsupervised multimodal pre-training step, as demonstrated in [18], to see if a cumulative improvement could be obtained.

A   Per-Class Results

Table 4. Per-class AUROC scores using different ResNet-50 initializations. The models are fine-tuned on the full training set (top) and on 10% of the training set (bottom).

100% training set						
Model	Attentive		MMBT			
Image Pre-Training	Supervised	MoCo	Random	Supervised	AE	MoCo
	ImageNet	CheXpert	Init.	ImageNet	CheXpert	CheXpert
Atelectasis	$73.5_{\pm1.0}$	$72.8_{\pm0.9}$	$71.8_{\pm0.6}$	$\mathbf{75.2_{\pm0.8}}$	$74.2_{\pm0.7}$	$74.9_{\pm0.7}$
Cardiomegaly	$77.1_{\pm0.5}$	$79.1_{\pm0.5}$	$80.0_{\pm0.4}$	$81.3_{\pm0.9}$	$81.6_{\pm0.4}$	$\mathbf{82.4_{\pm0.4}}$
Consolidation	$72.3_{\pm1.1}$	$75.0_{\pm0.6}$	$71.3_{\pm0.8}$	$\mathbf{77.2_{\pm1.8}}$	$74.3_{\pm0.6}$	$76.5_{\pm0.6}$
Edema	$82.2_{\pm0.7}$	$82.8_{\pm0.5}$	$80.9_{\pm0.8}$	$83.6_{\pm1.1}$	$82.7_{\pm0.4}$	$\mathbf{84.2_{\pm0.4}}$
Enlarged Card	$67.0_{\pm1.6}$	$68.7_{\pm0.9}$	$68.4_{\pm0.6}$	$73.3_{\pm2.1}$	$71.4_{\pm1.8}$	$\mathbf{75.0_{\pm1.8}}$
Fracture	$66.7_{\pm3.0}$	$69.7_{\pm1.6}$	$68.7_{\pm1.8}$	$70.0_{\pm1.2}$	$70.7_{\pm0.8}$	$\mathbf{72.3_{\pm0.8}}$
Lung Lesion	$68.9_{\pm2.2}$	$71.0_{\pm0.9}$	$69.6_{\pm0.6}$	$74.5_{\pm3.0}$	$70.2_{\pm0.6}$	$\mathbf{76.7_{\pm0.6}}$
Lung Opacity	$68.9_{\pm0.4}$	$70.8_{\pm0.9}$	$66.9_{\pm0.6}$	$71.8_{\pm0.5}$	$69.4_{\pm0.5}$	$\mathbf{72.0_{\pm0.5}}$
No Findings	$80.4_{\pm0.4}$	$80.9_{\pm0.9}$	$79.7_{\pm0.8}$	$82.5_{\pm1.2}$	$81.2_{\pm0.6}$	$\mathbf{82.6_{\pm0.6}}$
Pleural Effusion	$86.7_{\pm0.9}$	$86.8_{\pm0.6}$	$82.6_{\pm0.3}$	$\mathbf{87.6_{\pm0.6}}$	$85.0_{\pm0.2}$	$\mathbf{87.6_{\pm0.2}}$
Pleural Other	$78.8_{\pm1.7}$	$80.2_{\pm2.3}$	$89.4_{\pm1.2}$	$\mathbf{86.1_{\pm4.4}}$	$81.6_{\pm1.9}$	$86.1_{\pm1.9}$
Pneumonia	$70.8_{\pm0.9}$	$74.1_{\pm1.5}$	$69.7_{\pm0.9}$	$74.6_{\pm0.6}$	$71.8_{\pm0.6}$	$\mathbf{76.7_{\pm0.6}}$
Pneumothorax	$84.8_{\pm0.8}$	$86.9_{\pm0.9}$	$87.4_{\pm1.2}$	$\mathbf{87.9_{\pm0.4}}$	$86.9_{\pm1.0}$	$87.7_{\pm1.0}$
Support Devices	$90.4_{\pm0.2}$	$91.1_{\pm0.2}$	$89.3_{\pm0.2}$	$\mathbf{91.7_{\pm0.6}}$	$90.1_{\pm0.3}$	$\mathbf{91.7_{\pm0.3}}$
Average	$76.3_{\pm0.5}$	$77.8_{\pm0.6}$	$76.1_{\pm0.3}$	$79.8_{\pm1.1}$	$77.9_{\pm0.4}$	$\mathbf{80.4_{\pm0.3}}$
10% training set						
Model	Attentive		MMBT			
Image Pre-Training	Supervised	MoCo	Random	Supervised	AE	MoCo
	ImageNet	CheXpert	Init.	ImageNet	CheXpert	CheXpert
Atelectasis	$66.9_{\pm1.5}$	$69.3_{\pm1.3}$	$64.6_{\pm0.4}$	$65.5_{\pm0.9}$	$67.2_{\pm0.4}$	$\mathbf{71.4_{\pm1.3}}$
Cardiomegaly	$67.3_{\pm0.5}$	$72.4_{\pm0.8}$	$71.8_{\pm0.5}$	$70.7_{\pm0.7}$	$74.0_{\pm1.3}$	$\mathbf{77.0_{\pm0.9}}$
Consolidation	$61.3_{\pm0.3}$	$68.0_{\pm0.8}$	$66.3_{\pm1.1}$	$64.0_{\pm1.3}$	$67.7_{\pm0.8}$	$\mathbf{71.3_{\pm1.0}}$
Edema	$76.1_{\pm1.0}$	$78.4_{\pm1.4}$	$74.5_{\pm0.6}$	$76.5_{\pm1.1}$	$77.1_{\pm0.8}$	$\mathbf{80.7_{\pm1.3}}$
Enlarged Card	$58.5_{\pm2.5}$	$63.3_{\pm1.8}$	$62.6_{\pm3.3}$	$62.8_{\pm1.8}$	$61.5_{\pm5.0}$	$\mathbf{67.8_{\pm3.0}}$
Fracture	$52.2_{\pm3.4}$	$51.8_{\pm3.0}$	$61.6_{\pm4.5}$	$58.7_{\pm4.0}$	$60.1_{\pm2.4}$	$\mathbf{62.4_{\pm2.6}}$
Lung Lesion	$56.7_{\pm1.0}$	$64.5_{\pm2.9}$	$64.8_{\pm2.2}$	$60.7_{\pm2.0}$	$65.8_{\pm2.0}$	$\mathbf{67.2_{\pm1.4}}$
Lung Opacity	$60.4_{\pm0.7}$	$65.7_{\pm0.6}$	$61.7_{\pm0.8}$	$62.2_{\pm1.7}$	$62.2_{\pm0.8}$	$\mathbf{67.2_{\pm1.1}}$
No Findings	$72.1_{\pm1.4}$	$75.2_{\pm1.2}$	$74.5_{\pm0.8}$	$74.1_{\pm0.6}$	$75.8_{\pm0.9}$	$\mathbf{78.7_{\pm0.6}}$
Pleural Effusion	$80.0_{\pm0.9}$	$82.6_{\pm0.7}$	$73.0_{\pm0.8}$	$79.2_{\pm0.9}$	$76.8_{\pm0.4}$	$\mathbf{84.7_{\pm0.3}}$
Pleural Other	$60.0_{\pm1.3}$	$62.2_{\pm3.6}$	$61.2_{\pm1.2}$	$65.0_{\pm6.7}$	$62.1_{\pm3.2}$	$\mathbf{67.6_{\pm3.3}}$
Pneumonia	$57.6_{\pm1.5}$	$64.1_{\pm1.3}$	$66.4_{\pm1.5}$	$60.4_{\pm1.4}$	$66.0_{\pm0.7}$	$\mathbf{68.6_{\pm2.0}}$
Pneumothorax	$68.4_{\pm3.7}$	$78.7_{\pm2.8}$	$84.6_{\pm2.0}$	$79.9_{\pm2.0}$	$\mathbf{85.0_{\pm0.6}}$	$84.7_{\pm0.8}$
Support Devices	$78.0_{\pm1.9}$	$86.5_{\pm2.0}$	$87.1_{\pm0.6}$	$86.0_{\pm0.9}$	$86.9_{\pm0.5}$	$\mathbf{88.8_{\pm1.2}}$
Average	$65.1_{\pm1.1}$	$70.2_{\pm0.5}$	$69.6_{\pm0.7}$	$69.0_{\pm0.4}$	$70.5_{\pm0.4}$	$\mathbf{74.1_{\pm0.7}}$

References

1. Huang, S.C., Pareek, A., Seyyedi, S., Banerjee, I., Lungren, M.P.: Fusion of medical imaging and electronic health records using deep learning: A systematic review and implementation guidelines. Digital Medicine, no. 1 (2020)

2. Vaswani, A., et al.: Attention is all you need. In: Advances in Neural Information Processing Systems, vol. 30 (2017). https://proceedings.neurips.cc/paper/2017/file/3f5ee243547dee91fbd053c1c4a845aa-Paper.pdf
3. Jacenków, G., O'Neil, A.Q., Tsaftaris, S.A.: Indication as prior knowledge for multimodal disease classification in chest radiographs with transformers. In: 2022 IEEE 19th International Symposium on Biomedical Imaging (ISBI)
4. Hendricks, L.A., Mellor, J., Schneider, R., Alayrac, J.-B., Nematzadeh, A.: Decoupling the role of data, attention, and losses in multimodal transformers. Trans. Assoc. Comput. Linguistics **9**, 570–585 (2021). https://doi.org/10.1162/tacl_a_00385. https://aclanthology.org/2021.tacl-1.35
5. Anderson, P., et al.: Bottom-up and top-down attention for image captioning and visual question answering. In: Proceedings of the IEEE Conference on Computer Vision and Pattern Recognition, pp. 6077–6086 (2018)
6. Li, L.H., Yatskar, M., Yin, D., Hsieh, C.-J., Chang, K.-W.: VisualBERT: a simple and performant baseline for vision and language. arXiv preprint arXiv:1908.03557, 2019
7. Lu, J., Batra, D., Parikh, D., Lee, S.: ViLBERT: pretraining task-agnostic visiolinguistic representations for vision-and-language tasks. In: Advances in Neural Information Processing Systems, 32 (2019)
8. Ren, S., He, K., Girshick, R., Sun, F.: Faster R-CNN: towards real-time object detection with region proposal networks. In: Advances in neural information processing systems, 28 (2015)
9. Krishna, R., et al.: Visual genome: Connecting language and vision using crowdsourced dense image annotations. Int. J. Comput. Vis. **123**(1), 32–73 (2017)
10. Huang, Z., Zeng, Z., Liu, B., Fu, D., Fu, R.: Pixel-BERT: Aligning image pixels with text by deep multi-modal transformers. arXiv preprint arXiv:2004.00849(020)
11. Aditya Ramesh, A., et al.: Zero-shot text-to-image generation. In International Conference on Machine Learning, pp. 8821–8831. PMLR (2021)
12. Dosovitskiy, A., et al.: An image is worth 16×16 words: Transformers for image recognition at scale. arXiv preprint arXiv:2010.11929, 2020
13. Johnson, A.E.W., et al.: Mimic-cxr-jpg, a large publicly available database of labeled chest radiographs. arXiv preprint arXiv:1901.07042 (2019)
14. Johnson, A.E.W., et al.: MIMIC-CXR, a de-identified publicly available database of chest radiographs with free-text reports. Sci. Data **6**(1), December 2019. https://doi.org/10.1038/s41597-019-0322-0. https://doi.org/10.1038/s41597-019-0322-0
15. Goldberger, A.L., et al.: Physiobank, physiotoolkit, and physionet: components of a new research resource for complex physiologic signals. Circulation **101**(23), e215–e220 (2000)
16. Demner-Fushman, D., et al.: Preparing a collection of radiology examinations for distribution and retrieval. J. Am. Med. Inf. Assoc. **23**(2), 304–310 (2016)
17. van Sonsbeek, T., Worring, M.: Towards Automated Diagnosis with Attentive Multi-modal Learning Using Electronic Health Records and Chest X-Rays. In: Syeda-Mahmood, T., Drechsler, K., Greenspan, H., Madabhushi, A., Karargyris, A., Linguraru, M.G., Oyarzun Laura, C., Shekhar, R., Wesarg, S., González Ballester, M.Á., Erdt, M. (eds.) CLIP/ML-CDS -2020. LNCS, vol. 12445, pp. 106–114. Springer, Cham (2020). https://doi.org/10.1007/978-3-030-60946-7_11
18. Liao, R., Moyer, D., Cha, M., Quigley, K., Berkowitz, S., Horng, S., Golland, P., Wells, W.M.: Multimodal representation learning via maximization of local mutual information. In: de Bruijne, M., Cattin, P.C., Cotin, S., Padoy, N., Speidel, S., Zheng, Y., Essert, C. (eds.) MICCAI 2021. LNCS, vol. 12902, pp. 273–283. Springer, Cham (2021). https://doi.org/10.1007/978-3-030-87196-3_26

19. He, K., Fan, H., Wu, Y., Xie, S., Girshick, R.: Momentum contrast for unsupervised visual representation learning. In: Proceedings of the IEEE/CVF Conference on Computer Vision and Pattern Recognition, pp. 9729–9738 (2020)
20. Sowrirajan, J.Y., Ng, A.Y., Rajpurkar, P.: MoCo pretraining improves representation and transferability of chest X-ray models. In: Medical Imaging with Deep Learning, pp. 728–744. PMLR (2021)
21. Azizi, S., et al.: Big self-supervised models advance medical image classification. In: Proceedings of the IEEE/CVF International Conference on Computer Vision, pp. 3478–3488 (2021)
22. Chen, T., Kornblith, S., Norouzi, M., Hinton, G.: A simple framework for contrastive learning of visual representations. In: International Conference on Machine Learning, pp. 1597–1607. PMLR (2020)
23. Vu, Y.N.T.: Medaug: contrastive learning leveraging patient metadata improves representations for chest x-ray interpretation. In: Machine Learning for Healthcare Conference, pp. 755–769. PMLR (2021)
24. Selvaraju, R.R., Cogswell, M., Das, A., Vedantam, R., Parikh, D., Batra, B.: Gradcam: visual explanations from deep networks via gradient-based localization. In: Proceedings of the IEEE international Conference on Computer Vision, pp. 618–626 (2017)
25. Wang, X., Peng, Y., Lu, L., Lu, Z., Bagheri, M., Summers, R.M.: ChestX-ray8: Hospital-scale chest X-ray database and benchmarks on weakly-supervised classification and localization of common thorax diseases. In: Proceedings of the IEEE Conference on Computer vision and pattern recognition, pp. 2097–2106 (2017)
26. Kiela, D., Bhooshan, S., Firooz, H., Testuggine, D.: Supervised multimodal bitransformers for classifying images and text. arXiv preprint arXiv:1909.02950 (2019)
27. Devlin, J., Chang Kenton, M.-W., Toutanova, L.K.: BERT: pre-training of deep bidirectional transformers for language understanding. In: Proceedings of NAACL-HLT, pp. 4171–4186 (2019)
28. van den Oord, A., Li, Y., Vinyals, O.: Representation learning with contrastive predictive coding. arXiv preprint arXiv:1807.03748 (2018)
29. Irvin, J., et al.: CheXpert: large chest radiograph dataset with uncertainty labels and expert comparison. In: Proceedings of the AAAI Conference on Artificial Intelligence, vol. 33, pp. 590–597 (2019)
30. Singh, A., et al.: MMF: A multimodal framework for vision and language research (2020). https://github.com/facebookresearch/mmf
31. He, K., Zhang, X., Ren, S., Sun, J.: Deep residual learning for image recognition. In: Proceedings of the IEEE Conference on Computer Vision and Pattern Recognition, pp. 770–778 (2016)
32. Yijia, Z., Chen, Q., Yang, Z., Lin, H., lu, Z.: BioWordVec, improving biomedical word embeddings with subword information and MeSH. Sci. Data **6**, 05 2019. https://doi.org/10.1038/s41597-019-0055-0
33. Chung, J., Gulcehre, C., Cho, K., Bengio, Y.: Empirical evaluation of gated recurrent neural networks on sequence modeling. In: NIPS 2014 Workshop on Deep Learning, December 2014

Multi-scale Graph Neural Networks for Mammography Classification and Abnormality Detection

Guillaume Pelluet[1,2]([✉]) [ID], Mira Rizkallah[1] [ID], Mickael Tardy[2] [ID],
Oscar Acosta[3] [ID], and Diana Mateus[1] [ID]

[1] Nantes Université, École Centrale Nantes, CNRS, LS2N, UMR 6004,
F-44000 Nantes, France
[2] Hera-MI, SAS, Nantes, France
guillaume.pelluet@hera-mi.com
[3] Université de Rennes 1, LTSI, UMR 1099, Rennes, France

Abstract. Early breast cancer diagnosis and lesion detection have been made possible through medical imaging modalities such as mammography. However, the interpretation of mammograms by a radiologist is still challenging. In this paper, we tackle the problems of whole mammogram classification and local abnormality detection, respectively, with supervised and weakly-supervised approaches. To address the multi-scale nature of the problem, we first extract superpixels at different scales. We then introduce graph connexions between superpixels (within and across scales) to better model the lesion's size and shape variability. On top of the multi-scale graph, we design a Graph Neural Network (GNN) trained in a supervised manner to predict a binary class for each input image. The GNN summarizes the information from different regions, learning features that depend not only on local textures but also on the superpixels' geometrical distribution and topological relations. Finally, we design the last layer of the GNN to be a global pooling operation to allow for a weakly-supervised training of the abnormality detection task, following the principles of Multiple Instance Learning (MIL). The predictions of the last-but-one GNN layer result in a superpixelized heatmap of the abnormality probabilities, leading to a weakly-supervised abnormality detector with low annotations requirements (i.e., trained with image-wise labels only). Experiments on one private and one publicly available datasets show that our superpixel-based multi-scale GNN improves the classification results over prior weakly supervised approaches.

Keywords: Mammography · Superpixels · Graph · GNN · Classification · Detection · Segmentation

1 Introduction

Breast cancer is the most common cancer in women worldwide [7]. Early-stage screening through mammography has demonstrated strong efficacy in reducing

G. Yang et al. (Eds.): MIUA 2022, LNCS 13413, pp. 636–650, 2022.
https://doi.org/10.1007/978-3-031-12053-4_47

mortality caused by breast cancer. The detection of abnormal areas is a key step in the diagnosis process. However, since mammograms are 2D X-ray projections, the abnormal lesions can be overshadowed by superimposing high-density tissues.

Current deep learning methods built on Convolutional Neural Networks (CNN) have demonstrated good performances in the automated analysis of individual mammograms, e.g., for the tasks of malignant image or region classification [1,3]. To improve the ability to detect small lesions (e.g., calcifications) at higher resolutions, a common alternative are patch-wise classification or detection approaches [15,16]. For instance, Shen et al. [16] proposed converting a patch classifier into a whole image classifier by modifying the last layers of the network. Instead, Ribli *et al.* [15] opt for an object detector approach (Faster RCNN [8]). Fully supervised patch-wise approaches such as [15,16] require region-wise delineations of the lesions, which are not part of clinical protocols. Removing the need for lesion delineations, Choukroun *et al.* [4] proposed a weakly-supervised Multiple Instance Learning (MIL) approach, where the model for patch predictions is trained from image-wise labels only. Our approach is also weakly supervised but we rely on superpixels instead of patches which later allows for detailed abnormality region segmentation. To cope with the variability of both lesion's size and shape, we rely on a multi-scale graph representation of the mammogram where each node represents a superpixel at a specific scale, and each superpixel regroups neighboring pixels sharing common characteristics (e.g., pixel intensity) [2].

Despite mammograms being 2D uniform grids, abnormalities do not appear at a single scale, nor are uniformly distributed in the Euclidean space. Motivated by those two facts, we introduce an alternative representation of the image based on a multi-scale graph and model the classification task with a Graph Neural Network (GNN).

Graphs are powerful representation tools used to model the structure of the underlying domain in medical imaging [10]. GNNs contextualize patch-level information from their neighbors through message passing, thus enabling learning from both individual node features and the graph topological information. Few recent works have addressed the analysis of mammographic images with GNNs. In Du *et al.* [6], the authors introduced the fully supervised Graph Attention Networks (GAT) for mono-view mammography image classification. Their model relies on a multi-scale graph representation of the mammogram, where each node corresponds to a squared patch in a specific scale and zooming operations from radiologists are modeled as connections between neighboring scales. Graphs have also been useful for modeling intrinsic geometric and semantic relations between ipsilateral views (Liu *et al.* [12]).

In this paper, we propose the supervised learning of the mono-view mammogram classification task and the weakly-supervised learning of the abnormality detection task, both based on a single multi-scale graph and a Graph Convolutional neural Network (GCN) which only needs image-wise ground truth class labels for training. Unlike Du *et al.*'s graph [6], where relationships between scales are independent, our graph draws connections within and across scales, i.e., between each superpixel and its spatial neighbors in the same scale and between neighboring superpixels in different scales.

In practice, our method assigns a set of features for each node in the multi-scale graph by applying a customized encoder (denoted as Backbone). The multi-scale graph and the node features are then fed to a GCN which outputs a global classification of the mammogram along with multi-scale heat-maps used for lesion detection by adaptive thresholding.

The model is trained on an in-house private dataset (**PRV**) and then evaluated on both the private dataset and a public dataset (**INB**), both of them consisting of mammograms from different populations, countries of origin, and acquired with different mammography system vendors. The experimental validation shows that our proposed method yields competitive global classification results while outperforming state-of-the-art weakly-supervised methods for lesion detection on an unseen manufacturer dataset. To the best of our knowledge, our learning framework scheme is the first weakly supervised method reaching an AUC score of around 0.83 for breast-wise classification.

2   Methods

Let a breast imaging exam be composed of a mammogram $\mathcal{I}$, corresponding to a Craniocaudal (CC) or a Medio-lateral oblique (MLO) view. Our goal is to perform a breast cancer screening classification, intended to capture the presence of malignant regions on the mammogram. We treat a mammogram as benign when it has no or benign lesions only. We consider an image as malignant if it contains at least one malignant lesion. In this context, we propose a deep learning framework, as depicted in Fig. 1. The framework takes as input a breast image (mammogram) and an approximate range of possible lesion's sizes, then outputs a prediction of the probability of the presence of a malignant region in the image, and a region-wise prediction on different scales useful for lesion detection but also improving the interpretability of the model.

The framework is composed of three independent modules: the first module consists of a multi-scale over-segmentation of the mammogram based on the superpixels and a multi-scale graph generation. The second block is the feature extraction module, which computes the feature vectors of the nodes, i.e., the features assigned to each superpixel. Finally, the last module is a GCN taking as input both the node features and the multi-scale graph to output the probability of malignancy for every node and the whole mammogram. In the following, we give a detailed description of the three modules.

2.1   Multi-scale Graph Generation

Multi-scale Oversegmentation. To allow for better detection of malignant regions with variable sizes, we adapt the method proposed in Hang. *et al.* [9] to over-segment the mammogram $\mathcal{I}$ at several scales into superpixels. To generate the region candidates for each scale, we rely on a modified version [14]

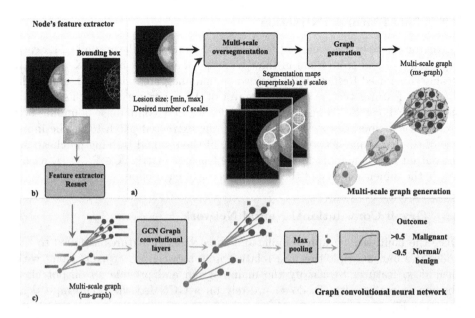

Fig. 1. Overview of the proposed learning framework consisting of three modules: a multi-scale graph generation module (a), a feature extraction module (b) and a graph convolutional neural network module (c). The framework requires as input a mammogram, the lesion's size range and the number of desired scales as input, and outputs a probability of malignancy for the whole image and an associated region-wise heatmap.

of the Scalable Simple Linear Iterative Clustering (SSLIC) algorithm proposed by Lowekamp *et al.* [13]. This modified version allows us to modulate the compactness parameter according to the variance of the superpixel features. As a result of this step, we obtain a multi-scale clustering $\mathcal{S} = \{S_1, S_2, \ldots, S_M\}$, with S_M the superpixel oversegmentation at scale m and M the number of scales. Equivalently, $\mathcal{S}$ can be seen as a collection of N superpixels s_i (with different sizes and shapes) resulting from all the scales such that $\mathcal{S} = \{s_i\}_{i=1}^N$.

Graph Generation. In order to capture intra-scale and inter-scale relationships in the mammogram $\mathcal{I}$, i.e., between sub-regions inside a specific scale and between corresponding superpixels in different scales respectively, we build a multi-scale graph. More precisely, given the image $\mathcal{I}$ and its multi-scale superpixel clustering $\mathcal{S}$, we build a graph $\mathcal{G} = \{\mathcal{V}, \mathcal{E}\}$ consisting of a finite set $\mathcal{V}$ of vertices and a set of edges $\mathcal{E}$. Each vertex in $\mathcal{V}$ corresponds to a superpixel $s_i \in \mathcal{S}$, therefore $\|\mathcal{V}\| = N$. To build $\mathcal{E}$, we connect each vertex in $\mathcal{V}$ with its 4 neighbors in the spatial (2D) domain (i.e., top, bottom, left, and right), and its 2 neighbors across scales (i.e., nearest smaller and the nearest larger scales). An illustration of the resulting multi-scale (ms-graph) is shown in Fig. 1.a. A binary adjacency matrix $\mathbf{A} \in [0, 1]^{N \times N}$ is associated to the multi-scale graph, such that each entry $a_{i,j}$ is set to 1 if there is an edge connecting the two vertices s_i and s_j, otherwise, $a_{i,j}$ is set to 0.

2.2   Node Features Extraction

Furthermore, we extract relevant features for each node in the graph i.e., for each superpixel s_i, and store them in the ith row $\mathbf{x}_i$ of a feature matrix $\mathbf{X}$. We use a weakly supervised Resnet22 [19], trained on mammograms with a MIL approach, to extract features vectors $\{\mathbf{x}_i\}$. In the rest of the paper, we denote this network as the Backbone $\mathcal{B}$. To apply $\mathcal{B}$ to a node, we first compute a bounding-box around each superpixel s_i. We then resize the extracted patch to fit the input size of the backbone network (i.e., the size of the original training patches). At the output of this module, we get the node features matrix $\mathbf{X} \in \mathbb{R}^{N \times D_{in}}$, where D_{in} is the dimensionality of the feature vector of each node.

2.3   Graph Convolutional Neural Network

Once the multi-scale graph is built, and the extracted features assigned to the nodes, we aim at exploiting the relationships between superpixels along with their deep features to classify the mammogram and provide an output class (benign or malignant). To do so, we rely on a GCN fed with the graph $\mathcal{G}$ as shown in Fig. 1.

From the architecture standpoint, the network is composed of four graph convolutional layers. Each layer GCN_n (with $n \in \{1, \ldots, 4\}$) is composed of a graph convolutional operator, as defined in Kipf et al. [11], followed by an activation function and a dropout layer. Each GCN_n gets as input the feature matrix from the previous layer $\mathbf{H}_{n-1}$ ($\mathbf{X}$ for the first layer) and provides as output the transformed matrix $\mathbf{H}_n$. The final output node feature matrix $\mathbf{H}_{out} = \mathbf{H}_4 \in \mathbb{R}^{N \times D_{out}}$ contains the node representation encoding both graph structural properties and node features. In our case, we fix D_{out} to 1 for binary malignancy probability. The feature matrix $\mathbf{H}_{out}$ is aggregated with a global maximum graph pooling layer, retaining only the node with the maximum value h_{max}. A non linear activation layer (a sigmoid function denoted as $\sigma(\cdot)$) is then applied on h_{max} to obtain the probability of malignancy. The prediction for the entire image is computed as:

$$\hat{\mathbf{y}} = \sigma(f_\theta(h_{max})) \tag{1}$$

where f_θ represents the whole GCN architecture with parameters θ trained with an image-wise weighted cross-entropy loss.

2.4   Implementation Details

The weakly-supervised backbone encoder is trained using a Resnet22 architecture respecting the MIL training strategy. In order to compute the features of a specific node in the graph, we use the backbone encoder and extract 256 features from the second but last layer. Our Multi-Scale Graph Convolutional Network ($\mathcal{MSGCN}$) model is trained following the same strategy (i.e., MIL) using the library DGL [20] with PyTorch [5] in backend. The training was performed using

Adam optimizer with an initial learning rate of $5 \cdot 10^{-4}$ and default parameters. For the graph convolutional layers, we used a weight decay factor of $1 \cdot 10^{-5}$. All the experiments were trained for at least 10000 epochs. While training the GCN, we apply a dropout with a probability of 0.1 at each layer and we used a batch size of 64. The model was trained on NVIDIA A100 GPU.

The input to our framework is a pre-processed mammogram. The preprocessing consists of the following steps: the right breasts are horizontally flipped to align the breast to the left of the image. The background is cleaned to remove labels using triangle thresholding; the cleaned mammograms are then cropped to the bounding box around the breast to avoid using background information; the cropped images are resized to a height of 3072 pixels. To increase the contrast of the resized mammogram, we perform histogram stretching between the intensities corresponding to the 2nd percentile and the 99th percentile. We finally normalize the intensity values between 0 and 1.

3   Experimental Results

3.1   Experimental Setup

Datasets. Experiments are performed on mammograms originating from different populations, locations (countries), and mammography system vendors. More precisely, we evaluate our model on two different datasets: a private dataset managed in-house, and a public dataset. The former, denoted as **PRV**, is composed of 3162 Full Field Digital Mammography (FFDM) images from four different vendors, namely Fujifilm, GE, Hologic, and Planmed. For all the malignant mammograms, pixel-level annotations of the lesions, drawn by the clinical experts, are provided (only used for evaluation). The publicly available INbreast dataset is composed of 410 FFDM images from the Siemens mammography system. Similar to **PRV**, images have pixel-level annotations for each lesion delineated by an expert radiologist. In the following, we refer to this dataset as **INB**. The distributions of the two classes (benign/normal or malignant) in both datasets are given in Table 1.

Table 1. Composition of the datasets

Dataset	Samples	Benign	Malignant	Train set	Test set
PRV	3162	1597 (50.5%)	1565 (49.5%)	2658	504
INB	410	310 (75.6%)	100 (24.4%)	0	410

In order to evaluate the proposed approaches, we used **PRV** for training and testing while keeping the same samples in the test set as done in the baseline. We split the remaining train set into 80–20 train/validation splits while keeping the validation set balanced. We used the full **INB** dataset for evaluation as well as a subset defined in [18] for a fair comparison to similar works.

The superpixels are generated at 4 different scales for both datasets, and their statistics are given in Table 2, and shown in Fig. 2.

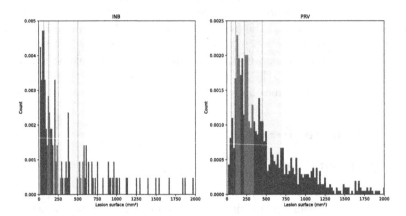

Fig. 2. Lesion's size's distribution in both datasets: **INB** and **PRV**. The red vertical lines and gray zones correspond to the average and standard deviation (in mm^2 of superpixel's size in each scale respectively) (Color figure online)

Table 2. Average and standard deviation (in mm^2) of the superpixel's size in each scale in both datasets.

Scales	PRV	INB
	Average size (std)	
0	56.57 (29.59)	63.36 (9.73)
1	113.09 (59.09)	126.52 (19.39)
2	226.15 (117.75)	252.04 (38.59)
3	452.17 (234.87)	502.67 (76.96)

Evaluation Protocol. We evaluate the performance of our learning framework for three tasks: global classification (image-wise and breast-wise), lesion detection, and lesion segmentation. We used breast-wise, image-wise, and pixel-level ground-truths to evaluate the proposed model for breast-wise/image-wise malignancy classification and local detection/segmentation. To evaluate our model at a breast-level, we average breasts' malignancy predictions when the breast is composed of several mammograms.

The Area Under the Curve (AUC) was used as a metric to assess the performance for image-wise classification. As for the local detection assessment, the Area under the Free-Response ROC Curve (AUFROC) and the TPR@FPPI metric were used. Dice Score was used to measure the malignant lesions segmentation performance.

3.2 Evaluation of the Proposed Framework

In this section, we focus on the analysis of the performance of our learning scheme in the context of two tasks: the global image/breast classification and abnormal region detection tasks.

Ablation Study of Multi-scale Features. In order to show the interest of the multi-scale representation, we start with an ablation study of the scales parameter given as input to our learning framework. More precisely, choosing one or more scales implies generating a one-scale graph or a multi-scale graph respectively. Node features are extracted accordingly. In each case, both the graph and the node features are fed to the GCN.

In Table 3, we report the image-wise classification AUC obtained with varying scale parameters. We observe that the scale 0 and 3 have the lowest AUC for image-wise classification, while the performance using scales 1 or 2 reaches 0.77. The difference in terms of performance can be explained by the fact that super-pixels in scales 0 and 3, with an average isotropic size of around 175 and 479 pixels (Table 2) respectively, had to be resized before being fed to the feature extractor module. The sub-optimal resizing procedure generates blur or noise artifacts in the interpolated patch. Moreover, exploiting the features originating from scale 1 and scale 2 simultaneously (i.e., 1&2) improves the classification performance to reach an AUC of 0.80, similarly to the performance with scales 1&2&3. This shows that the GCN is able to mix the information originating from multiple scales, leading to an improvement in the classification performance. With no benefit observed when adding scale 3, for the rest of the analysis, we will focus on scales 1 and 2 to generate the graph and node features.

Table 3. Scales ablation with $\mathcal{MSGCN}$ on **PRV** dataset.

Scales	0	1	2	3	1&2	1&3	2&3	1&2&3
Image-wise AUC	0.57	0.77	0.77	0.65	**0.80**	0.65	0.73	**0.80**

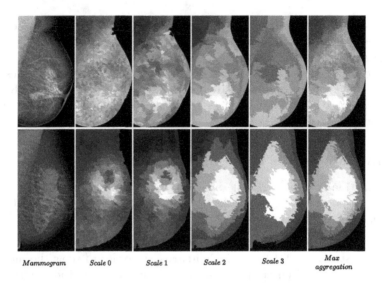

Mammogram　　Scale 0　　Scale 1　　Scale 2　　Scale 3　　*Max aggregation*

Fig. 3. Illustration of two types of lesions with different sizes (a calcification cluster in the first row, and a mass in the second row), along with their respective heatmaps generated at different scales and the aggregated $\mathcal{MSGCN}$ heat-map.

Patches vs Superpixels vs MSGCN. Having fixed the scales to consider in $\mathcal{MSGCN}$, we show here the interest of each of the modules in our framework by comparing the classification and detection performances against 2 related schemes:

- The Backbone ($\mathcal{B}$) scheme, based on the Backbone network, fed with square patches of size 256×256 and a stride of 128. This approach uses neither superpixels, the multi-scale graph, nor the GCN.
- The Superpixel-based Backbone ($\mathcal{BSP}$) scheme where we rely on the features extracted from the superpixels at two scales (1&2) (with our multi-scale graph generation module) and perform direct whole image classification, without entering the GCN module.

For the evaluation of the detection task, we rely on the intermediate computation of activation maps. Our $\mathcal{MSGCN}$ leverages the topological and textural information of the multiple scales to provide a node embedding that is suitable for both classification and detection tasks. Indeed, by design, the model does not only provide a malignancy probability for the whole image but also hands over a probability for each node in the multi-scale graph, yielding a set of activation maps $\mathcal{M}_G^{(m)}$ with m being the scale. We create the final activation map $\mathcal{M}_G$ for an image, by aggregating the activation maps with a maximum pooling across scales. To each pixel on the mammogram, we assign the maximum activation obtained for this pixel over the whole set $\mathcal{M}_G^{(m)}$. Examples of the resultant activation maps for two lesions are shown in Fig. 3. The superpixel-based scheme $\mathcal{BSP}$ provides also a set of activation maps $\mathcal{M}_S^{(m)}$ that are also aggregated into a single map $\mathcal{M}_S$ with a similar max pooling operation. The patch-based scheme $\mathcal{B}$ also gives, by design, the direct activation map for an image, corresponding to the patch-wise predictions before the last aggregation step of $\mathcal{B}$. Activation maps for $\mathcal{M}_S$ and $\mathcal{M}_B$ can be seen in Fig. 4.

From the above activation maps, we can detect the malignant regions using an adaptive thresholding procedure. In Table 4, we can see the results of image-wise, breast-wise classification, and abnormality detection obtained when using the three schemes: $\mathcal{B}$, $\mathcal{BSP}$ and our Multi-scale Superpixels Graph Neural Network denoted $\mathcal{MSGCN}$.

Classification. Table 4 shows that $\mathcal{MSGCN}$ allows a better classification (image-wise and breast-wise) compared to the backbone approach $\mathcal{B}$ on the public dataset **INB**. Indeed, in Pelluet *et al.* [14], we had shown that superpixels are suitable for a finer segmentation of lesions and thus we expect features extracted from the finer segmentation better capture the information about the lesion. Moreover, GNNs are efficient in summarizing and propagating information between different scales. The simpler patch-based backbone patches approach $\mathcal{B}$ gives a high AUC for global classification at the expense of lower detection performance.

Detection. In order to evaluate the detection performance i.e., the ability to detect and accurately localize malignant lesions, we evaluated the predicted heatmaps using the FROC curve on all findings (excluding distortions) on **INB**. To plot the curves, we applied thresholds on the probability values of the heatmaps $\mathcal{M}_B$, $\mathcal{M}_S$ and $\mathcal{M}_G$. Figure 4 shows the activation maps obtained with the 3 approaches: $\mathcal{M}_B$, $\mathcal{M}_S$, and $\mathcal{M}_G$. In the case of the method $\mathcal{B}$, only one activation map is provided. This is not optimal knowing the statistical distribution of the lesion's size shown in Fig. 2. Instead, aggregating the $\mathcal{MSGCN}$ heatmaps across scales provides a better detection, having learned the embedding of superpixels features at different scales simultaneously. Table 4 shows an improvement of the TPR, from 0.52 when using $\mathcal{M}_B$, to 0.73 with $\mathcal{M}_S$, at the expense of a higher FPPI. The best detection performance is obtained with $\mathcal{MSGCN}$ ($\mathcal{M}_G$) which reaches a TPR@FPPI of 0.98@1.01 increasing the initial backbone's TPR and FPPI by 88.4% and 71.2%, respectively. The increase of the FPPI can be explained by the communication of bad predictions between neighboring nodes in the multi-scale graph.

Comparative Performance Analysis Against State-of-the-Art Methods. We evaluate our methods against three state-of-the-art learning methods, two of which are fully supervised approaches [15,17] and one is a weakly supervised method [21]. The results are shown in Table 5.

- For the *abnormality detection task*, evaluation is only performed on the malignant images of the **INB** dataset for a fair comparison with the state-of-the-art. To generate the results for Shen *et al.* [17], the publicly available model

Table 4. Performance of $\mathcal{MSGCN}$, $\mathcal{B}$ and $\mathcal{BSP}$ in terms of image-wise and breast-wise classification on the full **INB** dataset.

Method	Test set	Supervision	Train data	TPR@FPPI	Image-wise AUC	Breast-wise AUC
$\mathcal{B}$	F	W	Private	0.52@0.59	0.8	0.8
$\mathcal{BSP}$	F	W	Private	0.73@0.74	0.80	0.82
$\mathcal{MSGCN}$	F	W	Private	**0.98@1.01**	**0.82**	**0.83**

was used. The TPR@FPPI was recomputed using their top 2% pooling, as suggested in the original paper.

– For the *classification task*, results of [21] are taken from [18] where they were also evaluated on the same subset of the **INB** dataset. The full dataset **INB** is used for evaluation against the fully supervised learning method [15]. For a fair comparison with the work of Wu et al. [21], Shen et al. [17], and Ribli et al. [15], we compute breast-wise AUC on an image subset of the test dataset **INB**.

Table 5. The performance of our scheme compared to state-of-the-art methods on the INBreast dataset. For the test set: F corresponds to the full INBreast dataset, and S is for the test subset defined in Stadnick *et al.* [18]. As for the supervision, the methods are fully supervised (Fully) if they need pixel-wise ground truth labels for training. They are weakly supervised (W) if they only require only image-wise ground truth labels.

Method	Test set	Supervision	Train data	TPR@FPPI	Breast-wise AUC
Wu [21]	S	Fully	Private	NA	0.80
Ribli [15]	S	Fully	Private & DDSM	NA	**0.97**
$\mathcal{MSGCN}$ (ours)	S	W	Private	NA	0.90
Ribli [15]	F	Fully	Private & DDSM	0.90@0.30	**0.95**
Shen [17]	F	W	Private	0.97@1.94	0.82
$\mathcal{MSGCN}$ (ours)	F	W	Private	**0.98@1.01**	**0.83**

Our method shows better results when compared to Wu et al. [21], with an improvement of 11.25% on the breast-level AUC while our method is weakly supervised. The best performance on the **INB** subset is yielded by the fully-supervised method of Ribli et al. [15], with a breast-wise AUC of 0.97.

Furthermore, the proposed method $\mathcal{MSGCN}$ improves the detection performance with a TPR@FPPI of 0.98@1.01, in comparison to other weakly and fully supervised methods, as shown in Table 5 and Fig. 5. However, Ribli *et al.* [15] achieves the lowest FPPI $= 0.3$, yielding a very low number of false positives. Finally, while the fully supervised model of [15] outperforms all the other methods with a breast-wise AUC of 0.95, our method performs relatively well with a TPR@FPPI of 0.98@1.01 on the **INB** among the three weakly supervised methods (relying only on whole-image labels), with a higher TPR and fewer false negatives. This shows that our model is generalizable to datasets from other manufacturers.

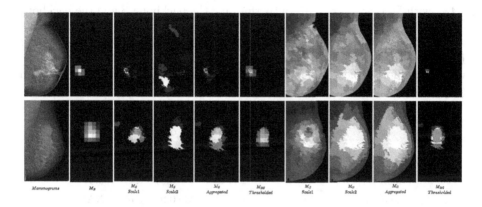

Fig. 4. Two examples of segmentation maps obtained from the merged heatmaps $\mathcal{M}_{BS}$ and $\mathcal{M}_{BG}$ with a threshold of 0.5. The second column corresponds to the Backbone heatmap extracted from the Backbone network. The 6th column corresponds to the merged heatmap resulting from aggregating $\mathcal{M}_B$ and $\mathcal{M}_S$ *Aggregated* (i.e., the 2nd and the 5th column). The last column illustrates the resulting heatmap after aggregating $\mathcal{M}_B$ and $\mathcal{M}_G$ (i.e., the second and the 9th columns).

3.3 A Finer Lesion Segmentation with Superpixels

To further illustrate the interest of using a superpixel-based segmentation, we evaluated the lesion segmentation which we can obtain by applying a merging operation on activation maps as explained below. More precisely, to exploit the superpixel ability to adhere to object boundaries for lesion segmentation, we generated two new activation maps $\mathcal{M}_{BG}$ and $\mathcal{M}_{BS}$, by merging the information from $\mathcal{M}_B$ with $\mathcal{M}_G$ or $\mathcal{M}_S$ (e.g. Fig. 4, 5th and 9th column) respectively. This is performed using a simple average aggregation as shown in Eq. 2.

$$
\begin{aligned}
\mathcal{M}_{BG} &= \frac{sum(\mathcal{M}_B, \mathcal{M}_G)}{2} \\
\mathcal{M}_{BS} &= \frac{sum(\mathcal{M}_B, \mathcal{M}_S)}{2}
\end{aligned}
\tag{2}
$$

In Fig. 4, we provide two examples of the obtained heatmaps for two different lesion's sizes. We can see that with heatmaps ($\mathcal{M}_{BG}$ and $\mathcal{M}_{BS}$), the merged information retains the boundaries of the superpixels which leads to a better loyalty to the lesion borders. This performance is also noticeable looking at the DICE score in Table 5. We can see that a better performance in terms of segmentation for all malignant lesions is obtained using our merged heatmap

$\mathcal{M}_{BS}$ with Dice Scores of 0.37, outperforming the backbone $\mathcal{B}$ and the backbone applied to superpixels bounding-boxes $\mathcal{BSP}$ which both have a DICE of 0.30. Although the $\mathcal{MSGCN}$ brings a better detection performance, it has a lower DICE score of 0.13. Indeed, the aggregation of the different scales appears to be not optimal for segmentation. This issue will be tackled in a future investigation (Table 6).

Table 6. Segmentation methods on **INB**

Methods	Supervision	Train data	TPR@FPPI	Dice
Shen [17]	W	Private	0.97@1.94	0.34
Agarwal [3]	Fully	OPTIMAM	0.95@1.14	NA
$\mathcal{B}$ (ours)	W	Private	0.52@0.59	0.30
$\mathcal{BSP}$ (ours)	W	Private	0.73@0.74	0.30
$\mathcal{MSGCN}$ (ours)	W	Private	**0.98@1.01**	0.13
$\mathcal{BG}$ (ours)	W	Private	0.94@1.03	0.28
$\mathcal{BS}$ (ours)	W	Private	0.93@1.03	**0.37**

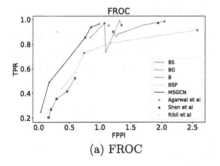

(a) FROC

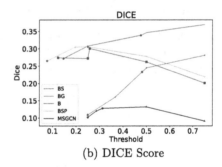

(b) DICE Score

Fig. 5. FROC curve and Dice Score representation of detection performance on the full INBreast dataset.

4   Conclusion

In this work we proposed a new learning framework for mammography classification and lesion detection/localization based on graph neural networks. We build our method on top of a backbone feature extraction module, and then improve its reliability in terms of classification, detection, and segmentation. To do so, we rely on three modules i) a novel multi-scale graph representation of the mammogram to model the zoom-in radiologist operation, allowing the backbone model to better capture relevant information at different scales; ii) deep features obtained for superpixels at different scales are then fed along with the graph; and iii) graph neural network to enable message passing between superpixels within and between scales. The lesion segmentation performance is improved when using superpixels which adhere well to object boundaries. Our weakly-supervised method based on a multi-scale graph improves the classification and detection results over the patch-based baseline, and compares well to state-of-the-art approaches, which do not consider graphs.

It is worth noting that the actual proposed model ($\mathcal{MSGCN}$) propagates the information uniformly through the local neighborhood without taking into account individual pair-wise correlations which can be different between neighboring superpixels. In order to improve the performance of the model, we will consider adding weights to the graph edges in future work.

References

1. Abdelrahman, L., Al Ghamdi, M., Collado-Mesa, F., Abdel-Mottaleb, M.: Convolutional neural networks for breast cancer detection in mammography: a survey. Comput. Biol. Med. **131**, 104248 (2021). https://doi.org/10.1016/j.compbiomed.2021.104248, https://www.sciencedirect.com/science/article/pii/S0010482521000421

2. Achanta, R., Shaji, A., Smith, K., Lucchi, A., Fua, P., Süsstrunk, S.: Slic superpixels. Technical report, EPFL, June 2010

3. Agarwal, R., Díaz, O., Yap, M.H., Lladó, X., Martí, R.: Deep learning for mass detection in Full Field Digital Mammograms. Comput. Biol. Med. **121**, 103774 (2020). https://doi.org/10.1016/j.compbiomed.2020.103774

4. Choukroun, Y., Bakalo, R., Ben-ari, R., Askelrod-ballin, A., Barkan, E., Kisilev, P.: Mammogram classification and abnormality detection from nonlocal labels using deep multiple instance neural network. Technical report (2017). https://doi.org/10.2312/VCBM.20171232

5. Collobert, R., Kavukcuoglu, K., Farabet, C.: Torch7: a MatLab-like environment for machine learning. In: BigLearn, NIPS Workshop (2011)

6. Du, H., Feng, J., Feng, M.: Zoom in to where it matters: a hierarchical graph based model for mammogram analysis (CC) (2019). http://arxiv.org/abs/1912.07517

7. Ferlay, J., et al.: Global cancer observatory: cancer today. International Agency for Research on Cancer, Lyon, France. https://gco.iarc.fr/today

8. Girshick, R.: Fast R-CNN. In: Proceedings of the IEEE International Conference on Computer Vision (ICCV), December 2015

9. Hang, M., Chandra, S., Crozier, S., Bradley, A.: Multi-scale sifting for mammographic mass detection and segmentation. Biomed. Phys. Eng. Express **5** (2019). https://doi.org/10.1088/2057-1976/aafc07

10. He, Y., Zhao, H., Wong, S.T.: Deep learning powers cancer diagnosis in digital pathology. Comput. Med. Imaging Graph. **88**, 101820 (2021). https://doi.org/10.1016/j.compmedimag.2020.101820, https://www.sciencedirect.com/science/article/pii/S0895611120301154

11. Kipf, T.N., Welling, M.: Semi-supervised classification with graph convolutional networks. CoRR abs/1609.02907 (2016). http://arxiv.org/abs/1609.02907

12. Liu, Y., Zhang, F., Chen, C., Wang, S., Wang, Y., Yu, Y.: Act like a radiologist: towards reliable multi-view correspondence reasoning for mammogram mass detection. IEEE Trans. Pattern Anal. Mach. Intell. **8828**(c), 1–15 (2021). https://doi.org/10.1109/TPAMI.2021.3085783

13. Lowekamp, B.C., Chen, D.T., Yaniv, Z., Yoo, T.S.: Scalable simple linear iterative clustering (SSLIC) using a generic and parallel approach. Kitware, Inc. (2018)
14. Pelluet, G., Rizkallah, M., Acosta, O., Mateus, D.: Unsupervised multimodal supervoxel merging towards brain tumor segmentation (2021)
15. Ribli, D., Horváth, A., Unger, Z., Pollner, P., Csabai, I.: Detecting and classifying lesions in mammograms with deep learning. Sci. Rep. **8**(1), 1–7 (2018). https://doi.org/10.1038/s41598-018-22437-z
16. Shen, L., Margolies, L., Rothstein, J., Fluder, E., McBride, R., Sieh, W.: Deep learning to improve breast cancer detection on screening mammography. Sci. Rep. **9**, 1–12 (2019). https://doi.org/10.1038/s41598-019-48995-4
17. Shen, Y., et al.: An interpretable classifier for high-resolution breast cancer screening images utilizing weakly supervised localization, February 2020. http://arxiv.org/abs/2002.07613
18. Stadnick, B., et al.: Meta-repository of screening mammography classifiers. CoRR abs/2108.04800 (2021). https://arxiv.org/abs/2108.04800
19. Tardy, M., Mateus, D.: Leveraging multi-task learning to cope with poor and missing labels of mammograms. Front. Radiol. **1**, 19 (2022). https://doi.org/10.3389/fradi.2021.796078
20. Wang, M., et al.: Deep graph library: a graph-centric, highly-performant package for graph neural networks. arXiv preprint arXiv:1909.01315 (2019)
21. Wu, N., et al.: Deep neural networks improve radiologists' performance in breast cancer screening. IEEE Trans. Med. Imaging **39**(4), 1184–1194 (2020). https://doi.org/10.1109/TMI.2019.2945514

TransSLC: Skin Lesion Classification in Dermatoscopic Images Using Transformers

Md Mostafa Kamal Sarker[1]([⊠]) [iD], Carlos Francisco Moreno-García[2] [iD], Jinchang Ren[1] [iD], and Eyad Elyan[2] [iD]

[1] National Subsea Centre, Robert Gordon University, Aberdeen AB21 0BH, UK
{m.sarker,j.ren}@rgu.ac.uk
[2] School of Computing Science and Digital Media, Robert Gordon University, Aberdeen AB10 7GJ, UK
{c.moreno-garcia,e.elyan}@rgu.ac.uk

Abstract. Early diagnosis and treatment of skin cancer can reduce patients' fatality rates significantly. In the area of computer-aided diagnosis (CAD), the Convolutional Neural Network (CNN) has been widely used for image classification, segmentation, and recognition. However, the accurate classification of skin lesions using CNN-based models is still challenging, given the inconsistent shape of lesion areas (leading to intra-class variance) and inter-class similarities. In addition, CNN-based models with massive downsampling operations often result in loss of local feature attributes from the dermatoscopic images. Recently, transformer-based models have been able to tackle this problem by exploiting both local and global characteristics, employing self-attention processes, and learning expressive long-range representations. Motivated by the superior performance of these methods, in this paper we present a transformer-based model for skin lesion classification. We apply a transformers-based model using bidirectional encoder representation from the dermatoscopic image to perform the classification task. Extensive experiments were carried out using the public dataset HAM10000, and promising results of 90.22%, 99.54%, 94.05%, and 96.28% in accuracy, precision, recall, and F1 score respectively, were achieved. This opens new research directions towards further exploration of transformers-based methods to solve some of the key challenging problems in medical image classification, namely generalisation to samples from a different distribution.

Keywords: Computer aided diagnosis · Skin lesion classification · Deep learning · Convolutional neural networks · Transformers

1 Introduction

Skin cancer is the most common type of cancer worldwide, responsible for $64,000$ fatalities in 2020 [16]. The majority of skin cancers can be treated if diagnosed

© The Author(s), under exclusive license to Springer Nature Switzerland AG 2022
G. Yang et al. (Eds.): MIUA 2022, LNCS 13413, pp. 651–660, 2022.
https://doi.org/10.1007/978-3-031-12053-4_48

early. However, visual inspection of skin malignancies with the human eye during a health screening is prone to diagnostic errors, given the similarity between skin lesions and normal tissues [12]. Dermatoscopy is the most reliable imaging method for screening skin lesions in practice. This is a non-invasive technology that allows the dermatologist to acquire high-resolution images of the skin for better visualisation of the lesions, while also enhancing sensitivity (i.e. accurate identification of the cancer lesions) and specificity (correct classification of non-cancerous suspicious lesions) when compared with the visual inspection. Nonetheless, dermatologists still confront hurdles in improving skin cancer detection, since manual assessment of dermatoscopic images is often complicated, error-prone, time-consuming, and subjective (i.e., may lead to incorrect diagnostic outcomes) [12]. Thus, a computer-aided diagnostic (CAD) system for skin lesion classification that is both automated and trustworthy has become an important evaluation tool to support dermatologists with proper diagnosis outcomes to finalise their decisions.

Over the last decades, several Convolutional Neural Network (CNN) based methods have been presented, delivering better CAD systems that identify the melanoma and non-melanoma skin lesions accurately. Deep neural networks are being used to classify skin cancer at the dermatological level. Examples include [9] using GoogleNet's Inception v3 model, which achieved 72.1% and 55.4% accuracy of the three and nine class respectively, on a Stanford Hospital private dataset. In [22], a fully convolutional residual network (FCRN) is proposed and evaluated on the IEEE International Symposium on Biomedical Imaging (ISBI) 2016 *Skin Lesion Analysis Towards Melanoma Detection Challenge* dataset. This model obtained the 1st place on the challenge leaderboard, yielding an accuracy of 85.5%. Moreover, an attention residual learning convolutional neural network (ARL-CNN) was introduced by [23] and evaluated on the ISBI 2017 dataset, achieving an average area-under-curve (AUC) of 91.7%.

Ensemble-based CNN models have also shown superior performance on medical image analysis [5,6] and skin lesion segmentation [15] and classification, as shown in the International Skin Imaging Collaboration (ISIC) datasets 2018 [3], 2019 [10], and the HAM10000 dataset [1]. However, these methods require training several deep learning models to create the ensemble, which requires huge computing power and is not suitable for real-time applications. In summary, it can be said that most methods used for medical image classification, including lesion classification are based on CNN models. However, it was reported that while such model's perform very well on datasets, cross-datasets generalisation is still considered as a key challenge for the computer vision research community [8].

To this end, we aim to address some of the issues above using a single deep learning model to classify skin lesions accurately. We propose the development of vision transformers-based models, as these have proven to be outperforming many image classification tasks [7,14]. In this study, we use a bidirectional encoder representation from the image transformers model to correctly diagnose the skin lesion. The rest of this article is organised as follows. Section 2

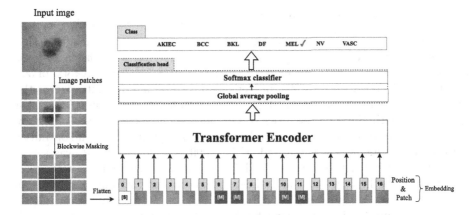

Fig. 1. The architecture of the proposed transformers model, *TransSLC*, input image, image patches. A special mask embedding [M] is replaced for some random mask of image patches (blue patches in the figure). Then the patches are fed to a backbone vision transformer and classify. (Color figure online)

describes the materials and the bidirectional encoder representation from the image transformers model in detail. The experimental findings of the CNN and transformer-based models are compared and examined in Sect. 3. Finally, Sect. 4 draws the research conclusions and suggests some future directions.

2   Methods and Materials

2.1   Image Transformer

In this work, we propose a bidirectional encoder representation from image transformers motivated by BEIT [2]. Figure 1 provides a schematic diagram of the proposed method.Initially, the input skin lesion 224×224 image is split into an array of 16 image patches, with each patch measuring 14×14 pixels, as shown in the top-left corner of Fig. 1. In BEIT, a masked image modelling (MIM) task to pretrain vision transformers is proposed for creating the visual representation of the input patches. Therefore, we used a block-wise masking forward by a linearly flatten projection to get the patch embeddings. A special token [S] is added to the input sequence for regularisation purposes. Furthermore, the patch embeddings include standard learnable 1D position embeddings as well. The input vectors of each embeddings are fed into transformers encoder. We then use vision transformers encoder as a backbone network of our model. The encoded representations for the image patches are the output vectors of the final layer of the transformers, which are then fed into the classification head which in turn classifies the input skin lesion image. The classification head consists of two layers: a global average pooling (used to aggregate the representations) and a softmax-based output layer that produces the classification of the distinct the categories.

2.2   Model Implementation Setup

As mentioned in the previous section, the proposed *TransSLC* model design is based on the BEIT model presented in [2]. In practice, we utilise a 12-layer transformer encoder, with 768 hidden size and 12 attention heads. A total of 307 feed-forward networks were also implemented for the intermediate size of the network. For our experiment, the input skin lesion image size is set to 224×224 resolution, with the 14×14 array of patches having some patches randomly masked. We trained our proposed model for 50 epochs, using the Adam optimiser [13] with parameters $\beta_1 = 0.5$ and $\beta_2 = 0.999$. The learning rate was set to 0.0001, and a batch size of 8 was used. To ensure a fair comparison with other CNN-based methods, we have used the same experimental settings. Experiments were carried out using Nvidia Tesla T4 16 GB Graphics Processing Unit (GPU) cards, and running the experiment for 50 epochs for all the models below took on average 24 h of training time.

2.3   Model Evaluation

Standard evaluation metrics were used to evaluate the performance of the models used in the experiments. These are accuracy, precision, recall, and F1 score. Definitions of these metrics are presented in Table 1.

Table 1. Model evaluation metrics to evaluate the models.

Metric	Formula
Accuracy (AC)	(TP+TN)/(TP+TN+FP+FN)
Precision (PR)	TP/(TP+FP)
Recall (RE)	TN/(TN+FN)
F1 Score (F1)	2.TP/(2.TP+FP+FN)

TP = True Positives,   TN = True Negatives,
FP = False Positives,   FN = False Negatives.

2.4   Dataset

The public and commonly used HAM10000 dataset was used [1] for evaluation purposes. The dataset contains 10,015 images. These images are labelled based on a discrete set of classes representing seven categories: actinic keratoses and intraepithelial carcinoma (AKIEC), basal cell carcinoma (BCC), benign keratosis (BKL), dermatofibroma (DF), melanoma (MEL), melanocytic nevus (NV), and vascular lesions (VASC). As can be seen in Table 2 the samples distributions is imbalanced. In other words, the number of training images in NV class is 4693 whereas DF and VASC classes have only 80 and 99 images, respectively. This is a common problem in most medical datasets, as well as health-related data [20] where various data sampling methods, as well as algorithmic modifications, are

Table 2. The image distribution per class and splits of the HAM10000 dataset.

Splits	AKIEC	BCC	BKL	DF	MEL	NV	VASC
Training	228	359	769	80	779	4693	99
Validation	33	52	110	12	111	671	14
Testing	66	103	220	23	223	1341	29
Total (10,015)	327	514	1099	115	1113	6705	142

employed to handle it [21]. However, for the purpose of this paper, we handled this problem using a simple data augmentation technique. This includes flipping the images horizontally and vertically, random cropping, adaptive histogram equalisation (CLAHE) with varying values for the original RGB images is used to change the contrast. To generate a range of contrast images, we set the CLAHE threshold for the contrast limit between 1.00 and 2.00

3   Experimental Results

For comparison purposes with our proposed *TransSLC* model, we have selected several state-of-the-art models, including ResNet-101 [11], Inception-V3 [18], the hybrid Inception-ResNet-V2 [17], Xception [4] and EfficientNet-B7 [19]. These models are considered state-of-the-art, and commonly used in medical image analysis. As can be seen in Table 3, *TransSLC* achieved the top performance reaching an accuracy of 90.22%, precision of 85.33%, recall of 80.62%, and F1 score of 82.53%. It can also be seen that among the selected CNN-based models, EfficientNet-B7 [19] achieved the best results with accuracy of 88.18%, precision of 83.66%, recall of 78.64%, and F1 score of 80.67%, respectively. Thus, our proposed model improves 2.04%, 1.67%, 1.98%, and 1.86% in terms of accuracy, precision, recall, and F1 score, respectively, comparing with CNN-based EfficientNet-B7 [19] model.

Table 3. Comparison of the performance (%) of the proposed transformers-based model against different CNN-based models in terms of the accuracy (AC), precision (PR), recall (RE), and F1 score (F1), respectively, on the test dataset.

Methods	AC	PR	RE	F1
CNN-based				
ResNet-101 [11]	83.04	68.86	68.06	68.06
Inception-V3 [18]	86.48	75.19	77.02	75.66
Inception-ResNet-V2 [17]	86.68	79.78	73.56	76.29
Xception [4]	86.98	79.55	74.08	76.07
EfficientNet-B7 [19]	88.18	83.66	78.64	80.67
Transformers-based				
Proposed *TransSLC*	**90.22**	**85.33**	**80.62**	**82.53**

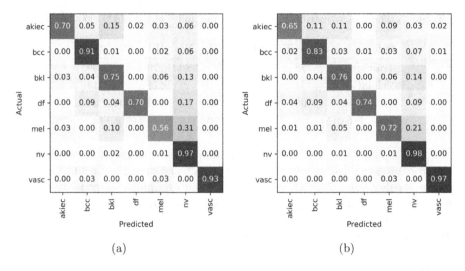

Fig. 2. Confusion matrix of (a) CNN-based EfficientNet-B7 Model (b) Transformers-based proposed model (*TransSLC*).

Moreover, Fig. 2 shows a confusion matrix of the 7 classes of the HAM10000 dataset with the test dataset. The confusion matrix in Fig. 2 shows (a) the EfficientNet-B7 [19] with the test dataset has some miss classification, particularly in the MEL types, and (b) that the proposed model, *TransSLC*, with the test dataset, is able to classify the skin lesion types in most of the classes. The CNN-based EfficientNet-B7 [19] model performs well in detecting AKIEC, BCC types of a skin lesion with 5%, and 8% higher than our proposed *TransSLC* model. To classify BKL, DF, MEL, NV, and VASC types of the lesions, the EfficientNet-B7 [19] model performs poorly and significantly fails in MEL types with 15% lower than our proposed model. This is a crucial flaw, as MEL types are deadly for patients. Therefore, CNN-based models have a considerable some limitations when used in real-world clinical settings. In contrast, our proposed model is capable of overcoming this limitation and could potentially be deployed in a real clinical setting. Still, *TransSLC* has some limitations when classifying MEL types, getting this class confused with 1% of AKEIEC, 1% of BCC, and 5% of BKL, 25% of NV types, respectively. Another drawback of the proposed transformers-based model consists of huge number of the parameters which requires large memory (computational capacity) in order to implement.

Figure 3 illustrates the comparison between CNN-based EfficientNet-B7 and proposed model using Receiver Operating Characteristic (ROC) curve. The EfficientNet-B7 yields the area of AKIEC class is 98% which is 2% higher than proposed model. The area of the rest of classes, DF, MEL, NV, and VASC achieved by *TransSLC* improves 1%, 2%, 2%, and 2%, respectively, compared with the EfficientNet-B7 model. The remain area of the BCC and BKL classes are the same for both EfficientNet-B7 and our proposed model. The class-wise

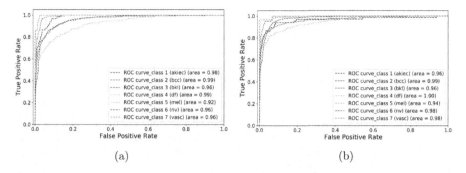

Fig. 3. ROC curve (receiver operating characteristic curve) of (a) CNN-based EfficientNet-B7 Model (b) Transformers-based proposed *TransSLC* model.

performance metrics of the proposed transformers-based, *TransSLC*, model is presented in Table 4. The proposed model yields the 86.00%, 78.90%, 84.77%, 89.47%, 79.60%, 93.70%, and 84.8% of accuracy to classify AKIEC, BCC, BKL, DF, MEL, NV, and VASC, respectively.

The performance analysis of several ablation experiments is likely insufficient to assess the benefits and behaviour of the proposed model. Thus, Fig. 4 we depict the activation maps of the CNN-based and transformers-based model. Notice that the EfficientNet-B7 rows show the activation maps, where the model can classify all these images correctly to the corresponding class but activated in over-all regions of the input skin lesion images. More preciously, the skin lesion types can be conformed through some lesion areas only on the dermatoscopic image. The activation maps by the proposed transformers-based *TransSLC* model can remarkably overlay with only the lesion regions, which could signify the presence of lesion type. Finally, we can infer that a transformers-based model would distinguish between important and non-relevant characteristics of skin lesion, as well as learning the appropriate features for each given class.

Table 4. The class-wise performance metrics of the proposed transformers-based, *TransSLC*, model for the seven classes of skin lesion classification in terms of the precision (PR), recall (RE) and F1 score (F1), respectively.

Class type	PR	RE	F1
Class 1 (akiec)	86.00	65.15	74.14
Class 2 (bcc)	78.90	83.50	81.13
Class 3 (bkl)	84.77	75.91	80.10
Class 4 (df)	89.47	73.91	80.95
Class 5 (mel)	79.60	71.75	75.47
Class 6 (nv)	93.70	97.54	95.58
Class 6 (vasc)	84.85	96.55	90.32

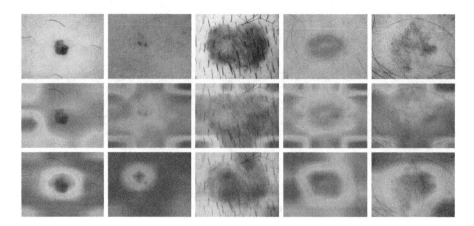

Fig. 4. Visualisation results of the activation maps. For every column, we show an input image, the corresponding activation maps from the outputs of EfficientNet-B7 and the proposed *TransSLC* model.

4   Conclusion

In this paper, we presented *TransSLC*, a transformers-based model able to classify seven types of skin lesions. The proposed method was compared with five popular state-of-the-art CNN-based deep learning models Using the HAM10000 public datasets. Our proposed model achieved the accuracy of 90.22%, precision of 85.33%, recall of 80.62%, and 85.53%, respectively on the test dataset. The proposed model shows the transformers-based model outperforms the traditional CNN-based model to classify different types of skin lesions which can enable new research in this domain. Future work will further explore transformers-based methods performances across other datasets, as well as carrying out cross-datasets evaluation to assess how well the model generalises.

Acknowledgment. This research has been supported by the National Subsea Centre in Robert Gordon University, United Kingdom.

References

1. Bansal, Nidhi, Sridhar, S..: Skin lesion classification using ensemble transfer learning. In: Chen, Joy Iong-Zong., Tavares, João Manuel R. S.., Iliyasu, Abdullah M.., Du, Ke-Lin. (eds.) ICIPCN 2021. LNNS, vol. 300, pp. 557–566. Springer, Cham (2022). https://doi.org/10.1007/978-3-030-84760-9_47
2. Bao, H., Dong, L., Wei, F.: Beit: Bert pre-training of image transformers. arXiv preprint arXiv:2106.08254 (2021)
3. Bissoto, A., Perez, F., Ribeiro, V., Fornaciali, M., Avila, S., Valle, E.: Deep-learning ensembles for skin-lesion segmentation, analysis, classification: Recod titans at ISIC challenge 2018. arXiv preprint arXiv:1808.08480 (2018)

4. Chollet, F.: Xception: deep learning with depthwise separable convolutions. In: Proceedings of the IEEE conference on computer vision and pattern recognition, pp. 1251–1258 (2017)

5. Dang, T., Nguyen, T.T., McCall, J., Elyan, E., Moreno-García, C.F.: Two layer Ensemble of Deep Learning Models for Medical Image Segmentation. ArXiv (2021). http://arxiv.org/abs/2104.04809

6. Dang, T., Nguyen, T.T., Moreno-García, C.F., Elyan, E., McCall, J.: Weighted ensemble of deep learning models based on comprehensive learning particle swarm optimization for medical image segmentation. In: IEEE Congress on Evolutionary Computing, pp. 744–751. IEEE (2021)

7. Dosovitskiy, A., et al.: An image is worth 16x16 words: transformers for image recognition at scale. arXiv preprint arXiv:2010.11929 (2020)

8. Elyan, E., et al.: Computer vision and machine learning for medical image analysis: recent advances, challenges, and way forward. Artificial Intelligence Surgery (2022). https://doi.org/10.20517/ais.2021.15

9. Esteva, A., et al.: Dermatologist-level classification of skin cancer with deep neural networks. Nature **542**, 115–118 (2017)

10. Gessert, N., Nielsen, M., Shaikh, M., Werner, R., Schlaefer, A.: Skin lesion classification using ensembles of multi-resolution efficientnets with meta data. MethodsX **7**, 100864 (2020)

11. He, K., Zhang, X., Ren, S., Sun, J.: Deep residual learning for image recognition. In: Proceedings of the IEEE Conference on Computer Vision and Pattern Recognition, pp. 770–778 (2016)

12. Jones, O., et al.: Dermoscopy for melanoma detection and triage in primary care: a systematic review. BMJ Open **9**(8), e027529 (2019)

13. Kingma, D.P., Ba, J.: Adam: a method for stochastic optimization. arXiv preprint arXiv:1412.6980 (2014)

14. Liu, Z., et al.: Swin transformer: hierarchical vision transformer using shifted windows. In: Proceedings of the IEEE/CVF International Conference on Computer Vision, pp. 10012–10022 (2021)

15. Sarker, M.M.K., et al.: Slsnet: skin lesion segmentation using a lightweight generative adversarial network. Expert Syst. Appl. **183**, 115433 (2021)

16. Sung, H., et al.: Global cancer statistics 2020: Globocan estimates of incidence and mortality worldwide for 36 cancers in 185 countries. CA Can. J. Clin. **71**(3), 209–249 (2021)

17. Szegedy, C., Ioffe, S., Vanhoucke, V., Alemi, A.A.: Inception-v4, inception-resnet and the impact of residual connections on learning. In: Thirty-first AAAI Conference on Artificial Intelligence (2017)

18. Szegedy, C., Vanhoucke, V., Ioffe, S., Shlens, J., Wojna, Z.: Rethinking the inception architecture for computer vision. In: Proceedings of the IEEE Conference on Computer Vision and Pattern Recognition, pp. 2818–2826 (2016)

19. Tan, M., Le, Q.: Efficientnet: Rethinking model scaling for convolutional neural networks. In: International Conference on Machine Learning, pp. 6105–6114. PMLR (2019)

20. Vuttipittayamongkol, P., Elyan, E.: Overlap-based undersampling method for classification of imbalanced medical datasets. In: Maglogiannis, I., Iliadis, L., Pimenidis, E. (eds.) Artificial Intelligence Applications and Innovations, pp. 358–369. Springer, Cham (2020). https://doi.org/10.1007/978-3-030-37734-2_36

21. Vuttipittayamongkol, P., Elyan, E., Petrovski, A.: On the class overlap problem in imbalanced data classification. Knowl.-Based Syst. **212**, 106631 (2021)

22. Yu, L., Chen, H., Dou, Q., Qin, J., Heng, P.A.: Automated melanoma recognition in dermoscopy images via very deep residual networks. IEEE Trans. Med. Imaging **36**, 994–1004 (2017)
23. Zhang, J., Xie, Y., Xia, Y., Shen, C.: Attention residual learning for skin lesion classification. IEEE Trans. Med. Imaging **38**(9), 2092–2103 (2019)

Image Enhancement, Quality Assessment, and Data Privacy

Privacy Preserving and Communication Efficient Information Enhancement for Imbalanced Medical Image Classification

Xiaochuan Li and Yuan Ke[(✉)] [iD]

University of Georgia, Athens, GA 30601, USA
{xiaochuan.li,yuan.ke}@uga.edu

Abstract. Deep learning methods, especially convolutional neural networks, have become more and more popular in medical image classifications. However, training a deep neural network from scratch can be a luxury for many medical image datasets as the process requires a large and well-balanced sample to output satisfactory results. Unlike natural image datasets, medical images are expensive to collect owing to labor and equipment costs. Besides, the class labels in medical image datasets are usually severely imbalanced subject to the availability of patients. Further, aggregating medical images from multiple sources can be challenging due to policy restrictions, privacy concerns, communication costs, and data heterogeneity caused by equipment differences and labeling discrepancies. In this paper, we propose to address these issues with the help of transfer learning and artificial samples created by generative models. Instead of requesting medical images from source data, our method only needs a parsimonious supplement of model parameters pre-trained on the source data. The proposed method preserves the data privacy in the source data and significantly reduces the communication cost. Our study shows transfer learning together with artificial samples can improve the pneumonia classification accuracy on a small but heavily imbalanced chest X-ray image dataset by 11.53% which performs even better than directly augmenting that source data into the training process.

Keywords: Deep learning · Generative models · Medical image classification · Privacy preservation · Transfer learning

1 Introduction

Since a deep Convolutional Neural Network (CNN) architecture won the ImageNet computer vision competition in 2012 [19], deep CNN model gain popularity in almost all computer vision related areas, such as image classification [26], feature extraction [31], face recognition [21], image segmentation [23,37], image understanding [28,30] and many more. Besides aforementioned promising applications, computer-aided diagnosis for medical images with CNN based classification algorithms have attracted intense research interests, see [8,9,12,20,42] and references therein.

© The Author(s), under exclusive license to Springer Nature Switzerland AG 2022
G. Yang et al. (Eds.): MIUA 2022, LNCS 13413, pp. 663–679, 2022.
https://doi.org/10.1007/978-3-031-12053-4_49

Unlike natural images, medical images, such as X-ray images, CT scans, stained tissue sections, and magnetic resonance imaging (MRI) images, have several salient features which may cause additional challenges in their analyzing processes. First, medical images are in general expensive and time-consuming to collect due to equipment availability, materials cost, and human labor expense. Thus, the sample sizes of many medical image datasets are not as large as the datasets we usually have in other computer vision applications. Second, it is common to observe class imbalance in medical image datasets. For example, in the pediatric chest X-ray image dataset we are going to study, the Normal class is much smaller than the Pneumonia class as healthy kids are less likely to visit doctors and take X-ray images. As a result of the first two salient features, training a deep CNN based classification model with randomly initialized weights can be a luxury for many medical image datasets as the process requires a large and well-balanced sample to output satisfactory results. Third, naive augmentation of medical image datasets from multiple sources may not always be a realistic option. On the one hand, the format, size, quality of medical images vary across multiple sources due to differences in equipment models, operation norms, and labeling standards. On the other hand, hospitals and medical institutes are usually not passionate about publishing or sharing their medical image data due to policy restrictions, privacy concerns, and communication issues. Therefore, researchers of medical image classification usually have no or restricted access to additional medical images data sources.

In this paper, we propose a privacy preserving and communication efficient information enhancement procedure for medical image classification. To reflect the salient features discussed above, we study the binary classification for a small and heavily imbalanced pediatric chest X-ray image dataset (target dataset). We assume there exists another X-ray image dataset (source dataset) that we can borrow additional information from. However, we prohibit ourselves from directly accessing the images in the source dataset to respect the privacy preserving concerns. The first component of our procedure is transfer learning. Transfer learning aims to re-use the parameters pre-trained on a large source dataset as the initial weights for the model training on a small target dataset. It allows the model training on the target dataset to have a "warm start", and hence alleviates the data insufficient problem. Existing transfer learning studies for deep CNN models are mainly focused on natural image analysis, where the source model is usually trained on a vast natural image database, such as ImageNet [38]. Recently, transfer learning has been a widely investigated method to improve the performance of various medical image classification applications, such as X-ray [22], MRI [47], skin lesion [14], CT scan [7], and more. However, transferring a deep CNN model pre-trained on a natural image dataset may not provide significant improvement for medical image classification problems, where pathology detection is based on local textures, like local white opaque patches in chest X-rays are signs of pneumonia and consolidation. In this paper, we investigate the transfer learning between two medical image datasets whose domains and class labels can be different. The second component of our procedure is artificial sampling with generative models. Naive data augmentation techniques like duplicating, rotating, flipping, zooming, and cropping of the existing images [5,39,41] are not suitable for medical image datasets as the generated sample are not interpretable. In recent years, generative networks, including AutoEncoder based and Generative Adversarial Networks (GANs) based models, have shown great potential in capturing the underlying distribution of data and generating images mimicking the existing ones [1,34]. In this paper, we explore several popular generative models and create artificial samples to address the class imbalance issue. Both components in our procedure do not require direct access to the medical images in the source dataset. Therefore, our procedure strictly preserves the privacy of the patient in the source dataset. Besides, our procedure is communication efficient as it only requires the transmission of model parameters rather than the raw medical images. The empirical advantage of our procedure is validated by extensive numerical experiments.

The rest of the paper is organized as follows. Section 2 describes the target and source datasets used in this study, and discusses the problem setup. Section 3 introduces the transfer learning technique and the generative models we use in our procedure. Section 4 presents the several experiments to validate our ideas. The empirical performance of several competing models will be carefully analyzed and compare. In Sect. 5, we concludes this paper. We submit the codes to replicate the experiments in this paper to the supplementary material.

2   Data Description and Problem Setup

2.1   Target Dataset

The target dataset is a collection of frontal chest X-ray images of pediatric patients under five years old, which are labeled by professionals in Guangzhou Women and Children's Medical Center, Guangzhou, China [16]. The dataset[1] consists of 5,910 frontal chest X-ray images. Among the X-ray images, 1,576 are labeled as Normal, and 4,334 are labeled as Pneumonia. The major research objective is to develop a computer-aided diagnosis method that can accurately and efficiently classify Normal and Pneumonia pediatric patients using their frontal chest X-ray images.

In this study, we randomly partition the target dataset into three sub-samples for training, validation, and testing. The validation and testing sets are designed to be balanced to evaluate the classification performance, while the training set is intentionally left severely imbalanced. The partition sample sizes are summarize in Table 1.

2.2   Source Dataset

To alleviate the information insufficiency in the target dataset, we introduce a supplement chest X-ray dataset[2] [44] released by the National Institutes of

---

[1] Available at https://data.mendeley.com/datasets/rscbjbr9sj/2.

[2] Available at https://nihcc.app.box.com/v/ChestXray-NIHCC.

Table 1. Target dataset splitting sample sizes.

	Training	Validation	Testing
Normal	800	334	442
Pneumonia	3500	390	444

Health Clinical Center (NIHCC). The NIHCC dataset consists of $112,120$ chest X-ray images collected from more than $30,000$ patients in all age groups, including many with one or more of 14 lung diseases, such as Infiltration, Atelectasis, Effusion, etc. In the dataset, $60,361$ images are labeled as No-Findings which means no lung disease can be diagnosed according to these images. Besides, $30,963$ images are labeled to have only one of the 14 lung diseases, while the others may be labeled by multiple lung diseases. Among the single disease classes, Infiltration, which indicates visible pulmonary infiltrates in the lung area, is the largest class with a class size of $9,547$ images.

In this paper, to match the binary classification problem of interest in the target dataset, we choose a bi-class subset of the NIHCC dataset as our source dataset. To be specific, the source dataset includes all $9,547$ Infiltration images plus $9,547$ No Finding images randomly sampled from the NIHCC dataset.

2.3   Problem Setup

In this paper, we design our experiments to mimic several typical challenges in medical image classification applications. First, the target dataset has a limited sample size which is insufficient to train a deep CNN model from scratch. Second, according to Table 1, the training sample in the target dataset is severely imbalanced as the ratio between Normal and Pneumonia is less than $1/4$. The label imbalance is a salient feature for many X-ray datasets since healthy, asymptomatic, and mild patients may not necessarily take X-ray images to assist their diagnoses. As a result, the performance of deep convolutional neural networks (CNN) on the target dataset is not ideal. For example, the classification accuracy of a VGG-16 [40] model is less than 85%, where nearly one-third of Pneumonia images in the testing set are misclassified to the Normal class. Such a high false negative rate may result in serious negligence and delay in the treatment of pneumonia patients.

According to the data description, there exists a clear domain adaption issue caused by transferring the information from the source dataset to the target dataset. The images in the source dataset are taken over all age groups while the target dataset only contains images of pediatric patients under five years old. In addition, the medical meaning of the disease label in the source dataset (Infiltration) is also different from the one in the target (Pneumonia). In Fig. 1, we list several images in each dataset, where the domain difference is visually recognizable. Therefore, we will show that directly augmenting the source dataset into the training process is not the best strategy to improve the classification accuracy in the target dataset.

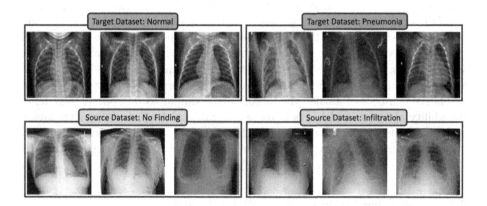

Fig. 1. Sample observations from target and source datasets.

In addition, we consider the scenario that direct access to the images in the source dataset is prohibited, which is, unfortunately, a widely encountered obstacle in medical image studies. Hospitals and medical institutes are usually reluctant to publish or share their medical image data due to policy restrictions and privacy concerns. Recent studies [36,45] have shown that traditional anonymization methods, like removing or shuffling IDs, may not truly preserve the privacy of patients. To avoid the risk of privacy leakage and reduce the communication cost, we propose to let the owner of the source data pre-train a deep CNN model they trust, and only share the trained model parameters to the researchers of the target dataset. In such an information sharing scheme, the privacy of patients is fully preserved and the transmission of gigantic raw medical image datasets is avoided.

3   Methods

3.1   Transfer Learning

In this paper, we first propose transfer learning as a viable solution to overcome the challenges discussed in Sect. 2.3. The intuition of transfer learning is to re-use a model pre-trained on a source dataset to a target dataset with a similar task. We can formulate a popular transfer learning scheme for image classification as follows. Let $\{X_i^s, Y_i^s\}_{i=1}^m$ be a source image dataset, where (X_i^s, Y_i^s) is the ith image and its corresponding class label. We pre-train a deep neural network model on the source dataset. Denote $T(\cdot; \theta^s)$ the trained model parametrized by an augmented coefficients vector θ^s. Then we propose to transfer $T(\cdot; \theta^s)$ to a target dataset $\{X_i^t, Y_i^t\}_{i=1}^n$, such that we predict Y_i^t by $T(X_i^t; \theta^s)$. Several modifications can be made to the transferred model such as layer selection, feature map screen, or model update by treating θ^s as initial estimates. Despite many attempts have been made by statisticians [6,29,43], a unified mathematical explanation to the success of transfer learning is still lacking. Nevertheless, an interesting phenomenon that has been repeatedly discovered in many computer vision studies [4,24,25,33,46]: the feature maps learned by the low-level layers of a CNN model are prone to represent some common visual notions like shapes, edges, geometric symmetry, effects of lighting, which are highly generalizable. On the other hand, feature maps on high-level layers are task-specific and hence can be useful when the target task is similar to the source. In general, the ability of lower-level layers is more general, and that of higher-level layers is more specific to the classification task. Therefore, a CNN model pre-trained on a large source dataset could help the learning for a similar target task with a small dataset through transfer learning.

3.2   Generative Models and Artificial Sample

The core idea behind generative models is to capture the underlying distribution of the input images and generate high-quality artificial samples. To address the class imbalance issue, we propose to boost the minority class with artificial images generated from a distribution learned by generative models. In this paper, we consider two representative types of generative models: Generative Adversarial Networks (GANs) [10] and AutoEncoders [13].

GAN: A GAN model simultaneously trains two neural networks: a generative (G) network and a discriminative (D) network. The two models are trained in an adversarial manner. G is an inverse neural network that takes a vector of random noise $z \sim p_z$ and up-samples it to an artificial image $x_a = G(z)$, which tries to mimic actual data $x \sim p_{data}$ and aims to fool D. In contrast, D is a feed-forward neural network that is trained to distinguish between real images x and artificial images x_a, returning the probability of input image being "true". So it gives us the following minimax optimization problem:

$$\min_{G} \max_{D} \{V(D,G)\} = \mathbb{E}_{x \sim p_{\text{data}}} [\log D(x)] + \mathbb{E}_{z \sim p_z} [\log(1 - D(G(z)))].$$

We train D to maximize $\log(D(x))$ the probability of assigning the correct label to both authentic and artificial images, and train G to minimize $\log(1 - D(G(z)))$ to foul D to commit misclassifications. By competing with D, G is gradually optimized to generate artificial images that are more and more indistinguishable from the authentic ones. In other words, we would expect the empirical distribution of x_a to be close to the population p_{data} if G is successful.

The innovative idea of GAN has motivated a large number of studies. In this paper, we adapt three widely used variations of GAN in our experiments, which are introduced as follows.

Deep Convolutional GAN: Compared to the original GANs that use fully connected layers, Deep Convolutional GANs (DCGAN) utilize convolutional architecture and thus have the ability to generate complicated images [35]. In addition, Batch Normalization [15] is used to make the learning process efficient and stable, and Leaky ReLU [27] is used to prevent gradients from vanishing.

Wasserstein GAN with Gradient Penalty: The optimization of GANs involves training two neural network models in an opposite direction and hence is well known to suffer from instability, mode collapse, and slow convergence [2]. Wasserstein GAN (WGAN) addresses these optimization challenges by using the 1-Wasserstein distance (also known as the Earth-Mover distance) as the loss function, and implementing a weights clipping trick [3]. In a follow-up work [11], the authors improve the training of WGAN by replacing the clipping with a gradient penalty term. The new method, named WGAN_GP, admits loss functions as

$$\mathcal{L}_D^{WGAN\_GP} = -\mathbb{E}_{x \sim p_{\text{data}}} \left[\log D(x) \right]$$
$$+\mathbb{E}_{z \sim p_z} \left[\log D(G(z)) \right] + \lambda \mathbb{E}_{\hat{x} \sim p_{\hat{x}}} \left[\left(\| \nabla D_{\hat{x}}(\hat{x}) \|_2 - 1 \right)^2 \right]$$
$$\mathcal{L}_G^{WGAN\_GP} = -\mathbb{E}_{z \sim p_z} \left[\log D(G(z)) \right],$$

where $\hat{x} = \alpha x + (1 - \alpha)G(z)$, and α is a random number uniformly distributed over the interval $[0, 1]$.

Conditional GAN: Conditional GANs (CGAN) modify the training process of the classical GANs by imposing priors drawn from exogenous information [32]. While training a CGAN model, both the generator and discriminator are conditioned on the exogenous information by concatenating it to the input of the layers. This information can be class labels, text, or data of other types. CGAN allows the generator to synthesize images of a specific class after training the model over images from multiple classes.

AutoEncoder: An AutoEncoder is an unsupervised learning neural network that compresses the underlying distribution in a lower-dimensional latent space [13]. It consists of two parts: Encoder and Decoder. The encoder encodes the input image into the latent space, while the decoder reconstructs the compressed representation to an output image with the same dimension as the input. The system is optimized with reconstruction error between the input and the output, say Mean Squared Error (MSE). The naive AutoEncoder is tailored to reconstruct the input rather than generate a near identically distributed but independent artificial observation. However, there are many variations of AutoEncoder which can be used as generative models.

Variational Autoencoder: One of the popular AutoEncoder based generative models is Variational Autoencoder (VAE), which enforces continuous latent spaces and allows random sampling [18]. Therefore, it can be a helpful technique for generative modeling. Unlike the classic AutoEncoder, VAE aims to compress an input image into a latent vector that follows a constrained multivariate latent distribution, such as multivariate normal. Then, the latent vector is passed to the decoder to reconstruct the image. In addition to the reconstruction loss (e.g. MSE), VAE also penalizes the KL-divergence between the real posterior and the estimated one. Such an architecture design allows us to sample the multivariate latent encoding vector from the constrained distribution and use a decoder to generate artificial images.

4   Experiments and Numerical Results

4.1   Classification Model

In our experiments, we unify X-ray images to a fixed size of 128 × 128 pixels and treat them as single-channel gray-scale images. We use a modified VGG16 [40] model for image classification whose architecture is visualized in Fig. 2. The main body of the architecture uses the convolutional layers of VGG16. An extra convolutional layer is added after the input layer to transform a single-channel gray-scale input into a 3-channel image compatible with the input of VGG16 architecture. The VGG16's fully connected layers have been replaced to produce the binary classification results. The final output is the probability of a specific chest X-ray image having Pneumonia. In the rest of this section, we call the above model the classification model for the simplicity of presentation. The classification models are trained with a batch size of 32 over 30 epochs using Adam optimizer [17] with a learning rate of 0.00002, unless otherwise specified.

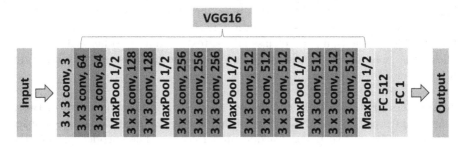

Fig. 2. Architecture of modified VGG16 for classification.

4.2   Training from Scratch on Imbalanced Dataset

First, we follow the sample partition scheme in Table 1, and train and test the classification model on the imbalanced target dataset from scratch. The weights of the classification model are randomly initialized. Notice that, the training sample (4, 300 images) is clearly insufficient to empower the classification model in Fig. 2 who has nearly 19 million trainable parameters. Therefore, during the training over 30 epochs, the model tends to overfit the training set and has an unsatisfactory generalization performance. As a result, the prediction accuracy measured over the 886 testing images is 84.42%. We treat this performance as our baseline, as this baseline model does not receive any information enhancement. The experiments were run on the Google colab Pro+ platform, which has 52 GB RAM and uses K80, T4 and P100 GPUs. It takes 389 s to fit the baseline model.

4.3   Information Enhancement by the Source Dataset

The source and target datasets are different in various aspects. The target dataset is collected and labeled by a hospital in China, which focused on pediatric patients aged under five. The source dataset is augmented by NIHCC from multiple sources, where most patients are adults. Besides, their class labels are of different meanings. To see this point, we use the baseline model trained in Sect. 4.2 to compute the probabilities of the images in the source dataset that belongs to the Pneumonia class. The histogram with smoothed density plots are presented in Fig. 3. Recall that the baseline model is trained to separate Pneumonia labeled X-ray image from the Normal class, and the output probability represents the possibility of an input X-ray image is likely to be labeled as Pneumonia. According to Fig. 3, both No Finding and Infiltration classes in the source dataset have histograms heavily skewed to 1, meaning that most of the images in the source data will be classified to the Pneumonia class, regardless they are labeled as No Finding or Infiltration. Although there is a clear domain difference, we show the source dataset can help improve the prediction of the target dataset by the following two approaches.

Augment No Finding Images to Normal Class: According to the label description in the source data, No Finding indicates that the X-ray image does not exhibit visible characteristics for a lung disease. Therefore, as the target training set is imbalanced and has a gap of 2, 700 images, we randomly sample 2, 700 No Finding images from the source dataset and add them to the Normal class to balance the two classes. Then, a classification model following the architecture in Fig. 2 is trained in a similar manner as described in Sect. 4.2 over the augmented balanced target training dataset. The model performance is measured over the same 886 testing images. To account for the variability, we repeat the random sampling for seven replications. For each replication, we randomly sample 2, 700 No Finding images and add them to the Normal class in the training set On average, the new model improves the prediction accuracy from the baseline model to 90.60%.

Transfer Learning: The experiment in the above section approved that directly borrowing similar images from the source dataset can improve the

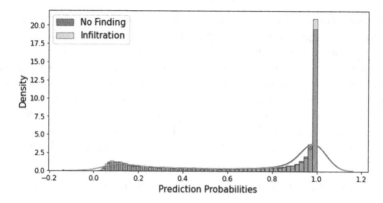

Fig. 3. Histogram and smoothed density plot for Pneumonia probabilities of the images in the source dataset.

prediction accuracy of the small and imbalanced target dataset. However, such a naive data augmentation approach may not always be available in practice due to the various challenges we have discussed in Sect. 2.3. In this experiment, we examine the performance of a transfer learning model where the target task has no direct access to the raw images in the source dataset. Instead, we pre-train the classification model on the source dataset as follows. The source dataset is randomly partitioned into two subsets: 90% for training and 10% for validation. A classification model with the same architecture as in Fig. 2 is trained on the source dataset to do a binary classification between No Finding and Infiltration. The training is over 100 epoch with a batch size of 64. The model with the highest prediction accuracy on the validation set is selected as the source model whose parameters are transferred to the target dataset. Then, we train the classification model on the target dataset and initialize the training with the source model parameters. After fine-tuning the weights over the imbalanced target training set following the same strategy in Sect. 4.2, the prediction accuracy on the target testing set is improved to 89.95%. The prediction accuracy by transfer learning has an increment of 5.53% over the baseline model and is fairly close to the performance of directly adding No Finding images to the target dataset.

Compared to the naive augmentation approach, transfer learning achieves a similar prediction accuracy improvement without transmitting any images from the source dataset. Thus, patients' privacy has been fully preserved. Besides, it is well known that the process of sharing medical images between institutes can be complicated and time-consuming, and the file sizes of high-quality medical images are usually large. The transfer learning approach avoids the transmission of the raw images but only requires a transfer of model parameters which can greatly reduce the communication cost. In our experiment, the file size of the images in the source dataset is over 7.7 GB. In contrast, the parameters of the pre-trained model can be stored and transferred by a single file of size around 200 MB. To sum up, in our experiments, transfer learning is a privacy preserving and communication efficient approach to improve the classification accuracy in a small and imbalanced X-ray image dataset. The performance of transfer learning is comparable to the naive augmentation approach, which directly adding the images in the source dataset to the target task.

4.4   Information Enhancement by Artificial Sample

Next, we consider an alternative information enhancement strategy to address the label imbalance issue in the target dataset that does not require any access to the source dataset. Classical image augmentation techniques that randomly rotate, zoom, or flip the training images are not suitable for medical image analysis as the generated images are often hard to interpret and not independent of the training sample. Instead, we propose to supplement the under-sampled Normal class with artificial images created by generative models. In this experiment, we train DCGAN, WGAN_GP, and VAE over 800 Normal images in the training set. CGAN is trained over 4,300 Normal and Pneumonia images in the training as it allows multi-class data.

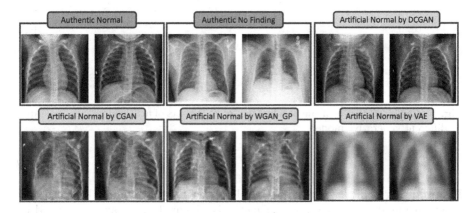

Fig. 4. Authentic images from Normal and No Finding classes, and artificial images generated by different generative models.

DCGAN, WGAN_GP, and CGAN: The three GAN based generative models share similar generator and discriminator architectures. A six-layer CNN generator takes a random noise vector of dimension 100 as input (except for CGAN, which also uses image labels as input), and outputs a single-channel image of size 128×128 pixels. The discriminator (critic for WGAN_GP), a five-layer CNN, takes artificial images generated by the generator and authentic Normal images as inputs, aiming to distinguish artificial images from true ones. The models' weights are randomly initialized and are trained with a batch size of 64 using Adam optimizer. Finally, the generator trained at the 300th epoch is saved to generate artificial images.

VAE: The encoder uses the same architecture as the discriminator for GAN based models, except for the output layer, which outputs two vectors of size 100, representing the means and variances. The decoder has the same architecture as the generator for GAN based models. Also, the VAE model is trained with the same batch size and optimizer. Finally, we save the decoder trained at the 300th epoch to generate artificial images. As we introduced in Sect. 3.2, VAE model uses the mean squared error as the loss function. As a result, VAE tends to "over-smooth" the output images compared with the ones generated by GAN-based models. This is shown in Fig. 4.

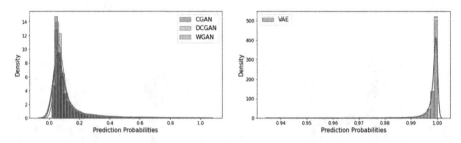

Fig. 5. Prediction results of the baseline model on the sets of artificial images generated by different generative models.

Results: Fig. 4 displays some artificial Norma images generated by the four generative models. Among the four methods, the artificial images generated by DCGAN are visually most clear and closest to the authentic Normal images. The images generated by VAE are blurred and not visually informative. We also evaluate the quality of artificial normal images by computing their prediction probabilities to be labeled as Pneumonia. Ideally, we expect a good artificial sample of the Normal class should have prediction probabilities concentrated around 0. Figure 5 visualizes these prediction probabilities for the artificial Normal samples generated by the four generative models. As we can see, three GAN based models work as expected as the empirical distributions of their artificial samples perform similarly to the true Normal images in the classification model. Further, the artificial sample generated by DCGAN has the smallest standard deviation. In contrast, the prediction probabilities of the artificial Normal images generated by VAE are concentrated around 1 which is not ideal.

According to the analysis above, we propose to use DCGAN to fill the sample size gap in two classes in the training set. In other words, we use DCGAN to generate 2,700 artificial images for the Normal class, such that the training sample is equally contributed by two classes. Similarly, the training process has been repeated seven times. Evaluating the models over the target testing set, we have the lowest prediction accuracy of 90.07%, and the highest one is 97.18%. The average prediction accuracy is 94.49%.

4.5 Privacy Preserving and Communication Efficient Information Enhancement Procedure

In previous experiments, we have separately demonstrated that transfer learning and artificial sample can improve chest X-ray image classification, preserve patients' privacy, and reduce or avoid communication costs. In this experiment, we combine these two ideas to form our privacy preserving and communication efficient information enhancement procedure, which can be illustrated by the following 3 steps: (1) Augment the minority class with 2,700 artificial images generated by DCGAN, so that the two classes are balanced. (2) Initialize the weights of the classification model by the parameters transferred from the model pre-trained on the source dataset. (3) Fine-tune all layers over the balanced target training set. We repeat this procedure 7 times to address the variability in random sampling. The prediction accuracy over the target testing set ranges from 93.34% to 97.63% with an average 95.95%, which improves the baseline model by 11.53%.

4.6 Comparison and Analysis of Experiment Results

Table 2 summarises and compares the prediction results of the five classification models over the 886 testing images. The five models, as introduced in Sects. 4.2–4.5, apply different transfer learning and data augmentation strategies.

Table 2. Summary of 5 models. There are three data augmentation (DA methods (DA) choices: no data augmentation (No); add No Finding to Normal (No Finding), and artificial sample (DCGAN). TL indicates if we use transfer learning. AUC stands for the area covered under a receiver operating characteristic curve. FP and FN are average number of false positives and false negatives over 7 replications.

DA	TL	Accuracy	AUC	FP	FN
No	No	0.8442	0.9829	1	137
No finding	No	0.9060	0.9859	1	82.29
No	Yes	0.8995	0.9857	4	85
DCGAN	No	0.9449	0.9927	3	45.86
DCGAN	Yes	**0.9595**	**0.9935**	4	31.86

The first row in Table 2 represents the baseline model which uses neither transfer learning nor data augmentation. The baseline model has a classification accuracy of 84.42%. Besides, baseline commits one false-positive (misclassify Normal to Pneumonia) and 137 false-negative (misclassify Pneumonia to Normal). The performance of the baseline model is not ideal as nearly one-third of Pneumonia pictures in the testing set are mistakenly diagnosed as Normal. Ignoring pneumonia patients as healthy people may delay their treatments and cause severe consequences in practice. The best model among the 5 utilizes both transfer learning and data augmentation with an artificial sample generated by DCGAN. It achieves a classification accuracy of 95.95% and reduces the average false-negative cases to 31.86.

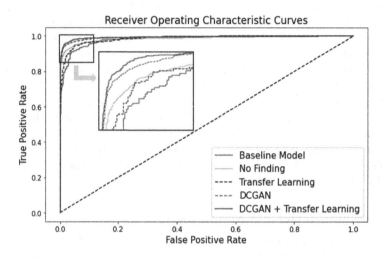

Fig. 6. ROC curves of five classification models over the target testing images.

Further, we plot Receiver Operating Characteristic (ROC) curves for the five models in Fig. 6. The areas under the curve (AUC) values are reported in Table 2. As we can see, the ROC curve of the baseline model is at the bottom, and hence the baseline model has the smallest AUC value. On the other hand, the ROC curve of the model that utilizes both transfer learning and an artificial sample is at the top, and hence it has the largest AUC value. The model that only utilizes transfer learning and the model that did data augmented by adding No Finding images to the training set has a similar performance. The model that did data augmented with an artificial sample generated by DCGAN ranks second among the 5.

5   Conclusion

In this paper, we study computer-aided diagnosis for a small and imbalanced pediatric chest X-ray image dataset. Training a deep CNN based classification model on this dataset from scratch does not work well as a lot of pneumonia kids can be misdiagnosed as normal. To improve the classification performance, we propose a privacy preserving and communication efficient procedure to enhance the information in model training on the target dataset. Additional information comes from a source dataset that contains X-ray images of patients over all age groups and labeled by 14 lung diseases. So, there is a clear domain adaption and target shift between the source and target datasets. Further, we prohibit ourselves from directly accessing the images in the source dataset to reflect the privacy concerns widely arising in medical data sharing. Our procedure has two key components: transfer learning and artificial sampling by generative models. The former one transfers the parameters of a deep CNN based model pre-trained on the source dataset to the target dataset as the initial weights. Transfer learning gives the training on the target dataset a warm start and improves the prediction accuracy by around 6%. The second component, artificial sampling, aims to supplement the minority class with artificial images generated from a distribution close to the minority population. The minority population is learned by several GAN based methods. The best generative model alone can increase another 6% to the prediction accuracy. Our procedure effectively combines these two components and can improve the prediction accuracy by more than 10%. Our procedure strictly preserves the privacy of the patients as no medical images in the source dataset will be released to the target dataset user. Our procedure is also communication efficient as it only requires the transmission of model parameters instead of the raw medical images. We expect our procedure to have broad impacts on a wide range of medical image classification problems where the researchers may suffer from insufficient sample size, imbalanced classes, and restricted access to additional data sources. We also aim to extend the research presented in this paper to multiple future directions. For example, we plan to work on the situations when data comes from multiple sources, the data has more than two class labels, or there is a strong correlation among classes.

References

1. Albahli, S., Rauf, H.T., Arif, M., Nafis, M.T., Algosaibi, A.: Identification of thoracic diseases by exploiting deep neural networks. Neural Netw. **5**, 6 (2021)
2. Arjovsky, M., Bottou, L.: Towards principled methods for training generative adversarial networks (2017)
3. Arjovsky, M., Chintala, S., Bottou, L.: Wasserstein GAN (2017)
4. Azizpour, H., Razavian, A.S., Sullivan, J., Maki, A., Carlsson, S.: Factors of transferability for a generic convnet representation. IEEE Trans. Pattern Anal. Mach. Intell. **38**(9), 1790–1802 (2015)
5. Buda, M., Maki, A., Mazurowski, M.A.: A systematic study of the class imbalance problem in convolutional neural networks. Neural Netw. **106**, 249–259 (2018)
6. Cai, T.T., Wei, H.: Transfer learning for nonparametric classification: minimax rate and adaptive classifier. Ann. Statist. **49**(1), 100–128 (2021)
7. Chowdhury, N.I., Smith, T.L., Chandra, R.K., Turner, J.H.: Automated classification of osteomeatal complex inflammation on computed tomography using convolutional neural networks. In: International forum of Allergy & Rhinology, vol. 9, pp. 46–52. Wiley Online Library (2019)
8. Gao, J., Jiang, Q., Zhou, B., Chen, D.: Convolutional neural networks for computer-aided detection or diagnosis in medical image analysis: an overview. Math. Biosci. Eng. **16**(6), 6536–6561 (2019)

9. Giger, M.L., Suzuki, K.: Computer-aided diagnosis. In: Biomedical Information Technology, pp. 359-XXII. Elsevier (2008)

10. Goodfellow, I.J., et al.: Generative adversarial networks (2014)

11. Gulrajani, I., Ahmed, F., Arjovsky, M., Dumoulin, V., Courville, A.: Improved training of Wasserstein GANs (2017)

12. Halalli, B., Makandar, A.: Computer aided diagnosis-medical image analysis techniques. In: Breast Imaging, p. 85 (2018)

13. Hinton, G.E., Salakhutdinov, R.R.: Reducing the dimensionality of data with neural networks. Science **313**(5786), 504–507 (2006)

14. Hosny, K.M., Kassem, M.A., Foaud, M.M.: Classification of skin lesions using transfer learning and augmentation with Alex-net. PLOS ONE **14**(5), e0217293 (2019)

15. Ioffe, S., Szegedy, C.: Batch normalization: accelerating deep network training by reducing internal covariate shift (2015)

16. Kermany, D.S., Zhang, K., Goldbaum, M.H.: Labeled optical coherence tomography (OCT) and chest x-ray images for classification (2018)

17. Kingma, D.P., Ba, J.: Adam: A method for stochastic optimization (2017)

18. Kingma, D.P., Welling, M.: Auto-encoding variational bayes (2014)

19. Krizhevsky, A., Sutskever, I., Hinton, G.E.: ImageNet classification with deep convolutional neural networks. In: Advances in Neural Information Processing Systems, pp. 1097–1105 (2012)

20. Krizhevsky, A., Sutskever, I., Hinton, G.E.: ImageNet classification with deep convolutional neural networks. In: Pereira, F., Burges, C.J.C., Bottou, L., Weinberger, K.Q. (eds.) Advances in Neural Information Processing Systems. Curran Associates, Inc. (2012)

21. Lawrence, S., Giles, C.L., Tsoi, A.C., Back, A.D.: Face recognition: a convolutional neural-network approach. IEEE Trans. Neural Netw. **8**(1), 98–113 (1997)

22. Lee, K.S., Jung, S.K., Ryu, J.J., Shin, S.W., Choi, J.: Evaluation of transfer learning with deep convolutional neural networks for screening osteoporosis in dental panoramic radiographs. J. Clin. Med. **9**(2), 392 (2020)

23. Long, J., Shelhamer, E., Darrell, T.: Fully convolutional networks for semantic segmentation. In: Proceedings of the IEEE Conference on Computer Vision and Pattern Recognition, pp. 3431–3440 (2015)

24. Long, M., Cao, Y., Wang, J., Jordan, M.: Learning transferable features with deep adaptation networks. In: Proceedings of the 32nd International Conference on International Conference on Machine Learning (ICML), vol. 13, pp. 97–105 (2015)

25. Long, M., Zhu, H., Wang, J., Jordan, M.I.: Unsupervised domain adaptation with residual transfer networks. In: Advances in Neural Information Processing Systems, pp. 136–144 (2016)

26. Lu, D., Weng, Q.: A survey of image classification methods and techniques for improving classification performance. Int. J. Remote Sens. **28**(5), 823–870 (2007)

27. Maas, A.L., Hannun, A.Y., Ng, A.Y.: Rectifier nonlinearities improve neural network acoustic models. In: ICML Workshop on Deep Learning for Audio, Speech and Language Processing (2013)

28. Mahendran, A., Vedaldi, A.: Understanding deep image representations by inverting them. In: Proceedings of the IEEE Conference on Computer Vision and Pattern Recognition, pp. 5188–5196 (2015)

29. Maity, S., Sun, Y., Banerjee, M.: Minimax optimal approaches to the label shift problem. arXiv preprint arXiv:2003.10443 (2020)

30. Maninis, K.-K., Pont-Tuset, J., Arbeláez, P., Van Gool, L.: Deep retinal image understanding. In: Ourselin, S., Joskowicz, L., Sabuncu, M.R., Unal, G., Wells, W. (eds.) MICCAI 2016. LNCS, vol. 9901, pp. 140–148. Springer, Cham (2016). https://doi.org/10.1007/978-3-319-46723-8_17

31. Mao, J., Jain, A.K.: Artificial neural networks for feature extraction and multivariate data projection. IEEE Trans. Neural Netw. **6**(2), 296–317 (1995)

32. Mirza, M., Osindero, S.: Conditional generative adversarial nets (2014)

33. Mou, L., et al.: How transferable are neural networks in NLP applications? arXiv preprint arXiv:1603.06111 (2016)

34. Qin, X., Bui, F.M., Nguyen, H.H.: Learning from an imbalanced and limited dataset and an application to medical imaging. In: 2019 IEEE Pacific Rim Conference on Communications, Computers and Signal Processing (PACRIM), pp. 1–6. IEEE (2019)

35. Radford, A., Metz, L., Chintala, S.: Unsupervised representation learning with deep convolutional generative adversarial networks (2016)

36. Rocher, L., Hendrickx, J.M., De Montjoye, Y.A.: Estimating the success of re-identifications in incomplete datasets using generative models. Nat. Commun. **10**(1), 1–9 (2019)

37. Ronneberger, O., Fischer, P., Brox, T.: U-Net: convolutional networks for biomedical image segmentation. In: Navab, N., Hornegger, J., Wells, W.M., Frangi, A.F. (eds.) MICCAI 2015. LNCS, vol. 9351, pp. 234–241. Springer, Cham (2015). https://doi.org/10.1007/978-3-319-24574-4_28

38. Russakovsky, O., et al.: ImageNet large scale visual recognition challenge. Int. J. Comput. Vision **115**(3), 211–252 (2015). https://doi.org/10.1007/s11263-015-0816-y

39. Sharma, H., Jain, J.S., Bansal, P., Gupta, S.: Feature extraction and classification of chest x-ray images using CNN to detect pneumonia. In: 2020 10th International Conference on Cloud Computing, Data Science & Engineering (Confluence), pp. 227–231. IEEE (2020)

40. Simonyan, K., Zisserman, A.: Very deep convolutional networks for large-scale image recognition (2015)

41. Stephen, O., Sain, M., Maduh, U.J., Jeong, D.U.: An efficient deep learning approach to pneumonia classification in healthcare. J. Healthcare Eng. 2019 (2019)

42. Stoitsis, J., et al.: Computer aided diagnosis based on medical image processing and artificial intelligence methods. Nuclear Instrum. Methods Phys. Res. Sect. A: Accel. Spectrom. Detect. Assoc. Equip. **569**(2), 591–595 (2006)

43. Tian, Y., Feng, Y.: Transfer learning under high-dimensional generalized linear models. arXiv preprint arXiv:2105.14328 (2021)

44. Wang, X., Peng, Y., Lu, L., Lu, Z., Bagheri, M., Summers, R.M.: ChestX-ray8: Hospital-scale chest x-ray database and benchmarks on weakly-supervised classification and localization of common thorax diseases. In: 2017 IEEE Conference on Computer Vision and Pattern Recognition (CVPR), July 2017

45. White, T., Blok, E., Calhoun, V.D.: Data sharing and privacy issues in neuroimaging research: opportunities, obstacles, challenges, and monsters under the bed. Human Brain Map. **43**(1), 278–291 (2022)

46. Yosinski, J., Clune, J., Bengio, Y., Lipson, H.: How transferable are features in deep neural networks? In: Advances in neural information processing systems (NIPS), pp. 3320–3328 (2014)

47. Zhang, C., et al.: A visual encoding model based on deep neural networks and transfer learning for brain activity measured by functional magnetic resonance imaging. J. Neurosci. Methods **325**, 108318 (2019)

Contrastive Pretraining for Echocardiography Segmentation with Limited Data

Mohamed Saeed$^{(\boxtimes)}$, Rand Muhtaseb , and Mohammad Yaqub

Mohamed bin Zayed University of Artificial Intelligence, Abu Dhabi, UAE
{mohamed.saeed,rand.muhtaseb,mohammad.yaqub}@mbzuai.ac.ae

Abstract. Contrastive learning has proven useful in many applications where access to labelled data is limited. The lack of annotated data is particularly problematic in medical image segmentation as it is difficult to have clinical experts manually annotate large volumes of data such as cardiac structures in ultrasound images of the heart. In this paper, We propose a self supervised contrastive learning method to segment the left ventricle from echocardiography when limited annotated images exist. Furthermore, we study the effect of contrastive pretraining on two well-known segmentation networks, UNet and DeepLabV3. Our results show that contrastive pretraining helps improve the performance on left ventricle segmentation, particularly when annotated data is scarce. We show how to achieve comparable results to state-of-the-art fully supervised algorithms when we train our models in a self-supervised fashion followed by fine-tuning on just 5% of the data. We show that our solution outperforms what is currently published on a large public dataset (EchoNet-Dynamic) achieving a Dice score of 0.9252. We also compare the performance of our solution on another smaller dataset (CAMUS) to demonstrate the generalizability of our proposed solution. The code is available at (https://github.com/BioMedIA-MBZUAI/contrastive-echo).

Keywords: Contrastive learning · Segmentation · Echocardiography · Ultrasound · SimCLR · BYOL · Self-supervised

1 Introduction

Echocardiography is a valuable diagnostic tool in cardiovascular disease as it can rapidly locate the presence of some abnormalities within the heart. This involves the quantification of heart structures such as the left ventricle. However, there is a lot of room for error in this process due to factors such as operator variability, patient's characteristics e.g. high body mass index, or low image quality compared to other imaging modalities [1].

M. Saeed and R. Muhtaseb—Contributed equally.

© The Author(s), under exclusive license to Springer Nature Switzerland AG 2022
G. Yang et al. (Eds.): MIUA 2022, LNCS 13413, pp. 680–691, 2022.
https://doi.org/10.1007/978-3-031-12053-4_50

Deep learning solutions can help automate the annotation process, but they are limited by the quantity and quality of labelled training data which can be difficult or expensive to obtain. For the problem of left ventricle segmentation in particular, previous works have had some success in detecting and quantifying heart abnormalities but there is room for improvement, potentially with the acquisition of more data [12]. Since annotation of the raw data is cumbersome, self-supervised learning helps make use of unlabelled data that does not require input from clinical experts. In similar tasks such as view classification of echocardiography images, contrastive pretraining on unlabelled data showed impressive improvements in results [3]. This indicates that there is a potential benefit for segmentation problems given that the features learned for classification should not be too dissimilar.

2   Related Work

In this section, we aim to give a brief revisit to important concepts which our paper investigates. We believe this is important to make our work clearer to a wide range of audiences.

2.1   Segmentation Networks

We investigate two well-known segmentation networks, UNet [17] and DeepLabV3 [5], which have demonstrated huge success in many segmentation problems and this is why we have chosen them. UNet is a fully convolutional network that consists of a contracting path (encoder) and an expanding path (decoder) in a U-shaped architecture. Features are extracted by the contracting path and then upsampled gradually by the expanding path, with skip connections between corresponding layers in the contracting and expanding paths. The second network is DeepLabV3 which has initially shown great performance on semantic segmentation of natural images. It introduces an Atrous Spatial Pyramid Pooling (ASPP) module [4] that utilizes atrous (dilated) convolutions at different rates to solve the problem of object scale variations in addition to expanding the receptive field while keeping the feature maps' spatial dimensions. ASPP consists of multiple dilated convolutions at different rates stacked in parallel followed by a concatenation of the outputs of said convolutions. Features from the encoder are passed through the ASPP module before upsampling back to the original resolution. In the following subsection, we review the use of these two networks in echocardiographic left ventricle segmentation.

2.2   Ventricular Segmentation

One example pertaining to the use of deep learning in ventricular segmentation made use of a UNet to segment the left ventricle in more than 1500 images from ultrasound videos of 100 patients [18]. The network was trained on the output of another segmentation algorithm that used a Kalman filter. Expert annotation was only available for 52 of the images, so the dataset was expanded by automatically annotating more examples using the Kalman filter based algorithm. Consequently, the UNet trained on this data was able to achieve a Dice score of 0.87, outperforming the previous algorithm.

Later work by [14] proposed a modification to the UNet architecture by combining it with a feature pyramid network. This was trained for left ventricle segmentation on the publicly available Cardiac Acquisitions for Multi-structure Ultrasound Segmentation (CAMUS) dataset [13] which consists of two- and four-chamber ultrasound images from 500 patients. Testing was then done on an external dataset of 137 four-chamber view images. Results showed that this architecture outperformed other state-of-the-art methods, achieving a Dice score of 0.953 on the test set.

Recent work proposed ResDUnet [2], which is a new deep learning method based on UNet, that integrates cascaded dilated convolution to extract features at difference scales, and deploys an improved version of the residual blocks instead of the standard UNet blocks to ease the training task. ResDUnet outperforms state-of-the-art methods on the CAMUS dataset with a Dice score of 0.951 compared to 0.939 with a standard UNet.

Furthermore, [16] attempted the same task, training on their large publicly available EchoNet-Dynamic dataset [15], containing 20,060 annotated images from 10,030 patients. A DeepLabV3 [5] network was chosen for this task and obtained a Dice score of 0.9211.

2.3   Contrastive Learning

Whilst there are multiple published contrastive learning algorithms in the literature, we have chosen to investigate two commonly used ones, namely SimCLR and BYOL.

SimCLR. SimCLR [7] is a popular framework for self-supervised contrastive learning, used to learn representations from unlabelled data. In essence, SimCLR creates two augmented versions of every input image. For each minibatch, one pair of augmented images coming from the same original image is chosen as the positive pair. All other pairs coming from different input images are considered negative pairs. The aim then becomes to maximize the agreement within the positive pair while simultaneously maximizing the disagreement between the positive pair and all the negative pairs. The framework begins with a base encoder which is a typical feature extractor such as a ResNet-50 [10]. A projection head is added on top of this to map the encoded representation to a new space in which a contrastive loss based on cosine similarity is applied. Figure 1 gives an overall view of how SimCLR works.

BYOL. Meanwhile, Bootstrap Your Own Latent (BYOL) [9] uses a similar contrastive approach to SimCLR but without negative pairs, and for this reason we chose it to compare the effect of this difference on the contrastive pretraining. It always uses a single pair of images which are transformed versions of

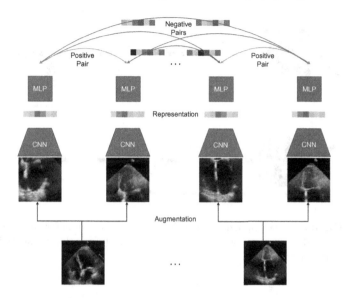

Fig. 1. SimCLR framework applied to the echo images. The goal of the contrastive loss is to attract the positive pairs by maximizing their agreement, while repelling the negative pairs by maximizing their disagreement.

the same input. The framework allows representation learning by making use of two networks (called the *online* and *target* network). The online network is trained to predict the output of the target network. Meanwhile, the target network's weights are updated with just an exponential moving average of the online network. The two networks are mostly identical, having an encoder (usually a ResNet-50), followed by a projection head which linearly projects the encoder's features onto a different space. The only difference is that the online network has an added predictor head, which is simply another linear projection. Figure 2 outlines the architecture. During training, the online network learns by attempting to maximize the agreement between the outputs from the two networks by minimizing a contrastive loss which simplifies to twice the negative of the cosine similarity between the two networks' outputs.

3 Methods

In this paper, we developed a solution to segment the left ventricle in echocardiographic images that is based on self-supervised contrastive learning. We argue why this could be a better approach than full supervision. This section describes the used data, the setup and the conducted experiments.

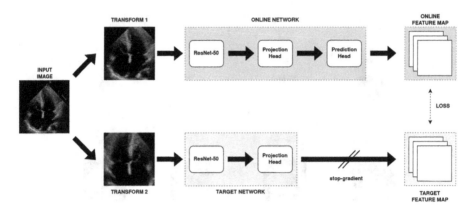

Fig. 2. BYOL framework applied to the echo images. The aim is for the two networks to eventually produce a common representation given differently augmented versions of the same input image.

3.1 Datasets

EchoNet-Dynamic. The EchoNet-Dynamic dataset [15] consists of 10,036 videos of apical four-chamber (A4C) view for patients who had an echocardiography between 2016 and 2018 at Stanford Health Care. Each video (encoded in RGB) consists of a sequence of 112×112 2D images extracted from the Digital Imaging and Communications In Medicine (DICOM) file and labeled with the corresponding left ventricle tracing, ejection fraction (EF), volume at end-systole (ES) and volume at end-diastole (ED) by expert sonographers. For each video, two frames (ES and ED) are annotated with manual segmentation. To the best of our knowledge this is currently the largest publicly available dataset for left ventricle segmentation, making it ideal for our contrastive task, given that it has a large amount of both labelled and unlabelled data.

CAMUS. The Cardiac Acquisitions for Multi-structure Ultrasound Segmentation (CAMUS) dataset [13] contains scans of 500 patients who underwent echocardiography at the University Hospital of St Etienne in France. Each patient's data is labelled with the corresponding left ventricle ejection fraction (EF) and volumes at end-systole (ES) and end-diastole (ED). Annotations include tracings of the left ventricle endocardium, myocardium and the left atrium (LA) for both apical two-chamber (A2C) and apical four-chamber (A4C) views of the heart. Training and testing sets consist of 450 annotated and 50 unannotated videos, respectively. We found that 50 patients are missing from the training set, resulting in data of only 400 patients for the training set. We have chosen this small dataset to investigate the importance of contrastive learning while experimenting with limited data.

3.2 Experimental Setup

We experiment with SimCLR and BYOL pretraining *(pretext task)* for left ventricle segmentation on the EchoNet-Dynamic and CAMUS datasets. First, we pretrained a DeepLabV3 backbone (ResNet-50 with atrous convolutions [5]) and a UNet backbone (original UNet encoder) with both SimCLR and BYOL. For the pretraining, unlabelled frames from the datasets are used. Thereafter, the pretrained backbones were used to train the segmentation networks, DeepLabV3 and UNet *(downstream task)*. Figure 3 outlines the overall experiment setup. The downstream segmentation experiments were done with 100%, 50% 25% and 5% of the available labelled data. In addition, we compare the SimCLR and BYOL pretrained backbones to randomly initialized and ImageNet pretrained (fully supervised) ones to see if self-supervision is beneficial. For evaluation, the Dice similarity coefficient (DSC) is used as a metric.

$$DSC = 2 * \frac{intersection}{intersection + union} \tag{1}$$

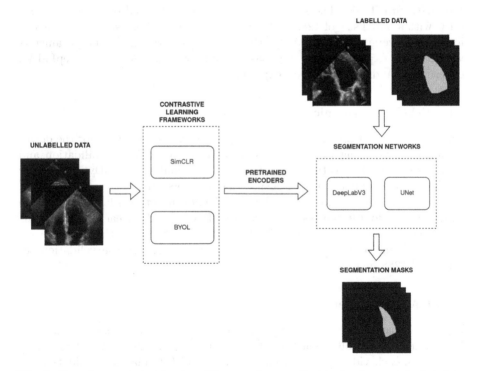

Fig. 3. Overall experimental setup: The encoders are first trained on unlabelled data using SimCLR and BYOL. The pretrained weights are then loaded into DeepLabV3 and UNet to train on labelled data for the task of left ventricle segmentation.

All images were resized to 224 × 224 pixels for both the pretext and downstream tasks, since we keep the same setup used in SimCLR [7]. Bilinear interpolation was used for the input images and nearest neighbour interpolation was used for the masks.

Pretext Task. All backbones were pretrained for 300 epochs on two NVIDIA A6000 GPUs. DeepLabV3 backbones were trained with a batch size of 128 (64 per device) and UNet backbones were trained with a batch size of 256 (128 per device). An Adam optimizer was used for the pretraining with a learning rate of 1e−3 for SimCLR and 0.2 for BYOL. These were chosen experimentally. For both SimCLR and BYOL, we use the augmentation strategy proposed in the SimCLR paper to see if these contrastive learning algorithms work out of the box for ventricular segmentation. The augmentations consist of random resized cropping (scales = [0.08, 1.0], aspect ratios = [0.75, 1.33]), color distortions (jittering with brightness = 0.8, contrast = 0.8, saturation = 0.8 and hue = 0.2), Gaussian blurring (kernel size = 23) and random horizontal flipping, following the default settings in [7].

Downstream Task. The segmentation tasks were trained on a single A6000 GPU with a batch size of 128. A Madgrad [8] optimizer was used because it was found to converge better and faster than other optimizers and hyperparameters were selected experimentally. The base learning rate was 1e−4 for DeepLabV3 experiments and 1e−5 for UNet experiments.

3.3   EchoNet-Dynamic Experiments

The two annotated ES and ED frames from every video were used for the downstream task, resulting in 14,920 images for training, 2,576 for validation and 2,552 for testing. This is the same setup as the original EchoNet-Dynamic paper to allow a fair comparison and ensure that the sets are separated by patient. Meanwhile, for pretraining, the unlabelled frames in between ES and ED were used. One random frame between ES and ED was used for each patient. This was done to avoid having frames that are too similar to each other. As a result, the pretraining training set consisted of 7460 images, and the validation set contained 1288 images.

3.4   CAMUS Experiments

For the downstream task, the 400 available *annotated* videos were split into 300 for training, 50 for validation and 50 for testing. Two frames (ES and ED) were taken from each video, leading to a training set of 600 images, a validation set of 100 images and a testing set of 100 images. For pretraining, a random frame (not including ES or ED frame) was taken from each of the 300 training videos. In addition, to create a validation set, a random frame from each of the videos in the *unannotated* CAMUS test set was used. These are samples from the held out CAMUS test set that were not used anywhere else in our experiments. Overall, the pretraining task used 300 training images and 50 validation images.

Table 1. Summary of experiments conducted on the EchoNet-Dynamic dataset with different fractions of data for the downstream task.

No.	Pretraining	Network	Dice (SD) 100%	Dice (SD) 50%	Dice (SD) 25%	Dice (SD) 5%
1	–	DeepLabV3	0.9204 (0.0483)	0.9164 (0.0490)	0.9090 (0.0559)	0.8920 (0.0718)
2	ImageNet	DeepLabV3	0.9229 (0.0461)	0.9175 (0.0605)	0.9142 (0.0625)	0.8968 (0.0778)
3	SimCLR	DeepLabV3	**0.9252** (0.0476)	**0.9242** (0.0452)	**0.9190** (0.0509)	**0.9125** (0.0548)
4	BYOL	DeepLabV3	0.9209 (0.0636)	0.9042 (0.1027)	0.8938 (0.0906)	0.8816 (0.1111)
5	–	UNet	0.9151 (0.0557)	0.9100 (0.0583)	0.9046 (0.0675)	0.8915 (0.0814)
6	SimCLR	UNet	0.9185 (0.0493)	0.9157 (0.0571)	0.9078 (0.0619)	0.9048 (0.0653)
7	BYOL	UNet	0.9070 (0.0718)	0.8959 (0.0775)	0.8768 (0.0997)	0.8318 (0.1284)

Table 2. Summary of experiments conducted on the CAMUS dataset with different fractions of data for the downstream task.

No.	Pretraining	Network	Dice (SD) 100%	Dice (SD) 50%	Dice (SD) 25%	Dice (SD) 5%
1	–	DeepLabV3	0.9095 (0.0272)	0.8941 (0.0369)	0.8731 (0.0646)	0.7803 (0.1517)
2	ImageNet	DeepLabV3	0.9286 (0.0250)	0.9217 (0.0420)	0.9120 (0.0456)	0.8539 (0.0930)
3	SimCLR (C)	DeepLabV3	0.9105 (0.0509)	0.8862 (0.0606)	0.8851 (0.0569)	0.8450 (0.1109)
4	SimCLR (E)	DeepLabV3	**0.9311** (0.0424)	0.9219 (0.0543)	0.9234 (0.0554)	**0.9123** (0.0490)
5	BYOL (C)	DeepLabV3	0.8189 (0.0777)	0.6202 (0.1275)	0.5727 (0.1263)	0.0084 (0.0269)
6	BYOL (E)	DeepLabV3	0.8347 (0.1303)	0.7552 (0.1318)	0.6321 (0.1363)	0.5729 (0.2316)
7	–	UNet	0.9125 (0.0263)	0.8921 (0.0415)	0.8883 (0.0506)	0.8006 (0.1864)
8	SimCLR (C)	UNet	0.9102 (0.0498)	0.8965 (0.0663)	0.8597 (0.1031)	0.8013 (0.1102)
9	SimCLR (E)	UNet	0.9296 (0.0506)	**0.9224** (0.0798)	**0.9248** (0.0596)	0.9077 (0.0574)
10	BYOL (C)	UNet	0.8162 (0.1304)	0.7810 (0.1263)	0.7063 (0.1417)	0.0520 (0.0907)
11	BYOL (E)	UNet	0.8824 (0.0746)	0.8366 (0.1073)	0.7984 (0.1418)	0.7256 (0.1720)

(E): Pretrained on EchoNet-Dynamic data, (C): Pretrained on CAMUS data

4   Results

Tables 1 and 2 show the quantitative results of the experiments that were conducted, for the EchoNet-Dynamic and CAMUS datasets respectively. Qualitative results from selected models are also shown in Fig. 4.

4.1   EchoNet-Dynamic

As Table 1 shows, our proposed self supervised method which uses DeepLabV3 with a SimCLR pretrained backbone outperformed all other methods (including the EchoNet-Dynamic [15] baseline - 0.9211 Dice), regardless of the amount of data. In fact, with only 5% of the data, our method produces results (0.9125 Dice) that are close to fully supervised training with all of the available data (0.9229 Dice). Furthermore, with the UNet architecture, SimCLR was found to be beneficial although the improvement was minor. We also found ImageNet pretraining to perform better than random initialization. However, BYOL did not have any significant benefit over ImageNet pretraining or even random initialization. Finally, DeepLabV3 performed better than UNet in the segmentation task.

Easy Case   Difficult Case

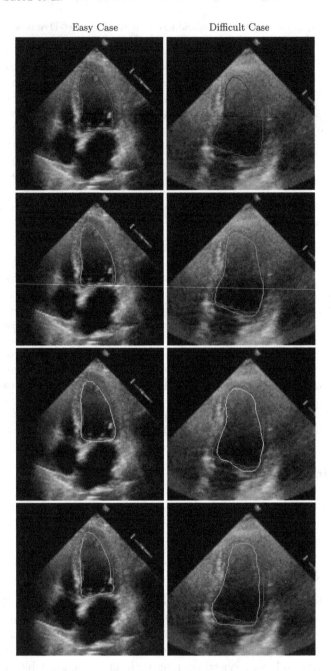

Fig. 4. Qualitative results using an ImageNet backbone with 100% data (blue), a Sim-CLR backbone with 100% data (green), a SimCLR backbone with 5% data (yellow) with DeepLabV3 and a BYOL backbone with 100% data (orange) with DeepLabV3 on the EchoNet-Dynamic dataset for two cases. **Right:** Case where predictions are close to the ground truth (red). **Left:** More difficult case where predictions have more discrepancy. (Color figure online)

4.2   CAMUS

Results on the CAMUS dataset are shown in Table 2. When pretrained on CAMUS, SimCLR backbones (0.9105 Dice) were found to perform worse than ImageNet pretrained backbones (0.9286 Dice). However, SimCLR backbones pretrained on the EchoNet-Dynamic dataset showed better performance (0.9311 Dice), exceeding both random initialization and ImageNet pretrained backbones. This was the case for both DeepLabV3 and UNet. Meanwhile, BYOL backbones continued to show worse performance on the CAMUS dataset as well, especially when pretrained on the CAMUS dataset itself. When finetuned on only 5% of the data, these backbones showed extremely poor performance, failing the downstream segmentation task. Pretraining with EchoNet-Dynamic improved the BYOL backbones, which achieved a Dice score of up to 0.7256 when finetuned on 5% of the data and up to 0.8824 when finetuned on 100% of the data.

5   Discussion

The experiments have shown that our proposed self supervised method with SimCLR outperforms the same method which uses BYOL when it comes to pretraining backbones for left ventricle echocardiography segmentation. We also noticed that BYOL is less stable than SimCLR. However, the purpose of the experiments was to study the use of these models with minimal changes and see how they perform out-of-the-box, without extensive tuning. This may be part of the reason why BYOL has shown suboptimal performance.

The main difference between the two self supervised frameworks is the fact that BYOL only uses positive pairs, trying to maximize agreement between two augmented versions of a single image (positive pair) and hence find a common representation for them. Conversely, SimCLR tries to maximize agreement between the differently augmented versions of an image (positive pair) while also maximizing disagreement between that image and augmented versions of other images (negative pairs). Meanwhile, BYOL's contrastive learning is implicit and indirectly dependent on the differences between the original images. In our experiments, we use a random frame from each video to introduce some dissimilarity between the original images, however it seems like this is not as effective as the transformations that SimCLR uses.

Furthermore, contrastive learning requires large amounts of data to produce good results, which is why pretraining on the CAMUS dataset with only 400 samples was not beneficial (rows 3 & 6 in Table 2). Hence, it makes sense for EchoNet-Dynamic pretraining to be more beneficial and its ability to work with a different dataset shows that generalizable features were learned from the pretraining (rows 4 & 9 in Table 2).

Apart from contrastive learning, the experiments also suggest that DeepLabV3 is more effective than UNet for echocardiography segmentation (compare rows 3 & 6 in Table 1). In general, what makes DeepLabV3 perform well is its ASPP module that captures multi-scale representations of high level features extracted by the encoder, making it more resistant to changes in object scales (in this case the size of heart structures), which do vary depending on the heart cycle and the anatomy of the patient's heart.

6 Conclusion

While contrastive learning is an open research problem, we conclude from our experiments that vanilla SimCLR pretraining could lead to an improvement in cardiac ultrasound segmentation, especially when annotated data for the downstream task is limited. However, it is crucial to pretrain on a large enough dataset to provide good results. Further experimentation could lead to a better understanding of contrastive learning frameworks in the context of cardiac ultrasound imaging. For example, there is room for improvement on the augmentation strategy used in the SimCLR paper because it targeted natural images not medical images. Optimizing the choice of augmentations might lead to significant improvements and is a good direction for future work in this area. Furthermore, it was out of the scope of this paper to investigate different UNet or DeeplabV3 variations such as nnUNet [11] and DeeplabV3+ [6] and hence this may be a good research direction to investigate. Additionally, both SimCLR and BYOL are sensitive to batch sizes and require very large batch sizes for optimal performance. Regardless, our work has shown that SimCLR does work with minimal changes and moderate resources.

References

1. Alsharqi, M., Woodward, W., Mumith, J., Markham, D., Upton, R., Leeson, P.: Artificial intelligence and echocardiography. Echo Res. Pract. **5**(4), R115–R125 (2018)
2. Amer, A., Ye, X., Janan, F.: ResDUnet: a deep learning-based left ventricle segmentation method for echocardiography. IEEE Access **9**, 159755–159763 (2021). https://doi.org/10.1109/ACCESS.2021.3122256
3. Chartsias, A., et al.: Contrastive learning for view classification of echocardiograms. In: Noble, J.A., Aylward, S., Grimwood, A., Min, Z., Lee, S.-L., Hu, Y. (eds.) ASMUS 2021. LNCS, vol. 12967, pp. 149–158. Springer, Cham (2021). https://doi.org/10.1007/978-3-030-87583-1_15
4. Chen, L.C., Papandreou, G., Kokkinos, I., Murphy, K., Yuille, A.: DeepLab: semantic image segmentation with deep convolutional nets, atrous convolution, and fully connected CRFs. IEEE Trans. Pattern Anal. Mach. Intell. **40**(4), 834–848 (2016). https://doi.org/10.1109/TPAMI.2017.2699184
5. Chen, L.C., Papandreou, G., Schroff, F., Adam, H.: Rethinking atrous convolution for semantic image segmentation. arXiv preprint arXiv:1706.05587 (2017)
6. Chen, L.-C., Zhu, Y., Papandreou, G., Schroff, F., Adam, H.: Encoder-decoder with atrous separable convolution for semantic image segmentation. In: Ferrari, V., Hebert, M., Sminchisescu, C., Weiss, Y. (eds.) ECCV 2018. LNCS, vol. 11211, pp. 833–851. Springer, Cham (2018). https://doi.org/10.1007/978-3-030-01234-2_49
7. Chen, T., Kornblith, S., Norouzi, M., Hinton, G.: A simple framework for contrastive learning of visual representations. In: International Conference on Machine Learning, pp. 1597–1607. PMLR (2020)

8. Defazio, A., Jelassi, S.: Adaptivity without compromise: a momentumized, adaptive, dual averaged gradient method for stochastic optimization. arXiv preprint arXiv:2101.11075 (2021)
9. Grill, J.B., et al.: Bootstrap your own latent: a new approach to self-supervised learning. arXiv preprint arXiv:2006.07733 (2020)
10. He, K., Zhang, X., Ren, S., Sun, J.: Deep residual learning for image recognition. In: Proceedings of the IEEE Conference on Computer Vision and Pattern Recognition, pp. 770–778 (2016)
11. Isensee, F., Jaeger, P.F., Kohl, S.A., Petersen, J., Maier-Hein, K.H.: nnU-Net: a self-configuring method for deep learning-based biomedical image segmentation. Nat. Methods 18(2), 203–211 (2021)
12. Kusunose, K., Haga, A., Abe, T., Sata, M.: Utilization of artificial intelligence in echocardiography. Circ. J. 83(8), 1623–1629 (2019)
13. Leclerc, S., et al.: Deep learning for segmentation using an open large-scale dataset in 2D echocardiography. IEEE Trans. Med. Imaging 38(9), 2198–2210 (2019)
14. Moradi, S., et al.: MFP-Unet: a novel deep learning based approach for left ventricle segmentation in echocardiography. Physica Med. 67, 58–69 (2019)
15. Ouyang, D., et al.: Echonet-dynamic: a large new cardiac motion video data resource for medical machine learning. In: NeurIPS ML4H Workshop, Vancouver, BC, Canada (2019)
16. Ouyang, D., et al.: Video-based AI for beat-to-beat assessment of cardiac function. Nature 580(7802), 252–256 (2020)
17. Ronneberger, O., Fischer, P., Brox, T.: U-Net: convolutional networks for biomedical image segmentation. In: Navab, N., Hornegger, J., Wells, W.M., Frangi, A.F. (eds.) MICCAI 2015. LNCS, vol. 9351, pp. 234–241. Springer, Cham (2015). https://doi.org/10.1007/978-3-319-24574-4_28
18. Smistad, E., Østvik, A., et al.: 2D left ventricle segmentation using deep learning. In: 2017 IEEE International Ultrasonics Symposium (IUS), pp. 1–4. IEEE (2017)

High-Quality 4D-CBCT Imaging from Single Routine Scan

Huihui Li[1], Pengfei Yang[2], Xin Ge[1], and Tianye Niu[1,2(✉)]

[1] Shenzhen Bay Laboratory, Shenzhen, Guangdong, China
niuty@szbl.ac.cn
[2] Zhejiang University, Hangzhou, Zhejiang, China

Abstract. The 4D-CBCT imaging from single routine scan can be used to address the respiratory-induced artifacts in image-guided radiation therapy. The sparse projections in each breathing phase degrade the image quality of 4D-CBCT. In radiotherapy, the CBCT scans are usually performed in multi-factions, which could be applied as the prior information to improve the image quality of 4D-CBCT images. We propose a novel method to obtain high-quality 4D-CBCT images from a routine scan in patients by utilizing multi-fraction projections. The multi-fraction projections are sorted according to the location of the lung diaphragm before being reconstructed to phase-sorted data. Oriented subsets simultaneous algebraic reconstruction technique (OS-SART) algorithm is used to reconstruct the intermediate phase-sorted data. The multi-phase and multi-fraction intermediate CBCT images are further used to estimate the deformable vector field (DVF) among breathing phases and fractions using the deformable image registration method. We propose a motion-compensated OS-SART approach to compensate the motion error among different breathing phases and fractions in the iterative reconstruction process. Results show that our method using multi-fraction projections significantly outperforms single-fraction based method in lung cancer patient studies. The proposed method enables a practical way for high-quality 4D-CBCT imaging from a single routine scan by using multi-fraction projections as prior.

Keywords: 4D cone beam CT · Multi-fraction projections · Motion compensation · Oriented subsets simultaneous algebraic reconstruction technique (OS-SART)

1 Introduction

Cone-beam computed tomography (CBCT) is developed as an image guidance tool to achieve accurate target localization during treatment, such as interventional surgery and radiation therapy [1]. The high-definition detector pixel used in CBCT allows for high spatial resolution imaging. However, due to its open-gantry geometry, the data acquisition time is much longer compared with multi-detector CT. For example, the typical scanning time for CBCT is about one minute, covering up to 20 human breathing cycles.

H. Li and P. Yang—Co-first authors.

G. Yang et al. (Eds.): MIUA 2022, LNCS 13413, pp. 692–702, 2022.
https://doi.org/10.1007/978-3-031-12053-4_51

Therefore, the image quality of the CBCT scan is severely degraded by the respiratory-induced motions. Even in the immobile state, respiratory movement constitutes the primary internal organ motion. The movement of organs makes a significant impact on the outcome of radiation therapy, which delivers a high level of radiation dose to the tumor site. The organ motion may reduce the initial planning dose to the target position while increasing radiation damage to normal tissues, especially in modern stereotactic body radiation therapy (SBRT). SBRT is a cancer treatment scheme that delivers a large amount of radiation dose to the tumor in a few single fractions while minimizing damage to healthy tissue. It requires image guidance techniques including CBCT that identifies the exact 3D location of the target to ensure the precise radiation dose delivery.

To compensate for the organ motion in CT imaging, four-dimensional (4D) technology has been developed by sorting acquired projection data into different phases according to the amplitude of the respiratory signal, which is usually defined as the signal of a motion-tracking device. The sorted projection data is used to reconstruct the CBCT images within each phase. The phase measurement techniques can be divided into two categories: invasive and non-invasive methods.

Invasive measurement methods insert fiducial markers into the body to track the movement of a specific organ. For example, gold particles are inserted into the body of a lung carcinoma patient to identify the location of the tumor after x-ray exposure [2, 3]. Invasive measurements directly locate the tumor while causing additional harm to the patient. Non-invasive measurements use a surrogate marker to monitor respiratory motion. A typical marker is the patient skin surface. Examples include the Real-time Position Management system (RPM, Varian Medical Systems, Palo Alto, CA) and the Vision RT system [4]. The other commonly used surrogate is the diaphragm. The diaphragm position in CBCT imaging can be obtained directly from the projection images. It is thus used in 4D CBCT respiratory phase-sorting, for example, the Amsterdam Shroud (A-S) method [5]. Currently, the majority of on-board CBCT scanners in radiation therapy do not include motion capture equipment. Consequently, the diaphragm measurements are used by researchers to sort projections into different phases, enabling the phase-sorting of projections in routine CBCT scans without additional sensors [5].

When CBCT projection data incorporate breathing phase information, 4D CBCT images can be reconstructed using phase-sorted projections acquired in a routine CBCT scan. Due to the limited number of projections and their non-equiangular distribution, 4D CBCT images reconstructed from phase-sorted projections in routine CBCT scans exhibit severely streaking and blurry artifacts. Multiple rotation cycles or slowing down the rotation speed in 4D CBCT scanning can improve image quality at the expense of increased imaging dose and scan time [6]. By slowing down the rotation speed, more projections are acquired in a single scan, increasing the number of projections in each breath phase accordingly. Prior knowledge-based and motion compensated reconstruction methods have been applied to suppress these artifacts in previous work.

The prior knowledge-based methods reconstruct CBCT images mainly from under-sampled projections within each phase. In this scheme, an iterative reconstruction framework with various regularization terms is used to incorporate prior knowledge into reconstruction. For example, the 4D CBCT iterative reconstruction framework has been combined with spatial-temporal constraints to take advantage of the spatiotemporal coherence of the patient anatomy in 4D images, such as nonlocal temporal means [7], spatial-temporal total-variation (TV) [8], and spatial-temporal tensor framelet [9]. Advanced algorithms, such as the prior image constrained compression sensing technique (PICCS) [10], have been developed to integrate the routine scanned CBCT images, reconstructed using all the acquired projection data, into the reconstruction framework. Over-regularization in these methods may misrepresent the region of the moving object [11].

Unlike the prior knowledge-based methods, which apply under-sampled projections in phase-sorted reconstruction, the motion-compensated methods incorporate all the projections for each phase-sorted reconstruction using a motion compensation scheme. Motion-compensated reconstruction strategies that use all the data acquired in a single routine scan are critical in obtaining high-quality 4D images, considering the limited number of projections within each phase. The motion-compensated reconstruction strategies aim to compensate for the breathing motion by estimating deformation vector fields (DVFs) within an iterative reconstruction framework [12].

Due to the naive assumption of regular breathing or image homogeneity, the previous two types of methods fail to depict clear patient anatomy in routine scanning conditions. The dose delivery in SBRT is usually performed within several fractions, usually in 1 to 10 fractions[13]. Due to the short treatment period, there are few changes on patient anatomy during the SBRT. The CBCT scans in the multi-fractions share the same anatomy but deformed internal organs. By compensating the deformation among the CBCT images within different fractions, the images in former fractions scan can be applied as the prior information to improve the image quality of CBCT images in current fraction.

In this study, we propose a novel method to obtain high-quality 4D-CBCT images from a routine scan in patients by utilizing multi-fraction projections. The breathing amplitude information is derived directly from the original projections to enable phase-sorting without additional sensors. The projections in multi-fractions are divided into different groups according to the breathing amplitude information. The ordered-subset simultaneous algebraic reconstruction (OS-SART) approach is applied to generate the initial phase-sorted image in each fraction. Then the initial images are used to generate DVF among different breathing groups and fractions using deformable registration approach. We propose a motion compensated OS-SART approach to reconstruct 4D-CBCT images in current fraction using the projections and DVFs from prior fractions. The proposed multi-fraction projections assisted motion-compensated OS-SART method is denoted as 'MFPMO' method for simplicity.

2 Materials and Methods

A. Workflow

Figure 1 depicts the workflow of the proposed MFPMO method. As shown in Fig. 1 (a), the measured projections acquired in a routine free-breathing 3D CBCT scan in n fractions are first respectively sorted into k groups according to the magnitude of the breathing motion at the diaphragm location in the acquired projection, resulting in a total of m groups of projections. The sorted projections are then reconstructed to generate the gated initial 4D CBCT images using OS-SART. The deformable image registration approach is used to estimate the DVFs among different respiratory periods and fractions from initial images. Then the phase-sorted projections and the estimated DVFs are used as the input of the motion-compensated iterative reconstruction. The scheme of motion compensated iterative reconstruction approach is shown in Fig. 1 (b). The projections in all the m phases are iteratively used to reconstruct the CBCT images in the h-th group. To update the image in the h-th group from the i-th group projection, the estimated DVF (i to h) is used to deform the image difference of the i-th group to that of the h-th group. The image difference in the i-th group is calculated using the backward projection operation on the difference between the virtual projections of the current group image and measured projections in the i-th group. The projections are generated using forward projection operation on the CBCT images in the related group. The CBCT images in the i-th phase are deformed from the images in the h-th phase using corresponding DVF (h to i). The iterative process is repeated over all k respiratory period to generate the final high-quality 4D CBCT images in current fraction.

B. Projection Breath-Sorting

The diaphragm location in x-ray projection is used to sort projections into different phases without additional sensors [14]. The flowchart of the proposed breath-sorting is shown in Fig. 2. Each projection is transformed using a logarithmic operation and first-order differentiation to increase the contrast between lung and liver. The contrast-enhanced projections are summed along the lateral detector direction to eliminate the fluctuation of the diaphragm locations on projections due to the view-angle variation within the scan for phase signal extraction. Each summed 1D vector is placed sequentially into a 2D matrix with the coordinates of rotation angle (i.e., data acquisition time) and the spatial position of the detector. The region of interest in the 2D matrix which covers the diaphragm region is used for breath signal extraction. The 2D matrix is firstly enhanced using the Hessian-based multiscale filtering operation. Then the breath curve is segmented from the enhanced image by a threshold method. A moving-average low-pass filter with a window width of five points is applied to smooth the motion signal. In this work, the breathing movement is divided into five groups according to the amplitude of diaphragm in the in-hale and ex-hale period. Accordingly, the projections in each fraction are sorted into five groups. The histogram normalization approach is also used to equal the number of projections in each group.

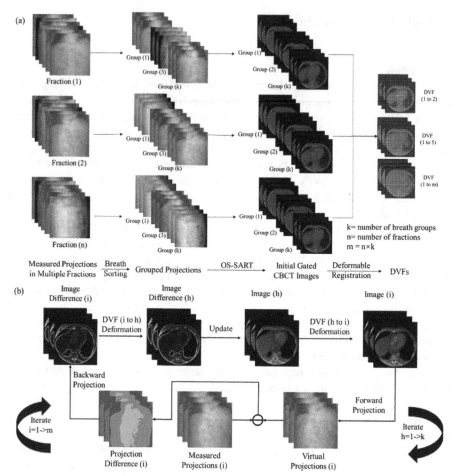

Fig. 1. The workflow of the proposed MPMP method. (a) the scheme of estimating DVFs among CBCT images in different breath period and fractions. (b) the scheme of motion compensated iterative reconstruction.

C. Initial Image Reconstruction and DVF Estimation

The OS-SART method is chosen in the proposed framework to reconstruct initial gated CBCT images due to its high computational efficiency when using the ordered subset strategy. The demons deformable image registration method is used to acquire the DVF within each group from the initial gated CBCT image within multiple fractions.

When the number of fractions is n, the projections in n fraction are sorted into $5n$ groups. Accordingly, $5n-1$ pairs of DVFs are derived from the $5n$ initial images by registering one to the other $5n-1$ for each of the five sets in the latest fraction. The DVFs are then applied to compensate for motion in the forward and backward projection processes within the iterative reconstruction.

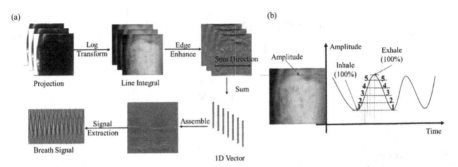

Fig. 2. (a) The workflow of breath signal extraction from projections. (b) The breath-sorting technique for projection assignment. The 1st and 6th phases represent end-inhalation and end-exhalation, respectively.

D. Motion Compensated Iterative Reconstruction

The basis for projection grouping, referred as ordered subset generation in the OS-SART algorithm, can be set as each respiratory phase to which the projections belong in the 4D mode. The goal of the proposed motion-compensated OS-SART algorithm is to solve the following equation:

$$A_k D_{o \to k}(x_o) = p^k, (i \in 1 \to m; o \in 1 \to 5), \tag{1}$$

where p^k denotes the line integral of the k-th group. x_o is the CBCT image in the o-th group. $D_{o \to k}$ represents the deformation operator that deforms from x_o to x_k. A_k is the projection operator in the k-th group. $A_k = \left(R_{ij}^k \right)$ is an $N_k \times M$ matrix, where N_k and M are the number of pixels in p^k and x_o, respectively. m is the total number of projection groups. The updating scheme of the proposed motion-compensated OS-SART is modified from OS-SART [15] and summarized in Eq. (2). x_o is the reconstructed image in the o-th group. x_o^l is the intermediate image at the l-th iteration. λ_n is the relaxation parameter for updating x_o. λ_n is initially set as one and decreased with a scale factor of 0.99 within each iteration. V is the diagonal weighting matrix for the forward projection, the entry of which is defined as the j-th element of A_k. W_k is the weighting matrix for backward projection and defined as the diagonal with the i-th entry of A_k [16]. $D_{o \to k}$ and

$D_{k\to o}$ are the deformation operators from the o-th to the k-th group image and inverse conversion, respectively.

$$\begin{cases} x_o^{l+1} = x_o^l + \lambda_n V_k^{-1} D_{k\to o}\left(A_k^T\left(W_k\left(p^k - A_k D_{o\to k}\left(x_o^l\right)\right)\right)\right) \\ V_k = diag\left\{ \sum_{i=1}^{n_k} R_{i1}^k, \sum_{i=1}^{n_k} R_{i2}^k, \ldots, \sum_{i=1}^{n_k} R_{im}^k \right\} \\ W_k = diag\left\{ \frac{1}{\sum_{j=1}^m R_{1j}^k}, \frac{1}{\sum_{j=1}^m R_{1j}^k}, \ldots, \frac{1}{\sum_{j=1}^m R_{1j}^k} \right\} \\ k = 1 \to m \\ l = 1 \to I \\ i = 1 \to N_k \\ j = 1 \to M \end{cases} \quad (2)$$

E. Evaluation

The proposed method is evaluated on patient datasets. To assess the capability of the proposed method, a set of CBCT projections from a patient with lung cancer who received 4-fraction routine CBCT scan and SBRT at our institution are used. During the CBCT scan, a total of 2095 projections is acquired in this dataset. Since no images are available as ground-truth to quantitatively evaluate the reconstructed image quality, planning CT (pCT) images of this patient are deformed to the 3rd group of CBCT images [29]. The deformed pCT images and 3D-FDK-reconstructed CBCT images serve as reference images in the comparison of organs and anatomy on the CBCT images.

The geometry of the Zhongneng On-Board Imager (OBI) CBCT system on the radiation therapy machine as shown in Table 1.

Table 1. The geometry of the Zhongneng system.

Scan protocol	
Scan mode	Full-fan
Source to detector distance	1560 mm
Source to rotation axis distance	1000 mm
Detector offset	1000 mm
Detector dimension	704 × 704
Reconstruction image size	512 × 512 × 512
Reconstruction voxel size	0.54 × 0.54 × 0.54
Number of views	523
Rotation	circular, 360°

The reconstructed image quality of the MFPMO method is compared with that using standard FDK, OS-SART, and motion-compensated OS-SART using single-fraction projection (MCOSSF) methods which is conventional motion-compensated 4D CBCT reconstruction model. As no ground truth is available for the clinical dataset, we evaluated the similarity between the histograms from CBCT images using different approach and the deformed pCT in the 3rd group.

F. Patient Study

As no ground truth is available in the patient study, the CBCT images reconstructed with 3D-FDK are used as the reference for bone and gas pockets in the abdomen which is less sensitive to the breathing motion. The deformed pCT images are included using the DVFs estimated from MSD-GAN processed images as the reference image for liver and kidney regions. Figure 3 shows the results reconstructed using different methods in the patient studies. Using a limited number of projections, the phase-sorted FDK approach generates CBCT images with strong streaking artifacts while preserving patient anatomy, as shown in the first row of Fig. 3. The OS-SART approach performs better than the FDK method. Nevertheless, it is prone to over-smoothing issues in the reconstructed images, as shown in the third row. The MCOSSP method presents more clear anatomy and image texture than the FDK and OS-SART methods. Nevertheless, the spine structure is not accurately visible in MSD-GAN processed images when compared with the true structure in CBCT images reconstructed using the 3D-FDK method, as pointed out by a red arrow in Fig. 3. The deformed pCT has clear organ boundaries.

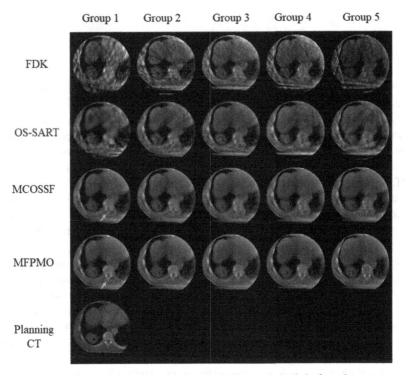

Fig. 3. Results of reconstructed images using different methods in five-phase groups.

Nevertheless, in the gas pocket region of the intestine, the deformed pCT is not accurate due to the different scanning times with CBCT images, as pointed out using a red arrow in Fig. 3. The proposed method achieves superior image quality as well as more accurate anatomy and image details. It produces CBCT images with image quality comparable with the deformed pCT images and presents accurate patient anatomy. The proposed method thus enables the 4D-CBCT imaging from a single routine scan in the clinic. Figure 4 shows the histograms for reconstructed image using different methods. It is indicated that the histogram using MFPMO method is more similar to the real pCT's histogram.

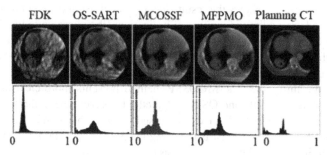

Fig. 4. Histograms for reconstructed image using different methods

3 Discussions

Improving the image quality of 4D CBCT is essential to facilitate the tracking and delineation of tumor/organ, calculation of treatment dose accumulation, and adaptive radiation therapy. In this study, a novel 4D CBCT imaging method from a single routine scan with multiple-fraction projections using a motion-compensated ordered-subset reconstruction framework is proposed. To improve motion compensation accuracy, the DVF applied in the proposed method is estimated using images reconstructed by OS-SART. The proposed method is evaluated using patient CBCT datasets. Improvement of the final reconstructed image quality is achieved using the proposed method compared with those using traditional OS-SART and FDK algorithms. The use of projections in former fractions as prior further improved the image quality than that only using the projections in single fraction.

We used the cone-beam CT projection of the pre-scan of the same patient to enhance the image quality of the current split-scan cone-beam CT. Here, our assumption is that the patient's body structure did not produce significant changes during the time of these scans. However, when certain body structures of the patient, such as tumors, appear to regress significantly with treatment, the introduction of projections from previous fractions can instead affect the observation of these areas. Therefore, the present method is suitable for scenarios where the scan interval is short and the patient's body structure does not change significantly. In addition, this study shows the improvement in reconstructed image quality brought by the introduction of projections from previous fractional scans through qualitative analysis on patient data only. We are conducting further modality experiments to quantitatively evaluate the improvement of the present method. Furthermore, MFPMO takes more times in computing than the MCOSSF. We will do more experiments in the future.

4   Conclusions

We propose a novel method named MFPMO to obtain high-quality 4D-CBCT images from a routine scan in patients by utilizing multi-fraction projections. Breath signal is extracted from projections. OS-SART method is chosen to reconstruct initial gated CBCT images. Furthermore, the updating scheme of the proposed motion-compensated OS-SART is modified from OS-SART and the deformation operators from one group image to another image were used. Our method using multi-fraction projections significantly outperforms single-fraction based method in lung cancer patient studies.

References

1. Goyal, S., Kataria, T.: Image guidance in radiation therapy: techniques and applications. Radiol. Res. Pract., 705604 (2014)
2. Harada, T., et al.: Real-time tumor-tracking radiation therapy for lung carcinoma by the aid of insertion of a gold marker using bronchofiberscopy. Cancer **95**, 1720–1727 (2002)
3. Harada, K., et al.: Evaluation of the motion of lung tumors during stereotactic body radiation therapy (SBRT) with four-dimensional computed tomography (4DCT) using real-time tumor-tracking radiotherapy system (RTRT). Physica Med. **32**(2), 305–311 (2016)
4. McClelland, J., et al.: Inter-fraction variations in respiratory motion models. Phys. Med. Biol. **56**, 251–272 (2011)
5. Chao, M., et al.: Robust breathing signal extraction from cone beam CT projections based on adaptive and global optimization techniques. Phys. Med. Biol. **61**(8), 3109–3126 (2016)
6. Chen, M., et al.: Motion-compensated mega-voltage cone beam CT using the deformation derived directly from 2D projection images. IEEE Trans. Med. Imaging **32**(8), 1365–1375 (2013)
7. Jia, X., et al.: Four-dimensional cone beam CT reconstruction and enhancement using a temporal nonlocal means method. Med. Phys. **39**(9), 5592–5602 (2012)
8. Choi, K., et al.: Enhancement of four-dimensional cone-beam computed tomography by compressed sensing with Bregman iteration. J. Xray Sci. Technol. **21**(2), 177–192 (2013)
9. Gao, H., et al.: 4D cone beam CT via spatiotemporal tensor framelet. Med. Phys. **39**(11), 6943–6946 (2012)
10. Qi, Z., Chen, G.H.: Extraction of tumor motion trajectories using PICCS-4DCBCT: a validation study. Med. Phys. **38**(10), 5530–5538 (2011)
11. Chee, G., et al.: McSART: an iterative model-based, motion-compensated SART algorithm for CBCT reconstruction. Phys. Med. Biol. **64**(9), 095013 (2019)
12. Brehm, M., et al.: Self-adapting cyclic registration for motion-compensated cone-beam CT in image-guided radiation therapy. Med. Phys. **39**(12), 7603–7618 (2012)
13. Hazelaar, C., et al.: Verifying tumor position during stereotactic body radiation therapy delivery using (limited-arc) cone beam computed tomography imaging. Radiother. Oncol. **123**(3), 355–362 (2017)
14. Vergalasova, I., Cai, J., Yin, F.F.: A novel technique for markerless, self-sorted 4D-CBCT: feasibility study. Med. Phys. **39**(3), 1442–1451 (2012)

15. Qiu, W., et al.: Evaluating iterative algebraic algorithms in terms of convergence and image quality for cone beam CT. Comput. Methods Programs Biomed. **109**(3), 313–322 (2013)
16. Kak, A.C., Slaney, M., Wang, G.: Principles of computerized tomographic imaging. Med. Phys. **29**(1), 107 (2002)

Non-iterative Blind Deblurring of Digital Microscope Images with Spatially Varying Blur

Furkan Kaynar[1]([✉]) [iD], Peter Geißler[2] [iD], Laurent Demaret[3] [iD],
Tamara Seybold[4], and Walter Stechele[5] [iD]

[1] Chair of Media Technology, Munich Institute of Robotics and Machine Intelligence, TU München, Arcisstr. 21 and Georg-Brauchle-Ring 60, Munich, Germany
furkan.kaynar@tum.de

[2] Munich Surgical Imaging, Türkenstr. 89, Munich, Germany
pgeissler@munichimaging.de

[3] Hochschule München, Dachauer Straße 98b, Munich, Germany
laurent.demaret@hm.edu

[4] ARRI Cine Technik, Herbert-Bayer-Str. 10, Munich, Germany
tseybold@arri.de

[5] Chair of Integrated Systems, TU München, Theresienstr. 90, Munich, Germany
http://www.ce.cit.tum.de/en/lmt/home/
http://www.munichimaging.de
http://www.me.hm.edu
http://www.arri.de
http://www.ce.cit.tum.de/en/lis/home

Abstract. One of the main limiting factors of image quality in surgical microscopy is of physical nature: resolution is limited by diffraction effects. The digitalisation of surgical microscopy allows computational solutions to partially compensate for this limitation of the involved optics. An inherent characteristic of microscope optics is that it is diffraction-limited which leads to blurred images of objects that do not lie in the (often very narrow) focus plane. Digital deblurring techniques can correct this during the surgical operation, however the point spread function is not constant spatially, making the problem complicated and extremely ill-posed. Most blind deblurring algorithms formulate an iterative solution to estimate the latent sharp image, which is not appropriate for processing high-resolution, high frame rate videos in real-time conditions. We propose a novel single-pass non-iterative blind deblurring method which estimates the spatially varying point spread function by evaluating structural details locally and performing deblurring only at pixels with significant structural information, avoiding noise amplification and decreasing computational cost. The quantitative and qualitative experiments showed the effectiveness and robustness of our method, indi-

---

F. Kaynar—This work was conducted as a Master Thesis at Arnold & Richter Cine Technik GmbH & Co. Betriebs KG, ARRI Medical GmbH and the Chair of Integrated Systems, TU München.

G. Yang et al. (Eds.): MIUA 2022, LNCS 13413, pp. 703–718, 2022.
https://doi.org/10.1007/978-3-031-12053-4_52

cating the promising nature of image enhancement for microscopy-based surgical operations.

Keywords: Blind deblurring · Image restoration · Digital surgical microscopy · Medical image enhancement

1   Introduction

One of the main challenges of digital microscopy is to obtain images which have simultaneously low noise and a high resolution. For a diffraction limited surgical microscope system like the ARRISCOPE developed at Munich Surgical Imaging and Arnold and Richter Cine Technik, the effective width of the PSF is typically larger than the pixel sensor. This results in a loss of fine details and microscope images which aren't as sharp as desired, even if they lie in the focal image plane.

The shallow depth of field causes objects to appear unsharp on the image as soon as they slightly deviate from the focal image plane. The dependency of the blurring kernel on the 3D distance between the objects and the lens makes the modelling of the local PSFs and the design of appropriate deblurring methods complex.

The main advantage of digital microscopes is to enable real-time processing to adaptively deblur the image. The design of the new deblurring method introduced in this work is driven by these properties:

Adaptiveness: The solution should be adaptive and valid for images with varying sharpness, contrast and brightness.
Spatially Selective Deblurring: The deblurring algorithm should focus on areas close to the focus plane as the surgeon is mainly interested in these regions.
Real-time compatibility: The algorithms should be as parallelizable as possible, hence allowing real-time application.

2   Related Work

Non-blind deconvolution often relies on a preliminary calibration procedure to obtain an accurate model of the shift-invariant PSF. The PSF can be estimated using images of point-like targets with system specific diffraction models [14], [9], or by adapting traditional knife-edge (or slanted edge) techniques to digital devices as done by Reichenbach et al. [11]. In the absence of precise knowledge of the PSF, a joint estimation of the unknown image and of the blurring kernel is required. This results in a severely ill-posed inverse problem called blind deconvolution, which often admits multiple solutions. In surgical microscopy, the relevant anatomy is often not situated on a single plane: the narrow depth of field common to most microscopes, thus generates a strong defocus for the parts of the scene situated away from the focal object plane, resulting in an optical blur which depends on the distance between object and microscope, hence changing spatially in the scene. Furthermore this spatial variation depends on the object and is therefore not constant over time in general, which makes it impossible to perform a pre-calibration. This leads to a new problem, the estimation of a spatially varying PSF which is extremely ill-posed. This problem has received some attention recently, often addressed in a more generic framework, not necessarily restricted to the microscopy application.

Over the last few decades, much research has been conducted on the minimisation of functionals with an image term and a PSF term for blind image deblurring. This leads to iterative methods which alternate *image restoration* steps with estimates of the blurring kernel, as in [3], where the classical Richardson-Lucy iteration [12] is applied to the problem of blind deconvolution. Sun et al. [17] use an image patch-based iterative optimization technique to estimate the spatially invariant PSF. Joshi et al. [5] estimate a spatially varying PSF from a single image. To this end, a cost function with a fidelity term and a penalty term for the smoothness of the PSF is minimized. After the PSF is estimated, the sharp image is recovered by using the Richardson-Lucy deconvolution algorithm. Michaeli et al. [7] propose an iterative minimisation where a patch-based image prior is added to a traditional data fidelity/smoothness functional.

In order to deal with the problem of spatially varying PSF, some authors used more classical edge extraction techniques, implicitly exploiting the valuable information contained in the local sharpness of edges. In [8] and [18], the original (unknown) edges are assumed to be ideal step edges. The spatially varying blur is modelled by a (spatially varying) Gaussian kernel: the estimate of the local PSF amounts to estimating the variance of the kernel which is done by using an unsharp masking approach. Smith [16] examines parametric models to fit on edge profiles through the gradient descent approach. Edge model fitting is preferred for estimating the PSF, because it reduces the noise amplification due to the differentiation step. A non-parametric and spatially invariant blur kernel is estimated using edge profiles in [2], leading to a Radon transform-based PSF estimation.

3   Image Blurring Model

Image blurring is usually modeled as the convolution of the ideal image with the point spread function (PSF), which describes how a point light source spreads on the image plane [15]. The degraded image additionally contains additive noise. The narrow depth of field typical of microscopy results in a PSF varying in space, which leads to the following image blurring model:

$$g(x,y) = \iint\limits_{m,n} I(x-m, y-n) \, p(m,n,x,y) \, dm \, dn + \eta(x,y) \qquad (1)$$

where g is the observed degraded image, I is the (unknown) ideal image, p is the PSF, η is the additive noise, and m, n denote the pixel indices. Due to the extreme ill-posedness of this problem, we will need to introduce some simplifying assumptions in order to obtain a solution:

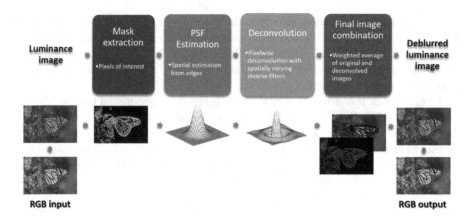

Fig. 1. Overview of the proposed deblurring scheme. The algorithmic steps are detailed in Sects. 4.1 to 4.4

Step Edge Assumption. It is assumed that the observed edges stem from ideal sharp edges, mathematically modelled as discontinuities along lines. In spite of some limitations in the biological context (e.g. intrinsically "unsharp" tissues), the approximation made by this model turns out to be accurate enough for practical purpose.

PSF Isotropy. Since we do not deal with motion blur, we assume that the PSF of the system can be approximated by an isotropic model. The optical PSF of lenses tend to be anisotropic at the image borders [6], however we assume that the regions of interest lie in the central areas of the image.

Use of Luminance Image. After applying a luminance/chrominance decomposition, the structural details are mostly concentrated in the luminance component. It is therefore straightforward to deblur exclusively the luminance channel, which also reduces chromatic aberration and color artefacts. Since the luminance image is a weighted average of the three color channels, the noise variance in the luminance image is smaller than the noise variances of each single individual color channel, which helps to avoid noise amplification as well.

4   Proposed Method

In order to recover the original image I from data g we need the blurring kernel at each pixel. The local condition of the problem is particularly bad in smooth areas, with no or few anatomical structure. Since in these areas deblurring is not necessary and leads to noise amplification, our method is designed such as performing no deblurring in the flat, information-sparse areas. Our local adaptive deblurring method is summarized in Fig. 1 and consists of the following steps:

A. Determination of the pixels of interest. The set of pixels on which the deblurring will be performed are extracted according to the (estimated) amount of information close to each pixel.

B. Local PSF estimates. The spatially varying PSF is estimated from the edges of the luminance image using an appropriate blur kernel model.

C. Deconvolution on the region of interest. The actual deconvolution applies the PSF estimates (step B) on the area selected at step A.

D. Formation of a global deblurred image. The deconvolved image is combined with the original image by using suitable weighting. This results in a coherent reconstruction of the image on the whole image domain.

4.1   Determination of the Pixels of Interest

The deconvolution of flat image areas leads to an amplification of noise without providing additional valuable information. In order to deblur only areas with structural information, we create a mask M which associates a value $M(p)$ between 0 and 1 with each pixel. The final recovered image is then obtained by combining the (locally) deconvolved image and the original image:

$$I_{final} = M \odot I_{deconvolved} + (1 - M) \odot I_{input} \qquad (2)$$

where $\odot$ is the element-wise multiplication.

In practice, images are noisy, which makes a naive use of gradients difficult: a preliminary edge-preserving denoising step is therefore necessary. The mask extraction should also be adaptive to the image contrast level which can differ from one input image to another. Hence, we apply an adaptive contrast stretching step to obtain the final mask. The proposed mask extraction algorithm consists of the following three steps:

- **Edge-preserving denoising** of the luminance channel by a modified non-iterative version of the anisotropic diffusion of Perona and Malik [10].
- **Structure map extraction.** The information on edges and textures is extracted by using the structure tensor of the image.
- **Adaptive contrast stretching** is applied to the structure map in order to take into account the contrast heteoregeneity over the image.

Edge-preserving Denoising. The preliminary denoising step needs to preserve the edges. To this end, we use the first iteration of a modified version of Perona-Malik non-linear diffusion method [10]. The Perona-Malik filtering relies on the use of a non-constant diffusivity, small at edge locations. The local amount of edge information is measured by the norm of the gradient $\|\nabla I\|$ and leads to a diffusion equation of the form:

$$\frac{\partial I}{\partial t} = \mathtt{div}\left(c\left(\|\nabla I\|^2\right)\nabla I\right) \qquad (3)$$

where $c : \mathbb{R}^+ \to \mathbb{R}^+$ is a positive decreasing function, for instance

$$c(s^2) = e^{-\frac{s^2}{\kappa}} \tag{4}$$

In this work we apply only the first iteration of a numerical procedure to solve the diffusion equation. Furthermore we modify the used diffusivity in order to take into account the local directionality in the image.

Structure Map Extraction. In order to generate a mask with high values in presence of structures and low values in the smooth image areas, we first compute the structure tensor [4] to analyse the local image anisotropy. The structure tensor $S_w(i,j)$ at a pixel (i,j) is defined as follows:

$$S_w(i,j) = \begin{bmatrix} \sum_w I_x^2 & \sum_w I_x I_y \\ \sum_w I_x I_y & \sum_w I_y^2 \end{bmatrix} \tag{5}$$

where $\sum_w$ indicates the weighted averaging of the values in the local neighborhood w, I_x and I_y are discrete approximations of the partial derivatives. The weighted averaging is done by applying a 2D Gaussian filter. The eigenvalues of the positive semidefinite symmetric matrix S_w describe the average contrast in the directions of its eigenvectors. The difference between the eigenvalues is a valuable quantitative indicator on how much structure is contained at this pixel [19]. We define the structure map $C(i,j)$ as follows:

$$C(i,j) = \lambda_1 - \lambda_2 \tag{6}$$

where $\lambda_1 \geq \lambda_2$ are the eigenvalues of the matrix $S_w(i,j)$. We do not normalize this coherence metric in order not to lose the global contrast information and not to amplify the noise in the flat image regions.

Adaptive Contrast Stretching. Once the structure map is obtained, we apply adaptive global contrast stretching in order to deal with different input image contrasts. To this end, we use unimodal thresholding (Rosin's method [13]) based on the histogram of the structure map. The obtained threshold T is used to decide whether a contrast level is significant or not. The final mask C_N is obtained by applying the following smooth thresholding strategy to the structure map C:

$$C_N(i,j) = \begin{cases} 1.0 & C(i,j) \geq T \\ C(i,j)/T & C(i,j) < T \end{cases} \tag{7}$$

It ranges in $[0,1]$ and allows for a smooth combination of the input and deconvolved images at the last step of our deblurring method. Our experiments show that the mask extraction is quite robust and stable under a wide range of contrast levels, as desired. We also tested the performance of mask extraction under simulated Gaussian noise and observed that the extraction remains robust also at noise levels higher than those measured in real images.

4.2   Spatially-Varying PSF Estimation

The actual PSF of a surgical microscope depends on the distance of the objects to the focus plane of the imaging system, which makes it impossible to perform a global 3D-calibration of the PSF. In this work, the PSF (varying spatially and in time) is estimated locally, in real time. Our model for the PSF relies on an isotropic and unimodal 2D function. We estimate the PSF at the locations where a blurred edge has been previously detected, based on the 1D profile perpendicular to the edge, which is also called the edge spread function (ESF).

Analytical PSF Modeling and Estimation. The line spread function (LSF), obtained by differentiating the ESF is the one dimensional equivalent of the PSF [20]. The reconstruction from the observed ESFs is ill-posed. We are facing the following issues:

- Direct reconstruction yields a noisy PSF due to the noise amplification by the differentiation of the ESF.
- The resolution of the reconstructed PSF is limited by the digital sensor resolution.

These observations led us to fit an edge model to the edge profile and reconstruct the PSF analytically as in [16], rather than directly reconstructing it via the observed ESFs. Since the ESF and the PSF have an analytical relation, we start with selecting the PSF model depending on the optical PSF of a diffraction-limited imaging system.

In order to model the PSF, we use a simple isotropic bivariate Gaussian function centered at the origin.

$$p(x, y) = \frac{1}{2\pi\sigma^2} e^{-\frac{x^2+y^2}{2\sigma^2}} \tag{8}$$

where x and y indicate the horizontal and vertical coordinates.

The PSF estimation problem thus amounts to estimating the spatially varying σ values along the image. The σ values are only estimated at pixels located on the edges at some pixels of the image and the initially estimated PSF map is called "sparse σ-map". After an outlier correction step, the sparse σ values are interpolated to obtain a continuous blur map. If the PSF model is an isotropic bivariate Gaussian function with a given σ, then the LSF of any orientation is a univariate Gaussian function with the same σ, and the ESF model to fit to the edge profiles is given as the cumulative distribution function of the normal distribution, given by

$$e(x) = \frac{1}{2}\left[1 + erf\left(\frac{x - x_0}{\sigma\sqrt{2}}\right)\right] \tag{9}$$

where erf is the error function.

Steps to Estimate the Sparse σ-map:
Let us summarize the main steps to estimate the sparse σ-map.

- Image edges are detected using an edge detector like Canny detector [1].
- For each pixel location on the edge map, the ESF values are calculated from the luminance image through bilinear interpolation for the locations on the perpendicular line to the edge.
- The extracted edge profile may include structural details not belonging to the edge. For robust model fitting, we isolate the central part of the edge profile as in [8].
- We use a threshold based on the total variation (TV) of the isolated edge: edge profiles below the threshold are dropped without estimating the σ at this image location.
- For model fitting, we compute the subpixel location m, corresponding to the middle point of the ESF model to be fitted. The local value of σ is then estimated by least square minimisation.

4.3   Deconvolution Filter Design

After estimating the spatially varying blur, we perform a non-blind deblurring step, by using non-linear locally adaptive filters based on the classical $2D$-Wiener deconvolution filter, together with a regularization factor. The proposed deconvolution filter is formulated in the frequency domain u, v as follows:

$$W(u,v) = \frac{1}{P(u,v)} \left[\frac{|P(u,v)|^2}{|P(u,v)|^2 + \frac{1}{SNR(u,v)^2}} \right] \tag{10}$$

where $P(u,v)$ is the Fourier transform of the PSF model $p(x,y)$ given in Eq. 8 with the locally estimated σ value. We need to take in to account that the SNR value varies spatially along the image, because the image sensor has a signal dependent noise. Hence, we use a regularized model for the SNR, given as:

$$SNR(u,v)_{I_m,\alpha} = \frac{I_m^2}{(u^2 + v^2)^{\alpha/2} \sigma_Y^2(I_m)} \tag{11}$$

where I_m indicates the local intensity value and $\sigma_Y^2(I_m)$ is the intensity dependent noise variance, obtained by camera specific modelling, and α is a regularization parameter.

4.4   Deconvolution and Final Image Composition

In this step, the regions of the luminance image where the mask has values larger than a small threshold are deconvolved pixelwise with the locally corresponding spatial domain filter. As explained in the previous section, the deconvolution filter depends on the intensity value of the center pixel, the estimated σ value at that pixel, the simulated noise power $\sigma_Y^2(i)$ and the selected α parameter. Finally, the deconvolved image is averaged with the input image using the mask weights as shown in Eq. 2.

5   Experiment Results

Quantitative and qualitative experiment results are discussed in this section. Quantitative analysis of estimation accuracy of the sparse σ-map for different inter-edge distances, orientations and noise levels are given. Only qualitative analysis can be performed on real word microscope images, since the sharp ground truth images are inherently non-accessible.

5.1   Quantitative Analysis of Blur Map Estimation

Ideal gray-scale patterns are blurred with isotropic bi-variate Gaussian kernels according to synthetic ground truth σ-maps. Based on the blurred images, we estimate the sparse σ-map and analyze the accuracy of the estimation under different conditions. Note that we analyze the accuracy of the sparse σ-map on the pixel locations where the PSF estimation was performed, and we do not analyze the interpolated σ-map since the edge-aware interpolation step depends on the image content. Test images with constant (bar type) or varying edge orientation (circle type) are used.

Influence of Inter-edge Distance. To test the accuracy of σ estimation under varying inter-edge distances, bar patterns with different bar widths are created and blurred using the ground truth σ-map given in Fig. 2d The ground truth σ values vary from 0.5 to 2.5.

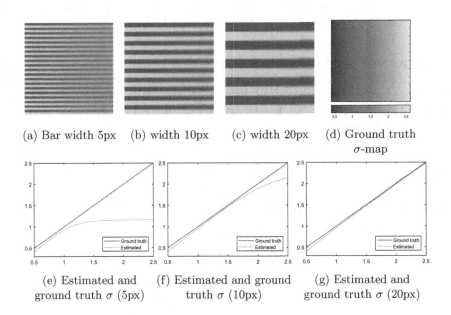

(a) Bar width 5px   (b) width 10px   (c) width 20px   (d) Ground truth σ-map

(e) Estimated and ground truth σ (5px)   (f) Estimated and ground truth σ (10px)   (g) Estimated and ground truth σ (20px)

Fig. 2. Influence of inter-edge distances on the σ estimation (Color figure online)

Blurry results are given in Figs. 2a,b,c and the corresponding estimation results are plotted underneath with red color, while the ground truth values are shown with blue color. We observe that there is an upper limit of correctly estimated blur kernel width, and this limit is determined by the inter-edge distances.

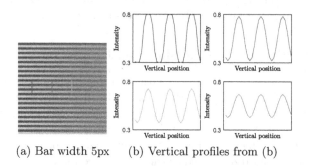

(a) Bar width 5px   (b) Vertical profiles from (b)

Fig. 3. Blurred bars with different widths and their profiles

If the PSF is wider than the inter-edge distance, the spread of an edge pixel affects the intensity values of neighboring edges and the edge contrasts decrease. In this case, PSF estimation yields smaller σ values due to edge contrast normalization in the next step. This effect is shown in Fig. 3 with the edge profiles extracted from the blurry image at different blur levels. Fortunately, this limitation does not lead to visible artifacts, on the contrary it yields better visual results than deblurring the close edges with large kernels.

Influence of Edge-Orientations. The blur estimation accuracy at different edge orientations is tested with a circle pattern, blurred with different kernels according to the σ-map in Fig. 4a. Edge map and sparse σ-map are estimated at edge locations. Estimation results at different orientation angles are shown in Fig. 4c with red color.

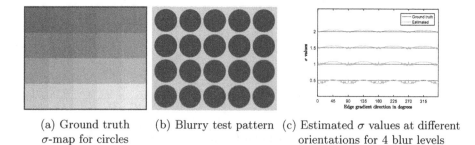

(a) Ground truth   (b) Blurry test pattern   (c) Estimated σ values at different
σ-map for circles   orientations for 4 blur levels

Fig. 4. Blur map, test pattern, and σ estimation for different edge orientations (Color figure online)

We observe that the estimation accuracy varies at different angles, due to the discrete grid nature of image pixels. We also observe that the estimation accuracy increases with increasing blur kernel size. This is reasonable because smaller kernels are discretized with fewer samples, leading to more severe discretization effects. We observe that the estimation errors remain at acceptable levels: The absolute deviation from the ground truth values is mostly smaller than 0.1.

Influence of the Additive Noise. In this section, the estimation accuracy will be tested using the blurred bar patterns contaminated with zero-mean additive white Gaussian noise.

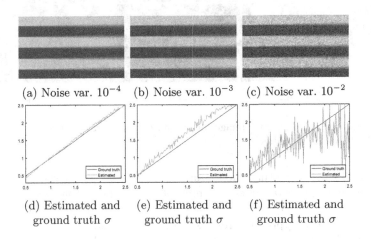

(a) Noise var. 10^{-4} (b) Noise var. 10^{-3} (c) Noise var. 10^{-2}

(d) Estimated and   (e) Estimated and   (f) Estimated and
   ground truth σ ground truth σ ground truth σ

Fig. 5. σ estimation with additive white Gaussian noise

In Fig. 5, we observe that the accuracy of σ estimation is acceptable for low-level and mid-level noise, and it decreases significantly for strong noise. Strong noise may cause false positive edge detections in flat areas, and it could affect the σ-estimation. These results indicate that the deblurring algorithm must be designed differently for the strong noise. However, deblurring strongly noisy images is out of our interest since the images obtained by the ARRISCOPE have much weaker noise than the high-level noise we used in the experiments.

5.2   Qualitative Analysis of Deblurring

In this section the experiment results for the real microscope images taken by the ARRISCOPE are given. We discuss results for a test image and a surgical image.

- **Test chart image:** This image shows the fine details printed on a flat test chart (Fig. 6). We can qualitatively estimate the original signal and assess the deblurring performance due to the basic structures in the image.

– **Surgery image:** This image was taken during a microsurgical operation and reflects the nature of images including biological tissues (Fig. 6).

5.3 Mask and σ-map Results

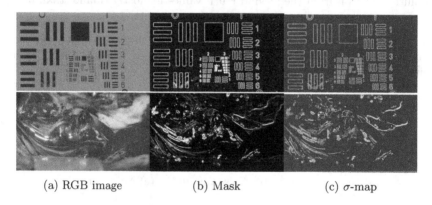

(a) RGB image   (b) Mask   (c) σ-map

Fig. 6. Test chart and surgery image, mask and σ-map. σ ranges from 0 (blue) to 2.5 (yellow). (Color figure online)

In Fig. 6 we observe that the extracted masks successfully select the regions to deblur. The sparse σ values are interpolated in the regions where the mask values ($\in [0,1]$) are larger than a small threshold (0.2 in our application). The obtained masked interpolation results are given alongside the masks. Note that smaller σ values are estimated on finer details, but results in less visual artefact as explained in Sect. 5.1.

In addition to the imaging parameters of the camera, we have many parameters for individual steps in the deblurring algorithm. As the performance of algorithm depends on the input image content, we cannot determine optimal parameter values valid for all possible images, but we can examine the effects of several critical parameters which cause remarkable difference in the final deblurring results. For this aim, we will examine the effects of selecting the frequency gain regularization parameter α of the Wiener deconvolution and the influence of increasing upper limit of the σ-map.

5.4 Influence of the Selection of α

As expressed in Sect. 4.3, the frequency attenuation parameter α is used to obtain the frequency dependent SNR functions and to have a better regularization of high frequency noise. This parameter changes the overall perceived sharpness level and it can be used as the single parameter to tune the deblurring strength during a surgical operation. For the analysis of α values, the upper limit of σ is set as 1.7, which is an intermediate value for the resolution of our test images. The effects of different upper limits for the σ-map will be analyzed in the subsequent section, for a selected α value.

In the Fig. 7 the experiment results are given using varying α values. As expected, small α values yield sharper images but with more visual artifacts. The experiments show that an α value of 0.8 yields good results for both test images.

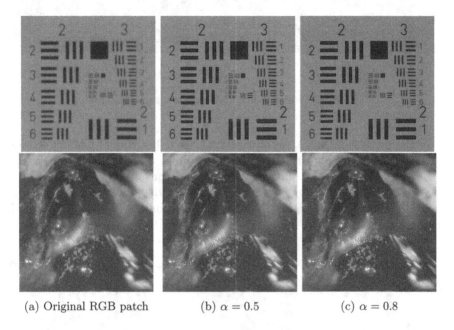

(a) Original RGB patch   (b) $\alpha = 0.5$ (c) $\alpha = 0.8$

Fig. 7. Test chart and surgery image patches with varying α values

5.5 Influence of the Upper Limit for σ-map

The estimated sparse σ-map values are clipped after outlier correction for several reasons. Too large σ values tend to be erroneous estimations and create visible artifacts in the image. Since our aim is not deblurring strongly blurred patterns, but to increase the visibility of fine details, very large σ values can be skipped. Clipping high σ values improves the robustness of the PSF estimation in shading areas. Based on experiments we chose a dual threshold method: all σ values above this shading threshold are eliminated, whereas σ values between the upper limit and the shading threshold are set to the upper limit. Results are given in Fig. 8. The shading threshold is constantly set at 3.5. The choice of the upper σ limit changes the deblurring results significantly, as different deconvolution filters are selected pixelwise. To reveal the effect of the upper limit, we first give the interpolated mask results for the surgery image with varying upper limits.

In the Fig. 8a, almost an uniform PSF is obtained, because the upper limit is very small and it clips most of the σ values in the map. As the upper limit increases in the further figures, clipping is observed on blurry edges which have higher σ values. The change in the deblurring results is exemplified with the patches in Fig. 9. For deblurring, alpha is set to 0.8.

(a) Upper σ limit = 1.2   (b) Upper σ limit = 1.7   (c) Upper σ limit = 2.5

Fig. 8. Estimated σ-maps with different upper limits

In the patches in Fig. 9, we observe that the deblurring of fine details does not change substantially with varying upper σ limit, while the more blurry areas in the southeast region are affected, as they are deconvolved using larger kernels with increasing upper limit. This is due to the fact that the original σ values on these blurry regions are higher than the clipping limit in every patch given in the figure.

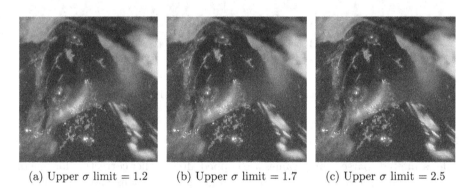

(a) Upper σ limit = 1.2   (b) Upper σ limit = 1.7   (c) Upper σ limit = 2.5

Fig. 9. Deblurred patches using σ-maps with different upper limits

6   Conclusion

In this work, we proposed a solution to improve the perceived resolution of a surgical microscope. It performs automatic selection of the regions of interest, spatially varying PSF estimation and regularized deconvolution in a non-iterative and adaptive way. The key (and most expensive) steps of the algorithm, the sparse σ-map estimation and the pixelwise deconvolution, both rely on local operations which make parallelization possible for a real-time implementation.

Quantitative and qualitative experiments indicate that the proposed algorithm can work in a stable way on a variety of images with different characteristics and increase the visual details without amplifying the image noise. The algorithm can be further optimized for a real-time blind deblurring application in order to increase the perceived visual information during the surgical operations. Its design allows easy porting to massively parallel computing devices such as GPUs.

References

1. Canny, J.: A computational approach to edge detection. IEEE Trans. Pattern Anal. Mach. Intell. **6**, 679–698 (1986)
2. Cho, T.S., Paris, S., Horn, B.K., Freeman, W.T.: Blur kernel estimation using the Radon transform. In: CVPR 2011, pp. 241–248. IEEE (2011)
3. Fish, D., Brinicombe, A., Pike, E., Walker, J.: Blind deconvolution by means of the Richardson-Lucy algorithm. JOSA A **12**(1), 58–65 (1995)
4. Jaehne, B.: Digital Image Processing. Springer, Heidelberg (2005). https://doi.org/10.1007/3-540-27563-0
5. Joshi, N., Szeliski, R., Kriegman, D.J.: PSF estimation using sharp edge prediction. In: 2008 IEEE Conference on Computer Vision and Pattern Recognition, pp. 1–8. IEEE (2008)
6. Kee, E., Paris, S., Chen, S., Wang, J.: Modeling and removing spatially-varying optical blur. In: 2011 IEEE International Conference on Computational Photography (ICCP), pp. 1–8. IEEE (2011)
7. Michaeli, T., Irani, M.: Blind deblurring using internal patch recurrence. In: Fleet, D., Pajdla, T., Schiele, B., Tuytelaars, T. (eds.) ECCV 2014. LNCS, vol. 8691, pp. 783–798. Springer, Cham (2014). https://doi.org/10.1007/978-3-319-10578-9_51
8. Nasonov, A., Nasonova, A., Krylov, A.: Edge width estimation for defocus map from a single image. In: International Conference on Advanced Concepts for Intelligent Vision Systems. pp. 15–22. Springer (2015)
9. Nasse, M.J., Woehl, J.C.: Realistic modeling of the illumination point spread function in confocal scanning optical microscopy. JOSA A **27**(2), 295–302 (2010)
10. Perona, P., Malik, J.: Scale-space and edge detection using anisotropic diffusion. IEEE Trans. Pattern Anal. Mach. Intell. **12**(7), 629–639 (1990)
11. Reichenbach, S.E., Park, S.K., Narayanswamy, R.: Characterizing digital image acquisition devices. Opt. Eng. **30**(2), 170–177 (1991)
12. Richardson, W.H.: Bayesian-based iterative method of image restoration. JoSA **62**(1), 55–59 (1972)
13. Rosin, P.L.: Unimodal thresholding. Pattern Recogn. **34**(11), 2083–2096 (2001)
14. Sarder, P., Nehorai, A.: Deconvolution methods for 3-D fluorescence microscopy images. IEEE Sig. Process. Mag. **23**(3), 32–45 (2006)
15. Sibarita, J.B.: Deconvolution microscopy. In: Microscopy Techniques, pp. 201–243 (2005)
16. Smith, E.H.B.: PSF estimation by gradient descent fit to the ESF. In: Image Quality and System Performance III, vol. 6059, p. 60590E. International Society for Optics and Photonics (2006)
17. Sun, L., Cho, S., Wang, J., Hays, J.: Edge-based blur kernel estimation using patch priors. In: IEEE International Conference on Computational Photography (ICCP), pp. 1–8. IEEE (2013)

18. Tang, C., Hou, C., Song, Z.: Defocus map estimation from a single image via spectrum contrast. Opt. Lett. **38**(10), 1706–1708 (2013)
19. Weickert, J.: Anisotropic Diffusion in Image Processing, vol. 1. Teubner Stuttgart (1998)
20. Zhang, X., et al.: Measuring the modulation transfer function of image capture devices: what do the numbers really mean? In: Image Quality and System Performance IX, vol. 8293, p. 829307. International Society for Optics and Photonics (2012)

Low-Effort Re-identification Techniques Based on Medical Imagery Threaten Patient Privacy

Laura Carolina Martínez Esmeral$^{(\boxtimes)}$ and Andreas Uhl

Paris Lodron University of Salzburg, Salzburg 5020, Austria
laura.martinez-esmeral@stud.sbg.ac.at, uhl@cosy.sbg.ac.at

Abstract. Deriving patients' identity from medical imagery threatens privacy, as these data are acquired to support diagnosis but not to reveal identity-related features. Still, for many medical imaging modalities, such identity breaches have been reported, however, typically employing a highly specialised image processing and pattern recognition pipeline. In this paper, we demonstrate that surprisingly, a simple and unified deep learning-based technique is able to determine patient identity from two exemplary imaging modalities, i.e., brain MRI and gastrointestinal endoscopic data. This demonstrates that almost anyone with limited resources and knowledge of the field would be able to perform this task, which indicates that according to GDPR, medical image data after pseudonymisation should be considered "information on an identifiable natural person" and thus must not be released to the public without further provisions.

Keywords: Endoscopy · MRI · Biometric recognition · Patient privacy

1 Introduction

Following the progress of computer-assisted diagnosis support systems relying on medical imagery and the corresponding quest for reproducible research, publicly available medical image datasets have become more widespread over the past years. Given these data, the creation of many different techniques that allow the (re-)identification of patients by employing such data sets has been possible. There are of course highly welcome application settings, like biometric authentication or forensic victim recognition using such data, but these developments also threaten patients' privacy as the medical data has been acquired to support diagnosis but not to enable patient identification. In fact, if one had access to a second (different) patient dataset containing identity information alongside the image data, one would be able to identify a patient in a public dataset by performing a biometric recognition with the not anonymized one.

The European Union's General Data Protection Regulation (GDPR) has to be applied to "personal data" only, thus it is crucial to determine if given data

© The Author(s), under exclusive license to Springer Nature Switzerland AG 2022
G. Yang et al. (Eds.): MIUA 2022, LNCS 13413, pp. 719–733, 2022.
https://doi.org/10.1007/978-3-031-12053-4_53

qualifies as personal data, in particular considering publicly available medical data sets that have undergone pseudonymisation. Article 4(1) GDPR defines personal data as "any information relating to an identified or identifiable natural person ('data subject')". Article 29 Working Party (the A29WP - now the European Data Protection Board-'EDPB') considers a data subject as being "identifiable" if it can be distinguished from others [7].

A legal test to discriminate personal and non-personal data is described in Recital 26 GDPR: "[p]ersonal data which have undergone pseudonymisation, which could be attributed to a natural person by the use of additional information should be considered to be information on an identifiable natural person." Thus, if we are able to re-identify a patient based on two different data items of the same medical imaging modality (i.e. one being stored after pseudonymisation in a public data set, the other used as additional information connected to the patients identity), the public medical data is personal data, and thus fall under GDPR and have to be treated accordingly.

Recital 26 GDPR further specifies what is meant by "identifiable": "To determine whether a natural person is identifiable, account should be taken of *all the means reasonably likely to be used* to identify the natural person directly or indirectly". Interestingly, this particular notion differs from that defined by the A29WP which states that there can be no remaining risk of identification for data to qualify as non-personal (anonymous) [7].

Recital 26 GDPR subsequently clarifies what is meant by "... all the means reasonably likely to be used ...": "..., account should be taken of all objective factors, such as the costs of and the amount of time required for identification, taking into consideration the available technology at the time of the processing and technological developments." This means, that one has to consider the actual risk that identification is (successfully) attempted, i.e. the GDPR suggests a risk assessment scheme [7].

Obviously, if patient re-identification relies on highly modality specific, rather complicated image processing pipelines (like those used in e.g. the MRI-based brain-print, see next section) that require highly skilled specialists for implementation and data-intensive atlas alignment operations, it is not very likely that a real-life identification attempt is conducted. On the other hand, technology has progressed and now eventually provides learning-based techniques that can be applied by any moderately skilled data scientist to the medical datasets in question. In fact, in this paper we show that a straight forward and unified transfer-learning approach is able to provide patient re-identification based on (i) brain MRI data, for which the currently available "brainprint" patient re-identification approach [33] relies on a complicated process involving atlas-based brain tissue segmentation and subsequent feature derivation and (ii) gastrointestinal endoscopic data, for which a potential link to patient identity has never been shown before. Therefore, we show that, even if one does not possess large quantities of data or even an expert knowledge of the field, it is possible to conduct re-identification, which makes its application much more likely.

In the next section of this paper, we give an overview on related work in patient identification based on medical signals. Subsequently, we provide a brief description of the image datasets, which were employed during our experiments, and the required steps for preparing these data will be given. In the fourth section, the implementation of the employed identification method for medical images, which tries to overcome the limitations in terms of specialised processing pipelines as described above, will be explained alongside its related experiments and results.

2   Related Work on Person Identification Using Medical Signals

There are biometric authentication methods that rely on biomedical signals, like the EEG-signal [28] or the ECG-signal [9]. Furthermore, retina recognition is based on fundus images [16] (which are used to assess diabetic retinopathy in ophthalmology) and sclera recognition [6] is based on imaging the conjunctival vasculature (which is utilized to assess and diagnose anemia [14] or erythema [26]).

Nonetheless, there also exist forensic recognition techniques based on such data, which are less known. In fact, one can identify human subjects by means of dental [11,25,36], hand [13], chest [5,12] or knee [31] X-Rays. For these two application cases, biometric authentication and forensic recognition, we observe an intended actual dual-use of the underlying medical data.

The situation is different for other modalities. Although never meant for biometric or forensic use, it has been shown that knee [30] or brain [17,33] MRIs, respectively, can be used as well to determine patients' identity.

No matter if intended for subject identification or not, the underlying algorithms of the techniques mentioned so far, are aimed to very specific body regions and lack uniformity among each other, since every single one of them follows a unique and rather complex (image) processing pipeline. From this fact, an obvious challenge arises, i.e. to find a simpler and more general approach, an eventually unified method for patient identification from medical images. Such an approach would increase the threat to privacy even more as described above, as this would significantly simplify the respective application in patient identification and thereby the likelihood of its application.

Even if the methods described are quite dissimilar from each other, they do share a common series of processing steps: image acquisition, image pre-processing, feature extraction and classification. Feature extraction is one of the most crucial steps and, because of this, it is important to create a robust model to obtain strong and discriminative features. Each of the techniques described so far, applies hand-crafted algorithms, which employ a combination of predefined features to describe an image (e.g. texture, shape, brightness, ...) [3].

In spite of the fact that the use of such types of algorithms often has adequate results, there is an alternative approach for extracting features: feature learning algorithms. The basic difference between the hand-crafted and these algorithms is that the feature extraction is not designed by human experts but there is a data-driven learning process similar to the one that humans have throughout their lives [24]. This has the potential to substantially simplify patient recognition from medical data sets. This family of algorithms are part of the Deep Learning [20] methodology.

In the field of biometric authentication, there are already several examples of Deep Learning based identification methods that range from face recognition, the use of the iris [1,22], to the finger or palm veins [18], or even the ears [2]. Nevertheless, in the area of determining identity from medical imagery this is not the case so far, probably also because of the lack of large quantities of data for this purpose. Nevertheless, we will show that this is still a reasonable approach if transfer learning is applied.

3   Data Selection and Preparation

To avoid complicated processing steps that often require data alignment (like those from "brainprint" [33] or "fiberprint" [17]), one goal is to perform patient-related identification based on data that has not to be registered or aligned at all. We aim to exploit unique texture features for identification. To do so, using datasets that contain texture rich data is fundamental. Moreover, since a recognition process is to be performed, the datasets had to contain at least two samples (i.e. images) belonging to the same person. Although there is a great amount of publicly available datasets, these requirements considerably narrowed our options. Eventually, we ended up with sufficient material for our target modalities, i.e. gastrointestinal endoscopic or brain MRI images, respectively.

The endoscopic datasets identified fulfil the described requirements. For this reason, sets of images were created by extracting frames from different surgical videos. Each of these 3-channel images depicts the interior of a cavity, e.g. the colon, and, therefore, contains walls covered by mucosal texture.

Ideally, the generated sets should have contained images from different dates (i.e. obtained from different sessions) to avoid having identifiers that might be influenced by biochemical or biomechanical processes that are unique for a precise period of time [31]. Nevertheless, it is still interesting to see the results for these intra-session comparisons since, as of today, (i) there has never been an attempt to perform patient identification that used endocopic images and (ii) the used images have strictly empty intersection, i.e. no overlap in terms of depicted mucosal area.

Particularly, we could find the *GLENDA* (*Gynecologic Laparoscopy ENdometriosis DAtaset*) dataset [21] that contained laparoscopy video frames, the *NBI-InfFrames* dataset [23] that was composed of different laryngoscopic frames and the *Nerthus* dataset [27] that consisted of frames taken from bowel videos that showed regions of the large intestine.

Furthermore, we got access to a dataset provided by the WaveLab of the University of Salzburg [35] that included esophago-gastroduodenoscopies depicting eventual patches of celiac disease in a group of patients. Since the images were recorded using the modified immersion technique, from now on, we will refer to the dataset as *Immersion*.

In addition to endoscopic data, we consider brain MRI data, since, as described in the introduction, there already exist patient identification techniques based on brain MRI, i.e. "brainprint" [8,33], that have very complex processing pipelines and depend on exact alignment of data. Because of this, we were interested to see if our simpler alternative was feasible for such images. Brain MRI slices were selected from *OASIS-3* (*Open Access Series of Imaging Studies*) [19] in the SWI, T1-weighted and T2-weighted modalities, and *ADNI-3* (*Alzheimer's Disease Neuroimaging Initiative*) [34] in the T1-weighted modality. In contrast to the endoscopic datasets, the brain MRI sets did not exclusively contain images from single sessions, but also images from the same patients at different points in time so that inter-session comparisons could be performed as well.

As soon as the datasets were selected, the images were prepared to be suitable for the planned method. In the subsections below, the specific steps followed for the data preparation of the different types of image sets will be described.

3.1   Endoscopic Datasets

In endoscopic images one can basically see interior organ walls covered by mucosa. If they are too far away from the camera, these regions might be too dark or unfocused, so using them has to be avoided. What is more, metallic instruments are sometimes used as an aid to the physician's tasks, but, again, if these are present inside the images, they would constitute a disturbance for our purpose. Consequently, we have to identify a region where none of these characteristics is exhibited, a Region of Interest (ROI) that exclusively consists of well illuminated focused walls so that square image blocks only containing useful information can be generated.

The irregularities of the images in question were not particularly helpful for employing an automatic method for locating the desired ROI. Although completely possible in principle, to reduce effort for this study, this process was done manually (cf. Fig. 1[1]). For each image, non-overlapping rectangles containing patches of clear and well-lit "walls" were extracted. Since location is not important for the prospective identification method, images were rotated to have maximally sized rectangles.

However, as explained before, medical image datasets are usually not large enough for Deep Learning applications, and these endoscopic datasets are no exception. Moreover, when feeding a dataset to a typical CNN, all images should have the same size. So, to augment the number of images and to have a uniform image size, the ROI rectangles were divided into non-overlapping square blocks of size 97×97 pixels. This particular size was selected so that could we could maximize the number of generated blocks when dividing our ROI rectangles, since the minimum length found among the generated rectangles was of 97 pixels.

---

[1] This figure has been designed using resources from [21].

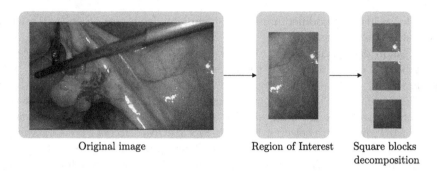

| Original image | Region of Interest | Square blocks decomposition |

Fig. 1. Overview of Endoscopic data preparation

After completing this task, it is highly unlikely that all patients end up with the same quantity of blocks. Nevertheless, when carrying out an experiment, one should be as fair as possible and, for avoiding on training bias, the number of blocks per subject (patient) was equalized by removing the excess of those with more blocks.

Table 1. Number of image blocks and patients for every endoscopic dataset and the total amount of blocks within a dataset for all patients

Dataset	N. Patients	Blocks per patient	Total blocks for all patients
Immersion	133	13	1,729
NBI-InfFrames	13	54	702
Nerthus	11	14	154
GLENDA	8	13	104

In the table above (cf. Table 1), one can see the number of image blocks extracted from each dataset. Unfortunately, although the original datasets had a considerable amount of images, there was a drastic reduction of these after the data preparation step. The reason for this is the fact that, since the images were frames from short videos and, thus, had large overlaps between each other, the majority of them had to be discarded.

3.2   Brain MRI Datasets

For the preparation of the brain MRI data, the endoscopies' line of though was followed: Square blocks containing texture from the brain were individuated for each person. Still, there is a huge difference from the initial pipeline. It was easily possible to create an automatic approach for finding the ROI rectangles in brain MRI slices (cf. Fig. 2[2]).

---

[2] This figure has been designed using resources from [19].

To do this, a global threshold was applied to the image to binarize it. This first binarization was not perfect, so a series of morphological operations were performed to enhance it. The binary image was firstly closed to fill some small gaps, then opened to get rid of useless regions. However, after the applied operation, these regions did not completely disappear, they remained as small islands around the brain region, which was the largest of them all. Thus, by only opening very small areas, these islands vanished. After that, a closing operation was applied to smooth the ROI borders.

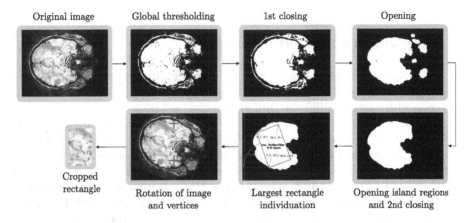

Fig. 2. Overview of Brain MRI data preparation

Once the ROI was found, the vertices and the angle of the largest rectangle within the ROI area were computed. Having these, the original image and the rectangle vertices were rotated according to the given angle. Subsequently, the rotated image was cropped according to the new vertices to obtain the rectangular ROI, which was once more divided into square blocks of size 97×97 pixels with the same procedure explained before.

In the table below (cf. Table 2), one can see the number of images extracted from each dataset. It is important to note that the *T1-ADNI* dataset did not have as much images as expected because, although the original set had huge amounts of data, the included images did not belong to the same sensor and, therefore, data uniformity was prioritized over quantity.

Table 2. Number of image blocks and patients for every brain MRI dataset and the total amount of blocks within a dataset for all patients

Dataset	N. Patients	Blocks per patient	Total blocks for all patients
SWI-OASIS 3	118	54	6,372
T1-OASIS 3	172	19	3,268
T2-OASIS 3	226	16	3,616
T1-ADNI	28	18	504

4   Implementation and Results

In the domain of biometric recognition, like in medical imaging, quantities of data that can be employed for training tend to be low (except for face recognition). To cope with this fact, different approaches can be followed.

To start with, it is possible to perform a simple subject classification (i.e. each subject/patient represents one class). Nonetheless, one has to consider that this might be inconvenient because as soon as new subjects (classes) are added to the set, the model might not be ready to handle them. Alternatively, a pretrained network can be used as a feature extractor so that a feature vector is obtained as an output of the network for each image. According to the similarity between two of these vectors, if they are sufficiently close, then they are considered to belong to the same person. Another possibility is the Siamese Networks Architecture that uses two networks [10] or its variant that employs the triplet loss [29]. With this kind of model, one does not look into the classes but the difference between samples (i.e. if they belong to the same class - subject - or not).

Having these general paths in mind, since the main issue of our datasets is the lack of huge quantities of images, using a Siamese Network implementation seemed like a good starting point for our experiments. As a consequence, we decided to test two types of Siamese Architectures, one the training of which was based on contrastive loss, and another one with triplet selection and a triplet loss training. The results obtained from both approaches were clearly inferior as compared to the third option (and are thus omitted). For the third option, we decided to evaluate a Feature Extraction Network (which led to the clearly most positive outcome). In the section below, this method will be presented with its related experiments and results.

4.1   Feature Extraction Network

To extract features by means of a neural network one way is to freeze all layers except the first linear layer. Once the images are fed to this network, a feature vector is returned as an output (cf. Fig. 3[3]).

---

[3] This figure has been designed using resources from [21].

Considering that not enough data is available to train such a network from scratch, VGG-16 [32] was used as a pretrained network. However, when using this type of model one must be careful. For example, VGG-16 was trained on Imagenet, which is an image dataset that contains pictures with certain characteristics that differ from those in our sets. Therefore, before using the net as a feature extractor, it is retrained and fine-tuned so that its weights capture relevant features in our space.

Since the original training was performed with the scope of having a certain classification, the retraining followed the same logic. A K-fold configuration was employed, where 80% of the image blocks were used as the new training set for each fold (data was partitioned to separate subjects/patients to avoid overfitting). Moreover, due to the fact that the original model was designed for the classification of 1000 different classes and our set does not present that quantity of subjects, the network was modified in such a way that it performed a classification of n classes, being n the number of subjects included in the training set.

As soon as the retraining was completed, the remaining 20% image blocks were tested by feeding them to the network for the feature extraction. The extracted feature vectors were then compared by means of the Euclidean distance. If this distance was small, the original blocks were considered to belong to the same patient.

After comparing all vectors, the results were used for three different metrics, the *Accuracy* (cf. Eq. 1), the *False Acceptance Rate (FAR)* (cf. Eq. 2) and the *False Rejection Rate (FRR)* (cf. Eq. 3), the last two being commonly used in the biometrics field.

$$Accuracy = \frac{Correct}{Total} \tag{1}$$

where *Correct* stands for the cases where the two blocks belonged or did not belong to same class (patient) and were considered as such.

$$FAR = \frac{Wrong\ people\ accepted}{Total} \tag{2}$$

where *Wrong people accepted* stands for the case where two blocks were considered from the same class but they were in fact not.

$$FRR = \frac{Right\ people\ rejected}{Total} \tag{3}$$

where *Right people rejected* stands for the case where two blocks were considered from two different classes but in reality they belonged to the same one.

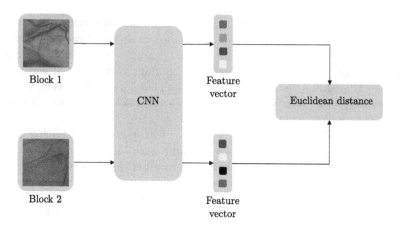

Fig. 3. Overview of Feature Extraction method

These metrics were applied to both the endoscopic and brain MRI datasets and, as one can observe, the outcome (cf. Table 3) turns out to be satisfactory. The *SWI-OASIS 3* dataset, which has the highest number of image blocks (6,372 blocks in total), got an accuracy over 90% and its *FAR* and *FRR* were, as desired, low and balanced. Nonetheless, one can also see that for smaller datasets results degraded, but still were above those obtained for the former network configurations. From the results obtained, we can deduce that identity-related features do exist in these data and results get more accurate when larger quantities of data are available for learning (which is obvious of course). In fact, to demonstrate this statement, we decided to take one of our datasets and artificially reduce the number of subjects/patients within it to see if the results got deteriorated. For this task, the Immersion dataset, which originally had 133 patients, was selected and reduced to a subset of only 20 patients. As one can see in the table below (cf. Table 4), this indeed was the case as results got clearly detoriated.

Moreover, our results suggest that, for the brain MRI sets, the different imaging modalities influence the results. For example, *T1-OASIS 3* and *T2-OASIS 3* have similar quantities of data (around 3000 blocks) but have very discordant outcomes.

On the other hand, if we compare the obtained results with those from the "brainprint", one can see that there are some noticeable differences. To start with, although, for our method and the "brainprint" one, the ADNI dataset was employed for assessing personal identification, their quantity of images was much larger. In fact, they utilized 3000 images, while we worked with only 504 blocks because, as previously explained, we prioritized data uniformity over quantity. Moreover, their results were higher. They performed a series of experiments with results ranging from around 80% to 99%, whereas our best result for ADNI reached a 63% accuracy. This outcome is not completely surprising, since their approach was brain MRI specific whilst ours is more general. What is more, it

Table 3. Results for Feature Extraction Network according to the number of epochs employed for training

Dataset	20 epochs	50 epochs	100 epochs
Immersion	Accuracy: 64.76 %	Accuracy: 88.22 %	Accuracy: 70.77 %
	FAR: 33.95 %	FAR: 9.88 %	FAR: 27.30 %
	FRR: 1.29 %	FRR: 1.90 %	FRR: 1.93 %
NBI-InfFrames	Accuracy: 62.20 %	Accuracy: 68.67 %	Accuracy: 68.88 %
	FAR: 22.77 %	FAR: 9.85 %	FAR: 5.83 %
	FRR: 15.02 %	FRR: 21.48 %	FRR: 25.29 %
Nerthus	Accuracy: 56.28 %	Accuracy: 61.38 %	Accuracy: 62.70 %
	FAR: 9.85 %	FAR: 20.05 %	FAR: 12.86 %
	FRR: 33.88 %	FRR: 18.57 %	FRR: 24.44 %
GLENDA	Accuracy: 57.77 %	Accuracy: 56.51 %	Accuracy: 55.55 %
	FAR: 33.80 %	FAR: 22.12 %	FAR: 5.70 %
	FRR: 8.43 %	FRR: 21.38 %	FRR: 38.76 %
SWI-OASIS 3	Accuracy: 93.11 %	Accuracy: 93.23 %	Accuracy: 93.20 %
	FAR: 3.52 %	FAR: 3.35 %	FAR: 3.43 %
	FRR: 3.37 %	FRR: 3.42 %	FRR: 3.37 %
T1-OASIS 3	Accuracy: 71.73 %	Accuracy: 71.97 %	Accuracy: 72.77 %
	FAR: 26.89 %	FAR: 26.69 %	FAR: 25.68 %
	FRR: 1.39 %	FRR: 1.34 %	FRR: 1.54 %
T2-OASIS 3	Accuracy: 43.27 %	Accuracy: 70.02 %	Accuracy: 48.80 %
	FAR: 56.26 %	FAR: 29.11 %	FAR: 50.54 %
	FRR: 0.47 %	FRR: 0.87 %	FRR: 0.66 %
T1-ADNI	Accuracy: 46.62 %	Accuracy: 61.22 %	Accuracy: 62.83 %
	FAR: 47.13 %	FAR: 29.11 %	FAR: 27.10 %
	FRR: 6.25 %	FRR: 9.68 %	FRR: 10.07 %

Table 4. Comparison of feature extraction results for the Immersion dataset containing 133 classes and 20 classes

Dataset	20 epochs	50 epochs	100 epochs
	Accuracy: 64.76 %	Accuracy: 88.22 %	Accuracy: 70.77 %
Immersion	FAR:	FAR:	FAR:
(133 classes)	33.95 %	9.88 %	27.30 %
	FRR:	FRR:	FRR:
	1.29 %	1.90 %	1.93 %
	Accuracy: 49.94 %	Accuracy: 73.54 %	Accuracy: 69.32 %
Immersion	FAR:	FAR:	FAR:
(20 classes)	44.42 %	12.35 %	15.86 %
	FRR:	FRR:	FRR:
	5.64 %	14.11 %	14.82 %

is highly probable that the huge gap between the amount of data employed for the experiments might have accentuated the difference with our results.

5   Conclusion

In the previous section, it was demonstrated that it is indeed possible to recognize persons through their medical images by means of our simple, unified deep-learning based identification method. This is remarkable, as for endoscopic visual data this outcome (i.e. that this is possible at all) was not necessarily to be expected, and for brain MRI existing techniques are much more complicated and do rely on data alignment.

Although the existence of this simple method may be useful in situations where easy patient identification is needed, it should also raise an alarm concerning patient privacy considering a release of medical imagery to the public. The reason for this is that, if one is able to perform the described identification, one would be able to do so for a person who, for example, participated in a study that resulted in a publicly available dataset of medical imagery. This identification would be done without the subject's consent, causing a serious privacy violation that would not only be in the responsibility of the researchers who directly conducted the study, but also their institution and the repository's organization. Given the discussion about corresponding GDPR regulations in the Introduction, it seems rather obvious that medical imagery even after pseudonymisation has to be considered personal data, given the simple algorithms that we have proven to facilitate patient identification.

From this, one can observe that, unless a method for obstructing this way of identification is developed, publicly accessible medical image data may cease to exist, as we know it today, in the future. For this reason, Anonymized Generative Adversarial Networks (AnomiGAN) [4] and Privacy-Preserving Semi-Generative Adversarial Network (PPSGAN) [15] have been introduced, which aim to ensure the privacy of personal medical data.

Although both methods for medical de-identification seem to fulfil the objective to protect patient privacy, they do this by creating synthetic data, which endangers the usage of the data for medical decision support. Therefore, it would be interesting in future work to investigate a technique where the original data is retained and only a spatial disentanglement of the identity features is performed. By doing this, the identifiers could be successfully concealed. However, extreme care has to be taken, because deteriorating the diagnosis related features in the process would be highly undesirable for obvious reasons.

References

1. Alaslani, M., Elrefaei, L.A.: Transfer learning with convolutional neural networks for iris recognition. Int. J. Artif. Intell. Appl 10(5), 47–64 (2019)
2. Alshazly, H., Linse, C., Barth, E., Martinetz, T.: Ensembles of deep learning models and transfer learning for ear recognition. Sensors 19(19), 4139 (2019)
3. Alshazly, H., Linse, C., Barth, E., Martinetz, T.: Handcrafted versus CNN features for ear recognition. Symmetry 11(12), 1493 (2019)
4. Bae, H., Jung, D., Choi, H.S., Yoon, S.: Anomigan: generative adversarial networks for anonymizing private medical data. In: Pacific Symposium on Biocomputing 2020, pp. 563–574. World Scientific (2019)
5. Cho, H., Zin, T.T., Shinkawa, N., Nishii, R.: Post-mortem human identification using chest x-ray and CT scan images. Int. J. Biomed. Soft Comput. Hum. Sci. Official J. Biomed. Fuzzy Syst. Assoc. 23(2), 51–57 (2018)
6. Das, A., Pal, U., Blumenstein, M., Ballester, M.A.F.: Sclera recognition-a survey. In: 2013 2nd IAPR Asian Conference on Pattern Recognition, pp. 917–921. IEEE (2013)
7. Finck, M., Pallas, F.: They who must not be identified-distinguishing personal from non-personal data under the GDPR. Int. Data Privacy Law 10(1), 11–35 (2020)
8. Fischl, B.: Freesurfer. Neuroimage 62(2), 774–781 (2012)
9. Fratini, A., Sansone, M., Bifulco, P., Cesarelli, M.: Individual identification via electrocardiogram analysis. Biomed. Eng. Online 14(1), 1–23 (2015)
10. Hadsell, R., Chopra, S., LeCun, Y.: Dimensionality reduction by learning an invariant mapping. In: 2006 IEEE Computer Society Conference on Computer Vision and Pattern Recognition (CVPR 2006), vol. 2, pp. 1735–1742. IEEE (2006)
11. Heinrich, A., et al.: Forensic odontology: automatic identification of persons comparing antemortem and postmortem panoramic radiographs using computer vision. In: RöFo-Fortschritte auf dem Gebiet der Röntgenstrahlen und der bildgebenden Verfahren. vol. 190, pp. 1152–1158. Georg Thieme Verlag KG (2018)
12. Ishigami, R., Zin, T.T., Shinkawa, N., Nishii, R.: Human identification using x-ray image matching. In: Proceedings of the International Multi Conference of Engineers and Computer Scientists, vol. 1 (2017)
13. Kabbara, Y., Shahin, A., Nait-Ali, A., Khalil, M.: An automatic algorithm for human identification using hand x-ray images. In: 2013 2nd International Conference on Advances in Biomedical Engineering, pp. 167–170. IEEE (2013)

14. Kent, A.R., Elsing, S.H., Hebert, R.L.: Conjunctival vasculature in the assessment of anemia. Ophtalmology **7**(2), 274–277 (2000)
15. Kim, T., Yang, J.: Selective feature anonymization for privacy-preserving image data publishing. Electronics **9**(5), 874 (2020)
16. Köse, C., İki, C., et al.: A personal identification system using retinal vasculature in retinal fundus images. Expert Syst. Appl. **38**(11), 13670–13681 (2011)
17. Kumar, K., Desrosiers, C., Siddiqi, K., Colliot, O., Toews, M.: Fiberprint: a subject fingerprint based on sparse code pooling for white matter fiber analysis. Neuroimage **158**, 242–259 (2017)
18. Kuzu, R.S., Maiorana, E., Campisi, P.: Vein-based biometric verification using transfer learning. In: 2020 43rd International Conference on Telecommunications and Signal Processing (TSP), pp. 403–409. IEEE (2020)
19. LaMontagne, P., et al.: Oasis-3: Longitudinal neuroimaging. Clinical, and Cognitive Dataset for Normal Aging and Alzheimer Disease. medRxiv (2019)
20. LeCun, Y., Bengio, Y., Hinton, G.: Deep learning. nature **521**(7553), 436–444 (2015)
21. Leibetseder, A., Kletz, S., Schoeffmann, K., Keckstein, S., Keckstein, J.: GLENDA: gynecologic laparoscopy endometriosis dataset. In: Ro, Y.M., et al. (eds.) MMM 2020. LNCS, vol. 11962, pp. 439–450. Springer, Cham (2020). https://doi.org/10.1007/978-3-030-37734-2_36
22. Minaee, S., Abdolrashidi, A.: Deepiris: Iris recognition using a deep learning approach. arXiv preprint arXiv:1907.09380 (2019)
23. Moccia, S., et al.: Learning-based classification of informative laryngoscopic frames. Comput. Methods Programs Biomed. **158**, 21–30 (2018)
24. Nguyen, K., Fookes, C., Ross, A., Sridharan, S.: Iris recognition with off-the-shelf CNN features: a deep learning perspective. IEEE Access **6**, 18848–18855 (2017)
25. Nomir, O., Abdel-Mottaleb, M.: Human identification from dental x-ray images based on the shape and appearance of the teeth. IEEE Trans. Inf. Forensics Secur. **2**(2), 188–197 (2007)
26. Papas, E.B.: Key factors in the subjective and objective assessment of conjunctival erythema. Invest. Ophthalmol. Vis. Sci. **41**, 687–691 (2000)
27. Pogorelov, K., et al.: Nerthus: a bowel preparation quality video dataset. In: Proceedings of the 8th ACM on Multimedia Systems Conference, pp. 170–174 (2017)
28. Poulos, M., Rangoussi, M., Kafetzopoulos, E.: Person identification via the EEG using computational geometry algorithms. In: 9th European Signal Processing Conference (EUSIPCO 1998), pp. 1–4. IEEE (1998)
29. Schroff, F., Kalenichenko, D., Philbin, J.: Facenet: a unified embedding for face recognition and clustering. In: Proceedings of the IEEE Conference on Computer Vision and Pattern Recognition, pp. 815–823 (2015)
30. Shamir, L.: MRI-based knee image for personal identification. Int. J. Biometrics **5**(2), 113–125 (2013)
31. Shamir, L., Ling, S., Rahimi, S., Ferrucci, L., Goldberg, I.G.: Biometric identification using knee x-rays. Int. J. Biometrics **1**(3), 365–370 (2009)
32. Simonyan, K., Zisserman, A.: Very deep convolutional networks for large-scale image recognition. arXiv preprint arXiv:1409.1556 (2014)
33. Wachinger, C., et al.: Brainprint: a discriminative characterization of brain morphology. Neuroimage **109**, 232–248 (2015)
34. Weiner, M.W., et al.: The Alzheimer's disease neuroimaging initiative: progress report and future plans. Alzheimer's Dementia **6**(3), 202–211 (2010)

35. Wimmer, G., Uhl, A., Vecsei, A.: Evaluation of domain specific data augmentation techniques for the classification of celiac disease using endoscopic imagery. In: 2017 IEEE 19th International Workshop on Multimedia Signal Processing (MMSP), pp. 1–6 (2017). https://doi.org/10.1109/MMSP.2017.8122221
36. Zhou, J., Abdel-Mottaleb, M.: A content-based system for human identification based on bitewing dental x-ray images. Pattern Recogn. **38**(11), 2132–2142 (2005)

Removing Specular Reflection in Multispectral Dermatological Images Using Blind Source Separation

Mustapha Zokay[(✉)] and Hicham Saylani

Laboratoire d'Électronique, Traitement du Signal et Modélisation Physique,
Faculté des Sciences, Université Ibn Zohr, BP 8106, Cité Dakhla, Agadir, Morocco
mustapha.zokay@edu.uiz.ac.ma, h.saylani@uiz.ac.ma

Abstract. In this paper we propose a new method for removing specular reflection from multispectral dermatological images which is based on blind source separation using Non-negative Matrix Factorization. The key idea of our method is based on a first step which consists to estimate the number of sources involved, by applying a Principal Component Analysis, then a first version of these sources by applying an Independent Component Analysis to our images. We exploit this first version of the sources in a second step to initialize our Non-negative Matrix Factorization algorithm instead of the random initialization that is used by most of the existing methods and that considerably affects their performances. In order to quantify numerically the performance of our method, we also propose a new protocol to artificially mix a specular reflection image with a diffuse reflection image. The tests effected on real and artificial multispectral dermatological images have shown the good performance of our method compared to two of the most used methods.

Keywords: Multispectral dermatological images · RGB images · Specular reflection · Diffuse reflection · Blind Source Separation (BSS) · Principal Component Analysis (PCA) · Independent Component Analysis (ICA) · Non-negative Matrix Factorization (NMF)

1 Introduction

Nowadays, medical imaging has become an essential tool to diagnose various human diseases, including those affecting the skin. Indeed, the dermatologists are increasingly using different imaging techniques for the early detection of skin diseases. One of these techniques that is increasingly used and has shown its effectiveness is multispectral imaging, which consists in acquiring different images of the same area of interest at different wavelengths [17]. The mutispectral images that are most commonly used in the field of dermatology are RGB colour images that are generally described by a so-called dichromatic mixing model. This model consists in expressing the total light reflected by the skin, called reflectance, as an additive mixture of the light immediately reflected by

© The Author(s), under exclusive license to Springer Nature Switzerland AG 2022
G. Yang et al. (Eds.): MIUA 2022, LNCS 13413, pp. 734–750, 2022.
https://doi.org/10.1007/978-3-031-12053-4_54

the skin, called specular reflection, and the light reflected after penetration into the skin, called diffuse reflection [28]. However, depending on its intensity, the specular reflection at the level of dermatological images can disturb the extraction of useful information for dermatologists and which are all contained in the diffuse reflection. Thus, the direct use of multi-spectral dermatological images is generally posed as a problem.

The classical solution that has always been adopted is one that consists basically in avoiding specular reflection by using two optical polarisers at the time of image acquisition [18]. However, this solution is no longer invetable since it needs a good adjustment of the equipment used and particular dispositions, things that are not accessible to most of the dermatologists. Thus, nowadays, a large part of the acquired dermatological images is affected by specular reflection, so that a pre-treatment to eliminate it is indispensable. Hence the necessity to use signal and image processing methods after a suitable modelling step. In this sense, following the optical model adopted by most researchers in the case of dermatological images [1,13,22,24], the reflectance detected by the multispectral camera at each wavelength λ at pixel $(x, y) = \boldsymbol{u}$, denoted $I_i(\boldsymbol{u})$, is written:

$$I_i(\boldsymbol{u}) = I_{i,d}(\boldsymbol{u}) + I_{i,s}(\boldsymbol{u}), \qquad 1 \leqslant i \leqslant M \tag{1}$$

$$= w_d(\boldsymbol{u}) \cdot \int_\Omega E(\lambda) F(\boldsymbol{u}, \lambda) q_i(\lambda) d\lambda + w_s(\boldsymbol{u}) \cdot \int_\Omega E(\lambda) q_i(\lambda) d\lambda \tag{2}$$

where:

- M is the number of spectral bands,
- $w_d(\boldsymbol{u})$ represents the variation of shading (which is related to the geometry of the skin),
- $E(\lambda)$ represents the intensity of the incident light,
- $F(\boldsymbol{u}, \lambda)$ represents the diffuse spectral reflectance function,
- $q_i(\lambda)$ represents the sensitivity of the camera sensor around the wavelength λ_i,
- Ω represents the spectral domain,
- $w_s(\boldsymbol{u})$ represents the specular component.

On the other hand, following the model adopted by most researchers [8], which consists to decompose the reflectance function $F(u, \lambda)$ in a set of basic functions, based on the colours of the image surface[1] we have:

$$F(\boldsymbol{u}, \lambda) = \sum_{j=1}^{N_d} \sigma_j(\boldsymbol{u}) \cdot f_j(\lambda), \tag{3}$$

where:

---

[1] As the reflectance function $F(u, \lambda)$ physically represents all phenomena produced by the interaction between light and skin, it is in principle described by an exponential model representing the absorption of the different components of the skin [14].

- N_d is the number of surface colours (diffuse colours),
- $f_j(\lambda)$ represents the basic functions of reflectance,
- $\sigma_j(\boldsymbol{u})$ are coefficients that depend on the surface colour.

Thus, using Eqs. (2) and (3), we finally obtain the following linear mixture model:

$$I_i(\boldsymbol{u}) = \sum_{j=1}^{j=N_d+1} a_{ij} \cdot S_j(\boldsymbol{u}), \qquad 1 \leqslant i \leqslant M, \tag{4}$$

where a_{ij} and $S_j(\boldsymbol{u})$ are defined respectively by the two following relations:

$$a_{ij} = \begin{cases} E(\lambda)f_j(\lambda)q_i(\lambda)d\lambda & \text{for} \quad 1 \leqslant j \leqslant N_d \\ \int_\Omega E(\lambda)q_i(\lambda)d\lambda & \text{for} \quad j = N_d + 1 \end{cases} \tag{5}$$

$$S_j(\boldsymbol{u}) = \begin{cases} \sigma_j(\boldsymbol{u})w_d(\boldsymbol{u}) & \text{for} \quad 1 \leqslant j \leqslant N_d \\ w_s(\boldsymbol{u}) & \text{for} \quad j = N_d + 1 \end{cases} \tag{6}$$

Over the past decade, the use of signal and image processing methods to remove specular reflection from multispectral images has attracted the interest of several researchers, whether for dermatological images [1,13,22,24] or for any other images [2,31]. This work has led to different methods which concern RGB images and which can be classified in two main families.

The methods of the first family are image processing methods which mainly use digital filtering techniques since they consider specular reflection as a noise image [1,13,22,31]. All based on a mixing model with only one component for the diffuse reflection (i.e. $N_d = 1$ in the Eq. (3)), they differ only in the filtering technique used. Indeed, to eliminate this noise, in [1] Abbas et al. used a high-pass filter. In [13], Gutenev et al. used a median filter. In [31], Yang et al. proposed using a bilateral filter. In [22], Liu et al. proposed to use the Yang method [31] and an interpolation technique. However, all these methods have constraints that limit their use to specific cases of dermatological images.

The methods of the second family are methods of signal processing more advanced that are also interested in the diffuse reflection as well as the specular reflection [2,24]. Indeed, by considering each of these two reflections as a full-fledged source of interest, they can finally estimate each of them separately, which allows to obtain an estimate of an RGB image containing only the diffuse reflection. These methods are then called methods of source separation which are more and more used to solve the inverse problems in the field of signal processing. Indeed, the objective of source separation is to estimate the sources from the only knowledge of their mixtures. When this estimation is done without any a priori information neither on the sources nor on the mixing coefficients, we call it Blind Source Separation (BSS)[2] [9]. In this sense, in [24], Madooei et al. were

---

[2] We show that the BSS problem is an ill-posed inverse problem which admits an infinity of solutions so that it is essential to add hypotheses on the sources and/or on the mixing coefficients, which gave rise to 3 families of methods. These three families are based respectively on *Independent Component Analysis (ICA)*, *Sparse Component Analysis (SCA)* and *Non-negative Matrix Factorisation (NMF)* (See [9] for more details).

based on a mixture model with a single component for diffuse reflection (i.e. $N_d = 1$ in the Eq. (3)) for dermatological images, then they used a BSS method based on *Non-negative Matrix Factorization (NMF)* with a sparsity constraint[3] on source images. In [2], Akhashi et al. proposed to test several values for the number N_d of components of the diffuse reflection (assumed unknown for any multispectral image) and then they used a BSS method based on *NMF* with sparsity constraints. In addition, these two methods suffer in their implementation from the problem of setting the parameter related to the degree of sparsity of the specular reflection in the image which is unknown and changes from one image to another. Moreover, both in [2] and in [24], the authors initialize their solution matrices with random matrices, which has an important impact on the performance of their methods.

In this paper, we propose a new method to remove specular reflection in dermatological images using BSS. For this, we adopt a mixing model in which we choose wisely the number of components of diffuse reflection N_d, then in a first step, we apply an *Independent Component Analysis (ICA)* to our images in order to estimate a first version of each component (diffuse and specular). We then exploit these first versions estimated by *ICA* for the initialization during a second step which consists to effect a *NMF* of our mixing matrix, contrary to the existing methods proposed in [2] and [24] which use a random initialization of the solution matrices. The rest of this paper is organized as follows. Section 2 presents our new method to remove specular reflection in dermatological images. Section 3 presents the results of the tests performed followed by a last section dedicated to a conclusion and perspectives for our work.

2   Proposed Method

In this section, we present our new method which aims to remove specular reflection present in dermatological images. This means that our proposed method allows us to estimate an image consisting only of the diffuse reflection that contains the pertinent information for the dermatologists. By adopting the mixing model described by the Eq. (4), we are first interested to determine the number of the diffuse reflection components N_d, which is primordial in this model, in order to make it the most adequate for modeling the real dermatological images. In this sense, we recall that according to the foundations provided in [8], which gave rise to the Eq. (3), and the mixing model proposed by Shafer in [28], the diffuse reflection is represented by the colours that relate to all the intrinsic information of the area of interest (taken in the image) while the specular reflec-

---

[3] A signal is said to be sparse in a given representation domain if there are some areas of that domain where it is inactive.

tion can be seen as an external factor that is represented only by the colour of the incident light. By exploiting these results for dermatological images, we concluded that the diffuse reflection of these images contains at least two main colours. In order to confirm this statement, we explored a database consisting of 30 real dermatological images which are 6-band multispectral images[4] [20], and which can be grouped into two classes, the images containing specular reflection and those without or with very low specular reflection. Indeed, by applying a Principal Component Analysis (PCA) [30], based on the computation of the covariance matrix of the spectral bands of each of these images, we could see that the number of principal components[5] of any image is equal to 3 when the latter contains specular reflection and equal to 2 otherwise. On the other hand, as most of the images provided by the databases in the field of dermatology are RGB images, i.e. 3-bands multispectral images (i.e. $M = 3$), for the following we rewrite the Eq. (4) as follows:

$$I_i(\boldsymbol{u}) = \sum_{j=1}^{j=3} a_{ij} S_j(\boldsymbol{u}), \qquad i \in \{1, 2, 3\}, \tag{7}$$

where $S_1(\boldsymbol{u})$ and $S_2(\boldsymbol{u})$ model the two sources that represent the two components of diffuse reflection and $S_3(\boldsymbol{u})$ models the source that represents the specular reflection. As with all BSS methods, we generate new one-dimensional mixtures (vectors), denoted $x_i(v)$, from the two-dimensional mixtures (matrices) $I_i(\boldsymbol{u})$ using the classical matrix vectorisation procedure[6] [10]. By adopting the following notations:

$$x_i(v) = \text{vec}(I_i(\boldsymbol{u})) \qquad \text{and} \qquad s_j(v) = \text{vec}(S_j(\boldsymbol{u})), \tag{8}$$

the equation (7) gives us:

$$x_i(v) = \sum_{j=1}^{j=3} a_{ij} s_j(v), \qquad i \in \{1, 2, 3\}. \tag{9}$$

The matrix formulation of these three linear mixtures described by the Eq. (9) gives us:

$$\mathbf{x}(v) = \mathbf{A} \cdot \mathbf{s}(v), \tag{10}$$

---

[4] That is 3 bands corresponding to the visible range (RGB) and 3 bands corresponding to the infrared range.

[5] We recall that this number of principal components is none other than the number of non-zero (or significant) eigenvalues of the covariance matrix associated to the image. In practice, we choose a threshold below which an eigenvalue is considered to be zero (see Results section).

[6] For example, for a matrix of size $m \times n$, this vectorisation consists in juxtaposing its rows one after the other which gives us a vector of length "$m \cdot n$".

where:

- $\mathbf{x}(v) = [x_1(v), x_2(v), x_3(v)]^T$,
- $\mathbf{s}(v) = [s_1(v), s_2(v), s_3(v)]^T$,
- $\mathbf{A} = (a_{ij})_{1 \leqslant i,j \leqslant 3}$.

Based on the *NMF*, the BSS method that we propose in this paper and that finally allows to separate the sources of diffuse reflection from that of specular reflection proceeds in two steps. The first step is to apply an *ICA* to our mixtures in order to estimate a first version of the source matrix $\mathbf{s}(v)$. We then exploit this first version in the second step for the initialization of our *NMF* algorithm. These two steps are detailed below.

Step 1: Preliminary separation using ICA

This step consists in applying an *ICA* to the mixtures $x_i(v)$ in order to obtain new mixtures which we note $y_i(v)$ that are as independent as possible. For this, we assume that the sources involved are independent. There are several BSS methods to achieve this objective[7]. We have opted here for the *AMUSE* method [29] for its simplicity, since it exploits the second-order statistics of the signals only, and because we assume that its working hypotheses are verified by the sources involved (i.e. the two components of the diffuse reflection and the specular reflection). These working hypotheses are as follows:

1. The sources $s_j(v)$ are *auto-correlated* and *mutually uncorrelated*, i.e.:

$$\forall \tau, \quad \begin{cases} E[s_j(v) \cdot s_j(v - \tau)] \neq 0, \ \forall \, j \\ E[s_i(v) \cdot s_j(v - \tau)] = E[s_i(v)] \cdot E[s_j(v - \tau)], \ \forall \, i \neq j \end{cases} \quad (11)$$

2. The *condition of identifiability* for the method is verified, i.e.:

$$\exists \, \tau \neq 0 \, / \quad \frac{E[s_i(v) \cdot s_i(v - \tau)]}{E[s_i^2(v)]} \neq \frac{E[s_j(v) \cdot s_j(v - \tau)]}{E[s_j^2(v)]}, \ \forall \, i \neq j \quad (12)$$

Here is the algorithm of this method which finally allows to estimate the separation matrix $\mathbf{A}^{-1}$ to a permutation matrix $\mathbf{P}$ and a diagonal matrix $\mathbf{D}$ [29].

---

[7] Indeed, BSS methods based on *ICA* can be classified into two families [9]. The first family includes the methods that exploit higher order statistics and assume that the source signals are statistically independent at higher orders (for example, the methods *JADE* [6] and *FasICA* [16]). The second family includes the methods that exploit second-order statistics and assume that the source signals are statistically independent at second order only (for example, the methods *AMUSE* [29] and *SOBI* [3]).

Algorithm 1 : *AMUSE* Method

---

1. Construction of the new vector of centred mixtures $\tilde{\mathbf{x}}(v)$:
   $\tilde{\mathbf{x}}(v) = [\tilde{x}_1(v), \tilde{x}_2(v), \tilde{x}_3(v)]^T$, where $\tilde{x}_i(v) = x_i(v) - E[x_i(v)]$, $i \in \{1, 2, 3\}$
2. Diagonalization of the matrix $\mathbf{R}_{\tilde{\mathbf{x}}}(0)$: $\mathbf{R}_{\tilde{\mathbf{x}}}(0) = E[\tilde{\mathbf{x}}(v).\tilde{\mathbf{x}}^T(v)] = \mathbf{V} \cdot \mathbf{E}_0 \cdot \mathbf{V}^T$
3. Spatial whitening of mixtures: $\mathbf{z}(v) = \mathbf{W} \cdot \tilde{\mathbf{x}}(v)$, where $\mathbf{W} = \mathbf{E}_0^{-\frac{1}{2}} \cdot \mathbf{V}^T$
4. Calculation of a matrix $\mathbf{R}_{\mathbf{z}}(\tau) = E[\mathbf{z}(v).\mathbf{z}^T(v - \tau)]$, $\tau \neq 0$ verifying the Eq. (12)
5. Diagonalization of the matrix $\mathbf{R} = \frac{1}{2} \{\mathbf{R}_{\mathbf{z}}(\tau) + \mathbf{R}_{\mathbf{z}}^T(\tau)\}$: $\mathbf{R} = \mathbf{U} \cdot \mathbf{E}_\tau \cdot \mathbf{U}^T$
6. Estimating the separation matrix : $\mathbf{C} = \mathbf{U}^T \cdot \mathbf{W} = \mathbf{PD} \cdot \mathbf{A}^{-1}$

Once the matrix $\mathbf{C}$ is estimated, we apply it to the matrix of non-centred mixtures $\mathbf{x}(v)$ instead of the matrix of centred mixtures $\tilde{\mathbf{x}}(v)$ as it is the case in the classical version of the *AMUSE* method [29]. Indeed, contrary to the classical case where the centred versions of the sources involved have generally the same interest as the non-centred versions[8], here we manipulate images whose pixels are all positive and whose centred versions have no interest. Thus, by noting $\mathbf{y}(v) = \mathbf{C} \cdot \mathbf{x}(v)$ we ideally obtain:

$$\mathbf{y}(v) = (\mathbf{PDA}^{-1}) \cdot (\mathbf{As}(v)) = \mathbf{PD} \cdot \mathbf{s}(v). \tag{13}$$

This relation (13) means that we would get ideally each source $s_j(v)$ to a scale factor $\mathbf{D}(j, j)$, with possibly permutations between them, which is not at all annoying for the most of applications [9]. However, as generally the working hypotheses of the method cannot be verified perfectly by our sources[9] the equalities in this Eq. (13) are never perfect, which means that we would instead have :

$$\mathbf{y}(v) \simeq \mathbf{PD} \cdot \mathbf{s}(v). \tag{14}$$

Hence the interest of a second step for our method which consists in considering the components of the matrix $\mathbf{y}(v)$ as the versions used as a basis for estimating new versions that are as close as possible to the optimal solutions.

Step 2: Estimation of diffuse reflection using NMF

This second step for our method consists in applying a *Non-negative Matrix Factorization* (*NMF*) in order to separate the different sources involved. This factorization consists in decomposing the matrix $\mathbf{x}(v)$ into the product of two matrices $\mathbf{B}$ and $\mathbf{h}(v)$ such that these two matrices approximate as well as possible the matrices $\mathbf{A}$ and $\mathbf{s}(v)$ respectively, i.e.:

$$\mathbf{x}(v) = \mathbf{A} \cdot \mathbf{s}(v) \tag{15}$$
$$= \mathbf{B} \cdot \mathbf{h}(v) \tag{16}$$

---

[8] This is for example the case of audio signals.

[9] This is the case for most of the real sources, using any BSS method.

where:
$$\mathbf{B} \backsimeq \mathbf{A} \quad \text{and} \quad \mathbf{h}(v) \backsimeq \mathbf{s}(v). \tag{17}$$

Note that this approach of BSS based on the *NMF* is particularly interesting in the sense that it allows to estimate the two matrices $\mathbf{A}$ and $\mathbf{s}(v)$ simultaneously[10]. The two indispensable hypotheses of this *NMF* approach are [7]:

1. $a_{ij} \geqslant 0$ and $s_j(v) \geqslant 0, \quad \forall i, j$
2. The number of mixtures available must be at least equal to the number of sources involved[11].

The determination of the two solution matrices $\mathbf{B}$ and $\mathbf{h}(v)$ using this approach amounts to minimize a criterion (or cost function) based on the measure of the deviation between the matrix $\mathbf{x}(v)$ and the product matrix $\mathbf{B} \cdot \mathbf{h}(v)$. Thus, the problem of *NMF* can be formulated as an optimization problem. Knowing that there are several criteria that allow us to measure this deviation [12], we have opted here for the most popular criterion which is the Euclidean distance, noted $D_{euc}(\mathbf{x}|\mathbf{Bh})$ and defined as follows:

$$D_{euc}(\mathbf{x}|\mathbf{Bh}) = \frac{1}{2}||\mathbf{x}(v) - \mathbf{B} \cdot \mathbf{h}(v)||^2. \tag{18}$$

To minimize this criterion, there are different algorithms in the literature, the most basic and popular of which have been proposed in [19,21,25]. Called the *Multiplicative Update algorithm (MU)*, the first one uses the gradient of the Lagrangian of our criterion [19]. The second algorithm, called the *Projected Gradient* algorithm (*PG*), exploits the gradient descent algorithm to realise the minimisation based on bounds constraints [21]. The third algorithm, which is called the *Alternate Least Squares algorithm (ALS)*, consists of decomposing the basic minimization problem into two distinct subproblems. The first sub-problem consists to minimize the criterion relative to the matrix $\mathbf{B}$ while the second consists to minimize this criterion relative to the matrix $\mathbf{h}(v)$ [25]. However, the major problem of *NMF* is that the factorization is not unique. Indeed, we can easily see that for any invertible matrix $\mathbf{M}$, the $\mathbf{B}$ and $\mathbf{h}(v)$ matrices defined by $\mathbf{B} = \mathbf{AM}^{-1}$ and $\mathbf{h}(v) = \mathbf{Ms}(v)$ are also solutions since we have:

$$\mathbf{x}(v) = \mathbf{A} \cdot \mathbf{s}(v) \tag{19}$$
$$= \mathbf{AM}^{-1} \cdot \mathbf{Ms}(v) \tag{20}$$

To solve this problem, the researchers were interested in reducing the set of solutions to a subset of admissible solutions, for which the matrix $\mathbf{M}$, called the indeterminacy matrix, is ideally written $\mathbf{M} = \tilde{\mathbf{P}}\tilde{\mathbf{D}}$, where $\tilde{\mathbf{P}}$ and $\tilde{\mathbf{D}}$ are respectively a permutation matrix and a diagonal matrix. In this case we have:

$$\mathbf{B} = \mathbf{AM}^{-1} = \mathbf{A}\tilde{\mathbf{D}}^{-1}\tilde{\mathbf{P}}^{-1} \tag{21}$$
$$\mathbf{h}(v) = \mathbf{M} \cdot \mathbf{s}(v) = \tilde{\mathbf{P}}\tilde{\mathbf{D}} \cdot \mathbf{s}(v) \tag{22}$$

---

[10] Indeed, for all other BSS approaches, the separation is performed in two steps: the estimation of the separation matrix, then that of the sources.

[11] In other words, in our case the number of spectral bands M of our image must be superior than or equal to the number of sources which is equal to $N_d + 1$.

For this, two solutions were adopted by these researchers. The first solution is to add a constraint to our criterion $D_{euc}(\mathbf{x}|\mathbf{Bh})$, as in [11,15] for the sparsity constraint, or in [27] for the constraint of the minimal determinant. The second solution consists to initialize $\mathbf{B}$ and/or $\mathbf{h}(v)$ by very particular matrices, as in [5], and this in order to avoid at best that the minimization algorithm converges to undesirable solutions, called local minima (which correspond to the cases where the indeterminacy matrix $\mathbf{M}$ is any).

On the other hand, the existing methods based on *NMF* that were interested in our topic [2,24] have used the algorithm *MU* [19] with sparsity constraint [11,15] since the specular reflection image is very sparse. Nevertheless, these methods suffer from an implementation problem due to the difficulty of setting the parameter related to the degree of sparseness of this reflection. Thus, in this paper, we are interested in the second solution by proposing to initialize the matrix $\mathbf{h}(v)$ by the matrix $\mathbf{y}(v)$ estimated by the *ICA* in the first step. For the choice of the minimization algorithm, we opted for the *ALS* algorithm which is known on the one hand by its rapidity, compared to the other algorithms of *NMF*, and on the other hand by its good performances in the case of sparse signals [4]. Here is the detail of this algorithm.

Algorithm 2 : *NMF-ALS*

---

1. Initialize $\mathbf{h}(v)$ by the matrix $\mathbf{y}(v)$ estimated by the *ICA* : $\mathbf{h}(v) = \mathbf{y}(v)$
2. **While** $D_{euc}(\mathbf{x}|\mathbf{Bh}) > \epsilon$, **do** :
   - $\mathbf{B} = \mathbf{xh}^T(\mathbf{hh}^T)^{-1}$
   - Set to zero all negative elements of $\mathbf{B}$
   - $\mathbf{h} = (\mathbf{B}^T\mathbf{B})^{-1}\mathbf{B}^T\mathbf{x}$
   - Set to zero all negative elements of $\mathbf{h}$
   - $D_{euc}(\mathbf{x}|\mathbf{Bh}) = \frac{1}{2}||\mathbf{x}(v) - \mathbf{B} \cdot \mathbf{h}(v)||^2$

After the convergence of the *ALS* algorithm, we obtain the two solution matrices $\mathbf{B}$ and $\mathbf{h}(v)$ which, from the Eqs. (22), are written ideally:

$$\mathbf{B} = \begin{pmatrix} b_{11} & b_{12} & b_{13} \\ b_{21} & b_{22} & b_{23} \\ b_{31} & b_{32} & b_{33} \end{pmatrix} = \mathbf{A} \cdot (\tilde{\mathbf{P}}\tilde{\mathbf{D}})^{-1}, \tag{23}$$

and

$$\mathbf{h}(v) = \begin{pmatrix} h_1(v) \\ h_2(v) \\ h_3(v) \end{pmatrix} = \tilde{\mathbf{P}}\tilde{\mathbf{D}} \begin{pmatrix} s_1(v) \\ s_2(v) \\ s_3(v) \end{pmatrix}. \tag{24}$$

Knowing that the specular reflection is easily identifiable visually[12] from the three components of the matrix $\mathbf{h}(v)$, it is sufficient to take it with the corre-

---

[12] Note that, we could very well propose a criterion exploiting the distribution of the specular reflection which is known for its sparseness, in order to identify it automatically.

sponding column of the matrix $\mathbf{B}$ to reconstruct the corresponding mixtures that we note $x_{i,s}(v)$. The two remaining components of the matrix $\mathbf{h}(v)$ as well as the corresponding columns of the matrix $\mathbf{B}$ will then be used for the reconstruction of the mixtures corresponding to the diffuse reflection that we note $x_{i,d}(v)$. In other words, if we consider for example that the component $h_3(v)$ corresponds to the specular reflection, then for each spectral band of index $i \in \{1,2,3\}$ we have:

$$x_{i,d}(v) = b_{i1} \cdot h_1(v) + b_{i2} \cdot h_2(v) \tag{25}$$

$$x_{i,s}(v) = b_{i3} \cdot h_3(v) \tag{26}$$

Finally, by the inverse operation of the vectorization adopted in (8), from the mixtures $x_{i,d}(v)$ and $x_{i,s}(v)$ we can reconstruct two images that we note $\hat{I}_{i,d}(\boldsymbol{u})$ and $\hat{I}_{i,s}(\boldsymbol{u})$, and which correspond respectively to an estimate of the RGB image of diffuse reflection and an estimate of the RGB image of specular reflection as follows:

$$\hat{I}_{i,d}(\boldsymbol{u}) = \mathrm{vec}^{-1}(x_{i,d}(v)) \tag{27}$$

$$\hat{I}_{i,s}(\boldsymbol{u}) = \mathrm{vec}^{-1}(x_{i,s}(v)), \tag{28}$$

knowing that what interests us in the end is the RGB image of diffuse reflection provided by the Eq. (27), which corresponds to an RGB dermatological image without specular reflection.

3   Results

In this section, we evaluate the performance of our method by comparing it to the two methods that have been proposed respectively in [31] and [2]. We recall that the first method [31] is a method based on image processing techniques while the second method [2] is a method based on BSS (see Sect. 1). We first evaluate these performances in the case of real multispectral dermatological images. In this case, we use the visual analysis of the area containing specular reflection before and after treatment as a criterion of measuring the performance. In order to quantify precisely the effectiveness of our method, we additionally evaluate its performance on artificial dermatological images that result from artificially mixing a real dermatological image that is proper (i.e. an image consisting only of the diffuse reflection) and a realistic specular reflection image. In this case, for the performance measurement we can use a numerical criterion which is based on the comparison between the estimated and the simulated source images. The test protocols as well as the results obtained for these two cases of dermatological images (real and artificial) are the subject of Sects. 3.1 and 3.2 respectively.

3.1   Real Dermatological Images

For our tests on real images, we used dermatological images provided by the database consists of 30 multispectral images with 6 bands that was developed by authors of [20] and which is accessible via [23]. First, we exploited the 6 available bands to ensure that the number of diffuse reflection components N_d is equal to 2 as mentioned in Sect. 2. Thus, after applying the PCA to all the images in this database, we can see that the number of principal components is equal to 3 for the images containing a strong specular reflection, and equal to 2 for the images without or with very low specular reflection[13].

Then, we were interested only to the three bands in the visible domain that form a dermatological RGB image. Knowing that we have tested our method on all the images and that the obtained results are similar, we present here only the obtained results for three images, due to lack of space. We have taken for these three images those which present the most specular reflection in order to make easier the quantification of the performances of three methods tested using as criterion the visual analysis of the areas where specular reflection is present before and after treatment. For the first step of our method, we have taken for the offset parameter $\tau = 10$. For the method 2, after having performed several tests[14], we have taken for the parameter which concerns the degree of sparseness of the specular reflection, noted α in [2], $\alpha = 2$, and for the number of components of the diffuse reflection[15], we have taken $N_d = 2$. the Fig. 1 groups into four columns the original images as well as the images obtained after processing using each of the three methods. The first column groups the original images while the three other columns group the images obtained using respectively the existing methods 1 and 2 and our method. We introduced in each original image a rectangle to point to one of the areas of the skin that contain specular reflection. This area serves as a marker to facilitate the visual analysis and the comparison between the three methods.

From the results illustrated by the images in Fig. 1, we can see that the elimination of specular reflection is significantly better using our method. In fact, the images provided by the other two methods still contain specular reflection. We also note that the processing done by these two methods greatly affects the image which is found degraded, which is not at all the case for the image provided by our method. We can explain the failure of these two methods mainly by the fact that their working hypotheses are not verified. We recall that method 1 proposed in [31], which consists to estimate the maximum diffuse chromaticity using a bilateral filter, assumes that the contribution of the specular reflection is the same in all the spectral bands of the image, which represents an unrealistic hypothesis Based on the NMF with sparsity constraint, method 2 proposed in [2], which also consists to separate the diffuse reflection from the specular reflection, is known for its sensitivity to the initialization of the solution matrices, in addition to its sensitivity to the setting of the parameter α related to the degree of sparsity of the specular reflection.

---

[13] In our computations, any eigenvalue of the covariance matrix (associated to the image) having a value less than 10^{-3} is considered as null.

[14] We used for that the source codes of the method [2] provided in [26].

[15] Knowing that, we performed tests for different values of N_d, and we found that the method [2] gives good results for $N_d = 2$.

3.2 Artificial Dermatological Images

It is usual in the field of BSS to study the performance of a method on artificial mixtures, in which case the source matrix as well as the mixing matrix are known in advance. This makes it possible to build a numerical criterion of performance measurement which is based on the comparison between the estimated and simulated matrices. Artificial images allow us to quantify in a precise way the performance of any method contrary to the case of real mixtures (i.e. real images) treated above[16]. On the other hand, it is usual to validate any BSS method first on artificial mixtures since it ensures that the working hypotheses of this method are well verified (since the sources are known).

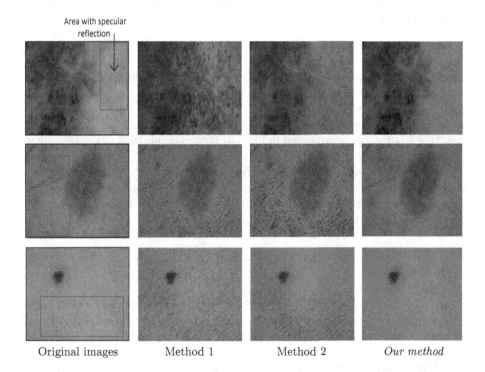

Original images   Method 1   Method 2   *Our method*

Fig. 1. Diffuse reflection estimated by our method and other methods.

As there is no protocol to generate artificial dermatological images, and in order to make these artificial images as close as possible to the real images, we proposed to use a real dermatological image from the database [23] which is proper (i.e. an image consisting only of the diffuse reflection) and then to

---

[16] Indeed, the criterion based on the visual analysis of the treated images is a qualitative criterion and it is difficult with the naked eye to compare in a precise way between two treated images. This comparison becomes even more difficult, if not impossible, when the two images are very close in terms of elimination the specular reflection.

add to it an artificial image of specular reflection. Furthermore, rather than generating this artificial specular reflection image randomly, we proposed to exploit the specular reflection estimates provided by the tests on real images in the previous section, in order to make this reflection image realistic. Once the separation has been achieved, the performance measurement will be focused only on the comparison between the simulated image and the one estimated from the specular reflection. The efficiency of methods 1, 2, and our method is shown by the closeness in appearance the estimated images from these methods and the original image. The proper dermatological image as well as the reflection image that was added to it to artificially generate different RGB images containing specular reflection are shown in Fig. 2. Indeed, in order to validate statically the performances of three methods we generated 20 RGB images, whose each spectral band $I_i(\boldsymbol{u})$ is written:

$$I_i(\boldsymbol{u}) = I_{i,d}(\boldsymbol{u}) + a_{i3}S_3(\boldsymbol{u}), \qquad i \in \{1,2,3\} \tag{29}$$

where $I_{i,d}(\boldsymbol{u})$ and $S_3(\boldsymbol{u})$ are respectively the proper RGB image[17] and the additive specular reflection image, and a_{i3} is the mixing coefficient which allows to change the contribution of this reflection, and which varies from one realization to another in a random way. We have taken for these tests $a_{i3} \in \,]0,1]$ and the resulting RGB image represented in Fig. 2-(c) corresponds then to the case where $[a_{13}, a_{23}, a_{33}] = [0.2, 0.3, 0.5]$.

For each test we will measure the performance of each method using as a criterion the Signal to Interference Ratio (SIR) which is based on the comparison between the estimated specular reflection vector $h_3(v)$ and the simulated one (i.e. $s_3(v) = \text{vec}(S_3(\boldsymbol{u}))$) and is defined as follows [9]:

$$SIR = 10 \cdot log_{10} \left(\frac{E[s_3'(v)^2]}{E[(s_3'(v) - h_3'(v))^2]} \right), \tag{30}$$

where $s_3'(v)$ and $h_3'(v)$ are respectively the normalized versions of $s_3(v)$ and $h_3(v)$. The more $h_3(v)$ tends to $s_3(v)$ (which means that the specular reflection is well estimated) the more the SIR is important. As we evaluate the performances on 20 realizations, we provide in Table 1 the mean and standard deviation of the SIR, noted respectively $\overline{SIR}$ and σ which are expressed in dB. Knowing that in [2] the authors of the method 2 proposed to test different values for the number of diffuse components N_d, we also tested this method for $N_d = 1$ and $N_d = 3$. Knowing that the resulting RGB image to be treated (containing specular reflection) is represented in Fig. 2-(c), the images estimated by the three methods are represented in Fig. 3.

---

[17] i.e. the real RGB image consisting only of the diffuse reflection.

Table 1. Mean and standard deviation of SIR obtained for the three methods.

	Method 1 [31]	Method 2 [2]			Our method
		$N_d = 1$	$N_d = 2$	$N_d = 3$	$N_d = 2$
$\overline{SIR}\,(dB)$	2.31	12.58	**18.60**	12.55	**41.60**
$\sigma\,(dB)$	7.38	5.51	**12.36**	11.37	**0.19**

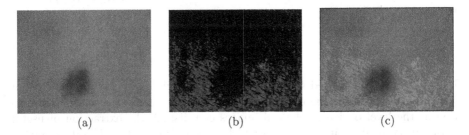

(a)   (b)   (c)

Fig. 2. (a) Proper RGB image, (b) Specular reflection image and (c) Resulting RGB image.

From the Table 1, we can see that our method performs much better than methods 1 and 2 in terms of SIR. In fact, we estimate the specular reflection with a mean of 41.6 dB and a standard deviation close to zero, while methods 1 and 2 do not exceed 19 dB with a very large standard deviation. We can also see that the performance of method 2 is better for $N_d = 2$, which confirms the validity of our working hypothesis (i.e. $N_d = 2$) which was supported by an

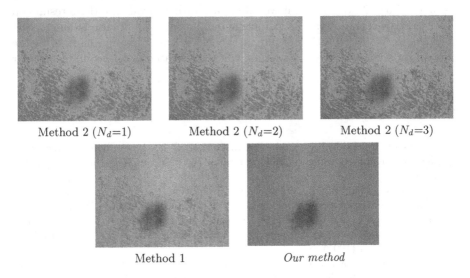

Method 2 (N_d=1)   Method 2 (N_d=2)   Method 2 (N_d=3)

Method 1   *Our method*

Fig. 3. Diffuse reflection estimated by our method and methods 1 and 2.

identification step of the number N_d based on *PCA*. On the other hand, the fact that the performance of method 2 is significantly better than method 1, which is an image processing method, allows us to deduce that the BSS approach is better adapted to achieve the objective of this work. Moreover, these obtained results are in perfect concordance with the images estimated by each of the three methods which are represented in Fig. 3. Indeed, from this figure, as in the case of real dermatological images, only our method allows to remove the specular reflection of the image without deforming it.

4   Conclusion

In this paper we proposed a new method for removing specular reflection from dermatological images. Indeed, depending on its intensity, the specular reflection at the level of dermatological images can disturb the extraction of useful information for dermatologists and which are all contained in the diffuse reflection. Based on BSS using *NMF*, our method proceeds in two steps. We first apply a *PCA* in order to estimate the number of sources and then an *ICA* in order to estimate a first version of the matrix sources, corresponding respectively to the two components of the diffuse reflection and the specular reflection. We exploit in a second step this first version for the initialization of our *NMF* algorithm, contrary to the existing methods [2,24] using a random initialization which affects considerably their performances. In order to be able to quantify numerically the performance of our method, we have also proposed a new protocol to artificially mix a specular reflection image with a diffuse reflection image. The results of the tests performed on real and artificial multispectral dermatological images have shown the relevance of our method compared to two existing methods [2,31]. Nevertheless, it would be interesting to validate these results on other multispectral dermatological image databases. It would also be interesting to evaluate the contribution of our method as a pre-processing method before applying any image processing method when the treated images contain specular reflection.

References

1. Abbas, Q., Celebi, M.E., Fondón García, I., Rashid, M.: Lesion border detection in dermoscopy images using dynamic programming. Skin Res. Technol. **17**(1), 91–100 (2011)
2. Akashi, Y., Okatani, T.: Separation of reflection components by sparse non-negative matrix factorization. Comput. Vis. Image Underst. **146**(C), 77–85 (2016)
3. Belouchrani, A., Abed-Meraim, K., Cardoso, J.F., Moulines, E.: A blind source separation technique using second-order statistics. IEEE Trans. Signal Process. **45**(2), 434–444 (1997)
4. Berry, M.W., Browne, M., Langville, A.N., Pauca, V.P., Plemmons, R.J.: Algorithms and applications for approximate nonnegative matrix factorization. Comput. Stat. Data Anal. **52**(1), 155–173 (2007)

5. Boutsidis, C., Gallopoulos, E.: SVD based initialization: a head start for nonnegative matrix factorization. Pattern Recogn. **41**(4), 1350–1362 (2008)
6. Cardoso, J.F., Souloumiac, A.: Blind beamforming for non-gaussian signals. In: IEE Proceedings F (radar and signal processing), vol. 140, pp. 362–370. IET (1993)
7. Cichocki, A., Zdunek, R., Phan, A.H., Amari, S.I.: Nonnegative Matrix and Tensor Factorizations: Applications to Exploratory Multi-way Data Analysis and Blind Source Separation. Wiley, New York (2009)
8. Cohen, J.: Dependency of the spectral reflectance curves of the Munsell color chips. Psychon. Sci. **1**(1), 369–370 (1964)
9. Comon, P., Jutten, C.: Handbook of Blind Source Separation, Independent Component Analysis and Applications, February 2010. https://doi.org/10.1016/C2009-0-19334-0
10. Dhrymes, P.J.: Matrix vectorization. In: Mathematics for Econometrics, pp. 117–145. Springer, New York (2000). https://doi.org/10.1007/978-1-4757-3238-2_4
11. Eggert, J., Korner, E.: Sparse coding and NMF. In: 2004 IEEE International Joint Conference on Neural Networks (IEEE Cat. No.04CH37541). vol. 4, pp. 2529–2533 (2004). https://doi.org/10.1109/IJCNN.2004.1381036
12. Févotte, C., Idier, J.: Algorithms for nonnegative matrix factorization with the β-divergence. Neural Comput. **23**(9), 2421–2456 (2011)
13. Gutenev, A., Skladnev, V., Varvel, D.: Acquisition-time image quality control in digital dermatoscopy of skin lesions. Comput. Med. Imaging Graph. **25**(6), 495–499 (2001)
14. Hecht, H.G.: The interpretation of diffuse reflectance spectra. J. Res. Natl. Bureau Stand. Sect. A, Phys. Chem. **80**(4), 567 (1976)
15. Hoyer, P.O.: Non-negative matrix factorization with sparseness constraints. J. Mach. Learn. Res. **5**(9), 1457–1469 (2004)
16. Hyvärinen, A., Oja, E.: Independent component analysis: algorithms and applications. Neural Netw. **13**(4–5), 411–430 (2000)
17. Jacques, S.L., Samatham, R., Choudhury, N.: Rapid spectral analysis for spectral imaging. Biomed. Opt. Express **1**(1), 157–164 (2010)
18. Kuzmina, I., et al.: Multispectral imaging of pigmented and vascular cutaneous malformations: the influence of laser treatment. In: Laser Applications in Life Sciences, vol. 7376, p. 73760J. International Society for Optics and Photonics (2010)
19. Lee, D., Seung, H.: Algorithms for non-negative matrix factorization. Adv. Neural Inform. Process. Syst. **13**, 556–562 (2001)
20. Lézoray, O., Revenu, M., Desvignes, M.: Graph-based skin lesion segmentation of multispectral dermoscopic images. In: International Conference on Image Processing (IEEE), pp. 897–901 (2014)
21. Lin, C.J.: Projected gradient methods for nonnegative matrix factorization. Neural Comput. **19**(10), 2756–2779 (2007)
22. Liu, Z., Zerubia, J.: Melanin and hemoglobin identification for skin disease analysis. In: 2013 2nd IAPR Asian Conference on Pattern Recognition, pp. 145–149. IEEE (2013)
23. Lézoray, O.: https://lezoray.users.greyc.fr/researchDatabasesDermoscopy.php
24. Madooei, A., Drew, M.S.: Detecting specular highlights in dermatological images. In: 2015 IEEE International Conference on Image Processing (ICIP), pp. 4357–4360. IEEE (2015)
25. Paatero, P., Tapper, U.: Positive matrix factorization: a non-negative factor model with optimal utilization of error estimates of data values. Environmetrics **5**(2), 111–126 (1994)

26. Ramos, V.: SIHR: a MATLAB/GNU Octave toolbox for single image highlight removal. J. Open Source Software **5**(45), 1822 (2020). https://doi.org/10.21105/joss.01822
27. Schachtner, R., Pöppel, G., Tomé, A.M., Lang, E.W.: Minimum determinant constraint for non-negative matrix factorization. In: Adali, T., Jutten, C., Romano, J.M.T., Barros, A.K. (eds.) ICA 2009. LNCS, vol. 5441, pp. 106–113. Springer, Heidelberg (2009). https://doi.org/10.1007/978-3-642-00599-2_14
28. Shafer, S.A.: Using color to separate reflection components. Color Res. Appl. **10**(4), 210–218 (1985)
29. Tong, L., Liu, R.W., Soon, V.C., Huang, Y.F.: Indeterminacy and identifiability of blind identification. IEEE Trans. Circuits Syst. **38**(5), 499–509 (1991)
30. Wold, S., Esbensen, K., Geladi, P.: Principal component analysis. Chemom. Intell. Lab. Syst. **2**(1–3), 37–52 (1987)
31. Yang, Q., Wang, S., Ahuja, N.: Real-time specular highlight removal using bilateral filtering. In: Daniilidis, K., Maragos, P., Paragios, N. (eds.) ECCV 2010. LNCS, vol. 6314, pp. 87–100. Springer, Heidelberg (2010). https://doi.org/10.1007/978-3-642-15561-1_7

A Multi-scale Self-supervision Method for Improving Cell Nuclei Segmentation in Pathological Tissues

Hesham Ali[1,2]([✉]) [iD], Mustafa Elattar[1,2] [iD], and Sahar Selim[1,2] [iD]

[1] Medical Imaging and Image Processing Research Group, Center for Informatics Science,
Nile University, Giza, Egypt
He.ali@nu.edu.eg
[2] School of Information Technology and Computer Science, Nile University, Giza, Egypt

Abstract. Nuclei detection and segmentation in histopathological images is a prerequisite step for quantitative analysis including morphological shape and size to help in identifying cancer prognosis. Digital pathology field aims to improve the quality of cancer diagnosis and has helped pathologists to reduce their efforts and time. Different deep learning architectures are widely used recently in Digital pathology field, yielding promising results in different problems. However, Deep convolutional neural networks (CNNs) need a large subset of labelled data that are not easily available all the time in the field of digital pathology. On the other hand, self-supervision methods are frequently used in different problems with the aim to overcome the lack of labelled data. In this study, we examine the impact of using self-supervision approaches on the segmentation problem. Also, we introduce a new multi-scale self-supervision method based on the zooming factor of the tissue. We compare the proposed method to the basic segmentation method and other popular self-supervision approaches that are used in other applications. The proposed Multi-scale self-supervision approach is applied on two publicly available pathology datasets. The results showed that the proposed approach outperforms Baseline U-Net by 0.2% and 0.02% for nuclei segmentation–mean Aggregated Jaccard Index (AJI), in TNBC and MoNuSeg, respectively.

Keywords: Nuclei segmentation · Histopathological images · Self-supervision · Transfer learning · Deep learning

1 Introduction

The revolution of cancer research that is led by the next generation sequence techniques, provides a lot of useful molecular insights of cancer. While the clinical diagnosis and prognosis of cancer are dominated by bioinformatics approaches like genomics epigenomic and transcriptomic, there is no dispensed with histopathological image data [1]. Tissues are stained with specific stain and used routinely in clinical purposes by observing important cellular components. And the most important molecular component is cell

© The Author(s), under exclusive license to Springer Nature Switzerland AG 2022
G. Yang et al. (Eds.): MIUA 2022, LNCS 13413, pp. 751–763, 2022.
https://doi.org/10.1007/978-3-031-12053-4_55

nucleus which enables pathologists to study mitotic actions and nuclear polymorphism in aims to provide a quantitative profile, that helps in studying disease prognosis.

Many tissue analysis techniques emerged in the last decade in the field of digital pathology, thanks to the improvement in computational aided assisted software tools (CAD), and the rich in the pathological data [2, 3]. Whole slide images are stained slides that are collected using automated scanners. These images provide us with a huge resource of information that could be used for studying the prognosis of many types of cancer diseases. However, the examination of the whole slide images that are stained with Hematoxylin and Eosin (H&E) is currently considered as the clinical gold standard of cancer diagnosis [4]. There are many problems that can be tackled using these stained slides.

Deep learning convolutional neural networks (CNN) have lately gained popularity in Digital pathology, with promising results, to assist pathologists in replacing the time-consuming manual process of inspecting slides on a daily basis. CNNs depend on finding visual patterns in tissue images. Therefore, many CNNs Architectures have been used in different tasks such as mitotic nuclei detection [3–5], and nuclear polymorphism (e.g. shape and size) segmentation using U-Net different architectures [6–8].

Nuclear component segmentation is the most essential and fundamental task in histology image analysis [11], as, pathologists take diagnostic and prognostic decision based on the morphological features of the nuclei. However, the segmentation of nuclei is a complex task as the shape of the nucleus may vary a lot due to slide preparation or staining, overlapping nuclei, and nuclei interaction with other cellular components. Many studies tried to overcome these problems with modified segmentation solutions. In [8] and [9], they calculated the Euclidian distance of each nuclei pixel from the nearest background pixel in the labelled masks, and dealt with overlapped objects task as regression and segmentation task. Meanwhile, others used modified architectures of U-net, (e.g. 2 staked U-net [12] for each U-net tried to segment different regions of the nuclei then merge them into the final product, and GB-UNet model with two stages. The first stage of GB U-net concatenated features maps from three U-net like DCNN (VGG-19, DenseNet-121, and ResNet-101 encoders), with the color normalized H&E image. The second stage of GB U-net passed the concatenated image through a final U-net (Lagree et al. 2021), Among the others instead of doing Semantic segmentation, they did Panoptic segmentation to extract local and global features for the neighborhood nuclei [13] and [14]. Also, [15] used blending loss to separate touching objects by giving different scores based on the contouring of predicted nuclei.

Deep learning architecture's success relays on the presence of large amount of labelled data, which is not available in most cases of pathological data. Therefore, in our study, our main goal is to try to find a solution for the limited labeled data which was a limitation in other works and we achieved this with commonly used method called Self-Supervision to improve results on small labeled pathology datasets. Self-Supervised Learning (SSL) is a machine learning technique which gets its information from unlabeled sample data. It's a kind of learning that's halfway between supervised and unsupervised. It is based on a neural network that has been artificially created. In order to learn, the neural network must go through two stages. The job is first solved using pseudo-labels, which aids in the initialization of network weights [16, 17]. The real work is then completed using either supervised or unsupervised learning.

In our study, we are the first to study the effect of different Self-supervision methods on Nuclei segmentation to address the problem of lack of labeled data. We proposed a new method that depends on multi-scaling of the tissue patches to classify each patch to its zooming factor class. The proposed approach improved the nuclear segmentation significantly compared to baseline U-Net. Also, we compared our self-supervision method of multi-scaling factor with two of the state of the art commonly used self-supervision methods in many fields. Denoising autoencoder is one of these methods that depends on adding noise on the image and then try to reconstruct the denoised image with Encoder-Decoder model [18]. The other method is relative positioning which works on unlabeled data by extracting random pairs of patches from each image and train convolutional neural net to predict the position of the second relative patch to the first [19]. Both methods improved the results but our method outperforms both methods in improving Nuclear segmentation.

We did our study on two publicity available different datasets (**MoNuSeg**: multi-organ fully annotated dataset of 44 images of 1000 * 1000 from 7 different organs of epithelial and stromal nuclei and **TNBC** dataset contained fifty H&E stained images taken at 40 X magnification from eleven TNBC patients).

Through this paper, we discuss methods that were used to help in overcome the problem of lack of data and how we set our hypothesis as shown in Sect. 2, then in Sect. 3, we show our results on both datasets and how our proposed method affected these results, finally, Sects. 4 and 5, discuss our finding and conclude the paper and outlines its impact on Digital pathology field.

2 Methods

Our proposed approach for Nuclear segmentation will be described in this section as illustrated in Fig. 1: (1) pre-processing of the data and creating the pseudo labels (Fig. 1. II); (2) self-supervision step as shown in (Fig. 1. III). which can be described as formulating Pseudo labels for doing an Auxiliary task in order to help the model identify some important features before Doing the segmentation task. In this step we used three different methods of self-supervision that we will be described in detail in (2.2 Self-supervision methods section); (2) transfer weights; (3) doing the actual task of Nuclear Segmentation using U-net Architecture (Fig. 1. IV)

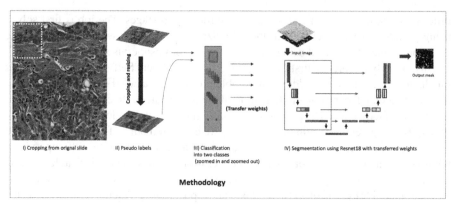

I) Cropping from orignal slide   II) Pseudo labels   III) Classification into two classes (zoomed in and zoomed out)   IV) Segmeentation using Resnet18 with transferred weights

Methodology

Fig. 1. Overview of our main pipeline that we follow in order to improve Nuclear component segmentation using U-Net and self-supervision techniques. First, we started by the preprocessing of the data in phase (I), then in phases (II) and (III), we created pseudo labels to do the Auxiliary task on them, then phase (IV) we transferred the method's weights into the encoder of the segmentation model to segment the nuclei.

In the rest of the subsections, we describe the Datasets that used in this study, all details of self-supervision methods, the segmentation step and the configurations, and the evaluation metrices that are used in this study to evaluate the segmentation results.

2.1 Dataset

To assess the effect of transfer learning in improving the performance of nuclear segmentation, two publicly available datasets were used. The first dataset is MoNuSeg2018 dataset from-Multi Organ Nucleus Segmentation (MoNuSeg) challenge [20, 21]. It is obtained from National Cancer Institute's cancer genome atlas [22] (TCGA). It includes 30 training and 14 testing images of high-resolution, H&E stained slides from nine tissue types, acquired at 40× magnification. The biopsy sites of all training images are breast, bladder, kidney, prostate, colon, and stomach. The 30 training slides contain almost 22,000 nuclei of epithelial and stromal nuclei and 7000 nuclei in the test set. The resolution of all images is (1000 * 1000) pixels and also its fully annotated masks (ground truth) are used in this study.

The second dataset is the Triple Negative Breast Cancer (TNBC) dataset which contains fifty H&E-stained images of breast cancer tissues taken at 40× magnification from eleven TNBC patients. The annotated nuclei include: normal epithelial cells, myoepithelial breast cells, invasive carcinoma cells, fibroblasts, -endothelial cells, adipocytes, macrophages, and inflammatory cells. Both datasets are used for training and testing separately without mixing in training or in testing.

2.2 Self-supervision Methods

Self-supervision learning is a form of supervised learning that doesn't require labelled data. It works by creating pseudo labels from the input data itself to help in extracting important features based on the desired task [17]. In our study, we created a new method named (Multi-scale) and compared it to another two common methods in literature (Denoising autoencoder and Relative positioning) (see Fig. 2) to assess the effect of self-supervision, and address how far these methods can help in improving the Nuclear segmentation. For all three self-supervised methods, MoNuSeg2018 dataset is used for training. Moreover, Resnet18 is the only Encoder that is used in all experiments. Three experiments are conducted. In each experiment only one self-supervised method is used as a starting point in the pipeline. The segmentation is done using a pre-trained CNN model.

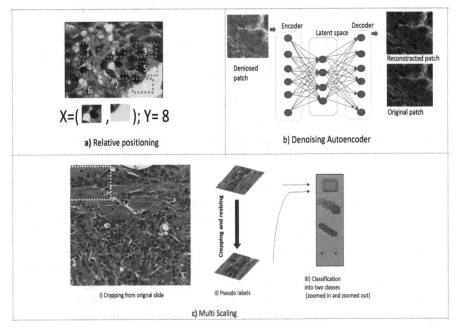

Fig. 2. All self-supervision methods that were used. **A)** Relative representation of the neighborhood patches to the randomly selected patch. **B)** Denoising autoencoder in aims to reconstruct the denoised image. **C)** Self-supervised method based on the zooming factor of the image. (Color figure online)

Relative Positioning Method

In this method, we tried to predict the relative position of patches within an image using a convolutional neural network, inspired by the context prediction method [19].

As shown in (Fig. 2. A), A patch relative representation involves in randomly sampling a patch (green). Then try to enforce the CNNs model to predict the correct one of eight neighborhoods (red). To achieve this, the fusion architecture introduced in [19] is used. A pair of Resnet18 architectures are used instead of AlexNet- style that is used in the original paper. only one-pixel gap has been left between each patch of nine patches.

Denoising Autoencoder Method

Autoencoders are a type of unsupervised learning technology that uses neural networks to learn representations from an input. A neural network architecture will be created in such a way that forces a compressed knowledge representation of the original input due to a bottleneck in the network. This compression transfers input into a latent space representation, then the decoder decompresses the reduced dimensions back to the original image [23]. Another method for creating a generalizable model is to slightly distort the input data while keeping the original data as our intended output (see Fig. 2. B). The results of this step are promising in terms of visualization and also in the MSE metric [24] result (Eq. 1), and we believe this method forced the model in finding important features from the shape and texture of the nuclei, and these weights can be used initially in the segmentation model to improve its performance.

$$MSE = \frac{1}{n} \sum (y - \hat{y}) \tag{1}$$

where y is actual image, $\hat{y}$ is the reconstructed output, and n is the number of sample images.

Multiscale Representation Method

After trying the previous two methods, we found that these self-supervised methods improved the segmentation, and gave weights that could be used initially in the segmentation step and are comparable with ImageNet weights. Therefore, we tried to create a method that depends on the zooming factor of the patch. This method is depending on the distinction between two patches zoomed in and zoomed out. So, we assume if the model is able to differentiate between these two patches then we can have weights that hold important features about the shape and the size of the nuclei. Therefore, we first extract small patches from MoNuSeg dataset and crop smaller patches from the extracted patches (see Fig. 2.C), A CNN model (Resnet18) is then trained until convergence to differentiate between every pair of patches and determine which one is zoomed out and which is zoomed in.

$$L = - \sum_{i=1}^{2} t_i \log(P_i) \tag{2}$$

where (t) is the ground truth image and (P) is the output of SoftMax function on the model output.

2.3   Segmentation

One baseline DCNNs with U-Net like architecture was trained for our study. The encoder used was Resnet18 [25]. The model started training with transferred weights that we get from self-supervision methods (see Fig. 1. IV.). For the decoder, an architecture called Feature Pyramid Network (FPN) [26] was used.

Both TNBC and MoNuSeg datasets were used separately with randomly applying a combination of horizontal flip, shifting, scaling, rotating, and Hue Saturation on H&E stained of training images. For TNBC the original size of (512 * 512) pixels was used while in MoNuSeg all images were tiled to size of (256 * 256) pixels with zero overlap. The ratio in both datasets between training and validation sets was (80:20). Adaptive moment estimation [27] (ADAM) was used to fine tune the U-Net model with cross entropy as loss function (see Eq. 2).

2.4 Evaluation Metrices

In this study, we used Aggregated Jaccard Index (AJI) and F1-score as Evaluation metrics. AJI is a concept proposed in 2017 in [21], which can be said to be an enhanced version of Intersection over Union (IOU), but compared to IOU, it has a stronger ability to measure the effect of strength division, because it is based on connected domains, not pixel-based [28] (Eq. 3, 4):

$$AJI = \sum_{i=1}^{N}\left|G_i \cap P_M^i\right| / \sum_{i=1}^{N}\left|G_i \cap P_M^i\right| + \sum_{F \in M}|P_F| \tag{3}$$

where (G) is the ground truth image, (P_F) is the output of SoftMax function on the model output, and (P_F) is all false positive pixels.

$$F1\ score = \frac{2TP}{2TP + FP + FN} \tag{4}$$

where TP is true positive, FP is false positive and FN is false negative.

3 Experiments and Results

The effect of the proposed Self-supervised Multi-scale method and other Self-supervised methods was evaluated on two datasets: MoNuSeg and TNBC.

Through this section we will discuss how self-supervision was performed and how it improved the segmentation results of both datasets, Also, all the setup configurations are discussed in details through this section.

3.1 Experiments Setup

All self-supervised methods were done on MoNuSeg dataset which each method has its own configuration, as each method requires data to be in a uniform shape. All configuration details will be discussed in this section.

To validate our proposed multiscale method and the other two self-supervision methods in improving nuclear segmentation, we used two datasets: MoNuSeg and TNBC. Both datasets were used separately with randomly applying combination of horizontal flip, shifting, scaling, rotating, and Hue Saturation on H&E stained of training images. For TNBC the original size of (512 * 512) pixels was used and the ratio between training and validation sets was (80:20). While in MoNuSeg all the 30 training images were tiled to size of (256 * 256) pixels with zero overlap, and the same was done for the 14 test images that we used to test the segmentation model in our study. Adaptive moment estimation [27] (ADAM) was used to fine tune the U-Net model with learning rate of $1\ e^{-3}$ and cross entropy as loss function (see Eq. 2). The U-Net model Encoder was Resnet18 [25] and the decoder was Feature pyramid Network [26].

3.2 Self Supervision Configurations

All the Self-supervision methods' configurations that were used during this study are discussed in detail through this section.

Relative Positioning Setup

We started our experiments with first unsupervised (Relative positioning) which was applied using all images of MoNuSeg dataset (30 images for training and 14 images for testing). each image was tiled into (256 * 256) pixels then two patches of (15 * 15) pixels were cropped from the original patch, one was randomly selected and the other was relatively selected from eight possible positions. A Resnet18 fusion architecture [19] then was trained until convergence to determine the position of the second patch with Cross entropy [29] as a loss function (Eq. 2) and ADAM optimizer with $3\ e^{-4}$ learning rate for fine-tuning.

Denoised Autoencoder Setup

In this method, all images of MoNuSeg dataset augmented with vertical and horizontal flipping and random rotation. The images are then tiled into (256 * 256) pixels. MSE loss was used [24] (Eq. 2) and Adaptive moment estimation (ADAM) optimizer with learning rate of $3\ e^{-4}$ was used to fine tune the model. All images were trained using autoencoder CNNs model until convergence.

Multi-scale Setup

We started by extracting random patches of size (256 * 256) pixels from the whole slide of MoNuSeg dataset, then crop smaller patches from the extracted patches and resize them into the same size (256 * 256) pixels (total of 4320 for training and 2016 for testing) (see Fig. 2.C). a CNNs model (Resnet18) then trained until convergence to differentiate between every pair of patches and determine which one is zoomed out and which is zoomed in. with Cross entropy [29] as loss function (see Eq. 2) and ADAM optimizer with $3\ e^{-4}$ learning rate.

3.3 Dataset 1 Results

TNBC dataset's segmentation results are shown in (Table 1), Despite the simplicity of our proposed method (multi-scale), it achieved great results in terms of extracting substantial features that could be transferred to the segmentation model to start with in nuclear segmentation task. The overall segmentation results with the multiscale method's weights also exceed ImageNet weights, which achieved an average AJI of 0.578 and F1 of 0.806 on TNBC dataset (Table 1), Also regarding to other methods and baseline, our method managed to segment the nuclei well on most of H&E stained images in terms of decreasing the percentage of overlapped regions (i.e. connected nuclei) (see

Fig. 3). Meanwhile the relative positioning had the lowest effect on improving the nuclear segmentation with AJI of 0.37 and F1 of 0.62. while Denoising autoencoder method improved the segmentation with better performance than relative positioning with AJI of 0.51 and F1 of 0.75 (Table 1).

Table 1. AJI and F1 results on TNBC dataset, Bolded values identify the highest scoring segmentation with respect the self-supervised method.

Method	AJI	F1
No pretraining	0.41	0.679
Pretraining with ImageNet	0.54	0.801
Pretraining with autoencoder	0.51	0.75
Pretraining with relative positioning	0.37	0.62
Pretraining with multiscale	**0.578**	**0.806**

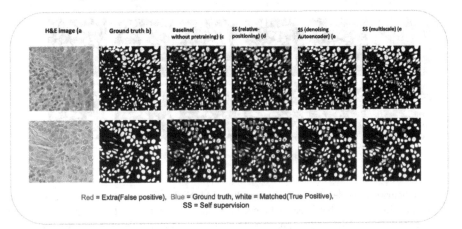

Fig. 3. Comparing Nuclei segmentation results of TNBC dataset. Annotations baseline to Self-supervision methods have been color coded. Such that red indicated false positive, blue false negative, and white indicated true positive. The original annotation Ground truth were released by [30].

3.4 Dataset 2 Results

While our proposed self-supervision method improved the segmentation results in both datasets, it boosted the segmentation in MoNuSeg with lower effect compared to TNBC (Table 2), but still gives better results than the baseline with AJI of 0.605 and F1 of 0.801. we could see that both Relative positioning and Denoising autoencoder methods have the same impact on improving the Nuclear segmentation with AJI of 0.58 and F1 of 0.77 (Table 2). Also, we can see in (Fig. 4) that the resulting nuclei are noticeably different between the three methods and the baseline with lowest proportion of False positives can be clearly found in last column of multi-scale method.

Table 2. AJI and F1 results on MoNuSeg dataset, Bolded values identify the highest scoring segmentation with respect the self-supervised method.

Method	AJI	F1
No pretraining	0.581	0.781
Pretraining with ImageNet	**0.61**	**0.805**
Pretraining with autoencoder	0.58	0.775
Pretraining with relative positioning	0.58	0.776
Pretraining with multiscale	**0.605**	**0.801**

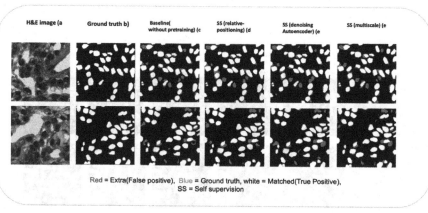

Fig. 4. Comparing Nuclei segmentation results of MoNuSeg dataset. Annotations baseline to Self-supervision methods have been color coded. Such that red indicated false positive, blue false negative, and white indicated true positive. The original annotation Ground truth were released by [21].

4   Discussion

The advancement in the computational pathology field and deep learning has opened a door to many for developing technologies to automate disease diagnosis and prognosis. Although WSIs are gigapixels-sized that is hard to handle and use it directly in deep learning models, so, they are split into patches and then annotated. This process is time consuming and requires a lot of field experts to annotate each patch. Transfer learning approaches [31] are used for addressing this problem. However, ImageNet [32] weights considered as from a different domain other than pathology, it has shown a great performance in many computational pathology tasks.

While transfer learning shows great success in the field of pathology [33] and other fields [31], in our study, we examined the impact of some of these methods and how the segmentation of the nuclei in H&E stained histopathology images can be improved by using pretrained weights other than ImageNet. Moreover, we introduced a state of art method that is based on multi-scale patches, which we get inspired by the multiscale CNNs models that have been used in the pathology field [34, 35].

The proposed methodology examined a new self-supervision method that is used for the first time in the segmentation of types of cancers, which depends mainly on the zooming factor of the patch, and as shown in (Table 1, 2). Our method greatly improved the Nuclear segmentation compared to other commonly used self-supervision methods and we assume that by trying different architectures the results could get better.

The data that were used to check the reliability of our approach are two publicly available datasets; TNBC dataset which represents triple negative breast cancer cases, and MoNuSeg dataset that contains nuclei of nine different tissue types, we first trained a classifier on MoNuSeg training set making two pseudo classes zoomed out images and zoomed in, then take this classifier to be the Encoder of The U-net for the segmentation step, and we can see that results comes from our approach is promising compared to other self-supervision methods that were used in this study (see Table 1, 2).

The Lack of enough data considers the biggest limitation of our study based on the publicly available datasets, as computational pathology field still needs more data for training and testing more Algorithms and models.

5 Conclusions

The use of AI in the pathology field, in general, increased recently trying to reduce pathologist's workload and time. The assessment of morphological features may take the lead in the next few years to replace other expensive techniques to predict cancer outcomes. In our proposed approach, we used AI to facilitate the process of cancer grading and mentioned the effect of transfer learning in improving the results.

Through our study, we formulate a new self-supervision approach to face the problem of lacking of data. the main goal of our method is to classify different patches based on the zooming factor of the patch to help the model in extracting important features to help in improving the segmentation.

We compared our newly proposed multi-scale self-supervision method to basic segmentation and other commonly used self-supervision methods in different applications.

Our proposed method outperformed other examined approaches.

Though our results are not the best compared to others in the literature that used larger architectures on the same data for segmentation, meanwhile, they are still comparable. also, our main focus was to prove that self-supervision could improve the nuclei segmentation and help in bringing weights from same domain that could be used other than ImageNet weights. Therefore, our further work is planned to investigate and compare the impact of our method on large scale of different architectures.

References

1. Komura, D., Ishikawa, S.: Machine learning methods for histopathological image analysis. Comput. Struct. Biotechnol. J. **16**, 34–42 (2018). https://doi.org/10.1016/J.CSBJ.2018.01.001
2. Cui, M., Zhang, D.Y.: Artificial intelligence and computational pathology. Lab. Investig. **101**(4), 412–422 (2021). https://doi.org/10.1038/s41374-020-00514-0
3. Barisoni, L., Lafata, K.J., Hewitt, S.M., Madabhushi, A., Balis, U.G.J.: Digital pathology and computational image analysis in nephropathology. Nat. Rev. Nephrol. **16**(11), 669–685 (2020). https://doi.org/10.1038/s41581-020-0321-6
4. He, L., Long, L.R., Antani, S., Thoma, G.R.: Local and global Gaussian mixture models for hematoxylin and eosin stained histology image segmentation. In: 2010 10th International Conference on Hybrid Intelligent Systems, HIS 2010, pp. 223–228 (2010). https://doi.org/10.1109/HIS.2010.5600019
5. Saha, M., Chakraborty, C., Racoceanu, D.: Efficient deep learning model for mitosis detection using breast histopathology images. Comput. Med. Imaging Graph. **64**, 29–40 (2018). https://doi.org/10.1016/J.COMPMEDIMAG.2017.12.001
6. Balkenhol, M.C.A., et al.: Deep learning assisted mitotic counting for breast cancer. Lab. Investig. **99**, 1596–1606 (2019). https://doi.org/10.1038/s41374-019-0275-0
7. Cireşan, D.C., Giusti, A., Gambardella, L.M., Schmidhuber, J.: Mitosis detection in breast cancer histology images with deep neural networks. In: Mori, K., Sakuma, I., Sato, Y., Barillot, C., Navab, N. (eds.) MICCAI 2013. LNCS, vol. 8150, pp. 411–418. Springer, Heidelberg (2013). https://doi.org/10.1007/978-3-642-40763-5_51. http://bit.ly/18681Km. Accessed 20 Mar 2022
8. Jung, H., Lodhi, B., Kang, J.: An automatic nuclei segmentation method based on deep convolutional neural networks for histopathology images. BMC Biomed. Eng. (2019). https://doi.org/10.1186/s42490-019-0026-8
9. Mahbod, A., et al.: CryoNuSeg: a dataset for nuclei instance segmentation of cryosectioned H&E-stained histological images. Comput. Biol. Med. **132** (2021). https://doi.org/10.1016/j.compbiomed.2021.104349
10. Naylor, P., Laé, M., Reyal, F., Walter, T.: Segmentation of nuclei in histopathology images by deep regression of the distance map. IEEE Trans. Med. Imaging **38**(2), 448–459 (2019). https://doi.org/10.1109/TMI.2018.2865709
11. Fuchs, T.J., Buhmann, J.M.: Computational pathology: challenges and promises for tissue analysis. Comput. Med. Imaging Graph. **35**(7–8), 515–530 (2011). https://doi.org/10.1016/J.COMPMEDIMAG.2011.02.006
12. Kong, Y., Genchev, G.Z., Wang, X., Zhao, H., Lu, H.: Nuclear segmentation in histopathological images using two-stage stacked U-nets with attention mechanism. Front. Bioeng. Biotechnol. **8** (2020). https://doi.org/10.3389/fbioe.2020.573866
13. Liu, D., et al.: Nuclei segmentation via a deep panoptic model with semantic feature fusion (2019)
14. Liu, D., Zhang, D., Song, Y., Huang, H., Cai, W.: Panoptic feature fusion net: a novel instance segmentation paradigm for biomedical and biological images. IEEE Trans. Image Process. **30**, 2045–2059 (2021). https://doi.org/10.1109/TIP.2021.3050668
15. Wang, H., Xian, M., Vakanski, A.: Bending loss regularized network for nuclei segmentation in histopathology images. In: Proceedings - International Symposium on Biomedical Imaging, vol. 2020, pp. 258–262, April 2020. https://doi.org/10.1109/ISBI45749.2020.9098611
16. Beyer, L., Zhai, X., Oliver, A., Kolesnikov, A.: S4L: self-supervised semi-supervised learning. In: Proceedings of the IEEE International Conference on Computer Vision, vol. 2019, pp. 1476–1485, October 2019. https://doi.org/10.1109/ICCV.2019.00156

17. Doersch, C., Zisserman, A.: Multi-task self-supervised visual learning. In: Proceedings of the IEEE International Conference on Computer Vision, vol. 2017, pp. 2070–2079, October 2017. https://doi.org/10.1109/ICCV.2017.226
18. Lee, W.-H., Ozger, M., Challita, U., Sung, K.W.: Noise learning based denoising autoencoder. IEEE Commun. Lett. **25**(9), 2983–2987 (2021)
19. Doersch, C., Gupta, A., Efros, A.A.: Unsupervised visual representation learning by context prediction, May 2015. http://arxiv.org/abs/1505.05192
20. Home - Grand Challenge. https://monuseg.grand-challenge.org/. Accessed 24 Nov 2021
21. Kumar, N., Verma, R., Sharma, S., Bhargava, S., Vahadane, A., Sethi, A.: A dataset and a technique for generalized nuclear segmentation for computational pathology. IEEE Trans. Med. Imaging **36**(7), 1550–1560 (2017). https://doi.org/10.1109/TMI.2017.2677499
22. The Cancer Genome Atlas Program - National Cancer Institute. https://www.cancer.gov/about-nci/organization/ccg/research/structural-genomics/tcga. Accessed 25 Nov 2021
23. Bank, D., Koenigstein, N., Giryes, R.: Autoencoders (2020)
24. Fürnkranz, J., et al.: Mean squared error. In: Encyclopedia of Machine Learning, p. 653 (2011). https://doi.org/10.1007/978-0-387-30164-8_528
25. He, K., Zhang, X., Ren, S., Sun, J.: Deep residual learning for image recognition. http://image-net.org/challenges/LSVRC/2015/. Accessed 27 Mar 2022
26. Lin, T.-Y., Dollár, P., Girshick, R., He, K., Hariharan, B., Belongie, S.: Feature pyramid networks for object detection (2017)
27. Kingma, D.P., Lei Ba, J.: Adam: a method for stochastic optimization (2014)
28. AJI (Aggregated Jaccard Index) enhanced version of IOU, based on connected domain image segmentation results evaluation - Fear Cat. https://blog.fearcat.in/a?ID=01600-351fda84-486d-4296-af30-6d8be0510161. Accessed 25 Nov 2021
29. Zhang, Z., Sabuncu, M.R.: Generalized cross entropy loss for training deep neural networks with noisy labels (2018)
30. Segmentation of Nuclei in Histopathology Images by deep regression of the distance map | IEEE DataPort. https://ieee-dataport.org/documents/segmentation-nuclei-histopathology-images-deep-regression-distance-map. Accessed 29 Mar 2022
31. Zhuang, F., et al.: A comprehensive survey on transfer learning. Proc. IEEE **109**(1), 43–76 (2020)
32. Deng, J., Dong, W., Socher, R., Li, L.-J., Li, K., Fei-Fei, L.: ImageNet: a large-scale hierarchical image database, pp. 248–255, March 2010. https://doi.org/10.1109/CVPR.2009.5206848
33. Sharma, Y., Ehsan, L., Syed, S., Brown, D.E.: HistoTransfer: understanding transfer learning for histopathology (2021)
34. Schmitz, R., Madesta, F., Nielsen, M., Krause, J., Werner, R., Rösch, T.: Multi-scale fully convolutional neural networks for histopathology image segmentation: from nuclear aberrations to the global tissue architecture, September 2019. https://doi.org/10.1016/j.media.2021.101996
35. Kosaraju, S.C., Hao, J., Koh, H.M., Kang, M.: Deep-Hipo: multi-scale receptive field deep learning for histopathological image analysis. Methods **179**, 3–13 (2020). https://doi.org/10.1016/J.YMETH.2020.05.012

Radiomics, Predictive Models, and Quantitative Imaging

Correlation Between IBSI Morphological Features and Manually-Annotated Shape Attributes on Lung Lesions at CT

Francesco Bianconi[1]([✉])[iD], Mario Luca Fravolini[1][iD], Giulia Pascoletti[2][iD],
Isabella Palumbo[3][iD], Michele Scialpi[4][iD], Cynthia Aristei[3][iD],
and Barbara Palumbo[5][iD]

[1] Department of Engineering, Università degli Studi di Perugia,
Via Goffredo Duranti, 93, 06125 Perugia, Italy
bianco@ieee.org
[2] Department of Mechanical and Aerospace Engineering (DIMEAS),
Politecnico di Torino, Corso Duca Degli Abruzzi, 24, 10129 Turin, Italy
[3] Section of Radiation Oncology, Department of Medicine and Surgery Università
degli Studi di Perugia, Piazza Lucio Severi 1, 06132 Perugia, Italy
[4] Division of Diagnostic Imaging, Department of Medicine and Surgery, Piazza Lucio
Severi 1, 06132 Perugia, Italy
[5] Section of Nuclear Medicine and Health Physics, Department of Medicine and
Surgery Università Degli Studi di Perugia, Piazza Lucio Severi 1, 06132 Perugia, Italy

Abstract. Radiological examination of pulmonary nodules on CT involves the assessment of the nodules' size and morphology, a procedure usually performed manually. In recent years computer-assisted analysis of indeterminate lung nodules has been receiving increasing research attention as a potential means to improve the diagnosis, treatment and follow-up of patients with lung cancer. Computerised analysis relies on the extraction of objective, reproducible and standardised imaging features. In this context the aim of this work was to evaluate the correlation between nine IBSI-compliant morphological features and three manually-assigned radiological attributes – *lobulation*, *sphericity* and *spiculation*. Experimenting on 300 lung nodules from the open-access LIDC-IDRI dataset we found that the correlation between the computer-calculated features and the manually-assigned visual scores was at best moderate (Pearson's r between -0.61 and 0.59; Spearman's ρ between -0.59 and 0.56). We conclude that the morphological features investigated here have moderate ability to match/explain manually-annotated lobulation, sphericity and spiculation.

Keywords: Morphological features · Lung cancer · Pulmonary nodules · Radiomics

This work was partially supported by the Department of Engineering at the Università degli Studi di Perugia, Italy, through the project *Shape, colour and texture features for the analysis of two- and three-dimensional images: methods and applications* (Fundamental Research Grants Scheme 2019).

1 Introduction

Pulmonary nodules (PN in the remainder) are common findings on Computed Tomography (CT). Results from low-dose CT screening programmes indeed indicate that 20% or more of the scans can lead to the detection of lung nodules requiring further assessment. The differential diagnosis includes benign and malignant causes, with the probability of cancer of PN detected on first screening CT between 3.7% and 5.5% [19]. The correct evaluation of PN is a challenge to the clinician, as recognising malignancies at an early stage is vital for timely treatment and, consequently, better prognosis. The management of pulmonary nodules may include regular follow-up, functional imaging and/or invasive procedures; the latter, however, are not exempt from major complications [1].

Radiological examination of PN involves the classification into solid, sub-solid or ground-glass nodules as well as the assessment of size, location, multiplicity and morphology [18]. As concerns morphology, roundness, spiculation and lobulation are considered major signs. Round solid nodules have lower probability of beign malignant than lesions with complex shape [26]; by contrast, lobulation and spiculation are known to be associated with malignancy [18,19]. One problem with the visual evaluation of morphological characteristics is that this is an intrinsically qualitative and subjective process. Furthermore, the presence of signs such as spiculation and/or lobulation is usually recorded in a binary manner only – i.e., present or absent.

In recent years the extraction of quantitative biomarkers from medical images (*radiomics*) has received increasing attention as a mean to overcome the above difficulties [7,8,14,21,23,24]. In previous works quantitative morphological features (also referred to as shape features in the remainder) such as compactness, convexity, rectangular fit, sphericity and surface-to-volume ratio have shown association with the nature of the lesion (benign vs. malignant [6,11,29]), overall survival [12] and response to treatment [10,29] in patients with lung cancer. There are, however, major hurdles before radiomics can find full application in the clinical practice. Two such obstacles are standardisation and explainability [5,16]. The first involves the establishment of unified procedures in all the steps of the radiomics pipeline, as for instance championed by the Imaging Biomarkers Standardisation Initiative (IBSI [15,28]). The second is related to the extent to which computer-generated results (including radiomics features) can be understood by humans and linked to physical, biological and/or clinical parameters [16,25]. Regarding the latter, it is to note that the ability of computer-generated shape features to match manually-assigned radiological scores on visual attributes has received little attention in the literature. Apart from [17], where the authors explored the link between radiomics shape parameters and spiculatedness on synthetic tumour models, the correlations between quantitative morphology features and manually-assigned radiological labels largely remain unexplored.

In this work we studied the relationship between IBSI-compliant morphological features and manually-assigned radiological scores characterising visual attributes of lung lesions at CT. Specifically, we investigated the correlations between nine computer-calculated shape features and three manually-assessed radiological attributes – i.e., lobulation, sphericity and spiculation. To avoid confusion, in the remainder of the paper we shall use camel case format to indicate the computer-calculated morphological features (e.g. AreaDensity, Sphericity) and lower case for the manually-assigned radiological scores (e.g. lobulation, sphericity).

2   Materials and Methods

2.1   Study Population

We retrospectively analysed a total of 300 lung nodules from a population of 158 patients (86 males, 62 females; age = 59.0 ± 14.5 [14.0–88.0 yr]) who underwent thoracic CT examination. All the data were collected from the open-access Lung Image Database Consortium image collection (LIDC-IDRI [3,4,9]). The inclusion criteria were: a) at the scan level, the presence of a complete data record as regards age, gender of the subject and basic image acquisition and reconstruction settings as listed in the next paragraph; b) at the nodule level, the availability of annotations from at least three independent radiologists.

The main image acquisition and reconstruction settings were: tube voltage 120–140 kVp, in-plane pixel spacing 0.53–0.98 mm, slice thickness 0.6–3.0 mm and inter-slice spacing 0.5–3.0 mm. Each nodule comes with annotated scores by different radiologists as regards *subtlety* (difficulty of detection), *calcification* (pattern of – if present), *sphericity*, *margin* (poorly or well defined), *lobulation*, *spiculation*, *texture* (solid, ground glass, or mixed) and estimated degree of *malignancy* as summarised in Table 1 (see also Fig. 1 for sample images). For the correlation analysis we considered the average score received by each attribute as the reference value.

2.2   Shape Features

We considered nine dimensionless morphological features as defined in the [28] reference document. These were: AreaDensity, Asphericity, Compactness1, Compactness2, Elongation, Flatness, SphericalDisproportion, Sphericity and VolumeDensity (see also Table 2 for details and formulae). The region of interest (ROI) was identified by the 50% consensus rule – that is, a voxel was considered in the ROI if it had been marked as such in at least half of the annotations available for that nodule, not in the ROI otherwise. Area and volume of the region of interest were computed on the boundary triangular mesh embracing the region

Table 1. Distribution of the manually-assigned radiological attributes in the study population (see also [13] for the complete definition of each attribute).

Attribute name	Score (mean ± std [range])	Scale [int. range]
calcification	5.66 ± 0.95 [1–6]	[1–6]
internal structure	1.02 ± 0.21 [1–4]	[1–4]
lobulation	1.93 ± 1.20 [1–5]	[1–5]
malignancy	2.98 ± 1.21 [1–5]	[1–5]
margin	4.19 ± 0.97 [1–5]	[1–5]
sphericity	3.91 ± 0.92 [1–5]	[1–5]
spiculation	1.77 ± 1.17 [1–5]	[1–5]
subtlety	4.13 ± 0.99 [1–5]	[1–5]
texture	4.70 ± 0.83 [1–5]	[1–5]

of interest. The mesh was generated using the marching cubes algorithm as implemented in scikit-image [27] at an iso-surface level of 0.5 (where 1 indicates ROI, 0 not ROI). No further pre-processing operation such as filtering, signal quantisation and/or spatial resampling was applied. For additional details on the implementations see also Sect. 2.4.

Table 2. Summary table of the IBSI-compliant morphological features considered in this study. In the formulae A and V denote the surface area and volume of the triangular mesh approximating the boundary of the region of interest; A_{aabb} and V_{aabb} the surface area and volume of the rectangular, axis-aligned bounding box; λ_{major}, λ_{minor} and λ_{least} ($\lambda_{\mathrm{major}} \geq \lambda_{\mathrm{minor}} \geq \lambda_{\mathrm{least}}$) the principal components (eigenvalues) of the ROI considered as a mass distribution with uniform density.

$$\mathrm{AreaDensity} = \frac{A}{A_{\mathrm{aabb}}} \quad (1)$$

$$\mathrm{Aspericity} = \left(\frac{1}{36\pi}\frac{A^3}{V^2}\right)^{1/3} - 1 \quad (2)$$

$$\mathrm{Compactness1} = \frac{V}{\pi^{1/2}A^{3/2}} \quad (3)$$

$$\mathrm{Compactness2} = 36\pi\frac{V^2}{A^3} \quad (4)$$

$$\mathrm{Elongation} = \sqrt{\frac{\lambda_{\mathrm{minor}}}{\lambda_{\mathrm{major}}}} \quad (5)$$

$$\mathrm{Flatness} = \sqrt{\frac{\lambda_{\mathrm{least}}}{\lambda_{\mathrm{major}}}} \quad (6)$$

$$\mathrm{SphericalDisproportion} = \frac{A}{(36\pi V^2)^{1/3}} \quad (7)$$

$$\mathrm{Sphericity} = \frac{(36\pi V^2)^{1/3}}{A} \quad (8)$$

$$\mathrm{VolumeDensity} = \frac{V}{V_{\mathrm{aabb}}} \quad (9)$$

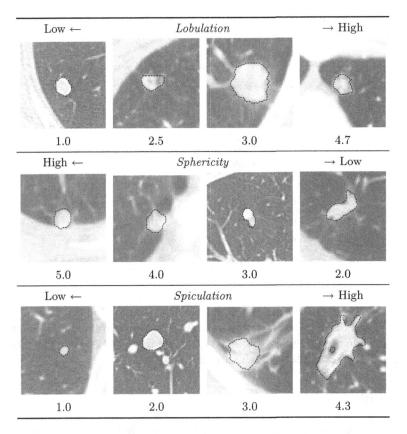

Fig. 1. Sample lesions from the population study displayed with lung window settings (width = 1500 HU, level = –600 HU). Each tile represents the central axial slice of the region of interest and corresponds to an area of approx. 50 mm × 50 mm. The value below each tile reports the average radiological score of the corresponding visual attribute – i.e., lobulation, sphericity or spiculation – over at least three annotations. The dashed line denotes the 50% consensus area.

2.3   Statistical Analysis

Linear and monotonic correlations between the computer-calculated shape features and the manually-assigned radiological scores were assessed using Pearson correlation coefficient (r) and Spearman rank-correlation coefficient (ρ). Qualitative interpretation of the results was based on Rowntree's scale [20] as shown in Table 3.

2.4   Implementation, Execution and Reproducible Research

We used Python 3.8.6 with functions from nibabel 3.2.1, Numpy 1.19.1, Pandas 1.0.5, pylidc 0.2.2, radiomics_pg 0.1.0-alpha, scipy 1.5.4 and Tabulate 0.8.9. The experiments were carried out on an ASUS ProArt Laptop PC with Intel®

Table 3. Qualitative interpretation of the correlation coefficients and related colourmap. Based on Rwontree's scale [20].

Range	Correlation strength	Correlation type	Colourmap
$0.9 < r, \rho \leq 1.0$	Very strong		
$0.7 < r, \rho \leq 0.9$	Strong		
$0.5 < r, \rho \leq 0.7$	Moderate	Positive	
$0.2 < r, \rho \leq 0.4$	Weak		
$0.0 < r, \rho \leq 0.2$	Negligible		
$-0.2 < r, \rho \leq 0.0$	Negligible		
$-0.4 < r, \rho \leq -0.2$	Weak		
$-0.7 < r, \rho \leq -0.4$	Moderate	Negative	
$-0.9 < r, \rho \leq -0.7$	Strong		
$-1.0 \leq r, \rho \leq -0.7$	Very strong		

Core^{TM} i7-9750H @ 2.60 GHz CPU, 36 Gb RAM and Windows 10 Pro 64-bit. The total execution time was approximately 1 h. For reproducible research purposes the code used for the experiments is freely available through the following repository: https://github.com/bianconif/miua_2022.

3   Results

The results reported in Table 4 and Fig. 2 indicate that the correlation between the morphological features and the manually-assigned radiological scores was, at best, moderate. Lobulation and spiculation showed very similar results: both attributes had moderate positive correlation with Asphericity and SphericalDisporportion; moderate negative correlation with Compactness (1 & 2), Sphericity and VolumeDensity; weak or negligible correlation with the remaining features. Manually-assigned sphericity had moderate positive correlation with Compactness (1 & 2), Flatness, Sphericity and VolumeDensity; moderate negative correlation with Asphericity and SphericalDisproportion; weak correlation with the remaining features

As expected, Compactess (1 & 2) and Sphericity gave identical results, and the same happened with Asphericity and SphericalDisproportion. Also note that Compactess (1 & 2) and Sphericity returned results symmetrical to those achieved by Asphericity and SphericalDisproportion. These findings are consistent with the mathematical definitions of the above features.

4   Discussion

The interpretability of radiomics models, and, in particular, the ability to explain computer-calculated features in terms of physical, biological and/or clinical

Table 4. Results of the correlation analysis. Rows represent the computer-calculated morphological features, columns the manually-assigned radiological scores. See Table 3 for qualitative interpretation of the correlation coefficient and related colourmap.

	lobulation	sphericity	spiculation		lobulation	sphericity	spiculation
Asphericity	0.55	−0.52	0.59	Asphericity	0.59	−0.51	0.56
AreaDensity	−0.21	0.29	−0.20	AreaDensity	−0.22	0.26	−0.20
Compactness1	−0.58	0.54	−0.61	Compactness1	−0.59	0.51	−0.56
Compactness2	−0.58	0.54	−0.61	Compactness2	−0.59	0.51	−0.56
Elongation	0.02	0.26	−0.01	Elongation	0.01	0.30	0.03
Flatness	−0.21	0.56	−0.26	Flatness	−0.19	0.53	−0.23
SphericalDisproportion	0.55	−0.52	0.59	SphericalDisproportion	0.59	−0.51	0.56
Sphericity	−0.58	0.54	−0.61	Sphericity	−0.59	0.51	−0.56
VolumeDensity	−0.46	0.41	−0.46	VolumeDensity	−0.49	0.40	−0.47

(a) Pearson's r (b) Spearman's ρ

parameters is a crucial step for translating radiomics into routine clinical practice [16,25]. Radiological evaluation of pulmonary nodules on CT requires manual assessment and scoring of morphological features [18]. In particular, it can be assumed that the margins of a PN (e.g. lobulation, sphericity or spiculation) can be considered a feature to differentiate benign from malignant nodules. We conducted this study not for this purpose (i.e. differentiation benign vs. malignant), but to investigate computer-calculated morphological characteristics and how they correlate with manually-assigned morphological scores.

Our results indicate that lobulation and spiculation correlated positively with Asphericity and SpericalDisproportion; negatively with AreaDensity, Compactness (1 & 2), Sphericity and VolumeDensity. This is consistent with spiculation and lobulation indicating deviation from a spherical shape, since a perfect sphere has no lobulation or spiculation. Likewise, sphericity correlated positively with AreaDensity, Compactness1, Compactness2, Sphericity and VolumeDensity; negatively with Asphericity and SphericalDisproportion. We also found positive correlation between flatness and Sphericity. Although this may appear contradictory, it is actually consistent with IBSI's defining flatness as an inverse ratio, thus 1.0 indicates a completely non-flat object (like a sphere), and smaller values objects which are increasingly flatter. Perhaps future versions of the IBSI could eliminate this inconsistency by adopting a more intuitive definition of flatness (with higher values indicating flatter objects) as for instance proposed in [2].

On the whole the strength of the correlation was at best moderate in our study. This contrasts with the results reported in [17], where the authors detected strong correlation ($r > 0.83$) between seven shape features (four of which also considered here – i.e., Compactness1 & 2, SphericalDisproportion and Sphericity) vs. spiculatedness on 28 synthetic (mathematically-generated) tumour models. This discrepancy may have different explanations. The first is that the

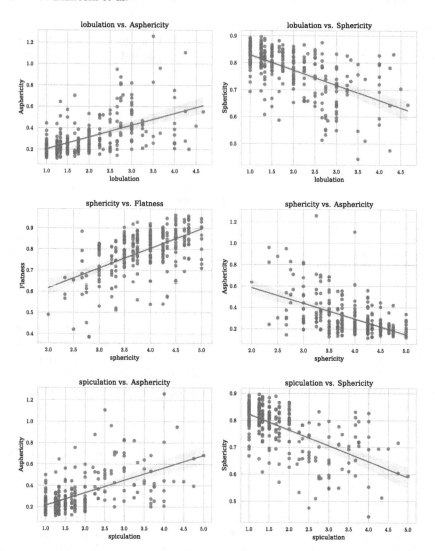

Fig. 2. Scatter plots with regression lines and 95% confidence intervals (shaded areas). Manually-assigned attributes are arranged by row – in top-down order: lobulation, sphericity and spiculation. For each of them we reported the scatter plots attribute vs. computer-calculated features that showed the strongest positive (first column) and negative correlation (second column).

IBSI-compliant shape features considered here could be not completely adequate to capture lobulatedness, spiculation and sphericity. Consequently, more involved parameters/methods may be required. Dhara et al. [11], for instance, proposed ad-hoc hand-crafted features for quantifying spiculation and lobulation; Qiu et al. [22] advocated the use of spiking neural P systems for evaluating spiculation. None of these however, are part of the IBSI at the moment, therefore they all lack standardisation. Secondly, manual radiological scoring is usually carried out on two-dimensional images (normally the axial slices); however, this procedure may not be adequate to capture the overall shape of the ROI as quantified by three-dimensional morphological factors. It is unclear, for instance, whether manually-assigned *sphericity* – as it is called in the LIDC-IDRI dataset – actually refers to three-dimensional sphericity or to two-dimensional *roundness*. Finally, lesion delineation is also a critical step and a source of potential bias.

5   Limitations and Future Work

Two main limitations apply to the present work. First, as a retrospective study based on a multi-centre dataset, we used CT images with heterogeneous scanning parameters as regards manufacturer, acquisition settings (tube voltage), image resolution (voxel size), reconstruction parameters and filtering. Future perspective studies may address this shortcoming by defining standardised imaging protocols. Second, the correlation analysis between manually-assigned visual scores and computer-based morphological features was carried on aggregated measures (average observer score) and 50% consensus ROI. Consequently, inter-observer variability as concerns attribute scoring and lesion segmentation was not considered here. This could be interesting subject of investigation for future studies.

6   Conclusions

Standardisation and interpretability are two major challenges in the clinical application of radiomics. In this work we investigated the correlation between standardised, IBSI-compliant morphological features and manually-assigned radiological scores about lobulatendess, spiculation and sphericity on pulmonary nodules at CT. We found that the correlation between the computer-calculated features and the manually-scored attributes was, in the best cases, moderate. Further studies will be needed to clarify the relationships between computerised imaging features and visual shape attributes as perceived by human operators.

Our study also confirms a high degree of redundancy among most of the features investigated here, which is consistent with their definition. Although this was largely expected, it nonetheless raises concerns about the potential risks related to the use and naming conventions of morphological features that are in fact equivalent. We believe additional standardisation effort is needed to minimise this kind of redundancy – for instance by choosing one representative among a set of equivalent features and declaring deprecated the others. This would help avoid confusion, improve across-centre study reproducibility and facilitate translation into the clinical practice.

Ethical Statement. The present study is based on publicly available data in anonymous form, therefore does not constitute research on human subjects.

Conflict of Interest. The authors declare no conflict of interest.

References

1. Aberle, D.R., et al.: Reduced lung-cancer mortality with low-dose computed tomographic screening. N. Engl. J. Med. **365**(5), 395–409 (2011)
2. Angelidakis, V., Nadimi, S., Utili, S.: Elongation, flatness and compactness indices to characterise particle form. Powder Technol. **396**, 689–695 (2022)
3. Armato III, S.G., et al.: Data from LIDC-IDRI, The Cancer Imaging Archive. https://doi.org/10.7937/K9/TCIA.2015.LO9QL9SX. Accessed 29 Jan 2022
4. Armato III, S.G., et al.: Data from LIDC-IDRI, The Cancer Imaging Archive. https://doi.org/10.7937/K9/TCIA.2015.LO9QL9SX. Accessed 29 Jan 2022
5. Baessler, B.: Radiomics and imaging: the need for standardisation. HealthManag. .l **20**(2), 168–170 (2020)
6. Balagurunathan, Y., Schabath, M.B., Wang, H., Liu, Y., Gillies, R.J.: Quantitative imaging features improve discrimination of malignancy in pulmonary nodules. Sci. Rep. **9**(1), 8528(2019)
7. Bianconi, F., Palumbo, I., Spanu, A., Nuvoli, S., Fravolini, M.L., Palumbo, B.: PET/CT radiomics in lung cancer: an overview. Appl. Sci. **5**(10) (Mar 2020)
8. Bianconi, F., Palumbo, I., Spanu, A., Nuvoli, S., Fravolini, M.L., Palumbo, B.: PET/CT radiomics in lung cancer: an overview. Appl. Sci. **5**(10) (Mar 2020)
9. Clark, K., et al.: The cancer imaging archive (TCIA): Maintaining and operating a public information repository. J. Digit. Imag. **26**(6), 1045–1057 (2013)
10. Coroller, T.P., et al.: Radiomic phenotype features predict pathological response in non-small cell radiomic predicts pathological response lung cancer. Radiot. Oncol. **119**(3), 480–486 (2016)
11. Dhara, A.K., Mukhopadhyay, S., Dutta, A., Garg, M., Khandelwal, N.: A combination of shape and texture features for classification of pulmonary nodules in lung CT images. J. Digit. Imag. **29**(4), 466–475 (2016)
12. Grove, O., et al.: Quantitative computed tomographic descriptors associate tumor shape complexity and intratumor heterogeneity with prognosis in lung adenocarcinoma. PLoS ONE **10**(3), e0118261 (2015)
13. Hancock, M.: Pylidc documentation. https://pylidc.github.io/index.html. Accessed 5 Feb 2022
14. Hassani, C., Varghese, B., Nieva, J., Duddalwar, V.: Radiomics in pulmonary lesion imaging. Am. J. Roentgenol. **212**(3), 497–504 (2019)
15. Hatt, M., Vallieres, M., Visvikis, D., Zwanenburg, A.: IBSI: an international community radiomics standardization initiative. J. Nucl. Medi. **59**(1 supp. 287) (2018)
16. Ibrahim, A., et al.: Radiomics for precision medicine: Current challenges, future prospects, and the proposal of a new framework. Methods **188**, 20–29 (2021)
17. Limkin, E.J., et al.:The complexity of tumor shape, spiculatedness, correlates with tumor radiomic shape features. Sci. Rep. **9**(1), 4329 (2019)
18. MacMahon, H., et al.: Guidelines for management of incidental pulmonary nodules detected on CT images: from the Fleischner Society 2017. Radiology **284**(1), 228–243 (2017)
19. McWilliams, A., et al.: Probability of cancer in pulmonary nodules detected on first screening CT. N. Eng. J. Med. **369**(10), 910–919 (2013)
20. Overholser, B.R., Sowinski, K.M.: Biostatistics primer: Part 2. Nutr. Clin. Prac. **23**(1), 76–84 (2008)

21. Palumbo, B., et al.: Value of shape and texture features from 18F-FDG PET/CT to discriminate between benign and malignant solitary pulmonary nodules: An experimental evaluation. Diagnostics **10**, 696 (2020)
22. Qiu, S., Sun, J., Zhou, T., Gao, G., He, Z., Liang, T.: Spiculation sign recognition in a pulmonary nodule based on spiking neural P systems. BioMed. Res. Int. **2020**, 6619076 (2020)
23. Rundo, L., et al.: A low-dose CT-based radiomic model to improve characterization and screening recall intervals of indeterminate prevalent pulmonary nodules. Diagnostics **11**(9), 1610 (2021)
24. Scrivener, M., de Jong, E., van Timmeren, Pieters, T., Ghaye, B., Geets, X.: Radiomics applied to lung cancer: a review. Trans. Cancer Res.**5**(4), 398–409 (2016)
25. Shaikh, F., et al.: Technical challenges in the clinical application of radiomics. JCO Clin. Cancer Inform. **2017**, 1–8 (2017)
26. Snoeckx, A., et al.: Evaluation of the solitary pulmonary nodule: size matters, but do not ignore the power of morphology. Insights into Imag. **9**(1), 73–86 (2017). https://doi.org/10.1007/s13244-017-0581-2
27. van der Walt, S., et al.: scikit-image: Image processing in Python. Peer J. **2**, e453 (2014). https://peerj.com/articles/453/
28. Various authors: The image biomarker standardisation initiative, https://ibsi.readthedocs.io/en/latest/index.html. Accessed 4 May 2021
29. Wu, W., Hu, H., Gong, J., Li, X., Huang, G., Nie, S.: Malignant-benign classification of pulmonary nodules based on random forest aided by clustering analysis. Phys. Med. Biol. **64**(3), 035017 (2019)

Large-Scale Patch-Wise Pathological Image Feature Dataset with a Hardware-agnostic Feature Extraction Tool

Zheyu Zhu[1], Ruining Deng[1], Quan Liu[1], Zuhayr Asad[1], Can Cui[1], Tianyuan Yao[1], and Yuankai Huo[1,2(✉)]

[1] Department of Computer Science, Vanderbilt University, Nashville, TN 37215, USA
yuankai.huo@vanderbilt.edu

[2] Department of Electrical and Computer Engineering, Vanderbilt University, Nashville, TN 37215, USA

Abstract. Recent advances in whole slide imaging (WSI) have transformed computer-aided pathological studies from small-scale (e.g., <500 patients) to large-scale (e.g., >10,000 patients). Moreover, a single whole slide image might yield Gigapixel resolution; thus, even basic preprocessing steps, such as foreground segmentation, tiling, and patch-wise feature extraction (e.g., via ImageNet pretrained models), can be computationally expensive. For example, it would take 2,400 h to simply obtain patch-level low-dimensional features (e.g., 1D feature with 2048 dimension) from all foreground patches (e.g., 512×512 images) in 10,000 WSI images. In this paper, we present a large-scale patch-wise pathological image feature dataset, covering 14,000 WSIs from TCGA and PAIP cohorts. The contribution of this study is five-fold: (1) We release a foreground patch-level feature dataset, saving 92.1% of storage space and 140 days of computational time; (2) The global spatial location of the patch-level features is provided to aggregate WSI-level results; (3) The feature dataset from two pretrained models (ImageNet and BiT) and two resolutions (1024 and 2048) are evaluated and released for flexible downstream analyses; (4) We containerize the foreground segmentation, tiling, and feature extraction steps as an operating system and hardware agnostic Docker toolkit, called PathContainer, to allow for convenient feature extraction; (5) The entire PathFeature dataset and the PathContainer software have been made publicly available. When performing a standard weakly supervised segmentation method on 940 WSIs, 85.3% of computational time was saved using the PathFeature dataset. The code and data have been made publicly available at https://github.com/hrlblab/PathContainer.

Keywords: Computational pathology · Feature extraction · Weakly supervised learning

© The Author(s), under exclusive license to Springer Nature Switzerland AG 2022
G. Yang et al. (Eds.): MIUA 2022, LNCS 13413, pp. 778–786, 2022.
https://doi.org/10.1007/978-3-031-12053-4_57

1   Introduction

With the development of digital pathology and deep learning techniques, the scale of whole slide imaging (WSI) based studies has been increased from small-scale (e.g., <500 patients) to large-scale (e.g., >10,000 patients) [1,4,7,8]. Moreover, a single whole slide image could be of Gigapixel resolution. Thus, the image data are typically processed at patch-level for downstream learning. However, processing large-scale Gigapixel images via deep learning can be resource intensive, even for preprocessing steps such as tiling and patch-wise feature extraction [9]. For example, it would take 2,400 h just to simply obtain patch-level low-dimensional features (e.g., 1D feature with 2048 dimension) from all foreground patches (e.g., 512×512 images) from 10,000 WSI images.

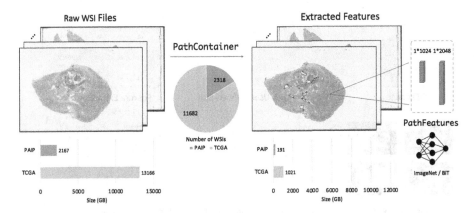

Fig. 1. This figure presents the proposed PathFeature dataset. The dataset consists of 14,000 whole slide images (WSIs) from TCGA and PAIP. The raw WSIs took about 15 Terabytes (TB), while the patch-wise feature dataset saved 92.1% of storage space. In the PathFeature dataset, both 1024 and 2048-dimensional patch level features are provided, from ImageNet and BiT pretrained models. The corresponding preprocessing approach has been containerized as a Docker image, named PathContainer.

To alleviate the time-consuming preprocessing steps, we present a large-scale patch-wise pathological image feature dataset called PathFeature, covering 14,000 WSIs from the Genome Atlas Program (TCGA) and Pathology AI Platform (PAIP) datasets (Fig. 1). Moreover, we release PathContainer, a containerized patch-wise tiling and feature extracting toolbox. Different from existing preprocessing toolkits (e.g., PyHIST [9] and CLAM [6]), PathContainer is hardware and operating system agnostic. For a consistent design, PathContainer can be used to reproduce the exact PathFeature dataset.

The contribution of this study is five-fold:

- We release a foreground patch-level feature dataset, saving 92.1% of storage space and 140 days of computational time.

- The global spatial location of the patch-level features is provided to aggregate WSI-level results.
- The feature dataset from two pretrained models (ImageNet and BiT) and two resolutions (1024 and 2048) are evaluated and released for flexible downstream analyses.
- We containerize the tiling and feature extraction steps as a hardware and operating system-agnostic Docker toolkit, called PathContainer, to allow for convenient feature extraction via one line of code.
- The entire PathFeature dataset and the PathContainer toolbox have been made publicly available at[1].

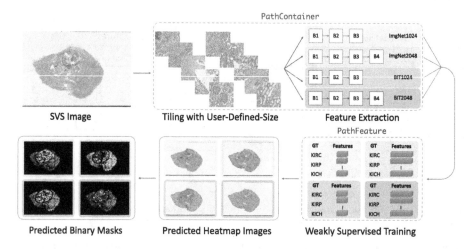

Fig. 2. This figure illustrates the experimental steps in this study. The first step conducts foreground segmentation and then crops the WSI into small patches. Next, the PathContainer toolbox extracts features from each patch via four different feature extraction models: ImageNet1024, ImageNet2048, BiT1024, and BiT2048. Then, the weakly supervised segmentation method, called CLAM [6], is employed as a downstream task for the usage of different types of features. Heatmaps, as well as tumor segmentation masks, are then created for visualization (red and blue colors indicate high and low probability of a tumor) and quantitative evaluation.(Color figure online)

2   Method

2.1   Tiling and Feature Extraction

Simple preprocessing (e.g., tiling and patch-level feature extraction) can be resource-intensive for large-scale Gigapixel WSIs. Moreover, most of the WSIs image regions are typically background, rather than the tissue foreground. To

---

[1] https://github.com/hrlblab/PathContainer.

obtain comprehensive foreground patch-level features, we implemented (1) foreground segmentation, (2) tiling, and (3) feature extraction using the proposed PathContainer preprocessing toolkit (Fig. 2). Briefly, the existing foreground segmentation and tiling algorithms are employed to achieve image patches (e.g., 256×256 or 512×512), following [6]. For the feature extraction stage, PathContainer incorporates different options that allow the users to choose the required (1) patch resolution (256×256 or 512×512), (2) pretrained models (ImageNet [2] or BiT [5]), and (3) feature dimension (1024 or 2028).

The ImageNet pretrained ResNet50 [3] model is employed, which utilizes adaptive mean-spatial pooling after the third block of ResNet50 in order to get feature vectors with a dimension of 1024 (i.e., ImageNet) or 2048 (i.e., ImageNet2048) after the fourth block. Beyond controlling the outputs' dimensionalities, we also employ the prevalent Big Transfer (BiT [5]) model as another pretrained model. Similar to ImageNet1024 and ImageNet2048, both 1024 (i.e., BiT1024) and 2048 (i.e., BiT2048) dimensional vectors are provided by PathFeature and PathContainer.

2.2   Containerization

To allow for convenient preprocessing with a single line of command, PathContainer is developed as a Docker image (Fig. 3). PathContainer consists of the following three steps: foreground segmentation, patch tiling, and feature extraction, as mentioned above. All the required libraries are included in the DockerFile, which is publicly available. The compiled Docker image has been pushed to DockerHub[2] for reproducible research.

In our Github Repository, PathContainer includes three major parameters: an input folder (input_dir) to save input WSI files, an output folder (output_dir) to save output features, and a configuration folder (config_dir) to specify both the Dockerfile and the configuration file. By defining the three parameters, PathContainer can be processed with the following command lines:

```
export  input_dir=./PathContainer/input_dir
export  output_dir=./PathContainer/output_dir
export  config_dir=./PathContainer/config_dir
sudo $config_dir/run_docker.sh ${input_dir} ${output_dir}
         ${config_dir} ${output_dir}/log
```

The config_dir contains a DockerFile to reproduce the Docker Image, as well as a configuration file (config.yaml) to specify all the custom parameters, such as desired patch size. The run_docker.sh is the root command to trigger the entire Docker. All files are available at[3].

---

[2] https://hub.docker.com.
[3] https://github.com/hrlblab/PathContainer.

2.3   Downstream Weakly Supervised Segmentation

To evaluate the efficiency and efficacy of the PathFeature dataset and the PathContainer Docker, we perform a downstream weakly supervised tumor segmentation task using the CLAM segmentation pipeline [6]. In the original CLAM design, ImageNet1024 was employed as the pretrained patch-level features model. In this study, we extend the design with ImageNet1024, ImageNet2048, BiT1024, and BiT2048. By only using the WSI-level weak classification label, CLAM classifies each image patch with a cancer score. Then, the heatmaps and tumor segmentation masks (following [6]) are utilized to evaluate different feature extraction strategies via PathContainer.

3   Data and Experiments

3.1   PathFeature Dataset

The PathFeature dataset consisted of WSIs from both the TCGA repository[4] and the PAIP dataset[5]. The TCGA repository included 11,682 WSIs of various types: Kidney, Liver, Prostate, Pancreas, etc. The PAIP dataset consisted of 2,318 WSIs of six types: Liver, Colon, Prostate, Kidney, Pancreas and Bile. We used PathContainer to extract features from all of the 14,000 WSIs with ImageNet1024, ImageNet2048, BiT1024, and BiT2048. It ultimately provided 56,000 .h5 files (each file saved all foreground patch-level features for a WSI).

3.2   Weakly Supervised Segmentation

940 WSIs of renal biopsies were employed from the TCGA dataset, which contained three subtypes of tumors for the kidney: 519 Kidney Renal Clear Cell Carcinoma (TCGA-KIRC) WSIs, 300 Kidney Renal Papillary Cell Carcinoma (TCGA-KIRP) WSIs, and 121 Kidney Chromophobe (TCGA-KICH) WSIs. Throughout the feature extraction process, PathContainer obtained four types of patch-wise features (only for foreground tissues) including: ImageNet1024, ImageNet2048, BiT1024, and BiT2048. This process generated 3,760 .h5 files containing both features and global coordinates for each patch. Following [6], the models were trained and applied to an external testing dataset with 44 renal cancer WSIs, from PAIP data. For the PAIP dataset, the tumor areas were manually traced by pathologists.

We used a ratio of 7:3 for splitting the training and validation data using the TCGA dataset. Then, the trained model was evaluated using 44 renal biopsies from the PAIP dataset as external validation.

---

[4] https://portal.gdc.cancer.gov/repository.
[5] http://www.wisepaip.org/paip.

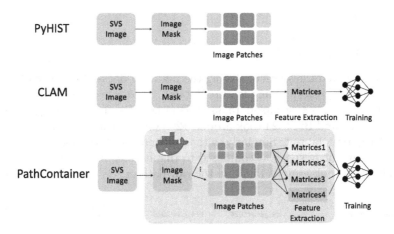

Fig. 3. This figure compares three different WSI processing pipelines. The upper panel represents the tissue segmentation and processing command-line tool called PyHIST; The middle panel represents the weakly-supervised method that uses an attention-based learning process called CLAM; The bottom panel represents our containerized PathContainer toolbox, which allows the users to customize the preprocessing step with different patch sizes (e.g., 256×256 or 512×512), feature extraction algorithms (e.g., ImageNet or BiT pretrained), and feature dimensionalities (e.g., 1024 or 2028).

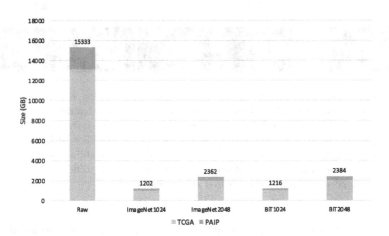

Fig. 4. This figure shows storage space consumption for 14000 features extracted from TCGA and PAIP datasets. The extraction methods include ImageNet1024, ImageNet2048, BiT1024, and BiT2048.

4   Results

4.1   Efficiency Analysis

Figure 4 compared the space of storing the raw WSI dataset for the entire PAIP dataset and the corresponding feature dataset via four feature extraction methods. The raw dataset occupied 15,333 GB (15.0 TB) of the disk spaces, while ImageNet1024 and BiT1024 took around 1200 GB, which is only approximately 7.8% of the raw dataset. Similarly, although ImageNet2048 and BiT2048 took twice the amount of space as compared to the features in the 1024 dimensions, they also only took around 15.5% of the raw dataset.

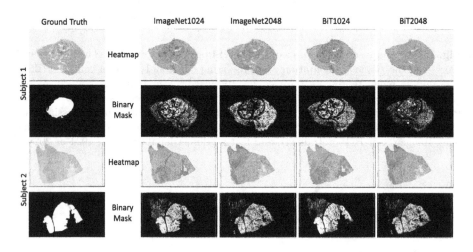

Fig. 5. This figure presents the qualitative tumor segmentation results on two randomly picked testing WSIs. 940 WSIs from TCGA were used as training and validation datasets, while 44 WSIs from PAIP were used as independent external validation. The heat maps and masks were computed using CLAM [6]. The different heatmap-based visualizations (red and blue colors indicate high and low probability of a tumor) and weakly supervised tumor segmentation masks were from using different feature types (from pretrained models) in PathFeature. (Color figure online)

For the downstream weakly supervised segmentation task, 940 renal biopsies were used to evaluate the efficiency and efficacy of using PathFeature and PathContainer. Directly learning from raw data, the preprocessing for feature extraction from 940 WSIs took 456 h. By contrast, downstream weakly supervised training only required around 20 h for the task of training each model. All the procedures were completed under the same workstation, with the NVIDIA Quadro P5000 GPU.

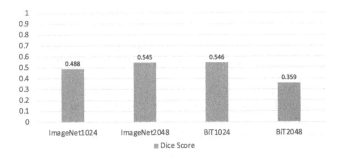

Fig. 6. This figure shows the Dice scores (the higher the better) of weakly supervised segmentation results of using different feature types (from pretrained models) in PathFeature, when the automated segmentation masks are compared with manual segmentation masks.

4.2 Efficacy Analysis

Figure 5 presented the qualitative testing results of weakly supervised segmentation using different pretrained models in PathContainer. Figure 6 shows the corresponding quantitative results (Dice) of weakly supervised tumor segmentation results that were trained by 940 WSIs. The ImageNet2048 and BiT1024 feature datasets achieved superior segmentation performance.

5 Conclusion

In this paper, we release and evaluate the PathFeature dataset, a large-scale patch-level image feature dataset from the TCGA and PAIP cohorts. Compared with processing from raw WSI files, PathFeature saves 92.1% of hardware storage space and 3360 h of computational time. Meanwhile, we release PathContainer, a containerized preprocessing toolbox for WSIs, that includes foreground segmentation, patch-wise tiling, and feature extraction. The prevalent ImageNet pretrained models as well as the recently developed BiT pretrained models are provided through PathContainer. Using a subset of 940 WSIs, the efficiency and efficacy of the PathFeature and PathContainer were evaluated via different feature types. The results indicated that ImageNet2048 and BiT1024 achieved superior segmentation performance.

Acknowledgments. This work has not been submitted for publication or presentation elsewhere. The results shown here are in whole or part based upon data generated by the TCGA Research Network: https://www.cancer.gov/tcga. Deidentified pathology images and annotations used in this research were provided by Seoul National University Hospital by a grant of the Korea Health Technology R&D Project through the Korea Health Industry Development Institute (KHIDI), funded by the Ministry of Health and Welfare, Republic of Korea (grant number: HI18C0316)"

References

1. Beck, A.H., et al.: Systematic analysis of breast cancer morphology uncovers stromal features associated with survival. Sci. Transl. Med. **3**(108), 108ra113–108ra113 (2011)
2. Deng, J., Dong, W., Socher, R., Li, L.J., Li, K., Fei-Fei, L.: Imagenet: a large-scale hierarchical image database. In: 2009 IEEE Conference on Computer Vision and Pattern Recognition, pp. 248–255. IEEE (2009)
3. He, K., Zhang, X., Ren, S., Sun, J.: Deep residual learning for image recognition (2015)
4. Kather, J.N., et al.: Deep learning can predict microsatellite instability directly from histology in gastrointestinal cancer. Nat. Med. **25**(7), 1054–1056 (2019)
5. Kolesnikov, A., et al.: Big transfer (bit): general visual representation learning (2020)
6. Lu, M.Y., Williamson, D.F.K., Chen, T.Y., Chen, R.J., Barbieri, M., Mahmood, F.: Data efficient and weakly supervised computational pathology on whole slide images. Nature Biomed. Eng. **5**, 555–57 (2020)
7. Mobadersany, P., et al.: Predicting cancer outcomes from histology and genomics using convolutional networks. Proc. Natl. Acad. Sci. **115**(13), E2970–E2979 (2018)
8. Moen, E., Bannon, D., Kudo, T., Graf, W., Covert, M., Van Valen, D.: Deep learning for cellular image analysis. Nat. Methods **16**(12), 1233–1246 (2019)
9. Muñoz-Aguirre, M., Ntasis, V.F., Rojas, S., Guigó, R.: PyHIST: a histological image segmentation tool. PLOS Comput. Biol. **16**(10), e1008349 (2020). https://doi.org/10.1371/journal.pcbi.1008349, https://doi.org/10.1371/journal.pcbi.1008349

Predicting Myocardial Infarction Using Retinal OCT Imaging

Cynthia Maldonado García(✉) ⓘ, Rodrigo Bonazzola ⓘ, Nishant Ravikumar ⓘ,
and Alejandro F. Frangi ⓘ

Centre for Computational Imaging and Simulation Technologies in Biomedicine,
School of Computing, University of Leeds, Leeds, UK
{C.Maldonado1,R.Bonazzola1,N.Ravikumar,A.Frangi}@leeds.ac.uk

Abstract. Late-stage identification of patients at risk of myocardial infarction (MI) inhibits delivery of effective preventive care, increasing the burden on healthcare services and affecting patients' quality of life. Hence, standardised non-invasive, accessible, and low-cost methods for early identification of patient's at risk of future MI events are desirable. In this study, we demonstrate for the first time that retinal optical coherence tomography (OCT) imaging can be used to identify future adverse cardiac events such as MI. We propose a binary classification network based on a task-aware Variational Autoencoder (VAE), which learns a latent embedding of patients' OCT images and uses the former to classify the latter into one of two groups, i.e. whether they are likely to have a heart attack (MI) in the future or not. Results obtained for experiments conducted in this study (AUROC 0.74 ± 0.01, accuracy 0.674 ± 0.007, precision 0.657 ± 0.012, recall 0.678 ± 0.017 and f1-score 0.653 ± 0.013) demonstrate that our task-aware VAE-based classifier is superior to standard convolution neural network classifiers at identifying patients at risk of future MI events based on their retinal OCT images. This proof-of-concept study indicates that retinal OCT imaging could be used as a low-cost alternative to cardiac magnetic resonance imaging, for identifying patients at risk of MI early.

Keywords: Retinal optical coherence tomography · Variational autoencoder · Myocardial infarction

1 Introduction

Cardiovascular diseases (CVD) remain a major cause of death globally [14]. In 2017 alone, there were ~17.8 million deaths worldwide of which more than

---

N. Ravikumar and A.F. Frangi—Joint last authors.

Supplementary Information The online version contains supplementary material available at https://doi.org/10.1007/978-3-031-12053-4_58.

G. Yang et al. (Eds.): MIUA 2022, LNCS 13413, pp. 787–797, 2022.
https://doi.org/10.1007/978-3-031-12053-4_58

three-quarters were in low- and middle-income countries [8]. Furthermore, this is projected to increase over the next decade. Therefore, it is crucial to identify patients at high-risk of CVD early on to deliver adequate preventive treatment, and improve patient quality of life and survival rates. Several statistical approaches for identifying patients at risk of CVD based on demographic and clinical data such as age, sex, gender, HbA1c, smoking status, etc. have been proposed previously [3]. Cardiac magnetic resonance imaging (CMR) is typically the imaging modality used to characterise cardiac structure and function, and can capture relevant information to identify patients at risk of CVD [11]. However, the infrastructure required to host a CMR imaging centre is expensive, limiting its availability in low- and middle-income countries. Thus, utilising cost-effective imaging solutions to identify patients at risk of CVD is essential to enable widespread screening of large populations in low- to middle-income countries.

Recently, retinal images have been used to assess changes in retinal vasculature and derive ocular biomarkers for predicting risk of CVD in patients [15]. Retinal imaging such as fundus photography and optical coherence tomography (OCT) are routinely used at opticians, eye clinics, and in hospitals to screen patients for several eye conditions (e.g. Glaucoma, age related macular degeneration, etc.) and are relatively inexpensive compared with CMR imaging. Poplin et al. [13] were the first to demonstrate that cardiovascular risk factors such as age, gender, smoking status, blood pressure, body mass index (BMI), glucose and cholesterol levels could be predicted directly from patients' fundus photographs. Following this study, Cheung et al. [1] proposed a CNN-based approach to measure retinal-vessel calibre from fundus photographs to improve subsequent CVD risk assessment. Son et al. [16] adopted a transfer learning approach, using an ImageNet-pretrained inception-v3 model, which was fine-tuned on retinal fundus photographs to identify patients with high Coronary artery calcium score (CACS) from those with no Coronary artery calcium (CAC). CACS is often used to help stratify patients' risk of CVD. Additionally, by visualising feature maps learned by their trained CNN, they demonstrated that discriminative features within correctly classified images were derived from, or in the vicinity of, retinal vasculature.

Most recently, Diaz-Pinto et al. [4] demonstrated for the first time that patients at risk of future myocardial infarction (MI) can be identified based on just their fundus images and minimal personal information (e.g. age, gender). They developed a multi-stage deep learning framework that utilised a convolutional multichannel variational autoencoder (mcVAE) to first learn a joint latent space of patients' fundus and short axis cine-CMR images. A regression network was trained separately to predict key cardiac functional indices i.e. left ventricular end-diastolic volume (LVEDV) and left ventricular mass (LVM) using cine-CMR images and basic metadata as inputs. Subsequently, during inference, the trained mcVAE was used to synthesise cine-CMR scans given just (unseen) fundus images as input, and the regression network was used to predict LVEDV and LVM using the synthesised cine-CMR scans and the patient's metadata. Finally, a logistic regression model was trained and used to predict future MI events given the predicted cardiac indices and patient metadata as inputs. While fundus images provide some insights to retinal vascular health, they are 2D images and do not capture detailed information of retinal microstructure and microvasculature in 3D. As highlighted by Farrah et al. [5] retinal OCT imaging provides ultra-high resolution 3D characterisation of retinal microstructure and microvasculature, and changes to the latter and biomarkers derived thereof, have been associated with pathological changes to other organs. Combining deep learning and OCT imaging therefore, could provide the means for screening patients at risk of CVD.

Therefore, the main aim of this study is to demonstrate that OCT images can be used to predict future myocardial infarction (MI) events. We propose a task-aware variational autoencoder (VAE) that jointly learns a latent representation patients' retinal OCT images, and to classify them into one of two classes - whether they are likely to undergo MI in the future or not. Here, as the latent space is learned, it is used to train a binary classifier in the form of a fully connected network (FCN). Both the VAE and FC are trained jointly, end-to-end, and henceforth we refer to this approach as a task-aware VAE. To the best of our knowledge, this is the first study to explore the prediction of MI using OCT images.

2 Methodology

An overview of the proposed task-aware VAE approach to identifying patients at risk of future MI is presented in the schematic shown in Fig. 1. Our approach comprises two components, namely, a self-supervised feature extractor based on a VAE and a FCN-based binary classifier. The inputs to the framework are 10 slices of OCT B-scans that are used to learn a compressed latent representation of the high-dimensional image data, which in turn is used by the FCN-classifier to distinguish between healthy subjects and those likely to suffer MI in the future.

2.1 Variational Autoencoder

Variational Autoencoders (VAEs) [10] are neural network-based generative models that comprise encoder-decoder network pairs, which are trained in a self-supervised fashion to learn latent representations of data. Here, the encoder is trained to approximate the posterior distribution of the latent variables given some input data, while, the decoder learns to reconstruct the input data by sampling from the resulting posterior distribution. Consider an observed data sample $\mathbf{x}$ which is modelled as $\mathbf{p}_\theta (\mathbf{x} \mid \mathbf{z})$ with parameters θ and latent variables $\mathbf{z}$. The prior distribution over the latent variables is modelled as $\mathbf{p}(\mathbf{z})$. The posterior distribution given the data $\mathbf{x}$ is denoted as $\mathbf{p}(\mathbf{z} \mid \mathbf{x})$, and since it is not always computable analytically, it is approximated as $\mathbf{q}_\phi (\mathbf{z} \mid \mathbf{x})$ with parameters ϕ, by maximising the evidence lower bound (ELBO) given by,

$$\mathbf{L}_{\mathbf{ELBO(x)}} = -\alpha \mathbf{D}_{\mathbf{KL}} \left[\mathbf{q}_\phi (\mathbf{z} \mid \mathbf{x}) \| \mathbf{p}(\mathbf{z}) \right] + \mathbf{E}_{\mathbf{q}_\phi(\mathbf{z}|\mathbf{x})} \left[\beta \mathbf{log} \mathbf{p}_\theta (\mathbf{x} \mid \mathbf{z}) \right], \quad (1)$$

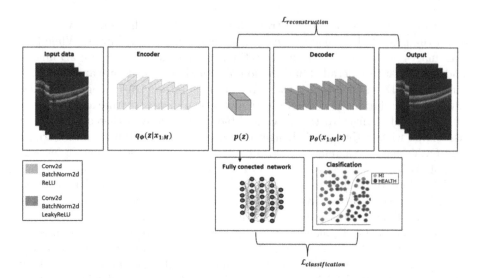

Fig. 1. Overview of the proposed model. Retinal OCT images as input data are encoded into a latent space which is trained to reconstruct the original input data. A fully connected network is trained from the latent space to classify MI events.

where, the Kullback-Leibler divergence between the distributions of the variational posterior **q** and the true posterior **p** is defined as:

$$\mathbf{D_{KL}}\left(\mathbf{q}_\phi\left(\mathbf{z}\mid\mathbf{x}\right)\|\mathbf{p}\left(\mathbf{z}\right)\right) = -\int\mathbf{q}_\phi\left(\mathbf{z}\mid\mathbf{x}\right)\log\left(\frac{\mathbf{p}\left(\mathbf{z}\right)}{\mathbf{q}_\phi\left(\mathbf{z}\mid\mathbf{x}\right)}\right). \tag{2}$$

The loss function used to train the proposed task-aware VAE is presented in Eq. 3, and is composed of: (1) the mean square error (MSE) $\mathcal{L}_{MSE}$ loss (see Eq. 4) for the reconstruction error between the original data ($\mathbf{y}_i$) and reconstructed data ($\hat{\mathbf{y}}_i$); (2) the binary cross-entropy loss $\mathcal{L}_{BCE}$ (see Eq. 5) for the classification task, where, y_i^g and y_i^p denote the ground truth class label and predicted class probability for the ith sample; and (3) the Kullback-Leibler divergence loss $\mathcal{L}_{KL}$ (see Eq. 6).

$$\mathcal{L}_{task-aware-VAE} = \mathcal{L}_{MSE} + \alpha\mathcal{L}_{BCE} + \beta\mathcal{L}_{KL} \tag{3}$$

$$\mathcal{L}_{MSE} = \frac{1}{N}\sum_{i=1}^{N}(\mathbf{y}_i - \hat{\mathbf{y}}_i)^2 \tag{4}$$

$$\mathcal{L}_{BCE} = -\frac{1}{N}\sum_{i=1}^{N}[y_i^g * \log(y_i^p) + (1 - y_i^g) * \log(1 - y_i^p)] \tag{5}$$

$$\mathcal{L}_{KL} = \frac{1}{2}\left[1 + \log(\sigma_i^2) - \sigma_i^2 - \mu_i^2\right] \tag{6}$$

3   Experiments and Results

3.1   Data Characteristics

In this study we used retinal OCT imaging data from the UK Biobank to train and evaluate the proposed approach. Approximately 85,000 patients' retinal images, including fundus and OCT imaging have been acquired to date within the UK Biobank, using the Topcon 3D OCT 1000 Mark 2 system. We utilised an automatic approach for quality assessment of retinal fundus images [6], based on the rationale that fundus and OCT images are acquired simultaneously and hence poor-quality fundus images are likely to be accompanied by poor quality OCT images. This quality assessment step was used to discard poor quality OCT images. This resulted in 31,791 images of the left eye, which we used in this study. Among these, only 683 images belonged to patients diagnosed with MI post image acquisition, while the remaining 31,108 images were from healthy subjects. Thus, the number of MI patients and correspondingly, the number of images in the MI group were significantly fewer than the healthy subjects group. To mitigate for this class imbalance we randomly selected an equal number of images from the healthy subjects group for training the task-aware VAE and classifier. Additionally, we used the first 10 slices (or B-scans) from each OCT image throughout this study.

3.2   Experimental Settings

Ten-fold cross-validation experiments were conducted to evaluate the performance of the models. We partitioned the dataset as $7 : 2 : 1$, for training, validation and testing, respectively. We kept the test set completely unseen and common across all folds. All experiments were performed using NVIDIA Tesla M60 GPUs. We adopted a grid search strategy to select suitable hyperparameters. The task-aware VAE model was implemented using PyTorch 1.10.2 [12] and comprised six 2D convolution layers in both the encoder and decoder networks. All convolution layers within the encoder used Rectified Linear Unit (ReLU) activations, while all convolution layers within the decoder using Leaky Rectified Linear Unit (LeakyReLU) activations. The bottleneck layer of the VAE representing the latent space, was connected to an FCN comprising three hidden layers with ReLU activations and a terminal layer with one output neuron and a Sigmoid activation function (acting as the classifier). The proposed task-aware VAE was trained using the Adam optimiser [9] with a batch size of 32 and a learning rate of $1e^{-6}$. Furthermore, to avoid overfitting, we pre-trained the encoder-decoder part of the proposed task-aware VAE model (i.e. without the FCN classifier) using 2228 healthy subjects' OCT images (where each image again comprised 10 slices/B-scans), enabling the VAE to learn rich representations in a self-supervised fashion. All subjects' images used for pre-training the VAE were excluded from subsequent experiments, where the task-aware VAE was trained and evaluated to identify patients at risk of future MI based on their OCT images.

We evaluated the performance of our task-aware VAE in two ways, namely, its reconstruction performance and its classification performance. The former evaluates the ability of the model to reconstruct OCT images not seen during training, and thereby assesses the richness of the latent representation learned. The latter meanwhile, quantitatively evaluates the ability of the model to identify patients at risk of future MI events. Reconstruction performance was quantitatively assessed using the structural similarity metric (SSIM). While, the classification performance of our approach was evaluated using standard metrics derived from the confusion matrix (e.g. precision, recall, F_1-score) and via ROC-AUC analysis. Additionally, we compare the classification performance of our task-aware VAE with two baseline CNN-based classifiers. For the first CNN-classifier, we used Densenet121 [7], based on the implementation available in MONAI [2], and followed their recommended training protocol for the same. For the second CNN-classifier, we utilised the encoder network from our task-aware VAE as the base feature extractor, and the 3-layer FCN from the task-aware VAE as the classification head. The activation functions of all layers in the encoder-FCN were kept identical to the corresponding layers in the task-aware VAE. The setting of this experiment is exactly the same as described for the task-aware VAE, except the learning rate was set to $1e^{-7}$ and the BCE loss was used for training CNN (see Eq. 3).

3.3   Results

OCT slices of unseen images from the test set (top row) and their corresponding reconstructions predicted by the trained task-aware VAE (bottom row) are depicted in Fig. 2. The reconstructed images indicate that the proposed model captures the global and local structure of the retinal layers, albeit with some visible smoothing artefacts which is not uncommon in VAEs due to the regularisation imposed by the KL-divergence term in the loss function used to train such models. The reconstruction performance of the proposed approach was also quantitatively assessed using SSIM. The average SSIM score estimated across all images in the test set was 0.988 ± 0.014.

We evaluated the classification performance of the proposed task-aware VAE model using standard classification metrics derived from the confusion matrix, namely, accuracy, precision, recall and the F_1-score, and compared the former with the Densenet121 and encoder-FCN classifiers. The confusion matrices depicted in Fig. 3 show that of the 260 test cases, 128 belonged to the MI group and the rest to the healthy group comprising 132 cases. The proposed approach correctly classified 83 MI samples, while, Densenet121 correctly classified 77 MI patients. Although, Densenet121 predicted more true negatives (82) than the proposed approach (79), our approach achieved fewer false negatives, which is especially relevant for this application as we want to minimise the number of patients at risk of future MI that go undetected. A summary of the classification performance on the unseen test set, across all models trained for both approaches, in the 10-fold cross-validation experiments conducted, is presented in Table 1.

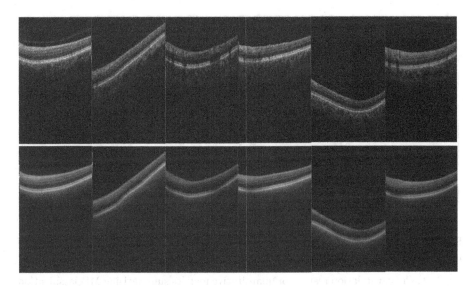

Fig. 2. Visual comparison of the reconstructed OCT images (bottom row) with their corresponding original (top row) counterparts. The OCT images were reproduced with permission from UK Biobank.

Table 1 indicates that our approach consistently outperforms the Densenet121 classifier on all four classification metrics. We also evaluated the performance of the encoder-FCN, which performed the worst out of all three approaches, achieving; accuracy: 0.501 ± 0.008; precision: 0.501 ± 0.008; recall: 0.509 ± 0.009; and F_1-score: 0.504 ± 0.003; which amounts to random guessing. For this reason, we omit the inclusion of the corresponding ROC curve and confusion matrix from the main text for brevity and include it in the supplementary material. Densenet121 achieves a lower mean accuracy score of 0.630 ± 0.014 than the task-aware VAE (0.674 ± 0.007). Similarly, as shown in Table 1 the proposed task-aware VAE outperformed both CNN-based techniques consistently across all classification metrics investigated, achieving a mean precision, recall and F1-score of 0.657 ± 0.012, 0.678 ± 0.017 and 0.653 ± 0.013, respectively. The poor overall performance of the encoder-FCN compared with Densenet121 and the task-aware VAE is attributed to the lack of pre-training of the former and the relatively small size of the dataset used for classification. Densenet121 and the task-aware VAE on the other hand, are both pre-trained networks, albeit in different ways, which highlights the benefit of transfer learning in the small data regime. While Densenet121 was pre-trained on the ImageNet database, our task-aware VAE was pre-trained as a conventional VAE (i.e. comprising just the encoder and decoder networks) on the complete left out data set of healthy individuals, as discussed previously.

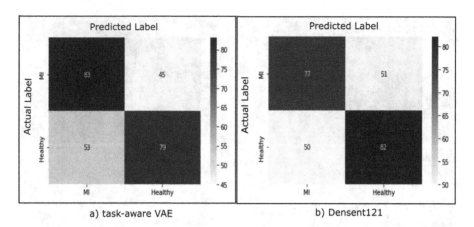

a) task-aware VAE   b) Densent121

Fig. 3. Confusion matrix using OCT images for a) task-aware VAE and b) Densenet121.

Table 1. Cross-validation results for quantitative metrics summarising MI classification performance of task-aware VAE and Densenet121.

Metric	k-Fold	Accuracy	Precision	Recall	F_1-score
Task-aware VAE	Fold 1	0.681	0.665	0.687	0.667
	Fold 2	0.678	0.663	0.687	0.657
	Fold 3	0.688	0.665	0.691	0.653
	Fold 4	0.677	0.666	0.686	0.664
	Fold 5	0.669	0.661	0.688	0.65
	Fold 6	0.672	0.666	0.696	0.654
	Fold 7	0.675	0.663	0.677	0.665
	Fold 8	0.667	0.633	0.644	0.633
	Fold 9	0.669	0.638	0.661	0.63
	Fold 10	0.666	0.652	0.661	0.665
	Mean 10-Fold	0.674 ± 0.007	0.657 ± 0.012	0.678 ± 0.017	0.653 ± 0.013
Densenet121	Fold 1	0.645	0.542	0.635	0.57
	Fold 2	0.622	0.506	0.615	0.539
	Fold 3	0.63	0.523	0.62	0.552
	Fold 4	0.646	0.545	0.632	0.56
	Fold 5	0.622	0.51	0.622	0.547
	Fold 6	0.612	0.523	0.616	0.552
	Fold 7	0.618	0.516	0.618	0.537
	Fold 8	0.63	0.525	0.622	0.555
	Fold 9	0.653	0.553	0.639	0.578
	Fold 10	0.618	0.504	0.618	0.542
	Mean 10-Fold	0.63 ± 0.014	0.525 ± 0.017	0.624 ± 0.008	0.553 ± 0.013

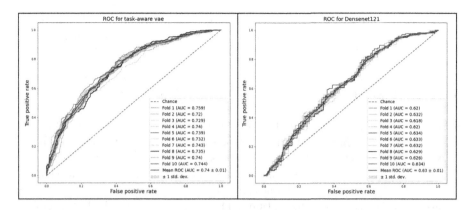

Fig. 4. Comparison of cross-validation ROC curves obtained for MI prediction using retinal OCT photographs for both methods

The ROC curves resulting from the 10-fold cross-validation experiments conducted to assess performance of the Densenet121 and task-aware VAE models is shown in Fig. 4. The AUC values of the task-aware VAE model was consistently higher than that of Densenet121 across all cross-validation folds, in accordance with the other classification metrics reported in Table 1. Our model achieved a mean AUC-ROC of 0.74 ± 0.01, which is significantly higher than that of Densenet121 (0.63 ± 0.01).

4   Discussion

Our results demonstrate that the latent representation learned for retinal OCT images using a task-aware VAE can be used to predict MI, which is supported by previous studies which suggest that retinal imaging contains relevant vascular biomarkers/information about cardiac health. Our method outperformed two conventional CNN classifiers, highlighting the advantage of semi-supervised learning, i.e. of leveraging unlabelled data to learn rich representations and relevant discriminative features through pre-training. This is a clear indication of the benefits of semi-supervised learning over fully-supervised learning, in the small data regime.

Despite the promising results, our study has several limitations and there are some open research questions we would like to address in our future work. For instance, can multi-organ data help improve understanding, diagnosis and management of cardiometabolic disease? Should OCT be used more broadly as a general screening and second referral tool for identifying patients at risk of cardiovascular diseases? What are the features in retinal images that are relevant for the identification of patients at risk of cardiovascular diseases? Our future work will look to answer these open research questions by combining multi-modal, multi-organ data within a cohesive representation learning framework to identify patients as risk of a variety of cardiovascular diseases. Additionally, incorporating recent advances in deep learning to enhance the interpretability/explainability of such systems will be explored and will be beneficial to accelerating their clinical adoption.

5   Conclusion

In this study, we propose a deep learning framework to predict future MI events using retinal OCT images. Modalities such as OCT have shown potential in detecting retinal microstructure and microvascular changes. However, to the best of our knowledge no study has demonstrated that retinal microvascular changes detected in OCT images, and biomarkers derived thereof, are powerful indicators of future cardiovascular complications. The results obtained in this proof-of-concept study demonstrate the potential for identifying such biomarkers using OCT images. This study is therefore, an important step towards facilitating cost-effective, early identification of patients at risk of MI, and potentially, other cardiovascular diseases.

Acknowledgements. This research was conducted using data from the UK Biobank under access application 11350. AFF is funded by the Royal Academy of Engineering (INSILEX CiET181919), Engineering and Physical Sciences Research Council (EPSRC) programs TUSCA EP/V04799X/1, and the Royal Society Exchange Programme CROSSLINK IESNSFC201380. CMG is funded by Consejo Nacional de Ciencia y Tecnología-CONACyT (scholarship no. 766588).

References

1. Lui Cheung, et al.: A deep-learning system for the assessment of cardiovascular disease risk via the measurement of retinal-vessel calibre. Nat. Biomed. Eng. (2020)
2. Consortium, M.: Monai: medical open network for AI, February 2022. https://doi.org/10.5281/zenodo.6114127. If you use this software, please cite it using these metadata
3. D'Agostino, R.B., et al.: General cardiovascular risk profile for use in primary care: the Framingham heart study. Circulation **117**, 743–753 (2008)
4. Diaz-Pinto, A., et al.: Predicting myocardial infarction through retinal scans and minimal personal information. Nat. Mach. Intell. **4**, 55–61 (2022)
5. Farrah, T.E., Webb, D.J., Dhaun, N.: Retinal fingerprints for precision profiling of cardiovascular risk. Nat. Rev. Cardiol. **16**, 379–381 (2019)
6. Fu, H., et al.: Evaluation of retinal image quality assessment networks in different color-spaces. In: Shen, D., et al. (eds.) MICCAI 2019. LNCS, vol. 11764, pp. 48–56. Springer, Cham (2019). https://doi.org/10.1007/978-3-030-32239-7_6
7. Huang, G., Liu, Z., Weinberger, K.Q.: Densely connected convolutional networks. 2017 IEEE Conference on Computer Vision and Pattern Recognition (CVPR), pp. 2261–2269 (2017)
8. Kaptoge, S., et al.: World health organization cardiovascular disease risk charts: revised models to estimate risk in 21 global regions. Lancet Glob. Health **7**(10), e1332–e1345 (2019)

9. Kingma, D.P., Ba, J.: Adam: A method for stochastic optimization. CoRR abs/1412.6980 (2015)
10. Kingma, D.P., Welling, M.: Auto-encoding variational Bayes. CoRR abs/1312.6114 (2014)
11. Littlejohns, T.J., Sudlow, C.L.M., Allen, N.E., Collins, R.: UK biobank: opportunities for cardiovascular research. Eur. Heart J. **40**, 1158–1166 (2019)
12. Paszke, A., et al.: Pytorch: an imperative style, high-performance deep learning library. In: NeurIPS (2019)
13. Poplin, R., et al.: Prediction of cardiovascular risk factors from retinal fundus photographs via deep learning. Nat. Biomed. Eng. **2**, 158–164 (2018)
14. Ruwanpathirana, T., Owen, A.J., Reid, C.M.: Review on cardiovascular risk prediction. Cardiovasc. Ther. **33**(2), 62–70 (2015)
15. Sandoval-Garcia, E., et al.: Retinal arteriolar tortuosity and fractal dimension are associated with long-term cardiovascular outcomes in people with type 2 diabetes. Diabetologia **64**(10), 2215–2227 (2021). https://doi.org/10.1007/s00125-021-05499-z
16. Son, J., Shin, J.Y., Chun, E.J., Jung, K.H., Park, K.H., Park, S.J.: Predicting high coronary artery calcium score from retinal fundus images with deep learning algorithms. Transl. Vision Sci. Technol. **9** (2020)

On the Feasibility of Radiomic Analysis for the Detection of Breast Lesions in Speed-of-Sound Images of the Breast

Andres F. Vargas⬤, Angie Hernández⬤, Ana Ramirez⬤, and Said Pertuz$^{(\boxtimes)}$⬤

Universidad Industrial de Santander, 680002 Bucaramanga, Colombia
spertuz@uis.edu.co

Abstract. Recent non-linear ultrasound imaging methods estimate acoustic tissue properties, such as speed-of-sound (SOS), density, and compressibility, among others. These methods can be used to generate 2D reconstructions of the properties of inner structures of the breast for further analysis. Due to differences in the acoustic properties between cancerous and normal tissues, these reconstructions are particularly attractive for computerized analysis. In this work, we explored the feasibility of using radiomic analysis on SOS images for breast lesion detection. We performed an in-silico analysis of SOS slices extracted from 120 3D virtual breast phantoms and built a system based on radiomic features extracted from SOS images for the detection of breast masses. We measured the performance of the system in terms of the area under the ROC curve (AUC) with 95% confidence intervals (CI). We also compared the performance of lesion detection from SOS images against a model trained with synthetic mammograms generated from the same breast phantoms. Radiomic analysis on SOS images yielded statistically significant results with AUCs of 0.73 (CI: 0.64–0.82), 0.89 (CI: 0.83–0.95), and 0.94 (CI: 0.89–0.98) at pixel-size of 1.5, 2.0 and 2.5 mm respectively. Radiomic analysis on mammograms showed lower performance with an AUC of 0.62 (CI: 0.52–0.72). Our evidence suggests that the use of SOS images, paired with radiomic analysis, could aid on the detection of breast masses that are hard to recognise using digital mammography. Further investigation on ultrasound-based reconstruction of SOS images of the breast is warranted.

Keywords: Ultrasound · Mammography · Full waveform inversion · Breast cancer · Lesion detection · Radiomic analysis

1 Introduction

As of 2021, breast cancer was the most diagnosed cancer in women in the United Kingdom and one of the leading causes of cancer-related deaths. Early cancer

This work was partially funded by MINCIENCIAS projects number 110284467139.
A. F. Vargas and A. Hernández—Equally contributing authors.

detection is crucial for better patient prognosis, and mammography is the primary screening modality used for this task. The utility of mammography screening has been reflected in a reduction on breast cancer mortality [5]. Despite its advantages, mammography has the downside of exposing the patient to ionising radiation, and has been shown to have a decreased sensitivity in radiologically dense breasts due to the overlaying of dense tissues [9]. As an alternative to mammography, ultrasound-based imaging is a non-invasive, radiation-free modality that uses high-frequency sound waves to retrieve information about the inner structures of the breast. Although breast ultrasound has a higher false positive rate, and often requires to be supplemented by mammography for screening purposes, it has shown a higher sensitivity in denser breasts and better diagnostic accuracy on younger patients than digital mammography [4,29].

Due to the advantages of ultrasound imaging, the research community has invested a lot of efforts in improving this technique as well as in developing new ultrasound-based imaging methods [23,26]. Ultrasound imaging uses high frequency sound waves to scan the interior of an organ. Reconstruction methods, such as full-waveform inversion (FWI) solve the wave equation using all the information in the recorded wavefield, including multiple scaterring, dispersion and diffraction effects [24,28]. As a result, modern ultrasound-based imaging techniques allow for a more accurate estimation of acoustic properties of the tissue. FWI has shown superior reconstruction capacities than other ultrasound techniques when tested on data representing a slice enclosing a cancerous mass [18].

For diagnosis and screening purposes, we believe that one of the main advantages of ultrasound imaging compared to mammography is the direct estimation of acoustic tissue properties that are more suitable for the detection of cancer-related anomalies. Specifically, ultrasound allows for the estimation of *speed-of-sound* (SOS) propagation in the tissue. Previous researchers have measured differences between the values of these properties in cancerous and non-cancerous tissues [13,20]. As a result, we hypothesise that ultrasound-based imaging is more suitable for fully-automated, quantitative analysis of the images. Specifically, we propose that *radiomic anaysis* of SOS images can be used to detect breast lesions. Radiomic analysis refers to computerised methods that use texture features extracted from medical images for quantitative analysis [12]. Radiomic analysis has shown encouraging performance for breast cancer diagnosis using mammography [1] and classic ultrasound images [15].

In order to test our hypothesis, we conduct an in-silico experiment to measure the performance of automatic lesion detection using SOS images of breasts by means of fully-automated, computerised radiomic features. For this purpose, we generated 3D digital breast phantoms corresponding to 60 healthy breasts and 60 breasts with lesions. Subsequently we build a lesion detection system based on radiomic features extracted from SOS images. For comparison purposes, we generated mammograms of the same breast phantoms by simulating X-ray propagation. Our results demonstrate that radiomic analysis on SOS images at pixel-size(Δ) of 1.5, 2.0 and 2.5 mm (AUCs of 0.73, 0.89, and 0.94) significantly outperforms radiomic analysis in the mammograms (AUC of 0.62). Our findings suggest that SOS images can be used for lesion detection via radiomics analysis. This highlights the potential of ultrasound based imaging and the exploration of imaging modalities that can characterise different acoustic properties of the tissue.

2   Materials and Methods

In this section we describe how we generated a virtual breast cohort for the in-silico experiments as well as the proposed method for the detection of breast lesions from SOS images. Specifically, the generation of 3D breast phantoms and SOS images are described in Sects. 2.1 and 2.2, respectively. Because we compare our approach with radiomic analysis in mammography images, we also describe the generation of synthetic mammograms in Sect. 2.3. Finally, in Sect. 2.4, we describe the extraction of radiomic features and the construction of the lesion detection model.

2.1   Virtual Breast Cohort

The generation of digital breast phantoms is an open problem in the community and several modelling systems have been developed to date [3,17,30]. The aim is to generate realistic and anatomically accurate models often utilised for the development and validation of new imaging techniques [10]. For our experiments, we used the simulation software developed for the Virtual Imaging Clinical Trial for Regulatory Evaluation (VICTRE). The VICTRE project was carried out by the U.S. Food and Drug Administration in order to reproduce virtual clinical trials, which are often expensive in time and resources [2,25]. We selected this simulator due to its adoption in the evaluation of X-ray breast imaging systems [10,19]. The VICTRE simulator generates voxelised breast phantoms with a pixel-size of 50 μm that contain the different tissues of the breast [7], with the possibility of inserting spiculated masses and calcifications. The phantoms are customisable in total volume, fat percentage, distance from the chest wall to the nipple, and other physiological characteristics. Figure 1 shows an example of a breast phantom and corresponding 2D slices. The different tissue types in the breast phantom and their properties are described in Sect. 2.2.

For our experiments, we generated a virtual cohort consisting of 120 subjects: 60 phantoms without a spiculated mass (controls) and 60 phantoms with a spiculated mass (cases) with a volume of $77.7\,mm^3$ and diameter of 5 mm. The only difference between cases and controls phantoms is the insertion of the spiculated mass in the cases. In order to conduct experiments in a realistic cohort, we simulated four types of breast phantoms, each reflecting different glandularity types. As reference, we used the distribution of glandurality types found in case-control studies of screening mammography (see [21]). Table 1 summarizes the main features of our virtual cohort.

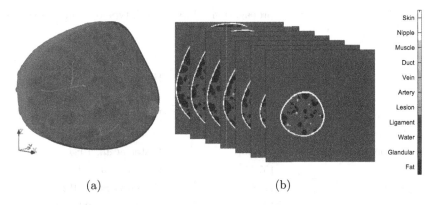

Fig. 1. (a) Visualisation of a virtual 3D breast phantom. (b) Slices taken at different positions along the X axis. Each colour identifies a different type of tissue in the slices.

Table 1. Summary of the virtual cohort.

Glandularity type	Mean percent density (%)	Mean volume (cm^3)	No. phantoms (%)
Dense	50	141.8	4
Heterogeneously dense	41	255.7	48
Scattered fibroglandular	25	497.7	56
Fatty	17	749.1	12

2.2   Speed-of-Sound Images

In order to assess the feasibility of using SOS images for lesion detection, we generate a stack of bidimensional SOS slices from each 3D breast phantom. Previous works have investigated and measured SOS values in both normal and cancerous breast tissue [6,14]. Therefore, we extract 2D SOS images by replacing each tissue type in the phantoms by their corresponding SOS values as reported in the literature. In Table 2, we summarise the SOS values used for each type of tissue. This approach assumes an ideal reconstruction process of the SOS images. In practice, the quality of the SOS slices obtained via ultrasound imaging will depend on several variables, such as the imaging architecture and the reconstruction techniques. The investigation of imaging architectures and reconstruction techniques for ultrasound-based imaging of the breast is beyond the scope of this work and the utilisation of ideally-reconstructed SOS images is sufficient for our feasibility study.

Table 2. Speed-of-sound (SOS) propagation values for each type of tissue. Tissues are ordered in increasing value of SOS.

Tissue	Speed-of-sound propagation [m/s]	Reference
Fat	1440.0	Hasgal *et al..*, 2012 [8]
Glandular	1505.0	Hasgal *et al..*, 2012 [8]
Water	1520.0	Ramirez *et al..*, 2017 [22]
Ligament	1525.0	Foster *et al.*, 1984 [6]
Lesion	1572.0	Foster *et al.*, 1984 [6]
Artery	1578.2	Hasgal *et al..*, 2012 [8]
Vein	1578.2	Hasgal *et al..*, 2012 [8]
Duct	1588.0	Klock *et al..*, 2016 [11]
Muscle	1588.4	Hasgal *et al..*, 2012 [8]
Nipple	1624.0	Hasgal *et al..*, 2012 [8]
Skin	1624.0	Hasgal *et al..*, 2012 [8]

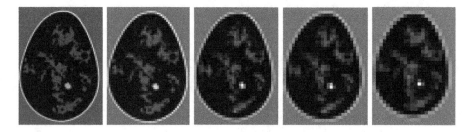

Fig. 2. SOS images for different pixel-sizes. From left to right: 1.0, 1.5, 2.0, 2.5 and 3.0 mm.

Previous work has demonstrated the generation of ultrasound-based reconstructions with pixel-size (Δ) down to 0.5 mm [16]. These pixel-sizes are an order of magnitude lower than in mammography, in which pixel-size of 0.05 mm are readily attainable by modern mammographic systems. In order to assess the impact of the pixel-size on the performance of the system, we generate SOS images at pixel-sizes between 1.0 mm and 3.0 mm (see Fig. 2).

2.3   Digital Mammography Simulation

Being the most widely used breast screening modality, we used radiomic analysis of mammograms for comparison. For this purpose, we generated digital mammograms from each of the virtual phantoms of the study cohort. Specifically, we used the open-source X-ray imaging simulation code MC-GPU [2], in order to simulate the image acquisition process of an actual mammography acquisition device, namely, a Siemens Mammomat Inspiration. MC-GPU is a GPU-accelerated Monte Carlo simulation of X-ray interaction with matter; the code models the source, primary radiation beam, scattering and absorption events, and direct-conversion detector, among other aspects that influence mammography acquisition. For each phantom, we simulated the physical compression of the breast in the craniocaudal direction using VICTRE, and obtained one craniocaudal mammography image, thus rendering a dataset of 120 mammograms, 60 cases, and 60 controls. Due to differences in breast volume, the image size of the mammograms were 1000×2010 pixels for dense and heterogeneous phantoms, and 1500×2010 pixels for scattered and fatty phantoms. The pixel size in every case was $85\,\mu$m.

2.4   Lesion Detection

We built a system for the detection of lesions in SOS images in two phases. In the training phase, we train a *slice classifier* that takes one SOS slice as input and generates a score with the likelihood of a lesion. In the second phase, the testing phase, the slice classifier is used to generate a score in each SOS slice of a test phantom, and a *greedy* classifier estimates the score at the breast level. We refer to this second phase as the *breast classifier*. To construction of the slice classifier and the breast classifier are detailed below.

Slice classifier: as shown in Fig. 3, the slice classifier is trained with SOS images extracted from the controls and the cases, with each phantom of the training set contributing with one SOS image. Because the lesions only occupy a very small volume of the 3D breast phantoms, SOS images in the cases are selected so that the lesion is visible. In the controls, the SOS images are selected on the same position as in the corresponding case. This allows to generate a training set of 2D SOS images with and without lesions. Figure 4 shows a pair of SOS images with and without lesions.

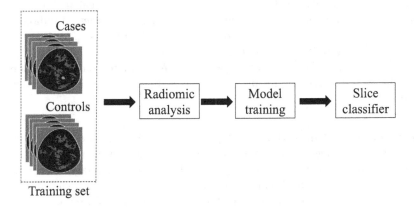

Fig. 3. Training of the slice classifier.

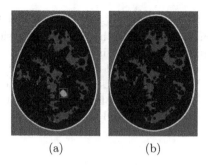

(a)   (b)

Fig. 4. Example of SOS images used to train the slice classifier. (a) SOS image from a case retrieved at a position where the lesion is visible. The lesion is highlighted by the red square. (b) SOS image from the control corresponding to the same case and position of (a). (Color figure online)

Back to the slice classifier in Fig. 3, each image in this training set goes through a *radiomic analysis* block in order to extract texture descriptors. The aim or radiomic analysis is to generate quantitative measures that describe the textural appearance of the image. In turn, these measures are used to build insightful models with supervised machine learning algorithms; in the case at hand, the model corresponds to a classification model to differentiate SOS images with and without lesions.

By their working principles, radiomic features can be categorised in five groups: statistical features, which describe the histogram of gray level values of the image; gray-level co-occurrence features that describe the statistical spatial distribution of co-occurrent pixel intensities; gray-level run-length features that describe the consecutive intensity values of the image (run-lengths); structural features that describe the topological and geometric elements that constitute the image; and finally, spectral features, which are features calculated from the frequency-spatial domain of the image. In this work, we extract 33 radiomic features from the breast region in our dataset using OpenBreast [21]. OpenBreast is an open source tool for radiomic analysis.

Finally, the *model training* block in Fig. 3 uses extracted radiomic features to build the slice classifier by means of logistic regression with sequential forward feature selection [27].

Breast classifier: from the training phase, the slice classifier should be able to classify SOS images with and without lesions. However, at testing time, each breast phantom is comprised of a full stack of 2D SOS images, whereas the potential location of the lesions is unknown. For this reason, the aim of the breast classifier is to analyse the full stack of SOS images of a phantom in order to generate a single estimate at the breast level.

Because SOS images are generated by slicing the 3D breast volume, not all SOS images in the stack have useful information. As shown in Fig. 5, the trailing 2D slices of a phantom correspond to the nipple region, whereas the leading slices correspond to the pectoralis muscle. For this reason, the slices at the trailing 10% and leading 30% of the breast volume are discarded, and only the SOS images of the remaining breast volume are processed.

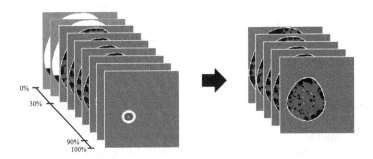

Fig. 5. Selection of slices between 30% and 90% for the subsequent analysis by the breast classifier.

Once the relevant slices have been selected by the procedure described above, the *slice classifier* that was trained in the previous stage is used to generate a classification score for each 2D slice in the breast. This generates an ordered sequence of scores, Score 1 to Score n in Fig. 6. In order to attenuate noise in the score estimate in individual slices, the *greedy classifier* of Fig. 6 works by computing a 3-tap moving average on the sequence of scores and retrieves the maximum score value of the sequence. This is a very simple method that yields a high score as long as the slice classifier detects at least one slice with a lesion in the full stack of slices of the breast.

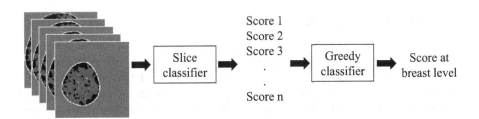

Fig. 6. Breast classifier. The input is a stack of n SOS images and the output is a single score for the breast.

Table 3. AUC of the slice classifier using different pixel-sizes of SOS images.

Pixel-size (Δ) [mm]	AUC (95% Confidence interval)
1.0	0.81 (0.74–0.89)
1.5	0.88 (0.81–0.94)
2.0	0.97 (0.94–1.00)
2.5	0.95 (0.90–0.99)
3.0	0.96 (0.93–1.00)

3   Experiments and Results

For all experiments, the results reported correspond to a randomised 5-fold cross validation. In each fold, the slice classifier is built using SOS images retrieved only from the training set and the breast classifier generates a score for each virtual breast in the test set. Performance was measured in terms of the area under the receiver operating characteristic (ROC) curve (AUC). The ROC curve is a graphical plot that illustrates the diagnostic ability of a binary classifier system.

3.1   Performance at the Slice Level

Because the breast classifier fully relies on the performance of the slice classifier, in this section we first report the performance in the classification of SOS images. At the image level, the greedy classifier is not used nor needed. Experiments are performed under the same conditions for each pixel-size of SOS images, namely 1.0, 1.5, 2.0, 2.5, and 3.0 mm. Results at slice level are presented in Table 3. As highlighted in that table, SOS images at 2.0 mm pixel-size yield the best performance at the image level.

3.2   Performance at the Breast Level

In this section, we report the results on lesion detection at the breast level. For comparison purposes, we also performed radiomic analysis of synthetic mammographic images generated as described in Sect. 2.3. For this purpose, in each mammogram, we process a region of 17×17 mm^2 enclosing the location of each lesion (i.e. see Fig. 7a) for the extraction of radiomic features and the construction of a *lesion classifier*, as shown in Fig. 7b. Performance results at the breast level are presented in Table 4. In this case, SOS images outperform mammography at all pixel-sizes, with the 2.5 mm pixel-size having the best performance. Figure 8 shows the ROC curve for the three top performing pixel-sizes using SOS images and the ROC curve of the model trained using mammography.

4   Discussion

The results show that the use of SOS images outperforms synthetic mammograms to detect breast lesions in pixel-sizes between 1.0 and 2.5 mm. The pixel-size that performs the highest at the breast level is 2.5 mm. Figure 9a shows

Table 4. AUC for the breast classifier using different pixel-sizes of SOS images and compared whit the mammography.

Modality	Pixel-size (Δ) [mm]	AUC (95% Confidence interval)
SOS image	1.000	0.67 (0.57–0.77)
	1.500	0.73 (0.64–0.82)
	2.000	0.89 (0.83–0.95)
	2.500	0.94 (0.89–0.98)
	3.000	0.59 (0.49–0.69)
Mammography	0.085	0.62 (0.52–0.72)

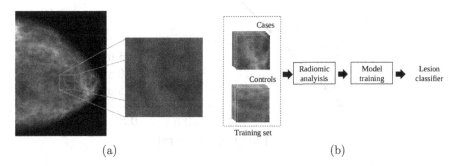

(a)   (b)

Fig. 7. Construction of lesion classifier for mammograms. (a) The region of interest corresponds to an area of $17 \times 17 \, \text{mm}^2$ surrounding the location of the spiculated mass. (b) Training of the classifier.

the distribution of case and control scores using the breast classifier at 2.5 mm pixel-size, and Fig. 9b shows the distribution of scores using the lesion classifier on digital mammograms. This figure shows that the scores estimated using SOS images allow for a more clear discrimination between cases and controls than mammograms. The lower performance obtained using mammography images can be explained by the overlapping of the different breast tissues: since mammography can be roughly described as a projection of the breast internal structures, overlapping can have a masking effect on small elements with similar radiation density to the surrounding tissues.

Figure 10 shows the output scores, after the 3-tap moving average, for each slice of the stack of images corresponding to a case and its respective control. In said figure, scores are very similar for most case and control slices. However, for the slices close to the centre of the lesion (vertical green line), there are notable differences. This behaviour clearly discriminates cases from controls.

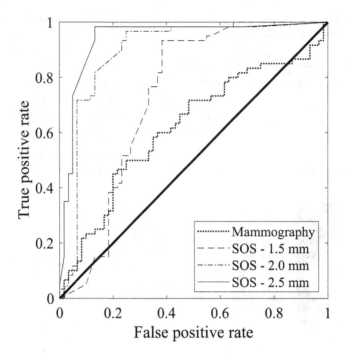

Fig. 8. ROC curves for the best-performing SOS images at breast level and mammography.

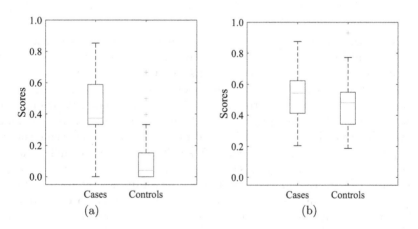

Fig. 9. Distribution of scores in cases and controls for: (a) the breast classifier using SOS images at pixel-size of 2.5 mm, and (b) the lesion classifier using mammograms.

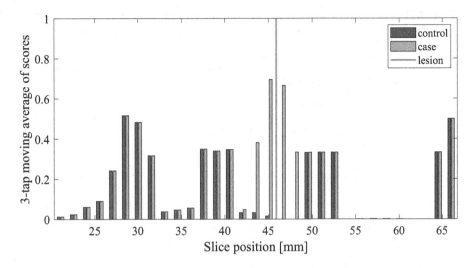

Fig. 10. Scores of the slice classifier for each slice of the stack of images corresponding to a case and its respective control. The green line represents the position of the lesion center. (Color figure online)

The sequential forward feature selection technique finds the most relevant features that the logistic regressor uses for the classification. Overall, when training the slice classifier using SOS images, the most relevant features were: statistical, gray-level co-occurrence, and gray level path length features, while for the lesion classifier using digital mammograms, the most relevant features were: structural and spectral features (see Table 5).

In this work we used SOS images that would be an ideal reconstruction of the speed of sound parameters for the breast tissues. In a real life scenario, different imaging architectures and reconstruction algorithms could affect the quality and noise level of the reconstructed images. In addition, we considered one type of lesion, spiculated masses with a volume of 77.7 mm^3; these lesions are among the most common malignant breast lesions. Future work should take into consideration the impact of the image quality on performance, as well as explore the impact of lesion size variability and consider the detection of other elements of interest, such as microcalcifications, which are typically more problematic in ultrasound imaging.

Table 5. Features selected by the model after the forward sequential feature selection, for each pixel-size of SOS images and mammography.

Feature group	Feature	SOS images					Mammography
		1.000 mm	1.500 mm	2.000 mm	2.500 mm	3.000 mm	0.085 mm
Statistical features	Minimum gray-level value				x		
	Maximum gray-level value	x	x	x	x		
	Mean gray-level value	x					
	Gray-level range	x			x	x	x
	Gray-level variance	x					
	Entropy						
	Skewness	x	x				
	Kurtosis	x	x	x	x		
	5th percentile		x				
	30th percentile					x	
	70th percentile	x					
	90th percentile						
	Balance 1	x	x				
	Balance 2	x	x				
Co-ocurrence features	Energy						
	Correlation	x	x				
	Contrast			x		x	
	Homogeneity					x	
	Entropy	x	x	x			
Run-length features	Run-length non-uniformity	x	x	x			
	Gray-level non-uniformity	x					
	Long run emphasis						
	Short run emphasis						
	Run percentage						
	High gray-level run		x				
	Low gray-level run		x				
Structural features	Gradient energy		x				
	Gradient variance	x					x
	Modified laplacian						
Spectral features	Wavelet sum						x
	Wavelet variance						
	Wavelet ratio						
	Fractal dimension						

5   Conclusions

In this work, we studied the feasibility of utilising speed-of-sound (SOS) propagation images of the breast for the detection of breast lesions via radiomic analysis. We performed an in-silico test, obtaining SOS images from a cohort of 120 3D synthetic phantoms, that were subsequently analysed at the breast level to detect breast lesions. We compared the performance of using SOS images against using the most common imaging modality for breast cancer diagnosis and detection, namely mammography. The results show that the performance using SOS images at the breast level outperforms mammography at pixel-sizes between 1.0 and 2.5 mm. This indicates that using these novel ultrasound-based imaging modalities as an adjunct for breast lesion detection would be feasible. It also shows the importance of exploring imaging modalities that can resolve tissue descriptors that are not classically used, such as speed SOS.

Novel methods for ultrasound-based medical imaging have recently been developed. These novel methods have the ability to construct a profile of some physical properties of the organ, such as SOS. More common imaging modalities for breast cancer screening, such as mammography or breast tomosynthesis, have the downside of being essentially projections of the breast; their capacity to resolve areas of interest depends on the attenuation contrast between breast elements, but the superposition of tissues, and the similar radio-density of interesting elements such as cancerous masses and fibroglandular tissue, can obscure these areas and result in missed cases. The use of novel technologies that allow for the characterisation of other properties of the breast, and other types of 2D visualisations such as SOS profiles at specific positions in the organ, could be explored to overcome the obstacles encountered with currently widespread modalities.

References

1. Al-Antari, M.A., Han, S.M., Kim, T.S.: Evaluation of deep learning detection and classification towards computer-aided diagnosis of breast lesions in digital x-ray mammograms. Comput. Methods Progr. Biomed. **196**, 105584 (2020)
2. Badal, A., Sharma, D., Graff, C.G., Zeng, R., Badano, A.: Mammography and breast tomosynthesis simulator for virtual clinical trials. Comput. Phys. Commun. **261**, 107779 (2021)
3. Barufaldi, B., et al.: Computational breast anatomy simulation using multi-scale Perlin noise. IEEE Trans. Med. Imaging **40**(12), 3436–3445 (2021)
4. Devolli-Disha, E., Manxhuka-Kërliu, S., Ymeri, H., Kutllovci, A.: Comparative accuracy of mammography and ultrasound in women with breast symptoms according to age and breast density. Bosn. J. Basic Med. Sci. **9**(2), 131 (2009)
5. Dibden, A., Offman, J., Duffy, S.W., Gabe, R.: Worldwide review and meta-analysis of cohort studies measuring the effect of mammography screening programmes on incidence-based breast cancer mortality. Cancers **12**(4), 976 (2020)
6. Foster, F., Strban, M., Austin, G.: The ultrasound macroscope: initial studies of breast tissue. Ultrason. Imaging **6**(3), 243–261 (1984)
7. Graff, C.G.: A new, open-source, multi-modality digital breast phantom. In: Medical Imaging 2016: Physics of Medical Imaging, vol. 9783, p. 978309. International Society for Optics and Photonics (2016)
8. Hassgal, P.A., et al.: IT'IS database for thermal and electromagnetic parameters of biological tissues version 4.1 (2022)
9. Ho, W., Lam, P.: Clinical performance of computer-assisted detection (CAD) system in detecting carcinoma in breasts of different densities. Clin. Radiol. **58**(2), 133–136 (2003)
10. Kiarashi, N., et al.: Development and application of a suite of 4-D virtual breast phantoms for optimization and evaluation of breast imaging systems. IEEE Trans. Med. Imaging **33**(7), 1401–1409 (2014)

11. Klock, J.C., Iuanow, E., Malik, B., Obuchowski, N.A., Wiskin, J., Lenox, M.: Anatomy-correlated breast imaging and visual grading analysis using quantitative transmission ultrasound^{TM}. Int. J. Biomed. Imaging **2016**, 7570406 (2016)

12. Lambin, P., et al.: Radiomics: the bridge between medical imaging and personalized medicine. Nat. Rev. Clin. Oncol. **14**(12), 749–762 (2017)

13. Li, C., Duric, N., Huang, L.: Clinical breast imaging using sound-speed reconstructions of ultrasound tomography data. In: Medical Imaging 2008: Ultrasonic Imaging and Signal Processing, vol. 6920, pp. 78–86. SPIE (2008)

14. Li, C., Duric, N., Littrup, P., Huang, L.: In vivo breast sound-speed imaging with ultrasound tomography. Ultrasound Med. Biol. **35**(10), 1615–1628 (2009)

15. Liu, B., Cheng, H.D., Huang, J., Tian, J., Tang, X., Liu, J.: Fully automatic and segmentation-robust classification of breast tumors based on local texture analysis of ultrasound images. Pattern Recognit. **43**(1), 280–298 (2010)

16. Lucka, F., Pérez-Liva, M., Treeby, B.E., Cox, B.T.: High resolution 3D ultrasonic breast imaging by time-domain full waveform inversion. Inverse Prob. **38**(2), 025008 (2021)

17. Omer, M., Fear, E.: Anthropomorphic breast model repository for research and development of microwave breast imaging technologies. Sci. Data **5**(1), 1–10 (2018)

18. Ozmen, N., Dapp, R., Zapf, M., Gemmeke, H., Ruiter, N.V., van Dongen, K.W.: Comparing different ultrasound imaging methods for breast cancer detection. IEEE Trans. Ultrason. Ferroelectr. Freq. Control **62**(4), 637–646 (2015)

19. Park, S., Villa, U., Su, R., Oraevsky, A., Brooks, F.J., Anastasio, M.A.: Realistic three-dimensional optoacoustic tomography imaging trials using the VICTRE breast phantom of FDA. In: Proceedings of the SPIE 11240, Photons Plus Ultrasound: Imaging and Sensing, vol. 11240, p. 112401H, March 2020

20. Pei, Y., Zhang, G., Zhang, Y., Zhang, W.: Breast acoustic parameter reconstruction method based on capacitive micromachined ultrasonic transducer array. Micromachines **12**(8), 963 (2021)

21. Pertuz, S., et al.: Clinical evaluation of a fully-automated parenchymal analysis software for breast cancer risk assessment: a pilot study in a Finnish sample. Eur. J. Radiol. **121**, 108710 (2019)

22. Ramirez, A.B., Abreo, S.A., van Dongen, K.W.: Selecting the number and location of sources and receivers for non-linear time-domain inversion. In: 2017 IEEE International Ultrasonics Symposium (IUS), pp. 1–3 (2017)

23. Ruiter, N., Zapf, M., Dapp, R., Hopp, T., Kaiser, W., Gemmeke, H.: First results of a clinical study with 3D ultrasound computer tomography. In: 2013 IEEE International Ultrasonics Symposium (IUS), pp. 651–654 (2013)

24. Sandhu, G., Li, C., Roy, O., Schmidt, S., Duric, N.: Frequency domain ultrasound waveform tomography: breast imaging using a ring transducer. Phys. Med. Biol. **60**(14), 5381 (2015)

25. Sharma, D., et al.: Technical note: in silico imaging tools from the VICTRE clinical trial. Med. Phys. **46**(9), 3924–3928 (2019). cited by: 16

26. Taskin, U., van der Neut, J., van Dongen, K.W.: Redatuming for breast ultrasound. In: 2018 IEEE International Ultrasonics Symposium (IUS), pp. 1–9 (2018)

27. Ververidis, D., Kotropoulos, C.: Sequential forward feature selection with low computational cost. In: 2005 13th European Signal Processing Conference, pp. 1–4. IEEE (2005)

28. Virieux, J., Operto, S.: An overview of full-waveform inversion in exploration geophysics. Geophysics **74**(6), WCC1–WCC26 (2009)

29. Ying, X., Lin, Y., Xia, X., Hu, B., Zhu, Z., He, P.: A comparison of mammography and ultrasound in women with breast disease: a receiver operating characteristic analysis. Breast J. **18**(2), 130–138 (2012)
30. Zastrow, E., Davis, S.K., Lazebnik, M., Kelcz, F., Veen, B.D., Hagness, S.C.: Development of anatomically realistic numerical breast phantoms with accurate dielectric properties for modeling microwave interactions with the human breast. IEEE Trans. Biomed. Eng. **55**(12), 2792–2800 (2008)

Oral Dental Diagnosis Using Deep Learning Techniques: A Review

Asmaa Elsayed[1], Hanya Mostafa[1], Reem Tarek[1], Kareem Mohamed[1],
Abdelaziz Hossam[1], and Sahar Selim[1,2(✉)]

[1] School of Information Technology and Computer Science, Nile University,
Giza, Egypt
sselim@nu.edu.eg
[2] Medical Imaging and Image Processing Research Group,
Center for Informatics Science, Nile University, Giza, Egypt

Abstract. The purpose of this study is to investigate the gradual incorporation of deep learning in the dental healthcare system, offering an easy and efficient diagnosis. For that, an electronic search was conducted in the Institute of Electrical and Electronics Engineers (IEEE) Xplore, ScienceDirect, Journal of Dentistry, Health Informatics Journal, and other credible resources. The studies varied with their tools and techniques used for the diagnosis while coping with the rapid deep-learning evolving base, with different types of conducting tools and analysis for the data. An inclusion criterion was set to specify the quality of the chosen papers. The papers included provided information about the neural network models used like model type, the targeted disease, and results evaluating parameters. The referenced databases ranged from 88 to 12600 clinical images. All the included studies used different neural network models with different outcome metrics. This inconsistency of the methods used makes them incomparable which makes reaching a reliable conclusion more complicated. The paper voiced some observations about the methods used with future recommendations. The goal is to review the deep learning methods that can be used in medical diagnosis.

Keywords: Deep learning · Machine learning · Dental health

1 Introduction

Dental healthcare is a major public health issue as well as the most widely prevalent chronic disease. It is a multi-factorial disease that is highly related to the patient's dietary, salivary fluoride level, sugar intake, and personal hygiene system. It is considered one of the most widely untreated disease that many disadvantaged populations believe can be endured since it is not life-threatening even if it profoundly diminishes the quality of life [1]. This poses a large problem as early detection of oral diseases can go a long way to help heal those diseases smoothly, quickly and without many complications.

Nile University.

G. Yang et al. (Eds.): MIUA 2022, LNCS 13413, pp. 814–832, 2022.
https://doi.org/10.1007/978-3-031-12053-4_60

The gradual incorporation of Artificial intelligence (AI) in the medical field for treatment and diagnosis procedures has offered more accurate results with a significantly low risk of complications. This encouraged the oral health sector to integrate AI in the rising wave of unraveling the prevalence of dental caries [2]. Using deep learning models for the detection and diagnosis of dental diseases as an alternative way of diagnosing dental disease can be very beneficial. The dental photography diagnosis brings a substantial improvement in the dental healthcare education and offer the clinical cases discussion at distance by sharing the diagnosis outcome with professionals or students in case of educational purposes [1].

The integration of Artificial intelligence in the oral health system has been in the work for years with many pioneering pieces of research paving the way for the future of this sector. These collective efforts for raising the awareness of this problem have opened so many possibilities. The purpose of this paper is to review papers that used deep learning and machine intelligence in dental diagnosis and inspect the effectiveness of using these models.

The most recent deep learning diagnosis methods were reviewed to assess their features and get more familiar with current trends and most used models. The papers were divided based on the type of the disease that they diagnosed and were evaluated to figure out their strengths and weaknesses in order to aid in any further development.

The rest of the paper is organized as follows: first the searching criteria that was used to collect the papers will be stated, then the results of our research will be mentioned and finally, the results will be discussed and our observations will be stated.

2 Materials and Methods

In this section, the used searching criteria and the questions that were asked when picked the suitable papers will be discussed.

2.1 Review Questions

- What are the deep learning models used to detect and diagnose dental health issues?
- How are multiple dental problems defined and diagnosed?
- What is the end result achieved by using deep learning?
- How and what databases are used in the construction of these models?
- Did deep learning help improve the dental healthcare system?

2.2 Search Strategy

An electronic research was conducted to select literature made on the inclusion of deep learning algorithms in dental care. The research was conducted up until 1 October 2021, in IEEE Conferences, Journal of Dentistry, Scientific Reports, Journal of Dental Disease, Health Informatics Journal, and multiple other credible sources in the field.

2.3   Inclusion and Exclusion Criteria

Inclusion. The study includes original work that incorporated the use of neural networks in the detection and diagnosis of multiple dental problems.

Exclusion. The study excluded systematic reviews, books, editorials, product advertisements, and social media in addition to any other sources written in a foreign language without English translation.

2.4   Study Selection

Included studies made attempts to diagnose various dental issues using deep learning algorithms fulfilling the inclusion criteria. The referenced data were manually reviewed and after that, some key items were observed and collected from the studies as follows:

- Publication source and year of publication
- Database characteristics like the number and type of images
- The neural network model used like model type and the targeted disease
- Evaluating parameters: the sensitivity and/or specificity of the model

2.5   Data Extraction

The data provided in the study was extracted from the methodology and results section of the referenced and reviewed papers. The data specified the requirements of the deep learning model and the information of the dental disease targeted. The data set was split into training and testing. The training set was used to train the deep learning classification model to detect the diseases, while the testing set was used to evaluate the model results sometimes by dental specialists annotation if provided.

2.6   Accuracy Measures

The paper depends on several metrics in the reviewed papers to define the accuracy of the results. Accuracy, Sensitivity, Precision, and Specificity were obtained if existed in the paper. The values were used to measure the diagnostic model accuracy.

3   Results

In this section, the study selection will be discussed, going through the steps took to pick the used papers. After that, relevant data and characteristics about the chosen papers will be stated.

3.1   Selection of the Study

The electronic research strategy led to around 523 potential resources in the screening process. After removing the duplicated files, 135 papers were left. Then a manual search was conducted to further analyze the referenced sources in the included papers. After reading the abstracts of those papers, not all results were deemed fit as a potential manuscript for the paper as some didn't fit the inclusion criteria mentioned above, which left 53 papers. Another sifting was done by reading through the whole body of each work and 27 papers were left to be reviewed in this paper. These steps can be clearly viewed in Fig. 1. Some examples for excluding some of the papers are shown in Table 1.

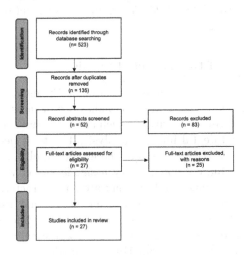

Fig. 1. Articles selection findings

Table 1. Elimination table

Author name	Elimination reason
L. Godlevsky [21]	The paper did not use a deep learning model
W. J. Park [1]	The paper tells the history of the usage of deep learning and is not a research paper
M. Ezhov [22]	The paper didn't offer sufficient information

3.2   Relevant Data About the Image Data Set

Tables 2, 3, 4, 5, 6, 7 and 8 show the main characteristics found in the researched papers; the tables are categorized according to the type of disease detection. In collected papers, the studies were conducted between 2014 and 2021 with most of them being conducted in 2019 or 2021.

The image data set ranged from 88 images to 12600 images with one paper not providing the number of images they collected in their data set.

Regarding the training and testing sets, 6 papers [5,7,10,16,17,20] used approximately 80% of their data set for training and validating, 4 papers [3,6,8,9] used about 68% of their data set, 3 papers [12,13,29] used 90% of their data set, 1 paper [25] used 53% of its data set, and 1 paper [24] used 88% of its data set. 11 papers [4,11,14,15,18,19,23,26–28,30] did not mention how they classed their training and testing sets.

3.3   Architectures of the Collected Studies

Artificial intelligence (AI) is a rapidly expanding in the medical field. Deep learning is a subset of machine learning that makes use of networks with computational layers. Deep learning algorithms, such as CNNs, have produced intriguing results in medical and dental imaging analysis. The term deep learning convolutional neural network (DNN) refers to the use of a multi-layer artificial neural network (ANN) to evaluate visual imagery, assign learnable weights and biases to different aspects of the image, and differentiate one characteristic from another. Support A vector machine is a statistical algorithm that uses an appropriate separation plane to divide datasets into subgroups with different characteristics. Decision Trees are a technique for classifying a statistical population based on a partition function. While Random Forest is made up of Decision Tree subsets that are combined to boost performance. U-Net is a semantic segmentation architecture. It is made up of a contracting path and an expanding path. The contracting path is designed in the manner of a convolutional network. YOLO is a clever convolutional neural network (CNN) for real-time object detection. The algorithm uses a single neural network to process the entire image, then splits it into regions and predicts bounding boxes and probabilities for each.

These architectures were used in the selected studies to diagnose different dental problems. 12 of the studied papers [8–11,13,17,19,20,23,25,29,30] used the deep Convolutional Neural Network model (CNN) with its different variations to train and test the data, 3 papers [7,27,28] used Support Vector Machine (SVM) and random forests, 3 papers [12,16,26] used U-shaped deep CNN (U-Net), and 2 papers [15,24] used You Only Look Once (YOLO). Figure 2 illustrates the number of models used in all of the papers and as viewed below, it can be deduced that CNN model was the most used model.

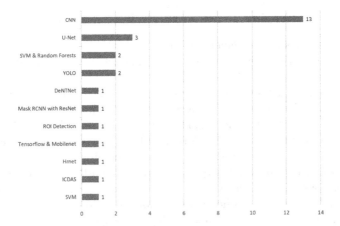

Fig. 2. Statistics of used models

In this review, most the papers that used convolutional neural network in the diagnosis process, showed a high accuracy rate and promising result despite targeting different diseases and using various imaging types demonstrated in [13], As by analysing patient hyper-spectral images, researchers created a deep learning algorithm for an automated, computer-aided oral cancer detection system. To validate the proposed regression-based partitioned deep learning algorithm, we compare its classification accuracy, specificity, and sensitivity to that of other methods. The paper demonstrated a new structure of partitioned deep Convolution Neural Network with two partitioned layers for labelling and classifying region of interest in multidimensional hyper-spectral image for a more accurate medical image classification. Classification accuracy was used to validate the partitioned deep CNN's performance. For 100 image data sets training for task classification of cancerous tumour with benign and task classification of cancerous tumour with malignant, the demonstrated a classification accuracy of 91.4% with sensitivity 0.94 and specificity 0.91 in comparison to normal tissue, an accuracy of 94.5 was obtained for 500 training patterns. Other work [25] traced the entire process of classification and segmentation, as well as pre-processing of dental images. During pre-processing, an adaptive histogram is used to stretch the contrast and equalise the brightness across the radiographic X-ray 2d dental image. This operation is useful for distinguishing between foreground teeth and background bone regions. A fundamental step in segmentation is the separation of dental 2d images into regions corresponding to the objects. To segment the oral cavity and its tissues, hybrid graph cut segmentation is used. In this study, a deep learning-based convolution neural network (CNN) was used to process dental images, yielding promising results with 97.07% accuracy. The findings of these and other reviewed studies indicate that deep learning CNN algorithms and their variants provide comprehensive, reliable, and accurate image assessment and disease detection, facilitating effective and efficient diagnosis and improving the prognosis of dental diseases in various imaging types.

3.4   Different Imaging Types in the Collected Studies

Dental imaging has made tremendous progress, with applications in many areas of dentistry. Imaging techniques being used dentistry are classified into several types.

Radiography with its types has been used is [10, 12, 16, 24], it comes in 2 forms. 2-D Conventional radiographs produce high-quality images for the majority of dental radiographic needs. Their primary purpose is to supplement clinical examinations by revealing caries, periodontal and periapical diseases. The superimposition of overlying structures, which conceals the object of interest, is a major restraint of conventional radiography also the diagnostic accuracy is limited in many situations. Meanwhile, Digital radiography is a method for obtaining a radiographic image with a solid-state technology sensor, separating it into electronic fragments, and presenting and storing the image with a computer. Obvious advantages include the ability to view the image more quickly due to the short processing time, the elimination of the darkroom, processing chemicals, and so on. However, it has drawbacks such as the thickness and rigidity of the digital detector, infection control, software as well as hardware maintenance, and the system's higher cost.

Using Digital Camera's is also a vital options in different diagnostic process reviewed [15, 17, 30]. But it was noticed that it rarely happened outside the clinical experiments due to the high quality camera usually required to obtain high resolution images and the different factors like lightening and stable images which opens a room for human error as well.

Smartphones [5, 10] facilitates the capture and storage of digital images. Utilising current technologies and dental professionals can digitally obtain and transmit diagnostic information to a faraway dentist for diagnosis, and referring patients. However, using a smart phone in the dental diagnosis sector is dependent on a variety of factors such as the phone's angle, picture resolution, phone type, associated lighting, and many others. All of these changes have the potential to completely alter the diagnosis or, at worst, provide no diagnosis, which defeats the purpose of the entire process. The reviewed studies suggest that smart phone diagnosis might be the future, but it still has a long way as there are too many factors that can affect it.

Another used mechanism used that does not require to move the patient during acquisition, is Dental Cone-beam Computed Tomography (CBCT). Its high resolution has aided in the detection of a wide range of cysts, tumours, and traumatic injuries involving the maxillo-facial structures [22]. The downsides of CBCT include higher doses than two-dimensional imaging, as well as the inability to properly reflect the internal structure of soft tissues and soft-tissue lesions.

3.5   Data Characteristics

The characteristics of the studied papers have been categorized into tables according to the disease that the paper diagnoses. These diseases are: dental caries, oral cancer, extent of periodontal bone loss, lesions, more than one disease and others.

4   Key Studies

The review targets a thorough analysis of the recent integration of neural networks in detecting and diagnosing various dental diseases. Reviewing the method each work used in the analysis process of the diseases like the symptoms that are analyzed and used in constructing the neural networks, the type of network used, the database type and features, and the results, were studied to construct a view of the structure and functionality of the model.

Formulating this review required a good understanding of each disease and its essential features to be used in the analysis and comparison process. The rest of this section is divided into 6 sections based on the type of diagnosed disease.

4.1   Dental Caries Detection

The authors in [7], aimed to introduce an algorithm that can recognize carious lesions on teeth using smartphone cameras. The data set consists of 620 unrestored molars and premolars extracted teeth that were cleaned and stored in thymol to prevent contamination. The data set was collected using a smartphone that was placed in a built-in LED light Photobox. The data set was then divided into three groups, no surface change (NSC), visually non-cavitated (VNC), and cavitated (C). A two-step automated Support Vector Machine (SVM) system was developed to detect caries. These consisted of, "C vs. (VNC + NSC)" classification and "VNS vs. NSC" classification [7]. The results were as follows: in the C vs. (VNC + NSC) classification, the accuracy, sensitivity and specify were 92.37%, 88.1%, and 96.6% respectively. As for the VNS vs. NSC classification, the accuracy, sensitivity and specify were 83.33%, 82.2%, and 66.7% respectively. These results show that there is a large possibility of using smartphone images for dental caries detection using machine intelligence.

Table 2. Dental caries

Authors	Target Condition	Data Acquisition	No. of Images	Training/Testing	Techniques	Performance	Published In
D. L. Duong [5] (2021)	Caries lesions	Collected 620 unrestored molar sand premolars extracted teeth from Hanoi Medical University and National Hospital of Odonto	589 images	C vs. (VNC + NSC): 80% of images for training and validation and 20% for testing. VNS vs. NSC: 60% of images for training, 20% for validation and 20% for testing	Support vector machine	C vs. (VNC + NSC): accuracy of 92.37%, sensitivity of 88.1% and specificity of 96.6%. VNS vs. NSC: accuracy of 83.33%, sensitivity of 82.2% and specificity of 66.7%	Health Informatics
S. Lee [6] (2021)	Dental caries	Randomly selected by two dentists from the archive of the Department of Conservative Dentistry, Yonsei University	354 bitewing radiographs	Training Set (304 radiographs), testing set (50 radiographs)	U-shaped deep CNN (U-Net)	Precision = 63.29%, recall = 65.02% and F1-score = 64.14%	-
L. Lian [20] (2021)	Caries Detection	Collected from Affiliated Stomatology Hospital, Zhejiang University School of Medicine	1160 images	-	nnU-Net	The model reached accuracy of 0.986	Diagnostics
A. G. Cantu [15] (2020)	Detect caries lesions of different radiographic extension on bi-tewings and hypothesizing it to be significantly more accurate than individual dentists	Collected from dental clinic at Charité -Universitätsmedizin Berlin (3016-2018)	3686 bitewing radiographs	Training Set (3293 images), validating set (252 images) and testing set (141 Images)	U-Net	Accuracy (0.80 versus 0.71), sensitivity (0.75 versus 0.36), specificity (0.83 versus 0.91)	Journal of Dentistry
X. Zhang [11] (2020)	Dental Caries	Collected from 625 volunteers with consumer cameras	3932 images	Training Set (2507 images), testing set (1125 Images)	Deep convolutional neural network model	AUC of 85.65%, localization sensitivities of 64.60% at the high-sensitivity operating point	Oral diseases
J.-H. Lee [7] (2018)	Premolar dental caries, molar dental caries and both	Collected from the authors'dental hospital's PACS system	3000 images	Training Set (2400 images), testing set (600 Images)	Deep convolutional neural network model	AUC of 0.917 on premolar, 0.890 on molar and 0.845 on both	Journal of Dentistry
E. K. Kohara [21] (2018)	Detecting caries lesions at different stages	Taking pictures of teeth in the human bank of the school of Dentistry	-	vitro and vivo	ICDAS and dentists	Sensitivity (Initial (30.1 to 40.7), Moderate (51.0 to 59.2), Extensive (90.0 to 100.0)). Specificity (Initial (83.3 to 100.0), Moderate (97.1 to 95.7), Extensive (91.9 to 93.9))	PloS One Journal

Table 3. Dental caries- cont

Authors	Target Condition	Data Acquisition	No. of Images	Training/Testing	Techniques	Performance	Published In
M. M. Srivastava [8] (2017)	Tooth caries detection	Collected from 100 clinics across USA	3000 images	Training Set (2500 images), testing set (500 Images)	FCNN (deep fully convolutional neural network)	Recall = 80.5, Precision = 61.5, F1-Score = 70	NIPS 2017 workshop on Machine Learning for Health (NIPS 2017 ML4H)
E. D. Berdouses [22] (2015)	Classification of occlusal caries	Collected from the Maxillofacial Surgery Clinic of the Denial School of the National and Kapodistrian University of Athen	103 images	-	Support Vector Machine and Random Forests	Accuracy = 83%, specificity = 80%, and sensitivity = 74%	Computers in biology and medicine
L. Ghaedi [23] (2014)	Dental caries detection	vitro images were taken by digital camera	88 Images	-	Support Vector Machine and Random Forest	Accuracy = 86.3%, specificity = 91.7%, and sensitivity = 83.0%	2014 36th Annual International Conference of the IEEE Engineering in Medicine and Biology Society

Table 4. Oral cancer

Authors	Target Condition	Data Acquisition	No. of Images	Training/Testing	Techniques	Performance	Published In
H. Lin [12] (2021)	Oral cancer	Collected from daily outpatient clinics and on patient of the First Affiliated Hospital, Zhejiang University	1448 images	Training Set (993 images), testing set (455 Images)	HRnet	Sensitivity of 83.0%, specificity of 96.6%, precision of 84.3% and F1 of 83.6%	Journal of Biomedical Optics
J. Quintero-Rojas [9] (2021)	Oral Cancer	-	-	80% Training set and 20% testing set	TensorFlow and Mobilenet V2 CNN	-	Revista Facultad de Ingenieria
P. R. Jeyaraj [16] (2019)	Oral Cancer	3 databases (BioGPS data portal=100, TCIA Archive=500, GDC Dataset=700)	1,300 image patches	The training partition varied from 10 to 90% and in testing phase	Deep convolutional neural network model	Accuracy=0.91, Specificity=0.94	Journal of cancer research and clinical oncology

Table 5. Multiple diseases

Authors	Target Condition	Data Acquisition	No. of Images	Training/Testing	Techniques	Performance	Published In
D. Kim [13] (2021)	Classifies tooth diseases and determines whether a professional dental treatment (NPDT) is required	Collected from 305 subjects from a private dental clinic in Korea	5251 images	Training Set(3357 images),validating set(946 images) and testing set (948 Images)	ROI detection model	The tooth disease accuracy was greater than 96% and NPDT accuracy was greater than 89%	Journal of Ambient Intelligence and Humanized Computing
Y. Liang [14] (2020)	Periodontal Disease, Caries, Soft Deposit, Dental Calculus, Dental Discoloration	Collected from 500 volunteers at a stomatology hospital by 6 dentists	3182 images	Training Set (2182 images), Testing set (1000 Images)	Deep convolutional neural network model (CNN)	Average Area Under the Curve (AUC) of 0.787, average sensitivity of 0.668	CHI Conference on Human Factors in Computing Systems
L. Liu [24] (2019)	Dental caries, Dental liuorisis, Periodontitis, Cracked tooth, Dental plaque, Dental calculus, Tooth loss	Collected from 10 private dental clinics	12 600 clinical images	-	Mask R-CNN with ResNet	Accuracy = 90% with high sensitivity and high specificity	IEEE journal of biomedical and healthinformatics
F. Casalegno [25] (2019)	Detection and localization of dental lesions in TI images ((background, enamel, dentin, proximal caries, occlusal caries)	Collected from Geneva university dental clinics (2013-2018)	217 grayscale images	-	Deep convolutional neural network model	Mean IOU=0.727, IOU (proximal caries) =0.495, IOU (occlusal caries) =0.490, AUC (proximal caries) =0.856, AUC (occlusal caries) =0.836	Journal of dentalreasearch

Table 6. Detecting the extent of periodontal bone lose

Authors	Target Condition	Data Acquisition	No. of Images	Training/Testing	Techniques	Performance	Published In
J. Krois [26] (2019)	Detecting the extent of periodontal bone lose	Randomly chosen digital panoramic dental radiographs collected using Orthophos XG 3	1750 images	Randomly and repeatedly split	Deep convolutional neural network model	Sensitivity = 0.81, specificity = 0.81	Scientific reports
J. Kim [27] (2019)	Periodontal Bone Loss (PBL) detection	Collected from Korea University of Anam Hospital	12,179 images	-	DeNTNet that applies CNN	F1 score = 0.75, average performance = 0.69	Scientific reports

Table 7. Detecting lesions

Authors	Target Condition	Data Acquisition	No. of Images	Training/Testing	Techniques	Performance	Published In
H. Askar [17] (2021)	Detect white spot lesions in dental photographs	Collected from the 1st Dental Unit of the Sapienza University Hospital (Rome, Italy)	2781 images	90% of dataset is for training and 10% for testing	Deep CNN	Mean accuracies between 0.81-0.84, Specificities were 0.85-0.86, sensitivities (0.58-0.66)	Journal ofDentistry
H. Yang [19] (2020)	Detecting the lesion at the early stages	Yonsei University Dental Hospital (2012-2019)	1603 images	Training set (1422 images), testing set (181 images)	YOLO, oral and maxillofacial surgeons, general practitioners	YOLO ranked highest with precision = 0.707, recall = 0.680	Journal of Clinical Medicine

Table 8. Other disease

Authors	Target Condition	Data Acquisition	No. of Images	Training/Testing	Techniques	Performance	Published In
T. Takahashi [28] (2021)	Recognizing dental prostheses and restorations of teeth	Osaka University Dental Hospital	1904 oral photographic images	-	You Only Look Once version 3 (YOLOv3)	More than 80% of metallic dental prostheses were detected correctly, but only 60% of tooth-colored prostheses were detected	Scientific Reports
W. You [10] (2020)	Dental plaque detection	Peking University School and Hospital of Stomatology in Beijing	886 groups of tooth photos	Training Set (709 images), testing set (177 Images)	Deep convolutional neural network model	The mean intersection-over-union (MIoU) was 0.726 ± 0.165	BMC Oral Health
M. Murata [29] (2019)	Diagnosis of maxillary sinusitis on panoramic radiography	Hospital's image database (2007-2018)	6000 image	-	CNN(AlexNet), Radiologist, Dental residents	CNN (Accuracy = 0.875, Specificity = 0.883, Precision = 0.881) Radiologist (Accuracy = 0.896, Specificity = 0.892, Precision = 0.893) , Dental residents(Accuracy = 0.767, Specificity = 0.750, Precision = 0.758)	Oral radiology
A. A. Al Kheraif [18] (2019)	Dental disease	-	1500 image	training set (800 images), testing set (700 images)	Hybrid graph-cut and Deep convolutional neural network	CNN showed accuracy of 97.07%	Measurement
J. Yang [30] (2018)	Propose a tool pipeline for automated clinical quality evaluation	Camera	196 pairs of periapical dental radiographs	-	6-layer CNN, Dentists, dental radiologists	Precision between (0.537 and 0.746), Recall between (0.49,0.66),F1 is 0.749	2018 IEEE 42nd annual computer software and applications conference

The authors of [10] discussed the evaluation of the efficacy of deep learning CNN in detecting and diagnosing dental caries. To achieve its goal the paper gathered a total of 3000 periapical radiographic images were divided into a training and validation data set (n = 2400 [80%]) and a test data set (n = 600 [20%]). A pre-trained GoogLeNet Inception v3 CNN network was used for preprocessing and transfer learning. The diagnostic sensitivity, accuracy, specificity, positive predictive value, negative predictive value, receiver operating characteristic (ROC) curve, and area under the curve (AUC) were calculated for detection and diagnostic performance of the deep CNN algorithm [10]. This lead to diagnostic accuracies of premolar, molar, and both premolar and molar models were 89.0% (80.4–93.3), 88.0% (79.2–93.1), and 82.0% (75.5–87.1), respectively. The deep CNN algorithm achieved an AUC of 0.917 (95% CI 0.860–0.975) on premolar, an AUC of 0.890 (95% CI 0.819–0.961) on molar, and an AUC of 0.845 (95% CI 0.790–0.901) on both premolar and molar models. The premolar model provided the best AUC, which was significantly greater than those for other models. This study highlighted the potential utility of deep CNN architecture for the detection and diagnosis of dental caries [10]. A deep CNN algorithm provided considerably good performance in detecting dental caries in periapical radiographs.

4.2   Oral Cancer

Lin et al. [6], sought to enable using a smartphone-based diagnosis that is propelled by deep learning algorithms. To achieve that, a centered rule image capturing approach was established to use the fixed region of interest method to crop the useless parts and filter the unnecessary background [6]. A data set of 1448 images was collected and categorized into normal (healthy), aphthous ulcer, low-risk OPMD, high-risk OPMD, and cancer. The authors also used the resampling method on images that are from another data set that was created from the original data set by a simulated image-capturing method [6]. They then compared the performance of both methods and found that the centered rule data set had about 8% higher F1 score than the random positioning data set. The results showed that the normal class had an F1 of 95% as compared with the lower F1 scores of the other classes. The results also showed that there were higher error rates for low-risk and high-risk lesions than on the other classes which is understandable since the two diseases are very similar looking [6].

The authors in [5] focus on developing a mobile application to identify oral lesions as an early sign of possible oral cancer by constructing a convolutional neural network. The model was built by using TensorFlow and Mobilenet V2 convolutional neural network. The images in the data set were divided into five categories/classes (Herpes Simplex Virus Type 1, Aphthous stomatitis, Nicotinic stomatitis, Leukoplakia, and No lesion). The Mobilenet V2 is considered the best floating-point model used for mobile vision. Along the process, TensorFlow lite API is used to make the model compatible with the mobile application form. The training of the model was conducted by transfer learning using the previously mentioned data set [5]. The recognition service offered by the mobile application prepares the images then loads them to the CNN model to be analyzed then displays the result. The results showed that the application had at least 80% score in recognizing four classes and higher than 75% for the recognition of three lesions but than 70% for identifying nicotinic stomatitis cases [5].

4.3 Multiple Disease

Liang et al. [9] presented OralCam, which is the first interactive app that enables patients to examine themselves from home using their smartphones. Their data set consists of 3182 images which were then categorized into five oral conditions; periodontal disease, caries, soft deposit, dental calculus, and dental discoloration. They used a mix of object localization and image classification; they enhanced the baseline model by giving it non-image information about the disease beforehand. They also used map-based reasoning to localize the conditions' regions [9]. The results of the testing data set found that the model achieves an average classification Area Under the Curve (AUC) of 0.787 for the five conditions and an average sensitivity of 0.668. The results showcase the capability of the model for accurately indicating the regions related to the five types of conditions [9]. They also had an experts' evaluation where two experts reviewed the application's data and found that the methods were clinically valid and agreed that the application gives reasonable results [9].

4.4 Detecting the Extent of Periodontal Bone Lose

Takahashi et al. [11], aim to detect periodontal bone loss on panoramic dental radiographs using convolutional neural networks (CNNs). A data set of 1750 images was collected and shuffled repeatedly in order to train and test the CNN model. A seven-layer deep neural network model was used using the TensorFlow framework and Keras. The model reached an accuracy, sensitivity and specificity of 81%. Six dentists were brought to detect the diseases to compare their results with the model's results. The dentists reached an accuracy of 76%, sensitivity of 92%, and specificity of 63% [11]. This shows that the developed model produced a more accurate result compared to the dentists.

4.5 Detecting Lesions

In [29], the authors aimed to implement deep learning models to detect white spot lesions. A data set of 2781 images of cropped teeth was collected and labeled by two different experts. The model aims to detect white spot lesions, fluorotic lesions, and other-than fluorotic lesions. SqueezeNet was the selected model as it's known for giving high accuracy. The model gave an accuracy that ranged between 81% and 84%, an F1 score that ranged between 68% and 77%, specificity ranging from 85% to 86%, sensitivity of 58% to 66%, and an AUC of 86% [29]. The model gave satisfactory results in the detection of white spots lesions that could be improved with a larger data set.

In [24], the authors aim to detect early-stage lesions by using the You Only Look Once (YOLO) v2 model that can both detect and classify objects simultaneously. A data set of 1603 images was collected and then categorized into dentigerous cysts, odontogenic keratocyst, ameloblastoma, and no lesion. The study compares three different groups, YOLO, oral and maxillofacial surgery (OMS) specialists, and general practitioners (GP) [24]. The results showed that YOLO came first with a precision of 70.7% and a recall of 68%. While the differences between the model and the human evaluation were not large, it still shows that there is a huge potential for computer-based detection [24].

4.6 Other Diseases

In [17], the authors designed a deep learning using an artificial intelligence model to detect plaque on primary teeth. To achieve this, they made a conventional neural network (CNN) to train 886 intraoral photos of primary teeth. 98 intraoral photos acquired by a digital camera of primary teeth were assessed by the model to further validate the clinical feasibility. An experienced pediatric dentist was hired to examine the photos of the primary teeth and mark the regions congaing plaque. Then, a plaque-disclosing agent was used on the teeth' areas where the plaque was identified [17]. After one week, the dentist was used again to diagnose the 98 photos again to evaluate the consistency of manual diagnosis. In addition, 102 intraoral photos of primary teeth were marked to denote the plaque areas obtained by the AI model and the dentist to evaluate the diagnostic capacity of every approach based on lower-resolution photos. The mean intersection-over-union (MIoU) metric was used to indicate detection accuracy. The MIoU for detecting plaque on the tested tooth photos was 0.726 ± 0.165 while, the dentist's MIoU was 0.695 ± 0.269 when first diagnosing the 98 photos taken by the digital camera and 0.689 ± 0.253 after 1 week. Compared to the dentist, the AI model demonstrated a higher MIoU (0.736 ± 0.174), and the results did not change after 1 week. When the dentist and the AI model assessed the 102 intraoral photos, the MIoU was 0.652 ± 0.195 for the dentist and 0.724 ± 0.159 for the model. The results of a paired t-test found no significant difference between the AI model and human specialist in diagnosing dental plaque on primary teeth [17]. The AI model results showed that a clinically acceptable performance in detecting dental plaque on primary teeth compared with the experienced pediatric dentist.

5   Discussion

The most recent work in the field showed a significant advancement in the medical science that had led to more portable diagnostic platforms in dental health. Results showed that this novel field is a promising area that has a scientific and commercial potential though challenging due to the different readability of each platform. Reviewing the recent work in the field led to some observations that might offer a useful insight to future work in the area.

It was noticed that while constructing a deep learning model, it must have a relatively large data set as it is an essential factor in the performance of any model. A big database is highly needed as the model learns directly from the data by an end-to-end process. And although it is considered a common knowledge in the field by now, some papers couldn't follow that due to the small sized data sets available. This resulted in a poor performance for training data and an optimistic and high variance estimation of the performance because of small test data. Most referenced work used a relatively small data set of images which affected the accuracy as most studies pulled less than 90% accuracy rate. These numbers are below the clinically expected accuracy which ranges between 98%–99%. A common misconduct regarding dealing with the data sets was that the images were taken by the same operator which goes against the common practices of telediagnosis. As it implies that images should be taken by different experts at different locations to ensure the most credible data set for the model. To avoid these mistakes, the research community needs to gather efforts to develop an open-source data set to collect and categorize the data to be used in medical applications. For this to happen, researchers in the field need to release their work data with support from big research institutions. This action will lead to a clinically meaningful high accuracy result. It was observed that, while preparing the data sets for the chosen model, some studies pre-processed images via manual cropping of the needed area which makes it more complicated to analyze and compare the results due to the possible human errors in the process.

A variety of deep learning architectures has been put to use in the referenced studies. It was noticed that the recent research papers have adapted recently developed models to increase the accuracy rates. In most of them, CNN was used as a main recognition and classification component with about 57.7% of the referenced papers implementing it. CNN has first appeared in the dental diagnosis world in 2016 and since then, it has dominated the field with more papers being published every year. Support Vector Machine which is a supervised machine learning algorithm, is used for both classification and regression challenges. The algorithm was used in around 11.6% of the reviewed papers. In addition to those, a variety of different models were used with smaller percentages.

A bias factor noticed while constructing this review, that most referenced studies used examiners/experts in labeling the training set images. Although all papers clearly emphasized that they used multiple experts with decent experience in the field, the dependency on a human opinion can not give a conclusive result as there is always room for human error. Some studied the detecting caries lesions at different stages of progression and concluded that the errors made while detecting the initial and moderate lesions demonstrated that although the inter-examiner reproducibility was high in the assessments, it did not lead to a good performance [4]. Furthermore, Artificial intelligence models trained with human input will always face a deficiency in the direct and constant dependency of the performance on the input accuracy. Also, systems based on this kind of model will never have the ability to exceed the trainer's input.

Dealing with smartphone diagnosis is a delicate process as the system is directly interacting with a person who is not familiar with the aspects that affect the accuracy of the deep learning model and any misdiagnosis could cause many complications. Multiple factors can affect the accuracy of the model, unfortunately, multiple papers overlooked them while a few did. Some observations from those papers that could help increase the accuracy were, taking multiple pictures from different angles while using natural lighting. Not relying solely on the images but adding a written section for the symptoms as well can help greatly in enhancing the accuracy and finally, not pre-processing the images before the training model will allow for a more realistic reference image. Another factor that was mildly mentioned is the significant variation in the coloring between phone models because of their different hardware structures. This factor can influence the results greatly if we are detecting a color-based disease like carries.

A limitation that presented itself while formulating this review was that some of the referenced grouped studies such as in Table 4 used different artificial intelligence methods to reach different purposes which should be put into consideration. Although these studies shared the same metrics, they are not to be compared due to different approaches and targets.

The wave of AI is taking over the medical field with big institutions like IBM investing in the field by developing "Watson" a medical program to support doctors' decision-making [31]. But the accuracy of these models still needs more verification by using a lot of cases and imaging modalities before the AI can take a more important role in the field. AI in dental healthcare is still emerging and still far from replacing the existing diagnostic tools. At present, it can serve as an addition to the existing tools with unlimited possibilities of crossovers with the new frameworks and methods in the future [32].

6 Limitations

This paper reviews some of the work done in the different diagnosis methods in dental health based on different methods and algorithms. Although they highlighted and deliberated some areas, there some aspects with some limitations that need to be improved in future works in the field. Some of the diagnosis techniques are addressed with no detailed mathematical representation that need some level of understanding of specific knowledge in some domains. Some aspects that provide a better understanding of the methods used in the paper are not mentioned thoroughly like learning rate, performance sensitivity, loss function, etc. However, the readers are welcome to read related references.

References

1. Park, W.J., Park, J.-B.: History and application of artificial neural networks in dentistry. Eur. J. Dent. **12**(04), 594–601 (2018)
2. El Tantawi, M., Aly, N.M., Attia, D., Abdelrahman, H., Mehaina, M.: Dentist availability in Egypt: a 20-year study of supply, potential demand and economic factors. Eastern Mediterr. Health J. **26**(9), 1078–1086 (2020)

3. Kim, D., Choi, J., Ahn, S., Park, E.: A smart home dental care system: integration of deep learning, image sensors, and mobile controller. J. Ambient Intell. Humanized Comput. 1–9 (2021). https://doi.org/10.1007/s12652-021-03366-8

4. Kohara, E.K., Abdala, C.G., Novaes, T.F., Braga, M.M., Haddad, A.E., Mendes, F.M.: Is it feasible to use smartphone images to perform telediagnosis of different stages of occlusal caries lesions? PLoS ONE **13**(9), e0202116 (2018)

5. Quintero-Rojas, J., González, J.D.: Use of convolutional neural networks in smartphones for the identification of oral diseases using a small dataset. Revista Facultad de Ingenierí **30**(55), e11846 (2021)

6. Lin, H., Chen, H., Weng, L., Shao, J., Lin, J.: Automatic detection of oral cancer in smartphone-based images using deep learning for early diagnosis. J. Biomed. Opt. **26**(8), 086007 (2021)

7. Duong, D.L., Kabir, M.H., Kuo, R.F.: Automated caries detection with smartphone color photography using machine learning. Health Inform. J. **27**(2) (2021)

8. Zhang, X., et al.: Development and evaluation of deep learning for screening dental caries from oral photographs. Oral Dis. **28**(1), 173–181 (2020)

9. Liang, Y., et al.: Proceedings of the 2020 CHI Conference on Human Factors in Computing System. Association for Computing Machinery, New York (2020)

10. Lee, J.-H., Kim, D.-H., Jeong, S.-N., Choi, S.-H.: Detection and diagnosis of dental caries using a deep learning-based convolutional neural network algorithm. J. Dent. **77**, 106–111 (2018)

11. Krois, J., et al.: Deep learning for the radiographic detection of periodontal bone loss. Sci. Rep. **9**(1), 1–6 (2019)

12. Cantu, A.G., et al.: Detecting caries lesions of different radiographic extension on bitewings using deep learning. J. Dent. **100**, 103–425 (2020)

13. Jeyaraj, P.R., Samuel Nadar, E.R.: Computer-assisted medical image classification for early diagnosis of oral cancer employing deep learning algorithm. J. Cancer Res. Clin. Oncol. **145**(4), 829–837 (2019). https://doi.org/10.1007/s00432-018-02834-7

14. Liu, L., Xu, J., Huan, Y., Zou, Z., Yeh, S.-C., Zheng, L.-R.: A smart dental health-IoT platform based on intelligent hardware, deep learning, and mobile terminal. IEEE J. Biomed. Health Inform. **24**(3), 1–7 (2021)

15. Takahashi, T., Nozaki, K., Gonda, T., Mameno, T., Ikebe, K.: Deep learning-based detection of dental prostheses and restorations. Sci. Rep. **11**(1), 99–110 (2016)

16. Lee, S., Oh, S., Jo, J., Kang, S., Shin, Y., Park, J.: Deep learning for early dental caries detection in bitewing radiographs. Sci. Rep. **11**(1), 1–8 (2021)

17. You, W., Hao, A., Li, S., Wang, Y., Xia, B.: Deep learning-based dental plaque detection on primary teeth: a comparison with clinical assessments. BMC Oral Health **20**, 1–7 (2020). https://doi.org/10.1186/s12903-020-01114-6

18. Kim, J., Lee, H.-S., Song, I.-S., Jung, K.-H.: DeNTNet: Deep Neural Transfer Network for the detection of periodontal bone loss using panoramic dental radiographs. Sci. Rep. **9**(1), 1–9 (2019)

19. Murata, M., et al.: Deep-learning classification using convolutional neural network for evaluation of maxillary sinusitis on panoramic radiography. Oral Radiol. **35**(3), 301–307 (2019). https://doi.org/10.1007/s11282-018-0363-7

20. Srivastava, M.M., Kumar, P., Pradhan, L., Varadarajan, S.: Detection of tooth caries in bitewing radiographs using deep learning. arXiv preprint arXiv:1711.07312 (2017)

21. Godlevsky, L., et al.: Application of mobile photography with smartphone cameras for monitoring of early caries appearance in the course of orthodontic correction with dental brackets. Appl. Med. Inform. **33**(4), 21–26 (2013)

22. Ezhov, M., et al.: Clinically applicable artificial intelligence system for dental diagnosis with CBCT. Sci. Rep. **11**(1), 1–16 (2021)
23. Casalegno, F., et al.: Caries detection with near-infrared transillumination using deep learning. J. Dent. Res. **98**(11), 1227–1233 (2019)
24. Yang, H., et al.: Deep learning for automated detection of cyst and tumors of the jaw in panoramic radiographs. J. Clin. Med. **9**(6), 18–39 (2020)
25. Al Kheraif, A.A., Wahba, A.A., Fouad, H.: Detection of dental diseases from radiographic 2D dental image using hybrid graph-cut technique and convolutional neural network. Measurement **146**, 333–342 (2019)
26. Lian, L., Zhu, T., Zhu, F., Zhu, H.: Deep learning for caries detection and classification. Diagnostics **11**(9), 1672 (2021)
27. Ghaedi, L., et al.: An automated dental caries detection and scoring system for optical images of tooth occlusal surface. Journal **2**(5), 99–110 (2016)
28. Berdouses, E.D., Koutsouri, G.D., Tripoliti, E.E., Matsopoulos, G.K., Oulis, C.J., Fotiadis, D.I.: A computer-aided automated methodology for the detection and classification of occlusal caries from photographic color images. Comput. Biol. Med. **62**, 119–135 (2015)
29. Askar, H., et al.: Detecting white spot lesions on dental photography using deep learning: a pilot study. J. Dent. **107**, 103615 (2021)
30. Yang, J., Xie, Y., Liu, L., Xia, B., Cao, Z., Guo, C.: 2018 IEEE 42nd Annual Computer Software and Applications Conference (COMPSAC), vol. 1, pp. 492–497. IEEE (2018)
31. Chen, Y., Argentinis, J.D.E., Weber, G.: IBM Watson: how cognitive computing can be applied to big data challenges in life sciences research. Clin. Ther. **38**(4), 688–701 (2016)
32. Alenezi, N.S.A.L.K.: A method of skin disease detection using image processing and machine learning. Procedia Comput. Sci. **163**, 85–92 (2019)

Computational Image Analysis Techniques, Programming Languages and Software Platforms Used in Cancer Research: A Scoping Review

Youssef Arafat$^{(\boxtimes)}$ ⓘ and Constantino Carlos Reyes-Aldasoro ⓘ

GiCentre, Department of Computer Science, School of Mathematics, Computer Science and Engineering, City, University of London, London, UK
{youssef.arafat,reyes}@city.ac.uk

Abstract. Background: Cancer-related research, as indicated by the number of entries in Medline, the National Library of Medicine of the USA, has dominated the medical literature. An important component of this research is based on the use of computational techniques to analyse the data produced by the many acquisition modalities. This paper presents a review of the computational image analysis techniques that have been applied to cancer. The review was performed through automated mining of Medline/PubMed entries with a combination of keywords. In addition, the programming languages and software platforms through which these techniques are applied were also reviewed.

Methods: Automatic mining of Medline/PubMed was performed with a series of specific keywords that identified different computational techniques. These keywords focused on traditional image processing and computer vision techniques, machine learning techniques, deep learning techniques, programming languages and software platforms.

Results: The entries related to traditional image processing and computer vision techniques have decreased at the same time that machine learning and deep learning have increased significantly. Within deep learning, the keyword that returned the highest number of entries was *convolutional neural network*. Within the programming languages and software environments, Fiji and ImageJ were the most popular, followed by Matlab, R, and Python. Within the more specialised softwares, QuPath has had a sharp growth overtaking other platforms like ICY and CellProfiler.

Conclusions: The techniques of artificial intelligence techniques and deep learning have grown to overtake most other image analysis techniques and the trend at which they grow is still rising. The most used technique has been convolutional neural networks, commonly used to analyse and classify images. All the code related to this work is available through GitHub: https://github.com/youssefarafat/Scoping-Review.

Keywords: Cancer · Data mining · Software · Image analysis

G. Yang et al. (Eds.): MIUA 2022, LNCS 13413, pp. 833–847, 2022.
https://doi.org/10.1007/978-3-031-12053-4_61

1   Introduction

Cancer has dominated the medical literature. At the time of writing of this paper (June 2022), there were 4,633,885 Cancer-related entries from the total 34,216,925, which represented 13% of all entries in PubMed (https://www.ncbi. nlm.nih.gov/pubmed), the search engine of the United States National Library of Medicine MEDLINE. These entries have risen from 6% of all yearly entries recorded in PubMed in the 1950s, to more than 16% seventy years later [19]. Among many technological innovations that have had an impact in medicine in general, and in Cancer in particular, computational data analysis techniques have been important, especially as new imaging technologies provide more and more data every year. Diagnostic images acquired with Magnetic Resonance Imaging [1], Computed Tomography [27], Ultrasound [8], and pathology staining [12,25] are routinely obtained and analysed, traditionally by experts that trained for many years to provide accurate diagnosis. In addition, computational techniques have been used to support decision-making [28], pre-operative planning [23] and predict survival based on the analysis of the images acquired [7].

In recent years, the computational techniques included under the umbrella term of Artificial Intelligence have grown at a very fast rate, but before that, a rich body of techniques developed under the areas of Image Processing and Computer Vision were applied to analyse data from a variety of Cancer data sets. Techniques like Fourier analysis [4], mathematical morphology [22], and fractals [13] among many others have been applied with success in the analysis of Cancer treatments or drug development [15,16,18]. The question that arises is then, are the artificial intelligence techniques displacing all the previous image processing and computer vision techniques as applied to the analysis of Cancer images?

In this paper, a review of the data analysis techniques that have been applied to Cancer data analysis is presented. Since the objective of the review is to map the literature, assess the volume of work, as reflected by the number of entries in PubMed, rather than compare outcomes or perform a precise systematic review and synthesis of the evidence [17,26], a scoping review, rather than a systematic review was performed. The review utilised data mining techniques to extract the entries related to different techniques that have been applied to the analysis of Cancer images. A series of keywords were used in combination to select different techniques, and their yearly entries in PubMed. In addition, the tools through which these techniques were applied, i.e. the software platforms or programming languages were also reviewed.

2   Materials and Methods

The scoping review followed the Preferred Reporting Items for Systematic Reviews and Meta-Analyses (PRISMA) [11,14] and the extension for Scoping Reviews (PRISMAScR) guidelines [17,26] and included the following stages: (1) Identify the research questions, (2) Identify data source and the combination of keywords that would retrieve the relevant entries, (3) Mine the number of entries per year of publication, (4) Display the trends graphically, (5) Interpret the findings. One notable difference of this review is that the screening and eligibility steps were performed automatically by sequentially adding a series of specific keywords to a basic search instead of excluding entries manually or with criteria other than the presence of keywords. The inclusion was solely based on the specific keywords being present in the query as described below.

2.1   Research Questions

The following questions were considered: *Which computational techniques of those considered traditional (i.e. not deep learning) and deep learning have been most widely employed in the analysis of images related to Cancer data sets?. Which tools have been most widely used to apply the computational techniques previously mentioned?*

2.2   Keywords and Data Source

The only database considered in this review was Medline/PubMed, which has been considered to be "the most widely used database of biomedical literature" [24]. The first keyword selected in the queries was *Cancer*, which returned more than 4 million entries (June 2022). With the addition of *Pathology* and a logical AND, entries were reduced to 1,668,363. To focus on image processing/analysis, *images AND imaging* were added and these reduced the entries to 283,702. Of these, 261,058 were published between 1990 and 2022, which were the basic sample to which particular keywords were further added.

Three groups of specific keywords were used to explore the landscape: traditional Image Processing and Computer Vision, Machine Learning and Deep Learning Techniques. The specific keywords are listed in Table 1.

The first group of specific keywords were used to investigate the traditional image processing/computer vision. Some of these keywords were specific enough to be used as a single word, like *Fractal*. Others required a combination of 2 or more terms, for instance, texture could be related to the texture of a sample and not to the specific technique of analysis and thus *texture analysis* was used.

Ambiguity is still possible, for instance, texture can be explored with Fourier transforms and an author under the name of Fourier could be included in the entries when no Fourier transforms or analysis were applied. However, the results from queries were manually observed and the keywords were refined to minimise these artefacts. The second and third group of keywords were related to Machine Learning and Deep Learning techniques, which have grown significantly in recent years.

The number of entries were analysed per year and in total for the period of analysis. To analyse the entries per year, in addition to absolute number of entries, a relative number was studied. There are 2 ways in which the relative numbers can be obtained. First, as a percentage of the total number of entries of all the keywords. That is, for a given year, the number of entries of all keywords are added and the ratio of the value of each keyword is divided by that total.

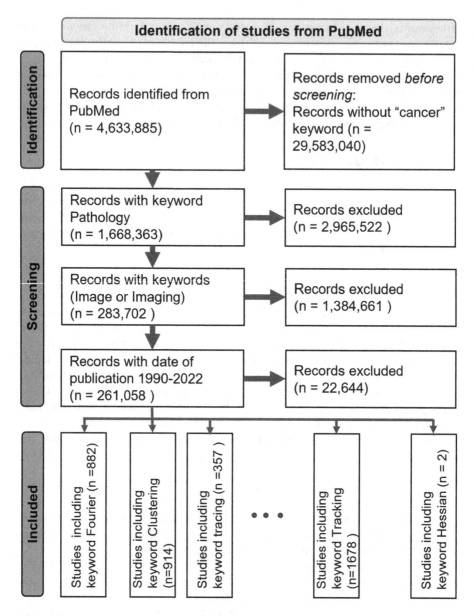

Fig. 1. PRISMA statement flowchart illustrating the details of the scoping review. Notably, the inclusion was given by the presence of keywords on PubMed for individual searches. Studies were not read individually.

Second, as a percentage of the total number of entries of the year irrespective of the specific keywords. In this way, if there are entries that do not include any of the keywords will also be counted to the total.

Table 1. Specific keywords used in the search strategy to explore image processing and computer vision, the machine learning and deep learning techniques.

Image processing/computer vision	Machine learning	Deep learning
Texture analysis	Classification	Deep belief
Fourier	Regression	Recurrent neural networks
Geometric	Dimensionality reduction	Auto-Encoders
Tracing	Ensemble learning	Multilayer perceptron
Linear discriminant analysis	Reinforcement learning	Generative adversarial network
Thresholding	Supervised learning	Convolutional neural network
Feature extraction	Bayesian	U-Net
Tracking	Decision tree	Transformer
Clustering	Linear classifier	Fully convolutional
Scale space	Unsupervised learning	ResNet (Residual
Hessian	Artificial neural networks	neural network)
Self-organizing	Hierarchical clustering	VGG
Region growing	Cluster analysis	Mask-RCNN (Region-Based
Mutual information	Anomaly detection	Convolutional Neural Networks)
Wavelet	Semi-supervised learning	LSTM (Long short-term
Multiresolution	Deep learning	memory)
Principal component analysis	Support Vector Machines	GoogleNet
Filtering	Naive Bayes	AlexNet
Active contour	Nearest Neighbor	Inception-v3
Fractal	Discriminant Analysis	DenseNet
Linear regression	K-Means	Inception-ResNet-v2
Ensemble	Hidden Markov Model	
Transfer learning	Feature Selection	
Convolutional neural	Feature Engineering	
Machine learning	Random Forest.	
Deep learning		

One final set of queries was performed to investigate the programming languages, softwares and environments that have been used for image analysis of cancer and pathological data sets. The most common options within the "point and click" and computational environments (as described in [5]) were considered: the general programming languages *Matlab, R, C* and *Python* and the specialised softwares *QuPath* [2], *CellProfiler* [9], *Fiji* [20], *ImageJ* [21] and *ICY* [3].

Several of these names can be directly keywords, like CellProfiler and QuPath, which referred exclusively to the tools to be investigated and did not imply any ambiguity. However, it was noticed that in some cases, the use of the keyword returned fewer entries than the number of citations to a specific paper. For instance searching for QuPath (https://pubmed. ncbi.nlm.nih.gov/?term=QuPath) returned 86 entries, yet the citations to the original paper describing QuPath (https://pubmed.ncbi.nlm.nih.gov/? linkname=pubmed_pubmed_citedin&from_uid=29203879) returned 780 entries. In other cases, like Matlab or R, would return entries as a keyword, but there was no original paper or reference that could be used.

Thus, two different search strategies were performed: the entries related to *Matlab, R, C and Python* were extracted directly through searches with specialised keywords in the URL. The entries related to *Fiji, ImageJ, ICY, QuPath* and *CellProfiler* were extracted from the citations. Whilst these comparisons are not exactly *like with like*, they provide a panoramic view of the tools used in the research reported in PubMed. In both cases the entries per year were available through the field *yearCounts* as described below in Mining Strategy.

To define the specific keywords of the programming languages the following considerations were taken into account. *Matlab* could refer to the programming environment of Mathworks and also to a rural area of Bangladesh and thus was queried as *(Matlab)) NOT ((rural) AND (bangladesh))*. The strategy to mine programming languages R and C was more complicated as a single letter cannot be queried effectively in PubMed, thus these keywords were expanded to the following, *(("R project") OR ("R package") OR (Rstudio) OR (R/Shiny))* and *("C programming") OR ("C language") OR ("C package")*. For Python, it was necessary to discard those entries that were related to python snakes and the keywords were formed as follows: *(Python) NOT (snake) NOT (python regius)*.

Whilst *Fiji* was not mined through keywords, this would have a high ambiguity and it would have been necessary to discard the entries related to the country, entries by authors of universities in Fiji, or cities. One search that would reduce these conditions would be: *(Fiji) NOT (suva) NOT (pacific) NOT (Samoa) NOT (Palau) NOT (Nausori)*.

2.3   Mining Strategy

To identify the main trends of these analysis techniques, the Medline/PubMed database was queried with a combination of keywords following the methodology previously described [6, 19].

The mining of PubMed was performed with a combination of keywords, which were combined into one Uniform Resource Locator (URL), e.g., a website address in which parameters are used to query the database. The first part of the URL was the address of PubMed (i.e. https://www.ncbi.nlm.nih.gov/pubmed/) and this was followed by search term, which started with *?term=* followed by the concatenation of keywords. Since URLs do not accept certain special characters like quotes or spaces, these need to be converted to the ASCII character set (space = %20, quotes = %22). The first keywords used were: *cancer* and *pathology*. Next, to restrict to those entries related with images, the following was used: *((image) OR (imaging))*. Next, the years of analysis were restricted, initially from 1990 to 2022, and later on, to focus on more recent entries, from 2010 to 2022. The concatenation of keywords with logical AND functions formed the **basic URL** (e.g. https://pubmed.ncbi.nlm.nih.gov/?term=(pathology)%20AND%20(cancer) %20AND%20((image)+OR+(imaging))%20AND%20(2010:2022[dp])) to which then specific keywords (e.g. *Fourier*) added to investigate the research questions.

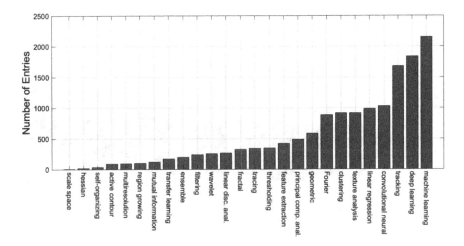

Fig. 2. Number of entries in PubMed corresponding to data analysis techniques as determined by specific keywords. The queries were formed with the combination of the following terms (*keyword*) AND (pathology) AND (cancer) AND ((image) OR (imaging)) AND (1990:2022[dp]). This last term corresponds to the date of publication.

Year-on-year entries were extracted directly from the query for all keywords as PubMed includes a field called *timelineData* with pairs of values [year, entries] for all the years that have entries. For example, the reader can try to search a term in PubMed, say *Cancer*, display the page source (*view-source:https://pubmed.ncbi.nlm.nih.gov/?term=cancer*) and search within that page for the string *yearCounts*.

All the code used in this paper was developed as Matlab® (The Mathworks™, Natick, USA) functions and Python Jupyter Notebooks, and both are available in the GitHub repository related to this publication (https://github.com/youssefarafat/Scoping-Review). The graphics used in this paper were generated in Matlab.

3   Results and Discussion

During the initial period of study, 1990–2022, the analysis techniques that had the higher number of entries were those identified by the keywords: *machine learning, tracking* and *deep learning* with more than 1,500 entries in PubMed. These were followed by five keywords with under 1,000 entries: *linear regression, convolutional neural, Fourier, texture analysis* and *clustering*. On the other side, the keywords which returned the lowest number of entries corresponded to: *mutual information, region growing, multiresolution, self-organizing, hessian* and *scale space* (Fig. 2).

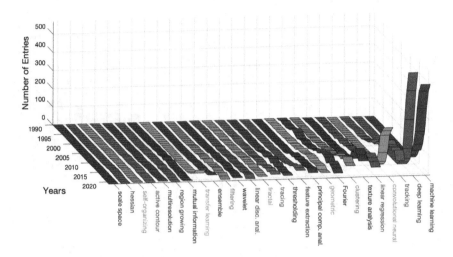

Fig. 3. Number of entries in PubMed corresponding to the specific keywords and the date of publication. Colours have been allocated to the ribbons and the names to aid visual discrimination of the computational techniques.

The year-on-year analysis of these same keywords showed some interesting trends and a rather different story (Fig. 3). Whilst it would be expected that the number of entries would increase for all keywords, as would be expected since the number of entries in PubMed have grown year on year, from 410,894 entries in 1990 to 1,763,742 entries in 2021 (https://pubmed.ncbi.nlm.nih.gov/? term=(1990[dp]), https://pubmed.ncbi.nlm.nih.gov/?term=(2021[dp])), some cases seem to grow faster. It is clear that some techniques, namely *machine learning, deep learning and convolutional neural*, have accumulated their entries quite recently as opposed to *tracking, linear regression* and *Fourier. Clustering, texture analysis* and *feature extraction* also seem to show an increase, but far less pronounced and difficult to appreciate in this graph. For this reason it is important to observe the trends in relative terms. The ratio of entries of every specific keyword divided by the sum of the entries of all the keywords in every year is shown in Fig. 4. This graph shows the relative contribution of each keyword against the rest for a particular year and emphasises the relative decrease of certain techniques, like *Fourier* and *linear regression*. It should be noticed that ratios of these two techniques were close to 30% in the early 90s. *Tracking* accumulated the majority of its entries in the 2000s s but has shown a steep decrease lately.

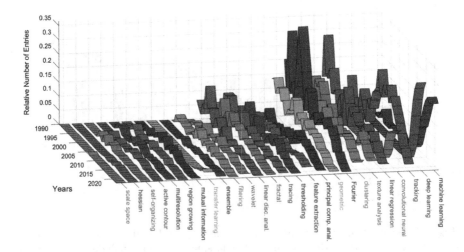

Fig. 4. Relative number of entries in PubMed per keyword and date of publication. The number of entries was divided by the sum of all the entries corresponding to the keywords of a given year and thus emphasises relative decrease of certain techniques. Colours have been allocated to the ribbons and the names to aid visual discrimination of the computational technique.

The number of entries for machine learning specific keywords is illustrated in Fig. 5. The first point to notice is that the vertical scale is logarithmic, as the number of entries for *Regression* and *Classification* was much higher than the rest, and this would be expected as these two terms encompass other terms, for instance, classification with random forests. However, these are useful to give perspective to the following entries. *Deep learning* is one order of magnitude above the next keywords; *Feature Selection, Random Forest, Discriminant Analysis* and *Cluster Analysis*. On the lower side, the keywords with fewer entries were *Feature Engineering, Reinforcement learning, Anomaly detection* and *Hidden Markov Model*. It is important to highlight at this stage, that the queries only returned what is indexed in PubMed. If the work of a certain entry did use a technique, say, feature engineering, but this appeared in the methods of the paper, but not in the fields of the PubMed entry, that entry would not be counted in the query. As an example of the data that was mined with the queries, i.e., title, abstract, MESH terms, etc., the following URL https://pubmed. ncbi.nlm.nih.gov/31783023/?format=pubmed corresponds to the work by Lee *et al.* [10].

When visualised per year, the trends are again very interesting (Fig. 6). In general, the entries corresponding to all specific keywords seem relatively stable, except for one, *deep learning*, which has grown significantly since 2010 and is very close to the entries corresponding to regression and classification. It can be speculated that in a few years, there will be more entries for deep learning than for the other keywords.

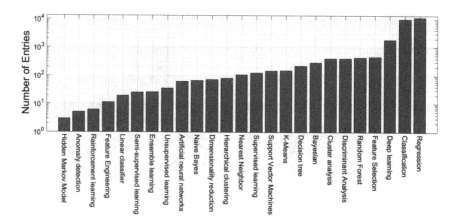

Fig. 5. Number of entries in PubMed per specific keyword related to Machine Learning Techniques. The terms "Regression" and "Classification" may include other keywords (e.g., Classification with Random Forest) and thus are more frequent. It can be seen that the term "Deep learning" is one order of magnitude higher than all others. The vertical axis is logarithmic.

The results for specific deep learning keywords are shown in Fig. 7, where the most common term is *convolutional neural network*, followed by *U-Net* and *ResNet*. Convolutional Neural Networks, commonly known as CNNs or Con-vNets, is almost one magnitude higher than all the other methods. The keywords with fewest entries were *Auto-Encoders, Transformers* and *Mask-RCNN*. It should be noticed that some of these terms are rather recent and thus would not be accumulating many entries in PubMed yet.

The entries corresponding to software and programming languages are shown in Fig. 8. These are shown in two ways, as total number of entries (a) and yearly (b), in both cases the vertical axes are logarithmic. *Fiji* and *ImageJ* returned the highest number of entries followed by *Matlab, R* and *Python*. One order of magnitude below were *QuPath, ICY, CellProfiler*, and this could be expected as the former are general platforms and languages that can be used for a variety of tasks, whilst the latter are more specialised for specific tasks on Quantitative Pathology, Bioimage Informatics and measuring and analysing cell images. As mentioned previously, the queries were performed in different ways and these did not include the keywords cancer, pathology and image analysis, thus they cover all entries indexed in PubMed.

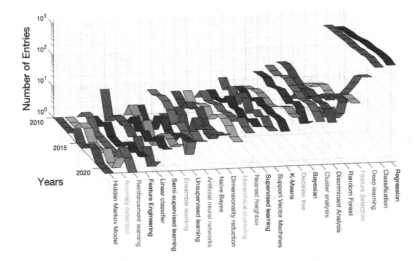

Fig. 6. Number of entries in PubMed per year and specific keyword related to Machine Learning Techniques. It should be noticed that entries related most techniques are fairly constant except for "Deep learning" which has increased constantly. It should be noticed that the vertical axis is logarithmic.

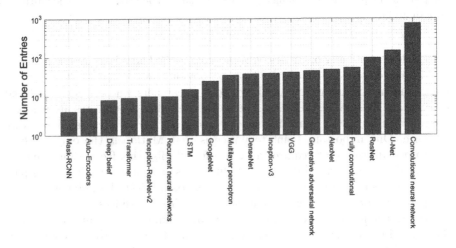

Fig. 7. Number of entries in PubMed per specific keyword related to Deep Learning Techniques and some specific architectures like AlexNet, VGG and U-Net. The vertical axis is logarithmic.

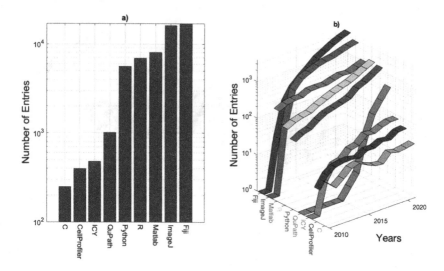

Fig. 8. Number of entries in PubMed related to eight programming languages: Fiji, ImageJ, Matlab, R, Python, QuPath, ICY, CellProfiler and C. Subplot a are the entries for the keywords for the programming languages and all the previous keywords *(pathology) AND (cancer) AND ((image) OR (imaging)) AND (2010:2022[dp])* and subplot b is just for the programming languages and the dates. The vertical axis is logarithmic in both graphs.

The lowest number of entries corresponded to *C*. The relatively low numbers could be due to several factors. The most obvious one is that the C programming language is not widely used by those researchers whose work is indexed in PubMed. It may also be that the work created in C may result in larger tools, which go under other names, for instance, ICY is java-based software platform. One important point to notice is that Matlab is the only of these software platforms that requires a license fee. Whilst this fee is significant for industry, academics can obtain it at reduced cost and in many times it is part of the universities site license. However, this could affect the number of users compared with other platforms that do not require license fees.

Yearly entries show how Fiji has been overtaking ImageJ in recent years. Although Fiji and ImageJ are very closely related, and for some people these are considered to be the same (the actual acronym of FIJI is a recursive Fiji Is Just ImageJ), with the addition of a set plugins that facilitate image analysis, in this publication they are being treated separately to identify the actual name being used in the entries that referred to them. A similar trend can be observed with R and Python overtaking Matlab. A very noticeable increase in entries is that related to QuPath, which has grown at a much faster rate than any other language/software. If this trend continues, it can be speculated that it will soon reach the same number of entries as the programming languages and eventually close to ImageJ and Fiji.

Whilst this review did not consider the actual biological/clinical tasks such as finding and counting nuclei, estimation of cellularity, semantic annotations, anomaly detection or segmenting organs, these could be investigated with the same methodology as described in this work.

4   Conclusions

This scoping review provides a panoramic view of the computational techniques that have been applied for the analysis of images produced in Cancer research. The techniques included in the areas of machine learning and deep learning have grown to dominate the recent works indexed in PubMed. Whilst other techniques are still recorded in the records of PubMed, most of these are decreasing their proportions as compared with machine and deep learning.

The tools with which these techniques have been applied, i.e. the software platforms and programming languages showed that general tools through which researchers programme their own solutions are popular, but some specialised softwares like ImageJ and Fiji are widely used, with some newer options like QuPath increasing their position in this area.

Acknowlegements. We acknowledge Dr Robert Noble for the useful discussions regarding this work.

Declaration of Interests Statement. The authors declare no conflicts of interest.

References

1. Abd-Ellah, M.K., Awad, A.I., Khalaf, A.A.M., Hamed, H.F.A.: A review on brain tumor diagnosis from MRI images: practical implications, key achievements, and lessons learned. Magn. Reson. Imaging **61**, 300–318 (2019). https://doi.org/10.1016/j.mri.2019.05.028

2. Bankhead, P., et al.: QuPath: open source software for digital pathology image analysis. Sci. Rep. **7**(1), 16878 (2017). https://doi.org/10.1038/s41598-017-17204-5

3. de Chaumont, F., et al.: Icy: an open bioimage informatics platform for extended reproducible research. Nat. Methods **9**(7), 690–696 (2012). https://doi.org/10.1038/nmeth.2075

4. Fourier, J.: Mémoire sur la propagation de la chaleur dans les corps solides. Nouveau Bulletin des sciences par la Société philomatique de Paris I, 112–116 (1808)

5. Jamali, N., Dobson, E.T.A., Eliceiri, K.W., Carpenter, A.E., Cimini, B.A.: 2020 bioimage analysis survey: community experiences and needs for the future. Biol. Imaging **1** (2022). https://doi.org/10.1017/S2633903X21000039. https://www.cambridge.org/core/journals/biological-imaging/article/2020-bioimage-analysis-survey-community-experiences-and-needs-for-the-future/9E824DC0C27568FE5B9D12FB59B1BB90

6. Kather, J.N., et al.: Large-scale database mining reveals hidden trends and future directions for cancer immunotherapy. Oncoimmunology **7**(7), e1444412 (2018). https://doi.org/10.1080/2162402X.2018.1444412

7. Kather, J.N., et al.: Predicting survival from colorectal cancer histology slides using deep learning: a retrospective multicenter study. PLoS Med. **16**(1), e1002730 (2019)

8. Ko, S.Y., et al.: Deep convolutional neural network for the diagnosis of thyroid nodules on ultrasound. Head Neck **41**(4), 885–891 (2019). https://doi.org/10.1002/hed.25415. https://onlinelibrary.wiley.com/doi/abs/10.1002/hed.25415

9. Lamprecht, M.R., Sabatini, D.M., Carpenter, A.E.: CellProfiler: free, versatile software for automated biological image analysis. Biotechniques **42**(1), 71–75 (2007). https://doi.org/10.2144/000112257

10. Lee, C.W., Ren, Y.J., Marella, M., Wang, M., Hartke, J., Couto, S.S.: Multiplex immunofluorescence staining and image analysis assay for diffuse large B cell lymphoma. J. Immunol. Methods **478**, 112714 (2020). https://doi.org/10.1016/j.jim.2019.112714

11. Liberati, A., et al.: The prisma statement for reporting systematic reviews and meta-analyses of studies that evaluate healthcare interventions: explanation and elaboration. BMJ **339**, b2700 (2009). https://doi.org/10.1136/bmj.b2700

12. Mahmood, F., et al.: Deep adversarial training for multi-organ nuclei segmentation in histopathology images. IEEE Trans. Med. Imaging **39**(11), 3257–3267 (2020). https://doi.org/10.1109/TMI.2019.2927182. conference Name: IEEE Transactions on Medical Imaging

13. Mandelbrot, B.B.: The Fractal Geometry of Nature. Freeman, San Francisco (1983)

14. Moher, D., et al.: Preferred reporting items for systematic review and meta-analysis protocols (PRISMA-P) 2015 statement. Syst. Control Found. Appl. **4**(1), 1 (2015). https://doi.org/10.1186/2046-4053-4-1

15. Oczeretko, E., Juczewska, M., Kasacka, I.: Fractal geometric analysis of lung cancer angiogenic patterns. Folia Histochem. Cytobiol. **39**(Suppl 2), 75–76 (2001)

16. Partin, A.W., Schoeniger, J.S., Mohler, J.L., Coffey, D.S.: Fourier analysis of cell motility: correlation of motility with metastatic potential. Proc. Natl. Acad. Sci. **86**(4), 1254–1258 (1989). https://doi.org/10.1073/pnas.86.4.1254

17. Peters, M.D.J., Godfrey, C.M., Khalil, H., McInerney, P., Parker, D., Soares, C.B.: Guidance for conducting systematic scoping reviews. JBI Evidence Implement. **13**(3), 141–146 (2015). https://doi.org/10.1097/XEB.0000000000000050

18. Reyes-Aldasoro, C.C., Williams, L.J., Akerman, S., Kanthou, C., Tozer, G.M.: An automatic algorithm for the segmentation and morphological analysis of microvessels in immunostained histological tumour sections. J. Microsc. **242**(3), 262–278 (2011). https://doi.org/10.1111/j.1365-2818.2010.03464.x

19. Reyes-Aldasoro, C.C.: The proportion of cancer-related entries in PubMed has increased considerably; is cancer truly "The Emperor of All Maladies"? PLoS One **12**(3), e0173671 (2017). https://doi.org/10.1371/journal.pone.0173671

20. Schindelin, J., et al.: Fiji: an open-source platform for biological-image analysis. Nat. Methods **9**(7), 676–682 (2012). https://doi.org/10.1038/nmeth.2019. https://www.nature.com/articles/nmeth.2019, number: 7 Publisher: Nature Publishing Group

21. Schneider, C.A., Rasband, W.S., Eliceiri, K.W.: NIH image to ImageJ: 25 years of image analysis. Nat. Methods **9**(7), 671–675 (2012). https://doi.org/10.1038/nmeth.2089

22. Serra, J.: Introduction to mathematical morphology. Comput. Vis. Graph. Image Process. **35**(3), 283–305 (1986). https://doi.org/10.1016/0734-189X(86)90002-2

23. Tang, J.H., Yan, F.H., Zhou, M.L., Xu, P.J., Zhou, J., Fan, J.: Evaluation of computer-assisted quantitative volumetric analysis for pre-operative resectability assessment of huge hepatocellular carcinoma. Asian Pac. J. Cancer Prev. APJCP **14**(5), 3045–3050 (2013). https://doi.org/10.7314/apjcp.2013.14.5.3045

24. Theodosiou, T., Vizirianakis, I.S., Angelis, L., Tsaftaris, A., Darzentas, N.: MeSHy: mining unanticipated PubMed information using frequencies of occurrences and concurrences of MeSH terms. J. Biomed. Inform. **44**(6), 919–926 (2011). https://doi.org/10.1016/j.jbi.2011.05.009

25. Tomita, N., Abdollahi, B., Wei, J., Ren, B., Suriawinata, A., Hassanpour, S.: Attention-based deep neural networks for detection of cancerous and precancerous esophagus tissue on histopathological slides. JAMA Netw. Open **2**(11), e1914645 (2019). https://doi.org/10.1001/jamanetworkopen.2019.14645

26. Tricco, A.C., et al.: A scoping review of rapid review methods. BMC Med. **13**(1), 224 (2015). https://doi.org/10.1186/s12916-015-0465-6

27. Xie, Y., Zhang, J., Xia, Y.: Semi-supervised adversarial model for benign-malignant lung nodule classification on chest CT. Med. Image Anal. **57**, 237–248 (2019)

28. Yung, A., Kay, J., Beale, P., Gibson, K.A., Shaw, T.: Computer-based decision tools for shared therapeutic decision-making in oncology: systematic review. JMIR Cancer **7**(4), e31616 (2021). https://doi.org/10.2196/31616

Image-Guided Intervention

A User Interface for Automatic Polyp Detection Based on Deep Learning with Extended Vision

Adrian Krenzer[1,2]([envelope]), Joel Troya[2], Michael Banck[1,2], Boban Sudarevic[2,3], Krzysztof Flisikowski[4], Alexander Meining[2], and Frank Puppe[1]

[1] Julius-Maximilians University of Würzburg, Sanderring 2,
97070 Würzburg, Germany
adrian.krenzer@uni-wuerzburg.de
[2] University Hospital Würzburg, Oberdürrbacher Straße 6,
97080 Würzburg, Germany
[3] Katharinenhospital, Heidelberg, Kriegsbergstrasse 60, 70174 Stuttgart, Germany
[4] Lehrstuhl für Biotechnologie der Nutztiere, School of Life Sciences,
Technische Universität München, Munich, Germany

Abstract. Colorectal cancer (CRC) is a leading cause of cancer-related deaths worldwide. To prevent CRC, the best method is screening colonoscopy. During this procedure, the examiner searches for colon polyps. Colon polyps are mucosal protrusions that protrude from the intestinal mucosa into the intestinal lumen. During the colonoscopy, all those polyps have to be found by the examiner. However, as the colon is folding and winding, polyps may hide behind folds or in uninvestigated areas and be missed by the examiner. Therefore, some publications suggest expanding the view of the examiner with multiple cameras. Nevertheless, expanding the examiner's view with multiple cameras leads to overwhelming and cumbersome interventions. Therefore, we suggest maintaining the examiner's classical endoscope view but extending the endoscope with side cameras. Those side camera views are only shown to an Artificial Intelligence (AI) trained for polyp detection. This AI system detects polyps on the side cameras and alarms the examiner if a polyp is found. Therefore, the examiner can easily move the main endoscope view on the AI detected area without being overwhelmed with too many camera images. In this study, we build a prototype of the endoscope with extended vision and test the automatic polyp detection system on gene-targeted pigs. Results show that our system outperforms current benchmarks and that the AI is able to find additional polyps that were not visualized with the main endoscope camera.

Keywords: Machine learning · Deep learning · Endoscopy · Gastroenterology · Automation · Object detection · Computer vision

G. Yang et al. (Eds.): MIUA 2022, LNCS 13413, pp. 851–868, 2022.
https://doi.org/10.1007/978-3-031-12053-4_62

1   Introduction

Colorectal cancer is one of the most common types of cancer globally. In most cases, the cause is unknown. Only three to five percent of all cases can be traced back to known genetic mutations that can be inherited and trigger colon cancer. Nevertheless, colorectal cancer almost always develops from growths that form in the mucosa of the colon, so-called intestinal polyps [8].

One of the most effective methods to prevent CRC is to detect the potential disease as early as possible using a colonoscopy. A colonoscopy inspects the large intestine (colon) with a long flexible tube inserted via the rectum. The tube carries a small camera to allow the physician to look inside the colon. The physician searches for polyps and analyses them carefully. Polyps are protrusions of the mucosal surface of various shapes and sizes that can be benign or malignant. Malignant polyps are at risk to turn into colorectal cancer. Polyps appear on the lining of the colon and rarely cause any symptoms. The two main types of polyps are non-neoplastic and neoplastic polyps. Non-neoplastic polyps are usually harmless, while polyps of type neoplastic can turn cancerous [6].

Therefore, even if many polyps are not cancerous, they always risk turning into colon cancer. In theory, the colonoscopist identifies all polyps of the patient during a colonoscopy and decides if it needs to be removed. However, there is always a potential risk of a polyp being missed during the colonoscopy. Previous studies showed that up to 27% of diminutive polyps are overlooked by physicians, which may be caused by the physician's lack of experience or fatigue and untypical appearance or bad visibility of the polyps [12,24]. Furthermore, a general error rate of 20%-24% during exams leads to a high risk for patients to die from CRC [18,25].

In conclusion, smaller polyps have a higher risk of being missed by the examiner than bigger polyps. Missed polyps are not removed and stay inside the colon, where they can have fatal consequences for the patient. Therefore, the colonoscopist must find and afterward remove all potential cancerous polyps to minimize the risk of colorectal cancer for the patient [1].

Additionally, there are challenges that increase the chance of polyps being missed. One of the fundamental challenges are folds in the colon. These folds can hide polyps from the examiner and increase the risk of developing CRC. In the literature are already different approaches to tackle the issue of hidden polyps by increasing the camera view of the examiner [10,28]. However, these approaches do always incorporate the additional views and monitors and therefore have the potential risk to overwhelm the examiner [11]. Accordingly, these procedures have not yet been implemented in practice. We propose an interface for automatic polyp detection, which includes an extended view. This extended view includes two additional side cameras to the endoscope. We run an artificial intelligence polyp detection system on these side-view cameras, which then alarms the examiner about missing a polyp. Therefore instead of the examiner being overwhelmed with different views, we let the AI handle the additional views, and the examiner can entirely focus on the classic view of the endoscope.

The main contributions of our paper are:

1) *We create an interface for automatic polyp detection with extends the vision of the endoscopists and shows seamless integration for the classic automatic polyp detection task.*

2) *We show that our system outperforms state of the art architectures on our dataset and present that additional polyps are found by the AI through adding extended vision to the system.*

3) *We create a prototype of an endoscope with side cameras and applied and test it during an animal trial with gene-targeted pigs.*

The interface with extended vision is publicly funded and developed by computer scienctists, engineers and endoscopists.

2   Data

One of the biggest problems in implementing deep learning methods is getting adequate qualitative data. Accordingly, getting high-quality colonoscopy video or image data is challenging for automated polyp detection. The challenge of data acquisition is caused by data protection issues and the expensive and time-consuming data annotation by experienced medical experts. We, therefore, used different technics to challenge these issues illustrated below. Further, we split our data into human and animal data to evaluate our system with extended vision. We could only apply our system to animal data as we did not have consent to use the system on humans. Nevertheless, all human data we got is used to pretrain our system for the polyp detection task.

2.1   Animal Data

Formerly, we published a framework that consists of two steps, a small expert annotation part and a large non-expert annotation part [16]. This moves most of the workload from the expert to a non-expert while ensuring high-quality data. Both annotation steps are supplemented with AI assistance to enhance the annotation efficiency further. We used the software Fast Colonoscopy Annotation Tool (FastCat) to process the entire annotation process. This tool supports the annotation process in endoscopic videos by enabling us to label these videos 20 times faster than traditional labeling techniques. The annotation process is split between at least two people. In the first step, an expert analyses the video and annotates a small set of video frames to verify the object's annotations.

In the second step, a non-expert has visual confirmation of the given object and annotates all following and preceding frames with AI assistance. To annotate individual frames, all video frames must be extracted first. Then, relevant frames can be pre-selected by an automated system, and this averts the expert from examining the entire video every single time. After the expert annotation, relevant frames are selected and can be passed on to an AI model. Then, the AI model detects and marks the desired object on all following and preceding frames with an annotation.

Afterward, the non-expert can adjust the AI annotations and further export the results used to train the AI model further. Additionally, the expert annotates the Paris classification [17], the size of the polyp and its location, as well as the start and end frame of the detected polyp, and one box for the non-expert annotators. Overall, as we were filming with extended vision, this data involved three camera angles. First is the classic endoscope view, the standard camera of the endoscope filming in front. It is an entire HD endoscope with a resolution of 1920 × 1080 px. Then we attached two side cameras to the endoscope. These side cameras capture other videos with a quality 320 × 320 px. The endoscope with extended vision is then inserted into four different pigs to create a dataset of 6185 side camera images. Those images are annotated by a medical expert, as illustrated in the previous paragraph. We pretrained our model on the human data illustrated below and then fine-tuned it on our collected animal data.

2.2 Human Data

We use our own data and all publicly available data for the development of our model. We merged the data from online resources and our own data to forge a data set of 506,338 images. The details about the creation of this training data set will are the same as presented in animal data. The data set is made of images and bounding box coordinates of boxes referring to the image. Here we list all the publicly available data we incorporated into the training: CVC-ColonDB [4] 2012, ETIS-Larib [27] 2014:, CVC-VideoClinicDB [3] 2017 CVC-EndoSceneStill [29] 2017, Kvasir-SEG [15] 2020, SUN Colonoscopy Video Database [21] 2020, CVC-Segementation-HD [30] 2017 and Endoscopy Disease Detection Challenge 2020 (EDD2020) [2]. Overall we built a team of advanced gastroenterologists, computer scientists, engineers and medical assistance staff. Together we produced a data set of 506,338 human images, including the open-source images listed above. Our data set includes 361 polyp sequences and 312 non-polyp sequences. This data set is then used for the pretraining of our model.

3 Methods

This section explains the software and hardware used in this work. Figure 1 illustrates the structure of our system. The illustration is split into three phases: video capture of endoscopic images with and without extended vision, AI detection system, and User interface. First, the endoscope coupled with two additional micro cameras captures the frames of the surface of the colon. Those frames are afterward input to the Artificial intelligence. This AI processes the frames in real-time and draws bounding boxes on the detected polyps. The detection results of the main camera are then shown to the endoscopist. The AI inspects only the extended views (side cameras) to avoid disturbing the endoscopist with the classical examination. If the AI detects a polyp in the extended views, the examiner is alarmed via an arrow on the screen on which camera (left camera or right camera) the polyp is detected. Afterward, the examiner can inspect

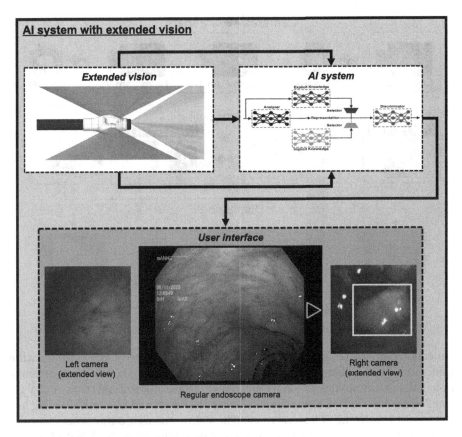

Fig. 1. Overview of the AI system with extended vision. This figure shows all the steps of the whole detection system. The start is an endoscope equipped with two additional micro cameras. The images taken from these cameras are then input into the AI system. If the AI detects a polyp in the extended views, the examiner is alarmed via an arrow on the screen. Afterward, the examiner can inspect the missed polyp with the main camera view. The examiner does never see the side camera views, just the arrows pointing him in the direction of the polyp.

the missed polyp with the main camera view. To further express the novelty of our approach using the YOLOR algorithm [31]. We like to highlight the combination of YOLOR and the side cameras. The architecture of YOLOR enables high detection accuracy while maintaining good detection speed, especially with low-resolution images. Therefore we consider it the best for detection of the side cameras, which operate in real-time with low resolution.

3.1 Video Processing System

As illustrated in Fig. 2, three types of optical camera signals were captured by our system in real-time: the endoscope image and the two lateral micro cameras.

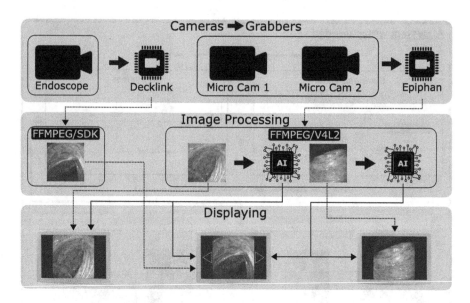

Fig. 2. Overview of the developed video processing system.

An endoscope can be described as a long, thin, illuminated flexible tube with a camera on the tip. They use fiber optics, which allow for the effective transmission of light to illuminate the inner mucosa of the gastrointestinal tract. A charge-coupled device (CCD) image sensor captures the image and transmits it using fine electrical wires to the video processor. The video processor outputs the image to display it on the screen, mainly using a serial digital interface (SDI) with Bayonet Neil-Concelman (BNC) connectors and/or digital visual interface (DVI). Image resolution has increased as technology has advanced. At the moment, most devices in the clinic can provide between 25–60 high-definition (HD) images per second, depending on the manufacturer and model. However, the first models with 4K resolution already appear on the market. In our case, the Olympus 180 CV endoscope processor was connected via SDI to a Blackmagic - DeckLink Mini Recorder 4K [20] on a 1080i signal.

The two micro cameras used for this study were the Osiris M from Optasensor GmbH. These micro cameras provide a resolution of 320 × 320 pixels and have the best focus point at 15mm. Their field of view is 90 degrees. Each microcamera was connected to an image processing system (Osiris M IPS, Optasensor GmbH.), providing a single output image of concatenated micro camera images. The final HDMI image output format is 8 Bit RGB 1080p. Therefore, only one grabber was needed for the micro cameras. To capture this signal, an Epiphan DVI2USB 3.0 grabber [13] was used. Both sources, the endoscope and the micro cameras, were processed by FFmpeg [7]. The micro cameras stream was captured within the V4L2 API. Since Blackmagic is not implementing V4L2, we compiled FFmpeg with the Decklink SDK to enable access to the device through FFmpeg. Processed by FFmpeg to BGR byte arrays, the data was converted to OpenCV [14] matrices for further steps. Since the data of the micro cameras are fused, splitting up and cropping is required to handle the two independent micro cameras individually. This results in a smaller BGR matrix for each camera and frame. The main matrix of the endoscope was forwarded as fast as possible to the main display pipeline. Since this is displayed to the monitor observed by the physician, keeping the delay is a priority for the best user experience. Each frame is forwarded to a second and third display pipeline for the micro cameras and simultaneously to the AI pipelines. The matrices are first cropped, scaled, and padded to the required 320×320 resolution to suit the convolutional neural network (CNN). Afterward, the color channels are swapped from BGR to RGB, before the data is normalized, uploaded to the GPU memory and injected into the CNN. Every microcamera uses its own copy of the CNN for inference. The outcome is a list of scored bounding boxes. If this list is not empty, an arrow is drawn on the main monitor, pointing to the direction of the camera in which the polyp has been detected. The boxes themselves are filtered by the confidence threshold. However, the boxes still contain relative coordinates based on the modified matrix. Therefore, coordinates are transformed to reverse the smaller matrix's crop-, scale-, and pad operations. The resulting boxes are added to the secondary displays to highlight the detected polyp. Since the boxes result from the AI pipelines, they are 1–3 frames delayed. This means bounding boxes are always drawn on a more recent frame. However, by a framerate of 50 frames per second, the delay is only 20 ms per frame. Since during the withdrawal, the camera moves slowly, the boxes are still accurate. The arrows and boxes are displayed until the next cycle of the AI pipeline has finished and passed to the display pipeline. In addition, at the same time, all streams are recorded as h264 encoded video files, together with all the polyp detections triggered by the two micro cameras. This asynchronously recording process opens the possibility for a retrospective system evaluation.

3.2   Endoscope Assembly

To assemble the micro cameras on the endoscope, an add-on-cap was 3D printed. This add-on-cap was inserted and fixed 5 mm from the tip of the endoscope. The cap dimensions were 27.3 mm long, the maximum radius was 10.5 mm, and the thickness was 5.5 mm. The material used was nylon PA12, and a selective laser sintering printer (Lisa Pro, Sinterit sp. Z o.o.) was used to produce it. The cap contained two openings to allow the integration of the micro cameras into the normal endoscope's axis. The micro cameras included four mini light-emitting diodes (OSRAM Opto Semiconductors GmbH) arranged around it that allowed the illumination of the mucosa. The total dimensions of the micro camera with the diodes was $3.8 \times 3.8 \times 2$ mm^3 ($height \times width \times depth$). The design of the add-on-cap incorporated cut-out areas to allow the micro cameras to have a full field of view. To secure the micro cameras on the add-on-cap, silicone epoxy was used. Additionally, a 2 m length cable has to be connected to use the micro cameras. A tube-like plastic foil was used to protect the cable of the micro cameras. This allowed the flexible endoscope could maintain its normal mobility. Figure 3 shows the 3D printed cap that was assembled to the endoscope. As illustrated, the micro cameras are fixed to each of the sides, thus extending the field of view of mucosa inspected. The position of the add-on-cap does not disturb the mobility of the endoscope because the bending section starts further back. The design does not alter any of the functions that endoscopists normally perform: the instrument channel remains free for therapeutic interventions as well as the illumination, and the suction and water irrigation channels.

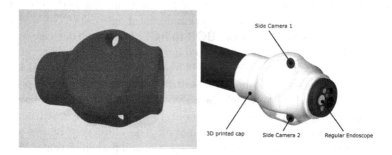

Fig. 3. Left: 3D printed cap used to assemble the micro cameras into the endoscope. Right: Assemble of the cap over the endoscope.

3.3   Polyp Detection System Using AI

Preprocessing and Data Augmentation. To ensure a fast processing speed while keeping up high detection accuracy, we rescale the images to 640 × 640 pixels. The change in image size allows the detection system to perform with high quality and a speed of 20 ms on an NVIDIA RTX 3080 GPU. In the clinical application subsection, we further define the use of different GPUs and the GPU requirements for a system able to process in real-time. Furthermore, we move the image and model to a half-precision binary floating-point (FP16). However, most machine learning models are in a precision binary floating-point (FP32). With FP16 the model calculates faster but also delivers high quality results. Afterwards, we normalize the image pixels in the following way: The min-max normalization function linearly scales each feature to the interval between 0 and 1. We rescale to the interval 0 and 1 by shifting the values of each feature with the minimum value being 0. Then, a division by the new maximum value is done to see the difference between the original maximum and minimum value.

The values in the column are transformed using the following formula:

$$X_{sc} = \frac{X - X_{\min}}{X_{\max} - X_{\min}}$$

After normalization, the data augmentation follows. In the context of deep learning, augmenting image data means using various processes to modify the original image data. We use the following augmentations: Vertical flip, horizontal flip, rotation, scaling mosaic. The most basic augmentation done is the flip augmentation. This is well suited for polyp images as the endoscope is often rotated during colonoscopy. Here, the image is flipped horizontally, vertically, or both. We use a probability of 0.3 for up and down flips and a vertical flipping probability of 0.5. In addition, we rescale the images with a probability of 0.638. Rescaling creates polyps in different sizes and therefore adds additional data to our data set. The translation moves the image along the horizontal axis. Furthermore, we apply a low probability of 0.1 to rotate the image with a random degree, e.g. 20-degree rotation clockwise. As the last augmentation step, we use mosaic data augmentation. Mosaic data augmentation merges four images into one image. Thereby, the image is rescaled, causing the images to appear in a different context. We use mosaic data augmentation with a probability of 0.944. These data augmentations are only applied to the training data.

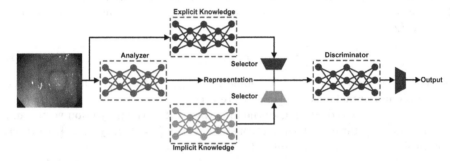

Fig. 4. Overview of the polyp detection system. Adopted from Wang et al. [31].

AI Architecture. For the AI architecture, we used a fast object detector system called YOLOR [31]. An overview of the network's architecture is illustrated in Fig. 4. Humans can look at the same piece of data from different perspectives. A trained CNN model, on the other hand, can generally only accomplish one goal. In general, the characteristics that may be recovered from a trained CNN are not well suited to other problems. The fundamental source of the aforementioned issue is that we extract features from neurons and do not employ implicit information, which is rich in CNN. YOLOR distinguishes between two different types of knowledge, implicit and explicit knowledge. The information directly corresponds to observation is referred to as explicit knowledge in the study. The authors of YOLOR call implicit knowledge that is implicit in the model but has nothing to do with observation. The implicit knowledge is represented as the deeper layers of the network and thereby contains more detail. This implicit and explicit information are especially useful in the case of real-time polyp detection as the structure of the network reduces the overall computational complexity and thereby allows the calculation to remain fast and accurate. This is an ideal scenario for real-time detection systems. To combine implicit and explicit information and enable the learned model to contain a generic representation, from which sub representations suited for particular tasks may be created, they propose a unified network, which is explained below.

What is unique about the unified network is that it can be effectively trained with implicit knowledge. To achieve this, explicit and implicit knowledge was combined to model the error term. The multi-purpose network training process can then be guided by it. This results in the following formula:

$$
\begin{aligned}
y &= f_\theta(x) + \epsilon + g_\phi(\epsilon_{ex}(x), \epsilon_{im}(z)) \\
&\text{minimize } \epsilon + g_\phi \phi(\epsilon_{ex}(x), \epsilon_{im}(z))
\end{aligned}
\tag{1}
$$

where ϵ_{ex} and ϵ_{im} are operations modeling the explicit error and implicit error from observation x and latent code z. g_ϕ here is a task-specific process for combining or selecting information from explicit and implicit knowledge. There are a few approaches for incorporating explicit knowledge into f_θ, now we can rewrite (1) into (2).

$$
y = f_\theta(x) \star g_\phi(z)
\tag{2}
$$

where $\star$ is the approach used to combine f_θ and g_ϕ. In the paper, manifold space reduction and kernel space alignment are used.

Manifold space reduction uses the inner product of the projection vector and implicit representation, which is a constant tensor $Z = \{z_1, z_2, ..., z_k\}$, to reach a reduction of the dimensionality of manifold space.

Kernel space alignment deals with the frequent misalignment problem in multi-task and multi-head networks. We may add and multiply output features and implicit representations to address this issue, allowing Kernel space to be translated, rotated, and scaled to match each neural network's output kernel space.

If we expand the error term derivation procedure to several tasks, we get the following equation:

$$
F(x, \theta, Z, \phi, Y, \psi) = 0
\tag{3}
$$

where $Z = \{z_1, z_2, ..., z_T\}$ denotes a collection of implicit latent codes for T separate jobs, and phi denotes the parameters that may be utilized to build implicit representation from Z. The final output parameters are calculated using ψ from various combinations of explicit and implicit representation.

We may use the following formula to get a prediction for all $z \in Z$ for various tasks.

$$
d_\psi(f_\theta(x), g_\phi(z), y) = 0
\tag{4}
$$

We begin with a common unified representation $f_\theta(x)$, then go on to task-specific implicit representation $g_\phi(z)$, and eventually accomplish various tasks with task-specific discriminator d_ψ.

We assume that it starts with no past implicit knowledge to train the model. It will not influence explicit representation $f_\theta(x)$. When the combining operator

$\star$ is an addition or concatenation, the first implicit prior is $z \sim N(0, \sigma)$, and when the combining operator $\star$ is multiplication, $z \sim N(1, \sigma)$. σ is an extremely tiny number that is nearly zero. Both z and x are taught using the backpropagation method during the training procedure.

The inference is relatively simple because implicit information has no bearing on observation x. Any implicit model g, no matter how complicated, may be reduced to a collection of constant tensors before the inference phase begins. That means that it has no negligible impact on the algorithm's computational complexity.

The resulting network thus achieves a better or comparable AP than state-of-the-art methods in object detection. In addition, the network can be used in real-time, to be more precise in 39 FPS, which makes it very attractive for polyp detection in endoscopy. Further, implicit representations can be added to the output layer for prediction refinement. This leads in object detection to the fact that although one does not provide any prior knowledge for the implicit representation, the proposed learning mechanism can automatically learn the patterns (x, y), (w, h), (obj), and (classes) of each anchor.

Training Details. For the training of the AI, we first have a pretraining process. This involves the training of the AI on the human data set of over 500.000 images. In this process, we run the AI for 110 epochs on the human dataset with a learning rate of 0.001. We implemented a learning rate schedule that slowly increases the learning rate. We use a batch size of 64 images and train on four NVIDIA Quadro RTX 8000 GPUs with 48 GB RAM each. The model is trained using stochastic gradient descent. Afterward, the AI is finetuned on the animal data. We use the pretrained checkpoint of the human data trained YOLOR as initialization. As the dataset involves smaller amounts of images with lower quality the AI is only trained for 40 epochs with a batch size of 128. In this case, only two of the NVIDIA Quadro RTX 8000 GPUs are used for training. We also implemented a learning rate schedule and slowly increased the learning rate in the initialization. Nevertheless, the learning rate increase was faster than with the human data and the learning rate is set to 0.0001. The model is also trained using stochastic gradient descent.

3.4   Animal Model

An animal model was used to test our concept and obtain all the data. Four gene-targeted pigs (*sus scrofa domesticus*) with the "truncating 1311" mutation in the adenomatous polyposis coli (APC) were endoscopically examined with our system [9]. This mutation is orthologous to the hotspot APC^{1309} mutation which causes human familial adenomatous polyposis with aberrant crypt foci and low- and high-grade dysplastic adenomas in the large intestine. As shown in previous studies, the $APC^{1311/+}$ pigs are a suitable model for experimental endoscopy [26,32]. All animal experiments were approved by the Government of Upper Bavaria (permit number ROB-55.2-2532.Vet_02-18-33) and performed according to the German Animal Welfare Act and European Union Normative for Care and Use of Experimental Animals.

4   Results

This section describes our results on our own created test dataset. For our evaluation, we compare our approach to two classic benchmarking algorithms and a newer approach called YOLOv4 [5]. The benchmarking algorithms are an SSD algorithm called YOLOv3 [22], and the ROI Proposal algorithm called Faster RCNN [23]. We train all algorithms on the same data listed in the data chapter. For the test data, we create a test set. The test set consists of three videos filmed in the colon of three different pigs. As in this example, we like to evaluate the detection of the extended view, our evaluation is only done on the side cameras of the endoscope. The three videos consist of 800 frames having a frame size of 320×320 px.

Table 1. Evaluation on the test data set. This table shows our comparison of four different polyp detection approaches on our benchmarking data. The YOLOv3 and Faster-RCNN are baseline models, the third as a model for comparison called YOLOv4 and the last is our polyp detection system. Precision, Recall, F1, and mAP are given in %, and the speed is given in FPS.

	Precision	Recall	mAP	F1	Speed	RT capable
YOLOv3	50.21	54.57	60.52	51.98	44	Yes
YOLOv4	52.02	56.76	62.49	53.99	**47**	Yes
Faster-RCNN	57.22	62.38	67.52	59.33	15	No
Ours	**61.87**	**66.80**	**72.13**	**63.93**	39	Yes

Table 2. Detailed evaluation on the test data set. This table shows our comparison of three different polyp detection approaches on our benchmarking data. The first two models are baseline models, and the third is our polyp detection system. Precision (P), Recall (R), F1, and mAP are given in %.

Video	YOLOv4				F-RCNN				**Ours**			
	P	R	mAP	F1	P	R	mAP	F1	P	R	mAP	F1
1	54.24	52.30	65.35	53.31	61.94	57.88	69.68	59.84	68.60	65.40	74.60	66.96
2	50.75	50.13	51.47	50.42	55.44	56.63	55.11	56.03	59.10	59.40	61.70	59.25
3	51.06	67.85	70.65	58.25	54.27	72.63	77.78	62.12	57.90	75.60	80.10	65.58
Mean	52.02	56.76	62.49	53.99	57.22	62.38	67.52	59.33	61.87	66.80	72.13	63.93

Table 1 presents the results on our test set for the detection task with YOLOv4, a fast detection algorithm, and Faster R-CNN, a FASTER R-CNN algorithm with a ResNet-101 backbone. For the evaluation, we provide the

F1-score. The F1-score consists of the harmonic mean of precision and the recall, as described in the following equations:

$$\text{Precision} = \frac{TP}{TP + FP} \quad \text{Recall} = \frac{TP}{TP + FN}$$

$$F_1 = \frac{2 * \text{Precision} * \text{Recall}}{\text{Precision} + \text{Recall}} = \frac{2 * TP}{2 * TP + FP + FN}$$

We consider an annotation as true positive (TP) when the predicted boxes and the ground truth boxes overlap at least 50%. In addition, we disclose the mean average precision (mAP) and the mAP50 with a minimum IoU of 0.5 [19]. We calculate the mAP using the integral of the area under the precision-recall curve. Thereby, all predicted boxes are first ranked by their confidence value given by the polyp detection system. Afterward, we compute precision and recall with different thresholds of the confidence values. When the confidence threshold is reduced, the recall increases while the precision decreases, resulting in a precision-recall curve. Finally, we measure the area under the curve precision-recall to receive the mAP value.

Table 2 presents a more detailed view of our results, showing the performance for every test video. Table 1 shows that our approach is outperforming classical benchmarks on our test data. Our approach increases the detection results by 4.6 % points compared to the F-RCNN algorithm. This is due to the architecture of the YOLOR algorithm, which allows fast but still accurate detections. Notably, the algorithm YOLOv4 is still 8 FPS faster than our approach to detect single images. Nevertheless, our approach yielded a huge recall increase of 12.23 % points compared to the fast YOLOv3 and 10.04 % compared to YOLOv4. A recall increase is beneficial for clinical practice as examiners care more about finding a missed polyp than getting distracted by a false positive detection. Figure 5 show a sequence of detection results with our algorithm on the test dataset provided.

Found Polyps Through Extended Vision: To test our extended vision user interface, we tried to test if polyps were missed by the classic front view endoscope but found them through a side camera of the extended view. Therefore we compared the detected polyps of our test set with the annotations of our polyps on the main view camera endoscopy. We then checked how many polyps were found through the extended view. We did this by comparing the polyp detections in the classic front view of the endoscope with the detections of the side camera. If there was no detection in the main camera before a true positive detection in the side camera appeared, we counted the polyp as being missed by the classic detection system but detected by our system with extended vision. Overall, the main view detected 84 different polyps in the test data. 13 polyps in the extended view were not seen in the classic endoscope view.

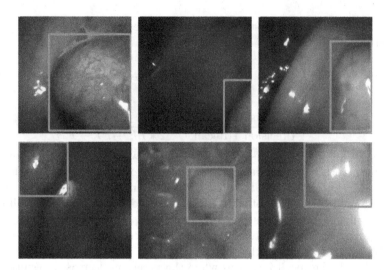

Fig. 5. Detection results. This figure shows some of the true positiv detection results of the side cameras used for extended vision. After the detection the examiner can visualize the polyp with the front camera.

5 Discussion

This chapter shows the limitations of our interface. We mainly show a failure analysis of our system, as well as showing potential risks and challenges that have to be addressed in future work. As our tests and data are based on animal trials, we also discuss the system's clinical application in human interventions.

5.1 Limitations

Fig. 6. Examples of errors in video 17 of the CVC-VideoClinicDB data set. The left image shows a clean detection of a rather flat polyp. The middle image shows a miss of the same polyp due to being blocked by a colon wall, while the right shows a (short) re-detection.

We initiate the discussion of our limitations with failure analysis of our model. First, we refer to Tables 1 and 2, specifically to video 2 which has significantly worse performance compared to the rest. Therefore the examples we choose for the failure analysis are exclusively from video 2. Nevertheless, they differ as some polyps are harder to detect than others. Different lighting in a camera place of the endoscope especially influences the side cameras' detection results (extended view). In addition, bad contrast, diagonal angles, and unusual shapes do enhance the detection difficulty. Hence, multiple reasons can be attributed to the worse performance in some situations.

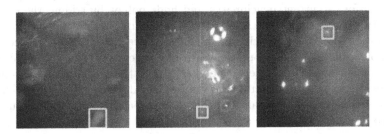

Fig. 7. Examples of errors in video 17 of the CVC-VideoClinicDB data set. The left image shows a clean detection of a rather flat polyp. The middle image shows a miss of the same polyp due to being blocked by a colon wall, while the right shows a (short) re-detection.

E.g., contrast and lighting are one of the main causes of missing or misidentifying a polyp. This is especially true with our extended vision, as the examiner does not see the side cameras. The view of the side cameras is impacted higher by bad lighting conditions. Figure 6 shows some of these bad lighting condition. The right polyps can not be detected because there is no light to make the polyp appear clear on the camera. In the image in the middle, the lighting is reflected very bright. This may be due to the camera being too close too the mucosa. Sometimes those lighting conditions cause FP detection, as seen in the last image on the left side.

Additionally, many FPs created by our system are due to feces and bubbles. Feces are high in contrast, and some polyps are too. Therefore, the neural network is making FP detections, as seen in the left picture of Fig. 7. The FP detection is set on the lower part of the screen; nevertheless, the top of the screen shows a polyp covered by feces and, therefore, is hard to detect. The algorithm is blinded by the lower feces and can not detect the polyp. Another problem is bubbles. Often, the endoscopist has to clean the bowel with water. While doing so, there are constantly emerging bubbles. The detection system sometimes detects these bubbles as their shape may be similar to the shape of polyps.

For clinical use, expanding the examiner's view results in more detected polyps. Therefore, such a system could help the examiner during an actual intervention. Nevertheless, we could only show new detections in animal examples. Our user interface can help the examiner without having to change classical procedures. Nevertheless, first the endoscope with extended vision has to be developed to apply to humans and tested there in future work.

6 Conclusion

We present a prototype that maintains the examiner's classical endoscope view but extends the endoscope with side cameras and AI polyp detection. This AI system detects polyps on the side cameras and alarms the examiner if a polyp is found. The prototype is created by adding two micro cameras to the sides of a classic endoscope. The AI system is trained on human data and fine-tuned with animal data. Then we test the prototype with gene-targeted pigs. The AI outperforms current benchmarks and finds polyps by adding the extended vision to the system. Nevertheless, there are limitations to the system. First, the position and light condition of the side cameras have a high impact on the detection results. If light conditions are bad or cameras are too close to the mucosa, the system cannot detect polyps. Second, the system sometimes detects bubbles, feces, or light reflections as polyps. Third, the system is not ready for clinical interventions in humans. Further development and medical product tests have to be done to allow the system to be applied to the human body.

References

1. Ahn, S.B., Han, D.S., Bae, J.H., Byun, T.J., Kim, J.P., Eun, C.S.: The miss rate for colorectal adenoma determined by quality-adjusted, back-to-back colonoscopies. Gut Liver **6**, 64–70 (2012). https://doi.org/10.5009/gnl.2012.6.1.64
2. Ali, S., et al.: Endoscopy disease detection and segmentation (edd2020) (2020). https://doi.org/10.21227/f8xg-wb80
3. Bernal, J., Sánchez, F.J., Fernández-Esparrach, G., Gil, D., Rodríguez, C., Vilariño, F.: WM-DOVA maps for accurate polyp highlighting in colonoscopy: Validation vs. saliency maps from physicians. Computerized Medical Imaging and Graphics 43, 99–111, July 2015. https://doi.org/10.1016/j.compmedimag.2015.02.007
4. Bernal, J., Sánchez, J., Vilarino, F.: Towards automatic polyp detection with a polyp appearance model. Pattern Recogn. **45**(9), 3166–3182 (2012)
5. Bochkovskiy, A., Wang, C.Y., Liao, H.Y.M.: Yolov4: optimal speed and accuracy of object detection. arXiv preprint arXiv:2004.10934 (2020)
6. Colucci, P.M., Yale, S.H., Rall, C.J.: Colorectal polyps. Clin. Med. Res. **1**(3), 261–262 (2003)
7. Fabrice Bellard, F.t.: Ffmpeg 4.4 (2000). http://www.ffmpeg.org/, [Online; Stand 25.03.2022]
8. Favoriti, P., Carbone, G., Greco, M., Pirozzi, F., Pirozzi, R.E.M., Corcione, F.: Worldwide burden of colorectal cancer: a review. Updat. Surg. **68**(1), 7–11 (2016). https://doi.org/10.1007/s13304-016-0359-y
9. Flisikowska, T., et al.: A porcine model of familial adenomatous polyposis. Gastroenterology **143**(5), 1173–1175 (2012)
10. Gralnek, I.M., et al.: Standard forward-viewing colonoscopy versus full-spectrum endoscopy: an international, multicentre, randomised, tandem colonoscopy trial. Lancet Oncol. **15**(3), 353–360 (2014)
11. Hassan, C., et al.: Full-spectrum (fuse) versus standard forward-viewing colonoscopy in an organised colorectal cancer screening programme. Gut **66**(11), 1949–1955 (2017)

12. Heresbach, D., et al.: Miss rate for colorectal neoplastic polyps: a prospective multicenter study of back-to-back video colonoscopies. Endoscopy **40**(04), 284–290 (2008). https://doi.org/10.1055/s-2007-995618
13. Inc, E.S.: Epiphan dvi2usb 3.0. https://www.epiphan.com/products/dvi2usb-3-0/tech-specs/, [Online; Stand 25.03.2022]
14. Intel Corporation, Willow Garage, I.: Opencv (2000). https://opencv.org/, [Online; Stand 25.03.2022]
15. Jha, D., et al.: Kvasir-SEG: a segmented polyp dataset. In: Ro, Y.M., Cheng, W.-H., Kim, J., Chu, W.-T., Cui, P., Choi, J.-W., Hu, M.-C., De Neve, W. (eds.) MMM 2020. LNCS, vol. 11962, pp. 451–462. Springer, Cham (2020). https://doi.org/10.1007/978-3-030-37734-2_37
16. Krenzer, A., et al.: Fast machine learning annotation in the medical domain: a semi-automated video annotation tool for gastroenterologists (2021)
17. Lambert, R.F.: Endoscopic classification review group. update on the Paris classification of superficial neoplastic lesions in the digestive tract. Endoscopy **37**(6), 570–578 (2005)
18. Leufkens, A., van Oijen, M., Vleggaar, F., Siersema, P.: Factors influencing the miss rate of polyps in a back-to-back colonoscopy study. Endoscopy **44**(05), 470–475 (2012). https://doi.org/10.1055/s-0031-1291666
19. Lin, T.-Y., et al.: Microsoft COCO: common objects in context. In: Fleet, D., Pajdla, T., Schiele, B., Tuytelaars, T. (eds.) ECCV 2014. LNCS, vol. 8693, pp. 740–755. Springer, Cham (2014). https://doi.org/10.1007/978-3-319-10602-1_48
20. Ltd, B.D.P.: Blackmagic - decklink mini recorder 4k. https://www.blackmagicdesign.com/pl/products/decklink/techspecs/W-DLK-33, [Online; Stand 25.03.2022]
21. Misawa, M., et al.: Development of a computer-aided detection system for colonoscopy and a publicly accessible large colonoscopy video database (with video). Gastrointestinal Endoscopy **93**(4), 960–967 (2021)
22. Redmon, J., Farhadi, A.: Yolov3: an incremental improvement. arXiv preprint arXiv:1804.02767 (2018)
23. Ren, S., He, K., Girshick, R., Sun, J.: Faster R-CNN: towards real-time object detection with region proposal networks. In: Advances in Neural Information Processing Systems 28 (2015)
24. Rex, D., et al.: Colonoscopic miss rates of adenomas determined by back-to-back colonoscopies. Gastroenterology **112**(1), 24–28 (1997). https://doi.org/10.1016/s0016-5085(97)70214-2
25. van Rijn, J.C., Reitsma, J.B., Stoker, J., Bossuyt, P.M., van Deventer, S.J., Dekker, E.: Polyp miss rate determined by tandem colonoscopy: a systematic review. Am. J. Gastroenterol. **101**(2), 343–350 (2006). https://doi.org/10.1111/j.1572-0241.2006.00390.x
26. Rogalla, S., et al.: Biodegradable fluorescent nanoparticles for endoscopic detection of colorectal carcinogenesis. Adv. Func. Mater. **29**(51), 1904992 (2019)
27. Silva, J., Histace, A., Romain, O., Dray, X., Granado, B.: Toward embedded detection of polyps in WCE images for early diagnosis of colorectal cancer. Int. J. Comput. Assist. Radiol. Surg. **9**(2), 283–293 (2014)
28. Triadafilopoulos, G., Li, J.: A pilot study to assess the safety and efficacy of the third eye retrograde auxiliary imaging system during colonoscopy. Endoscopy **40**(06), 478–482 (2008)

29. Vázquez, D., et al.: A benchmark for endoluminal scene segmentation of colonoscopy images. J. Healthcare Eng. **2017**, 1–9 (2017). https://doi.org/10.1155/2017/4037190

30. Vázquez, D., et al.: A benchmark for endoluminal scene segmentation of colonoscopy images. J. Healthcare Eng. **2017**, 4037190 (2017). https://doi.org/10.1155/2017/4037190

31. Wang, C.Y., Yeh, I.H., Liao, H.Y.M.: You only learn one representation: Unified network for multiple tasks. arXiv preprint arXiv:2105.04206 (2021)

32. Yim, J.J., et al.: A protease-activated, near-infrared fluorescent probe for early endoscopic detection of premalignant gastrointestinal lesions. Proceedings of the National Academy of Sciences 118(1) (2021)

Using Deep Learning on X-ray Orthogonal Coronary Angiograms for Quantitative Coronary Analysis

Laura Busto[1]([✉])[ID], José A. González-Nóvoa[1][ID], Pablo Juan-Salvadores[1], Víctor Jiménez[2], Andrés Íñiguez[2], and César Veiga[1]

[1] Cardiology Research Group, Galicia Sur Health Research Institute, Vigo, Spain
{laura.busto,cesar.veiga}@iisgaliciasur.es
[2] Cardiology Department, Álvaro Cunqueiro Hospital (SERGAS), Vigo, Spain

Abstract. Coronary Artery Disease is developed when the blood vessels are narrowed, hindering the blood flow into the heart. An accurate assessment of stenosis and lesions is key for the success of Percutaneous Coronary Intervention, the standard procedure for the treatment of this pathology, which consists in the implantation of a stent in the narrowed part of the artery, allowing the correct blood flow. This is the aim of Quantitative Coronary Analysis (QCA), namely the measurement of the arteries diameter in the angiographies. Therefore, the automatic analysis of the QCA from angiograms is of interest for the clinical practice, supporting the decision making, risk assessment, and stent placement. This work proposes a set of tools required for the computation of the QCA, which include the application of deep learning and image processing techniques to angiograms for the automatic identification of contrast frames and the measurement of the diameter along the artery. The first stage of the work addresses the segmentation of the coronary tree, using a U-Net model trained with a self-built dataset, whose annotations have been semi-automatically obtained using edge-detection filters. This model is used for different applications, including the automatic identification of contrast frames, suitable for the QCA study, and the extraction of the vessels centerlines and the measurement of the diameter, useful for the analysis of possible lesions. Results of this process, obtained for a set of sequences captured from several patients are provided, demonstrating the validity of the methodology.

Keywords: Coronary angiograms · Deep learning · Quantitative Coronary Analysis (QCA) · U-Net

1 Introduction

Coronary Artery Disease (CAD) develops when the blood vessels (coronary arteries) that supply blood, oxygen, and nutrients to the heart, become diseased and narrowed, often leading to a decrease in blood flow to the heart [10].

© The Author(s), under exclusive license to Springer Nature Switzerland AG 2022
G. Yang et al. (Eds.): MIUA 2022, LNCS 13413, pp. 869–881, 2022.
https://doi.org/10.1007/978-3-031-12053-4_63

The most common symptoms of CAD include chest pain, pressure or tightness, and shortness of breath. Sometimes there are no symptoms [16], and a complete blockage can cause a heart attack. CAD is the most common type of heart disease in Europeans, representing the 27% of the cerebrovascular diseases, and 20% of the overall Cardiovascular Diseases costs [15].

Treatment for CAD usually includes lifestyle changes, medications, and, if necessary, medical procedures [11]. Lifestyle changes often include quitting smoking, exercising, controlling weight, eating healthy, and reducing stress. Medications may include cholesterol-modifying medications, blood thinners, beta blockers, calcium channel blockers, and medications to control chest pain. Concerning the medical procedures, Percutaneous Coronary Intervention (PCI), sometimes called angioplasty with a stent, is a minimally invasive procedure where a haemodynamist (cardiology specialist) inserts a catheter (long, thin tube) into the narrowed part (lesion) of the artery. A wire with a deflated balloon is inflated to push the blockage aside. Often, a coronary stent -a small, metal structure- is placed in the artery to help keep the narrowed artery open. Research reveals that almost 1 in 3 patients receiving a stent may not have needed one [8].

Angiography is a diagnostic procedure that uses X-rays to make the coronary arteries visible in an imaging sequence [17], also called angiogram, widely used at the cathlab. The assessment of the coronary stenosis severity by a visual estimation from the angiogram has traditionally served as the cornerstone for the diagnosis of patients with known or suspected CAD. In contrast to visual assessment, Quantitative Coronary Analysis (QCA) allows a more accurate estimation of both the diameter stenosis and length of a coronary lesion, parameters proved to contribute to resistance to blood flow [8].

The morphology of coronary arteries could be obtained from real-time interpretation at the catheterisation room, and quantitative analysis as QCA. This technique is used to provide objective quantitative measures from angiographies [20]. QCA-based diagnostic methods have been introduced, such as the SYNTAX score for the evaluation of multi-vessel diseases [13], angiography-derived Fractional Flow Reserve (FFR) [18], and prediction of plaque vulnerability [14]. All those applications rely on a previous task, which is the precise determination of the coronary vessels on X-ray angiographic sequences [4,20].

Nowadays, the use of coronary physiology to assess coronary stenosis severity is gaining importance and is recommended by international revascularisation guidelines to guide revascularisation strategies [11,16]. In this physiology, QCA-based percentage diameter stenosis has proved to be valuable to detect the presence of obstructive CAD [20].

This work presents a set of tools required for the automatic QCA computation from angiographic imaging. Firstly, a deep learning architecture is used for the segmentation of the coronary tree, by training a model with an annotated dataset. Afterwards, the predictions obtained by the model are processed for further applications, as the automatic identification of frames with contrast and the extraction of the centerline and walls of the arteries, allowing the width measurement along the vessel. The remainder of the document is structured as follows: Sect. 2 introduces the required background for this work, Sect. 3 presents the methodology, Sect. 4 gathers the obtained results, and Sect. 5 presents the conclusions of this work.

2   Background

This section includes the background required for this work in terms of image processing techniques used for the dataset semi-automated annotation and posterior analysis of the predictions, U-Net architecture for image segmentation, and QCA fundamentals.

2.1   Image Processing Tools

The extraction of information from images is very data-specific and diverse, as the required tools would depend on the image characteristics and the problem to solve [3]. In the particular case of vessel-like structures segmentation there are several important steps, which are considered down below.

– Noise reduction

Noise reduction is often employed in these tasks as a prior stage [7], before applying suitable operators for the image characteristics. Among the plethora of noise filters in the literature, Median filter [2] is a simple and well-known one. It is a non-linear, smoothing technique that computes the local median in neighboring pixels, using a sliding window, whose size and shape can be a filter parameter. As a smoothing technique, it is effective when removing noise in smooth regions while preserving edges, under certain conditions.

– Ridge detection

Ridge operators are filters used in computer vision to detect edges and ridge-like structures by means of second-order differential operators. Specifically, they use the eigenvalues of the Hessian matrix of the image intensity values. Different filters may be suited for detecting different structures. In particular, Frangi filter [6] has been designed for vessel enhancement filter, using simultaneously all the eigenvalues of the Hessian of the image. The computations for this filter, as others ridge operators, involve a Gaussian kernel with a σ parameter that acts as a smoothing scale. This σ must be tuned taking into account the width of the tubular structure of interest and the imaging modality.

– Skeletonisation

Skeletonisation [21] is the process of reducing binary objects in an image to one pixel wide representations. It can be performed by making successive modifications on an image, identifying and removing the border pixels in each iteration until no more pixels can be removed.

2.2   U-Net

U-Net is a convolutional neural network developed for biomedical image segmentation [12]. It has a symmetric structure, consisting of a contracting path followed by an expanding path. The first half follows the typical architecture of a convolutional network, capturing the context and gradually reducing the spatial resolution dimension. After that, the expansive path gradually recovers the object details, enabling precise localisation. A main characteristic in U-Net is the use of skip connections between paths, which concatenate features from the contracting path to the expanding path to improve object details recovery, allowing faster convergence.

U-Net relies on the use of data augmentation, this is using modified version of the training images by applying elastic transformations. By using data augmentation, the dataset is enlarged with the aim of enhancing the invariance and robustness properties.

With respect to the training, the stage when the network weights are adjusted in each epoch such that a cost function is optimised, several optimisers and cost functions can be employed. One widely used optimiser in Deep Learning applications is Adam [9], an extension to classical stochastic gradient descent. One of the most frequent cost functions used in image segmentation is cross-entropy, defined as follows for an image binary classification:

$$CE = - \sum_{i=1}^{N \times M} y_i \log(p_i) + (1 - y_i) \log(1 - p_i), \qquad (1)$$

where i is an index over all the pixels of an image of size $N \times M$. $y_i \in \{0, 1\}$ corresponds to the pixel classification in the image annotation, background or foreground respectively. p_i is the probability of the pixel i to belong to foreground, predicted by the model.

2.3   QCA Basis

Computer-Assisted QCA was initiated around 1985 by Brown and colleagues [17], who magnified 35-mm cineangiograms obtained from orthogonal projections and hand-traced the arterial edges on a screen. After computer-assisted correction for pincushion distortion, the tracings were digitised, and the orthogonal projections were combined to form a 3D representation of the arterial segment, assuming an elliptical geometry. Although the accuracy and precision were enhanced compared to visual methods, the time the image required to be processed limited the clinical use.

Several automated edge-detection algorithms were then developed and applied to directly acquired digital images or to 35-mm cinefilm digitised images using a cine-video converter. Subsequent iterations of these first-generation devices used enhanced microprocessing speed and digital image acquisition to render the end-user interface more flexible, and they substantially shortened the time required for image analysis.

QCA is divided into several distinct processes, including film digitisation (when applicable), image calibration, and arterial contour detection. For estimation of absolute coronary dimensions, the diagnostic or guiding catheter usually serves as the scaling device. A non-tapered segment of the catheter is selected, and a centerline through the catheter is drawn. Linear density profiles are constructed perpendicular to the catheter centerline, and a weighted average of the first and second derivative functions is used to define the catheter edge points. Individual edge points are connected using an automated algorithm, outliers are discarded, and the edges are smoothed. The diameter of the catheter is used to obtain a calibration factor, which is expressed in millimeters per pixel. The injection catheter dimensions may be influenced by whether contrast or saline is imaged within the catheter tip and by the type of material used in catheter construction. As high-flow injection catheters have been developed, more quantitative angiographic systems have been using contrast-filled injection catheters for image calibration. Automated algorithms are then applied to a selected arterial segment. Absolute coronary dimensions are obtained from the Minimal Lumen Diameter (MLD) reference diameter, and from these, the percentage diameter stenoses are derived.

3   Method

The methodology involves three main parts, namely the acquisition of the angiographic sequences, the identification of the coronary tree in such sequences, and the analysis of these segmentations for applications of interest for the QCA study.

3.1   Image Acquisition

The images used to evaluate the method presented in this work belong to five patients undergoing PCI procedures, performed according to the local protocol at the participating site. Several X-ray angiographic sequences were captured for each patient, from two orthogonal projections, making a total of 999 frames. The sequences have been filmed using conventional fluoroscopy and cine at 15 or 25 fps. During the intervention, a contrast agent is injected to make the arteries perceptible, yielding angiograms in the dataset both with and without contrast. Each frame is a grayscale image, of 512×512 pixels, with a pixel resolution of 8 bits, in DICOM format.

3.2   Coronary Segmentation

The automatic coronary segmentation in the angiograms is the first step for the computations required for the QCA. In this work, this task is accomplished by training a U-Net model with a self-built dataset. The architecture has been fed using a reduced dataset, constructed by randomly selecting 30 images with contrast from the original dataset. This reduced dataset has been split into training and test sets, of 10 and 20 images respectively, randomly selected with the only consideration that frames belonging to a same patient are not used both for training and test.

The annotations of the training set have been semi-automatically obtained by means of an annotation pipeline, which includes image processing components described in Sect. 2.1, in addition to a minimal manual work. These annotations allow to train the model, which is afterwards used to make predictions for the test set.

Annotation Pipeline. The semi-automatic annotation pipeline used in this work includes five stages, namely noise reduction, ridge detection, image thresholding, small elements removal, and manual data curation. Figure 1 provides examples of the outputs of each of the pipeline steps.

Noise reduction has been performed using Median filter with a size of 3×3 (Fig. 1b), and ridge detection used Frangi filter with $\sigma = 5$ (Fig. 1c). Note that Scikit-image [19] implementations of these filters have been used for the computations, the parameters not specified in this section are set to their default values. After that, a threshold of 6×10^{-7} was applied for the binarisation of the Frangi filter output (Fig. 1d). Next, the sets of connected foreground pixels with size under 70 pixels have been removed (Fig. 1e).

The final step, unlike the previous ones, involves manual work, dealing with the curation of the frames, in this case performed by experienced members of the research team using GNU Image Manipulation Program (GIMP) software. This curation mainly consists in removing speckles and joining discontinuities, solving the most noticeable classification errors of the automatic process (Fig. 1f).

U-Net Implementation. The original frames of the training set and their annotations obtained by the pipeline are used to train the U-Net model. The implementation of the architecture in this work has 64 filters in the first convolutional layer, as in the original paper [12], and it has been trained employing Adam optimiser [9], with binary cross-entropy (1) as the cost function, for 120 epochs, and with a batch size of 2. Data augmentation has been used, applying transformations of width and height shifts, shear, zoom, and rotation. The expected inputs are 512×512, 8-bit (integer values from 0 to 255), grayscale images and their corresponding labels as binary masks for the training. The outputs are 512×512 matrices representing the predicted probability of each pixel to belong to the foreground. The trained model has been used to obtain predictions of the test set, which allow the implementation of further applications, as the described in following the subsection.

For the implementation of the U-Net, Keras [5] and Tensorflow [1] Python libraries have been employed. The training of the model has been performed using NVIDIA TESLA A100 GPUs.

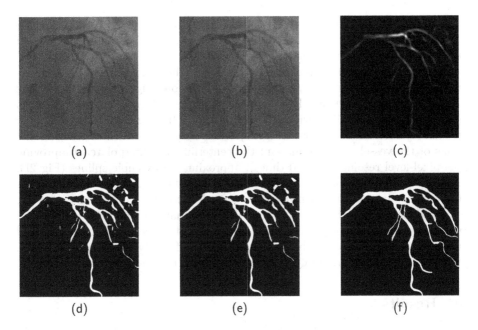

Fig. 1. Examples of the outputs of each of the pipeline steps. (a) Original angiogram, (b) Median filter output (noise reduction), (c) Frangi filter output (ridge detection), (d) Binarisation output, (e) Removal of small objects, (f) Result of the manual correction (final annotation).

3.3 Applications

Once the coronary arteries have been successfully segmented for the test set, the following applications, with interest for the QCA, have been implemented. These applications are the automatic identification of contrast frames and the analysis of regions of interest (ROIs) for the study of the variations in the vessel diameter.

Identification of Frames with Contrast Agent. The segmentation model has been used for the automatic identification of the angiograms with contrast agent, using the original complete dataset. This is accomplished by analysing the number of foreground pixels in the binarisation of the U-Net predictions. In order to estimate the number of foreground pixels to expect in contrast frames, this number has been computed for the training set annotations, obtaining an average of 17558 foreground pixels (6.7% of the image pixels). In case of optimal segmentation, the non-contrast frames would have null foreground, therefore a threshold could be established regarding this feature.

ROI Analysis. For the computation of the QCA it is required to obtain the width along the vessel, identify a narrowing and evaluate the gravity of the possible lesion. With this purpose, reduced ROIs are analysed, computing the vessel width from the U-Net predictions. Figures 2 and 5 provide examples of the results of each step of the process, described below.

In first place, the ROI is manually defined in the original angiogram, determining a part of the artery suspected to be a lesion (Fig. 2c). Afterwards, the vessel centerline is extracted by skeletonising the binary U-Net segmentation (Fig. 2d). Then, the bifurcations (if any) in the ROI are removed, keeping only the artery interest to analyse (Fig. 2e). Next step is the identification of the walls of the vessel. These walls and the centerline are interpolated (improving the pixel-level resolution by 10 times), approximated by cubic splines (Fig. 2f). At each point of the centerline, the orthogonal line is determined, measuring the distance in that direction from the centerline to each of the walls (Fig. 5a). These distances allow to obtain the width fluctuations along the artery. All those steps implemented on a single algorithm that process two orthogonal and matched projections, could be further automated for a QCA analysis tool and, thus, facilitating the use of QCA-based diagnostic methods.

4   Results

Several results are obtained for different stages of the work using the self-built dataset previously described, namely the coronary segmentation, contrast frames identification, and the measurement of the diameter variation.

4.1   Coronary Segmentation

In order to assess the U-Net model performance for the coronary segmentation, the predictions obtained for the test set have been analysed and compared to their corresponding gold standard. This gold standard has been generated in a manual way by experienced members of the research group, using GIMP. Table 1 gathers the results obtained in average and standard deviation after having segmented the test set in terms of conventional classification metrics, such as accuracy, precision, recall, specificity, F1 score, Area under the Receiver operating characteristic curve (AUROC), Dice Coefficient, and Jaccard Index. The metric values in average achieve high values, such as an accuracy of 0.99.

Table 1. Metric results of the segmentations of the test set, in average and standard deviation.

Metric	Accuracy	Precision	Recall	Specificity	F1 score	AUROC	Dice	Jaccard
Average ± std	0.99 ± 0.01	0.89 ± 0.07	0.93 ± 0.06	0.99 ± 0.01	0.94 ± 0.04	0.97 ± 0.03	0.06 ± 0.04	0.89 ± 0.07

An example of the obtained segmentations is provided in Fig. 3.

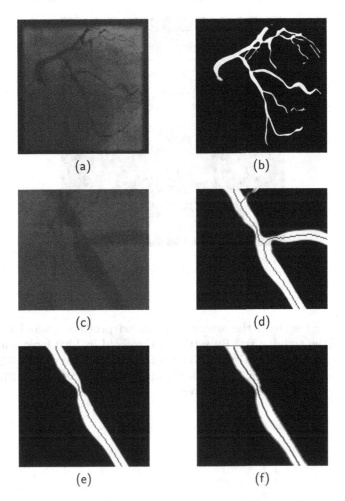

Fig. 2. Examples of the steps of the ROI analysis. (a) Original angiogram, (b) U-Net segmentation of the angiogram, (c) Manually defined ROI with a possible lesion, (d) Segmentation of the ROI and vessel centerline (red), (e) Removal of the segmentation of the ROI and vessel centerline (red), (f) Extraction of the centerline (red) and walls (green) of the vessel. (Color figure online)

4.2 Applications

Contrast Frames Identification. In order to evaluate the ability of the model to distinguish contrast and non-contrast angiograms, the whole original dataset has been segmented, excluding the training frames, and the number of foreground pixels in the predictions have been analysed. This dataset includes 475 frames with contrast and 514 without contrast. Figure 4 shows the histogram of the feature obtained for these frames. The figure shows two noticeable peaks, one closer to 0 (which corresponds to the non-contrast frames) and another around

Fig. 3. Original frame with the binarised U-Net prediction overlaid in red. (Color figure online)

1750, which agrees with the average foreground pixels computed in the gold standard of the training set. By setting a threshold in 1300 foreground pixels, this approach would correctly detect all the non-contrast frames and 452 contrast frames, which means a 100% and 95.16% of the non-contrast and with contrast frames correctly identified, respectively.

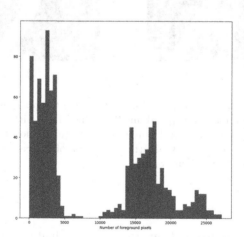

Fig. 4. Histogram of the number of foreground pixels.

ROI Analysis. In order to test the methodology for the measurement of the vessel diameter in a narrowed part of the coronary, an experienced cardiologist

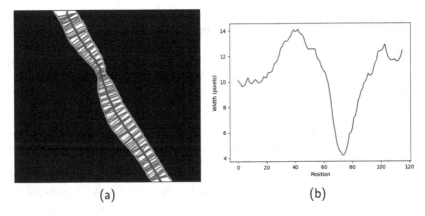

Fig. 5. Coronary width measurement in a ROI extracted from the original frame in Fig. 2a. (a) Perpendicular cuts along the narrowed artery, (b) Graphical representation of the width evolution measured in the cuts in (a) (from distal to proximal).

identified a possible lesion in Fig. 2a, determining the ROI shown in Fig. 2c. The method obtained the orthogonal cuts along the artery depicted in Fig. 5a, whose width evolution (from distal to proximal) can be seen in Fig. 5b. It is noticeable the narrowing in the vessel.

Repeating the process in an orthogonal projection of the ROI, correctly matched, would allow a 3D reconstruction of the vessel and the computation of the coronary section, required for the QCA analysis.

5   Conclusion

This work proposes a set of tools for the extraction of information from coronary angiograms that can be used for the QCA analysis. The methodology includes the coronary tree segmentation, accomplished by the training of a deep learning (U-Net) model with a dataset, which was annotated using a proposed semiautomatic pipeline. This annotation pipeline involves several image processing techniques, such as denoising filters, ridge operators, and skeletonisers.

In addition, this work presents a way of analysing the segmentation results that permits to implement new applications such as the identification of contrasted agent frames or the extraction of the width variation along a narrowed part of an artery. Results presented in this work demonstrate the validity of the proposed methodology, that, when performed on orthogonal matched projections, could be used for the automatic QCA computations, allowing QCA-based diagnosis.

References

1. Abadi, M., et al.: TensorFlow: Large-Scale Machine Learning on Heterogeneous Systems (2015). http://tensorflow.org/, software available from tensorflow.org

2. Bovik, A.C., Huang, T.S., Munson, D.C.: The effect of median filtering on edge estimation and detection. IEEE Trans. Patt. Anal. Mach. Intell. PAMI-9(2), 181–194 (1987). https://doi.org/10.1109/TPAMI.1987.4767894

3. Busto, L., et al.: Automatic identification of bioprostheses on X-ray angiographic sequences of transcatheter aortic valve implantation procedures using deep learning. Diagnostics 12(2) (2022). https://doi.org/10.3390/diagnostics12020334, https://www.mdpi.com/2075-4418/12/2/334

4. Cervantes-Sanchez, F., Cruz-Aceves, I., Hernandez-Aguirre, A., Hernandez-Gonzalez, M.A., Solorio-Meza, S.E.: Automatic segmentation of coronary arteries in x-ray angiograms using multiscale analysis and artificial neural networks. Appl. Sci. 9(24) (2019). https://www.mdpi.com/2076-3417/9/24/5507

5. Chollet, F., et al.: Keras. https://keras.io (2015)

6. Frangi, A.F., Niessen, W.J., Vincken, K.L., Viergever, M.A.: Multiscale vessel enhancement filtering. In: Wells, W.M., Colchester, A., Delp, S. (eds.) MICCAI 1998. LNCS, vol. 1496, pp. 130–137. Springer, Heidelberg (1998). https://doi.org/10.1007/BFb0056195

7. Gupta, S., Gupta, A.: Dealing with noise problem in machine learning datasets: a systematic review. Proc. Comput. Sci. 161, 466–474 (2019). https://doi.org/10.1016/j.procs.2019.11.146, https://www.sciencedirect.com/science/article/pii/S1877050919318575, the Fifth Information Systems International Conference, Surabaya, Indonesia, 23–24 July 2019

8. Kern, M., Samady, H.: Current concepts of integrated coronary physiology in the catheterization laboratory. J. Am. Coll. Cardiol. 55, 173–185 (2010)

9. Kingma, D.P., Ba, J.: Adam: a method for stochastic optimization (2014). http://arxiv.org/abs/1412.6980, cite arxiv:1412.6980 Comment: Published as a conference paper at the 3rd International Conference for Learning Representations, San Diego (2015)

10. Mendis, S., Puska, P., Norrving, B.E., Organization, W.H., et al.: Global atlas on cardiovascular disease prevention and control. World Health Organization (2011)

11. Stone, P.H., et al.: Prediction of progression of coronary artery disease and clinical outcomes using vascular profiling of endothelial shear stress and arterial plaque characteristics. Prediction study. Circulation 126, 172–181 (2012). https://doi.org/10.1161/CIRCULATIONAHA.112.096438

12. Ronneberger, O., Fischer, P., Brox, T.: U-Net: convolutional networks for biomedical image segmentation. In: Medical Image Computing and Computer-Assisted Intervention - MICCAI 2015, May 2015

13. Sianos, G., et al.: The syntax score: an angiographic tool grading the complexity of coronary artery disease. EuroIntervention J. EuroPCR Collab. Working Group Intervent. Cardiol. Eur. Soc. Cardiol. 1(2), 219–227 (2005)

14. Stone, P.H.E.A.: Prediction of progression of coronary artery disease and clinical outcomes using vascular profiling of endothelial shear stress and arterial plaque characteristics: the prediction study. Circulation 126, 172–181 (2012)

15. Timmis, A., et al.: European society of cardiology: cardiovascular disease statistics 2019. Eur. Heart J. 41(1), 12–85 (2019). https://doi.org/10.1093/eurheartj/ehz859

16. Tonino, P.A., et al.: Fractional flow reserve versus angiography for guiding percutaneous coronary intervention. New England J. Med. 360(3), 213–224 (2009)

17. Topol, E.J., Teirstein, P.: Textbook of Interventional Cardiology, 8th Edition. Qualitative and Quantitative Coronary Angiography. Elsevier, ISBN: 9780323568142 (2019)

18. Tu, S., et al.: Fractional flow reserve calculation from 3-dimensional quantitative coronary angiography and TIMI frame count: a fast computer model to quantify the functional significance of moderately obstructed coronary arteries. JACC: Cardiovasc. Interv. **7**(7), 768–777 (2014). https://doi.org/10.1016/j.jcin.2014.03.004, https://www.sciencedirect.com/science/article/pii/S1936879814007912
19. van der Walt, S., et al.: The scikit-image contributors: scikit-image: image processing in Python. PeerJ **2**, e453 (2014). https://doi.org/10.7717/peerj.453
20. Yang, S., et al.: Deep learning segmentation of major vessels in X-ray coronary angiography. Sci. Rep. **9**(1), 1–11 (2019)
21. Zhang, T.Y., Suen, C.Y.: A fast parallel algorithm for thinning digital patterns. Commun. ACM **27**(3), 236–239 (1984)

Efficient Pipeline for Rapid Detection of Catheters and Tubes in Chest Radiographs

Hossam Mohamed Sarhan[1]([✉]), Hesham Ali[1], Eman Ehab[1], Sahar Selim[1,2], and Mustafa Elattar[1,2]

[1] Medical Imaging and Image Processing Research Group, Center for Informatics Science, Nile University, Giza, Egypt
h.mohamedgamaleldin@nu.edu.eg

[2] School of Information Technology and Computer Science, Nile University, Giza, Egypt

Abstract. Catheters are life support devices. Human expertise is often required for the analysis of X-rays in order to achieve the best positioning without misplacement complications. Many hospitals in underprivileged regions around the world lack the sufficient radiology expertise to frequently process X-rays for patients with catheters and tubes. This deficiency may lead to infections, thrombosis, and bleeding due to misplacement of catheters. In the last 2 decades, deep learning has provided solutions to various problems including medical imaging challenges. So instead of depending solely on radiologists to detect catheter/tube misplacement in X-rays, computers could exploit their fast and precise detection capability to notify physicians of a possible complication and aid them identify the cause. Several groups attempted to solve this problem but in the absence of large and rich datasets that include many types of catheters and tubes. In this paper, we utilize the RANZCR-CLiP dataset to train an EfficientNet B1 classification model to classify the presence and placement of 4 types of catheters/tubes. In order to improve our classification results, we used Ben Graham's preprocessing method to improve image contrast and remove noise. In addition, we convert catheter/tube landmarks to masks and concatenate them to images to provide guidance on the catheter's/tube's existence and placement. Finally, EfficientNet B1 reached a ROC AUC of 96.73% and an accuracy of 91.92% on the test set.

Keywords: Catheter · Tube · Deep learning · Segmentation · Multiclass classification

1 Introduction

The Catheters and tubes are devices that have many uses in daily medical practice. They are frequently used for delivery of intravenous fluids, chemotherapeutic agents, total parenteral nutrition, and drug administration. In addition, tubes could be used for fluid and pus drainage in body cavities such as the lung and pleural cavity. Catheters are also essential for neonates who were born with birth defects or with low body weight, which requires precise positioning. There are numerous types of catheters and tubes including endotracheal tubes (EET), nasogastric tubes (NGT), central venous catheters (CVC), umbilical arterial catheters (UAC), umbilical venous catheters (UVC), and Swan Ganz Catheter (SGC).

CVC is inserted in veins for many purposes such as administration of vasoactive medications, insertion of devices, hemodialysis, and plasmapheresis [1]. Misplacement of CVC could lead to several complications like arrhythmias, pneumothorax, airway obstruction, thrombosis, and internal hemorrhage [1]. NGT is used in standard health-care practice for dealing with intestinal obstruction and as a feeding tube [2]. Incorrect positioning of NGT could lead to perforation and esophageal trauma [2]. At the same time, prolonged inaccurate use of NGT result in gastrointestinal irritation and electrolyte imbalance [2]. EET is utilized to secure airway for patients with ventilation problems such as COVID-19 patients [3]. Mispositioning of EET could result in perforation, aspiration, bleeding, or infection [3]. SGC is used to monitor cardiac function and blood flow.

Due to the numerous severe complications that could result from misplacement of catheter and tubes, a fast and accurate bedside catheter/tube mispositioning detection method is seriously needed to aid healthcare professionals and provide quicker intervention to avoid further damage. Deep learning offers a successful solution to this problem due to its ability to learn complex patterns in medical images and provide fast and accurate classification of catheters and tubes. In this paper, we propose an end-to-end pipeline for detection of catheters and tubes in a chest radiograph in addition to whether each of them is placed correctly, incorrectly or borderline. We introduce the use of optimized Ben Graham's method to preprocess images before training and inference. This method decreases noise and enhances the contrast of the image. We also exploit catheter/tube annotation to create binary masks of the tracks of catheters and tubes and generate masks for unannotated images using self-supervised learning. Finally, we use both images and masks for classification, and we use a hybrid weighted loss function of cross entropy and binary cross entropy to improve classification results.

2 Methods

In this section, we introduce the methodology of this paper first by describing the dataset used in the analysis and its properties. Then, we illustrate the proposed data preprocessing technique. Finally, we outline the experimental design of our pipeline in details.

2.1 Dataset

The dataset we used in our analysis is RANZCR-CLiP dataset. It is provided by the Royal Australian and New Zealand College of Radiologists (RANZCR) [4]. The data consists of 30,083 chest X-ray images with each radiographic image containing a catheter or a tube or more than one at the same time. The data are labelled into 11 labels categorized into 4 main types of catheters/tubes: namely, central venous catheter (CVC), endotracheal tube (EET), nasogastric tube (NGT), and Swan Ganz catheter (SGC). Each of CVC, EET, and NGT can either be normally positioned, abnormally positioned, or borderline. There is an additional label for NGT, and it is being incompletely imaged. All the radiographs are RGB images, and each radiograph is taken form 1 patient only. Data augmentation was randomly applied using *Albumentations* to the images to increase the robustness of the model to shifts and variations in input X-rays [5]. Augmentation techniques include horizontal flipping, rotation, distortion, and altering saturation, brightness, and contrast.

2.2 Data Preprocessing

The images are preprocessed by cropping the uninformative areas at the edge of the X-ray radiograph. They are then further preprocessed by Ben Graham's method for the purpose of improving the contrast of the image and removing noise. The method works by adding a weighted Gaussian blur to the image, which lessens the noise in noisy images and improves the lighting condition for the poorly lit images. Finally, all the images were resized to the size of (224×224) before using in segmentation and classification (Fig. 1).

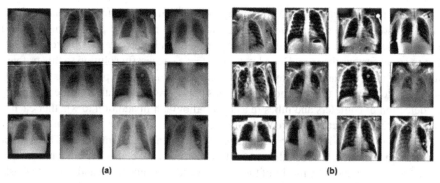

Fig. 1. Ben Graham preprocessing results. A sample of 12 images taken form RANZCR-CLiP dataset is represented in (a) without preprocessing and in (b) after preprocessing.

2.3 Experimental Analysis

In this section, we introduce the experimental design of our proposed pipeline. The pipeline consists of 2 main stages, segmentation, and classification. We go through each stage in details in this section.

2.3.1 Segmentation

Of the 30,083 images found in the RANCR-CLiP dataset, only 9000 images have corresponding annotations for the XY coordinates of the position of catheter/tube. These annotations were constructed into binary masks with ones in the trail of each catheter/tube and zeros for the background. The 9000 reconstructed masks alongside their corresponding chest radiographs, were divided into a training set (8000 samples) and a validation set (1000 samples). Three segmentation models were then trained on the training set for 30 epochs and validated by calculating accuracy, Jaccard index and dice coefficient. The model with the highest accuracy and Jaccard index was saved in order to be used for the prediction of weak labels for the remaining 21,083 images with no corresponding annotations.

2.3.2 Classification

The whole dataset is divided randomly into training set, validation set and test set with sizes of 23983 samples, 100 samples, and 6000 samples, respectively. After that, each RGB image is concatenated to an RGB mask to form an input image of 6 channels for the multi-label classification model. Since there can only be either 1 EET in the trachea in a given radiograph or none, the placement and existence of EET could be treated as multi-class classification problem instead of a multi-label classification problem. Thus, an additional label (No EET) is added to classify the 4 labels pertaining EET using one classification head. The loss function is was a weighted hybrid loss of the cross-entropy loss (for EET) and the binary cross entropy loss (for the rest of the labels) with weights 1:9, respectively. The weights are obtained by experimenting with a grid of various weight ratios and evaluated on validation set.

Three classification models, namely *EfficientNet*, *SE-ResNeXT*, and *Inception-ResNet* are trained and then tested by calculating the following metrics: accuracy, F1 score, and the area under the receiving operative characteristics curve (AUC) [6–8]. MADGRAD algorithm is used to optimize the loss function [8]. Furthermore, learning rate scheduler is utilized to reduce learning rate on plateau, with a starting learning rate of 3×10^4. Finally, the validation set was used for hyperparameter tuning, which includes searching for the most suitable initial learning rate and weights for the hybrid loss function (Fig. 2).

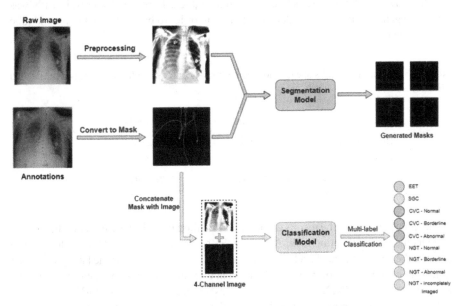

Fig. 2. Catheter/tube misplacement detection pipeline

3 Results

The segmentation step was carried out by experimenting with 3 different segmentation models. ResUNet 18 is similar to the regular UNet-like architecture with the addition of using ResNet 18 as the UNet's encoder. Pyramid Attention Network (PAN) was also used, as it exploits the enhanced ability to attend to pixel-level contextual information by incorporating the feature pyramid attention module (FPA) and the global attention upsample module (GAU) [9]. Furthermore, we included the Feature Pyramid Network (FPN) segmentation architecture [10]. FPN operates by including various scales of the input image, thus forming the encoder feature pyramid. After producing masks at each encoder scale, the masks are then rescaled to original size and combine to 1 final output mask [10]. The advantage of FPN is that it leverages the multi-scale pyramid structure to extract more sematic features at different levels, not just at the level of the input image [10]. The encoders of both PAN and FPN are based on the EfficientNet B1 architecture [7, 9, 10].

The segmentation performance results of the 3 models are shown in Table 1 in terms accuracy and Jaccard scores. All the models demonstrate remarkably high accuracy and Jaccard scores, which indicates the capability of the models to predict accurate synthetic masks for images with no corresponding catheter/tube annotations. ResUNet 18 and PAN exhibit very close performance in terms of both accuracy and Jaccard. While the segmentation accuracy of FPN is still quite close to the other 2 models, it stands out by achieving a higher Jaccard score with a noticeable difference. As a result, FPN was utilized to generate masks for unlabeled images in order to be used for catheter and tube misplacement classification.

Table 1. Segmentation results of each model in terms of accuracy and Jaccard index on the labeled validation set.

Model	Accuracy	Jaccard
ResUNet 18	98.29%	75.23%
PAN	98.34%	75.26%
FPN	**98.40%**	**76.30%**

In Table 2, we show the results of the 3 classification models we used for catheter/tube misplacement classification task. Accuracy, F1 score, and ROC AUC are calculated to measure the performance of each model. Average F1 and AUC across the labels are robust indicators of model performance in the presence of imbalance in the dataset. While the accuracy of both ResNeXT and Inception ResNet are similar, EfficientNet stands out with a considerable margin. In addition, EfficientNet also achieves higher F1 score, and ROC AUC compared to the other 2 models with much less trainable parameters. The superior performance of EfficientNet depends on the compound scaling technique. Commonly used CNN architectures like ResNet and DenseNet use arbitrary scaling of depth, width, and resolution. Some techniques focus on scaling in one direction, either width, depth, or resolution, which leads to higher performance with only images of specific qualities. Whereas images with different properties lead to much lower performance. The EfficientNet family of architectures solve this problem by scaling in all 3 areas using compound scaling coefficients, which adjust the network depth, width, and resolution to the input data.

Table 2. Classification results of each model in terms of accuracy, F1 score and ROC AUC along with the number of parameters for each model on RANZCR test set.

Model	Accuracy	F1	AUC	Parameters
EfficientNet B1	**91.92%**	**90.21%**	**96.73%**	**4.02 M**
ResNeXT	85.59%	88.30%	95.79%	25.54 M
Inception ResNet	86.49%	89.04%	96.16%	54.33 M

The ROC AUC of each label during the training of EfficientNet B1 for 30 epochs is displayed in the box plot in Fig. 3. Swan Ganz Catheter, abnormally placed NGT, normally placed NGT and normally placed EET demonstrate the highest scores (close to 100%) with a notably low interquartile range. Furthermore, normally placed NGT and incompletely imaged NGT still perform remarkably high with almost no outliers and substantially low variance. This leaves borderline NGT with fairly less AUC and wider interquartile range, which can be explained by the subtlety of borderline NGT classification. Borderline NGT may be easily misclassified because it might be either more similar to normal NGT or abnormal NGT. The difference between borderline NGT and the other NGT classes is not well-defined, thus it can be misclassified as either normal or abnormal. Although the AUC score of abnormally placed EET and borderline EET is not as high as normally placed EET, their scores are still comparable to that of normal EET with a median AUC above 85% and 90%, respectively. Finally, CVC catheters are clearly more misclassified than the rest. This could be explained by the relatively low contrast of CVC due to vascular blood flow. Nonetheless, ROC AUC of CVC is still above 70%, which indicates a reasonable performance of the classifier on all labels.

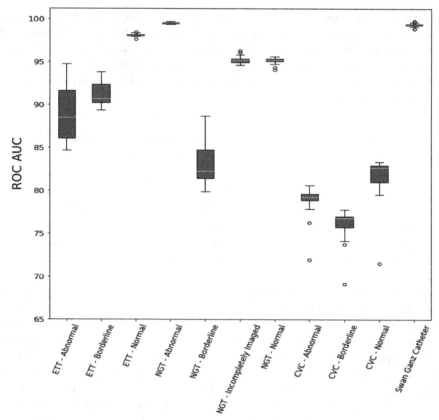

Fig. 3. Box plot of ROC AUC of each label in the dataset; including all the catheters and tubes involved and their placement condition

4 Discussion

We have presented a new pipeline for catheter/tube detection in X-ray images. We first preprocess the image using Ben Graham's preprocessing method, which enhances the image contrast and lessens the effect of noise. This method has not been used before in the problem of catheter/tube detection. It improves classification accuracy by making catheters/tubes more visible in radiographs compared to the background and the internal organs. Furthermore, we converted landmark catheter/tube annotations present only for some images in the dataset into binary masks that are later used to train a segmentation model. The highest-performing segmentation model, which achieved an accuracy of 98.40% and a ROC AUC of 76.30%, is used to generate masks for unlabeled images.

This self-supervised approach ensures accurate prediction of additional masks and provides more data without the need for more human expertise for annotation. Moreover, the concatenation of 1-channel masks and 3-channel images creates 4-channel images that contain the enhanced X-ray radiographs and mask annotations, which guide the model by outlining each catheter/tube's path in addition to its entry and exit points.

This technique greatly improves the classification results without the need for additional labelling or training remarkably more parameters like the teacher-student learning scheme. Despite not being a common practice in the literature, the concatenation of masks and images may be favorable because the mask is added as an additional channel, which allows the model to extract more useful features for classification and does not simply lay off annotations on the image. Besides, the use of EfficientNet B1 achieved high performance scores on all the type of catheters and tubes without being highly computationally expensive. Finally, the weighted hybrid loss function of cross entropy and binary cross entropy does not only improve classification accuracy but also incorporates multi-class classification for EET and multi-label classification, seamlessly. The efficiency of our proposed pipeline is based on the ability to train a model that classifies a number of catheters and their placement with high performance, relatively low computational power, and minimal human annotation.

The problem of catheter and tube detection has not been mentioned many times in the literature probably due to the lack of sufficiently large datasets. However, a few groups attempted to provide a solution to this problem by creating synthetic data [11]. Other groups attempted to increase the size of the training data by classify catheters or tubes in addition to other observations that are typically monitored in X-rays such as effusion, congestion, and consolidation [12]. Direct comparison between the proposed solutions for the problem of catheter and tube detection can be very difficult to achieve due to the wide variety of used methodologies, the difference in datasets, and the diversity of catheters and tubes involved in the analysis. Nonetheless, the available methods could still be analyzed and contrasted in terms of their performance, experimental design, and inclusiveness of numerous catheter/tube labels.

In the absence of labeled data, Yi et al. used synthetic on 100 chest radiographs and achieved a ROC AUC score of 87% using ROI segmentation and support vector machines (SVM). The reliability on synthetic labels may be questionable despite the high performance [11]. The small dataset included EET and NGT like RANZCR in addition to umbilical venous catheters (UVC) and umbilical arterial catheters (UAC) that are only present in neonates [11]. Besides, their dataset also lacked CVC and Swan Ganz catheters. The same group later used a slightly larger dataset of 777 images with the same labels as in their previous contribution [12]. The dataset was labelled by radiologists, but the sample size is still clearly small to train a robust generalizable model [12]. Lakhani et al. [13] trained a GoogleNet classifier on 300 adult chest radiographs to classify the presence of EET and their positioning status. However, beside the small dataset and the lack of ability to classify catheters and tubes other than EET, their model's AUC (80.9%) is remarkably less than our average AUC for EET (97%) [13].

Furthermore, NLP algorithms were used to label part of a chest X-ray dataset by Niehues et al. [14]. They also used human-in-the-loop approach to train their model to classify several occurrences and objects in chest radiographs including NGT and CVC and reached considerably high AUC scores [14]. However, their scores cannot be compared to ours for 2 main reasons: (i) their problem is different since most of the dataset does not contain catheters, (ii) they only classify whether NGT or CVC exist in the X-ray image but not whether they are misplaced or not, thus serving a different purpose. Although Khan et al. [15] used a similar approach to ours, the did not use any data preprocessing techniques, which may affect the classification accuracy on unseen noisy data [15]. X-rays taken in suboptimal conditions in underprivileged regions are usually very noisy, thus they need an effective preprocessing methods to enhance image contrast and lessen the effect of noise. Moreover, their methodology and results of Khan et al. are very poorly described, and they report their results in terms of public and private scores but fail to mention the interpretation of these scores [15]. Nonetheless, we still reached slightly greater ROC AUC than their cross-validation AUC using the same architecture (EfficientNet B1) [15]. Finally, the other architectures achieve cross-validation AUC higher than ours by a margin of less than 0.2% but at a much larger computational cost [15].

Despite the high performance and the significant practicality of our proposed pipeline, several modifications and enhancements could be carried out to further improve the model's accuracy and generalizability as well as provide more effective aid to the healthcare practitioners. Model interpretability and explainability could largely help physicians understand the deep learning model's prediction instead of dealing with a black box model that takes a chest radiograph as input and outputs the predicted catheters/tubes and their position. Explainable Artificial Intelligence is an active area of research with a room for improvement and it has not been yet applied to many problems including catheter/tube detection. Furthermore, the inclusion of more catheters and tubes and more types of medical devices may raise the adaptation power of the model to unseen data that contain different object than in the training data. Moreover, real-time catheter segmentation and detection could present a radical solution for monitoring procedures that involve catheters and tubes as it detects wrong placement during the procedure itself, thus greatly lessening possible complications Finally, with the availability of more large, annotated datasets, including various datasets in the analysis may boost the generalizability and robustness of the deep learning model.

5   Conclusion

In this work, we have built a pipeline for catheter and tube detection in chest radiographs. We enhanced the X-ray images by Ben Graham's preprocessing methods and converted catheter/tube landmark annotations into masks. Segmentation was conducted to use the trained model (FPN) to predict masks for unannotated images. Images and masks were then used together to improve classification results. Our classifier (EfficientNet B1) detects 4 types of catheters/tubes and predict if any requires repositioning. This pipeline is fast and accurate at detecting misplaced catheters, thus helping both healthcare professionals and patients avoid complications due to incorrect catheter placement.

References

1. Seifert, H., Jansen, B., Widmer, A.F., Farr, B.M.: Central venous catheter. In: Catheter-Related Infections, 2nd edn., pp. 293–326, December 2021. https://doi.org/10.5005/jp/books/12452_12
2. Sigmon, D.F., An, J.: Nasogastric tube. StatPearls, November 2021. https://www.ncbi.nlm.nih.gov/books/NBK556063/. Accessed 16 Apr 2022

3. Ahmed, R.A., Boyer, T.J.: Endotracheal tube. StatPearls, November (2021). https://www.ncbi.nlm.nih.gov/books/NBK539747/. Accessed 16 Apr 2022

4. RANZCR CLiP - Catheter and Line Position Challenge | Kaggle. https://www.kaggle.com/competitions/ranzcr-clip-catheter-line-classification/. Accessed 15 Apr 2022

5. Buslaev, A., Iglovikov, V.I., Khvedchenya, E., Parinov, A., Druzhinin, M., Kalinin, A.A.: Albumentations: fast and flexible image augmentations. Information **11**(2) (2020). https://doi.org/10.3390/INFO11020125

6. Hu, J., Shen, L., Albanie, S., Sun, G., Wu, E.: Squeeze-and-excitation networks. IEEE Trans. Pattern Anal. Mach. Intell. **42**(8), 2011–2023 (2017). https://doi.org/10.48550/arxiv.1709.01507

7. Tan, M., Le, Q.V.: EfficientNet: rethinking model scaling for convolutional neural networks. In: 36th International Conference on Machine Learning, ICML 2019, vol. 2019, pp. 10691–10700, May 2019. https://doi.org/10.48550/arxiv.1905.11946

8. Defazio, A., Jelassi, S.: Adaptivity without compromise: a momentumized, adaptive, dual averaged gradient method for stochastic optimization (2021). https://doi.org/10.48550/arxiv.2101.11075

9. Li, H., Xiong, P., An, J., Wang, L.: Pyramid attention network for semantic segmentation. In: British Machine Vision Conference 2018, BMVC 2018, May 2018. https://doi.org/10.48550/arxiv.1805.10180

10. Lin, T.Y., Dollár, P., Girshick, R., He, K., Hariharan, B., Belongie, S.: Feature pyramid networks for object detection. In: Proceedings - 30th IEEE Conference on Computer Vision and Pattern Recognition, CVPR 2017, vol. 2017, pp. 936–944, November 2017. https://doi.org/10.1109/CVPR.2017.106

11. Pitts, T., Gidopoulos, N.I., Lathiotakis, N.N.: Performance of the constrained minimization of the total energy in density functional approximations: the electron repulsion density and potential (2018)

12. Henderson, R.D.E., Yi, X., Adams, S.J., Babyn, P.: Automatic detection and classification of multiple catheters in neonatal radiographs with deep learning. J. Digit. Imaging **34**(4), 888–897 (2021). https://doi.org/10.1007/S10278-021-00473-Y/FIGURES/5

13. Lakhani, P.: Deep convolutional neural networks for endotracheal tube position and X-ray image classification: challenges and opportunities. J. Digit. Imaging **30**(4), 460–468 (2017). https://doi.org/10.1007/S10278-017-9980-7/FIGURES/10

14. Niehues, S.M., et al.: Deep-learning-based diagnosis of bedside chest X-ray in intensive care and emergency medicine. Investig. Radiol. **56**(8), 525–534 (2021). https://doi.org/10.1097/RLI.0000000000000771

15. Khan, A.B.M., Ali, S.M.A.: Early detection of malpositioned catheters and lines on chest X-rays using deep learning. In: ICAICST 2021 - 2021 International Conference on Artificial Intelligence and Computer Science Technology, pp. 51–55, June 2021. https://doi.org/10.1109/ICAICST53116.2021.9497809

FCN-Transformer Feature Fusion for Polyp Segmentation

Edward Sanderson[✉][ID] and Bogdan J. Matuszewski[ID]

Computer Vision and Machine Learning (CVML) Group,
University of Central Lancashire, Preston, UK
{esanderson4,bmatuszewski1}@uclan.ac.uk
https://www.uclan.ac.uk/research/activity/cvml

Abstract. Colonoscopy is widely recognised as the gold standard procedure for the early detection of colorectal cancer (CRC). Segmentation is valuable for two significant clinical applications, namely lesion detection and classification, providing means to improve accuracy and robustness. The manual segmentation of polyps in colonoscopy images is time-consuming. As a result, the use of deep learning (DL) for automation of polyp segmentation has become important. However, DL-based solutions can be vulnerable to overfitting and the resulting inability to generalise to images captured by different colonoscopes. Recent transformer-based architectures for semantic segmentation both achieve higher performance and generalise better than alternatives, however typically predict a segmentation map of $\frac{h}{4} \times \frac{w}{4}$ spatial dimensions for a $h \times w$ input image. To this end, we propose a new architecture for full-size segmentation which leverages the strengths of a transformer in extracting the most important features for segmentation in a primary branch, while compensating for its limitations in full-size prediction with a secondary fully convolutional branch. The resulting features from both branches are then fused for final prediction of a $h \times w$ segmentation map. We demonstrate our method's state-of-the-art performance with respect to the mDice, mIoU, mPrecision, and mRecall metrics, on both the Kvasir-SEG and CVC-ClinicDB dataset benchmarks. Additionally, we train the model on each of these datasets and evaluate on the other to demonstrate its superior generalisation performance.
Code available: https://github.com/CVML-UCLan/FCBFormer.

Keywords: Polyp segmentation · Medical image processing · Deep learning

1 Introduction

Colorectal cancer (CRC) is a leading cause of cancer mortality worldwide; e.g., in the United States, it is the third largest cause of cancer deaths, with 52,500 CRC deaths predicted in 2022 [27]. In Europe, it is the second largest cause of cancer deaths, with 156,000 deaths in 27 EU countries reported in 2020 [7].

© The Author(s) 2022
G. Yang et al. (Eds.): MIUA 2022, LNCS 13413, pp. 892–907, 2022.
https://doi.org/10.1007/978-3-031-12053-4_65

Colon cancer survival rate depends strongly on an early detection. It is commonly accepted that most colorectal cancers evolve from adenomatous polyps [26]. Colonoscopy is the gold standard for colon screening as it can facilitate detection and treatment during the same procedure, e.g., by using the resect-and-discard and diagnose-and-disregard approaches. However, colonoscopy has some limitations; e.g., It has been reported that between 17%–28% of colon polyps are missed during colonoscopy screening procedures [18,20]. Importantly, it has been assessed that improvement of polyp detection rates by 1% reduces the risk of CRC by approximately 3% [4]. It is therefore vital to improve polyp detectability. Equally, correct classification of detected polyps is limited by variability of polyp appearance and subjectivity of the assessment. Lesion detection and classification are two tasks for which intelligent systems can play key roles in improving the effectiveness of the CRC screening and robust segmentation tools are important in facilitating these tasks.

To improve on the segmentation of polyps in colonoscopy images, a range of deep learning (DL) -based solutions [8,13,14,17,19,22,28,30,32,37] have been proposed. Such solutions are designed to automatically predict segmentation maps for colonoscopy images, in order to provide assistance to clinicians performing colonoscopy procedures. These solutions have traditionally used fully convolutional networks (FCNs) [1,9,10,13–15,17,25,28,39]. However, transformer-based architectures [24,32–34,36] have recently become popular for semantic segmentation and shown superior performance over FCN-based alternatives. This is likely a result of the ability of transformers to efficiently extract features on the basis of a global receptive field from the first layers of the model through global attention. This is especially true in generalisability tests, where a model is trained on one dataset and evaluated on another dataset in order to test its robustness to images from a somewhat different distribution to that considered during training. Some studies have also combined FCNs and transformers/attention mechanisms [3,8,19,22,30,37] in order to combine their strengths in a single architecture for medical image segmentation, however these hybrid architectures do not outperform the highest performing FCN-based and transformer-based models in this task, notably MSRF-Net [28] (FCN) and SSFormer [32] (transformer). One significant limitation of most the highlighted transformer-based architectures is however that the predicted segmentation maps of these models are typically of a lower resolution than the input images, i.e. are not full-size. This is due to these models operating on tokens which correspond to patches of the input image rather than pixels.

In this paper, we propose a new architecture for polyp segmentation in colonoscopy images which combines FCNs and transformers to achieve state-of-the-art results. The architecture, named the Fully Convolutional Branch-TransFormer (FCBFormer) (Fig. 1a), uses two parallel branches which both start from a $h \times w$ input image: a fully convolutional branch (FCB) which returns full-size ($h \times w$) feature maps; and a transformer branch (TB) which returns reduced-size ($\frac{h}{4} \times \frac{w}{4}$) feature maps. The output tensors of TB are then upsampled to full-size, concatenated with the output tensors of FCB along the channel

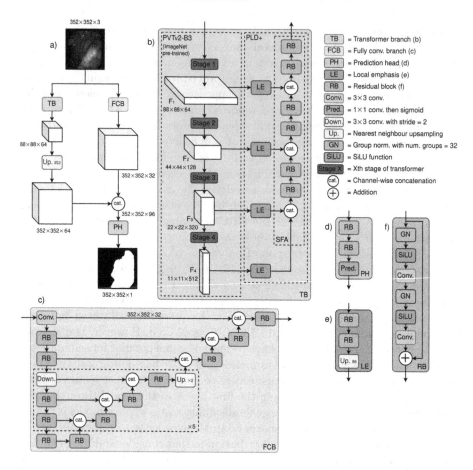

Fig. 1. The architectures of a) FCBFormer, b) the transformer branch (TB), c) the fully convolutional branch (FCB), d) the prediction head (PH), e) the improved local emphasis (LE) module, f) the residual block (RB).

dimension, before a prediction head (PH) processes the concatenated tensors into a full-size segmentation map for the input image. Through the use of the ImageNet [5] pre-trained pyramid vision transformer v2 (PVTv2) [34] as an image encoder, we encourage the model to extract the most important features for segmentation in TB. We then randomly initialise FCB to encourage extraction of the features required for processing outputs of TB into full-size segmentation maps. TB largely follows the structure of the recent SSFormer [32] which predicts segmentation maps of $\frac{h}{4} \times \frac{w}{4}$ spatial dimensions, and which achieved the current state-of-the-art performance on polyp segmentation at reduced-size. However, we update the SSFormer architecture with a new progressive locality decoder (PLD) which features improved local emphasis (LE) and stepwise feature aggregation (SFA). FCB then takes the form of an advanced FCN architecture, composed of a modern variant of residual blocks (RBs) that include group normalisation

[35] layers, SiLU [12] activation functions, and convolutional layers, with a residual connection [11,29]; in addition to dense U-Net style skip connections [25]. PH is then composed of RBs and a final pixel-wise prediction layer which uses convolution with 1×1 kernels. On this basis, we achieve state-of-the-art performance with respect to the mDice, mIoU, mPrecision, and mRecall metrics on the Kvasir-SEG [16] and CVC-ClinicDB [2] datasets, and on generalisability tests where we train the model on one Kvasir-SEG and evaluate it on CVC-ClinicDB, and vice-versa.

The main novel contributions of this work are therefore:

1. The introduction of a simple yet effective approach for FCNs and transformers in a single architecture for dense prediction which, in contrast to previous work on this, demonstrates advantages over these individual model types through state-of-the-art performance in polyp segmentation.
2. The improvement of the progressive locality decoder (PLD) introduced with SSFormer [32] for decoding features extracted by a transformer encoder through residual blocks (RBs) composed of group normalisation [35], SiLU activation functions [35], convolutional layers, and residual connections [11].

The rest of this paper is structured as follows: we first define the design of FCBFormer and its components in Sect. 2; we then outline our experiments in terms of the implementation of methods, the means of evaluation, and our results, in Sect. 3; and in Sect. 4 we give our conclusion.

2   FCBFormer

2.1   Transformer Branch (TB)

The transformer branch (TB) (Fig. 1b) is highly influenced by the current state-of-the-art architecture for reduced-size polyp segmentation, the SSFormer [32]. Our implementation of SSFormer, as used in our experiments, is illustrated in Fig. 2. This architecture uses an ImageNet [5] pre-trained pyramid vision transformer v2 (PVTv2) [34] as an image encoder, which returns a feature pyramid with 4 levels that is then taken as the input for the progressive locality decoder (PLD). In PLD, each level of the pyramid is processed individually by a local emphasis (LE) module, in order to address the weaknesses of transformer-based models in representing local features in the feature representation, before fusing the locally emphasised levels of the feature pyramid through stepwise feature aggregation (SFA). Finally, the fused multi-scale features are used to predict the segmentation map for the input image.

PLD takes the tensors returned by the encoder, with a number of channels defined by PVTv2, and changes the number of channels in the first convolutional layer in each LE block to 64. Each subsequent layer, except channel-wise concatenation and the prediction layer, then returns the same number of channels (64).

The rest of this subsection will specify the design of TB in the proposed FCB-Former and how this varies from this definition of SSFormer. The improvements resulting from our changes are then demonstrated in the experimental section of this paper.

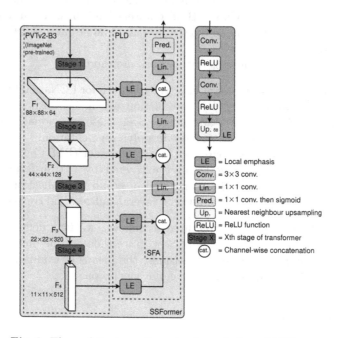

Fig. 2. The architecture of our implementation of SSFormer.

Transformer Encoder. As in SSFormer, we used the PVTv2 [34] for the image encoder in TB, pre-trained on ImageNet [5]. The variant of PVTv2 used is the B3 variant, which has 45.2M parameters. This model demonstrates exceptional feature extraction capabilities for dense prediction owing to its pyramid feature representation, contrasting with more traditional vision transformers which maintain the size of the spatial dimensions throughout the network, e.g. [6,24,31]. Additionally, the model embeds the position of patches through zero padding and overlapping patch embedding via strided convolution, as opposed to adding explicit position embeddings to tokens, and for efficiency uses linear spatial reduction attention. On this element we do not deviate from the design of SSFormer.

Improved Progressive Locality Decoder (PLD+). We improve on the progressive locality decoder (PLD) introduced with SSFormer using the architecture shown in Fig. 1b (PLD+), where we use residual blocks (RBs) (Fig. 1f) to overcome identified limitations of the SSFormer's LE and SFA. These RBs take inspiration from the components of modern convolutional neural networks which have seen boosts in performance due to the incorporation of group normalisation [35], SiLU activation functions [12], and residual connections [11]. We identified SSFormer's LE and SFA as being limited due to a lack of such modern elements, and a relatively low number of layers. As such, we modified these elements in FCBFormer to form the components of PLD+. The improvements resulting from these changes are shown through ablation tests in the experimental section of this paper.

As in SSFormer, the number of channels returned by the first convolutional layer in the LE blocks 64. Every subsequent layer, except channel-wise concatenation, then returns the same number of channels (64).

2.2 Fully Convolutional Branch (FCB)

We define the fully convolutional branch (FCB) (Fig. 1c) as a composition of residual blocks (RBs), strided convolutional layers for downsampling, nearest neighbour interpolation for upsampling, and dense U-Net style skip connections. This design allows for the extraction of highly fused multi-scale features at full-size, which when fused with the important but coarse features extracted by the transformer branch (TB) allows for inference of full-size segmentation maps in the prediction head (PH).

Through the encoder of FCB, we increase the number of channels returned by each layer by a factor of 2 in the first convolutional layer of the first RB following the second and fourth downsampling layers. Through the decoder of FCB, we then decrease the number of channels returned by each layer by a factor of 2 in the first convolutional layer in the first RB after the second and fourth upsampling layers.

2.3 Prediction Head (PH)

The prediction head (PH) (Fig. 1d) takes a full-size tensor resulted from concatenating the up-sampled transformer branch (TB) output and the output from the fully convolutional branch (FCB). The PH predicts the segmentation map from important but coarse features extracted by TB by fusing them with the fine-grained features extracted by FCB. This approach for the combination of FCNs and transformers for dense prediction to the best of our knowledge has not been used before. As shown by our experiments, this approach is highly effective in polyp segmentation and indicates that FCNs and transformers operating in parallel prior to the fusion of features and pixel-wise prediction on the fused features is a powerful basis for dense prediction. Each layer of PH returns 64 channels, except the prediction layer which returns a single channel.

3   Experiments

To evaluate the performance of FCBFormer in polyp segmentation, we considered 2 popular open datasets, Kvasir-SEG [16][1] and CVC-ClinicDB [2][2], and trained our models using the implementation detailed in Sect. 3.1. These datasets provide 1000/612 (Kvasir-SEG/CVC-ClinicDB) ground truth input-target pairs in total, with the samples in Kvasir-SEG varying in the size of the spatial dimensions while all samples in CVC-ClinicDB are of 288 × 384 spatial dimensions. All images across both datasets contain polyps of varying morphology. These datasets have been used extensively in the development of polyp segmentation models, and as such provide strong benchmarks for this assessment.

3.1   Implementation Details

We trained FCBFormer to predict binary segmentation maps of $h \times w$ spatial dimensions for RGB images resized to $h \times w$ spatial dimensions, where we set $h, w = 352$ following the convention set by [8,32,37]. We used PyTorch, and due to the aliasing issues with resizing images in such frameworks which have recently been brought to light [23], we used anti-aliasing in our resizing of the images. Both the images and segmentation maps were initially loaded in with a value range of $[0, 1]$. We then used a random train/validation/test split of 80%/10%/10% following the convention set by [8,15,17,28,32], and randomly augmented the training input-target pairs as they were loaded in during each epoch using: 1) a Gaussian blur with a 25×25 kernel with a standard deviation uniformly sampled from $[0.001, 2]$; 2) colour jitter with a brightness factor uniformly sampled from $[0.6, 1.4]$, a contrast factor uniformly sampled from $[0.5, 1.5]$, a saturation factor uniformly sampled from $[0.75, 1.25]$, and a hue factor uniformly sampled from $[0.99, 1.01]$; 3) horizontal and vertical flips each with a probability of 0.5; and 4) affine transforms with rotations of an angle sampled uniformly from $[-180°, 180°]$, horizontal and vertical translations each of a magnitude sampled uniformly from $[-44, 44]$, scaling of a magnitude sampled uniformly from $[0.5, 1.5]$ and shearing of an angle sampled uniformly from $[-22.5°, 22°]$. Out of these augmentations, 1) and 2) were applied only to the image, while the rest of the augmentations were applied consistently to both the image and the corresponding segmentation map. Following augmentation, the image RGB values were normalised to an interval of $[-1, 1]$. We note that performance was achieved by resizing the segmentation maps used for training with bilinear interpolation without binarisation, however the values of the segmentation maps in the validation and test sets were binarised after resizing.

We then trained FCBFormer on the training set for each considered polyp segmentation dataset for 200 epochs using a batch size of 16 and the AdamW optimiser [21] with an initial learning rate of 1e−4. The learning rate was then reduced by a factor of 2 when the performance (mDice) on the validation set

---

[1] Available: https://datasets.simula.no/kvasir-seg/.
[2] Available: https://polyp.grand-challenge.org/CVCClinicDB/.

did not improve over 10 epochs until reaching a minimum of $1e-6$, and saved the model after each epoch if the performance (mDice) on the validation set improved. The loss function used was the sum of the binary cross entropy (BCE) loss and the Dice loss.

For comparison against alternative architectures, we also trained and evaluated a selection of well-established and state-of-the-art examples, which also predict full-size segmentation maps, on the same basis as FCBFormer, including: U-Net [25], ResUNet [38], ResUNet++ [17], PraNet [8], and MSRF-Net [28]. This did not include SSFormer, as an official codebase has yet to be made available and the model by itself does not predict full-size segmentation maps. However, we considered our own implementation of SSFormer in an ablation study presented at the end of this section. To ensure these models were trained and evaluated in a consistent manner while ensuring training and inference was conducted as the authors intended, we used the official codebase[3] provided for each, where possible[4] and modified this only to ensure that the models were trained and evaluated using data of 352×352 spatial dimensions and that the same train/validation/test splits were used.

Some of the codebases for the existing models implement the respective model in TensorFlow/Keras, as opposed to PyTorch as is the case for FCBFormer. After observing slight variation in the results returned by the implementations of the considered metrics in these frameworks for the same inputs, we took steps to ensure a fair and balanced assessment. We therefore predicted the segmentation maps for each assessment within each respective codebase, after training, and saved the predictions. In a separate session using only Scikit-image, we then loaded in the targets for each assessment from source, resized to 352×352 using bilinear interpolation, and binarised the result. The binary predictions were then loaded in, and we used the implementations of the metrics in Scikit-learn to obtain our results. Note that this was done for all models in each assessment.

3.2 Evaluation

We present some example predictions for each model in Fig. 3. From this, it can be seen how FCBFormer predicts segmentation maps which are generally more consistent with the target than the segmentation maps computed by the existing models, and which demonstrate robustness to challenging morphology, highlighted by cases where the existing models are unable to represent the boundary well. This particular strength in segmenting polyps for which the boundary is less apparent is likely a result of the successful combination of the strengths of transformers and FCNs in FCBFormer, leading to the main structures of polyps being dealt with by the transformer branch (TB), while the fully convolutional

---

[3] ResUNet++ code available: https://github.com/DebeshJha/ResUNetPlusPlus.
  PraNet code available: https://github.com/DengPingFan/PraNet.
  MSRF-Net code available: https://github.com/NoviceMAn-prog/MSRF-Net.

[4] For U-Net and ResUNet, we used the implementations built into the ResUnet++ codebase (available: https://github.com/DebeshJha/ResUNetPlusPlus).

branch (FCB) serves to ensure a reliable full-size boundary around this main structure. We demonstrate this in Fig. 4, where we show the features extracted by TB and FCB, and the predictions, for examples from the Kvasir-SEG [16] test set. The predictions are shown for the model with FCB, as defined, as well as for the model without FCB, where we concatenate the output of TB channel-wise with a tensor of 0's in place of the output of FCB. This reveals how the prediction head (PH) performs with and without the information provided by FCB, and in turn the role of FCB in assisting with the prediction. The most apparent function is that FCB highlights the edges of polyps, as well as the edges of features that may cause occlusions of polyps, such as other objects in the scene or the perimeter of the colonoscope view. This can then be seen to help provide a well-defined boundary, particularly when a polyp is near or partly occluded by such features.

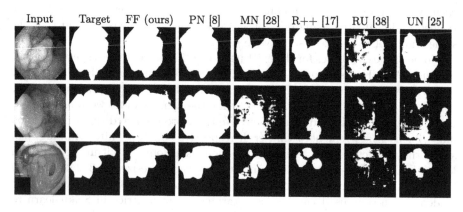

Fig. 3. Example inputs and targets from the Kvasir-SEG test set [16] and the predictions for FCBFormer and the considered existing architectures. FF is FCBFormer, PN is PraNet, MN is MSRF-Net, R++ is ResUNet++, RU is ResUNet, and UN is U-Net. Each model used for this was the variant trained on the Kvasir-SEG training set.

Primary Evaluation. For each dataset, we evaluated the performance of the models with respect to the mDice, mIoU, mPrecision, and mRecall metrics, where m indicates an average of the metric value over the test set. The results from these primary assessments are shown in Table 1, which show that FCB-Former outperformed the existing models with respect to all metrics.

We note that for some of the previously proposed methods, we obtain worse results than has been reported in the original papers, particularly MSRF-Net [28]. This is potentially due to some of the implementations being optimised for spatial dimensions of size 256 × 256, as opposed to 352 × 352 as has been used here. This is supported by our retraining and evaluation of MSRF-Net [28] with 256×256 input-targets, where we obtained similar results to those reported in the original paper. We therefore present the results originally reported by the authors of each model in Table 2. Despite the potential differences in the experimental

Input	Target	TB output	FCB output	with FCB	without FCB

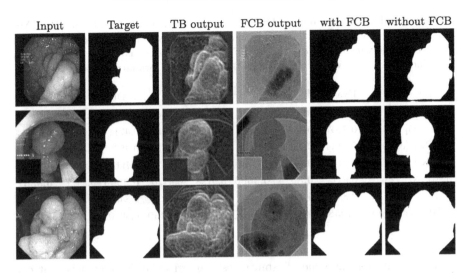

Fig. 4. Visualisation of the features returned by TB and FCB (channel-wise average), and the with/without FCB predictions for examples from the Kvasir-SEG [16] test set.

set up, it can be seen that FCBFormer consistently outperforms other models with respect to the observed mDice, one of the most important metrics out of those considered, and also outperforms other models with respect to mRecall on the Kvasir-SEG dataset [16], and mPrecision on the CVC-ClinicDB dataset [2]. FCBFormer can also be seen to perform competitively with respect to the mIoU.

Table 1. Results from our primary assessment.

Dataset	Kvasir-SEG [16]				CVC-ClinicDB [2]			
Metric	mDice	mIoU	mPrec.	mRec.	mDice	mIoU	mPrec.	mRec.
U-Net [25]	0.7821	0.8141	0.7241	0.8450	0.8464	0.7730	0.8496	0.8796
ResUNet [38]	0.5133	0.3792	0.5937	0.5968	0.5221	0.4120	0.6151	0.5895
ResUNet++ [17]	0.8074	0.7231	0.8991	0.7874	0.5211	0.4126	0.5633	0.5693
MSRF-Net [28]	0.8586	0.7906	0.8933	0.8774	0.9198	0.8729	0.9222	0.9308
PraNet [8]	0.9011	0.8403	0.9034	0.9272	0.9358	0.8867	0.9370	0.93888
FCBFormer (ours)	**0.9385**	**0.8903**	**0.9459**	**0.9401**	**0.9469**	**0.9020**	**0.9525**	**0.9441**

Generalisability Tests. We also performed generalisability tests following the convention set by [28, 32]. Using the same set of metrics, we evaluated the models trained on the Kvasir-SEG/CVC-ClinicDB training set on predictions for the full CVC-ClinicDB/Kvasir-SEG dataset. Such tests reveal how models perform with respect to a different distribution to that considered during training.

Table 2. Results originally reported for existing models. Note that U-Net and ResUNet were not originally tested on polyp segmentation, and as such we present the results obtained by the authors of ResUNet++ [17] for these models. For ease of comparison, we include the results we obtained for FCBFormer in our primary assessment.

Dataset	Kvasir-SEG [16]				CVC-ClinicDB [2]			
Metric	mDice	mIoU	mPrec.	mRec.	mDice	mIoU	mPrec.	mRec.
U-Net [25]	0.7147	0.4334	0.9222	0.6306	0.6419	0.4711	0.6868	0.6756
ResUNet [38]	0.5144	0.4364	0.7292	0.5041	0.4510	0.4570	0.5614	0.5775
ResUNet++ [17]	0.8133	0.7927	0.7064	0.8774	0.7955	0.7962	0.8785	0.7022
MSRF-Net [28]	0.9217	**0.8914**	**0.9666**	0.9198	0.9420	**0.9043**	0.9427	**0.9567**
PraNet [8]	0.898	0.840	–	–	0.899	0.849	–	–
FCBFormer (ours)	**0.9385**	0.8903	0.9459	**0.9401**	**0.9469**	0.9020	**0.9525**	0.9441

The results for the generalisability tests are given in Table 3, where it can be seen that FCBFormer exhibits particular strength in dealing with images from a somewhat different distribution to those used for training, significantly outperforming the existing models with respect to most metrics. This is likely a result of the same strengths highlighted in the discussion of Fig. 3.

Table 3. Results from our generalisability tests.

Training data	Kvasir-SEG [16]				CVC-ClinicDB [2]			
Test data	CVC-ClinicDB [2]				Kvasir-SEG [16]			
Metric	mDice	mIoU	mPrec.	mRec.	mDice	mIoU	mPrec.	mRec.
U-Net [25]	0.5940	0.5081	0.6937	0.6184	0.5292	0.4036	0.4613	0.8481
ResUNet [38]	0.3359	0.2425	0.5048	0.3307	0.3344	0.2222	0.2618	0.8164
ResUNet++ [17]	0.5638	0.4750	0.7175	0.5908	0.3077	0.2048	0.3340	0.4778
MSRF-Net [28]	0.6238	0.5419	0.6621	0.7051	0.7296	0.6415	0.8162	0.7421
PraNet [8]	0.7912	0.7119	0.8152	0.8316	0.7950	0.7073	0.7687	**0.9050**
FCBFormer (ours)	**0.8735**	**0.8038**	**0.8995**	**0.8876**	**0.8848**	**0.8214**	**0.9354**	0.8754

As in our primary assessment, we also present results reported elsewhere. Similar generalisability tests were undertaken by the authors of MSRF-Net [28], leading to the results presented in Table 4. Again, we observe that FCBFormer outperforms other models with respect to most metrics.

Ablation Study. We also performed an ablation study, where we started from our implementation of SSFormer given in Fig. 2, since an official codebase has yet to be made available, and stepped towards FCBFormer. We refer to our implementation of SSFormer as SSFormer-I. This model was trained to predict segmentation maps of $\frac{h}{4} \times \frac{w}{4}$ spatial dimensions, and its performance in predicting

Table 4. Results from the generalisability tests conducted by the authors of MSRF-Net [28]. Note, ResUNet [38] was not included in these tests. For ease of comparison, we include the results we obtained for FCBFormer in our generalisability tests.

Training data	Kvasir-SEG [16]				CVC-ClinicDB [2]			
Test data	CVC-ClinicDB [2]				Kvasir-SEG [16]			
Metric	mDice	mIoU	mPrec.	mRec.	mDice	mIoU	mPrec.	mRec.
U-Net [25]	0.7172	0.6133	0.7986	0.7255	0.6222	0.4588	0.8133	0.5129
ResUNet++ [17]	0.5560	0.4542	0.6775	0.5795	0.5147	0.4082	0.7181	0.4860
MSRF-Net [28]	0.7921	0.6498	0.7000	**0.9001**	0.7575	0.6337	0.8314	0.7197
PraNet [8]	0.7225	0.6328	0.7888	0.7531	0.7293	0.6262	0.7623	0.8007
FCBFormer (ours)	**0.8735**	**0.8038**	**0.8995**	0.8876	**0.8848**	**0.8214**	**0.9354**	**0.8754**

full-size segmentation maps was then assessed by upsampling the predictions to $h \times w$ using bilinear interpolation then binarisation. We then removed the original prediction layer and used the resulting architecture as the transformer branch (TB) in FCBFormer, to reveal the benefits of our fully convolutional branch (FCB) and prediction head (PH) for full-size segmentation in isolation of the improved progressive locality decoder (PLD+), and we refer to this model as SSFormer-I+FCB. The additional performance of FCBFormer over SSFormer-I+FCB then reveals the benefits of PLD+. Note that SSFormer-I and SSFormer-I+FCB were both trained and evaluated on the same basis as FCBFormer and the other considered existing state-of-the-art architectures.

The results from this ablation study are given in Tables 5 and 6, which indicate that: 1) there are significant benefits of FCB, as demonstrated by SSFormer-I+FCB outperforming SSFormer-I with respect to most metrics; and 2) there are generally benefits of PLD+, demonstrated by FCBFormer outperforming SSFormer-I+FCB on both experiments in the primary assessment and 1 out of 2 of the generalisability tests, with respect to most metrics.

Table 5. Results from the primary assessment in the ablation study. For ease of comparison, we include the results we obtained for FCBFormer in our primary assessment.

Dataset	Kvasir-SEG [16]				CVC-ClinicDB [2]			
Metric	mDice	mIoU	mPrec.	mRec.	mDice	mIoU	mPrec.	mRec.
SSFormer-I	0.9196	0.8616	0.9316	0.9226	0.9318	0.8777	0.9409	0.9295
SSFormer-I+FCB	0.9337	0.8850	0.9330	**0.9482**	0.9410	0.8904	**0.9556**	0.9307
FCBFormer	**0.9385**	**0.8903**	**0.9459**	0.9401	**0.9469**	**0.9020**	0.9525	**0.9441**

Table 6. Results from the generalisability test in the ablation study. For ease of comparison, we include the results we obtained for FCBFormer in our generalisability tests.

Training data	Kvasir-SEG [16]				CVC-ClinicDB [2]			
Test data	CVC-ClinicDB [2]				Kvasir-SEG [16]			
Metric	mDice	mIoU	mPrec.	mRec.	mDice	mIoU	mPrec.	mRec.
SSFormer-I	0.8611	0.7813	0.8904	0.8702	0.8691	0.7986	0.9178	0.8631
SSFormer-I+FCB	**0.8754**	0.8059	**0.8935**	**0.8963**	0.8704	0.7993	0.9280	0.8557
FCBFormer	0.8735	**0.8038**	0.8995	0.8876	**0.8848**	**0.8214**	**0.9354**	**0.8755**

4 Conclusion

In this paper, we introduced the FCBFormer, a novel architecture for the segmentation of polyps in colonoscopy images which successfully combines the strengths of transformers and fully convolutional networks (FCNs) in dense prediction. Through our experiments, we demonstrated the models state-of-the-art performance in this task and how it outperforms existing models with respect to several popular metrics, and highlighted its particular strengths in generalisability and in dealing with polyps of challenging morphology. This work therefore represents another advancement in the automated processing of colonoscopy images, which should aid in the necessary improvement of lesion detection rates and classification.

Additionally, this work has interesting implications for the understanding of neural network architectures for dense prediction. The method combines the strengths of transformers and FCNs, by running a model of each type in parallel and concatenating the outputs for processing by a prediction head (PH). To the best of our knowledge, this method has not been used before, and its strengths indicate that there is still a great deal to understand about these different architecture types and the basis on which they can be combined for optimal performance. Further work should therefore explore this in more depth, by evaluating variants of the model and performing further ablation studies. We will also consider further investigation of dataset augmentation for this task, where we expect the random augmentation of segmentation masks to aid in overcoming variability in the targets produced by different annotators.

Acknowledgements. This work was supported by the Science and Technology Facilities Council grant number ST/S005404/1.

Discretionary time allocation on DiRAC Tursa HPC was also used for methods development.

References

1. Ali, S., et al.: Deep learning for detection and segmentation of artefact and disease instances in gastrointestinal endoscopy. Med. Image Anal. **70**, 102002 (2021)
2. Bernal, J., Sánchez, F.J., Fernández-Esparrach, G., Gil, D., Rodríguez, C., Vilariño, F.: WM-DOVA maps for accurate polyp highlighting in colonoscopy: Validation vs. saliency maps from physicians. Comput. Med. Imaging Graph. **43**, 99–111 (2015)
3. Chen, J., et al.: TransuNet: transformers make strong encoders for medical image segmentation. arXiv preprint arXiv:2102.04306 (2021)
4. Corley, D.A., et al.: Adenoma detection rate and risk of colorectal cancer and death. N. Engl. J. Med. **370**(14), 1298–1306 (2014)
5. Deng, J., Dong, W., Socher, R., Li, L.J., Li, K., Fei-Fei, L.: ImageNet: a large-scale hierarchical image database. In: 2009 IEEE Conference on Computer Vision and Pattern Recognition, pp. 248–255. IEEE (2009)
6. Dosovitskiy, A., et al.: An image is worth 16×16 words: transformers for image recognition at scale. In: ICLR (2021)
7. Dyba, T., et al.: The European cancer burden in 2020: incidence and mortality estimates for 40 countries and 25 major cancers. Eur. J. Cancer **157**, 308–347 (2021)
8. Fan, D.-P., et al.: PraNet: parallel reverse attention network for polyp segmentation. In: Martel, A.L., et al. (eds.) MICCAI 2020. LNCS, vol. 12266, pp. 263–273. Springer, Cham (2020). https://doi.org/10.1007/978-3-030-59725-2_26
9. Guo, Y.B., Matuszewski, B.: Giana polyp segmentation with fully convolutional dilation neural networks. In: Proceedings of the 14th International Joint Conference on Computer Vision, Imaging and Computer Graphics Theory and Applications, pp. 632–641. SCITEPRESS-Science and Technology Publications (2019)
10. Guo, Y., Bernal, J., J Matuszewski, B.: Polyp segmentation with fully convolutional deep neural networks-extended evaluation study. J. Imaging **6**(7), 69 (2020)
11. He, K., Zhang, X., Ren, S., Sun, J.: Deep residual learning for image recognition. In: 2016 IEEE Conference on Computer Vision and Pattern Recognition (CVPR), pp. 770–778 (2016). https://doi.org/10.1109/CVPR.2016.90
12. Hendrycks, D., Gimpel, K.: Gaussian error linear units (gelus). arXiv preprint arXiv:1606.08415 (2016)
13. Huang, C.H., Wu, H.Y., Lin, Y.L.: HardNet-MSEG: a simple encoder-decoder polyp segmentation neural network that achieves over 0.9 mean dice and 86 fps. arXiv preprint arXiv:2101.07172 (2021)
14. Jha, D., et al.: Real-time polyp detection, localization and segmentation in colonoscopy using deep learning. IEEE Access **9**, 40496–40510 (2021)
15. Jha, D., Riegler, M.A., Johansen, D., Halvorsen, P., Johansen, H.D.: Doubleu-net: a deep convolutional neural network for medical image segmentation. In: 2020 IEEE 33rd International Symposium on Computer-Based Medical Systems (CBMS), pp. 558–564. IEEE (2020)
16. Jha, D., et al.: Kvasir-SEG: a segmented polyp dataset. In: Ro, Y.M., et al. (eds.) MMM 2020. LNCS, vol. 11962, pp. 451–462. Springer, Cham (2020). https://doi.org/10.1007/978-3-030-37734-2_37
17. Jha, D., et al.: Resunet++: an advanced architecture for medical image segmentation. In: 2019 IEEE International Symposium on Multimedia (ISM), pp. 225–2255. IEEE (2019)

18. Kim, N.H., et al.: Miss rate of colorectal neoplastic polyps and risk factors for missed polyps in consecutive colonoscopies. Intestinal Res. **15**(3), 411 (2017)

19. Kim, T., Lee, H., Kim, D.: UacaNet: Uncertainty augmented context attention for polyp segmentation. In: Proceedings of the 29th ACM International Conference on Multimedia, pp. 2167–2175 (2021)

20. Lee, J., et al.: Risk factors of missed colorectal lesions after colonoscopy. Medicine **96**(27) (2017)

21. Loshchilov, I., Hutter, F.: Decoupled weight decay regularization. In: International Conference on Learning Representations (2018)

22. Lou, A., Guan, S., Ko, H., Loew, M.H.: CaraNet: context axial reverse attention network for segmentation of small medical objects. In: Medical Imaging 2022: Image Processing, vol. 12032, pp. 81–92. SPIE (2022)

23. Parmar, G., Zhang, R., Zhu, J.Y.: On aliased resizing and surprising subtleties in GAN evaluation. In: CVPR (2022)

24. Ranftl, R., Bochkovskiy, A., Koltun, V.: Vision transformers for dense prediction. In: Proceedings of the IEEE/CVF International Conference on Computer Vision, pp. 12179–12188 (2021)

25. Ronneberger, O., Fischer, P., Brox, T.: U-net: convolutional networks for biomedical image segmentation. In: Navab, N., Hornegger, J., Wells, W.M., Frangi, A.F. (eds.) MICCAI 2015. LNCS, vol. 9351, pp. 234–241. Springer, Cham (2015). https://doi.org/10.1007/978-3-319-24574-4_28

26. Salmo, E., Haboubi, N.: Adenoma and malignant colorectal polyp: pathological considerations and clinical applications. Gastroenterology **7**(1), 92–102 (2018)

27. Siegel, R.L., Miller, K.D., Fuchs, H.E., Jemal, A.: Cancer statistics, 2022. CA Cancer J. Clin. (2022)

28. Srivastava, A., et al.: MSRF-net: a multi-scale residual fusion network for biomedical image segmentation. IEEE J. Biomed. Health Inform. (2021)

29. Srivastava, R.K., Greff, K., Schmidhuber, J.: Highway networks. arXiv preprint arXiv:1505.00387 (2015)

30. Tomar, N.K., et al.: DDANet: dual decoder attention network for automatic polyp segmentation. In: Del Bimbo, A., et al. (eds.) ICPR 2021. LNCS, vol. 12668, pp. 307–314. Springer, Cham (2021). https://doi.org/10.1007/978-3-030-68793-9_23

31. Touvron, H., Cord, M., Douze, M., Massa, F., Sablayrolles, A., Jegou, H.: Training data-efficient image transformers & distillation through attention. In: Meila, M., Zhang, T. (eds.) Proceedings of the 38th International Conference on Machine Learning. Proceedings of Machine Learning Research, vol. 139, pp. 10347–10357. PMLR, 18–24 July 2021. https://proceedings.mlr.press/v139/touvron21a.html

32. Wang, J., Huang, Q., Tang, F., Meng, J., Su, J., Song, S.: Stepwise feature fusion: local guides global. arXiv preprint arXiv:2203.03635 (2022)

33. Wang, W., et al.: Pyramid vision transformer: a versatile backbone for dense prediction without convolutions. In: Proceedings of the IEEE/CVF International Conference on Computer Vision, pp. 568–578 (2021)

34. Wang, W., et al.: Pvtv 2: improved baselines with pyramid vision transformer. Comput. Vis. Media **8**(3), 1–10 (2022)

35. Wu, Y., He, K.: Group normalization. In: Proceedings of the European Conference on Computer Vision (ECCV), pp. 3–19 (2018)

36. Xie, E., Wang, W., Yu, Z., Anandkumar, A., Alvarez, J.M., Luo, P.: SEG-Former: simple and efficient design for semantic segmentation with transformers. In: Advances in Neural Information Processing Systems, vol. 34 (2021)

37. Zhang, Y., Liu, H., Hu, Q.: TransFuse: fusing transformers and CNNs for medical image segmentation. In: de Bruijne, M., et al. (eds.) MICCAI 2021. LNCS, vol. 12901, pp. 14–24. Springer, Cham (2021). https://doi.org/10.1007/978-3-030-87193-2_2
38. Zhang, Z., Liu, Q., Wang, Y.: Road extraction by deep residual U-net. IEEE Geosci. Remote Sens. Lett. **15**(5), 749–753 (2018)
39. Zhou, Z., Rahman Siddiquee, M.M., Tajbakhsh, N., Liang, J.: UNet++: a nested U-net architecture for medical image segmentation. In: Stoyanov, D., et al. (eds.) DLMIA/ML-CDS -2018. LNCS, vol. 11045, pp. 3–11. Springer, Cham (2018). https://doi.org/10.1007/978-3-030-00889-5_1

Correction to: Faster Diffusion Cardiac MRI with Deep Learning-Based Breath Hold Reduction

Michael Tänzer⑩, Pedro Ferreira⑩, Andrew Scott⑩,
Zohya Khalique⑩, Maria Dwornik⑩, Ramyah Rajakulasingam,
Ranil de Silva, Dudley Pennell⑩, Guang Yang⑩,
Daniel Rueckert⑩, and Sonia Nielles-Vallespin⑩

Correction to:
Chapter 8 in: G. Yang et al. (Eds.): *Medical Image*
Understanding and Analysis, **LNCS 13413,**
https://doi.org/10.1007/978-3-031-12053-4_8

In an older version of this paper, the names and details of the authors Ramyah Rajakulasingam and Ranil de Silva had been omitted from the header. They have now been added as co-authors.

The updated version of this chapter can be found at
https://doi.org/10.1007/978-3-031-12053-4_8

© The Author(s), under exclusive license to Springer Nature Switzerland AG 2024
G. Yang et al. (Eds.): MIUA 2022, LNCS 13413, p. C1, 2024.
https://doi.org/10.1007/978-3-031-12053-4_66

Author Index

Acosta, Oscar 636
Ahamed, Md. Atik 298
Ahmed, Sheraz 46, 139
Alahdab, Yesim Ozen 157
Ali, Hesham 751, 882
Aljabar, Paul 398
Almakky, Ibrahim 234
Alsharid, Mohammad 187
Annappa, B. 578
Arafat, Youssef 833
Aristei, Cynthia 767
Arya, Zobair 398
Asad, Zuhayr 778
Ashburner, John 271
Atug, Ozlen 157
Aviles-Rivero, Angelica I. 130
Azarmehr, Neda 357

Balada, Christoph Peter 46
Balbastre, Yaël 271
Banck, Michael 851
Bashir, Raja Muhammad Saad 425
Basty, Nicolas 3
Bawazir, Ameera 234
Bernander, Karl Bengtsson 283
Bianconi, Francesco 767
Bise, Ryoma 609
Bonazzola, Rodrigo 482, 787
Brady, Sir Michael 28, 398
Brudfors, Mikael 271
Busto, Laura 869

Cao, Kunlin 253
Cardoso, M. Jorge 271
Chen, Xin 262
Cheng, Nina 482
Connell, John 398
Cresswell, Emily 3
Cui, Can 778

Dalla Serra, Francesco 623
Dalton, Jeff 623
de Silva, Ranil 101
Deligianni, Fani 623

Demaret, Laurent 703
Deng, Ruining 778
Dengel, Andreas 46, 139
Dodia, Shubham 578
Dong, Bo 116
Drukker, Lior 187
Duvieusart, Benjamin 13
Dwornik, Maria 101

Edlund, Christoffer 139
Edwards, A. David 469
Ehab, Eman 882
Elattar, Mustafa 339, 751, 882
Elgohary, Kareem 339
Elsayed, Asmaa 814
Elyan, Eyad 651
Ergenc, Ilkay 157
Esmeral, Laura Carolina Martínez 719

Fan, Di 223
Fawaz, Abdulah 469
Fernandes, Carolina 28
Ferreira, Pedro 101
Fetit, Ahmed E. 443
Fitzgerald, Kerr 535
Flisikowski, Krzysztof 851
Francis, Susan T. 262
Frangi, Alejandro F. 482, 787
Fravolini, Mario Luca 767

Ge, Xin 692
Geißler, Peter 703
Ghoshal, Bhargab 565
Ghoshal, Biraja 565
Gollini Navarrete, Ivo 234
Gong, Zhendi 262
González-Nóvoa, José A. 869
Gordon, Isobel 28
Goyal, Manu 199
Gyires-Tóth, Bálint 412

Hasan, S. M. Kamrul 371
Hayashi, Hideaki 609
He, Hongjian 116

Herlihy, Amy   28
Hernández, Angie   798
Higazy, Mahmoud   339
Hobson, Kezia   398
Hong, Chenyang   130
Hossam, Abdelaziz   814
Hu, Peng   65
Hu, Xi   116
Huang, Baoru   75
Hunsicker, Eugenie   172
Huo, Yuankai   778

Ibrahim, Samar   339
Imran, Abdullah Al Zubaer   298
Íñiguez, Andrés   869
Insalata, Ferdinando   412

Jacenków, Grzegorz   623
Jackson, Timothy R   139
Jiménez, Víctor   869
Juan-Salvadores, Pablo   869

Kadota, Takeaki   609
Kani, Haluk Tarik   157
Karpe, Fredrik   3
Kaynar, Furkan   703
Ke, Yuan   663
Khalid, Nabeel   139
Khalique, Zohya   101
Khurram, Syed Ali   357, 425
Kim, Kyungsang   328
Kong, Bin   253
Koochali, Mohammadmahdi   139
Krenzer, Adrian   851
Krones, Felix   13

Law, Meng   535
Li, Baihua   172
Li, Hao   313
Li, Huihui   692
Li, Quanzheng   328
Li, Xiaochuan   663
Li, Yue   87
Lian, Dankun   87
Lim, Ngee Han   75
Lindblad, Joakim   283
Linte, Cristian   371
Lió, Pietro   65
Liu, Huafeng   87, 328
Liu, Lihao   130

Liu, Quan   778
Lu, Chenxi   116
Lu, Yi   253
Lucieri, Adriano   46

Mahdi, Adam   13
Mahmood, Hanya   357
Maldonado García, Cynthia   787
Mandujano-Cornejo, Vittorino   519
Marimont, Sergio Naval   387
Mateus, Diana   636
Matuszewski, Bogdan   535
Matuszewski, Bogdan J.   892
Meining, Alexander   851
Mohamed, Kareem   814
Mohannad, Thanaa   339
Montoya-Zegarra, Javier A.   519
Moreno-García, Carlos Francisco   651
Mostafa, Hanya   814
Muhtaseb, Rand   680
Munir, Mohsin   139

Nachev, Parashkev   271
Nan, Yang   313
Nicholas, Rosemary   262
Nielles-Vallespin, Sonia   101
Niu, Tianye   692
Noble, J. Alison   187
Núñez, Luis   398
Nyström, Ingela   283

O'Neil, Alison Q.   623
Ourselin, Sébastien   271

Padukudru, Mahesh A.   578
Palumbo, Barbara   767
Palumbo, Isabella   767
Papageorgiou, Aris T.   187
Papież, Bartłomiej W.   13, 75
Parsons, Guy   13
Pascoletti, Giulia   767
Pelluet, Guillaume   636
Pennell, Dudley   101
Pertuz, Said   798
Polat, Gorkem   157
Puppe, Frank   851

Qi, Haikun   65
Qian, Pengfang   65
Qin, Pinle   508

Rajakulasingam, Ramyah 101
Rajbhandari, Satyan 199
Rajpoot, Nasir 357, 425
Ralli, George 28
Ramirez, Ana 798
Ravikumar, Nishant 482, 787
Raza, Shan E. Ahmed 425
Rees, Geraint 271
Reeves, Neil D. 199
Ren, Jinchang 651
Reyes-Aldasoro, Constantino Carlos 833
Ridzuan, Muhammad 234
Rizkallah, Mira 636
Robinson, Emma C. 469
Rohling, Robert 594
Rohr, Karl 212
Rueckert, Daniel 101

Saeed, Mohamed 680
Salcudean, Septimiu 594
Sanderson, Edward 892
Sarhan, Hossam Mohamed 882
Sarker, Md Mostafa Kamal 651
Saylani, Hicham 734
Schmeisser, Fabian 46, 139
Schönlieb, Carola-Bibiane 130
Scialpi, Michele 767
Scott, Andrew 101
Seah, Jarrel 535
Selim, Sahar 339, 751, 814, 882
Seybold, Tamara 703
Shaban, Muhammad 425
Sharma, Harshita 187
Shephard, Adam 357
Siddiqui, Shoaib Ahmed 46
Sjögren, Rickard 139
Song, Qi 253
Song, Weihu 223
Stechele, Walter 703
Strand, Robin 283
Sudarevic, Boban 851

Tanaka, Kiyohito 609
Tang, Jennifer 535
Tänzer, Michael 101
Tarassenko, Lionel 13
Tardy, Mickael 636
Tarek, Reem 814
Tarroni, Giacomo 387

Temizel, Alptekin 157
Troya, Joel 851
Trygg, Johan 139
Tucker, Allan 565

Uchida, Seiichi 609
Uhl, Andreas 719
Unyi, Dániel 412

Vargas, Andres F. 798
Veiga, César 869
Veličković, Petar 412
Vincent, Tonia 75
Vogt, Nora 398
Voiculescu, Irina 494

Wagner, Royden 212
Wang, Jing 116
Wang, Xin 253
Wang, Ziyang 75, 494
Watts, Todd 547
Williams, Logan Z. J. 469

Xie, Yiming 443
Xu, Pengcheng 328

Yang, Guang 101, 313, 547
Yang, Hao-Yu 253
Yang, Junwei 65
Yang, Pengfei 692
Yao, Tianyuan 778
Yap, Moi Hoon 199
Yaqub, Mohammad 234, 680
Ye, Lei 172
Yeung, Michael 547
Yin, Hujun 458
Yin, Youbing 253
Yu, Heng 223

Zeng, Jianchao 508
Zhang, Jinjing 508
Zhao, Lijun 508
Zhao, Yang 116
Zheng, Jian-Qing 75, 494
Zhou, Diwei 172
Zhou, Qifan 458
Zhu, Hongzhi 594
Zhu, Zheyu 778
Zokay, Mustapha 734

Printed in the United States
by Baker & Taylor Publisher Services